The Yale Edition of the Complete Works of St. Thomas More

VOLUME 12

A DIALOGUE OF COMFORT AGAINST
TRIBULATION

Published by the St. Thomas More Project, Yale University,
under the auspices of Gerard L. Carroll and Joseph B. Murray,
Trustees of the Michael P. Grace, II, Trust,
and with the support of the
National Endowment for the Humanities

to remissyon / many a man shuld stand w it so
moche / in very pilouse case

Anthony

wh an so shuld in dede Cosyn / & in dede many so do,
And the old saynt wrote very sore in this poynt
honore? Misericordia domini super omnia opera eius ~

————— the mercie of god is above all his workes:
and he standith not boundyn wt no rewle
Et ipse cognouit figmentu suu, & propiciatur
infirmitatibus nostris And he knows the
frayltie of his erthey vessell that is of his
owy makyng & is mercifull & hath pitie vppon
o feble infirmytees, & shall not expect of vs
above the thyng that we may do /

But yet Cosyn he that findeth hym selfe in that case /
in that he is myndid to do well hereafter let hym
geve god thanke that he is no worse / but in that he may
not be sory for his sinne passed, let hym be sory hardely
that he is no better / And as saint Jherome biddith hym,
that for his sinne sorowth in his hart be glad & reioyce
in his sorow / so wold I counsayle hym that w not be

sorry for he

The Complete Works of
ST. THOMAS MORE

VOLUME 12

Edited by

LOUIS L. MARTZ
and
FRANK MANLEY

Yale University Press, New Haven and London, 1976

Designed by Crimilda Pontes
and set in Baskerville type.
Printed in the United States of America by
The Murray Printing Company, Westford, Massachusetts.

Published in Great Britain, Europe, Africa and Asia
(except Japan) by Yale University Press, Ltd., London.
Distributed in Latin America by Kaiman & Polon,
Inc., New York City; in Australia and New Zealand by
Book & Film Services, Artarmon, N.S.W., Australia; in
Japan by John Weatherhill, Inc., Tokyo.

EDITORIAL COMMITTEE

Louis L. Martz, *Chairman* · Richard S. Sylvester, *Executive Editor*
Franklin L. Baumer · Gerard L. Carroll · Richard J. Schoeck
David R. Watkins · William K. Wimsatt

ADVISORY COMMITTEE

A. F. Allison, Catholic Record Society
The Rev. Roland H. Bainton, Yale
Arthur E. Barker, Western Ontario
Leicester Bradner, Brown
R. W. Burchfield, Oxford
Douglas Bush, Harvard
Marie Delcourt-Curvers, Liège
William H. Dunham, Jr., Yale
G. R. Elton, Cambridge
O. B. Hardison, Jr., Director, Folger Shakespeare Library
Denys Hay, Edinburgh
Hubertus Schulte Herbrüggen, Düsseldorf
J. H. Hexter, Yale
N. R. Ker, Oxford
Chester Kerr, Director, Yale University Press
Stephan Kuttner, University of California, Berkeley
The Rev. Germain Marc'hadour, Université Catholique, Angers
Jean-Claude Margolin, Renaissance Institute, Tours
Thomas E. Marston, Yale
The Rev. Walter J. Ong, S. J., St. Louis
Cornelis Reedijk, Director, Royal Library, The Hague
E. E. Reynolds, President, Amici Thomae Mori
Lewis Spitz, Stanford
Craig R. Thompson, University of Pennsylvania
J. B. Trapp, Director, Warburg Institute
Louis B. Wright, Director Emeritus, Folger Shakespeare Library

IN MEMORIAM
WILLIAM KURTZ WIMSATT
AMICO ET CONSILIARIO
1907–1975

ACKNOWLEDGMENTS

The work on this edition has been often interrupted by other responsibilities, until at the end it was finished, like the *Utopia*, only in those hours we were able to steal from leisure and rest. What seemed in the process like a journey without end allowed us to remain with Thomas More longer than we expected, and we came to know him better and feel the impress of his spirit more clearly. We also came to know the other members of the More edition—friends and fellow editors who helped along the way —better than we had in the past. Their help and friendship will remain with us. Like Don Quixote, we tend to start off with the idea of righting all wrongs and restoring the age of gold, only to realize in the end that it is the people we meet along the way that make the real adventures.

Our first debt is to one another, for mutual advice in what has proved to be a true collaboration, although each editor's responsibilities have been clearly defined. The work of establishing the text and preparing the textual apparatus has been performed by Louis Martz. The Commentary is primarily the work of Frank Manley, with Louis Martz adding perhaps five or six percent of the materials, chiefly in the form of verbal glosses, or comments on textual problems. The Introduction has been equally divided: Martz has written Part I, "The Text," Part II, "The Tower Works," and Part V, "A Note on the Text"; Manley has written Part III, "The Argument of the Book," and Part IV, "Audience." Martz has also selected and written the captions for the illustrations. As for the remaining materials, Martz has prepared Appendix A, Part I, Manley has prepared Appendix B, and the staff of the Thomas More Project has compiled the rest of the matter at the back, under the supervision of the editors of the volume and of the executive editor.

Both editors wish to express their deep gratitude to Richard Sylvester, the executive editor, whose patient, friendly, acute, and firm advice has been indispensable at every stage of the work on this volume. And many warm thanks are due to the dedicated staff of the More Project, particularly to Paula Barbour, Elizabeth Coffin, Patrick O'Connell, Robert Scavone, Michael Schwartz, Helen Whall-Seligman, and David Yerkes, for a great variety of work, including the process of verification, and the preparation of the Index and the Glossary.

With special regard to his portion of the work, Louis Martz wishes to extend his warm gratitude to the following: to the President and Fellows of Corpus Christi College, Oxford, for their gracious permission to reproduce the manuscript belonging to their College; to the Bodleian Library, especially to Robert Shackleton, R. W. Hunt, David Rogers, and the staff of Duke Humphrey's, for many favors generously extended during several happy periods of study at Oxford; to the staff of the Manuscript Room of the British Library, along with thanks for permission to reproduce a page from one of their manuscripts; to the Library of Lincoln's Inn, for permission to consult the volumes that once belonged to William Rastell, now in that library, and also for permission to photograph and reproduce here certain parts of those volumes; to the Paul Mellon Centre for Studies in British Art (London), for arranging to photograph the volumes in Lincoln's Inn, particularly to Douglas Smith, who expertly performed the photography, and to Mrs. Patricia Barnden, who made the arrangements with her usual courtesy.

He also wishes to thank *Moreana* and the Yale University Press for permission to include in the Introduction materials from two essays that were originally published in *Moreana* (November, 1967) and in *St. Thomas More: Action and Contemplation. Proceedings of the Symposium Held at St. John's University, October 9–10, 1970*, ed. Richard Sylvester (New Haven, 1972). Gratitude is also extended to the Kupferstichkabinett der Öffentlichen Kunstsammlung of Basel, for permission to reproduce the drawing of the More family by Holbein; to T. Cottrell-Dormer, Esq., for permission to reproduce the portrait of Lady Jane Dormer in his possession, and to the Courtauld Institute of Art (particularly to Caroline Pilkington) for supplying the photograph of this painting; to the Metropolitan Museum of Art for permission to reproduce the two engravings of Suleiman the Magnificent; to the Bodleian Library for supplying photographs of the Corpus Christi manuscript; and to the Beinecke Rare Book and Manuscript Library and the Photographic Department of the Yale University Library for supplying photographs from More's *Workes* and from his *Supplycacyon of soulys*. He is also grateful to the staff of the Beinecke Library for many favors performed, both before and after he became a member of the staff of that library. He is particularly grateful to the Rockefeller Foundation for a generous grant that enabled him to spend most of a year at work upon this project. Thanks are also due to J. B. Trapp for valuable advice and for admission to the facilities of the Warburg Institute; to Fred Robinson for valuable advice on linguistic matters; to his fellow editors of the "Tower Works," Clarence Miller and Garry Haupt, for many helpful suggestions; to Egbert Begemann, for advice concerning portraits of the Great Turk; to Susan Engberg, who typed most of the transcription;

and to Sara Van den Berg, who prepared the materials contained in Appendix A, Parts II and III. A great debt of thanks is due to the patient and dedicated work of Mrs. Fannie Gillette, who typed and retyped the textual footnotes in various forms, over a period of several years; indeed, without her accurate help and unfailing good humor, the textual footnotes might never have been completed. Finally, as she already knows, Louis is grateful to Edwine, whose experience as an editor of eighteenth-century texts has been a constant help in every aspect of this edition.

Frank Manley, with special regard to his portion of the work, wishes to thank Gordon N. Ray and the Board of Trustees of the Guggenheim Foundation for a fellowship which freed him from other responsibilities for a year and allowed him to begin work on the edition. He also wishes to acknowledge the assistance of the Emory University Research Committee for typing and travel grants. On a much more personal level, he is deeply indebted to his colleagues, Louis Martz and Richard Sylvester, not only for their friendship over the years, from the time when he was a young instructor fresh out of graduate school and alien to Yale and New Haven, but also for their open-mindedness and tolerance of strange opinions and sudden gusts of enthusiasm. They will know what he thanks them for, but they will not know how much he is indebted to them for their generosity in going over his portions of the manuscript and doing what they could to check his natural tendency toward excess. His portions of the edition are stronger for their help. A number of students at Emory also lent their assistance at one time or another, and their help is gratefully acknowledged: Richard Beard and John Mebane, who labored on the Commentary, and Robert Holland and Stephen Whitner, who helped in the research for the Introduction. Virginia Trombley in particular did exceptionally fine work on the Turks. He also wishes to thank Mary Lou Grabbe, a former student, for her assistance in proofreading the manuscript of the Commentary and checking cross-references. Lucy Sheffield did most of the typing, learning to read a difficult hand. Very special thanks are due to Helen Whall-Seligman and Elizabeth Coffin, whose real friendship and encouragement were more important and more meaningful than their invaluable check of the manuscript for errors. They also will know what he thanks them for. And to Joy, for her warm hospitality with little opportunity to repay her; to Sara, whose godfather failed her in religious instruction, but who carries, along with Paul and Peter, his heartfelt prayers; to William and Margaret Wimsatt, Clarence Miller, Richard Marius, Garry Haupt, Thomas Lawler, Richard Schoeck, and Germain Marc'hadour, friends he came to know through More, to William Dillingham and Floyd Watkins, who kept him going at home; and finally to those he loves the most, Carolyn and Evelyn and Mary, who were willing to hole up with him in the mountains, haul the water and tend the garden, who lived in a quiet house, listened to endless anecdotes about More, and kept him alive—house cats and yard dogs—his sincerest gratitude and love.

L. L. M. and F. M.

New Haven and Atlanta, 1976

CONTENTS

ILLUSTRATIONS

INTRODUCTION

INTRODUCTION

I. THE TEXT

1. Preliminary Survey

The text of the present edition is based upon the manuscript of *A Dialogue of Comfort* given to Corpus Christi College, Oxford, in the seventeenth century, and now deposited in the Bodleian Library. The body of this manuscript consists of a basic text that appears to be a scribal copy very close to More's original manuscript; this basic text has, however, been carefully edited and expanded by a second hand, also of the sixteenth century, with the evident purpose of preparing a definitive manuscript, presumably for printing. The Corpus Christi manuscript, as the following discussion will show, constitutes a fresh text that takes precedence, both in time and in authority, over the one other extant manuscript and the three printed texts of the sixteenth century.

The materials that are potentially important for establishing the text of *A Dialogue of Comfort* are five in number: two manuscripts and three printed editions:

Manuscripts

1. Ms. C.C.C. D. 37 in the Bodleian Library: a folio paper-book, in a leather binding of the sixteenth century, originally consisting of 207 leaves (fols. 8 and 9 have been cut out). The leaves measure 205 × 287 mm. and are neatly ruled with a plum-colored ink into a writing-space that measures on the average 131 × 205 mm. The number of lines per page varies greatly, ranging from a generously spaced twenty lines in the earlier part to a crowded thirty-three lines in the latter part. The basic text is written throughout in the same hand, with a light-to-medium brown ink; this is a secretarial hand of the first half of the sixteenth century, using a cursive script for English and italic for Latin; the hand is hereafter designated by the symbol *A*. Alterations and additions in a second hand, dating from the middle of the sixteenth century, are clearly distinguishable by dark ink, a thin pen, and distinctive letter-formation; this hand, hereafter designated by the symbol *B*, has edited and expanded the text throughout. The margins contain summaries and occasional marks and remarks of emphasis

written in at least three different hands, all from the sixteenth century and all clearly distinct from hands *A* and *B*.[1]

The manuscript is made up in twenty gatherings of ten leaves each (i.e., five sheets folded in folio), plus a final gathering of six conjugate leaves and one unconjugate (fol. 201). Some of the gatherings are numbered in the lower right-hand corner of the verso of the last leaf: 2–10, xi–xiiij, the arabic and the roman series being apparently the work of two different hands. The outer pages in some of these gatherings are heavily soiled, as though they had become dirty by separate use of the gatherings.[2] Further evidence of such use is found in the foliations made in the top right-hand corners, which undergo frequent changes, always in relation to groupings of ten.[3] The fact that the marginalia are frequently clipped at the outer edges indicates that many of them were written before the book was given its present binding; the leaves must have been originally at least 8 mm. wider. The manuscript, then, was used for some time before it received its present binding and, for a while, it was used without any binding at all. The volume is bound in fine calf, with the edges of the paper gilded and tooled in a design of grapevines. In the middle of the outer side of each cover is embossed a star of David, with the initials G and P stamped in gold on either side of the star.[4] This whole volume will hereafter be designated by the symbol *CC*.

II. Ms. Royal 17 D. XIV in the British Library, folios 5–192: part of a collection of treatises by More, all from the era 1533–35, along with letters and miscellaneous materials by or related to More, forming a total of 455 leaves, written in various hands on various kinds of paper.[5] *A Dialogue of*

---

[1] The marginalia are printed in Appendix A, Part I; the different hands are there distinguished only when two hands clearly are combined to form a single marginal comment.

[2] See especially folios 130ᵛ, 131, 140ᵛ, 141.

[3] Folios 41–49 appear to have been originally misnumbered 21–29; then 4 has been written over 2 to correct the numbering (the original 2 is not evident on all these leaves, but is clearly there for 21–26). Folios 70–159 were originally misnumbered 80–169; furthermore, the erroneous series 160–169 has itself been written over an earlier erroneous set of numbers now illegible. Folios 160–207 were originally misnumbered 180–228 (with the erroneous series skipping from 193 to 195).

[4] The binding appears to be English, rather than continental, in the opinion of Dr. David Rogers. The star is 38 mm. in width, 43 mm. in height; it is formed of brown strips with gold edges. The rosette in the center of the star has a brown center with gold rays. Seven similar rosettes are stamped along the spine, separated by ridges. The boards of the binding measure approximately 204 × 295 mm. A gold line along the outer edges forms a frame measuring approximately 188 × 283 mm. The stubs of four ties (i.e., two pairs) remain, along with one metal clasp near the right-hand upper edge. See Plate VI.

[5] For the entire contents of Ms. Royal 17 D. XIV, see the Introduction to *Treatise on the Passion*, etc., ed. Garry Haupt, *The Yale Edition of the Complete Works of St. Thomas More*

Comfort is here treated with special care, as though the manuscript represented a presentation copy; it appears to be the work of a professional scribe. It is written throughout in a large and elegant cursive hand of the mid-sixteenth century which does not appear elsewhere in the collection.[1] It is furnished with large, decorative initial letters at the beginning of each chapter, and with large, broadly inked letters for the opening words of each chapter-heading and chapter-opening, as well as for the names of the two speakers. Letters are frequently formed with decorative flourishes. It is the only work in this collection to be written in a ruled-off space. Leaves are approximately 198 × 277 mm., with the writing-space (ruled in red ink) measuring approximately 146 × 221 mm. From the almost complete reliance on the comma, and the corresponding absence of virgule-punctuation, the manuscript would appear to date from the middle, rather than from the earlier part, of the sixteenth century. This manuscript will hereafter be designated by the symbol *L*.

Printed Texts

III. *A dialoge of comfort against tribulacion, made by Syr Thomas More Knight, and set foorth by the name of an Hungarien, not before this time imprinted. Londini in aedibus Richard di Totteli. Cum Privilegio ad imprimendum solum.* Colophon: "Imprinted at London in fletestrete within Temple barre at the signe of the hand & starre by Richarde Tottel ye xviii. day of Nouembre in ye yere of our lord. 1553. Cum priuilegio ad imprimendum solum." First edition, quarto in 8s. *STC*. 18082.[2] Referred to hereafter as *1553*.

IV. *The workes of Sir Thomas More Knight . . . Printed at London at the costes and charges of Iohn Cawood, Iohn Waly, and Richarde Tottell. Anno. 1557. A dyalogue of comforte* occupies sigs. CC₆–LL₄ (pages 1139–1264). Edition

---

(New Haven, 1976), *13*. Cited hereafter as "*CW 13*." Full titles of all works frequently cited in this Introduction will be found in the Bibliography preceding the Commentary.

[1] At first glance one might conclude that *A Dialogue of Comfort* and the English *Treatise on the Passion* were written in the same hand, for they are indeed remarkably similar. But close examination indicates that they can hardly be the work of the same scribe. The *Treatise on the Passion* is almost entirely punctuated with the virgule, whereas the *Dialogue* relies almost entirely upon the comma—even at the ends of paragraphs. The characteristic formation of certain letters is different: e.g., small "d" and capital "I." In the *Treatise on the Passion* individual paragraphs are usually begun with a word or two in large, broad lettering, but this is not so in the *Dialogue*. Finally, the *Treatise on the Passion* is not ruled off into a writing-space.

[2] Cf. R. W. Gibson and J. Max Patrick, *St. Thomas More: A Preliminary Bibliography of His Work and of Moreana to the Year 1750* (New Haven, 1961), no. 51. Cited hereafter as "Gibson."

sponsored by William Rastell. *STC.* 18076. Gibson, no. 73. Referred to
hereafter as *1557*.[1]

V. *A Dialogve of Cumfort against Tribulation, made by the right Vertuous, Wise
and Learned man, Sir Thomas More . . . Now newly set foorth, with many places
restored and corrected by conference of sundrie Copies . . . Antverpiae, Apud
Iohannem Foulerum, Anglum. M. D. LXXIII.* Octavo. *STC.* 18083. Gibson,
no. 52. Referred to hereafter as *1573*.

Only the first four of these potential sources prove to be of value in a
study of the text: the collations show that Fowler for *1573* has simply
compared the two previously printed texts. His statement on the title-page
(repeated in his dedication) that he has made a "conference of sundrie
Copies" has led to the conjecture that Fowler may have used manuscripts.
Since he was married to the daughter of John Harris, More's secretary, and
Dorothy Colley, Margaret Roper's maid, and since it is known that Harris
had a collection of More's writings in manuscript,[2] there would be strong
reason to believe that Fowler might have had access to manuscripts de-
riving from More or the More family. Nevertheless, the collations make it
plain that Fowler based his text upon *1553*, with frequent adoption of
readings from *1557*, and frequent changes of his own, none of them
requiring manuscript authority. The edition of *1573* has therefore no
claim to textual authority, and it will not play a significant part in the
subsequent discussion. Aside from its admirably clear printing and the
handiness of its octavo format, the main importance of Fowler's edition
lies in its dedication and preface, which have a literary and historical
value of their own, and in the marginal notes, which often give lively
polemical comment and which also provide helpful clues to More's
biblical and other references. These materials have therefore been reproduced in Appendix A, Part III, and in Appendix B.

2. The Corpus Christi Manuscript:
Dating and Provenance

The dating and provenance of the Corpus Christi manuscript (*CC*)
present complicated problems. Joseph Delcourt, who in 1914 gave a brief,
but in some ways astute, description of *CC*, concluded that it was anterior
to all the editions and to the British Library manuscript (*L*), on the basis
of a few examples of the kind of evidence that will be set forth here in

---

[1] That is, when this edition is being considered from a textual point of view. In other
contexts it will be cited as "*EW.*"

[2] See the Introduction to *The History of King Richard III*, ed. Richard S. Sylvester, *The
Yale Edition of the Complete Works of St. Thomas More* (New Haven, 1963), 2, xlviii–xlix.
Cited hereafter as "*CW 2.*"

greater detail.[1] But, wishing to bring the manuscript as close to More as possible, he theorized that both the original text of scribe A and the additions of scribe B might have been dictated by More himself—dictated, because both hands are clearly scribal, not holograph. In support of this theory Delcourt reports Falconer Madan's opinion,[2] based on the handwriting, that CC dates from the second quarter of the sixteenth century. Madan's dating is right, as the subsequent evidence will show, but Delcourt's theory of dictation cannot be sustained. One objection is that both hands A and B give every evidence that they are copying from prior manuscripts; and in any case the watermarks make a dating from More's lifetime impossible. The paper of the text bears the watermark of C. Pinette, Briquet 8518, a paper of Troyes which made its earliest recorded appearance in 1546, and was widely current in the 1550s, especially in the Low Countries.[3] Both pastedowns of the binding show a watermark of the arms of the city of Troyes, related to Briquet 1048–54, and indicating paper current between 1524 and 1549. It seems, then, that the manuscript and its binding are not widely separated in time.

The binding is of the utmost importance in suggesting the provenance of the volume, particularly because of the initials GP stamped on both covers. A clue to the identity of GP is found at the top of the front pastedown, where an inscription has been nearly erased; Delcourt shrewdly deciphered this to read, possibly, "Liber Galfredi (?) Pe (?)."[4] The last name is unfortunately cut short because the pastedowns have been cut off about 60 mm. from the spine. But the ultra-violet machine shows the inscription to be: "Liber Galfredi Po." Could this be Sir Geoffrey Pole (d. 1558), the recusant brother of Cardinal Pole, who suffered imprisonment and threats of torture under Henry VIII? There is evidence that Sir Geoffrey Pole was collecting More's manuscripts, for in 1530 he possessed a manuscript of More's *History of King Richard III*, which he lent to George Croftes.[5] He also possessed at least one printed book by More, for a copy of More's *Answer to the first part of a poysened book* (1534) in the Oscott College library bears the following inscription on its title page: "Sū liber gulielmi Dawkey ex dono galfridi pooli militis."[6]

---

[1] Joseph Delcourt, *Essai sur la langue de Sir Thomas More* (Paris, 1914), pp. 372–76. Cited hereafter as "Delcourt."

[2] *Ibid.*, p. 376.

[3] Charles M. Briquet, *Les Filigranes: Dictionnaire Historique des Marques du Papier*, 4 vols., Geneva, 1907 (facsimile, ed. Allan Stevenson, "with Supplementary Material," 4 vols., Amsterdam, 1968).

[4] Delcourt, p. 372.

[5] See *CW 2*, xxvii.

[6] This information has been provided by Dr. David Rogers, who was the first to suggest that the initials GP might represent Sir Geoffrey Pole.

The name of Sir Geoffrey Pole also becomes significant in view of an inscription that appears in the middle of the front pastedown: "Liber C.C.C. ex dono Edmundi Orson qui eiusdem collegij quondam in artibus magistri." Orson is identified in *Alumni Oxonienses*: "Orson, Edmund, of co. Lincoln, pleb. Corpus Christi Coll., matric. 10 July, 1593, aged 17; B.A. 1 Feb., 1594–5, M.A. 26 June, 1598, rector of North Marden, Sussex, 1607."[1] The publications of the Sussex Record Society further inform us that on May 8, 1603, Edmund Orson, then vicar of Eastmarden, Sussex, married Elizabeth Purslowe, daughter of Francis Purslowe, rector of Trotton, Sussex.[2] Now it is a remarkable coincidence that the villages of Eastmarden and Northmarden lie, respectively, three and four miles north of Lordington, the home of Sir Geoffrey Pole, who in 1558 was buried nearby in Stoughton Church. Trotton, the home of Orson's wife, lies about four miles north of the Mardens; since she came from this region, the manuscript could have reached Orson through his wife.

Another name is written in an Elizabethan hand on the back pastedown: "Elyne Henslowe."[3] This is a strong clue, since Ellen Henslow, daughter of Ralph Henslow, from Hampshire, became the wife of John Fortescue, grandson of Sir Geoffrey Pole and son of Sir Anthony Fortescue and Katherine Pole, daughter of Sir Geoffrey.[4] But "Elyne" has signed her maiden name; thus the manuscript could not have descended to her directly from Sir Geoffrey, through the Fortescues, but somehow reached her before her marriage to John Fortescue. Significant light is cast on this problem by the will of Sir Geoffrey Pole's widow, Dame Constance (d. 1570), which designates "Rawffe Henslowe" as one of the two overseers named to assist her son Thomas in his function as executor:

> All the Resydewe of my goodes not given and bequeathed I give vnto Thomas Poole my Sonne whome I make my sole Executor of this my laste wyll and Testamente he to doe for me as shalbe thowghte good by hym for the moste profytte he maye devyse for my Sowle . . . And I do ordayne and make for the comforte of my sayde Executor for his better advyse in performing my wyll my welbeloved Cosen

---

[1] Joseph Foster, *Alumni Oxonienses: the Members of the University of Oxford, 1500–1714*, 4 vols. (Oxford, 1891–92), *3*, 1092.

[2] *Sussex Record Society*, *9* (1909), 31.

[3] Delcourt (p. 372) read the first name as "Elyce (?)"; this reading is possible, though unlikely.

[4] See Marquis of Ruvigny and Raineval, *The Plantagenet Roll of the Blood Royal* (London, 1905), Table LXVI; and Thomas Fortescue, Lord Clermont, *Sir John Fortescue, Knight, His Life, Works, and Family History*, 2 vols. (London, 1869), *2*, 310. Clermont here identifies Ralph Henslow as living in "Barrald, in Hampshire," but "Barrald" must be a misreading of one of the several variant spellings of "Boarhunt" in the sixteenth century, such as "Barrant" or "Burrunt."

> Henrye Marvyn Esquyer and my Frende Rawffe Henslowe gent
> Overseers . . . [1]

Ralph Henslow must have been a close and trusted friend of the Pole family. He was a prosperous landowner who held the manor of West Boarhunt (Westburhant), Hampshire, only about eleven miles across the county border from the seat of the Pole family at Lordington.[2] From the family monument in the church at Boarhunt, it appears that Ralph Henslow died in 1577 and that he had two wives, one of whom was a member of the Pole (Poole) family. These, at least, are the conclusions to be drawn from the description of this monument in the *Victoria History*:

> Against the north wall of the chancel is set a monument dated 1577, with no inscription except the initials C P, R H, and K P of the persons commemorated.
> The upper part has three panels surmounted by a flat cornice on which are three pediments, one of rounded form between two which are angular . . . the panels below are divided from each other by Corinthian columns carrying an architrave, on which over the columns is the date 1577, one figure over each column, and over the panels the initials already noted. In the panels are shields, as follows:—
> Under C P, the arms of Pound . . . under R H, the arms of Henslow . . . and under K P, the arms of Poole, Party or and sable a saltire engrailed counterchanged. The central shield is that of Ralph Henslow . . . [3]

---

[1] Prerogative Court of Canterbury, 28 Lyon: Public Record Office, vol. Prob. 11/52, fol. 193. The will was made on August 12, 1570, and registered in probate on September 20, 1570.

[2] For an excellent account of Boarhunt, the manor of West Boarhunt, and the significance of Ralph Henslow (or Henslowe) in the community, see *The Victoria History of Hampshire and the Isle of Wight*, ed. H. Arthur Doubleday and William Page, 6 vols. (London, 1900–14), *3*, 144–47: "After the Dissolution the manor of West Boarhunt was granted to Thomas Wriothesley, earl of Southampton, in order that he might alienate it to Ralph Henslowe" (p. 145).

[3] *Ibid.*, p. 147. The account goes on to say that Ralph Henslow "married a sister of John White, the grantee of Southwick Priory," but this must be an error, unless Ralph had a third wife, not entered on the monument. The *Victoria History* (*ibid.*, p. 346) says that Ralph Henslow died in 1578, a date not hard to reconcile with the 1577 on the monument. Additional evidence of Henslow's prominence in the region is found in the fact that in 1555 (and again in 1570) he was granted the lease of the rectory at Burpham (Burgham), Sussex, near Arundel; see *Sussex Record Society, 58* (1959) nos. 545, 749 (pp. 25, 74). The Henslow family had strong Roman Catholic affiliations. Stephen Henslow, of West Boarhunt, was removed from his fellowship at New College, Oxford, in 1566, on the grounds of "papistical heresy" (see Hastings Rashdall and Robert S. Rait, *New College*, London, 1901, pp. 118–19; and Foster, *Alumni Oxonienses, 2*, 694, where Stephen is identified as coming from "West Burrant," wrongly interpreted by Foster to mean "Westbourne").

The description of the Poole shield here is almost exactly that of the arms of the Pole family at Lordington: "Party sable and or a chevron engrailed counterchanged."[1] The exact identity of K (Katherine?) Poole remains uncertain.[2] The other wife, however, was certainly named Clare Pound, from a family prominent in the nearby parish of Farlington.[3] Thus it seems that the manuscript passed from Geoffrey or Constance or Thomas Pole to their friend Ralph Henslow, and from Ralph to his daughter Ellen, and then, perhaps through some intermediary, to the neighboring clergyman, Edmund Orson, who gave it to Corpus Christi College, probably during the first half of the seventeenth century.[4]

Sir Geoffrey Pole, after being broken under threat of torture, went abroad in 1541 and ultimately settled in Liège. William Rastell and his wife, along with John Clement and his wife, were living in exile in Louvain during the latter half of the reign of Edward VI. There can be little doubt

Ralph's son Thomas and the son's wife are both listed as recusants in the rolls for 1592/93 (see *Publications of the Catholic Record Society*, *18* [1916], 279, 290, 334; also *idem*, *57* [1965], 174, 179, where Thomas Henslow is associated with "Thomas Pownde," also a recusant).

[1] See *The Victoria History of the County of Sussex*, ed. William Page and L. F. Salzman, 9 vols. (London, 1905–53), *4*, 116.

[2] Katherine was a common name in the Pole family. Sir Geoffrey's brother Henry (Lord Montague) had a daughter named Katherine, who married the second earl of Huntingdon and is buried with him at Ashby-de-la-Zouch. Sir Anthony Fortescue, husband of Sir Geoffrey's daughter Katherine, was still living as late as 1608 or 1611. The only other candidate that appears in the genealogical tables is a daughter of the Thomas Pole for whom Ralph Henslow was named overseer in Dame Constance Pole's will. There would have been a great difference in ages, but it is not unlikely that, after the death of his first wife, Ralph Henslow could have married a woman many years younger than he. See next footnote.

[3] Her first name and further evidence of her family's name appear in a record of 1559 that states her claim to several properties near Littlehampton, Sussex, particularly in West Preston, Kingston, and Wick. She is here described as "Clare Henslow, wife of Ralph Henslow, esq.," with the legal details following: "and as to manor of Wyke remainder to Thomas Pound and heirs of his body, remainder to Richard Pound and heirs of his body, remainder to said Clare and heirs of her body, remainder to right heirs of William Pound." *Sussex Record Society*, *20* (1915), 484–85.

[4] One may be struck by the similarity of the names "Henslowe" and "Purslowe." It may seem conceivable that some parish clerk, copying off the record of Edmund Orson's marriage, misread "Hen" as "Pur" or "Per." But the ms. Diary (1601–13) in which Orson's marriage is entered, now in the West Sussex Record Office (STC III/E, fol. 33ᵛ), clearly reads "Elizabetham Purslowe," and the father's name, twice mentioned, is spelled "Purslowe" and "Purslow." Mrs. Patricia Gill, Archivist of the West Sussex Record Office, has supplied a copy of this record, along with the information that "no bonds or affidavits have survived before 1605." Evidence of a connection between the Purslowe family and the family of Sir Geoffrey Pole may be found in the fact that on November 24, 1599, Nicholas Diggons, vicar of Stoughton (where Sir Geoffrey was buried), was married to Mary Purslowe of Trotton—presumably a sister of Orson's wife (*Sussex Record Society*, *9*, [1909], 26).

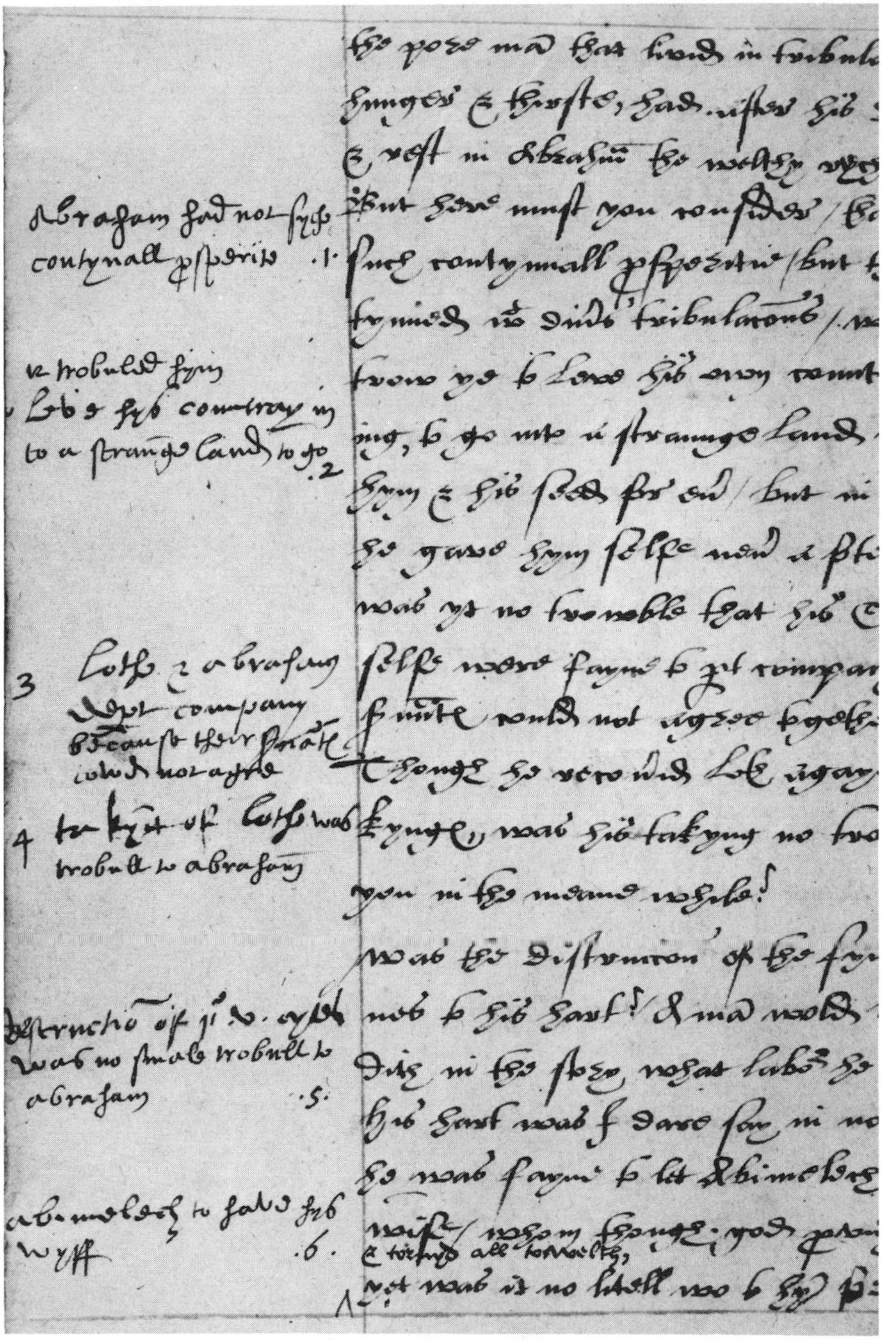

PLATE II. Corpus Christi College MS: fol. 42^{v} (detail: reduced)

that Pole would have been in touch with these close friends and relatives of Thomas More, at that time, if not earlier. Considerable evidence, set forth below, suggests a close association between *CC* and the text of this work as it appears in Rastell's folio of 1557. Rastell says, in his dedication of the folio, that he had, before the reign of Mary, been collecting More's English works, published and unpublished, for the purpose of making this collected edition. It is possible that Pole may have lent this manuscript to Rastell for editing; or Rastell may have given it to Pole after it had served Rastell's own purposes.

The latter possibility seems the more likely, in view of certain aspects of the marginalia in *CC*. The marginalia are written in several hands, with broad pens and sharp pens, in faint ink and dark ink, in large, sprawling script and in small, neat script—all intermingled in a way that suggests several different readers at work over a considerable period of time. But at least three hands can be distinguished. Hand *E* is neat and small, usually making brief notes. *E* is of special importance because he has also corrected the text in a few places, at some time before the extensive revision of *B*: for the corrections of *E* are cancelled and emended by *B* in two significant places.[1] Hand *F* is usually large and sprawling; he is also an early annotator, who seems to have made his remarks before the revision of *B*, since in a few places he seems to be following the unrevised text of *A*.[2] Strong proof of the priority of *F* is found in at least fifteen places where the brief notes of *F* have been incorporated within the longer notes of hand *G*, whose writing is fairly neat and usually of moderate size.[3]

---

[1] See textual notes and Commentary for 130/15, and textual notes for 130/18. It should be noted that the identification of hand *E* is sometimes precarious, since his corrections of the text occasionally consist of a brief word, a few letters, or even a single letter. In some cases all one can say with certainty is that the hand (from the color of ink and the letter formation) does not look like that of *B*. The symbol *E* might best be regarded as indicating changes in the text made by some person or persons other than *B*.

[2] The clearest instance occurs at 24/10, where the marginal note follows the reading "profit" (*A*), instead of "profe" (*B*). See also 14/15, 17/29, 25/18, 85/20.

[3] See Appendix A, Part I, where angle brackets denote hand *F* in composite marginalia found at 26/24, 54/9, 13, 15, 17, 20, 26; 55/1, 108/16, 18; 109/19, 130/4, 166/18, 169/18. In the reproduction here of fol. 42ᵛ (54/4–22) one can see three, perhaps four, stages of marginalia. The larger writing, also distinguishable by lighter ink, is that of *F*; nearly all other writing is that of *G*. One exception occurs in the marginal note numbered 5, where, at the beginning, a third hand has written "de" over "e" to replace an original "d" clipped off in the process of binding (only one other clear instance of such a late emendation is found: at 150/14 [fol. 112ᵛ], where an opening "d" has been clipped off, the remaining "ull" is cancelled and "dull" written above). A more important exception occurs in the numerals, which appear to be the work of a late hand, inserting numbers in vacant spaces after the other marginalia have been completed. The numbers in *CC* (fols. 42ᵛ, 43) run from 1 through 9 and are made according to the marginalia; they thus do not agree with the numbers found in all the other texts, which run from 1 through 8. In the printed texts the

Hand *G* is the most copious writer of the marginalia. It is clear that *G* is writing after *B* has performed his revision, for the notes of *G* are sometimes derived from the corrected version of *B*.[1] Since the notes of *G* (as well as *F*) are frequently clipped as the result of binding, it would appear that the binding occurred at a relatively late stage in the transmission of the manuscript.[2]

Finally, after the volume had received its present binding, someone cut out folios 8 and 9, containing all of More's second chapter: "That for a foundacion men must needs begyn with fayth"—a chapter which appears in all the other texts. The stubs are still in the binding, and the chapter-heading remains at the bottom of folio 7ᵛ. The most likely reason that one can conjecture for such an excision is that GP or a later reader found the chapter objectionable, perhaps even dangerous, on theological grounds, for it may have seemed to give an undue emphasis to the doctrine of faith, and thus to play into the reformers' hands. The worry is of course completely unwarranted, for More is placing faith as a "foundacion," not as a sole necessity for salvation. It would appear that only someone of extremely orthodox affiliation would have made such an excision. Sir Geoffrey Pole was such a person. It may seem rather unlikely that the excision would have been made after the chapter had already appeared in print, but an extremely sensitive person might of course have removed the chapter at any time—though presumably not after the manuscript had been given to Corpus Christi College.[3]

3. The Corpus Christi Manuscript: Priority and Authority of the *A* Text

The strongest single piece of evidence for the priority of the *A* text is found in one passage that does not occur in the body of any of the other texts, although *1557* prints it in the form of two marginal notes. It is found at 246/31–32, where the following words are written by *A* and cancelled by *B*: "Romanus that shuld haue bene beheddid as Eusebius tellith /

---

numbers occur at the beginnings of separate paragraphs. In *L* the numbers 1 through 8 were written in the margin, although 3 and 4 no longer appear, since the edge of the page where they must have been written has been torn away.

[1] See the example represented in Plate VII (fol. 145), where the words "trouth of fayth" and "trouth of Iustice" in the margin are clearly derived from the long interlineation of *B*. For other examples see 21/5, 36/11, 143/28, 198/29, 293/12.

[2] A striking proof of this point is found on fol. 187 (281/23), where the marginal note "the affection of the mynd" accords with the elaborate revision by *B*; the final "d" of this note is partly clipped. On the same folio, at 282/2, the marginal note by *G* has the plural "affections," following *B*, and the word "men" in this note has the "en" clipped off.

[3] In the present edition this excised portion (12/8–14/12) has been supplied from *1557*.

as he found the S. John the evangelist, which let his clothe fall
fro him/ wherevppon they caught hold, & so fled hym selfe
naked away & escaped fro them/ or though they hold hym &
bryng hym to prison/ yet god sometyme delyuereth them thens.
as he did saynt Peter/ And sometyme he taketh them to hym
out of the prison into heven, & suffreth them not to come to
their turment at all/ as he hath done by many a good holy man/
And some he suffreth to be brought into the tourmentes and yet
suffreth them not to dye therin, but lyve many yeres after
and dye their naturall deth/ as he did by ~~Romanus that shuld~~
~~have bene beheded as Eusebius telleth/~~ Blondina & apud S
~~Cipr quidam & relictus pro mortuus~~/ Saynt John the evangelist
& by many a nother mo/ as we may well see both by sundry
storyes & in the pistles of S. Cypriane also/
And therfor which way god will take wt vs, we can not tell/

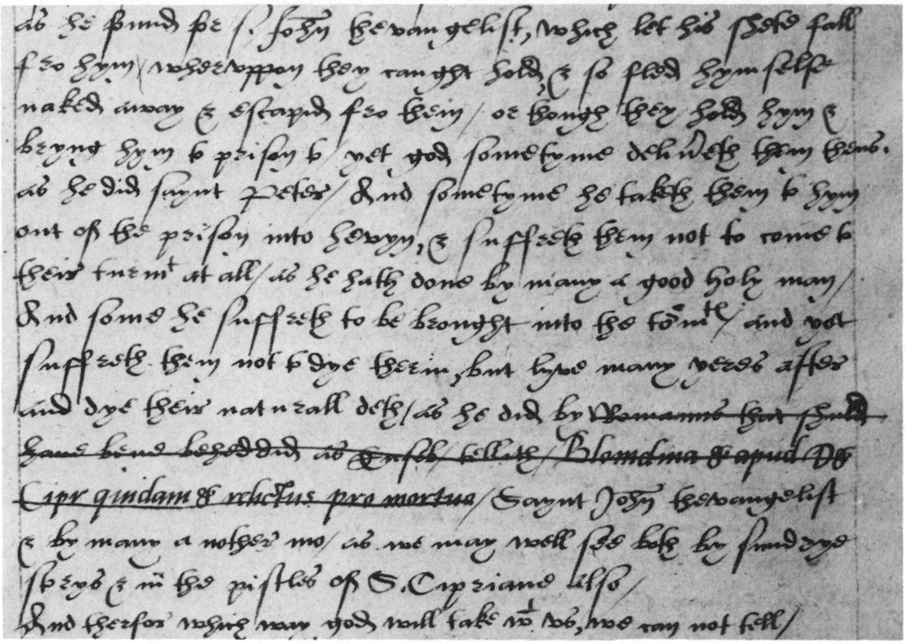

A. Corpus Christi College MS: fol. 169ᵛ (detail: reduced)

B. More's *Workes* (1557), p. 1235, col. 2 (detail: reduced)

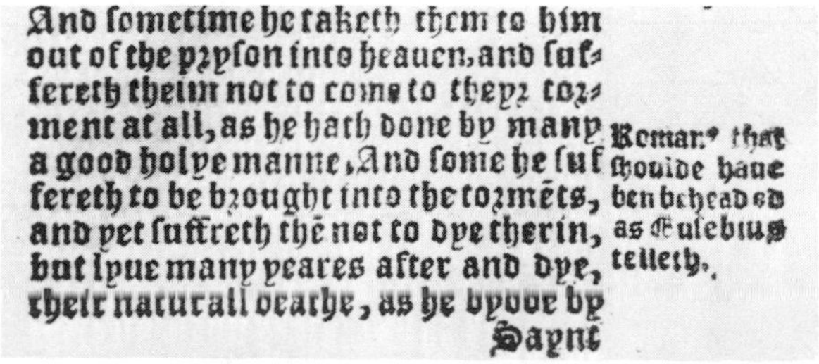

And sometime he taketh them to him
out of the pryson into heauen, and suffereth theim not to come to theyr torment at all, as he hath done by many
a good holye manne, And some he suf
fereth to be brought into the tormẽts,
and yet suffreth thẽ not to dye therin,
but lyue many yeares after and dye,
their naturall deathe, as he dydde by
Saynt

Roman.* that shoulde haue ben beheaded as Eusebius telleth.

C. More's *Workes* (1557), p. 1236, col. 1 (detail: reduced)

1236 The thirde booke o

A Sainte John the Euaungelyste, and
by manye a nother moe, as wee maye
wel see both by sundrye storyes, and
in the pistles of Saint Cipriane also.
And therfore which way God wyll
take with vs, we can not tel. But sure
ly if we be true Christen menne, thys
can we wel tel, that without any bold
warrauntise of our selfe, or foolyshe
truste in oure owne strengthe, we be
bounden vpon paine of dampnacion,
that we be not of the contrary minde,

Blondina, & apud S Cipr. quidam relictus pro mortuo.

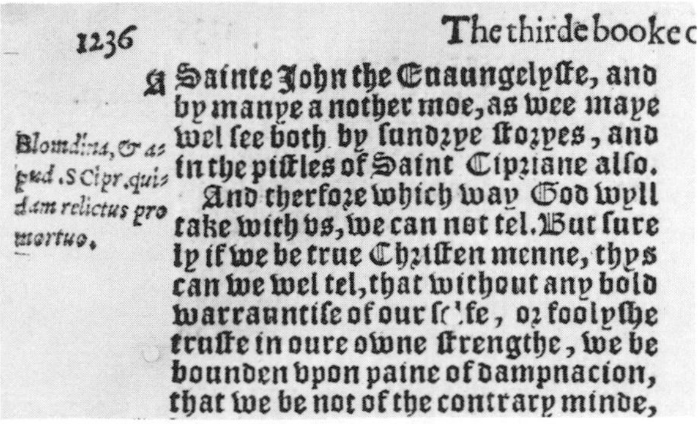

PLATE III. Romanus and "Blonidina": the cancelled passage

Blonidina & apud Divus Ciprianus quidam & relictus pro mortuo."[1] Scribe *A* has written the part about Romanus in his normal cursive hand, but he has written the rest in the italic reserved for Latin. It would appear from this that the part in cursive script was intended to form a regular part of the text; but the remainder looks like a note that More wrote to suggest the possible inclusion of other examples. More wrote exactly this kind of cryptic note in Latin at the bottom of half a dozen pages in the Valencia holograph of the *De Tristitia;* these are, Clarence Miller says, "jottings" that More made as suggestions to himself.[2] Notes in Latin are also found at three points in the British Library manuscript of the English *Treatise on the Passion,* giving directions for the addition of biblical and patrological materials.[3] Whether these are More's own notes we do not know, but the additions are certainly part of his plan.

In any case the part written here in italic could not have been designed in its present form for More's text; this cryptic Latin could play no part in a conversation between Antony and Vincent. What we have here seems to be a brief glimpse into a text that underlies the *A* text: a tantalizing glimpse of something in More's holograph. Rastell printed the cancelled passage in the form of marginal notes in *1557.* Where did he find it? The peculiar correlation suggests that he may have had this very manuscript before his eyes.[4]

Other evidence strongly indicates the closeness of the *A* text to More's holograph. In eighteen places scribe *A* has left blank spaces in the manuscript. Ten of these seem to indicate a word or words that the scribe could not decipher in the manuscript from which he was copying. Four others allow blank spaces for precise biblical references. Two others allow space for biblical quotations.[5] And two more are caused by uncertain allusions to saints. All but four of these have been filled in by other hands, usually by *B.*

At 71/22 the word "those" has been supplied by *B* to fill a blank. At 82/19 *B* has written εὐτραπελϊα in the blank space (with modern accents, εὐτραπελία). At 94/1 *B* has written "austere" in the space, while at 123/11

---

[1] Abbreviations expanded: see reproduction here, and textual notes and Commentary for 246/28–32.

[2] *De Tristitia Christi,* ed. Clarence Miller, *The Yale Edition of the Complete Works of St. Thomas More* (New Haven, 1976), *14,* Introduction, pp. 748–51. The jottings occur on folios [A1], [A1ᵛ], 13ᵛ–15, 23ᵛ, 29, and 116 of the Valencia manuscript.

[3] See Ms. Royal 17 D. XIV (*L*), fols. 302ᵛ, 314, 314ᵛ.

[4] This conjecture is strengthened by the reading "Blomdina" in *1557;* unless one notices the rather faint dot after the third minim in *A,* one could easily read "Blonidina" in this way, as the reproduction here shows.

[5] More left blank spaces for such additions in four places of the Valencia holograph: see *CW 14,* 263/10, 265/6, 513/5, 565/3–5.

B has written "sybbe." At 130/15 *A* has written "a fry," with space left
for about four more letters; the combined efforts of marginal hand *E* and
of *B* have resulted in the interlineation "Afryque" by *B* (see Commentary).
At 140/2 the word "kynde" has been supplied by *B*. At 143/27 the word
"Carvers" has been supplied, probably by *B*, possibly by marginal hand
E. At 146/12 space for about seven letters has been allowed after "Here
must the"; *B* has simply altered "the" to "they" and has drawn a line
across the rest of the space; but from the size of the space it looks as though
scribe *A* has seen some other word or words that he could not read. At
239/22, 24 two blank spaces have both been filled in with the word
"mothe" by *B*.[1]

    At 62/24 two blank spaces are filled in by *B* to read: "the ⌜.x.ᵗʰ⌝ chapiter
of the ⌜first⌝ boke."[2] At 70/1 the name "s. paule" is written by *B* in the
blank space. At 97/17–18 space amounting to an entire line is left for a
Latin quotation from the Bible, before the English version (see the
Frontispiece, fol. 79); *B* fills in the words in italic, "*Misericordia domini
super omnia opera eius,*" and then draws lines through the remaining space.
At 102/14 scribe *A* evidently expected a longer quotation than "*deprehendere
omnes artes,*" and so left the remaining three-fifths of the line blank before
continuing with the English version. At 104/6 a blank space of six or seven
letters is left for filling in an exact reference to a passage from Matthew; *B*
writes "the" in the first half of the space and interlineates "chapiter," but
the exact reference is still left blank (it remains blank in *L*, but is filled in
by *1553* and *1557*: "the .xxiii. Chapter"). Finally, at 181/14–16 two blank
spaces appear in a complicated passage that seems to reflect something in
the holograph that baffled the scribe; it involves a confusing series of
references to Augustine (or Paul) and Christ (see textual notes and Commentary). The other texts, in resolving these eighteen blanks, nearly always
use the same words and references as those supplied in *CC*. The only
significant exceptions occur in *L*, and these are very few in number.[3]

    These blank spaces, then, lead to two important conclusions. First, *A* is
a scribe so scrupulous that he does not wish to venture upon guesses.

---

[1] At 42/26 the use of italic for the word "puncto" makes it hard to be absolutely sure
about the hand, but, from the crowding of the letters and the lack of slant in the writing,
this also appears to be a word filled in by *B*.
[2] Here, and throughout the text of this edition, half-brackets indicate words added by *B*
(except for a very few cases where the textual footnote indicates an addition by *E*).
Throughout the Introduction, however, these half-brackets have been omitted in quotations, except in a few places where they are especially relevant to the discussion.
[3] At 71/22 *L* reads "these" instead of "those"; at 140/2 *L* omits the phrase "kynde of";
at 181/14 the name of the saint is also left blank in *L*. At 62/24 an unusual situation is
found: the two precise biblical references, filled in by *B*, are left blank by *L*.

Secondly, taken together with the passage about Romanus and "Bloni-dina," these spaces serve to suggest that the *A* text is closer to More's holograph than any other text. Is the *A* text a copy made directly from the holograph? The blank spaces would argue strongly that it is. Furthermore, although the copy has been carefully and neatly made throughout, there are a sufficient number of slips and false starts to indicate that scribe *A* is copying from a manuscript that is not always clear. This is especially true in the last quarter of *CC*, where scribe *A* makes a greater proportion of errors than elsewhere. This is not because he is writing less carefully; on the contrary the writing is particularly neat, since in the latter half of *CC* the scribe has reduced the size of his writing in order to save space, especially from folio 144 to the end. It seems likely that More himself was writing more hastily, or in a hand that was for some reason less clear, toward the end of the work, with the result that the copyist had more difficulty in his task.

For the priority of the *A* text, in relation to the other texts, further evidence can be found. One important strand of evidence lies in significant individual words that are unique in *A* (or, in one important case, found also in *L*), and that have a strong ring of authenticity, in their context. One example is found in the climactic word "vnkyndnes" in the following passage (8/8–15):

> Howbeyt yf the prynces of Cristendome euery where about, wold where as nede was haue set to their handes in tyme, the Turk had neuer taken any one place of all thes places / but partly dyscencions fallen among our selfes, partly that noman carith what harm other folke felc, but cch part suffer other to shifte for yt selfe / The Turke is in few yeres wonderfully encreasid, & cristendome on the other side very sore decayid / And all this worketh our vnkyndnes, with which god ys not content.

The word is not changed by *B*, but all other texts read "wickednes." Yet "vnkyndnes," in the old sense of "unnatural behavior," is quite appropriate here, and entirely in accord with More's use of the same word in other places of this work (48/16, 244/8, 278/9). A marginal commentator in *CC* finds the word so important that he writes it in the margin. The reading "wickednes" may well represent a scribal error.

Three of the best examples of this kind occur, along with other interesting readings, in the following passage of *A*, where Antony is describing his illness in advanced old age (85/19–86/4):

> For surely Cosyn I can not liken my selfe more metely now than to the snofe of a candell that burneth with in the candell styk nose / for as

that snofe burneth down so low / that who that loketh on it, wold
wene it were quyte owt / And yet sodenly lyfteth a leme halfe an Inch
aboue the nose, & giveth a praty short light agayne / and thus playeth
diuers tymes till at last or it be lokyd for out it goeth all together / so
haue I cosyn dyuers such dayes together / as euery day of them I loke
evyn for to dye / And yet haue I than after that some such few dayes
agayne / as you see me now haue your selfe / in which a man wold
wene that I might yt ⌜well⌝ contynew. But I know my lingryng not
likly to last long / but out will my sowle sodenly some day within a
while.

The textual notes for these lines show a surprising number of variants
here, none of them necessary, one certainly wrong, others probably wrong,
and all adding up to a marked diminution of the colloquial effect. Near
the beginning "selfe" ("I can not liken my selfe") is not changed by *B*,
but is changed to "lyfe" in all other texts, apparently in an effort to make
the comparison more strictly logical. Near the end of the passage "sowle"
("out will my sowle") is cancelled by marginal hand *E* and also by *B*, with
"snuff" interlineated by *E* and approved with clarifying strokes by *B*; all
other texts agree with this revision, which is also apparently made to carry
out the consistency of the simile. But "sowle" seems more richly consistent
with the context; for "out will my sowle" says that his life ("lingryng") on
earth will end with the release of his soul. This is the kind of quick and
witty shift of meaning that is characteristic of More. It seems unlikely that
scribe *A* could have mistaken "snuff" or "snofe" for "sowle."

But most significant of all is the reading "leme," also preserved by *L*
("leame"), and not changed by *B*. This is the Middle English word for
"light, flame; a flash, ray, or gleam of light" (*OED*, "leam," *sb.*[1]). The
printed texts all change this to "flame," evidently a modernizing substitution for a word that was passing out of general use by 1550. But "leme"
must be More's word, the word of a man whose basic habits of speech were
formed before 1500, the precise word for this context.

Similarly, the old-fashioned "or" (not changed by *B*) is changed to
modern "ere," in *L* as well as in the printed texts. Other changes include
the possessive "candelstyckes" in the printed texts; "the snuffe" for "that
snofe"; the addition of "some time" before "burneth"; "who so" for "who
that" (evidently to avoid the repetition of "that"), in all other texts; and
the change of "now haue" to the more formal "now to haue" in *L* and
1553. Meanwhile the crisp alliterative phrase "lyfteth a leme" is further
changed in *1557* by the addition of "vp" to read: "lifteth vp a flame." It
is important to notice that *B* has made only one of all these substantive
changes. Aside from accepting the alteration of "sowle" to "snuff," *B* has
been content to clarify the word "now" by writing a "w" over a wrong or

poorly-formed letter, to modernize the spelling of "snofe" to "snuff," to add an enhancing "well," to clarify the meaning of "yt" by emending to "yet" (see Commentary for 86/2), and to add punctuation.[1]

In other cases of unique readings in *A* the variations in the other texts may have a plausible claim to validity, as in the following passage, dealing with the threat of the Great Turk, where *A* reads thus: "And yet which we more feare than all the remenant, no small part of our own folke that dwell even here about vs, are (as we here) fallen to hym, or all redy confeteryd with hym /" (7/1–3). No words are changed by *B*, but in all other texts the passage "are (as we here) fallen" reads "are (as we feare) falling." The phrase "as we here [hear]" is appropriate to the context of rumor in which the words are spoken, though one might argue that "here" is a corrupt reading caused by the word "here" six words earlier; or one might argue that the variant reading "feare" is influenced by the occurrence of that word at the outset of the passage. The words "all ready" may be taken to justify a change to the present participle: "falling" for "fallen"; unless we take Vincent to be making a distinction between those who have gone over completely to the Turk's sect, and those who have simply agreed to accept the Turk's rule, while remaining nominal Christians. The readings of *A*, unquestioned by *B*, seem strong enough to be authentic.

A few additional examples of major substantive readings unique to *A* (chosen from among 228 such examples) are listed here, with the hope that the reader will wish to examine them closely in their context. All of the following are defensible as authentic readings, though the variants in the other texts are always plausible (the symbol *B* indicates that *B* has changed the word, while Z indicates agreement of all the other texts):

1/2	very *A* : sory *B* Z (see Commentary)[2]
27/28	paciently *A* : mekely Z
48/5	pleasure *A* : prosperitie Z
48/22	shewith *A* : sendyth *B* Z
50/4	further *A* : furnysh *B* Z (see Commentary)
63/10	sower *A* : sowce *B* Z (see Commentary)
76/30	goodnes *A* : good will *B* Z
101/31	seeth *A* : feleth Z

---

[1] While this passage is under scrutiny it may be useful to describe the punctuation. *B* adds two commas, which are not needed; two virgules, one after "agayne" and another after "yourselfe," neither of which is strictly needed, though both provide appropriate pauses; and two periods, both at places where *A* comes to the end of a line. The first period is well-placed, but the second forces somewhat too strong a stop: *A* continues with "and therfor." The punctuation is typical of the sensible but excessive punctuation provided by *B* throughout *CC*.

[2] Spelling variants in the four other texts are not recorded in this list.

109/22	rehersid *A*: remembryd *B Z*
118/8	husband *A*: good man *B Z*
128/13	fede *A*: fode *Z* (see Commentary)
143/23	depe *A*: dead *Z*
148/20	wayes *A*: meanes *Z*
150/20	maliciouse *A*: melancolyous *B Z* (see Commentary)
150/27–28	concience *A*: conflyct *B Z*
185/3	possessing *A*: dysposing *Z*
198/29	conserue *A*: confyrme *B Z*
204/17	swarve *A*: fal *Z*
206/5	substance *A*: sustenaunce *Z*
237/1	very *A*: fyry *B Z*
281/7	fele *A*: fynde *B Z*
281/23	menys myndes *A*: the mynde *B Z*
289/14	raylyng *A*: vilanous *B Z*
297/5	holdyth *A*: byddyth *B Z*
305/11	very *A*: mervelouse *B Z*
314/13	willyngly *A*: wittingly *Z*
315/13	yon *A*: there *B Z*

The strength of such readings in *A* increases the probability that minor examples of unique substantive readings (verb endings, pronouns, prepositions, etc.—running to more than six hundred examples) are also likely to be authentic.

Beyond such unique readings we have the continuous, pervasive evidence found in other aspects of the *A* text. The punctuation depends primarily upon the virgule, with occasional use of parentheses and periods, and, perhaps, a comma here and there.[1] The *A* text, that is to say, has the kind of punctuation characteristic of the earlier years of the sixteenth century, before the virgule had fallen into disuse. It is the kind of punctuation found in More's holograph letter in English written to Henry VIII in 1534, where More uses primarily the virgule, along with parentheses and periods.[2] And it is the kind of punctuation found throughout the Valencia holograph of More's *De Tristitia*.[3]

Supporting this sense of a manuscript style belonging to the earlier years of the century are the frequently peculiar word-forms and spellings of the *A* text—forms and spellings that apparently often seemed archaic, or strange, or improper to scribe *B*, who has altered them in many instances. These peculiarities are emphasized by the tendency toward modernization

---

[1] See below, p. xxxvi.

[2] British Library, Ms. Cleo. E vi, fols. 176–177ᵛ.

[3] Commas occur very seldom in the Valencia MS; about twenty examples can be found.

in the printed texts, and also, to a lesser extent, in *L*. The following examples will suggest the variations, of which many more examples may be found in the glossary and in the textual notes: "keuer" (cover), "lovyer" or "lovier" (lover), "hit" (it), "sowneth" (soundeth), "be" (by), "abought" (about), "dought" (doubt), "weder" (weather), "childhed" (childhood), "shryng" (shrink), "hundreth" (hundred), "ye" (you). The *A* text also shows a number of metathetic forms recognized by the *OED*: "tharldome" (thralldom), "shirle" (shrill), "thurst" (thrust). *A* also contains many examples of aspirated spellings: "heres" (ears), "habundaunce," "habraham," "prehemynaunce," as well as a strong preference for "tone" (one) and "tother" (other). Many of these are of course instances of colloquial usage, similar to the use of the popular form of the noun "colletes," instead of the learned form "collectes" employed by all the other texts (46/17). Such examples shade into doublet-forms or synonyms: "riall" (royal), "scriple" (scruple), "scripelous" (scrupulous), "or" (ere), "sample" (example), "aferd" (afraid), "boysteouse" (boisterous), "seld" (seldom), "brede" (breadth), "egall" (equal).

At the same time the *A* text shows a tendency to cling to verb-forms more characteristic of the fifteenth century than of the middle of the sixteenth. These are therefore frequently modernized in the printed texts (especially in *1553* and *1573*), and also in *L*, though less frequently: "heng" ("dyd hange" *L*, "honge" *1553 1557 1573*), "commen" (come), "shotten" (shot), "had be" (had been), "chese" ("choose" *L*, "chose" *1553 1557*, "chuse" *1573*), "bode" (bade). Many of these usages are part of the informal, colloquial manner of the dialogue, a manner shown also in *A* by the much greater frequency, as compared with the other texts, of colloquial ellipses: omission of pronouns and connectives, neglect of formal parallelisms, lack of proper agreement between singular subject and plural verb, or vice versa.

Finally, it is essential to note that *CC* and *1557* agree in dividing Book II into seventeen chapters, whereas *L* and *1553* divide the book into nineteen chapters. In *CC* and *1557* chapters 16 and 17 are inordinately long. Chapter 16 runs to thirty-seven pages (129–166) in the present text, while Chapter 17 runs to twenty-two pages (166–187). *L* and *1553* sensibly begin a new chapter (17) at 157/5, about three-fourths of the way through Chapter 16 of *CC*, and they also, much less sensibly, begin a new chapter (19) at 175/26, about halfway through Chapter 17 of *CC*. (Fowler in *1573* accepts the first division of *L 1553*, but rejects the second, giving eighteen chapters for Book II.) It seems clear that the chapter-division of *CC* (the division of the *A* text, unchanged by *B*), here represents an earlier stage in the transmission of the text than the divisions shown in *L* and *1553*. Here, as in many other places, *1557* has preferred the text as represented in *CC*.

From all this varied mass of evidence, it seems fair to conclude that the text of *A* is closer to More's holograph than any other extant text, and we have therefore made it the basis of the present edition.

4. The Corpus Christi Manuscript: Additions and Alterations by Scribe *B*

The changes made by scribe *B* in the Corpus Christi manuscript run the full range of editorial possibilities: the addition of long phrases and clauses, with the insertion of one passage seven lines in length; additions and cancellations involving hundreds of single words and short phrases; changes in word-order; changes in verb-endings; changes from singular to plural and vice versa. Revisions of this kind, one might conjecture, could have been made by someone who, finding the *A* text faulty in places, wished to create a complete and accurate text for his own use, and therefore sought out another copy of the work and brought the *A* text into conformity with that other text. But *B* seems to have a larger aim, for his editorial work goes far beyond the sort of alterations thus far mentioned. The editor repunctuates the entire manuscript with remarkable care. The *A* text, as we have said, depends primarily upon the virgule, with occasional use of parentheses and periods. Whether *A* used the comma at all is uncertain; usually the commas are clearly added by *B*, as one can tell from the dark ink and the evidence of crowding into a space where no punctuation was intended by *A*. But in a relatively few cases, extending to no more than five or six per cent of the thousands of commas in *CC*, the presence of a lighter ink makes absolute determination impossible. Scribe *B*, however, unlike the scribe of *L*, does not give up the use of virgules; on the contrary he adds them by the hundreds, as one can see from the dark ink, the less-slanted and shorter stroke, and the evidence of crowding between words. *B* also adds many parentheses, frequently writing them over the virgules of *A*. He not only adds commas, but also many colons, periods, and question-marks; these can usually be identified by the dark ink and the crowding, but they are also identifiable from the way in which *B* frequently cancels a virgule by *A* and substitutes different punctuation. Periods added by *B* may also be identified by the fact that *B* often alters the following letter to a capital. This repunctuation is scrupulous, insistent, and highly intelligent. Though excessive by modern standards, it helps to clarify many passages, and it has therefore been preserved in the present text, except in cases where it replaces satisfactory punctuation by *A*.

Beyond repunctuation the care of scribe *B* for clarity extends to the frequent expansion of abbreviations and to the respelling of words in a more modern or a more clearly comprehensible form. At the same time *B* often changes or clarifies individual letters within a word, when he evidently thinks that a letter is not clearly formed, or is not in accord with modern spelling. And finally, he worries very often about the clarity of words when they are broken at the end of a line; he will often cancel the part of the word carried over and attach it to the end of the preceding line (or vice versa); or he will cancel both divided parts and rewrite the whole word.

It seems that such pains would be taken only if one wished to guarantee that the manuscript would be absolutely clear for the purpose of producing copies: *CC* looks like a manuscript edited for the purpose of publication.

Before proceeding further, it is essential to ascertain, if possible, the degree of authority that may be found in the substantive additions and alterations made by *B*. For, with one major exception[1] and a few minor exceptions, *all* of the substantive changes made by *B* appear in *all* of the other texts. That is, the materials that appear as substantive additions and alterations in the hand of *B*, even the changes in word-order, have with very few exceptions become part of the standard text. In view of this, one is faced with the question: could not these additions and alterations have been copied by *B* from *L*, or from a manuscript closely resembling *L*, or from one of the printed texts? The collations, however, provide strong evidence against this possibility.

A tabulation of the variants in Book I (75 pages) reveals 285 substantive readings shared by all four other texts (as indicated by the symbol $\mathcal{Z}$), but not found anywhere in *CC*, that is, not found either in the *A* text or in the revisions of *B*. At the same time Book I shows 126 substantive variants shared by *L* and *1553*, but not found in *CC* and *1557*. In addition Book I shows 80 substantive variants peculiar to *L*, 80 original in *1553* (shared by *1557* in 29 cases), and 45 original in *1557*. In the equivalent number of pages at the outset of Book II (pp. 78–152) drastic changes appear in some of these categories, but the number of substantive variations from *CC* remains substantial. These figures are best displayed in tabular form:

Substantive Variants from Text of *CC* (*A* and *B*)

	Book I	Book II (pp. 78–152)
$\mathcal{Z}$ variants (agreement of *L 1553 1557 1573*)	285	112
L 1553 (shared) against *CC 1557*	126	381
L (unique)	80	92
1553 (original)	80	142
1553 1557 (shared)	29	15
1557 (original)	45	38

---

[1] See below, p. xxxviii.

If scribe *B* is comparing the *A* text with one of the other extant texts, it is hard to see why he would omit so many other variants, similar in nature to the changes which he in fact does make. Consequently, if *B* is copying materials from another source, it seems that this source must be a manuscript anterior to any of the other extant texts, a manuscript that did not contain the additional variants shown in *L, 1553, 1557,* or *1573.*

Finally, we come to the basic question: to what extent do the substantive additions and alterations of *B* represent the authentic words of Thomas More? This is a complex problem, with different answers possible for different instances. In order to make the issues plain, the present text, wherever possible, prints the additions of *B* in half-brackets, which serve to alert the reader to the fact that these words are additions by a second hand, and that they deserve special scrutiny, in order to ascertain whether they do, or do not, constitute words essential to the text.

It seems best to begin discussion of this problem with the longest addition, which is written by *B* in the bottom margin of folio 194 and is marked for insertion at 295/10, near the close of More's fable concerning the hart who is frightened by a hunter's bitch (see plate IX,C):

> (here it must be known of some man that can skyll of huntyng, whither that we mystake not our termys / for than are we vtterly shamyd ye wot well. And I am so connyng, that I cannot tell whither among them, a bych be a bych or no. But as I remember she is no bych, but a brache. This is a hye poynt in a low howse. Beware of barkyng / for there lakkyth a nother huntyng term. At a fox it is called cryeng. I wot not what they call it at a hart / but it shall make no mater of a fart)

This "merry" note of direction does not appear in *1557,* but it is included, without parentheses, as an integral part of the text in both *L* and *1553.* *L* gives it a separate paragraph, while *1553* prints it within the body of a long paragraph. Fowler's edition of 1573 puts the passage in parenthesis within the body of a long paragraph; but Fowler evidently found the last phrase too indecorous, for he omitted the last three words, even though he thus spoiled the rhythm and the rhyme of the pentameter couplet with which this note concludes.

But the question must be raised: is this really More's note? Could it not be the work of scribe *B?* Against this one should point to a cancellation in the note: at 295/22 *B* originally wrote "whither that he," but then cancelled "he" and continued with "we mystake not our termys." Here is an indication that the scribe is copying from another manuscript, for *B* has apparently written "he" through association with "some man" in the preceding clause; but then the scribe realizes that his text goes on to read "we" and "our" and he therefore corrects accordingly. Even so, could it not be the work of some previous scribe?

Perhaps the best evidence of authenticity is internal. Surprising as it may seem in the context of More's imprisonment, the whole note is quite in line with the humor of the fable to which it refers, and its crackling, sardonic wit is in every way characteristic of More—and of many passages in *A Dialogue of Comfort*, such as the fable of Mother Maud or the tale of the great man of the church who took such pride in his oration. It is accepted as authentic in three of the four other texts. But why, then, does Rastell omit the whole passage in *1557*? Perhaps he thought it indecorous, but one doubts that he would be more delicate than Fowler, who at least prints nearly all of the passage. One can conceive a better justification for Rastell's omission: he rightly recognized that it was not a part of the text, but was a note of direction to an amanuensis or a future editor, and he took the editorial privilege of omitting it, as scribe *A* (or a predecessor) had also done. The fact that *A* did not include it, and the visual position of the passage as a footnote in *CC*, would serve to stress the extraneous nature of the passage and encourage its omission. Here again we have some evidence, however slight, that Rastell may have had *CC* under his eye.

The conclusion that this passage is authentically More's and is derived, directly or indirectly, from his holograph, has immense consequences for the many other substantive additions and alterations made by scribe *B* in *CC*. Are we to regard all his other substantive revisions as derived, directly or indirectly, from More's holograph? One must set this problem within a broad view of the entire editorial process as performed by *B*. In his repunctuation, respelling, expansion of abbreviations, and uniting of divided words he would appear to be operating on his own, to produce a clear, readable text. Would he not also, here and there, be likely to add or cancel words, change the word-order, or suggest an alternative reading, in places where he found the text obscure or awkward? Many of his changes involve propriety in syntax: changes of tense, changes from singular to plural or vice versa, addition of pronouns, and so on. Other changes involve the creation of parallelisms where the *A* text does not show this kind of phrasing. Still others involve the simple addition of an adverb or a preposition, or a simple shift in word-order, with an effect of greater smoothness in the phrasing. Still other words that are added have an effect of embellishment or intensification. All such revisions could have been made without reference to any other manuscript, simply as a part of copy-editing.

But when one turns to consider the longer additions, one discovers that these often occur in places where a repeated word or phrase has apparently caused the most common of scribal errors: the skipping ahead to the repeated word or phrase and the omission of the intervening material. Some of these additions are found in places where it is obvious that a scribal slip has occurred, as at 183/1–2, where Antony is speaking of one's duty to assist the sick: "For whan god hath by such chaunce sent hym to me, & there ones matchid me with hym / ⌐I reken my self surely chargyd with him,¬ till I may without perell of his life be well & conveniently dischargid of hym." Similarly, at 263/20–21 a comparison needs to be completed: "And that there is also no prince lyvyng vppon earth, but he is in worse case prisoner by this generall ymprisonment that I speke of / ⌐than is many a lewd simple wrech by that speciall imprisonment that you speke of.¬" Such corrections have the ring of authenticity, but it is conceivable that an editor could have invented them from the context.

On the other hand, in at least a dozen examples where such eye-skipping seems to have occurred, it is doubtful whether any error would have been suspected in the ordinary course of reading, for the passage in *A* makes sense as it stands. Thus at 169/12–14 the reading of *A* causes no difficulty: "they wold not rest them self but runne on styll vnto more payne & more." But *B* adds a passage apparently omitted by skipping to the second "still": "they wold not rest them self but runne on styll ⌐in theyr werynes / & put them self still¬ vnto more payne & more." Similarly at 261/21–23 a passage apparently omitted through the repetition of "els" would hardly be missed; and indeed the omission might even be regarded as an improvement in the sense: "and we shall fynd that the straytest kept of them both / yf he get the wisedome & the grace to quyet his own mynd, & hold hym selfe content with that place / & long not like a woman with child for her lustes to be gaddyng out any where ⌐els, is by the same reson of yours, while his will is not longyng to be any where¬ els / he is I say at his fre libertie to be where he will / & so is out of prison to." And at 199/8 –10 the repetition of "in the case" creates an awkward sentence through the addition: "How be yt many a man may wene hym selfe far therefro / that yet may fortune by some one chaunce or other / to fall in the case / ⌐that eyther for the trouth of fayth, or for the trouth of Iustice, which go almost all alyke, he may fall in the case.¬"[1] It is hard to see why the scribe would have made additions of this kind unless he were comparing his text with another source.

The probability of such a procedure is strengthened by the fact that in making these long additions the scribe shows virtually no signs of the sort of hesitation or rewriting that one would expect to find in long additions that the scribe was himself composing to fill out an omission. He seems to know that the addition will fit into the space available, and he writes his

[1] See Plate VII.

addition with hardly any signs of correction within his added words. In short, his additions look like fair copies.

Against this hypothesis, however, one needs to set the unusual example of a necessary addition made at 130/17–18, where Antony is speaking of the suicide of Cato Uticensis: "S Austyn well declarith in his worke *de ciuitate dei* / ⌐that there was no strength nor magnanimyte⌐ therin but playne pusillanimite & impotency of stomake." The addition in half-brackets is first crowded into the margin by *E*; this is then cancelled and rewritten more carefully between the lines by *B*. This is the only instance of such a long addition by *E*, but its presence may be explained by the glaring evidence that something has been omitted. Did *E* invent the addition by simply matching the nouns "pusillanimite & impotency"? Or did *E* also consult another source on this occasion? Has *B* verified the addition by consulting another source? Such questions cannot be answered.

One is left, then, with signs that point in two directions. There is in some places very strong evidence that *B* is copying from another source, for one cannot see why the addition should have been made unless it was prompted by its presence in another source. Some of the short additions may also come from another source, but here one must always be in doubt, for most of them could have been added without authority, just as the spelling has been changed.

Further guidance in this problem may be sought in thirty-two places where *B* has written a different word as an alternative above the reading of *A*, without any cancellation: the reader is left to choose. Is the alternative offered because *B* has found it in another manuscript? Or is it simply the suggestion of the editor as a possible improvement? There is also the possibility that these double readings represent unresolved alternatives in More's holograph, for the Valencia manuscript of the *De Tristitia* shows four examples of exactly such unresolved variants, and there is evidence of this practice in other writings of More.[1] To clarify the problem and to suggest some answers, a listing of some of these alternative readings may be of help, along with brief comments on some items and a record of their appearance in the other texts:[2]

24/12	latter *A*: last *B Z*
36/5	release *A*: relief *B Z*
47/21	perceve *A*: prove *B Z*
49/20	your *A L 1553*: my *B 1557* (see Commentary)

---

[1] See *CW 14*, 327/3, 417/10, 421/5, 589/8. See also *CW 2*, xxxviii–xliii.

[2] To simplify the table, separate references to the readings of *1573* have not been included.

51/5   paynes *A :* pangys *B Z*[1]
51/14   bestly *A :* bodely *B Z*[2]
59/17   full *A :* dull *B Z*[3]
69/12   homo *A :* hominum *B Z*
87/3   willyngly *A :* afterwarde *B Z*
91/22   laboraui *A 1557 :* cucurri *B L 1553*[4]
        laboryd *A 1557 :* ronne *B L 1553*
104/9   quemadmodum *A 1557 :* sicut *B L 1553*
114/13 litell *A 1557 :* gret dele *B L 1553*
121/9   man *A 1557 :* men *B L 1553*
137/13 of *A 1557 :* in *B L 1553*
146/10 goodly *A L 1557 :* godly *B 1553*
154/7   life *A :* blisse *B Z*[5]
258/15 yf *A :* whither *B Z*
265/21 leuer *A Z :* rather *B*
        sorely *A 1553 1557 :* soryly *B L*
269/27 parcell *A :* pecys *B Z*[6]
279/10 that *A 1557 :* if *B L 1553*
314/5   Peter *A :* Paule *B Z*[7]

In their treatment of these alternatives the texts show an interesting variety of "choices." Out of the twenty-three instances given so far, the suggestion of *B* is found in all other texts twelve times, and is rejected by all other texts only once.[8] In the cases where the texts divide in their "choices," *A* and *1557* agree seven times, *A*, *L*, and *1557* agree once, while *B*, *L*, and *1553* agree seven times. *A*, *L*, and *1553* agree only once, as against *B* and *1557* (at 49/20). *A*, *L*, and *1557* agree once against *B* and *1553* (at 146/10). The "choice" between "sorely" and "soryly" (at 265/21) shows *A*, *1553*, and *1557* in agreement against *B* and *L ;* but this is a rather

[1] This occurs in the phrase "such paynes as payne the body"; perhaps the suggested change was prompted by the wish to avoid this repetition.

[2] The reading of *A* seems right, in view of More's use of the word "bestes" in the preceding line; again the suggestion of *B* may have been prompted by the wish to avoid a repetition.

[3] This occurs in the phrase "full of welth"; *L* and *1553* read "dull of wealth," but the phrase "of welth" is omitted by *1557*, evidently because it does not make very good sense if one prefers the reading "dull."

[4] The word "cucurri" represents a departure from the Vulgate.

[5] The change to "blisse" creates an antithesis.

[6] The change from "a very grete parcell" to "very grete pecys" may have been made to accord with the plural subject preceding.

[7] "Paule" is correct: see Commentary.

[8] For additional (minor) examples where all other texts adopt the alternative offered by *B* see 28/31, 34/7, 40/23, 48/10 and 60/19.

dubious example, since "sorely" might have been regarded as a variant spelling of "sorily." An additional and anomalous case occurs at 59/14, where *B* has written "fet" over an illegible word in *A* (probably "for"); *B* has then written "seke" above as an alternative; *1557* reads "fet," while *L* and *1553* read "seke."[1]

It is important to note that in 25 out of 29 examples *L* and *1553* agree with the interlinear suggestion of *B*. One explanation of this lopsided preference might be that these readings were in a manuscript, resembling *L*, that provided the text for *1553;* if this is so, then *B* is copying these variants from a manuscript resembling *L* in these instances. A second explanation might be that this hypothetical manuscript resembling *L* (call it *Y*) has descended from *CC*, as edited by *B*, and that the scribe of *Y* has simply decided to follow the interlineated choice in nearly every case.

The results of examining the substantive additions and alterations of *B* may be summed up in a series of inferences. First of all, scribe *B*, in his editing, is doing everything in his power to create what he regards as a complete, accurate, clear, and readable manuscript. Thus he appears to have compared the *A* text with another manuscript in order to be sure that all of More's authentic words are given—even to that seven-line direction omitted by *A*. Next, his revisions attempt to "improve" the manuscript by changes in word-order and by the addition of single words and brief phrases, in the interests of clarity, grammatical agreement, current usage, smoothness, embellishment, or intensification; such "improvements" may be his own invention, or they may be copied from another manuscript. Finally, he has paid careful attention to clarity and accuracy in all the accidentals of spelling and punctuation. He has performed the whole duty of an editor, and he has done it, by sixteenth-century standards, quite conservatively.

5. Relationships among the Texts

The Corpus Christi manuscript, then, looks like a manuscript ready to go to the printer, with everything clarified for the typesetter's eye. But there is no sign that *CC* has passed through a printer's hands; there are no printer's marks, and the smudging that appears on the outside leaves of certain gatherings[2] is not of the kind that would suggest a printer's shop. Moreover, as our tabulation has shown, *CC* bears no exact accord with any

---

[1] An anomalous case also occurs at 69/16, where *B* writes "after" above "yet" (uncanc.); the *Z* reading keeps both words: "And after yet." Another anomalous case occurs at 87/6, where "to" is altered to "for" by *B*, and then "to" is written as an alternative above "for" (uncanc.); the other texts read "for." An additional case, perhaps only a spelling variant, is found at 171/9: "havour" *A*, "haver" *B Z*.

[2] See above, p. xx.

of the three printed texts of the sixteenth century. It is closest to *1557*, as the evidence already put forward has indicated. The tabulation based upon the first 150 pages[1] (Book I plus the equivalent number of pages in Book II) shows 507 substantive readings where *CC* and *1557* agree *against* the shared readings of *L* and *1553*. And the textual notes show that this proportion is maintained and even increased throughout the remainder of the work. Yet *1557* could not have been set up from *CC* or from an unaltered copy of *CC*: the tabulation shows that in 397 instances *1557* shares substantive readings with *L* and *1553* (taken together) which do not appear in *CC*. Furthermore (again in the first 150 pages) *1557* agrees with *1553* in 44 substantive readings that do not appear in *L* or *CC*, while *1557* has 83 readings of its own. A further process of extensive editing has clearly occurred between the text represented in *CC* and all four other texts.

The manuscript in the British Library (*L*) substantially represents that process, so far as *1553* is concerned, for the agreements between these two texts are persistent and impressive, as the textual notes constantly indicate. Nevertheless, additional editing has been performed independently in both *L* and *1553*. The tabulation of the first 150 pages shows 172 unique readings in *L* and 266 original readings in *1553*. One must therefore hypothesize an earlier manuscript (*Y*) from which both *L* and *1553* derive.

We are left, then, with the problem of the close, though by no means complete, accord between *CC* and Rastell's edition of 1557—a relationship that may be reinforced by the hybrid punctuation of *CC*, as edited by *B*. This combination of virgules with commas, colons, parentheses, periods, and question-marks does not of course appear in *1557*, or in the other printed editions of *A Dialogue of Comfort;* but it is the kind of transitional punctuation that was practiced by printers in the earlier part of the century, and was practiced by William Rastell in the editions of Thomas More's works that he published during the years 1532–34.[2] That is why the punctuation of the present text bears a very close resemblance to the punctuation of More's *Confutation of Tyndale's Answer* in the present series of the *Complete Works* (Vol. 8), for there the text has been based upon Rastell's edition of 1532/33. This resemblance may be more than coincidence, for *CC* may well be a manuscript that was prepared by Rastell himself with a view toward publication.

It is important, first of all, to remember Rastell's words in the dedication of his great folio to Queen Mary:

> and when I further considered, that those workes of his were not yet all imprinted, and those that were imprinted, were in seuerall

---

[1] See above, p. xxxvii.

[2] Gibson, nos. 45, 46, 48, 49, 50, 66.

volumes and bokes, whereby it were likely, that aswell those bokes of
his that were already abrode in print, as those y^t were yet vnprinted,
should in time percase perish and vtterly vanish away (to the great
losse and detriment of many) vnlesse they were gathered together and
printed in one whole volume, for these causes (my most gracious liege
Lady) I dyd diligently collect and gather together, as many of those
his workes, bokes, letters, and other writinges, printed and vnprinted
in ye English tonge, as I could come by, and the same (certain yeres
in the euil world past, keping in my handes, very surely and safely)
now lately haue caused to be imprinted in this one volume, to thintent, not onely that euery man y^t will now in our dayes, maye haue
and take commoditie by them, but also that they may be preserued for
the profit likewise of our posteritie.

Rastell indicates here that his collection of More's English writings,
"printed and vnprinted," had been made some years before Mary's
accession, for he says that he has kept them in his hands "very surely and
safely" during "certain yeres in the euil world past"—years when it was
impossible to publish the works of Thomas More in England. Among the
English works that he "dyd diligently collect," a manuscript of *A Dialogue
of Comfort* would have been among the foremost. In the case of the *History
of King Richard III* Rastell tells his reader explicitly that he is printing from
More's own manuscript.[1] Since he does not say so with regard to *A
Dialogue of Comfort*, we must assume that he is printing from a copy or from
the printed text of *1553*. But it seems fair also to assume that during the
process of gathering More's manuscripts he tried to come as close to the
holograph as possible, and that he may have had a copy made for himself
directly from the holograph, which may have remained in the possession
of Margaret Roper until her death in 1544 and after that in the possession
of her immediate family.

But More's holograph does not appear to have been available in the
More circle during Mary's reign, when Rastell was actively preparing for
the printing of his folio. One may infer this from certain remarks made by
Nicholas Harpsfield, in the life of More that he was writing in or near
1556. At one point he speaks of the imminent appearance of Rastell's
collected edition: "we trust shortlye to haue all his englishe workes, as well
those that haue beene sett forth ere this, as some others, in print, wherin
Master Sargeant Rastell doth nowe diligently trauell, and imployeth his
good and carefull indeuour to the furthering of the saide good purpose."[2]

---

[1] *CW 2*, 2. Rastell speaks of earlier editions as "muche varying fro the copie of his own hand, by which thys is printed."

[2] Nicholas Harpsfield, *The Life and Death of Sir Thomas More*, ed. E. V. Hitchcock (London, 1932), p. 100. Cited hereafter as "Harpsfield."

Harpsfield was in close touch with Rastell and with other members of the
More family, yet it appears from what he says a little later that he does not
know where the original manuscript of *A Dialogue of Comfort* is, and that
he may never have seen it, for he makes an apparently unwarranted
statement about its manner of writing:

> there is one thing wherin these bookes of Sir Thomas More [i.e.,
> the three books of *A Dialogue of Comfort*] by an especiall prerogatiue
> surmounte, or els I am deceaued, all other of this sort, and that is,
> that they were for the moste part written with none other penne in
> the worlde then with a coale, as was also his Treatise vpon the
> passion; which copie, if some [men] had, they might and would more
> esteeme then other bookes written with golden letters, and woulde
> make no lesse accompt of it then St Jerome did of certaine bookes of
> the learned martyr Lucian written with his owne hande, that per-
> chaunce he happed [vpon] and esteemed them as a pretious iewell.[1]

His reference to the "Treatise vpon the passion" is certainly wrong: part
of the English treatise, we now know, was written before More entered the
Tower;[2] and the discovery of the Valencia holograph of the *De Tristitia*
makes it plain that More had sufficient supplies of pen and ink to write that
entire treatise.[3] There is no need, then, to accept Harpsfield's statement
that the *Dialogue* was mostly written with a coal. Harpsfield's assertion is
probably based on his knowledge of certain letters from the Tower which,
as we know from statements by More, Margaret Roper, and Rastell, were
certainly written with a coal.[4] The important point to be made here, however, is that Harpsfield seems not to know where the holograph is, and his
ignorance on this crucial point would suggest that Rastell did not have it
available for use in the final preparation of his folio. Rastell would, then,
have had to depend upon a manuscript resembling *CC* for the passage
concerning Romanus and "Blonidina."

That *CC* is in fact a manuscript prepared by Rastell himself seems to be
put almost beyond doubt when all the preceding evidence is combined
with additional evidence drawn from what appear to be examples of
Rastell's handwriting in other documents. The key evidence here is found
in four volumes of law books that once belonged to Rastell and are now

[1] Harpsfield, pp. 134–35.
[2] Cf. *St. Thomas More: Selected Letters*, ed. E. F. Rogers (New Haven, 1961), pp. 185–88
(cited hereafter as "*SL*") and *CW 13*, Introduction.
[3] Cf. *CW 14*.
[4] *EW*, sigs. XX$_7$v-XX$_8$, XX$_8$, ZZ$_3$v-ZZ$_5$, ZZ$_5$-ZZ$_5$v (Rogers, nos. 201, 204, 209, 210,
217, 218).

preserved in the Library of Lincoln's Inn.[1] These four "Year Books" were left to Lincoln's Inn by Ranulph Cholmeley, who purchased them from William Rastell in the year 1538, as we know from a note written by Rastell in one of these volumes:

> *Memorandum* that I William Rastell the xvj day of March in the xxx yere of kyng Henry the viij haue solde to Randall Cholmeley my fyve gret bokes of yeres wherof this is one / for the some of xxxiiij[s] viij[d] which the same day he hath payd me[2]

Four of these five volumes can be identified by the fact that Rastell has written his name in Greek at or near the beginning of each volume, and his name in English on the last page of each volume.[3] All four of these volumes contain copious manuscript annotation in the margins, summing up the law cases and giving cross-references; these notes are written in several different hands, representing several generations of law students. Rastell, who entered Lincoln's Inn on September 12, 1532,[4] may have been the original owner of these books. Two hands predominate throughout, one of which is certainly that of Ranulph Cholmeley, for his signature, accompanied with comments, occurs on several pages in such a way as to identify his rather idiosyncratic hand beyond doubt.

The other chief hand in the marginal annotations appears to be that of

---

[1] The existence of these books was pointed out by A. W. Reed at the end of his essay, "The Printer of Heywood's Plays: William Rastell," included in Reed's *Early Tudor Drama* (London, 1926), pp. 72–93. Reed here transcribes the memorandum of sale.

[2] See reproduction in Plate IX, A. This appears at the beginning of the volume that opens with the years Edw. IV, 21–22; it is written on a leaf that has been cut out and pasted on a blank leaf for preservation. This leaf bears the heading, "The fyfte volume," along with a table of contents, written in a large italic hand that cannot be identified. The signature "Ranulphus Cholmeley" appears in the lower left-hand corner of the leaf. Evidently this was the last of the five volumes sold to Cholmeley by Rastell.

[3] The four identified volumes are as follows: (1) Edw. III, 7–50; this has the Greek signature of Rastell on the engraved title-page, and the English signature of Rastell on the engraved leaf at the end. (2) Hen. IV, 7–14, Hen. V, 9, Hen. VI, 1–18; this has the Greek signature of Rastell on the first printed page, and also on fol. 1 of Hen. IV, 11; the English signature of Rastell appears on the last printed page. (3) Hen. VI, 11, 19–39; here the Greek signature of Rastell appears at the opening of the second treatise (Hen. VI, 19, fol. 1), in the same light brown ink that appears in the marginal notes on this page, written in the hand which seems to be Rastell's, and which appears copiously in the margins of this particular section of 80 folios; the English signature of Rastell appears on the last printed page of the volume. (4) Edw. IV, 21–22, Edw. V, Rich. III, Hen, VII, 1–21, Hen. VIII, 12–14; the Greek signature of Rastell appears on the first printed page of this volume; the English signature of Rastell appears on the last printed page.

[4] *The Records of the Honorable Society of Lincoln's Inn: Admissions*, 2 vols. (Lincoln's Inn, 1896), *1*, 46. "Randle" Cholmeley was admitted on June 22, 1535 (p. 49).

William Rastell, for it bears a considerable resemblance to the memorandum of sale written by Rastell himself. The resemblance is not complete, because the memorandum has been written in a loose scrawl, on what may have been a blank page; at least there is plenty of space for writing. Most of the marginal notes that may be ascribed to Rastell are written in a very small, very precise hand that is taking great pains to pack a great many words into a narrow marginal space. These conditions of writing in the margins, however, provide a favorable field for comparison, when we turn to compare the neat and small handwriting of these notes with the neat and small handwriting in the alterations and additions made by hand B in *CC*. Here the similarity in the neat, sharp, angular formation of letters is striking, as the examples here reproduced will show.[1]

Meanwhile, a third source of manuscript evidence must be brought into the comparison: the marginal notes and brief interlinear corrections written in one of the Yale copies of William (or possibly John) Rastell's edition of More's *Supplycacyon of soulys* (second edition, 1529). This very book served as printer's copy in setting the type for Rastell's folio: the printer's casting-off marks match throughout with *1557*. At the same time the marginal notes in manuscript match exactly the marginal glosses actually printed in *1557*. Did Rastell himself write these glosses in the printer's copy for *1557*? Or was it perhaps Thomas Paynell, who compiled the summary index for *1557*?[2] Examination of Paynell's notebooks in the library of St. John's College, Oxford, makes it clear that the hand in the marginalia of the printer's copy cannot be Paynell's; nor does Paynell's hand bear any resemblance to hand B of *CC*. But there is a very close resemblance between hand B and these marginal glosses in the printer's copy of the *Supplycacyon*—especially after allowance has been made for the different conditions of writing. Hand B is neat and small, using a finely sharpened pen, because the words must be fitted into a small interlinear space. The marginal hand in the *Supplycacyon* has plenty of room for writing, since only brief notes are being provided, with wide margins available; the writer can therefore use a broad pen and write with much less care in letters of a larger size than B can use. In the one place (fol. xxiiii^v) where significant interlinear alterations occur in this printer's copy, the hand and pen indeed seem identical with B. (See Plate X.)

We have, then, three sources of manuscript material, all closely associated with William Rastell on grounds other than handwriting: the Year

---

[1] It is especially helpful to compare Rastell's memorandum with the one place in *CC* where B has plenty of space to write: the long addition at the bottom of fol. 194. Compare reproductions A and C in Plate IX.

[2] See *EW*, sig. C$_4$: "A table of many matters conteined in this booke. Collected and gathered together by Thomas Paynell preist."

Books, the printer's copy for the *Supplycacyon,* and hand *B* of the Corpus Christi manuscript. When allowance has been made for the different conditions of writing, the resemblances among these three sources are sufficient to indicate the strong probability that all three are the work of Rastell himself.

But if *CC* is a manuscript prepared by Rastell, why does the text of *1557* show so many agreements with *L* and *1553,* in places where no such reading appears in *CC?* The answer probably lies in the publication of the separate edition of *A Dialogue of Comfort,* printed by Richard Tottel, with a colophon dated November 18, 1553. The date is significant: barely five months after Mary's accession. Little time was lost in putting this major work of More into print at last. Could Rastell have had a hand in this publication? He had returned to England by April 1553,[1] and relations between Tottel and Rastell seem to have been cordial, for Tottel was one of the three printers of *1557.* Furthermore, Tottel was the sole printer of the thick quarto law-book edited by William Rastell and published with a colophon dated October 16, 1557: *A colleccion of all the statutes (from the begynning of Magna Carta vnto the yere of our Lorde, 1557) which were before that yere imprinted.*

The important study of Richard Tottel's career by H. J. Byrom[2] has made it clear that Tottel, from the early 1550s on, had a very close connection with an influential group at Lincoln's Inn that included Ranulph Cholmeley, William Rastell, William Roper, and Richard Heywood—the last three of course all being intimate members of the More circle. From evidence provided by Ranulph Cholmeley's will, Byrom gleans the fact that Tottel "had succeeded to the printing-house of Henry Smithe—like Redman, Middleton, and Powell, a printer of law books— soon after Smithe's death in 1550."[3] On April 12, 1553, Tottel was granted an unprecedented monopoly on the printing of law-books pertaining to the common law. In 1553 he produced three such books. How did so young a man, still in his early twenties, manage to gain so valuable a privilege? Byrom's interpretation of the evidence puts the matter beyond doubt, and at the same time suggests why Tottel became the printer for More's unpublished *Dialogue of Comfort:* "all Tottell's associates at this time were Catholics—the Cholmeley group with which he had been connected from his youth, and John Brende, John Wilkinson, Ferdinando

---

[1] See A. B. Emden, *A Biographical Register of the University of Oxford A.D. 1501 to 1540* (Oxford, 1974), p. 475: "returned a widower by Apr. 1553 when he took 'Crosbies Place,' Bishopgate Street on a 90 yrs. lease."

[2] H. J. Byrom, "Richard Tottell—His Life and Work," *The Library* (4th series), *8* (1927–28), 199–232.

[3] *Ibid.,* p. 200.

Pulton, Nicholas Grimald (who became a Catholic about 1554), John
Cawood, and William Rastell."[1]

> It is probable that by 1550, when Smithe died, Ranulf Cholmeley and
> his friends regarded law-printing as a preserve of their own. They
> would have had no difficulty in securing through the judges from the
> Privy Council a monopoly of law-printing—for there could be no
> surer guarantee of good quality than that they, experienced lawyers
> having extensive connexions with reputable law-printers, should
> control the printing of law books: also it was an obvious way of putting
> an end to the chaotic conditions which had hitherto prevailed in
> law-printing, when each stationer was free to print any legal treatise
> in any way he chose. Tottel, therefore, would be the nominee of the
> Lincoln's Inn group and would depend on them for his texts.[2]

Since William Rastell had returned to England from Louvain by April
1553, he was in England at about the time when Tottel received his
monopoly. But more important for our purpose here, Rastell had returned
to England at least seven months before Tottel's edition of *A Dialogue of
Comfort* was published, on November 18, 1553. It seems, then, that Rastell
must have known of and approved the plans for publication. Tottel, whose
welfare was so heavily dependent on the Lincoln's Inn group, would
never have ventured to publish the *Dialogue* if Rastell had wished to
reserve publication for his projected edition of the collected English works.
But Rastell must have been a very busy man in 1553, involved in re-
establishing his position in the law, involved also in re-establishing the
revenues of his estate: he would have had little time in 1553 to think about
carrying his great project to any quick conclusion. Why, then, would he
wish to delay the publication of this work, already withheld from the
public for nearly two decades? Probably the whole More circle wished to
see it published as soon as possible.

But the manuscript that Tottel used for printing was not the Corpus
Christi manuscript. Undoubtedly other copies were circulating.[3] The *L*

---

[1] *Ibid.*, p. 204.

[2] *Ibid.*, pp. 222–23.

[3] J. B. Trapp has pointed out to us the listing of the manuscript of "A large Dialogue of
Comfort against Tribulation, Translated out of an *Hungarian* MS." in *Bibliotheca Illustris:
sive Catalogus Variorum Librorum* . . . (London, 1687), p. 89, lot 19. This is the catalogue for
an auction that began "on *Monday* the 21 day of *November* next, 1687. at the Sign of the
Bear in *Ave-Mary-Lane*, near the West-end of St. *Paul's* Church" (Preface). The Preface
informs the Reader of two important "Circumstances" concerning the catalogue: "The
first is, That it comprises the main part of the Library of that Famous Secretary *William
Cecil*, Lord *Burleigh* . . . The second is, That it contains a greater number of Rare Manuscripts than ever yet were offer'd together in this way, many of which are rendred the

manuscript is one example of the type that provided the basic copy for *1553*. Manuscript *L* is an elegant piece of writing, apparently a presentation copy prepared by a professional scribe; moreover, as its many unique variants indicate, it was subjected to considerable editorial polishing. Another fair copy seems clearly to lie behind it. One can believe that many members and friends of the More circle would have sought to have a copy, during the nearly twenty years that elapsed between its writing and its appearance in print. Several copies may have been made directly from the holograph, and other copies made from these copies. One of these, closely resembling *L*, was evidently given to Tottel for printing: perhaps a copy that belonged to Roper, or Heywood, or Harpsfield, or some other member of the circle. Rastell would have had no reason to doubt its accuracy, and no time to examine it carefully.

But when he came to the actual preparation of copy for his folio, he would have had time, occasion, and reason to examine Tottel's edition quite closely. Rastell's usual practice for *1557* was to send to the printer the separate editions of More's works that he (or his father) had published in the years 1529–34. The printer's copy for the *Supplycacyon* shows how he did it: with brief glosses written in the margins of the book and a few passages corrected here and there. Did he use Tottel's edition as printer's copy? Here we must return to examine the tabulation presented earlier.[1] One notices at once a striking shift in the figures, when one compares Book I with the equivalent number of pages in Book II. Somewhere near the beginning of Book II the printer of *1557* has begun to follow the readings of *CC* much more closely than he has done in Book I. In Book I *1557* departs from *CC* to agree with *1553* in 314 substantive readings; in Book II that figure is reduced to only 127 such agreements with *1553*. Or, to take another set of figures; in Book I *L* and *1553* agree in 126 readings that do not appear in *CC* and *1557* (taken together); whereas in Book II this figure

---

more valuable by being remark'd upon by the hand of the said great Man." This has led to the listing of the book under the name of Lord Burghley. But the *National Union Catalogue* lists the book under "Ailesbury, Robert Bruce, 1st earl of, d. 1685" with this explanation: "the collection in fact was owned by Robert Bruce, 1st earl of Ailesbury, who had inherited the mss. and possibly some of the printed books through his wife, Lady Diana Grey, Lord Burghley's great-great-granddaughter." Sears Jayne (*Library Catalogues of the English Renaissance*, Berkeley, 1956, p. 132) suggests that most of the 249 manuscripts were "probably Burghley's." The provenance of the above manuscript may be indicated by another manuscript in the sale (p. 89, lot 31), closely associated with the daughter of Margaret Roper: "*Eusebius* his Ecclesiastical History, *Engl.* and *Lat.* Translated by *Mary Clarke* [Basset] Daughter to *Will. Roper*, Esq; dedicated to Queen Mary." This appears to be the manuscript now in the British Library (Ms. Harley 1860). Perhaps, then, the manuscript of the *Dialogue of Comfort*, here listed, also made its way into the British Library and is in fact our MS. *L*.

[1] See above, p. xxxvii.

rises sharply to 381 readings shared by *L 1553* against *CC 1557*. Finally, to take a third set of figures: in Book I *1553* shows 80 original variants, of which 29 appear in *1557;* in Book II *1553* shows 142 original variants, of which only 15 appear in *1557.* This drastic reduction in agreement with *1553* continues throughout the remainder of the work, as the textual notes constantly indicate, although agreement still exists on a scale that shows the presence of what might be called "contamination" from *1553.*

Another set of statistics will throw further light on this issue. In the present edition reliance on the *A* text has produced, as acceptable unique readings, 228 major instances and 612 minor instances. The count of "major" unique readings has been made in conservative fashion, limiting the term "major" to cases of significant words or passages that are completely different, or, in cases of word order, to variants that involve the transposition of two or more words. The count of "minor" unique readings therefore contains a good many important cases, for this count includes variants in verb form: variants in tense and variants from regular verb to participle, as well as variants from singular to plural or vice versa. To be "major" the instance must involve a completely different word, and moreover a significant word, not simply a variant from "this" to "his" or from "of" to "at," or the insertion or removal of a minor adverb such as "yet." The term "minor" includes variants in pronouns, conjunctions, prepositions, and articles, along with variants from singular to plural and vice versa, and variants in word order that involve the transposition of only one word. Obviously some of these "minor" instances have a considerable effect upon the sense, especially when they occur in combination. The results of the count of accepted unique readings shows an interesting distribution throughout the treatise:

Accepted Unique Readings of the *A* Text

	Major	Minor
Book I (pp. 3–77: 75 pages)	106	269
Book II (pp. 78–152: 75 pages)	48	125
Books II and III (pp. 153–227: 75 pages)	34	91
Book III (pp. 228–320: 92 pages)	40	127
Totals	228	612

The drastic reduction in the number of unique readings between Book I and Book II is the result of the fact that *1557* has begun to adopt the readings of *CC* much more frequently as Book II proceeds. The tabulation indicates that *1557* has moved rapidly away from the reliance on *1553* that marks Book I, and has relied more and more upon the authority of *CC.*

These facts can be explained by the following hypothesis. Rastell began the printing of *1557* by following his usual practice: setting up type from

the separate edition, with corrections here and there. But somewhere near
the beginning of the second book he became aware that the text of *1553*
was not reliable, that it differed in many places from the text that he had
himself collected and corrected some years before (presumably the text of
CC). Consequently, although the printer's copy was still based on *1553*,
that copy was subjected, from the early portion of Book II onward, to a
much more rigorous comparison and correction, with the result that the
agreement between *CC* and *1557* becomes much more pronounced and
indeed predominant in nearly all significant readings. The difference
between the editorial practice in Book I and that followed in the remaining
two books can be fairly estimated by comparing the textual footnotes for
pages 43 and 46 with those for page 115. The pages of *1553* allowed plenty
of space for the writing of extensive editorial alterations, as one may see
from a copy of *1553* at Yale; for in this copy a contemporary reader has
covered the wide margins of the book with copious remarks.

One can see what might have caused Rastell gradually to lose faith in
the text of *1553*, in the earlier part of Book II. At 81/13–22 the conclusion
of the merry tale about the "kynswoman" who loved to talk, and whose
husband was frequently absent with a friend at mealtime, is drastically
altered by *1553*, far beyond the minor alterations made by *L*. In *CC* and
1557 the conclusion of the tale runs thus (after the friend has explained
that he lets the husband have "all the wordes" in their conversations):

> All the wordes quoth she / mary that am I content he shall haue all
> the wordes with good will as he hath euer had / but I speke them all
> my selfe, & give them all to hym / & for ought that I care for them
> so shall he haue them styll / but otherwise to say that he shall haue
> them all / you shall kepe hym still rather than he get the halfe.
>   Anthonye
> For soth Cosyn I can sone gesse which of our kyn she was / I wold
> we had none therin for all her mery wordes / that lesse wold lett
> there husbandes for to talke /

In *1553* the ambiguous wording is "clarified" with great liberty (the
changes in *1553* are here italicized and noted in brackets):

> Al the wordes quoth she? mary y^t am I content, he shall haue all the
> wordes with *a* good will, as he hath euer had. *For* I speake them *not* al
> my selfe, *but* geue them al to hym, and for ought that I care for them,
> [*so om.*] *he shall* haue them still: but *yet* to saye that he shall haue them
> all, you shall *then rather* kepe him stil, than he *shal* geat y^e *one* half
> *at my handes.*
> *Anthony.* Forsoth Cosin I can soone gesse whiche of our kinne she was:

> *but yet the fewer of that kinde, the quieter is the many* (for all her mery wordes) that *thus* would let *her husbande* [for *om.*] to talke. (sig. F₃)

By adding the word *not* in the second sentence *1553* has made nonsense out of the passage, and through his creation of a formal parallelism in the close of the paragraph *1553* has destroyed the colloquial vigor and bite of the wife's retort. In the uncle's response the long substitution in *1553* has created grammatical confusion in the whole sentence, while attempting to simplify the sense of the uncle's enigmatic reply. The wit in the text of *CC 1557* seems to lie in the ambiguity of "for all her mery wordes": we may take "for" to mean "in spite of" or "because of." In the latter sense the comment sounds like an affectionate compliment: "I wish we had no kinswomen (because of all her merry words) that would less prevent their husbands from talking"—that is, "I wish all the women were as merry as she is." Vincent takes the phrase in this sense, answering: "Forsoth she is not so mery but she is as good." But the uncle's response may contain a hidden sting: "In spite of all her merry words, I wish we had no kinswomen with this habit of preventing their husbands from talking." The drastic revision of *1553* has taken all the fun out of the passage, along with the crisp colloquial vigor.

Then at 91/22 *CC* offers a "choice" in the biblical quotation between *laboraui* (*A*, uncanc.) and *cucurri* (interl. *B*). *1557* rejects the suggestion of *B* and keeps *laboraui*, the Vulgate reading, along with "laboryd" instead of "ronne" in the following translation. On the contrary *L* and *1553* have the alternate readings, *cucurri* and "runne." Since Rastell has frequently brought the biblical quotations into conformity with the Vulgate,[1] he would have discovered here that *A* had the more accurate reading.

At 92/1–2 a passage of nine words is omitted by *1553*, apparently by eye-skipping; this creates a nonsensical account of the parable of the workers in the vineyard which requires correction. At 101/1–2 a passage of eight words is omitted in *L 1553*, again producing an obvious error in the text.

Such an accumulation of variants in *1553* could well have led Rastell to correct the text more carefully from the early part of Book II onward. And then in the latter part of Book II the difference in chapter-divisions would have reinforced a feeling that *1553* could not be relied upon in cases of major disagreement, although in small matters of "touching up," its readings could be retained. There is no absolute proof that *1557* is being set up from *1553*, but the agreement in very small variants throughout Book I and occasionally thereafter strongly indicates that this is so. There is always, of course, the possibility that Rastell is using the manuscript that

---

[1] Cf. Germain Marc'hadour, "Three Tudor Editors of Thomas More," *Editing Sixteenth Century Texts*, ed. R. J. Schoeck (Toronto, 1966), pp. 59–71.

provided copy for *1553*, or one like it, although it is hard to see why he would have done this, with the printed text available.

To sum up, one may construct the following hypotheses. Rastell had prepared *CC* for publication, as part of his projected edition of More's collected English works. Then, with his approval, *1553* was published from another manuscript which Rastell assumed was reliable, but he kept in his possession the manuscript which he had already prepared for his own edition. When the time came to send copy to the printers of the folio, it would have been convenient to allow Tottel and his colleagues (Tottel seems to have been the chief printer)[1] to set up from Tottel's own edition. This was done, but as Rastell compared the text of *1553* more and more closely with the manuscript in his possession (*CC*), he discovered that more and more correction was necessary, perhaps as the printing proceeded. The result is that *1557* represents a conflation of *1553* and *CC*. Then, when all his corrections had been made, and the printing perhaps completed, Rastell gave *CC* to Sir Geoffrey Pole as a memento very close to More's holograph, and Pole at once had it bound and stamped with his initials. Although Sir Geoffrey Pole died in November 1558, the printing of the folio was completed in April 1557,[2] thus allowing time for *CC* to become a part of his library.

On the basis of all the evidence, then, one might construct two, alternative, stemmae:

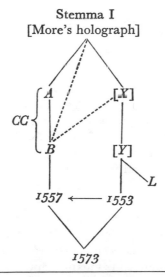

Stemma I
[More's holograph]

CC { A [X]
       B [Y] }

1557 ← 1553 L

1573

---

[1] See *The Carl H. Pforzheimer Library: English Literature 1475–1700* [Catalogue compiled by Emma Va. Unger and William A. Jackson], 3 vols. (New York, 1940), 2, 753–54 (item 743).

[2] See *EW*, sig. ZZ₅v, the colophon: "Finished in Apryll, the yere of our Lorde God ·1557·."

Here the assumption is that *L* and *1553* descend from *X*, a hypothetical independent copy made from More's holograph, containing passages not found in *A*. Scribe *B* could thus have copied his additions and alterations either from *X* or from the holograph. The symbol *Y* represents a hypothetical intermediate manuscript, containing extensive revisions (not found in *CC*), from which *L* and *1553* immediately descend. It is important to note that in this theory virtually all the substantive additions and alterations made by *B* in *CC* would need to have been copied from *X* or from More's holograph; otherwise they would not appear so consistently in *L* and *1553*. Since such an assumption may be unwarranted, it seems wise to suggest an alternative, though perhaps less likely, stemma:

Stemma II
[More's holograph]

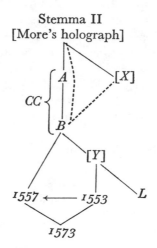

The second stemma assumes that *L* and *1553* descend from *CC*, for it is possible that copies were made from *CC* after it had been edited. Additional alterations would then have accrued in the process of transmission. Objections to the second stemma may be found in the fact that in a place related to a specific biblical reference, two spaces are left blank in *L*, whereas they are filled in by *B* in *CC*; and in another case of this kind, the word left blank by *A* and supplied by *B* has been omitted (along with the subsequent word) by *L*.[1] But these isolated instances cannot bear much weight; and in any case one must allow for the possibility that Rastell (if, as we assume, he kept *CC* with him for many years) made further corrections in *CC* after his major work of editing had been performed, and after the hypothetical copies had been made of his edited manuscript.

One important conclusion would follow from either stemma: that the substantive readings of *L*, *1553*, and *1557* which are not supported by *CC*

---

[1] See textual notes for 62/24 and 140/2.

are probably invalid, the result of editorial tampering. At the same time, many of the substantive additions or alterations made by *B* in *CC* may also be invalid, for either of two reasons: (1) if stemma II is adopted, they may represent editorial tampering on the part of *B*, or (2) in either stemma, they may represent editorial tampering already performed in the hypothetical manuscript *X*. The substantive additions and alterations of *B* cannot with confidence be traced directly to More's holograph.

From all the above evidence one is led to conclude that the Corpus Christi manuscript represents the two earliest strata in the available levels of the textual history of *A Dialogue of Comfort*. In places where *B* has altered *A*, preference has been given to *A*—always provided that the *A* reading makes sense and does not show evidence of scribal error. The *A* text is the earliest text available to us; it is the closest to More's holograph; and it deserves the respect due to its evident priority.

II. THE TOWER WORKS

1. The Art of Improvisation

Volumes 12, 13, and 14 of the present edition are devoted to those writings of More that have come to be called "The Tower Works." These are the writings contained in the last 320 pages of Rastell's great folio of 1557—those works which the editor specifically identifies with the statement: "made in the yere of our lorde, 1534. by syr Thomas More knyghte, while he was prysoner in the tower of London,"[1] or words to that effect. These are, in the order of their folio printing: "A dyalogue of comforte"; "A treatice to receaue the blessed body of our lorde, sacramentally and virtually bothe" (a very short work, less than six pages); "A treatice vpon the passion of Chryste (vnfinished)"—in Rastell's title—"To which," says the editor, More "made this tytle folowing. A treatyce hystorycall, conteyning the bytter passion of our sauioure Christe, after the course and order of the fowre euangelistes, with an exposicion vppon theyr woordes . . . begynnyng at the fyrst assemblye of the byshopps, the priestes, and the seniours of the people, about the contriuing of Christes death . . . And it endeth in the committing of hys blessed body into his sepulchre . . . ."[2] This last is the English treatise on the Passion, which of course breaks off long before the scene at the sepulchre; it ends with More's long exposition of the meaning of the sacrament established at the Last Supper. And as it breaks off, in the midst of "The thirde lecture of the sacrament,"

---

[1] *EW*, sig. CC$_6$. The "Tower Works" occupy sigs. CC$_6$-ZZ$_5$v.

[2] *Ibid.*, sig. LL$_7$v.

the editor notes: "Syr Thomas More wrote no more in englishe of thys treatice of the passion of Chryst. But he (still prisoner in the tower of London) wrote more therof in latine (after the same order as he wrote thereof in englyshe:) the translacion wherof here foloweth."[1] Then follows Mary Basset's translation of her grandfather's Latin treatise, formerly known as the *Expositio Passionis*, but, as the Valencia holograph makes clear, properly entitled *De tristitia, tedio, pavore et oratione Christi ante captionem eius*.[2]

But at this point one must cast doubt upon the validity of some of the editor's statements concerning the Tower Works in the edition of 1557. (We shall call the editor "Rastell," though we cannot be sure that he made all the editorial remarks and titles.) Garry Haupt has found a letter from More to his secretary, John Harris, written from Willesden (then of course a separate village outside of London).[3] In this letter More asks Harris to correct a certain learned matter concerning the paschal feast which occurs about half-way through the English treatise on the Passion. "I put you in remembrance of this," says More to Harris, "because I have mistaken it in the paper that you have." The paper in Harris's possession, one would assume, must be a draft of More's treatise on the Passion, of which Harris was perhaps making a fair copy. Clearly then, as Haupt points out, some part, if not all, of this English treatise had been written before More entered the Tower; and one might wish to speculate that it was the inter-vention of More's imprisonment that caused the breaking off of the English treatise and the change to Latin for its sequel. Since the two are in such close sequence, Rastell could well have assumed that they were written under the same conditions—especially since More might have taken the English treatise, or a part of it, into the Tower with him, intend-ing to complete it there. However this may be, Rastell is highly circum-stantial concerning the Latin treatise which follows. In a prefatory note he says that More began the Latin treatise, "beyng then prisoner, and coulde not atchieue and finishe the same, as he that ere he could goe thorow therwith (eauen when he came to thexposicion of these wordes, *Et in[i]ecerunt manus in Iesum*) was bereaued and put from hys bookes, pen, inke and paper, and kepte more strayghtly than before, and soone after also was putte to death hymselfe."[4] (Note how the word *hymselfe* stresses the parallel between Jesus and More.)

Finally, we have the miscellany gathered together by Rastell at the

---

[1] *Ibid.*, sig. QQ₇.

[2] See *CW 14*. The title *Expositio Passionis* derives from the collected edition of More's Latin works, Louvain, 1565.

[3] *SL*, pp. 185–88. See also *CW 13*, Introduction.

[4] *EW*, sig. QQ₇v.

close of the great folio: "certaine deuout and vertuouse instruccions, meditacions, and prayers made and collected"[1] by More, and the great series of last letters written from the Tower.[2]

The last letters are of the utmost importance, because they constitute the best account of More's conduct during his interrogations and imprisonment, the best account of his state of mind, and, it is not perhaps too much to say, some of his finest works of art. They are indeed works of *art* in every sense of that word, for they show the most artful regard for the presence of two or three or more different audiences. More could have no doubt that every letter he wrote might be carefully read by his keepers, perhaps even sent to Cromwell himself, who was, as More well knew, alert to every phrase which might entrap More into a confession or a recantation. One has the sense that when, for example, More is writing his account of his interrogation at Lambeth,[3] he is concerned with more than sending a clear account to his daughter Margaret and thus to all his family. He is also taking the occasion to clarify and stake out his position to anyone who might happen to read the letter; meanwhile, he engages in some sharp plays of wit: "In that time saw I Maister Doctour Lattemer come in to the gardein, and ther walked he with diuers other doctours and chapleins of my Lorde of Caunterbury, and very mery I saw hym, for he laughed, and toke one or tweyne aboute the necke so handsomely, that if they had been women, I wolde have went he had ben waxen wanton."[4] Or note the apparent touch of irony in his account of how he was temporarily dumbfounded by Cranmer's argument that, in doubtful matters, one is bound to obey the king: "yet this argument semed me sodenly so suttle and namely with such authorite comminge out of so noble a prelate's mouth, that I coulde againe answere nothinge therto but only that I thought myself I might not well do so, because that in my conscience this was one of the cases, in which I was bounden that I shoulde not obey my prince."[5] Or consider the incongruously gentle compliments that More so ceremoniously pays, while recording the rough oath of Cromwell: "Vpon this Maister Secretary (as he that tenderly fauoreth me), saide and sware a gret oth that he had leuer that his owne only sonne (which is of trouth a goodly yonge gentilman, and shall I trust come to much worship) had lost his hedde, than that I shoulde thus haue refused the oth."[6] Later on, in a

---

[1] *Ibid.*, sig. XX$_3$. A few items in this miscellany are identified as having been written before More's imprisonment: see *ibid.*, sigs. XX$_1$v–XX$_6$v.

[2] *Ibid.*, sig. XX$_6$v–XX$_8$v, and Rogers, pp. 501–63.

[3] Rogers, no. 200.

[4] Rogers, p. 503.

[5] *Ibid.*, p. 505.

[6] *Ibid.*, p. 506.

long letter[1] to Dr. Wilson, his fellow-prisoner in the Tower, one feels that More's verbosity is a way of conveying the fact that he is really unwilling to say anything to Wilson about the problem that they both face.

Most artful of all, and most important for More's *Dialogue of Comfort*, is that letter allegedly written by Margaret Roper to Alice Alington,[2] giving an account of the conversation with her father, by way of answer to Alice's letter relating the two fables she has been told by Audley.[3] In a letter to Margaret in August 1534, Alice (More's stepdaughter) says that Audley had come to hunt deer on her estate, and the next day, at a neighbor's house, she took the opportunity to ask him to use his good offices to help her father. Audley was friendly enough, but evaded the plea for help: "he merueyled that my father is so obstinate in his owne conceite, as that euery body wente forthe with all saue onely the blynde Bisshopp [Fisher] and he. And in goode faithe, saied my Lord, I am very glad that I haue no lerninge but in a fewe of Esoppes fables of the which I shall tell you one."[4] He then told her the following story:

> There was a countrey in the which there were almoste none but foolys, sauynge a fewe which were wise. And thei by their wisedome knewe, that there shoulde fall a greate rayne, the which shoulde make theym all fooles, that shoulde so be fowled or wette therewith. Thei seing that, made theym caues vnder the grounde till all the rayne was paste. Than thei came forthe thinkinge to make the fooles to doe what thei liste, and to rule theym as thei woulde. But the fooles woulde none of that, but would haue the rule theimselfes for all their crafte. And whan the wisemen sawe thei coulde not obteyne their purpose, thei wished that thei had bene in the rayne, and had defoyled their clothes with theim.[5]

Audley laughed "very merily" at the tale, but when Alice continued to plead for help for More, he told her plainly: "I woulde not haue your father so scrupulous of his conscience. And than he tolde me an other fable of a lion, an asse, and a wolfe and of their confession."

> Fyrste the lion confessed him that he had deuoured all the beastes that he coulde come by. His confessor assoyled him because he was a kinge and also it was his nature so to doe. Than came the poore asse and saide that he toke but one strawe owte of his maisters shoe for hunger, by the meanes whereof he thought that his maister did take colde. His confessor coulde not assoile this great trespace, but by

---

[1] *Ibid.*, no. 208.　[2] *Ibid.*, no. 206.
[3] *Ibid.*, no. 205.　[4] *Ibid.*, p. 512.
[5] *Ibid.*, pp. 512–13.

and by sente him to the bisshoppe. Than came the wolfe and made his confession, and he was straightely commaunded that he shoulde not passe vi^d at a meale. But whan this saide wolfe had vsed this diet a litle while, he waxed very hungrye, in so much that on a day when he sawe a cowe with her calfe come by him he saied to himselfe, I am very hungrye and fayne would I eate, but that I am bounden by my ghostely father. Notwithstandinge that, my conscience shall iudge me. And then if it be so, than shall my consciens be thus, that the cowe dothe seme to me nowe but worthe a groate, and than if the cowe be but worthe a groate than is the calfe but worth ii^d. So did the wolfe eate both the cowe and the calfe.[1]

"I wiste not what to saye," Alice concludes, "for I was abashed of this aunswere. And I see no better suyte than to Almightie God, for he is the comforter of all sorrowes, and will not faile to sende his comforte to his seruauntes when thei haue moste neede."[2]

Of the letter that Margaret sent in answer to these fables, Rastell's comment gives the right clue: "But whether thys aunswer wer writen by syr Thomas More in his daughter Ropers name, or by her selfe, it is not certaynelye knowen."[3] The arguments of More in this letter are so circumstantially given, and the language has such a resonance of his own style, that I think one ends up with very little doubt that this letter is primarily More's own composition. One can imagine More and Margaret planning it together and speaking much of it aloud in More's Tower room. But its art seems to be all More's.

This letter is a prime example of More's art of improvisation, his art of exploration, displayed at length in *A Dialogue of Comfort*. It is an art that seems informal, extemporaneous, spontaneous. It allows for long digressions, excursions, and familiar asides, but in the end it reveals, lying under and within all its apparent wandering, a firm and central line, a teleological structure, based on a goal never forgotten. The chief goal of this letter is a defense of what people call More's "scruple of conscience," as described in the opening lines: "if he stande still in this scruple of his conscience (as it is at the lest wise called by manie that are his frendes and wise) all his frendes that seme most able to do hym good either shall finally forsake hym, or peraduenture not be hable in dede to doe hym any good att all."[4] "Conscience" is the key word, more than forty times repeated. The drama of the letter is set in terms of a temptation scene, with

---

[1] *Ibid.*, p. 513.
[2] *Ibid.*
[3] *EW*, sig. YY₁v; Rogers, p. 514 (with the reading "hym self" instead of "her selfe").
[4] Rogers, p. 514.

daughter Margaret in the role of "maistres Eue": "hath my daughter
Alington played the serpent with you, and with a letter set you a worke to
come tempt your father again, and for the fauour that you beare hym
labour to make hym sweare against his conscience, and so sende hym to
the deuill?"[1]

More is thoroughly prepared to meet the temptation, for, as he says:
"I haue ere I came here, not left vnbethought nor vnconsidered, the very
worst and the vttermost that can by possibilite fall. And al be it that I
know mine owne frailtie full well and the naturall faintnes of mine owne
hart, yet if I had not trusted that God shoulde geue me strength rather to
endure all thinges, than offend hym by sweringe vngodly against mine
owne conscience, you may be very sure I wold not haue come here."[2]
After three pages carefully setting up the situation, we then find Margaret
giving More her sister's letter to read: "Therupon he read ouer your
letter. And when he came to the ende, he began it afresh and read it ouer
again. And in the reading he made no maner hast, but aduised it laisorly
and poynted euery word." "And after that he paused, and than thus
he said . . . "[3] Here is More in the very process of creating one of his
artful improvisations. He does not speak or write spontaneously; he
speaks and writes only after the line and goal of his work have been firmly
established.

More now begins his answer by showing his warm appreciation of
Alice's effort to help, and especially of her "good counsell"[4] at the end of
her letter, where she expresses her faith that God "will not faile to send his
comforte"[5] in time of need. Then he shows his awareness of a possibly
wider audience by declaring his confidence in the good will of both Audley
and Cromwell and by pointedly urging them never to help him if he "be
founde other than a true man to my prince."[6]

He next turns to deal with Audley's first fable, which he knows all too
well, because, he says, Wolsey often used it in the King's Council when
anyone advised against meddling in the disputes "betwene the Emperour
and the French Kynge." More retells the fable in Wolsey's version and
concludes wryly: "But yet this fable for his parte, did in his daies helpe the
Kynge and the realme to spende many a faire peny."[7] As for the implications of the fable in Audley's version, More now spends over a page in

---

[1] *Ibid.*, p. 515.
[2] *Ibid.*, p. 516.
[3] *Ibid.*, p. 517.
[4] *Ibid.*
[5] *Ibid.*, p. 513.
[6] *Ibid.*, pp. 517–18.
[7] *Ibid.*, p. 518.

showing the folly of attempting to overcome fools by becoming a fool oneself, or of hoping that a few wise men can rule a crowd of fools, or indeed of placing ultimate value upon any sort of rule except self-rule.

Then he proceeds to deal with Audley's second fable, beginning with consideration of its authorship in a tone of ironic solemnity and puzzlement that leads digressively but certainly toward a slowly dawning apprehension that he must be the scrupulous ass in Audley's view:

> The second fable, Marget, semeth not to be Esopes. For by that the matter goeth all vpon confession, it semeth to be fayned since Christendome began. For in Grece before Christes daies they vsed not confession, no more the men than, than the beastes nowe. And Esope was a Greke, and died long ere Christ was borne. But what? who made it, maketh litle matter. Nor I enuy not that Esope hath the name. But surely it is somwhat to subtil for me. For wham hys Lordship vnderstandeth by the lyon and the wolfe, which both twaine confessed them selfe, of rauin and deuowringe of all that came to their handes, and the tone enlarged his conscience at his pleasure in the construction of his penaunce, nor whom by the good discrete confessor that enioyned the tone a little penaunce, and the tother none at all, and sent the pore asse to the bishoppe, of all these thinges can I nothinge tell. But by the folish scrupelous asse, that had so sore a conscience, for the taking of a strawe for hungar out of his maisters shoo, my Lordes other wordes of my scruple declare, that his Lordship meryly meant that by me: signifieng (as it semeth by that similitude) that of ouersight and folye, my scrupulous conscience taketh for a great perilous thing towarde my soule, if I shoulde swere this othe, which thinge as his Lordship thinketh, were in dede but a trifle.[1]

The whole movement of this passage is characteristic of More's mode of apparently extemporaneous chattering which leads the audience by irony and indirection into the very heart of the issue.

Then, after asserting his need to rely upon his own individual conscience, he launches into a two-page "merry" anecdote about "a poore honest man of the countrey that was called Company,"[2] but who would not follow the lead of "gude cumpany" and instead followed his own conscience—a tale that Margaret enlivens at the outset with her show of utter ignorance concerning legal terms ("a quest of xii men, a iury as I remember they call it, or elles a periury").[3] This comic interlude, situated in the middle of the letter, proves to be the pivot on which the tone moves

---

[1] *Ibid.*, p. 520.
[2] *Ibid.*, p. 521.
[3] *Ibid.*, p. 522.

from comic to solemn, as Margaret continues to press her argument "that ye well ought and haue good cause to chaunge your owne conscience, in confirming your owne conscience to the conscience of so many other."[1] Here is the crux of the problem, and in answer More gives a long and precise analysis of the proper relationship between the law of the land and the individual conscience, a discourse that rises in eloquence until at last he reaches his ultimate declaration of faith:

> But as concerninge mine owne self, for thy coumfort shall I say, Daughter, to the, that mine owne conscience in this matter (I damne none other mans) is such, as may well stand with mine owne saluacion, therof am I, Megge, so sure, as that is, God is in heauen. And therfore as for all the remenaunt, goodes, landes, and lyfe both (if the chaunce sholde so fortune) sith this conscience is sure for me, I verelie trust in God, he shall rather strenght me to bere the losse, than against this conscience to swere and put my soule in peryll, sith all the causes that I perceyue moue other men to the contrary, seme not such vnto me, as in my conscience make any chaunge.[2]

Finally, he rounds out the dramatic framework by returning to the image of a temptation, saying: "how now, doughter Marget? What how mother Eue? Where is your mind now? sit not musing with some serpent in your brest, vpon some newe perswasion, to offer father Adam the apple yet once againe."[3] And so the letter concludes with the temptation firmly overcome and with Thomas More displaying, to the comfort of his friends and family, his cheerful, resolute, and loving spirit:

> And with this, my good childe, I pray you hartely, be you and all your sisters and my sonnes too comfortable and seruisable to your good mother my wyfe. And of your good husbandes mindes I haue no maner doute. Commende me to them all, and to my good daughter Alington, and to all my other frendes, sisters, neces, nephewes, and alies, and vnto all our seruauntes, man, woman and childe, and all my good neighbours and our acquayntaunce abrode. And I right hartely praye both you and them, to serue God and be mery and reioyce in hym.[4]

This entire letter bears a very close relation to the literary method and to the contents of More's *Dialogue of Comfort*. For the letter is in itself a dialogue of comfort, an answer to Alice Alington's plea for comfort at the

---

[1] *Ibid.*, p. 524.

[2] *Ibid.*, pp. 528–29.

[3] *Ibid.*, p. 529; the question-mark at the end in Rogers' text has been omitted.

[4] *Ibid.*, p. 532.

close of her letter, and a summation of previous conversations between
More and Margaret on this very subject, as More here says near the
beginning of the letter: "Doughter Margaret, we two haue talked of this
thinge ofter than twise or thrise, and that same tale in effect, that you tel
me now therin, and the same feare to, haue you twise tolde me before, and
I haue twise answered you too . . . "[1] No wonder then that the dialogue
between father and daughter bears much the same tone and manner that
we find in the longer dialogue between those two fictional Hungarians,
old Uncle Antony and young Nephew (or "Cousin") Vincent, as the
Great Turk threatens to overwhelm Hungary with his persecutions. The
general subject of this dialogue-letter and *A Dialogue of Comfort* is basically
the same: how should the Christian behave when persecutors test his
strength to endure for what he believes, in his conscience, to be the true
faith?

A particular analogy between the two dialogues is found in "Mother
Maud's" elaborate fable of the fox, wolf, and ass, and their scruples of
conscience, as told at length in the second book of *A Dialogue of Comfort*.[2]
This seems to be the direct result of More's reading the similar fable in
Alice Alington's letter; and More's witty and cautious reworking of the
fable (omitting the Lion-King: too dangerous a topic) may be taken to
represent a further and even more carefully considered answer to Audley
and all others who accuse him of excessive "scrupulosity." This particular
collocation lends very strong support to Rastell's statement that *A Dialogue
of Comfort* was a Tower Work, as indeed its whole tenor would lead us to
believe. But the parallels between this great letter and *A Dialogue of
Comfort* form only one strand of the many affiliations that tie together the
Tower Works into the one central work that is the ultimate achievement
of all these varied writings: the preparation of More's mind to meet his
death, if God so wishes.

2. The Design of *A Dialogue of Comfort*

As we have noted earlier, Harpsfield's statement that *A Dialogue of
Comfort* was "for the moste part written with none other penne in the
worlde then with a coale"[3] has no adequate basis in the available evidence.
There is no reason, then, to assume poor conditions of composition for the
Dialogue, but rather, for More, an unusual opportunity for careful planning
and writing—made available by his fifteen months of lonely imprisonment. Furthermore, if we consider that the *Dialogue* bears every mark of

---

[1] *Ibid.*, p. 516.
[2] 114/14–120/6.
[3] Harpsfield, p. 134.

being an ultimate spiritual testament, we may well believe that More would have lavished upon it all the care that his time would allow. The *Dialogue* itself bears out this conjecture, for it displays all the signs of More's finest literary skill, both in the details of its language and in the total command of its development. But we must, to appreciate its skill, adjust ourselves to its unhurried, deliberate pace, and to its highly colloquial style, which the Corpus Christi manuscript accentuates.

Let us start with the setting in Hungary, where two Hungarians, Uncle Antony and Nephew Vincent, discuss the problems of human suffering, under the threat of an imminent invasion of their country by the Turks. We cannot read these affectionate conversations between the older and the younger Hungarian without thinking of More's letters from the Tower to his daughter Margaret, and of the conversations of this kind which actually occurred between More and this daughter in the Tower—and perhaps also with other members of his family, before his imprisonment. Thus at the outset of the *Dialogue* More has the nephew say:

> You be not ignorant good vncle what heps of hevynes hath of late fallen among vs all redye / with which some of our pore famely be fallen into suche dumpes, that scantly can any such comfort as my pore wyt can give them, any thyng asswage their sorow / And now sith the tydynges haue come hether so brymme of the great Turkes interprise into these parties here: we can almost neyther talke nor thynke of any other thyng els, than of his might & our mischefe. (6/15–21)

Yet at the same time, as we point out in section IV below, More describes the Turkish threat with such exact reference to the historical conditions that we are never allowed to think of this setting as only a device: "Than hath he taken Belgrade the fortres of this realme / And syns hath he destroyid our noble yong goodly kyng / And now stryve there twayne for vs / our lord send the grace / that the third dogg cary not away the bone from them both" (8/1–5). Such allusions to the contemporary situation in Hungary make the setting operate both historically and metaphorically, at one and the same time, with a result that is well stated by John Fowler in the preface to his edition of 1573:

> The inuention in dede of the Authour seemeth to respect some particular cases, which was of him wonderful wittily deuised, applyng his whole discourse to that peece of Christendome, to wit, the land of Hungarie, which hath bene these many yeares (and yet is) sore persecuted and oppressed by Turks. But vnder this particular case of Turks persecution he generally comprehendeth al kinds of afflictions and persecutions both of body and mind, that may any way be suffred,

either by sicknes or health, by frind or fo, by wicked & wrongful
oppressors, by Miscreants and Turks, and the very fiends and diuels
of hel also. And that was done for this entent (as it may wel seeme)
that vnder this one kind of Turkish persecution, the benefit of y^e
booke might be the more common to al Christen folke, as the which
could iustly of none be reiected nor reprooued, but if themselues were
very Turkes to, or woorse.[1]

He adds that the book would also be very good for the Turks themselves to
read, since they are sometimes taken prisoner by the Christians.

In his universal application of the book, Fowler has the right key to its
spirit and its strategy. It is a book of comfort against all kinds of tribulation, not only against that kind which Thomas More himself is suffering.
The treatise seems written at random only if we insist on limiting its
concerns to the special situation of More's own treatment at the hands of
Henry VIII. More is aware of larger issues than his own fate. He sees his
plight as involved in mankind's universal condition. At the same time, as
Fowler seems to discern, the generalizing tendency of the treatise serves
wittily to disguise its personal implications. "What are you writing there,
Thomas?" "A book of comfort for those who are sick, or who are tempted
by the devil, or who are living in Hungary." So the book escaped suspicion,
and somehow made its way out of the prison cell.

This general application and disguise is accomplished by means of
deliberate garrulity and conscious digression, with the result that the
topic of persecution for the faith is held in abeyance during the first two
books of the treatise, while all the lesser kinds of tribulation are being
covered. Then in the final book all strands are drawn together in a subtle,
surprising, and powerful way that fulfills the underlying design. Let us see
how this design is developed.

Each of the three books has its own peculiar decorum, with a lapse in
time before each renewal of the conversation: each book has the effect of a
fresh attack upon the universal problem. Book I is chiefly composed of the
reassertion of familiar, traditional views. The main point is, simply, tribulation is good for you, if you keep faith. It cures past sins and prevents sins
to come. It is a gift of God, the mark of God's favor. But for all his wise
utterances here, Uncle Antony finds his nephew hard to convince.
Vincent listens respectfully and seems to be taking in the arguments, and
yet about three-fifths of the way through the first book he suddenly enters
a startling objection:

But yet good vncle though that some do thus / this answereth not
full the mater / For we se that the whole church in the comen

---

[1] See below, Appendix B, pp. 485–86.

seruice, vse diuers colletes / in which all men pray specially for the princes and prelattes, & generally euery man for other, & for hym selfe to / that god wold vouchsafe to send them all perpetuall helth & prosperitie / And I can se no good man pray god send an other sorow, nor no such praers are there put in the prestes portuouse as far as I can here /

And yet yf it were as you say good vncle / that perpetuall prosperitie were to the sowle so perilouse, & tribulacion therto so frutefull / than were as me semeth euery man bound of charitie, not onely to pray god send their neibours sorow / but also to help therto them selfe / & when folke are sike, not pray god send them helth / but when they come to comfort them they shuld say I am glad good gossep / that ye be so syk / I pray god kepe you long therin / (46/15–47/1)

Antony quells this and other objections with an effect of main force, since in the end he takes the floor for twelve pages of an unbroken dissertation, closing with a ritual affirmation and "summary comfort" that lists all the gracious benefits of tribulation. One might think that after this resounding catalogue (see chapter 20) there would not be much more to say. This effect of a formal conclusion to a formal discourse (carried on primarily by Uncle Antony) is emphasized by the way in which Book I is set forth in twenty chapters, reasonably divided and of reasonably similar length. Twenty is a "perfect number," a multiple of ten.

Yet an uneasy feeling persists that the problems of human suffering cannot be adequately met by the delivery of traditional apothegms. The wisdom of Book I, however eloquent, however sound, is not enough, we feel (as Vincent feels), to cover all the experiences of man in tribulation. The positions set forth by Antony remain too theoretical, too far removed from actual existence. Such wisdom is a basis to build upon, no more. Book I is appropriately the shortest of the three.

As the dialogue resumes in Book II, after a lapse of several days, we find ourselves abruptly moved out of the orderly world of theory and plunged into the chaotic world of everyday. Now Antony and Vincent begin by swapping worldly jests, and Antony at once signals a drastic change in tone and technique when he apologizes in a jocular way for having talked too much the other day, saying that he wished "the last tyme after you were gone / when I felt my selfe (to sey the trowth) evyn a litell wery / that I had not so told you styll a long tale alone / but that we had more often enterchaungid wordes / & partid the talke betwene vs, with ofter enterparlyng vppon your part / in such maner as lernid men vse between the persons / whom they devise disputyng in their faynid diologes" (79/20–26). He immediately demonstrates the change in tone by an anecdote, comparing himself with the nun who lectured her brother at length at the convent grate, and then berated him for not giving her the benefit of his wisdom. Vincent responds with the "merye tale" concerning the "kynswoman" who loved to talk, which we have cited earlier, and which is worth quoting complete here as an introduction to the more concrete and worldly atmosphere of this entire book:

> Her husband had mych pleasure in the maner and behavour of an other honest man, & kept hym therfor mych company / by the reason wherof he was at his meale tyme the more oft from home / So happid it on a tyme, that his wife and he together dynid or soupid with that neybour of theirs / And than she made a mery quarell to hym, for makyng her husband so good chere out at dore that she could not haue hym at home / For soth mastres quod he (as he was a dry mery man) In my company nothyng kepeth hym but one / Serve you hym with the same, & he will neuer be from you / what gay thyng may that be quoth our Cosyn than / forsoth mastres quoth he your husband loveth well to talke / & whan he sittith with me I let hym haue all the wordes / All the wordes quoth she / mary that am I content he shall haue all the wordes with good will as he hath euer had / but I speke them all my selfe, & give them all to hym / & for ought that I care for them so shall he haue them styll / but otherwise to say that he shall haue them all / you shall kepe hym still rather than he get the halfe. (81/2–18)

While they are thus jesting Antony declares that he will from now on force his nephew to talk half the time. This turns out to be quite a jest in itself, since some of Antony's unbroken disquisitions are in fact even longer than in the first book. Nevertheless, Book II works in quite a different way from Book I. It is thirty-five pages longer, and that extra length, we might say, is filled out with a remarkable array of racy, vivid, colloquial anecdotes. What we are watching here is a gradual process of adjusting theory to the world as it is, a process that More wittily heralds in the first chapter of Book II by having the nephew ask whether Antony really meant, in the previous day's conversation, to rule out all forms of worldly comfort, such as "a mery tale with a frend" or "proper plesaunt talkyng." Antony allows that his theories cannot in fact be so strictly applied, considering that men are as they are: "A man to take now & than some honest worldly myrth / I dare not be so sore as vtterly to forbyd yt" (83/11–13). True, we ought to find all our joy and comfort in talking of heaven, but somehow men seem to be easily wearied by this topic, as Cassian, he says, shows in one of his *Collations*:

> a certen holy father in makyng of a sermon, spake of hevyn & of hevynly thynges so celestially that much of his audience with the

> swete sowne therof began to forget all the world & fall a slepe / which
> whan the father beheld he dissemblid their slepyng & sodenly said vnto
> them I shall tell you a mery tale / at which word they lyft vp their hedes
> & herknid vnto that / And after the slepe therwith broken, herd hym
> tell on of hevyn agayne / . . . But thus much of that mater suffisith for
> our purpose / that where as you demaund me whether in tribulacion
> men may not sometyme refresh them selfe with worldly myrth &
> recreacion / I can no more saye / but he that can not long endure to
> hold vpp his hedd & here talkyng of hevyn except he be now & than
> betwene (as though hevyn were hevynes) refreshid with a folish mery
> tale / there is none other remedy, but you most let hym haue yt /
> better wold I wish it but I can not help it. (84/6–23)

Shortly after this Antony becomes so involved in recounting the strange
tale of a tertian fever of his, in which he felt hot and cold at once, that he
loses his train of thought: "But se now what age is lo / I haue bene so long
in my tale / that I haue almost forgotone / for what purpose I told yt / Oh
now I remember lo" (90/8–10).

We are moving ever more clearly and concretely into the world of
actuality—the story of the fever includes an allusion to a young woman
trained in medicine that almost certainly is a reference to More's adopted
daughter, Margaret Clement.[1] Now the world's stage opens out suddenly
with two long and brilliant tales involving religious satire. The first occurs
when Vincent narrates at length his recent experiences in Saxony, during
the early days of Luther's revolt ("nor Luther was not than weddid yet").
Vincent proceeds to give a brilliant parody of a Lutheran sermon that he
has heard, in words that bring directly home the powerful appeal of the
Reformers:

> he cried euer owt vppon them to kepe well the lawes of christ / let go
> their pevysh penaunce & purpose them to amend, and seke nothyng to
> saluacion but the deth of christ / for he is our iustice, & he is our
> saviour, & our hole satisfaccion for all our dedly synnes / he did full
> penaunce for vs all vppon his paynfull crosse / he wasshid vs there all
> clene with the water of his swete side, & brought vs out of the devilles
> daynger with his dere preciouse bloude / Leve therfor leve I besech
> you these invencions of men, your folysh lenton fastes & your pevish
> penaunce, minysh neuer christes thankes nor loke to save your selfe.
> It is Christes deth I tell you that must save vs all. Christes deth I tell
> you yet agayne & not our own dedes. Leve your own fastyng therfor
> & lene to christ alone good christen people for christes dere bitter
> passion.

---

[1] See the Commentary at 88/4–90/7.

Now so lowd & so shirle he cried christ in theire heres & so thikke
he came forth with christes bitter passion, & that so bitterly spoken /
with the sweate droppyng down his chekes, that I merveylid not
though I saw the pore women wepe / For he made myne heare stand
vp vppon myne hed / And with such prechyng were the people so
brought in, that some fell to breke the fastes on the fastyng dayes / not
of frayltie or of malice first / but almost of deuocion, lest they shuld
take fro christ the thanke of his bitter passion / But whan they were
a while noselid in that poynt first, they could endure & abyde after
many thynges mo / with which had he begone, they wold haue pullid
hym downe. (94/5-28)

Twenty pages later, however, we find the other side of the picture in
the longest and most brilliant tale of the entire treatise, the five-page
beast-fable which Antony says he heard from his old nurse, Mother Maud
—More's complete and carefully considered answer to Audley's similar
fable about conscience. This is, among other things, a hilarious piece of
anti-clerical satire, presenting the Ass who suffers from an excessively
scrupulous conscience, Father Reynard the confessor, the worldly priest
who never worries about fasting, and the Wolf, who represents the utterly
unscrupulous and rapacious tendencies of man. When the Wolf comes late
to his lenten confession, on Good Friday, he explains:

I durst come no soner / for fere lest you wold for my glotony haue
givyn me in penaunce to fast some part of this lent / Nay Nay quod the
father Fox I am not so vnreasonable / for I fast none of yt my selfe / For
I may say to the sone here in confession betwene vs twayne / it is no
commaundement of god this fasting, but an invencion of man / The
prestes make folke fast & put them to payne about the mone shyne
in the water, & do but make foke foles / but they shall make me no
such fole I warrant the sone / For I eate flessh all this lent my self I.
Howbeit in dede because I will not be occasion of slaunder, I therfor
eate it secretely in my chamber out of sight of all such folysh brethren
as for their weke scrupulouse conscience wold wax offendid with all /
And so wold I counsayle you to do. (116/1-12)

Thus far, nearly halfway through the second book, we have been within
the realm of comical satire, but now, with chapter 15, we move into a
darker realm of tales concerning self-destruction. Some of these are
savagely comic in their way, such as the opening anecdote of the carpenter's wife who was so fiendish that the devil tempted her to taunt her
husband into chopping off her head with his axe: "There were standyng
other folke by / which had a good sport to here her chide / but litell they

lokyd for this chaunce till it was done ere they cold let it / They said they
herd her tong bable in her hed & call horson horson twise after that the
hed was fro the bodye" (125/24–27).

Although some of the examples are thus touched with grim humor, the
major part of this thirty-five-page discussion of suicide or self-destruction
is given over to a serious discussion of the ways by which a man can distinguish the illusions of the devil from the true revelations of God (chapter
16). One may wonder why More devotes so much space to this problem of
devilish delusions, with special reference to the temptation of self-
destruction. It may be relevant to remember that More was, in his last
years, very closely concerned with the question of the truth or falsehood of
the revelations allegedly experienced by the Nun of Kent.[1] This question
of temptation by demons was a real and pressing issue for More, as we may
see from the frequent notation *contra demones* which More wrote in the
margins of the book of Psalms which he had with him in the Tower.[2] In
this connection it is interesting to note that here in the *Dialogue* More says:
"Speciall verses may there be drawen out of the *psalter* / agaynst the
devilles wikked temptacions" (156/17–18). There is no evidence that More
was tempted toward suicide, in the ordinary sense of that word; but in a
subtler way the possibility of such a devilish temptation may indeed have
been close to More's mind. He dwells at some length upon the case of the
"very specall holy man" who was by the devil "brought into such an high
spirituall pride" that he became convinced it was God's will that he should
destroy himself, "& that therby shuld he go strayt to hevyn" (129/20–25).
More in the Tower had chosen a course that was almost certain to lead to
his death. How could he be sure that he was not being assailed by the
temptation of spiritual pride? (One thinks of the temptations of Thomas à
Becket in Eliot's play.) But of course the whole section on self-destruction
is part of More's effort to make his book useful in comfort against all
tribulations for everyman.

Finally, for the last twenty pages of Book II, the discussion turns toward
a very practical examination of the role of *business* in this world, a term
under which More includes the busy search for pleasures of the flesh,
along with business in the sense of seeking worldly wealth. In this connection More takes the occasion to explain the necessity of having men of

---

[1] For a full account see R. W. Chambers, *Thomas More* (London, 1935), pp. 294–300,
and J. Duncan M. Derrett, "Sir Thomas More and the Nun of Kent," *Moreana*, *15–16*
(1967), 267–84.

[2] *Thomas More's Prayer Book*, ed. L. L. Martz and R. S. Sylvester (New Haven, 1969),
pp. 27, 29, 31, 32, 50, 59, 66, 67, 100, 101, 106, 111, 115. Cited hereafter as "*Prayer
Book.*"

substance in this world, in a passage that sounds like a rebuke to those who would take his *Utopia* as a blueprint for society:

> Men can not you wot well lyve here in this world, but yf that some one man prouide a meane of lyvyng for some other many. Euery man can not haue a ship of his own, nor euery man be a merchaunt without a stoke / And these thinges you wote well must nedes be had / nor euery man can not haue a plough by hym selfe / And who might live by the taylours crafte yf no man were able to put a gowne to make? who by the masonry / or who could live a carpenter, yf no man were able to bild neyther church nor howse? (180/14–21)

It is appropriate that after this reconciliation with the ways of the busy world, Book II should end with the bringing in of a good dinner.

These materials have been reviewed at length in order to stress their rich variety. In Book II nearly every aspect of the world as More knew it is vividly brought before us, in colloquial terms, until we may feel that the turmoil of human existence is in some danger of overwhelming the unity and the direction of the dialogue. This sense of disorder is mirrored in the gradual disintegration of the chapter-divisions, so reasonably maintained in Book I. The first chapter of Book II belongs with the prologue, rather than in a division by itself, while chapter 2 marks the beginning of the argument of the book, as the closing words of Vincent in chapter 1 indicate: "But now I pray you good vncle vouchsafe to procede in our principall mater." The summary of chapter 3 shifts to the third person—a manner not used before: "He devidith tribulacion into / 3 / kyndes of which / 3 / the last he shortly passith ouer." Chapter 4 has no real division in topic from the preceding chapter, and, significantly, it is not provided with any summary—the first example of such an omission. There is no convincing division of topic between chapters 10 and 11, nor between 13 and 14. Finally, the chapter-divisions break down completely, as chapter 16 runs to 37 pages and chapter 17 runs to 22 pages—a discrepancy that is the more notable because seven of the earlier chapters have run to only a page or a little more. One has the impression that the whole book has been written without regard to chapter-divisions—an impression that continues throughout Book III, where the chapter-divisions are, however, more reasonably made, both in topic and in length. One begins to wonder whether the chapter-divisions in the last two books are the work of More, or whether they have been imposed by another hand.[1]

In any case, the breakdown in the chapter-divisions indicates a shift to a different principle of organization. As the danger of disunity threatens, More quietly and firmly brings in the counterforce of reason to control

---

[1] See the discussion of this problem in the Commentary at 9/17.

these follies and evils. About a quarter of the way through the second book
he brings in the great central text from Psalm 90 which runs like a refrain
throughout the rest of Book II and on throughout Book III, forming the
basis for a sustained set of considerations on the comfort to be found in
"the truth of God":

> The prophet sayth in the psalme / *Scuto circumdabit te veritas eius /
> non timebis a timore nocturno / a sagitta volante in die, a negocio perambulante in
> tenebris, ab incursu & demonio meridiano:* The trouth of god shall com-
> passe the about with a pavice, thow shalt not be aferd of the nightes
> feare, nor of the arrow fleying in the day, nor of the bysynes walkyng
> about in the darknesses / nor of the incursion or invacion of the devill
> in the mydde day. (105/17–23)

The intricacy of the discussion that lies ahead is at once shown here as
More now proceeds to repeat, ten times within the space of one page, that
key word *pavis:* the ancient term for a long shield protecting the whole
body:

> as god hath faythfully promisid to protect & defend those that fayth-
> fully will dwell in the trust of his help / so will he truly perform yt /
> And the that such one art, will the trouth of his promise defend, not
> with a litell round buckeler that scant can couer the hed, but with a
> long large pavice, that couereth all along the bodye, made as holy
> saynt Barnard sayth brode above with the godhed, & narrow beneth
> with the manhed / so that this pavice is our saviour christ hym selfe.
> And yet is not this pauice like other pauices of this world, which
> are not made but in such wise, as while it defendith one part, the man
> may be woundid vppon the tother / but this pavise is such / that as the
> prophet sayth / it shall rownd about enclose & compase the / so that
> thyn ennymye shall hurt thy sowle on no side. For *scuto* sayth he /
> *circumdabit te veritas eius* / with a pauise shall his trouth environ &
> compasse the rounde aboute. (106/4–18)

With this winding, repetitive method of discourse, More then dissects
the text, part by part, seeing in it four kinds of temptations or tribulations
by which we are beset by the devil.

1) "*Non timebis a timore nocturno,* thow shalt not be aferd of the fere of the
night" (107/3–4)—which includes temptations that come from an overly
scrupulous conscience, from the "pusillanimity" of a "timorous mind."
This is a fear that in its worst form leads to the temptation of suicide.

2) "*a sagitta volante in die*": "from the arrow fleyng in the daye"— that
is, "the arrow of pride, with which the devill temptith a man" in prosperity (157/18–21).

3) *"negocium perambulans in tenebris"*: "bysines walkyng in the darknes"
(166/8–9)—business which includes both the busy seeking after fleshly
pleasures and the busy seeking after worldly wealth.

Such are the three lesser fears that constitute the matter of Book II.
This whole part of the treatise is pursued in a tantalizing manner of
deliberate digression and casual divagation that is foreshadowed in
chapter 11, where the basic text is introduced, with Antony saying: "And
therfor I shall peraduenture / except any ferther thyng fall in our waye,
with treatyng of those ij verses fynysh & end all our mater" (105/14–16).
What falls in our way from here on happens to be about two-thirds of the
entire treatise! This consciously ambling and rambling manner is openly
maintained by many different asides, such as the explanation that occurs
in the middle of the discussion of devilish delusions: "That were somwhat
out of our purpose Cosyn," says Antony, "sith as I told you before, the
man were not than in sorow and tribulacion wherof our mater speketh /
but in a perilous mery mortall temptacion / so that yf we shuld besid our
own mater that we haue in hand, entre into that to / we might make a
lenger warke betwene both, than we could well finish this day / How be it
to be short . . . " (131/21–26). Then he continues the admittedly "irrelevant" discussion for a dozen more pages. Similarly, Antony promises to
"touch one word or twayn of the third temptacion . . . & than will we
call for our dener." At this suggestion Vincent, always concerned for his
uncle's health, pleads: "for our lordes sake take good hede vncle that you
forbere not your dener ouer longe." "Fere not that cosyn I warrant you,"
Antony replies, "for this piece will I make you but short" (165/24–166/7).
The piece of course runs on for twenty more pages.

The whole of Book II thus serves as a variegated interlude, or as a
leisurely prologue, before the main event, which now rushes upon us in
the form of the fourth temptation, to which More devotes the whole of
Book III, the longest book of all:

> The fourth temptacion Cosyn that the prophet speketh of in the fore
> remembrid psalme . . . ys playne open persecucion / which is touchid
> in these wordes / *Ab incursu & demonio meridiano* / And of all his
> temptacions this is the most perilouse, the most bittre sharpe, & the
> most rigorouse / . . . for in this temptacion he shewith hymselfe such
> as the prophet nameth hym, *Demonium meridianum* / the mydday
> devill / he may be so lightsomely seen with the yie of a faythfull soule
> by his fierce furyouse assawt & incurcion / for therfor sayth the
> prophet, that the trouth of god shall compasse that man round about /
> that dwellith in the faythfull hope of his helpe / with a pavice *Ab
> incursu & demonio meridiano* from the incursion & the devill of the
> mydday / (200/5–29)

Here, twelve pages along in Book III, is the climax of the mode of repetitious winding by which More pursues his tenacious explication of the basic text; we are now ninety-five pages away from the point at which the text was introduced, and yet the word *pavis* is still ringing, and will continue to ring, as the keynote of the faithful man's belief. In this way the last two books are firmly tied together, while More's explication of the text gradually develops, through its network of repetitions, into an abiding proof that the *pavis* of God is always present to protect the faithful amid the apparent chaos of ordinary life. As the explication weaves its way among the illustrative, gossipy anecdotes of Book II, we come to feel that the disorder of life is being brought under the steady control of reason. More's biblical explication, we might say, gradually weaves a net that subdues the unruly world of anecdote. Yet even this is not enough for full comfort. The reasoning mind of man may do much, More seems to say, but the most difficult problem and the richest comfort remain to be explored.

As the third book opens, the problem is abruptly brought before us, as Vincent enters with the news (just received in a letter from Constantinople) that the Turk is preparing a mighty army which may in all likelihood be aimed at Hungary. We have returned with a jolt to the threat with which the treatise had begun, a threat whose imminence has gradually receded as More's discourse has turned to lesser matters. But now the historical situation, both for the Hungarians and for Thomas More, is brought in hard upon us, especially when Vincent says: "I here at myn eare some of our owne here among vs, which with in these few yeres could no more haue born the name of a Turke than the name of the devill, begyn now to fynd litle faute therin / ye and some to prayse them to, litle & litle as they may / more glad to fynd fawtes at euery state of christendome, prestes, princes / rites / ceremonies / sacramentes laues and custumes spirituall temporall & all" (192/3–9). And there are, he says, even some who "talke as though they loked for a day whan with a turne vnto the Turkes fayth, they shulbe made maisters here, of trew christen mennys bodies, & owners of all their goodes" (195/9–11).

Here, then, in this incursion of the mid-day devil, lies the ultimate temptation by which the soul of a man will stand or fall. In such a plight the theoretical wisdom of the ages, as presented in Book I, will not suffice; nor will the toughest reasoning powers of man, struggling to subdue the world about him, as represented in Book II. There is, in this ultimate danger, only one resource: to turn within the self and give the mind to meditation on the great central facts of the faith: the vanity of worldly things, the facts of death, judgement, hell, and heaven, and above all the great central fact of Christ's Passion.

Thus in Book III More presents what might be called a treatise on the art of meditation. He advises what topics to seek out, and he shows by brief examples how to meditate upon these ancient themes: *contemptus mundi*, the Last Things, and the Passion. By such meditation, More shows, a man may move with the help of reason into a realm that includes and yet transcends reason: the realm of the affections, the emotions, where man may find his ultimate comfort in his love of God. All this More explains in two powerful passages: one, very early in Book III (chapter 3), and the other near the end, in chapter 24. These two passages enclose all the intervening matter within the love of God and sum up the culminating purpose of More's final book:

> yf a man had in his hart / so diepe a desiere & love longyng to be with god in hevyn to haue the fruicion of his gloriouse face, as had those holy men that were martires in old tyme / he wold no more now styke at the payne that he must passe betwene / than at that tyme those old holy martirs did / But alas our faynt & feble fayth, with our love to god lesse than luke warm, by the fyery affeccion that we bere to our own filthy flesh, make vs so dull in the desiere of hevyn, that the sodayne drede of euery bodely payne, woundeth vs to the hart & strikith our devocion ded / And therfor hath there euery man Cosyn / (as I said before) mich the more nede to thinke vppon this thing many tyme & oft aforehand, ere any such perell fall / & by mich devisyng thervppon before they se cause to fere yt, while the thing shall not apere so terrible vnto them / reason shall bettre entre, & thorow grace workyng with their diligens / engendre & set sure, not a sodayne sleyght affeccion of sufferaunce for godes sake / but by a long contynuaunce, a strong depe rotid habit / (204/28–205/14)

> why should not than reason I say thus fortherid with fayth & grace, be mych more able, first to engendre in vs such an effeccion / and after by long & depe meditacion therof, so to contynew that affeccion, that it shall tourne into an habituall fast & depe rotid purpose, of pacient suffryng the paynfull deth of this body here in earth, for the gaynyng of euerlastyng welthy lyfe in hevyn, & avoydyng of euerlastyng paynefull deth in hell / (294/5–12)

For this purpose, then, he proceeds to develop these affections: contempt of the world, leading gradually to a withdrawal of the mind into its interior citadel, where it is free to meditate upon the three most important facts: the pains of hell, the joys of heaven, and the Passion of Christ. The Passion, indeed, is never out of More's mind, from beginning to end of this final book. Meditation on this theme is briefly mentioned in the first chapter (198/15–17) as the essential exercise to fortify the heart, with the result that the theme thus lies in the background of the discussion of the *contemptus mundi;* and then it comes forward into dominance throughout the latter half of Book III, beginning with the sixteenth chapter and culminating in the detailed memorials of the Passion, the mental communion, of chapters 23 and 27:

> So say I now / for paynefull deth also, that yf we could & wold with dew compassion, conceyve in our myndes a right Imagynacion & remembraunce of Christes byttre paynefull passion, of the many sore blody strokes that the cruell tourmentours with roddes & whyppes gaue hym vppon euery part of his holy tendre body / the scornefull crowne of sharp thornes beten down vppon his holy hed, so strayght & so diepe, that on euery part his blyssid blode yssued owt & stremyd down / his lovely lymmys drawen & strechid out vppon the crosse to the Intollerable payne of his forebeten & sorebeten vaynes and synewes / new felyng with the cruell strechyng & straynyng payne far passyng any crampe, in euery part of his blyssid body at ones / Than the greate long nayles cruelly dryven with hamers thorow his holy handes and fete / & in this horryble payne lyft vpp & let hang with the payce of all his body beryng down vppon the paynfull woundid places so grevously percyd with nayles / & in suche tourment / without pitie, but not without many dispightes / suffred to be pynyd & paynid the space of more than three long howres / tyll hym selfe willyngly gave vpp vnto his father his holy soule / after which yet to shew the myghtenes of their malice after his holy soule departid / perced his holy hart with a sharpe spere / at which issued out the holy blode & water, wherof his holy sacramentes haue Inestymable secrete strength / yf we wold I say remembre these thinges in such wise, as wold god we wold / I verely suppose that the consideracion of his incomparable kyndnes, could not fayle in such wise to inflame our kay cold hartes, & set them on fire in his love / that we shuld fynd our selfe not onely content, but also glad & desierouse to suffre deth for his sake / that so mervelously lovyngly lettid not to sustayne so farre passyng paynfull deth for ours.
> (312/10–313/7)

As the minds of uncle and nephew move toward this affectionate meditation, we notice that the nephew comes to play a greater part throughout the final book. He does not talk half the time, but he comes near to sharing a quarter of the talk; and there is throughout the final book much more true engagement and "enterparlyng" of minds than we have seen in the first two books. There, Vincent was presented as callow, naive, badly in need of instruction. But here in Book III we note that it is the nephew who tells, with subtle insight, that story of the great man of the

church who was never "saciate of heryng his own prayse" (ch. 10). One
has the feeling from this tale of flattery, and from the nephew's frequent,
vigorous, and highly intelligent intervention in the last book, that his mind
has been aroused and strengthened, and that young and old have been
truly brought together within the flexible and all-inclusive movement of
the dialogue. This final accordance of human minds within the pavis of
truth represents the carefully designed fulfillment of the anguished plea
for help with which the nephew has entered upon the scene:

> And sith that I now se the lyklyhod, that when ye be gone, we shalbe
> sore destytute of any such other lyke / Therfor thynketh me / that
> god of dewtie byndeth me to sew to you now good vncle, in this short
> tyme that we haue you, that yt may like you agaynst these grete
> stormes of tribulacions / with which both I and all myne are sore
> beten alredy / And now vppon the comyng of this cruell Turke, fere
> to fall in ferre mo / I may lern of you such plentie of good councell &
> comfort, that I may with the same layd vp in remembrauns, gouerne
> and staye the ship of ower kyndred, & kepe yt a flote from perill of
> spirituall drounnyng. (6/5–14)

3. Treatises upon the Passion

After these exhortations to meditate upon the sufferings of Christ,
More's English treatise on the Passion might seem to form a natural sequel.
But in Rastell's folio the *Dialogue of Comfort* is immediately followed by the
brief treatise entitled by More (so Rastell tells us): "To receaue the
blessed body of our lorde, sacramentally and virtually bothe."[1] There is,
however, strong evidence that this brief treatise is misplaced in the folio
and that it may in fact constitute the final portion of the incomplete
"third lecture" with which the English treatise on the Passion breaks off
in Rastell's printing.

This "third lecture" is introduced with the declaration, "I haue in the
first lecture (good readers) expowned you the wordes of our sauiour at the
institucion of ye blessed sacrament. And after haue I in the second, shewed
you somwhat of the sacramentall signes, & of the sacramentall thinges,
that are either conteined therin, or signified thereby."[2] And then he adds,
"Now is it conuenient that we somewhat speake, in what maner wyse we
ought to vse our self in the receiuinge. We must vnderstand that of this
holye sacrament, there are three maner of receiuing. For some folke
receiue it only sacramentally, and some only spiritually and some receiue

---

[1] *EW*, sig. LL$_4$v.
[2] *Ibid.*, sig. QQ$_6$v.

it both."[1] Clearly this third lecture is planned as a short treatise on how to receive the sacrament. More then describes for two columns in the folio the state of those who receive the sacrament only sacramentally, that is, those who receive it "unworthily":

> But because they receyue it in dedely sinne, y^t is to witte, eyther in will to committe dedely sinne againe, or impenitent of y^t they haue committed before, therefore they receiue it not spiritually: that is to say, they receiue not the spiritual thing of the sacrament, whiche as I before haue shewed, is the sacramentall thing that is signified therby, that is to wit, ye societe of holy saintes, y^t is to say, he is not by the spirite of God vnyd with holy saintes as a liuely membre of Christes misticall body.[2]

Then, in a short paragraph that ends the English treatise as here printed, More explains the second manner of receiving:

> Some as I sayde before, receiue this blessed sacrament only spiritually, and not sacramentally, and so dooe all they receiue it whiche are in cleane lyfe, and are at their high masse devoutely. For there the curate offreth it for him & them too. And although that only himselfe receiue it sacramentally, that is to witte, the uery bodye & bloud vnder the sacramentall sygnes the fourmes of bread & wyne, yet as manye of them as are present at it, & are in cleane lyfe, receyue it spiritually: that is to wit, the fruitefull thing of the sacrament, that is to saye, they receiue grace, by which they be by the spirite of Christ more firmely knyt and vnyd quicke liuely membres in the spirituall societie of sayntes.[3]

Is it possible that More would thus leave the treatise without the essential third way of receiving, that is, sacramentally and spiritually both? Now consider the opening of the brief treatise on receiving the sacrament: "They receyue ye blessed bodi of our lord both sacramentally and virtuallye, whiche in dew maner and worthely, receyue the blessed sacrament."[4] And then he goes on to warn against taking the sacrament when we are "unworthy":

> In remembrance and memorial wherof, he disdaineth not to take for worthie suche men, as wilfully make not theim selfe vnworthy, to receiue the selfe same blessed body into their bodies, to the inestimable

---

[1] *Ibid.*
[2] *Ibid.*
[3] *Ibid.*, sig. QQ$_7$.
[4] *Ibid.*, sig. LL$_4$v.

welthe of their soules. And yet of his high soueraigne pacience, he
refuseth not to entre bodili into yᵉ vile bodies of those, whose filthye
mindes refuse to receue him graciously into their soules. But than do
such folke receiue him onely sacramentally, and not virtually: that
is to witte, they receiue his very blessed body into theirs, vnder the
sacramental sygne, but they reciue not the thinge of the sacrament,
that is to wit, the vertue and theffecte thereof, that is to saye, the grace,
by whiche they shulde bee lyuely membres incorporate in Christes
holye mysticall body: but in stede of that liue grace, they receiue
their iudgment, and their dampnacion.[1]

The echo of certain phrases and concepts in the passage quoted from the
beginning of the third lecture may suggest that this opening of the
"treatice to receaue the blessed body" is firmly welded to the third
lecture. And this effect is reinforced by the way in which, on the next page
of the treatise on the blessed body, More repeats in his characteristic way
an allusion to St. Paul's statement in the first epistle to the Corinthians,
concerning those who "eat the bread and drinke yᵉ cuppe of our lord
unworthyly."[2]

Why, then, does More use here the word "virtually," when we would,
perhaps, after reading the fragment of the third lecture, expect him to say
"sacramentally and spiritually"? But there are clear reasons for using the
word "virtually" with reference to the basic meaning of "virtue" as
"essential power" or "effective essence." In the third lecture the "spiritual"
receiving occurs when one attends mass devoutly, but does not personally
take the sacrament. In More's usage one receives the sacrament "virtually" when he receives the actual sacrament in a spiritual way. All this is
made clear by More's use of this same word "virtually" in a passage of his
Answer to a Poysoned Booke, written a year or so earlier. Here, in explaining
the workings of the sacrament, he speaks of "effectual receyuing, by which
a man not onely receiueth Chrystes blessed body into hys owne sacramentally, but also virtually, and effectually so receiueth therwith the
spirite of god into his soule, yᵗ he is incorporate thereby with our sauiour."[3]
From this and similar passages in the *Answer to a Poysoned Booke*, we can see
that the terms *virtually, effectually,* and *spiritually* are all referring to the
same essential action of the sacrament. And indeed this is clear on the
second page of the treatise on the blessed body, where More goes on to
urge that we "in suche wyse receiue the bodye and blud of our lord, as god
may of his goodnesse accepte vs for worthy, and therfore not only entre

---

[1] *Ibid.*

[2] *Ibid.*, sig. LL₅.

[3] *Ibid.*, sig. Y₁v. The whole of Chapter 18 in Book I of the *Answer to a Poysoned Booke*
helps to clarify the meaning: see *EW*, sigs. Y₁–Y₂v.

with his blessed flesh and blud sacramentally and bodily into our bodies, but also with his holy spirit graciously and effectually into our soules."[1]

Read in this way, the "treatice to receaue the blessed body" becomes not separate at all, but indeed the missing treatment of the third way of receiving promised by More at the outset of his third lecture on the sacrament. And read thus, this section forms a most satisfying and appropriate conclusion to the English treatise on the Passion, for the treatise on receiving works toward a deeper and stronger vehemence until, in the closing page and a half, it exhorts us to maintain the "inward speaking of Christ" in a manner that reminds one of the third and fourth books of the *Imitation of Christ*. As More says, "Let vs by deuout prayer talke to him, by deuout meditacion talke with him. Let vs say with the prophete: *Audiam quid loquatur in me dominus*, I will heare what our lord will speake within me."[2] Then the treatise on receiving closes with the example of Zacchaeus (used also at length in *A Dialogue of Comfort*),[3] ending with a passage that provides an apt and beautiful conclusion to the entire English treatise on the Passion:

> With such alacritie, with such quicknes of spirite, with such gladdenes, and such spirituall reioysing, as thys man receiued our Lorde into hys house, our lord geue vs the grace to receue his blessed body and bloud, his holye soule, and his almighty godhed both, into our bodyes and into our soules. . . . And then shal god geue a gracious sentence and saye vpon our soule, as he sayd vpon Zacheus: *Hodie salus facta est huic domui*. Thys day is helth and saluacion come vnto thys house: whiche that holye blessed persone of Chryste, whiche we verely in the blessed sacramente receyue, through the merite of hys bytter passion (whereof he hath ordeined hys owne blessed body, in that blessed sacrament to be the memorial) vouchsafe good christen reders, to graunt vnto vs all.[4]

How could this treatise on receiving the sacrament have become detached from the remainder of the English treatise, and have been provided with a separate title, given, according to Rastell, by More himself? Here we are utterly in the realm of conjecture, but one might make a few suggestions. Perhaps More was interrupted in his writing and taken off to the Tower before he had time to write this final portion of the third lecture. Being separated from the rest of his papers, he would naturally indicate the subject of the writing by giving it a heading, "To receaue the blessed

---

[1] *Ibid.*, sig. LL₅.
[2] *Ibid.*, sig. LL₆v.
[3] 176/7–178/21.
[4] *Ibid.*, sig. LL₇.

body of our lorde, sacramentally and virtually bothe," in order to remind
himself or John Harris that this belonged at the end of the other "paper
that you have." Or perhaps, since this was a matter of supreme importance, More decided to emphasize it by giving this final portion a subtitle
within the body of the third lecture itself, just as he provided subtitles for
two portions of the *De Tristitia*.[1] Standing in this way, with a separate
title, the treatise could well have been interpreted as an entirely separate
work, particularly with the reading of that word *virtually*, which had not
occurred in the earlier part of the third lecture. In any case, whether
attached or separate, the treatise on receiving follows naturally and
indeed inevitably from the arguments that have been presented in the
published fragment of this third lecture and in the earlier portion of the
entire English treatise on the Passion. And with the third lecture thus
completed by the climactic treatise on receiving the sacrament, the entire
English treatise on the Passion comes to an appropriate conclusion.

But can we speak of such a conclusion, in view of that very long title
given to the English treatise, with its promise to proceed as far as the
sepulchre of Christ? First of all we should note that no such long title
appears in either of the two manuscripts of this treatise.[2] And secondly, we
must remember More's art of improvisation, his art of exploratory writing.
More begins with a goal, but he will not commit himself to any inflexible
procedure. Consequently, as the treatise proceeds, More is free to vary and
conclude as he wishes, according to interior and exterior conditions. The
English treatise on the Passion appears to have been written, either in
whole or in part, before More entered the Tower of London, and therefore,
chronologically, it appears to come before the *Dialogue of Comfort*. Although
it follows the *Dialogue* in Rastell's edition, it is not in fact the kind of
meditative writing that we should expect to follow after the vehement
exhortations to meditate upon the Passion that are found in the last book
of the *Dialogue*. Indeed, More's English treatise on the Passion is not, for the

---

[1] Clarence Miller has provided the following explanation and suggestion: "The last
two gatherings (F and G) of the [Valencia Ms] begin with subsidiary titles or headings
('De amputata Malchi auricula' and 'De fuga discipulorum') which were also written on
the last pages of the preceding gatherings (E and F) instead of the ordinary catchwords
in order to ensure the correct sequence of the gatherings [see *CW 14*, 467, 557]. Now
consider what might have happened if gathering F (which includes all of the section
entitled 'De fuga discipulorum' and nothing but that section) had somehow been separated from the other gatherings and the last page of the preceding gathering (E) had
been mutilated or damaged so that the subtitle 'De fuga discipulorum' had been lost. Then
gathering F, 'De fuga discipulorum,' might have been printed as a separate short essay
with its own title, like the Blessed Body."

[2] See *CW 13*, 3/1–30 and textual note.

most part, a meditation, although, as Haupt points out, it contains meditative aspects.[1] But basically it is what the repeated headings call it, a series of *lectures* in the old sense of that word: readings, interpretations, "omelies," as we read in one heading.[2] It is a set of theological and moral sermons, expositions of the sacred text; and they have a completeness of their own.

The Latin treatise on the Passion gradually reveals itself as a work of another order and kind: a continuation, yes, a sequel, but transposed, in the musical sense, into another key. That transposition is marked by the change to another language, the language in which More wrote the most intimate writings of his that have come out of the Tower: the marginal annotations to the Psalms written in Latin in the Prayer Book preserved from those last days—the marginalia in which we come to the quick of More's spiritual being. Thus, as we have pointed out in the facsimile edition of the Prayer Book, certain verses from Psalm 37 form the basis for More's actions throughout all his interrogations and trial, as this marginal comment shows: "A meek man ought to behave in this way during tribulation; he should neither speak proudly himself nor retort to what is spoken wickedly, but should bless those who speak evil of him and suffer willingly, either for justice' sake if he has deserved it or for God's sake if he has deserved nothing."[3]

So now, in the intimacy and sanctuary of this Latin, we find More moving gently and gradually away from the lecture-like manner of the English treatise and ever more deeply into the hearing of that "inward speaking" of his Lord, so strongly urged in the treatise on receiving the sacrament. Throughout the Latin work we find numerous occasions, long and short, in which the speaker hears the voice of his Redeemer answering his meditation:

> O faint of heart, take courage and do not despair. You are afraid, you are sad, you are stricken with weariness and dread of the torment with which you have been cruelly threatened. Trust me. I conquered the world, and yet I suffered immeasurably more from fear, I was sadder, more afflicted with weariness, more horrified at the prospect of such cruel suffering drawing eagerly nearer and nearer. Let the brave man have his high-spirited martyrs, let him rejoice in imitating a thousand of them. But you, my timorous and feeble little sheep, be content to have me alone as your shepherd, follow my leadership; if you do not trust yourself, place your trust in me.[4]

---

[1] *Ibid.*, Introduction.
[2] *EW*, sig. DD₂.
[3] *Prayer Book*, p. 194.
[4] *CW 14*, 101–105.

These inward sayings of the Lord are answers to the personal problem raised at the outset of the Latin work, where More draws a long and careful distinction between two kinds of martyrs. On the one hand are those who offer their lives bravely and quickly, and on the other are those, much more fearful, who seek to escape suffering and death, if possible, but who ultimately are given the strength to face death as resolutely as the more stalwart souls have done. This is the question that underlies the entire Latin treatise on the Passion. It is the question evoked by the Agony in the Garden and by Christ's cry, "Let this cup pass from me." More interprets this as a scene of encouragement to the second, faint-hearted kind of martyr, a sign that it is not wrong to seek, as More did, all honorable and faithful methods of escape, every loophole of the law. St. Paul himself, More notes,

> not only managed skillfully to escape from the snares of the Jews by means of the tribune, but also freed himself from prison by declaring that he was a Roman citizen, and once again he eluded the cruelty of the Jews by appealing to Caesar, and he escaped the hands of the impious King Aretas by being let down from the wall in a basket.[1]

It is no sin to seek escape, so long as faith is not broken: "And so the fear of death and torments carries no stigma of guilt but rather is an affliction of the sort Christ came to suffer, not to escape. We should not immediately consider it cowardice for someone to feel fear and horror at the thought of torments, not even if he prudently avoids dangers (provided he does not compromise himself)."[2] There is the essence of More's position.

So the inward speaking of the Lord comes to comfort the fearful martyr, fulfilling the counsel found at the close of the *Dialogue of Comfort*, where Antony assures his nephew that meditation upon the Agony of Christ will bring the necessary comfort to sustain a Christian under the utmost threat of persecution.[3] These three great treatises are tied together inseparably: the *Dialogue of Comfort*, the English treatise on the Passion, including as its end the treatise on receiving the sacrament, and finally, the Latin treatise. The first two works converge upon and prepare the way for the meditative action of the Latin work. The *Dialogue of Comfort* exhorts the reader to meditate upon the Agony, in order to comfort the faint-hearted man, while the treatise on the blessed body counsels the reader to seek interior colloquies with the Lord, saying, "And let us with Mary also sit in deuout

---

[1] *Ibid.*, p. 77.

[2] *Ibid.*, p. 83.

[3] "In our fere let vs remembre Christes paynfull agonye, that hym selfe wold for our comfort suffre before his passion, to thentent that no fere shuld make vs dispayre / & euer call for his help, such as hymselfe lyst to send vs" (318/26–29).

meditacion, and hearken wel what our sauior, beyng now our geast, wil inwardly say vnto vs."[1]

Meanwhile, the Latin meditation on the Agony has a wholeness and integrity that implies a goal and design from beginning to end. That goal is plainly indicated in the title that the work bears in all three of its manuscripts, including the title arrived at after several revisions in the Valencia holograph.[2] The treatise bears the title *De tristitia, tedio, pavore, et oratione Christi ante captionem eius,* or in Mary Basset's version: "Of the sorowe, werinesse, feare, and prayer of Christ before hys taking."[3] It is not, at heart, an *Expositio:* this is an editorial title better suited to describe the English treatise. More has written here his meditations on the Agony, while he prepares his fearful soul to meet his own taking. The work reaches its goal and the height of its personal application as Christ emerges from His Agony to face the approach of His captors, saying, "This is your hour, and the power of darkness." Upon this text, near the close of the treatise, More creates his long, climactic speaking of the Lord, as Christ says to His persecutors:

> You are in the dark when you ascribe my death to your strength. So too the governor Pilate will be in the dark when he takes pride in possessing the power to free me or to crucify me. For, even though my people and my high priests are about to hand me over to him, he would not have any power over me if it were not given to him from above. And for that very reason, those who will hand me over to him are the greater sinners. But this is the hour and the brief power of darkness.[4]

We can hardly doubt that More continued these meditations to the Cross and to the Sepulchre. But this continuation perhaps existed only in the realm of mental prayer: to write it down would be too intimate a revelation for anyone to know except his Lord.

III. THE ARGUMENT OF THE BOOK

1. Conversation and Argument

"Comfort," Antony tells us,

> is properly taken by them that take it right / rather for the consolacion of good hope, that men take in their hart / of some good growing toward them / than for a present pleasure with which the body is

---

[1] *EW*, sig. LL₆v. [2] See *CW 14*, 789–90.
[3] *EW*, sig. QQ₈. [4] *CW 14*, 539–40.

delitid & tyklyd for the while / . . . And therfor . . . I speke but of such
comfort as is very comfort in dede, by which a man hath hope of
godes favour & remission of his synnes, with mynyshyng of his payne
in purgatorye or reward els in hevyn / & such comfort cometh of
tribulacion & for tribulacion well taken / (68/12–27)

Here is an epitome of what we shall call "the argument of the book"—the
most consciously formed and most readily accessible portion of the work,
designed for the widest audience. One might assume that it would be
relatively easy to follow. It is surprising, therefore, to discover that it has
been so little understood. E. E. Reynolds, for example, an excellent
scholar and the author of the most recent critical biography of More,
echoes general critical opinion when he writes that "any attempt to
summarize the contents of the *Dialogue of Comfort* would not be helpful; it
lacks a carefully developed argument that can be systematically set down."[1]
    The major difficulty lies in the form in which the work is written. As in
the *Utopia*, More has taken some pains to convince us of the literary fiction
of the dialogue. "And therfor wished I . . . when I felt my selfe," says
Antony, looking back at their first day's conversation,

evyn a litell wery / that I had not so told you styll a long tale alone /
but that we had more often enterchaungid wordes / & partid the
talke betwene vs, with ofter enterparlyng vppon your part / in such
maner as lernid men vse betwene the persons / whom they devise
disputyng in their faynid diologes. (79/21–26)

This is no feigned dialogue, More seems to insist. It took place in the city of
Buda in the year 1527/28, after the death of Louis II at Mohács, when
Hungary was divided by dissent from within over rival claimants to the
throne and threatened from without by renewed Turkish invasion. It was
written by a Hungarian in Latin and translated from Latin into French
and from French into English.[2] We learn a good bit about the personal
characteristics of each of the participants. Antony, for example, loves to
tell stories of his youth, such as the anecdotes about Vladislav II and his
Queen, Anne de Candale (218/13–23; 124/15–126/23), or about the time
he was camped "within the Turkes grownd many a mile beyond Belgrade"
and a group of Hungarian scouts mistook a hedge at night for the Turkish
army (109/29–110/26). As an old man who is esteemed by his family for

---

[1] *The Field is Won* (London, 1968), p. 349. The only attempt at a full-scale outline of the
argument of *A Dialogue of Comfort* is in Leland Miles' abbreviated, modernized version of
the text (Bloomington, Ind., 1965), pp. 243–51. Cited hereafter as "Miles."

[2] So in the title (1/2–6). In the text itself Vincent says that he will record the conversation in Hungarian and German. See 320/15–16 and n. How it supposedly came to be
written in Latin first is never explained, but see Commentary, n. to 1/2–6.

his wisdom and experience, he nevertheless has some of the failings of age. He loves to talk, and in at least one place loses his train of thought, as old men are wont to do, in the middle of a story.[1] In another place Vincent is instructed to play the part of a great lord who is loath to give up his possessions in a time of persecution. In this small drama within the larger drama of the *Dialogue*, Vincent is addressed as "your lordship" for almost an entire chapter, until he runs out of reasons for the defense of his folly and so can play the part no longer (229/2–237/24). Long digressions are recognized as such, but as in real conversations, they are never avoided.[2] Antony will often set up an extremely rational structure, divided into precise parts, and then ignore all except one because the others do not really pertain to the problem (86/15–87/15).

The dialogue form modifies the argument of the book and keeps it from being presented as logically and straightforwardly as it might have been in a regular treatise or discourse. The argument disappears at times into the deliberate garrulity of the dialogue. At other times it is carried forward by the conversation itself in a kind of crabwise progress through objection. Antony presents a certain point of view, and Vincent offers a number of objections. Antony stops the forward motion of the argument to meet the objections. And so on. In the discussion of the world as a prison in Book III, for example, Vincent is dissatisfied with Antony's initial demonstration and calls it sophistry. Antony is pleased with Vincent's spirit, but the accusation hurts, and he reverts to the idea of sophistry on more than one occasion as he goes to work to shift his nephew's perspective so that he may see without sophistry that the world is truly a prison for all men born into it (262/11–280/14). Within the dialogue, Antony is usually responsible for sustaining the argument. Vincent's primary function is rhetorical.[3] He serves as the voice of our response, articulating objections likely to be present in the reader's mind. Vincent's objections make concrete the abstract nature of the discourse and give it an air of reality it would not

---

[1] See above, p. lxx.

[2] See, for example, the long digression on suicide in chapters 15 and 16 of Book II. Many cases of suicide, Antony recognizes, are "out of tribulacion" and therefore "out of our mater that is to treate of comfort in tribulacion" (129/4–5). He nevertheless goes on with the discussion. See also 130/1–7 and 145/20–146/2.

[3] I do not mean to imply, as P. E. Hallett in his edition of the *Dialogue* (London, 1937, p. vi; cited hereafter as "Hallett") and Miles in his edition (p. xliv) have done, that Antony is a surrogate for More and Vincent for Margaret Roper, or other members of More's family, or the reader himself. That seems to me inappropriate to the nature of the dialogue form. For in a very real sense More is both the old man whose purity of heart is such that he does not fear the Turks and at the same time the young man who is anxious and uncertain of how he will conduct himself should the time of trial come. In this respect the dialogue may be seen as taking place in More's own heart.

otherwise possess. The argument itself is entirely orthodox, and this process of embodying the traditional form in a concrete experience is a significant part of More's overall intention and meaning.

Since the argument flows from point to point in the haphazard, random fashion of ordinary conversation, it is a measure of More's art that he is able to sustain it and at the same time make it seem as though it is emerging directly from a particular moment in time.[1] Hence arises one of the most distinguishing features of the work, one of its most peculiar tonal characteristics. Beneath the loose conversational flow, the vagaries of two particular people in a particular time at a particular place, is a firm sense of order that outcrops throughout the book like what geologists call *country rock*, the underlying strata of a region. Chapter 7 of Book I (23/10–24/13), for example, chapter 3 of Book II (86/15–87/15), chapter 8 of Book II (99/21–100/22), and chapter 3 of Book III (203/7–204/10) are given over almost entirely to the purpose of formulating sets and subsets outlining and focusing the work.

This combination of dialogue and argument, conversational ease and underlying design, is entirely characteristic of the man himself and the literary style exhibited in all his Tower works. More's ability to sustain the argument within the casual form of a dialogue is a prime example of what has earlier been described as "More's art of improvisation," an art that "reveals, lying under and within all its apparent wandering, a firm and central line, a teleological structure, based on a goal never forgotten."[2] That teleological structure is what is here termed the argument of the book. It is largely a function of the major drift, the overall purpose and goal of each book and of all three books taken together. It is a demonstration of the meaning of that inner trinity, faith, hope, and charity.

2. Faith

The first book is focused on faith and is divided into three primary sections: (1) a consideration of faith itself; (2) a catalogue of the major kinds of tribulation; (3) a series of objections by which our perspective is adjusted to accept tribulation in the light of faith as a gift of God. The prologue is concerned primarily with setting the scene of the dialogue and establishing the fact that God alone, through the indwelling of the Holy Spirit in the church and in each individual soul through grace, is the

---

[1] For More's views on the nature of dialogue see the Commentary at 9/17.

[2] See above p. lxi f. and Martz, "Thomas More: The Tower Works" in *St. Thomas More: Action and Contemplation, Proceedings of the Symposium Held at St. John's University, October 9–10, 1970*, ed. R. S. Sylvester (New Haven, 1972), pp. 63–64, 75. Cited hereafter as "*More Symposium.*"

source of our only true comfort (4/28–5/13). Chapters 1–6 are then given over to a consideration of faith itself.

Chapter one is essentially negative. Ancient moral philosophers attempted to show men how to rise above the miseries of this world. They emphasized, More says, the freedom of the mind. By its very nature tribulation must affect either the body or the mind. Nothing can be done about bodily pain, but the mind has a freedom of its own: "Now the body not to fele that it feleth: all the wit in the world can not bryng about / But that the mynd shuld not be grevid neyther with the payne that the body felyth, nor with the occasions of heuynes offrid & given vnto the sowle yt selfe: this thing laborid the philosophers very much about" (10/8–12). More himself later, in the third book, uses this distinction extensively when he comes to consider the most fearful of all tribulations, the possibility of a shameful and painful death, for the teachings of the ancient philosophers are not to be despised: "some good drugges haue they yet in their shops" (11/2–3). The difficulty is that they do not go far enough. They lack "the chief comfort of all / ... without which ... all other comfortes are nothyng." Since they lived before the coming of Christ, they lack the necessary faith to refer "the fynall end of their comfort vnto god" and the willingness to suffer tribulation on earth so as to obtain God's favor and eternal reward in heaven (10/19–24). The ancient philosophers also lacked the special means by which this comfort could be obtained: the "gracious" assistance of God Himself moving men through obscure impulses of the heart.

More makes it absolutely clear here at the beginning of the book that he is dealing not with the consolation of philosophy, but with supernatural sources of comfort beyond the reach of reason alone. He is speaking not of man in a state of nature, but man in a state of grace. For although faith is an act of the intellect directing the will to the true and the good, as Aquinas said, it is nevertheless the first of the supernatural or theological virtues "because natural knowledge cannot reach God as the object of heavenly bliss, which is the aspect under which hope and charity tend towards Him." True faith is a supernatural desire implanted in our hearts by God. Even intellectual assent, which is the primary act of faith according to Aquinas, "is from God moving man inwardly by grace."[1] Considered as a theological virtue, faith is much more than mere intellectual assent to Christian doctrine. It is an operative power in which

---

[1] *Summa Theologica*, ed. Instituti Studiorum Medievalium Ottaviensis (Ottawa, 1941) II–II, Q. 4, a. 1. Cited hereafter as *ST*. Translations are by the Fathers of the English Dominican Province, rev. D. J. Sullivan, *Great Books of the Western World*, ed. R. M. Hutchins (Chicago, 1952), vol. 20.

all the natural links of the world remain intact . . . ; but a principle, an inward finality, one might almost say an additional soul is super-imposed upon them. Under the influence of our faith, the universe is capable, without outwardly changing its characteristics, of becoming more supple, more fully animate—of being 'suranimated.' . . . If we believe, then everything is illuminated and takes shape around us: chance is seen to be order, success assumes an incorruptible plenitude, suffering becomes a visit and a caress of God.[1]

The overall purpose of Book I is to lead us to the reversal of ordinary, worldly judgment, to the peculiar paradoxes that occur in the light of operative faith, where suffering is truly seen as "a visit and a caress of God."

Since reason alone is insufficient, one must begin, More explains in chapter 2, with a firm foundation of faith. "For likewise as it wer vtterlye vayne to lay natural resons of coumfort, to him that hath no witte, so were it vndoutedlye frustrate to laye spirituall causes of coumforte, to hym that hath no faythe" (12/14–17). Faith, however, is not in man's possession. One man cannot give it to another or even to himself. It is "the gracious gift of god" alone, the result of the inspiration of the Holy Spirit. If a man feels his faith weak, all he can do is to pray to God that it may please Him to increase it. The argument of the first book, therefore, is in a sense oblique and curiously circular. Given its basic premise, it is eminently reasonable, but all its reason is based on the obscure motion of grace in the soul, which lies beyond the power of man to achieve. More can show us, in other words, how tribulation may be viewed by one whose life has been "suranimated" by the supernatural gift of faith. But he can do nothing to give the grace necessary to achieve it. What More attempts instead is to supply the reader with a realization, a full exploration of truths that the reader had perhaps given mere verbal or intellectual assent to for most of his life. "Comfort" is to be found by confronting the mystery of suffering and realizing that it becomes transfigured by faith.

The next three chapters are a further exploration of the nature of faith. The first comfort a man may expect to find in tribulation, we learn from chapter 3, is simply the act of faith itself and the longing and desire to be comforted by God that arise from it. Those who seek comfort in God alone rather than in the things of this world cannot fail to be consoled for two reasons. "The one is that they see them self seke for their comfort where they can not fayle to fynd yt / For god both can give them comfort & will" (15/26–28). It is faith and faith alone that assures us of this and

---

[1] Pierre Teilhard de Chardin, *The Divine Milieu* (New York, 1960), pp. 116–17. Cited hereafter as "Teilhard."

gives us the necessary comfort, peace, and contentment in suffering and tribulation. As Teilhard has said, we have only to believe and all our fears vanish:

> If we do not believe, the waves engulf us, the winds blow, nourishment fails, sickness lays us low or kills us, the divine power is impotent or remote. If, on the other hand, we believe, the waters are welcoming and sweet, the bread is multiplied, our eyes open, the dead rise again, the power of God is, as it were, drawn from Him by force and spreads throughout all nature.[1]

The second reason is again somewhat paradoxical and proceeds from the mysterious nature of faith itself. If one has faith of this sort in God, it is a sign that he is not utterly cast out of God's favor, for it is He who inspires men to turn to Him in tribulation and to desire to be comforted by Him. It is His love that draws men toward Him in the time of their true desperation and need. Out of this same love, moreover, God often sends tribulation in order to call men away from the things of this world. Unless they turn to Him in faith and desire to be comforted by Him, "ther can in tribulacion none other good cumfort come forth" (18/23–24). The first and only source of all true spiritual consolation is the desire God Himself implants within us to turn to Him in faith.

The sixth chapter presents the first of Vincent's objections. If we turn to God for comfort in tribulation, he asks, what if we pray to Him to have the tribulation taken away? "Ys not this a good desier of godes comfort" (19/18–19)? Antony replies that tribulations vary and that although in some of them, such as hunger or sickness, one may legitimately pray to God to have them taken away, there are nevertheless others which we may not pray to have removed. Temptations such as the goading of the flesh by sensual desire are part of man's essential nature and will remain with him till death as a test of his love and merit. "For the salvacion of our sowle may we boldly pray," Antony continues in a passage that catches up the structure, argument, and overall intent of *A Dialogue of Comfort:* "For grace may we boldly pray / for fayth / for hope / and for charitie / & for euery such vertew as shall serue vs to hevyn ward" (21/9–11). For the rest, we should leave it up to God's will, knowing that what He desires for us, even temptation and tribulation, will be to our greater spiritual benefit.

The discussion of faith that occupies the first six chapters of *A Dialogue of Comfort* ends not on faith itself, which is beyond man's ability to attain, but on man's willing acceptance of tribulation within the framework of faith. The next three chapters proceed, therefore, into a consideration of

---

[1] Teilhard, p. 115.

the nature of tribulation itself. Chapter 7 is one of the brief organizational chapters that outcrop throughout the book and give it a momentary focus which gradually drifts away in the course of the conversation only to be caught up once again and given a new direction. The chapter is brief and rigid enough to be almost an outline. Every tribulation is designed by God, Antony says, "to be medicinable yf men will so take yt / or may become medicynable yf men will so make it / or is better than medicynable but yf we will forsake yt" (23/23–25). Vincent replies, with a flash of humor, that that is indeed very consoling if we could but understand it. And Antony elaborates. All tribulations are sent either (1) as a punishment for sins we are aware of in the past; or (2) as punishment for sins in the past we do not remember or as a means of preserving us from sins in the future that we might otherwise fall into; or (3) not as a punishment for sin at all, but as a test of our patience and merit.

Since the saying still remains, as Vincent says, "somewhat obscure and darke," the next three chapters—8, 9, and 10—constitute a further elaboration. More begins with the first: we suffer these tribulations for what we did to offend God in the past. But we may turn them to good by entering into them and taking them upon us willingly, accepting them "in trew fayth & good hope" (25/13–14). This willing acceptance of punishment, through the operative power of faith, changes the very nature of the suffering into an act of love. And in a general sense that is what the first book of *A Dialogue of Comfort* does for all tribulation. It takes what in the eyes of the world would be regarded as intolerable pain and suffering and transforms it into an occasion of joy and rejoicing. The miracle of the transformation is the miracle of faith.

The ninth chapter examines tribulation sent without any known cause. Some of these tribulations may fall into the first category and may be activated and turned to our own benefit in the way described in the preceding chapter. The difference is that in the first category we are aware of the faults we have committed. In the second case we are not conscious of the specific offenses but accept the tribulation anyway. To those who have a clear conscience, however, this second kind of tribulation has within it a further source of consolation, for they may believe that it was perhaps sent to restrain them from sins they would otherwise commit. Thus tribulation is transformed once again through operative faith into a sign of God's favor.

The tenth chapter treats the final cause of tribulation, that which is sent as a test of one's love for God. Of the three this comes closest to More's own situation, and in the context of his imprisonment the chapter takes on considerable weight and meaning. At first Vincent objects to the whole idea, as well he might, for it would seem impossible for one to know for certain which of these categories a particular tribulation would fall into. Antony replies that of course it is difficult since all men are sinners, but that there are many men who live with a clear conscience. Some men, says Antony, are aware that the tribulations they endure were sent by God to test their patience. The tribulations themselves often indicate as much, as when a man suffers "for the mayntenaunce of iustice or for the defence of godes cause" (32/1–2). If such a man of clear conscience were to fall into the hands of the Turks and remained true to his faith despite torture, Antony continues, "I wold not faile to bid hym boldly (while I shuld se him in his passion) cast synne & hell and purgatorie & all vppon the devilles pate / and dowt not but like wise as yf he gave ouer his hold all his merite were lost & he tournid into misery / so yf he stand & percever still in the confession of his fayth, all his hole payne shall tourne all into glorye" (32/14–19). In these few sentences much of the future development of Books II and III is anticipated: the linking of justice and the defense of the faith with the fear of torture and bodily pain, and the further association of such suffering with the passion of Christ.

The remainder of Book I has as its organizational pattern a series of objections posed by Vincent and responded to by Antony. The chapter headings alone indicate the pattern:

A certeyne obieccion agaynst the thynges
aforesaid /
The xij chapiter

A certeyne obieccion & the answere therto
The xiiij Chapiter

Other obieccions /
The / 15 / chapiter

The answere to the obieccions
The xvj chapiter

An answere to the second obieccion
The seventene chapiter

An other obieccion with the answere therunto
The xix[th] Chapiter

There is little need to summarize these various objections. They are all designed to bring concrete reality to the incomprehensible nature of faith and the acceptance of suffering faith affords. Each objection adjusts the perspective a little more carefully. In their overall effect, chapters 11–19 constitute an encomium of tribulation that explores its fundamental benefits, which are not apparent except paradoxically to one who has the gift of faith to perceive them.

The twentieth chapter is a summary statement of the entire first book. It emphasizes faith as the first source of comfort in tribulation and the necessary precondition from which all other comforts are derived:

> If we lay first for a sewer grownd a very fast fayth / wherby we beleve to be trew all that the scripture sayth, vnderstondyng trewly as the old holy doctours declare it, and as the spirit of god instructith his catholique church / than shall we consider tribulacion as a graciouse gyfte of god: A gyfte that he specially gaue his speciall frendes / . . . A thyng wherof the contrary long contynued is perilous / A thyng which but yf god send it, men haue nede by penaunce to put vppon them selfe and seke it / A thyng that helpith to purge our synnes passid / A thyng that preserueth vs fro sinne that els wold come / A thyng that causeth vs set les by the world, . . . The thyng by which our saviour entrid his own kyngdom / The thyng with which all his apostelles folowid hym thether, The thyng which our saviour exortith all men to / The thyng without which (he sayth) we be not his dicyples, The thyng without which no man can get to hevyn. (75/7–24)

Remembering these things, men should not complain if they fall into tribulation. Rather they should turn it to their spiritual advantage by finding in it not anguish, diminishment, and desolation, but the glorification of their spirit. Even if it is God's will that they die in tribulation, they should give Him thanks and long to go to Him: "And than shall hope of hevyn comfort our hevines / & out of our transitory tribulacion shall we go to euerlastyng glory" (76/31–77/1). At a certain point faith is imperceptibly transformed into hope.

3. Hope

Book II is divided into four disproportionate parts: (1) an introduction that sets the tone for the conversation that follows and defends the use of merry tales and anecdotes; (2) a discussion, largely through objections, of penance or tribulation willingly assumed for the forgiveness of sins; (3) a discussion of tribulation not chosen, but accepted willingly, divided into two parts, temptation and persecution; and finally (4) the formal meditation on the 90th Psalm, which begins here and extends throughout the remainder of the book. The overall drift of the argument in Book II, its major tendency and direction in the course of its leisurely progress, is to capture some glimpse of the infused theological virtue of hope. Hope in general, Aquinas says, must have certain conditions accompanying it. It must be directed toward something good that lies in the future; the good must be arduous and difficult to obtain; and it must be possible to obtain.[1] Considered not in general terms, but as a theological virtue, the good that men hope for is eternal happiness in heaven. It is not therefore something already possessed. And although it is arduous and difficult to gain, it is possible to obtain by means of God's assistance.[2] The object of hope, in other words, is eternal happiness with God, and the means by which men obtain this hope is, paradoxically, the supernatural gift of hope itself, by which they trust in God's assistance to enable them to achieve it. "Now the object of hope is, in one way, eternal happiness, and, in another way, the divine assistance."[3] "Accordingly," Aquinas continues, "it is unlawful to hope in any man, or any creature, as though it were the first cause of movement towards happiness. It is, however, lawful to hope in a man or a creature as being the secondary and instrumental agent, through whom one is helped to obtain any goods that are ordered to happiness."[4] Hope, then, is inseparable from sanctifying grace, the strength men are given to see them through the trials and temptations of this world; and at the same time it is also the supernatural trust that God will give them that strength.

More also thinks of the virtue of hope in this dual sense. But the first aspect—the hope of eternal happiness in heaven—is posited, as it were, outside the book as its final cause. What More insists on within the work itself, in Book II and in large portions of Book III, is the second aspect of hope—God's willingness to give us the strength to resist temptation so that we may at last attain the final object of our hope. For that is where More himself was located in the course of writing his book. Considered from a biographical standpoint, *A Dialogue of Comfort* is a work in progress. It catches that moment between two great temptations—the past, before More resolved to enter the Tower, and that still to come, in his trial and death. At the time of writing, he was not yet facing the full test. What would happen if he were brought to the torture? How would he be able to endure physical pain of an intensity he had never known before, and what would that do to him and his relationship with God? Faith was obviously no problem. The problem was that he might betray his beliefs because of his physical nature. Until he was brought to that point he could never be certain of how he would conduct himself. As his imprisonment drew on and the noose of the king's new laws and purposes became increasingly tighter, all this became a cause of more and more concern. In the last act of his life, as he asked for assistance to ascend the difficult steps to the scaffold,

---

[1] *ST*, I–II, Q.40, a. 1.

[2] *ST*, II–II, Q.17, a. 1 and a. 7.

[3] *ST*, II–II, Q.17, a. 7. See also II–II, Q.17, a. 6 and a. 4.

[4] *ST*, II–II, Q.17, a. 4.

he could be confident that once he got there and the executioner's ax fell, his body and soul could shift for themselves. But meanwhile, he was responsible for them both, and the comfort that sustained him during the course of his imprisonment was "the consolation of good hope" that God would either take the fear and temptation away from him or give him the grace to endure it. But of course the work is written so as to encompass more than the author's personal career.

The introduction and the first two chapters of Book II are designed primarily to prepare for the change in tone to come in the remainder of the dialogue. Some time has passed since Antony and Vincent have been together, and Antony immediately signals the new tone that will prevail when he speaks of himself as an old fool who loves "to sit well & warm with a cupp & a rostid crabb & dryvill & drinke & talke" (78/25–26). It was ever his nature, he says, to be "evyn halfe a giglot & more" (83/4–5). Moreover, he is aware that in their previous conversation he did most of the talking. In the future he will share the words, and in the changed mood of the book he proceeds to tell an anecdote about a nun in the cloister who talked too much. Quoting Aquinas, Vincent goes on to observe that "a mery tale with a frend, refresheth a man much / & without any harm lightith his mynd & amendith his courage & his stomake / so that it semeth but well done to take such recreacion" (82/13–16). Antony agrees, so long as it is realized, as we learned in the first book, "that our chiefe comfort must be of god, & that with hym we must begyn, & with hym contynew, & with hym end also." That understood, "a man to take now & than some honest worldly myrth / I dare not be so sore as vtterly to forbyd yt" (83/10–13).

From this point on the merry tales and anecdotes crowd the conversation and on the whole form one of the most inexplicable features of the work— a genuine sense of wit and humor rising discordantly from the grim circumstances of fear, suffering, and death— tales of humorous suicide and prideful martyrdom side by side with playful anecdotes, thinly disguised, about the vagaries of Dame Alice, More's second wife, or the precocious brilliance of his adopted daughter, Margaret Giggs. According to what Antony says in the introduction, the merry tales and anecdotes that fill Book II with their strange levity have been designed as a form of relief, to compensate for human weakness, but they are entirely superficial when compared with the grim business underneath the laughter. But surely this is wrong, for the anecdotes are not a superficial overlay. They are part of the very process of thought, inextricably fused with the material presented. They rise primarily from More's complex view of his own and of all human nature.

More's mirth, which gives his literary works and his life their unique

and most characteristic quality, is one of the most mysterious elements in
the man, overwhelmingly easy to enjoy, but difficult to understand and
fully comprehend. In one sense it is a matter of personal style, a mask with
which to face the world, an intellectual strategy employed in the
brilliant, complex ironies of *Utopia*, in conversation with his wife and the
king's good servants—Wolsey, Cromwell, and the Lords at Lambeth—
and even in his last, graceful remarks on the scaffold that so outraged the
chronicler Edward Hall.[1] But it also had to do with his relationship with
God, which allowed him to see the world with sufficient detachment to be
aware of its insignificance in the face of eternity. Viewed from this perspective, the merry tales and anecdotes in *A Dialogue of Comfort* would seem
to proceed directly from the formal structure of the work. The argument of
Book II reasons the need in times of tribulation for the infused theological
virtue of hope. But all the while the tone itself, created by the merry tales
and anecdotes, demonstrates even more graphically than the argument
itself the experiential realization of the hope and trust in God More is
speaking of in the *Dialogue*. In the argument of the book the theological
virtue of hope is presented in intellectual terms; in the anecdotes and
merry tales it is realized as an emotional experience. The tone of Book II,
in other words, the essential tone of *A Dialogue of Comfort* in all its complexity, is a clear expression of the hope and trust in God and the detachment from worldly things that the *Dialogue* itself is working to effect. As
John Donne once said in another context, it is both the object and the wit.

The second part of Book II begins in chapter 3 and continues through
chapter 7. Chapter 3 is very brief, but it is one of the granite outcroppings
that give the work its hard structural core. Reverting to chapter 7 of Book
I, More once again divides all tribulation into three primary categories:
"either is it such as hym selfe willyngly taketh, or secondly such as hym
selfe willyngly suffreth / or fynally such as he can not put from hym"
(86/20–22). The third category includes such items as "siknes, imprisonment, losse of good, losse of frendes, or such bodely harm as a man hath
all redy caught & can in no wise avoyd" (86/26–87/1).[2] Since nothing can
be done about these things except to endure them in good spirits and not
displease God, More passes over them in silence. No comfort can help,
only faith and reason, which have already been sufficiently explained in
Book I: "as to the man that laketh wit & fayth, no comfort can serue what
so euer counsayle be gevyn / so to them that haue both, I haue as to this
kynd said in maner ynough all redye" (87/4–6). More concentrates instead on the other two. The first of these forms the material of the next

---

[1] Chambers, *Thomas More*, pp. 347, 349.

[2] More later treats a number of these in Book III, but only insofar as they constitute
temptations, where a man has a choice, not as here, where they are inflicted by God.

four chapters, and the final category, the category of temptation, which More is most interested in, occupies the remainder of Book II and all of Book III.

The first of these two categories, the tribulation which a man willingly takes on himself, is the act of penance. It differs from the medicinable tribulations in chapter seven of Book I by being willingly chosen. Punishment for sin is inflicted by God, and one can turn it into remorse and sorrow for one's sins by willingly accepting it. Penance, on the other hand, is tribulation that a man deliberately takes on himself. No consolation is needed for such an individual since the pleasure of his soul far exceeds the pain of his body. And it is at this point that we catch our first glimpse of the underlying form of Book II. For penance (and consequently this entire section) has to do with the first of the two primary aspects of the theological virtue of hope: the hope of eternal happiness in heaven. Through true repentance for sin and the tribulation inflicted to demonstrate remorse, men hope to attain God's forgiveness and eternal joy: "yea and while he [the penitent] hath in hart also some great hevynes for his synne / yet when he considereth the ioy that shall come of it, his sowle shall not fayll to fele than that straunge case, which my body felt ones in a grete feuer" (88/2–5). After a charming anecdote describing how he felt both hot and cold at once, designed in part as a compliment to his adopted daughter, Margaret Giggs,[1] More concludes with a powerful image of suffering and hope: the image of Christ crucified, His arms spread on the cross, open to receive all men. This is the first in a series of images of Christ's passion that become increasingly insistent as the *Dialogue* proceeds.

The section on penance effectually ends at that point. Vincent, however, has a number of objections which extend the discussion beyond what Antony thought was necessary. One objection has to do with deathbed confessions, another with the Protestant rejection of penance, another with the inability to feel remorse for sin. None of these is particularly important for the progress of the argument. They primarily clear the way for what follows.

The third major section of Book II begins at chapter 8, and after only two brief chapters it is almost immediately absorbed into the formal meditation on the 90th Psalm, which occupies the remainder of the book. Since these two sections are so closely related, one merging imperceptibly into the other, it is difficult to determine whether they are to be considered separately or grouped together. For the sake of clarity, they can be viewed as two separate sections.

Chapter 8 is essentially organizational; it takes up the last of the three

---

[1] See the Commentary at 88/4–90/7.

categories of tribulation introduced in chapter 3: tribulation willingly
endured, but not willingly chosen. This form of tribulation may be further
divided into two parts, temptation and persecution. By persecution, More
makes it clear, he means only that kind "which though the sufferer wold
be loth to fall in / yet will he rather abyde it & suffer, than by the fletyng
from yt, fall in the displesure of god / or leve godes pleasure vnprocurid"
(100/9–11). Persecution of this sort may be seen as a form of temptation.
In the case of temptation proper, the devil usually attacks through subter-
fuge, trickery, and illusion. In persecution, however, he comes out in the
open and reveals himself clearly, attempting to overwhelm his victim by
violence. "The first," More says, "shall I call the devilles traynes the
tother his open fight" (100/21–22). The remainder of Book II will
consider temptation in its more subtle forms, whereas the temptations
inherent in persecution, the fiercer, more deadly, and more difficult to
resist, will be reserved for Book III, in accordance with the overall
structure of the work. Brief as it is, then, chapter 8 is one of the major
organizational watersheds in *A Dialogue of Comfort*. More has finally
narrowed his subject from tribulation in general to the specific tribulation
of temptation. As the book proceeds, the focus will become ever sharper
and more intense as More approaches the temptations threatening him
personally and all men who are persecuted for the sake of conscience and
defense of their beliefs.

Chapter 9 considers temptation in general as it is common to both
temptation and persecution. It serves, therefore, as a general introduction
to the remainder of the book. Although we are tempted by many things,
More says—by the world, the flesh, and the devil, by our enemies, and
even by our friends—in all these various temptations there is "one
mervelous cumfort." The more we are tempted, the happier we should be,
for it is through wrestling and struggling with the devil that we achieve
the victor's crown of eternal bliss: "And therfor may it be a greate comfort/
as S Iames sayth, to euery man that seeth hym selfe chalengid & prouokyd
by temptacion / For therby percevith he that yt commeth to his course to
wrestle / which shalbe / but yf he willyng will play the coward or the fole,
the mater of his eternall reward" (101/29–102/3). The first comfort to be
derived in all temptation, in other words, is the first aspect of the theological virtue of hope—the hope of eternal happiness in heaven.

In the next chapter More turns to the second aspect of hope—the trust
in God's assistance. If a man has faith and his faith does not fail him, there
is a further "inestimable cumfort" in all temptation: the knowledge that
God is ready to assist him in his struggles with the devil (102/6–9). Citing
Psalm 117:14, James 1:5, Ephesians 3:18, and Psalm 36:24 to illustrate
the point, More concludes the *catena* with the initial verse of Psalm 90,

alluding to the peace and quiet of mind of those who dwell in the divine protection: "*Qui habitat in adiutorio altissimi, in protectione dei celi comorabitur:* who so dwellith in the help of the hiest god, he shall abide in the proteccion or defence of the god of hevyn" (102/26–103/2). In More's artful handling of the dialogue form, the psalm appears almost casually, as though it were stumbled upon by accident at the end of a series of other scriptural quotations and only then grasped and used as the primary structural principle of the remainder of the book. Once arrived at the psalm, More immediately elaborates on it:

> Who dwellith now good Cosyn in the help of the high god? Surely he that thowrow a good faith abydith in the trust and confidence of goddes helpe, & neuer for lacke of that fayth & trust in his helpe,[1] falleth desperat of all helpe / nor departeth from the hope of his helpe, to seke him selfe helpe as I told you the tother daye of the flesh the world or the devill.
>
> Now he than that by fast fayth & sure hope, dwellith in godes helpe & hangeth alway thervppon, neuer fallyng fro that hope / he shall sayth the prophet euer dwell and abyde in godes defence & proteccion / that is to saye that while he fayleth not to beleve well & hope well, god will neuer fayle in all temptacion to defend hym / (103/2–12)

The virtue of hope is here seen clearly emerging from the foundation of faith in Book I. From this point on the words "faithful hope" reverberate together throughout the dialogue.

The fourth and final section of Book II, the formal meditation on the 90th Psalm, begins in earnest at chapter eleven. The shield of God's truth, mentioned in verse five of Psalm 90, is said to protect us against four specific dangers, which More translates as "the nighten feare, the arrow fleyng in the day, . . . the bysynes walkyng about in the darknesses / . . . [and] the incursion or invacion of the devill in the mydde day" (105/20–23). Following Jerome, Augustine, Bernard, Nicholas de Lyra, and other scriptural commentators,[2] More interprets each of these four metaphors as a specific form of temptation. Taken together, they constitute "all the tribulacion that we shall now speke of, & also some part of that which we haue spoken of before" (105/12–14).

---

[1] In the Vulgate, which More used, the term for *hope* is *spero*, which means not only *hope*, but also *trust*. In hoping in God (*sperare*), we also trust (*sperare*) that He will come to our assistance.

[2] For More's use of these traditional commentaries, see the notes to specific passages in the Commentary. The psalm was regarded particularly as a song of hope and trust in God. See n. to 103/3–12.

Chapter 12 considers the first of these four temptations, "the nightes feare," which More interprets as "the tribulacions by which the devyll thorow the suffraunce of god, eyther by hym selfe or other that are his instrumentes, temptith good folke to impacience / as he did Iob" (107/11–13). The only real danger in this temptation is that fear itself will cause men to lose the virtues of faith and hope, which are the only defense against it: "and therfor the depe darknes of the myd night, maketh men that standith out of fayth & out of good hope in god, to be in their tribulacion far in the greter fere, for lak of the light of fayth, whereby they might perceve that the vtter must of their perill is a far lesse thyng than they take yt for" (108/21–25).

After considering in chapter 12 the nature of the first temptation, More divides it into its various sub-species in chapters 13 to 16, descending into the depths of the temptation, exploring by degrees the intensity of the various manifestations of despair, from pusillanimity to scrupulosity to suicide and death by demonic illusion. These are some of the richest and most complex chapters in the book, full of long, leisurely stories, like the brilliant Mother Maud's tale or the strange case of the old monk in Cassian who was led to suicide by what he believed to be the command of God. Anecdotes of paradoxical self-destruction—suicide for revenge and martyrdom for pride—appear side by side with astute psychological observation, such as the list of rules for the discernment of spirits derived in part from Jean Gerson, while underneath it all runs a strong subcurrent of autobiographical revelation as More probes the question of his own fears and motives in the Tower.[1] The argument dissolves into the dialogue at this point and is carried forward by Vincent's objections and Antony's rambling reminiscences. Much of the progress is through digression.

In each of the various temptations considered, however, the remedy is the same: to hope and trust in God's protection. In the case of pusillanimity, for example, in which "a man for faynt hart, is a ferd where he nedeth not" (111/13–14), More concludes by saying: "And therfor let vs faythfully dwell in the good hope of his helpe, & than shall the pavice of his trouth so compas vs about, that of this nightes feare we shall haue no fere at all" (112/11–14). And the same is true of scrupulosity:

who so hath such a trowble of his scrupulouse conscience: let hym for a while forbere the iugement of hym selfe, . . . & percever in prayour for grace, & abyde & dwell faythfully in the sure hope of his helpe / and than shall he fynd without any dout, that the pauice of godes

---

[1] See Paul D. Green's excellent discussion in his "Suicide, Martyrdom, and Thomas More," *Studies in the Renaissance*, *19* (1972), 135–55.

trouth shall (as the prophet sayth) so compasse hym about, that he
shall not dreade this nightes fere of scrupulositie. (121/14–25)

And suicide and death by demonic illusion:

he that in such a temptacion will vse good counsayle & prayour, . . . &
abide in the faythfull hope of godes helpe, shall haue the trowth of
god (as the prophet sayth in the verse afore rehersid) so compase hym
about with a pavice, that he shall not nede to drede this nightes feare
of this wikkid temptacion / (156/27–157/1)

The effect is repetitive, but it is also cumulative as we come to realize in
temptation after temptation that man is sustained by hope and that in a
very real sense chance and necessity give way before it. More never loses
sight of the form of his book, its teleological goal, despite all the anecdotes,
all the digressions, all the vagaries of ordinary conversation.

The second temptation, the arrow flying in the day, is introduced
toward the end of chapter 16. In More's interpretation, it is the opposite
of fear, just as day is the opposite of night:

[by] the arrow fleyng in the daye / I vnderstond the arrow of pride,
with which the devill temptith a man / not in the night / that is to wit in
tribulacion & aduersite / for that tyme is to dyscomfortable & to
fearefull for pride / but in the day that is to wit in prosperite / for that
time is full of lightsome lust & corage. (157/19–24)

Such a temptation may very well seem like no tribulation at all, but to a
man of good conscience "the devilles temptacion vnto pride in prosperite,
ys a greter tribulacion, & more nede hath of good comfort & good
counsayle both, than he that neuer felt it wold wene" (160/16–19). Many
a good man who has arrived at high position and authority in the world
and is aware of the dangers of pride falls into the opposite extreme of
pusillanimity through scrupulosity and fear of displeasing God. Once
again, as in all temptations, the remedy is hope:

Let such a man therfor temper his fere with good hope / and thynke /
that sith god hath set hym in that place . . . god will assist hym with
his grace to the well vsyng therof / . . . And so dwellyng in the faythfull trust of godes help, he shall well vse his prosperite & perseuer in
his good profitable bysynes, And shall haue therin the trowth of god
so compasse hym about with a pavice of his hevenly defence / that of
the divilles arrow flying in the day of worldly welth, he shall not nede
to drede. (162/10–13, 165/13–17)

The third temptation—the last in Book II—is *negocium perambulans in
tenebris*. *Negocium*, More says, is the name of a devil tempting men to evil

"besynes." The darknesses he walks in are the spiritual equivalents of dawn and dusk, the time before the light of grace appears in the soul and the time after it has begun to fade. The "besynes" itself is a form of covetousness for worldly things, for the pleasures of the flesh or worldly possessions. Most men who set their hearts on transient things, losing sight of God and their eternal goal, have no need for consolation since they are not aware of being troubled. Others, however—"very good folke & vertuouse"—are tempted by such things, "& sith they se plenty of worldly substaunce fall vnto them & fele the devill in likewise bisily tempt them to set their hart thervppon / they be sore trowblid therwith / & begynne to fere therby that they be not with god" (170/1–4). The fear itself is a temptation, and "withdraweth the mynd of a man far fro the spirituall consolacion of the good hope that he shuld haue in godes helpe" (170/16–17). For it is not the having, but "the will & the desire / and affeccion to haue & the longyng for it" that constitute covetousness (171/11–12). The consolation once again in this temptation, as in all others, is the consolation of good hope:

> Let euery man fere and thynke in this world that all the good that he doth or can do is a great deale to litle but yet for all that fere / let hym dwell therwith in the faythfull hope of godes helpe / and than shall the trouth of god so compas hym about (as the prophet sayth) with a pavice / that he shall not so nede to drede the traynes of & the temptacions of the devill, that the prophet calleth bysynes walkyng about in the darknesses / but that he shall for all the havyng of riches & worldly substaunce, so avoyd his traynes & his temptacions, that he shall in conclucion by the greate grace & almightie mercie of god, gete into hevyn well inough / (186/16–25)

And the second book ends in effect at that point. The fourth temptation of Psalm 90, "the incursion or invacion of the devill in the mydde day" is reserved for Book III. The emphasis on temptation continues until the very end and with it the theological virtue of hope. At the same time, however, the last book develops its own internal form. Through the use of reason operating within the argument itself, hope is absorbed into love.

4. Charity

Book III returns us to the scene at the beginning of the *Dialogue*: Hungary in the year 1527/28. After considering the general nature of tribulation in Book I and the specific tribulation of temptation in Book II, More is now in a position to confront directly the initial problem posed, the question of persecution for the faith. In the structure of the work, this is what the two preceding books have been leading up to, and within

Book III the same structure will prevail. Matters of most pertinence will be held off till last. The book begins in a leisurely way, and most of the introductory chapter is given over to a renewal of scene, discussion of the internal problems of Hungary and the Turks in their ravages of other lands, as though More were pausing to refocus the work and prepare for a final assault. The first mention of the threat that hangs over the entire book occurs almost at once in passing. Should the Turks invade, one may be forced "to forsake the fayth of christ, & turne to the profession of their shamfull supersticiouse sect / or els will they put hym vnto deth with cruel intolerable tormentes" (191/22–24). This is the starkest and most dangerous temptation of all—the simple choice between life itself and the love of God or charity.

The overall form of the argument, the structural use of the three theological virtues, continues in Book III, but in a somewhat unexpected fashion. For charity is not approached directly like hope in Book II, with its circular, repetitive patterns. Although it suffuses the book and remains its teleological goal throughout, charity emerges fully only in the last, cumulative chapter, in the affective meditation on Christ's passion and death. It is as though More, faced with the overwhelming question of violent death, felt that some new beginning must be made and extensive preparation laid down first. Hence the emphasis on reason and will, structure and logical organization throughout the book. The realization of charity in Book III, in other words, emerges from a rational process, from the very structure and organization of the work itself—the movement of the mind through rational forms, categories, and distinctions, attempting to control fear and direct one's desires toward God. By considering all the possibilities clearly and foreseeing all the probable torments—even the chance that one might not be able to endure them— one is in a better position to control his instinctive fear of pain and death. But reason alone is not enough. It must be illuminated by the supernatural light of grace. At a certain point the mind proceeds beyond itself, the choice is made, and reason is absorbed in charity. More constructs a rational structure in Book III so as to contain fear and subject it to the will, and at the same time within that structure, within the rational subdivisions and organization of the argument itself, one is aware of another, emergent pattern that makes its appearance subliminally at first, in flashes of apprehension and insight, and finally becomes more and more insistent as the book proceeds—first as a series of brief meditations on various aspects of Christ's passion, and ultimately in the highly emotional, vivid meditation on the passion as a whole that concludes the book.

Charity in its simplest terms is the love of man for God. Aquinas defines it as a form of friendship:

not every love has the character of friendship, but that love which is together with benevolence, when, that is, we love someone so as to wish good to him. . . . Yet neither does well-wishing suffice for friend-ship, for a certain mutual love is requisite, since friendship is between friend and friend: and this mutual well-wishing is founded on some kind of communication. Accordingly, since there is a communication between man and God, in so far as He communicates His happiness to us, there must be some kind of friendship based on this same communication. The love which is based on this communication is charity. And so it is evident that charity is the friendship of man for God.[1]

Friendship of this sort is a gift of God and "can be in us neither naturally, nor through acquisition by the natural powers, but by the infusion of the Holy Spirit."[2] But it is not exactly created or infused in the soul entirely from without since that would remove man's volition, and "love, of its very notion, implies an act of the will." Charity is, instead, "the Holy Spirit Himself dwelling in the mind. . . . The will must be so moved by the Holy Spirit to the act of love, that the will itself also is the efficient cause of that act."[3]

In *A Dialogue of Comfort* More moves by degrees toward the final per-fection of charity, the "desire to be dissolved and to be with Christ,"[4] but he proceeds through stages of fear. One is the natural corollary of the other, and as love emerges in the course of the book, fear is put aside—fear that despite the use of reason, despite faith and the hope of God's help, reason itself will desert man in the end, and his powers of rational control will give way to irrational pain and anguish. Hope continues that even if that happens and one falls, he will be given the grace to rise again. But the current of fear is very strong. The image of St. Peter, in his denial of Christ, alternates for pages with its opposite, the image of the crucified Christ. But eventually even that fear falls away toward the end of the book as the ardor of charity increases and consumes the mind.

Charity in Book III, therefore, is to be seen as cumulative, the result of the overall process of the book. *A Dialogue of Comfort* proceeds by degrees to a love of God for Himself alone. But the *Dialogue* itself is part of a larger continuum, and the ultimate act of charity lies outside the work in More's ascent of the scaffold and humble acceptance of death. The execution casts its shadow over the entire book, as it does over More's entire life. It

---

[1] *ST*, II–II, Q.23, a. 1.

[2] *ST*, II–II, Q.24, a. 2. See also II–II, Q.23, a. 2.

[3] *ST*, II–II, Q.23, a. 2.

[4] *ST*, II–II, Q.24, a. 9.

is impossible to read *A Dialogue of Comfort* without seeing in it the integrity of More's death and the victory he achieved. But as long as he remained a prisoner in the Tower and had the power of free will and the opportunity to deny himself, he was not entirely free of the burden of fear. *A Dialogue of Comfort*, therefore, rises to charity, but in a crucial way the work remains centered on hope. Book III is in a sense a continuation of Book II. They are linked together by scene (the conversation takes place on the same day) and by the formal meditation on the 90th Psalm. Book III, in other words, remains based on hope while advancing tentatively beyond it.

Chapter 2 begins a consideration of the last of the four temptations mentioned in Psalm 90, "the incursion or invacion of the devill in the mydde day." Of all temptations, More says, "this is the most perilouse, the most bittre sharpe, & the most rigorouse" (200/8–9). In other temptations the devil lures man with illusory pleasures or uses hidden traps to capture him in darkness. But in this temptation all disguise is thrown off, and one is fully aware of the circumstances. The temptation itself is twofold. On the one hand the devil threatens man with the fear and terror of unbearable pain and torment, and on the other, he entices him with the promise of rest and quiet, surcease from pain and the immediate threat of death. Moreover, this is not an ordinary fight in which we are in a position to inflict injuries on our enemies. The suffering is passive, helpless and powerless. Pain is inflicted, and one must bear it as courageously as possible. More does not disguise the case. He presents the threat clearly for what it is, in all its stark brutality.

After the introduction and a clear definition of the temptation to be considered, More presents in chapters 3 and 4 the specific means a man assisted by the grace of God may use to resist it. Again one has the sense of a new beginning, signalled by a return to basic principles, as though all the previous portions of the book were preamble to this. Both chapters are brief. Chapter 4 consists of one short paragraph only. But they are extremely important to the organization and overall movement of the book. In fact, they are the primary organizational chapters in Book III.

In searching for the ground on which to begin the final movement of the *Dialogue*, More reverts to the position of the ancient moral philosophers mentioned briefly at the beginning of Book I. Using natural reason only, unenlightened by grace, these philosophers attempted to deal with suffering and tribulation through a form of stoical self-control, the discipline of the mind and power of the will. More had stated earlier that this is not sufficient, that other avenues of consolation are available far exceeding these. But he also said that the arguments of the ancients were not to be rejected entirely since, in Augustine's metaphor, they had many good medicines to cure the wounds of original sin.[1] More now reverts to the consolation of philosophy and begins with man's essential nature. By this point in the *Dialogue*, however, natural reason is illuminated by faith, and philosophy operates within the realm of grace.

In times of persecution, as at any other time, nothing can harm the soul unless it declines in inordinate love to the body. As for the body, one must first take into account the possible loss of the "owtward thinges of fortune" that serve to maintain it, such as wealth, possessions, and positions of power and authority. Second, one must consider the torments the body itself may suffer, such as "losse of libertie / labour / imprisonament, paynfull and shamfull deth" (204/9–10). All these things are real physical losses and must be regarded carefully before the time comes so that one fully understands the claims they make on man's nature. In chapters 5 through 16 More takes up one by one the loss of the outward goods of fortune, and in chapters 17 through 26, the tribulations suffered by the body itself.

Chapter 4—certainly one of the briefest chapters in the book—simply reiterates the fact that if subjected to reason, all the terrors of persecution previously mentioned are not so dreadful as they might otherwise seem to be. Having used reason to control the body in chapter 3, More articulates here the method he will use in the remainder of the book. But reason itself is not the goal. Reason leads to an act of will, and will in turn reveals where one's true love and affection should lie. In chapters 5 through 26, More uses reason to weigh the body and its needs so as to arrive at an act of will. And having made the choice reason presents, the will turns to its proper object in love and desire for God. As Aquinas noted, "the object of charity is not a sensible good, but the divine good, which is known by the intellect alone. Therefore the subject of charity is not the sensitive, but the intellectual appetite, that is, the will. . . . The subject of charity is none other than the rational mind."[2]

Chapters 5 through 16 explore the loss of the outward goods of fortune—lands and possessions, riches, fame, offices, and authority. More follows very carefully the outline presented in chapter 3. The approach is entirely rational, and much of the material is drawn from the traditional consolation of philosophy. In chapter 7, however, another brief organizational unit no more than a few sentences in length, More introduces a new, specifically Christian element into the discussion: Augustine's famous distinction between *uti* and *frui*, use and enjoyment, at the heart of his system of ethics.[3] Our relation to the goods of fortune, More says, is

---

[1] See 10/15–12/4 and Commentary.
[2] *ST*, II–II, Q. 24, a. 1 and a. 5.
[3] See the Commentary, n. to 223/14–26.

essentially a question of the overall direction of our lives and what we set our love on. We either love the things of this world as "comodiouse vnto vs for the state & condicion of this present life / or els as thinges that we purpose by the good vse therof, to make them mater of our merite with goddes helpe in the life after to come" (209/21–24). The ancient philosophers, who arrived at a somewhat similar attitude, rejected excessive concern with material things so as to achieve a greater freedom of the mind, avoiding the fever, anxiety, and foredoomed, hectic activity that the pursuit of power and wealth entails. All this More adopts as his own, but he adds to it the knowledge that the mind finds its proper freedom and rest not in itself as its own end, but only in the love of God. The traditional Augustinian distinction between *uti* and *frui* echoes throughout the remainder of the discussion of the goods of fortune as faith is added to the teachings of philosophy. The chapter headings alone indicate as much:

The litle commoditie of richesse being set by but
for this present life /
The / 8 / chapitre

The litle comoditie of fame being desirid but
for worldly pleasure /
The / 9 / chapitre

The litle commoditie that men haue of romes, offices,
& aucthorite / yf they desire them but for their
worldly comoditie /
The xj chapitre

Each of these is not rejected in its essential nature. What More identifies as wrong is the excessive love of worldly things in and for themselves, esteeming them as more valuable than the love of God they beckon us to In times of persecution, More concludes, one can easily discern what value men set on these things and how much of their love is centered on them. As Christ said,

vbi thesaurus tuus ibi est & cor tuum / where as thy tresour is / there is also thyne hart / yf we laye vpp our tresours in earth / in earth shalbe our hartes / yf we send our tresour into hevyn / in hevyn shall we haue our hartes . . . Yff thyne hart were in dede out of this world & in hevyn, all the kyndes of torment that all the world cold devise, coud put the to no payne here // let vs than send our hartes hens thether. (241/11–19)

In line with the overall process of Book III, More's analysis of the goods of fortune leads inevitably to a form of charity. But at this point in the book the contrast between the love of God and love of the things of this world is not as strong as the emphasis on reason itself. In the next section the virtue of charity becomes increasingly more insistent and more powerful as More turns to the more brutal, physical aspects of persecution.

The second major section of Book III is concerned with the suffering of the body itself and is divided into two main, interlocking parts. In chapters 17 through 20 More considers various kinds of bodily pain: captivity, imprisonment, and torture. In chapters 21 through 26 he takes up the fear of death itself, its degradation, suffering, and torment, weighed against the eternal torment of hell and the joys of heaven. Chapter 17 serves as a general introduction to the entire section and sets the overall framework or context in which it is to be viewed. In many respects it is one of the most significant chapters in the book. Vincent begins: "surely good vncle, whan I bethynke me ferther on the greefe & the payne that may tourne vnto my flesh: here fynd I the feare that forceth myne hart to tremble" (245/13–15). It is not the pain itself that Vincent stresses, but the fear and horror of the anticipation of pain, the slackening of resolve and interior collapse of the will induced by fear. The consideration of physical suffering in the chapters to come is set against this background of fear. In chapter 27, for example, after the section on physical suffering is complete, fear still persists. And it is this fear that More eventually identifies as the primary incursion of the noonday devil, the fourth and most deadly of all temptations mentioned in Psalm 90:

> Thus may we see that in such persecucions, it is the mydday devill hym selfe that maketh such incursion vppon vs, by the men that are his ministers to make vs fall for feare / For till we fall, he can neuer hurt vs. And therfor sayth S. Peter / *Resistite Diabolo et fugiet a vobis* / Stand agaynst the devill, & he shall flye fro you / for he neuer runneth apon a man to seas on hym with his clawes, tyll he see hym down on the grownd willyngly fallyn hym selfe / for his fasshion ys to set his seruauntes agaynst vs, & by them to make vs for feare or for Impacyence to fall / And hym selfe in the meane while compasseth vs, runnyng & roryng like a rampyng lyon abowt vs, lokyng who will fall, that he than may devoure hym / (317/24–318/5)

Against such fear, More says, there are two primary means of defense. One is reason leading to charity. The other is hope in God's assistance. Reason is More's primary method of dealing with the temptation in chapters 18 through 26. In the general introduction in chapter 17, however, this emphasis on reason is set against a backdrop of hope:

> surely yf we be trew christen men / this can we well tell, that without any bold warrantyse of our selfe / or folysh trust in our own strength /

we be bound vppon payne of dampnacion, . . . that we will with his help / how loth so euer we fele our flesh therto / rather yet than forsake hym or his fayth afore the worlde . . . we wold with his help endure & sustayn for his sake, all the turmentry that the devill with all his faythles tourmentours in this world wold devise / And than whan we be of this mynd / & submit our will vnto his, & call & pray for his grace: we can tell well inough, that he will neuer suffre them to put more vppon vs / than his grace will make vs hable to bere / but will also with their temptacion prouide for vs a sure waye / (247/4–17)

Similarly, in chapter 27, in the last few pages of the book, More concludes the section on physical suffering by reiterating once again the importance of hope, as he did at the end of each temptation considered in Book II:

let vs well consider these thynges, & let vs haue sure hope in the helpe of god / & than I dowt not, but that we shalbe sure, that as the prophet sayth, the truth of his promise shall so compace vs with a pavise, that of this incursion of this mydday devill / this Turkes persecucion / we shall neuer nede to fere / for eyther yf we trust in god well, & prepare vs therfor / the Turke shall neuer medle with vs / or els yf he do, harm shall he none do vs / but in stede of harme inestimable good / (316/1–8)

After the general introduction in chapter 17 identifying the nature of the temptation and the primary need to offset fear by hope in God's assistance, More turns in chapters 18 through 20 to the various kinds of bodily pain. Chapter 18 takes up captivity and servitude, chapter 19 imprisonment, and chapter 20 "hard handlyng" or mistreatment and torture in prison. In each case More defines the essential nature of the suffering involved and by the use of reason, distinguishing essentials from accidentals, draws from it a new perspective based on the fundamental features of the thing itself. Captivity, for example, is to be defined as "the violent restraynt of a man, beyng so subdued vnder the domynyon rule & power of an other / that he must do what the tother lyst to commaund hym, & may not do at his libertie such thinges as he lyst hym selfe" (252/7–10). That being the case, certain conclusions logically follow. The first and most important is that the liberty we think lost in captivity must not be exaggerated. No man is entirely free from restraint. God restrains us by His commandments; law restrains us; other men have authority over us; and finally all men are in bondage to themselves through sin. Similarly, imprisonment in chapter nineteen is defined as "but a lak of libertie to go yf we lyst" (258/15), and considered in that light, the entire world is a prison and all men in it prisoners.

Chapters 21 through 26 take up "the last & vttermost poynt of the drede, that maketh / *incursum & demonium meridianum* / this incursion of this mydday devyll," the fear of shameful and painful death (280/24–25). The first of these chapters once again serves as a general introduction to the entire section. The very thought of death, More admits, is enough to cause many men to forget all forms and modes of consolation. It makes even "the fervour of our fayth wax so cold, & our hartes so faynt, that we fele our selfe at the poynt to fall evyn therfro for feare" (281/6–8). But fear has various degrees, depending upon our "affeccions." And at this point More's insistence on reason and his overall intent and purpose in Book III begin to come clear. The term *affections* is a somewhat difficult one for most of us today. Although More does not define it precisely, he seems to use it in a sense common at the time meaning desires, values, emotional attachments and tendencies—all the conscious and unconscious urges created by the entire course and tenor of our lives.[1] The affections, More says, are implanted in the mind in various ways. One of these is by means of the senses and the experience of pleasure and pain, which causes us to avoid one and seek the other. This is common to both beasts and man. It is entirely physical. Another method is through the reason,

> which both ordenately tempereth those affeccions that the bodely five wittes ymprent / and also disposeth a man many tymes to some spirituall vertues, very contrary to those affeccions, that are fleshly & sensuall / And those resonable dispositions bene the affeccions spirituall, & propre to the nature of man, & above the nature of best / Now as our goostly ennymye the devill, enforseth hym selfe to make vs lene vnto the sensuall affeccions and bestly / So doth almighty god of his goodnes by his holy spirite, inspire vs good mocions, with ayd & help of his grace toward the tother affeccions spirituall / And by sundry meanes instructith our reason to lene vnto them / (282/4–13)

In chapters 22 through 26, therefore, More attempts by the use of reason to put down the sensual fear of death. In chapter 22 he considers the essential nature of death itself defined as "a bare levyng of this life onely" (283/2). In chapters 23 and 24 he examines the accidents of shame and pain, and in chapters 25 and 26, the contrast of such a death with the

---

[1] See Glossary. Cf. also John Donne's "Love is a Possessory Affection, it delivers over him that loves into the possession of that that he loves; it is a transmutatory Affection, it changes him that loves, into the very nature of that that he loves, and he is nothing else" (*Sermons*, ed. G. R. Potter and E. Simpson [Berkeley and Los Angeles, 1953–62], *1*, 184–85). For More's use of the term in this same archaic sense in other works, see *The Confutation of Tyndale's Answer*, ed. L. A. Schuster, R. C. Marius, J. P. Lusardi, and R. J. Schoeck, *The Yale Edition of the Complete Works of St. Thomas More* (New Haven, 1973), *8*, 511/19–27, 826/1 (cited hereafter as "*CW 8*"); and *Poisoned Book, EW*, sig. X₃v.

pains of hell and the joys of heaven. The overall purpose of the entire
section is to control fear and present to the will a clear and distinct,
logical choice. Although reason cannot change the nature of pain ("for
but yf it be felt yt is perdye no payne" [293/1]), it can nevertheless lead
the will to the realization that transitory pain and even death itself are
preferable to an eternity of suffering in the life to come. In times of sickness,
for example, men do not hesitate to be lanced and have their flesh cut or
drink poisonous medicines in order to get well. For "reason may make a
reasonable man . . . not to shryng therefro & refuse yt to his more hurt &
harm / but for his far greater avantage & commoditie, content & glad to
sustayne yt / And this doth reason alone in many cases, where it hath mich
lesse help to take hold of, than it hath in this mater of fayth" (293/4, 8–12).

Reason is thus capable of directing the will toward God, but without
grace it can go no further. In the tale of the cowardly hart, for example, in
chapter twenty-four, More comments that in Aesop's time animals were
given the power to talk, "& in ther talkyng power to talke reason to / yet to
folow reason & rule them selfe therby / therto had they neuer geven them
the powre / And in good fayth Cosyn / as for such thynges as perteyne
toward the conductyng of resonable men to salvacion / I thinke without
help of grace, mennys reasonyng shall do litle more" (296/6–10). And yet
reasoning of the sort that More is carrying on in these pages is itself a sign
of grace and the sure hope of God's assistance: "as for grace yf we desire
yt / god is at such reasonyng alway present, & very redy to give yt / & but
yf that men will afterward willyngly cast it away / he is euer still as redy to
kepe yt / & fro tyme to tyme glad to encrese it" (296/11–14).

Reason, then, directs our affections. It allows us to control our sensual
love for the things of this world, including the demands of the body and
the capacity for suffering it contains within it. Reason creates in us a
yearning for God and the enjoyment of eternal happiness with Him in
heaven. And in their final reaches, assisted by grace, rational affections of
this sort are inseparable from the love of God or charity:

> Now than yf reason alone be sufficient to move a man to take payne
> for the gaynyng of some worldly rest or pleasure, & for the avoydyng
> of a nother payne throwgh peradventure more / yet endurable but
> for a short season / why shold not reason growndid vppon the sure
> fowndacion of fayth, & holpen also forward with ayd of goddes grace /
> . . . why shuld not than reason I say thus fortherid with fayth & grace,
> be mych more able, first to engendre in vs such an effeccion / and
> after by long & depe meditacion therof, so to contynew that affeccion,
> that it shall tourne into an habituall fast & depe rotid purpose, of
> pacient suffryng the paynfull deth of this body here in earth, for the

gaynyng of euerlastyng welthy lyfe in hevyn, & avoydyng of euerlastyng paynefull deth in hell / (293/24–294/1, 5–12)

Charity is a gift of God Himself, but, as Aquinas said, "the will must be so
moved by the Holy Spirit to the act of love, that the will itself also is the
efficient cause of that act."[1] Love does not destroy reason, but in a sense
completes it.

Through the use of reason and the movement of the mind through the
rational forms, categories, and distinctions of the argument itself, More
attempts to control fear and direct the will toward the acceptance of pain
and death. At the same time, however, within that rational process something else occurs, like the mysterious motion of grace in the soul, which
leads directly to the full emergence of the theological virtue of charity in
the final chapter of the book. Beginning with chapter 16, the conclusion
to the long, middle section on the goods of fortune, More ends each step in
the rational process with a formal allusion to an aspect of Christ's passion
and death appropriate to the matter at hand. The pattern seems somewhat casual at first, but it soon becomes a structural principle, as though
Christ's passion were the ultimate goal of the rational process itself. After
considering the goods of fortune, for example, More refers in chapter 16
to Christ's voluntary poverty and His lack of worldly power. "Vnto a
warme faythfull man," More concludes, the memory of this thing alone
"were comfort inough in this kynd of persecucion, agaynst the losse of all
his goodes" (242/26–243/1–3). From this point on both these forces, the
power of reason in the frame and argument, and the power of love in the
allusions to Christ's passion, operate alternately to affect the will and turn
the mind and heart toward God. Reason remains the primary form or
organizing principle, but as the book proceeds the recollection of Christ's
passion becomes increasingly insistent. In chapter 17, on fear, More refers
to Christ's fear and anxiety in the agony in the garden; in chapter 18, on
captivity and servitude, to Christ's assumption of the form of a servant,
"obedient unto death, even death on the cross";[2] in chapters 19 and 20,
to Christ's imprisonment; and in chapter 24, on shame, to the crown of
thorns, the mockery of the Roman soldiers, and the degradation of death on
the cross. Finally, in chapter 26 More concludes the series by identifying
Christ's passion with the suffering of all those called upon to die in defense
of the faith:

Our hed is Christ / & therfor to hym must we be Ioynid / & as
membres of his must we folow hym / yf we will come thither. He is

---

[1] *ST*, II–II, Q.23, a. 2.

[2] Phil. 2:5–8. The quotation is from 2:8: "factus obediens usque ad mortem, mortem
autem crucis."

> our Guyde to guyde vs thyther & is entryd in before vs / & he therfor
> that will enter in after, *Debet sicut ille ambulauit et ipse ambulare* / the
> same way that Christ walkyd, the same way must he walke / ...
> *Nesciebatis quia oportebat Christum pati, & sic introire in regnum suum?*
> knew you not that Christ must suffre passion, & by that way entre
> into his kyngdome? Who can for very shame desire to entre into the
> kyngdom of Christ with ease, whan hym selfe entrid not into his own
> without payne / (311/15–28)

These recollections of the passion appear in conjunction with a parallel
series of allusions to St. Peter, who denied Christ through fear. Both
series of allusions reenact metaphorically the same tension and movement
of mind that is taking place on a different level within the rational exposition of the argument itself. St. Peter represents one who loves God but
falls suddenly through weakness of the flesh despite all his promises to the
contrary. It is the archetype of fear that appears throughout *A Dialogue of
Comfort*, in More's last letters to Margaret, and all his Tower works.[1]
Christ, on the other hand, represents the conquest of fear and the willing
acceptance of suffering and death. As the argument proceeds in chapters
17 through 26, the references to Christ's passion increase in fervor and
intensity while the allusions to St. Peter fall away until in the final chapter
of the book only Christ remains.

The formal meditation on the passion in chapter 27 is a continuation of
the series of allusions in the previous section. More points to this fact at
the very beginning: "as I said before in beryng the losse of worldly goodes,
in suffryng of captyuytie thraldome & Imprisonment, & in the glad
susteyning of worldly shame, that yf we wold in all those poyntes, dyepely
pondre the sample of our saviour hym selfe / It were of yt selfe alone
sufficyent, to encorage euery kynd christen man & woman, to refuse none
of all those calamytees for his sake / So say I now / for paynefull deth
also ... " (312/5–11). This is the structural recollection of the passion,
omitted earlier in the section on painful death, but it is also the culmi-
nation of the entire book, in which all its diverse strands are brought
together. As a meditation, it reflects the traditional process of late
medieval meditation, precursor to the Ignatian method. The first step
More performs is to release the imagination[2] so as to recall as graphically

---

[1] See, for example, 196/13–14, 245/3–7, 246/16–18, 297/19–21, 299/27–300/11; and
Commentary, n. to 146/23–29.

[2] We must, More says, meditate on Christ's death "with dew compassion" so as to
"conceyve in our myndes a right Imagynacion & remembraunce" (312/11–12). More's
"Imagynacion" is comparable to Ignatius' use of memory in the composition of place.
More was not of course influenced by Ignatius' *Spiritual Exercises*, which were not in
common use until after More's death. Rather, both drew upon traditional Augustinian

as possible the intolerable pain and torment Christ suffered on the cross:

> his lovely lymmys drawen & strechid out vppon the crosse to the
> Intollerable payne of his forebeten & sorebeten vaynes and synewes /
> new felyng with the cruell strechyng & straynyng payne far passyng
> any crampe, in euery part of his blyssid body at ones / Then the greate
> long nayles cruelly dryven with hamers thorow his holy handes and
> fete . . . (312/18–23)

The purpose is to open the door to fear and at the same time contain it by
focusing on the crucifixion. The second step is to apply the reason or
understanding to what the imagination presents so as to arrive at an act of
will. By understanding fully what his imagination has visualized, More
arrives at a sense of God's love, which arouses the will with desire:

> yf we wold . . . remembre these thinges in such wise, as wold god we
> wold / I verely suppose that the consideracion of his incomparable
> kyndnes, could not fayle in such wise to inflame our kay cold hartes,
> & set them on fire in his love / that we shuld fynd our selfe not onely
> content, but also glad & desierouse to suffre deth for his sake / that so
> mervelously lovyngly lettid not to sustayne so farre passyng paynfull
> deth for ours.
>
> Wold god we wold here to the shame of our cold affeccion, agayne
> toward god for such fervent love & Inestimable kyndness of god
> toward vs / wold god we wold I say but consider, what hote affeccion
> many of thes fleshly lovers haue borne & dayly do, to those vppon
> whome they dote. (313/1–12)

If we were to love God with the same hot affection as these earthly lovers,
we would be willing to die for His sake. "And how cold lovers be we than
vnto god / yf rather than dye for hym ones, we will refuse hym & forsake
him for euer, that both dyed for vs before / & hath also prouidid, that yf
we dye here for hym, we shall in hevyn euerlastyngly both live & also
reigne with hym" (313/30–314/4). If the remembrance of Christ's passion,
the pains of hell and the joys of heaven

> had so dyepe a place in our brest as reason wold they shuld . . . , than
> shuld they so take vpp our mynd, & ravish yt all an other way, that
> as a man hurt in a fray, feleth not sometyme his wound / nor yet is not

---

psychology and the three powers of the rational soul—memory, understanding, and will.
See Louis L. Martz, *The Poetry of Meditation* (New Haven, 1954), pp. 35–39. In orthodox
scholastic psychology the imagination received the impression of the various senses and
combined them by means of the *sensus communis*, passing the image of the thing perceived
on to the storehouse of the memory. Thus memory and imagination were closely allied.
One had to do with the immediate perception of images, the other with their remembrance.

ware therof, till his mynd fall more theron / so farforth that some tyme
an other man shewith hym that he hath lost an hand, before that he
perceveth it hym selfe: so the mynd ravishid in the thinkyng diepely
of those other thinges, Christes deth / hell & hevyn, were lykly to
mynish & put away of our paynefull deth, foure partes of the felyng,
eyther of the feare or the payne. For of this am I very sure / yf we
had the fyfteneth part of the love to Christ, that he both had and
hath to vs: all the payne of this Turkes persecucion, could not kepe
vs from hym / (314/21–315/3)

In the act of meditation, such as More performs here, the mind rises to
the emotional apprehension of the love of God and the "desire to be dissolved and to be with Christ," which Aquinas describes as the most perfect
form of charity,[1] but it inevitably subsides and falls away. Only in the
actual moment of death can one fully lose himself in the darkness of
Christ's love. Until then, fearful and anxious, one remains in hope:

And therfor . . . let vs well consider these thynges, & let vs haue sure
hope in the helpe of god / . . . In our fere let vs remembre Christes
paynfull agonye, that hym selfe wold for our comfort suffre before his
passion, to thentent that no fere shuld make vs dispayre / & euer call
for his help, such as hymselfe lyst to send vs / & than nede we neuer
to dowt / but that eyther he shall kepe vs from the paynfull deth / or
shall not fayle so to strength vs in yt, that he shall ioyously bryng vs
to hevyn by yt / (315/30–316/2, 318/26–32)

As More's definition of "comfort" suggests, the ultimate consolation of *A
Dialogue of Comfort* is "the consolacion of good hope, that men take in their
hart / of some good growing toward them" (68/13–14).

5. The Tradition of Comfort

From the title and the circumstances of composition, it might be
expected that *A Dialogue of Comfort* would bear a close relation to the
ancient tradition of comfort and literary consolation, most notably
represented by Boethius' *De Consolatione Philosophiae*.[2] And indeed there are

---

[1] *ST*, II–II, Q.24, a.9.

[2] More's career and Boethius' were remarkably similar. Both were literary men who
had placed their talents at the disposal of the state and entered government service. Both
had risen to high positions, and at the peak of their worldly success and power both were
accused of treason—a charge to which men of integrity and strong principle are particularly vulnerable. While imprisoned, awaiting execution, both men universalized their
experience in works of lasting literary value. In addition to the *consolatio* and comfort
tradition More's *Dialogue* also participates in the tradition of prison literature, looking
back to such works as Plato's *Crito* and Paul's Epistles written from prison, as well as
Boethius. More seems particularly aware of his indebtedness to Paul.

a number of similarities between More's *Dialogue* and other works of a traditional nature which seek to confront the mystery of suffering that plays so large a part in every man's experience. Generally speaking, there are two main lines of tradition. One is essentially rational and philosophical, looking back to Boethius and behind him to the ancient moral philosophers of Greece and Rome.[1] Works within this tradition usually emphasize the ability of the human mind to detach itself from both pleasure and pain and, through the use of reason, withdraw into its own isolation and splendor. At their best, as in the *De Consolatione Philosophiae*, the symbol of that perfection and splendor is the form of the work itself, produced by the mind to image itself and its own activity.

The other main line of tradition is fundamentally religious, drawing upon the Christian scheme of salvation and biblical promises of eternal reward for suffering endured on earth.[2] Works of this sort were usually addressed to a popular audience and rarely rose above their doctrinal content. Their purpose was essentially didactic, and whatever literary distinction they achieved was derived primarily from interweaving orthodox themes and traditions, such as the imitation of Christ, the way of the cross, the *contemptus mundi*, and the *ars moriendi*.[3] As the Renaissance proceeded and religious dissension increased in intensity, many of these Christian books of comfort became increasingly polemical and were used

---

[1] See, for example, H. R. Patch, *The Tradition of Boethius: A Study of His Importance in Mediaeval Culture* (New York, 1935); E. K. Rand, *Founders of the Middle Ages* (Cambridge, Mass., 1929); and H. M. Barrett, *Boethius: Some Aspects of His Time and Work* (Cambridge, 1940). An extremely useful edition for the Renaissance is *Boetius de consolatu philosophico cum duplici commento sancti Thome, videlicet & Ascensii* (n.p., 1503).

[2] The comfort tradition has not yet been fully explored. For a pioneering study of English works in the sixteenth century, see Beach Langston's *Tudor Books of Consolation*, unpub. diss., Univ. of N. Carolina, 1940. Cited hereafter as "Langston." Typical examples of the genre as it existed before the Reformation are *The Boke of Comforte Agaynste All Tribulacyons* (a title remarkably similar to More's), printed by Wynken de Worde in 1505, and *The Remedy Agenst the Troubles of Temptacyons*, printed by de Worde in 1508. One of the most famous continental examples was Luther's *Tessardecas Consolatoria pro Laborantibus*, which went through eight German editions between 1520 and 1536 and was twice translated into English in the sixteenth century, once in 1564 and again in 1578.

[3] For the way of the cross, see, for example, the dialogue between Christ on the cross and the "poor sinner" in *The Boke of Comforte Agaynste All Tribulacyons* (London, 1505), sigs. A₂–D₂v, and chapter 30 of John Downame's *Consolations for the Afflicted* (London, 1613). For the *contemptus mundi* theme, see Erasmus, *De Contemptu Mundi*, trans. Thomas Paynell (London, 1533). The *ars moriendi* is combined with the comfort tradition in *The Doctrynall of Dethe* (London, 1498 and 1532), *A Newe Book, Conteyninge an Exhortation to the Sycke* (Ipswich, 1548), and Peter de Luca's *A Dialogue of Dying Well*, trans. R. V. (Antwerp, 1603). For the *ars moriendi* proper, see Nancy L. Beaty, *The Craft of Dying: A Study in the Literary Tradition of the Ars Moriendi* (New Haven, 1970), and Mary C. O'Connor, *The Art of Dying Well: The Development of the Ars Moriendi* (New York, 1942).

by Protestant and Catholic alike to strengthen the faithful against persecution.[1]

The overall purpose of both these traditions was "to rationalize the universe; to render it, in the writer's and reader's minds, conformable to reason . . . , in accordance with some just and reasonable pattern."[2] More's *Dialogue of Comfort* shares this broad purpose and thus, even with its essential differences, may be seen as part of the tradition. Langston defines it as a Renaissance imitation of the classical *consolatio*, written in the form of a Platonic dialogue.[3] But More's work differs from the usual *consolatio* in its reliance not on reason, but on faith. It begins at the point where Boethius and the ancient moral philosophers left off and proceeds into sources of consolation beyond the reach of man's natural faculties. True comfort, More explicitly says at the very beginning of the book, is derived not from man's rational powers, but from the supernatural assistance of God (9/17–12/14). Reason is not, of course, entirely rejected. More makes extensive use of it, particularly in Book III, but the emphasis on reason in the classical *consolatio* is subordinated to faith, and philosophy functions within the state of grace. More incorporates, in other words, elements of the classical *consolatio* within a Christian frame of reference.

A *Dialogue of Comfort* would seem therefore to be closely related to the Christian tradition of comfort. But it is different from all other comfort books both in the way in which it incorporates the classical *consolatio* and in its superior literary technique, which carries with it More's whole manner and mode of thought—the complexity of the dialogue form, the artistic structure and design, the various levels of audience address, and the strange, Menippean combination of merry tales and anecdotes side by side with the grim realities of mental and physical torture.[4] The only real resemblance between *A Dialogue of Comfort* and other works in the comfort tradition is its shared doctrinal content, its use of Christian themes and

---

[1] Typical Catholic examples are John Scory, Bishop of Hereford's *Epistle Wrytten vnto All the Faythfull that be in Pryson in Englande, or in Any Other Troble for the Defence of Goddes Truth* (1555) and Robert Southwell's *Epistle of Comfort*, written in 1587–89, while Southwell was a member of the English Mission. The Protestant position is upheld by George Joye in his *Present Consolacion for the Sufferers of Persecution for Ryghtwisenes* (London, 1544). Joye assisted Tyndale in his translation of the bible and refers to More in passing as "that traytor," the former Lord Chancellor, who persecuted fellow Englishmen.

[2] Langston, p. ix.

[3] Langston, pp. 256–58.

[4] More's merry tales serve a function similar to the verse interludes in Boethius' *De Consolatione*. Both look back to the mixture (*satura*) of verse and prose in the anatomy or Menippean satire. See Northrop Frye, *An Anatomy of Criticism* (Princeton, 1957), pp. 309–11; Frye identifies the *consolatio* as an offshoot of the tradition of Menippean satire.

traditions, and the fervor of its faith. Very few writers of comfort books had artistic aspirations. *A Dialogue of Comfort*, however, is an intensely personal work of great power and a masterpiece of Renaissance devotional literature. The nature of More's originality has, we hope, become apparent from our discussion of the argument of the book. The word "argument" has come to mean something as simple as the outline and paraphrasable content of the work—its overall purpose, drift, and direction—and at the same time something as complex as the obscure process by which More attempted in the last remaining months of his life to prepare himself for death. It is the means by which More attempted to objectify and embody in some external form his fears for himself and his family during the fifteen months of his imprisonment—the destitution of those he loved and felt responsible for, the very real possibility of torture at the hands of Cromwell and other agents of the king, the fear that he would deny himself and destroy his spiritual nature, and finally the fear of death itself.

IV. AUDIENCE

1. The General Reader: The Turkish Threat

In writing *A Dialogue of Comfort* More used the various literary means at his disposal to arrive at a sense of God's presence in his own life, along with a simultaneous sense of detachment from all the things of this world, including the literary creation he was at the moment in the process of making. And he was doing this not only for himself, but for generations of other men who might conceivably at one time or another be placed in a similar situation or in some fashion see their own lives and their own tribulations reflected in what he had written. The work itself, the literary fiction, is a symbolic action or outward sign of an interior process. The overall structure and organization, the literary motifs, the merry tales and anecdotes—all these are designed to convey and to create the obscure motion of the soul, an inward teaching and prompting of the spirit. It is for this that Antony prays at the very end of the book, in the last few sentences: "I besech our lord to breth of his holy spirite into the readers brest, which inwardly may tech hym in hart, without whome litle availeth all that all the mowthes of the world were able to tech in mens eares" (320/23–26).

The relation of an author to his work, however, is extremely complex. *A Dialogue of Comfort* is undercut throughout by fear, but despite the threat of torture and death by disembowelling, the tone is remarkably serene—

humorous in places, wry and ironic in others, controlled and almost non-chalant. There is a sense in which every author both participates in his own work and stands outside it as an observer, engaged in detachment in the very process of writing. But for a variety of reasons this seems to be particularly true of *A Dialogue of Comfort*. More deliberately plays with the literary aspects of the work so as to produce different effects and different dimensions of meaning for different kinds and varieties of audience, depending on how much the individual reader knew about More himself, the circumstances of composition, and the nature and application of the material he was dealing with. This complex use of the literary aspects of a work and the development within it of a variety of levels of address seem to have been typical of More's approach to composition throughout his literary career. As Stapleton points out, "More was as clever in hiding his virtues as he was in feigning the circumstances in which his books were written . . . ; in artifices of this nature he was resourceful, and indeed a past master." In the *Utopia*, there is the fictitious tale of discovery and the factual description of Utopian culture and the interior peace that arises from it, in contrast to the continued barbarism, pride, and avarice of Europe. But there are also numerous clues built into the work that make it clear that something more complicated than a mere factual account is going on. As Stapleton says, "the artifice is not too difficult to detect, but the reader is beguiled." Similarly, in the *Ad Lutherum*, More "introduces Ross as travelling in Italy and, at the instigation of his host, replying to Luther. Without Ross's knowledge, his reply is then published by his questioner." "With no less skill," Stapleton concludes, More

> pretends that his book *A Dialogue of Comfort against Tribulation* was written in Hungary. . . . His references to Henry's cruelty, to the disturbances in England, to the fear and expectation of the spread of heresy there, to what comfort the good may have in view of such evils, present or to come, are all disguised cleverly and naturally . . . , so that you would be convinced that a Hungarian is speaking of his own land and not More of England.[1]

---

[1] Thomas Stapleton, *The Life . . . of Sir Thomas More*, tr. P. E. Hallett (London, 1928), pp. 65–66. Cited hereafter as "Stapleton." Along the same lines, in speaking of the *Utopia*, Harpsfield (p. 103) noted that "many great learned men, as Budaeus and Johannes Paludanus, [seemed to take the same storie as a true storie. And Paludanus] vpon a feruent zeale wisshed that some excellent diuines might be sent thither to preache Christes Gospell; yea, then were here amonge vs at home sundry good men and learned diuines very desirous to take that voyage, to bring that people to Christes fayth, whose maners they did so well like vpon. And surely this saide iollye inuention of Sir Thomas More seemed to beare a good countenaunce of truth."

In each case the simultaneous disguise and revelation is part of the essential form and meaning of the work.

The primary level of address in *A Dialogue of Comfort* is to the general reader who presumably had no way of identifying the author of the book as the ex-Lord Chancellor of England, the friend of Erasmus, discoverer of Utopia, and the scourge of heretics, and therefore had no reason to doubt the statement on the title page that the book had been written "by an hungaryen in laten, & translatyd out of laten into french, & out of french into Englysh." The general reader would tend to locate the work within the historical circumstances of the dialogue itself: the Christian bulwark of Hungary on the eve of a Turkish invasion. For this audience the literary surface would be perfectly intelligible and completely sufficient within itself. More never departs from the fictional scene, and in Europe at the time, with its entire civilization threatened for almost a century by the increasing military power of the Turks and their steady, almost inexorable, encroachment on European territory, it would have had great emotional reverberation.

In 1452 Mahomet II, surnamed the Conqueror, sacked Athens, "the Uniuersitie and Nurce of all worthy Artes & Disciplines,"[1] and on May 29, 1453, he took Constantinople itself, renaming it Istambul and proclaiming it the new capital of the Ottoman empire.[2] Half of Christendom had fallen, and Hagia Sophia was converted to a mosque. Mahomet then turned his face toward Europe. In 1464, he conquered the Adriatic coast of Yugoslavia, in 1464–79 northern Albania, and on August 11, 1480, established a foothold in Italy itself, at Otranto.[3] Pope Sixtus IV summoned all Christendom to the defense of Rome and made ready to flee to France. Mahomet II died, however, before his preparations for the full-scale invasion of Italy were complete, and his successor, Bagazeth II, was concerned primarily with consolidating his rule, modernizing the army and navy, and creating the firm political and economic base for the further conquests of Selim I and Suleiman the Magnificent.

Selim I marched first against Persia, and after defeating Shah Ishmail on the plain of Chaldiran, on August 23, 1514, turned against the Mameluke empire of Syria and Egypt. On August 24, 1516, he defeated Kansuh Ghuri, Sultan of the Circassian Mamelukes of Syria, and occupied Aleppo, Damascus, and Jerusalem. A little more than a year later, on January 22, 1517, at the battle of Reydaniyya, he took Egypt, and the remaining

[1] Thomas Newton, *A Notable History of the Saracens . . . Drawen out of Augustine Curio and sundry other good Authours* (London, 1575), fol. 131. Cited hereafter as "Newton."

[2] For a detailed, graphic account of the fall of Constantinople, see Robert Schwoebel, *The Shadow of the Crescent* (Nieuwkoop, 1967), pp. 1–24. Cited hereafter as "Schwoebel."

[3] Again Schwoebel, pp. 131–34, has an excellent account of the siege of Otranto.

Mameluke strongholds in Arabia and North Africa fell shortly afterwards.
The Turks were now in firm control of all Asia Minor and North Africa.
In Europe, they occupied the Grecian peninsula and a good part of the
Balkans. Only Hungary stood in the way of further expansion toward the
west.

At this precise moment in history Europe was in no way prepared to
meet the Turkish threat. The "common corps of Christendom," as More
so fondly spoke of it,[1] the *respublica Christiana*, was internally divided by
what can only be described as a form of civil war. Beginning in March
1521, the decade was marked by a constant struggle for power and control
among the rising national states. Savage wars of ambition and revenge
broke out between the Holy Roman Emperor, Charles V, and Francis I of
France, with Henry VIII and Wolsey attempting to affect the balance of
power through adroit political maneuvering and direct military aid. After
being taken prisoner at the battle of Pavia, on February 24, 1525, Francis I
even went so far as to negotiate an alliance with the Turks against his
fellow Christians, telling the Venetian ambassador that only in that way
could he be assured of guaranteeing national sovereignty in Europe against
Charles V.[2] Wolsey, on the other hand, stated that as far as he was
concerned the real Turk was the king of France.[3] At the instigation of the
French, the Turkish Sultan, Suleiman the Magnificent, approached the
Schmalkaldic League of Protestant princes in Germany, fighting against
Charles V, and urged them to cooperate with France against the Pope
and Emperor, promising them amnesty if the Turks should happen to take

---

[1] The phrase is a rendering of the Latin *corpus Christianum*. For the continuation of this
essentially medieval notion despite the new diplomacy of the Renaissance, which allowed
for negotiating with the infidel for purposes of dynastic or national expediency, see F. L.
Baumer, "England, the Turk, and the Common Corps of Christendom," *American
Historical Review, 50* (1944), 26–48. Baumer's conclusions, working with historical records,
are similar to those of Samuel C. Chew in *The Crescent and the Rose* (New York, 1937), who
relied primarily on evidence from literary sources. See also R. H. Schwoebel, "Coexistence, Conversion, and the Crusade against the Turks," *Studies in the Renaissance, 12*
(1965), 164–87, and C. A. Patrides, "'The Bloody and Cruell Turke': the Background of
a Renaissance Commonplace," *Studies in the Renaissance, 10* (1963), 126–35. Medieval
concepts of the Turk, many of which survived after more extensive contact in the Renaissance, are best surveyed in N. A. Daniel, *Islam and the West: The Making of an Image*
(Edinburgh, 1960), and R. W. Southern, *Western Views of Islam in the Middle Ages* (Cambridge, Mass., 1962).

[2] Halil Inalcik, *The Ottoman Empire: The Classical Age, 1300–1600*, trans. N. Itzkowitz
and C. Imber (London, 1973), p. 35. Cited hereafter as "Inalcik." For French treaties,
pacts, and agreements with the Turks, see C. D. Rouillard, *The Turk in French History,
Thought, and Literature, 1520–1660* (Paris, 1961).

[3] R. P. Adams, *The Better Part of Valor: More, Erasmus, Colet, and Vives on Humanism, War,
and Peace, 1496–1535* (Seattle, 1962), p. 273. Cited hereafter as "Adams."

over Europe.[1] Humanist pleas for unity against the common enemy, such as Vives' *De Europae dissidiis, & republica* (Bruges, 1526), *De concordia & discordia in humano genere* (Antwerp, 1529), and Erasmus' *De Bello Turcis* (1530), were totally ineffectual.[2] The Popes, Julius II and Leo X, were themselves warlords, and their repeated calls for a unified Christian crusade against the Turks, promising plenary indulgences to all participants, were undercut by their own political self-seeking and rejected offhand by Protestant princes, who refused to rally under the menstruous rag of the Whore of Babylon. Luther's position in his early works, such as the *Resolutiones* (1518) and *Assertio 34* (1521), was that the Turks were the scourge of God intended to punish Europe for its sins; therefore to unite in a common crusade under the leaders of the church was directly opposed to God's will—a position which was, of course, condemned in turn by the church in the bull of 1520, *Exsurge Domine*.[3] As Erasmus wrote in the *Colloquies*, summing up the condition of Europe in the 1520s, "the three monarchs of the world [Henry VIII, Charles V, and Francis I] . . . [are] bent upon one another's destruction with a mortal hatred . . . ; [there is] no part of Christendom free from the ravage of war; for these three have drawn all the rest to be engaged in the war with them. Nor are the Turks at quiet, but are preparing to make a dreadful havoc."[4]

It was precisely at this low point of Christian discord and disunity that the new Ottoman Sultan, Suleiman the Magnificent, chose to make his move. On August 29, 1521, he took Belgrade, that "sure fortresse and defense, not onlye of Hungary, but also of all Christentie,"[5] which had successfully resisted in the past the siege of both Amurath II in 1442 and Mahomet II in 1456. On January 21, 1522, after a five-month siege, Suleiman succeeded in capturing the island of Rhodes, the key to the eastern Mediterranean, defended by the Christian Knights of St. John of Jerusalem. As the papal legate to England pointed out to Henry VIII, "Rhodes and Belgrade were the 'outworks of Christendom' and . . . after their collapse, all Hungary or, alternately, Sicily and Italy lay open to conquest. Indeed he said that 'the rest of Christendom and England itself are in the greatest danger.'"[6] And in the summer of 1526, it would have

---

[1] Inalcik, p. 37. For the use of the Turkish threat as a bargaining point by Protestant princes in Germany in their dealings with Charles V, see S. Fischer-Galati, *Ottoman Imperialism and German Protestantism, 1521–1555* (Cambridge, Mass., 1959).

[2] These treatises are admirably paraphrased in Adams, pp. 262–64, 285–91, 298–99.

[3] *CW 8*, n. to 123/31–35. For More's ridicule of Luther's position, see Adams' excellent discussion, pp. 274–75.

[4] The title of the colloquy is *Charon*, quoted in Adams, p. 278.

[5] Paulus Jovius, *A Shorte Treatise vpon the Turkes Chronicles*, tr. P. Ashton (London, 1546), fol. 103^v.

[6] Adams, p. 273.

seemed as though his prophecy was about to come true. Invading Hungary, Suleiman defeated Louis II at the disastrous battle of Mohács on August 28, 1526, and occupied Buda. The bulwark of Hungary, which had successfully resisted the Turks for almost a century, had fallen. The wall had been breached, and Europe lay open to the infidel.

In 1526, at the time of Suleiman's invasion of Hungary, More had been in the service of the king for nine years. From September 1525 to October 1529, he held the chancellorship of the Duchy of Lancaster, but he also assisted in the negotiation of extremely important foreign alliances, such as the Treaty of the More (1525), in which Wolsey shifted allegiance from Charles V to Francis I after the battle of Pavia, and the Treaty of Cambrai (1529), in which peace in Europe was finally ratified. More was regarded as an expert in foreign policy, particularly in French affairs, but, as G. R. Elton has shown, his primary, though unofficial, position was that of personal secretary to the king and humanist in residence at the English court. "The king enjoyed his company and conversation, kept him close to his person, and when the occasion offered exploited his intellectual gifts and his pen. Henry liked to have intellectuals around him: he took pleasure in talking about their concerns, and his interest in books and writers was genuine, though haphazard. . . . With such men his relationship was more personal than usual: one may speak of friendship."[1] The official secretariat was held first by Richard Pace and later, after Pace went mad, by William Knight, but from the middle of 1519 to late 1526, Wolsey employed indifferently both More and the principal secretary as the normal channel through which to convey written information to the king. "The minute Pace is off again on diplomatic missions, More acts in effect as secretary, getting the king's signature on papers, reading Wolsey's letters to him, conveying his instructions."[2] Between August and November 1523, thirteen letters survive in which More acts as intermediary between Wolsey and the king, and in September 1526, William Knight, the principal secretary, declined to open in his absence official correspondence addressed to More. Later, at More's request, he overcame his diffidence[3] and on October 11, 1526, wrote to Wolsey from Ampthill: "Your letters to More, dated Hampton Court, the 8th [reached this] on the 9th; and as More was gone to London, I opened the packet. I read to the King the news of Hungary and its overthrow, which he lamented as lost by the folly of Christian princes thus giving way to the Turk, who would now easily overrun Germany, where Lutheranism was so obstinately

---

[1] "Thomas More, Councillor (1517–1529)" in *More Symposium*, pp. 109–10.

[2] *Ibid.*, p. 105.

[3] *Ibid.*, pp. 105–106.

supported."[1] All the items in the packet were of considerable importance. Besides the news from Hungary, there was a letter from the Pope, Wolsey's draft of a letter of consolation in reply, which the king proceeded to amend, approval of Wolsey's advice to the Pope not to leave Rome and his promise of 30,000 ducats in aid, along with further advice on how to deal with the Papal and French ambassadors. During the years of his unofficial secretariat, More was close enough to the king to be trusted with matters such as this and thus had access to detailed information on the international situation. More's knowledge, of course, was not automatically that of Wolsey or the king, but it is difficult to believe that he did not absorb in this way a thorough background in contemporary Hungarian history, which he later drew upon when he came to write A Dialogue of Comfort. Of the nine hundred state papers that are preserved from the year 1526, more than seventy deal with the Turks and the situation in Hungary, most of them arriving in England through the agency of the Pope, who kept Henry fully informed so as to gain his assistance against the infidel.[2] More could hardly have avoided picking up the information.[3]

The letters themselves were galvanizing enough to attract anyone's attention. On February 4, 1525, Louis II of Hungary wrote to the Pope from Cracow: "The Turk does not fear the Christians; he believes that the practice of arms has grown to desuetude among them, as he found no opposition at the siege of Taurinus or Albanevander (Belgrade), and in his attack upon Rhodes was encouraged by the indifference of Christendom. He is ever active, whilst the Christians are sluggish;—intends to attack Italy;—is aware of the disputes of Christian princes."[4] By March 27 of the following year Baron de Burgio, the Papal Nuncio at Buda, advised the Pope that Hungary was in confusion on the approach of the Turks. The king was penniless; no one would lend him money; and the king admitted that he was more afraid of the Turks of Hungary, as he called them, than he was of the real Turks. "There is no preparation, no

---

[1] *Letters and Papers, Foreign and Domestic of the Reign of Henry VIII*, ed. J. S. Brewer (London 1870), *4*, pt. 2, 1137 (item 2558). Cited hereafter as "*LP*." Elton, *More Symposium*, p. 106, notes a similar instance in which Knight opened an official letter addressed to More and read it to the king.

[2] See, for example, *LP*, *4*, items 2120, 2122, 2373, and 2466.

[3] More may also have been familiar with the Turks from having read such items as Cochlaeus' *Dialogus de bello contra Turcos* (Leipzig, 1529), Sebastian Franck's *Türkenchronik* (1530), Felice Petanzio (of Ragusa)'s *Quibus itineribus Turci aggrediendi sint?* (1502), *Genealogia Turcorum imperatorum* (1508-12), and *Historia Turcica* (1508-12). See R. J. Schoeck, "Thomas More's 'Dialogue of Comfort' and the Problem of the Real Grand Turk," *English Miscellany, 20* (Rome, 1969), 23-37. Cited hereafter as "Schoeck." Works such as these would have given More the larger picture, but not the specific details of the contemporary situation in Hungary in the period of 1526-28.

[4] *LP*, *4*, pt. 1, 463 (item 1061).

order, and, what is worse, many have no wish to defend themselves."[1] On July 5th the Archbishop of Colacza relayed the information to Louis II that spies had seen the Turkish army enter Belgrade; they were waiting only for their artillery to catch up with them before proceeding further.[2] Four months later the Archbishop's head was impaled on a spear in the Turkish camp on the racecourse between Buda and Thales.[3] On August 5th de Burgio describes the fall of Petra Varadin: "when the Turks had taken the castle by a mine, the garrison fought in the courtyard until the blood of Turks and Christians reached to their knees . . . [The Turks] cut off the heads of the wounded and flung them into the Danube." On August 6th he reports that in the same battle the Turks were repulsed six or seven times. "Their corpses filled the ditches. The Hungarians could not bear the stench." Of the thousand defenders only one hundred escaped to a small rock, where they were surrounded and forced to surrender.[4] And finally, a tense statement with no superscription, merely the note "Nova Hungarica allata ex Pettovia die xx Septembris," announcing the defeat of the Hungarian forces at Mohács:

> The Turk entered Buda on the 9th, and killed everyone over 13 or 14 years of age. He kept no prisoners, but sent those under age to Turkey. He has burnt many towns. The King, after his defeat, was drowned in a marsh, whither his horse had carried him. Those lords of Hungary who have escaped are not making any attempt to recruit the army, but are committing worse cruelties than the Turks, spoiling and burning their own domains . . . The Turk had in his army 300,000 men, and sent forward to the first engagement 70,000 men . . . For a whole hour the firing was furious, and the Hungarians were routed, with great slaughter of bishops, lords, and great men. After the victory, the Turks refreshed themselves three days, and then went about carrying rapine and slaughter to the confines of Germany.[5]

Sir John Wallop, writing to Wolsey from Cologne on October 8, described the battle in similar terms. He noted that "the Hungarians are utterly broken" and added that the Turk had 20,000 mercenary Lutheran *Landsknechte* serving on double wages in his army.[6] At the end of the campaign season, the Turk withdrew. "He had on the Danube 3,000 boats laden with Hungarian spoil. Among other things, bells of brass and

[1] *LP*, *4*, pt. 1, 925–26 (item 2096).

[2] *LP*, *4*, pt. 1, 1033 (item 2301).

[3] *LP*, *4*, pt. 2, 1147 (item 2589).

[4] *LP*, *4*, pt. 2, 1064–65 (items 2380 and 2381).

[5] *LP*, *4*, pt. 2, 1114 (item 2496).

[6] *LP*, *4*, pt. 2, 1136 (item 2554).

all kinds of iron goods, 5,000 Hungarian prisoners, and 30 ships laden with
Jews. . . . Of the 72 counties of Hungary, 12 have been plundered, and
Buda and the other places visited by the Turk have been burnt."[1] "Next
spring," the Lord Chancellor of Hungary prophesied on October 3rd,
"the Turk intends to attack the rest of Hungary, which is without means
of defence, and then Transylvania and the remainder of Europe. Can
hardly hope for help, as Europe is in such discord."[2] A few years later,
when Sir Francis Bryan was asked in Paris what Henry VIII intended to
do about the Hungarian situation, he told the king he replied, "I could
not tell, but that, if all agreed, you would act like a Christian prince."[3] In
More's analysis of the situation, that was precisely the problem.

The Turkish threat to Europe and the invasion of Hungary, which
seemed to forecast what was in store for the remainder of Christendom,
were matters of deep and lasting concern for More. While walking with
his son-in-law, William Roper, on the banks of the Thames at Chelsea,
More once told him, Roper reports: "Nowe wold to our Lord, sonne
Rooper, vppon condicion that three things were well established in
Christendome, I were put in a Sack, and here presently caste into the
Thames." Roper solemnly asked what those three great things might be.
And More replied in effect: the unity of Christendom. The first of the
three wishes was "that where the moste parte of Christen princes be at
mortall warre, they were all at an vniuersall peace."[4] The remark is
pressured in part by an awareness of recent Turkish victories in Hungary,
Belgrade, and Rhodes. If Europe were united and at peace, More knew—
as did all his fellow humanists—Christendom would no longer be threatened by the Turk. As he remarked in 1531 to Eustache Chapuys, the
Spanish Ambassador to England, it was only the "blindness" of Christian
princes that allowed them to refuse aid to the Emperor in driving back the
Turk, "so cruel and implacable an enemy."[5] Almost ten years after the
first invasion of Hungary, while imprisoned in the Tower, More still
remembered the event in moments of private reflection. In his prayer

---

[1] *LP, 4*, pt. 2, 1146–47 (item 2588).

[2] *LP, 4*, pt. 2, 1147 (item 2589).

[3] *LP, 4*, pt. 3, 2674 (item 6007).

[4] William Roper, *The Lyfe of Sir Thomas Moore, Knighte*, ed. E. V. Hitchcock, *EETS*,
Original Series, no. 197 (London, 1935), pp. 24–25. Cited hereafter as "Roper." The
other two wishes were (1) that the Church "were settled in a perfecte vniformity [of]
religion" and (2) that the King's great matter of his marriage were "brought to a good
conclusion." Roper does not give the date, but the conversation undoubtedly occurred
after 1527, when the question of the divorce first arose.

[5] *Calendar of Letters, Despatches, and State Papers, . . . Between England and Spain, Preserved
. . . at Simancas and Elsewhere* [1485–1553], ed. G. A. Bergenroth (London, 1862–1954), *4*,
ii, 114. Cited hereafter as "*Spanish Calendar*."

book, opposite Psalm 68:7–21, he wrote: "in tribulacione dicendum fidelibus a Hungaris inualescentibus turcis et multis hungarorum in turcarum perfidiam desciscentibus (to be said in [time of] tribulation by the faithful among the Hungarians when the Turks grow strong and many Hungarians fall away into the false faith of the Turks)."[1] The annotation is clearly related to *A Dialogue of Comfort*; besides this there are six other more general references in the prayer book to verses in the psalter to be used "pro populo christiano contra turcas."[2] Clearly, the Turks were much on More's mind toward the end of his life, not only in *A Dialogue of Comfort*, but also in his most personal, private meditations and prayers. Besides the fact that he considered himself persecuted by a form of renegade Christian, More was preoccupied with the Turk because of his life-long belief in the preeminence of the Church and the common bond thus formed among all Christian nations—the ancient dream of the *respublica Christiana*, united under God on earth. At his trial, when Audley evoked the authority of the learned men of the realm—bishops, theologians, and professors—who had acceded to the Act of Supremacy, More replied:

> [I am] not bounden, my Lorde, to conforme my conscience to the Councell of one Realme against the general Councell of Christendome. For of the foresaide holy Bisshopps I haue, for euery Bisshopp of yours, aboue one hundred; And for one Councell or Parliament of yours (God knoweth what maner of one), I haue all the Councels made these thousande yeres. And for this one kingdome, I haue all other christian Realmes.[3]

It is this same vision of Christianity, threatened by the bloody conquests of the infidel and divided within by political and spiritual disharmony, that More evokes in *A Dialogue of Comfort*. "There falleth so contynually before the eyen of our hart," Vincent says at the beginning of the book,

> a fearcfull imaginacion of this terryble thyng / his [the Turk's] myghty strength and power, his high malice and hatryd, & his incomparable crueltie, with robbyng, spoylyng, burnyng, and layng wast all the way that his armye commeth / . . . so that such as are here & remayne styll / shall eyther both lese all & be lost to / or forcid to forsake the fayth of our savyour christ, and fall to the false sect of machomete. (6/22–7/1)

---

[1] *Prayer Book*, pp. 197, 114.
[2] The annotations occur opposite Ps. 16:8; 79:4; 79:14; 82:2; 84:2; and 93:2. See *Prayer Book*, pp. 191, 199–201.
[3] Harpsfield, p. 196. "The Paris News Letter" (Harpsfield, pp. 263–64) and Roper (p. 95) give a somewhat abbreviated version of the speech. For a distant echo in *A Dialogue of Comfort*, see 289/5–9 and n.; 315/6–30.

"And therfor," Antony later concludes, "albeit I wold advise euery man pray still & call vnto god to hold his graciouse hand ouer vs, & kepe away this wrechidnes yf his pleasure be / yet wold I ferther advise euery good christen body, to remembre & consider, that it is very likely to come, & therfor make his rekenyng & cast his peny worthes before / & euery man & euery woman both, appoynt with goddes helpe in their own mynd beforehand / what thyng they intend to do yf the very worst fall" (195/24–31). This is the primary level of address in *A Dialogue of Comfort*, and read in this way the book is similar to Vives' somber essay attached to his *De concordia & discordia in humano genere* in June 1529, as the Turks were marching westward toward Vienna: "Since it might be useful for Christians to know what to expect and how earlier men had endured such oppression, he reviewed some histories of the martyrs."[1]

The second level of address proceeds directly from the first. The book turns inward and without altering in any way the historical circumstances of the Turkish invasion of Hungary, something else appears. The date More chose for the scene of the dialogue is alone almost sufficient to indicate as much. The fictional conversation does not take place, as one would expect, in 1526, immediately after the battle of Mohács, when Hungary was defeated and lay open to the Turks. This would have been the most logical and most dramatic moment to have chosen if More were interested only in exhibiting the Turkish threat to Europe. He chose instead the years 1527–28, the interval of relative calm between the first Turkish invasion and the second. And the choice complicates considerably the impact and meaning of the book.

After the battle of Mohács, Suleiman went on to occupy Buda, inadvertently burning the town. The coming of winter put an end to the campaign season, and the Turks withdrew their forces from the European side of the Danube, retaining only Shem. Since Louis II had died without issue, the surviving Hungarian nobility assembled in Diet at Alberegalis to elect a new king. They chose John Zapolya, Voivode of Transylvania. Another faction, however, supported the brother of Charles V, Ferdinand of Austria, who claimed the throne by right of inheritance. In 1527, the issue led to civil war. Ferdinand invaded Hungary, and after defeating Zapolya, occupied the capital. Zapolya fled to Poland and negotiated with Suleiman for the restoration of his throne, promising fealty as a vassal and annual tribute in return for Turkish assistance. Ferdinand attempted to ratify a truce, but in the spring of 1529, Suleiman once again invaded Hungary. Zapolya met him at Belgrade "with a great companie of the Hungarian Nobilitie, which he brought with him. . . . He found him

---

[1] Adams, p. 291.

sitting vnder a Canapie where he gaue him his right hand in signe of
amitie, the which he kissed, and after some courtesies, *Solyman* said to him;
that he doubted not but with ease to reconquer all that which vniustly had
been taken from him."[1] By September, Suleiman was at the gates of Vienna.
After only a three week siege, he withdrew his forces on the coming of
winter and bestowed the kingdom of Hungary as a fief to John Zapolya.
From that point on, the city of Buda was occupied by a garrison of
Turkish Janissaries and remained in Turkish hands for the next one hundred and forty-five years.[2]

By placing the scene of the dialogue sometime after Ferdinand's coronation in 1527 and before Suleiman's invasion on behalf of Zapolya in 1529,
More is able to catch up not only the external threat of the Turks, but also
the internal threat of those false Christians who both literally and figura-
tively allied themselves with the Turks: the Turks of Hungary, as Louis II
called them—Zapolya and his followers, the noblemen after the battle of
Mohács who ravaged their own domains, the 20,000 Lutheran *Landsknechte*
who were reported to have served in the Turkish army, the princes of
Europe who sought out Turkish alliances to redress the balance of power,
and, by implication, the growing Protestant sects who in More's opinion
had betrayed the faith, turned to false gods, and were in the process of
dismembering the mystical body of Christ through war and persecution.
At the beginning of *A Dialogue of Comfort*, after describing fully the horrors
of Turkish rule, More goes on to emphasize the danger these false Christians present:

> And yet which we more feare than all the remenant, no small part of
> our own folke that dwell even here about vs, are (as we here) fallen
> to hym, or all redy confoteryd with hym / which yf yt so be, shall
> happely kepe this quarter fro the Turkes incursion / but than shall
> they that torne to his law, leve all their neybors nothyng / but shall
> haue our goodes given them, and our bodies both / but yf we turn as
> they do, & forsake our saviour to / And than (for there ys no born

---

[1] M. Fumée, *The Historie of the Troubles of Hungarie*, trans. R[ooke] C[hurche], (London,
1600), p. 44. Cited hereafter as "Fumée."

[2] The Turks remained a constant threat to Western civilization throughout the remainder of the sixteenth century. After the death of Zapolya in 1540, Ferdinand invaded
Hungary once again and offered to pay the Turks an annual tribute for the grant of the
entire kingdom. Suleiman instead transformed the portions of the country he occupied
into a Turkish Province under the direct control of a Pasha. Suleiman died at the siege of
Szigeth, and his successor, Selim II, inherited the Hungarian conflict. After 1568, however, the fighting degenerated to a series of border clashes, for by that time the major
Turkish threat had shifted to the Mediterranean. The last significant Turkish victory in
the sixteenth century was the conquest of Cyprus in 1571.

Turke so cruell to christen folke, as is the false christen that falleth fro
the fayth) we shall stand in perill yf we percever in the truth, to be
more hardely handelyd & dye more cruell deth by our own countremen at home / than yf we were taken hens and caried into Turkey /
(7/1–12)

In the introduction to Book III, he stresses the point once again: "my
thinke I here at myn eare some of our owne here among vs, which with in
these few yeres could no more haue born the name of a Turke than the
name of the devill, begyn now to fynd litle faute therin / ye and some to
prayse them to, litle & litle as they may / more glad to fynd fawtes at euery
state of christendome, prestes, princes / rites / ceremonies / sacramentes
laues and custumes spirituall temporall & all" (192/3–9). Behind these
statements stands the memory of such astounding events as the sack of
Rome on May 6, 1527, when the Christian troops of the Emperor, unpaid
and mutinous, pillaged the city as wantonly as any barbarians or Turks,
destroying the capital of Christendom.[1] In his graphic, highly charged
description in *A Dialogue Concerning Heresies* (1529) More blames the
mercenary, Lutheran *Landsknechte*, and the accusation takes on symbolic
proportions: "Of this sect [the Lutherans] was the great part of those
vngracious people also, which late entered in to Rome with the Duke of
Burbon, not onely robbing and spoyling the cite as well theyr owne frindes
as the contrary part, but like very beastes dyd also violate yͤ wyues in the
syght of their husbandes, slew the children in the syght of the fathers."
Children were roasted alive, and old men were brought out naked with a
cord tied to their genitals, by which they were drawn toward levelled
pikes. "Nowe, than was all their cruel sporte and laughter eyther to see the
sely naked men in shrinking from yͤ pykes to teare of their membres, or for
pain of that pulling, to runne their naked bodies in depe vppon the pikes."[2]
They violated the churches, "spoyled the holy reliques, cast out the
blessed sacrament, pulled the chalice from the auter at masse, slaine
priestes in the church, left no kind of cruelte or spite vndone, but from
howse to howse embruinge theyr handes in bloude, & yͭ in such wyse as
any Turke or Saricine would haue pytyed, or abhored." The symbolic
equation between Protestant and Turk is made even stronger in the final

---

[1] The Turks were generally regarded as contemporary counterparts of the ancient
barbarians who destroyed Greece and Rome. See Schwoebel, "Coexistence, Conversion,
and the Crusade against the Turks," 164, 183.

[2] Cf. Wolsey's somewhat more prudish account of the sack of Rome, quoted in Adams,
p. 266: "like as the King in hunting time hath slain 300 deer, and the garbage and paunches
be cast round about, in every quarter of the park, so (said the Cardinal) every street lay
full of the privy members and genitures of the Cardinals and holy prelates: the whole
history were too abominable to tell."

summing up: "thoughe men in warre waxe furiouse and cruel, yet was ther neuer none y^t went therin so farre, & specially in such kinde of cruelty as hath ben amonge christen men in their warre alway forborne, as is the dispites done to the blessed sacrament, wherein the bestes wer more hote and more busye, than woulde the great Turke, and that because theyr sect is yet in maner worse than his." [1]

The analogy seems perfectly natural, given the times and More's belief in a united Christendom founded on a universal church. Over and over, throughout his polemical works, More equates Protestant and Turk, heretic and infidel. The remarks in *The supplycacyon of soulys* (1529) are typical: "Then shall ye not neede to feare the great Turke & he came to morowe, except ye suffer among you to grow in great nomber these Lutherans that fauour hym. For we dare make you the warantyse that if hys lye be trewe, there be mo men a great meany in London & within .iiii. shyrcs next adioyning, than the greate Turke bringeth in to Hungary." [2] In *A treatice upon the passion* More speaks of the Protestants, who denied their baptism, as worse than any Turks. [3] And in the *De Tristitia Christi*, More's last work, he indicates explicitly the way in which the analogy functions in *A Dialogue of Comfort*:

> I think we would not be far wrong if we were to fear that the time approaches when the son of man, Christ, will be betrayed into the hands of sinners, as often as we see an imminent danger that the mystical body of Christ, the church of Christ, namely the Christian people, will be brought to ruin at the hands of wicked men. And this, alas, for some centuries now we have not failed to see happening somewhere, now in one place, now in another, while the cruel Turks invade some parts of the Christian dominion and other parts are torn asunder by the internal strife of manifold heretical sects. [4]

The analogy between Protestant and Turk, heretic and infidel, is never directly insisted on in *A Dialogue of Comfort*. More is careful to keep the implications oblique and ambiguous—flexible, suggestive, and rich in possibility—so that they seem to rise spontaneously from the reader himself and not from any conscious intent on the part of the author. The metaphoric correspondence between persecution for the faith in Hungary and persecution for the faith in England, under the Great Turk, Henry VIII, is built into the very structure and meaning of the work as part of

---

[1] *EW*, sigs. r₅v–r₆.

[2] *EW*, sig. v₂v; see also *Heresies*, *EW*, sigs. s₆–s₆v, s₈; *Confutation*, *CW 8*, 94/27–29, 252/31–253/29, 266/9–10, and 466/29–467/2.

[3] *EW*, sig. OO₆v.

[4] *CW 14*, 345–47.

its original conception and design, but it is intended for a somewhat more
intimate, more limited audience than the broader historical scene of the
Turkish threat to Europe. It constitutes a second level of address, directed
primarily to those who knew of More's authorship and were aware of the
general circumstances of composition or, more broadly, those who, like
More, recognized the Protestant sects as a threat to the universal church,
who felt the tempo of persecution for the faith increase throughout Europe
from the beginning of the Reformation, and were thus able to apply the
analogy themselves. For these readers the simultaneous disguise and
revelation were part of the essential form and meaning of the work. As
R. W. Chambers has pointed out, More chose "a really dangerous
subject. . . . The *Dialogue* had to be kept very secret; it was a denial of the
thesis that the head of the State might dictate the religious belief of his
subjects."[1] Some protective covering was obviously necessary to attack the
king in the king's own prison, but it is an oversimplification to skim over or
otherwise dismiss the powerful scene of Turkish invasion in order to get at
what one presumes to be the "real" meaning underneath the fiction. The
book is not to be read simply as a veiled conceit in which everything that
is said really stands for something else. The Hungarian setting is important
in its own right at the same time that it serves as an extended metaphor.
The Turk burns, pillages, imprisons, tortures, and kills in order to destroy
the faith. Ironically, though (and the resemblances to *Utopia* are dim, but
perceptible),[2] Christians do the same to Christians. An analogy is set up
whereby Christian disunity is stripped to its essential form and seen in its
proper perspective. Like the Turks, Christians themselves pose a threat
not only to the universal peace envisioned by the church, but to the
universal church itself.

Rather than an allegory More creates a loose, metaphoric analogy. But
beneath that—beneath the historical setting and its metaphoric extension
—is the more basic, fundamental problem of persecution for the faith,
whether by true Turk or false Christian, and the overwhelming question
of how to maintain one's integrity in the face of pain and death. On this
level, the level of the individual conscience, beyond history, More equates
Protestant and Turk, heretic and infidel, in such a way as to make them
more than mere metaphoric equivalents. The enemy within is identical
with the enemy without, and both are to be seen as masks—agents or
representatives—of a more ancient power of evil. "Our wrestlyng is not
agaynst flesh & bloud," More says, quoting St. Paul, at the end of *A*

---

[1] *Thomas More*, p. 314.

[2] Schoeck, for example, comments briefly on the force of the argument *a fortiori* in both
works (pp. 32–33).

Dialogue of Comfort (317/24). "The Turke is but a shadow" compared with this ancient power of evil, "the world ruler of this present darkness,"[1] that uses men as agents of its will—whether they be Suleiman, Henry, Cromwell, Audley, Norfolk, or the more immediate manifestations in our own lives and time. "Thus may we see," More says,

> that in such persecucions, it is the mydday devill hym selfe that maketh such incursion vppon vs, by the men that are his ministers to make vs fall for feare. . . . The devill it is therfor, that yf we for fere of men will fall, is redy to rone vppon vs & devoure vs. And is it wisedome than, so mych to thinke vppon the Turkes, that we forgete the devill / . . . Therfor whan he roreth out vppon vs by the threttes of mortall men / let vs tell hym that with our inward yie, we see hym well ynough, & intend to stand & fight with hym evyn hand to hand. (317/24–27, 318/8–10, 12–15)

2. Family and Friends

In addition to the levels of address described in the previous section, certain portions of the work would have had a more specific meaning for More's immediate family and circle of friends than they did for the general reader. For this more limited audience of his kinsmen and friends More deliberately dissolves at times the literary artifice of the dialogue and speaks to them directly from behind the mask of his fiction. These brief flashes of intense personal recognition do not come together to form a consistent pattern; they are not part of the structure and architectonic design of the work; they do not change or alter in any way the surface of the text. They simply extend it momentarily, and the book becomes richer for it and at the same time full of a plain, homely humanity. This deliberate manipulation of literary surface that occurs on various levels of address throughout the book forms one of the most remarkable features of the work. It springs in part from a sense of creative exuberance and play, but it is also related to More's fundamental freedom and detachment of mind that allowed him to assume an ironic, humorous, almost casual indifference to what at the same time was eminently fearful and harrowing to him. *A Dialogue of Comfort* happens to work in the way it does partly because of the kind of man More was, with his liking for jokes and his amused awareness of the rich involutions and possibilities for irony present in this world. As Erasmus once wrote to the German humanist Ulrich von Hutten, shortly after the publication of *Utopia:* "Even from boyhood . . . [More] was

---

[1] Eph. 6:12, the continuation of the passage More quotes from St. Paul. The Vulgate reads: "mundi rectores tenebrarum harum."

always so amused by jokes that he seems almost born for them."[1] The use
of humorous anecdote was one way in which he might convey his deep
affection for his family.[2]

Take, for example, the various anecdotes in the book identified by
Harpsfield and other sixteenth-century biographers with Dame Alice
Middleton, More's second wife. The evidence is not entirely conclusive,
but there is good reason to believe that most of these identifications drew
upon family history. Harpsfield, with whom most of them originate, wrote
in the reign of Queen Mary, using Roper's notes. His work was intended
as the official family biography, and it presumably voices family opinion
on Dame Alice and other matters as well. Moreover, the anecdotes Harpsfield identifies with Dame Alice are entirely in keeping with what we
know of her from other sources, particularly Roper's remarkably life-like
descriptions in his *Life of More*. She was a strong-willed, ignorant woman
who was not easily put down. Erasmus, who never learned to like her,
called her a *mater familias*, "acrem et vigilantem,"[3] and another friend,
Andrew Ammonio, spoke of her nose in one of his letters to Erasmus as
"the hooked beak of the harpy."[4] More seems to have had a genuine
affection for her. She was, after all, good-hearted, loving toward him and
his children, and full of a real if sometimes overwhelming gusto. But in
learning to live amicably with her, More adopted a particular manner and
tone that was quickly turned into a private family joke.[5] While seeking his
real companionship from his children, he relished his wife's outrageous
pronouncements and treated her with a somewhat condescending, amused

---

[1] *Opus Epistolarum Des. Erasmi Roterodami*, ed. P. S. Allen, H. M. Allen, *et al.* (Oxford,
1906–58), *4*, 16: "Iam inde a puero sic iocis est delectatus vt ad hos natus videri possit."
Cited hereafter as "Allen." The letter is dated July 23, 1516.

[2] Identifications and ages of each person in the Holbein drawing are written in Latin
in a hand that was once thought to be More's, but is now presumed to be that of Nicolas
Kratzer. Chambers (p. 220) translates the inscriptions as follows, running from left to
right: "Elizabeth Dauncey, Thomas More's daughter, in her 21st year—Margaret Gigs
[or Giggs], Clement's wife, fellow student and kinswoman of More's daughters, in her
22nd year—John More, the father, in his 76th year—Anne Grisacre [or Cresacre],
betrothed to John More, in her 15th year—Thomas More in his 50th year—John More,
son of Thomas, in his 19th year—Henry Patenson, Thomas More's fool, in his 40th year—
Cecily Heron, Thomas More's daughter, in her 20th year—Margaret Roper, Thomas
More's daughter, in her 22nd year—Alice, Thomas More's wife, in her 57th year." For
an account of the drawing and of the painting related to it, see Stanley Morison, *The
Likeness of Thomas More*, ed. Nicolas Barker (New York, 1963), pp. 18–21.

[3] Allen, *4*, 19.

[4] Allen, *1*, 476; Chambers, *Thomas More*, p. 111.

[5] As early as 1519 Erasmus describes More's customary method of handling her: "Vix
vllus maritus a sua tantum obsequii impetrat imperio atque seueritudine quantum hic
blanditiis iocisque" (Allen, *4*, 19).

PLATE IV. Thomas More and his Family, by Hans Holbein the Younger, 1527 (reduced)

awareness of the differences between them, pretending to be in awe of her. And this is the tone we find in the anecdotes identified with her in *A Dialogue of Comfort*.

In the twentieth chapter of Book III More considers the nature of imprisonment. Many members of contemplative orders are content to live all their lives imprisoned in their cloisters. To have a door shut on us and be confined, therefore, is no real punishment; it is only "an horrour enhauncid of our own fantasye" (277/4–5). To illustrate the point More tells the following anecdote:

> I wist a woman ones that came into a prison, to visit of her charite a pore prisoner there, whom she found in a chamber / to say the trouth metely feyre / & at the lest wise it was strong ynough / But with mattes of straw the prisoner had made yt so warme / both vnder the fote & round about the walles, that in these thinges for kepyng of his helth, she was on his behalfe glad & very well comfortid / But a mong many other displeasures that for his sake she was sory for / one she lamentid much in her mynd / that he shuld hauc the chamber dore vppon hym by nyght made fast by the gaoler that shuld shit hym in / For by my trouth quod she / yf the dore shuld be shit vppon me, I wold wene yt wold stopp vpp my breeth / At that word of hers / the prisoner laughed in his mynd / but he durst not laugh a lowde nor say nothing to her / For somewhat in dede he stode in awe of her / & had his fyndyng there mich part of her charite for almoyse / but he could not but laugh inwardly / while hc wist well inogh that she vsid on the in- side to shit euery night full surely her own chamber to her, both dore & wyndowes to / & vsid not to open them of all the long night / (277/6–23)

Harpsfield identifies the characters in this story as More and Dame Alice,[1] and the more we know of the circumstances, the more humorous and involved it becomes. The irony moves in a number of different ways at once. In a letter to Henry VIII, dated Christmas 1534, Dame Alice complains to the king of the poverty her husband's willful ways had plunged her into. By refusing the Oath of Allegiance he had earlier for- feited to the crown "all his goodis and cattells and the profytt of all his landes, anuities and fees," leaving her only "his moveable goodes and the reuenewes of his landis." After the Act of Supremacy and the Act of Treasons in November 1534, even that pittance was taken away. "And thus . . . your saide pore bedewoman his wyffe . . . ys likelie to be vtterlye vndone." Later, in a letter to Cromwell, dated May 1535, she complains

---

[1] Harpsfield, pp. 97–98.

once again of her "great and extreme necessyte." Besides her own household expenses, she has to pay fifteen shillings a week "bord-wages" for the
maintenance of More and his servant, John à Wood, in the Tower.[1] Thus,
like the poor prisoner, More was in fact dependent on his wife's charity
for his "fyndyng" in prison, though in the circumstances *charity* is not
exactly the right word for it. If More was poor, Dame Alice may very well
have thought, it was all his own fault. A number of details in the anecdote
itself would seem to corroborate Harpsfield's identification, particularly
the fact that the prisoner knew the intimate details of his visitor's sleeping
arrangements, though she was presumably only a casual acquaintance.
The personal nature of the anecdote not only has the authority of Harpsfield and thus the force of family tradition behind it, it also rings true
within itself. If the anecdote is in fact autobiographical, it perhaps affords
us the only glimpse we have of the interior of More's cell and the actual
conditions of his confinement in the Tower. Members of More's family
who had visited him in prison may very well have been startled by the
realistic detail of the "mattes of straw" lining the floor and walls of the
room to keep out the cold as the summer of 1534 lengthened into winter,
though it is doubtful that Dame Alice, like the woman in the anecdote,
thought the chamber was "metely feyre" and as a result was "glad & very
well comfortid." Harpsfield associates the anecdote with Roper's celebrated account of Dame Alice's visit to More in the Tower;[2] there she
blusters in and greets her husband bluntly with, "What the good yere,
master Moore, . . . I mervaile that you, that have bine alwaies hitherto
taken for so wise a man, will nowe so play the foole to lye heare in this
close, filthy prison, and be content thus to be shut vpp amongst mise and
rattes, when you might be abroade at your libertye"—at home in his fair
house at Chelsea with his wife and children.[3] The doubling of irony on
irony, the woman's illogic, the poor prisoner's quiet contentment, the awe
in which he held his visitor, and the ironic distance he maintained,
laughing inwardly but afraid to say anything—all these illuminate the
passage, but they depend for much of their meaning on things outside the
text.

     In other cases More draws the joke out, prolonging the enjoyment. In
the fourteenth chapter of book two, for example, in the middle of the
Mother Maud's tale, More tells the story of a "shrewed wife" who came
in from confession and told her husband of her good resolution: "Be mery
man quoth she now / for this day I thanke god was I well shreven / and I
purpose now therfor to leve of all myn old shrewdnes & begyn evyn a

---

[1] Rogers, pp. 547–48, 554.
[2] Harpsfield, pp. 95–97.
[3] Roper, p. 82.

fresh" (118/3–5). The anecdote is once again identified by Harpsfield with More and Dame Alice,[1] and the language More catches—the vividness and verve of Dame Alice's stout nature—jibes with the language Roper uses for her and the language that appears in all her reported conversations. After the anecdote, however, the speakers in the *Dialogue* continue, and the real Dame Alice enters the fiction and becomes an inhabitant of Hungary:

Vyncent

Ah well vncle can you report her so. That word hard I her speke / but she said yt in sport to make her husband laugh.

Anthonye

In dede it semyd she spake yt halfe in sport / For that she said she wold cast away all her shrewdnes / therin I trow she sportid / but in that she said she wold begin it all a fressh, her husband found that good ernest.

Vincent

Well I shall shew her what you saye I warrant you.

Anthonye

Than will you make me make my word good.

What More seems to have done here was to take a jest of Dame Alice's own, or perhaps a slip of the tongue that More made into a jest for her, and add another on top of it. When Vincent threatens to "shew" her what Antony has said, Antony portrays for us the flinching, frightened husband. He seems to know what he is talking about when he says "her husband found that good ernest." The rather enigmatic or difficult phrase Antony ends with seems to mean that if Vincent shows her what he has said, she will be so angry that she will start up all her old shrewishness again. And yet More presumably expected her to read this or have it read to her. He increases the humor by increasing the sense of fiction.[2]

The portrait of Dame Alice that More draws in these anecdotes was probably a truthful portrayal of her as she functioned in the society of the family. But it was also a quasi-literary creation of More's own, related to the anti-feminist literature of the Middle Ages. The resemblance to the Wife of Bath is more than coincidental, for it is often difficult to distinguish an individual from the stereotypes of his culture which help shape him into what he then becomes. The personality of Dame Alice portrayed by More and Roper was, no doubt, a caricature that the family created and enjoyed in their daily lives, and it was for the sake of the family that More

---

[1] Harpsfield, p. 94.

[2] Other anecdotes identified with Dame Alice occur at 81/1–24, 168/31–169/7, and 219/20–220/12.

continued the customary joking here, keeping the tone light, toying with the surface of the book in order to maintain an air of normalcy in a period of abnormal separation and danger. But it was also a rough and gruffly affectionate gesture toward Dame Alice herself. She is the butt of all these anecdotes, and More, for all his pretended fear, comes off distinctly better than she does—less immured and isolated in an insensitive nature. He knew these things would be shown to her, and he knew, in the relationship they had established, that she would be aware, if not of his love, at least of his affection and broad tolerance of her eccentricities.[1]

Other anecdotes of a similar nature are addressed to the same audience for slightly different purposes, as when Antony wishes to explain how repentance makes us experience joy and sorrow at once and tells the story of a curious fever he once had that made him feel both hot and cold at the same time. The doctors did not know what to make of it until a young girl of his acquaintance, who was beginning to be taught medicine by a kinsman of hers, identified the fever in *De Differentiis Febrium*, a work of Galen's "redy to be sold in the boke sellers shopps."[2] More's early biographers identify the young girl as Margaret Giggs, who was raised and educated in More's household as one of his own daughters.[3] The kinsman who taught her physic was More's protégé and the former tutor to his children, John Clement, who had married her early in 1526. After leaving More's employ, Clement had lectured in Greek at Oxford and studied medicine at Louvain and Siena. In 1525, the same year he received the degree of doctor of medicine, he was thanked for his assistance in the *editio princeps* of Galen, published by the Aldine Press, and this is probably the work More refers to as just coming out. More's close friendship with the Clements continued for the rest of his life. It was at their house on Sunday, April 12, 1534, that More was summoned to appear before the Lords at Lambeth prior to being incarcerated in the Tower. The full significance of the anecdote is perhaps not entirely accessible; much has been lost in the passage of time. Why More chose to remember only Margaret Clement in this way is not known. All that remains is this affectionate farewell, the compliment to Margaret's erudition, More's fond memory of the humanistic education he had given

---

[1] Elton, *More Symposium*, sees it somewhat differently: "Centuries of adulation [of More] have accustomed us to regard his treatment of Dame Alice as affectionate, and so, up to a point, it was. But it was also mildly contemptuous, and he did not scruple to print tales about women which everybody knew were aimed at her. He did not disguise his conviction that his second wife was a bit of a fool. . . . Yet, in truth, every time that we learn of an argument between them, it seems to me that she had sense and unselfishness on her side" (p. 113).

[2] The anecdote occurs at 88/9–90/13. For further information on Margaret Giggs and John Clement, see the Commentary at that point.

[3] Harpsfield, pp. 90–91.

to all his children, and the bond of learning between husband and wife. For More, it reaches back to the memory of a shared life together. But the main effect is one of wry humor and surprise at seeing real people from a remembered past projected into the imaginary scene of the *Dialogue* in Hungary.[1]

In addition to anecdotes and shared memories, More also draws upon certain information held in common with his family, and in the areas of the book in which this information is used the text once again becomes charged with additional meaning. In the fourteenth chapter of Book II, a chapter which considers the "nightes feare" of scrupulosity, More remembers old Mother Maud, who "was wont whan she sat by the fier with vs, to tell vs that were children many childish tales," and proceeds to retell one of her stories about an ass and a wolf who went to confession to Father Reynard, the fox. The story is retold with humor and gusto. It is probably More's most famous anecdote—and justly so. But as the members of More's family would have known, Mother Maud is pure invention. The origin of the story was a conversation between More's step-daughter, Alice Alington, and Sir Thomas Audley, Lord Chancellor of England after More's resignation, in which Audley, by his fable of "a lion, an asse, and a wolfe and of their confession," accused More of excessive scrupulosity of conscience.[2]

Audley was not the only one to accuse More of scrupulosity. It was a common explanation of his obstinacy in refusing the Oath of Allegiance. As Margaret wrote in her reply to Alice Alington, who told her of Audley's accusation, "if he stande still in this scruple of his conscience (as it is at the lest wise called by manie that are his frendes and wise) all his frendes that seme most able to do hym good either shall finally forsake hym, or per-aduenture not be hable in dede to doe hym any good att all."[3] Even as late as Christmas, 1534, in her letter to the king, Dame Alice described her husband as the victim of a sort of neurotic compulsion. His offence did not proceed from "eny malice or obstinate mynde, but of suche a longe contynued and depe rooted scrupple, as passethe his power to avoyde and put away."[4] The accusation was obviously one of great concern to More and considerable perplexity. If he had an overly scrupulous conscience,

---

[1] Other anecdotes which are said to have been based on real people would have been comprehensible not only to the family, but to a somewhat wider audience. One such involves Cardinal Wolsey's "vaineglorious, scabbed, itching follye to heare his owne prayse," as Harpsfield called it (p. 35). Another has to do with the time Wolsey called More a fool (Chambers, *Thomas More*, pp. 161–62). See 213/6–216/23, 217/11–218/4 and n.

[2] See above, pp. lx-lxi.

[3] Rogers, p. 514.

[4] Rogers, p. 548.

it was bound to cast him into further doubts, and even if he did not, the possibility was still something he could not afford to overlook. It was related to his fear of spiritual pride and demonic illusion, a subtle form of temptation in which a man's faith and his love of God are used against him. "There is something of this worm in the hearts of all religious men," Thomas Merton has written. "Who can escape the secret desire to breathe a different atmosphere from the rest of men? Who can do good things without seeking to taste in them some sweet distinction from the common run of sinners in this world? . . . And the secret voice of pleasure sings in his heart: '*Non sum sicut caeteri homines.*' Once he has started on this path there is no limit to the evil his self-satisfaction may drive him to do in the name of God and of His love, and for His glory." [1]

For the family the whole point of the Mother Maud's tale would have been seen as an answer to the accusation of excessive scrupulosity.[2] More takes a story, which he indicates he had never heard before,[3] designed to illustrate the asininity of his own conscience, and turns it upside down, using it to prove that it is better to have some conscience than no conscience at all. The moral of the fable as More tells it is that "a conscience somwhat scriplouse, thoughe it be paynfull and troubelows to hym that hath it like as this pore asse had here / is lesse harm yet than a consciens ouer large / or such as for his own fantasye the man list to frame hym selfe / now drawying yt narow now strechyng it in bredth after the maner of a cheuerell poynt, to serue on euery side for his own comoditie, as did here the wyle wolfe" (119/32–120/6). For those who knew how the Mother Maud's tale originated, this elaborate retelling of Audley's fable would have reverberated with a subtle and richly humorous inversion, and humor is not a characteristic of a man with an overly scrupulous conscience. If More is an ass, Audley and the others are wolves, just as in the original version, More perhaps remembered, the lion devoured all the beasts he came by, but was absolved because he was the king, and it was his nature to do so.

For those who knew More closely, this conscious play in which the author peers out from behind the mask of his own creation would have been only a part of the autobiographical dimension of the book. There were also the pervasive reminders of the man himself and their former life together—habits, customs, likes and dislikes, turns of phrase and modes of thought—all the accumulated knowledge that comes from simply

---

[1] *The Seeds of Contemplation* (New York, 1949), pp. 23–25.

[2] More also answers the accusation more fully and more directly, without literary disguise, in Margaret's letter to Alice Alington, referred to above, one of the most remarkable documents to come out of More's imprisonment. See Rogers, pp. 520–32.

[3] Rogers, p. 520.

knowing an individual so well and living intimately with him. This is
the true autobiographical dimension of the book, and it is strong and
pervasive. But it is not play. More reveals himself in this way because of
the nature of what he is writing. *A Dialogue of Comfort* grows out of
the total context of More's life. It is the final summing up, and for
those who knew him well, it would have been impossible at times to
distinguish it from the man himself.

Toward the end of Book II, for example, in considering the second
temptation in Psalm 90, "the arrow fleyng in the daye," More speaks of
the danger pride presents to a good man who has arrived at a position of
great power and wealth in the world. A man in such a position is often
afraid of losing God's favor, but unless the fear causes him to leave his
duty undone, he must accept God's will and realize that as long as he
remains in prosperity he will always be tempted to pride and ambition.
To combat the temptation he should so order his life as to be able to step
outside it frequently and in solitude call to mind the real nature of his
existence:

> Let hym also chose hymselfe some secret solitary place in his own
> house / as far fro noyse & companye as he conveniently can / And
> thyther lett hym some tyme secretely resort alone / ymagynyng hym
> selfe as one goyng out of the world evin strayt vnto the gevyng vpp his
> rekenyng vnto god of his sinfull lyvyng / Than let hym there before
> an altare or some pitifull image of christes bitter passion / . . . knele
> downe or fall prostrate as at the fete of almighty god / . . . There let
> hym declare vnto god, the temptacions of the devill / the suggestions
> of the flesh / thoccasions of the world, & of his worldly frendes much
> worse many tymes in drawing a man from god than are his most
> mortall enymyes / which thyng our saviour witnesseth hym selfe where
> he sayth: *Inimici hominis domestici eius* / the enymyes of a man, are they
> that are his own famyliers / (164/15–165/3)

To the members of More's family this passage would have come with a
shock of recognition, for in discussing this good man More was in part
describing himself. Before he had chosen imprisonment and demonstrated
where his deepest love and affection lay, More had been disturbed almost
all his adult life over the problem of his own high position and authority
in the world. The means he suggests for combating the temptation to pride
and ambition in *A Dialogue of Comfort* were the same means he employed
in his own life. As Roper describes it:

> And because he was desirous for godlye purposes sometyme to be
> solitary, and sequester himself from worldly company, A good dis-
> taunce from his mansion house builded he a place called the newe

buildinge, wherein there was a Chappell, a library, and a gallery; In which, as his vse was vppon other dayes to occupy himself in prayer and study together, So on the Fridaie there vsually contynewed he from morning till evening, spending his time only in devoute praiers and spirituall exercises.[1]

More's reference to a man's familiars as being far worse "in drawing a man from god than are his most mortall enymyes" is picked up later in a conversation with Margaret. While in the Tower, sequestered and withdrawn at last more fully from the world than in the chapel in the New Building, More explained that if it had not been for his wife and children, "whom I accompte the cheife parte of my charge, I wold not haue fayled longe ere this to haue closed my self in as straighte a roome, and straighter too. But since I am come hither without myne owne deserte, I trust that god of his goodnes will discharge me of my care, and with his graciouse helpe supply my lack amonge you. I find no cause, I thanck god, Megge, to reckon my self in wors case heare then in my owne house. For me thinckethe god makethe me a wanton, and settethe me on his lappe and dandlethe me."[2]

Similarly, at the end of Book II, More describes a man who had no love for wealth ("yf there be a man such"), even though it fell abundantly to him. He took no pleasure in it, "but as though he had it not, kepeth him selfe in like abstynence & penaunce prively, as he wold do in case he had it not / & in such thinges as he doth openly, bestow somewhat more liberally vppon hym selfe in his howse after some maner of the world / lest he shuld give other folke occasion to merveyle & muse & talke of his maner & misse report hym for an hipocryte" (184/22–28). Again the family would have recognized that More was in part describing himself. When he was Lord Chancellor, Roper reports, "for the avoiding of singularity, wold he appeare none otherwise then other men in his apparell and other behaviour. And albeit outwardly he appeared honorable like one of his callinge, yeat inwardly he no such vanityes esteeming, secreatly next his body ware a shirte of heare."[3] The day before he died, he sent the shirt to his daughter Margaret, "not willinge to haue it seene."[4] It was wrapped up in the same cloth as "the scourge with which he had been wont to give himself the discipline." Thirty years later Stapleton examined the shirt at Margaret Clement's home in Bergen, near Antwerp. It was

[1] Roper, pp. 25–26.
[2] Roper, p. 76.
[3] Roper, p. 48; see also Stapleton, p. 74.
[4] Roper, p. 99.

"knotty, like a net, much rougher, I should think than are commonly the hair-shirts of religious." The scourge had been lost.[1]

A similar effect would have occurred in chapter fifteen of Book II, on suicide, where Antony admits to having had some experience on the subject: "many haue I herd of / & with some haue I talkid my selfe, that haue bene sore combrid with that temptacion, & markid haue I not a litell the maner of them" (123/4–6). In the next chapter, on the same general subject, he cites a few case histories he has known. One was paranoid and believed everyone thought he was a fool. Two others were afraid that they would kill themselves, but neither knew why. Neither of them had any reason to die, but both were constantly tempted. One even went so far as to have his friends tie him up for fear of what he might do to himself (148/25–149/16). In reading this, More's family may have remembered the hours he himself had spent in counseling potential suicides, and after More's death, their memory of the citizen of Winchester would have been particularly vivid.[2]

Even words and turns of phrase, habitual ideas and modes of expression would have recalled the memory of the man. In the chapter on captivity in Book III, More argues that it does not matter into what strange country one is conveyed: "for sith I am very sure, that whether so euer men convey me / god is no more verely here than he shalbe there / yf I get (as I may yf I will) the grace to set my hole hart vppon hym / & long for nothyng but hym / yt can than make me no greate mater to my mynd / whether they cary me hensc or leve me here" (251/7–12). As some of the family may have recollected, he had said almost precisely the same thing to Dame Alice on her visit to the Tower, referring to his own captivity there. When she told him that he might be at home with his wife and children if he chose to, he replied,

> "Is not this house [referring to the Tower] . . . as nighe heauen as my owne?"
> To whom shee, after hir accustomed homely fashion, not liking such talke, awneswered, "Tylle valle, Tylle valle!"
> "Howe say you, mistris Alice," quoth he, "is itt not so?"
> "Bone deus, bone deus, [man], will this geare neuer be lefte?" quoth shee.
> "Well then, mistris Ales, if it be so," [quoth he], "it is very well. For I see no great cause why I should much Ioye [either] of my gay

---

[1] Stapleton, p. 75.

[2] For this anecdote, see the Commentary at 123/4-5. The story was first printed by Stapleton (pp. 71–72); Chambers (*Thomas More*, p. 349) speculates that Stapleton's source was Margaret Giggs.

house or [of] any thinge belonginge thereunto; when, if I should but seuen yeares lye buried vnder the ground, and then arise and come [t]hither againe, I should not faile to find some therein that wold bid me get [me] out of doores, and tell me it were none of mine. What cause haue I then to like such an house as wold so soone forgett his master?"[1]

On another occasion he also expressed the same idea to Margaret. Once again the conversation was in the Tower, and More referred to his imprisonment: "I find no cause, I thanck god, Megge, to reckon my self in wors case heare then in my owne house."[2] In the conversation with Dame Alice, the reference to the house forgetting its master would also have had its reverberation. More uses the same idea in the chapter on lands and possessions in the third book of the *Dialogue*. The ground is imagined to speak to its proud owner, who had built on it a fine mansion for his pleasure:

> ah thow sely pore soule, that wenest thow were halfe a god / & art a midd thy glory / but a man in a gay gowne / I that am the grownd here ouer whome thow art so prowde, haue had an hundred such owners of me as thow callest thy selfe / mo than euer thow hast hard the names of / And some of them that prowdly went ouer my hed / lye now low in my bely & my side lieth ouer them / And many one shall as thow doost now / call hym selfe myn owner after the, that neyther shalbe sibbe to thy blode / nor eny word here of thy name. Who ought your Castell Cosyn three thowsand yeres agoo? (208/3–11)

The idea is a commonplace, of course, but it is a commonplace that More habitually used. The same is true of the reference to suffering at the end of the chapter on the joys of heaven:

> Our hed is Christ / & therfor to hym must we be Ioynid / . . . He is our Guyde to guyde vs thyther & is entryd in before vs / and he therfor that will enter in after, *Debet sicut ille ambulauit et ipse ambulare* / the same way that Christ walkyd, the same way must he walke / . . . Who can for very shame desire to entre into the kyngdom of Christ with ease, whan hym selfe entrid not into his own without payne / (311/15–28)

For the members of More's family this passage would have had strong associations going back a number of years. As Roper explains: "If his wife or any of his children had bine diseased or troubled, he wold say vnto

---

[1] Roper, pp. 83–84.
[2] Roper, p. 76.

them: 'We may not looke at our pleasure to goe to heaven in fetherbeds: it is not the way, for our lord himself went thither with greater payne and by many tribulacions, which was the path wherein he walked thither; [for] the servaunt may not looke to be in better case then his master."[1] More's family would have realized that this was one of the keys to his spirituality and, in the context of *A Dialogue of Comfort*, a clear indication of what he was prepared to undergo.

For More's family and close friends, these personal references would have increased considerably the tension between the imaginary scene of a conversation in Hungary and the real scene of a man alone in a cell in the Tower of London. The art More used in these instances was an art that moved beyond itself toward an intensity of close, personal experience.

3. The Self

Still other portions of the work—other kinds and dimensions of meaning —are perhaps not intended for any audience except the author himself engaged in what was for him the symbolic act of writing the book. They have to do with still more complex relations of the author to his work and his own reactions to it in the process of writing. They were obviously not intended as part of the literary effect, and it is difficult to say precisely what they are. They seem to be additional dimensions of meaning that arise from knowing the context of a particular quotation from scripture More uses or the emphasis and warping he gives to specific aspects of the exegetical tradition of the 90th Psalm.[2] As with the fragments of auto-biography addressed to his family, they do not come together to form a unified whole. But the totality of *A Dialogue of Comfort* and its uniqueness would be incomplete without them. Just how far we can proceed in this direction remains to be seen. The farther one goes, the more problematical the evidence seems to be. Ultimately, perhaps, the best one can do is to suggest possibilities, for the way leads downward into the depths and secret recesses of the human personality, after the manner described by Teilhard de Chardin:

Leaving the zone of everyday occupations and relationships where

---

[1] Roper, pp. 26–27; see also *Heresies*, *EW*, sig. k₄.

[2] More follows Bernard, for example, in interpreting all the temptations itemized in Ps. 90 except the last, where he switches to Augustine. To read Augustine's interpretation of the noonday devil against what More chose to select from it and, more important, what he chose to omit is to realize the extent of More's fear of torture. Similarly, he uses Bernard's interpretation of the noonday devil in association with the first temptation, not the last. The warping is extremely significant for what it says about More's own fears of demonic illusion. See the Commentary, notes to 132/25–133/1, 200/5–8, 201/3–11, and 318/5–8.

everything seems clear, I went down into my inmost self, to the deep
abyss whence I feel dimly that my power of action emanates. But as
I moved further and further away from the conventional certainties by
which social life is superficially illuminated, I became aware that I
was losing contact with myself. At each step of the descent a new
person was disclosed within me of whose name I was no longer sure,
and who no longer obeyed me. And when I had to stop my exploration because the path faded from beneath my steps, I found a bottomless abyss at my feet and out of it came—arising I know not from
where—the current which I dare to call *my* life.[1]

There are almost five hundred quotations from and specific references to
scripture in *A Dialogue of Comfort*, an average of almost two to a page.[2]
Most of them seem to be used in the fashion of the time to prove or to
exemplify a point. But as the book proceeds and the quotations accumulate,
one begins to suspect that scripture stands in some more complex relation
to the work. If one considers not only the particular verse cited—usually
brief, hardly ever more than a sentence or so in length—but also the
general context in which the verse appears, it soon becomes apparent that
More's scriptural references are often linked together so as to form complex
chains of association. Yet the links that bind them together are not usually
present in the brief fragments of scripture More quotes, nor in the text of
the *Dialogue* itself. The associative links are usually found in the context in
which the quotations appear. The evidence seems weak and inconclusive
at first, more like a shadow cast by one's own reflections on scripture
rather than an actual part of More's meaning. And yet it seems to happen
too regularly and too consistently to be entirely accidental, and one
eventually comes to believe that what is going on in his own mind as he
turns the pages of scripture had probably also been going on in More's
mind as well.

These chains of association tend to revolve about a number of crucial
concerns of More in prison, but they do not come together to form a
consistent pattern of meaning or "secret teaching" such as Leo Strauss
suggests is to be found in all works written under the threat of persecution.[3]

---

[1] Teilhard, p. 48.

[2] See G. Marc'hadour's scriptural index to *A Dialogue of Comfort* in *The Bible in the Works
of St. Thomas More* (Nieuwkoop, 1969–71), 5, 191–95.

[3] *Persecution and the Art of Writing* (Glencoe, Illinois, 1952). Strauss' thesis is that "the
influence of persecution on literature is precisely that it compels all writers who hold
heterodox views to develop a peculiar technique of writing, the technique which we have
in mind when speaking of writing between the lines. . . . An exoteric book contains then
two teachings: a popular teaching of an edifying character, which is in the foreground;
and a philosophic teaching concerning the most important subject, which is indicated only

They flare out at times and then subside. Most often they run along concurrently with the text, within or below it. At times, however, they emerge more fully and become incorporated in the literary surface of the work, usually in the form of a quotation from scripture which contains within itself an overt reference to the contextual allusions underlying the previous quotations. And these are usually the places where *A Dialogue of Comfort* seems most autobiographical, where More seems to be speaking most directly of his own situation: his imprisonment, the isolation from his family, his ambivalent attitude toward the king, his fear of torture and demonic illusion, and the probability of a shameful and painful death.

In writing *A Dialogue of Comfort*, More objectified these fears and universalized them, seeing his own particular experience in the light of Christ's suffering and death and the suffering and pain other men are called upon to deal with in their lives. And he turned to scripture for comfort. "For except a man first belieue," More wrote, "that holye scripture is the woorde of God, and that the woorde of God is true, how can a man take any coumforte of that, that the scripture telleth him therin? ... This fayth as it is more faynte or more strong, so shall the coumfortable woordes of holye scripture stande the man in more stede or lesse" (12/17–24). In turning to scripture for comfort, however, More frequently turned to those passages that spoke most directly of his own needs. In doing so he inadvertently reveals certain kinds of meaning that are not part of the public intent and purpose of the work. They indicate something of More's deepest fears and the extent of his hope and trust in God. They constitute the most personal and private part of the work and are best seen perhaps as a prayer or prayerful meditation in which More applies what he is writing to his own tribulation and his own need for spiritual comfort at the same time he is writing it. In becoming aware of these scriptural contexts we seem to step into More's cell more than four hundred years ago and participate to some degree in the actual process by which he prepared himself to die.[1]

---

between the lines" (pp. 24, 36). Although *A Dialogue of Comfort* participates to some degree in this technique, particularly in the autobiographical references and allusions More addressed to his family and circle of friends, these instances of multiple audience in the work are sporadic and inconsistent, proceeding more from a sense of creative play than a significant technique or vehicle of meaning. Even the overall metaphor of the Turk and its application to Henry VIII is too imprecise in detail to constitute anything like a "secret teaching." In his use of the 90th Psalm and other passages of scripture, More reveals certain private, personal dimensions of meaning, but these are not designed as part of the public intent and purpose of the work.

[1] In the marginal comments in his Psalter, written during this same period in the Tower, More reveals a process of scriptural meditation extremely similar to that which I attempt to describe in *A Dialogue of Comfort*. The emphasis on tribulation, temptation by

The method is similar to a form of meditation described by Jean Leclercq,[1] who notes that among the contemplatives in medieval monasteries *lectio divina* referred not to matters of *quaestio* and *disputatio*, as in the universities, but to the act of reading itself. The emphasis was not on objective truth, but on the subjective benefit derived by the reader. The goal was *oratio* and *meditatio*. Reading of this kind was often referred to by the graphic metaphor of *ruminatio*. In the phrase of Augustine, Gregory, and others, it was the means by which one tasted scripture in *palatum cordis* so as to incorporate it like food into the very fiber of one's being. After years of such absorption of scripture, the reader achieved an almost total recall, and, according to Leclercq: "It is this deep impregnation with the word of Scripture that explains the extremely important phenomenon of reminiscence whereby the verbal echoes so excite the memory that a mere allusion will spontaneously evoke whole quotations and, in turn, a scriptural phrase will suggest quite naturally allusions elsewhere in the sacred books." Leclercq goes on to suggest that this quality of reminiscence had considerable influence on the methods of composition among the fathers of the church and monastic authors of the Middle Ages. Thus Augustine is said to compose poorly because his structure is not always based upon a detailed outline determined in advance, but rather upon a psychological process within a loose framework in which one association leads to another through a series of apparent digressions. The leisurely, offhand tempo and structure of *A Dialogue of Comfort* are perhaps related to a similar psychological process in which the scriptural associations play a significant role.[2]

---

demons, Turkey and Hungary, the king, and the fear of death are precisely the same in both. In fact, Sylvester and Martz suggest that the "annotations concerning the 'Turks' seem to provide the germ from which the dramatic setting of the *Dialogue of Comfort* has developed" (*Prayer Book*, p. xxxvi; see also pp. xxxiv–xxxv). Not knowing the relative dates, however, it is difficult to say which came first. For an excellent, comprehensive discussion of the marginalia, see *Prayer Book*, pp. xxvii–xlv.

[1] *Love of Learning and the Desire for God: A Study of Monastic Culture* (New York, 1961), pp. 88–92.

[2] More seems to have achieved something near total recall of at least certain portions of scripture—much of the New Testament and a number of the Psalms. One is reminded, for example, of the anecdote in More's *Letter to a Monk* about an actor who gave an impersonation of a friar preaching a sermon. The peculiar thing about the performance was that it was made up entirely of phrases of scripture arranged precisely in such a way that they carried a meaning directly opposite to the one originally intended. The *cento* was so cleverly done, More says, that no one could keep from laughing, though no one was foolish enough not to be angry at seeing scripture used in that way. More uses the anecdote to condemn the monk, John Batmanson, for doing the same thing in his attack on Erasmus' New Testament: "You think you have done something really spectacular when you mock Erasmus with *centos* scraped together here and there from the Sacred Books. You play the fool with the words of Sacred Scripture as the parasites in the comedies used to play with

A typical example of More's use of scripture in *A Dialogue of Comfort* occurs toward the beginning of Book I.[1] More is discussing the need for faith in times of tribulation. Our only true comfort is from God. No one can turn to God without faith, however. And yet faith is a mystery, "the gracious gift of god himself" (12/29). More then proceeds to quote James 1:17: "*Omne datum optimum & omne donum perfectum de sursum est descendens a patre luminum.* Euery good gyft & euery perfit gyft, is geuen from aboue, descending from the father of lightes" (12/30–32). The choice of the verse is in no way unusual. The gift James speaks of *de sursum descendens* was traditionally associated with grace—by Walafrid Strabo, for example, in the *Glossa Ordinaria* and Nicholas de Lyra in his *Postilla*.[2] Yet the verse occurs toward the end of a passage that speaks of the need for faith in times of trial and temptation that one suspects would have had particular application to More himself. The epistle is addressed to the twelve tribes of Israel in the Diaspora, and the passage More refers to begins:

> Count it all joy, my brothers, when you fall into various temptations, for you know that the testing of your faith produces patience. And patience produces this work of perfection: that you may be whole and complete, lacking in nothing . . . Blessed is the man who suffers temptation, for when he has stood the test, he will receive the crown of life, which God has promised to those who love him. (1:2–4, 12)[3]

The text of More's *Dialogue* refers only to faith as it is applicable to all men. The context in James would seem to apply that general statement to More's own faith in a time of trial and temptation. Moreover, in the next verse More quotes from scripture (Mark 9:23), we can see the same underlying concern for temptation and the testing of one's faith. The associative link is not in the text, but in the context.

Since faith is dependent on grace, More says, we must pray to God to increase our faith, like the father of the child possessed by an evil spirit, who cried out: "*Credo domine, adiuua incredulitatem meam.* I belieue good Lorde, but helpe thou the lacke of my beliefe" (13/3–5). More quotes the

---

witty sayings. There is nothing worse than that, and nothing easier to do" (Rogers, p. 193). The most important phrase for our purposes is the last: "ita nihil est vsquam facilius." For a scriptural *cento* of More's own, drawn from the Psalms, see *EW*, sig. VV₄v. See also the discussion in *Prayer Book*, p. xxxi.

[1] Because of the limitations of space, it is impossible to give more than a brief suggestion of the range and complexity of More's scriptural allusions in *A Dialogue of Comfort*. The Commentary attempts to indicate those passages of scripture in which allusion to context seems most important, but even there, because of their number, it has been impossible to mention them all or discuss them in detail.

[2] *Biblia Latina*, 6, sig. H₁.

[3] Translations are from the Revised Standard Version, corrected where necessary by reference to the Vulgate.

version in Mark 9:23. The same story is told in Matthew 17:14–21 and Luke 9:38–43. From this point on to the end of the chapter More weaves these three accounts together: the apostles' inability to cure the child, Jesus' telling them that this kind of demon can be driven out only by prayer, the father's cry of faith, the boy freed of demonic possession, and finally Jesus' parable comparing faith to a mustard seed. Beneath this harmonizing of the gospels, however, are other associative links of a more private nature. The next verse More quotes after the father's cry for faith is taken from Luke 17:5, a passage which contains the parable of the mustard seed. After we have prayed to God to help our unbelief, More says, "lette vs pray with the Apossles. *Domine, adauge nobis fidem.* Lord encrease oure fayth" (13/5–6). The immediate context of this quotation speaks of the impossibility of avoiding temptation or inducements to sin. The passage reads:

> Temptations to sin [*scandala*] are sure to come, but woe to him through whom they come. It would be better for him if a millstone were hung around his neck and he were cast into the sea than that he should cause one of these little ones to sin. Take heed to yourselves: if your brother sins against you, rebuke him; and if he repents, forgive him. And if he sins against you seven times a day and turns to you and says, I repent, you must forgive him. And the apostles said to the Lord, Increase our faith. (Luke 17:1–4)

Beginning with the first reference to James, More seems to move in this series of contextual allusions from the realization of the need for faith in a time of trial and temptation, to a warning against those like Cromwell and Henry VIII through whom temptations come, and finally to the need to increase one's faith so as to forgive one's enemies. All the while the text of the *Dialogue* simply has to do with faith and the necessity to pray for it.

In the case of these contextual allusions the associative links are not many, nor are they complex. In other portions of the work, however, they are much more involved and carry over a number of pages until they assume as it were the force of their own mass and emerge fully on the surface of the work. A fairly good example occurs a little further on in Book I. God is our only source of true comfort. But what if a man desires God to comfort him by taking his tribulation away? Is that a reasonable thing to pray for? More's answer is that some tribulations are intended by God for our greater good, and therefore we cannot pray to have them taken away. Paul, for example, asked to have his suffering removed and was told by God that he was "but a fole in askyng that request" (22/18). The reference is to 2 Corinthians 12:7–10, where Paul speaks of a thorn in his flesh: "Three times I besought the Lord about this, that it should leave

me, but he said to me, My grace is sufficient to you, for my strength is made
perfect in weakness" (12:8–9). These verses were extremely important
to More; he refers to them repeatedly in all his Tower works.[1] Throughout
his imprisonment he seems to have been strengthened by the hope that
God's grace would be sufficient and that he would not be allowed to suffer
more than he could endure. The context itself is not particularly significant
except perhaps in its final acceptance of suffering and persecution. "For
the sake of Christ, then," Paul continues, "I am content with weakness,
insults, hardships, persecution, and danger, for when I am weak, then am
I strong" (12:10). In the next few quotations from scripture the personal
dimension of the context becomes increasingly stronger until we seem to
hear More's own voice merge with Paul's. For this is the first oblique
allusion to persecution and suffering of a specific kind which More develops
with increasing intensity over the next few chapters of the work, moving
from a sense of hope and trust in God to an acceptance of death and
martyrdom.

Shortly after alluding to 2 Corinthians, More goes on to quote from
Paul's Epistle to the Romans. We can trust God to look after us, "For his
own holy sprite so sore desierith our weale / that as man might say, he
groneth for vs in such wise as no tong can tell. *Nos autem* / sayth saynt
paule / *quid oremus* / *vt oportet nescimus, sed ipse spiritus postulat pro nobis
gemitibus inenarrabilibus* / what may we pray that were behoueable for vs,
can not our selfe tell / but the sprite hym self desiereth for vs with vnspeakable groninges" (22/24–30). The quotation is from Romans 8:26. In
context, the assistance of the Holy Spirit is associated specifically with
those who suffer for the sake of Christ and with the need for hope and
patience:

> For the Spirit himself bears witness with our spirit that we are sons
> of God. And if sons, then heirs: heirs of God and fellow heirs with
> Christ, provided that we suffer with him in order that we may be
> glorified with him. I think that the sufferings [*passiones*] of this present
> time are not worth comparing with the glory that is to come, which
> will be revealed in us . . . We ourselves, who have the first fruits of
> the Spirit, groan inwardly as we await adoption as sons of God, the
> redemption of our body. For we were saved by hope. But hope that
> is seen is not hope. For who hopes for what he sees? But if we hope for
> what we do not see, we wait for it in patience. (8:16–18, 23–25)

---

[1] For specific references and further discussion, see n. to 25/15–19. In his gloss on these
verses in his New Testament, Erasmus, following Ambrose, notes that Paul's tribulation
had to do with the persecution of evil men, which would make the passage even more
closely applicable to More. See n. to 22/15–20.

In the next paragraph More turns once again to this same section from Romans, as though he were still reflecting on it. If God is dwelling with us, More argues in the text, what trouble can come to us? *"Si deus nobiscum quis contra nos |* yf god be with vs | sayth saynt paule | who can stand agaynst vs" (23/7–8). The verse is from Romans 8:31, but the entire passage is significant and seems to proceed not from the text, but from the underlying context, which has been building steadily in the last two quotations. The reference to criminal charges and justice seems like a direct allusion to More's own interrogations by Cromwell and the king's commission leading directly to his trial. "If God is with us," Paul says,

> who can stand against us? . . . Who shall bring any charge against God's elect? It is God who justifies; who is to condemn? Christ Jesus who died, yes, and who rose again from the dead, who is seated at the right hand of the Father, and who indeed intercedes for us. Who therefore shall separate us from the love of Christ? Tribulation? Or distress, or hunger, or nakedness, or danger, or persecution, or the sword? (As it is written: For your sake we are put to death all the day long; we are regarded as sheep for the slaughter). But in all those things we overcome because of him who loved us. For I am sure that neither death, nor life, nor angels, nor principalities, nor powers, nor things present, nor things to come, nor might, nor height, nor depth, nor any other creature will be able to separate us from the love of God, which is in Christ Jesus our Lord. (8:31, 33–39)

After demonstrating the need for faith and the patient acceptance of God's will, More goes on to outline three kinds of tribulation that benefit the soul. The second of these is tribulation sent without known cause to keep men from sins they might otherwise commit. Since even men of clear conscience are sinners, we should regard this sort of tribulation as a means both of punishing us for our known faults and of preserving us from future sin. More quotes in illustration 1 Corinthians 4:4: *"Nullius mihi conscius sum | sed non in hoc iustificatus sum |* My conscience grugeth me not of any thing | but yet am I not therby iustified" (28/6–8). The quotation supports the point More is making, but the context looks back to the chain of associations forged in the previous references to 2 Corinthians 10 and Romans 8. Specifically, it seems to continue the allusion to criminal charges and justice in Romans 8. "And to me," the passage reads,

> it is a very small thing that I be judged by you or by any human court. But neither do I judge myself. My conscience does not convict me of anything, but yet I am not thereby justified. It is the Lord who judges me. Do not, therefore, pronounce judgment before the time comes,

before the Lord comes, who will bring to light the things now hidden
in shadows and disclose the secrets of the heart. Then every man will
receive his praise from God. (1 Cor. 4:3–5)

A short while later, at 29/21–30/2, More once again alludes to 2 Corinthians 12:1–10, the passage which began this series of scriptural quotations,
in which Paul prays to God to have his tribulation taken away and is told
that God's grace is sufficient. More returns to it again at 31/9–15, where
Paul serves as an example of a man of clear conscience who nevertheless
suffered tribulation like Job as a test of his love for God. The similarity to
More's own suffering in prison becomes even clearer as the argument
proceeds.

The third kind of tribulation More discusses is that which is sent by God
not to punish faults nor to keep men from sins they might otherwise
commit, but to exercise their patience and increase their merit, as when,
in More's words, "a man falleth in tribulacion for the mayntenaunce of
iustice or for the defence of godes cause" (32/2–3). It is at this point that
More draws close to his own situation, and the autobiographical pressure
behind the text becomes most intense. "Surely," he writes,

> yf a man may . . . haue grete cumfort in the clerenes of his conscience,
> that hath a false cryme put vppon hym, & by false witnes provid
> vppon hym, & he falsely punyshid & put to worldly shame & payne
> therfor / an hundred tymes mor comfort may he haue in his hart /
> that where white is callid blak / & right is callid wrong / abidith by
> the trouth & is persecutid for iustice / (33/20–26)

> I wold not faile to bid hym boldly (while I shuld se him in his passion)
> cast synne & hell and purgatorie & all vppon the devilles pate / and
> dowt not but like wiso as yf he gave ouer his hold all his merite were
> lost & he tournid into misery / so yf he stand & percever still in the
> confession of his fayth, all his hole payne shall tourne all into glorye.
> (32/14–19)

More explains that he is not speaking of worldly justice, where one defends
himself for "temporall availe" (34/5), and to support his position he uses
a quick series of scriptural quotations. "Saynt paule counceilith / *Non
vosmet defendentes charissimi* / defend not your selfes most dere frendes / and
our saviour counsailith: *Si qui vult tecum in iudicio contendere & tunicam tuam
tollere dimitte ei & pallium* / yf a man will strive with the at law & take away
thy cote / leve hym thy gown to" (34/5–10). And so on. The quotations
are taken from Romans 12:19, Matthew 5:40, and Philippians 2:4. The
contexts of all these verses refer, however, not simply to justice, but in a
very particular way to the underlying references to criminal charges in the

scriptural allusions immediately preceding. In Romans 12, Paul urges us to present our bodies as a living sacrifice and not to conform to the world, but to bless those who persecute us and leave vengeance to God:

> And so I beg of you, brothers, to present your bodies as a living sacrifice, holy, pleasing to God, your reasonable worship. And do not conform to this world . . . Rejoice in your hope, be patient in tribulation, be constant in prayer . . . Bless those who persecute you: bless, and do not curse them . . . Do not repay evil for evil . . . Do not defend yourselves, dear friends, but give place to anger. For it is written: vengeance is mine, I will repay, says the Lord. But if your enemy is hungry, give him food; if he is thirsty, give him drink. Doing this you will heap coals on his head. Do not be overcome by evil, but overcome evil by good. (12:1–2, 12, 14, 17, 19–21)

The context in Matthew 5 also refers to the need to pray for those who persecute and bring false charges against us, emphasizing particularly the refusal to swear a false oath:

> You have heard what was said by the men of old: you shall not swear falsely, but render your oaths to the Lord. But I say to you, do not swear at all . . . You have heard it said, an eye for an eye, and a tooth for a tooth. But I say to you, do not resist evil, but if any one strikes you on the right cheek, turn the other also to him. And if anyone would take you to court to take away your shirt, let him have your coat as well . . . You have heard it said, love your neighbor and hate your enemy. But I say to you, love your enemies and bless those who hate you and pray for those who persecute you and bring false charges against you, that you may be sons of your Father, who is in heaven. (5:33–34, 38–40, 43–45)

The final quotation in this series is a conflation of Philippians 2:4 and 1 Corinthians 10:24. The syntax and most of the phrasing is from Philippians. Corinthians adds only one word. The meaning of both verses is essentially the same, but the context of Philippians is more in keeping with the chain of associations that tie these quotations together. Writing from prison, Paul urges the Philippians not to be frightened by their opponents,

> for this is to them a cause of their damnation, but of your salvation, and that from God. For it has been granted to you for the sake of Christ that you not only believe in him, but also that you suffer for him, engaged in the same conflict that you saw in me and now hear from me. So if there is any consolation in Christ and comfort in charity, any companionship with the Spirit, any compassion in your

bowels, complete my joy by being of the same mind, having the same charity, being in full accord and of one mind. (1:28–30, 2:1–2)

Up to this point the chapter has been extremely autobiographical. Few of us could read these pages without suspecting that More had his own case clearly in mind. At the same time another, still more specific form of personal reference has been going on in the context of the verses of scripture More quotes. At the end of the chapter, in a final quotation from the Sermon on the Mount, these two dimensions of meaning draw together. The concern with persecution underlying the scriptural quotations for the last twelve pages or so emerges fully on the surface of the text. One who is called upon to suffer, More says, for the defense of God's cause or the sake of justice can comfort himself with the words of Christ: "*Beati misericordes | quia misericordiam consequenter |* Blessid be the mercifull men, for they shall haue mercie given them | *Beati qui persecutionem patiuntur propter iustitiam, quoniam ipsorum est regnum celorum |* Blessid be they that suffer persecution for iustice | for theirs ys the kyngdome of hevyn" (34/22–26). The verses are taken from the beginning of the Sermon on the Mount, the same general passage as the previous reference to Matthew (above, 34/7–9). More quotes verses 7 and 10, but he was no doubt also aware of the verse that immediately follows, the last of the Beatitudes, for it catches up the idea of calumny or false accusation persistently alluded to in this chain of scriptural allusion: "Blessed are you when men curse you and persecute you and utter all kinds of evil against you falsely on my account. Rejoice and be glad, for your reward is great in heaven, for so men persecuted the prophets before you" (Matthew 5:11–12).[1]

Except for the Psalms, the Book of Proverbs, and Job, More's quotations from the Old Testament do not carry with them the same sort of awareness of context as his quotations from the New Testament.[2] One of the most significant and most revealing of all the scriptural allusions in *A Dialogue*

---

[1] Similar chains of scriptural allusion occur throughout the text; see, for example, 48/13–49/8, 101/3–103/2 and 306/14–319/25. For specific scriptural references and brief discussion, see the Commentary.

[2] More's references to the Old Testament do not seem to have been specifically verbal. He apparently did not have the words of whole passages echoing in his mind as he did in his references to the New Testament. He seems instead to refer to the total configuration of the lives of outstanding individuals, such as David, Saul, Abraham, Solomon, and Jonah; and he seems to regard these lives as figures and types. Thus Abraham is a type of the rich man who nevertheless loved God more than his worldly wealth (54/1–56/12). Achan is a type of sinner whose suffering on earth was a blessing from God because it led to his repentance (26/9–25). And so on. Very few allusions of this sort carry an autobiographical dimension. Notable exceptions are the reference to Queen Esther at 184/29 and the chain of allusions to Joseph, Daniel, and John the Baptist at 279/12–25. Even in these, however, the allusions are not verbal.

of Comfort, however, and one of the most starkly autobiographical, occurs in a series of recurrent quotations from the Apocryphal Book of Sapientia, which was thought to have been written by Solomon and is therefore located in the Vulgate immediately after the Song of Songs and before Ecclesiasticus. More alludes to the passage on three separate occasions, each in relation to one of the temptations described in Psalm 90. The first allusion occurs in Book II. More is speaking of the second temptation, the arrow that flies by day, which he interprets as pride:

> vpp we fle like an arrow that were shott vp into the ayer / & yet whan we be sodanly shotten vpp into the hiest / ere we be well warm there, down we come vnto the cold ground agayne, & than evyn there stikk we styll / And yet for the short while that we be vpward & aloft / lord how lustye & how proud we be, buzzyng above bysily like as a bumble bee fleeth about in somer, neuer ware that she shall die in wynter / (157/27–158/6)

Then, by a process of association, More links the arrow in Psalm 90 with a similar image in Sapientia, where an arrow is used explicitly as a metaphor for pride. Although More quotes Sapientia 5:8–9 and 12–14, he seems to have had in mind, here and in his subsequent allusions, the entire passage, in fact the entire first six chapters, which tell a continuous story. The Book of Sapientia is addressed to all the rulers of the earth and instructs them in the ways of wisdom. The instruction consists primarily of a moral exemplum, contrasting the just man with the rich and powerful of this world, who live their lives disbelieving in God. "The breath of our nostrils is smoke," they say, "and speech is a spark kindled by the beating of our hearts. When it is extinguished, our body will be ashes, and our spirit will dissolve like gentle air" (2:2–3). They resolve, therefore, to live for this world only and enjoy the good things of the earth (2:6–11). And they turn against the just man because he rebukes them. "Let us see if his words are true," they say,

> and let us test what will happen to him and see what his last days will be. For if he is the true son of God, He will help him and deliver him from the hand of his enemies. Let us examine him with insults and torture so that we may see how gentle he is and test his patience. Let us condemn him to a most shameful death, for according to what he says, he will be protected. (2:17–20)

If More remembered such an insignificant detail in this section of Sapientia as the metaphor of pride as an arrow, it is difficult to believe that he was not also aware of the startling resemblance between himself and the just man whose only hope was in God. After persecuting the man of God and condemning him to an early death, the wicked eventually die themselves and descend into hell. They see the man of God in glory and finally come to understand the vanity of their existence. Then follow the verses More quotes, as the wicked lament their folly:

> What has our pride profited us, and what good has our boasted wealth brought us? All those things have vanished like a shadow . . . or like an arrow shot at a mark: the divided air presently comes together again, so that no one knows its passage. So we also, as soon as we were born, ceased to be, and we had no mark of virtue to show, but were consumed in our wickedness. (5:8–9, 12–13)

After connecting the arrow in Psalm 90 with the arrow of pride in Sapientia, More makes another associative link that proceeds partially from the text and partially from the context. In the text More moves from the arrow of pride to Lucifer, who committed the first sin of pride:

> For whan hym selfe was in hevyn & began to fly vpp a copp high, with that lusty light flight of pride sayng: *Ascendam super astra, & ponam solium meum ad latera Aquilonis, & ero similis altissimo* / I will stye vpp above the steres, & set my trone on the sides of the north, and wil be lyke vnto the hiest / long ere he could fly vpp half so high as he said in his hart he wold / he was tournid from a bright gloriouse Angell, into a darke deformid devill / and from flying any ferther vpward / downe was he throwen into the diepe dongeon of hell / (159/26–160/4)

The quotation is taken from the so-called "taunt" of the people of Israel over the King of Babylon in the 14th chapter of Isaiah, traditionally interpreted as an account of the fall of Lucifer. Although he makes use of this allegorical interpretation in the text, More also seems aware of its literal significance, referring to the fall of an unjust king. For the scene in Isaiah is surprisingly similar to that of Sapientia: a mighty king whose power knew no limits on earth awakens in hell. Those who see him ponder his fate and remark on the vanity of his life. As More uses it, the entire passage is applicable both to Lucifer and to temporal monarchs like Henry VIII, joint rulers of this world of shadows.[1] As the verses in Isaiah continue, they seem strangely reminiscent, almost prophetic, of the reign of Henry VIII:

> Is this the man who disturbed the earth and shook kingdoms, who made the world a desert and overthrew its cities, who did not let his prisoners go home? . . . You have destroyed your land, you have

---

[1] For More's belief in the relationship between the devil and the men who act as his agents, see 317/12–27 and note to 317/24–27.

slain your people: the heirs of the wicked will nevermore be named. Prepare his sons for slaughter because of the iniquity of their fathers. They will not rise up; they will not inherit the land. (14:16–17, 20–21)

A page or so later, in the next scriptural quotation, More once again alludes to kingship. The general discussion in the text concerns wealth and authority. If a man feels that the possession of great power and wealth endangers his soul, he should be willing to give them up and turn to God alone. In any case it is always good to stand in moderate fear, as it says in scripture: "*Beatus homo qui semper est pauidus:* Blessid is the man that is alway ferefull" (162/4–5). The quotation is from Proverbs 28:14. The context is almost identical to the sections of Sapientia and Isaiah we have been looking at, and its application to Henry VIII seems inescapable. The entire passage reads:

> Blessed is the man who is always fearful, but he who hardens his heart will fall into evil. Like a roaring lion[1] or a hungry bear is a wicked king over a poor people. A ruler who lacks understanding will oppress many through false accusations . . . A man who brings false accusations against the blood of the soul, even if he flees to the pit, no one will help him. He who walks in simplicity of heart will be saved, but he who walks in crooked ways will fall at once. (28:14–18)

The second allusion to Sapientia occurs about seven pages later, in relation to the third temptation in Psalm 90, *negotio perambulante in tenebris,* which More translates as "besines walkyng about in the darkenessis" (166/17). The allusion simply catches up the weariness and pain attendant on the excessive pursuit of the things of this world: "They that now lye in hell for their wrechid livyng here / do now perceve their foly in the more payne that they toke here for the lesse pleasure / There confesse they now their foly & cry owt / *Lassati sumus in via iniquitatis* / we haue bene weryed in the way of wikkednes" (169/8–11). The quotation is taken from the speech of the wicked in Sapientia 5:7, when they see the man of God in glory. The context is no different from before, but the fact that More turns to it once again indicates something of its importance to him, as though it were held in suspension and all the intervening pages were to be read against it.

The final allusion to Sapientia occurs toward the end of Book III, in relation to the last of the four temptations in Psalm 90, the assault of the noonday devil, which More interprets as open persecution for the faith. In his previous references to Sapientia More emphasized the fate of the wicked when they awaken in hell. In this last quotation he stresses instead

---

[1] For More's use of the lion-king metaphor, see the Commentary at 108/1–6 and 318/5–8.

the glory of the just man in heaven. In chapters twenty-five and twenty-six (302/19–311/28) More contrasts the pains of hell with the joys of heaven. "Let vs not so mich with lokyng to haue describid what maner of Ioyes they shalbe," More says, "as with heryng what our lord telleth vs in holy scripture" (306/26–28). He then quotes Sapientia 3:7: "*fulgebunt Iusti sicut sol, & qui erudiunt ad iustitiam tanquam scintille in arudineto discurrent |* Ryghteus men shall shyne as the sone, & shall run about like sparkes of fyre among redes" (307/6–8). The verses immediately preceding More's quotation mention a time of trial or testing of the righteous, such as More himself was going through, whereby God finds them worthy:

> The souls of the just are in the hand of God, and the torment of death will not touch them. In the eyes of the foolish they seem to have died, and their departure was thought to be an affliction and their going from us utter destruction. But they are at peace. For though in the sight of men they suffered torture, their hope is full of immortality. Having suffered a little, they will receive great reward because God tested them and found them worthy of himself. Like gold in the furnace he tried them, and like a sacrificial offering he accepted them. And in time they will be respected. Just men will shine and run about like sparks of fire among reeds. (3:1–7)

The passage continues by contrasting the reward of the righteous with the punishment of the wicked, whose offspring will be accursed, and again the verses seem like a direct warning to Henry VIII:

> But the wicked, who despised the just man and turned away from God will receive the punishment they devised for themselves. For whoever rejects wisdom and discipline is miserable; their hope is vain, their labor unprofitable, and their work useless. Their wives are foolish and their children evil. Their offspring are accursed. For blessed is the barren woman who is undefiled, who has not entered into a sinful union. She will have fruit when God examines the souls of saints . . . But the children of adulterers will not come to maturity, and the seed of an unlawful union will perish . . . The prolific brood of the wicked will be of no use, and none of their legitimate offshoots will strike deep root or take firm hold . . . For children born of unlawful unions are witnesses of evil against their parents when God examines them. But the just man, though he die early, will be at rest. (3:10–13, 16; 4:3, 6–7)

The entire passage in Sapientia, one must remember, is a moral exemplum addressed to kings, urging them to rule with justice. Within or below the fictional conversation of *A Dialogue of Comfort* in Buda on the eve of a

Turkish invasion, we seem to hear in all these allusions to Sapientia the
voice of Thomas More's own heart in meditation, murmuring to his former
friend, remembering perhaps, in Robert Lowell's phrase, "the great king's
bluff arm on his neck, / feeling that friend-slaying, terror-ridden heart /
beating under the fat of Aretino"—[1]saying:

> Listen, therefore, O kings, and understand; learn, O judges of the
> ends of the earth . . . For your power was given to you by the Lord,
> and your strength from the Most High, who will inquire into your
> works and read your thoughts because as ministers of his kingdom
> you did not judge rightly, nor guard the law of justice, nor walk
> according to the will of God. He will appear to you terribly and
> swiftly, for severe judgment awaits those who rule . . . To you then,
> O kings, my words are directed, that you may learn wisdom and not
> depart from it. (6:2, 4–6, 10)

Perhaps the reason we are able to identify the account of the just man
in Sapientia with the suffering and death of Thomas More is that both
seem to us like instances of the same archetypal action. For More, however,
the identity would have been much more explicit and much more mysterious and powerful. In More's own time, in the great Froben Bible,
Nicholas de Lyra interprets the account of the man of God in Sapientia
as a prefiguration of the passion and death of Christ.[2] De Lyra's interpretation is dependent on the notion of biblical typology, in which figures in
the Old Testament are to be regarded as shadowy forms of truth and
types of Christ. In this instance, however, the typology is dependent not
on an obsolete form of biblical interpretation, but on a central feature of
Hebraic-Christian religious experience. For the death of the just man in
Sapientia and the passion and death of Christ are both instances of the
same paradox, reenactments of the same ancient Hebrew tradition, which
describes a man who is cast out of his society by the rich and powerful of
his day and is reborn through suffering and death, miraculously giving
hope to other men:

> It has to do with the idea that the new man gets born under the
> mysterious circumstances of what the Hebrews called the *anaw* . . .
> That very rich conception was translated historically in different

---

[1] "Sir Thomas More" in *Notebook 1967–68* (New York, 1969), p. 41. Lowell later
revised the lines to read: "feeling that friend-slaying, terror-dazzled heart / baloooning
[*sic*] off into its awful doom" (*History* [New York, 1973], p. 61). A change for the worse.

[2] *Biblia Latina*, *3*, sig. ss₅v. The interpretation did not, of course, originate with Nicholas
de Lyra. The *Glossa Ordinaria*, for example (*op. cit.*, sig. ss₆), interprets the just man as
Christ's church and the ungodly who persecute him as heretics and schismatics who
adulterate the divine doctrine and produce illegitimate offspring who cannot survive.

ways, depending upon the culture; but it had to do quite generally with the redemptive possibilities which become incarnate in one who is despised and considered worthless by the rich and powerful people of his time. Often the man's life was pressed to the point of extreme anguish—such as we read in, say, the forty-ninth chapter of Isaiah or the twenty-first Psalm . . . But it is instructive that this man, so far as we can trace his spiritual physiognomy, is so repeatedly (in various religious traditions) a human reject, a man who finds himself some-what like Job: there, left and alone, at the gate of the city, cast out, without recourse—and so one whose final hope became the absurdity of believing beyond belief and hoping beyond hope . . . Israel has never really quite been able to forget that magnificent explosion in its ancient literature—of Isaiah and Jeremiah; and neither has Christianity, because it seems to me Christ declared so explicitly His own solidarity with that tradition at the hour of His death.[1]

In *A Dialogue of Comfort* and his other Tower works, More declares his own solidarity with that tradition. In the choice he made and the suffering that choice entailed, More saw himself called upon to reenact Christ's suffering and death. Earlier, in *A Dialogue Concerning Heresies* (1529), More wrote:

What ease also cal you this, yᵗ we be bounden to abide all sorowe and shameful death & al martirdome vppon pain of perpetual damnacion for the profession of our faith. Trowe ye that these easy wordes of his easy yoke & light burdein wer not aswel spoken to his apostles as to you, & yet what case called he them to. Called he not them to watching, fasting, praying, preching, walking, hunger, thirst, colde, & heate, beating, scourging, prisonment, painful & shamefull death. The ease of his yoke standeth not in bodily ease, nor the lightnes of his burden standeth not in the slacknes of any bodily payn (except we be so wanton, that wher himself had not heauen without pain, we loke to come thither with playe) but it standeth in the swetenes of hope, whereby we fele in our pain a pleasaunt taste of heauen.[2]

More discovered nothing new about his faith in the Tower. He was forced to experience it, however, in a new way, testing his long-standing convictions and proving them true with his own life. If in *A Dialogue of Comfort*, therefore, we seem to hear the voice of More's deepest, most

---

[1] Daniel Berrigan and Robert Coles, *The Geography of Faith* (New York, 1971), pp. 203–204.

[2] *EW*, sig. k₄. For an echo of this same idea, attributed to More by Roper, see n. to 43/7–9.

inward self blend with the words of Christ in the gospels and the words of St. Paul and the other apostles in scripture, it is because More has consciously claimed them for his own, having become transformed through the love of God into the outcast, the failure, the human reject. The shape More's life assumed in prison was the shape of the suffering man on the cross he worshipped at the altar. In the *De Tristitia Christi*, the last work More wrote in the Tower, Christ is imagined to say to those like More, who are called to martyrdom and are afraid:

> O faint of heart, take courage and do not despair. You are afraid, you are sad, you are stricken with weariness and dread of the torment with which you have been cruelly threatened. Trust me . . . See, I am walking ahead of you along this fearful road. Take hold of the border of my garment.[1]

When More was led to execution on July 6, 1535, dressed in the cheap gown of his servant, he carried before him a cross painted red.[2] In the liturgy of More's time such a cross had particular significance. In the processions held each Sunday in Lent, the customary *Crux processionalis* was forbidden to be used. The procession was headed instead by a cross of plain wood painted red in memory of Christ's blood shed on the cross.[3] In *A Dialogue of Comfort* More waited in hope. In his last walk to the scaffold, with the bloody cross in his hand, he stepped forth and grasped the hem of Christ's garment.

V. A NOTE ON THE TEXT

The text that follows represents a moderately conservative transcription of the Corpus Christi College manuscript of *A Dialogue of Comfort*. When the corrections of scribe *B* replace the readings of scribe *A*, the readings of *A* (including his spellings) have been retained, except in places where scribe *A* seems to have made an obvious error, or in a few places where the reading of *A*, though possibly right, creates serious confusion or difficulty even for an experienced reader of sixteenth-century texts. The basic principle has been to follow the readings of *A* even when the corrections

---

[1] *CW 14*, 101–105.

[2] Stapleton, pp. 208–209. Stapleton got most of his information on More's death from the eyewitness account of Margaret Clement, who was the only member of More's household present at the execution. See Chambers, *Thomas More*, pp. 346–50.

[3] F. A. Gasquet, *Parish Life in Medieval England* (London, 1909), p. 171. In carrying the red cross More also seems to have considered his execution in larger liturgical terms, coalescing the death signified by Lent into the resurrection at Easter.

of *B* provide a more grammatical, more polished, or more immediately comprehensible version, for such corrections are exactly what one would expect to find if *B*, or his source in another manuscript, were performing the work of a copy-editor. The assumption has been that, if the reading of *A* makes sense, it may represent what More really wrote, even though the reading of *A* is rougher and less precise. The effect of·colloquial style is, indeed, greatly enhanced by following *A*, in most instances.

In places where *B* has added words or phrases, these additions have been printed within half-brackets (⌐yet¬). When emendations made by the present editor constitute an entire word, these have been printed within square brackets; other emendations are of course recorded in the textual notes. In some cases of capitalization or of obvious scribal misspelling, no source is recorded for an emendation: such emendations have been made by the present editor, usually in accordance with the other texts. Foliations have also been printed in square brackets, at the beginning of the page concerned. Abbreviations have been silently expanded, except for the ampersand, and superscript letters have been brought down. Expansion of abbreviations has usually been guided by places in the manuscript where the word, or a similar word, is found fully spelled. Fortunately, both *A* and *B* are not much given to abbreviations, and examples of fully spelled words are thus quite frequent. One big exception is the word here transcribed as "mervailouse" (or some variation of this spelling), where the "er" is always abbreviated. The expansion "mer" has been chosen as characteristic of More's usage elsewhere and as being in line with the French derivation of the word. Abbreviations involving the superscript letter "r," such as yor, o^r, hono^r, favo^r, to^{r}ment, etc., have consistently been expanded by "our," although "or" readings are sometimes found in fully spelled versions of words such as "torment" and "favor." Capitalization has been normalized at the beginnings of paragraphs and at the beginnings of chapter headings. Modern indentation has been provided for paragraphs, whereas the manuscript indicates paragraphs only by the blank space at the end of the preceding line. When no punctuation occurs at the end of a paragraph, a period has been silently added. The phrases indicating the chapter number ("The ij Chapiter") have been given a normalized placement at the center of the page, in a separate line, whereas in the manuscript these phrases are sometimes written in the same line after the summary, with separation by virgules. It should be noted that in *1553* these phrases indicating the chapter numbers are placed before the summary, whereas in the other four texts the numbering almost always follows the summary; this sort of variation has not been recorded in the textual footnotes.

Scribe *B* is a remarkably scrupulous editor whose corrections frequently extend to the clarification of a letter that is already quite clear; he will, for example, extend the first minim of a "w" to avoid any possibility of mistake. And *B* will also often add connecting dashes (=) when a word is broken over the end of a line. Such clarifications are not usually recorded in the textual footnotes.

Normally, spelling-variants in the secondary texts have not been recorded, but exceptions have been made in places where spellings have some special, intrinsic interest, or when the spellings may help to cast some light upon relationships among the various texts. On the other hand, differences in word-forms have usually been recorded. The chief exception here is found in the variations, "thorough," "through" ("thorowe," "throwe"), as preposition or adverb; these variations, running into the hundreds, have not been recorded, in order to avoid encumbering the already heavy mass of textual footnotes. In the textual notes, where agreement is recorded among the secondary texts, the spelling of the variant is normally that of the earliest printed text involved.

In general the punctuation of the text represents the original punctuation of *A*, heavily supplemented by the additions of *B*. But the punctuation presents a number of special problems. Scribe *B* has very frequently cancelled the punctuation of *A*, and has then added new punctuation; in other places the punctuation of *A* has been left intact, while new punctuation has been added in the same place; thus *B* may write a question-mark or a period before or after an uncancelled virgule. In all such cases the principle has been to follow *A*, if his punctuation is satisfactory. Parentheses, however, are erratic in *A*; for *A* will often give a virgule (or a stroke with so slight a curve that it looks like a virgule) at one end of what appears to be a parenthetical passage, and in such cases *B* very frequently writes a parenthesis over the virgule (or near-virgule). Since the use of parentheses is a marked characteristic of More's style, the corrections or clarifications of *B* have usually been followed in such cases. Editorial choices of this kind in the punctuation have been recorded in the footnotes, and editorial alterations in the punctuation (very few in number) have also been noted, except for the periods added at the ends of paragraphs.

As we have said earlier (above, p. xxxvi) the punctuation of *A* consists primarily of the virgule, with some parentheses and periods, and perhaps a few commas. Scribe *B* adds hundreds of virgules and commas, but he clearly sees a difference between the comma and the virgule, since he very frequently cancels a virgule in *A* and substitutes a comma. Apparently, to scribe *B* the comma indicates a slighter pause. Scribe *B* also adds many colons, question-marks, and parentheses. In the great majority of cases it is possible to distinguish the punctuation of *A* from that of *B* by color of ink, slant of virgule, crowding between words, and so on. But a complete listing of such identifications would require an unbearable mass of foot-notes, with very little profit. Hence such identifications have not been recorded. The reader should assume that nearly all of the commas, and all of the colons and question-marks, are added by *B*.

The following sigla have been used:

CC The Corpus Christi College manuscript, now in the Bodleian Library (Ms. C.C.C. D. 37)

A The basic scribal hand in *CC*.

B The chief correcting hand in *CC*.

E A minor correcting hand and one of the hands in the margin of *CC*.[1]

F An early hand in the margin of *CC*.

G A later hand in the margin of *CC*.

L Ms. Royal 17 D. XIV in the British Library.

1553 Tottel's edition of *A Dialogue of Comfort*, London, 1553.

1557 The edition of *A Dialogue of Comfort* contained in Rastell's collected edition of More's English *Workes*, London, 1557.

1573 John Fowler's edition of *A Dialogue of Comfort*, Antwerp, 1573.

Z Agreement of readings in *L*, *1553*, *1557*, and *1573*.

---

[1] The marginalia in *CC* and in the early editions are reproduced in Appendix A (below, pp. 445–80).

A DIALOGE OF COMFORT AGAYNST
TRYBULACION, MADE BY AN HUNGARYEN
IN LATEN, & TRANSLATYD OUT OF LATEN
INTO FRENCH, & OUT OF FRENCH INTO
ENGLYSH.

A dialoge of comfort agaynst trybulacion, made by an hungaryen in laten, & translatyd out of laten into french, & out of french into Englysh.

5

Antony & Vyncent

[Vyncent]

Who wold haue went / O my good vnckle / afore a few yeres passed, that such as in this countrey wold visit their frendes lying in desease 10 & siknes, shuld come (as I do now) to seke & fetch comfort of them / or in gevyng comfort to them, vse the wey that I may well vse to you / For albeit that the prestes and freres be wont to call vppon sik men to remember deth / yet we worldly frendes for feare of discomfortyng them, haue euer had a gise in hungarye / to lyft vp 15 their hartes and put them in hope of lyfe / But now my good vncle the world is here wexen such / & so gret perilles appere here to fall at hand that me thynketh the gretest comfort that a man can haue, ys when he may see that he shall sone be gone. And we that are lykely long to lyve here in wrechidnes, haue nede of some comfortable 20 councell agaynst trybulacion / to be gevyn vs by such as you be good vncle, that haue so long lyvid vertuously, & are so lernyd in the law of god, as very few be better in this countrey here / and haue had of such thynges as we now do feare, good experyence & assay in your selfe, as he [f. 1ᵛ] that hath bene taken prisoner in Turkey ij tymes 25 in your dayes / & now lykely to depart hens are long / But that may

---

1–6 *1557 adds the following before this title*: A dyalogue of comforte agaynste tribulacyon, made in the yere of our lorde, 1534. by syr Thomas More knyghte, while he was prysoner in the tower of London, whiche he entitled thus as foloweth.; made . . . Englysh] made by the right Uertuous, wise & Learned man, Sir Thomas More sometime L. Chanceller of England. *1573*   6 Englysh.] *period added B?* above dash A   7 Antony & Vyncent] *added* E? *See note*   8 Vyncent] *added* Z   9 vnckle] vnckcle A   10 wold] here would L 11 (as] *parenth. wr. over* / B   13 freres] the fryars L   15 gise] guyse here L   16 in hope] in good hope Z; my] *flourish above* m *canc.* B?   18 thynketh] thynck L; minim *canc. after* a   19 *bar of separation added* B? *after* be   24 now do] do now Z 26 are] *canc. and* ere *interl.* B, ere Z; long /] / *canc. and period added* B; may] a *wr. over* e? B

3

be your great comfort good vncle, sith you depart to god / But vs
here shall you leve of your kyndred a sort of very comfortles orphanes /
to all whom your good help & counsaile & comfort hath longe bene
a great staye / not as an vncle vnto some, & to some as one ferther
5 of kyn / but as though vnto vs all, you had bene a naturall father.

Antony

Myn own good Cosyn I can not much say nay, but that there is
in dede, not here in hungery onely, but almost in all places of
christendome, such a customable maner of vncristen comfortyng /
10 which albeit that in any sik man yt doth more harm than good /
withdrawyng hym in tyme of sikenes with the lokyng & longyng for
lyfe, fro the meditacion of deth, iugement, heven, & hell, wherof he
shuld beset much part of his tyme / even all his whole lyfe in his best
helth / yet is that maner in my mynd more than mad, where such
15 kynd of comfort ys vsid to a man of myn age / for as wee well wot that
a yong man may dye sone / so be we very sure, that an old man can
not lyve long / And yet sith there is as Tullye sayth no [f. 2] man for
all that so old but that he hopeth ⌈yet⌉ that he may lyve one yere
more / and of a frayle folye, deliteth to thynke theron, & comfort
20 hymselfe therwith / other mens wordes of lyke maner comfort addyng
mo stykes to that fyer / shall in a maner burn vp quyt, the plesaunt
moysture that most shuld refresh hym / the holsom dew I meane of
goddes grace, by which he shuld wish with goddes will to be hens,
& long to be with hym in heven / Now where you take my departyng
25 fro you ⌈so hevely⌉ / as of hym of whom ye recognise of your goodnes
to haue had here before help & comfort: Wold god I had to you &
other mo, done halfe so much as my selfe rekeneth had bene my
dewtie to do / But when so euer god take me hens, to reken your selfe
then comfortles / as though your chiefe comfort stode in me / therin

1 great] graat *A*: e *wr. over first a B* 2 very] *canc. and* sory *interl. B*, sory *Ƶ* 3 &
counsaile & comfort] *first* & *canc. B?*, coumforte and counsell *Ƶ* 4 to] vnto *L*
5 though vnto] though that vnto *Ƶ* 8 almost in] almoste also in *Ƶ* 9 such] *om. L*
1553 1573 11 with the] the *om. Ƶ* 12 fro] from *L* 18 that he may lyve] to
lyve *L* 19 to thynke theron] thereon to thinke *1553 1573*; comfort] comfort-
ing *L 1553 1557*, cumforteth *1573* 21 mo] no *1553*; quyt] *final e added B*
24 departyng] yng *wr. by A over orig.* ure? 25 fro] from *Ƶ*; *comma after* hevely *B*; ye]
you *Ƶ* 26–27 & other] and to other *1557* 27 done halfe so much] halfe so muche
doone *1553 1573* 28 selfe] es *wr. over final e B*, selues *Ƶ*

make ye me thinketh a rekenyng ⌜very⌝ much like, as though ye wold
cast a way a strong staff, & lene vppon a rotten rede / for god ys
& must be your comfort & not I. And he is a sure comfort / that as
he said to his disciples, neuer leveth his seruauntes in case of comfortles orphanys, not even when he departid from his disciples by 5
deth / but both as he promisid, sent them a comforter, the holy spryt of
his father & hym selfe, & made them also sure that to the worldes
end, he wold euer dwell with them hym selfe / And therfor yf ye be part
of his floke, & beleve his [f. 2ᵛ] promyse: how can ye be comfortles
in any trybulacion / when christ & his holy spryte, & with them 10
their vnseparable father, yf you put full trust & confidens in them /
be neuer one fynger brede of space, nor one mynute of tyme from
you /

Vyncent

O my good vncle, even these same selfe wordes wherwith ye well 15
prove, that because of goddes own gracious presence, we can not be
left comfortles / make me now fele & perceve, what a mysse of much
comfort we shall haue, when ye be gone / for albeit good vncle, that
while ye do tell me this, I can not but graunt yt for trew / yet yf I
now had not hard yt of you: I had not remembryd yt / nor yt had 20
not fallen in my mynd. And ouer that, like as our trybulacions shall
in weight & nomber encrease / so shall we nede, not onely one such
good word or twayne, but a greate hepe therof, to stable & strength
the walles of our hartes, agaynst the great sourges of the tempestious
see. 25

Antony

Good cosyn trust well in god, & he shall prouide you techers abrode
convenient in euery tyme / or els shall hym selfe suffyciently teche
you within. [f. 3]

1 ye] interl. A, clar. B, you Ƶ; ye] you Ƶ   2 god] yod A: g wr. over y B   3 And] and
A; sure comfort /] sure comforter / B: ter wr. over t and /, new / added B, sure coumforter Ƶ
4 to] vnto 1553 1557 1573   6 sent] send L   7 made them also] them also made 1553
1573   8 selfe /] / canc. and period added B; ye] you Ƶ   9 floke] second k inserted before
e B; ye] you Ƶ   12 neuer one] neuer neyther one Ƶ; brede] breadth Ƶ   15 ye]
you Ƶ   16 gracious] om. L   18 ye] you Ƶ; gone / for] period added after gone and f
alt. to F B   19 ye] you Ƶ   22-23 onely one such good] onely suche one good L,
onely suche a good 1553 1573   23 greate] graate A: e wr. over first a B?   24 sourges
of] of om. L; the] is wr. over e B, this Ƶ

Vyncent

Very well good vncle / But yet yf we wold leve the sekyng of
outward lernyng, where we myght haue yt / and loke to be inwardly
towght onely by god / then shuld we therby tempt god & displease
5 hym / And sith that I now se the lyklyhod, that when ye be gone,
we shalbe sore destytute of any such other lyke / Therfor thynketh
me / that god of dewtie byndeth me to sew ⌐to⌐ you now good vncle, in
this short tyme that we haue you, that yt may like you agaynst these
grete stormes of tribulacions / with which both I & all myne are sore
10 beten alredy / And now vppon the comyng of this cruell Turke, fere
to fall in ferre mo / I may lern of you such plentie of good councell
& comfort, that I may with the same layd vp in remembrauns,
gouerne and staye the ship of ower kyndred, & kepe yt a flote from
perill of spirituall drounnyng.
15   You be not ignorant good vncle what heps of hevynes hath of late
fallen among vs all redye / with which some of our pore famely be
fallen into suche dumpes, that scantly can any such comfort as my
pore wyt can give them, any thyng asswage their sorow / And now
sith the tydynges haue come hether so brymme of the great Turkes
20 interprise into these parties here: we can almost neyther talke nor
thynke of any other thyng els, than of his might & our mischefe.
[f. 3ᵛ] There falleth so contynually before the eyen of our hart, a
fearefull imaginacion of this terryble thyng / his myghty strength and
power, his high malice and hatryd, & his incomparable crueltie, with
25 robbyng, spoylyng, burnyng, and layng wast all the way that his
armye commeth / than kyllyng or carying away, the people far hens
fro home / and there seuer the couples & kyndred asonder, euery
one far from the other / some kept in thrauldome, & some kept in
prison / & some for a tryumph tormentyd and kyllid in his presens
30 / Than send his people hether & his fals fayth therwith / so that such
as are here & remayne styll / shall eyther both lese all & be lost to /
or forcid to forsake the fayth of our savyour christ, and fall to the

---

3 myght] maye *Z*   5 the] *om. L 1553 1573*; ye] you *Z*   6 lyke / Therfor] *colon*
added before / *and* T *alt. to* t B   9 grete] *interl. A*; tribulacions] s *canc.* B, tribulacion *Z*
11 ferre] a *wr. over first* e B, farr many L; *comma added and canc. after* councell B
14 drounnyng] ro *wr. over illeg. letters A*   15 heps] i *ins. before* s B   19 sith the] sith
these *Z*; come] comen *1557*   20 parties] partes *Z*   26–27 far hens fro] farre thence
farre from *1553 1573*, farre thence from *1557*, farr thence far fro L   27 & kyndred]
& the kinred *Z*   28 the other] the *om. Z*   31 are here] here are *1553 1573*

false sect of machomete. And yet which we more feare than all the remenant, no small part of our own folke that dwell even here about vs, are (as we here) fallen to hym, or all redy confeteryd with hym / which yf yt so be, shall happely kepe this quarter fro the Turkes incursion / but than shall they that torne to his law, leve all their 5 neybors nothyng / but shall [f. 4] haue our goódes given them, and our bodies both / but yf we turn as they do, & forsake our saviour to / And than (for there ys no born Turke so cruell to christen folke, as is the false christen that falleth fro the fayth) we shall stand in perill yf we percever in the truth, to be more hardely handelyd 10 & dye more cruell deth by our own countremen at home / than yf we were taken hens and caried into Turkey /

These ferefull heps of perill, lye so hevy at oower hartes, whyle we wot not into which we shall fortune to fall, & therfore fere all the worst / that as our sauiour prophesied of the people of Ierusalem, 15 many wysh among vs all redye before the perill come, that the montayns wold ouerwhelm them / or the valeys open & swallow them vpp & keuer them.

Therfor good vncle, agaynst thes horrible feres of thes terrible tribulacions / of which some you wot well our howse all redye hath, 20 & the remnant stand in dread of / give vs while god lendith you vs, such plentye of your confortable councell, as I may wryte and kepe with vs, to staye vs when god shall call you hens. [f. 4ᵛ]

Antonye

Ah my good cosyn, this is an hevy heryng / & likewise as we that 25 dwell here in this part, fere that thyng so sore now / which few yeros passid ferid yt not at all / so dowt I, that ere yt long be, they shall fere yt as much, that thinke them selfe now very sure, because they dwell ferther of. Grece ferid not the Turke when that I was born / & within a while after all the hole Empier was his / The gret Sowdan 30 of Syry thought hym selfe more than hys match / and long syns ye

---

1 false] om. L 1553 1573; machomete] Machomett L, Machomette 1553, Mahomete 1557, Mahomet 1573   3 here] feare Z; fallen] falling Z; confeteryd] d wr. over t B 4 this] his 1557; fro] from Z   6 goodes] es canc. B, good Z   8 (for] parenth. wr. over / B   9 fro] from Z   13 heps] i ins. before s B; perill] perils 1573; oower] canc. and our interl. B (first o separately canc. B?)   18 keuer] couer 1553 1557 1573   20 you] ye Z   25 Ah] Z, A A   26 so] canc. B, om. Z; now /] / canc. and comma added B   30 all the hole] that whole Z   31 ye] you Z

were born, hath he that Empire to / Than hath he taken Belgrade the
fortres of this realme / And syns hath he destroyid our noble yong
goodly kyng / And now stryve there twayne for vs / our lord send
the grace / that the third dogg cary not away the bone from them
5 both / What shuld I speke of the noble strong Citie of Roodes, the
wynnyng therof he countith as a victory agaynst the hole corps of
Cristendome / sith all cristendome was not hable to defend that
strong Towne agaynst hym / Howbeyt yf the prynces of Cristendome euery where about, wold where as nede was haue set to their
10 handes in tyme, the Turk had neuer taken any one place of all thes
places / but partly dyscencions fallen among our selfes, partly that
noman carith what harm other folke fele, but ech part suffer other
to shifte for yt selfe / The [f. 5] Turke is in few yeres wonderfully
encreasid, & cristendome on the other side very sore decayid / And
15 all this worketh our vnkyndnes, with which god ys not content.

But now where as you desier of me some plentie of comfortable
thynges / which ye may put in remembrauns, and comfort therwith
your companye / verely in the rehersyng and hepyng of your
manyfold feres / my selfe began to fele, that there shuld much nede
20 agaynst so many troubles, many comfortable counsayles / for surely
cosyn a lytell before your comyng, as I dyvisid with my selfe vppon
the Turkes comyng / yt happed my mynd to fall sodenly from that,
into the dyvisyng vppon myn own departyng / wherin albeit that I
fully put my trust and hope to be a savid sowle, by the great mercye
25 of god / yet sith there ys here noman so sure, that without revelacion
may clene stond out of drede: I bethought me also vppon the paynes
of hell / and after I bethought me than vppon the Turk agayne / And
first me thought his terrowre nothyng, when I comparid yt with
the ioyfull hope of heven / Then comparid I it on the tother side with
30 the fearefull dreade of hell / & therin castyng in my mynd those terry-

---

1 that] that whole L   4 from] | partly covered by f A, fro 1573   5 of Roodes] of the
Rhodes Z   6 therof] wherof Z; countith] compteth L, counted 1553 1557 1573
7 hable] h canc. B, able L 1553 1573   9 comma after haue B (evidently meant to be after was)
10 place] om. 1573; thes] those Z   11 selfes] selvys L, selfe 1553 1557 1573   12 other]
ather A: o wr. over a B?; suffer] suffreth Z   13 The] canc. and the ins. B   14 other]
tother L 1557   15 vnkyndnes] wickednes Z   16 as] interl. A   20 counsayles / for]
period added before | and f alt. to F B   21 cosyn] om. Z   22 happed] hapned 1553 1573
23 myn] my 1553 1557 1573   25 there] canc. and no man interl. B; noman] canc. B; sith
there ys here noman so] sith no man is here so Z   26 paynes] paine Z   28 yt with]
with it Z   29 tother] other 1553 1557 1573

ble develysh tourmentours, with the depe consideracion of that
feryouse endles fyer / me thought that yf the Turke with all his hole
[f. 5ᵛ] host, & ⌜all⌝ trumpettes & his tumbrelles ⌜to,⌝ were to kyll me
in my bed come to my chamber dore, in respect of the tother
rekenyng, I regard hym not a rish /   5
And yet when I now hard your lamentable wordes, layng forth as
yt were present before my face, that hepe of ⌜hevy⌝ sorofull trybulacions / that beside thos that are alredy fallen, are in short space lyke
to folow / I wexid therwith my selfe sodenly somwhat a flyght / And
therfore I well alow your request in this behalfe, that wold haue 10
store of comfort afore hand redy by you, to resort to & ⌜to⌝ lay vp in
your hart, as a treacle agaynst the poyson of all desperat dreade, that
myght rise of occacion of sore trybulacion / And herein shall I be
gladd (as my pore wit will serue me) to call to mynd with you, such
thynges as I before haue rede hard or thought vppon, that may 15
convenyently serue vs to this purpose.

The first chapter

That the cumfortes devisid by the old
paynym philosophers, were insufficient /
And the cause wherfore   20
[f. 6]

First shall ye good Cosyn vnderstond this, that the naturall wise
men of this world, the old morall philosophers, laborid much in this
mater / & many naturall resons haue they written / wherby they might
encourage men to set litell by such goodes, or such hurt eyther, the 25
goyng & comyng wherof are the mater & cause of trybulacion / as

---

2 feryouse] furious Z; all his] all *om.* Z 3 all trumpettes] al his trumpets *L 1553 1573*;
his] *om. L 1553 1573*; were to] were come to *A*: come *canc. B*   4 come] comming
1553 1573; tother] other *1553 1557 1573*   5 regard] id *added B*, regarded *L*; rish] ryshe
1553 1557, rushe *L*   7 that] the *1573*   7–8 trybulacions] tribulacion *L 1553 1573*
10 that wold] that you would *1573*   12 treacle] y *wr. over first* e *B*, tryacle *L*,
triacle *1553 1557 1573*   15 rede] de *wr. over final* e *B*   18 cumfortes] coumfort *1557*
19 philosophers] Z, philosopher *A: final* s *added B*; insufficient] vnsufficient Z 22 ye]
you Z 24 mater /] | *wr. over comma B*   25 hurt] hurtes Z 26 goyng &] goyng
or the Z; mater &] matter & the Z

are the goodes of fortune / reches, favour, & frendes, fame, worldly
worship, & such other thynges / or of the body / as bewtie, strength,
agilitie, quiknes, & helth / These thynges ye wot well comyng to vs,
are mater of worldly welth / and taken from vs by fortune or by
5 force / or the fere of the losyng, ˹be˺ mater of aduersitie or tribulacion.
For tribulacion semeth generally to signifie nothyng els, but some
kynd of grefe eyther payne of the body or hevynes of ˹the˺ mynd.
    Now the body not to fele that it feleth: all the wit in the world
can not bryng about / But that the mynd shuld not be grevid neyther
10 with the payne ˹that the body felyth,˺ nor with the occasions of
heuynes offrid & given vnto the sowle yt selfe: this thing laborid the
philosophers very much about / & many goodly saynges haue they
toward the strength & comfort agaynst tribulacion / exirtyng men to
the full contempt [f. 6ᵛ] of all worldly losse, & dispisyng of syknes, &
15 all bodely grefe, paynfull deth and all / Howbeit in very dede, for
any thyng that euer I red in them, I neuer could yet fynd, that euer
these naturall resons, were able to give sufficient comfort of them
selfe / for they neuer strech so ferre, but that they leve vntouchid for
lak of necessarye knolege, that speciall poynt, which is not onely the
20 chief comfort of all / but without which also, all other comfortes are
nothyng / that is to wit the referryng the fynall end of their comfort
vnto god, & to repute & take for the speciall cause of comfort, that
by the pacient suffraunce of their tribulacion, they shall attayne his
favour / & for their payne receve reward at his hand in heven / And
25 for lak of knolege of this end: they did (as they nedes most) leve
vntouchid also the very speciall meane / without which we can neuer
attayne to this comfort / that is to wit the graciouse help & ayd of god,
to move styre and gide vs forward, in the referryng all our gostly
comfort / yee and our worldly comfort to, all vnto that hevenly end /
30 And therfor as I say for lak of thes thinges, all their comfortable
counsaylles are very farre [f. 7] vnsufficient / Howbeit though they

---

1 the goodes] the *om. 1553*; reches] y *wr. over first* e *B*; & frendes] & *om.* Ƶ   3 helth /]
period after | *B*; ye] yow *L*   5 or the fere] or by feare *1553 1573*; the losyng] thm
losyng *1553*, losing them *1573*; be] by *A*: *canc. and* be *interl. B*; or] and Ƶ   7 the body]
the *om. L*; the mynd] the *om. L*   9 grevid neyther] grevid the body felith neyther
A: the body felith *canc. B*, that *interl. after* grevid *and canc. B*   10 the occasions] the *om.*
Ƶ, o̅c̅c̅o̅n̅s̅ *A*: *canc. and* occasions *interl. B*   13 exirtyng] cy *wr. over* ir *B*, excityng Ƶ
14 worldly] *first* l *interl. B*, wordly *A*   17 these] those Ƶ   18 for] f *alt. to* F *B*; ferre]
a *wr. over first* e *B*   21 referryng the] referring of the *1573*   27 help & ayd] ayde
and helpe Ƶ   30 for lak] for the lacke Ƶ

be farre vnable to cure our desease of them selfe / & therfor are not
suffycyent to be taken for our phisicions / some good drugges haue
they yet in their shops / for which they may be suffrid to dwell among
our poticaryes / yf the medycyns be not made of their own braynes,
but after the billes made by the great phisicion god / prescribyng 5
the medycyns hymselfe, & correctyng the fautes of their erronyouse
receyptes / for without this way taken with them, they shall not fayle
to do as many bold blynd potycaries do / which eyther for lucre or of
a folysh pride, give sik folke / medisins of their own devisyng / and
therwith kyll vp in corners, many such symple folke, as they fynd 10
so folysh to put their lyves in such lewdd & vnlernid blynd bayerdes
handes.

We shall therfor neyther fully receve those philosophers resons in
this matter / nor yet vtterly refuse them / but vsyng them in such
order / as shall beseme them / the principall & the effectuall medisyns 15
agaynst these diseases of trybulacion, shall we fetch from the high
great & excelent phisicion, without whom we could neuer be helid
of our very dedly decease of damnacion, for our [f. 7ᵛ] necessitie
wherin the sprit of god spiritually spekith of hym ꜟselfꜞ to vs, &
byddith vs of all our helth give hym the honour / & therin ꜟthusꜞ 20
sayth vnto vs / *honora medicum* / *propter necessitatem* / *enim ordinauit eum*
altissimus. Honour thow the phisicion / for hym hath the high god
ordeynid for thy necessitie /

Therfore let vs requier that high phisicion ower blessid savyour
crist / whose holy manhed god ordeynyd / for our necessitie to cure our 25
dodly woundes with the medisyn made of the most holsome blode
of his own blessid body, that lykewlse as he curid by that incomparable medisyn our mortall maladye / yt may like hym to send vs &
put in our myndes such medysins at this tyme / as agaynst the siknes
of sorowes & trybulacions, may so comfort & strength vs in his grace / 30

1 selfe] selves *L*   4 poticaryes] Apoticaryes *1553*, Apothecaries *1573*; yf the] if theyr *Z*;
not] *canc. and interl. after* made *B, comma after* made *B*; be not made] bee made not *L 1557*
6 fautes] faultes *Z* (*this spelling variant not hereafter listed*)   8 potycaries] Apoticaries *1553*,
Apothecaries *1573*   9 folke /] | *canc. B*   11 lewdd] *final* d *canc. B*   13 receve] i
interl. before v *B*; those] these *Z*   15 order /] | / *canc. B*   16 the] that *Z*   18 decease]
disease *Z*; *period added after* necessitie *B*   19 spiritually] *Z*, spirituall *A*   21 vnto] to
1553 1573   21–22 honora . . . altissimus] *ital. ed.*   21 necessitatem /] | / *canc. B*; enim]
etenim *1557 1573*; ordinauit] di *interl. B*   22 *illeg. marks canc. after* Honour *B*   24 that]
the *1573*   25 manhed] manhod *L 1557*   27 by that] by the *1557*   30 of] *canc.
and* & *interl. B*; &] *canc. and* of *interl. B*; of sorowes &] & sorowes of *Z*

as our dedly enemy the devyll, may neuer haue the power by his
poysonid dart of murmure, gruge, and inpacyence, to turn our short
siknes of worldly tribulacion, into the endles euerlastyng deth of
infernall damnacion /

5   The second chapiter

That for a foundacion men must nedes
begyn with fayth

[Syth all our principall coumforte must come of God, we must first
presuppose in hym to whome we shall with anye ghostely counsell
10 geue any effectuall coumfort, one ground to begyn withall: where-
uppon, all that we shall build must be supported and stand, that is
to witte, the grounde & foundacion of fayth, without which had
ready before, all the spiritual coumfort that any man maye speake
of, can neuer auaile a flye. For likewise as it wer vtterlye vayne to
15 lay natural resons of coumfort, to him that hath no witte, so were it
vndoutedlye frustrate to laye spirituall causes of coumforte, to hym
that hath no faythe. For except a man first belieue, that holye scripture is the woorde of God, and that the woorde of God is true, how
can a man take any coumforte of that, that the scripture telleth him
20 therin? Nedes must the man take little fruit of the scripture, if he
either belieue not that it were the woorde of God, or els wene that
though it wer, it might yet be for al that vntrue. This fayth as it is
more faynte or more strong, so shall the coumfortable woordes of holye
scripture stande the man in more stede or lesse. This vertue of fayth,
25 can neither any man geue himselfe, nor yet any one manne another:
but though men maye with preaching be ministers vnto God
therein, & the man with hys own free will obeying freely the inward
inspiracion of God, be a weake woorker with almighty god therin:
yet is the faith in dede the gracious gift of god himself. For as Saynt
30 Iames saith. *Omne datum optimum & omne donum perfectum de sursum
est descendens a patre luminum.* Euery good gyft & euery perfit gyft, is
geuen from aboue, descending from the father of lightes. Therfore

---

2 inpacyence] impacience ℨ   8 Syth—14/12 desperate,] *text from 1557, folios 8 and 9*
cut out of ms.   22 yet be] be yet L   31 luminum.] *period ed.*; perfit] perfect L *1553 1573*

feelyng our fayth by manye tokens very faynt, lette vs praye to him
that geueth it, that it may please him to helpe & encrease it. And
lette vs first saye with him in the ghospel. *Credo domine, adiuua incredu-*
litatem meam. I belieue good Lorde, but helpe thou the lacke of my
beliefe. And after lette vs pray with the Apossles. *Domine, adauge nobis* 5
fidem. Lord encrease oure fayth. And finallye, lette vs consider by
Chrystes saying vnto them, that if we woulde not suffer the strength
and feruour of our fayth to waxe luke warme, or rather key cold,
and in maner lese his vigor by scatteryng our mindes abrode about
so many tryfling thinges, that of the matters of our faith, we very 10
seldom thinke but that we woulde withdrawe our thought fro the
respect and regard of all worldly fantasies, & so gather our fayth
together into a little narrowe rowme. And lyke the lyttle grayne of
musterde seede, whiche is of nature hote, sette it in the garden of our
soule, all weedes pulled out for the better feding of our faith, then shall 15
it growe, and so spreade vppe in heyght, that the byrdes, that is to
wit the holy Aungelles of heauen shal brede in our soule, and bring
furth vertues in the branches of our fayth, and then with the faithfull
trust, that through the true beliefe of Goddes woorde, we shall putte
in his promyse, we shall be well hable to commaund a great mountayn 20
of tribulacion, to voyde from the place where he stode in our hert,
whereas with a verye fieble fayth & a faynte, we shall be scant hable
to remoue a lyttle hillocke. And therefore, as for the fyrst conclusion,
as we must of necessitie before any spirituall coumfort presuppose the
foundacion of fayth: So syth no man can geue vs faith but only God, 25
lette vs neuer cease to cal vpon God therefore.

Vyncent

For sooth good vncle, me thynketh that this foundacion of fayth,
which as you saye must be layde first, is so necessarily requisite, that
withoute it, all spirituall coumforte wer vtterly geuen in vayn. And 30
therfore now shal we pray God for a full and a fast fayth. And I pray

---

3 with him] with the man *L 1553 1573*   11 thinke but that] thinke it that *1553*
11 fro] from *L 1573*   13 grayne of] graine of a *1553 1573*   20 hable] able *1553 1573*
21 where he stode] wher it stood *1573*   22 be scant hable] scant be able *L*   24 as]
om. *1573*   27 Vyncent] *1557 places name of speaker (in italic, followed by a period) in first line*
of paragr.; the position of the names has here been brought into accord with A   28 good] my good
L 1553 1573

you good vncle, procede you farther in the processe of your matter
of spirituall coumfort, agaynst tribulacyon.

Antony

That shall I cosin with good wille.

5   The first coumforte in tribulacion, may a
        man take in this. When he feleth in himself
      a desyre and longyng to be coumforted by God.

The .iij. Chapiter.

I wil in my poore mind assigne for the fyrst comfort, the desire and
10 longing to be by god comforted, and not withoute some reson call I
this the first cause of coumfort. For like as the cure of that persone,
is in a maner desperate,] [f. 10] that hath no will to be curid / so
is the discumfort of that person desperat, that desierith not his own
cumfort /
15   And here shall I note you .ij. kyndes of folke, that are in trybulacion
& heuynes / one sort that will seke for no cumfort / A nother sort that
wyll / And yet of thes that will not, are there also ij sortes / for first
one sort there are that are so drownyd in sorow, that they fall into
a careles dedly dulnes, regardyng nothyng / thynkyng almost on
20 nothyng, no more than yf they ley on a letarge / with which yt may
so fall, that wit and remembraunce will were awaye, & fall even faire
from them / And this cumfortles kynd of hevynes in trybulacion, ys
the hieghest kynd of the dedly synne of slowth / A nother ⌐sort⌐ are
there that will seke for no cumfort, nor yet none receve, but ⌐are⌐
25 in their trybulacion (be it losse or siknes) so testie, so fvmysh, & so
ferre out of all pacyence, that yt boteth no man to speke to them.
And thes are in a maner with inpacyence so furyouse, as though they

---

8 iij] thyrde *L*   15 kyndes] es *added B?*   16 cumfort /] *period wr. on* / *B*; A nother] an
other *L 1553 1573*, another *1557* (*this variant not hereafter listed*)   17 thes] those *Z*
17-18 for . . . are] *bracketed and underlined by marginal annotator*   19 dulnes, regardyng]
dulnes. ¶ *Regarding 1553 1573*; on] of *Z*   20 on] in *Z*   23-24 A nother . . .
cumfort,] *bracketed and underlined by marginal annotator*   24 are] all *A*: all *canc. and* are
interl. B   26 ferre] a *wr. over first* e *B*   27 And] and *A*: a *alt. to* A *B*; inpacyence so]
impacience, as *Z*

were halfe in a frenesey / and may with a custome of such fassionid
behaviour, fall in therto full & hole. And this kynd of hevynes in
tribulacion, is even a myschevose high braunch of the mortall synne
of ire / [f. 10ᵛ] And than ys there as I told you a nother kynd of folke,
which fayne wold be comfortid / and yet are they of ij sortes to. One 5
sort are those / that in their sorow, seke for worldly comfort / And
of them shall we now speke the lesse / for the dyuers occasions that
we shall after haue to touch them in mo places than one / But this
will I here say that I lernid of saynt Barnard / he that in tribulacion
turneth hymselfe vnto worldly vanyties, to get help & comfort by 10
them, fareth lyke a man that in perill of drownyng, cacheth what so
euer cometh next to hand, and that holdith he fast be yt neuer so
symple a styke. But than that helpith hym not / for that styk he
draweth down vnder the water with hym, and there lye they drownyd
together.   15

So surely yf we custome our sclfe to put our trust of comfort in
the delite of these pevesh worldly thynges / god shall for that fowle
faute, suffer our tribulacion to grow so grete, that all the plesure
of this worlde, shall neuer bere vs vp / but all our pevesh pleasure,
shall in the depth of tribulacion drown with vs /   20

The tother sort ys I say of those that long & desier to be comfortid
of god / And as I told you before, they haue an vndowtid greate
cause of cumfort, evyn in that poynt a lone, that they consider them
selfe to desier & long to be of almightie god cumfortid. [f. 11]

This mynd of theirs may welbe cause of great comfort vnto them 25
for ij great consideracions / The one is that they see them ˹self˺ seke
for their comfort where they can not fayle to fynd yt / For god both
can give them comfort & will / he can for he is almightye / he will
for he is all good & hath promisid hym selfe / *petite & accipietis* / aske
and you shall haue / He that hath fayth (as he must neades haue 30

---

1 halfe in a] in *canc. and interl. before* halfe *B*, in halfe a Z 4 And] *canc. B, om.* Z; than]
T *wr. over* t *B*; ire / And than] yre. ¶ Than Z 5-6 One . . . that] *bracketed and underlined
by marginal annotator*   7 occasions] o͞cc͞o͞ns *A: canc. and* occasyons *interl. B?*   13 styke]
e *canc. B*   14 draweth] *written twice: first word canc. because of faulty* w *A*; drownyd]
drowned bothe *1553 1557 1573*   18 faute] e *added B?*; plesure] pleasures Z
19 worlde] worldle *A: second* l *canc. B?*; but] but that *L*   21 tother] other *1553 1557
1573*   22 of god] by god *L*   24 of] by Z 25 welbe] *canc. and* well be *interl. B*
26 one] tone *L 1557 1573*   28 will] i *interl. B?*; he will] And he wyll *L*   29 promisid
hym selfe] himselfe promised Z 30 you] ye Z

that shall take comfort) can not dought but god will surely kepe this
promise / and therfor hath he a great cause to be of good cumfort
(as I say) in that he considerith that he longeth to be comfortid by
hym / which his fayth maketh hym sure he will not fayle to comfort
5 hym.
    But here consider this that I speke here of hym that in tribulacion
longeth to be cumfortid by god / And that ys he that referryth the
maner of his comfortyng to god / holdyng hym selfe content / whether
yt be by takyng away or mynyshment of the tribulacion it selfe / or
10 by the givyng of hym pacience & spirituall consolacion therin / For
hym that onely longeth to haue god take his trowble fro hym: we
can not so well warant that mynd for a cause of so grete comfort / for
bothe may he desier that that neuer myndeth to be the better / [f.
11ᵛ] and may misse also theffect of his desier, because his request
15 is happely not good for hymselfe / And of this kynd of longyng &
requyryng we shall haue occasion ferther to speke hereafter / But he
that referryng the maner of his cumfort vnto god / desierith of god to
be cumfortid, asketh a thyng so laufull & so plesaunt vnto god / that
he can not fayle to spede / and therfor hath he (as I say) greate cause
20 to take cumfort in the very desier yt selfe / A nother cause hath he
to take of that desier a very great occasion of comfort / for sith his
desier ys good, & declarith vnto hym selfe that he hath in god a good
fayth, it is a good token vnto hym, that he is not an abiect cast out
of godes gracious favour / while he perceveth that god hath put such
25 a vertuouse well ordred appetite in his mynd / For as euery evill mynd
cometh of the world & our selfe and the devill / so is euery such good
mynd, eyther immediatly or by the meane of our good angell or other
graciouse occasion, inspirid into mans hart by the goodnes of god
hymselfe / And what a cumfort may than this be vnto vs, when we
30 by that [f. 12] desier, perceyve a sure vndowtid token, that toward
our fynall saluacion our saviour is hym selfe so graciously besy abowt
vs /

---

1 dought] *canc. and* dowt *interl. B*; but] but that *1553 1557 1573*; this] his *1553 1557 1573*
4 he] *canc. B, om.* 𝒵   7 that ys] it is *1553 1557 1573*   9 by] by the 𝒵; away
or] away or the 𝒵   10 of] *canc. B, om.* 𝒵; For] For of 𝒵   11 fro] from 𝒵   15 good]
good / *A*   16 occasion] occōn *A: canc. and* occasion *interl. B*   17 that] which 𝒵
28 occasion,] occōn *A: canc. and* occasion, *interl. B*   29 may than] than may 𝒵
31 besy] busy 𝒵

That tribulacion is a meane to draw man
to that good mynd, to desier and long
for the cumfort of god /

The / 4 / chapiter

Vyncent   5

Forsoth good vncle / this good mynd of longyng for godes comfort /
is a good cause of greate cumfort in dede / our lord in tribulacion
send it vs / But ⌐by⌐ this I se well / that woo may they be, which in
tribulacion lak that mynd, & that desierith not to be comfortid by
god / but are eyther of slouth or impacyence discumfortles / or of 10
foly seke for their cheef ease & cumfort eny where elles.

Anthonye

That is good Cosyn very trew as long as they stand in that state /
but than must ye consider that trybulacion ys yet a meane to dryve
hym fro that state / And that is one of the causes for the which [f. 12ᵛ] 15
god sendith it vnto man / for albeit that payne was ordeynyd of god
for the punyshment of synne (for which they that can neuer now but
synne, can neuer be but ever punyshid in hell) yet in this world in
which his high mercye giveth men space to be better / the pvnysh-
ment by trybulacion that he sendith, servith ordinarily for a meane 20
of amendment /

Saynt paule was hym selfe sore agaynst crist, till Crist gave hym
a great fall / and threw hym to the grownd & streke hym sterke blynd /
And with that tribulacion he turnid to hym at the first word / and
god was his phisicion & helyd hym sone after ⌐both⌐ in body and 25
sowle / by his mynister Ananias / & made hym his blessid apostle.

Some are in the begynnyng of tribulacion very stoubourn and styff
agaynst god / & yet at length tribulacion bryngeth them home / The
prowd kyng pharow did abyde and endure ij or iij of the first plages,

---

1 man] men *1553 1557 1573*   4 4] fourth *L 1553 1573*   6 godes] *second* d *ins. before*
e *B*   9 desierith] ith *canc. B,* desyre *Z*   13 good] *om. L*   14 ye] you *Z*   15 fro]
from *Z*; the] *canc. B, om. Z*   17 synne] *final* s *added B,* synnes *Z*   18 can neuer] neuer
can *Z*   21 amendment] *orig.* a mendment: *connecting stroke added B?*   23 streke] a *wr.*
over first e *B*; sterke] *first* e *alt. to* a *B*   28 agaynst] *wr. twice A: first word canc. B*
29 pharow] pharao *B*: w *canc. and* a *interl. before* o

& wold not ones stope at them / but then god laid on a sorer lash that
made hym crye to hym for help / and then sent he [f. 13] for Moyses
and Aron, and confessid hymselfe for a synner / and god for good
& rightouse / & praid them to pray for hym and to withdraw that
5 plage / and he wold let them go / but when his tribulacion was
withdrawen, then was he nought agayne / So was his tribulacion occasion of ⌐his⌐ profit / and his help agayn cause of his harm / For his
tribulacion made hym call to god / and his help made hard his hart
agayne //

10   Many a man that in an easye tribulacion falleth to seke his ease in
the pastyme of worldly fantasies / fyndeth in a greater payne all these
comfortes so feoble, that he ys fayne to fall to the sekyng of godes
help / And therfor ys (as I say) the very tribulacion yt selfe, many
tymes a meane to bring the man to the takyng of the afore remembrid
15 cumfort therin / that is to wit to the desire of cumfort given by god /
which desier of godes cumfort / is (as I haue provid you) greate cause
of cumfort it selfe //

The speciall meanes to get this first cumfort
in Tribulacion /

20   The / v / chapiter [f. 13ᵛ]

How be it though the tribulacion it selfe be a meane often tymes to
get man this first cumfort in it / yet it selfe some tyme alone bringeth
not a man to it / And therfor sith without this cumfort first had, ther
can in tribulacion none other ⌐good⌐ cumfort come forth: we must
25 labour the meanes that this first cumfort may come. And therto semeth me, that yf the man of slouth or impacyence or hope of worldly
cumfort, haue no mynd to desier & seke for cumfort / of god / those
that are his frendes that come to visit & comfort hym, must a fore
all thynges put that poynt in his mynd / & not spend the tyme as they
30 comenly do in triflyng & turnyng hym to the fansies of the world /

---

1 stope] u *interl. after* o B   2 help /] *comma added and* / *wr. over comma* B   3 hymselfe for]
for *om.* Ƶ   11 these] those Ƶ   13 as] *om.* Ƶ   18 meanes] meane *1573*   20 v] vth
L, fifthe *1553 1573*   24 come forth] *wr. as one word* A   25 therto] vn *interl. before*
to B, thervnto Ƶ   26 me] one L *1553*   27 cumfort /] / *canc.* B   29 thynges]
thinge Ƶ   30 fansies] fantasies Ƶ

They must also move hym to pray god to put this desier in his mynd /
which when he gettith ones, he than hath the first cumfort / & without
dout yf it be well considerid, a cumfort mervilouse greate. His frendes
also that thus counsaile hym must vnto the attaynyng therof, help
to pray for hym them selfe & cause hym to desier good folke to help 5
hym to pray therfor. And than yf these wayes be taken for the
gettyng / I nothyng dowt but the goodnes of god shall give yt. [f. 14]

Hit suffisith not that a man haue a desier
to be cumfortid by god / onely by the
takyng away of the Tribulacion / 10

The vj chapiter

Vincent

Verely me thynketh good vncle that this counsaile is very good /
For except the person haue first a desier to be comfortid by god / els
can I not see what can availe to give hym any ferther counsail of 15
any spirituall cumfort. How be it what yf the man haue this desier
of goddes cumfort / that is to wit that it may please god to cumfort
hym in his trybulacion by takyng that tribulacion from hym / ys not
this a good desier of godes comfort, & a desier sufficient for hym that
is in tribulacion? 20

Antony

No Cosyn that is it not / I touchid before a word of this poynt, &
passid yt ouer / because I thought it wold fall in our way agayne /
and so wote I well yt will ofter than ones / And now am I glad that
ye move yt me here your selfe / 25
A man may many tymes well & without synne, desier of god the
tribulacion to be taken from hym / but neyther may we desier ⌐that⌐
in euery case / nor yet very well in no [f. 14ᵛ] case (except very few)
but vnder a certeyne condicion eyther expressid or implied / for trybulacions are / ye wot well / of many sundrye kyndes / some by losse 30

---

of goodes or possessions, & some by the siknes of oure selfe / & some
by the losse of frendes / or by some other payne put vnto our bodies /
some by the drede of the losyng of those thynges that we fayne wold
save / vnder which feare fall all the same thynges that we haue spoken
5 before / For we may feare losse of goodes or possessions / or the losse
of our frendes / their grefe and trouble / or our own / by siknes
imprisonment or other bodely payne / we may be troubled with the
drede of deth / and many a good man ys troublid most of all with the
feare of that thyng / which he that most nede hath, fearith lest of all /
10 that is to wit / the feare of lesyng thorow dedly synne the life of his
silly sowle / And this last kynd of trybulacion / ys the sorest tribulacion of all / though we towch here & there some pieces therof before /
yet the chiefe part and pryncipall poynt will I reserue to treate a part
effectually that matter in the last end / [f. 15]
15   But now as I said, where the kyndes of tribulacions are so divers /
some of these tribulacions a man may pray god to take from hym /
and take some comfort in the trust that god will so do / And therfor
agaynst hunger siknes & bodely hurt, and agaynst the losse of eyther
body or sowle / men may laufully many tymes pray to the goodnes
20 of god eyther for them selfe or for their frend / And toward this
purpose / are expressly prayed many devout orisons in the comen seruice of our mother holy church / And toward ᴦourᴧ help in some of
these thynges / serve some of the peticions in the pater noster / wherin
we pray for our daily foode, & to be preseruid from the fall in temp-
25 tacion and to be deliuerid from evill.
    But yet may we not alway pray for the takyng away from vs of euery
kynd of temptacion / For yf a man shuld in euery sicknes / pray for his
helth agayne / whan shuld he shew hym self content to die & depart
vnto god. And that mynd a man must haue (ye wot well) or els yt
30 will not be well /
    One tribulacion is it vnto good men, to fele in them selfe the

1 &] om. Z; oure] one A: re wr. over e B, our Z   3 the losyng of] the om. L 1573, of
om. Z; those] these 1557   4 spoken] spoken of L   10 lesyng] loosyng L, losinge 1553
1557 1573   11 silly] sely Z; ys] as Z   13 and] & the Z   15 tribulacions are]
tribulacion are Z   16 these tribulacions a man] this tribulacion. A man 1553; to] om.
1553 1557 1573   20 or for] for om. Z   21 prayed] prayers A: s canc. and d wr. over
r B   22 our] one A: canc. and our interl. B   24 pray] praye daylye 1553 1557 1573
28 hym self] hym sell A; & depart] and to depart Z   29 a man must] must a man Z;
ye] yow L   31 vnto] to Z

conflyte of the flessh agaynst the sowle / the rebellion of sensualitie
agaynst the rule & gouernaunce of reson [f. 15ᵛ] the reliques that
remayne in mankynd of our old original syn of which saynt paule
so sore compleynyth in his epistle to the Romaynes / And yet may we
not pray while we stand in this lyfe to haue this kynd of tribulacion 5
vtterly ⌜taken⌝ from vs / For yt is lefte vs by godes ordynaunce to
strive agaynst yt & fight with all / & by reason & grace to master
yt / and vse it for the matter of our meryte /

   For the salvacion of our sowle may we boldly pray. For grace may
we boldly pray / for fayth / for hope / and for charitie / & for euery such 10
vertew as shall serue vs to hevyn ward / But as for all other thynges
before remembryd in which is conteynid the matter of euery kynd of
tribulacion, we may neuer well make prayer so presisely, but that we
must expresse / or imply a condicion therin / that is to wit / that yf
god se the contrary better for vs, we referre it whole to his will / and in 15
stede of our grefe taken away / pray that god of his goodnes may send
vs eyther spirituall cumfort to take yt gladly, or strength at the lest
way to take yt pacyently. For yf we detcrmyn with our selfe / that
we will take no cumfort in no thyng but in the takyng of our tribulacion [f. 16] from vs / then eyther prescribe we to god that we will 20
he shall no better tourne do vs though he wold, than we will our selfe
apoynt hym / or els do we declare that what thyng ys best for vs / our
selfe can better tell than he.

   And therfor / I say / let vs in tribulacion desier this help & cumfort,
& let vs remit the maner of that cumfort vnto his own high pleasure / 25
which whan we do: let vs nothyng dowt / but that like as his high
wisedome better seeth what is best for vs than we can see our selfe /
so shall his souerayne goodnes give vs the thyng ⌜that⌝ shall in dede
be best / for els yf we will presume to stand vnto our own choyse /
except it so be that god offer vs the choyse hymself / as he did to 30
David in the choyse of his own punyshment after his high pride

---

1 conflyte] conflicte Z   3 our] om. Z   7 strive] strue A: iv wr. over u B   9 pray.]
period ed.   12 before] before / A: / canc. B   13 prayer] prayers 1553 1557 1573, owr
prayour L   14 expresse /] / canc. B; imply] imploy 1553 1557   16 taken] takyng Z
16–17 may send vs] canc. and interl. after god B, god maie send vs of his goodnes Z   17 the]
om. 1573   18 way] canc. and wise interl. B, waies 1553, wyse L 1573, wsie 1557 (mispr.);
take] beare Z   24 this] canc. and his interl. B, his Z; help & cumfort] comforte and
helpe L 1553 1573   25 remit] submytt L   26 like] like / A   28 his] his high 1557
1573; the thyng] that thing 1573   29 for] f alt. to F B; vnto] to Z   30 hymself]
hymsell A

concevid in the nombryng of his people / we may folyshly chose the
worse / and by the prescribyng vnto god our selfe so presisely what
we will that he shall do for vs / except that of his gracious favour he
reiect our foly / he shall for indignacion graunt vs our own request /
5 and after shall we well fynd that it shall tourne vs to harm. How
many men atteyne helth of bodye / that were better for their sowle
helth, their body were sike styll / [f. 16ᵛ]

How many men get owt of prison / that hap on such harms abrode /
as the prison shuld haue kept them from. How many haue there
10 bene loth to lese their worldly goodes, haue in kepyng of them sone
after lost their life. So blynd ys our mortalitie, & so vnware what will
fall / so vnsure also what maner mynd we will our selfe haue to morow /
that god could not lightly do man a more vengaunce / than in this
world to graunt hym his own folysh wishes /

15   What wit haue we pore foles to wit what will serue vs / whan the
blessid apostell hym selfe in his sore tribulacion praying thrise vnto
god to take yt away from hym / was answerid agayne by god in a
maner that he was but a fole in askyng that request / but that the
help of godes grace in that tribulacion to strength hym, was ferr
20 better for hym than to take the tribulacion from hym. And therfor
by experience perceivyng well the trouth of that lesson, he givith
vs good warnyng not to be to bold of our own mynd when we
requier ought of god, nor to be precise in our askyng, but refer the
choise [f. 17] to god at his own pleasure / For his own holy sprite so
25 sore desierith our weale / that as man might say, he groneth for vs
in such wise as no tong can tell. *Nos autem* / sayth saynt paule / *quid
oremus* / *vt oportet nescimus, sed ipse spiritus postulat pro nobis gemitibus
inenarrabilibus* / what may we pray that were behoueable for vs, can
not our selfe tell / but the sprite hym self desiereth for vs with vnspeak-
30 able groninges.

And therfor I say for conclucion of this poynt, let vs neuer aske of

---

2 worse] worste *1553 1557 1573*   6 sowle] soules *Z*   7 body] bodies *Z*; sike] e *canc. B*
8 men] *canc. B, om. Z*; harms] harme *Z*   9 from.] fro *1557 1573, period ed.*; many haue
there] there *canc. B, om. Z*, that *interl. after* many B, many that *Z*   10 them] yr *wr.
over* m *and* goodes *interl. before* sone B, theyr goods *Z*   11 their] their / A: / *canc. B*
12 maner] manour *of L*; will] shall *L*; our selfe] *om. L 1553 1573*   20 hym.] *period ed.*
22 own] *om. 1557*; mynd] mindes *Z*   23 nor] not *L 1553*; askyng] askinges *L 1553 1573*
25 man] *canc. and* men *interl.* B, men *Z*   26 tell.] *period ed.*   28 what may we pray]
we *interl. before* what, may *and* pray *canc. and* may pray for *interl. after* we B, We what we
maye praye for *Z*   29–30 vnspeakable] vnspeable *A*

god precisely our own ease by deliuere from our tribulacion / but pray
for his ayd and cumfort by which wayes hymselfe shall best like /
And than may we take comfort evyn of our such request / for both
are we sure that this mynd cometh of god / & also be we very sure
that as he begynneth to work with vs / so / but ýf our selfe flyt from 5
hym, he will not fayle to tarye with vs / And than he dwellyng with
vs, what trouble can do vs harm / *Si* ⌈*deus*⌉ *nobiscum quis contra nos* /
yf god be with vs / sayth saynt paule / who can stand agaynst vs /
[f. 17ᵛ]

A grete comfort it may be in tribulacion,   10
that euery tribulacion ys (yf we will our
selfe) a thyng eyther medicinable, or
els more than medicinable /

The vij chapiter

Vincent   15

You haue good vncle well openid & declarid the question that
I demaunded you / that is to wit / what maner comfort a man might
pray for in tribulacion / And now procede forth good vncle / & shew
vs yet ferther some other spirituall comfort in tribulacion.

Antonye   20

This may be thynkith me good Cosyn great comfort in tribulacion / that euery tribulacion which any tyme falleth vnto vs / ys eyther
sent to be medicinable yf men will so take yt / or may become
medicynable yf men will so make it / or is better than medicynable
but yf we will forsake yt.   25

Vincent

Surely this is very comfortable yf we may well perceyve yt /

---

1 deliuere] delyuerye *1557*, deliuering us *L 1553 1573*   3 evyn] *om. L 1553*; of our]
of our own *L 1553*   4 are] *canc. and* be *interl.* B, be Ƶ   5 so /] / *canc.* B   6 hym]
hym fyrst *L*   7 deus] dominus *A: canc. and* deus *interl.* B; nobiscum] pro nobis *1573*
8 paule /] paule) *A:* / ed.   10 it] om. *1553*   11–12 will our selfe] our selfe wyl Ƶ
13 *extra* the *canc. after* medicinable / *A*   14 vij] vij^th *L*   17 maner] maner of *L 1553*
1573   22 which] whych at *L*

Anthony

These thre thynges that I tell you we shall consider thus / euery
tribulacion that we fall in / cometh eyther by our own knowen deseruyng dede bryngyng vs therunto, [f. 18] as the siknes that foloweth
5 our intemperat surfet / or the prisonment or other punyshment put
apon a man for his heynouse cryme / or els yt is sent vs by god without any certeyne deservyng cause open & knowen vnto our selfe, eyther
for punyshment of some synnes passid, we certenly know not for which /
or for preseruyng vs from some synnes in which we were els lyke to
10 fall / or fynally for no respect of the mans synne at all, but for the profit
of his pacience & encrease of his merite / In all the former causes,
tribulacion ys (yf we will) medicinable / in this latter case of all, it
is yet better then medicinable /

The declaracion larger concernyng them
15   that fall in trybulacion by their own well
knowen fawt, & that yet such tribulacion
ys medicinable

The viij Chapiter

Vincent

20   This semeth me very good / good vncle / savyng that it semeth somwhat brefe & short / and therby me thynketh sumwhat obscure and
darke.

Antony

We shall therfor to give it light withall, towch euery member
25 somwhat more at large /
One member is / ye wot well, of them that fall in tribulacion,
[f. 18ᵛ] through their own certeyne well deserving dede open and

---

6 yt is] is it Z   8 passid, we certenly] passid *comes at end of line without punct.* A, passed,
certaynly we L, passed. Certainly we *1553 1557*, passed (certainly we *1573*   9 preser-
uyng] v *wr. over* u B; from some synnes] from synne *1557*   10 profit] *canc. and* profe
interl. B, profe Z   11 causes] cases Z   12 we] he *1553 1573*, ye *1557*; will)] *parenth. added*
B; latter] last *interl.* B *above* latter (*uncanc.*), last Z   13 yet] *om.* Z   15 well] *om.* L
1553 1573   18 viij] viijᵗʰ L   21 sumwhat] h *interl.* A   26 ye] you Z

knowen to them selfe / as where we fall in a siknes / folowyng vppon
our own gloutonouse festyng / or a man that is punysshid for his own
open fawt /

These tribulacions lo & such other like / albeit that they may seme
discomfortable, in that a man may be sory to thynke hym selfe the 5
cause of his own harm / yet hath he good cause of comfort in them /
yf he consider / that he may make them medicinable for hym self /
yf hym selfe will /

For where as ther was dew to that synne (except it were purgyd
here) a farre greter punyshment after this world in an other place / 10
this worldly tribulacion of payne and punyshment by godes good provision for hym / put vppon hym ⌐here⌐ in this world before, shall
by the meane of christes passion (yf the man will in trew fayth &
good hope by meke & pacient sufferaunce of his tribulacion so make
yt) serue hym for a suer medicyn to cure hym & clerely discharge hym, 15
of all his siknes & desease of those paynes, that els he shuld suffer
after / for [f. 19] such is the ⌐gret⌐ goodnes of ⌐almighty⌐ god that
he punyshith not one thyng twyse / And albeit so that this punyshment is put vnto the man, not of his own eleccion & fre choyse / but
so by force as he wold fayne avoyd ⌐it⌐ / & fallith in yt agaynst his 20
will / & therfor semeth worthy no thanke / yet so far passeth the grete
goodnes of god, the pore vnperfit goodnes of man / that though men
make their rekenyng one here with an other such / god yet of his
bowntie in mans accompt toward hym ⌐allowyth⌐ it farr otherwise.
For though that a man fall in his payne by his own faute / and also 25
first agaynst his will / yet as sone as he confessith his fawte / &
applyeth his will to be content to suffer that payne and punyshment
for the same / and waxith sory, not for that onely that he shall
susteyne such punyshment / but for that also that he hath offendid
god / & therby deseruid much more / our lord from that tyme 30
comptith it not for payne taken agaynst his will / but yt shalbe a mervelouse good medisyn & worke as a willingly [f. 19ᵛ] taken payne /
the purgacion & clensyng of his sowle with gracyouse remission of

1 to] vnto Z   7 for hym self] self om. L 1553   8 yf hym selfe] if he himself 1557 1573
13 (yf] / yf A: parenth. wr. over / B   14 by] Z, be A   15 yt)] parenth. added B   16 his]
the Z   17 for] f alt. to F B   18 punyshith] i ins. B   21 semeth] scantly L 1553
22 of god] of almighti god 1557   23 his] his high Z   24 allowyth] although A: canc.
and allowyth interl. B; farr] for 1553   25 For] for A: f alt. to F B; that] om. L 1553, that
otherwise 1557 1573   31 comptith] counteth 1553 1557 1573

his synne / & of the far greater payne that els had bene preparid therfor peradventure for euer in hell /

For many there are vndoutydly, that wold els dryve furth & die in their dedly synne / which yet in such tribulacion fealyng their own
5 frayeltie so effectually / and the false flateryng world faylyng them so fully / turn goodly to god & call for mercye / & by grace make vertew of necessitie / & make a medisyn of ther maladye, takyng their trowble mekely & make a right godly end //

Consider well the story of Acam that committid sacrilege at the
10 great Citie of hierico / wheruppon god toke a great vengeaunce vppon the children of Israell, and after told them the cause, & bode them go seke the fawte & try yt owt by lottes / when the lot fell vppon the very man that did yt, being tried by the fallyng first vppon his trybe / & than vppon his famylie, & than vppon his howse, and fynally vppon
15 his person: he might well see [f. 20] that he was deprehendid & taken agaynst his will. But yet at the good exortacion of Iosue saying vnto hym / *fili mi da gloriam deo Israell, & confiteri & indica mihi quid feceris, & ne abscondas* / Myn own sonne give glory to the god of Israell & confesse & shew me what thow hast done & hyde it not / he confessid
20 humbly the thefte, & mekely toke his deth therfor, and had I dowt not both strenghth and comfort in his payne, & died a very good man / which yf he had neuer commen in the tribulacion, had bene in perell neuer happely to haue had iust remorse therof in all his whole lyfe / but might haue died wrechidly & gon to the divell
25 eternally / And thus made this thefe a good medicyn of his well deseruid payne and tribulacion / Consider the well convertid thefe that heng on christes right hand / did not he bi his meke suffraunce & humble knolege of his fawte, askyng forgivenes of god, & yet content to suffer for his sinne, make of his iust punyshment & well deseruid tribula-
30 cion, a very good speciall medisyn, to cure hym of all the payne in the tother world, & wyn [f. 20ᵛ] hym eternall salvacion / And thus I say that this kynd of tribulacion though yt seme the most base and

---

2 for euer in hell /] *period before* / B, in hel for euer *1553 1573*   6 goodly] *om.* L
11 bode] bad Z   14 & than vppon his famylie] *om.* L *1553 1573*   17 mi] Z, mei A : e
canc. B?; deo] Domino Deo *1573*; confiteri] confitere Z; & indica] ac indica *1573*   18 &
ne abscondas] & *om. 1573*; god] Lord God *1573*   19 done & hyde] & *om. and comma
substituted 1573*   22 commen] come Z; the] *om.* Z   26 the] *interl.* A; heng] dyd hange
L, honge *1553 1557 1573*   27 christes] es *added* B; bi] y *wr. over* i B   30 all the]
the *om.* Z   31 the tother] thother *1553 1557*, th'other *1573*

the lest cumfortable / is yet (yf the man will so make it) a very mervelouse holsome medisyn, and may therfor be to the man that will so
consider it, a great cause of cumfort & spirituall consolacion.

The second poynt that ys to wit, that
tribulacion that ys sent vs by god without   5
any open deseruing cause knowen vnto
our selfe / And that this kynd of tribulacion /
is medicinable yf men will so take it &
therfor great occasion of Comfort /

The ix chapter   10

Vyncent

Verely myn vncle this first kynd of tribulacion haue you to my
mynd openid sufficiently / & therfor I pray you resort now to the
second /

Antonye   15

The second kynd was ye wot well, of such tribulacion as is so sent
vs by god, that we know no certeyne cause deservyng that present
trowble / as we certenly know that vppon such a surfet, we fell in such
a siknes / or as the thefe knowith, that for such a certeyne thefte he
is fallen into such a certeyne punyshment. [f. 21]   20

But yet sith we seldome lacke fautes agaynst god worthy & well
deseruyng great punyshment in dede / we may well thynke / & wisedome is so to do, that with synne we haue deservid yt / and that god
for some synne sendith it, though we certenly know not our selfe for
which. And therfor as yet thus farforth is this kynd of tribulacion 25
somwhat in effect in comfort to be taken like vnto the other / for this
as ye see yf we will thus take it well / rekenyng it to be sent for our
synne & suffryng it paciently therfor / is medicinable against the

---

4–5 that tribulacion] of that tribulation *1573*   6 open] open certaine Z; vnto] to Z
7 that] *om. L 1553*   10 ix] ix^th L 16 ye] you Z 19 siknes /] / *wr. over comma* B
22 punyshment in dede /] punyshmentes in dede, *L*, punishment: in dede *1553 1557 1573*
22–23 wisedome is] wisdom it is Z 26 other] tother L 27 ye] you Z; thus] *canc. and*
interl. before will *B*, thus wil Z; it well /] it, wel Z; our] *om.* Z 28 paciently] mekely
Z; is medicinable] imedicinable *1553*

payne in the tother world to come / for our synnes in this world passid,
which is as I shewed you a cause of right greate comfort /

But yet may than this kynd of tribulacion be to some men of more
sobre lyvyng, & therby of the more clere conscience / sumwhat a
5 litell more cumfortable / for though they may none otherwise reken
them selfes then synners / for as saynt paule sayth / *Nullius mihi
conscius sum | sed non in hoc iustificatus sum* / My conscience grugeth me
not of any thyng / but yet am I not therby iustified / & saynt Iohn
saith / *Si dixerimus quia peccatum non habemus, ipsi nos seducimus, &*
10 *veritas in nobis non est* / yf we say ⌈that⌉ we haue no synne in vs, we
begil [f. 21ᵛ] our selfes & trouth is there not in vs / yet for asmuch as
the cause is to them not ⌈so⌉ certeyne as it is to the other afore remembrid in the first kynd / and that it is also certeyne, that god some tyme
sendith tribulacion for kepyng & preservyng a man fro such synne as
15 he shuld els fall in, and some tyme also for exercise of their pacience
& encrease of merite: greate cause of encrease in comfort have these
folke of the clerer conscience in the fervour of thir tribulacion, in
that they may take the comfort of a double medicyn, & of a thyng
also that is of the kynd, which we shall ⌈fynally⌉ speke of, that I call
20 better than medicinable / But as I haue before spoken of this kynd of
tribulacion, how it is medicynable in that it cureth the synne passid,
and purchaseth remiscion of the payne dew therfor / so let vs somwhat consider how this tribulacion sent vs by god, is medicinable, in
that it preserueth vs fro the synne into which we were els like to
25 fall /

Iff that thyng be a good medicyn, that restorith vs our helth when
we lese yt / a good medicyn must this nedes be, that preserueth our
helth while we haue it, & suffreth vs not to fall in to that paynfull
siknes that must after drive [f. 22] vs to a paynfull plaster.

30 Now seeth god some tyme, that worldly welth is with one that is
yet good comyng vppon hym to fast / that forseyng how much weight

---

1 tother] other *1553 1557 1573*   6 selfes] selvys *L*, self *1553 1557 1573*; Nullius] Nihil
1573   8 &] And as *Z*   11 begil] *final* e *added B*; selfes] self *Z*   12 other] tother *L*
14 fro] from *Z*   16 these] those *Z*   18 may take] make *L 1553*; a double] a *om. 1573*
18–19 a thyng also] *om. L 1553 1573*, that thing also *1557*   19 is of] of *om. L 1553*
1573; fynally] spirituall *A: canc. and* fynally *interl. B*   24 fro] from *1553 1557 1573*;
synne] sinnes *Z*   27 a good] a *canc. and* as *interl. B*, a *interl. after* good *B*, as good a *Z*;
that] tha *A*: t *added B*   28 to that] to the *1553 1573*   30 seeth] sith *A*: ee *wr. over*
i *B*   31 to] so *interl. B above* to (*uncanc.*), so *Z*

of worldly welth the man may bere / & how much will ouer charge
hym / & enhaunce his hart vp so high that grace shuld fall from hym
low / god of his goodnes I say preventith his fall and sendith hym
tribulacion be tyme while he is yet good, to garr hym to kenne his
maker, & by lesse lykyng the false flateryng world set a crosse vppon 5
the shypp of his hart, & bere a low saile theron, that the boysteouse
blast of pride blow hym not vnder the water.

Some yong lovely lady lo that is yet good inough, god seeth a storm
comyng toward her / that wold (yf her ⌐helth & her⌐ fat fedyng shuld
a litell lenger lest) strik her into some lecherouse love / and in stede 10
of her old acquentyd knyght / lay her a bed with a new acquentid
knave / But god lovyng her more tenderly / than to suffer her fall
into such shamfull [f. 22ᵛ] bestly synne, sendith her in season a goodly
fair fervent fever, that maketh her bones to ratle, & wastith away
her wanton flesh, & bewtifyeth her faire fell with the colour of the 15
kites claw / & makith her loke so lovely, that her lovier wold haue
litell lust to loke vppon her / and maketh her also so lustyc, that yf her
lovyer lay in her lapp, she shuld so sore long to breke vnto hym the
very botom of her stomak, that she shuld not be able to refrayne it
from hym, but sodenly lay it all in his nek. 20

Did not as I before shewid you, the blessid apostel hym selfe
confesse / that the high revelacions that god had given hym, might
haue enhaunced hym into so high pride, that he might haue caught
a fowle fall, had not the provedent goodnes of god providid for his
remedy / And what was his remedie / but a paynfull tribulacion, 25
so sore that he was fayne to call thrisse to god to take the tribulacion
from hym. And yet wold god not graunt his request / but let hym
lye so long therin / till hym selfe that saw more [f. 23] in saynt paule,
than saynt paule saw ⌐in⌐ hym selfe, wist well the tyme was come
in which he might well without his harm take it from hym. 30

And thus ye see good Cosyn, that tribulacion is dowble medicyn /

2–3 hym low /] him. Loe, *1553*   4 be] y *wr. over* e *B*; to kenne] to *om.* ⟨Z⟩   6 shypp]
shepes *A*: ypp *wr. over* epe *and final* s *canc. B*; boysteouse] boystuouse *L*, boisterous *1553*
1557 1573   9 comyng] come ⟨Z⟩   10 lest] last ⟨Z⟩   14 fervent] v *wr. over* u? *B*
15 bewtifyeth] *apparently A first wrote* bewtie, *then wrote* f *over* e, fy *clar. B*; of the] of a ⟨Z⟩
16 lovier] *canc. and* lover *interl. B*, louer ⟨Z⟩   17 to loke] *om. 1553*; maketh] make ⟨Z⟩
18 lovyer] *canc. and* lover *interl. B*, louer ⟨Z⟩   23 so] such *L 1553 1573*   24 provedent]
y *wr. over first* e *B*   25 remedy /] *question-mark added before* | *B*   26 to call thrisse]
thrisse *canc. and* thryse *interl. before* to call *B*, thrise to cal ⟨Z⟩   27 god not] not god ⟨Z⟩
31 ye] you ⟨Z⟩

both a cure for the synne passid, & a preseruative fro the synne that
is to come / And therfor in this kynd of tribulacion, is there good
occasion of ⌈a⌉ dowble comfort / but that is I say / diuersly to sondry
diuers folke, as their own conscience is with synne combrid or
5 clere.

How beit I will advise no man to be so bold, as to think that their
tribulacion ys sent them to kepe them fro the pride of their holynes /
let men leve that kynd of comfort hardely to saynt paule, tyll theyre
lyvyng be like / but of the remnent may men well take grete comfort
10 and good biside.

Of the third kynd of tribulacion, which is not sent a man for his synne / but for exersice of his pacience & encrease of his merite / which is better then medicynable /

15   The / x / chapiter

Vyncent

The third kynd vncle that remaynith now behynd, [f. 23ᵛ] that is
to wit / which is sent a man by god, & not for his synne neyther
committid nor which wold els come / and therfor is not medicynable
20 ⌈but sent for exercise of our pacyens & encrese of our meryte, &
therfore better than medicinable⌉ though it be as you say (and as
in dede it is) better for the man than any of the tother ⌈ij⌉ kyndes in
a nother world where the reward shalbe receivid / yet can I not see
by what reson a man may in this world, where the tribulacion is
25 suffrid, take any more comfort therin, then in any of the tother twayne
that are sent a man for his syn / sith he can not ⌈here⌉ know, whether
yt be sent hym for synnes before commyttid or sinne that els shuld
fall, or for increase of merite & reward after to come ⌈namely⌉ sith

---

1 for] of Ƶ; fro] from L   3 a] om. 1553   4 folke] folkes Ƶ; conscience] conciece A
7 fro] from L   15 x] xᵗʰ L   17 remaynith now] nowe remayneth L   18 sent] sent
to L 1553   19 which] wᵗʰ A : ch wr. over th, then word canc. and which interl. B   22 is)]
is / A : parenth. wr. over / B; tother] other Ƶ   23 the] their 1553   25 tother] other
1553 1557 1573   26 here] he A : re added B, then word canc. and here interl. B   27 synnes]
sin Ƶ

euery man hath cause inough to feare & to thynke, that his synne
al redy passid hath deservid yt, and that it is not without perell a man
to thynk otherwise.

Antony

This that ye saie cosyn, hath place of trouth in farr the most part 5
of men / and therfor must they not envye nor disdayne (sith they
maie take in their tribulacion consolacion for their part sufficient)
that some other that more be worthye, take yet a gre dele mo. [f. 24]
For as I told you cosyn, though the best man must confesse hym selfe
a sinner / yet be their many men (though to the multitude few) that 10
for the kynd of their lyvyng, and therby the clerenes of their conscience, may well and without synne, haue a good hope that god sendith them some greate grefe, for exercyse of their pacience & for
cncrease of their merit / as it apperith not ⌐onely⌐ by saynt paule in
the place before remembrid / but also by that holy man Iob / which 15
in sondry places of his dispicions with his burdenouse comfortours /
lettid not to say, that the clerenes of his own conscience declarid &
shewid vnto hym selfe, that he deservid not the sore tribulacion that
he than had / How be it (as I tollid you before) I will not advise euery
man at adventure to be bold vppon this maner of cumfort. But yet 20
some men know I such / as I durst for their ⌐more⌐ ease & comfort
in their great & grevouse payne, put them in right good hope, that
god sendith it vnto them, not so much for their punyshment as for
exercise of their pacience / And some tribulacions are there also,
that [f. 24ᵛ] grow vppon such causes / that in thes cases I wold neuer 25
let, but alway ⌐wolde⌐ without any dowt give that councell and
comfort to any man.

Vincent

What causes good vncle be those?

---

1 & to] to *om.* Ƶ   5 ye] you Ƶ   7 maie] make *A*: k *canc. and* i *interl. B*   8 yet a gre]
y *wr. over illeg.* i *? and a added after* gre *B, then whole phrase cànc. and* yet a grete *interl.* B; mo]
re *added B* (r *may be A*); gre dele mo] great deale more Ƶ   9 For] *catchword f. 23ᵛ, for*
in text; man] *om. 1557*   10 (though] *parenth. ed.,* / though *A*; multitude] number *L 1553*
11 for the] for that *1557*   15 that] the *1553 1557 1573*   16 of his] his *om. L 1553*;
comfortours] s *added B*   18 vnto] to Ƶ; the] that Ƶ   19 tollid] *canc. and* tolde *interl. B*
20 cumfort.] *period ed.*   21 know I] I know *L 1553*   22 payne] paines Ƶ   25 thes]
o *wr. over* e *B*, those Ƶ   29 those?] *question-mark ed.*

Anthonye

Mary Cosyn / where so euer a man falleth in tribulacion for the
mayntenaunce of iustice or for the defence of godes cause / For yf I
shuld hap to fynd a man that had long livid a ⌐very⌐ vertues lyfe /
5 and had at last happenid to fall into the Turkes handes / and there
did abide by the trouth of his fayth, & with the suffryng of all kynde
of Tormentes taken vppon his bodye / still did tech and testifie the
trouth / yf I shuld in his pacion give hym a spirituall cumfort / might
I be bold to tell hym no ferther, but that he shuld take paciens in
10 this payne / and that god sendith it hym for his synne, and that he is
well worthie to haue it all though it were ⌐yet⌐ much more / he might
well answere me & such other cumfortours as Iob answerid [f. 25]
his / *Onerosi consolatores estis vos* / Burdenouse & hevy comfortours be
you. Nay I wold not faile to bid hym boldly (while I shuld se him in
15 his passion) cast synne & hell and purgatorie & all vppon the
devilles pate / and dowt not but like wise as yf he gave ouer his hold
all his merite were lost & he tournid into misery / so yf he stand &
percever still in the confession of his fayth, all his hole payne shall
tourne all into glorye.
20   Yee more shall I yet saye you than this / that if there were a cristen
man that had among those infidelles comittid a very dedly cryme /
such as were worthy deth / not onely by their law but by christes to /
as manslawter advltery / or such other thyng like / yf when he were
taken / he were offrid pardon of his life, vppon condicion that he shuld
25 forsake the fayth of christ / yf this man wold now rather suffer deth
than so do / shuld I comfort hym in his payne but as I wold a
malefactour / Nay this man though he shuld haue died for his sinne /
dieth now for christes sake / while he might live still yf he wold forsake
hym / The bare pacient takyng of his deth, shuld haue seruid for
30 the satisfaccion of his synne / thorow the merite of christes passion / I

---

5 at] at the *L*; happenid] happed *Z*   6 his *canc. A*? *after* all   7 Tormentes] Torm^{tes}
A, canc. and turmentes *interl. B*   8 pacion] ss *wr. over* c *B*; a] *om. Z*   10 this] his *Z*
11 yet] it *A: canc. and* yet *interl. B*, yet *Z*; might] might then *Z*   13 Onerosi
consolatores estis vos] Consolatores onerosi omnes vos estis *1573*   16 devilles] v *wr. over*
illeg. letter and i *ins. B*; wise] *om. Z*   17 into] to *Z*   19 tourne all] all *om. L*   20 Yee]
Yet *A: second* e *wr. over* t *B*; you] *om. Z*   22 / not] (not *A:* / *ed.*; onely by their law]
by their lawes only *Z*   23 manslawter] manslaughter, or *Z*   29 The] the *A*
30 synne /] synne) *A:* / *wr. over parenth. B*; thorow] h *wr. over illeg. letter B*; passion /] /
canc. B

meane, without help of which no payne of our own could be satisfactorye. [f. 25ᵛ] But now shall christ for his forsakyng of his own
life in the honour of his ⌐fayth,¬ forgive the payne of all his sinnes of
his mere liberalytie / and accept all the payne of his deth for merite
of reward in heven / & shall assigne no part therof to the payment 5
of his det in purgatory / but shall take it all as an offryng, & requite
⌐it¬ all with glory. And this man among christen men, all had he bene
⌐before¬ a Divell, nothyng wold I after dowt to take hym for a martire.

Vincent

Verely good vncle me thynketh this is said mervelouse well / and 10
it specially deliteth and comforteth me to here it, because of our
principall feare that I first spake of the Turkes cruell incursion into
this countrey ⌐of ours.¬

Antony

Cosyn as for the matter of that feare, I purpose to touch last of all / 15
nor I ment not here to speke therof / had it not bene that the vehemence of your obieccion brought it ⌐in¬ my way / But rather wold I
els haue put some sample for this place / of such as suffer tribulacion
for mayntenaunce of right & iustice / & that rather chose to take harm
than do wrong in any ⌐maner of¬ matter. For surely yf a man may 20
(as in dede he may) haue grete cumfort in the clerenes of his conscience, that hath [f. 26] a false cryme put vppon hym, & by false
witnes provid vppon hym, & he falsely punyshid & put to worldly
shame & payne therfor / an hundred tymes mor comfort may he haue
in his hart / that where white is callid blak / & right is callid wrong / 25
abidith by the trouth & is persecutid for iustice /

Vincent

Than yf a man sue me wrongfully for my land in which my selfe

---

1–2 satisfactorye.] *period ed.*   3 *comma added after first* his, *then canc. by caret B*   7–8 bene
before a] bene a *A*: before a *wr. over orig.* a *and in margin B*   8 wold I after] after woulde
I *Z*   10 mervelouse] meruelously *L 1553 1573*   13 of ours.] *wr. over | at end of line B*
16–17 that the vehemence] for the vehemencie *1553*, that the vehemency *1557*, for that
the vehemencie *1573*   17 obieccion] abieccion *A*: o *wr. over* a *B*   18 sample] exaumple
Z; tribulacion] tribulacions *L 1553*   19 chose] choose *L*   20 For] for *A*   24
hundred] hundreth *Z*   26 & *interl. before* for *B*   28 for my] for my owne *1553 1557*
1573, for myne owne *L*

haue good right / it is a comfort yet to defend it well sith god shall
give me thanke therfor /

Antonye

Nay ⌜nay⌝ Cosyn nay there walke ye sumwhat wide / for ther you
5 defend your ⌜own⌝ right for your temporall availe / And sith saynt
paule counceilith / *Non vosmet defendentes charissimi* / defend not your
selfes most dere frendes / and our saviour counsailith: ⌜*Si*⌝ *qui vult
tecum in iudicio contendere & tunicam tuam tollere dimitte ei & pallium* /
yf a man will strive with the at law & take away thy cote / leve hym
10 thy gown to / the defence therfor of our right askith no reward / Say
you spede well yf ye get leve / loke hardely for no thanke.

But on the other side / yf ye do as saynt paule biddith, *Querentes
non quae sua sunt sed quae aliorum* / Seke not for your own profit but
for other folkes / but defend therfor of pitie a pore widow, ⌜or⌝ a por
15 fatherles child, & rather [f. 26ᵛ] suffer sorow by some strong extorcion /
than suffer them take wrong / or yf ye be a guge & will haue such
zele to iustice that ye will rather abyde tribulacion by the malice
of some mightie man / than iuge wrong for his favour / such tribulacions lo be those / that are better than onely medicinable / and euery
20 man vppon whom they fall may be bold so to reken them / & in his
depe trouble may well say to hym selfe the wordes that crist hath
taught hym for his comfort / *Beati misericordes* / *quia misericordiam
consequentur* / Blessid be the mercifull men, for they shall haue mercie
given them / *Beati qui persecutionem patiuntur propter iustitiam, quoniam
25 ipsorum est regnum celorum* / Blessid be they that suffer persecution for
iustice / for theirs ys the kyngdome of hevyn. Here ys an high comfort
lo, for them that are in the case. And in this case their own conscience
can shew it them, & so may fulfill their hartes with spirituall ioy, that

---

4 Nay nay] *second* nay *may be interl.* A; ye] you Z   6 vosmet] vosmetipsos *1573*;
charissimi] Z, charisimi A   7 selfes] selfe my *1553 1557 1573*, owne self my L; Si] *interl.*
B *above* Ei A *(uncanc.)*; qui] quis *1557 1573*   8 in] *om.* Z; dimitte] demitte *1557*   9 at]
at the Z   10 our] *wr. twice* A, *second* our *canc.* B, our owne Z   11 ye] you Z
12 other] tother L; ye] you Z; biddith,] *comma ed.*; Querentes] *om. 1573*   13 non quae]
1573, non que L *1553 1557*, non quia A; sunt] sunt singuli considerantes *1573*; sed quae]
quia A: *canc. and* quae *interlin.* B, sed que L *1553 1557*, sed ea quae *1573*   14 but defend]
and defend *1573*; por] *final* e *added* B   15 extorcion] er *added* B, extorcyoner Z   16 ye]
you Z; guge] *canc. and* Iudge *interl.* B   17 ye] you Z   22 quia] quoniam L *1553*
1557, quoniam ipsi *1573*; misericordiam] misercordiam A   24 persecutionem] per-
sequntionem L   26 hevyn.] *period ed.*   27 the case] that case *1573*   28 ey? *canc.*
A *before* ioy

the pleasure may far surmounte the hevines & the grefe of all their
temporall trowble. But godes nerer cause of faith agaynst the Turkes,
hath yet a farr passyng comfort, & by many digrees farre excellith
this / which as I haue said I purpose to treat last / & for this tyme
this suffiseth concernyng the speciall comfort that men may take in 5
the third kynd of tribulacion. [f. 27]

A nother kynd of comfort yet in the base
kynd of tribulacion sent for our synne /

The xj Chapiter

Vincent 10

Of trowth good vncle, albeit that euery of these kyndes of tribulacion haue cause of comfort in them as ye haue well declarid / yf men
will so consider them / yet hath this third kynd above all a speciall
prerogative therin.

Antonye 15

That ys vndowtidly trew / But yet is there not good Cosyn the most
base kynd of them all, but that ⌐yet⌐ hath mo causes of comfort than
I haue spoken of yet / for I haue ye wot well in that kynd that is sent
vs for our synne / spoken of no nother comfort yet, but twayne / that
is to wit / one that it refraynith vs from the synne that els we wold 20
fall in / & in that seruoth vs thorow the merite of cristes passion, as
a meane by which god kepeth vs from hell, & serueth for the satisfaccion of such payne as els we shuld endure in purgatorye. [f. 27ᵛ]

Howbeit there is therin a nother greate cause of ioy besides this /
for surely these paynes sent vs here for our synnes, in what so euer 25
wise they hap vnto vs / be our own synne neuer so sore / nor neuer
so open & evident vnto our self & all the world to / yet yf we pray

3 hath] haue *1553*; & by] that by Z   6 the] this Z   7 caret wr. in margin above comfort
9 xj] xjᵗʰ L   11–12 tribulacion] tribulacions Z   12 ye] you Z; men] A's abbrev. canc. and
men interl. B   16 yet] orig. yit: e wr. over i A   17 base] e added B?; yet] it Z   18 ye]
you Z   19 no nother] none other Z   20 from the] the om. *1557 1573*   24 besides]
besyde L   25 these] those Z; sent vs here] here canc. and interl. before sent B, here sent
vs Z; synnes] synne *1557 1573*   26 hap] happen Z; own] om. Z

for grace to take it mekely & paciently / & confessyng to god that it
is ⌐farre˥ ouer litle for our fawte / besech hym yet neuertheles that
sith we shall come hens so void of all good workes wherof we shuld
haue any reward in hevyn, to be not onely so mercifull vnto vs as to
5 take that our present tribulacion in release of our payn in purgatory /
but also so gracyouse vnto vs as to take our pacience therin for a mater
of merite & reward in heven / I verely trust & nothyng dowt it, but
god shall of his high bowntie, graunt vs our bone / For likewise as
in hell payne serveth onely for punyshment without any maner of
10 purgyng, because all possibilitie of purgyng is past / ⌐& in purgatory
punyshment servith for onely purgyng, because the place of deservyng
is passyd:˥ so while we be yet in this world in which is our place &
our time of merite & well deservyng / the tribulacion that is [f. 28]
sent vs here for our sinne shall yf we faythfully so desire, beside the
15 clensyng & purgyng of our payne, serve vs also for encrease of
rewarde /

And so shall I suppose and trust in godes goodnes, all such penaunce
& good workes as a man willyngly performeth enioynid by his gostly
father in confession / or which he willingly ferther do of his own
20 devocion beside / for though mans penaunce with all the good workes
that he can do / be not hable to satisfie of them selfe ⌐for˥ the lest
synne that we do / yet the liberall goodnes of god thorow the merite
of christes bitter passion (without which all our workes could neyther
satisfie nor deserue / nor yet do not in dede neyther merite nor satisfie
25 so much as a sponefull to a great vessell full, in comparison of the
merite and satisfaccion that christ hath meritid & satisfied for vs hym
selfe) this liberall goodnes of god I say / shall yet at our faithfull
instaunce & request, cause our penaunce & tribulacion paciently
taken in this world, to serue vs in the tother world both for relese
30 & reward tempered after such rate, as his high goodnes & wisedome
shall se convenyently for vs / wherof our blynd mortalitie can [f. 28ᵛ]
not here imagine nor devise the stynt / And thus hath yet evyn the

1 it] *interl. A*   2 is] *canc. and is farre interl. B*; ouer] ouer to *1557 1573*   4 vnto vs]
to vs *1553 1557 1573*   5 release] relief *interl. B above* release *A (uncanc.),* reliefe *Ƶ*; payn]
paynes *Ƶ*   9 serveth onely] onely serueth *1557*   12 so while] *canc. after* past *and interl.*
after passyd *B*   14 here for our sinne] here *canc. and* here, *interl. after* sinne *B,* for oure
sinne here *Ƶ*   19 do] th *added B, then erased, then word canc. and* doth *interl. B,* doth *Ƶ*
21 hable] h *canc. B,* able *Ƶ*   27 selfe)] selfe / *A*   29 tother] other *1553 1557 1573*
31 convenyently] ly *canc. B,* convenient *L 1557 1573*   32 extra the *canc. B after* devise;
yet evyn] evyn yet *L*

Howbeit there is therin a nother great cause of ioy
beside this / for surely these paynes (here) sent vs for
our synnes, in what so euer wise they say vnto vs / be I
euer synne neu so sore / nor neu so oppen ... euident vnto
my self & all the world to / yet yf we the for geue
take it mekely & pacuently & confessyng to god
that (it is farre) on litle for our fautes / besides them yet may we
lo that syth we shall come hens so voide of all good
worke, wherof we shuld haue any reward in
heuyn, to be not onely so mersifull vnto vs as to
take that & these tribulacion in release of our payny
in purgatory / but also so gracyous vnto vs as to
take & pacience therin for a mater of merite &
reward in heuy / I surely trust & nothyng dout
it, but god shall of his hygh bountie, graunt vs
to do / for likewise is it in that payne swete
onely, for puny shent without any mau of ... (purgyng)
(C in purgatory punyshent that for onles purgyng, because the place of)
(deseruyng is passid: so wicked)
because all possibilitie of purgyng is past ... ...
we be yet in this world in which is our place & our time
of merite & well deseruyng / the tribulacion that is
                                                                    sent vs here

first kynd of tribulacion & the most base, though not fully so grete
as the second, & very far lesse then the third / far greter cause of
comfort yet than I spake of before.

A certeyne obieccion agaynst the thynges
aforesaid /
5
The xij chapiter

Vincent

Verely good vncle this liketh me very well / but yet is there ye wot
well some of thes thynges now brought in question / for as for any
payne dew for our synnes to be minished in purgatory by the pacient 10
sufferaunce of our tribulacion here / ther ar ye wot well / many that
vtterly deny that / & affirm for a suer trowth, that ther is no purgatory
at all / and than is (yf they say trew) the cause of that comfort gone /
yf the comfort that we shall take, be but in vayne & nede not / They
say ye wot well also, that men merite nothyng at all / but god giveth 15
all for fayth alone / & that it were sinne & sacrilege to loke for any
reward in hevyn, yether for our pacient & glad suffryng for goddes
sake / or for any other good dede / and than is there gone yf this be
thus, the tother cause of our ferther comfort to. [f. 29]

Anthony
20

Cosyn / yf some thynges were as they be not, than shuld some
thynges be as they shall not / I can not in dede say nay but that some
men of late haue brought vp some such opynyon / & many mo than
these beside, & haue spred them abrode / And albeit that it is a right
hevy thyng to se such variaunce in our beleve rise & grow among our 25
self / to the grete encouragyng of the comen enymies of vs all / wherby

6 xij] xij^th L   8 very] v wr. over u B; ye] yow L   10 synnes] sinne Z; by] orig. bi: i
alt. to y B?   11 ye] yow L   13 trew)] parenth. ed., comma B   14 shall] shoulde Z;
but] om. L 1553 1573   15 ye] yow L   16 any] om. Z   17 yether] y canc. B; pacient]
pacience Z   19 tother] other Z   23 of late haue] haue canc. and interl. before of B,
haue of late Z; opynyon] final s added B, opinions Z   23–24 than these] interl. A, than
those L   24 beside] besydes Z; it] om. 1557   25 variaunce] final s added B, varyaunces
Z; fayth canc. A and B before beleve; beleve] beliefe Z   26 self] selvys L

they haue our fayth in dirision & cach hope to ouerwhelm vs all /
yet do there iij thynges not a litle recomfort my mynd.

The first is, that in some communicacions had of late together,
hath aperid good liklyhod of some good agrement to grow in one
5 accord of our fayth /

The second, that in the meane while till this may come to pas,
contencions, dispicions, with vncharitable behaviour, is prohibitid
& forboden in effect vppon all partes / all such partes I meane as
fell before to fight for it.

10 The Third is, that all germanye for all their diuers opynions / yet
as they agre together in profession of christes name / so agre they
now together in preparacion [f. 29ᵛ] of a comen power in defence
of cristendome ageinst our comen ennymy the Turke / And I trust
in god that this shall not onely help vs here to strength vs in this
15 warr / but also that as god hath causid them to agre together in the
defence of his name / so shall he graciously bryng them to agree
together in the truth of his fayth.

Therfor will I let god worke & leve of contention, & nothyng shall
I now say / but that with ⌜which⌝ they that are them selfe of the con-
20 trary mynd shall in reason haue no cause to be discontent / For first
as for purgatory, though they thynke ther be none / yet sith they deny
not that all the corps of christendome by so many hundred yeres,
haue belevid the contrary, & among them all the old interpretours
of scripture from the apostelles daies downe to our own tyme, of
25 whome they deny not many for holy sayntes / that I dare not ⌜now⌝
beleve these men agaynst all those: these men must of their curtsy
hold my pore fere excusid / And I besech our lord hartely for them,
that whan they depart out of this wrechid world, they fynd no
purgatory at all / so god kepe them [f. 30] from hell / And as for the
30 merite of man in his good workes / neyther ar they that deny yt, full

---

1 cach] cacheth *A*: eth *canc. B*   2 recomfort] re *interl. A*   4 grow] growe together *Z*
6 second] second ys *L*   7 contencions, dispicions] contentious dispicious*1573* (*see note*);
vncharitable] oncharitable *A*: o *alt. to* v *B*; is prohibitid] are prohibited *1573*   8 for-
boden] forbodden *L*, forbydden *1553 1573*   11 they] *Z*, the *A*   13 trust] thrust *A*:
canc. and trust *interl. B*   14 in] to *L 1553 1573*   16–19 of his name . . . are them selfe]
om. 1573   16 name /] | *canc. and comma added B*   17 truth] ruth *1557* (*letter dropped out*)
19 which] wish *A*: *canc. and* which *interl. B*   20 discontent] discontented *Z*   21 for]
om. L   22 hundred] hundredth *1553*   23 interpretours] interpretorus *A*   24 own]
om. 1557; tyme,] *comma ed.*   25 now] *om. L 1553 1573*   27 And] *om. 1557*   29 for
the] the *om. L*

agreed among them selfe / nor any man is there almost of them all,
that sith he began to write, hath not somwhat chaungid & varied from
hym selfe. And far the more part are thus farr agreed with vs, that
like as we graunt them that no good worke is ought worth to hevyn
ward without fayth / and that no good worke of man is rewardable 5
in hevyn of his own nature, but through the mere goodnes of god that
list to set so high a price vppon so pore a thyng, and that this price god
settith thorough cristes passion / and for that also that they be his own
workes with vs (for good workes to god ward worketh no man without
god worke with hym) And as we graunt them also that no man may 10
be proude of his workes for his own vnperfit workyng / & for that that
in all that man may do / he can do god no good / but is a servaunt
vnprofitable & doth but his bare dewtie / As we I say graunt vnto
them these thynges / so this one thyng or twayne do they graunt vs
agayne / that men are bound to worke good workes yf they haue tyme 15
& power [f. 30ᵛ] and that who so workith in trew fayth most, shalbe
most rewardid / But than set they therto, that all his rewarde shalbe
gevyn hym for his fayth alone, & nothyng for his workes at all / because
his fayth is the thyng (they sey) that forceth hym to worke well. Strive
will I not with them for this matter now / but yet this I trust to the 20
great goodnes of god, that yf the question hang on that narrow poynt,
while crist sayth in the scripture in so many places, that men shall
in hevyn be rewardid for their workes, he shall neuer suffer our sowles
that are but meane wittid men, & can vnderstond his wordes but as
hym selfe hath set them, & as old holy saintes hath constrewed them 25
before, and as all christen people this thowsand yere haue belevid /
to be dampnid for lack of perceyving such a sharpe subtill thyng /
specially sith some men that haue right good wittes, & are beside
that right well lernid to / can in no wise perceve for what cause or
whye, these folke that fro good workes take away the reward and 30
give the reward all hole to fayth alone / give the reward to faith rather
[f. 31] than to charitie / for this graunt they them selfe / that fayth
serueth of nothyng / but yf she be companid with her sister charitie.

---

1 selfe] selvys *L*   2 he] they *Z*   3 far] for *L 1553 1573*   7 list] lust *1553 1557*; price]
orig. pride: de *canc. and* ce *interl. A, word canc. and* price *interl. B*   9 (for] / for *A: parenth.*
wr. over / *B*   10 hym)] *parenth. added B*   11 vnperfit] vnperfecte *Z*; for that
that] *second* that *om. Z*   13 doth] dooeth *1553*   16 power] powes *A:* r *wr. over* s *B*
17 rewarde] rewardes *L 1553*   19 (they] *parenth. added B?*   20 this] *Z,* thus *A*
30 good] goodes *A:* es *canc. B*   31 give the reward] gyve yt *L*   32 selfe] selvys *L*
33 companid] accompanyed *L*

And than sayth the scripture ⌐to⌐ / *fides* / *spes* / *charitas* / ⌐*tria haec,*⌐
maior autem horum / *charitas* / of the thre vertues fayth hope and
charitie, of all these / 3 / the greaest is charite, and therfor as worthy
to haue the thanke as fayth. Howbeit as I said I will not strive therfor /
5 nor in dede as our matter standith, I shall not greatly neade. For yf
they say that he which suffreth tribulacion or martirdome for the
fayth, shall haue his high reward, not for his worke but for his well
workyng fayth / yet sith they graunt that haue it he shall / the cause
of the high comfort in the third kind of tribulacion standith / And that
10 is ye wot well the effect of all my purpose /

Vincent

Verely good vncle this is trewly driven & tried out to the vttermoste
as it semeth me. I pray you procede at your pleasure /

That a man ought to be comfortable to
15   hymself & haue good hope & be ioyfull
also in tribulacion, aperith well by this
that a man hath greate cause of ⌐fere &⌐
hevines, that continueth alwey still in
welth discontinued with no tribulacion /

20   The / 13 / chapiter [f. 31ᵛ]

Antonye

Cosyn it were to long worke to peruse euery comfort that a man
may well take in tribulacion / for as many comfortes ye wot well may a
man take therof, as there be good comodities therin / and that be there
25 ⌐surely⌐ so many, that it woldbe very long to reherse & treat of them /
But me semeth we can not lightly better perceve what profit &

<hr>

2 charitas] est charitas *Z*; the] these *Z*   3 greaest] greateste *Z*; charite,] *comma ed.*
(*period added B*)   4 to haue the] *om. L 1553*   6 *extra* for yf *canc. before* they *B?*
7 haue his] his *om. Z*; not] nor *A*, t *wr. over* r *B*   8 sith] sith that *Z*   9 of the] the *om. Z*
10 ye] you *Z*   12 out] *om. Z*; to] vn *interl. before* to *B*, vnto *Z*   13 I pray] And
therfore I pray *Z*   20 13] xiiijᵗʰ *L*   22 to long] a long *Z*   23 in] of *interl. B above*
in (*uncanc.*), of *Z*; comfortes] comforth *A*: h *alt. to* es *B*; ye] you *Z*   24-25 be there
surely] there be surely *1553*   25 them /] *period before* / *B*

comoditie & therby what comfort they may take of it that haue yt, than yf we well consider what harm the lak ys, & therby what discumfort the lak therof shuld be to them that neuer haue yt / So it is now that all holy men agree, & all the scripture is full, & our own experience proveth at our eye / that we be not ⌐come⌐ into this wrechid 5 world to dwell here / nor haue not as saynt paule sayth our dwellyng citie here / but we be sekyng for that citie that is to come, and therfor saynt paule shewith vs that we do seke for it, because he wold put vs in mynd that we shuld seke for it, as they that are good folke and fayne wold come thyther / ⌐do.⌐ 10

For surely who so settith so litell therby, that he lusteth not to seke therfor / yt wilbe I feare me long [f. 32] er he come therat, & mervelouse great grace yf euer he come thither. *Sic currite* (seyth saynt paule) *vt comprehendatis* / runne so that ye may get yt / yf it most than begotten with runnyng, when shall he come at it that list not ones to 15 steppe toward it?

Now because this world is as I tell you, not our eternall dewellyng but our litell while wandryng / god wold that we shuld in such wise vse it, as folke that were wery of yt / and that we shuld in this vale of labour, toyle / teares, & miserye / not loke for rest and ease / game, 20 pleasure / welth, and felicitie / for they that so do / fare like a fond felow that goyng toward his own house where he shuld be welthye / wold for a tapsters pleasure become an hosteler by the way / & die in a stable & neuer come at home.

And wold god that those that drown themselfe in the desier of this 25 wouldeo wrechid welth, were not yet more foles than so / but alas their foly as farre passeth the folishnes of that other fond felow, as ther ys distance betwene the height of hevyn & the very depth of hell, for as our saviour sayth / *ve vobis qui ridetis nunc, quia lugebitis & flebitis* / ⌐wo⌐ may you [f. 32ᵛ] be that laugh now / for you shall 30 wayle & wepe / *Est tempus flendi* / sayth the scripture / *& est tempus*

---

3 it is] is it *Z*   7 that citie] the citie *1557 1573*; come,] *comma ed., period added B*; and] a *alt. to* A B   8–9 because . . . for it] *om.* L *1553 1573*   10 thyther /] / *canc. and* do. *added in space at end of paragr.* B; do] to *1557*   11 lusteth] lysteth *Z*   12 wilbe I feare me] wyll I feare me be *Z*   13 euer he] he euer L *1553 1573*; (seyth] / seyth A   14 ye] you *Z*; most] o *canc. and* u *interl.* B   15 his *canc.* A *after* at; ones to] *om.* L *1553*, to *om. 1557 1573*   16 toward] towardes *Z*; it?] *question-mark ed.*   17 because] because that *Z* 20 game,] game and L   22 toward] towardes *Z*   23 tapsters] *Z*, tapters A   25 themselfe] themselues *1573*   29 hell,] *comma ed. (period added B);* for] f *alt. to* F B; as] *canc.* B, *om. Z*   30 wo] who A: *canc. and* wo *interl.* B

ridendi. There is tyme of wepyng, & there is tyme of laughyng / but as
you see / he settith the wepyng tyme before / for that is the tyme of
this wrechid world, and the laughing ⌐tyme¬ shall come after in hevyn /
There is ⌐also¬ a tyme of sowyng & a tyme of repyng to / Now must
5 we in this world sow, that we may in the tother world repe / and in
this short sowyng tyme of this wepyng world, must we water our sede
with the showers of our teares and than shall we haue in hevyn a mery
laughing hervest for euer / *Euntes ibant & flebant* sayth the prophet
mittentes semina sua / They went forth sowyng their sedes wepyng /
10 but what ⌐saith¬ he shall folow therof / *venientes autem venient cum*
exultatione portantes manipulos suos / They shall come agayne more than
laughyng with greate ioy & exultacion with their handfulles of corn
in their handes.

Lo they that in their goyng home toward hevyn sow their sedes
15 with wepyng, shall at the day of iugement come to their bodys agayne
with euerlasting plentifull laughing. And for to proue that this life
is no laughing tyme but rather the tyme of wepyng / we fynd that
our saviour hym selfe wept twise or thrise / but neuer fynd we that
[f. 33] he laughed so much as ones / I will not swere that he neuer
20 did / but at the lest wise he left vs no samples of it. But on the other
side he lefte vs ensample of wepyng. Of wepyng haue we mater Inow
both for our own sinnes & other folkes to / for surely so shuld we do
bewaile their wrechid sinnes, & not be glad to detract them nor envy
them nother / Alas sely soules what cause is there to envy them, that
25 are euer welthy in this world & euer out of tribulacion / which as
Iob sayth / *Ducunt in bonis dies suos & in* ⌐*puncto*¬ *ad inferna descendunt* /
lede all ther dayes in welth, & in a moment of an houre descend into
their grave & be paynfully buried in Hell / saint Paule sayth to the
hebrewes that god those that he loveth he chastiseth / *Et flagellat omnem*
30 *filium quem recipit*: and he scourgeth euery sonne of his that he
recevith. Saynt paule sayth also / *per multas tribulaciones oportet nos*

1 ridendi.] *period ed.*   3 tyme] *om.* L *1553*   4 Now] N *wr. over* n *A?*   5 tother]
other *Z*   9 & *interl. after* forth *B*; sowyng] sowyd *B*: g *canc. and* d *wr. over* n, and
sowed *Z*   12 handfulles] handes full L *1553*   14 Lo] Lo nowe L; toward] towardes
Z; sedes] sede L *1553 1573*   16 plentifull] plentye *1553 1573*, plenty of L; that] *interl.* A
17 tyme *canc.* A *before* life   20 samples] *final* s *canc.* B, sample L, ensample *1553 1557*
1573; But] but A; other] tother L   22 other] for other *Z*   24 nother] neyther *Z*
26 puncto] *appears to be wr. by* B *in blank space left by* A   28 grave] graues *1557 1573*; to]
vnto *Z*   29 that *canc.* B *after* god; chastiseth] chasteth A   30 recipit:] *colon ed.*
31 recevith.] *period ed.*

introire in regnum dei / by many tribulacions must we go into the
kyngdome of god / And no merveyle / for as our saviour said of hym
selfe vnto his ij disciples that were goyng into the castell of Emaus /
An nesciebatis quia oportebat Cristum pati & sic introire in regnum suum /
know you not that christ must suffer [f. 33ᵛ] & so go into his kyng- 5
dome / And wold ⌈we⌉ that are seruauntes loke for more previlege in
our masters house than our master hym selfe / wold we get into his
kyngdome with ease, when hym selfe got not into his own but by
payne? His kyngdome hath he ordeynid for his disciples, & he sayth
vnto vs all / *Qui vult meus esse discipulus* / *tollat crucem suam & sequatur* 10
me / yf any man wilbe my disciple let hym lerne at me to do as I haue
done / take his crosse of tribulacion vppon his bake & folow me. He
sayth not here lo let hym laugh & make mery.

Now yf hevyn serue but for cristes disciples & they be those that
take their crosse of tribulacion / when shall these folke come there 15
that neuer haue tribulacion. And it be trew that saint paule sayth /
that god chastesith all them that he loveth, & scourgith euery childe
that he recevith / ⌈& to heven shall none come but such as he lovyth
& receyvyth,⌉ when shall they than come thyther whome he neuer
chasteseth, nor neuer do vouch safe to file his handes vppon them & 20
give them so much as one lassh / and yf we can not (as saynt paule
sayth we can not) come to hevyn but by many tribulacions: how shall
they come thether than that neuer haue none at all / [f. 34]

Thus see we well by the very scripture yt selfe how trew the wordes
are of the old holy sayntes, that with one voise in a maner say all one 25
thyng / that is to wit / that we shall not haue both contynuall welth
in this world & in the tother to / And therfor sith that they that in
this world without any tribulacion enioy their long continuall course
of neuer interuptid prosperitie, haue a great cause of fere & of discomfort, lest they be farre fallen out of godes favour, & stand depe 30

---

2 as] *canc.* B, *om.* Z; said] Christ sayd *1553 1557 1573*   3 disciples] is *wr. over illeg. letter*
(e?) B; into] vnto *1573*   4 nesciebatis] neciebatis *1557*   5 know] knew *1573*
6 *comma after* seruauntes B   7 selfe /] *question-mark added before* / B   8 when] when he
1553 1557 1573   9 His] his A   10 meus esse] esse meus Z   11 disciple] s *ins.* B?
12 bake] k *wr. over* e B   13 lo] lo / A   14 disciples] disciplies A   16 And] and A:
a *alt. to* A B; And it] And if it Z   17–18 childe that] chylde whome Z   19 than] *om.*
L *1553*   20 do] dooeth *1553*, doth L *1557 1573*; &] nor *1557 1573*   21 (as] / as A
24 very] *om.* L; *comma after* selfe B   25 of the] the *om.* Z; that] / that A   27 tother]
other *1553 1557 1573*; sith that] that *om.* Z   29 & of] of *om.* L

in his indignacion & displeasure, while he neuer send them tribulacion / which he is euer wont to send them whom he loveth / they
therfor I say / that are in tribulacion haue on the tother side a greate
cause to take in their grief gret inward comfort & spirituall consola-
5 cion.

A certeyne obieccion & the answere therto

The xiiij Chapiter

Vyncent

Verely good vncle this semeth so in dede / how beit yet my thynketh
10 that you say very sore in some thyng, concernyng such persons / as
are in contynuall prosperitie / & they be ye wot well / not a few /
And those are they also that haue the rule & aucthoritie of [f. 34ᵛ]
this world in their hand / and I wot well ⌐that¬ when they talke with
such greate conyng ⌐men¬ / as I tro can tell the trouth / & when they
15 aske them whether / while they make mery here in erth all their life,
they may not ⌐yet¬ for all that haue hevyn after to / they do tell them /
yes / yes well inow / for I haue herd them tell them so my selfe.

Anthonye

I suppose good Cosyn that no very wise men, and specially none
20 that very good is therwith, will tell any man fully of that fassion /
but surely such as so say to them / I feare me that they flatter them
either for lucre or feare / Some of them thinke peradventure thus /
This man makith much of me now, & giveth me money also to fast &
watch & pray for hym / but so I fere me wold ⌐he¬ do no more, yf I
25 shuld go tell hym now / that all that I do for hym will not serue hym /
but yf he go fast & watch & pray for hym selfe to / for if I shuld set
therto & say ferther, that my diligent intercession for hym, shuld I

---

1 send] yth *added* B, sendeth *Z*   3 tother] other *1553 1557 1573*   4–5 consolacion.]
period ed., comma B   6 therto] therunto L   7 xiiij] xiiijᵗʰ L   9 my thynketh] me
thynke *1553 1557 1573*, me thyncketh L   10 that] *om.* L *1553 1573*; thyng] thynges L
1553 1573; persons /] / *canc.* B   11 ye] you *Z*   14 I tro can] can I trowe *Z*
15 whether] *om. after* them *and placed after* life L; whether /] / *canc.* B   17 inow]
ynough *Z*   19 men] man *Z*   21 surely] *interl.* A; to] vnto L   22 or] or for L
24 he] I A: *canc. and* he *interl.* B

trust be the meane that god shuld the soner give hym grace to amend,
& fast & watch & pray & take affliccion [f. 35] in his own body for the
betteryng of his synfull sowle / he wold be wonderouse wroth with
that / for he wold be loth to haue any such grace at all as shuld make
hym go leve of any of his myrth & so sit & morn for his sinne / Such 5
mynd as this is lo / haue their some of those that are not vnlernid &
haue worldly wit at will / which tell grete men such tales as pere-
lousely begile them / rather than the flaterar that so tellith them,
wold with a trew tale iebard to lose his lucre.

Some are there also, that such tales tell them for consideracion of 10
a nother fere / for seyng the man so sore set on his pleasure that they
dispayre any amendment of hym what so euer they shuld shew hym /
And than seyng also besides, that the man doth no great harm / but
of a gentill nature doth some good men some good: they pray god
them selfe to send hym grace / & so they let hym lye lame still in his 15
fleshly lustes / *Ad probaticam piscinam expectantes aque motum* / At the
pole that the gospell spekith of / biside the temple wherin they
wasshid their shepe for the sacrafice / & they tary to se the water
stiryd / and when his good angell comyng from god shall ones begyn
to stire [f. 35ᵛ] the water of his hart, & move hym to the lowly 20
mekenes of a simple shepe / than yf ⌐he¬ call them to hym / they will
tell hym an other ⌐tale,¬ & help to bere hym & plunge hym into the
pole of penaunce ouer the hard cares / But in the meane while / for
feare lest when he wold wex neuer the better, he wold wax much the
worse / and ⌐fro¬ gentle smoth swete and curtuouse, wax angry rough 25
froward and sower, & ther uppon be troubelouse & tedious to the
world / to make fair wether withall, they give hym faire wordes for
the while, & put hym in ⌐good¬ comfort / & let hym for the remenant
stand at his own aduenture / And in such wise deale they with hym,
as the mother doth somtime with her child / which whan the litell 30
boy wold not rise for her in tyme but lye still a bed and slougge / &

1 amend] a *canc. B*   5 go] to *1553*; sinne] e *canc. and* es? *added B*; Such] Sush *A: canc.
and* Such *interl. B*   6 is] *om.* Z   9 lose] lese *L 1553*, leese *1557 1573*   11 fere /]
period before | *B*; so] *om.* L *1553*; sore set] sette sore *L 1553*   13 besides] besyde Z
16 aque] *hook added to* e *B*   17 wherin] *divided*: whe-rin *A*, rin *canc. and* rein *added after*
whe *B*   18 their] the Z   21 he] He *A: canc. and* he *interl. B*   22 tale] take *A:* k *alt.*
to l *B, then word canc. and* tale, *interl. B*   23 But in the meane while] *repeated after* while | *A*,
repetition canc. A?   24 when] *interl. A*   25 fro] for *A: canc. and* fro *wr. by B in space at end
of line, from 1553 1557 1573*   31 wold] will Z; for her in tyme] for her *canc. and* for her,
interl. after tyme *B*, in time for her Z

whan he is vp wepith because he hath lien so long / fering to be betten
at scole for his late commyng thether / she tellith hym it is but erly
dayes / & he shall come tyme inough / & biddith go good sonne I warrant the I haue sent to thy master my selfe / take thy brede & butter
5 with the / thow shallt not be betyn at [f. 36] all / & so thus she may
send hym mery forth at dore that he wepe not in her sight at home /
she studith not much vppon the matter, though he be taken tardy
& beten when he cometh to scole / Surely thus I fere me fare their
many freres & states chapleyns to, in comfort gyvyng to grete men /
10 when they be loth to displease them / I can not commend their thus
doyng / but surely thus I fere me they do.

Other obieccions /

The / 15 / chapiter

Vincent

15   But yet good vncle though that some do thus / this answereth not
full the mater / For we se that the whole church in the comen seruice,
vse diuers colletes / in which all men pray specially for the princes and
prelattes, & generally euery man for other, & for hym selfe to / that
god wold vouchsafe to send them all perpetuall helth & prosperitie /
20 And I can se no good man pray god send an other sorow, nor no such
praers are there put in the prestes portuouse as far as I can here /
     And yet yf it were as you say good vncle / that perpetuall prosperi-
tie were to the sowle so perilouse, [f. 36ᵛ] & tribulacion therto so
frutefull / than were as me semeth euery man bound of charitie, not
25 onely to pray god send their neibours sorow / but also to help therto
them selfe / & when folke are sike, not pray god send them helth /
but when they come to comfort them ⌜they shuld say⌝ I am glad good

---

2 hym] hym then that *Z*   3 biddith] byddeth hym *Z*   5 so] *canc. and interl. after* thus
B, thus, so *Z*   6 forth] *second* o *ins. before* r *B*; at] at the *Z*   7 studith] e *interl. after* i *B*
11 thus I fere me] I feare me thus *1553 1557 1573*   13 15] xvᵗʰ *L*   15 though that]
that *om. L 1553 1573*   16 full the] the ful *1557*   17 vse] vseth *1573*; colletes] collectes *Z*   18 prelattes] the prelates *Z*   20 can] cannot *1553*   21 there] *om. L
1553 1573*; portuouse] portas *L*, portes *1553 1557*, Portesse *1573*   24 bound] bounden *Z*
25 neibours] neyghbor *Z*

gossep / that ye be so syk / I pray god kepe you long therin / and
neyther shuld any man give any medicyne to other / nor take any
medicyn hym selfe neyther / for by the mynyshyng of the tribulacion,
he taketh away part of the profit from his sowle, which can by no
bodely profit be sufficiently recumpensid.   5

And ⌐also¬ this wote ye well good vncle, that we rede in holy scripture, of men that were welthy & rich & yet very good withall. Salamon was / ye wot well / the rechest & welthyest kyng that any man
could in his tyme tell of / & yet was he well belovid with god.

Iob was also no begger perdye / nor no wrech otherwise / nor lost 10
⌐his ryches¬ & his welth, for that god wold not that his frend shuld
haue welth / but for the shew of his pacience to thencrese of his [f.
37] merite & confucion of the devill / & for profe that prosperite may
stand with godes favour / *Reddidit deus Iob omnia duplicia* / god restorid
hym dowble of all that euer he lost, & gave hym after long life to take 15
his pleasure long. Abraham was eke / ye wot well / a man of great
substans / & so contynued all his life in honour & in welth / yee &
when he died to, he went vnto such welth, that Lazarus which died
in tribulacion & pouertie, the best place that he came to, was that
rich mans bosome / Fynally good vncle this we find at our eye, & euery 20
day we perceve it by playne experience, that many a man is right
welthy, & yet therwith right good / and many a man a myserable
wrech as evill as he is wrechid / And therfor it semith ⌐harde¬ good
vncle, that betwene prosperitie & tribulacion, the mater shuld go thus,
that tribulacion shuld alwey be given by god to all those he loveth for 25
a signe of salvacion / & prosperitie sent for displeasure as a token of
eternall dampnacion.

1 ye] you Z   2 other] an other Z   4 by] with Z   6 ye] you Z   7 very] were
Z .   8 ye] you Z; rechest] y *wr. over first* e B; welthyest] est *canc. and* the most *interl. before
altered word* B, the most welthy Z   16 eke /] / *canc.* B; ye] you Z   20 bosome] *first* o
wr. over u? B   21 perceve] prove *interl.* B *above* perceve (*uncanc.*), proue Z   22 therwith]
with *interl.* A; man a] *om.* Z   23 wrechid /] *period before* / B   25 alwey be given] be
gyven by god allwaye L, be geuen alwaye *1553 1557 1573*; all] *om.* Z; those] those that Z
26 as] and *1553*

The answere to the obieccions
The xvj chapiter

Anthonye

Eyther I said not Cosyn, orels ment I not to say, that for an vndou-
5 tid rule / worldly pleasure were [f. 37ᵛ] alwey displesaunt to god /
or tribulacion euermore holsome to euery man / For well wote I that
our lord giueth in this world, vnto euery sort of folke eyther sort of
fortune. *Et facit solem suum oriri super bonos & malos | & pluit super iustos
& iniustos* / he makith his sonne to shyne ⌈bothe⌉ vppon the good &
10 the bad, & the rayne to rayne ⌈bothe⌉ vppon the iust & vniust. And
on the tother side *flagellat omnem filium quem recipit*: he scourgith euery
sonne that he recevith. And yet he betith not ⌈onely⌉ good folke ⌈that
he lovyth⌉ / but *multa flagella peccatoris* ⌈to,⌉ ther are many scourges
for synners also /
15   He giueth evill folke good fortune in this world, both to call them
by kyndnes, & yf they therby come not the more is their vnkyndnes /
and yet where welth will not bryng them / he giueth them sometyme
sorow. And some that in prosperite can not to god crepe forward /
in tribulacion they runne toward hym a pace / *Multiplicate sunt infir-*
20 *mitates eorum postea accelerauerunt* / their infirmities were multiplied /
sayth the prophet, & after that they made hast.
    To some that are good men, god shewith welth ⌈here⌉ also, [f. 38]
and they give hym greate thanke for his gyft / and he rewardith them
for that thanke to / To some good folke he sendith sorow / & they
25 thanke hym therof to. Yf god shuld give the goodes of this world onely
to evill folke / than wold men wene that god were not lord therof /
yf god wold give the goodes onely to good men, than wold folke take
occasion to serue hym but for them.
    Some will in welth fall to foly / *homo cum in honore esset non intellexit* /

1 obieccions] obieccion *L 1553*   2 xvj] xvjᵗʰ *L*   4 I said] sayd I *L*   5 pleasure]
prosperitie *Z*   7 euery] eyther *Z*   8 fortune.] *period ed.*   10 the rayne] his *interl. B
above* the (*uncanc.*), his raine *Z*; to rayne] *om. 1557*; vppon] on *Z*; & vniust] and on the
vniust *Z*   11 tother] other *1553 1557 1573*   12 recevith.] *period ed.*   17 and] a *alt.
to* A *B*   19 they runne toward hym] toward him they runne *Z*; Multiplicate] *hook
added to* e *B*   20 accelerauerunt] accelarauerunt *A*: le *wr. over second* a *B*   22 shewith]
canc. and sendyth *interl.* B, sendeth *Z*   24 that thanke] the thanke *1573*   25 Yf] yf *A*
26 lord] the lord *Z*   28 occasion] occõ *A*: *canc. and* occasion *interl.* B   29 to] into *Z*

comparatus est iumentis insipientibus, & similis factus est illis / when man
was in honour, his vnderstandyng failid hym / than was he comparid
with bestes & made like vnto them.

Some man with tribulacion will fall into synne / & therfor sayth
the prophet / *Non relinquet dominus virgam peccatorum super sortem iustorum* 5
vt non extendant iusti ad iniquitatem manus suas / god will not leue the rod
of wiked men vppon the lotte of rightouse men / lest the rightouse
peradventure happe to extend & strech out their handes to iniquitie.

So say I not nay / but that in eyther state / [f. 38ᵛ] welth or
tribulacion, may be mater of vertu & mater of vice also / but this is 10
the poynt lo / that standith here in question betwene you & me /
not whether euery prosperitie be a perilouse token / but whether
contynuall welth in this world without any tribulacion, be a fearefull
ᵣsigne˥ of godes indignacion / And therfor this marke that we must
shote at set vp well in our sight, we shall now mete for the shote, and 15
consider how nere toward or how far of your arrows ar from the
prik.

Vincent

Some of my boltes vncle will I now take vp my selfe, & pretely
put them vnder your belt agayn, for some of them I se well be not 20
worth the metyng / and no greate merveyle though I shote wide,
while I somwat mystake the marke.

Antonye

These that make toward the marke & light farre to short / when
the shote is met shall I take vp for you. To prove that perpetuall welth 25
shold be no evill token, you lay first that for princes & prelattes &
euery man for other, we pray all for perpetuall prosperite, [f. 39]
& that in the comen prayers of the church to.

---

1 insipientibus] incipientib *A*: s *wr. over* c *and abbrev. sign added after* b *B*   6 leue] *interl.
above canc.* leve *A*; rod] rodes *L*   7 rightouse] righouse *A*; the rightouse] they *L*   9 or]
interl. above canc. & *A*   10 may] there maye *L*; &] *interl. above canc.* or *A*   14 signe]
sing *A*: *canc. and* signe *interl. B*   15 now] not *A*: w *wr. over* t *B*; shote] e *canc. B*   16 or]
and *L*   19 now] *om. L 1553*   20 your] my *interl. B above* your *(uncanc.)*, my *1557 1573
(see note)*; agayn,] *comma ed., period B*   21 worth] worthy *L*   24 These] Those *Z*
25 To prove] 1 To proue *1553 1573 (this and the three following Arabic numerals are wr. in
margin of CC ms., prob. by B)*

Than say you secondly that if prosperite were so perilous, & tribulacion so profitable / euery man ought than to pray god to send other
sorow.

Thirdly ye further your obieccions with ensamples of Salomon Iob
5 & habraham.

And fourthly in the end of all, you prove by experience of our own
tyme daily before our face, that some welthy folke are good, & some
nedy very nought. That last bolt sith I lye the same myselfe you may
be content to take vp, it lieth so far wide.

10   Vincent

That will I with good will vncle.

Anthony

Well do so than cosyn / & we shall mete for the remenaunte. First
must you Cosyn be sure / that you loke well to the marke / & that
15 can you not, but yf ye know what thing tribulacion ys / for sith that is
one of the thinges that we principally speke of / but yf you consider
well what thyng that is / you may mysse the marke agayne.

I suppose now that you will agre that tribulacion [f. 39ᵛ] is euery
such thing, as trowbleth & greveth the man, eyther in body or in
20 mynd / & is as it were the prik of a thorn, a bramble / or a brere thurst
into his flesh or into his mynd / And surely Cosyn the prik that very
sore priketh the mynd / as far almost passeth in payne the grefe that
payneth the body / as doth a thorn that stikketh in the hart, passe and
excede in payne the thorn that is thrust in the hele.

25   Now Cosyn yf tribulacion be this that I call it / than shall you sone
consider this / that there be ⌈mo⌉ kyndes of tribulacion than peradventure ye thought on before / And thervppon yt foloweth also, that

---

1 Than say] 2 Than saye *1553 1573*   4 Thirdly] 3 Thirdely *1553 1573*; ye] you *Z̧*;
further] *canc. and* furnysh *interl.* B, furnishe *Z̧ (see note)*   5 habraham] Abraham *Z̧*
6 And] 4 And *1553 1573*; fourthly] r *interl.* A   8 lye] *ed.,* kye A: sith I kye *canc. and* I
think lo that syth I say *interl.* B: *reading of B followed by Z̧ (see note)*; may] *om. Z̧*   11 with
good] wyth a good *Z̧*   13 cosyn] good Cosin L *1553 1573*; First] first A: f *alt. to* F B
15 you not] you not doe L *1553 1573*; ye] you *Z̧*; that is] that it is L *1553 1573*
16 thinges] chiefe thynges L *1553 1573*   17 thyng] *om. Z̧*   19 the man] a man *Z̧*
19–20 in mynd] in *om. Z̧*   20 thurst] thrust *Z̧*   23 stikketh] ȳg *wr. over* eth, *then whole
word canc. and* stykkyng *interl.* B, styckyng L *1553 1557*, is sticking *1573*   24 excede] *orig.*
exede: c *wr. over first* e A   25 such *canc. before* this A   26 mo] no A: *canc. and* mo *wr.
after* B   26–27 peradventure ye] you peraduenture *1553 1573*, peradeuenture you L *1557*

sith euery kynd of tribulacion is an interupcion of welth / prosperitie
which is but of welth another name, may be discontynued by mo
wayes than you wold before haue went /

Than say I thus vnto you Cosyn / that sith tribulacion is not onely
such paynes as payne the body, but euery trouble also that greveth 5
the mynd / many good men haue many tribulacions that euery man
markith not / & consequently their welth interuptid therwith whan
other men arc not ware / for trow [f. 40] you Cosyn that the temptacions of the devill the world and the flesh, solicityng the mynd of a
good man to syn, is not a great inward trowble & secret grefe in his 10
hart?

To such wrechis as care not for their conscience, but like vnresonable bestes folow their fowle affeccions / many of these temptacions
be no trowble at all / but matter of their bestly pleasure / But vnto
hym Cosyn that standith in the drede of god / the tribulacion of 15
temptacion is so paynfull / that to be ridd therof or sure of the victorye
therin / be his substaunce neuer so grete he wold gladly give more
than halfe.

Now yf he that careth not for god, thynk this trouble but a trifle,
& with such tribulacion prosperitie not interruptid: let hym cast in 20
his mynd / yf hym selfe happe vppon a fervent longyng for the thyng
which get he can not / & as a good man will not / as percase his
pleasure of some certen good woman that will not be nought / and
than let hym tell me whither the ruffle of his desier, shall so torment
his mynd, as all the pleasure that he can take beside, shall for lak of 25
that one, not please hym of a pynne / And I dare [f. 40ᵛ] be bold to
waraunt hym, that the payne in resistyng, and the grete fere of fallyng,
that many a good man hath in his temptacion, is an anguysh & a
griefe euery deale as great as his /

Now saye I ferther Cosyn / that yf this be trew as in very dede trew 30
it is, that such trouble is tribulacion / & therby consequently an interupcion of prosperouse welth / noman precisely meaneth to pray for

---

1–2 welth / prosperitie which ... name,] welth and prosperitie, (which ... name) *Z*,
prospery *mispr. 1557*   3 before] afore *L 1553 1573*   4 thus] this *L 1553*; tribulacion]
la *repeated in breaking over line A*   5 paynes] pangys *interl. B above* paynes (*uncanc.*),
panges *Z*   10 to] vn *interl. before* to *B*, vnto *Z*; trowble] trowle *A*, trouble *Z*; grefe in]
grief to *1553 1557 1573*, greyf vnto *L*   14 bestly] bodely *interl. B above* bestly (*uncanc.*),
bodily *Z*   15 the drede] the *om. Z*; the tribulacion] the *om. L 1553*   22 &] *om. L 1553*
25 pleasure] *final* s *added B*, pleasures *Z*   28 an] *Z, as A*   32 noman] *vertical line wr.*
after no *B*

other to kepe hym in contynuall prosperitie, without any maner of
discontynuaunce or chaung in this world / for that prayer without
any other condicion addid or implied, were inordinate & ⌈were⌉
very childysh / for it were to pray that eyther they shuld neuer haue
5 temptacion / orels that yf they had, they might folow it & fulfill their
affeccion.

Who dare good Cosyn / for shame or for synne, for hym selfe or any
man els, make this maner kynd of prayer. Besides this Cosyn the
church / ye wot well / advisith euery man to fast to watch and pray,
10 both for tamyng of his fleshly lustes, & also to morn and lament his
synne before comyttid, & to bewayle his offences done agaynst god.
And as they did at the Citie of Ninive [f. 41] and as the prophet David
did / for their synne put affliccion vnto their flesh / And whan a man
so doth Cosyn, is this no tribulacion to hym because he doth yt hym
15 selfe / for I wot well ye wold agree that it were yf an other man did it
agaynst his will / Than is tribulacion / ye wot well tribulacion still,
though it be taken well in worth / ye and though it be taken with very
right good will / yet is payne / ye wot well payne / and therfor so is it
though a man do it hym selfe.

20 Than sith the church advisith euery man to take tribulacion for
his synne, what so euer wordes you fynd in any prayour / they neuer
meane ye may be fast and sewer, to pray god to kepe euery good man
nor euery bad man neyther, from euery maner kynd of tribulacion.

Now he that is not in some kynd of tribulacion, as peradventure
25 in siknes or ⌈in⌉ losse of goodes, is not yet out of tribulacion, yf he
haue his ease of bodye or of mynd inquietid, & therby his welth
interuptid with an other kynd of tribulacion / as is eyther temptacion
to a good man, or voluntary afflicion, eyther of body by penaunce
or of mynd by contricion & hevenes for his synne & offence agaynst
30 god. [f. 41ᵛ]

And thus I say / ⌈that⌉ for precise perpetuall welth & prosperite
in this wrechid world / that is to say / for the perpetuall lak of all

2 for] so L 1553   3 any] om. Ƶ; implied] L 1573, imployed 1553 1557, implued A   3–4
were very] were om. L   5 that yf] if that 1553   7 any] for anye L 1553 1573   9 ye]
you L 1553 1573; to watch] & watch L 1553 1573   10 lament] lament for L 1553 1573
11 offences] offence 1557   13 vnto] to Ƶ   14 comma after because B   15 selfe /]
question-mark before / B; ye] you Ƶ   16 will /] period before / B; ye] you Ƶ; ye wot well]
interl. A   17 taken] taken to Ƶ   18 ye] you Ƶ   22 ye] you Ƶ; to kepe] to om. L
1553   26 inquietid] vnquieted L 1553 1573   32 wrechid] om. Ƶ

trowble & all tribulacion / there is no wise man that eyther prayeth
for hym selfe or for any man els / And thus answere I your first
obieccion.

Now before I medell with your second / your third will I ioyne vnto
this / for vppon this answere will the solucion of your ensamples 5
conveniently depend / As for Salamon was as you saye all his dayes
a mervelouse welthy kyng / & mich was he belovid with god I wote
well in the begynnyng of his reigne / but that the favour of god perseverd with hym as his prosperite did, that can I not tell / And therfor
wil I not waraunt yt / But surely we se that his contynuall welth, 10
made hym fall first into such wanton folye, in multipliyng wives to
an horrible nombre, contrary to the commaundment of god given
in the law by moyses / and secondly takyng to wife among other such
as were infidels, contrary to an other commaundment of goddes written law also / that fynally by the meane of his miscreant wife / he fell 15
ʳin˥ to the mayntenaunce of Idolatry hym selfe / and of [f. 42] this
find we none amendment or repentaunce / as we ʳfynde˥ of his father /
And therfor though he were beried where his father was / yet whether
he went to the rest that his father did, thorough some secret sorow for
his synne at last / that is to say / by some kynd of tribulacion, I can 20
not tell / & am therfor content to trust well, & pray god he did so.
But surely we be not sure / And therfor the ensample of Salamon can
very litell serue you / for you might as well ley it for a profe that god
favorid Idolatry / as that he favorid prosperitie / for Salamon was
ye wot well in both. 25

As for Iob, sith our question hangeth vppon perpetuall prosperitie /
the welth of iob that was with so grete aduersitie so sore interuptid,
can as your selfe seeth serue you for no sample / And that god gave
hym here in this world all thyng dowble that he lost, litell tocheth
my mater / which ded deny not prosperite to be godes gyfte & given 30
to some good men to, namely such as haue tribulacion to.

---

4 vnto] to Ƶ   5 your] yours A: s canc. A   9 with] om. 1553 1557; can I not] cannot
I 1553 1573   13 by] of Ƶ   16 in] added at end of line B; to the] the om. Ƶ   17 none]
no 1553 1557 1573; repentaunce] superfluous superscript a wr. above unc A; fynde] find
A: n lacks minim: i added and de wr. over d B, then word canc. and fynde interl. B   21 therfor
content] content therefore Ƶ   24 favorid] th wr. over d B, fauoureth Ƶ; favorid] th wr.
over d B, fauoureth Ƶ   25 ye] you Ƶ   26 perpetuall prosperitie] prosperitie perpetual
1553 1557 1573   28 sample] ensample Ƶ   29 tocheth] u interl. after o B   30 ded]
canc. A?, om. Ƶ

But Abraham Cosyn / I suppose is all your chief hold / because that
you not onely shew riches & prosperite perpetuall in hym thourough
the course of all his ⌜hole⌝ life in this world, but that after his deth
also Lazare [f. 42ᵛ] the pore man that livid in tribulacion & died for
5 pure hunger & thirste, had after his deth his place comfort & rest
in Abraham the welthy reche mans bosome / But here must you
consider / that Abraham had not such contynuall prosperitie / but
that [yet] it was discontynued with diuers tribulacions / Was it nothyng to hym trow ye to leve his own countrey / & at godes sending,
10 to go into a straunge land which god promisid hym & his seed for
euer / but in all his whole life he gave hym selfe neuer a fote?

Was yt no trowble that his Cosyn Loth & hym selfe were fayne
to part companye, because their seruauntes could not agree together /

Though he recouerid Loth agayne from the thre kynges, was his
15 takyng no trowble to hym trow you in the meane while?

Was the distruccion of the fyue Cities, none hevynes to his hart /
A man wold wene / yes / that redith in the story what labour he made
to save them.

His hart was I dare say in no litell sorow when he was fayne to let
20 Abimelech the kyng haue his wife / whom though god providyd to
kepe vndefilid ⌜& tornyd all to welth,⌝ yet was it no litell wo to hym
for the meane tyme? [f. 43]

What a contynuall grefe was it to his hart many a long day, that
he had no childe of his own body begotton? He that dowteth therof
25 shall fynd it in genisis of his own mone made vnto god.

No man dowtith but Ismaell was great comfort ⌜to⌝ hym at his
birth / & was ⌜it⌝ no grefe than whan he was cast out the mother &
the child both.

---

1 But] But in Z   2 thourough] *first* u *canc. B*   4 also Lazare the] also. Lazare that
1553 1557   5 place] place of *1553 1557 1573*, best place of *L*   6 reche] y *wr. over first*
e *B*; bosome] *first* o *wr. over* u? *B?*   8 yet] *ed.*, it *A: canc. B, om.* Z (*see note*); tribulacions /] *period after* / *B*; Was] was *A*, 1 Was Z (*see Appendix A, Part I for numbering in margin
of CC ms.*)   9 ye] you Z   11 but] but yet *L*; fote?] *question-mark ed.*   12 Was yt] 2
Was it Z   13 together /] *question-mark wr. over* / *B*   14 Though] 3 Though Z   16 Was
the] 4 Was the Z; none] no Z; hart /] *question-mark before* / *B*   19 His hart] 5 His
heart Z   21 tornyd] turned at length *L*   22 for the] in the Z; tyme?] *question-mark
ed.*   23 What a contynuall] a *canc. B: catchwords on f. 42ᵛ read* What continuall, 6
What continual Z; long] *interl. A?* (*see note*)   24 He] he *A*   25 vnto] to Z   26 No
man] 7 No man Z; to] vnto Z   27 it] yet *A: canc. and* it *interl. B*; was] *canc. and* must
interl. B, must Z (*see note*)

Isaac that was the child of promiscion, although god kept his life which was vnlokyd for / yet while the lovyng father bownd hym & went abowt to behed hym, & offre hym vp in sacrifice / who but hym selfe can conceve what hevynes his hart had than? I wold wene in my mynd, because you speke of Lazare, that Lazaris own deth pangid 5 not hym so sore / Than as Lazaris payne was paciently borne / so was Abrahams taken not onely paciently / but which is a thyng much more meritoriouse / of obediens willyngly / And therfor though Abraham had not / as he did in dede, farre excell Lazare in merite of reward for many other thynges beside / and specially for that he was a speciall 10 patriark of the fayth / yet had he far passid hym evyn by the merite of tribulacion well taken here for godes [f. 43ᵛ] sake to / And so serueth for your purpose no man lesse than Abraham.

But now good Cosyn let vs loke a litell lenger here vppon the rich Abraham / & Lazare the pore / and as we shall see Lazare sit in 15 welth somewhat vnder the rich Abraham / so shall we se an other rich man lye full low byneth Lazare, criyng and callyng out of his fyry cowch, that Lazare might with a dropp of water fallyng from his fyngers end, a litell cole & refresh the tipp of his burnyng tong.

Consider ʳwellᵔ now what Abraham answerid to the rich wretch / 20 *fili recordare, quia recipisti bona in vita tua / & lazarus similiter mala / nunc autem hic consolatur tu vero cruciaris* / sonne remember that thow hast in the lyfe recevid welth, & Lazare in likewise payne / but now recevith he comfort, & thow sorow payne and turment.

Christ discribeth his welth & his prosperitie / gay & softe apparell, 25 with riall delicate fare continually day by day / *Epulabatur* sayth our saviour / *quotidie splendide* / he did fare rially every day / his welth was contynuall lo / no tyme of tribulacion betwene. [f. 44] And Abraham tellith hym the same tale that he had taken his welth in this world, & Lazarus in likewise his payne / & that they had now 30 chaungid ech to the clene contrary / pore Lazare from tribulacion into welth, & the rich man from this contynuall prosperitie into perpetuall payne.

---

1 Isaac] 8 Isaac Ƶ; promiscion] s *ins. after* s *and* i *wr. over* c *B*   2 which] that Ƶ   6 not hym] hym not half *L*, him not *1553 1557 1573*   9 excell] excelled *1573*   10 and] And *A*   15 sit] set Ƶ   21 recipisti] recepisti Ƶ   22 consolatur] u *interl. B*   23 the lyfe] thy lyfe Ƶ   24 turment] turmᵗ *A*: *superl.* t *canc. and* ent *added B*   26 riall] royall Ƶ   27 saviour /] / *ed.*; rially] royally Ƶ   30 Lazarus in] in *om.* Ƶ, Lazar *L*   32 this] his Ƶ

Here was laid expresly to Lazare no very greate vertew by name /
nor to this rich glotone no greate heynous cryme / but the takyng
of his own continual ease & pleasure, without any tribulacion or grefe /
Wherof grew slowth & negligence to thynke vppon the pore mans
5 payne / for that euer hym selfe saw Lazrus & wist hym die for hunger
at his dore, that laid neyther christ nor Abraham to his charge. And
therfor Cosyn this story lo / of which by occasion of Abraham & Lazare you put me in remembraunce, well declarith what perell is in
contynuall worldly welth / & contrarywise, what comfort cometh of
10 tribulacion. And thus as your other samples of salamon & Iob
nothyng for the mater further you: so your ensample of the rich Abraham and pore Lazare, haue not a litell hyndred you. [f. 44ᵛ]

An answere to the second obieccion
The seventene chapiter

15   Vincent

Surely vncle you haue shaken myn example sore, and haue in
metyng of your shote removed me thes arrows me thynke ferther from
the prik then me thought they stak when I shot them / and I shall
now be content to take them vp agayne / But yet me semeth surely
20 that my second shafte may stand / for of trewth yf euery kynd of tribulacion be so profitable, that it be good to haue it as you say it is: I
can not se wherfor any man shuld ⌈wyssh⌉ or pray or any maner thyng
do, to haue any kynd of tribulacion withdrawen, eyther from hym
selfe or any frend of his.

25   Antonye

I thynke in very dede tribulacion so good & so profytable / that
I shuld hapely dowt as ye do / wherfor a man might labour or pray

---

3 own] *om. Z*   5 Lazrus] a *interl. after* z *B*, Lazar *L*   7 occasion] o͞cc͞on *A: canc. and*
occasion *interl. B*   10 samples] ensamples *Z*   11 the rich] the *om. Z*   14 seventene]
xvij^th *L*   16 example] ensamples *Z*; sore] very sore *L*   17 metyng] your meting *Z*;
your] y *canc. B*; removed] moued *1573*; thynke] thinketh *Z*; from] of fro *Z*   18 shall]
shall therefore *Z*   20 shafte] shalte *1553*, shotte *1557*, shoot *1573*   22 wyssh] which
A: canc. and eyther wyssh *interl. B*, eyther wyshe *Z*; maner] maner of *Z*   26 & so] so
om. Z   27 ye] you *Z*

to be deliuerid of it / saving that god which techeth vs the one, techeth
vs also the tother / and as he biddeth vs take our payne pacyently,
& exort our neybour to do also the same / [f. 45] so biddith he vs also
not let to do our devour, to remove the payne from vs both / And
then when it is god that techeth ⌈both⌉ / I shall not nede to breke 5
our brayne in devisyng wherfor he wold bydd vs do both, the tone
semyng to resist the tother.

Yff he send the scourge of scarsitie & greate famyn / he will we
shall bere it paciently / but yet wold he that we shuld eate our meate
when we can hap to get it / 10

Yf he send vs the plage of pestilence / he will we shall paciently take
it / but yet will he that we let vs bloud & lay plasters to draw it / &
ripe it / & launce it / & so get it away / Bothe these poyntes teacheth
god in scripture in mo than many places.

Fastyng is better than eatyng, & more thanke hath of god / and 15
yet will god that we shall eate. Praying is better than drynkyng, &
much more plesaunt to god / and yet will god that we drynke. Wakyng in good bissines is moch more acceptable to god than slepyng /
and yet will god that we shall slepe / [f. 45ᵛ]

God hath given vs our bodies here to kepe, & will that we man- 20
teyne them to do him seruice with / till he send for vs hens / Now can
we not surely tell how mich tribulacion may marre it / or peradventure hurt the sowle also / wherfor the apostell after that he had
comaundid the Corrynthians to deliuer to the devill, the abomynable
fornicatour that forbare not the bed of his own fathers wife, yet after 25
that he had bene a while accursid & punyshid for his synne / the apostell commaundid them charitably to receve hym agayne, & give hym
consolacion / *Vt non a magnitudine doloris absorbeatur* / that the greatnes
of his sorow, shuld not swalow hym vpp.

And therfor when god sendith the tempest / he will that the ship 30
men shall get them to their takelyng & do the best they can for them

---

1 one] tone *L*; techeth] thecheth *A*: *canc. and* techyth *interl. B*   2 tother] t *added B?*
other *1553 1557 1573*   3 neybour] neighbours *Z*   6 our] *canc. and* my *interl. B*, my *Z*;
do] to dooe *Z*   7 tother] other *1553 1557 1573*   8 greate] of greate *Z*   9 wold]
wyll *Z*; shuld] shall *Z*   13 so] *om. Z*; Bothe] bothe *A*   16 Praying] praying *A*
17 that] *interl. A*; we] we shall *Z*   17–18 Wakyng] wakyng *A*   20–21 manteyne] i
interl. after a *B*   22 surely tell] tell surely *Z*   28 Vt non a magnitudine doloris ab-
sorbeatur] Ne fortè abundantiori tristitia absorbeatur *1573*; greatnes] greanes *A*: t *ins. B*
28–29 that the greatnes . . . hym vpp] Least peradventure the greatnes of his sorow should
swalow him vp *1573*

selfe / that the see eat them not vpp / for help our selfe as well as we
can / he can make his plage as sore & as long lastyng as hym selfe
lyst / And as he will that we do for our selfe, so will he that we do
for our neybour to / and that we shall in this [f. 46] world be ech to
5 other pyteouse ⌐& not sine affectione⌐ / For which the apostell rebuk-
eth them / that lak their tender affeccions / so that of charitie sory
shuld we be for their paynes to / vppon whom for cause necessary
we be driven our selfe to put yt / And who so sayth that for pitie of
his neybours sowle he will haue none of his body / Let hym be sure
10 that as saynt Iohn sayth / he that loveth not his neybour whom he
seeth / loveth god but a litell whom he seeth not / so he that hath no
pitie on the payne that he feleth his neybour fele afore hym, pitieth
litell what so euer he sayeth / the payne of his sowle that he seeth not
yet. God sendith vs also such tribulacion sometyme / because his
15 pleasure is to haue vs pray vnto hym for help / And therfor when
saynt Peter was in prison, the scripture shewith that the whole church
without intermission prayd incessantly for hym / And at their fervent
praour god by miracle delyuerd hym /

When the deciples in the tempest stode in feare of drownyng, they
20 prayd vnto christ and sayd / *Salua nos domine / perimus* / save vs lord we
perish / & then at their prayour he shortly seasid the tempest / And
now se we provid often that in sore weder or siknes, by generall processions [f. 46ᵛ] god giveth graciouse helpe / And many a man in his
grete payne & siknes by calling vppon god, is mervelously made hole.
25 This is godes goodnes, that because in welth we remember hym
not but forget to pray to hym, sendith vs sorow & siknes to force vs
to draw toward hym, and compellith vs to call vppon hym & pray
for relese of our payne, wherby when we lerne to know hym & seke
to hym, we take a good occasion to fall after into a ferther grace.

1 see] seas L *1553 1573*; selfe] selfes *1553*, selues L *1557 1573*   3 lyst] luste *1553 1557*
4 in this world be] be in thys world L *1553 1573*   5 & not sine affectione / For] for
Sine affeccione L *1553*   6 their] *om.* L *1553*; affeccions] affeccyons here Ƶ; hart *interl.*
B *after* affeccions (*uncanc.*): *see note*   7 paynes] s *canc.* B, payne Ƶ; *blot in purple ink above*
cause (*not a cancellation*)   8 pitie] piety *1553*   12 on] of L *1553 1573*; feleth] seeth Ƶ
13 sayeth] saye Ƶ   13–14 not yet. God] not, Yet god L, not: yet God *1553*, not yet: God
1557, not. ¶God (yet *om.*) *1573*   14 his *repeated before* pleasure A   17 hym / And at]
him: and that at *1573*   19 deciples] is *wr. over first* e B; drownyng] downyng A: r *ins.* B
22 weder] weather Ƶ; by] *orig.* be: y *wr. over* e A   27 to draw] to *om.* L *1553*;
toward] towardes L   28 lerne to] *interl.* A; & seke] and to seke *1557*   29 occasion]
occõn A: *canc. and* occasion *interl.* B; into a] a *om.* Ƶ

Of them that in tribulacion seke not vnto
god, but some to the flesh & some to the
world, & some to the devill hym selfe.

The xviij chapiter

Vyncent 5

Verely good vncle with this good answere am I well content.

Antonye

Ye / Cosyn but meny men are there, with whome god ys not
content / which abuse this great high goodnes of his / whom neyther
faire tretyng nor hard handlyng can cause them to remember their 10
maker / but in welth they be wanton / forget god & folow their lust.
And when god with tribulacion draweth them toward hym / than
wax they woode & draw bak all that euer [f. 47] they may / &
rather runne & seke help at any other hand, than to go fet it at his.

Some for comfort seke to the flessh, some to the world, & some to 15
the devill hym selfe.

Some man that in worldly prosperite is very full of welth, & hath
depe steppid into many a sore sinne which sinnes when he did them,
he counptid for part ⌐of⌐ his pleasure / god willyng of his goodnes to
call the man to grace, castith a remors into his mynd among after his 20
first slepe / & maketh hym ly a litell while and bethinke hym / Than
begynneth he to remember his lyfe / & from that he falleth to thynke
vppon his deth, & how he must leve all this worldly welth within a
while behynd here in this world / & walk hens alone he woteth not
wether, nor how sone he shall take his iourney thither, nor can tell 25
what companye he shall mete there / And than begynneth he to thynke
that it were good to make sure & to be mery so that we be wise

4 xviij] xviijᵗʰ L   6 am I] I am Z   9 high] om. L 1553 1573   10 them] om. Z
11 forget] and forgett Z   13 wax they] Z, wax thy A   14 fet] for? A: et wr. over or?
B, seke interl. B above fet (uncanc.), seke L 1553   15 flessh,] fleshe, and L   17 full] dull
interl. B above full (uncanc.), dull Z; of welth] om. 1557 1573   18 sinne] i alt. to y B?;
sinnes] i alt. to y B?   21 maketh] make A: th added B   24 walk] l interl. A
25 wether] h interl. after w B, whither Z   27 to be] to om. 1553; we canc. before
were A; comma after so B; we] canc. and he interl. B, he 1557 1573

therwith lest there hap to be such blak bugges in dede / as folke call
devilles whose tormentes he was wont to take for poetes talis.

These thoughtes yf they sinke depe, are a sore [f. 47ᵛ] tribulacion /
& surely yf he take hold of the grace that god therin offreth hym, his
5 tribulacion ys holsome & shalbe full comfortable to remember that
god by this tribulacion callith hym & biddith hym come ⌐home⌐
out of the countrey of synne that he was bred & brought vpp so long
in, & come into the land of byhest that floweth milke and hony /
And than yf he folow this callyng (as many one full well doth) ioyfull
10 shall his sorow be / & glad shall he be to chaunge his lyfe, leve his
wanton lustes, & do penaunce for his synnes, bestowyng his tyme
vppon better bisynes. But some men now when this callyng of god
causeth them to be sad, they be loth to leve their synfull lustes that
hang in their hartes, & specially yf they haue any such kynd of lyvyng
15 as they must leve of or fall deper in sinne / or yf they haue done so
many great wronges, that they haue many ⌐amendes⌐ to make that
must (yf they folow god) mynish myche there money / than are those
folke alas wofully bewrapid / for god pricketh vppon them oft of his
grete goodnes styll / & the grief of this grete pang pyncheth them by
20 the hart, & of wikkednes they [f. 48] wry away / & fro this tribulacion
they turne to their flessh for help & labour to shake of this thought /
And than they amend their pillow & ley their hed softer & assay
to slepe / & whan that will not be, than they find a talk a while with
them that lye by them / Yf that can not be neyther, than they lye &
25 long for day, & than get them forth about their worldly wrechednes /
the mater of their prosperitie, the selfe same sinnfull thynges with
which they displease god most. And at lenghth with many tymes
vsyng this maner, god vtterly castith them of / & than they set nought

---

2 tormentes] tormᵗᵉˢ *A: superl. letters canc. and* entes *added* B   3 These] Those *1557*
1573   6 this] *om. 1553*   9 doth)] doth / *A: parenth. wr. over* / B   14 hang]
a *wr. over orig.* u? *A?*   15 must] must nedes *Ƶ*   15–16 done so many great
wronges] suche great wronges done *L 1553*   16 amendes] ames *A: canc. and*
amendes *interl.* B, myndes *1553*, mendes *L 1557 1573*   16–17 that must] (that must
A   17 god)] god / *A: parenth. wr. over* / B; myche] *divided:* my-che: che *canc. and* ch
added to my B, much of *L 1553 1573*; there] i *interl. before* r B   17–18 those folke]
these folkes *L 1553 1557*, these folke *1573*   18 oft] *canc.* B, *om. Ƶ*   19 pang] payne
1553; by] at *interl.* B *above* by (*uncanc.*), at *Ƶ*   20 &] *interl. A*; they] *Ƶ,* thy *A*; fro]
from *L,* for *1553 1573*   21 flessh] ssh *wr. over illeg. letters A?*; labour] *interl.* B *above*
canc. laboʳ? *A (letter after orig.* b *blotted out)*   22 amend] mend *Ƶ*   23 whan] then
1553; talk] talke? *A*   24 Yf] yf *A*   26 sinnfull] y *wr. over* i B, *final* l *added* B?

neyther by god nor devill / *peccator quum in profundum venerit / contempnit* / whan the sinner commeth into the depth than he contymneth ⌐& settyth nought⌐ by no thyng savyng worldly fere that may fall by chaunce or that nedes must (they wot well) fall ones by deth.

But alas when deth commeth / than cometh agayn their sorow / than will no soft bed serue, nor no company make hym mery / than must he leve his vtward worship & comfort of his glory, & lye pantyng in his bed as he were on a pyn banke. Than commeth his feare of his evill lyfe, & of his [f. 48ᵛ] drefull deth / than cometh the torment his combrid conscience & fere of his hevy iugement / Than the devill draweth hym to dispaire with imaginacion of hell / & suffreth hym not than to take it for a ⌐fable. And yet if he do, than fyndyth it the wrech no⌐ fable / Ah wo worth the while that folk thinke not of this in tyme /

God sendith to some man grete trowble in his mynd, and great tribulacion abought his worldly goodes, because he wold of his goodnes take his delite & his confidence from them / & yet the man withdraweth no part of his fond fantasies / but falleth more fervently to them than before, & settith his whole hart like a fole ⌐more⌐ vppon them / and than he taketh hym all to the devises of his worldly councelours, & without any councell of god or any trust put in hym, maketh meny wise wayes as he wencth / & all turne at lenghth to foly / & one subtill dryfte driveth an other to nought.

Some haue I sene evyn in their last siknes, sit vpp in their deth bed vnderproppid with pillowes, take their playfelowes to them, & comfort them selfes with cardes / And this they said did ease them well to put fansies owt of their hed / And what [f. 49] fantasies now you / such as I told you right now, of their own lewd lyfe & perell of their sowle, of hevyn & of hell that irked them to thynke of / And therfore

---

1 neyther] nother *1553 1573*   2 commeth] cometh euyn *Z*; contymneth] mn *wr. over illeg. letters E?, word canc. and* contemneth *interl. E (see note)*   3 worldly] world? *A*: ly *added B?, then word canc. and* worldly *interl. B*   5 their sorow] his sorow *1573*   6 serue,] *see note*   7 must he] he muste *L 1553 1573*   8 he] *canc. and* it *interl. B*, it *Z*   9 drefull] dreadeful *Z*   10 torment] torment of *1553 1573*   12–13 fable. And ... wrech no] *om. L 1553*   13 fable *interl. and canc. after* no *B*   15 trowble] *orig.* towbee?: l *wr. over first e A*   16 abought] ght *canc. and* t *ins. after* u, *then whole word canc. and* abowt *interl. B*; his worldly] t *ins. before* h *B*   18 fantasies] fansyes *L*   20 than] *om. L 1553*; devises] deuyll *L 1553*   22 to] vn *interl. before* to *B*, vnto *Z*   24 sit] set *1557*   25 pillowes] *divided*: pill=lowes *A*   26 selfes] selves *L*, selfe *1553 1557 1573*   27 fansies] fantasies *1553 1557 1573*; hed] des *added B*, heades *Z*; fantasies] fansyes *L*   29 of /] *period after* / *B*

cast yt owt with cardes playe as long as euer they might till the pure
panges of deth pullid their hart fro their playe, & put them in the
case they could not reken their game / And than left them their
gameners and slyly slonke awaye, & long was it not ere they galped
5 vp the goost. And what game they came than to / that god knowith
& not I / I pray god it were good / but I fere it very sore /

   Some men are there also, that do as did kyng saule, In their
tribulacion go seke vnto the devill / This kyng had commaundid all
such to be destroyid as vse the false abhominable supersticion of this
10 vngraciouse wichcrafte & necromancy / And yet fell he to such foly
afterward hym selfe / that ere he went to batayle, he sought vnto a
wich and besought her to reyse vp a ded man to tell hym how he
shuld spede.

   Now had god shewid hym before by samuell, that he shuld come
15 to nought, & he went abought [f. 49^v] none amendment / but waxed
wurse & wurse / so that god lyst not to loke to hym / & whan he
sought by the prophet to haue answere of god, there came none answere to hym / which thyng he thought straunge / & because he was
not with god hard at his pleasure / he made sute to the devill /
20 desiering a woman by wychcrafte to rayse vp ded samuell. But spede
had he such therof as commonly they haue all that in their besines
medill with suche maters / for an evill answere had he & an evill spede
therafter / his army discomfit & hym selfe slayne / And as it is rehersid
in paralypomenon the ⌐.x.th⌐ chapiter of the ⌐first⌐ boke, one cause of
25 his fall was, for lacke of trust in god / for which he left to take councell
of god & fell to seke counsayle of the wich, agaynst godes prohibicion
in the law / & agaynst his own good dede by which he punysshid &
put out all wiches so late ⌐afore⌐ / Such spede let them loke for that
play the same part / as I se many do / that in a grete losse, send to
30 seke a coniurere to get there gere agayne & mervelous thinges there
they see / sometyme, but neuer grote of their good. [f. 50]

---

1 cardes] carde L *1553 1573, comma after* cardes B; euer] *interl.* A   2 fro] from L
3 left them] left they *1573*   4 slonke] slong *1553*; galped] gasped *1573*   7 their] *om.*
L *1553 1573*   9 vse] vsed *1573*   14 before by samuell] by Samuell before *1557*
15 abought] ght *canc. and* t *ins. after* u B   16 lyst] *orig.* lest: y *wr. over* e A, lust *1553 1557*
1573   17 prophet] Prophetes *1553 1573*; none] no L   18 hym /] *comma before* / B
23 discomfit] discomfited ℤ   24 .x.th] *wr. by* B *in blank space left by* A, *blank space* L, .x.
1553 1557; first] *wr. by* B *in blank space left by* A, *blank space* L; the .x.th chapiter of the first
boke] *om. 1573 and* Lib. 1. cap. 10. *placed in margin*   28 afore] b *interl. and canc. before* afore
B   30 seke] seke to L; there] i *interl. before* r B   31 good] good agayne L *1553 1573*

And many fond foles are there / that when they be sik, will medill
with no phisike in no maner wise / nor send his water to no connyng
man / but send his cap or his hose to some wise woman otherwise
callid a wich / Than sendith she word agayne / that she hath spied
in his hose / where when he toke none hede he was taken with a 5
spryte betwene ij dores as he went in the twylight / but the sprite
wold not let hym fele it in five dayes after / & yt hath the while
feystrid in his bodye / and that is the greefe that payneth hym so sore /
but let hym go to no lech crafte / nor any maner phisike other than
good mete & strong drinke / for siropes shuld sower hym vpp / but 10
he shall haue five leves of valerian, that she enchauntid with a charm
& gatherid with her left hand / let hym lay those / v / leves to his
right Thombe / not byndid fast to / but let it hang lose therat, by a
grene threde / he shall neuer nede to chaunge yt / loke it fall not
away, but let yt hang till he be hole / ⌈&⌉ he shall nede no more. 15

In such wise witches / & in such mad medisins haue their soles more
fayth a great deale than in god. And thus Cosyn as I tell you all these
kynd of [f. 50ᵛ] folke in their tribulacion, call not vppon god / but
seke for their ease & help otherwise / to the flesh & the world & to
the flyngyng fend / The tribulacion that goddes goodnes sendith 20
them for good, them selfe by their foly torn into their harm / And
they that on the tother side seke vnto god therin, both comfort &
profit they gretly take thcrby /

---

1 fond foles] a fond foole *1573*; are there] there are *L 1553*, there is *1573*; they be] they
lye *L 1553 1557*, he lyeth *1573*   3 some] a *Z*   5 none] no *Z*   7 hath] hathe all *Z*
9 maner] maner of *L 1553 1573*   10 mete &] meate or *L 1553*; siropes] y *wr. over* i *B*;
sower] *canc. and* sowce *interl.* B, sowce *Z*   13 byndid] binde it *Z*; hym *canc. after* let *A*
14 / loke] (loke *A*: / *wr. over parenth.* B   16 their] re *wr. over* ir *B*, many *interl. after* their
B; soles] s *alt. to* f *B* (*to read*: there many foles *B*), there in many fooles *1553*, there manye
fooles *L 1557*, many fooles (there *om.*) *1573* (*see note*)   17 god.] *period ed.*   18 folke]
folke that *Z*   19 for their ease & help] helpe and for their ease *L 1553 1573*; otherwise]
otherwhere *Z*; & to] and some to *L 1553 1573*   20 fend] fiende him self *L 1553 1573*
21 into] vnto *L 1553 1573*   22 they that] them that *L 1553*; the tother] thother *1553*
1573, the other *1557*

An other obieccion with the answere therunto

The xix^th Chapiter

Vincent

I like well good vncle all your answere herein. But one dowt yet
5 remayneth there in my mynd which risith vppon this answere that
you make / & that dout soylid / I will as for this tyme myn own good
vncle encomber you no ferther / for my thynke I do you very much
wrong to give you occasion to labour your selfe so much / in mater of
some study with long talkyng at ones / I will therfor at this tyme move
10 you but one thyng / & seke some other tyme for the remenaunt at
your more ease.

My dowt good vncle is this / I perceve well by your answeres gatherid
& considerid to gether, that you will well agre, that a man may both
haue [f. 51] worldly welth, & yet well go to god / And that on the
15 tother side a man may be misirable & live in tribulacion, & yet go
to the devill / And as a man may plese god by pacience in aduersitie,
so may he please god by thankes givyng in prosperitie.

Now sith you graunt these thynges to be such, that eyther of them
both may be mater of vertew orels mater of synne / mater of damp-
20 nacion or mater of saluacion / they seme neyther good nor bad of their
own nature / but thinges of themselfe egall & indeferent / tornyng to
good / or the contrary, after as they be taken / And than yf this be
thus, I can perceve no cause / why you shuld gyve the prehemynaunce
vnto tribulacion / or wherfor you shuld rekyn more cause of comfort
25 therin, than you shuld rekyn to stand in prosperitie / but rather a
greate deale lesse by in a maner halfe, sith that in prosperitie the man
is well at ease, & may also by givyng thanke to god get good vnto his
soule / where as in tribulacion though he may merite by pacience / as

---

2 xix^th] xix *1553 1557 1573*   4 answere] aunswers Z 5 my] *om. L 1553 1573*
6 / *wr. after* you *for separation A*   6–7 myn own good vncle] *om. L*   7 my thynke] me
thinke Z 8 occasion] occōn *A: canc. and* occasion *interl. B*   10 some] *om. 1553 1573*
10 for the remenaunt] *canc. B*   11 *after* ease B *adds* at (*canc.*) for the remenant. *in space at*
end of paragr., at your more ease for the remnaunte Z 15 tother] other *1553 1557 1573*
17 givyng] geuen *L 1553 1557*   20 neyther] nother *1553 1573*   21 egall] equal Z
22 good /] god *L 1553,* / *canc. B*   23 prehemynaunce] h *canc. B*   26 a maner] a *om.*
1553 1573; that] *om. L 1553 1573*   28 / as] *parenth. wr. over* / B

in aboundaunce [f. 51ᵛ] of worldly welth the tother may by thanke / yet
laketh he much comfort that the welthy man hath, in that he is sore
grevid with hevynes & payne / beside this also that a welthy man well
at ease, may pray to god quietly & meryly with alacrite & grete quiet-
nes of mynd / where as he that lieth gronyng in his grefe, can not 5
endure to pray nor thynk almost vppon nothyng but vppon his payne /

Anthonye

To begyn Cosyn where you leve / the prayours of hym that is in
welth / and hym that is in wo / yf the men be both nought, their
prayours be both lyke. For neyther hath the tone list to pray nor the 10
tother neyther / and as the tone ys let with his payne / so is the tother
with his pleasure / savyng that the payne stirith hym some tyme ᴦto
call vppon godᴴ in his grief though the man be right bad / where the
pleasure pulleth his mynd an other way, though the man be metly
good.   15
And this poynt / I thynke there are few / that can [f. 52] yf they
say trew / say that they fynd it otherwise. For in tribulacion which
commeth you wot well in many sondry kyndes / any man that is not
a dull best or a desperat wretch, callith vppon god, not houerly but
right hartely, & settith his hart ᴦfullᴴ hole vppon his request / so sore 20
he longeth for ease & helpe of his hevynes.
But when men are welthy and well at there ease, while our ᴦtongᴴ
patereth apon our prayours apace, good god how many mad wayes
our mynd wandreth ᴦthe whileᴴ.
Yet wot I well that in some tribulacion, the while such sore 25
sicknes ther is / or other grevous bodely payne / that hard it wore for a
man to say a long payre of mattyns / And yet some that lye a diyng
say full devoutly the vij psalmes and other prayours with the preste
at their own anelyng / But those that for the grefe of their payne can

---

1 the tother] thother *L 1553*, the other *1557 1573*; by] be *A*; y *wr. over* e *B*; thanke /]
parenth. wr. over | *B*   2 is] *canc. and interl. after* sore *B*, sore is *Z*   3 beside] besides *Z*
4–5 quietnes] *first* e *wr. over illeg. letter B*   10 For] for *A*: f *alt. to* F *B*; tone list] one lust
1553 1557, one lyste *L 1573*   10–11 the tother] thother *1553 1573*, the other *1557*
11 the tone] the one *L 1553 1573*, that one *1557*; tother] other *L 1553 1573*   13 right]
righe? *A*, t *wr. over* e? *B*   14 metly] e *interl. after* t *B*   16 few] very fewe *L 1553 1573*;
parenth. added before yf *B?*   17 trew /] *parenth. wr. over* | *B?*; For] for *A*: f *alt. to* F *B*
19 houerly] v *wr. over* u *B*   22 there] i *interl. before* r *B*   24 the while] *added in space*
at end of paragr. B   25 the while] *canc. B*, *om. Z*   28 psalmes] psamles *A*   29 own]
om. Z; grefe] giefe? *A*: r *wr. over* i? *B*

not endure to do yt / or that be more tender & lak that strong hart
& stomak that some other haue / god requireth no such [f. 52ᵛ] long
praours of them / but the liftyng vp of their hart alone without any
word at all / is more acceptable to hym of one in such case / than long
5 seruice so said as folke vse to say it in helth.

The martirs in their agony made no long prayours aloud / but one
ynch of such a prayour so prayd in that payne, was worth an hole ell
& more evyn of their own prayours prayd at some other tyme /

Grete lernid men say that christ, albeit / that he was very god, & as
10 god was in eternall ⌐equall⌐ blysse with his father / yet as man, meritid
not for vs onely but for hym selfe to / For profe wherof they lay in these
wordes the aucthorite of saynt paule / *Cristus humiliauit semet ipsum
factus obediens vsque ad mortem / mortem autem crucis, propter quod & deus
exaltauit illum, & donauit illi nomen quod est super omne nomen / vt in nomine
15 Iesu omne genu flectatur celestium terrestrium & infernorum, & omnis lingua
confitiatur, quia dominus Iesus cristus in gloria est dei patris.* Christ hath humbled hym selfe, & became obedient vnto the deth, and that vnto the
deth of the crosse / for which thyng god hath also exaltid hym & given
hym a name which is above all [f. 53] names, that in the name of Iesus
20 euery knee be bowed both of the celestiall creaturs & the terrestriall
/ & of the infernall to / and that euery tong shall confes that our Lord
Iesus christ is in the glory of god his father.

Now yf it so be as these greate lernid men vppon such auctoritie of
holy scripture sey / that our saviour merytid as man / and as man
25 deseruid reward, not for vs onely but for hym selfe also / then were
there in his dedes as it semyth, sundrye degrees & defference of deseruyng / & not his maundy like merite as his passion / nor his slepe like
merite / as his watch & his prayour / no nor his prayours peradventure all of like merite neyther / but though there none was nor none
30 could be in his most blessid person / but exelent & uncomparable
passyng the prayour of any pure creature / yet his own not all alike /

---

3 of their] of *om. L 1553,* of the *1573*   6 aloud] aloue *A*: wd *wr. over* ue *B*   7 an hole
ell] a whole ealne *L 1553,* a whole elle *1557 1573*   9 albeit /] / *canc. B*; that he] that
om. Z   12 / *after* Cristus *A*   16 confitiatur] confiteatur *Z*; patris.] *period ed.*   18 also]
interl. A   21 & of] of *om. L 1553 1573*   22 in] into *L 1553*   23 auctoritie]
auctorities *Z*   24 merytid] so merited *Z*   26 defference] differences *Z*   27 maundy]
divided: mau-ndy: v *wr. over* u *B?, then whole word canc. and* mawndy *interl. B*   28 merite /] /
canc. B; his prayour] his *om. L*   30 uncomparable] y *wr. over* e *B,* incomparably *Z*
31 yet his] yet wer his *1573*; a *canc. after* own *A*

but some one farre above some other / And than yf it thus be, of all his holy prayours the chiefe semeth me those that he made in his grete agony & payne of his bitter passion / [f. 53ᵛ]

The first when he thrys fell prostrate in his agony, whan the hevynes of his hart with fere of deth at hand so paynefull & so cruell 5 as he well beheld it, made such a fervent commotion in his blissid bodye, that the bloudy swete of his holy flessh droppyd down on the grownd.

The tother were the paynfull prayours that he made vppon the crosse / where for all the torment that he hangyd in / of beatyng / 10 naylyng / & strechyng out all his lymmes / with the wrestyng of his synews / & brekyng of his tender vaynes / & the sharpe crown of thorn so prickyng hym into the hed that his blessid bloude stremyd down all his face / In all [these] hidious paynes / In all their cruell despites / yet ij very devout & fervent prayours he made / the tone for their 15 pardone that so dispituously put hym to this payne / & the tother about his own deliueraunce, commendyng his own sowle vnto his holy father in hevyn. These prayours of his among all that euer he made / made in his most payne / reken I for the chief / And these prayours [f. 54] of our saviour at his bitter passion / & of his holy martirs in the 20 fervour of theire torment / shall serve vs to see that there is no prayour made at pleasure, so strong and effectuall as in tribulacion.

Now come I to the touchyng of the reason you make, where you tell me that I graunt you, that both in welth & in woo some man may be nought & offend god, the tone by inpacience the tother by fleshly 25 lust / & on the tother side both in tribulacion & prosperitie to, some man may ʳalsoʰ do very well & deserue thanke of god by thankes giv yng to god as well of his gifte of riches worship & welth, as of nede / penurye / prisonement / siknes & payne / & that therfor you can not see for what cause I shuld give eny preemynence in comfort vnto 30 tribulacion, but rather alow prosperitie for the thing more comfortable / & that not a litell but in a maner by dowble, sith therin hath

1 some other] other some *1553*   4 thrys] e *interl. after* y *B*; thrys fell] fel thrise *L 1553 1573*   9 tother] other *Z*   14 these] *Z*, this *A*; paynes /] paynes, and *L*   15 tone] one *Z*   16 this] his *Z*; tother] other *Z*   17 deliueraunce] *superl.* ā *wr. above* anc *A*   21 theire] i *interl. A*   23 reason] reason that *L 1553 1573*   24 wh *canc. before* woo *A*; man] men *1553 1573*   25 tone] one *Z*; inpacience] impacience *Z*; tother] other *Z*   26 tother] other *1553 1557 1573*   27 also *interl. after* do *and canc. B*   27–28 givyng] geuen *Z*   28 nede] nede and *Z*   30 vnto] *interl. above canc.* in *A*   32 that] the *1557*; a maner] a *om. Z*.

the sowle comfort & the body both / the sowle by thanke givyng vnto
god for his gyfte, & than the body by beyng well at ease / where the
person paynid in tribulacion, taketh no comfort but in his sowle
alone / [f. 54ᵛ]

5   First as for your dowble comfort Cosyn / you may cut of the tone
/ for a man in prosperitie / though he be bound to thanke god of his
gyfte / wherin he feleth ease / & may be glad also that he giveth
thanke to god / yet for that he taketh his ease here, hath he lytell
cause of comfort / except that the sensuall felyng of bodely pleasure,
10 you lyst for to call by the name of comfort / nor I say not nay / but
that sometyme men vse so to take yt / when they sey this good drynke
comforteth well my hart / but comfort Cosyn / is properly taken by
them that take it right / rather for the consolacion of good hope, that
men take in their hart / of some good growing toward them / than for
15 a present pleasure with which the body is delitid & ˻tyklyd˼ for the
while / Now though a man without pacience can haue no reward
for his payne / yet when his payne is paciently taken for godes sake,
& his will confirmyd to godes pleasure therin / god rewardith the
sufferer after the rate of his payne / And this thing aperith by many a
20 place in scripture / of which some haue I shewid you & yet shall I
shew you [f. 55] mo / But neuer found I any place in scripture that I
remember / in which though the welthy man thanke god for his gyfte /
our lord promisid any reward in hevyn because the man toke his ease
& pleasure here / And therfor sith I speke but of such comfort ˻as is
25 very comfort˼ in dede, by which a man hath hope of godes favour
& remission of his synnes, with mynyshyng of his payne in purgatorye
or reward els in hevyn / & such comfort cometh of tribulacion & for
tribulacion well taken / but not for pleasure though it be well taken /
therfor of your comfort that you dowble by prosperitie / you may as I
30 told you cut very well awaye the halfe /
    Now why I give prerogatyue in comfort vnto tribulacion, far above

---

1 givyng] *canc. and* gyven *interl. B*   1–2 givyng vnto god for his gyfte] for his gyfte gyven
vnto god *L*, (for his gyft) geuen vnto god *1553 1573*, geuen vnto god for his gift *1557*
5 tone] tone half *L*, one *1553 1573*   6 though] thoug *A*; bound] bounden *L 1553 1573*
10 lyst for to] lyste to *L 1573*, lust to *1553*, lust for to *1557*   11 sey] a *wr. over* e *B*
12 my] mine *1557*   15 tyklyd] killid *A*: *canc. and* tyklyd *interl. B*, tickeled *Z*   18
confirmyd] conformed *Z*   22 the welthy] thys welthy *1553*; thanke] thanked *L 1553
1573*   23 man] welthy man *L*   24 &] & his *1557*   26 payne] paynes *L 1553 1573*

prosperitie / though a man may do well in both / of this thyng will I
shew you causes ij or iij / for as I before haue at length shewid you
/ out of all question contynuall welth interruptid with no tribulacion,
is a very discomfortable token of euerlastyng dampnacion / whervppon it foloweth that tribulacion is one [f. 55ᵛ] cause of comfort vnto a 5
mans hart, in that it dischargith hym of the discomfort that he might
of reason take of ouer long lastyng welth /

A nother ys / that scripture much commendith tribulacion, as
occasion of more profit / than welth & prosperite / not to them onely
that are therein, but to them to, that resort vnto them / And therfor 10
sayth Ecclesiastes / *Melius est ire ad domum luctus quam ad domum con-*
uiuii. In illa enim finis cunctorum admonetur homo, & viuens cogitat quid
futurum sit: better yt is to go to the howse of wepyng & waylyng for
some mans deth, than to the howse of a fest / for in that house of hevynes is a man put in remembrans of the end of euery man / & while he 15
yet liveth he thinketh what shall come after / & yet he ferther sayth /
Cor sapientium vbi tristitia est, & cor stultorum vbi letitia / the hart of wise
men is there as hevines ys / and the hart of folis is there as is mirth &
gladnes / And verely there as you ⌐shall⌐ here worldly mirth seme to
be commendid in scripture, it is eyther commenly spoken [f. 56] as in 20
the person of some worldly disposid people / or vnderstonden of reioyc-
yng spirituall / or ment of some small moderat refresshyng of the
mynd, agaynst an hevye discomfortable dulnes /

Now where as prosperitie was to the children of Israell promisid in
the old law, as a speciall gifte of god / that was for their inperfeccion 25
at that tyme, to draw them to god with gay thynges & plesaunt / as
men to make children lerne, give them cakebrede & butter / for as
the scripture maketh mencion, that people were much after the
maner of children in lak of wit & in waywardnes / and therfor was
their master Moyses callid *pedagogus* / that is ⌐a⌐ teacher of children / 30
or as they ⌐call⌐ such one in the grammer scoles, an vssher / or a master

---

2 for] First *Z*   8 scripture] the scripture *Z*   9 profit /] / *canc. B*   11 ire] iri *A*: e
wr. over i *B*   11–12 conuiuii. In illa] En, illa *1553*, conuiuii in illa *1557*   12 homo]
hominum *interl. B above* homo (*uncanc.*), hominum *Z*   13 sit:] *colon ed.*; yt is] is it *1557*
14 that house] the house *1573*   16 *first* yet] it *A*: ye *wr. over* i *B*, yet *Z*; after *interl. B*
above second yet (*uncanc.*), And after yet *Z*   17 sapientium] sapientum *L 1553 1573*
20 commendid in] commended: in *1553*   21 vnderstonden] vnderstondyng *A*: en *wr.*
over yn *and* g canc. *B*, vnderstaund *L*   25 inperfeccion] *first* n *alt. to* m *B*   30 a]
interl. B and then canc.

of the petites / for as ⌐s. paule⌐ sayth: *Nihil ad perfectum duxit lex* / the old law brought nothing to perfeccion.

And god also threteneth ⌐folk⌐ with tribulacion in this world for synne / not for that worldly tribulacion ys evill / but for that we shuld 5 be well ware [f. 56ᵛ] of the siknes of synne / for feare of that thyng to folow / which though it be in dede a very good holsome thyng / yf we will well take it / is ⌐yet⌐ because it is paynfull the thyng that we be loth to haue.

But ⌐this⌐ I say yet agayne& agayne, that as for the farr better 10 thyng in this world toward the gettyng of the very good that god giveth in the world to come, the scripture vndoutidly so commendith tribulacion / that in respect & comparison therof, it discommendith this worldly wrechid welth & discomfortable comfort vtterly / for to what ⌐other⌐ thyng sowneth the wordes of Ecclesiastes that I rehersid you 15 now / that it is better to be in the howse of hevynes than to be at a fest / wherto sowneth this comparison of his, that the wise mans hart draweth thyther as folke are in sadnes, & the hart of a fole is there as he may fynd mirth? wherto draweth this thret of the wise man, that he that delitith in welth, shall fall into woo / *Risus* (sayth [f. 57] he) 20 *dolore miscebitur, & extrema gaudij luctus occupat* / laughter shalbe menglid with sorow, & thend of mirth is taken vpp with hevynes / And our saviour sayth hym selfe *ve vobis qui ridetis, quia lugebitis & flebitis* / woo be to you that laugh / for you shall wepe & wayle. But he sayth on the tother side *Beati qui lugent, quoniam illi consolabuntur* / Blessid be they 25 that wepe & wayle, for they shalbe comfortid / and he sayth to his discyples / *Mundus gaudebit* / *vos autem dolebitis* / *sed tristitia vestra vertetur in gaudium* / the world shall ioy & you shalbe sory / but your sorow shalbe tournyd in to ioy / and so is it you wot well now, & the mirth of many that than were in ioy, is now tournyd all to sorow / And 30 thus you see by the scripture playne, that in mater of very comfort / tribulacion is as farre above prosperite, as the day is above the night.

---

1 petites /] *period after* / *B*; s.paule] *wr. by B in blank space left by A*   2 to] *canc. and* vnto *interl. B*, vnto *1557*   5 that thyng] the thing *1573*   7 will] *om. L 1557*; well] *om. 1553 1573*; yet] it *A*: y *added before* i *E?*, yit *canc. and* yet *wr. in margin B*, yet *Z*   9 the farr] farre the *Z*   14 sowneth] soundeth *Z*; Ecclesiastes] Eccliastes *A*   15 now] right nowe *L* 16 fest /] *question-mark before* / *B*; sowneth] soundeth *Z*   18 this wherto draweth *canc. B after* draweth (*repetition A*)   19 (sayth] / sayth *A*   22 ridetis] redetis *1557*   24 tother] other *1553 1557 1573*; be] *canc. and* are *interl. B*, are *Z*   25 to] vnto *L 1553 1573* 26 discyples] s *ins. B*; gaudebit] u *interl. A*   27–28 your sorow] *after* your *A first wrote* soroʳ, *then wrote final* w, *then canc. word and wrote* sorow

A nother prehemynaunce of tribulacion ouer welth in occasion of
merite and reward shall well apere vppon certeyne consideracions well
markid in them both. [f. 57ᵛ]

Tribulacion meritith in pacience, & in the obedient confirmyng
of the mans will vnto god, & in thankes givyng to god for his visitacion. 5

Yf you reken me now agaynst these / many other good dedes that
a welthy man may do / as by riches give almes / by aucthorite labour
in doyng meny men iustice / or yf you fynd ferther eny such other
thyng like / first I say that the pacyent person in tribulacion, hath in
all those vertues of a welthy man an occasion of merite to, the which a 10
welthy man hath not agaynward in the fore rehersid vertues of his /
for it is easy for the person that is in tribulacion, to be well willyng
to do the selfe same yf he could / & than shall his good will where the
power lacketh, go very nere to the merite of the dede.

But now is not the welthe man in a like case, with the will of 15
pacience & confirmyte & thankes geven to god for tribulacion / sith
it is not so redye for the welthy man to be content to be in the tribulacion, that is the occasion of the pacientes desert / as for the trowbled
to be content to [f. 58] be in prosperite / to do the good dedes that
the welthy ˹man˺ doth. 20

Besides this / all that the welthy ˹man˺ doth, though he cold not do
them without ˹those˺ thynges that are accomptid for welth & callid
by that name / as not do greate almes without greate ryches / nor do
those many men right by his labour without aucthoritie / yet may he
do these thynges beyng not in welth in dede / as where he taketh his 25
welth for no welth / nor his riches for no riches / nor in hart settith by
neyther nother / but secretly liveth in a contrite hart & a lifo penytentiall / as many tymes did the prophet David beyng a greate kyng /
so that worldly welth was no welth vnto hym / And therfor it is not
of necessitie worldly welth to be cause of these good dedes, sith he may 30

1 prehemynaunce] h canc. B   2 apere] extra final e canc. B   4 confirmyng] conforming
Ƶ   5 the mans] the om. L 1553; givyng] geuen Ƶ   7 almes] allmoyse L, almose 1553
1557 1573   10 those] these Ƶ; a welthy] the wealthy L 1553 1573; to, the which a] to,
whiche the Ƶ   15 welthe] y wr. over final e B; man] om. 1553   16 confirmyte] conformyte L, conformitie 1553 1557 1573   18 the occasion] the om. L 1553; trowbled]
troubled persone Ƶ   22 those] wr. by B in blank space left by A, these L; thynges] es added B
23 not do] not to doo L; almes] allmoyse L, almose 1553 1557 1573   24 those] these
Ƶ; without] without the 1553, without great 1557 1573   29 vnto] to Ƶ; it] canc. B, om. Ƶ
30 to be] to canc. B, th wr. over b B; to be cause] called the cause L 1553, the cause 1557
1573; these] those Ƶ

do them & doth them best in dede / to whom the thyng that worldly
folke call welth is yet for his godly set mynd drawen fro the delight
therof, no pleasure in maner nor no welth at all.

Fynally whan so euer the welthy man doth those good vertues dedes
5 / yf we consider the nature [f. 58ᵛ] of them right / we shall perceyve
that in the doyng of them, he doth euer for the rate & porcion of those
dedes, mynish the mater of his worldly welth / as in givyng greate
almouse, he departeth ⌐with¬ so much of his worldly goodes which
are in that part the mater of his welth / In laboryng about the doyng
10 of many good dedes, his labour minysheth his quiet & his rest / & for
the rate of so much / it mynysheth his welth / yf payne and welth be
ech to other contrary / as I wene ye will agree they be.

Now who so euer than will well consider the thing / he shall I dowt
not perceyve & see therin / in thes good dedes that the welthy man
15 doth / though he doth it be that / that his welth makith hym able,
yet in the doyng of them he departith for the porcion from the nature
of welth, toward the nature of some part of tribulacion / And therfor
evyn in thos good dedes themselfe that prosperitie doth in goodnes
the prerogatyue of tribulacion above welth aperes / Now yf it happ
20 that some man can not perceve this [f. 59] poynt, because the welthe man for all his almes abidith rich still, and for all his good labour
abydith still in his aucthorite / let hym consider that I speke / but
after the porcion / And because the porcion of all that he giveth of his
goodes, is very litell in respect of that he leveth / Therfor is the
25 reson happly with some folke litell percevid / but yf it so were that he
went forth with givyng / till he had given out all, & lefte hymselfe
nothyng / than wold a very blynd man see it / for as he were from
riches come to pouertie / so were he from welth willyngly fallen
into tribulacion / And betwene labour and rest the reason goeth alike

---

2 is yet] (is yet) *A*; fro] from *L 1553 1573*   4 vertues] vertuouse *L*, verteous *1553*, vertuous *1557 1573*   5 / yf] (yf *A*   6 the doyng] the *om. L 1553 1573*   9–10 doyng of] of
om. 1557   12 other] the other *L*; ye] you *Z*; will] wyll well *L*   14 in thes] that *interl.
above* in (*uncanc.*) *B*, that in these *Z*   14–15 man doth] manne dooeth *1553*; it] *canc. and*
them *interl. B*; be] y *wr. over* e *B*; doth it be] dooe them by *L 1553 1573*, doth them by *1557*;
that /] | *canc. B*   16 in the] the *om. L 1553*   18 dedes] dedes / *A*; doth in] dooeth:
dooeth in *1553*, doth: doth in *1557*, doth, doth in *L 1573*   19 aperes] aperee *A*:
final e *canc. and correction wr. over penult.* e *B*, appeare *Z* (*see note*)   20–21 welthe] y
wr. over final e *B*, wealthy *Z*   21 almes] allmoyse *L*, almose *1553 1557 1573*
22 speke /] | *canc. B*   28 riches] rychesse *1553*; come] ceme *1557*   29 alike] all
alyke *Z*

/ which who can so consider, shall see that for the porcion in euery good dede done by the welthy man, the mater is all one. Than sith we haue somwhat weyed the vertues of prosperitie / let vs consider on the tother side the afore namyd thynges that are the mater of merite & reward in tribulacion / that is to wit pacience confirmyte / & 5 thankes.

Pacyence, the welthy man hath not in that that he is welthy / for yf he be pynched in any poynt / wherin he taketh pacyence, in that part he suffreth some tribulacion / & so not by his prosperite but by his tribulacion hath the man that merite. [f. 59ᵛ]   10

Lyke ys it yf we wold saye / that yf the welthye man hath a nother vertew in the stede of pacience / that ys to wit to kepe hym selfe from pride, & from such other synnes as welth wold bryng ⌐him⌐ to / for the resistyng of such mocions is as I before told you, without any dowt a mynyshyng of fleshly welth / & is a very trew kynd & one of the 15 most profitable kyndes of tribulacion / so that all that good merite groweth to the welthy man, not by his welth but by the mynishyng of his welth with holsome tribulacion /

The most colour of comparison is in the tother tweyn, that is to wit in the confirmyte of mans will vnto god, & in the thankes givyng vnto 20 god / for like as the good man in tribulacion sent hym by god, conformeth his will to godes will in that behalfe, & giveth god thanke therfor / so doth the welthy man in his welth which god giveth hym, conforme his will to godes in that poynt / sith he is well content to take it of his gyfte / and giveth god agayne also right harty thanke 25 therfor.

And thus as I said in these two thynges may you catch the most colour to compare the welthy mans merite with the merite of tribulacion. But [f. 60] yet that they be not matches / you may sone see by this / for in tribulacion can there none confirmc his will vnto godes 30 & give hym thanke therfore / but such a man as hath in that poynt a very speciall good mynd / But he that is very nought / or hath in

---

1 who can so] whoso canne Ƶ   4 tother] other *1553 1557 1573*   5 confirmyte] conformyte L, conformitie *1553 1557 1573*   7 that that] *second* that *om. 1553 1573*
8–9 that part] the parte *1557*   11 that yf] yf *om.* Ƶ   12 to kepe] the kepyng of Ƶ
13 from such] from *om. 1557*   14 of] *om.* L *1553*   19 tother] other *1553 1557 1573*
20 confirmyte] conformyte L, conformitie *1553 1557 1573*   20 the thankes] the *om.* Ƶ;
givyng] geuen *1553 1557 1573*   22 to godes will] *om.* L *1553*   24 godes] goddes wyll
L *1553 1573*   27 you] u *wr. over illeg. letter* B; the most] the *om.* L *1553 1573*   30
confirme] conforme Ƶ

his hart but very litell good, may well be content to take welth at
godes hand / and say mary I thanke you ⌜sir⌝ for this with all myn
hart, & will not fayle to love you well while you let me fare no worse.
⌜Confitebimur tibi cum benefeceris ei.⌝

5   Now yf the welthy man be very good / yet in confirmyte of his
will & thankes given to god for his welth, his vertue is not like yet to
his that doth the same in tribulacion / For as the phylosophers said in
that thyng very well of old / vertue standith in thynges of ⌜hardnes
& difficulty. And than as I told you much lesse⌝ hardnes / & lesse
10 dificultie there is ⌜by⌝ a greate deale to be content & to confirm our
will to godes will & to give hym thankes to / for our ease / than for our
payne / for our welth than for our woo / And therfor is the confirmyng
of our will vnto godes / & the thankes that we give hym for our tribulacion, more worthy thanke agayne, and more rewarde meritith in
15 the very fast welth & felicite of hevyn / than our confirmyte with our
thankes givyn for & in our worldly welth here. [f. 60ᵛ]
    And this thyng saw the devyll when he said vnto our lord of Iob /
that it was no mervayle though Iob had a reverent feare vnto god /
god had done so much for hym & kept hym in prosperite / but the
20 devill wist well that it was an hard thyng for Iob to be so lovyng &
so to give thankes to god in tribulacion & aduersitie. And therfor was
he glad to get leve of god to put hym in tribulacion / & therby trustid
to cause hym murmour & gruge agaynst god with impacience / But
the devill had there a fall in his own tourne. For the pacience of Iob
25 in the short tyme of his aduersitie, gat hym much more favour &
thanke of god, & more is he renowmed & commendid in scripture for
that / than for all the goodnes of his long prosperouse lyfe /
    Our saviour sayth hymselfe also, that yf we say well by them or yeld
them thanke that doth vs good, we do no grete thyng therin / & therfor
30 can we with reason loke for no greate thanke agayne.
    And thus haue I shewid you lo no litell prehemynence, that tribula-

---

2 myn] my Z   3 worse.] period ed.   4 Confitebimur . . . ei] added by B in space at end
of paragr., Confitebitur Z   5 confirmyte] o wr. over i B, conformyte L, conformitie 1553
1557 1573   6 yet] e interl. A   10 to] om. L 1553 1573; confirm] o wr. over i B, conforme Z   11 thankes] thanke Z   12 confirmyng] o wr. over i B, conforming Z
13 vnto] to L, into 1553   15 confirmyte] o wr. over i B, conformyte L, conformitie 1553
1557 1573   17 vnto] to Z   18 that] om. Z   26 he] om. L 1553; & commendid in
scripture] in Scripture, & commended there L 1553 1573   27 goodnes] goones A: od
wr. over second o B   29 doth] th canc. B, doe Z   31 prehemynence] h canc. B, pre-
eminence Z

cion hath in merite / & therfor no litell prehemynence of comfort in hope of hevenly rewarde above the vertues / the merite / & cause of good hope & comfort that commeth of welth & prosperitie / [f. 61]

A summary comfort of tribulacion

The xxth Chapiter 5

And therfor good Cosyn to fynish our talkyng for this tyme / lest I shuld be to long a let vnto your other besines / If we lay first for a sewer grownd a very fast fayth / wherby we beleve to be trew all that the scripture sayth, vnderstondyng trewly as the old holy doctours declare it, and as the spirite of god instructith his catholique church / than shall we consider tribulacion as a graciouse gyfte of god: A gyfte that he specially gaue his speciall frendes / the thyng that in scripture is highly commendid & praysid / A thyng wherof the contrary long contynued is perilous / A thyng which but yf god send ˹it,˺ men haue nede by penaunce to put vppon them selfe and seke it / A thyng that helpith to purge our synnes passid / A thyng that preserueth vs fro sinne that els wold come / A thyng that causeth vs set les by the world, A thyng that excitith vs to draw more toward god, A thyng that much mynysheth our paynes in purgatory, A thyng that mych encreseth our fynall reward in hevyn, The thyng by which our saviour entuid his own [f 61ᵛ] kyngdome / The thyng with which all his apostelles folowid hym thether, The thyng which our saviour exortith all men to / The thyng without which (he sayth) we be not his dicyples, The thyng without which no man can get to hevyn.

Who so these thynges thynketh on, & remembreth well, shall in his tribulacion neyther murmur nor gruge / but first by pacience take his

---

1 prehemynence] h *canc. B*, preeminence *Ƶ*   2–3 vertues / the merite / . . . comfort that] vertues (the merite . . . comforte) that *1553 1557 1573, no punctuation L*   4 comfort] commendacion *Ƶ*   5 xxth] xx *1553 1557 1573*   9 vnderstondyng] vnderstanden *Ƶ* 10 spirite] spririte *A*, Scripture *L 1553*; instructith] u *interl. A*   11 god:] *colon ed.* 12 specially gaue] gaue speciallye *1553 1573*, gave specyally to *L*, geveth *canc. before* gaue *A*; speciall] *Ƶ*, speall *A*   15 to put] to *om. L 1553*   16–17 fro sinne] from synnes *L 1553 1573*, fro synnes *1557*   17 set] to set *Ƶ*   18 world,] *comma ed.*; god,] *comma ed.* 19 purgatory,] *comma ed.*   20 hevyn,] *comma ed.*   22 thether,] *comma ed.*   24 di- cyples,] s *ins. before* c *B, comma ed.*   25 on,] *comma erased?*

payne in worth / and than shall he grow in goodnes & thynke hymselfe well worthy / than shall he consider that god sendith it for his
well / and therby shall he be movid to give god thanke therfor.

Therwith shall his grace encrease / & god shall give hym such com-
5 fort by consideryng that god is in his trowble euermore nere vnto hym
/ *Quia deus iuxta est ijs qui tribulato sunt corde* / god is nere sayth the
prophet to them that haue their hart in trowble / that his ioy therof
shall mynysh much of his payne. And he shall not seke for vayne
comfort els where / but specially trust in god & seke for help of hym
10 submyttyng his own will wholy to godes pleasure, and pray to god in
his hart, & pray his frendes to pray [f. 62] for hym, and specially
the prestes as saynt Iames biddith / And begyn first with confession,
& make vs clene to god & redy to depart & be glad to go to god, puttyng purgatory in his pleasure / Yf we this do / this dare I boldly
15 say / we shall neuer live here the lesse of halfe an houre / but shall
with this comfort fynd our hartes lightid, & therby the grefe of our
tribulacion lessid, & the more likelyhed to recouer & to lyve the lenger
/ Now yf god will we shall hens / than doth he much more for vs / for
he that this way taketh, can not go but well / for of hym that is loth to
20 leve this wrechid world, myn hart is much in feare lest he dye not well
/ hard it is for hym to be welcome that cometh agaynst his will / that
sayth vnto god whan he cometh to fetch hym, welcome my maker
mawgre my tethe / but he that so loveth hym that he longeth to go to
hym / myn hart can not give me but he shalbe welcome / all were it so
25 that he shuld come or he were well pourgid, for charite couerith a
multitude of synnes / and he that trustith [f. 62ᵛ] in god can not be confoundid / And christ sayth / he that cometh to me I will not cast hym
out. And therfor let vs neuer make our rekenyng of long life / kepe it
while we may because god hath so comaundid / but yf god give the
30 occasion that with his goodnes we may go / let vs be glad therof &
long to go to hym / And than shall hope of hevyn comfort our hevines /

---

3 well] weale Z 6 ijs] hijs L 7 his] is A: h *added B*   8 payne.] *period ed.*
9 specially] specyall L 11 to pray] to *canc. B*, *om. 1553 1557 1573*   14 in] to Z;
Yf] yf A; this do] thus doe Z 15 h *canc. A before* halfe   16 this] his *1553*; h *canc. A
before* lightid   17 likelyhed] likelyhod L *1553 1573*, likelyhoode *1557*   19 well /] / *ed.*
(*end of line A*)   20 myn] my L *1553 1573*; is] Z, in A 21 agaynst] *divided*: agay-nst:
nst *canc. and added to* agay B 22 vnto] to L *1553 1573*   24 myn] my Z 25 or]
ere Z; pourgid,] *comma ed.*; couerith] *divided*: couer-ith (*with redundant superl.* r): *canc. and*
coveryth *interl. B*   27 of *wr. after* hym *and canc. A*   28 out] w *wr. over* u? B 30
goodnes] nes *canc. and* will *interl. B*, good wyll Z

& out of our transitory tribulacion shall we go to euerlastyng glory /
to which my good Cosyn I pray god bryng vs both /

Vincent

Myne own good vncle I pray god reward you / And at this tyme
will I no lenger troble you / I trow I haue this day done you mych 5
tribulacion with myne importune obiections of very litell substaunce /
And you haue evyn shewid me a sample of sufferaunce in beryng my
foly so long & so paciently / And yet shalbe so bold vppon you
ferther, as to seke some tyme to talke forth of the remenaunt, the
most profitable poynt of tribulacion which you said you reseruid to 10
treat of last of all. [f. 63]

Anthony

Let that be hardely very shortly Cosyn, while this is fresh in mynd /

Vyncent

I trust good vncle so to put this in remembrans, that it shall neuer 15
be forgotton with me / our lord send you such comfort as he knowith
to be best.

Anthonye

That is wel said good Cosyn / and I pray the same good for you, &
for all our other frendes that haue nede of comfort / for whom I 20
thinke more than for your selfe / you nedid of some counsayle.

Vincent

I shall with this good counsaill that I haue hard of you, do them
some comfort I trust in god / to whose kepyng I commyt you /

Anthonye   25

And I you also / Fare well myn own good Cosyn.

---

6 myne] my Z 7 a sample] an ensample Z 8 shalbe] e *canc. and* b *alt. to* l B, I be
interl. B, shall I be Z 13 hardely very shortly Cosyn] verye shortelye Cosin hardely
L *1553*   19 good] *canc.* B, *om.* Z 21 your selfe /] / *canc.* B   26 myn] my *1553*

The second boke

Vyncent [f. 63ᵛ]

Hit is to me good vncle no litell comfort / that as I came in here,
I herd of your folke / that you haue had syns my last beyng here (god
5 be thankid) metely good rest / & your stomake somwhat more come
to you / For verely albeit I had hard befor, that in respect of the
greate greef / that for a moneth space had holden you / you were a
litell before my last comyng to you some what easid & relevid / for
els wold I not for no good haue put you to the payne to talke so much
10 / as you than did / yet after my departyng from you, remembring how
long we taried together, and that we were all that while in talkyng /
And all the labour yours in talkyng so long together without interpawsyng betwene / & that of mater studiouse & displesaunt, all of
desease & siknes & other payne & tribulacion: I was in good fayth
15 very sory & not a litell wroth with my selfe for myn ˹own˺ ouer sight,
that I had so litell considerid your payne / & very ferd I was till I herd
other word, lest you shuld haue waxid weker & more sik therafter /
But now I thanke our lord that hath sent the contrary / for els [f. 64]
a litell castyng bakke, were in this greate age of yours no litell daynger
20 & perell.

Anthonye

Nay nay good Cosyn / to talke mych / except some other payne let
me / ys to me litell griefe / A fond old man is often so full of wordes as
a woman. It is you wot well / as some poetes paynt vs / all the lust of
25 an old foles lyfe / to sit well & warm with a cupp & a rostid crabb
& dryvill & drinke & talke.

But in earnest Cosyn our talkyng was to me great comfort, &

---

1 The second boke] The Seconde booke of trybulacion and comforte there agaynst. *L*, The
.ii. Boke *1557*, OF CVMFORT AGAINST TRIBULATION THE SECOND BOOKE.
1573   3 Hit] It *Ƶ*   7 moneth] moneths *L 1573*   9 I not] not I *1553 1573*
11 that we were] that while we were *1573*   12 And all] And *om. L 1553 1573*; labour
yours] labour was yours *1553 1573*   15 myn] my *L*   17 waxid] waxen *1573*; therafter]
hereafter *1553*   18 our lord] god *1553*   23 so] *canc. and* as *interl. B*; is often so] is as
often *1553*, is often as *L 1557 1573*   24 wh *canc. before* woman *A*

nothyng displesaunt at all / for though we communid of sorow &
hevynes / yet was the thyng that we cheefly thought apon / not the
tribulacion yt selfe, but the comfort that may grow theron / And
therfor am I now very glad that you be come to fynish vpp the
remanaunt.   5

Vincent

Of trowth my good vncle it was comfortable [f. 64ᵛ] to me & hath
byn syns to some other of your frendes, to whom as my pore wit &
remembraunce wold serue me / I did / and not nedeles / report & reherse your most comfortable counsayle / and now come I for the 10
remenaunt / & am very ioyfull that I fynd you so well refresshid & so
redy therto / But yet this one thyng good vncle I besech you hartely,
that yf I for delyte to here you speke in the mater, forget my selfe &
you both, & put you to to mych payne / remember you your own
ease and / when you lyst to leve, commaund me ⌜to⌝ go my way & 15
seke some other tyme.

Anthony

Forsoth Cosyn many wordes yf a man were very weke / spokyn
(as you said right now) without interpawsyng, wold peradventure at
length somwhat wery hym / And therfor wished I the last tyme after 20
you were gone / when I felt my selfe (to sey the trowth) evyn a litell
wery / that I had not so told you styll a long tale alone / but that
we [f. 65] had more often enterchaungid wordes / & partid the talke
betwene vs, with ⌜ofter⌝ enterparlyng vppon your part / in such
maner as lernid men vse betwene the persons / whom they devise 25
disputyng in their faynid diologes. But yet in that poynt I sone
excusid you, & layd the lak evyn where I found yt / and that was evyn
vppon myn own nekke / For I remembrid that betwene you & me, it
farid as yt did ones betwene a none & her brother.

---

1 communid] commoned *1553 1557 1573*   12 But yet] yet *om. Z*   13 yf I for] I *om.*
L 1553 1573; forget] I forgeat *L 1553 1573*   15 when] then if *1553*; lyst] lust *1553*
1557 1573   16 seke] to seke *1553 1573*   18 were very] very *om. 1553 1573*   19 (as]
/ as *A: parenth. wr. over* / *B*   21 felt] left *1553*; trowth] trewth *L*, trueth *1553 1557 1573*
23 enterchaungid] *one minim lacking in* un *A*; talke] yng *added B*: y *wr. over* e, talking *Z*
24 ofter] other *A: canc. and* ofter *interl. B* (*see note*); enterparlyng] y *wr. over blotted* y *B*,
enterpausing *1553*   26 diologes] *first* o *alt. to* a *B*   28 remembrid] remembre *L*

Very vertuouse was this ladye, & of a very vertuous place, a close
religion, & therin had be long. In all which tyme she had neuer
seen her brother / which was in like wise very vertuouse to, & had bene
farr of at an vniuersite, & had there take the degre of doctour in
5 diuynitie / When he was come home, he went to see his sister / as he
that highly reioycid in her vertue / So came she to the grate that they
call I trow the locutory / And after their holy watch word spoken on
both the sides, after the maner vsid in that place, the tone toke the
tother by the typp of the finger for hand wold ther [f. 65ᵛ] none be
10 wrongyn through the grate / and forwith began my ladye to give her
brother a sermon of the wrechednes of this world, & the frayelte of
the flesh, & the subtill sleight of the wikked fend / & gaue hym surely
good counsayle (savyng somwhat to long) how he shuld be well ware
in his lyvyng, & master well his body for savyng of his sowle / And yet
15 ere her own tale came all at an end / she began to fynd a litell fawt
with hym / and sayd / In good fayth brother I do somewhat mervayle,
that you that haue bene at lernyng so long, & are ⌐a⌐ doctour, & so
lernid in the law of god / do not now at our metyng (while we mete
so seld) to me that am your syster & a symple vnlernid sowle, give
20 of your charitie some frutfull exortacion / And as I dowt not but you
can sey some good thyng your selfe / By my trouth good sister / quoth
her brother I can not for you / for your tong haue neuer ceasid, but
said inough for vs bothe. And so Cosyn I remembrid that whan I
was ones fall in, I lefte you litell space to say ought betwene / But now
25 will I therfor take an other way with you / for I shall of our talkyng
drive you to the tone halfe / [f. 66]

Vincent

Now forsoth vncle this was a merye tale. But now yf you make me
take the tone halfe / than shall you be contentid / fare otherwise than

---

1 place,] *comma ed.*, place in *1553 1573*   2 be long] bene long *Z*   3 to] *om. 1553 1573*
4 take] taken *Z*   5 When] when *A*   8 both the] the *om.* L *1553 1573*; the tone] one
(the *om.*) *1553*, the one *1557 1573*   9 tother] other *1553 1557 1573*; none be] be none
L *1553 1573*   10 forwith] forthwyth *Z*   12 sleight] sleightes *Z*; surely] sure L
13 to long] to *om. 1553*   17 a] *om. Z*   18 while] seing *1553 1573*   19 seld)] *parenth.*
added B, seldom *1553 1557 1573*   20 And as I dowt] For I doubt *1553 1573*   21 good]
om. L   22 haue] hath *Z*   23 remembrid] remember *1553 1557 1573*   24 fall]
fallen *Z*   26 tone] one *1553 1557 1573*   29 take] l *ins. before* k *B*, talke *Z*; tone]
one *1553 1557 1573*; contentid /] | *canc. B*; fare] e *canc. B*

there was ⌐of late⌐ a kynswoman of your own / but which will I not tell
you, gesse there and you can / Her husband had mych pleasure in the
maner and behavour of an other honest man, & kept hym therfor
mych company / by the reason wherof he was at his meale tyme the
more oft from home / So happid it on a tyme, that his wife and he 5
together dynid or soupid with that neybour of theirs / And than she
made a mery quarell to hym, for makyng her husband so good chere
out at dore that she could not haue hym at home / For soth mastres
quod he (as he was a dry mery man) In my company nothyng kepeth
hym but one / Serve you hym with the same, & he will neuer be from 10
you / what gay thyng may that be quoth our Cosyn than / forsoth mastres quoth he your husband loveth well to talke / & whan he sittith
with me I let hym haue all the wordes / All the wordes quoth she /
mary [f. 66ᵛ] that am I content he shall haue all the wordes with
good will as he hath euer had / but I speke them all my selfe, & give 15
them all to hym / & for ought that I care for them so shall he haue
them styll / but otherwise to say that he shall haue them all / you
shall kepe hym still rather than he get the halfe.

Anthonye

For soth Cosyn I can sone gesse which of our kyn she was / I wold 20
we had none therin for all her mery wordes / that lesse wold lett there
husbandes for to talke /

Vincent

Forsoth she is not so mery but she is as good / But where you fynd
faute vncle that I speke not ynough / I was in good fayth asshamyd 25
that I spake so much / & movid you such questions / as I found vppon

---

1 there] re *wr. by B over faulty* r *in A*; of late] *interl. E*   2 you,] *comma ed.*; gesse] gest
A: se *wr. over* t *B*; there] *canc. and* her *interl. B*, her *Z*; can] *abbrev. form canc. and* can *interl. B*
4 the reason] the *om. L*   4–5 the more] the *om. 1553*   5 oft] often *L 1553 1573*; happid]
happened *1553 1573*   8 at dore] a dore *Z*; For] for *A*   9 man)] *parenth. added B*
10 from] fro *L*   14 am I] I am *L*; with] with a *1553 1573*   15 but] For *1553 1573*;
them all] them not al *1553*, them not al to *1573*; & give] but geue *1553 1573*   16 so
shall he] he shall (so *om.*) *1553 1573*   17 otherwise] yet *1553*   18 kepe hym still
rather] then rather kepe him stil *1553*, rather kepe him stil *1573*; he get the halfe] he shall
gett the tone half *L*, he shal geat the one half at my handes *1553 1573*   20–21 I wold we
had none therin] but yet the fewer of that kinde, the quieter is the many *1553*   21 lesse]
thus *1553*; there] i *interl. before* r *A?*, her *1553*   22 husbandes] husbande *1553*; for to
talke] for *om. Z*   25 speke] spake *L*   26 as I] which I *1553*

your answere might better haue bene sparid / they were so litell worth /
But now sith I se you be so well content, that I shall not forbere boldly
to shew my foly / I will be no more so shamfast / but aske you what me
lyst. [f. 67]

5   Whether a man may not in tribulacion vse some
worldly recreacion for his comfort

The first chapiter

And first good vncle ere we procede ferther, I will be bold to move
you one thyng more / of that we talkid when I was here before / For
10 whan I revolvid in my mynd agayne, the thynges that were here concludid by you / me thought you wold in no wyse that in any tribulacion, men shuld seke for comfort eyther in worldly thyng or fleshly,
which mynd vncle of yours semeth somwhat hard / For a mery tale
with a frend, refresheth a man much / & without any harm lightith
15 his mynd & amendith his courage & his stomake / so that it semeth
but well done to take such recreacion / And Salamon sayth I trow,
that men shuld in hevines give the sory man wyne to make him forget
his sorow / And saynt Thomas sayth that proper plesaunt talkyng
which is callid ⌜εὐτραπελία,⌝ is a good vertew, servyng to refresh the
20 mynd & make it quikke & lusty to labour & study agayne / where
contynuall fatigacion wold make it dull and dedly /

Anthonye

Cosyn I forgat not that poynt / but I longid not much [f. 67ᵛ] to
towch it / For neyther might I well vtterly forbere it where the case
25 might happe to fall that yt shuld not hurt / And on the tother side yf
the case so shuld fall / me thought yet it shuld litell nede to give any
man counsayle to yt: folke are prone inough to such fansies of their

---

4 lyst] lust *1553 1557*   9 one] *interl. A*; thyng] othyng *A*: o *canc. A?*; here before] before
om. *L 1553*; For] *om. L 1553*   10 here] *canc. and interl. after* concludid *B*, concluded here *Z*
11 you] ye *Z*   15 his courage] his *om. L 1553*; his stomake] his *om. 1573*   19 εὐτραπελία,] *wr. by B in blank space left by A*   23 longid] long *1553*   24 well] *interl. A*;
forbere] forbidde *L 1553 1573*; case] cause *Z*   25 tother] other *1553 1557 1573*
26 yet it] yet I *L 1553 1573*   27 man] *om. L 1553 1573*; yt:] *colon ed., period? B?*;
fansies] fantasies *1553 1557 1573*

own mynd / you may se this by our selfe, which commyng now
together to talke of as ernest ⌐sad¬ mater as men can devise / were fallen yet evyn at the first into wanton idell talys / And of trouth Cosyn /
as you know very well my selfe am of nature evyn halfe a giglot &
more / I wold I cold as easly mend my faute as I well know yt / But 5
scant can I refrayne yt as old a fole as I am / how beit so parciall will I
not be to my fawte as to prayse it. But for that you require my mynd
in the matter whither men in tribulacion may not laufully seke
recreacion, & comfort them selfe with some honest myrth: First agreed
that our chiefe comfort must be of god, & that with hym we must 10
begyn, & with hym contynew, & with hym end also / A man to take
now & than some honest worldly myrth / I dare not be so sore as vtterly to forbyd yt / sith good men & well lernid haue in some case alowid
it, specyally for the diuersitie of diuers mens myndes / for els yf we
were [f. 68] all such as I wold god we were, & such as naturall wyse- 15
dome wold we shuld be, & is not all clene excusable that we be not in
dede, I wold than put no dout / but that vnto any man the most comfortable talkyng that could be, were to here of hevyn / where as now
(god help vs) our wrechednes ys such, that in talkyng awhil therof,
men wax almost werye / & as though to here of hevyn were an 20
hevy burdeyne / they must refresh them selfe after with a folysh
tale /

Our affeccion toward hevenly ioyes waxith wonderfull cold / yf
drede of hell were as far gone / very few wold fere god / but that yet a
litell styketh in our stomakes / marke me cosyn at the sermon / & 25
commonly toward the end somewhat the precher spekith of hell &
of hevyn / now whille he precheth of the paynes of hell styll they stand
& yet give hym the heryng / but as sone as he cometh to the ioyes of
hevyn, they be buskyng them bakward & flokmele fall away / It is in
the sowle somewhat as it is in the bodye / Som are there of nature / or 30
of evill custome come to that poynt / that a worse thyng some tyme
more stedeth them then a better / Some man yf he be sik / ⌐can away

---

1 our] your A: y canc. B   2 mater] matters L 1553   5 cold] u interl. before l B;
I well] I can wel L 1553 1573   10 of] canc. and in wr. after B, in Z   15 I] canc. B,
om. Z (I also canc. in catchwords, f. 67ᵛ)   19 awhil] final e added B   26 toward] towardes Z   26–27 of hell & of hevyn] of heaven & hell L, of hell and heauen 1553 1557
1573   27 paynes of hell] paynes in hell L 1553; they] thye A   28 & yet] yet and
L 1553 1573; cometh] coneth A: minim added before n B   29 away /] period after / B
32 more stedeth them] stedeth them more 1553 1573

with[1] no holsome mete [f. 68ᵛ] nor no medicyn can go down with
them / but yf it be temprid with some such thing for his fancye as
maketh the meate or the medisin lesse holsome then it shuld bee / And
yet ⌐while⌐ yt will be no better, we must let hym haue it so.

5 Cassianus that very good vertuose ⌐man⌐ rehersith in a certen col-
lacion of his, that a certen holy father in makyng of a sermon, spake
of hevyn & of hevynly thynges so celestially that much of his audience
with the swete sowne therof began to forget all the world & fall a
slepe / which whan the father beheld he dissemblid their slepyng &
10 sodenly said vnto them I shall tell you a mery tale / at which word
they lyft vp their hedes & herknid vnto that / And after the slepe
therwith broken, herd hym tell on of hevyn agayne / In what wise
that good father rebukid than their vntoward myndes so dull vnto the
thyng that all our life we labour for / & so quikke & lusty toward
15 other trifles / I neyther bere in mynd nor shall here nede to reherse /
But thus much of that mater suffisith for our purpose / that where as
you demaund me whether in tribulacion men may not [f. 69] sometyme refresh them selfe with worldly myrth & recreacion / I can no
more saye / but he that can not long endure to hold vpp his hedd &
20 here talkyng of hevyn except he be now & than betwene (as though
hevyn were hevynes) refreshid with a folish mery tale / there is none
other remedy, but you most let hym haue yt / better wold I wish it but
I can not help it.

How be it let vs by myne advise at the lest wise, make these kyndes
25 of recreacion as short & seld as we can / let them serue vs but for
sawce & make them not our meate / and let vs pray vnto god & all
our good frendes for vs, that we may fele such a savour in the delite of
hevyn / that in respect of the talkyng of the ioyes therof, all worldly
recreacion be but a grief to thinke on / And be sure Cosyn that yf we
30 myght ones purchase the grace to come to that poynt / we neuer of

---

1–2 with them] with him Z   2 fancye] fantasie 1553 1557 1573   3 meate] matter L
1553   4 while] will A: canc. and while interl. B   5 good] canc. B, om. Z; man] interl. E
7 & of hevynly] of om. Z   8 sowne] sounde Z   9 comma after father B   11 herknid]
hernid A: k ins. E, word canc. and harkenyd interl. B; lyft] lifted 1573   12 herd] they
hard L   15 illeg. letter interl. and canc. after neyther B   16 that mater] the matter
1553 1573; suffisith] second s wr. over illeg. letter (c?) B; as] interl. A   18 sometyme
canc. after selfe A   20 parenth. before except A; (as though] Z, no parenth. A, (as though
to heare of L 1553 1573   21 mery] canc. and interl. before folish B, mery folishe Z; tale /]
parenth. wr. over / B   22 most] must Z   24 these] those Z   25 seld] as selde Z   30
we neuer] fownd interl. after neuer B, we found L, we neuer founde 1553 1557 1573

worldly recreacion had so much comfort in a yere, as we shuld fynd in
bethynkyng vs of hevyn in lesse than halfe an howre / /

Vyncent

In fayth vncle / I can well agre to this / & I pray god [f. 69ᵛ] bring
vs / ones to take such a savour in it / And surely as you began the 5
tother daye / by fayth must we com to it / and to fayth by prayour /
But now I pray you good vncle vouchsafe to procede in our principall
mater.

Of the short vncerteyne life in extreme age or siknes /

The ij Chapiter

Anthonye

Cosyn I haue bethought me somewhat of this mater syns we were
last together / & I fynd yt (yf we shuld go some way to worke) a thyng
that wold require many mo dayes to treat of / than we shuld happely 15
fynd mete therto / in so few as my selfe wene that I haue now to lyve /
while euery tyme is not like with me / & among many paynfull in
which I loke euery day to depart / my mendyng dayes come very
seld & are very shortly gone / For surely Cosyn I can not liken my
selfe more metely now than to the snofe of a candell that burneth 20
with in the candell styk nose / for as that snofe burneth down so low /
that who that loketh on it, wold wene it were quyte owt / And yet
sodenly lyfteth a leme [f. 70] halfe an Inch aboue the nose, & giveth
a praty short light agayne / and thus playeth diuers tymes till at last
or it be lokyd for out it goeth all together / so haue I Cosyn dyuers 25
such dayes together / as euery day of them I loke evyn for to dye / And

1 recreacion] recreatyon never L; had] canc. B, om. Z   1-2 in bethynkyng] in the bethynkyng Z   6 tother] other 1553 1557 1573   11 ij] ij / A   13 of] canc. and vppon
interl. B, vpon Z   14 a] A wr. over t A   15 of] therof Z   16 therto /] / canc. B
20 selfe] lyfe Z; now] w wr. over illeg. letter B; snofe] canc. and snuff interl. B   21 candell
styk] candelstyckes 1553 1557 1573; that snofe] snofe canc. and snuff interl. B, the snuffe Z;
burneth] some time burneth Z   22 who that] who so Z   23 lyfteth a] lifteth vp a
1557; leme] leame L, flame 1553 1557 1573   25 or it] ere it Z

yet haue I than after that some such few dayes agayne / as you see me
now haue your selfe / in which a man wold wene that I might yt ⌈well⌉
contynew. But I know my lingryng not likly to last long / but out will
my sowle sodenly some day within a while. And therfor will I with
5 godes help (seme I neuer so well a mendid) neuerthelesse rekyn euery
day for my last / for though that to the repressyng / of the bold
courage of blynd youth / ther is a very trew proverbe / that as sone
commeth a yong sheps skyn to the market as an old / yet this differens
ther is at the lest betwene them / that as the yong man may happ some-
10 tyme to dye sone / so the old man can neuer live long / And therfor
Cosyn in our mater here, levyng out many thynges that I wold els
treate of / I shall for this tyme speke but of very few / howbeit hereafter
yf god send me mo such dayes / than will we whan you list ferther talke
of mo. [f. 70ᵛ]

15   He devidith tribulacion into / 3 / kyndes of which / 3 /
                      the last he shortly passith ouer

                           The third Chapiter

       All maner of tribulacion Cosyn that any man can haue, as far as for
this tyme cometh to my mynd, falleth vnder some one at the lest of
20 these three kyndes / either is it such as hym selfe willyngly taketh, or
secondly such as hym selfe willyngly suffreth / or fynally such as he can
not put from hym //
       This third kynd I purpose not much more to speke of now / for
therof shall as for this tyme suffice these thynges that we haue
25 treatid betwene vs this other day / what kynd of tribulacion this is I
am sure your selfe perceve / For siknes, imprisonment, losse of good,
losse of frendes, or such bodely harm as a man hath all redy caught

2 now haue] now to haue L 1553 1573; yt] e interl. after y B, yet 1557 1573, om. L 1553
4 sowle] canc. B, underlined for cancellation and snuff interl. E with clarifying strokes by B, snuffe
Z; And] and A   6 repressyng /] | canc. B   8 old /] old) A   12–13 hereafter yf god]
if god hereafter Z   13 yf god] canc. and yet if god interl. before hereafter B; tyme canc. A
before mo such; list] luste 1553 1557   15 / 3 /] second / ed.   16 shortly passith] passeth
shortly L 1553 1573   17 third] iii Z   20 either is it] either it is L 1553 1573   23 not
much] not not moche L   24 these] those Z; haue] om. Z   26 good] es added B,
goodes Z   27 frendes,] frendes / A: comma wr. over / B

& can in no wise avoyd / These thynges & such like are the third kynd
of tribulacion that I speke of, which a man neyther willyngly taketh
in the begynnyng / nor can though he wold put willyngly away /

Now thynke I that as to the man that laketh wit [f. 71] & fayth, no
comfort can serue what so euer counsayle be gevyn / so to them that 5
haue both, I haue as to this kynd said in maner ynough all redye.

And consideryng that suffer it nedes he must / while he can by no
maner of mene put it from hym / the very necessitie is halfe counsayle
inough to take it in good worth & bere it pacyently & rather of his
pacience to take both ease & thanke / than by freting & by fumyng 10
to encrease his present payne / & by murmur & gruge to fall into
ferther daynger after, by displeasing of god with his froward behaviour. And yet albeit that I thynke that that is said suffiseth / yet
here & there I shall in the second kynd, shew some such comfortes
as shall well serue vnto this last kynd to /   15

The iiij Chapiter

The first kynd also will I shortly passe / for the tribulacion that a
man taketh hym selfe willyngly which no man puttith vppon hym
agaynst his own will / is you wot well / as I somwhat touchid the last
day, such affliccion of the flessh or expence of his [f. 71ᵛ] goodes as a 20
man taketh hym selfe / or willyngly bestoweth in punyshment of his
own synne & for devocion to god.

Now in this tribulacion nedeth the man none to comfort hym / for
while no man troubleth hym but hym selfe (which feleth how farrforth
he may convenyently bere / & of reason and good discrecion shall 25
not passe that / wherin yf any dowt arise counsaile nedeth & not comfort) the corage that for godes sake & his sowle helth kyndleth his hart
& enflamyth it therto, shall by the same grace that put it in his mynd /

---

3 put willyngly] afterward *interl.* B above willyngly (*uncanc.*), put afterwarde Z   6 as to]
to *alt.* to for B, with to *interl.* B above for (*uncanc.*), as for Z   9 pacyently] *comma added*
B, then canc. B by stroke that may be virgule   10 & by fumyng] by *canc.* B, om. Z   11 to
fall] to om. Z; into] in Z   12–13 behaviour.] bhaviour A: e *and period ed.*   13 that
that is] that that which is L *1553 1573*   14 I shall] shall I L *1553 1573*; comfortes]
comfort Z   16 iiij] *superl.* th *added* B, Fowrth L   17 passe] passe ouer to Z
18 willyngly] *canc. and interl. before* taketh B; taketh hym selfe willyngly] willingly taketh
himself Z   19 own] om. L   23 the man none] he no man Z   24 (which) / which A

give hym such comfort & ⌐such¬ ioy therin, that the pleasure of his
sowle shall passe the payne of his body / yea and while he hath in hart
also some great hevynes for his synne / yet when he considereth the
ioy that shall come of it, his sowle shall not fayll to fele than that
5 straunge case, which my body felt ones in a grete feuer.

Vincent

What straunge case was that vncle?

Anthonye [f. 72]

Forsoth Cosyn evyn in this same bed / it is now more than fiften
10 yeres agoo / I lay in a tercian & had passid I trow iij or iiij fittes / But
after fell ther on me one fitte out of course / so straunge & so mervelouse, that ⌐I¬ wold in good fayth haue thought it vnpossible / for
I sodenly felt my selfe verely both hott & cold thorowgh out all my
body / not in some part the tone & in some part the tother (for that
15 had bene / you wot well / no very straung thing, to fele the hed hote
while the handes were cold) but the self same partes I say / so god
saue my sowle / I sensibly felt & right paynfully to / all in one instant
both hote and cold at ones.

Vincent

20 By my fayth vncle this was a wonderfull thyng, & such as I neuer
herd happen any man els in my dayes. And few men are there of whose
mowthes I could haue belevid it /

Anthony

Curtesye Cosyn peradventure lettith you to say / that you beleve
25 it not yet of my mowth neyther / And surely for fere of that / you shuld
not haue hard it of me neyther / had there not happid me a nother
thyng sone after / [f. 72ᵛ]

---

1 *second* such *om.* Z   3 yet when] yet then *1553*   5 in a grete feuer] in gret a feuer *1557*
7 vncle?] *question-mark ed.*   9 evyn] *om. 1553*   10 yeres] yere Z   11 on me one
fitte] one fitte on me L *1553 1573*   12 vnpossible] impossible Z   13 hott] e *wr. over
final* t *B*   14 tone] one *1553 1557 1573*; tother] other *1553 1557 1573*; (for] *parenth.
added B*   15 bene /] / *canc. B*; well /] / *canc. B*   16 cold)] *parenth. wr. over* / *B*, a colde L
1553   17 saue my sowle] my soule saue *1553 1573*   20 fayth] trouth L *1553 1573*
25–26 shuld not] not *om. 1553*   26–27 happid me a nother thyng] an other thing happed
me Z

Vincent

I pray you what was that vncle?

Anthonye

Forsoth Cosyn this / I askyd a phisicion or twayne that than lokyd
vnto me / how this shuld be posible / and they tweyne told me both 5
that it could not be so / but that I was fallen in some slumber and
dremyd that I felt yt so /

Vincent

This happ hold I litell cause / you to tell the tale the more boldly /

Anthony   10

No Cosyn that is trew lo / but than happid there a nother, that a
yong girle here in this towne / whom a kynsman of hers had begone
to tech phisike, told me that there was such a kynd of feuer in dede.

Vincent

By our lady vncle save for the credence of you, the tale wold I not 15
tell agayne vppon that happ of the maid / For though I know her now
for such, as I durst well beleve her / yt might happe her very well at
that tyme to lye / because she wold ye shuld take her for cunnyng //
[f. 73]

Anthonye   20

Ye but yet happid there an other happe theron cosyn that a worke
of galien / *De differentijs febrium* / is redy to be sold in the boke sellers
shopps / in which worke she shewid me than the chapiter where galyen
sayth the same.

---

2 that vncle?] *question-mark ed.*, that good vncle *1557 1573*   4 phisicion] phision *A*
5 posible] *second* s *ins. before* i *B*   6 not be so] so *om. L 1553*; in] into *1553 1557 1573*
7 yt] *om. L*   9 cause] causeth *1573*; the more] the *om. 1557*   11 a nother] an other
happe *L*   15 vncle] *wr. twice by A, second word canc. B*   15–16 not tell] not yet tell *Z*
17 well] well yet *L*   18 ye] you *Z*   21 yet] *canc. and* than *interl. B*, yet *interl. after* there
B; yet happid there] than happed there yet *Z*   23 worke] workes *1553 1557*; the
chapiter] that Chapter *1573*

Vincent

Mary vncle as you say / that happe happid well / and that maid
had as happ was, in that one poynt more connyng than had both
your phisicions beside / and hath I wene at this daye in many poyntes
5 mo.

Antonye

In fayth so wene I to / and that is well wared on her / For she is very
wise & well lernid & very vertuose to / But se now what age is lo / I
haue bene so long in my tale / that I haue almost forgotone / for
10 what purpose I told yt / Oh now I remember lo / likewise I say as my
selfe felt my body than both hote and cold at ones / so he that is con-
tryte & hevy for his synne / shall haue cause to be & shalbe in dede /
both sad & glad & both twayne at ones / & shall do as I remember
holy saynt hierome biddeth, [f. 73ᵛ] *Et doleas & de dolore gaudeas //* both
15 be thow sorye (sayth he) and be thow also of thy sorow ioyfull / and
thus as I began to say of comfort to be gyuyn vnto hym that is in this
tribulacion / that is to wit in frutefull heuines and penaunce for his
synne, shall we none nede to give, other than onely to remember &
consider well the goodnes of goddes eccellent mercie, that infynitely
20 passeth the malice of all mens synnes / by which he is redy to receve
euery man / And did spred his armes abrode vppon the crosse lovyng-
lye to enbrace all them that will come / And evyn there acceptid the
thefe at his last end, that turnid not to god till he might stele no lenger /
And yet maketh more fest in hevin at one that fro synne turneth, than
25 ⌜of⌝ foure score & nynetene good men that synnid not at all / And
therfor of that first kynd will I make no lenger tale /

2–3 maid had] maide hath *1573*   3 one poynt] one *om. 1553*   4 your] our *L 1553
1573*; beside] besides *Z*   9 forgotone] *divided:* forgo-tone: tone *canc. and* tten *added to*
forgo *B*   10 remember lo] remember me loe *1553 1557 1573*   12 cause to] cause
for to *1553 1573*; shalbe in dede] shall in dede be *Z*   13 sad & glad] glad and sadd *L*,
merye and sadde *1553*   14 biddeth,] *comma ed.*; dolore] *Z*, dolere *A*   15 (sayth] /
sayth *A*; also of thy sorow ioyfull] of thy sorowe ioyfull also *L 1553 1573*; thy] *orig.*
the *A*, y *wr. over* e *A*   19 eccellent] x *wr. over first* c *B*; well the goodnes . . . mercie] the
goodnes . . . mercye wel *L 1553*   20 malice] malice / *A*; synnes] sinne *L 1553 1573*;
receve] *divided:* rece-ve: ve *canc. and added to* rece *B*   23 lenger] longar *L*, longer *1553
1573*   24 fest] *final* e *added B*; fro] from *Z*   25 foure score & nynetene] lxxxxix *L*,
xcix *1553 1557*, ninetie & nine *1573*   26 lenger] longar *L*, longer *1553 1557 1573*

An obieccion concernyng them that turne not
to god till they come at the last cast

The v Chapiter

Vincent

Forsoth vncle this is vnto that kynd comfort very grcte / & so gret 5
also that it may make many a man ⌐bolde⌐ to abide in his synne evyn
vnto his end / trustyng to be than savid as that thefe was. [f. 74]

Anthonye

Very soth you say Cosyn / that some wretches are there such, that
in such wise abuse the great goodnes of god, that the better that he is 10
the worse agayne bc they / But Cosyn though there be more ioye made
of his tournyng / that from the poynt of perdicion commeth to saluacion / for pitie that god had & his sayntes all of the perill of perishyng
that the man stode in / yet ys he not set in like state in hevyn, as he
shuld haue bene yf he had livid better before / except it so fall that he 15
live so ⌐well⌐ after, & do so mych good / that he therin out runne in the
shorter tyme, those good folke that yet did not so mych in mych lenger.

As it provid in the blessid apostell saynt paule, which of a percecut-
our became an Apostell, & last of all came in into that office / and yet
in the labour of sowyng the seede of christes fayth / owt ranne all the 20
remenaunt and so farrforth that he lettid not to saye of hym selfe:
plus omnibus luboruui / I haue laboryd more than all the remenaunt
haue.

But yet my Cosyn though god I dowt not be so mercifull vnto them,
that in any tyme of their life torne & aske his mercie & trust therin / 25
though it be at the last end of a mans lyfe / And hireth hym as well
for hevyn that cometh to [f. 74ᵛ] worke in his vynyard toward night,

---

3 v] v.ᵗʰ L   7 end] last ende L 1553 1573   11 be they] they be 1553   13 had] om.
1553   14 yet ys he] yet he is L 1553   17–18 lenger. ¶ As] lenger, as Z   18–19 perce-
cutour] s wr. over first c B   19 into] v wr. over i B, vnto Z   20 labour of] labour &
of A: & canc. A?; the seede] that sede 1553   21 and so] and om. Z   22 plus omnibus
laboraui] Ego added in margin after selfe, cucurri interl. B above laboraui (uncanc.), Ego plus
omnibus cucurri L 1553, Abundantius illis omnibus laboraui 1557 1573; laboryd] ronne
interl. B above laboryd (uncanc.), runne L 1553   25 in any tyme of] at anye time in L
1553 1573   27 worke] warke? A: a? alt. to o B?

at such tyme as workmen leve warke & go home, beyng ⌐than⌐ in will
to worke yf the tyme wold serue, as he hireth hym that cometh in the
mornyng / yet may there no man vppon the trust of this parable, be
bold all his life to ly styll in synne / For let hym remember that into
5 goddes vinyard ther goeth no man but he that is callid thether / Now
he that in hope to be callid toward night, will slepe out the mornyng,
& drinke out the day, ys full likely to pass at night vnspoken to / &
than shall he with shrewid rest go souperlesse to bedd /

They tell of one that was wont alwey to sey, that all the while he
10 livid he wold do what he lyst / For three wordes whan he died shuld
make all safe inough / But than so happid it that long or he were old,
his hors ones stumblid vppon a broken bryge / & as he laborid to
recouer hym, whan he saw it wold not be / but down into the flode
⌐hedling⌐ nedes he shuld / in a soden flight he cried out in the fallyng /
15 haue all to the divell / And there was he drownid with his iij wordes
ere he died, wheron his hope hong all his wrechid life / And therfor
[f. 75] let no man sinne in hope of grace / grace cometh but at goddes
will / and that mynd may be the let that grace of frutfull repentyng
shall neuer after be offred hym / but that he shall eyther gracelesse
20 go lynger on careles, or with a care fruteles fall into despayre /

An obieccion of them that say the tribulacion of penaunce nedith not but is a supersticiouse folye

The sixt Chapiter

Vyncent

25 Forsoth vncle in this poynt me thinkyth you say very well. But than
are there some agayne that say on the tother side / that heuynes

---

1 workmen] men L 1553   1–2 & go home, beyng than in will to worke] om. 1553
4 styll] styill? A: canc. and styll interl. B   6 toward] interl. A above canc. at   7 at night]
as nyghte 1553   8 bedd /] period before / B   9 that all] t canc. before all A   10 lyst]
luste 1553 1557 1573   11 safe] sauf L, saue 1557; or] ere Z   12 bryge] d interl.
before g B   14 hedling] added in margin B, headlong 1553 1557 1573   17 grace / grace]
grace, for grace L 1553 1557, grace: for grace 1573   18 frutfull] a frutefull 1553
19 he shall] shall om. 1553   21 say the] saye that 1553 1557 1573   22 comma after
nedith B   23 sixt] vjᵗʰ L, vi 1553 1557 1573   26 are] ere A: a wr. over e B; tother]
other 1553

for our synnes we shall nede none at all, but onely chaunge our intent
and purpose to do better / & for all that that is past, take no thought
at all /

And as for fasting & other affliccion of the body, they say we shuld
not do it, but onely to tame the flesh whan we fele it wax wanton & 5
begyn to rebell / for fastyng / they say serueth to kepe the bodye in
temperaunce / But for to fast for penaunce, or to do any ⌐other¬ good
worke, almes dede or other, [f. 75ᵛ] toward satisfaccion of our own
synne / this thyng they call playn iniury to the passion of christ / by
which onely are our sinnes forgevyn frely without any recompence 10
of our own / And they that wold do penaunce for their owne sinnes /
loke to be their own Christes & pay their own raunsoms, & save their
soules them self / And with these resons in saxony many cast fastyng
of, & all other bodely affliccion, save onely where nede requireth to
bryng the body to temperaunce / for other good they say can it none 15
do to our selfe, & than to our neybour can yt do none at all / And
therfor they condempn it for supersticiouse folye /

Now hevines of hart & wepyng for our sinnes, this they rekyn shame
almost & womannysh peuyshnes / how be it thankid be god ther women wax there now so mannyshe / that they be not so pevish nor so 20
pore of sprite, but that they can synne on as men do, & be neyther
aferd nor ashamyd, nor wepe for their synnes at all /

And surely myn owncle I haue mervelid the lesse euer syns I hard
the maner of their prechers [f. 76] there / for as you remember when I
was in Saxonye these maters were in maner but in a mameryng / nor 25
Luther was not than weddid yet / nor religiouse men out of their
habite / but suffred were those that wold be of the sect, frely to preach
what they wold vnto the people / And forsoth I hard a religiouse man
there my selfe / one that ⌐had¬ bene reputid & taken for very good /
and which as farre as the folke percevid was of his own lyvyng 30

1 for our] of our *1553 1573*   1–2 intent and purpose] purpose and intent L *1553*, purpose
and intend *1573*   2 all] *om.* L *1553*; that that] that which L *1553 1573*   4 & other]
or other L *1553 1573*   6–7 in temperaunce] in a temperaunce L *1553 1573*   8 almes]
allmoyse L, almose *1553 1557 1573*; dede or] dede and *1553 1573*; of] *canc. and* for *interl.*
B, for L *1557 1573*   13 self] selvys L   19 peuyshnes] v *wr. over* u B   19–20 women]
wemen? A: e? *alt. to* o B   22 aferd] afrayde *1553 1557 1573*   23 owncle] o *and first
minim of* w *canc.,* w *alt. to* v B; mervelid] merueled much L *1553 1573*; syns] since that Z
25 in maner] in a maner L *1553 1557*   26 weddid] wedde L *1553 1573*   27 were
those that] where those that *1553*, where those were that *1573*   28 vnto] to *1573*

somwhat ⌜austere⌝ & sharpe. But his prechyng was wounderfull / me
thynke I here hym ⌜yet⌝ / his voyce was so lowd & shirle / his lernyng
lesse than meane / But where as his mater was mych part agayne
fastyng & all affliccion for any penaunce which he callid mens inven-
5 cions / he cried euer ⌜owt⌝ vppon them to kepe well the lawes of
christ / let go their pevysh penaunce & purpose them to amend,
and seke nothyng to saluacion but the deth of christ / for he is our
iustice, & he is our saviour, & our hole satisfaccion for all our dedly
synnes / he did full penaunce for vs all vppon his paynfull crosse / he
10 wasshid vs there all clene with the water of his swete side, & brought
vs out of the devilles daynger with his dere preciouse bloude / Leve
therfor leve I besech you these invencions [f. 76ᵛ] of men, your folysh
lenton fastes & your pevish penaunce, minysh neuer christes thankes
nor loke to save your selfe. It is Christes deth I tell you that must save
15 vs all. Christes deth I tell you ⌜yet⌝ agayne & not our own dedes. Leve
your own fastyng therfor & lene to christ alone good cristen peoplé for
christes dere bitter passion.

   Now so lowd & so shirle he cried christ in theire heres / & so
thikke he came forth with christes bitter passion, & that so bitterly
20 spoken / with the sweate droppyng down his chekes, that I merveylid
not though I saw the pore women wepe / For he made myne heare
stand vp vppon myne hed / And with such prechyng were the people
so brought in, that some fell to breke the fastes on the fastyng dayes /
not of frayltie or of malice first / but almost of deuocion, lest they shuld
25 take fro christ the thanke of his bitter passion / But whan they were a
while noselid in that poynt first, they could endure & abyde after
many thynges mo / with which had he begone, they wold haue pullid
hym downe.

---

1 austere] *wr. by B in blank space left by A*; sharpe.] *period ed.*   2 yet] it *A: canc. and* yet
interl. B, yet *Ƶ*; so] *om. L 1553*; shirle] shryll *Ƶ*; lernyng] *divided*: lerny-ng: ng *canc. and*
macron wr. above y, *with* g *added in margin B*   3 agayne] against *Ƶ*   6 them] thē *L 1553,*
then 1557 1573; amend] a *canc. B*, mend *Ƶ*   10 brought] boughte *L 1553 1573*   12 in-
vencions] invencons *A*   13 thankes] es *canc. B*, thanke *Ƶ*   14 selfe] selvys *L*
18 shirle] shryll *Ƶ*; heres] h *canc. and* y *wr. over second* e *B, then whole word canc. and* earys
interl. B, eares *Ƶ*   21 myne] myne owne *L*, my owne *1553 1557 1573*   22 stand] to
stand *L 1553*; myne] my *Ƶ*   23 breke the] the *canc. and* theyr *interl. B*, breake their *Ƶ*
25 fro] from *Ƶ*   26 endure & abyde] abide & endure *Ƶ*   27 begone] than begonne
L 1553 1573; *comma added and then canc. after* haue *B*

Antonye

Cosyn god amend that man what so euer he be [f. 77] and god kepe
all good folke fro such maner of prechours / Such one prechour mich
more abuseth the name of christ & of his bitter passion than / v /
hundered hasardours / that in their Idell besines swere and forswere 5
them selfe by his holy bitter passion at the dice.

They cary the myndes of the people fro the percevyng of their crafte,
by the contynuall naming of the name of christ, & crying his passion
so shirle into their eares /

They forget that the church hath euer taught them that all our 10
penaunce without christes passion were not worth a pease / And they
make the people wene that we wold be savid by our own dedes without cristes deth / where we confesse that his onely passion meritith
incomparable more for vs than all our own dedes do / But his pleasure
is that we shall also take payne our own selfe with hym. And therfor 15
he biddith all that wilbe his deciples, take their crosses on their bakke,
as he did & with their crosses folow hym.

And where they say that fastyng serueth but for [f. 77^v] temperaunce to tame the flesh & kepe it from wantonnes / I wold in good
fayth haue went that Moyses had not bene so wild / that for tamyng 20
of his flesh he shuld haue nedid to fast hole .xl. dayes together / No
nor hely neyther / nor yet our saviour hymselfe / which began & the
appostelles folowid & all cristendome haue kept the lenton .xl. dayes
fast that these folke now call so folish. Kyng Achas was not disposid to
be wanton in his flesh, when he fastid & went clothid in sake cloth & 25
all bisprent with asshes.

Nor no more was in Nynive the kyng and all the Citie / but they
waylid & did paynfull penaunce for their synne, to procure god to
pitie them and withdraw his indignacion. Anna that in her widowhed
abode so many yeres with fastyng & praying in the temple till the 30

---

3 fro] from Z; Such] Suth A: t $alt.$ to c B 4 & of his] of $om.$ L 1553 5 hundered]
hundreth 1553; hasardours /] | $canc.$ B, hasardes 1557 6 selfe] selvys L, selues 1573;
at the dice] the $om.$ Z 7 fro] from Z; ch $canc.$ $before$ crafte A   9 shirle] shryll Z;
eares / ¶ They] eares, they 1553 1557 1573 14 incomparable] incomparably L 1553
1573 15 selfe] selvys L; hym.] $period$ $ed.$ 16 deciples] is $wr.$ $over$ $first$ e B; on
their] vpon theyr L 1553 1573; bakke] backes Z 20 tamyng] the taminge Z
21 nedid] nede 1553 1557 1573 24 now call] cal nowe Z; folish.] $period$ $ed.$; Achas] h
$interl.$ A? and $clar.$ B, who $also$ $writes$ Acab $above$, Achab L 1557 1573 25 sake] e $canc.$ B
27 Nor no] Z, No no A

birth of christ, was not I wene in her old age so sore disposid to the
wantonnes of her flesh, that she fastid all therfor / ⌐Nor⌐ Saint paule
that fastid so mych / fastid not all therfor neyther / The scripture is
full of places that proue the fastyng not to be the invencion of man /
5 but the institucion of god & that it hath many mo prophetes than one.
[f. 78]
    And that the fastyng of one man may do good to an other our
saviour shewith hym selfe, where he sayth that some kynd of devilles
can not be by one man cast out of an other / *Nisi in oratione & ieiunio* /
10 without prayour & fastyng / And therfor I mervayle that they take
this way agaynst fastyng & other bodely penaunce.
    And yet much more I mervayle that they myslike the sorow &
hevines & displeasure of mynd, that a man shuld take in forthynkyng
of his sinne / The prophet sayth / *Scindite corda vestra & non vestimenta* /
15 teare your hartes (sayth he) & not your clothes. And the prophet David
sayth / *Cor contritum & humiliatum deus non despicies* / A contrite hart &
an humblid / that is to say an hart broken toren & with tribulacion
of hevynes for his synne layd a low vnder fote, shall thow not good lord
dispice / He sayth also of his own contricion / *laboraui in gemitu meo,*
20 *lauabo per singulas noctes lectum meum, lachrimis meis stratum meum rigabo* /
I haue laborid in my waylyng / I shall euery night wash my bed with
my teares / my cowch will I water.
    But what shuld I nede in this mater lay forth [f. 78ᵛ] one place or
twayne / the scripture is full of those places / by which it playne aper-
25 ith / that god loketh of dewtie not onely that we shuld amend & be
better in the tyme to come / but also be sory and wepe & bewayle our
synnes commyttid before / And all the old holy doctours be full &
whole of that mynd that men must haue for their synnes contricion
& sorow in hart.

---

1 I wene in her old age] in her old age I wene *L*   4 proue] prouethe *1553 1557*; the
fastyng] the *om. 1553 1557 1573*   5 prophetes] *canc. and* profyttes *interl. B*, profytes *Z*;
comma after one *B*   7 to an other] vnto another *L 1557*   8 shewith] saieth *L 1553*;
sayth] sheweth *L 1553*   14 Scindite] Sindite *1553 1557*   15 (sayth he)] *first parenth.
ed.*, he sayeth *Z*; clothes.] *period ed.*, garmentes or clothes *L*   16 despicies] dispicies *A*:
e *wr. over first* i *B*?   17 an hart] a heart *Z*   18 synne] sinnes *Z*; shall] shalte *Z*
19 dispice] s *wr. over* c *B*   22 teares / my] tearys, and my *L*   23 lay] to laye *Z*
24 playne] playnlye *Z*   24–25 aperith /] | *canc. B*   26 the tyme] the *om. L*

What yf a man can not wepe nor in his hart be
sory for his synnes

The seven Chapiter

Vincent

Forsoth vncle yet semeth me this thing somewhat a sore sentence / 5
not for that that I think otherwise, but that there is good cause &
greate wherfor a man so shuld / but for that of trouth some man can
not be sory & hevy for his synne that he hath done, though he neuer
so fayne wold / But though he can be content for godes sake to forbere
it from thens forth / yet for euery synne that is passid, can he not onely 10
not wepe / but some were happely so wanton / that whan he happeth
to remember them, he can scantly forbere to laugh / Now yf contricion
& sorow of hart be so requisite of necessite [f. 79] to remission / many
a man / shuld stand as it semeth / in very perilouse case.

Anthonye 15

Many so shuld in dede Cosyn / & in dede many so do, And the old
sayntes write very sore in this poynt. Howbeit ⌈*Misericordia domini
super omnia opera eius*⌉ the mercie of god is above all his workes and he
standith not bounden vnto comen rewle / *Et ipse cognouit figmentum
suum, & propiciatur infirmitatibus nostris* / And he knowith the fraylte of 20
his erthen vessell that is of his own makyng, & is mercifull & hath
pitie vppon our feble infirmytles, & shall not exact of vs above the
thyng that we may do /
But yet Cosyn he that findeth hymselfe in that case / in that he is
myndid to do well hereafter / let hym give god thanke that he is no 25
worse / but in that he can not be sory for his sinne passid, let hym be
sory hardely that he is no better / And as saint Iherome biddith hym,

---

1 *comma after* nor B 3 seven] th *added* B, vij^th L 6 for that that I] for that I *Z*
14 as] as / *A*; in very] in a very *Z* 17 poynt.] *period* ed. 17–18 Misericordia . . . eius]
wr. by B *in large blank space left by* A, *extra blank space filled by dashes* 18 *period after* workes B
19 not] *om.* *Z*; bounden] bound *1553 1573*; vnto] to no *Z* 20 infirmitatibus] infir-
memitatibus *1557* 21 his erthen] this earthen *Z* 22 pitie] pitye and compassyon
1553 1557 1573 22–23 the thyng] that thing *1573* 25 thanke] thankes *1553 1557*
1573 26 sinne] synnes L

that for his sinne soroweth in his hart be glad & reioyce in his sorow /
so wold I counsayle hym that can not be [f. 79ᵛ] sad for his sinne, to be
sory yet at the lest that he can not be sory /

Besides this, though I wold in nowise any man shuld dispayre /
5 yet wold I counsayle such a man while that affeccion lastith, not to be
to bold of corage but live in dowble feare.

First for it is a token eyther of faynt fayth / or of a dull diligence /
for surely if we well beleve in god, & therwith depely consider his maiestie, with the perill of our synne & the great goodnes of god also /
10 eyther shuld drede make vs tremble & breke our stony hart / or love
shuld for sorow relent it into teares.

Besides this sith I can scant beleve, but sith so litell mislikyng of
our old sinne, is an affeccion not very pure & clene, & none vnclene
thyng shall enter into hevyn: clensid shall it be & purified before that
15 we com there. And therfor wold I ferther advise one in that case,
the counsaile which master Gerson giveth euery man / that sith the
body & the sowle together make the hole man / the lesse affliccion that
he felith in his sowle, the more payne in recompence let hym put vppon
his body, & pourge [f. 80] the spirite by the affliccion of the flesh /
20 And he that so doth I dare lay my life / shall haue his hard hart after
relent into teares / & his sowle in an holsome hevynes & hevenly gladnes to / specially yf (which must be ioynid with euery good thyng) he
ioyne faythfull prayour therwith /

But cosyn as I told you the tother day before / In these maters with
25 these new men I will not dispute / but surely for myn own part I can
not well hold with them, for as far as myn owne pore wit can perceve,
the holy scripture of god is very playne agaynst them / And the whole
corps of cristendome in euery cristen region / and the very places in
which they dwell them self, haue euer vnto their own dayes clerely
30 belevid agaynst them / And all the old holy doctours haue euer more
taught agaynst them / And all the old holy interpretours haue construed the scripture agaynst them. And therfor yf these men haue now
percevid so late / that the scripture hath be misse vnderstanden all this

---

4 nowise] *vertical line after* no B   5 while] wlile A: hi *wr. over* li B   8 beleve] B, beleye?
A, v *wr. over* y? B   8–9 his maiestie] his high maiestye Z   9 synne] sowle L   12 this
sith I] sith *om.* 1573   15 we] yt L, we *interl.* L; com there.] *period ed.,* come thether L
1553 1573   20 after] *interl.* A   21 into] in L   24 tother] other 1553 1557 1573
25 I will] nowe wyll I L, wil I 1553 1573; for as farre as *canc. before* but surely A   26 far
as] *om.* 1553   29 self] selvys L, selues 1573   33 hath be] hathe bene L 1553 1573

while / & that of all those old holy doctours / no man could vnderstand yt / than am I to old at this age to begyn to study it now / and
trust these mens connyng Cosyn that dare I not in no wise / sith I
can not se nor perceve no cause wherfor I shuld thynke that these
men might not now in the vnderstandyng of scripture, as [f. 80ᵛ] well 5
be decevid them selfe / as they bere vs in hand that all those other
haue bene all this while before.

Howbeit Cosyn yf it so be that their way be not wrong, but that
they haue found out so easy a way to hevyn, as to take no thought /
but make mery / nor take no penaunce at all / but sit them down & 10
drynke well for our saviours sake / sett cokke a hope & fill in all the
cupps at ones, & than let christes passion pay for all the scott / I am
not he that will envye their good happe / but surely counsayle dare I
give no man to adventure that way with them / But such as fere
lest that way be not sure, & take vppon thcm willyngly tribulacion of 15
penaunce: what comfort they do take & well may take therin / that
haue I somwhat told you all redye / And sith these other folke sit so
mery without such tribulacion, we nede to talke to them / you
wot well of no such maner comfort / And therfor of this kynd of tribulacion will I make an end /   20

Of that kynd of tribulacion which though they not
willyngly take / yet they willyngly suffer

The / 8 / chapiter

Vyncent

Verely good vncle so may you well do / for you haue brought it 25
vnto a very good passe / And now I requier you come to the tother
kynd, of which you purposid alway to treate last / / [f. 81]

---

1 doctours] enterpretors *L*   4 that] *interl. A*   6 selfe] selvys *L*   10 sit] set *1557*
11 hope] hoope *L 1557 1573*   12 scott] shot *L 1553 1573*   17 I *canc. before* haue *A*
19 maner comfort] maner of comforte *1557*   23 8] viij^th *L*   26 vnto a very] a *om. Z̧*;
you come] you to come *L 1553 1573*; the tother] that other *1553 1573*

Anthonye

That shall I Cosyn very gladly do / The tother kynd ys this which
I rehersid second, & sortyng out the tother ⌐twayn⌐ haue kept it for
the last / This kynd of tribulacion is you wot well, of them that willyng-
5 ly suffre tribulacion though that of ther own choyce they toke yt not
at the first / This kynd Cosyn devide we shall into twayne. The first
might we call temptacion, the second persecucion. But here must you
consider, that I mene not euery kynd of persecucion / but that kynd
onely, which though the sufferer wold be loth to fall in / yet will he
10 rather abyde it & suffer, than by the fletyng from yt, fall in the displesure of god / or leve godes pleasure vnprocurid / Howbe it yf we
well consider thes two thynges, temptacion & persecucion we may
fynd that eyther of them is incedent to the tother / For both by temptacion the devill persecuteth vs, & by persecucion the devill ⌐also⌐
15 temptith vs / and as persecucion is tribulacion to euery man, so is
temptacion tribulacion to euery good man / Now though the devill
our spirituall enemye fight agaynst man in bothe, yet this difference
hath the comen temptacion from the persecucion, that temptacion
ys as it were the fendes trayne / and [f. 81ᵛ] persecucion his playne open
20 fight / & therfor will I now call all this kynd of tribulacion here, by the
name of temptacion / & that shall I devide into two partes. The first
shall I call the devilles traynes the tother his open fight.

First of temptacion in generall, as it is comen to
both /

25   The ixᵗʰ chapiter

To speke of euery kynd of temptacion particulerly by it selfe, this
were ye wot well in maner an infinite thing / for vnder that as I told

---

1 *catchword on f.80ᵛ wr. by* E: Antho (*in faint ink*), *followed by* Anthonye   2 tother] other
1553 1573   3 tother] other *1553 1573*   5 though that of] that *om. 1573*; ther] i *interl.*
before r B   10 suffer] suffer it L *1553*; fletyng] flitting L *1553 1573*, flyttynge *1557*
11 Howbe] *cap. ed.*   12 well consider thes two thynges] considre these two thinges wel
1553 1573   13 incedent] y *wr. over first* e B; to] in *interl. before* to B, into *1557*; tother] other
L *1553 1573*   15 euery] *canc. and* a *interl.* B, a Z   18 that temptacion] that temptacion
playn *1553*   19 trayne] traynes L; his] ys L; playne] *om. 1553*   22 tother] other L
1553 1573   25 ixᵗʰ] ix Z   27 ye] you L *1553 1573*

you fall persecucions & all / And the devill hath of his traynes a thowsand subtill wayes / & of his open fight as many poysenyd dartes.

He tempteth vs by the world / he temptith vs by our own flesh / he
temptith vs by pleasure / he temptith vs by payne / he temptith vs by
our foes / he temptith vs by our own frendes / & vnder colour of kynd- 5
red, he maketh many tymes our next frendes our most foes / For as
our saviour sayth, *Inimici hominis domestici eius.*

But in all maner of so diuers temptacions, one mervelous cumfort
is this / that with the mo we be temptid, the [f. 82] glader haue we
cause to be / for ⌈as⌉ S Iames sayth, *omne gaudium existimate fratres quum* 10
in tentationes varias incideritis / estime it & take it sayth he my brethren
for a thyng of all ioy whan you fall into diuers & sundry maner of temptacions / And no mervel, for there is in this world set vpp as it were a
game of wrestelyng, wherin the people of god come in on the tone
side, & on the tother side come mighty strong wresteters & wily, that 15
is to wit, the devilles the cursid prowd dampnid sprites. For it is not
our flesh alone that we must wrestell with, but with the devill to /
Non est nobis colluctatio aduersus carnem & sanguinem | sed aduersus principes
& potestates tenebrarum harum, aduersus spiritalia nequitie in celestibus / our
wrestelyng is not here sayth S paule agaynst flesh and bloude / but 20
agaynst the princes & potestates of these darke regions, agaynst the
spirituall wikkid goostes of the ayer.

But as god vnto them that on his part giue his aduersary the fall,
hath preparid a crowne / so he that will not wrestle shall none haue /
for as [f. 82ᵛ] saynt paule sayth / *Nemo coronabitur nisi qui legitime certau-* 25
erit / ther shall no man haue the crown but he that doth his devour
therfor icordyng to the law of the game. And than as holy saynt Barnard sayth / how couldest thow fight or wrestell therfor, yf there were
no chalenger agaynst the that wold provoke the therto / And therfor
may it be a greate comfort / as S Iames sayth, to euery man that 30
seeth hym selfe chalengid & prouokyd by temptacion / For therby

---

1–2 of his traynes a thowsand subtill wayes / &] *om. L 1553*   2 many] many sundry *Z*
5 foes /] / *wr. over* s *B*   7 sayth,] *comma ed.*; eius] eius. A mans owne familiar frindes are
his enemies *1573*   10 as] *om. L 1553 1573*; fratres] fratres mei *1557 1573*   11 estime]
wr. in italic A   13 mervel] *second* l *added B*   14 tone] one *1553 1573*   15 tother]
other *1553*   19 potestates tenebrarum] potestates adversus mundi rectores tenebrarum
1557 1573; aduersus spiritalia] contra spiritalia *1557*, contra spiritualia *1573*; nequitie]
hook added to final e *B*   21 princes] r *ins. B (orig.* r *blurred)*   25 Nemo coronabitur]
Qui certat in agone non coronabitur *1557 1573*; qui] *om. 1557*   27 icordyng] accordyng
wr. above and then blotted out A?, according Z   31 seeth] feleth *Z*

● percevith he that yt commeth to his course to wrestle / which shalbe / but yf he willyng will play the coward or the fole, the mater of his eternall reward.

A speciall comfort in all temptacion

5   The tenth Chapiter /

But now must this nedes be to man an inestimable cumfort in all temptacion, yf his fayth fayle hym not / that is to wit / that he may be sure that god is allway redy to gyve hym strength agaynst the devilles might, & wisdome agaynst the devilles traynes. For as the
10   prophet sayth / / *fortitudo mea & laus mea ⌐est⌐ dominus, factus est mihi in salutem* / my strenghth & my prayse is our lord / he hath bene my safe gard / And the scripture sayth [f. 83] *pete a deo sapientiam & dabit tibi* / aske wisedome of god & he shall give it the / *vt possitis* (as saynt paule sayth) *deprehendere omnes artes*: that you may spye & perceve all
15   the craftes.

A grete comfort may this be in all kyndes of temptacion, that god hath so his hand vppon hym that is willyng to stand & will trust in hym & call vppon hym / that he hath made hym sure by many fayth-full promyses in holy scripture, that eyther he shall not fall / or yf he
20   sometyme thorow fayntnes of fayth stager or hap to fall / yet yf he call vppon god betymes, his fall shalbe no sore brosyng to hym / but as the scripture sayth / *Iustus si ceciderit non collidetur, quia dominus supponit man-um* / the Iust man though he fall, shall not be brusid for our lord holdeth vnder his hand.

25   The prophet expressith a playne comfortable promise of god agaynst all temptacion, where he sayth / / *Qui habitat in adiutorio altissimi, in protectione dei celi comorabitur*: who so dwellith in the help of the

2 willyng] ly *added B*, willingly Ƶ; will] *om. L*   3 reward] reward in heauen *L 1553 1573*
5 tenth] x Ƶ   6 cumfort] cumfo (*end of line*) *A*, rt *added in margin B*   10 mea est] est
om. Ƶ; factus] et factus *1557 1573*   12 safe gard] safegarder *L 1553 1557*   14 deprehendere omnes artes] *wr. at beginning of line with rest of line left blank A*; artes:] *colon ed.*
14–15 that you . . . craftes] *wr. on next line after blank space A*   20 stager or] stagger & Ƶ
21 betymes] by tymes *B* (y *wr. over first* e, *with vertical line before* t)   22–23 manum] manum
suam *1557 1573*   26 temptacion] temptacions *L 1557*   27 comorabitur:] *colon ed.*,
commorabitur Ƶ

hiest god, he shall abide in the proteccion or defence of the god of
hevyn. Who dwellith now good Cosyn in the help of the high god?
Surely he that thowrow a good faith [f. 83ᵛ] abydith in the trust and
confidence of goddes helpe, & neuer for lacke of that fayth & trust
in his helpe, falleth desperat of all helpe / nor departeth from the 5
hope of his helpe, to seke him selfe helpe as I told you the tother
daye of the flesh the world or the devill.

Now he than that by fast fayth & sure hope, dwellith in godes helpe
& hangeth alway thervppon, neuer fallyng fro that hope / he shall
sayth the prophet euer dwell and abyde in godes defence & protec- 10
cion / that is to saye that while he fayleth not to beleve well & hope
well, god will neuer fayle in all temptacion to defend hym / For vnto
such a faythfull well hopyng man, the prophet in the same psalme
sayth further / *Scapulis suis obumbrabit tibi, & sub pennis eius sperabis*:
with his sholders shall he shadow the, & vnder his fethers shalt thow 15
trust / Lo here hath euery faythfull man a sure promise / that in the
fervent hete of temptacion or tribulacion (for as I haue said diuers
tymes before they be in such wise concident that euery tribulacion the
devill vseth for temptacion to bryng vs to impacience & therby to
murmur and grudge & blasphamye / And euery kynd of temptacion 20
to a good man that fightith agaynst yt & will not folow yt, is a very
paynfull tribulacion) [f. 84] In the fervent hete I say therfor of euery
temptacion, god geveth the faythfull man that hopeth in hym, the
shadow of his holy shulders, which are brode & large, sufficient to
refrigerate & refresh the man in that hete / & in euery tribulacion he 25
putteth his shulders for a defence betwene. And than what weapon of
the devill may give vs any dedly wound, while that impenetrable
pavice of the shulder of god standeth alway betwene /

Than goeth the verse ferther & sayth vnto such a faythfull man:
Et sub pennis eius sperabis / Thyne hope shall be vnder his fethers / that 30
is to wit / for the good hope thow hast in his helpe, he will take the so
nere hym into his proteccion that as the henne to kepe her yong chekyns from the kyght, nestelith them together vnder her ʳownˡ wynges /

2 How *canc. before* Who A   4 neuer] neyther Z   6 fayth *canc. before* helpe A;
tother] other *1553 1573*   9 fro] from L *1553 1573*   10 dwell and abyde] abyde and
dwell *1553 1573*   14 further] farther Z; sperabis:] colon ed.   18 concident] *canc. and*
coincydent *interl.* B, coincydent Z   20 murmur and] and *om.* L *1553 1573*
20–21 temptacion to] temptacion ys to A, ys *canc.* B, temptacion is to L *1553 1573*
21 is a very] is *om.* L *1553 1573*   22 tribulacion)] *parenth. added* B   23 faythfull]
fayfull A, faythful Z   30 Thyne] Thy L *1553 1573*   33 own] *wr. at end of line* B

so fro the devilles claues the revenouse kyte of this darke ayer, will the
god of hevin gather the faythfull trustyng folke nere vnto his own
sides, & set them in surety very well & warm, vnder the coueryng of
his hevenly wynges.

5   And of this defence & proteccion, our saviour spake hymselfe vnto
the iewes, as mencion is made in ⌈the⌉   ⌈chapiter⌉ of saynt
mathew, to whome he said in this wise: *Hierusalem Hierusalem quae
occidis prophetas et lapidas eos qui ad te* [f. 84ᵛ] *misi sunt quoties volui congre-
gare te quemadmodum gallina congregat pullos suos sub alas suas & noluisti* |
10 that is to say hierusalem hierusalem that kyllest the prophetes & ston-
est vnto deth them that are sent vnto the, how often wold I haue
gatherid thy sones together as the henne gathereth her chikyns vnder
her wynges, & thow woldest not?

Here are Cosyn Vincent wordes of no litell comfort vnto euery
15 cristen man | by which we may see with how tender affeccion god
of his grete goodnes longeth to gather vnder the proteccion of his
wynges, & how often like a lovyng henne he clokketh home vnto hym,
evyn those chekyn of his that wilfully walkith abrode into the
kightes dainger, & will not come at his clokkyng | but euer the more
20 he clokketh for them, the ferther they go from hym. And therfor can
we not dowt yf we will folow hym, & with faythfull hope come run to
hym, but that he shall in all mater of temptacion, take vs nere vnto
hym & set vs evyn vnder his wyng | And than are we safe yf we will
tary there | for agaynst our will can there no power pull vs thens |
25 nor hurt our sowles there | *Pone me* sayth the prophet | *iuxta te, &
cuiusuis manus pugnet contra me* | set me nere vnto the, & fight agaynst
me whose hand that will.

---

1 claues] w *wr. over* u *B*; revenouse] *first* e *alt. to* a *B*   1–2 will the god of hevin] the
God of heauen wyll *L 1553 1573*   2 gather the] gather his *L 1553 1573*   3 coueryng]
c *dotted by error A*   4 hevenly] owne heauenly *L 1553 1573*   6 iewes] I *wr. over* i *B*;
the] *wr. by B in part of blank space left by A*; chapiter] *interl. above of* saynt *B*; *blank space
after the L*, the .xxiii. Chapter *1553 1557*, the Gospel *1573* (Matth. 23. *in margin*)
7 *middle stop before second* Hierusalem   8 misi] missi *Z*   9 quemadmodum] sicut *interl.
B above* quemadmodum (*uncanc.*), sicut *L 1553 1573*; sub alas suas] *om. L 1553*, suas *om.
1573*; noluisti |] *question-mark added before* | *B*; *comma after* is *B?*   11 vnto deth] to death
1573; vnto] *om. L*   12 thy sones] the *Z*   12–13 vnder her wynges] *om. L 1553*
14 Here are Cosyn Vincent wordes] Here are wordes Cosyn Vincent, wordes *L 1553 1573*
18 chekyn] *final* s *added B*, chickens *Z*; walkith] walke *B* (th *canc. and* i *alt. to* e), walke *Z*;
abrode into] abrode in *L 1553 1573*   21 run to] runne vnto *L 1553 1557*   23 wyng]
wynges *L 1553 1573*   24 | for] (for *A*   25 sowles] *orig.* sowes: le *wr. over* e *A?*; *parenth.
added before* sayth *B*; prophet |] *parenth. wr. over* | *B*

And to shew the great savegard & suerty that we shall [f. 85] haue while we sit vnder his hevenly fethers, the prophet sayth yet a greate deale ferther / *sub vmbra alarum tuarum exultabo* / that is to wit, that we shall not onely whan we sit by his swete side vnder his holy wyng / sit in safe garde / but that we shall also vnder the coueryng of his 5 hevenly wynges with greate exultacion reioyce.

Of iiij kyndes of temptacion, & therin both the partes
of that kynd of tribulacion, that men willyngly suffre
touchid in the ij verses of the psalter /

The xj chapiter   10

Now in the two next verses folowyng, the prophet brefely comprehendith iiij kyndes of temptacion, & therin all the tribulacion that we shall now speke of, & also some part of that which we haue spoken of before / And therfor I shall peraduenture / except any ferther thyng fall in our waye, with treatyng of those ij verses fynysh & end all our 15 mater.

The prophet sayth in the psalme / *Scuto circumdabit te veritas eius* / *non timebis a timore nocturno* / *a sagitta volante in die, a negocio perambulante* *in tenebris, ab incursu & demonio meridiano*: The trouth of god shall compasse the about with a pavice, thow shalt not be aferd of the nightes 20 feare, nor of the arrow fleyng in the day, nor of the bysynes walkyng about in the darknesses / nor of the incursion or [f. 85ᵛ] invacion of the devill in the mydde day.

First Cosyn in these wordes / the trouth of god shall compas the about with a pavise / the prophet for the comfort of euery good man 25

---

1 savegard] safegarde Z   3 sub vmbra] In velamento *1557 1573*   4 holy] heauenly
L *1553*   7 temptacion] temptacions Z; partes] partyes *1557*   9 the ij] the *om.* L *1553*
1573   10 xj] xjᵗʰ L   11 two next] two *om.* L *1553*   12 temptacion] *final* s *added* B,
temptacions *1557*   14 / except] (except A   15 with treatyng] with the treating L
1553 1573   17 the psalme] *blank space before* psalme L, the .xc. psalme *1557*, Psal. 90
in margin 1573   18 nocturno /] *comma after* / B; negocio] io *added* B; perambulante] u
added and lante *interl.* B   19 tenebris] ris *interl.* B; incursu] *interl.* B *above canc.* in;
demonio] onio *added* B; meridiano:] *interl.* B *above canc.* mer   20 about] o *interl.* A;
shalt]Z, shall A; aferd] afraid *1553 1573*   21 fleyng] flyeng L, flying *1553 1557 1573*
22 about in the] the *om. 1553 1573*; incursion] in cursion A: *connecting line added* B; invacion] si *wr. over* c B   22–23 of the] & of the A: & *canc.* B (*same corrections made for*
invacion & *in catchwords on f. 85*)

in all temptacion & in all tribulacion, beside those other thynges
that he said before, that the sholders of god shuld shadow them, &
that also they shuld sit vnder his wyng / here sayth he farther that the
trouth of god shall compase the with a pavice / that is to wit that as
5 god hath faythfully promisid to protect & defend those that faythfully will dwell in the trust of his help / so will he truly perform yt /
And the that such one art, will the trouth of his promise defend, not
with a litell round buckeler that scant can couer the hed, but with a
long large pavice, that couereth all along the bodye, made as holy
10 saynt Barnard sayth brode above with the godhed, & narrow beneth
with the manhed / so that this pavice is our saviour christ hym selfe.

    And yet is not this pauice like other pauices of this world, which
are not made but in such wise, as while it defendith one part, the
man may be woundid vppon the tother / but this pavise is such / that
15 as the prophet sayth / it shall rownd about enclose & compase the /
so that thyn ennymye shall hurt thy sowle on no side. For [f. 86]
scuto sayth he / *circumdabit te veritas eius* / with a pauise shall his trouth
environ & compasse the round aboute. And than contynently
folowyng, to thentent that we shuld se that it is not without necessitie /
20 that the pavice of god shold compasse vs about vppon euery side,
he shewith in what wise we be by the devill with traynes and as-
sautes, by iiij kyndes of temptacions & tribulacions environid vppon
euery side / agaynst all which compasse of temptacions & tribulacions
/ that round compasyng pavice of godes trouth shall in such wyse
25 defend vs & kepe vs safe, that we shall nede to drede none of them
all /

---

1 tribulacion] tribulacon *A*   2 shuld] shal *L 1553 1573*   3 wyng] wynges *L*; farther
that the] that *om. L 1553 1573*, farther, The *L*, farther. The *1553*, farther: The *1573*
5–6 faythfully will] wyll faythfully *L*   7 the that] thou that *B*: e *alt. to* o *and* u *added,
with vertical line before* that, thou that *Z*   9 holy] *om. L 1553*   11 manhed] manhod
1557   12 not this pauice] this pauice not *L 1553 1573*   13 it defendith] they defende
L 1553 1573   14 the tother] another *L 1553 1573*, an other *1557*   16 wise *canc.
before* side *A*   18 contynently] incontynently *B* (in *interl.*), continently *Z*   19 thentent]
the entent *1553 1573*   22 vppon] on vpon *L 1553*

The first kynd of the iiij temptacions
The xij Chapiter

First he sayth / *Non timebis a timore nocturno,* thow shalt not be aferd
of the fere of the night / By the night is there in scripture sometyme
vnderstanden tribulacion, as apperith in 34 chapiter of Iob: *Nouit* 5
enim deus opera eorum, idcirco inducet noctem / god hath knowen the worke
of them, & therfor shall he bryng night vppon them, that is to wit
tribulacion for ther wikednes.

And well you wot that the night is of the nature selfe [f. 86ᵛ] discumfortable & full of fere / And therfor by the nightes feare, here I vnder- 10
stond, the tribulacions by which the devyll thorow the suffraunce of
god, eyther by hym selfe or other that are his instrumentes, temptith
good folke to impacience / as he did Iob / But he that (as the prophet
sayth) dwellith & contynueth faythfully in the hope of godes help,
shall so be clipid in on euery syde with the shild or pauice of god, 15
that he shall haue no nede to be a ferd of such tribulacion that is here
callid the nightes feare. And it may be also conveniently callid the
nightes feare for ij causes / the tone for that many tymes the cause of
his tribulacion, is vnto hym that suffreth, darke & vnknowen / &
therin varieth yt & differith fro that tribulacion by which the devill 20
temptith a man by open fight & assaut / for a good knowen thing
from which he wold withdraw hym / or for some knowen evil thing,
into whIch he wold dreve hym by force of such persecucion / A nother
cause for which it is callid the nightes feare, may be for that that the
night is so far out of corage, & naturally so casteth folke in feare, that 25
of euery thing wherof they perceve ⌜any maner⌝ drede, their fantasye
dowbleth their feare, & maketh them often wene that it were much

---

2 xij] xijᵗʰ *L*   3 aferd] afrayd *1553*   5 vnderstanden] vnderstand *1553 1573*; in 34]
in the .xxxiiii. *L 1553 1573,* in the .34 *1557*; Iob:] *colon ed.*   6 idcirco] iccirco *A*;
worke] s *added B,* workes *Z*   8 ther] yr. *wr. over* r *B*   9 nature selfe] nature of itselfe
L 1553 1573   11 the] that *1573*; tribulacions] tribulacion *Z*   13 / as] / *ed.,* (as *A*
15 clipid] becleped *L 1553 1573*; shild] e *wr. over* i *B*   16 a ferd] afrayde *1553*; is] *interl. A*
17 nightes] es *added B,* nightes *Z*   18 tone] one *1553 1573*   19 suffreth] suffereth it
L 1553 1573   20 differith] dyfferith yt *L*; fro] from *L 1553 1573*   21 by open] wyth
open *Z*; a good knowen] knowen *canc. and* known *interl. before* good *B,* a knowen good *Z*
22 evil] *second* l *added B*   23 dreve] driue *Z*; persecucion /] *period before* / *B*   24 for
that that the] *one* that *om. L 1553 1573*   26 any maner] *interl.* B *above canc.* euery man,
any maner *L 1553 1573,* euerye maner *1557*; fantasye] fansy *L*   27 dowbleth] th *added B*

worse than in dede it is / The prophet sayth in the psalter / *Posuisti
tenebras, et facta est nox, in illa pertransibunt omnes bestie siluarum, catuli*
[f. 87] *leonum rugientes querentes a deo escam sibi* / Thow hast good lord set
the darknes, & made was the night / & in the night walken all the
5 bestes of ⌜the⌝ woodes / the whelps of the lions roryng & calling vnto
god for their meate.

Now though that the lions whelps walke about roryng in the night
& seke for their pray / yet can they not get such meate as they wold
all way / but must hold them selfe content with such as god suffreth
10 to fall in their waye / and though they be not ware therof, yet of god
they aske yt / and of hym they haue it.

And this may be comfort to all good men in their nightes feare, in
their darke tribulacion, that though they fall into the clawes or the
teth of those lions welps / yet shall all that they can do, not pas beiond
15 the body / which is but as the garment of the soule / For the soule it
selfe which is the substaunce of the man, is so surely fensid in round
about with the sheld or pauice of god, that as long as he will
abide faythfully in *adiutorio altissimi* / in the hope of godes help, the
lions whelpes shall not be able to hurt it / for the grete lion hym selfe
20 could neuer be suffrid to go ferther in the tribulacion of Iob, than
god from tyme to tyme gave hym leve / And therfor the depe darknes
of the myd night, maketh men that standith out of fayth & out [f.
87ᵛ] of good hope in god, to be in their tribulacion far in the greter
fere, for lak of the light of fayth, whereby they might perceve that the
25 vtter must of their perill is a far lesse thyng than they take yt for.

But we be so wont to set so much by our body which we se & fele,
& in the fedyng & fostryng wherof we set our delight & our welth / &
so litle (alas) & so seld we thynke vppon our soule, because we can
not se that but by spirituall vnderstandyng, & most speciall by the
30 yee of our fayth (in the meditacion wherof we bestow god wot litle

2 in illa] in ipsa *1557 1573*; bestie] *hook added to final* e B; siluarum] sylue *1557*, syluae 1573;
catuli] catali A: u *wr. over second a* B, Catuli Ƶ   3 leonum] leones A: es *alt. to* um B (*same
correction in catchwords on 86v*), leonum Ƶ   4 walken] walke L *1553 1573*   5 woodes]
wood L *1553 1573*   8 meate *added after* such *and canc.* L   12 nightes] night *1553 1573*
14 welps] h *interl. before* e B; beiond] y *wr. over* i B   17 or pauice] or the pauyce *1557*
19 for] f *alt. to* F B   21 from] fro *1557*   22 standith] stande Ƶ   23 greter] *final* r
added B   25 vtter must] vttermoste Ƶ   26 *comma added and canc. after* se B   27 our
delight] our whole delight L *1553*; (alas) *parenth. added* B   28 vppon] on *1573*
29 speciall] specially Ƶ   30 yee] eye B (*final* e *canc. and* e *ins. before* y), eye L *1573*, iye
1553, yie *1557*

tyme) that the losse of our body we take for a sorer thyng & for a greter tribulacion a greate dele / than we ⌐do⌐ the losse of our soule. And
where our saviour biddith vs that we shuld not fere those lions whelps
that can but kyll our bodies, & whan that is done / haue no ferther
thing in their power wherwith they can do vs harm / but biddith vs 5
stand in drede of hym which whan he hath slayne the body / ys able
than beside to cast the sowle into euerlastyng fier / we be so blynd in
the darke night of tribulacion, for lak of full & fast belive of godes word
/ that where as in the day of prosperitie we very litle fere god for our
soule / our nightes fere of aduersitie, maketh vs very sore to fere the 10
lyon [f. 88] and his whelps for drede of losse of our bodies /

And where as saynt paule in sundry places shewith vs, that our body
is but as the garment of the soule / yet the fayntnes of our fayth to the
scripture of god, maketh vs with the nightes feare of tribulacion, more
to drede, not onely the losse of our body than of our soule / that is to 15
wit of the clothyng / than of the substaunce that is clothid therwith /
but also of the very outward goodes that serue for the clothyng of the
body / And mych more folysh are we in that dark nightes fere, than
were he that wold forget the savyng of his bodye, for fere of lesyng of
his old rayne beten cloke that is but the coueryng of his gown or his 20
cote.

Now consider ferther yet, that the prophet in the fore rehersid
verses, sayth not that in the night walke onely the lions whelpes but
also / omnes bestie siluarum / all the bestes of the wode. Now wote you
well that yf a man walke thowrow the wode in the night, many 25
thynges may make hym a ferd, of which in the day he wold not be
a ferd a whit. For in the night euery bush to hym that waxeth ones
a ferd semeth a thefe.

I remember that [when] I was a yong man, I was ones in the
[f. 88ᵛ] warre with the kyng than my master (god assoyle his soule) 30
& we were campid within the Turkes grownd many a mile beyond

1–2 & for a greter] for om. L 1553   3 where] wheras Z; those] these L 1553 1573
8 for lak] for the lacke L 1553 1573; belive] ef wr. over v B, belief Z   11 bodies] body
L 1553   17 goodes] es canc. B   19 wold] coulde L 1553 1573; lesyng of] of om. Z,
loosyng L, losing 1553 1573, leesing 1557   20–21 his cote] his om. L   22 rehersid] canc.
and remembryd interl. B, remembred Z   23 walke] walks 1553   24 bestie] hook added to
final e B, besties 1553; wode.] period ed.   26 hym a ferd] him afrayde 1553 1573   27 a
ferd a whit.] period ed., afrayde of a whit 1553, afraid a whit 1573   28 a ferd] afrayde
1553 1573   29 when] Z, was A   30 soule)] soule/A: parenth. wr. over / B   31 were]
interl. B above canc. we A

Belgrade (which wold god ⌜were⌝ ours now as well as it was than)
but so happid it that in our camp about midd night, there sodenly
rose a rumour & a scrye that the Turkes whole armye was secretly
stelyng vppon vs / wherwith our whole host was warnid to arm them
5 in hast, & set them selfe in array to fight / & than were the Scurers of
ours that brought those sodayn tidinges examinid more leasurely by
the counsayle / what suretye / or what likelyhed they had percevid
therin. Of whom one shewid that by the glimeryng of the mone, he
had espied & percevid & sene them hym selfe comyng on softely &
10 soberly in a long range all in good ordre / not one farther forth than
the other in the fore front / but as even as a therede & in bredth ferther
than he could see in lenghth.

His felowes beyng examynid said that he was somwhat prikkyd
forth before them, & cam so fast bak to tell it them, that they thought
15 it rather tyme to make hast & give warnyng to the camp / than to go
nere vnto them / For they were not so farr of, but that they had yet
them selfe some what an vnperfit sight of them to / [f. 89]

Thus stode we watching all the remenaunt of the night, euermore
harkenyng whan we shuld here them come / with husshe / stand still,
20 me thynke I here a tramplyng / so that at last many of vs thought we
herd them our selfe also / But when the day was sprongen & that we
saw no man / out was our Scurer sent agayne / & some of our capi-
taynes with hym to shew where about the place was in which he
percevid them. And when they came thether, they found that the
25 greate ⌜ferefull⌝ army of the Turkes so soberly comyng on, turnid
(god bethankyd) into a fayre long hedge standyng evyn stone stil.
And thus fareth yt in the nightes feare of tribulacion / in which
the devill to bere down & ouerwhelme with drede, the faythfull
hope that we shuld haue in god, casteth in our imaginacion mych
30 more fere than cause / for while there walke in that night, not onely
the lions whelps, but ouer that all the bestes of the wode beside / the

1 than)] parenth. ed., than / A 5 selfe] selvys L; the Scurers] the canc. B, om. Z
6 those] these L 1553 1573 7 likelyhed] likelyhode Z 8 Of] of A: O wr. over o B
9 espied &] & om. L; & sene] & wr. over / A 9–10 softely & soberly] sobrely and softly L
10 range] rayne A: ng wr. over yn B; in good] in a good 1553 11 a therede] the threde
1553 1573; bredth] d interl. A 16 nere] nerer Z 17 selfe] selvys L 18 the] yᵗ
1557 19 husshe] hushte Z 20 many] minim lacking in ny A 21 selfe] selvys L
23 shew where] shewe them where 1553 1573 24 them.] period ed. 24–25 the greate]
the om. L 1553 1573 26 stil] second l added B 30 in that] in the L 1553 1573
31 wode beside / the] wood, beside the 1553, wood: byside the 1573

beest that we here rore in the dark night of tribulacion, & fere it
for a lyon, we sometyme fynd well afterward in the day, that it was
no lyon at all / but a sely rude roryng asse. And the thyng that on
the see semeth sometyme a rokke, ys in dede nothyng els but a
myst / How be it as the prophet sayth, he that faythfully dwellith in 5
the hope of [f. 89ᵛ] godes help / the pauice of his trouth shall so fence
hym round about / that be it an asse / colt / or a lions whelpe / or a
rok of stone or a miste / *Non timebit a timore nocturno* / The nightes feare
therof shall he nothyng nede to drede /

Of pusillanimite 10
The / 13 / chapter

Therfore fynd I that in the nightes feare, one grete part is the faute
of pusillanimite / that is to wit faynt & feble stomake / by which a
man for faynt hart, is a ferd where he nedeth not / by the reason wherof he fleeth often tymes for fere of that thyng / of which (yf he fled 15
not) he should take none harm / And some man doth sometyme by
his fleyng, make his ennymy bold on hym / which wold yf he fled not /
but durst abide therbye / geve ouer and fle from hym.

This faute of pusillanimite maketh a man in his tribulacion for
feble hart first impacient, & afterward often tymes drevith hym by 20
impacience into a contrary affeccion / makyng frowardly stubbourn
& angry agaynst god, & therby to fall into blasphamye as do the dampnid soules in hell. This faute of pusillanimite & tymerouse mynd,
lettith a man also many tymes from the doyng of many good thynges /
which yf he toke a good stomake to hym in the trust of godes help, 25
he were well hable to do / But the devill castith hym in a cowardice,
& maketh hym take it for humilite, to thynke [f. 90] hym selfe vnmete

1 beest] beastes *1553 1573*; rore] roaring *1553 1573*   7 round] in round *L 1553 1573*
7–8 or a rok] or *om. L 1553 1573*   9 drede] dreade at all *L 1553 1573*   11 13] xiij^th *L*
12 the] this *L 1553 1573*; part] parte thereof *L 1553 1573*   13 faynt & feble] feble,
and faynte *L 1553 1573*; feble] feble / *A*   14 a ferd] afrayed *1553 1573*; by the reason]
the *om. L 1553 1573*   15 fleeth] flyeth *L 1553 1557*; tymes] tyme *1557*   16 none
harm] no harme *L 1553 1573*   17 fleyng] flyeng *1557*   18 fle] flye *1557*   20 drevith]
driueth *Z*   21 makyng frowardly] makyn hym froward *L*, makyng hym frowardly *1557
1573*; stubbourn] stubbour *A*: n *added B*   26 well] wall *A*; hable] h *canc. B*, able *Z*

& vnhable therto, & therfor ⌈to⌉ leve the good thyng vndone, wherof
god offerith hym occasion & had made hym convenient therto.

But such folke haue nede to lyft vpp their hartes & call vppon god /
& by the counsayle of other good goostly folke, cast away the coward-
5 ice of their ⌈own⌉ conceyte, which the nightes feare by the devill hath
framid in their fantasye / & loke in the gospell vppon hym which layd
vpp his talent & left it vnoccupied, & therfor vtterly lost it, with a
greate reproch of his pusillanimite / by which he had went he shuld
haue excusid hym selfe in that he was a ferd to put it forth in vre &
10 occupie yt / & all this feare commeth by the devilles dryft, wherin he
taketh occasion of the fayntnes of our good & sure trust in god / And
therfor let vs faythfully dwell in the good hope of his helpe, & than
shall the pavice of his trouth so compas vs about, that of this nightes
feare we shall haue no fere at all.

15   Of the dowghter of pusillanimite a scripelous conscience /

The / 14 / chapiter

This pusillanimite bringeth furth by the nightes feare, a very timerouse doughter a sely whrechid girle & euer pulyng, that is callid
scrupulositie or a scrupulouse conscience / This girle is a metely good
20 posill in an house, neuer idell but euer occupied & besy / but albeit
she hath a very gentle ⌈mastres⌉ that loveth her well, & is well content
with that she doth / or yf it be not all well / as all can not alway be
well, content [f. 90ᵛ] to pardon her, as she doth other of her felowes /
& so lettith her know that she will / yet can this pevish girle neuer
25 ceace whynyng & pulyng for fere, lest her ⌈mastres⌉ be alway angry
with her, & that she shall shrewdly be shent / Were her ⌈mastres⌉
wene you like to be content with this condicion / nay surely /

1 vnhable] h canc. B, vnable Z   2 made hym] made hym mete and L 1553 1573
6 fantasye] fansye L   8 reproch] final e added B   9 a ferd] afrayde 1553 1573
15 scripelous] scrupulous Z   17 furth] o wr. over u B; nightes] es added B   18 whrechid]
r wr. over e A   20 posill] pussell L 1553 1573; an house] a house L 1553 1573
21 hath] haue 1553 1573; mastres] interl. B above canc. abbreviation   22 alway be]
alwayes 1553 1573   26 shrewdly] shredly A: w interl. before d B; Were] ed., were A;
mastres] interl. B above canc. abbreviation   27 condicion /] question-mark added before | B;
surely] verely 1553 1573   27–p.113, l.1 nay surely / ¶ I] Naye surely, I L, Naye verely,
I 1553, nay surely. ¶ I 1557, Nay verily. I 1573

I knew such one my selfe whose ⌜mastres⌝ was a very wise woman /
which is in women very rare / very mylde also & meke & likid very
well such seruice as she did her in the house / but this contynuall discomfortable fasshion of hers / she so mich mysse likyd that she wold
sometyme saye Eye what eileth this girle / the elvish vrchene weneth 5
I were a devill I trow / Surely yf she did me ten tymes better service
than she doth / yet with this fantasticall fere of hers, I wold be loth
to haue her in my house.

Thus fareth lo the scriplouse person, which frameth hym selfe many
tymes dowble the feare that he hath cause / & many tymes a greate 10
feare where ther is no cause at all / And of that that is in dede no
synne, maketh a veniall / & that that is venyall, imageneth to be dedly
/ & yet for all that falleth in them beyng namely of their nature such as
no man long liveth without / And than he fereth that he be neuer full
confessid, nor neuer full contrite, & than that his synnes be neuer full 15
forgeven hym / & than he confessith & confessith agayne, & cumbreth
hym selfe & his confessour both / & than euery prayour that he sayth
though he say it as well as the frayle infyrmyte of the man wil [f. 91]
suffre, yet is he not satisfied, but yf he say it agayne & yet after that
agayne / & whan he hath said one thyng thrise: as litell is he satisfied 20
at the last as with the first / & than is his hart euermore in hevynes
vnquiat & in fere, full of dout & of dulnes without comfort or spirituall
consolacion.

With this nightes feare the devill sore trobleth the mynd of many
a right good man, & that doth he to bryng hym to some greate incon- 25
venience / For he will yf he can, dreve hym so mich to the myndyng
of godes rigorouse iustice, that he will kepe hym from the comfortable
remembraunce of godes greate mightie mercie, & so make hym do
all his good workes werely, & without consolacion or quyckenes.

---

1 mastres] *interl. B above canc. abbreviation*   2 which is] and (whiche thing is *Z*; very
rare] very *om.* 1553 1573; also &] also *om.* L, and also 1553 1573   3 her in the] her in
her L 1553 1573; contynuall] *om.* L   4 of hers] of hers contynually L   5 Eye] *final*
e *canc. B*, Eighee L, Eygh 1553 1573   6 ten tymes] ten an tymes 1573   8 in my house]
in myne house 1557   9 scriplouse] e *interl. before* l B, scrupulous *Z*   11 of that that]
of that whiche L 1553 1573   12 is venyall] is no venial L 1553   13 of their nature
such] such of theyr own nature L 1553 1573   14 liveth] *om.* L   18 infyrmyte] in
fyrmyte A; wil] *second* l *added B*   21 at the last] wyth the laste *Z*   22 & of dulnes]
of *om. Z*; spirituall] *Z*, spiall A   25 right] *om.* L; doth] doeth 1553   26 dreve] driue
Z; the myndyng] the fearefull mindinge *Z*   28 greate mightie] mightie *om.* L 1553
29 consolacion or] consolacion and 1553 1573

More ouer he maketh hym to take for synne, some thyng that is
none / & for dedly, ⌜some⌝ such as are but veniall / to the entent that
whan he shall fall into them, he shall be reson of his scriple synne,
wherels he shuld not / or synne dedly while his conscience in the dede
5 doyng so gave hym / where in dede he had offendid but venially.
Yee & further the devill longeth to make all his good workes &
spirituall exersice so paynfull & so tedious vnto hym, that with some
other suggestion or false wily doctryne [f. 91ᵛ] of a false spirituall
libertie, he shuld for the false ease & pleasure that he shuld sodenly
10 fynd therin, be easely conveyd from that evill faute into a much
worse / & haue his consciens ⌜as wide &⌝ as large after, as euer it was
narow & strayt before. For better ys yet of trouth a conscience litle
to strayt than a litell to large /
    My mother had whan I was a litell boye, a good old woman that
15 toke hede to her children, they callid her mother mawd / I trow you
haue hard of her.

Vincent

Yee yee very much.

Anthonye

20 She was wont whan she sat by the fier with vs, to tell vs that were
children many childish tales / but as *plinius* sayth that there is no
boke lightely so bad, but that some good thyng a man may pyk
out therof / so thinke I that there is al most no tale so folysh, but that
yet in one mater or other, to some purpose it may hap to serue / for I
25 remember me that among other ⌜of⌝ her fond tales, she told vs ones
that the asse & the wolfe cam vppon a tyme to confession to the
Fox / The pore Asse cam to shrift in the shroftide a day or two before
Asshwensday / but the wolfe wold not come to confession till he saw

---

1 hym to take] to om. *L 1553 1573*   2 the entent] thentent *L 1557*   3 fall into] fall
in *L 1553 1573*; shall be] shal by *Z*; scriple] u *wr. over* i *B*, scruple *Z*   4 wherels]
vertical line before els *B*   5 where in] where els in *L 1553*, wher as els in *1557 1573*; had
offendid but] had but offended *1553 1573*   6 further] farther *Z*; good] *interl. A*
8 other] other subtyll *Z*   12 conscience litle] conscience a lytle *Z*   13 litell] gret
dele *interl. B above* litell (*uncanc.*), greate deale *L 1553*, litle *1557 1573*   21 childish]
chidish *A*: ld *wr. over* d *B*   22 pyk] *final* e *added B*   23 I that there] that om. *1553
1573*; is al most no] al most om. *1553 1573*   25 fond] fonde chyldyshe *L 1553 1573*;
ones] one *L 1553*   26 cam vppon] came on *L 1553 1573*   28 till] until *1553 1573*

first palme sonday past, & than fodid yet forth farther till good friday /
The [f. 92] fox askyd the Asse before he began *benedicite* wherfor
he came to confession before lent began so sone / The pore best answerid hym agayne for fere of dedly synne, yf he shuld lese his part of any
of those prayours that the prest in the clensing dayes pray for them 5
that are than confessid all redy. Than in his shrifte he had a mervelouse growge in his inward conscience, that he had one day gevyn his
master a cause of anger, in that that with his rude roryng before his
master arose, he had awakyd hym out of his slepe / ⌐& byrevyd him
of his rest.¹ The Fox for that faut like a good discrete confessour, 10
chargid him to do so no more but lye styll & slepe like a good sone
hym selfe, till his master were vpp & redy to go to warke / & so shuld
he be sure that he shuld not wake hym no more.

To tell you all the pore Assis confession it were a long worke / for
euery thyng that he did was dedly sinne with hym / the pore soule 15
was so scrupulouse. But his wise wile confessour accomptid them for
trifles as they were / & sware after vnto the hageard that he was so wery
to sit so long & here hym, that savyng for the maner sake he had leuer
haue sitten all that while at brekefast with a good fat gose.

But when it came to the penaunce givyng, the Fox found that the 20
most weighty synne in all his shrifte, was glotony / & therfor he discretely gave hym in penaunce, that he shuld neuer for gredines of his
mete, do eny other best eny harm or hinderans / & than eate his
meate & study for no more / [f. 92ᵛ]

Now as good mother mawde told vs, whan the wolfe cam to father 25
Raynart (that was she said the fox name) to confession vppon good
friday / his confessour shoke his greate payre of hedes vppon hym
almost as bigg as bolles / & askyd hym wherfor he cam so late / Forsoth
father Raynard quoth he, I must nedes tell you the trouth / I come

---

1 farther] farder L *1553 1573*; till] untyll *Z*; friday] frydaye came L *1553 1573*   3 began]
begyn B: y *wr. over* a, begin *1557*; so sone] *canc. and interl. after* confession B, confession
so soone *Z*   4 yf] and for feare L *1553 1573*   5 pray] prayeth L *1553 1573*   6 are
than] than *om.* L *1553 1573*; Than] than A: T *wr. over* t B   7 growge] great grudge L
1553 1573   11 so] / *added* B; no] *wr. twice by* A, *first* no *canc.* A; sone] *bar wr. above* o B
16 But] but A: B *wr. over* b B; wile] y *wr. over* e B, wyly *Z*   17 were /] were in dede
L *1553 1573*; after] afterwarde L *1553 1573*   18 maner] maners *1573*   19 all that]
all the L *1553 1573*   22–23 his mete] hys owne meate L *1553 1573*   25 cam] came
to confession *1553 1573*   26 Raynart] d *wr. over* t B; (that] *parenth. wr. over* / B, for
that L *1553 1573*; fox] foxis B: is *added*, foxes *Z*; to confession] *om. 1553 1573*   28 bolles]
canc. and bowlys, *interl.* B, bowles L *1553 1557*, boules *1573*   29 he] the woulfe L *1553
1573*

you wot well therfor / I durst come no soner / for fere lest you wold for
my glotony haue givyn me in penaunce to fast some part of this lent /
Nay Nay quod the father Fox I am not so vnresonable / for I fast
none of yt my selfe / For I may say to the sone here in confession be-
5 twene vs twayne / it is no commaundement of god this fasting, but an
invencion of man / The prestes make folke fast & put them to payne
about the mone shyne in the water, & do but make foke foles / but they
shall make me no such fole I warrant the sone / For I eate flessh all
this lent my self I. Howbeit in dede because I will not be occasion of
10 slaunder, I therfor eate it secretely in my chamber out of sight of all
such folysh brethren as for their weke scrupulouse conscience wold
wax offendid with all / And so wold I counsayle you to do / Forsoth
father Fox quoth the wolfe, & so I thank god I do as nere as I can /
for whan I goo to my meate I take non other companye with me,
15 but such sure brethren as are of myn own nature / whose conscience
are not weke I warant you / but their stomakes as strong as myn / Well
than no forse quod father Fox. [f. 93]

   But when he hard after by his confession, that he was so grete a
ravenour, that he devowrid & spent some tyme so much vitayle at
20 one meale, as the price therof wold well fynd some pore man with his
wife and his children al most all the weke / than he prudently reprouid that poynt in hym, & prechid hym a processe of his own
temperaunce, which neuer vsid as he said to passe vppon hym selfe
the valure of six pens at a meale / no nor yet so mych neyther / For
25 whan I bryng home a gose quoth he not out of the powlters shop
where folke find them out of the fethers redy pluckyd, & se which is
the fattest & yet for vj^d bye & chose the best / but out of the huswivis
howse / at the first hand, which may somwhat bettre chepe aforth
them / you wot well than the powltre may / nor yet can not be suffrid
30 to se them plukkid & stand & chese them by day / but am fayn by

1–2 for my] for any *1557*   3 quod] quodth *A* (th *a misreading of the* ?); the] *om.* L *1553*
1573; am not] *Z*, am no *A*   4 sone] *bar wr. above* o *B*   4–5 betwene vs twayne] *canc.
and* betwene vs twayn *interl. before* here *B*, betweene vs twayne here *Z*   7 shyne] shene
1557   8 sone] *bar wr. above* o *B*   9 occasion] occōn *A*: *canc. and* occasion *interl. B*; in
dede] *om. after* Howbeit, *placed after* will not be *1553*   14 companye *canc. A before*
brethren   15 myn] my *1553*; conscience] consciences *Z*   16 stomakes] stomake *1553*;
Well] well *A*   20 wold well] well *om. 1553*   21 prudently] ly *blotted in ms., clarified B*
21–22 reprouid] v *wr. over* u *B*   26 the fethers] theyr feathers L *1553 1573*
27 chose] chuse *1573*; huswivis] huswyves L, houswifes *1553 1573*, huswiues *1557*   28
somwhat] *om.* L; aforth] aforde L *1553 1573*   30 stand] *faulty* n *A*; chese] choose L,
chose *1553 1557*, chuse *1573*

night to take at a venture, & whan I come home am fayne to do the
labour to plukk her my selfe to / yet for all this though it be but lene /
& I wene not well worth a grote, serueth yt me sometyme for all that
both dener & sowper to / And therfor as for that you live of ravyn:
therin can I find no faut / you haue vsid it so long that I thinke you 5
can do none other. And therfor were it folye to forbid it you / & to
say the trouth agaynst good conscience to / for live you must I wote
well & other craft can you none / And therfor (as reason is) must you
live by that / But yet you wot well to much is to much / & measure is
a mery meane / which I perceve by your [f. 93ᵛ] shrifte you haue neu- 10
er vsid to kepe / and therfor surely this shalbe your penaunce / that
you shall all this yere neuer passe vppon your selfe the price of vjᵈ
at a meale as nere as your conscience can gesse the price.

   Their shrift haue I shewid you as mother mawd shewid it vs / But
now serueth for our mater the conscience of them both in the trew 15
performyng of their penaunce.

   The pore Asse after his shrifte whan he waxid an hungerd, saw a
sow lye with her pigges well lappid in new straw, & nere he drew &
thought to haue eaten of the straw / but anone his scripelouse conscience began therin to grudge hym / for while his penaunce was, that for 20
gredines of his meate, he shuld do none other body none harm / he
thought he might not eate one straw there, lest for lak of that straw,
some of those pygges might happ to dye for cold / so held he still his
hunger tell one brought hym meate / but when he shuld fall therto,
than fell he yet in a far ferther scruple. For than it cam in his mynd 25
that he shuld yet breke his penaunce, yf he shuld eate any of that
eyther / sith he was comaundid by his goostly father, that he shuld
not for his own meate, hyndre any other best / for he thought that yf
he eate not that meate, some other best might happ to haue yt / & so
shuld he by the eatyng of it, peradventure hinder a nother / And 30
thus stode he still fastyng till when he told the cause, his gostly father
came & enformyd hym bettre, & than he cast of that [f. 94] scruple
& fell manerly to his meate, & was a right honest asse many a fayre
day after.

1 at] om. 1553; a venture] aduenture Z   2 to plukk her my selfe to] to om. at end 1573,
myselfe & plucke her 1553   5 faut /] period wr. on / B   6 forbid it] it om. L   8 (as]
parenth. added B   14 shewid it] shevid it A   15 trew] w clarified B   19 scripelouse]
scrupulous Z   20 grudge] divided gru-dge, dge canc. and added after gru B; that] om. 1553
21 body none] beast no L, bodye no 1553, none om. 1573   22 straw there] there om. L
1553, straw thereof 1573   25 than] interl. A   30 a nother] some other L 1553 1573,
another 1557

The wolfe now comyng from shrifte clene soylid from his synnes /
went a bout to do as a shrewed wife ones told her husband that she
wold do when she cam from shrifte. Be mery man quoth she now /
for this day I thanke god was I well shreven / and I purpose now ther-
5 for to leve of all myn old shrewdnes & begyn evyn a fresh.

Vyncent

Ah well vncle can you report her so. That word hard I her speke /
but she said yt in sport to make her husband laugh.

Anthonye

10   In dede it semyd she spake yt halfe in sport / For that she said she
wold cast away all her shrewdnes / therin I trow she sportid / but in
that she said she wold begin it all a fressh, her husband found that
good ernest.

Vincent

15   Well I shall shew her what you saye I warrant you.

Anthonye

Than will you make me make my word good / but what so euer
she did at the lest wise, so farid now this wolfe, [f. 94ᵛ] which had
cast out in confession all his old ravyn, & than hunger prikkid hym
20   forward that (as the shrewid wife said) he shuld begyn all a fresh /
But yet the prike of consciens withdrew & held hym bake, because
he wold not for brekyng of his penaunce take any pray for his meale
tide that shuld passe the price of vjᵈ.

Hit happid hym than as he walkid prollyng for his gere about, he
25   cam where a man had in few dayes before cast of two ʳolde˥ lene &
lame horses, so sike that no flesh was there left vppon them / And the

---

1 now *canc. B before* from   3 shrifte.] *period ed.*   5 old] *interl. A*; shrewdnes] shrewenes
A: second e *alt. to* d *B*   6 *letter* A *canc. A before* Vyncent   8 husband] *canc. B,* god
interl. and canc. B, good man *then interl. B,* good man *Z*   11 all her] all her olde *Z*
12 fressh] *orig.* fresch: s *wr. over* c *A*   15 I warrant you] *placed after* shew her *1553*
18 at the lest] *the om. L 1553*   19 in confession] *placed after* ravyn *L 1553*   20 that
(as] *parenth. canc. and comma wr. after that B*; said)] *parenth. ed.*; he] *Z,* she *A*; shuld] dyd in
dede *L 1553 1573*   21 prike] k *wr. over* e *B*; bake] k *wr. over* e *B*   24 Hit] It *Z*
26 sike] k *wr. over* e *B*; there] there almoste *L 1553 1573*; vppon] on *L 1553 1573*

tone whan the wolfe cam by, could scant stond on his legges / & the
tother alredy ded & his skynne ripped of & caried away / And as he
lokyd vppon them sodenly, he was first about to fede vppon them, and
whet his teth on their bones / But as he lokyd a side, he spied a fayre
cow in a close walkyng with her yong calf by her side / & as sone as 5
he saw them his conscience began to grudge hym agaynst booth
those two horsis / And than he sighed & said to hym selfe, alas wikkid
wretch that I am / I had almost broken my penaunce ere I was ware.
For yonder ded horse because I neuer saw ded horse sold in the
market / & I shuld die therfor by the way that my sinfull soule shall 10
to, I can not devise what price I shuld set vppon hym, but in my
conscience I set hym farre above vj^d, & therfor I dare not medle with
hym /

Now than is yonder quik horse of likelyhed worth a gret dele of
money / For horse be dere in this countrey, specially such soft amblers 15
/ for I se by his pase he troteth not / nor [f. 95] can scant shift a fote,
& therfor I may not medle with hym for he very fer passeth my vjd /
But kyne this countrey here hath inough / but money haue they very
litell / And therfor consideryng the plentye of the keen & the scarcite
of the money / ⌜as⌝ for yonder pevish cow semeth vnto me in my con- 20
science worth not past a grote & she be worth so mich / Now than as
for her calf, is not so mych as she by halfe / & therfor while the cow is
in my consciens worth but iiijd, my consciens can not serue me for
sinne of my soule to prayse her calfe aboue ijd / & so passe they not
vjd betwene them both. And therfor they twayne may I well eate at 25
this one meale & breke not my penaunce at all. And so thervppon he
did without any scruple of conscience. If such better could speke now
as mother maud said they could than / some of them wold I wene tell
a tale almost as wise as this / wherin saue for the menisshing of old
mother mawdes tale, els wold a shorter proces haue servid. 30

But yet as pevish as the parable is / in this it serueth for our purpose,
that the nightes fere of a conscience somwhat scriplouse, thoughe it

---

1 tone] one *1553 1573*; stond] stande *Z*; on] vpon *L 1553 1573*   2 tother] other *1553
1573*; ded] *final* e *added B*   7 to] vnto *Z*   8 I am /] *period wr. before* / *B*   9 saw] sawe
no *Z*   10 shuld] shoulde euen *Z*; shall] *interl.* A *above canc.* shuld go   13 hym /] *period
wr. after* / *B*   14 likelyhed] likelihode *Z*   15 horse] horses *1573*   17 fer] a *wr.
over* e *B*   18 inough] w *wr. over* u *and* gh *canc.* B   23 consciens] conscieens *A*
25 they] them *Z*   26 so thervppon] therevpon so *1573*   29 saue] v *wr. over* u *B*
32 scriplouse] i *alt. to* u *and* e *interl. after* p *B*, scrupulouse *Z*; thoughe] *Z*, thoughte *A*

be paynfull and troubelows to hym that hath it like as this pore asse
had here / is lesse harm yet than a consciens [f. 95ᵛ] ouer large / or
such as for his own fantasye the man list to frame hym selfe / now
drawyng yt narow now strechyng it in bredth after the maner of a
5 cheuerell poynt, to serue on euery side for his own comoditie, as did
here the wyle wolfe /

But such folke are out of tribulacion / & comfort nede they none /
& therfor are they out of our mater /

But those that are in ⌈the⌉ nightes feare of their own scripelouse
10 conscience, let them be well ware as I said, that the devill for werines
of the tone, draw them not into the tother / & while he wold fle ⌈fro⌉
scilla dreve hym into *charibdis* / He must do as doth a shipp that shuld
come into an haven, in the mouth wherof lye secret rokkes vnder the
water on both the sides / yf he be by misse happe entrid in a mong
15 them that are on the tone side & can not tell how to get out / he must
get a substanciall conyng pylote, that so can conduce hym from the
rokkes on that side, that yet he bryng hym not into those that are on
the tother side / but can guide hym in the myd way / Let them I say
therfor that are in the troubelouse feare of their own scripelouse con-
20 science, submit the rule of their own conscience, to the counsayle of
some other good man, which after the varietie & the nature of the
scriples may temper the advise / yee although a man [f. 96] be very
well lernid hym selfe / yet let hym in this case lern the custume vsid
among phisitiens / For be one of them neuer so conyng, yet in his own
25 decease & siknes, he neuer vseth to trust all to hym selfe / but send
for such of his felows as he knowith mete, & puttith hym selfe in
there handes for many consideracions wherof they assigne the causes /
And one of the causes is fere / wherof vppon some tokens, he may con-

3 list] lust *1553*   6 wyle] y *wr. over* e *B*   9 feare] feal *canc. A before* feare; scripelouse]
u *wr. over* i *B*, scrupulous *Z*   11 tone] one *1553 1573*; tother] other *1553 1573*; fle] flye
1557; fro] from L *1553 1573*   12 dreve] y *wr. over first* e *B*, dryue L *1553 1573*, drew
1557; He] *ed.*, he *A*; do] & *canc. after* do *A*   13 an haven] a hauen *1553*   14 on]
orig. in: o *wr. over* i *A*, on *Z*; the sides] the *om.* L *1553 1573*   15 tone] one *1553 1573*
16 conduce] conduct *1573*   17 on] in *A*, o *wr. over* i *B*, on *Z*   18 tother] other *1553
1573*; them] hym *A*: t *ins. and* e *interl. over* y *(uncanc.) E*   19 therfor that are] that are therfore *1553*; scripelouse] u *wr. over* i *B*, scrupulous *Z*   20 own] *om. 1573*   22 scriples]
scriplous *A*: u *wr. over* i, es *wr. over* ou *and* s *canc. B*, scrupulous L *1553*, scruples *1557 1573*;
comma wr. before may *B*; the] *canc. and* his *interl. B*, his *Z*   22–23 be very well] be well
catchwords f. *95ᵛ*   25 decease] disease *Z*; selfe] f *wr. over blotted letter, then whole word canc.
and* self *interl. B*; send] ith *added B*, sendeth *Z*   27 there] i *interl. before* r *B*

ceyue in his own passion a greate deale more than nedeth / & than were good for his helth / that for the tyme, that he knew no such thyng at all.

I knew ones in this town, one of the most conyng men in that facultie & the best expert, & therwith the most famouse to, & he that the 5 greatest cures did vppon other men / And yet when he was hym selfe ones very sore sike / I hard his felows that than lokyd vnto hym, of all which euery one wold in their own decease haue vsid his helpe before any other man, wish yet that for the tyme of his own siknes beyng so sore as it was, he had knowen no phisike at all / he toke so 10 greate hede vnto euery suspiciouse token, & fearid so farre the worst, that his feare did hym some tyme much more harm than the siknes gave hym cause /

And therfor as I say who so hath such a trowble of his scrupulouse conscience: let hym for a while forbere the iugement of hym selfe, 15 & folow the counsaylc of some other, whom he knowith for well lernid & vertuouse, & specially in the place of confession / For there is god specially present [f. 96ᵛ] with his grace assistyng his sacrament / & let hym not doute to aquiete his mynd, & folow that that he is there bode, & thinke for a while lesse of the fere of godes iustice, & be more 20 mery in remembraunce of his mercie, & percever in prayour for grace, & ʳabyde &ꜞ dwell faythfully in the sure hope of his helpe / aud than shall he fynd without any dout, that the pauice of godes trouth shall (as the prophet sayth) so compasse hym about, that he shall not dreade this nightes fere of scrupulosite, but shall haue his conscience stablysh- 25 id in good quiet & rest.

1–2 & than were] & that were *1553*   2 were good] were it good *1573*; helth /] | *canc.* B; tyme, that] that *canc.* B, om. Ƶ   3 at] *interl.* A   5 famouse] famoust A: e *wr. over* t B   8 decease] ys *wr. over* ec B, disease Ƶ   9 man] men *interl.* B *above* man (*uncanc.*), men L *1553 1573*   14 And] A *clarified* B   18 his sacrament] his holy Sacramente L *1553 1573*   19 folow that that] *one* that *om.* Ƶ; is there] there is Ƶ   20 bode] bidden L *1553 1573*, bounden *1557*   21 in remembraunce] in the remembraunce L *1553 1573*   24 not dreade] not nede to dreade L *1553 1573*   25 haue] haue afterwarde Ƶ

A nother kynd of the nightes feare, a nother doughter of
pusillanimite, that is to wyt that horrible temptacion by
which some folke are temptid to kyll
& destroy them selfe /

5   The xv chapiter

Vincent

Verely good vncle you haue in my mynd well declarid these kyndes
of the nightes fere.

Anthonye

10   Surely Cosyn but yet are there many mo than I can eyther remember ⌈or⌉ fynd / howbeit one yet cometh now to my mynd, of which I
before nothyng thought, & which is yet in myn opinion of all the
other feres the most horrible / that is to wyt cosyn, where the devill
temptith a man to kyll & destroy hym selfe.

15   Vincent

Vndowtidly this kynd of trybulacion is mervelouse & straunge &
the temptacion is of such a sort, that some men haue opinion, that
such as ones fall in that fantasye, can neuer [f. 97] full cast it of /

Anthonye

20   Yis yis Cosyn many an hundred & els god forbede / But the thing
that maketh men so say / is because / that of those which finally do
destroy them selfe / there is much spech & much wondryng (as it is
well worthy) but many a good man & woman hath some tyme / ye
diuers yeres one after other continually be temptid therto / &
25 yet haue by grace & good counsayle well and vertuously withstand

---

2 wyt] wete *1553*; that horrible] the horrible *1573*   4 selfe] selvys *L*   5 xv] xv^th *L*
11 or] *interl. B above canc.* to, or *Z*; now to my mynd] to my minde now *L 1553 1573*
16 straunge] *divided* stra-unge: unge *canc. and* nge *added after* stra *B*   18 as ones fall] as fall
once *L 1553 1573*; neuer] neuer after *L 1553 1573*   20 an hundred] an hundreth *L*, a
hundreth *1553*, a hundred *1573*; & els] or els *1573*   22 selfe] selvys *L*; spech] *final* e
added B   23 & woman] and many a good woman *L 1553 1573*   24 one] *canc. and*
eche *interl. B*, eche *Z*; be] bene *1573*   25 withstand] withstanden *1573*

yt, & bene in conclucion clerely deliuerid of hit / & there tribulacion
nothyng knowen abrode & therfor nothyng talkyd of. But surely
Cosyn an horrible sore trowble it is, to any man or woman that the
devill tempteth therwith / many haue I herd of / & with some haue
I talkid my selfe, that haue bene sore combrid with that temptacion, 5
& markid haue I not a litell the maner of them.

Vincent

I require you good vncle shew me somwhat of such thinges as you
perceyve therin /

For first where you call this kynd of temptacion the doughter of 10
pusillanimite & therby so nere of ⌐sybbe⌐ vnto the nightes fere, me
thinketh on the tother side that it is rather a thing that cometh of a
greate courage & boldnes / whan they dare their own handes put them
selfe to deth / from which we see al most euery man shrynke & fle /
& that many such, as we know by good profe & playne experience 15
for men of greate [f. 97ᵛ] hart & excellent hardy corage.

Anthonye

I said Cosyn Vincent that of pusillanimite cometh this temptacion /
& very trouth it is / that in dede so it doth / but I ment it not that
of onely faynt hart & fere it cometh & groweth alway / for the devill 20
temptith sondry folkes by sondry wayes / But the cause wherfor I
spake of none other kynd of that temptacion, than of onely that ⌐which
is the doughter, that⌐ the devill begettith vppon pusillanimite / was for
that / that those other kyndes of that temptacion fall not vnder the
nature of tribulacion & fere / & therfor fall they far out of our mater 25
here / & are such temptacions as onely nede counsayle & not comfort
or consolacion / for that the persons therwith temptid, be with that
kynd of temptacion not troublid in there mynd, but verely well content both in the tempting & folowyng / For some hath there bene
cosyn such, that they haue be temptid therto by meane of a folish 30

---

1 hit] it *Z*; there] i *interl. before* r *B*   5 combrid] encombred *L 1553 1573*   11 sybbe]
wr. by B in blank space left by A   12 thinketh] *minim lacking for* in *A*; tother] other *1553*
1573   14 selfe] selvys *L*; fle] flye *1557*   15 & that] as that *L 1553*   16 excellent
hardy] of an excedyng hardie *L 1553 1573*   18 that of] that *om. L*, of that *1553*
19 is /] | *canc. B*; so it] it so *1553 1573*; but I] but yet I *Z*   22 of that temptacion]
that *om. 1553*   23–24 for that /] | *canc. B*   28 temptacion] *interl. A above canc.*
tribulacion; there] i *interl. before* r *B*; mynd] myndes *L*; verely] very *L*   29 in the
tempting] the *om. L 1553*; hath] haue *1573*   30 cosyn] *interl. A*; be] bene *1573*

pride / & some by the mene of Angre without any drede at all / & very
glad to go therto / to this I say not nay / But where you wene that
none fall thereto by fere / but that they haue all a strong mighti stomake, that shall ye well see the contrary, & that peradventure in those
5 of whom you wold wene the stomake most strong & theire hart &
courage most hardye /

Vincent

Yet is it merveyle vnto me that it shuld be as you say it is / that this
temptacion is vnto them that do it for pride or for Angre no tribula-
10 cion, nor ⌈that⌉ they shuld nede in so [f. 98] greate a distres & perell
both of body & soule to be lost, no maner of good goostly comfort /

Anthony

Let vs therfor Cosyn consider a sample or two / for therby shall we
the better perceve it /
15   There was here in Buda in kyng Ladislaus dayes, a good pore honest mans wife / This woman was so fendich / that the devill percevyng
her nature, put her in the mynd that she shold angre her husband,
so sore that she might give hym occasion to kyll her / & than shuld
he be hangid for her.

20   ### Vincent

This was a straunge temptacion in dede / what the devill shuld she
be the better than /

Anthonye

Nothyng / but that / it easid her shrewid stomake before, to thynke
25 that her husband shuld be hangid after / And peradventure yf you
loke aboute the world / & consider it well / you shall find mo such
stomakes than a few / Haue you neuer hard no furiouse body

---

2 glad to go] to go *om. L 1553*; where] where as *L 1553 1573*   3 mighti] y *wr. over* i *B*
4 ye] you *Z*; well see] well *om. L 1553*   5 theire] i *interl. A*   8 merveyle vnto me]
maruayle Uncle to mé *L 1553 1573*, merueyl vncle vnto me *1557*   11 comfort] comforte at al *L 1553 1573*   16 fendich] s *wr. over* c *B*   18 sore that] *Z*, sore the *A*; hym]
him an *L 1553*   18–19 shuld he] he should *L 1553 1573*   24 that /] | *canc. B*
27 Haue] *ed.,* haue *A*

playnly saye / that to se some such man haue a mischiefe, he wold
with good will be content to lye as long in hell as god liveth in hevyn.

Vincent

Forsoth & some such haue I hard ⌈of.⌉

Anthonye   5

This mynd of his was not mich lesse mad than hers / but rather
happely more mad of the twayne / for the woman peradventure did
not cast so ferre perell therin / But to tell you now to what good passe
the charitable [f. 98ᵛ] purpose cam / As her husband (the man was
a carpenter) stode hewyng with his chippe axe vppon a pece of tymber   10
/ she began after her old guise so to revile hym, that the man waxid
wroth at last / & bode her get her in / or he wold lay the helm of
his axe about her bakke / & said also that it were litle sinne, evyn
with that axe hed to chopp of that vnhappy hed of hers that caried
such an vngraciouse tonge therin. At that word the devill toke his   15
tyme & whettid her tonge agaynst her tethe / & when it was well
sharpid, she sware to hym in very fiers angre / by the masse horson
husband I wold thow woldest / here lieth myn hed lo / and therwith
down she laid her hed vppon the same timber logge / yf thow smyte
it not of, I beshrew thyn horsons hart / with that likewise as the devill   20
stode at her elbow / so stode (as I hard say) his good angell at his, &
gave hym goostly corage, & bode hym be bold & do it / And so the
good man vpp with his chipp axe & at a choppe choppid of her
hed in dede / There were standyng other folke by / which had a good
sport to here her chide / but litell they lokyd for this chaunce till it was   25
done ere they cold let it / They said they herd her tong bable in her
hed & call horson horson twise after that the hed was fro the bodye /
At the lest wise afterward vnto the kyng thus they reportid all except
onely one / & that was a woman / & she said that she hard it not /
[f. 99]   30

---

1 playnly saye] saye playnly L *1553*   2 hevyn] n *added B after faulty* yn A   4 of.] *wr.*
by B at end of line, om. L *1553*   7 more] the more Z   8 therin /] *period wr. after* / B
9 the] *canc. and* her *interl.* B, her Z   12 bode] bade L *1553 1573*; helm] helue L *1553*
1573   17 sware to] sware vnto L *1553 1573*   18 myn] my L *1553 1573*; lo /] *parenth.*
wr. over / B   19 logge /] *parenth. wr. over* / B   20 thyn] thy L *1553 1573*   21 say)]
parenth. wr. over / B   22 bode] bade L *1553 1573*   25 sport] *orig.* spore: t *wr. over* e A
27 that] *om.* L *1553 1573*; fro] from L *1553 1573*   28 At the] the *om.* L *1553*; except]
(except A   29 one /] *parenth. wr. over* / B

Vinsent

Forsoth this was a wonderfull worke / What becam vncle of the man?

Anthony

5   The kyng gaue hym his pardon.

Vincent

Verely he might in conscience do no lesse.

Anthonye

But than was ferther al most at an other poynt / that there shuld
10 haue bene a statute made, that in such case there shold neuer
after pardon be grauntid / but the trouth ⌈being⌉ able to be prouid,
none husband shuld nede any pardon / but shuld haue lefe by the law
to folow the sample of the carpenter & do the same.

Vincent

15   How happid it vncle that that good law was left vnmade?

Anthonye

How hapid yt / as it happith Cosyn that many mo be left vnmade /
as well as yt / & within a litell as good as it to / bothe here and in
other countreys, & some tyme ⌈some⌉ worse made in their stede /
20 But as they say the let of that law was the quenes grace (god forgive
her soule) It was the greaste thyng I wene good ladye that she had to
answere for when she died / For surely save for that one thyng, she was
a full blessid woman.

But lettyng now that law passe, this temptacion in procuring her
25 own deth, was vnto this Carpenters wife no tribulacion at all, as far as
euer men could perceve / for it liked her well to thynke theron, & she
evyn longid therfor / And therfor yf [f. 99ᵛ] she had told you or me

---

2 What] *ed.*, what *A*; becam] came *1557*   3 man?] *question-mark ed.*   9 was] *interl. A
above canc.* were, was it *Z*; al most] *om. L 1553*; at an other] at nother *1553*   12 none] no
L 1553 1573; lefe] *canc. and* leve *interl. B*, leaue *Z*   17 yt /] *question-mark wr. before | B*;
many] *minim lacking in* ny *A*   21 soule)] *parenth. wr. over | B*; greaste] greatest *Z*
25 vnto] *Z*, vn *A*   26–27 she evyn] l *canc. after* she *A*

before her mynd, & that she wold so fayne bryng it so to pas / we cold haue had none occacion to comfort her as one that were in tribulacion, but mary counsayle her (as I told you before) we might / to refrayne and amend that maliciouse devilish mynd /

Vincent

Verely that is trewth / but such as are well willyng to do any purpose that is so shamfull, will neuer tell their mynd to no body for very shame /

Anthonye

Some will not in dede / & yet are there some agayne that be their intent neuer so shamefull / fynd some yet whom ⌐theyr¬ hart serueth them to make of their counsell therin. Some of my own folke here can tell you that no lenger ago than evyn yister day, one that came out of vienna shewid vs among other talkyng / that a rich wydow (but I forgate to aske hym where it happid) havyng all her lyfe an high prowd mynd & a fell (as those ij vertuose are wont allwey to kepe companye together) was at debate with a nother neighbour of hers in the town / And on a tyme she made of her counsayle a pore neybour of hers, whom she thought for money she might induce to folow her mynd. With hym she secretly brake & offrid hym / x / ducates for his labour to do so much for her / as in a mornyng erely to come to her howse, & with an axe vnknowen prively strik of her hed / & whan he had so done than convey the blody axe [f. 100] into the house of hym with whome she was at debate, in some such maner wise as it might be thought that he had murdred her for malice / & than she thought she shuld be taken for a marter / And yet had she ferther devisid, that a nother some of money shuld after be sent to Rome & there shuld be meanes made to the pope that she might in all haste be canonisid /

<hr>

1 before] *canc. and interl. after* had *B,* had before tolde *Z;* so fayne bryng it so] brynge it so fayne *L 1553*   2 none] no *1553 1573*   3 we might] we well might *L 1553 1573*
4 maliciouse] *om. L 1553;* mynd] mynde of hyrs *L 1553 1573*   11 theyr] *interl. B after canc.* yⁱʳ *A*   12 counsell] counsell / *A* : / *canc. B;* own] *canc. B, om. Z*   13 lenger] longer *L 1553 1573*   17 together)] *parenth. ed.,* together / *A*   20 With] *ed.,* with *A;* she secretly] secretly she *L 1553 1573*   21 in a mornyng erely to come] come in a morninge early *L 1553*   22 strik] to stryke *L 1553 1573*   24 maner] maner of *L 1553*   25 for malice] of malyce *L 1553 1573*   26 be taken] betaken *A*   27–28 & there] and that there *L 1553 1573*

This pore man promisid / but intendid not to perform it / howbeit
whan he deferrid it, she prouidid the axe her selfe & he apoyntid
with her the mornyng when he shuld come & do it & thervppon into
her howse he came / But than set he such other folke as he wold shuld
5 know her frantik fantasie, in such place appoyntid as they might well
here her & hym talke together / And after that he had talkyd with
her therof / what he wold, so much as thought was inough / he made
her lye down & toke vpp the axe in his one hand & with the tother
hand he felt the edge & found a faut that it was not sharpe / & that
10 therfor he wold in nowise do it till he had grownden yt sharper / he
cold not els he said for pitie / it wold put her to so much payne / And
so full sore agaynst her will for that tyme she kept her hed styll / but
because she wold no more suffre eny mo deceve her so / & fede her
forth with delayes, ere it was very long after, she hong her selfe her
15 own handes.

Vincent

Forsoth here was a tragicall story, wherof I neuer herd the like.

Antone

Forsoth the partie that told yt me, sware that he knew it for [f.
20 100ᵛ] a trouth / And hym selfe is I promise you such, as I reken for
right honest & of substanciall trewth /
Now here she lettid not / as shamfull a mynd as she had, to make
one of her counsayle yet / & yet as I remember a nother to, whom
she trustid with the money that shuld procure her canonisation.
25 And here I wot well that her temptacion cam not of fere, but of
high malice & pride / But than was she so glad in the plesaunt devise
therof / that as I shewid you / she toke it for no tribulacion / & therfor

---

1 not] no *A*, t *added B*   3–4 & do it & thervppon into her howse he came] *om. L 1553,*
& thervppon into her howse he came] *om. 1573*   5 fantasie] fansye *L*   7 therof /] | /
canc. B; as thought] as he thought *Z*   8 one] owne *1557*; tother] other *1553*   10 till
he] tyll that he *L 1553 1573*; grownden] ground *L 1553 1573*; sharper] sharpe *1557*
13 no more suffre] not suffer *L 1553 1573*; eny mo] any moe to *L 1553 1573*; fede] fode *Z*
14 hong] hanged *1553 1573*; selfe her] selfe with her *L 1553 1573*   18 Antone] y *wr.*
over e *B*   21 right] *interl. A*   22 lettid not /] | *canc. B*   23 yet / & yet as] *second* yet
om. 1573; comma wr. after nother *and erased B*   27 tribulacion] tribulacion, but for a
maruelous mery mortall temptacion. *1553,* trybulacion but *L: after* but *in L follows a blank
half-page, the lower half of f. 80 recto; 80ᵛ then begins with the opening words of Ch. 16:* But lest
you; *apparently a page was missing in the ms. from which L was copying*

comfortyng of her could haue no place / but yf men shuld any thyng
geve her toward her help, it must haue bene as I told you good counsayle / And therfor / as I said / this kynd of temptacion to a mans own
destruccion which requireth counsayle / & is out of tribulacion / was
out of our mater that is to treate of comfort in tribulacion. 5

Of hym that were movid to kyll him selfe by Illucion of
the devill, which he rekeneth for a revelacion
The / xvj / chapiter /

But lest you might reiect bothe these samples, wening they were
but faynid tales: I shall put you in remembraunce of one which I 10
reken your selfe haue redd in the Collacions of Cassianus / & yf you
haue not, there may you sone fynd yt / For my selfe haue halfe forgotton the thyng it is so long syns I redd it / but thus much I remembre
that he tellith there, of one that was many dayes a very specall holy
man [f. 101] in his lyuing / & among the other vertuouse monkes & 15
ankers that livyid there in wildernes, was mervelously much estemid /
savyng that some were not all out of fere of hym, lest his revelacions
wherof he told many by hym selfe, wold proue illusions of the devill /
And so provid it after in dede / For the man was by the divylles subtill
suggestions brought into such an high spirituall pride, that in con- 20
clucion the devill brought hym to that horrible poynt, that he made
hym go kyll hym selfe / And as far as my mynd giveth me now without
new sight of the boke / he broght him to it by this perswasion / that
he made hym beleve that it was godes will he shuld so do / & that
therby shuld he go strayt to hevyn. 25
And than yf it were by that perswacion with which he toke very
great comfort in his own mynd hymselfe / than was it as I said out of
our case / & nedid not comfort, but counsayle agaynst givyng credence to the devilles perswasion.

---

5 treate] wete *1553*   6 Illucion] sy *wr. over* c B   7 rekeneth] reckoned *1553*   9 these]
those *1553 1573*   10 shall put you] shal but put you L *1553*, shal put you but *1573*
12 there may you] ther you may *1557*   14 there, of one] of one there *1553*; many] all
his L *1553*; specall] *om.* L *1553 1573*   16 there] *om.* L *1553*   20–21 conclucion] sy
wr. over third c B   22 go kyll] to kyll L *1553 1573*   23 him] *interl.* A *above canc.* it
24 beleve that] that *om.* L *1553*   25 shuld he] he should L   27 than was it] was it
then L *1553*   28 case] case here L *1553 1573*; agaynst] *divided* agay-nst, nst *canc. and*
added after agay B

But mary yf he made hym first perceve how he had bene deludid /
& than temptid hym to his own deth by shame & by dispayre, than
was it within our mater lo / for than was his temptacion fallen down
fro pride to pusillanimite / & was waxen that kynd of the nightes fere
5 that I speke of, wherin a good part of the counsayle that were to be
gevyn hym shuld haue nede to stand in good comfortyng / For than
was he brought into right sore tribulacion. [f. 101ᵛ]
But as I was about to tell you, strength of hart & corage is there
none there in / not onely for that very strength as it hath the name of
10 vertew in a resonable creature / can neuer be without prudence / but
also for that (as I said) even in them that seme men of most hardines /
it shall well apere to them that well way the mater, that the mynd
wherby they be led to destroye them selfe, groweth of pusillanimite &
very folysh fere /
15 Take for the sample *Cato vticensis* which in ⌐Afryque⌐ killid hym
selfe, after the ⌐great⌐ victory that Iulius Cezar had / S Austyn well
declarith in his worke *de ciuitate dei* / ⌐that there was no strength nor
magnanimyte⌐ therin but playne pusillanimite & impotency of stomake / wherby he was forcid to the distruccion of hym selfe / because
20 his hart was to feoble for to bere the beholdyng of an other mans glory /
or the suffryng of other worldly calamyties that he ferid shuld fall on
hym selfe / So that as saint Austen well proueth, that horrible dede
is none act of strenghth but an act of a mynd eyther drawn from the
consideracion of it selfe with some develysh fantasie, wherin the man
25 hath nede to be callid home by good counsayle / or ⌐els⌐ oppressid by
faynt hart & fere / wherin a good part of the counsayle must stand in
leftyng vpp his corage with good consolacion and comfort.
And therfor if we found eny such religiouse person as was that

---

2 by dispayre] by *om. L 1553 1573*   3 within] in *L 1553*; fass *canc. before* fallen *A*   4 fro]
from *L 1553 1573*   5 speke] spake *Z*   6 *comma wr. after* gevyn *B*   7 brought into]
brought to *L 1553*   11 seme] some *1553*   13 they] yᵉʸ *A: canc. and* they *interl. B*
13–14 & very] and of very *L*   15 the sample] example *1573*; which in] who in *1573*;
Afryque] *interl. B*, *A has a* fry *followed by blank space, E amends to* Afryuyke, *which is canc. B*:
see note   16 victory that] victory of *1553*   18 therin] *occurs at end of line, above and in*
margin E has ins. that ther was no strength nor [*mg canc.*] magnanimite, *B has canc. this*
insertion along with original therin *and interl. above next line* that there was no strength nor
magnanimyte therein /   19 was forcid] has forced *1573*   20 for to] for *om. L 1553*
1573   21 worldly] *om. L 1553 1573*   22 as] *om. L 1553*   23 none act] no acte *L 1553*
1573; a mynd] the mind *L 1553 1573*   24 fantasie] fansy *L*   25 home by] home with *Z*
27 leftyng] y *wr. over* e *B*; corage] *divided* cora-ge *A*, ge *canc. and added after* cora *B*

father which Cassian writeth of, that were of [f. 102] such austerite &
apparant goostly livyng / that he were with such as well knew hym
reputid for a man of singuler vertew / and that it were percevid that
he had many straunge visions appering vnto hym / if it shuld now be
percevid after that / that the man went about secretly to destroy hym   5
selfe / who so shuld happe to come to the knolege therof, & entendid
to do his devour in the lett / first must he fynd the meanes to serch &
fynd out / whether the man be in his maner & his countenaunce,
lightsome glad & ioyfull / or dumpish hevy and sad / & whether he go
therabout as one that were full of the glad hope of hevyn / or as one   10
that had his brest farcid full of tediousnes & werynes of the world /
Iff he were found in the first fassion, it were a token that the devill
hath by his fantasticall apparicions, puffid hym vpp in such a pevish
pride that he hath finally perswadid hym by some illusion shewid
hym for the profe, that godes pleasure is / that he shall for his sake   15
with his own handes kill him selfe /

Vincent

Now yf a man so fownd it vncle / what counsayle shuld a man give
hym than /

Anthony   20

That were somwhat out of our purpose Cosyn / sith as I told you
before, the man were not than in sorow and tribulacion wherof our
mater speketh / but in a perilous mery mortall temptacion / so that
yf we shuld besid our own mater that we haue in hand, entre into that
to / [f. 102ᵛ] we might make a lenger warke betwene both, than we   25
could well finish this day / How be it to be short, it is sone sene that
therin / the sum & theffect of the counsaile, must in maner rest in
gevyng hym warnyng of the devilles sleyghtes / & that must be done
vnder such swete plesaunt maner, as the man shuld not abhorre to

2 well] *om. L 1553*   4 straunge] *om. L 1553*; visions] *first s wr. over illeg. letter B*
8 maner &] maner and in *L 1553 1573*   9 ioyfull /] *comma wr. after | B*; and sad] or
sadde *L 1553*   12 found in] founden of *Z*   15 *repeated* that godes pleasure is that
canc. A B and that *interl. B*   18 Now] What *L 1553 1573*   19 than /] | *canc. and*
question-mark ins. B   24 haue in] haue taken in *L 1553*   25 might make] might happe
to make *L 1553 1573*; lenger] longer *L 1553 1573*   26 day /] *period wr. after | B*
27 sum & theffect of the counsaile] counsayle and the effecte therof *L 1553*, sum &
effect of the counsayle *1557 1573*   29 swete] *interl. A*; swete plesaunt] pleasante swete
L 1553

here it / for while it could lightly be none other, but that the man
were rokkyd and song a slepe by the devilles crafte / & his mynd
occupied as it were in a delectable dreme / he shuld neuer haue good
audience for hym, that wold rudely & boystuously / shogge hym &
5 wake hym, & so shake hym out therof / Therfor must you fayre &
easly towch hym, & with some plesaunt spech awake hym / so that
he wax not wayward as children do that are waked ere they list
to rise /

But whan a man hath first begonne with his prayse / for yf he be
10 proud ye shall mich better please hym with a commendacion than
with a dirige / than after favour wonne therwithall, a man may a litle
& litle insinuate the dovt of such reuelacions / not at the first / as it
were for any dout of his / but of some other that men in some other
places talke of / And peradventure it shall not misse content hym selfe,
15 to shew great perilles that may fall therin in a nother mans case than
his own, & shall begyn to prech vppon it. [f. 103]

Or yf you were a man that had not so very greate scrupulouse conscience of an harmlesse lye devisid to do good withall, which kynd
S Austyne / though he take alway for synne / yet he taketh but for ven-
20 iall, & S Hierom (as by diuers places in his bokes apperith) taketh not
fully for so much / than may you fayne some secret frend of yours to
be in such case, & that your selfe somewhat fere his perill / & haue
made of charitie this viage for his sake, to aske this good fathers
counsell. And in that communicasion vppon these wordes of saynt
25 Iohn / *Nolite omni spiritui credere / sed probate spiritus si ex deo sint* / give
not credence to euery spirite, but proue the spirites whether they be
of god / And these wordes of saynt paule / *Angelus sathane transfigurat
se in angelum lucis* / the Angell of Sathan, transfigureth hym selfe in to

1 be none] by none *1557*   2 song] songen *Z*; & his] and therby his *L 1553 1573*
4 for] *canc. and of interl.* B, of *Z*; boystuously /] / *canc.* B; shogge] shugge *L 1553*
5 therof /] *period wr. before* / B   6 hym / so that] / *canc. and comma added after* so B, *then
comma canc.* B, him so, that *Z*   7 list] lust *1553*   8 rise /] *period wr. after* / B
10 proud] w *wr. over* u B   11 a litle] a *om. Z*   12 dovt] u *wr. over* v B   13 were for]
were, that it were for *L 1553*; that men] men that *L 1553*   15 than] rather than *1573*
17 so very greate scrupulouse] a scrupulouse *L 1553*, so very a scrupulous *1573*   19 taketh
but] taketh it but *L 1553 1573*   20 places in] places of *L 1553*; apperith)] h *and parenth.
added* B; taketh] taketh yt *L*   24 counsell. And] / *erased? under period* B, and *A*: a *alt.
to* A B; vppon these] maye you bringe in these *L 1553 1573*   25 sint] sunt *L 1553 1573*
26 to euery] vnto euery *L 1553 1573*; the spirites] *om. L 1553*   27 sathane] *hook added
to* e B

the angell of light: you shall take occasion the bettre yf they happ to
com in on his side / but yet not lak occasion neyther / yf those textes /
for lak of his offre, come in vppon your own / occasion I say you
shall not lak, to enquire by what sure & vndeceveable tokens, a man
may decern the trew reuelacions from the false Illusions / wherof a 5
man shall fynd many both here & there in diuers other authoures /
& whole together diuers goodly tratice of that good godly doctour
master Iohn Gerson, intitlid *de probatione spirituum.* [f. 103ᵛ]

As whether the party be naturall wise, or eny thing seme fantastic-
all /   10

Whether the partie be pore spiritid or proude / which will somwhat
apere, by his delite in his own prayse / or yf of wilines / or of a nother
pride for to be praysid of humilite / he refuse to here therof / yet any
litle faut found in hym selfe / or diffidence declarid & missetrust of his
own reuelacions & doutfull tokens told / wherfor hymselfe shuld feare 15
lest they be the devilles illusions / such thinges (as master Gerson sayth)
will make hym spett out somwhat of his spirite, yf the devill lye in his
brest.

Or yf the devill be yet so sotill, that he kepe hym selfe close in his
warm denne, & blow out neuer an hote word / yet is it to be con- 20
siderid / what end his revelacions draw to / whether to any spirituall
profitt to hym selfe or other folke / or onely to vayne mervayles &
wonders.

Also whether they withdraw hym from such other good vertuouse
busines, as by the comen rules of christendom, or any rules of his 25
profession, he was wont ⌐to⌐ vse or were bound to be occupied in.

Or whether he fall into any singularite of opinions, agaynst the
scripture of god, or agaynst the comen fayth of christes catholique
church.

Many other tokens are there in that worke of master Gerson spoken 30
of, to consider by, whether the person neuer havyng revelacions of

---

2 his side] his owne side *L 1553 1573*; textes /] / *canc. B*   3–4 you shall] you *canc. and
interl. after* shall *B*, shall you *Z*   5 false] / *canc. B after* false (/ *prob. meant as separation A*)
6 both] *om. L*; other] *om. L*   7 tratice] (*sp. with superl. a*) *canc. and* treatice *interl. B*; treatises
Z   9 whether] if *L 1553 1573*   11 Whether] or whither *L 1553 1573*   13 for to be]
for *om. L*   15 wherfor] wherof *L 1553 1573*   16 illusions] *final* s *canc. B*, illusion *1557*
17 spett] to spette *L 1553 1573*; his spirite] his spitefull spirite *L 1553 1573*   20 an
hote] a hote *L 1553 1573*   21 whether to] *blotted* to *canc. A? after* whether   26 were]
was *1573*; bound] bounden *1557*   31 neuer] nether *B*: th *wr. over* uer *and* er *added B*,
neyther *Z*

god, nor illucions fro the devill / do eyther for wining of money or
worldly favour [f. 104] fayne his revelacions hymselfe, & delude the
peple withall. But now for our purpose, if among any of the markes
by which the trew revelacions may be knowen from false illucions,
5 that man hym selfe bryng ⌐forth for one mark, the doyng or techyng
of⌐ any thyng agaynst the scripture of god, or the comen fayth of the
church: than haue you an entre made you, by which whan you list
you may entre into the speciall mater, wherin he can neuer well flyt
from you.

10   Orels may you yet / yf you list, fayne that your secret frend (for
whose sake you come to hym for counsaile) is brought in that mynd,
by a certeyne apparition shewid vnto hym (as hym selfe sayth) by an
angell (as you fere) by the devill / that he can be by you none otherwise perswadid as yet / but that the pleasure of god is, that he shall go
15 kyll hym selfe / & that yf he so do, than shall he be therby so specially
participant of christes passion, that he shall forwith, be caried vpp
with angelles into hevyn / For which is he so ioyfull, that he fermly
purposith vppon it / no lesse glad to do it / than an other man wold
be glad to avoyd it / & therfor may you desier his good counsayle, to
20 instruct you with some substanciall good advise, wherwith you may
tourne hym from this errour, that he be not vnder hope of godes trew
revelacion, in body & soule destroyid by the devilles false illucion /

    If he will in this thing study & labour to instruct you, [f. 104ᵛ] the
thing that hym selfe shall find of his own invencion, though they be
25 lesse effectuall, shall peradventure more worke with hym selfe toward
his own amendment, sith he shall of likelyhed better lyke them / than
shall dowble so substanciall told hym by an other man /

    If he be loth to thinke vppon that side, & therfor shrinke fro the

1 illucions] sy wr. over c B; fro] from L 1553 1573   2 comma wr. after favour B; & delude]
to delude 1553 1573   4 revelacions] reuelacion 1553; false] the false L 1553 1573;
illucions] si wr. over c B   5 that man] that maye L 1553; bryng] r wr. over illeg. letter B
7 list] luste 1553   10 yet /] | canc. B, yet om. L 1553; list] luste 1553; (for] parenth.
added B   11 in] into L 1553 1573   13–14 otherwise] other waye L, other wayes 1553
14 go] om. 1553   15 that yf] thas A: t wr. over s B; be] interl. A; specially] speciall 1553
16 forwith] th interl. after r B, forthwith Z   17 is he] is canc. and interl. after he B, he is Z
19 avoyd] a canc. B, voyde Z   20 substanciall good] good substancyall L 1553 1573
22 illucion] si wr. over c B, delusion L 1553   24 thing] thinges Z; find of] fynd out of
L 1553 1573   26 likelyhed] lykelyhod Z   27 dowble so substanciall] the double
substanciall thinges L 1553, double so substancial thinges 1573; hym] om. L 1553 1573
28 fro] from L 1553 1573

mater / than is there none other way, but adventure after the playne fasshion, to fall into the mater, and shew what you here, & to give hym counsayle & exortacion to the contrary / but if you list to say, that thus & thus hath the mater bene reasonid all redy betwene your frend & you. And therin may you reherse such thinges as shuld prove, 5 that the vision which moveth hym, is no trew revelacion, but a very false illucion.

Vincent

Verely vncle I well alow this, that a man shuld as well in this thing, as euery other wherin he longeth to do a nother man good / seke such 10 a plesaunt way, as the partie shulbe likely to like / or at the lest wise, well to take in worth his communicacion / & not so to entre in ther unto, as he whom he wold helpe, shuld abhorre hym & beloth to here hym, & therfor take no profit by hym / But now vncle yf it come by the tone way or the tother, to the poynt / that here me he will or shall / 15 what be the reasons effectuall, with which I shuld by my counsayle convert hym /

Anthonye

All those by which you may make hym perceyve, that hym selfe is decevid, & that his visions be no godly revelacions, but very develysh 20 illucions. [f. 105] And those resons must you gather of the man, of the mater, & of the law of god, or of some one of these. Of the man, if you can peradventure shew hym, that in such a poynt or such, he is waxen worse sins such revelacions haue hauntid hym than he was before / as in those that are deludid who so be well acquentid with 25 them, shall well marke & perceve / for they wax more prowd, more wayward, more enviouse / suspiciouse / misse iugyng & depravyng other men, with the delyght of their own prayse, & such other spirituall vices of the soule /

---

3 list] luste *1553 1573*   5 as shuld] y^t shoulde *L 1553*   6 very] *om. L 1553*   7 illucion] sy *wr. over* c *B*   11 shulbe] d *ins. after* l *B*, shoulde be *Z*   12 well to take] to take wel *1573*   13 beloth] *vertical line wr. after* be *B*   14 take] to take *1553*   15 tone] one *1553*; tother] other *1553*; that here] to heare *L 1553*   16 my] *om. L 1553 1573* 21 illucions.] *period ed.*, si *wr. over* c *B*, illusion *1557*   22 Of] of *A*: O *wr. over* o *B* 24 revelacions] s *added B*   25 that] *interl. A*   28 delyght] y *wr. over* i *B?*

Of the mater may you gather, if it haue happid his revelacions before to prove false / or that they be thinges rather strange than profitable / for that is a good marke betwene godes miracles & the devilles wonders / for christ & his sayntes haue their miracles alway
5 tendyng to frute & profit / the devill & his wiches & necromancers all their wonderfull workes, draw to no frutfull end, but to a frutles ostentacion & shew / as it were a iugeler that wold for a shew before the people, play maistreys at a fest /

Of the Law of god you must draw your resons, in shewyng by the
10 scripture, that the thyng which he weneth god by his angell biddith / god hath his own mouth forbidden, And that is you wot well in the case that we speke of so easely to find, that I nede not to reherse it to you, sith there is playne among the commaundementes forbidden, the vnlawfull kyllyng of any man / And therfor of hym selfe / as S Austen
15 sayth / all the church techeth / except hym selfe be no man /

Vincent

This is very trew good vncle / nor I will not dispute vppon any glosyng of that prohibicion / but sith we fynd not the contrary but that god may dispence with that commaundement hymselfe, and both licence
20 & commaund also, if hym selfe list any man [f. 105ᵛ] to go kyll either an other man or hym selfe either: this man that is now by such a mervelouse vicion inducid to beleve that god so biddith hym, & therfor thynketh hym selfe in that case / of that prohibicion dischargid, & chargid with the contrary commaundment / with ⌐what⌐ reason
25 may we make hym perceve that his vicion is but an illucion & not a trew reuelacion?

Antonye

Nay Cosyn Vincent ye shall in this case not nede to require those

---

1–2 if it haue happid his revelacions before to prove false] yf yow have proved hys revelacions false before *L*, if you haue proued his revelacion before false *1553*   3 godes] d
interl. before d *B*   5 necromancers] s *added B*, Necromancer *L 1553*   8 maistreys] r
wr. over illeg. letter B   10 thyng] tyng *A*: h *interl. B*   12 easly] easy *Z*   12–13 to
you] vnto you *1553 1573*   13 the commaundementes] the x commaundementes *Z*;
forbidden] forboden *L 1557*   15 sayth / all] sayeth, and all *L 1553 1573*   18 *comma
added after* contrary *B*   20 hym selfe] him *L 1553*; list] lust *1553*; hym selfe *canc. after*
kyll *A*   22 vicion] s *wr. over* c *B*   23 case /] | *canc. B*   25 his] this *L 1553*; vicion]
s *wr. over* c *B*; illucion] si *wr. over* c *B*   28 ye] you *L 1553 1573*; in this case not nede]
not nede in this case *L 1553 1573*

reasons of me / but takyng the scripture of god for a grownd for this
mater / you know very well your selfe, you shall go somwhat a shorter
way to worke, if you aske this question of hym / that sith god hath ones
forboden the thyng hym selfe / though he may dispence therwith if he
will, yet sith the devill may fayne hym selfe god, & with a mervelouse 5
vision delude one, & make as though god did it / and sith the devill
is also more likely to speke agaynst godes commaundement / than god
agaynst his own: you shall ⌐haue⌐ good cause I say / to demaund of
the man hym selfe, wherby he knowith that his vision is godes trew
revelacion & not the devilles false delusion /   10

Vincent

In dede vncle I thinke that wold be an hard question to hym. May
a man vncle haue in such a thing evyn a very sure knolege of his own
mynd /

Anthonye   15

Ye Cosyn god may cast into the mynd of man I suppose, such an
inward light of vnderstandyng, that he can not faile but be sure therof
/ And yet he that is deludid by the devill, may think hym selfe as sure,
& yet be decevid in dede / And such a difference is there in a maner
betwen them, as is betwene the sight of a thing while we be wakyng 20
& loke theron, & the sight with which we se [f. 106] a thing in our
slepe while we dreme therof /

Vincent

This is a pretty similitude vncle in this thing / & than is it easye for
the monke that we speke of, to declare how he knowith his vision for 25
a trew revelacion & not a false dilucion / if there be so grete deference
betwene them /

---

1 for this] in thys *L 1553 1573*   3 ones] *canc. and interl. after* forboden *B*   3–4 hath ones
forboden the thyng] hath forbidden the thyng once *L 1553 1573*, hath forboden once the
thing *1557*   6 vision] yllusyon *L*   7 is also] also is *L 1553 1573*; godes] d *interl. before*
d *B*   8 haue] *interl. E*   9 godes] d *interl. before* d *B*   12 an hard] a hard *L*; to] for
L 1553 1573   13 vncle haue] haue vncle *L 1553 1573*; evyn] *abbrev. A, canc. and* evyn
interl. B, om. L; of] in *interl. above* of *(uncanc.) B*, in *L 1553 1573*   14 mynd /] question-
mark *wr. before / B*   16 into] in *L 1553*; of man] of a man *Ƶ*   17 of] and *L 1553 1573*
19 a difference] *wr. together A, separated by /* after a *B*   22 dreme] e *added B?*   24 simili-
tude] *abbrev. A*, li *interl. B*   25 speke] spake *L 1553*   26 dilucion] si *wr. over* c *B*

Anthonye

Not so easy cosyn as you wene it were. For how can you now proue
vnto me that you be a wake /

Vincent

5   Mary lo do I not now wagge my hand, shake my hed, & stampe
with my fote here in the flore /

Anthonye

Haue you neuer dremyd ere this, that you haue done the same?

Vincent

10   Yis that haue I / & more to than that / for I haue ore this in my
slepe dremyd, that I dowtid whether I were a slepe or a wake, & haue
in good fayth thought that I did therevppon, evyn the same thinges
that I do now in dede / & therby determynid that I was not a slepe /
And yet haue I dremyd in good fayth ferther, that I haue bene after-
15   ward at dener & there makyng mery with good companye, haue told
the same dreme at the table, and laughed well therat / that while I
was a slepe I had by such meanes of movyng the parties of my bodye,
& consideryng therof, so verely thought my selfe wakyng.

Antonye

20   And will you not now sone trow you whan you wake & rise, lawgh
as well at your selfe / whan you see that you lye now in your warm
bed a slepe agayne, & dreme all this tyme, while you wene so verely
that you be wakyng & talkyng of these maters with me /

Vincent

25   Goddes lord vncle / you go now merely to worke with me [f. 106ᵛ]

---

2 Not] t *added B?*; as] *yet as* Ƶ; For] for *A*: f *alt. to* F *B*; you now] *om. L*, now *om. 1553*;
proue] v *wr. over* u *B*   3 a wake] a wake, nowe *L*   5 now] *om. L 1553*   6 fote]
feete *L 1553 1573*; flore /] *question-mark wr. before* / *B*   10 haue I] I haue *L 1553*; ore] e
wr. over o *B*, ere Ƶ   11 a slepe or a wake] awake or aslepe *L 1553 1573*   15 dener] y
wr. over first e *B*; good] *om. L 1553 1573*   17 parties] es *wr. over* i *and* es *canc. B?*, partes Ƶ
18 thought] thoughe? *A*: t *wr. over* e? *B*, thought *L 1553 1557*, though *1573*   20 now
sone] now as sone *1573*; wake &] *interl. A*   23 talkyng] *divided* tal-kyng: *extra* ky *canc.*
at end of line A; these] Ƶ, the *A*; me /] *question-mark wr. before* / *B*

in dede / when you loke & speke so saddly, & wold make me wene I
were a slepe /

Antonye

It may be that you be so, for eny thyng that you can say or do,
wherby you may with any reason that you make, dreve me to confesse 5
that your selfe be sure of the contrary / sith you can do nor say nothyng
now / wherby you be sure to be wakyng / but that you haue ere this or
hereafter may, thinke your selfe as surely to do the selfe same thinges
in dede, while you be all the while a slepe, & nothyng do but lye dremyng /   10

Vincent

Well well vncle though I haue ere this thought my selfe awake while
I was in dede a slepe / yet for all that, this I know well inough, that I
am a wake now / & so do you to / though I can not fynd the wordes /
by which I may with reason force you to confesse it / but that alway 15
you may dreve me of, be the sample of my dreme /

Antonye

This is cosyn as me semeth very trew / And likewise / semeth me the
maner & diference, betwene some kynd of trew revelacions, & some
kynd of false illucions as it standith betwene the thinges that are 20
done wakyng, & the thinges that in our dremis seme to be done while
we be slepyng / that is to wit, that he which hath that kynd of revelacion fro god, is as sure of the trouth, as we be of our own dede while
we be wakyng / & he that is illudid by the devyll, is in such wise
decevid & worse to, than be they by their dreame / and yet rekcnyth 25
for the tyme hymselfe as sure as the tother / savyng that the tone
falsely weneth, the tother trewly knowith / [f. 107]

---

5 you make] you can make *L 1553 1573*; dreve] dryve *L*, driue *1553 1557 1573*   13 that,
this] that *om. Z*   15 force] enforse *L 1553 1573*   16 be] y *wr. over* e *B,* by *Z*   19
maner] matter *L 1553*   20 illucions] si *wr. over* c *B; comma added after* illucions *and
then canc. B (canc. stroke meant as* / ?); standith] standith / *A*   21 dremis] drenis *A:* n
alt. to m *B*   22 wit] wete *1553*   23 fro] from *L 1553 1573*   26 for the tyme hymselfe
as sure] hym self for the tyme as sure *L,* him self as sure for the tyme *1553 1573*; tother]
other *1553 1573*; tone] one *1553 1573*   27 weneth, the] weneth, and the *L 1553 1573*;
tother] other *1553 1573*

But I say not Cosyn that this kynd of sure knolege cometh in euery
ᴦkyndeᴵ of revelacion / for there are many kyndes / wherof were
to long to talke now / but I say that god doth or may do to man in
some thyng certenly send some such.

5   Vincent

Yet than may this religiouse man of whom we speke, whan I shew
hym the scripture agaynst his revelacion, & therfor cal it an illucion / bid me with reason go care for my selfe / For he knowith well &
surely hym selfe, that his revelacion is very good & trew / & not any
10 false illucion / sith for all the generall commaundment of god in the
scripture / god may dispence wher he will & whan he will, & may
commaund hym to do the contrary, as he commaundid Abraham to
kyll his own sonne / And as sampson had by inspiracion of god, commaundment to kill him selfe, with pulling down the howse vppon his
15 own hed at the fest of the phelisties.
Now yf I wold than do as you bode me right now, tell hym that
such apparicions may be illusions / & sith goddes worde is ᴦin the
scriptureᴵ against hym playne / for the prohibicions / he must proue
me the trewth of his revelacion, wherby that I may know it is not a
20 false illusion: than shall he bid me agayne tell hym, wherby that I
can proue my selfe to be a wake & talke with hym, & not to be a slepe
and dreame so / sith in my dreme I may as surly wene so as I know
ᴦthatᴵ I do so / And thus shall he dreve me to the same bay, to which
I wold bryng hym.

25   Antonye

This is well said Cosyn but yet could he ᴦnotᴵ scape you so. For
the dispensacion of goddes comen precept / which dispensacion [f.

---

2 kynde] *wr. by B in blank space left by A*; kynde of] *om. L*   6 speke] spake *1553*   7 cal]
second l *added B*   7–8 illucion] si *wr. over* c? *B*   9 very] *om. L 1553 1573*   10 illucion] s
wr. over c, *then word canc. and* illusion *interl. B*   12 to] *om. 1557*   13 And as] And as / *A*
14 vppon] on *L 1553 1573*   15 phelisties] Philistines *1553 1573*   16 than do] doe
than *L 1553 1573*; bode] bade *1553*; now, tell] now, goe tell *L 1553 1573*   17 may be]
were *L 1553 1573*; & sith] and sith that *L 1553*, and that sith *1573*   18 scripture]
scrupture *B*; prohibicions] s *canc. B*, prohibicion *Ƶ*; proue] perceiue *1557*   19 me] *om.*
1557; that I may] that *om. 1553 1573*; know it] know that it *1553 1573*   20 bid] aske
L 1553 1573; tell hym] *om. L 1553 1573*   22 surly] sury *A*: ly *wr. over* y *B*   23 dreve]
y *wr. over first* e *B*   26 *period after* Cosyn *B*

107ᵛ] he must say that he hath by his private revelacion / is a thing of such sort, as shewith it selfe nought & false / For it neuer hath had any sample like, sins the world began vnto now, that euer man hath redd or hard of among faythfull people commendid /

First in Abraham towching the deth of his sone, god intendid it not 5 / but onely temptid the towardnes of the fathers obediens. In Sampson all men make not the mater very sure, whether he be savid or not / but yet therin some mater apperith / For the philisties being enimies to god, & vsing Sampson for their mokkyng stokke in scorne of god / it is well likely that god gaue hym the mynd / to bestow his own life 10 vppon the revengyng of the displeasure that thos blasphemous philisties did vnto god / And that aperith metely clere by this / that though his strength faylid hym whan he wantid his here / yet had he not as it semeth that strength euermore at hand / while he had his heare / but at such tymes as it pleasid god to give it hym / which thing 15 aperith by these wordes that the scripture in some place of that mater sayth: *Irruit virtus domini in sampsonem* / the power or might of god russhed into Sampson / And so therfor while this thing that he did in the pullyng down of the house, was done by the speciall gifte of strength than at that poynt gevyn hym by god / it well declarith that 20 the strength of god & therwith the spirite of god, entrid into hym therfor.

S. Austyn also rehersith, that certeyne holy vertuouse virgyns in time of persecucion, being by godes ennimies infidelis [f. 108] pursued vppon to be deflorid by force, ran into a water & drownid them selfe, 25 rather than they wold be birevid of their virginite / And albeit that he thinketh it is not laufull for any other maid to folow their sample / but rather suffer other to do her any maner violence by force, & commit sinne of his own vppon her agaynst her will / than willingly & therby sinfully her selfe become an homicide of her selfe / yet he 30 thinketh that in them it happid by the speciall instingte of the spirite

1 private] om. L 1553   2 such] suche a L   3 vnto] tyll L 1553 1573; euer] any L 1553
5 towching] as touchyng L 1553 1573; sone] bar wr. above o B   8 some mater] some
matter & cause Z; apperith /] period after / B; philisties] Philistines 1553 1573   11–12 philisties] Philistines 1553 1573   12 clere] clerely L 1553   14 hand /] / canc. B   17
sayth:] colon ed.   18 into] nto A, i added B   21 entrid into] wr. together A, vertical line before
into B   21–23 hym therfor. S. Austyn] him. Therefore S. Austen L 1553 (L has comma after
him)   24 godes] d interl. before d B; by godes ennimies infidelis] by (Infidels) Gods enemies
1573; infidelis] divided infide-lis: catchwords on f. 107ᵛ read: lis in   25 selfe] selvys L   27
thinketh] thinketh that 1553 1573   28 maner] manour of L   31 instingte] c wr.
over g B

of god, that for causes seen vnto hym selfe, wold rather that they
shuld avoid it with their own temporall deth, than abide the
defoylyng & violacion of their chastite /

But now this good man neyther hath any of godes enymis to be by
5 his own deth revengid on, nor any woman that violently pursew hym
beforce to berive hym of his virgynite / nor neuer find we that god
prouid any mans obedient mynd by the commaundment of his own
slaughter of hym selfe / therfor is his case both playne agaynst goddes
open precept / & the dispensacion straunge, & without sample, no
10 cause apering or well imagynable / but yf ⌐he⌐ wold thinke that ⌐he⌐
could neyther any lenger live without hym, or take hym to hym in
such wise as he doth other men / but commaund hym to come by a
forboden way, by which without other cause we neuer hard that euer
he bode eny man els before.

15   Now whether you thynke if you shuld after this bid hym tell you,
by what way he knowith that his intent risith [f. 108ᵛ] vppon a trew
revelacion & not vppon a false illusion / he wold bid you than agayne
tell hym by what meane you know that you be talkyng with hym
well wakyng, & not drem it slepyng / you may tell hym agayne / that
20 men thus to talke together as you do, & in such maner wise, & to
proue & perceve that they so do by the movyng of them selfe, with
puttyng the question therof vnto them selfe for their pleasure, & the
markyng & consideryng therof, is in wakyng a dayly comen thyng,
that euery man doth or may do whan he will / & when they do it,
25 they do it but of pleasure / but in slepe it happeth very silde, that
men dreame they so do / nor in the dreme neuer put the question
but for dout / And therfor it is more reson, that sith his revelacion is
such also, as happeth so seld, & ofter happeth that men dreme of such

---

3 defoylyng] defyling *1553 1573*; chastite /] *period added after* / B   5 woman] women L;
violently] i *interl.* A?; pursew] pursueth *1573*   6 beforce] *first alt. to* before *by* B?, *then
canc. and* by force *interl.* B, by force Z   7 prouid] v *wr. over* u B   10 or] *canc. and* nor
interl. B, nor Z; that he] he *om. 1557,* that God *1573*   11 neyther any lenger] no longre
L, no lenger *1553 1573*; l *canc.* A *before* any; or] *canc. and* nor *interl.* B, nor Z   13 for-
boden] forbydden *1553 1573*; euer] *om.* L *1553*   14 bode] bad L *1553 1573*; els] *om.*
L *1553*   15 whether] where Z; if you] that you L *1553*, that if you *1573*   16 comma
added and canc. after* knowith B   18 meane] meanes L *1553 1573*   19 drem] *canc. and*
dreme *interl.* B   20 to talke] to *om.* L *1553 1573*   20–21 maner wise, & to proue]
maner of wyse they maye proue L *1553 1573*   21 with] and wyth L *1553 1573*
25 silde] e *wr. over* i B   26 dreame] dreame that Z; in the] in their L *1553 1573*; the
question] they question *1553 1573*   27 it is] ys yt L; sith] whyle L *1553*; his] this *1557*
28 as happeth] that happeth L *1553 1573*

than haue such in dede / therfor is it more reason you may tell hym, that he shew you wherby he knowith in such a rare thyng, & a thing more like a dreame / that hym selfe is not a slepe, than you in such a comen thyng among folke that are wakyng and so seldome happing in a dreme, shuld nede to shew hym wherby you know that you be not 5 a slepe.

Besides this hym selfe to whom you shuld shew it, seeth and per- cevith the thing that he wold bid you proue / but the thing that he wold make you belive, the truth of his revelacion, which you bid hym proue, you se not he woteth well hym selfe / And therfor ere you 10 beleve it agaynst the scripture, it were well consonaunt vnto reson that he shuld [f. 109] shew you wherby he knowith it for a trew wakyng revelacion, & not a false dremyng delusion /

Vincent

Than shall he peradventure say to me agayne, that whether I 15 beleve hym or not, maketh hym no mater, the thing tocheth hym selfe & not me / & hym selfe is in hym selfe as sure that it is a trew revela- cion / as that he can tell that he dremeth not but talketh with me wakyng /

Antonye   20

Without dout cosyn yf he abide at that poynt, & can be by no reason brought to do so much as dout / nor can by no meanes be shoggid out of his depe slepe, but will nedes take his drem for a very trewth / & as some by night rise & walke about their chamber in their slepe / will so rise & hang hym selfe: I can than none other way see, 25 but eyther bynd hym fast in his bed / or els assay whether that might happ to help hym with which the comen tale goeth that A ⌜Carvers⌝ wife in such a frantike fantasye holp her husband / to whom when

1 is it] it is L 1553 1573   2 wherby he knowith] om. L 1553, om. after shew you and placed after like a dreame 1573   3 dreame /] | canc. B   4 that] Z, than A   5 wherby] divided whe-rby A, rby canc. and added after whe B   9 belive,] comma ed.   13 not a] not for a L 1553 1573   16 tocheth] canc. and touchyth interl. B   22 nor can] and can L 1553 1573; meanes] meane 1557   23 shoggid] shugged L 1553; depe] dead Z; drem] final e added B   25 none other way] no other wayes 1553 1573   26 whether] abbrev. A: er added B   27 A Carvers] bracketed thus: ⌞ by E; Carvers] wr. by B in blank space left by A   28 fantasye] fansye L

he wold apon a good friday nedes haue killid hym selfe for christes sake
as christ was kyllid for hym, she wold not in vayne plede agaynst his
mynd / but well & wisely put hym in remembrans, that yf he wold
dye for christ as christ did for hym, it were then convenient for hym
5 to dye evyn after the same fasshion / & that might not be by his own
handes, but by the hand of some other / for christ perdie killid not
hym selfe / [f. 109ᵛ]

And because her husband shuld nede to make no mo of counceyle
(for that wold he not in nowise) she offrid hym that for goddes
10 sake, she wold secretly crucify hym her selfe vppon a greate crosse
that he had made to nayle a new carvid crucifyx vppon / wherof
whan he was very glad / yet she bethought her that christ was
bounden to a piller & beten first, & after crownyd with thorn / wheruppon whan she had by his own assent bound hym fast to a post /
15 she left not beting with holy exortacion to suffre so much & so long,
that ere euer she left worke & vnbound hym, praying neuer the lesse
that she might put on his hed & dreve it well down, a crown of thorn,
that she had wrethen for hym, & brought hym / he said / he thought
this was inough for that yere, he wold pray god forbere hym of the
20 remenaunt till good friday come agayne / but when it came agayne
the next yere / then was his lust past, he longid to folow christ no
ferther /

Vincent

In dede vncle if this help hym not, than will nothing helpe hym I
25 trow /

Anthony

And yet Cosin the devill may peradventure make hym toward such

---

1 he wold] he tolde he woulde L *1553 1573*   1–4 for christes sake as christ was kyllid
for hym . . . that yf he wold dye] *om. 1557* (*printer ended p. 1193 with* haue killed himself,
then at beginning of next p. dropped eye to l.4: for christ *etc.*)   4 christ] chrystes sake L;
did] dyed L *1553 1573*   6 but by the] by *om. 1557*   8 shuld] shud *A:* l *ins. B*
9 wold he] he woulde *1553*   10 crucify hym her selfe] her selfe crucifye him L *1553*
1573; vppon] on *1553 1573*   11 new carvid] great L *1553*   13 bounden] bounde
L *1553*   16 ere] or *1553;* praying] praying him L *1553 1573*   19 this] that L *1553;*
forbere] to forbeare L *1553 1573*   20 come] cam L   27 the devill may peradventure]
paraduenture the deuill might L *1553 1573*

a purpose, first gladly to suffre other payne, yee & minish his felyng to
therin, that he may therby the lesse fere his deth / And yet are peradventure some tyme such thynges & many mo to be assayed / for as
the devill may happe to make hym suffre: so may he hap [f. 110] to
misse / namely yf his frendes fall to prayour for hym agaynst his   5
temptacion / for that can hym selfe neuer do while he takith it for
none / But for conclucion, yf the man be surely provid so inflexibly
set vppon the purpose to destroy hym selfe, as commaundid therto
by god, that no good counsaile that men can give hym / nor any other
thing that men may do to hym can refrayne hym, but that he wold 10
surely shortly kyll hym selfe / than except onely good prayour by his
frendes made for hym / I can find no ferther shift, but eyther haue hym
euer in sight, or bynd hym fast in his bed / And so must he nedes of
reason be content to be ordred / For though hymselfe take his fantasye
for a trew revelacion / yet sith he can not make vs perceve it for such / 15
likewise as he thinketh hym selfe by his secret commaundment
bounden to folow yt, so must he nedes agre, that sith it is agaynst the
playne open prohibicion of god, wc be by the playne open precept
bounden to kepe hym from it /

Vincent   20

In this poynt vncle I can go no ferther / But now yf he were vppon
the tother side, percevid to mynd his distruccion & go therabout with
heuines of hart / & thought & dulnes: what way were there to be vsid
to hym than /

Antonye   25

Then were his temptacion as I told you before, properly perteynyng

---

1 to] canc. and furst interl. B; first gladly to suffre] first gladly suffer (to om.) L 1557 1573,
first gladly firste suffer 1553; payne] minim lacking for ne A: ne wr. over fault B; yee] om.
L 1553   2 yet are] yet are there 1573   5 for hym] om. L 1553   7 conclucion] sy
wr. over last c B; provid so] proued, & so L 1553   10 to] vnto L   11 surely] om. L 1553
11–12 by his frendes made] made by his frendes L 1553 1573   12–13 eyther haue hym
euer] euer haue him L 1553   14 content to] content so to L 1553; fantasye] fanstasye
A, fansye L   18 open prohibicion] open om. L 1553   19 bounden] bound 1553 1573;
hym canc. A after from   21 vppon] on L 1553 1573   22 tother] r wr. over illeg. letter
B?, other 1553 1573; & go] & to goe Z   23 heuines] v wr. over u B; hart /] / canc. B;
& thought] & om. L 1553 1573   24 to hym] with him L 1553 1573; than /] question-
mark wr. before / B

to our mater / for than were he in a sore tribulacion [f. 110ᵛ] & a very
perilous / for than were it a token that the devill had eyther by
bringyng hym in to some grete sinne, brought hym in dispayre / or
peradventure by his revelacions founden false & reprouid / or by some
5 secret synne of his deprehendid, & divulgid, cast hym both in despayre
of hevyn thorow fere, & in a werynes of this lyfe for shame / sith he
seeth his estymacion lost among other folke, of whose prayse he was
wont to be proude. And therfor Cosyn in such case as this is, the
man is to be fayre handled, & swetely, & with dowce & tendre lovyng
10 wordes to be put in good corage & comfort in all that men goodly
may.

Here must the   put hym in mynd, that yf he despaire not,
but pull vpp his corage & trust in godes greate mercie / he shall haue
in conclucion greate cause to be glad of this fall. For before he stode
15 in greater perell than he was ware of, while he toke hym selfe for
better than he was / And god for favour that he bereth hym, hath
suffred hym to fall diepe into the devilles daynger, to make hym
therby know what he was, while he toke hym selfe for so sure / And
therfor as he suffred hym than to fall for a remedy agaynst ouer bold
20 pryde: so will god now (yf the man meke hym selfe, not with frutles
dispayre, but with frutfull penaunce) so set hym vp agayne vppon
his fete / & so strength hym with his grace / that for this one fall that
the devill hath gevyn hym, he shall gyve the divill an / C. / And here
must he be put in remembrans of Mary Magdalyn, of the prophet
25 david, & specially of s. peter / whose high bold corage toke a fowle
fall / & yet because he despairid not of godes mercie, but wept & callid vppon it / how highly god [f. 111] toke hym into his favour agayne,
in his holy scripture ⌈is⌉ well testified, & well thorow christendom
knowen /
30   And now shall it be charitably done yf some good vertuouse folke /

---

3 in dispayre] into dispayre L *1553 1573*   4 by his] by *om. L 1553*; founden] foounden
A: f *canc. and* f *wr. over first* o B   5 deprehendid, & divulgid] diuulged and deprehended
L *1553*   6 this] hys L   8 proude] w *wr. over* u B   9 dowce] doulce *1573*
10 comfort] id *added B,* comforted *Z*; goodly] godly *interl.* B *above* goodly (*uncanc.*), godly
1553 1573   12 Here] And here L *1553 1573*; the] *blank space before* put A: the *alt. to* they
and line drawn across space B, they *Z* (*no blank space*); despaire] i *interl.* A?   13 godes] d
interl. before d B   14 conclucion] si *wr. over last* c B   16 bereth] bare L *1553 1573*
20 meke] meken L *1553 1573*; frutles] vnfrutefull L *1553 1573*   22 strength] strengthen
1553 1573   23 an / C. /] An hundreth L *1553,* an hundred *1557 1573*   25 corage]
u *ins. after* o B   29 knowen /] *period before* / B

such as hymselfe somwhat estemith / & hath afore longed to stand in
estimacion with / do resorte sometyme vnto hym / not onely to give
hym counsayle / but also to aske advise & counsayle of hym in some
casis of their own conscience / to let hym therby perceve, that they
no lesse esteme hym now / but rather more than they did before / sith 5
they think hym now by his fall, bettre expert of the devilles crafte / &
therby not onely better instructid hym selfe / but also better hable to
give good advise & counsaile vnto other. This thing will in my mynd
well amend & lift vpp his corage from the perell of that desperat
shame. 10

Vincent

Me thinke vncle that this were a perilouse thing / for it may peradventure make hym set the lesse by his fall, & therby cast hym into
his first pride or into his other synne agayne / the fallyng wherinto
drave hym into this dispaire / 15

Anthonye

I do not meane cosyn that euery fole shuld ⌈at⌉ adventure fall in
hand with hym / for so lo might it happe for to do harm in dede / But
Cosyn if a conyng phisicion haue a man in hand / he can well decerne
whan & how long some certen medicyne is necessarye, which at an 20
other tyme ministred / or at that tyme ouer long contynued, might
put the pacient to perell /
Iff he haue his pacient in an ague, to the cure wherof he nedeth his
medicynes in there workyng cold / yet yf he happ ere that fever be full
curid, to fall in some such other [f. 111ᵛ] disease / as except it were 25
holpen with hote medicyns, were likely to kill the bodye before the
fever could be curid, he wold for the while haue his most care to the
cure of that thyng / wherin were most present perell & whan that

---

6 they] yᵉʸ A: *canc. and* they *interl.* B; his] this Z   7 onely better] onely the better L;
hable] h *canc.* B, able Z   8 advise & counsaile vnto] counsaile and aduise to L *1553*,
aduise and counsel to *1573*   12 thinke] thinketh Z   14 wherinto] wherunto L *1553*
18 hym /] *period wr. before* / B; for] *om.* L *1573*   20 certen] *om.* L *1553*   22 to] *canc.*
and in *interl.* B, in Z; perell /] *period before* / B   22–23 perell / ¶ Iff] peryll, For yf L,
peryl, for if *1553*, perill. If *1557*, peril. For if *1573*   24 there] i *interl. before* r B; yet]
yet / A: / *canc.* B   25 fall in] fall into Z

were ones out of iuberdy do than the more exact diligence after about the ferther cure of the fever /

And likewise if the ship were in perell to fall into Scilla / the fere of fallyng into Charibdis on the tother side / shall neuer let any wise
5 master therof to draw hym from Scilla toward charibdes first in all that euer he maye / But when he hath hym ones so far away fro Scilla, that he seeth hym safe out of that dainger / than will he begyn to take good hede to kepe hym well fro the tother / And in likewise while this man is fallyng down to despaire, & to the fynall destruccion of hym
10 selfe / a good wise spirituall leche will first loke vnto that, & by good comfort lyft vp his corage / & whan he seeth that perell well past, care for the cure of his other fautes after / How beit evyn in the gevyng of his comfort / he may fynd wayes inough in such wise to temper his wordes, that the man may take occasion of good Corage, & yet far
15 from occasion gevyng of new recidivacion into his formar synne / sith the greate part of his counsayle shalbe to corage hym to amendment / & that is perdye far fro fallyng vnto synne agayne /

Vincent

I thinke vncle that folke fall into this vngraciouse mynd, thorow the
20 devilles temptacion by many mo wayes than one.

Antonye

That is cosyn very trew / for the devill taketh his occasion as he seeth them fall mete for hym. Some he styreth to it for werynes [f. 112] of them self after some great losse / some for fere of horrible
25 bodely harm / And some as I said for fere of worldly shame / One wist I my selfe that had bene long reputid for a right honest man, which

---

1 iuberdy] i *first alt. to* I, *then word canc. and* Ieberdy, *interl. B*, ieobardy *L*, ieopardye *1553 1557*, ieopardie *1573*; than] om. *1573*; cure *canc. A before* more; exact] except *1553*   4 tother] other *1553 1573*   5 from] fro *1557*; first in all] first of al, in al *L 1553 1573*   6 away] *om. L 1553*; fro] from *L 1553 1573*   7 safe] selfe *L 1553*, self safe *1573*   8 good] *om. L 1553*; fro] from *L 1553 1573*; tother] other *1553 1573*; And in likewise while] & likewise when *L 1553*, And in likewise when *1573*   10 leche] e *added B*   12 evyn] *om. L* 15 new] more *L 1553*   17 fro] from *L 1553 1573*; vnto] to *L 1553 1573*   20 wayes] meanes *Ζ*   22 occasion] occasions *Ζ*   23 for werynes] through werynes *L 1553 1573* 24 horrible] *om. L 1553 1573*   26 that] which *L 1553 1573*; a right honest] an honest *L 1553 1573*

was fallen in such a fantasie that he was well nere worne away therwith / but what he was temptid to do / that wold he not tell no man /
but he told vnto me that he was sore combred, and that it alway ran
in his mind that folkes fantasies were fallen from hym / & that they
estemyd not his witt as they were wont to do / but euer his mynd gave 5
hym that the people began to take hym for a fole / And folke of trouth
nothyng so did at all / but reputid hym both for wise & honest /

Two other knew I that were mervelouse ferd that they shuld kill
them selfe & could tel me no cause wherfor they so ferid it / but onely
that their own mynd so gave them / neyther losse had they any had / 10
nor no such thing toward them / nor none occasion of any worldly
shame / the tone in body very well lykyng & lustye / but wonderouse
wery were they both twayne of that mynd / And alwey they thought
that do it they wold not for nothyng / And neuertheles euer they ferd
they shuld / and wherfor they so ferid, neyther of them both could 15
tell / and the tone lest he shuld do it desirid his frendes to bynd hym.

Vincent

This is vncle a mervelouse straunge maner.

Antonye

Forsoth cosyn I suppose many of them are in this case. The divill 20
as I said before / seketh his occasions / for as saint peter sayth /
Aduersarius vester diabolus quasi leo rugiens [f. 112ᵛ] *circuit querens quem
deuoret*: your aduersary the devill, as a roryng lyon goth about sekyng
whom he may devour / He marketh well therfor the state & condicion
that euery man standith in / not onely concernyng these owtward 25

1 fantasie] fansye L; worne] *divided* wor-ne A: ne *canc. and added after* wor B   2 he not
tell] not *om.* L *1553 1573*   3 vnto] *om.* L   4 fantasies] fansyes L   5 they] yᵉ A:
canc. and they *interl.* B   6 fole /] *period after* / B   7 nothyng so did] did no thing so
L *1553 1573*; all /] *comma after* / B   8 mervelouse] marueilouslye L *1553 1573*; ferd]
afeard L, afrayde *1553 1573*   9 selfe] selves L   9-10 *extra* onely *canc. before* that B
10 any had] had *om.* L *1553*   12 tone] one L *1553 1573*; very] *interl. above canc.* vely A;
but wonderouse] & wonderous L *1553 1573*   14 And neuertheles] but neuerthelesse L
1553 1573; euer they] they euer L *1553 1573*   15 so ferid] so both feared L *1553 1573*
16 tone] one L *1553 1573*   18 mater *canc. before* maner A   20 suppose] suppose that L
1553 1573; case.] *period ed.*   22 Aduersarius vester diabolus quasi leo rugiens] Diabolus
tanquam leo rugens L *1553*, (rugiens L, rugens *1573*)   23 deuoret:] *colon ed.*; your
aduersary] *om.* L *1553*   24 devour] devoᶠre A: re *canc.* B; well therfor] therfor *om.* L
1553, therefore well *1573*; condicion] the condicion *1553 1557 1573*

thynges / londes, possessions, goodes, auctorite / fame, favour / or
hatred of the world / but also mens complexcions within them, helth
or siknes, good humours or badd / by which they be light hartid or
lumpish / strong hartid / or faynt & feble of spirite / bold & hardy / or
5 timerouse & ferefull of corage / And after as these thinges minister
hym mater of temptacion, so vseth he hym selfe in the maner of his
temptacion.

Now likewise as such folke as are full of yong warm lusty blode &
other humours excityng the flesh to filthy voluptuouse livyng, the
10 devill vseth to make those thinges his instrumentes in temptyng them
& provokyng them thervnto / And where he findeth some folke full of
hote blode & colour, he makith those humours his instrumentes to set
their hart on fier in wrath & fierce furiouse anger: so where he findith
some folke which thorow some dull malencolious humours are natur-
15 ally desposid to feare / he castith sometyme such a fearefull imaginacion
in ther mynd that without help of god they can neuer cast it out of
their hart / Some at the sodayne fallyng of some horrible thought
into their mynd, haue not onely had a great abomynacion therat
(which abomynacion they well & vertuously [f. 113] had there at)
20 but the devill vsing their maliciouse humour, & therby their naturall
inclinacion to fere / for his instrument, hath causid them to conceve
therwith such a diepe drede beside, that they wene them selfe with
that abominable thought, to be fallen into such an outragiouse sinne,
that they be redye to fall into despayre of grace / wenyng that god hath
25 gevyn them ouer for euer / where as that ⌐thought⌐ (were it neuer so
horrible & neuer so abomynable) ys yet vnto them that neuer like it
but euer still abhorre yt & stryve still there agaynst, mater of conscience & merit, & not any synne at all /

Some haue with holdyng a knyfe in their hand, sodaynly thought

---

1 londes] as landes L *1553 1573*   2 helth] as helth L *1553 1573*   4 faynt &] faynt,
or *1553*; bold &] & *om. 1553 1573*   8 as such folke as] as in such folke that L *1553
1573*, as in such folke as *1557*   10 in temptyng] *vertical line after* in B   11 & provo-
kyng] & in prouoking *1553 1573*   13 hart] hartes L *1553 1573*; & fierce] & very fierce
L *1553 1573*   15 imaginacion] imaginacions A: s *canc.* B   16 ther] yr *wr. over* r *and*
comma added B   17 hart] heartes L *1553 1573*; fallyng] fall L *1553*   19 at)] *parenth.*
wr. over / B   20 maliciouse] *canc. and* melancolyous *interl.* B, melancolious Ƶ   21 to
fere] te fere A: o *wr. over* e *of* te B; instrument,] *comma ed.*   26 neuer so] *om.* L; abomynable)] *parenth. ed.*, abomynable / A; neuer] *om. 1553*   27-28 conscience] *canc. and*
conflyct *interl.* B, conflict Ƶ   29 hand] handes L *1553 1573*; sodaynly thought]
thought sodeynlye L *1553*

vppon the kyllyng of them selfe / & forthwith in devisyng what an horrible thing it were / if they shuld mishap so to do, haue fallen in a fere that they shold so do in dede / & haue with long & often thynk-yng theron, imprintid that fere so sore in their imaginacion / that some of them haue not after cast it of without great difficultie / & some 5 could neuer in their lyfe be rydd therof / but haue after in conclucion miserably done yt in dede / But likwise as where the devill vseth the blode of mans own bodye toward his purpose, in prouokyng hym to lechery, the man must and doth with grace & wisedome resist it: so must that man do, whose maliciouse humours the devill abuseth to- 10 ward the castyng of such a desperat drede into his hart.

Vincent

I pray you vncle what advise were to be gevyn hym in such case? [f. 113ᵛ]

Antonye   15

Surely me thinketh his help standeth in two thynges / counsayle and prayour / First as concernyng counsayle, likewise as it may be that he hath ij thinges / that hold hym in his temptacion / that is to wit some evill humours of his own bodye, and the cursid divill that abuseth them to his perniciouse purpose / so must he nede agayne 20 them twayne / the counsayle of ij maner of folke / that is to wit phisitions for the bodye & phisitions for the soule / The bodely phisition shall consider what abundaunce the man hath of those evill humours that the devill maketh his instrument in movyng the man toward that ferefull affeccion / And as well by diet convenient 25 & medicyns mete therfor to resist them, as by purgacions to disburden the body of them / Nor let no man thinke straunge, that I wold advise a man to take

---

1 selfe] selves *L*; forthwith] th *interl. A*   2 fallen in] fallen into *L 1553 1573*   3 long &] *om. L 1553 1573*   5 them] yᵉᵐ *A*: *canc. and* them *interl. B*; after] *om. L 1553 1573* 6 rydd] quite ridde *L 1553*; in conclucion] *vertical line after* in *B*, sy *wr. over third* c *B* 7 likwise] e *ins. after* k *B*; as] *interl. A*   8 mans] a mannes *Z*; own] *om. L 1553*; prouok-yng] v *wr. over* u *B*; hym] *om. L 1553*   10 maliciouse] *canc. and* melancolyous *interl.* *B*, melancolyous *Z*   13 I pray] But I praye *L 1553*   18 thinges /] / *canc. B*   19 wit] wete *1553*   20 agayne] against *L 1553 1573*   21 twayne] *divided word canc. and* twayn *interl. B*; wit] wete *1553*   24 instrument] instrumentes of *L 1553 1573*, instrumentes *1557*

counsayle of a phisicion for the body in such a spirituall passion /
For sith the soule & the bodye be so knyt and ioynid together, that
they both make betwene them one person / the distemperaunce of
either other, engendreth some tyme the distemperaunce of both
5 twayne /

And therfor like as I wold advise euery man in euery siknes of the
bodye, be shreven & seke of a good spirituall phisicion the sure helth
of his soule, which shall not onely serue agaynst perell that may
peradventure ferther grow by that siknes than in the begynnyng
10 men wold wene were lykely / but the comfort therof & godes favour
increasyng therwith, shall also do the body good / for which cause
the blessid apostell saynt [f. 114] Iames exorteth men that they shall
in their bodely siknes induce the prestes / and sayth that yt shall do
them good both in body and soule / so wold I sometyme advise some
15 men in some siknes of the soule, beside their spirituall lech, take
also some counsayle of the phisicion for the bodye. Some that are
wrechidly disposid & yet long to be more viciouse than they be / go
to phisicions & poticaries & enquire what thynges may serue to make
them more lustye to their fowle fleshly delight / And were it than
20 any foly vppon the tother side, yf he that feleth hym selfe agaynst his
will much movid vnto such vnclennes, shold enquire of the phisicion,
what thyng without mynishyng of his helth were mete for the
minishyng of such fowle fleshly motion /

Of spirituall counsayle the first is to be shrevyn, that by reason of
25 his other synnes, the devill haue not the more power vppon hym.

Vincent

I haue hard some say vncle, that whan such folke haue bene at
shrifte, their temptacion hath bene the more brymme vppon them
than it was before /

---

1 spirituall] spīall A: canc. and spirytuall interl. B   7 be] to be L 1553 1573; seke of] of
om. L 1553   8 serue] v wr. over u B   9 ferther] furder L   11 do] d wr. over t A
12 saynt Iames] om. L 1553 1573; exorteth] h interl. after x B; shall] should L 1553 1573
13 shall] should L 1553 1573   15 lech] final e added B   16 bodye.] period ed.
18 serue] v wr. over u B   20 tother] other 1553 1573   22 thyng] thinges Z
23 minishyng] minishment Z; motion /] question-mark before / B   24 spirituall] spīall?
A: ua wr. over ia? B   28 the more] the om. L 1553 1573

Antony

That thinke I very well / but that is a speciall token that shrifte is holsome for them, while the devill is with that most wroth / You fynd in some places of the gospell, that the devill / the person whom he possessid, ⌈dyd⌉ most trowble, whan he saw that christ wold cast hym 5 out / We must els let the devill do what he will / yf we fere his angre / for with euery good dede will he wax angry /

Than is it in his shrifte to be shewid hym / that he not onely fereth more than he nedeth / but also fereth where he [f. 114ᵛ] nedeth not / And ouer that is sory of that thing wherof / but yf he will willyngly 10 tourne his good into his harm, he hath more cause to be glad.

First yf he haue cause to fere / yet fereth he more than he nedeth / For their is no divill so diligent to destroy hym / as god is to preserue hym / nor no devill so nere hym to do hym harme / as god is to do hym good / nor all the divelles in hell so strong to invade & as- 15 sawte hym / as god is to defend hym / yf he distrust hym not but fayth-fully put his trust in hym /

He fereth also where he nedeth not / for where he dredeth that he were out of godes favour because such horrible thoughtes fall in his mind agaynst his will, they be not imputid vnto hym / / / He is fynally 20 sad of that he may be glad. For sith he taketh such thoughtes dis-plesauntly & striveth & fighteth agaynst them / he hath therby a good token that he is in godes favour / & that god assistith hym & helpeth hym / and may make hym selfe sure, that so will god neuer sease to do / but if hym selfe faile & fall from hym first / And ouer that / this 25 conflict that he hath agaynst his temptacion shall (yf he will not fall where he nede not) be an occasion of his merite, & of a right greate reward in hevin / and the payne that he taketh therin / shall for so much (as master Gerson well shewith) stand hym in stede of his purgatory / The maner of the fight agaynst this temptacion, must 30

---

3 You] ed., you A   5 dyd] interl. B above canc. & A, dyd Z   6 We] ed., we A   7 will he] he wyl 1553   8 fereth] om. L   10 extra butt canc. A? after wherof /   13 their] re wr. over ir B   14 is] his A: h canc. A   15 invade] inuade hym L 1553   19 / canc. B after horrible; fall in] fall into L 1553 1573   20 mind] mynde, let hym consider, that syth they fal into hys mynde L 1553, minde, he must understand that whyle they fall in his mind 1557, minde, he must understand, that sith they fal into his mind 1573; be not] be therfore not L 1553 1573   21 thoughtes] thougthes A   27 nede] nedeth L 1553 1573; not)] parenth. added B; & of a] of om. L 1553 1573   30 this] hys 1557

stand in iij / thinges that is to wit / in resistyng, & in contempnyng
& in the invocacion of helpe.

    Resist must a man for his own part with reason, consideryng [f.
115] what a foly it were to fall where he nede not / while he is not
5 dreven to hit in avoydyng of any other payne, or in hope of wynnyng
eny maner of pleasure / but contrary wise, shuld by that payne lese
euerlastyng life & fall into euerlastyng payne / And yf it were in avoydyng of other great payne / yet could he void none so greate therby
as he shuld therby fall into /

10   He must also consider that a great part of this temptacion, is in
effect but the fere of his own fantasie / the drede that he hath lest he
shall ones be driven to it / which thing he may be sure that (but if
hym selfe will of his own foly) all the devilles in hell can neuer drive
hym to / but his own folish Imaginacion may / For likewise as some
15 man going ouer an high bridge, waxith so ferd thorow his own fantasie
that he falleth down in dede / which were els able inough to passe
ouer without any daingour / And as some man shall vppon such a
bridge / yf folke call vppon hym / you fall / you fall, fall with the
fantasye that he taketh therof / which bridge yf folke lokid merely vp-
20 pon hym & said ther is no dainger therin, he wold passe ouer well
inough / & wold not let to run theron yf it were but a fote from the
grownd / thus fareth it in this temptacion / The devill findeth the man
of his own fond fantasye aferd / & than crieth he in the eare of his hart
/ thow fallest / thow fallest / & maketh the fond man a ferd that he
25 shuld at euery fote fall in dede / And the devill so werieth hym with
that contynuall fere (yf he give the eare of his hart vnto hym) that
at the last he withdraweth his mynd from dew remembraunce of
god, & than driveth hym to that [f. 115ᵛ] dedly myschiefe in dede /
Therfor like as agaynst the vice of the flesh, the victorye standith not
30 all hole in the fight / but sometyme also in the flight, savyng that it is

---

1 wit] wete *1553*   2 invocacion] invacocion *A*: o *wr. over* a *and first* o *alt. to* a *B*
3 with] by *L 1553 1573*   4 nede] nedeth *L 1553 1573*   5 hit] yᵗ *L*, it *1553 1557 1573*
7 life] blisse *interl. B above* life (*uncanc.*), blisse *Z*   11 fantasie] fansye *L*   12 ones]
interl. A   13 foly)] *parenth. wr. over* | *B*   14 likewise] lyke *L 1553 1573*   15 ferd]
fraide *1553 1573*   16 inough] h *added B*   17 man] men *1553 1573*   18 fall, fall]
comma ed.   19 fantasye] fansye *L*   21 yf] though *L 1553*   21–22 from the grownd]
brode *L 1553*, fro the ground *1557 1573*   23 fantasye] fansy *L*; aferd] afraide *1553 1573*
24 a ferd] afrayde *1553 1573*   25 devill] *final* l *added B?*   26 eare] care *1553*; hym)]
parenth. added B   27 withdraweth] draweth *L 1553 1573*; dew] the due *L 1553 1573*
30 sometyme also] also some tyme *L 1553*

in dede a part of a wise warriours fight / to fle from his ennymies trayns:
so must a man in this temptacion to, not onely resist it alway with
resonyng ther agaynst / ⌐but sometyme set it clere at right nought¬
& cast it of when it cometh / & not ones regard it so much as to vouch-
saufe to thinke theron. Some folke haue bene clerely ridd of such pesti- 5
lent fantasies with very full contempt therof / makyng a crosse vppon
their hart, & biddyng the devill avaunt, & some tyme laugh hym to
scorne to / & than torne theire mynd to some other mater / And when
the devill hath seen that they haue set so litell by hym after certeyne
assayes / made in such tymes as he thought most mete / he hath geven 10
that temptacion quiet ouer / both for that / the prowd spirite can
not endure to be mokqued / and also leste with much temptyng the
man to the synne wherto he could not in conclusion bryng hym, he
⌐shuld¬ mich encrease his merite.

The fynall fight is by invocacion of help vnto god both praying for 15
hym selfe & desieryng other also to pray for hym, both pore folke for
his almoise & other good folke of their charite / specially good preestes
in that holy sacred seruice of the masse / And not onely them / but
also his own good Angell & other holy sayntes such as his devocion
specially stand vnto / or yf he be lernid, vse than the letany with the 20
holy suffrages that folow / which is a prayour in the church of mervelouse old antyquite / not made first as some wene it were by that holy
man [f. 116] saynt Gregorye, which opynion rose of that that in the
tyme of a greate pestilence in Rome / he causid the whole Citie go in
solempne procession therwith / but it was in vse in the church many 25
yeres before S Gregoryes dayes, as well apperith by the bokes of
other holy doctours & sayntes that were ded hundredes of yeres before

---

1 a part] the parte L 1553 1573; fle] flie 1553; from] alway from 1573   3 clere] cleane
L 1553 1573   4 it so] it, nor so 1573; as to] to om. L 1553 1573   6 fantasies] fansyes L
7 hart] heartes Z; & biddyng] & om. L 1553; laugh] divided lau-gh A: gh canc. and wr.
after lau B   8 theire] i interl. A; to some] vnto some Z   9 certeyne] many L 1553 1573
11 quiet] quite Z; that /] / canc. B   12 mokqued] ky wr. over qu, then word canc. and
mokked interl. B   13 synne] same 1553 1573; wherto] whereunto L 1553 1573
14 shuld] such A: canc. and shuld interl. B, shoulde Z; encrease] therby encrease L 1553
1573   15 help vnto] om. L 1553 1573; praying] by praying L 1553 1573   17 almoise]
almose 1553 1573, almes 1557; other good folke of] other for L 1553, other good folke
for 1573   19 own] om. L; Angell] aungels 1553   20 specially stand] standeth specially
L 1553 1573; or yf] And if L 1553 1573; vse than] let him vse L 1553 1573   23 man]
abbrev. A: canc. and man interl. B; Gregorye,] first r interl. B, comma ed.   24 greate canc.
before tyme A; go] to goe L 1553 1573   26 yeres] yere 1557   27 holy] olde holy L
1553 1573; hundredes] hundrethes 1553

S Gregory was borne / And holy saynt Bernard geveth counsayle that euery man shuld make sute vnto Angelles & sayntes to pray for hym to god in the thynges that ⌈he⌉ wold haue sped at his holy hand / Yf any man will styk at that, and say it nede not because god can here vs
5 hymselfe, & will also saye that it is perilouse so to do / because ⌈they say⌉ we be not so counsaylid by no scripture / I will not dispute the mater here / he that will not do it / I let hym not to leve it vndone. But yet for myn own part I will as well trust to the counsaile of saynt Barnard, & reken hym for as good & as well lernid in the scripture /
10 as any man that I here say the contrary / And bettre dare I iuberd my soule with the soule of saint Bernard, than with his that fyndeth that faut in his doctryne /

Vnto god hym selfe euery good man counsaylith to haue recorse above all / And in this temptacion to haue speciall remembrans of
15 christes passion, & pray hym for the honour of his deth the ground of mans saluacion, kepe this person thus temptid fro that dampnable deth. Speciall verses may there be drawen out of the *psalter* / agaynst the devilles wikked temptacions as for example / *Exurgat deus & dissipentur inimici eius, & fugiant qui oderunt eum a facie eius* / and many
20 other which are in such horrible temptacion to god plesaunt, & to the devill very terrible / But none more terrible nor more odiouse to the devill, than the wordes with which [f. 116ᵛ] our saviour drave hym away hym selfe / *vade sathana* / nor no prayour more acceptable vnto god / nor more effectuall for the mater / than those wordes which
25 our saviour hath taught vs hymselfe: *Ne nos inducas in tentationem* / *sed libera nos a malo* /

And I dout not by godes grace, but he that in such a temptacion will vse good counsayle & prayour, & kepe hym selfe in good vertuouse bysynes & good vertuouse companye, & abide in the faythfull
30 hope of godes helpe, shall haue the trowth of god (as the prophet sayth in the verse afore rehersid) so compase hym about with a pavice, that

---

2 vnto] to *L 1553 1573*   4 nede] nedes *L 1553 1573*   9 in the] the *om. L 1557*; scripture] holy Scripture *L 1553 1573*   10 iuberd] iubd *A: canc. and* Ieobard *interl.* B, ieobard *L*, ieopard *1553 1557 1573*   13 good] *om. L 1553 1573*; recorse] u *interl. after* o *B*   15 deth] neath *1557*   16 kepe this person] to kepe the parson *L 1553 1573*; fro] from *L 1553 1573*   17 agaynst] *divided* ag-aynst *A:* ag *canc. and added before* aynst *B* 19 many] *minim lacking in* ny *A*   20 plesaunt] *minim lacking in* un *A,* most pleasaunte *L 1553 1573*   21 nor more] nor none more *L 1553 1573*   25 taught vs] vs *om. L 1553 1573*; hymselfe:] *colon ed.*   31 *extra* pavice *canc. after* a *A*

he shall not nede to drede this nightes feare of this wikkid temptacion /
And thus will I fynish this piece of the nightes feare / And glad am I
that we be passed it & comen ones vnto the day, to those other wordes
of the prophet / *A sagitta volante in die* / for me thynketh I haue made
it a long night /   5

Vincent

Forsoth vncle so haue you / but we haue not slept in it but byn very
well occupied / But now I fere that except you make here a pause till
you haue dined, you shall kepe your selfe from your dener ouer
longe /   10

Anthonye

Nay Nay cosyn / for both brake I my fast evyn as you came in / &
also you shall find this night & this day like a winter day & a winter
night / for as the winter hath short dayes & long nightes: so shall you
fynd that I made you not this ferefull night so long / but I shall make 15
you this light coragiouse day as short / And so shall the mater require
well of it selfe indede / for in [f. 117] those wordes of the prophet /
scuto circumdabit te veritas eius a sagitta volante in die / The trouth of god
shall compasse the round about with a pavice from the arrow fleyng
in the daye / I vnderstond the arrow of pride, with which the devill 20
temptith a man / not in the night / that is to wit in tribulacion & aduersite / for that tyme is to dyscomfortable & to fearefull for pride /
but in the day that is to wit in prosperite / for that time is full of
lightsome lust & corage. But surely this worldly prosperite wherin a
man so reioyceth & wherof the devill maketh hym so proud is but 25
evyn a vyry short winter day / /
For we begyn many full pore and cold, & vpp we fle like an arrow

3 comen] come *1553 1573*   5 night /] L *1553 1573 begin a new chapter here*: The xvijth
Chapter L, The .xvii Chapter *1553*, Of the arrow flying in the day, which is, the spirite
of pride in prosperitie. The XVII. Chapter *1573*   8 that] *om.* L *1553 1573*; pause] w
wr. over u B   9 dener] y *wr. over* e B   13–14 winter day & a winter night] wynter
night and a wynter daye L   15 made you] you *om.* L *1553 1573*   17 indede] *om.*
L; those] these *Z*   19 round] *om.* L *1553*; fleyng] flyeng L, flying *1553 1573*, fleing *1557*
21 that is to wit] *om.* L *1553*; in tribulacion] in all tribulacion L *1553*   23 wit] wete
1553; prosperite] *divided with error*: pros-properite, pros *canc. and* s *ins. before* perite B
23–24 full of lightsome lust & corage] lightsome, lusty, & full of courage L *1553 1573*
25 so reioyceth] *comma added* B, so *om.* L *1553*; proud] w *wr. over* u B   26 vyry] *canc.
and* very *interl.* B   27 fle] flye L *1553 1557*, flie *1573*

that were shott vp into the ayer / & yet whan we be sodanly shotten
vpp into the hiest / ere we be well warm there, down we come vnto
the cold ground agayne, & than evyn there stikk we styll / And yet
for the short while that we be vpward & aloft / lord how lustye &
5 how proud we be, buzzyng above bysily like as a bumble bee fleeth
about in somer, neuer ware that she shall die in wynter / And so fare
many of vs (god help vs) for in the short wynter day of worldly welth
& prosperite, this fleyng arrow of the devill this high spirite of
pride, shot out of the devilles bow & persing thorow our hart, bereth
10 vs vpp in our affeccion a loft into the clowdes where we wene we sit
on the rayne bow / & ouer loke the world vnder vs / accomptyng in
the regard of our own glory / such other pore soules as were peradventure wont to be our felowes, for sely pore pismeres & Antes. [f.
117ᵛ]
15   But this arrow of pride fly yt neuer so high in the clowdes, and be
the man that it carieth vpp so high neuer so ioyfull therof / yet let hym
remember / that be this arrow neuer so light, it hath ⌈yet⌉ an hevy
iron hed / and therfor fly it neuer so high / down must it nedes come
& on the grownd must yt light / and falleth sometyme, nott in a very
20 clenly place / but the pride turneth into rebuke & shame, & there is
than all the glory gone /
      Of this arrow spekith the wise man in the vᵗʰ chapter of Sapience /
wher he sayth in the person of them that in pride & vanite passid the
tyme of this present life, & after that so spent / passed hens into hell /
25 *Quid profuit nobis superbia aut diuitiarum iactantia, quid contulit nobis, transier-*
unt omnia illa tanquam vmbra &c aut tanquam sagitta emissa in locum destina-
tum, diuisus aer continuo in se reclusus est, vt ignoretur transitus illius. Sic &
nos nati continuo desinimus esse, & virtutis quidem nullum signum valuimus
ostendere | in malignitate autem nostra consumpti sumus | Talia dixerunt in
30 *inferno ij qui peccauerunt /* What hath pride profitt vs, or what good hath

---

1 shotten] shotte *Z*   2 vpp] *Z*, vppon *A*   5 proud] w *wr. over* u *B*; fleeth] flyeth *L*, flieth
1553 1557 1573   6 she] he *L 1553 1573*   7 may *canc. before* many *A*; (god) *parenth. ed.*, |
god *A*   8 prosperite] s *ins. B*; fleyng] flyeng *L*, flying *1553 1557 1573*   10–11 sit on]
sit vpon *L 1553 1573*   11 ouer loke the] ouerloke al the *L 1553 1573*   15 high in] high
into *L 1553 1573*   17 yet] it *A*: it *canc. and* yet *interl. B*, yet *Z*   18 come] come at
last *L 1553 1573*   19 nott] *canc. and* not *interl. B*   20 but] & then *L 1553 1573*; &
there] so that there *L 1553 1573*   22 vᵗʰ] .v. *1553 1557 1573*   24 hell /] *flourish in*
place of | *A, space left at end of line*   27 transitus] transiens *L 1553*; Sic] *ed.*, sic *A*
28 desinimus] desi uimus *1553 1573*   30 profitt] profyted *Z*

the glory of our riches done ⌐vnto⌐ vs / Passed are all those thinges
like a shadow &c or like an arrow shot out into the place appoyntid.
The aer that was devidid, is by & by retournid into the place, & in
such wise closid together agayne, that the way is not percevid in which
the arrow went. And in like wise we, as sone as we were bourne, ⌐be⌐ 5
by & by vinishid away, & haue left no token of any good vertue behind
vs, but are consumid & wastid & come to nought in our malignite /
[f. 118]

They lo / that haue livid here in sinne, such wordes haue they
spoken whan they lay in hell.   10

Here shall you good cosyn considre, that where as the scripture
here speketh of the arrow shot into his place appoyntid or intendid /
in shotyng of this arrow of pride there be diuers purposynges and
appoyntynges / for the proud man hym selfe hath no certeyne purpose or appoyntment / at any marke / butte / or prikke vppon erth / 15
wherat he determineth to shote & there to stikke & tary / but euer he
shoteth as children do that love to shote vpp a copp high, to see how
high their arrow can fly vpp.

But now doth the divell entend & appoynt a certeyne prikk surely
set in a place into which he purposeth / flye this arrow neuer so high 20
& the proud hart theron, to haue them light both at last. And that
place is in the very pitte of hell / Ther is set the devilles well acquentid
pricke & his very iust marke downe / vppon which pricke with his
prickyng shaft of pride, he hath by hym selfe a playne profe & experi-
ens that (but yf it be stoppid by some grace of god by the way) the 25
soule that flieth vpp therwith, can neuer fayle to fall / For whan hym
selfe was in hevyn & began to fly vpp a copp high, with that lusty light
flight of pride sayng: *Ascendam super astra, & ponam solium meum ad
latera Aquilonis, & ero similis altissimo* / I will stye vpp above the steres,
& set my trone on the sides of the north, and wil be lyke vnto the 30

<hr />

1 vnto] *om. L 1553 1573*; those] these *L 1553 1573*   2 appoyntid] *faulty* app *canc. after*
place *A*; appoyntid.] *period ed.*   3 thy? *canc. A before* that   5 we were] we be *L 1553*
6 vinishid] a *wr. over first* i *B*; good] goog *A*: d *wr. over final* g *B*   7 our] our own *L
1553 1573*   12 into his] in his *L 1553*   13 in shotyng] in the shoting *Z*; this arrow]
his arrow *1553*; there be] therby *1553*   14 appoyntynges] appointmentes *1553*   15
erth] thearth *L*, the heartes *1553*, the earth *1573*   21 proud] w *wr. over* u *B*; last.] *period ed.*
22 is *canc. A before* place; is in] is euen in *L 1553 1573*; acquentid] i *interl. before* n *B*
24 *faulty* he *canc. after* pride *A*   25 by] *canc. and in interl. B, in Z*   28 sayng:] *colon ed.*
29 similis] similis ero *L 1553 1573*; altissimo /] *period before* / *B*; stye] flie *1553*; steres] r
interl. after r *B*   30 wil] *second* l *added B*

hiest / long ere he could fly vpp half so high as he said in his hart he
wold / he was tournid from a bright gloriouse Angell, into a darke
deformid devill / and from flying any ferther vpward / downe was he
[f. 118ᵛ] throwen into the diepe dongeon of hell /

5   Now may it peradventure Cosyn seme, that sith this kynd of
temptacion of pride is no tribulacion or payne, all this that we speke
of this arrow of pride, flying forth in the day of prosperite, were beside
our mater /

Vincent

10   Verely myn vncle & so semed it vnto me, & somwhat was I myndid
so to say to you to / savyng that were it proprely perteynyng to the
present mater or somwhat disgressing therfro / good mater methought
it was, & such as I had no lust to let.

Antonye

15   But now must you cosyn consider / that though prosperite be contrary to tribulacion, yet vnto many a good man the devilles temptacion vnto pride in prosperite, ys a greter tribulacion, & more nede
hath of good comfort & good counsayle both, than he that neuer felt
it wold wene. And that is the thyng cosyn that maketh me speke ther-
20 of, as ⌐of⌐ a thyng proper to this mater / For cosyn as it is a thing right
hard to towch pich & neuer file the fingers, to put flex vnto fier &
yet kepe them fro burnyng, to kepe a serpent in thy bosome & yet be
safe fro stingyng / to put yong men with yong women without daynger of fowle fleshly desier: so is it hard for any person eyther man
25 or woman, in great worldly welth & mich prosperite, so to withstand
the suggestions of the devill & [f. 119] occasions geven by the world,
that they kepe them selfe from the dedly desier of ambiciouse glorye /
whervppon there foloweth (yf a man fall therto) an whole floode of
all vnhappy mischief, arrogant maner / high soleyne solempne port /

---

1 vpp] *om. L 1553 1573*; he said in his hart] in his hearte he sayd *L 1553 1573*   2 bright
gloriouse] gloryous bryght *L 1553 1573*; darke] blacke *L 1553 1573*   4 diepe] depe
darke *L 1553 1573*   10 somwhat] *orig.* somwaat: h *wr. over first* a *A*   17 vnto pride]
to pryde *L*; greter] greater more *1553*; more] *om. 1553*   18 good comfort & good
counsayle] good counsaile and good comfort *L 1553 1573*   22 them fro] it from *L 1553
1573*   23 fro] from *L 1553 1573*   26 &] and the *L 1553 1573*   27 kepe] should
kepe *L 1553 1573*; selfe] selves *L*

ouerlokyng the pore / in word & countenaunce displesaunt, & disdaynouse behavour / ravyn / extorcion / oppression / hatred and crueltie /
  Now many a good man cosyn comen into great authorite, castyng
in his mynd the perell of such occasions of pride, as the devill taketh
of prosperite to mak his instrumentes of, wherwith to move men to 5
such ⌐high⌐ poynt of presumpcion as ingendreth so many great in-
conveniences / & felyng the devill therwith offryng to them selfe
suggestions thervnto: they be sore trowblid therwith / & some fall so
ferd therof, that evyn in the day of prosperite, they fall into the
nightes feare of pusillanimite / & dowtyng ouermuch lest they shuld 10
misse vse them selfes, leve the thinges vndone wherin they might vse
them selfe well / & mistrustyng the ayd & help of god in holdyng them
vpp right in their temptacions / geve place to the divill in the contrary temptacion / wherby for faynt hart they leve of good besynes,
wherin they were well occupied / & vnder pretext (as it semeth to 15
them self) of humble hart & mekenes, & servyng god in contemplacion & silence, they seke their own ease & erthly rest vnwar / [f. 119ᵛ]
wherwith (yf it so be) god is not well content.
  Howbeit yf it so be that a man fele hym selfe such in dede, as by
thexperyence that he hath of hym selfe, he percevith that in welth & 20
aucthoryte he doth his own soule harm, & can not do there in the good
that to his part apperteynyth / but seeth the thinges that he shuld set
his hand to sustayne, decay thorow his defaut & fall to ruyne vnder
hym / and that to thadmendment therof he leveth his own dewtie vndone / than wold I in any wise aduise hym to leve of that thing / beit 25
spirituall benefice that he haue / parsonage / or bisshopperike / or
temporall rome & aucthorite / and rather give it ouer quyte & draw
hym selfe aside, & serve god, than take the worldly worship & commodite for hym selfe, with incommoditie of them whom his dewtie
were to profit / But on the tother side yf he se not the contrary, but that 30
he may do his dutie conveniently well / & fereth nothyng but that

7 selfe] selvys L   8 trowblid] trowlid A   9 ferd] fraide 1553 1573   10 dowtyng]
doubteth L 1553, doubt 1573   11 them selfes] theym selvys L, themselfe 1553 1557
1573; they might] the night 1553 (mispr.)   12 selfe] selves L; & help om. L 1553 1573
14 temptacion] temptacions L 1553 1573   15 vnder] vnder / A   16 self] selvys L
17 vnwar] final e added B   18 wherwith (yf] ed., (wherwith yf A   20 thexperyence]
experience L 1553   23 hand] es added B, handes 1557   24 thadmendment] the
amendment L 1553 1573, thamendment 1557   29 with] with the L 1553 1573
30 tother] other 1553 1573   31 but that] but only that 1573

⌐the⌐ temptacions of ambicion & pride, may peraduenture tourne
his good purpose, & make hym declyne vnto synne / I say not nay
but that well done it is to stand in moderate feare alway / wherof the
scripture·sayth: *Beatus homo qui semper est pauidus*: Blessid is the man
5 that is alway ferefull / and saynt paule sayth / *Qui stat videat ne cadat* /
he that standeth / let hym loke that he fall not: yet is ouer mich fere
perilouse / & draweth toward the mistrust of godes graciouse helpe /
which immoderate fere and faynt hart, holy scripture forbedith
saying / *Noli esse* [f. 120] *pusillanimis*: be not feble hartid or timerouse /
10 Let such a man therfor temper his fere with good hope / and thynke /
that sith god hath set hym in that place (yf he thinke that god haue
set hym therin) god will assist hym with his grace to the well vsyng
therof / How be it yf he came therto by simony or some such other
evill meane / than were that thing one good reason wherfor he shuld
15 the rather leve it of / But els let hym contynew in his good bysynes /
& agaynst the devilles prouocacion vnto evill / blesse hym selfe &
call vnto god & pray / And loke what thing the devill temptith hym to
/ lene the more to the contrary / / Let hym be pytuouse & comfortable
to those that are in distresse & affliccion / I mene not / to let euery
20 malefactour passe forth vnpunyshid & frely run out & robb at rouers /
but in his hart be sory to see that of necessitie for feare of decaying the
comen weale, men are dryven to put malefactours to payne. And yet
where he fyndeth good tokens & likelyhed of amendment / there in all
that he may / help / that mercie may be had. There shall neuer lakke
25 desperatly desposid wrechis inough beside / vppon whom for ensample
iustice may procede / Let hym thynke in his own hart euery pore
begger his felow /

Vincent

That wilbe very hard vncle for an honorable man to do / whan

---

1 temptacions] themptacions *A*: t *wr. over* h *and first* t *canc.* B, temptacyon *1553 1573*;
peraduenture torne] turne peraduenture L *1553 1573*   3 wherof] wherfore L *1553*
4 sayth:] *colon ed.*; pauidus:] *colon ed.*   8 which] with L *1553*; holy] and holy L *1553*
9 pusillanimis:] *colon ed.*   11 that] *interl. A*; haue] hath *1553 1573*   12 therin)]
parenth. ed., therin / *A*; assist] st *wr. over illeg. letter* B   13 came] come L *1553*; or some]
or by some L *1553 1573*   14 thing] *om.* L   18 lene] leaue L *1553*; to the] towarde
the *Z*   19 to let] to *om. 1553 1573*   22 weale] wealth L *1553*; payne.] *period ed.*
23 likelyhed] likelyhode *Z*   23–24 all that] all that ever L   24 help /] / *canc.* B; may
be had] may *om. 1573*

he beholdeth hymselfe richly apparilid & the begger riggid in his
ragges / /

Anthonye

Iff here were Cosyn ij men that were beggers both, & afterward a
greate rich man wold take the tone vnto hym & tell hym [f. 120ᵛ] 5
that for a litle tyme he wold haue hym in his howse / & thervppon
arrayed hym in silke & give hym a greate bagge by his side fillid evyn
full of gold / but givyng hym this knott therwith, that within a litell
while, out he shuld in his old ragges agayne, & bere neuer a peny with
hym / Iff this beggar mett his felow now while his gaye gowne were 10
on / might he not for all his gay gere, take hym for his felow still /
And were he not a very fole, yf for a welth of a few wekes, he wold
wene hym selfe far his bettre /

Viucent

Yes vncle / yf the difference of their state were none other.   15

Anthony

Surely Cosyn me thinketh that in this world, betwene the rychest
& the most pore, the differense is scant so much / For let the hiest
loke on the most bace / and consider how pore they came both into this
world, & than consider ferther therwith, how rich so euer he be now / 20
he shall yet within a while peradventure lesse than one weke, walke
out agayne as pore as that begger shall / And than by my trowth me
thynketh this rich man mych more than madd / yf for the welth of a
litell while, happely lesse than one weke, he reken hym selfe in erenest
eny bettre than the beggers felow / And lesse than thus can no man 25
thynke that hath any naturall wyt & well vseth yt.

But now a christen man Cosyn that hath the light of fayth, he can
not fayle to thynke on this thing mich ferther / For he will not thynke
onely vppon his bare comyng hether & his bare goyng hens agayne /

1 apparilid] e wr. over first i B   4 afterward] divided afterwa-rd A: rd canc. and added
after afterwa B   5 tone] one 1553 1573   8 gold] good interl. and then canc. B above gold
13 far] a wr. over illeg. letter, then word canc. and farre interl. B; bettre /] question-mark before
/ B   15 Yes] Yes by my trouth L 1553 1573   23 mych] om. L   25 thus] this 1553
1573   26 well vseth] wyl vse L 1553 1573   27–28 he can not] he om. 1573   28 not
thynke] thinke not Z

but also vppon the dredfull iugment of god, & vppon the ferefull
paynes of hell / and the inestimable ioyes of hevyn / And in the consideryng of these thinges, [f. 121] he will call to remembraunce, that
peraduenture whan this begger & he be both departid hens / the beg-
5 gar may be sodanly set vpp in such royaltie / that well were hymselfe that euer was he borne / yf he might be made his felow / And
he that well bethinketh hym Cosyn vppon these thinges / I verely
thinke / that the arrow of pride flying forth in the day of worldly
welth, shall neuer so wound his hart / that euer yt shall bere hym vpp
10 one fote.

But now to thentent he may thinke on such thynges the bettre, let
hym vse often to resort to confession / & there open his hart / & by
the mouth of some vertuouse goostly father, haue such thinges oft
renued in his remembraunce.

15 Let hym also chose hymselfe some secret solitary place in his own
house / as far fro noyse & companye as he conveniently can / And
thyther lett hym some tyme secretely resort alone / ymagynyng hym
selfe as one goyng out of the world evin strayt vnto the gevyng vpp
his rekenyng vnto god of his sinfull lyvyng / Than let hym there be-
20 fore an altare or some pitifull image of christes bitter passion / the
beholdyng wherof may put hym in remembraunce of the thing &
move hym to devout compassion / knele downe or fall prostrate as at
the fete of almighty god / verely belevyng hym to be there invisibly
present / as without ᒿenyᒿ dowt he is / There let hym open his hart
25 to god & confesse his fautes / such as he can call to mynd & pray god
of forgivenes / Let hym call to remembraunce the benefittes that god
hath gevyn hym, eyther in generall among other men, or privatly to
[f. 121ᵛ] hym selfe, and geve hym humble hartye thankes therfor.
There let hym declare vnto god, the temptacions of the devill / the
30 suggestions of the flesh / thoccasions of the world, & of his worldly
frendes much worse many tymes in drawyng a man from god than

2 and] and of L *1553*   3 these] those L *1553*   6 was he] he was *1573*; borne /]
/ *canc.* B   8 flying] fleyng L   9 vpp] *orig.* vppo: o *canc.* A   11 thentent] the entent
1553 1573   13 some] some good L *1553 1573*   15 chose] choose *1553 1557 1573*
16 fro] from L *1553 1573*   18 evin] *orig.* evil: l *corr. to* n A, evin *canc. and* even *interl.* B
18–19 vpp his] vp of hys L *1553 1573*   20 passion /] *parenth. wr. over* / B   22 compassion /] *parenth. wr. over* / B; knele] and there knele L *1553*   26 call] also cal L *1553*
1573; remembraunce] *minim lacking in* au A   27 eyther] eiyther? A: iy *alt. to* y B?;
extra hym *canc. after* to B   28 therfor.] *period ed.*   30 thoccasions] thoicasions A (*first*
o *wr. over* e?), the occasyons L

are his most mortall enymyes / which thyng our saviour witnesseth
hym selfe where he sayth: *Inimici hominis domestici eius* / the enymyes
of a man, are they that are his own famyliers /

There let hym lament & bewayle vnto god his own fraylte negligence & slouth in resistyng & withstandyng of temptacion, his redines 5
& pronite to fall therunto.

There let hym lamentably besech god of his gracyouse ayd & helpe,
to strength his infirmite withall / both in kepyng hym selfe fro fallyng
/ & whan he by his own faute misfortuneth to fall, than with the
helpyng hand of his mercifull grace, to lyft hym vp & set hym on his 10
fete in the state of his grace agayne.

And let this man not dowt, but that god hereth hym and graunteth
hym gladly hys bone / And so dwellyng in the faythfull trust of godes
help, he shall well vse his prosperite & perseuer in his good profitable
bysynes, And shall haue therin the trowth of god so compasse hym 15
about with a pavice of his hevenly defence / that of the divilles arrow
flying in the day of worldly welth, he shall not nede to drede /

Vincent

Forsoth vncle I like this good counsayle well / & I wold wene that
such as are in prosperite & take such order therin, may do both to 20
them selfe & other folke abowt mich good / / [f. 122]

Anthonye

I besech our lord cosyn put this & bettre in the mynd of euery man
that nedeth it / And now will I touch one word or twayn of the third
temptacion (wherof the prophet speketh in these wordes) *A negocio* 25
perambulante in tenebris: from the besines walkyng in the darknes / &
than will we call for our dener levyng the last temptacion that is to
wit / *Ab incursu & demonio meridiano* / from the incursion & the devill
of the midd day / till after none / & than shall we therwith god willyng make an end of all this mater. 30

---

2 sayth:] *colon ed.*   7 lamentably] *om.* Z   8 strength] strengthen *L*; selfe] *canc. B?*,
om. Z; fro] from *L 1553 1573*   9 faute] faultes *L 1553*   13 hys] this *L 1553 1573*;
his *canc. B before* gladly   25 wordes)] *parenth. ed.*, wordes / *A*   26 perambulante]
perambulanti *A*: *illeg. letter after i erased and e wr. over i B*; the] the / *A*; tenebris:] *colon ed.*;
darknes] sses *wr. over* s *B*, darkenesses *L 1557 1573*; &] *canc. and interl. B*   28 wit]
wete *1553*

Vincent

Our lord rewarde you good vncle for your good labour with me /
But for our lordes sake take good hede vncle that you forbere not
your dener ouer longe.

Antonye

Fere not that cosyn I warrant you / for this piece will I make you
but short /

Of the devill namid *negocium perambulans in tenebris* /
that is to wit bysines walkyng in the darknes /

The xvij chapiter

The prophet sayth in the said psalm / *Qui habitat in adiutorio altissimi,
in protectione dei celi commorabitur* / *scuto circumdabit te veritas eius, non
timebis a timore &c A negotio perambulante in tenebris* / He that dwellith
in the faythfull hope of godes helpe, he shall abyde in the proteccion
& safegard of god of hevyn. And thou that art such one / shall the
trouth of hym so compasse about with a pavice that thow shallt not
be aferd of the besines walkyng about in [f. 122ᵛ] the darkenessis /
Negocium is here cosin the name of a devill that is euer ful of besynes
in temptyng folke to mich evill besynes / his tyme of temptyng is in
the darknessis / For you wot well that beside the very full night,
which is the diepe darke / there are ij tymes of darkenessis / the tone
ere the mornyng wax light, the tother whan the evenyng waxeth
darke /
Two tymes of like maner darknesse are there also in the soule of
man / the tone ere the light of grace be well in the hart sprongen

---

4 dener] y *wr. over first* e *B*   8 perambulans in tenebris] *om. L 1553 1573*   9 walkyng]
walking about *L 1553 1573*; darknes] ssys *wr. over* s *B*, darkenesses *L 1557 1573*   10 xvij]
xviijᵗʰ *L*, xviii *1553 1573*; *long flourish after* chapiter *A*   13 a timore] *om.* 𝒵   15 &]
or 𝒵; safegard] sauegard *1557*; god] the god *1553 1573*; hevyn.] *period ed.*; thou] the *A*:
ou *wr. over* e, *then word canc. and* thow *interl. B*   17 aferd] afrayed *1553 1573*   21 tone]
one *1553 1573*   21–22 *Two passages marked for emphasis by marginal annotator*: the tone
ere the *underlined with vertical at beginning*; the tother when *marked in same way*   22
tother] other *1553 1573*   25 tone] one *1553 1573*

vpp / the tother when the light of grace out of the soule begynneth
to walke fast awaye /

In these ij darknesses the devill that is callid bisines bisily walketh
about / & such folke as will folow hym, he carieth about with hym,
& settith them a worke with many maner bumblyng bysynes /   5

He settith I say some to seke the pleasures of the flesh / in eatyng
drinkyng & other filthy delite / And some he settith about incessaunt
sekyng for these worldly goodes.

And of such bisy folke whom this devill callid bysines walkyng about
in the darknessis settith aworke with such besynes / our saviour sayth   10
in the gospell / *Qui ambulat in tenebris nescit quo vadit* / he that walketh
in darknessis woteth not whyther he goth / And surely in such case
are they / They neyther wote which way they go nor whyther / For
verely they walke round about as it were in a round mase / whan
they wene them selfe at an end of their besynes they be but at the   15
begynnyng agayne / For is not the goyng about the servyng of the
[f. 123] flesh a bysines that hath none end / but euermore from
the end commeth to the begynnyng agayne / go they neuer so ful fed
to bed / yet euermore on the morow as new be they to be fed agayne
as they were the day before /   20

Thus fareth it by the bely / thus fareth it by those partes that are
byneth the bely / And as for covetice fareth like the fyer / the more
wode that cometh therto the more fervent & the more gredy it is /

But now hath this mase a centre or a mydle place, into which some
tyme they be conveyed sodaynly / whan they wene they were not yet   25
far fro the brynke.

The centre 'or' mydle place of this mase is hell / & into that place
be these bysy folke that with this devill of besynes walke about in this
besy mase in the darkenessis sodanly sometyme conveyd / nothyng

1 tother] other *1553 1573*   3 the devill] this deuil *Z*   4 such] such fond *Z*
6 eatyng] eatyng and *L*   7 about] about the *L 1553 1573*   9-10 walkyng about in
the darknessis settith aworke with such besynes] *om. L 1553*   12 darknessis] darkenes
1553   13 they / They] they, for thei *L 1553 1573*   15 selfe] selvys *L*   16 agayne]
om. 1573   16-18 For is not the goyng about . . . commeth to the begynnyng agayne]
om. L 1553   17 none end] no end *1573*   18 agayne /] *question-mark added and / canc.*
B; begynnyng agayne / go] *beginning: agayn, goe 1553, beginning againe? For go 1573;*
ful] *second* l *added B*   20 before /] / *canc. and period added B* (/ *ends with flourish A*)   21 by
those] with those *L 1553*   22 fareth] it fareth *1573; comma after* more *B*   24 centre
or a] centry or *L 1553*, a *om. 1553 1573*   26 fro] from *L 1553 1573*   27 centre] centrye
L, contrey *1553*; or] of *canc. and* or *interl. B*, or *Z*   29 sodanly] e *wr. over a B*

ware whyther they be goyng / & evyn while they wene that they were not far walkyd fro the begynnyng / & that they had yet a greate way to walke abowt before they shuld come to thend / But of these fleshly folke walkyng in this bisy plesaunt mase, the scripture declareth
5 thend: *Ducunt in bonis dies suos, & in puncto ad inferna descendunt* / They lede their life in pleasure / & at a poppe down they descend into hell.

Off the covetouse men sayth S paule / *Qui volunt diuites fieri, incidunt in tentationem & in laqueum diaboli, & desideria multa inutilia & nociua, quae mergunt homines in interitum & perditionem* / They that long to be
10 rich / do fall [f. 123ᵛ] into temptacion, & into the grynne of the devill, & into many desieres vnprofitable / & harmfull / which drowne men into deth & into destruccion.

Lo here is the midle place of ᴿthisᴸ besy mase / the grenne of the devill the place of perdicion & destruccion that they fall & be caught
15 & drownyd in ere they be ware.

The covetouse rich man also that our saviour speketh of in the gospell / that had so greate plenty of corn, that his barnes wold not receve it / but intendid to make his barnes larger, & said vnto hym selfe / that he wold make mery many dayes / had went you wot well
20 that he had had a greate way yet to walke / but god said vnto hym *Stulte / hac nocte ᴿtollentᴸ a te animam tuam, quae autem parasti cuius erunt.* Fole this night shall they take thy soule from the / & than all this good that thow hast gatherid, whose shall it be. Here you se that he fell sodanly into the diepe centre of this bysy mase / so that he was
25 fallen full therin long ere euer he had went he shuld haue come nere therto.

Now this wote I very well, that those that are walkyng about in this besy mase, take not their besines for eny tribulacion / And yet are there many of them foreweried as sore / & as sore pangid & paynid
30 therin / their pleasures beyng so short / so litle & so few, & their displeasures & their griefes so greate / so contynuall & so many, that maketh me thinke vppon a good worshipfull man / which whan he

---

2 fro] from L *1553 1573*   3 thend] the end *Z*   4 fleshly] flesly *A*; bisy plesaunt] pleasaunte busi L *1553 1573*   5 thend:] colon *ed.*, the ende *Z*   6 *elaborate flourish after* hell *A*   7 men] man L *1553*   10 grynne] r *interl. A and strengthened by B*   11 vnprofitable /] / *canc. B*; drowne] drounde *1553*, drownd L *1557*   13 midle] d *wr. over* l *A*; grenne] gryn L, grinne *1553 1557*, grin *1573*   20 he had had a] he had a *1573*   24 centre] centry L *1553*   25 full] ful & whole L *1553 1573*   29 foreweried] *vertical line after* fore *B?*   32 maketh] it maketh *Z*

diuers tymes byheld his wife what payne she toke in strayte byndyng
vpp her here to make her [f. 124] a fayre large forhed, & with strayt
bracyng in her body to make her mydle small / both twayne to her
great payne / for the pride of a litle folysh prayse / he said vnto her
forsoth madame / if god give you not hell, he shall do you greate 5
wronge / For it must nedes be your own of very right / for you by it
very dere, & take grete payne therfor /

They that now lye in hell for their wrechid livyng here / do now
perceve their foly in the more payne that they toke here for the lesse
pleasure / There confesse they now their foly & cry owt / *Lassati sumus* 10
in via iniquitatis / we haue bene weryed in the way of wikkednes / And
yet while [they] were walking therin, they wold not rest them self but
runne on styll ⌜in theyr werynes / & put them self still⌝ vnto more
payne & more, for that litle pevish pleasure short & sone gonne, that
they toke all that labour & payne for, beside the euerlastyng payne 15
that folowid it for their ferther avantage after /

So help me god & none other wise but as I verely thinke, that
many a man bieth hell here with so mich payn, that he might haue
bought hevyn with lesse than the tone halfe /

But yet as I saye / while these fleshly & worldly bysy folke are walk- 20
yng ⌜abowt⌝ in this round bisy mase of this divill that is callid besynes
that walketh about in these two tymes of darknes, their wittes are so
by the secret inchauntment of the devill bewychid, that they marke
not the greate long miserable werynes & payne that the devill maketh
them take [f. 124ᵛ] & endure about nought / & therfor they take it for 25
no tribulacion, so that they nede no comfort / and therfor it is not for
their sakes that I speke all this / sayyng that it may serue them for
counsayle / toward the percevyng of their own folysh myserye thowrow the good helpe of godes grace begynnyng to shyne vppon them
agayne / But there are very good folke & vertuouse that are in the 30
day light of grace / & yet because the devill temptith them bysyly to

---

1 *Virgule canc. after* his *B*   7 grete] verye greate *Z*   9 the more] theyr more *L 1553
1573*   12 they were] *Z*, we were *A*; self but] selves but *L*   13 self still] selves still *L*
15 the euerlastyng] theverlastyng *L*   16 avantage] advauntage *L*, aduantage *1553 1557
1573*; after /] *virgule wr. with flourish A, period placed before* / *B*   17 thinke] ke *wr. over* g *A*
19 lesse] *final* e *added B?*; tone] one *1553 1573*   20 fleshly] *divided* fle-shly *A*: shly *canc.
and added after* fle *B*   21 abowt] *wr. by B over blotted word* (about?) *interl. by A*; this divill]
the deuil *1553*   22 darknes] darkenesses *L 1553*   23 marke] make *A*: r *interl. B*,
marke *Z*   25 them take] them to take *L 1553*   26 and] a *alt. to* A *B*; it is] s *wr. over*
t *and* t *wr. over* s *B*, is it *Z*

such fleshly delight / & sith they se plenty of worldly substaunce fall
vnto them & fele the devill in likewise bisily tempt them to set their
hart thervppon / they be sore trowblid therwith / & begynne to fere
therby that they be not with god in the light / but with this devill that
5 the prophet calleth *Negocium* / that is to say besynes walkyng about in
these ij tymes of darknesses /

How be it as I said before of those good folke & graciouse, that are
in the worldly welth of great power & aucthorite / & therby fere the
devilles arrow of pride: so say I now here agayne of these that stand
10 in drede of fleshly fowle synne & covitice / sith they be but temptid
there with & folow it not / Albeit that they do well to stand euer in
moderate fere, lest with waxyng ouer bold & settyng the thyng ouer
light, they might peradventure mishapp to fall in therto / yet sore to
vexe & trowble [f. 125] them selfe with the fere of losse of godes favour
15 therfor, is without necessite & not alway without perell / For as I said
before / yt withdraweth the mynd of a man far fro spirituall consolacion of the good hope that he shuld haue in godes helpe / And as for
those temptacions, while he that is temptid foloweth them not / the
fight agaynst them serueth a man for mater of merite and reward in
20 hevyn / yf he not onely fly the dede the consent & the delectacion, but
also in that he conveniently may, flye from all occasions therof / And
this poynt is in those fleshly temptacions, eth to perceve & metely
playne inough / But in these worldly besynes perteynyng vnto covetice,
therin ys the thing somewhat more darke, & in the percevyng more
25 difficultie / And very greate troubelouse fere doth there often tymes
arise therof, in the hartes of very good folke, when the world falleth
fast vnto them / because of the sore wordes & terrible threttes that god
in holy scripture speketh agaynst those that are rich, as where saynt
paule sayth / *Qui volunt diuites fieri incidunt in tentationem, & in laqueum*
30 *diaboli*: They that wilbe rich, fall into temptacion & into the grenne
of the divill. And where our saviour sayth hym selfe: *facilius est camel-*
um per foramen acus transire / *quam diuitem intrare in regnum dei*: It is more

---

1 delight] delght *A* 2 & fele] &, fele *B*; bisily tempt] busy abowt to tempte *L*, busily
about to tempt *1553* 4 this devill] the deuil *L 1553* 5 about] *extra* about *canc. A*
after walkyng 6 these ij] the two *Z*; darknesses] darknes *1573* 16 fro] from *L 1553*
1573 18 those] these *L 1553 1573* 20 fly] flee *1557 1573* 21 flye] flee *1557*
1573; all] al the *L 1553 1573* 22 eth] *final* e *added B*, a thing eth *Z* 23 besynes]
businesses *L 1553 1573* 28 rich] *final* e *added B* 30 diaboli:] *colon ed.*; rich] made
rytche *L*; grenne] grynn *L*, grynne *1557*, grin *1553 1573* 31 selfe:] *colon ed.* 32
transire] *om. L 1553*

easy for a camell or as some say (for *camelus* so signifieth in the greke [f. 125ᵛ] tong) for a greate cable rope to go thorow an nedilles ye / than for a rich man to entre into the kyngdome of god /

No merveyle now though good folke that fere god / take occasion of greate dreade at so dreadfull wordes / whan they se the worldly goodes 5 fall to them / And some stand in dout whether it be lefull for them to kepe any good or no / But euermore in all those places of scripture, the havyng of the worldly goodes, ys nott the thyng that is rebukyd & thretenid / but theffection that the havour vnleifully bereth therto / For where saynt paule sayth: *Qui volunt diuites fieri* ⌐&c⌐ / they that wil- 10 be made rich / he speketh not of the havyng / but of the will & the desire / and affeccion to haue & the longyng for it / For that can nott be lightely without synne. For the thing that folke sore long for / they will make many shyftes to gete & iubard them selfe therfor / And to declare that the havyng of richesse is not forboden / but the inordinate 15 affeccion of the mynd sore set ther uppon / the prophet sayth: *Diuitie si affluant nolite cor apponere* / Iff riches flow vnto you, set not your hart thervppon / And albeit that our lord by the said ensample of the cam- ell or cable rope to come thorow the nedlys yie / said that it is not onely hard but also impossible for a rich man to entre into the 20 kyngdome of hevyn: yet he declarid that though the rich man can not get in to hevyn of hymselfe / yet god he said can get him in well inough / For vnto men he said it was impossible, but not vnto god / / for vnto god (he said) all thinges are possible / yet ouer that he told of which maner rich men he ment, that could not get into the kyng- 25 dome of hevyn: saying *Filioli quam difficile est confidentes, in pecunijs regnum dei introire* / my babis how hard is it for them that put theire trust & confidence in their money, to entre into the kyngdome [f. 126] of god /

---

1 (for] *parenth. wr. over* / *B*; camelus so] so Camelus *L 1553 1573*   2 cable] gable *L*; rope] rope) *A*; an nedilles] a nedles *Z̧*; ye] e *added before* y, *then word canc. and* eye *interl. B* 5 the worldly] the *om. 1573*   6 to them] vnto them *L 1553 1573*; lefull] lawful *L 1553 1573*, lyefull *1557*   7 good] goodes *L 1553 1573*   9 theffection] *first* e *alt. to* a *B*, the affeccion *Z̧*; havour] haver *interl. B above* havour (*uncanc.*), hauer *Z̧*   10 sayth:] *colon ed.*; fieri &c / they] fieri / and they *A*: and *canc. and* &c *interl. B before* they   11 rich] rytche &c *L*   12 desire /] / *canc. B*; to haue] *om. L 1553*   13 extra the *canc. after* For *B* 14 iubard] ieobard *L*, ieopard *1553 1557 1573*; selfe] selvys *L*   15 richesse] rytches *L*, riches *1553 1557 1573*; forboden] forbydden *L 1553 1573*   16 sayth:] *colon ed.*; Diuitie] *hook added to* e *B*   17 hart] harts *L 1553 1573*   18 albeit] abbeit *A*: *first* b *alt. to* l *B* 19 or cable] or gable *L*, or the cable *1553 1573*   22 him] *orig.* yim: h *wr. over* y *A* 24 yet] And yet *Z̧*   27 regnum] in regnum *L 1553 1573*; babis] babes *Z̧*

Vincent

This I suppose very trew / & els god forbede / for els were the worlde in a very hard case / yf euery rich man were in such dainger & perell /

⁵
Antonye

That were it Cosyn in dede / & so I wene is it yet / For I fere me that to the multytude, there be very few but that they long sore to be rich / & of those that so long to be, very few reseruid also but that they set their hart very sore theron /

¹⁰
Vincent

This is vncle I fere me very trew / but yet not the thing that I was about to speke of / But the thing that I wold haue said was this / that I can not well perceve (the world beying such as yt is / & so many pore people therin) how any man may be rich & kepe hym rich, ¹⁵ without dayngour of dampnacion therfor / for all the while that he seeth pore peple so many that lak, while hym selfe hath to give them, and whose necessite (while he hath therwith) he is bound in such case of dutie to releve / so ferforth that holy S Ambrose sayth, that who so that die for defaut where we might help them, we kyll them / I can ²⁰ not see / but that euery rich man hath greate cause to stand in greate fere of dampnacion / nor I can not perceve / as I say how he can be deliuerid of that fere, as long as he kepeth his reches / And therfor though he might kepe his riches yf their lakkid pore men, & yet stand in goddes favour therwith / as Abraham did & many an other ⌐holy¬ ²⁵ rich man syns / yet in such abundaunce of pore men as there be now in euery countrey, eny man that kepeth any riches, it must nedes be that he hath an inordinate affeccion therunto, while he giveth it not out vnto the pore [f. 126ᵛ] nedy persons / that the dewtie of charitie bynd-

---

2 This I suppose] This is I suppose vncle *Z*   3 worlde] *Z*, worldle *A*; very] full *Z*
6–7 me that to] that *om.* L *1553*   7 they] the *A*, y *added B*   8 so long] longe so L
1553 1573; reseruid] v *wr. over* u *B*   9 hart] heartes L *1553 1573*; theron] thereuppon L
11 This] That L *1553 1573*   14 rich] *final* e *added B*; rich] *final* e *added B*   16 thei
canc. A before lak   17 therwith)] *parenth. added B*, wherwith L *1553 1573*; bound]
bounden *1557*   19 kyll them] kyl them our selfe L *1553 1573*   22 reches] y *wr. over*
e *B*, richesse *1557*   23 riches] richesse *1557*   24 / *canc. B after* &   26 riches]
richesse *1557*   28 *comma added and erased after* pore *B*

eth & straynneth hym to / And thus vncle in this world at this daye
me semeth your comfort vnto good men that are rich & trowblid
with fere of dampnacion for the kepyng, can very scantly serve /

Antonye

Hard is it Cosyn in many maner thinges, to bid or forbede, afferm 5
or denye, reprove or alow, a mater nakidly proponid & put forth /
or presisely to say this thing is good or this thyng is nought, without
consideracion of the circumstaunces /

Holy s Austeyne tellith of a phisicion, that gave a man a medicyne
in a certeyne disease / that holpe hym / The selfe same man at a 10
nother tyme / in the selfe same disease toke the selfe same medycyne
hym selfe, and had therof more harm than good / which thing whan
he shewid vnto the phisicion, & askyd hym wherof that harme shuld
happe / That medicyne quod he did the no good but harm, because
thow tokest it whan I gave it the not. This answere / s Austyne very 15
well aloweth / For that though the medicyne were one / yet might
ther be peradventure in the siknes some such deference as the
pacyent percevid not / ye or in the man hym selfe or in the place / or
the tyme of the yere, many thinges might make the let / for which the
phisicion wold not than haue gevyn hym the selfe same medicyne that 20
he gavc hym before. To peruse euery circumstaunce that might
cosyn in this mater be towchid & were to be considerid & waycd,
wold in dede make this part of this devill of bysines a very bysy [f.
127] piece of worke & a long / But I shall a litle open the poynt that
you speke of / & shall shew you what I thinke therin, with as few 25
wordes as I conveniently can / & than will we go to dener

First Cosyn he that is a rich man & kepeth all his good / he hath I
thynke very good cause to be very ferd in dede / And yet I fere me that
such folke fere lest / For they be very far fro the state of good men /
sith yf they kepe styll all / than are they very far fro charite / & do 30
you wot well allmoise either litle or none at all / But now is our question cosyn / not in what case the rich man standith that kepeth all /

---

2 comfort] *extra stroke of* m *canc.* A?   3 fere] the feare L   5 is it] it is *canc. before* is it
A; Hard is it] Hard it is *1573*   9 Holy] Holy / A   10 disease /]/ *canc.* B   11 tyme /]
/ *canc.* B   18–19 or the tyme] in the time L *1553 1573*   21 peruse] v *wr. over* u B
28 ferd] frayd *1553 1573*   29 fere lest] feare it least *Z*; fro] from L *1553 1573*   30 fro]
from L *1553 1573*   31 allmoise] almose *1553 1573*, almes *1557*   32 the rich] that
riche L *1553 1557*

but whether we shuld suffre men to stand in a perilouse drede & fere
for the kepyng ⌐of any gret part / for that if [by] the kepyng¬ styll of
so mich as maketh a rich man styll / they stand in the state of dampnacion / than are the curattes bounden ⌐playnly¬ to tell them so /
5 accordyng to the commaundment of god gevin vnto them all in the
person of Ezechiell / *Si dicente me ad impium morte morieris non annuncia-*
ueris ei &c / yf when I say to the wikkid man thow shalt dye, thow do
not shew it vnto hym / nor speke vnto hym / that he may be tornid
from his wikkid waye & may live / he shall sothely die in his wikked-
10 nes, & his bloode shall I verily require of thyn hand.

But Cosyn though god invitid men vnto the folowing of hym selfe
in wilfull pouertie, by the levyng of all together at ones for his sake,
as the thing whereby with beyng out of the sollicitude of worldly
bysynes & far fro the desire of erthly commodities / they may the
15 more [f. 127ᵛ] spedely get / and attayne the state of spirituall perfeccion, & the hungrye desire & longyng for celestiall thinges / yet
doth he not commaund euery man so to do vppon the perell of dampnacion / For where he sayth / *Qui non renunciauerit omnibus quae possidet*
non potest meus esse dissipulus / he that forsake not all that euer he hath,
20 can not be my disciple / he declarith well by other wordes of his own
in the selfe same place a litell before, what he meaneth / for there sayth
he more / *Si quis venit ad me, & non odit patrem suum & matrem, &*
vxorem & filios & fratres & sorores, adhuc autem & animam suam, non
potest meus esse discipulus / he that cometh to me, & hateth not his
25 father & his mother, ⌐&¬ his wife & his children, & his brethern &
his sisters / yee and his own lyfe to, can not be my disciple.

Here meneth our saviour christ, that none can be his disciple but
yf he love hym so far above all his kynne, & above his own lyfe to,
that for the love of hym rather than to forsake hym / he shall forsake
30 them all / And so meneth he by those other wordes / that who so
euer do not renounce & forsake all that euer he hath in his own hart
and affection, that he will rather lese it ⌐all¬ & let it go euery whit /

---

2 of . . . kepyng] of *wr. in space at end of line and rest of insertion interl.* B; for that . . .
kepyng] For if that by the kepyng Ⱬ   8 shew it vnto hym] shew it to him *1573*; speke]
speake it *1553 1573*   10 verily] *om. 1557*; require] *divided* requi-re A: re *canc. and added*
after requi B; thyn] thy *1573*; hand] handes L *1553*   14 fro] from L *1553 1573*   15 &
canc. before and B   19 meus esse] esse meus L *1553 1573*; forsake] th *added* B, forsaketh Ⱬ
23 filios] filies? A   24 meus esse] esse meus L *1553 1573*   25 & his wife] *om.* L *1553*
30 his *canc. after* by B   31 do not] doe not so Ⱬ

than dedly displese god with the reseruyng of any one part therof /
he can not be christes disciple (sith christ techeth vs to love god
above all thing) ⌐& he lovyth not god above all thing⌐ that contrary
to goddes pleasure, kepeth any thing that he hath / for that thing he
shewith hymselfe to set more by than by god / while he is bettre con-   5
tent to lese god than yt / But as I said to give away all / or that no man
shuld be rich or haue substance, that fynd I no commaundement of.
[f. 128] There are as our saviour sayth in the house of his father
many mansions / And happy shall he be that shall haue the grace to
dwell evyn in the lowest /   10

Hit semeth veryly by the gospell, that those which for godes sake
pacyently suffre penury, shall not onely dwell above those in hevyn
that live here in plentye in erth, but also that hevyn in some maner of
wise more properly belongeth vnto them, & is more specially preparid for them / than it is for the rich / by that ⌐that⌐ god in the gospell /   15
counsaylith the rich folke to bye in a maner hevyn of them where he
sayth vnto the rich men / *facite vobis amicos de mammona iniquitatis, vt*
quum defeceritis recipiant vos in aeterna tabernacula / make you frendes of
the wikked riches / that whan you fayle here, they may receve you
into the euerlastyng tabernacles.   20

But now although this be thus in respect of the riches & the pouertie
comparid together / yet they beyng good men both, there may be
some other vertue beside, wherin the rich man may so peraduenture
excell, that he may in hevyn be far above that pore man that was
here in erth in other vertues far vnder hym / as the profe apperith   25
clere in Lazarus & Abraham.

Nor I say not this to thintent to comfort rich men in heping vpp of
riches / For a litele comfort is bent inough therto for them that be not
so proud hartid & obstynate, but that they wold I wene to that counsayle be with right litle exortacion very conformable / but I say this   30

1 displese] *divided* disp-lese *A*: p *canc. and wr. before* lese *B*   3 thing)] *parenth. ed.,* / *after*
thing *B*   5 *middle stop after* by *A*   7 haue] haue any *L 1553 1573*; of.] *period ed.*
11 Hit] It *Z*; veryly] very *A*: ly *added B*   12 pacyently] *om. L 1553*   15 gospell /] /
canc. B   18 defeceritis] ce *interl. B*, defeceritis *Z*; frendes] ferndes *A*: re *wr. over* er *B*
20 into the] the *om. Z*   21 riches] rychesse *1557*   24 in hevyn be] be in heauen *L*
1553 1573; that pore] the poore *1573*   26 clere] clerely *L 1553 1573*; Abraham] *L and*
1553 begin new chapter here: The xix^th Chapyter *L*, The .xix. Chapter *1553*   27 thintent]
the entent *1553 1557 1573*   28 riches] richesse *1557*; / For] *period after* / *B*; litele] *canc.*
and lytill *interl. B*; / *ins. after* them *B*; that] ey *wr. over* at *B*, They *Z*   29 proud] w *wr.*
over u *B*

for those good men, to [f. 128ᵛ] whom god giveth substaunce & the
mynd to dispose it well, and yet not the mynd to give it all away at
ones / but for good causes to kepe some substaunce styll / shold not
dispayre of godes favour / for the not doyng of the thyng which god
5 hath geven them no commaundment of / nor drawen by any speciall
callyng therunto /

Zacheus lo that clymyd vpp into the tree for desire that he had to
behold our saviour, at such tyme as christ callid aloude vnto hym
and said / Zacheus make hast & come down / for this day must I
10 dwell in thyn howse / was so glad therof & so towchid inwardly with
speciall grace to the prophet of his soule / that where as ˹all˺ the
people murmurid mich that christ wold call hym and be so famyliar
with hym as of his own offre to come vnto his house, consideryng that
they knew hym for the chiefe of the publicanes, that were custumers
15 or toll gatherers of the emperours dewties (all which whole companye
were amonge the people sore infamid of ravyn extorcion & brybery)
and than Zacheus not onely the cheef of that feleship / but also growen
greately rich, wherby the people accomptid hym in their own opinyon
for a man very synfull & nought / he forthwith by thinstinct of the
20 spirite of god, in reproch of all such temerariouse bold & blynd iugment / given vppon a man, whose inward mynd & sodayne chaunge
they can not se, shortly prouid them all deceyvid / & that our lord
had at [f. 129] those few wordes owtewardly spoken to hym / so
wrought in his hart within / that what so euer he was before, he was
25 than vnware vnto them all, sodaynly waxen good. For he made hast
& came downe, & gladly recevid christ and said / Lo lord the tone
halfe of my goodes here I give vnto the pore people / And yet ouer
that / yf I haue in any thyng decevid any man: here am I redye to
recompence hym fooure fold as mich / /

---

1 for those] for that those *1573*   6 therunto /] *period before* / B   8 aloude] w *wr. over*
u B   10 thyn] thy Z; was] zacheus was L *1553*, he was *1573*   11 speciall] spīall A;
prophet] *canc. and* profyt *interl.* B   15 the emperours] themperours L *1553 1573*; (all]
parenth. added B   16 brybery)] *parenth. wr. over* / B   19 thinstinct] y *wr. over second* i
B, the instinct *1553 1573*   22 prouid] v *wr. over* u B   23 to hym /] to him, so touched
him, that his grace L *1553 1573*   24 wrought] *divided* wro-ught A: ught *canc. and added*
after wro B   25 vnware] vnwares *1553 1573*   26 tone] one *1553 1573*   27 goodes]
good *1557*; the pore] the *om.* Z   29 fooure] f *wr. over first* o *and orig.* f *canc.* B

Vincent

This was vncle a graciouse heryng / But **I** merveyle me somwhat / wherfor Zacheus vsid his wordes in that maner of ordre / / For me thinketh he shuld first haue spoken of makyng restitucion vnto those whom he had begilid / and speke of givyng of his almes after / For 5 restitucion is you wote well dutie, & a thing of such necessitie, that in respect of restitucion almes dede is but voluntarye / Therfor it might seme that to put men in mynd of their dewtie in makyng restitucion first & doyng their almes after / Zacheus shuld haue said more conveniently / yf he had said first that he wold make euery man 10 restitucion whom he had wrongid, & than give halfe in almes of that that remaynid after / for onely that might he call clerely his own /

Anthonye

This is trew cosyn, wherc a man hath not inough to suffice both / But he that hath / is not bounden to leve his almes vngevyn to the 15 pore man that is at his hand, & peradventure [f. 129ᵛ] calleth vppon hym / till he go seke vpp all his creditours & all those that ⌐he⌐ hath wrongid / so far peradventure a sundre that levyng the tone good dede vndone the while, he may before they come together, chaunge that good mynd agayne, & do neyther the tone nor the tother. It is 20 good alway to be doyng some good out of hand while we thinke theron / grace shall the bettre stand with vs & encrease also to go the ferther in the tother after / And this I answere yf the man had there done the tone out of hand / the givyng **I** meane alfe in almes / and not so mich as speke of restitucion till after / where as now though 25 he spake the tone in ordre before the tother / & yet all at one tyme / the thing remaynid still in his libertie to put them both in execucion after such ordre as he shuld than thinke expedient / But now Cosyn

---

2 But] but yet *Z*   4 restitucion] tu *interl. B*   5 speke] than speake *Z*; giving of] of om. *Z* (geuen *1557*); almes] allmoyse *L*, almose *1553 1573*   6 restitucion] tu *interl. A*
7 restitucion] tu *interl. B*; almes] allmoyse *L*, almose *1553 1573, comma after* almes *B*
9 almes] allmoyse *L*, almose *1553 1573*; said] sad *A*   11 almes] allmoyse *L*, almose
1553 1573   14 both] for bothe *Z*   15 bounden] bound *1553 1573*; almes] allmoyse
L, almose *1553 1573*; *comma added and erased after* man *B*   18 tone] one *L 1553 1573*
20 tone] one *1553 1573*; tother] other *1553 1573*   21 alway] alway therfore *L 1553 1573*
23 in] into *L 1553*; tother] other *1553 1573*   24 tone] one *1553 1573*; alfe] ha *wr. over*
a *B*; almes] allmoyse *L*, almose *1553 1573*   26 tone] one *1553 1573*; tother] other *1553
1573*   28 after] after, *B*

did the spirite of god temper the tonge of Zacheus in the vtteraunce
of these wordes, in such wise / as it may well apere / the saying of the
wise man to be veryfied in them where he sayth / *Domini est gubernare*
linguam: To god it belongeth geverne the tong / For here when he said
5 he wold give halfe of his whole good vnto pore peple / and yet beside
that not onely recompence any man whom he had wrongid / but more
& recompence hym by thre tymes as mich agayne / he dowble reproui-
id the false suspicion of ⌐the⌐ peple that accomptid hym for so evill /
that they rekenid in [f. 130] their mynd all his good gotten / in effect
10 with wrong because he was growen to substaunce in that office that
was commenly misvsid extorsiously / But his wordes declarid that he
was ripe inough in his rekenyng / that yf halfe his good were gevyn
away / yet were he well able to yeld euery man his dewtie with the
tother halfe, & yet leve hym selfe no begger neyther / for he said not
15 he wold give away all /

   Wold god Cosyn that euery rich christen man that is reputid right
worshipfull / ye & (which yet in my mynd more is) rekenid for right
honest to / wold & were able to do the thing that litle Zacheus that
same greate publicane (were he iew / or were he paynym) said / that
20 is to wit with lesse than halfe his goodes recompence euery man whom
he had wrongid iiij tymes as much / ye ye Cosyn / as mych for as mych
/ hardely / And than they shall receve it, shalbe content I dare promise
for them / to let the tother thrise as mich goo & forgive it, because it
was one of the hard poyntes of the old law / where as christen men
25 must be full of forgevyng & not vse to require & exact their amendes
to the vttermost. But now for our purpose here, not withstandyng
that he promisid not neyther to give away all / nor to becom a beggar
neyther / no nor yet to leve of his office neyther, which albeit that he
had not vsed before [f. 130ᵛ] peradventure in euery poynt so pure as
30 S Iohn the baptist had taught them the lesson: *Nihil amplius quam con-*

---

1 spirite] spririte *A*   2 wise /] / *canc. B*   4 linguam:] *colon ed.*; geverne] to gouerne *Z*
5 yet] it *A*: yet *wr. over* it *B*, yet *Z*   6–7 more &] more than *Z*   7 agayne] *divided*
ag-ayne *A*: ag *canc. and added before* ayne *B*   7–8 reprouid] v *wr. over* u *B*   8 so evill]
so *om. L 1553*   9 they] than *L 1553*; gotten /] / *canc. B*   10 office that] office, which *L*
1553 1573   12 ripe] diepe *1557*; good] goodes *L 1553 1573*   13 able] hable *1557*;
dewtie] dewtite *A*: y *wr. over* i *and* te *canc. B*   14 tother] other *1553 1573*   15 away all]
al away *1553 1573*   17 is)] *parenth. ed.*, is / *A*   18 to /] *parenth. wr. over* / *B*; able] well
able *L*, hable *1557*; did *canc. B after* Zacheus   19 iew] I *wr. over* i *B*; paynym)] *parenth.*
added B   20 wit] wete *1553*   22 shall receve] that shal receiue *Z*   23 tother]
other *1553 1573*   30 the baptist] the *om. L 1553 1573*; lesson:] *colon ed.*

stitutum est vobis faciatis: Do no more than is appoyntid vnto you /
yet for as mich as he might both laufully vse his substaunce that he
myndid to reserue, & laufully might vse his office to, in receving the
princes dewtie accordyng to christes expres commaundment: *Red-*
dite quae sunt Caesaris Caesari / Geve the Emperour those thynges that 5
be his / refusyng all extorcion and brybery beside / our lord well al-
lowyng his good purpose, & exactyng no fertherforth of hym concernyng his worldly behavour, answerid & said: *Hodie salus facta est*
huic domui, eo quod & ipse filius sit habrahae / This day is helth comen to
this house, for that he to, is the sone of Abraham.   10

But now forget I not cosyn that in effect thus far you condecendid
vnto me / that a man may be rich & yet not out of the state of grace
nor out of godes favour. Howbeit you thynke that though it may be
so in some tyme / or in some place, yet at this tyme & in this place
or eny such other like, wherin be so many pore people vppon whome 15
they be (you thinke) bounden to bestow their good, they can kepe no
riches with conscience.

Verely Cosyn if that reason wold hold, I wene the world was neuer
such any where, in which any [f. 131] man might haue kept any
substaunce without the dainger of dampnacion / As for syns Christes 20
dayes to the worldes end, we haue the witnes of his own word, that
there hath neuer lakkyd pore men nor neuer shall, for he said hymselfe: *pauperes semper habebitis vobiscum, quibus quum vultis benefacere*
potestis, pore men shall you alway haue with you, whom whan you
will you may do good vnto / So that as I tell you yf your rule shuld 25
hold / than were there I wene no place in no tyme syns christes dayes
hether / nor as I thynke in as long before that neyther / nor neuer
shall there here after, in which there wold abyde any man rich,
without the daynger of eternall dampnacion, evyn for his riches alone
though he demeaned it neuer so well / But Cosyn men of substaunce 30

---

1 faciatis:] *colon ed.*   2 substaunce] *minim lacking in* un *A*   5 the Emperour] themperour
L 1553   6 be] are *Z*   7 fertherforth] *vertical line after* ferther *B*   8 said:] *colon ed.*
9 quod &] & *om. L 1553*; habrahae] Abrahae *L 1573*, Abrahe *1553 1557*   10 sone]
bar added above o *B*   11 condecendid] s *ins. before* ce *and* id *canc. B*, condiscende *L 1553*
1573   14 in some tyme] at some time *1573*   15 wherin] where *canc. B before* wherin
16 (you thinke)] *first parenth. wr. over* / *and final parenth. added B*; kepe] therfore kepe *L*
1553 1573   17 with] with good *L 1553 1573*   21 wo *canc. A at end of line before*
worldes   22 shall,] *ed.*, shall. *B*   23 habebitis] habetis *L*   26 syns] sin *1557*
27 hether] to *added to* hether *B*, hetherto *Z*   28 wold] *canc. and* could *interl. B*, could *Z*;
abyde any man] any man abide *Z*   30 substaunce] / *canc. B after* substaunce

must there be / for els mo beggers shall you haue perdy then there
be, & no man left able to releve an nother. For this I thinke in my
mynd a very sure conclucion / that yf all the money that is in this
countrey were to morow next brought to gether out of euery mans
5 hand, & laid all vppon one hepe, and than devidid out vnto euery
man a like: it wold be on the morow after worse than it was the day
before. For I suppose whan yt were all egally thus devidid among all /
the best shuld be left litle bettre than than almost a beggar is now /
And yet he that was a begger before, all that he shall be the richer for
10 [f. 131ᵛ] that he shuld therby receyve, shall not make hym mych
above a beger still / but many one of the rich men yf their riches stode
but in moveable substans, shalbe safe inough from riches happely
for all their life after /

　　Men can not you wot well lyve here in this world, but yf that some
15 one man prouide a meane of lyvyng for some other many. Euery man
can not haue a ship of his own, nor euery man be a merchaunt without a stoke / And these thinges you wote well must nedes be had / nor
euery man can not haue a plough by hym selfe / And who ⌜might⌝ live
by the taylours crafte yf no man were able to put a gowne to make?
20 who by the masonry / or who could live a carpenter, yf no man were
able to bild neyther church nor howse? who shuld be the makers of
eny maner cloth, yf their lakyd men of substaunce to set sondry sortes
a worke / Some man that hath not two ducates in his howse, were
bettre forbere them both & leve hym selfe not a ferthing but vtterly
25 lese all his own, than that some rich man by whome he is wekely set a
worke, shuld of his money lese the tone halfe / for than were hym selfe
like to lacke worke. For surely the rich mans substaunce is the well
spring of the pore mans livyng. And therfor here wold it fare by the
pore man, as it farid by the woman in one of Esops [f. 132] fables,

---

1 there be] ther nedes be L *1553 1573*; mo beggers] *canc. and* mo beggars *interl. after* haue
B; mo beggers shall you haue] shal you haue moe beggars Ƶ　　2 For] for A: f *alt.*
to F B; I thinke] thinke I *1553 1573*　　3 conclucion] sy *wr. over last* c B　　4 *comma after*
countrey B　　7 For] for A: f *alt. to* F B; egally] equally L　　8 than] *first* than *canc.*
B, one than *om. 1553 1573*; almost a beggar] a begger almost *1553 1573*　　11 beger]
g *added before* g B; riches] richesse *1557*　　13 after /] *following this A leaves space and writes*
on same line: Men can not you wot well life, *this is then canc. A and new paragraph begun on*
next line.　　15 prouide] v *wr. over* u B　　17 stoke] k *wr. over* e B; must nedes] nedes
must *1557*　　18 might] *interl. B above canc.* my A　　20 the masonry] the *om.* L *1553 1573*
21 able] hable *1557*; the makers] the *om.* L *1553 1573*　　22 cloth] of cloth *1553 1573*
23 hath not] hath but L *1553 1573*　　24 ferthing] y *wr. over* i B　　26 tone] one *1553*
1573　　27 For] *ed.,* for A

which had an henne that laid her euery day a golden egge / till on
a day she thought she wold haue a grete many egges at ones / &
therfor she killid her henne & found but one or twayne in her bely /
so that for a few she lost many /

But now cosyn to come to your dowt, how it may be that a man 5
may with conscience kepe riches with hym, whan he seeth so many
pore men vppon whom he may bestow it / veryly that might he not
with conscience do, yf he must bestow it vppon as many as he may /
And so must of trouth euery rich man do / yf all the pore folke that
he seeth, be so specially by godes commaundment committid vnto 10
his charge alone / that because our sauiour sayth / *omni petenti te da* /
give euery man that asketh the, therfor he be bounden to give out
still to euery beggar that will aske hym, as long as any peny lasteth
in his purse / But verely cosyn that saying hath (as s   sayth
other places in scripture hath) nede of interpretacion for as saynt Aus- 15
tyn sayth   Though christ sayth
Geue euery man that asketh the / he sayth not yet, give them all that
they will aske the. But surely all were one if he ment to bind me by
commaundment to give euery man without excepcion som what / for
so shuld I leve my selfe nothyng.   20

Our saviour in that place of ⌐the¬ vj chapiter of S luke speketh [f.
132ᵛ] bothe of the contempt that we shuld in hart haue of these worldly thinges / & also of the maner that men shuld vse toward their
ennymyes / for there he biddith vs love our ennymyes / give good
wordes for evill / & not onely suffre iniuryes paciently, both by takyng 25
away of our good / & harm done vnto our body / but also be redy to
suffre the dowble, & ouer that to do them good agayne that do vs the
harm / And among these things he biddith vs give euery man that

1 her euery] her *om*. L *1553*   2 egges] of egges L *1553*   4 a few] couetise of those
fewe L *1553 1573*   12 he be bounden] he be bownd L, should he be bound *1553 1573*
14 (as] *parenth. ed.*, | *wr. over* s A; *blank space*] A L, S. Paule *1553*, saint Austine *1557*; s⟨   ⟩
sayth] *om. 1573*   14–15 hath (as . . . interpretacion] hath, as S. Paule saith, and other
places in Scripture, neede of interpretacion *1553*, hath (as saint Austine saith other places
in scripture hath) nede of interpretacion *1557*, hath (as other places in Scripture, haue) neede
of interpretation *1573*   15 other] and other *1553*; scripture hath] hath *om. 1553*, haue
1573; saynt] holy .S. Z   15–16 Austyn sayeth] *A leaves blank space of half-line and begins
new line with* Though christ, *other texts ignore blank space*: saith, Though L, saith: Though *1553
1573*, saith: though *1557*   16 christ sayth] Christ say Z   17 not] no A, t *added* B   21
vj] *superl.* th *added* B, vjᵗʰ L, sixth *1557*; of the vj chapiter] *om. 1573*; chapiter] r *added* B   24
for] f *alt. to* F B   26 away of] of *om*. L *1553 1573*; good] goodes L *1553 1573*; body] bodies
L *1553 1573*   27 ouer that] *vertical line after* ouer B; good] good | A: | canc. B

asketh / menyng that in the thing that we may conveniently do a man
good, we shuld not refuse it, what maner of man so euer he be, though
he were our mortall ennymye / namely where we se that but yf we
helpe hym our selfe, the person of the man shuld stand in perell of
5 perishing / & therfor sayth *si esurierit inimicus tuus, da illi cibum*: yf thyn
enymy be in hungre geve hym mete / But now though I be bound to
give euery maner man in some maner of his necessitie were he my
frend or my fo, christen man or hethen / yet am I not vnto all men
bound a like, nor vnto any man in euery case a like / but as I began to
10 tell you, the differences of the circumstances make greate chaunge
in the mater. Saynt paule sayth / *Qui non prouidet suis, est infidelis de-*
terior / he that prouideth not for those that are his, is worse than an
infidell / Those are ours that are [f. 133] belongyng to our charge eyther by nature or by law / or any commaundment of god / by
15 nature as our children / by law as our seruauntes in our howsehold /
so that albeit these ij sortes be not ours all a like / yet wold I thinke
that the lest ours of the twayne / that is to wit our seruauntes / yf they
nede or lake / we be bounden to loke to them & prouide for their
nede / & see so forforth as we may / that they lak not the thinges
20 that shuld serue for their necessite while they dwell in our seruice /
Me semeth also yf they fall sik in our seruice, so that they can not do
the seruice that we reteyne them for / yet may we not in any wise torn
them than out of dores / & ˹cast˺ them vp comfortles, while they be
not able to labour & helpe them selfe / for this were a thing agaynst
25 all humanite / And surely yf he were but a way faryng man that I
recevid into my house as a gest / yf he fall sik therin & his money
gonne, I reken my selfe bounden to kepe hym still / & rather to begge
about for his relefe, than cast hym out in that case to the perell of his
life / what losse so euer I shuld happe to sustayne in the kepyng of
30 hym. For whan god hath by such chaunce sent hym to me, & there

---

2 of man] a man *L*   5 therfor] there *L 1553*; sayth] sayth S. Paule. *1557 1573*;
esurierit] *Z*, esuierit *A*; cibum:] *colon ed.*   6 in hungre] an hungred *1573*; bound]
bounden *1557*   7 man] a man *L*, of man *1553 1573*   8 fo,] *colon canc. B after*
comma   9 bound] bounden *L 1557*   10 differences] difference *L 1553*   11
Saynt] saynt *A*: S *wr. over* s *B*; infidelis] infideli *Z*, s *canc. A and B*   14 by law] by *om.*
L 1553 1573   17 ours] to be ours *L 1553*; wit] wete *L 1553*   18 nede or] nede
& *Z*; lake] k *wr. over* e *B*; & prouide] and to provyde *L*   19 forforth] farforth *L 1553*
1573, farre furth *1557*; they] yᵉʸ *A*: *canc. and* they *interl. B*   21 Me] me *A*: M *wr. over*
m *B*; yf] that if *Z*   23 out of] owt a *L*   24 selfe] selvys *L*   26 revc *canc. A before*
recevid   29 happe to sustayne] take thereby *1553*; in the kepyng] the *om. 1553 1573*;
30 For] for *A*: f *alt. to* F *B*

ones matchid me with hym / ⌐I reken my self surely chargyd with
him,⌐ till I may without perell of his life be well & conveniently dischargid of hym.

By godes commaundment are in our charge our parentes / for by
nature we be in theirs sith / as / s / paule sayth / it is not the childrens 5
part to provide for the parentes, but the parentes [f. 133ᵛ] to prouide
for the children / prouide I mene conveniently good lernyng / or good
occupacions to gete their livyng by with trewth & the favour of god /
but not to make prouicion for them of such maner livyng, as to
godward they shuld live the worse for / but rather yf they se by their 10
maner that to much wold make them nought / the father shuld than
give them a greate deale the lesse / But although that nature put not
the parentes in the charge of the children / yet not onely god commaundith, but the order of nature also compellith, that the children
shuld both in reuerent behauour / honour their father & mother / 15
& also in all their necessite manteyne them / And yet as mich as god
& nature both hyndeth vs to the sustenaunce of our own father / his
neade may be so litle / though it be somewhat / and a fremde mannes
so greate / that both nature & god also wold I shuld in such vnequalle
nede, releve that vrgent necessitie of a straunger, ye my foo & goddes 20
ennymye to, the very Turke or sarecen / before a litle nede & vnlikely
to do great harm in my father & my mother to / For so ought they
both twayne them selfe to be well content I shuld /

But now Cosyn out of the case of such extreme nedes well percevid
& knowen vnto my selfe / I am not bound to geve euery begger that 25
will aske / nor to belive euery faytour that I mete in the strete that
will say hym selfe that he is very sik / nor to reken all the [f. 134]
pore folke commyttid by god onely so to my charge alone, that none
other man shuld give them nothyng of his, till I haue first given out all
myn / nor am not bounden neyther to haue so evill opynion of all 30
other folke save my selfe / as to thinke that / but yf I helpe, the pore
folke shall all fayle at ones / for god hath lefte in all this quartre no mo
good folkes now but me / I may thinke bettre by my neybours &

---

9 prouicion] v *wr. over* u, sy *wr. over* c *B*; livyng] of liuing *L 1553 1573*   13 in the charge]
the *om. 1557*   16 in all their] all *om. 1573*   18 fremde] frende *A L* (d *clarified B*),
fremd *1553 1557 1573*   19 nature & god] god & nature *1553 1573*   20 straunger,]
comma ed.   21 to,] *comma ed.*; sarecen] az *wr. over* ec *B*   22 & my mother] and in my
mother *L 1553 1573*   23 selfe] selvys *L*; shuld /] *period before* / *B*   24 nedes] nede
L 1553   25 bound] bounden *Ƶ*   31 selfe /] *comma before* / *B*; that /] / *canc. B*
33 folkes] folke *Ƶ*; neybours] neyghbour *L 1553*

worse by my selfe than so / & yet come to heven by godes grace well inough / /

Vincent

Mary vncle but some man will peradventure be right well content
5 in such case, to thinke his neybours very charitable / to thentent that he may thinke hym selfe at libertie to give nothing at all /

Antonye

That is Cosyn very trew / so will their some be content eyther to thinke or make as though they thought / but those are they that are
10 content to give nought because they be nought / But our question is Cosyn not of them / but of good folke that by the kepyng of worldly good, stand in greate feare to offend god / For the acquietyng of their conscience speke we now, to thentent that they may perceve what maner of havyng of worldly good & kepyng therof, may stand with
15 the state of grace / Now thinke I cosyn that yf a man kepe riches aboute hym for a glory & rialtie of the world, in the consideracion wherof he taketh a greate delight, & liketh hym selfe therfor / takyng the porer for the lak therof / as one farre worse than hym selfe: such a mynd is very vayne folysh pride, & such a man is very nought in dede / But on
20 the tother side / yf [f. 134ᵛ] there be a man such as wold god were many, that hath vnto riches no love / but havyng it fall habundantly vnto hym, taketh to his own parte no greate pleasure therof / but as though he had it not, kepeth him selfe in like abstynence & penaunce prively, as he wold do in case he had it not / & in such
25 thinges as he doth openly, bestow somewhat more liberally vppon hym selfe in his howse after some maner of the world / lest he shuld give other folke occasion to merveyle & muse & talke of his maner & misse report hym for an hipocryte / therin betwene god & hym doth truly protest and testifie as did the good quene hester, that he doth it

---

4 peradventure be] be paradventure *L*   5 case] cases *Z*; thentent] the entent *1553*
1573   12 good] goodes *L 1553 1573*   13 thentent] the entent *1553 1573*   14 good]
goodes *L 1553 1573*   15 riches] richesse *1557*   16 rialtie] royalty *L 1553*, ryaltie *1557*,
roialty *1573*; in the] the *om. 1553 1573*   17 therfor] the better therfore *L*, therfore the
better *1553 1573*; porer] poore *L 1553*   18 therof /] | *canc. B*   19 pride] proud *L*
1553 1573   20 tother] other *1553 1573*; god were] god ther were *Z*   21 riches]
rychesse *1557*; habundantly] abundantly *Z*   28 hipocryte] ypochryte *L*, ipocrite *1553*

not for any desire therof in the satisfiyng of his own pleasure / but
wold with as good will or bettre forbere the possession of riches, savyng
for the commoditie that other men haue by his possessing therof / as
percase in keping a good howsehold in good christen ordre & fasshion
/ & in settyng other folke aworke with such thinges as they gayne 5
ther livyng the bettre by his meanes / this mans havyng of riches I
might me thinketh in merite match in a maner, with an other mans
forsakyng of all / yf there were none other circumstaunce more plesaunt
vnto god addid ferther vnto the forsakyng beside / as percase far the
more fervent contemplacion, by reson of the sollicitude of all worldly 10
bysines left of / which was the thing that made Mary mawdeleyns
part the bettre / For els wold christ haue cannid her mich more
thanke to go about & be bisy in the helpyng her sister [f. 135] Martha
to dresse his dener, than to take her stole & sit down at her ease & do
nought /   15
    Now yf he that haue this good & riches by hym, haue not hapely
fully so perfit a mynd / but somwhat loveth to kepe hym selfe from
lacke / & not so fully as a pure christen fasshion requireth, determynid
to abandon his pleasure / well / what will you more / the man is so
much the lesse perfitt than I wold he were, and happely than hym 20
selfe wold wish if it were as easy to be it / as to whysh it / but yet not
by & by in state of dampnacion for all that / no more than euery
man is forthwith in state of dampnacion, that forsakyng all & entryng
into religion / ys not yet allway so clere depurid from all worldly affeccions / as he hym selfe wold very fayne he were and mych bewayleth 25
that he is not / of whom some man that hath in the world willyngly
forsaken the likelyhed of right worshipfull romes / hath afterward
had mich a do / to kepe hym selfe from the desire of thoffice of cellerer
or sexten / to bere ⌐yet⌐ at the lest wise some rule and aucthoryte though
it were but among the belles / But god is more mercifull to mannes 30

---

3 possessing] dysposing Z 4 keping] keping of L *1553 1573*   5 thinges] thing *1553*
6 livyng] lil *canc. before* livyng A   8 circumstaunce] circumstaunces L *1553 1573*;
plesaunt] *superfluous superl.* a *wr. above* un A   9 addid ferther] farther added L *1553
1573*; far] for Z 13 in the helpyng] the *om.* L *1553 1573*   14 dener] y *wr. over first* e B
15 nought /] *period before* | B   16 riches] rychesse *1557*   17 a mynd] a *om. 1553 1573*
18 lacke /] | *wr. over comma* B   21 selfe] *om.* L; whysh] *canc. and* wyssh *interl.* B   22 by
& by] by an by L; in state] in the state L *1553*; for all that] *om.* L *1553 1573*; than]
than he L *1553 1573*   22–23 euery man is forthwith in state of dampnacion] *om.* L
1553 1573   24 clere] clerely L   25 as he] he *om.* Z 27 likelyhed] likelihode Z
28 thoffice] the office Z 29 yet] it A: *canc. and* yet *interl.* B, yet Z

imperfection / yf the man know it & knolege it & misse like it / & litle
& litle labour to amend it / than to reiect & cast to the devill, hym that
after as his frayltie can bere & suffre / hath a generall entent & purpose to please hym, & to preferre or set by nothing in all this world
5 before hym / And therfor Cosyn to make an end of this pece with all /
A negocio perambulante in tenebris, of this devill I [f. 135ᵛ] meane / that
the prophet calleth besynes walkyng in the darknesses / yf a man
haue a mynd to serue god & please hym, & rather lese all the good
he hath / than wittyngly to do deddly synne, & wold without mur-
10 mur or gruge give it euery whitt away in case that god shuld so commaund hym, & intend to take it paciently / yf god wold take it from
hym, & glad wold be to vse it vnto godes pleasure, & do his diligence
to know & to be taught what maner vsing therof god wold be pleasid
with, & therin fro tyme to tyme be glad to folow the counsayle of
15 good vertuouse men: though he neyther give away all at ones nor give
euery man that asketh hym neyther / Let euery man fere and thynke
in this world that all the good that he doth or can do is a greate deale
to litle but yet for all that fere / let hym dwell therwith in the faythfull
hope of godes helpe / and than shall the trouth of god so compas
20 hym about (as the prophet sayth) with a pavice / that he shall not so
nede to drede the traynes of & the temptacions of the devill, that the
prophet calleth bysynes walkyng about in the darknesses / but that he
shall for all the havyng of riches & worldly substaunce, so avoyd
his traynes & his temptacions, that he shall in conclucion by the
25 greate grace & almightie mercie of god, gete into hevyn well inough /
And now was I Cosyn about lo after this piece thus endid, to bidd them
bring in our dener / but now shall I not nede lo / for here thei come
with it all redy / [f. 136]

Vincent

30 Forsoth good vncle god disposeth & tymeth your mater & your
dener both I trust / For thend of your good tale (for which our lord

---

2 amend] mend *L 1557;* cast to] of *wr.* over to *and to interl.* B, cast of *L 1553 1573,* caste
of to *1557;* the devill] *om. L 1553 1573*   7 darknesses] darknes *1553 1573*   9 to do]
to *om.* Ƶ   10 gruge] d *interl. after* u B   14 fro] from *L 1553 1573*   15 men] folke *L;*
all *canc. A? before* away   20 sayth)] *parenth. added* B   21 traynes of] of *canc. B?, om.*
Ƶ; & the] the *om. L;* the devill] this deuil Ƶ   24 & his] his *om. L;* conclucion] sy *wr.*
over last c B   25 grace] *om. L 1553 1573*   27 bring] to bringe *1553;* dener] y *wr. over*
first e B; thei] yᵉⁱ A: *canc.* and they *interl.* B; thei come] com they *L*   31 dener] y *wr.*
over first e B; thend] the end *1553 1573;* (for] *parenth ed.,* / for A

reward you) and the begynnyng here of your good dener to (from which it were more than pitie that you shuld any lenger haue taried) mete evyn at the close to gether /

Antonye

Well Cosyn now will we say grace / & than for a while wyll we 5
leve talkyng / & assay how our dener shall leke vs, & how fayre we can fall to fedyng / which done, you know my custumable guise (for maner I may not call it / because the guise is vnmanerly) to bid you not fare well / but stele away fro you to slepe / But you wote well I am not wont at after none to slepe long / but evyn a litle to forget the 10
worlde / and whan I wake, I will agayne come to you / & than is / god willyng all this long day ours / wherin we shall haue tyme inough to talke much more than shall suffice for the fynishyng of this one part of our mater, which onely now remayneth /

Vincent   15

I pray you good vncle kepe your custumable maner / for maner may you call it well inough / for as it were agaynst good maner to loke that a man shuld knele doune for curtesye whan his knee is sore : so is it very good maner that a man of your age, agrevid with such [f. 136ᵛ] sundry siknesses beside, that suffre you not alway to slepe 20
whan you shuld / let this slepe not slypp away but take it when you may / And I will vncle in the meane while stele from you to, & spede a litle erand & retourne to you agayne.

Antonye

Tary while you will / & whan you haue dinyd goo at your pleasure / 25
but I pray you tarry not long.

Vincent

You shall not nede vncle to put me in mynd of that / I wold so fayne haue vpp the remenaunt of our mater /

---

1 dener] y *wr. over first* e B; (from] *comma added and then parenth wr. over comma* B   5 wyll]
y *wr. over* e A   6 dener] y *wr. over first* e B; shall] hall A, s *added* B; leke] lyke L *1557*,
like *1553 1573*   8 vnmanerly)] *parenth.* *1557 1573, no parenth.* A   9 fro] from Ƶ
12 tyme] *divided* ty-me A : me *canc. and added after* ty B   13 talke] take *1557*; much more]
much *om.* L *1553 1573*   20 / *canc.* B *after* siknesses   21 not *canc.* B? *after* let   21–22
you may] he maye Ƶ   28 mynd *canc.* A *after* not; me] *om.* L

The third boke & the last
of consolacion and comfort
in tribulacion

Vincent

5   Somwhat haue I taried the lenger vncle / partly for that I was loth
to come ouer sone / lest my sone comyng might haue happid to haue
made you wake to sone / but specially by reason that I was lettid with
one that shewid me a lettre datid at Constantinople / by which lettre
[f. 137] it apperith that the greate Turke preparith a mervelouse
10 mighty army / And iet whether he will therwith / that can there yet
no man tell / But I fere in good fayth vncle that his vyage shalbe
hyther / How be it he that wrote the lettre, sayth that it is secretly
said in Constantinople that great part of his army shalbe shippid &
sent either into Naples or into Cicile.

15   Anthonye

    It may fortune Cosyn that the lettre of the venetian datid at Con-
stantinople, was devisid at venice / from thens come there some
among, & some tyme fro Rome to / & sometyme also fro some other
places letters all farcid full of such tydynges / that the Turke is redy
20 to do some greate exployt / which tydynges they blow aboutte for the
furderaunce of some such affayres as they then haue them selfe in
hand.
    The Turke hath also so many men of armes in his retynue at his
contynuall charge, that lest they shuld lye styll & do nothyng / but
25 peradventure fall in devysyng of some newelties among them selfe /
he is fayne yerely to make ⌐some¬ assemblies, & some chaungyng
of them from one place vnto a nother / & parte some sorte [f. 137ᵛ]

---

1 boke] om. *1573*; & the last] AND LAST BOOKE *1573*   5 lenger] longer *1553 1573*
7 by reason] by the reason *1553 1557 1573*; that I] that om. L *1553*   10 iet] y *wr. over* i B
11 in] *interl.* A   14 Cicile] *1553 1557*, Cycylye L, Cicilie *1573*, Cilile A   18 fro Rome]
from Rome L *1553 1573*; also fro] also from L *1553 1573*; some other] some om. *1553 1573*
19 Turke] greate Turcke L   21 furderaunce] fartherance L *1553*, furtherance *1557*
1573; then] *orig.* them: m *alt. to* n A; selfe th *canc.* A *before* haue; selfe] selvys L
25 newelties] noveltyes L, nouelties *1553 1573*; selfe] selvys L   26 assemblies] assembles
1557

a sondre, that they wax not ouer well acquayntid by dwellyng ouer
long together /

By these wayes also he makyth those that he myndeth sodaynly to
envade indede / the lesse to loke therfor / & therby the lesse preparacion to make before / while they see hym so many tymes make a 5
greate visage of warre / whan he myndeth it not / But than at one tyme
or other, thcy sodenly fele it whan they fere yt not.

Howbeit full likely Cosyn it is of very trouth, that into this realme
of Hungary he will not fayle to come / for neyther is there any countrey thorow Christendome that lieth for hym so mete / nor neuer was 10
there any tyme till now in which he myght so well & surely wynne
it.

For now call we hym in our selfe (god save vs) as Esope tellith that
the shepe toke in the wolfe vnto them to kepe them fro the dogges.

Vincent 15

Than are there very like good vncle all those tribulacions to fall
vppon vs here, that I spake of in the begynnyng of our first communicacion here the tother day / [f. 138]

Anthonye

Very trouth it is Cosyn that so there will of likelyhed in a while / 20
but not forthwith all at the first / For while he commeth vnder the
colour of ayd for the tone agaynst the tother / he will somwhat see the
profe before he fully shew hym selfe / But in conclucion yf he be hable
to get it for hym / you shall se hym so handle it / that he shall not fayle
to gete it from hym, & that forthwith out of hand ere euer he suffre 25
hym setle hymselfe ouer sure therin.

Vincent

Yet say they vncle that he vseth not to force any man to forsake
his fayth /

---

6 visage] Z, viage A: *see note*   13 vs)] *parenth. wr. over* | B 14 fro] from L *1553 1573*
16 those] these *1553 1573*   18 tother] other *1553 1573*   20 likelyhed] likelihod L
1553 1573, lykelyhoode *1557*   22 tone] one *1553 1573*; tother] other *1553 1573*
23 conclucion] sy *wr. over last* c B; hable] h *canc.* B, able Z 25 ere] or *1553*

Anthonye

Not any man Cosyn / they say more than they can make good that tell you so / He maketh a solempne othe among the ceremonyes of the fest in which he first taketh vppon hym his aucthorite / that he shall 5 in all that he possible may, minysh the fayth of Christ, & dilate the fayth of Mahumet / But yet hath he not vsid to force euery whole countrey at ones to forsake their fayth / for of some countreyes hath he bene [f. 138ᵛ] content onely to take a tribute yerely, & let them than live as they lyst.

10   Out of some he taketh the whole people away / disparsyng them for slaves among many sundry countreyes of his very far fro their own, without any sufferaunce of regresse.

Some Countrey so great & populose that they can not well be caryed & conveyd thens / he destroyeth the gentill men, & giveth 15 the landes, part to such as he bringeth / & part to such as willyngly will reney their fayth / and kepeth the tother in such misery, that they were in maner as good be ded at ones / In rest he suffreth els no christen man almost / but those that resort as merchauntes / or those that offre them selfe to serue hym in his warre /

20   But as for those christen countreyes that he vseth not for onely tributaries / as he doth Chio Cipris or candy / but rekenith for clere conquest & vtterly taketh for his own / as morea Grece & Macedonye, & such other like ⌈& as I verely think, he will Hungary if he get it⌉ / in all those vseth he christen people after sundry fasshions / he 25 lettith them dwell there in dede, because they were to many to cary all away, & to many [f. 139] to kyll them all to / but if he shuld either leve the land dispepled & desolate / or els some other countreys of his own from whens he shuld (which wold not well be done) convey the people thether / to peple that land withall /

30   There lo those that will not be turnyd fro theyr faith, of which

---

3 He] *ed.*, he *A*   3–4 the fest] that feast *Ƶ*   5 possible] possibly *1573*   6 Mahumet] Machomett *L*, Machomet *1553 1573*, Mahomet *1557*   8 *comma after* onely *B*   9 than live] liue than *L 1553 1573*; lyst] lust *1553*   11 fro] from *L 1553 1573*   12 regresse] *orig.* redresse?: d? *alt. to* g *A?*   13 *middle stop? after* Countrey *B*   14 thens /] *comma before* / *B*   15 the landes] their landes *L 1553 1573*; such] such / *A*: / *canc. B*   16 reney] *canc.* and renye *interl. B*; tother] other *1553 1573*   17 be ded] to be dead *1553 1573*   19 selfe] selvys *L*   20 for onely] onely for *L*   22 morea] M *wr. over* m *B*   23 of *canc. B before* if   27 his] *interl. A above canc.* their   28 done)] *parenth. added B*   30 fro] from *L 1553 1573*

god kepeth (lawdid be his holy name) very many he suffreth to dwell
styll in peace / but yet is there peace for all that not very pesable /
For landes he suffreth them to haue none of their own / office or
honest rome they bere none / with occasions of his warres he pilleth
them with taxis & tallages vnto the bare bonys / Their children he 5
choseth where he list in their vth & taketh them fro their parentes,
conveyyng them whither he list where theire frendes neuer see them
after, & abuseth them as he lyst / some yong maydens maketh har-
lottes / some yong men he bryngeth vpp in warre, & some yong
children he causeth to be geldid / not their stones cut out as the 10
custome was of old / but cutteth of their whole membres by the body /
how few scape & live he litle forceth / for he will haue inough. And
all that he so taketh yong to any vse of his own, are betaken [f. 139^v]
to such Turkes or false Renegates to kepe, that they be turnid fro the
fayth of christ euery chone / or els so handlid that as for this worlde 15
they come to an evill cheving / For by side many other contumelies &
dispightes that the Turkes & the false renegate christyens many tymes
do to good christen people that still perseuer & abyde by the fayth /
they fynd the meane some tyme to make some false shrewis say / that
they hard such a christen man speke obprobrious wordes agaynst 20
Mahumete. And vppon that poynt falsely testified, will they take
occasion to compell hym forsake the fayth of christ, & turne to the
profession of their shamfull supersticiouse sect / or els will they put
hym vnto deth with cruel intolerable tormentes.

Vincent   25

Our Lord vncle for his mightie mercie, kepe those wrechis hens /
For by my trouth yf they happe to come hether, me thinke I se many
mo tokens than one, that we shall haue of our own folke here redy to

---

1 lawdid be] Z, lawdid by A; name)] *parenth. 1553 1557 1573*, name / A, B adds *parenth.
after many   2 is *canc. A before* yet; there] i *interl. before* r B; pesable] pesably A: e *wr.
over* y B, peacible Z 5 bare] a *wr. over* e A?   6 list].lust *1553*; vth] *canc. and* youth
interl. B; fro] from L *1553 1573*   7 list] lust *1553*   8 lyst] lust *1553*; maketh] he
maketh *1573*   12 inough.] w *wr. over* u *and* gh *canc.* B, *period ed.*; *second that canc. before
he* B 14 to such] vnto such Z; for *canc. A before* fro; fro] from L *1553 1573*   15 worlde]
worldle A: le *canc.* B 20 obprobrious] opprobrious *1553 1573*   21 Mahumete] Machomett L, Machomet *1553 1573*, Mahomet *1557*   22 turne to] turne vnto L *1553 1573*
24 vnto deth] to death L *1553 1573*; intolo^r *canc. A before* intolerable   26 mightie]
might L 28 mo] *orig. no*: n *alt. to* m A?

fall in vnto them / For like as before a greate storm, the see begynneth
⌜sometyme⌝ to worke & rore in hym selfe ere euer the wynd waxeth
boystuouse / so my thinke I here at myn eare some of our owne here a-
mong vs, which with ⌜in⌝ these few yeres could no more haue [f. 140]
5 born the name of a Turke than the name of the devill, begyn now to
fynd litle faute therin / ye and some to prayse them to, litle & litle as
they may / more glad to fynd fawtes at euery state of christendome,
prestes, princes / rites / ceremonies / sacramentes laues and custumes
spirituall temporall & all.

10   Anthonye

In good fayth Cosyn so begynne we to fare here in dede / & that
but evyn now of late / For sinnes the title of the crowne hath comen
in question, the good rule of this realme hath very sore decayed / as
litle while as it is / And vndowtidly Hungary shall neuer do well, as
15 long as it standeth in this case / that mens myndes harken after newelties, & haue their hartes hangyng vppon a chaunge / And much the
worse I like it, whan their wordes walke so large toward the favour of
the Turkes sect / which they were euer wont to haue in so greate a-
bomynacion, as euery trew myndid christen man & christen woman
20 to must haue.

I am of such age as you see / & verely from as farre as I can remember, it hath bene markyd & often tyme provid trew, that whan
children haue in Bowda fallen in a fantasye by them selfe to draw
together, & in their [f. 140ᵛ] playing make as it were corsis caried to
25 church / and sing after their childish fasshion the tewne of the dirige,
there hath greate deth there shortly folowid after / And twyse or thrise
I may remembre in my dayes, whan children in diuers partes of this
realme haue gatherid them selfe in sundry companyes, & made as it
were parties & batayles / & after their batayls in sport wherin some
30 children haue yet taken grete hurt, there hath fallen very batayle &
dedely warr in dede.

These tokens were somwhat like your ensample of the see / sith they

---

2 hym selfe] it selfe *Z*; wynd] windes *1557 1573*; waxeth] waxe *Z*   5 the devill] a deuill
L 1553 1573   8 laues] w *wr. over* u *B*   9 spirituall] spīall? *A*, ua *wr. over* ia? *B*,
spirituall and *L 1553 1573*   12 hath] haue *A*: th *wr. over* ue *B*, hath *Z*; comen] come
L 1553 1573   15–16 newelties] nouelties *L 1553 1573*, neweltie *1557*   22 often tyme]
tyme *om. Z*   23 fantasye] fansye *L*; selfe] selvys *L*   28 selfe] selvys *L*   31 dedely]
very deadly *L 1553 1573*

be of thinges that after folow tokyns foregoyng, thorow some secret
mocion or instinct, wherof the cause is vnknowen. But by S mary
Cosyn these tokens like I mych worse / these tokens I say / not of
childrens playes / nor of childrens songes / but old shrewes large open
wordes, so boldly spoken in the favour of Machometes sect in this 5
realme of Hungary, that hath bene euer hetherto a very sure kay of
christendome / And out of dout yf Hungary be lost, & that the
Turke haue it ones fast in his possession / he shall ere yt be long after,
haue an open redy way into almost the remenaunt of all christendome, though he wynne it not all in a weke / the greate part wilbe 10
wonne after I fere me within very few yeres / [f. 141]

Vincent

But yet euer more I trust in Christ good vncle, that he shall not
suffre that abhomynable sect of his mortall ennymyes, in such wise
to prevayle agaynst his christen countrey.   15

Anthony

That is very well said Cosyn / Let vs haue our sure hope in hym /
and than shall we be very sure, that we shall not be deceyvid / for
eyther shall we haue the thyng that we hope for, or a better thyng in
the stede / for as for the thyng it selfe that we pray for, & hope to haue: 20
god will not alway send vs / And therfor as I said in our first communycacion, in all thing save onely for hevyn, our prayour nor our
hope may neuer be to precise, although the thing be leifull to require /

Verely yf we peple of the christen nations, were such as wold god
we were: I wold litle fere all the preparacions that the great Turke 25
could make. No nor yet ⌐beyng¬ as bad as we be, I nothyng dowt at
al, but that in conclucion how bace so euer christendom be brought,
it shall spring vp agayne till the tyme be come very nere to the day
of dome / wher of some tokens as me thinketh are not comen yet /
But som [f. 141ᵛ] what before that tyme shall christendome be straytid 30
sore, & brought into so narrow a compas, that according to christes
wordes / *Filius hominis quum venerit putas inueniet fidem in terra / /* Whan

---

2 vnknowen.] *period ed.*   4 but old] but of old *L*   5 boldly] d *wr. over* l *A*   15 coun-
trey] countreyes *Z*; *flourish after* countrey *A*   22 hevyn] *interl. A above canc.* givyng
27 that] th *wr. over* m *A*   29 comen] come *L 1553 1573*   31 to] vnto *1553 1573*
32 quum] *om. 1557 1573*; venerit] veniens *1557 1573*; terra / /] *question-mark ins. before* / / *B*

the sonne of man shall come agayne, that is to wit to the day of generall iudgement, wenest thow that he shall fynd fayth in the erth / as who say but a litle / for as apperith in thapocalips & other places of scripture, the fayth shalbe at that tyme so far vaded that he shall for the
5 love of his electes, lest they shuld fall & perish to, abbredge those dayes, & accelerate his comyng.

But as I say me thinketh I mysse yet in my mynde, some of those tokens, that shall by the scripture come a good while before that / and among other, the comyng in of the iewes, & the delatyng of
10 christendome agayne before the world come to that strayght / So that I saye for myn own mynd, I litle dout / but that this vngraciouse sect of Machomete, shall haue a foule fall, & christendome spryng and sprede, floure and increace agayne / How be yt the pleasure and the comfort shall they see, that shalbe born after that we be beryed / I
15 fere me both twayne / For god giveth vs greate lykelyhed, that for our sinfull wrechid lyvyng, he [f. 142] goeth about to make these infidelys that are his open professid enymyes, the sorowfull scourge of correccion, ouer evill christen people that ⌐shuld be⌐ faythfull, & are of trouth his falsely professid frendes. And surely cosyn, albeit that me
20 thinketh I see diuers evill tokens of this mysery comyng to vs / yet can there not in my mynd be a worse pronosticacion therof ⌐than⌐ this vngraciouse token, that you note here your selfe / For vndowtedly cosyn this new maner here of mens favorable fasshion in their language toward these vngraciouse Turkes / declareth playnely, that
25 not onely their myndes give them that hether in shall he come / but also that they can be content both to live vnder hym, & ouer that, fro the trew fayth of christ, to fall into machometes false abomynable secte /

---

2 iudgement] *divided* iud-gem^t *A: canc. and* iugement, *interl. B* (*comma before* wenest *canc. B*); erth /] *question-mark ins. before* / *B*   3 thapocalips] the Apocalyppes *L 1553 1573*   4 the fayth] he sayth *1553*; vaded] *canc. and* fadyd, *interl. B,* faded *Z*   7 thinketh] thnketh *A,* thinke *L 1553 1573*   9 comyng in of] in *om. 1573;* iewes] I *wr. over* i *B;* delatyng] dilating *Z*   10 come to] come vnto *1553*   11 myn] my *1553;* dout /] / *canc. B;* but that this] that *om. 1557;* Machomete] h *wr. over* o *A*   13 the pleasure] that pleasure *1573* 14 the comfort] the *om. L 1553 1573;* beryed /] / *canc. B*   15 lykelyhed] likelihode *L 1553 1573,* likelyhoode *1557*   16 goeth] *catchword 141ᵛ,* goth *A, with* e *interl. B before* t; these] those *L*   17 scourge] *interl. B above heavily canc. and corrected* sco--ge   18 shuld be] *interl. B above canc.* shulbe *A*   18-19 are of trouth] of truth are *L 1553 1573* 21 pronosticacion] prognosticacion *Z*   25 give] geueth *1553 1573*   26 *middle stop after* content *B*   27 fro] from *L 1553*

Vincent

Verely myn vncle as I go more about than you: so must I nedes
more here / which is an hevy heryng in myn eare, the maner of men
in this mater, which encreasith about vs here / I trust in other places
of this realme ⌐by goddes grace⌐ it is other wise / but in this quarter 5
here about vs, many of thes felowes that are mete for the warre, first
were wont as it were in sport / & in a while after halfe betwene game
& ernest / & by our lady now not far from fayre flatt ernest in dede,
talke as though they loked for a day whan with a turne vnto the
Turkes fayth, they shulbe made [f. 142ᵛ] maisters here, of trew 10
christen mennys bodies, & owners of all their goodes /

Antonye

Though I go litle abrode Cosyn, yet here I sometyme whan I say
litle almost as mich as that / But while there is noman to complayne
to for the redresse: what remedy but paciencc, & fayne to sit still & 15
hold my peace / For of these two that strive whyther of thcm both shall
raygne vppon vs, & ech of them calleth hym selfe kyng / & both
twayne put the people to payne / the tone is you wote well to farre
from our quarter here to help vs in this behalfe / And the tother while
he loketh for the Turkes ayd / either will not or I wene well dare not / 20
fynd any faute with them that favour the Turke & his sect / For of
Turkes naturall this countrey lakketh none now, which are here
conuersaunt vnder diuers pretextes, & of euery thing aduertise the
greate Turke full surely / And therfor Cosyn, albeit I wold advise
cuery man pray still & call vnto god ⌐to hold⌐ his graciouse hand 25
ouer vs, & kepe away this wrechidnes yf his pleasure be / yet wold I
ferther advise euery good christen body, to remembre & consider,
that it is very likely to come, & therfor make his rekenyng & cast his
peny worthes before / & euery man & euery woman both, appoynt
with goddes helpe in their own mynd beforehand / what thyng they 30
intend to do yf the very worst fall. [f. 143]

---

2 myn] my *1553 1573*   2–3 nedes more here] more heare nedes *L 1553*   3 myn] my
L 1553 1573   7 sport /] / *canc. and comma added B*   10 Turkes] Turke his *1553*; shulbe]
d *ins. after* l B, should be *Ӡ*   14 almost as mich as that] as much as that almost *L 1553*
18 tone] one *1553 1573*   19 tother] other *1553 1573*   20 I wene well dare not] well
dare not I wene *L 1553 1573*   24 albeit] albeit that *Ӡ*   25 god ... hand] god his
graciouse to hold his hand *A*: to hold his *canc. B*   29 before /] / *wr. over comma B*; both]
om. L 1553 1573   30 beforehand /] *comma before* / *B*

Whither a man shuld cast in his mynd and
appoynt in his hart before, that yf he were taken
with Turkes, he wold rather dye than forsake the fayth /

The first chapiter

5   Vincent

Well fare your hart good vncle, for this good counsayle of yours /
For surely me thinketh that this is mervelouse good. But yet hard **I**
ones, a right connyng & a very good man saye / That it were greate
folye & very perilouse to, that a man shuld thinke vppon any such
10 thyng, for fere of dowble perell that may folow theruppon / for either
shall he be likely to answere hym selfe to that case put by hym selfe,
that he will rather suffre any paynfull deth than forsake his fayth, &
by that bold appoyntment shuld he fall in the fawte of saynt Peter /
that of ouersight made a proud promise & sone had a fowle fall / or
15 els were he likely to thynke, that rather than abyde the payne / he
wold forsake god in dede / & by that mynd shuld sinne dedly thorow
his own folye where as he nedeth not / as he that shall peradventure
neuer come in the perell to be put therunto. And that therfor it were
most wisedome, neuer to thinke vppon any such maner case.

20   Anthonye [f. 143ᵛ]

I beleve well Cosyn that you haue hard some man that wold so
saye / For I can shew almost as much as that, left of a very good man
& a greate solempne doctour in writyng / But yet Cosyn allthough **I**
shuld happe to fynd one or two mo as good men & as well lernid to,
25 that wold both twayne say and wryte the same / yet wold **I** not fere
for my part to counsayle my frend to the contrary / for Cosyn yf his
mynd answere hym as S. peter answerid christ / that he wold rather
dye than forsake hym: though he say therin more vnto hymselfe than
he shuld be peradventure able to make good if it came to the poynt /

---

3 forsake] sake *interl. A*   4 first] i *1557*; *flourish after* chapiter *A*   7 But] but *A*: B *wr.*
over b *B*   8 saye /] | *canc. and comma added* B; That] T *canc. and* t *ins.* B   10 thyng,
for] thing, or imagine any such case in his mynd for *Z*   13 Peter /] | *canc. and comma
added* B   14 proud] w *wr. over* u B, *then word canc. and* prowd *interl.* B; *period wr. over*
| *B*   16 shuld sinne] should he synne *Z*   22 very good] very *om.* L *1553 1573*   27
wold] wil *Z*

yet perceve I not that he doth in that thought, eny dedely displeasure
vnto god / nor S. peter though he said more than he cold performe /
yet in his so sayng offendid not god gretly neyther / But his offence
was, whan he did not after, so well as he said before / But now may
this man be likely neuer to fall in the perell of brekyng that appoynt- 5
ment / sith of some tenne thowsand that so shall examyne themselfe,
neuer one shall fall in the perell / and yet to haue that good purpose
all their life, semeth me no more harm the while / than a pore beggar
that hath neuer a peny / to thinke that yf he had greate substaunce,
he wold give grete almes for goddes sake. 10

But now is all the perell / yf the man answere hymselfe, that he wold
in such case rather forsake the fayth of christ with his mouth, & kepe
it still in his hart / than for the confessyng [f. 144] of it, to endure a
paynfull deth / for by this mynd he falleth in dedly synne, while he
ncuer cometh in the case in dede / yf he neuer had put hym selfe the 15
case, he neuer had fallen in / But in good fayth me thinketh that he
which vppon that case put vnto hym selfe by hym selfe, will make
hym selfe that answere / hath the habit of fayth so faynt & so cold,
that to the bettre knolege of hym selfe & of his necessite, to pray
for more strenghth of grace he had nede to haue the question put 20
hym either by hym selfe or some other man. Besides this, to
counsayle a man neuer to thinke on that case, is in my mynd as much
reason / as the medicyne that I haue hard taught one for the toth
ache, to go thrise about a chirchyard / & neuer thynke on a fox tayle /
For yf the counsayle be not given them / yt can not serue them / and 25
yf it be gyven them, it must put the poynt of the mater in their mynd /
which by and by to reiect & thinke therin neyther one thyng nor
other / is a thyng that may be sonner bidden than obeyid.

I wene also that very few men can escape yt / but that though they
wold neuer thinke theron by them selfe / but that yet in one place or 30
other where they shall hap to come in companye, they shall haue the

---

2 cold performe] performe *canc. and* performe: *interl.* B, did perfourme *1573*   6 sith
of some] of *om. 1557*   7 perell /] / *canc. and period added* B; and] a *alt. to* A B   8 while /]
/ *canc. and comma added* B   10 almes] almose *1553 1557 1573*   14 he falleth] falleth
he L *1553 1573*; while] which while Z   15 neuer] *interl.* A; dede /] / *wr. over comma* B
16 fallen in] fal in *1553*   22 that case] the case *1573*; *erron. caret canc.* A? *after* case; in
my mynd] *interl.* A   23 reason /] / *canc. and comma added* B   24 chirchyard] chirch-
ayrd A; on a] vpon a L *1553 1573*   25 serue] v *wr. over* u B   26 the poynt] that
point *1573*   27–28 nor other] or other *1553 1573*   28 sonner] *alt. by* B *to* soner, *then
canc. and* soner *interl.* B   30 but that yet] but that *om. 1557 1573*

question by adventure so proponid & put forth / that like as while he
hereth one talkyng to hym, he may well wynke yf he will / but he
cannot make hym selfe slepe / so shall he whether he will or no, thinke
one thyng or other there in.

5   Fynally whan christ spake so often & so playne of the mater, that
euery man shuld vppon payne of dampnacion, openly confesse his
fayth, yf men toke hym & by drede of deth wold [f. 144ᵛ] drive hym
to the contrary / it semeth me in a maner implied therin, that we be
bounden condicionally to haue euermore that mynd actually some
10 tyme, & euermore habitually, that yf the case so shuld fall, than
with goddes helpe so we wold / And thus mich thinketh me necessarye for euery man and woman, to be alway of this mynd, and often
to thinke theruppon / & where they fynd in the thynkyng theron,
their hartes agrice, & shrynke in the remembraunce of the payne
15 that their imaginacion representith to the mynd / than must they
call to mynd & remembre, the greate payne & torment that christ
suffred for them, and hartely pray for grace / that yf the case shuld so
fall, god shuld give them strength to stand / And thus with exercise
of such medytacion, though men shuld neuer stand full out of feare
20 of fallyng / yet must they percever in good hope / & in full purpose of
standyng / And this semeth me cosyn so ferforth the mynd that euery
christen man and woman must nedes haue, that me thinketh euery
curat shuld often counsayle all his parishons, and euery man & woman
their seruauntes & their children, evyn begynnyng in their tender
25 youth, to know this poynt and thinke theron, and litle & litle fro their
very childhed, to accustume them dulcely & plesauntly in the meditacion therof / wherby the goodnes of god shall not fayle so to asspire
the grace of his holy sprite into their hartes, in reward of that vertuose
diligence, that thorow such actuall meditacion he shall conserue them
30 in such a sure habit of spirituall faythfull strength, that all the devilles
in hell with all the wrestlyng that they can make, shall neuer be hable
to wrest it out of their hart /

---

2 will /] | canc. and comma added B   6 man] interl. A; dampnacion canc. A before payne
9 bounden] bound L 1553 1573   22 thinketh euery] thinketh that euery 1553 1573
23 parishons] parishions 1553, parishioners 1573   25 and thinke] and to thinke Z; fro]
from L   26 childhed] childhode L 1553 1573, childhoode 1557   28 sprite] spirite Z
29 conserue] v wr. over u B, then word canc. and confyrme interl. B, confirme Z   31 hable]
able Z   32 hart] hartes L

Vincent

By my trouth vncle me thinketh that you say very well. [f. 145]

Antonye

I say surely Cosyn as I thinke / and yet all this haue I said, con-
cernyng them that dwell in such places, as they be neuer like in their 5
lives to come in the daynger to be put to the profe / How be yt
many a man may wene hym selfe far therefro / that yet may fortune
by some one chaunce or other / to fall in the case / ⌐that eyther for
the trouth of fayth, or for the trouth of Iustice, which go almost all
alyke, he may fall in the case.⌐ But now be you & I Cosyn and all 10
our frendes here far in an other poynt / For we be so likely to fall in
thexperience therof so sone / that it had bene more tyme for vs all
other thinges set a side / to haue devisid vppon this mater, & fermly
to haue setlid our selfe vppon a fast poynt long ago / than to begynne
to comen & counsayle vppon yt now /   15

Vincent

In good fayth vncle you say therin very trouth / & wold god it had
come soner in my mynd / But bettre is it ⌐yet⌐ late than neuer / And I
trust god shall yet give vs respite and tyme / wherof vncle that we
lese no part, I pray you procede now with your good counsayle therin. 20

Antonye

Very gladly Cosyn shall I now go forth in the fourth temptacion,
which onely remayneth to be treatid of, & properly perteynyth whole
vnto this present purpose /

---

2 thinketh that you] that om. L *1553 1573*   7 far] farther *1553 1573*; therefro] fro *1553*
9 all] om. L *1553 1573*   12 thexperience] the experience *1553 1573*   14 fast]
stedfast *1553*   15 to comen] and comme L, to common *1553 1557 1573*   17 good]
God *1553*   18 is it] it om. L *1553 1573*

Of the fourth temptacion which is persecucion for
the fayth, towchid in these wordes of the prophet / *Ab*
incursu & demonio meridiano / /

The second chapiter

5   The fourth temptacion Cosyn that the prophet speketh of in the
fore remembrid psalme, *Qui habitat in adiutorio altissimi* &c ys playne
open persecucion / which is touchid in these wordes / *Ab incursu & de-*
monio meridiano / And of all his temptacions this is the most perilouse,
the most bittre sharpe, & the most rigorouse / For where as in other
10 temptacions, he vseth either pleasaunt allectives vnto [f. 145ᵛ] synne /
or eyther secret sleightes & traynes / & cometh in the night, & stelith
on in the darke vnware / or in some other part of the day flyeth &
passeth by like an arrow / so shapyng hymselfe some time in one
fasshion sometyme in an other / & so dissimulyng hymselfe & his
15 high mortall malice, that a man is therby so blyndid & bygilid, that
he may not some tyme perceve well what he is / in this temptacion
this playne open persecusion for the fayth / he cometh evyn in the
very mydd day / that is to witt evyn vppon them that haue an high
light of fayth shynyng in their hart, & ⌐openly⌐ suffreth hym selfe
20 so playnely be percevid by his fierce maliciouse persecucion agaynst
the faythfull christiens for hatrid of christes trew catholike fayth /
that no man havyng fayth, can doute what he is / for in this temptacion he shewith hymselfe such as the prophet nameth hym, *Demonium*
meridianum / the mydday devill / he may be so lightsomely seen with
25 the yie of a faythfull soule by his fierce furyouse assawt & incurcion /
for therfor sayth the prophet, that the trouth of god shall compasse
that man round about / that dwellith in the faythfull hope of his
helpe / with a pavice *Ab incursu & demonio meridiano* from the incursion
& the devill of the mydday / because this kynd of persecucion is not
30 ⌐a⌐ wily temptacion / but a furiose force & a terrible incursion / In
other of his temptacions he stelith on like a fox / but in this Turkes

3 meridiano /] *period after* / B   4 second] ii *1557*   11 eyther] *canc. and* other *interl.* B,
other *Z*   16 is /] | *canc. and colon added* B   18 witt] wete *1553*   19 hart] hartes *L*
20 fierce] fierce furious *L 1553 1573*   21 christiens] chrystyan *L*, christen *1553 1573*
25 incurcion /] *period before* / B   26 for] f *alt. to* F B   30 incursion /] | *canc. and*
period added B

persecucion for the fayth, he runnyth on roryng with assawt lyke a
rampyng lyon /

This temptacion is of all temptacions also the most perilouse / for
wheras in temptacions of prosperite, he vseth onely delectable allectyves to move a man to synne / and in other kyndes of tribulacion & 5
aduersite, he vseth onely grife and payne to pull a man into murmure
impacience and blaspamye / in this kynd of persecucion for the
[f. 146] fayth of christ he vseth both twayne / that is to wit both his
allectiue of quyete & rest by deliueraunce from deth & payne, with
other pleasures also of this present life / and beside that the terrour 10
& infliccion of intollerable payne and turment.

In other tribulacion, as losse, or siknes, or deth of our frendes,
though the payne be peradventure as greate & some tyme greater to,
yet is not the perell no where nygh halfe so much / for in other tribulacions as I said before / that necessitie that the man must of fyne force 15
abide & indure the payne, wax he neuer so wroth & impacient therwith / is a greate reason to move hym to kepe his pacyence therin / &
be content therwith, and thanke god therof / & of necessite to make a
vertue, that he may be rewardid for / But in this temptacion, this
persecucion for the fayth, I meane not by fight in the feld by which 20
the faythfull man standith at his defence, & putteth the faythlesse in
halfe the fere & halfe the harme to / but where he is taken & in hold /
& may for the forsweryng or the denying of his fayth, be deliuerid &
suffred to live in rest & ⌐some in⌐ greate worldly welth also / In this
case I say / this thing that he nedeth not to suffre this trowble and 25
payne but he will / is a mervelouse greate occasion for hym to fall
into the synne that the devill wold dreve hym to / that is to wit the
forsakyng of the fayth. And therfor as I say of all the devilles temptacions, is this temptacion this persecucion for the fayth, the most
perilouse. 30

Vincent

The more perilouse vncle that this temptacion is / as in dede of all

5 tribulacion] tribulacions L 1553 1573   7 for the] catchwords on f. 145ᵛ, omitted at
beginning of f. 146   9 allectiue] allectiues Z   12 or siknes] of sickenesse 1553   13 &
some tyme] interl. A; or canc. A before greater   15 before /] comma before / B; that
necessitie] the necessitie L 1553 1573   17 reason] occasion L 1553, reason & occasion
1573   24 some] sometime 1573   27 wit] wete 1553   28 the fayth] his faith L
1553 1573

temptacions the most perilouse it is: the more nede haue they that
stand in perell therof, to be before with substanciall advise & good
counsayle well armyd agaynst it / that we may with the comfort &
consolacion therof, the bettre bere that tribulacion whan yt commeth,
5 & the bettre withstand the temptacion. [f. 146ᵛ]

Antonye

You say Cosyn Vincent therin very trewth, & ⌈I⌉ am content to
fall therfor in hand with it / But for as much cosyn as me thinketh,
that of this tribulacion somewhat you be more ferd than I / and of
10 trouth somewhat more excusable it is in you than it were in me, myn
age considerid / and the sorow that I haue suffrid all redy / with some
other consideracions vppon my part beside / reherse you therfor the
grifes & the paynes that you thinke in this tribulacion possible to fall
vnto you / and I shall agaynst ech of them, give you counsayle, &
15 reherse you such occasion of comfort and consolacion, as my pore wit
& lernyng can call vnto my mynd.

Vincent

In good fayth vncle I am not althyng aferd in this case onely for
my selfe / but well you wote I haue cause to care also for many mo, &
20 that folke of sundry sortes, men and women both / & that not all of
one age /

Antonye

All that you haue cause to fere for Cosyn / for all them haue I cause
to fere with you to, sith all your kynnes folke & alies within a litle,
25 be likewise vnto me / howbeit to say the trewth, euery man hath cause
in this case to fere both for hymselfe, & also for euerye other / For
sith as the scripture sayth / *Vnicuique dedit deus curam de proximo suo*, god
hath givin euery man cure & charge of his neighbour: there is no man
that hath any sparke of christen love & charite in his brest / but that in
30 a mater of such perell as this is / wherein the soule of man standith

---

8 with it] therwith *Z*   9 ferd] frayde *1553 1573*   10 myn] my *L 1553 1573*
12 vppon] on *1553 1573*   13 the paynes] the *om. L 1553 1573*   16 call vnto] call to
1553 1573   18 aferd] afraid *1553 1573*   19 also] *interl. A*   24 kynnes folke]
kinsfolkes *L 1553 1573*   27 dedit deus] deus dedit *L 1553*

in so greate dainger to be lost / he must nedes care & take thought /
not for his frendes onely / but also for his very foes / we shall therfor
Cosyn not reherse your harmes or myn that may be fall in this persecucion, but all the greate harmes in generall as nere as we can call
[f. 147] to mynd / that may hap vnto any man /   5

The third chapiter

Sith a man is made of the bodye & the soule: all the harm that
any man may take / it must nedes be in one of these two / eyther immedyatly / or by the meane of ⌐some¬ such thing as serveth for the
pleasure / weale, or comoditie of the tone of these two / As for the   10
soule / first / we shall nede no rehersall of any harm, that by this
kynd of tribulacion may attayne therto / but yf that by some inordinate love & affeccion that the soule bere to the bodye / she consent
to slyde fro the fayth, & therby doth her harm her selfe /
Now remayne there the bodye & these owtward thinges of fortune   15
which serue for the mayntenaunce of the bodye, & mynister mater
of pleasure to the soule also, thorow the delite that she hath in the
body for the while that she is matchid therwith.
Consider than first the losse of those outward thinges, as somewhat
the lesse in weight / than is the body it selfe / In them what may a   20
man lese, & therby what payne may he suffre /

Vincent

He may lese vncle (of which I shuld somewhat lese my selfe) mony /
plate / & other moveable substaunce / than offices, authorite, &
fynally all the landes of his enheritaunce for euer / that hymselfe &   25
his heires perpetually might elles enioy / And of all these thinges
vncle / you wote well that my selfe haue some / litle in respect of that /
that some other haue here / but somewhat more yet than he that hath
most here wold be well content to lese /

---

3 be fall] be *om. L*   6 third] iii *1553 1557 1573*   10 pleasure /] *comma wr. on* / *B*;
tone] one *1553 1573*   11 first /] / *canc. B*   12 therto / but] / *ed.,* therto but / *A*
14 fro] from *L*; doth] doe *Z*   21 lese] lose *1553 1573*   23 lese] lose *L 1553 1573*;
lese] lose *L 1553 1573*   25 euer /] / *canc. B*   27 of that /] / *canc. B*   29 lese] lose
1553 1573

Vppon the losse of these thinges folow nedines & pouertie / the payne of lackyng / the shame of beggyng / of which twayne I wote not well which is the most wrechid necessitie / beside the griefe of hart & hevines, in beholdyng good men & faythfull, & his deare
5 [f. 147ᵛ] frendes, bewrappid in like misery, & vngraciouse wretchis & infidelles & his mortall enymyes, enioy the commodities that hym selfe and his frendes haue lost /

Now for the bodye very few wordes shall serue vs / For therin I se none other harme but losse of libertie / labour / imprisonament, payn-
10 full and shamfull deth /

Anthonye

There nedeth not mich more Cosyn as the world is now / for I fere me that lesse than a fourth part of this, will make many a man sore staggar in his fayth, & some fall quiet therefro / that yet at this day
15 before he come to the profe, weneth hym selfe that he wold stand very fast / And I besech our lord that all they that so thinke, & wold yet whan they were brought vnto the poynt, swarve therefro for fere or for payne, may get of god the grace to wene still as they do, & not to be brought to thassay, where payne or fere shuld shew them (as it
20 shewid S peter) how farre they be deceyvid now /

But now Cosyn agaynst these terrible thinges, what way shall we take in givyng men counsayle of comfort / Yf the fayth were in our dayes as fervent, as it hath bene ere this in tyme before passid / litle counsayle & litle comfort wold suffice / We shuld not much nede
25 with wordes & resonyng to extenuate & mynish the vigour & asperite of the paynes / but the greater, the more bittre that the passion were / the more redy was of old tyme the feruour of fayth to suffre yt.

And surely Cosyn I dowt ⌜it⌝ litle in my mynd / but that yf a man had in his hart / so diepe a desiere & love longyng to be with god in
30 hevyn to haue the fruicion of his gloriouse face, as had those holy

---

3–4 griefe of hart & hevines] griefe and heauynes of heart *Z*   6 mortall] most mortal *L 1553 1573*   8 serue] v *wr. over* u *B*   12 nedeth] nede *L 1553*; mich] *extra minim added B to read* much   13 will make] *second* will *canc. B before* make   14 some] some man *Z*; quiet] *canc. and* quyte *interl. B*, quite *Z*   17 vnto] to *1573*; swarve] fal *Z*
19 them (as] them then. And (as *1553*, theym then, (as *L*, them then (as *1573*   22 of] or *L 1553 1573*; comfort /] *period before | B*; Yf] *ed.*, yf *A*   23 tyme before passid] tymes past *L 1553 1573*   26 the more] & the more *1557*   27 feruour] v *wr. over* u *B*
28 dowt] dowtid *A*: id *canc. B*

men that were martires in old tyme / he [f. 148] wold no more now
styke at the payne that he must passe betwene / than at that tyme
those old holy martirs did / But alas our faynt & feble fayth, with
our love to god lesse than luke warm, by the fyery affeccion that we
bere to our own filthy flesh, make vs so dull in the desiere of hevyn, 5
that the sodayne drede of euery bodely payne, woundeth vs to the
hart & strikith our devocion ded / And therfor hath there euery man
Cosyn (as I said before) mich the more nede to thinke vppon this
thing many tyme & oft aforehand, ere any such perell fall / & by
mich devisyng thervppon before they se cause to fere yt, while the 10
thing shall not apere so terrible vnto them / reason shall bettre entre,
& thorow grace workyng with their diligens / engendre & set sure,
not a sodayne sleyght affeccion of sufferaunce for godes sake / but by
a long contynuaunce, a strong depe rotid habit / not like a ride redy to
wave with euery wind / nor like a rotelesse tre scant vpp an end in a 15
lose hepe of light sand, that will with a blast or two be blowen
down /

The fourth chapitre /

    For yf we now consider Cosyn, these causes of Terrour and drede
that you haue recitid / which in this persecucion for the fayth / this 20
mydday devill may by these Turkes reare agaynst vs to make his incurcion with / we shall well perceve waying them well with reason,
that albeit somewhat they be in dede / yet euery part of the mater
pondred, they shall well apere in conclucion, thinges nothing so
much to be dred & fled fro, as to folke at the first sight they do 25
sodaynly seame /

---

1 in old] in the old L *1553 1573*   5 make] maketh Z   7 ded] *final* e *added B*, starke
dead L *1553 1573*   8 before)] *parenth. ed., comma added B*   9 many tyme] many a
tyme Z; fall /] *comma before* / B   10 se cause] see the cause L *1553 1573*   13 godes
sake] god his sake *1553*   14 ride] e *wr. over* i B, reede Z   15 wind] *final* e *added B*;
scant vpp] scant set vp L *1553 1573*   18 fourth] iiii *1553 1557*   20 in this] in hys Z
24 shall well apere *canc. A after* they; apere] aperee A: *last* e *canc. B*; thinges] thinges /
A: / *canc. B*

Of the losse of the goodes of fortune
The fift Chapiter [f. 148ᵛ]

For first to begynne at the owtward goodes, that neither are the
proper goodes of the soule nor of the bodye / but are callid the
5 goodes of fortune, that serve for the substaunce & comoditie of man,
for the short season of this present life / as worldly substaunce, offices,
honour, and aucthorite: what greate good is there in these thinges of
them selfe / for which they were worthye so mich as to bere the
name, by which the world of a worldly favour custumably callith
10 them / For yf the havyng of strength make a man strong / & the
havyng of heate make a man hote / and the havyng of vertew make a
man vertuouse: how can those thinges be verely & trewly good, which
he that hath them, may by the havyng of them, as well be the worse
as the bettre / and as experience proveth more ofte is the worse than
15 the bettre / What shuld a good man greatle reioyce in that / that he
dayly seeth moost habound in the handes of many that be nought /
Do not now the greate Turke & his Bassawes in all these avaunce-
mentes of fortune, surmount very far above any christen estate, &
eny lordes livyng vnder hym / And was there not yet hens vppon /xx/
20 yeres, the greate Sowdan of Siry, which many a yere together bare as
greate a port as the greate Turke / And after in one somer vnto the
greate Turke the whole Empier was lost / And so may all his empier
now, & shall hereafter by goddes grace, be lost into christen mens
handes likewise, whan christen peple shalbe mendid & grow in goddes
25 favour agayne / But whan that whole kyngdomes & mighty greate
Empieres are of so litle suretye to stand / but be so sone translatid
from one man vnto a nother / what greate thyng can you or I / yea
or any lord the greatest in this land, reken hymselfe to haue by the

---

2 fift] v *1553 1557 1573*   3 at the] at these L *1553 1573*   5 substaunce] sustenaunce
Ƶ: *see note*   10 make a] make a a a A   12 those] these L *1553 1573*   14 ofte]
often *1553 1573*   15 What] Whan *1573*   16 habound] abounde Ƶ; nought /] *question-
mark ins. before* / B   17 the] is *wr. over* e B, this Ƶ   19–20 vppon / xx / yeres,] *periods
before and after* xx B, vppon a xxᵗʰ yere a go L, vpon a .xx. yere agoe *1553 1573*
22 the whole] the *alt. to* that B (at *wr. over* e), that whole Ƶ   23 goddes] God his *1553*
24 handes] handes / A: / *canc.* B; in goddes] into god his *1553*, into Gods L *1573*
26 but be so] be *om. 1553*, and be so *1573*; translatid] tranlatid A: s *wr. over second minim
of* n *and minim added after first* a B   27 vnto] to L

possession of an hepe of syluer or gold whight & yelow metall, not so profitable of their own nature save for a litle glistryng, as the rude rusty metall of yron. [f. 149]

Of the vnsewertie of landes & possessions

The vj Chapitre 5

Landes & possessions many men yet mich more esteme than money / because the landes seme not so casuall as money is or plate / for that though their other substaunce may be stolen & taken away / yet euermore they thinke that their land will lye still where yt laye / But what are we the bettre that our land can not be stirid but will 10 lye still where it lay / while our selfe may be removid & not suffrid to come nere yt /

What great difference is there to vs whither our substaunce be moveable / or vnmoveable, sith we be so moveable our selfes, that we may be removid from them both, & lese them both twayne / sav- 15 yng that sometyme in the money / is the suerty somewhat more / For whan we be fayne our selfe to fle, we may make shifte to cary some of our money with vs / where of our land we can not cary one ynch /

Yf our land be of more suertye than our money / how happeth it 20 than that in this persecucion, we be more ferd to lese it / for yf it be a thing of more suertie, than can it not so sone be lost /

In the translacion of these two greate Empircs Grece firot / sith my selfe was borne / and after Syry / syns you were borne to / the land was lost before the money was found. 25

Oh Cosyn Vincent / yf the whole world were anymatid with a re- sonable soule, as plato had went it were / & that it had wit & vnder- stondyng to marke & perceve all thing / lord god how the ground on which a prince bildeth his palice, wold lowd lawgh his lord to scorne, whan he saw hym prowd of his possession, & herd hym bost hym 30

1 whight] *canc. and* whyte *interl.* B　5 vj] syxth *L*　7 casuall] casuall / *A*　8 sub- staunce] *one minim lacking in* un *A*; virgule? *before* may *A*; stolen] n *canc.* B, stole *1557* 14 selfes] selfe *Z*　18 where] where / *A*: / *canc.* B　20 be of] be a thing of *Z* 21 ferd] frayde *1553 1573*　24 Syry /] / *canc.* B　27 virgule? *after* soule *A*

selfe, that he & his blowde are for euer the very lordes & owners of
that land / for than wold the grownd thinke the while in hym selfe /
ah thow sely pore soule, that wenest [f. 149ᵛ] thow were halfe a god /
& art a midd thy glory / but a man in a gay gowne / I that am the
5 grownd here ouer whome thow art so prowde, haue had an hundred
such owners of me as thow callest thy selfe / mo than euer thow hast
hard the names of / And some of them that prowdly went ouer my
hed / lye now low in my bely & my side lieth ouer them / And many
one shall as thow doost now / call hym selfe myn owner after the, that
10 neyther shalbe sibbe to thy blode / nor eny word here of thy name.
Who ought your Castell Cosyn three thowsand yeres agoo?

Vincent

Three thowsand vncle / nay / nay / in any kyng christen or hethen,
you may streke of a third part of that well inowgh / & as farre as I
15 wene halfe of the remenaunt to / In far fewer yeres than / 3 / M / it
may well fortune, that a pore plowgh mannes blode, may come vpp
to a kyngdome / & a kynges right roiall kynne on the tother side, fall
downe to the plowgh and cart / and neyther that the kyng know
that euer he came fro the carte / nor the carter know that euer he
20 came fro the crowne /

Anthonye

We fynd Cosyn Vincent in full antique storis, many straunge
chaunges / as mervelouse as that, come about in the compas of very
few yeres in effect / And be such thinges than in reson so greatly to be
25 set by, that we shuld esteme the losse at so greate, whan we see that in
the kepyng our suertie is so litle?

---

1 blowde] *canc. and* blode *interl. B*; lordes] Lorde *L 1553*   2 the while] *interl. A*, that
while *1553*   4 glory /] | *canc. B*   5 hundred] hundreth *1553*   7 *flaw in paper
resembling virgule canc. B after* ouer   7–8 my hed] mine head *1557*   10 nor eny] or any
L 1553   11 thw? *canc. A before* thowsand; yeres] yere ℨ   14 streke] strike ℨ
15 3 / M /] M / *wr. as superscript A*   16 well *canc. A before* may   17 tother] other *1553
1573*; *extra* fall *canc. B before* fall downe   18 the kyng] the *om.* ℨ   19 fro] from *L*;
the carter] that carter ℨ   20 fro] from *L 1553 1573*   22 antique] Autentique *L 1553
1573: see note*   23 chaunges /] | *canc. B*; chaunges] chaunces *L 1553 1573*   25 at]
om. 1573   25–26 in the] the *om. 1557*

Vincent

Mary vncle but the lesse suerty that we haue to kepe it, sith it is
a greate commoditie to haue it / the ferther by so mich & the more
loth we be to forgo it /

Antony

That reason shall I Cosyn turne agaynst youre selfe. [f. 150] For
yf it be ⌈so⌉ as you say, that sith the thinges be commodiouse / the
lesse suerty that you see you haue of the keping / the more cause you
haue to be a ferd of the losyng / Than on the tother side / the more
that a thing is of his nature such / that the commoditie therof bringeth
a man litle suertie & mich fere / that thing of reason the lesse haue we
cause to love / And than the lesse cause that we haue to love a thing /
the lesse cause haue we to care therefor / or fere the losse therof, or be
loth to go there from.

These owtward goodes or giftes of fortune are by two maner wise to be considerid

The / 7 / chapitre

We shall yet Cosyn considre in these owtward goodes of fortune,
as riches / good name / honest estymacion / honorable fame, & au-
torite / in all these thinges we shall I say consider / that either we
love them & set by them as thinges commodiouse vnto vs for the state
& condicion of this present life / or els as thinges that we purpose by
the good vse therof, to make them mater of our merite with goddes
helpe in the life after to come / Let vs than furst consider them as
thinges set by & belovid for the pleasure & commoditie of them for
this present life /

---

2 se *canc. A before* suerty   3 ferther] fearder *L 1553 1573*   4 it /] *period before* / *B*
6 selfe.] *period ed.*   9 a ferd] afrayde *1553 1573*; losyng /] *colon before* / *B*; tother] other
1553 1573   14 there from] therefro *1573*   15 by] *om. L 1553 1573*   16 maner]
manour *of L*   17 7] vij^th *L*   22 as thinges] as by thynges *L 1553 1573*   23 goddes]
god his *1553*

The litle commoditie of richesse being set by but
for this present life /

The / 8 / chapitre /

Now riches lovid & set by for such, yf we consider it well, the com-
5   moditie that we take there thereof, is not so greate as our own fond
affeccion & fantasye maketh vs imagine it. It maketh vs (I say not
nay) go mich more gay & gloriouse in sight, garnishid in silke / but
cloth is within a litle as warme. Hit maketh vs haue greate plentye of
many kynd of delicate & deliciouse vitayle, & therby to make more
10 excesse / but lesse exquisyte & lesse superfluouse fare, with fewer
surfittes & fewer fevers growyng there on to, were within a litle as
holsome / Than [f. 150ᵛ] the labour in the gettyng / the fere in the
kepyng, & the payne in the partyng fro / do more than contrepayse
a greate part of all the pleasure & commoditie that they bring /
15 Beside this, that riches is the thinge, that taketh many tymes from
his maister all his pleasure and his life to / for many a man is for his
richesse slayne / And some that kepe their richesse as a thing plesaunt
& commodiouse for their life / take none other pleasure in a maner
thereof in all their life, than as though they bare the kay of an other
20 mans cofer / & rather are content to live in nedines miserably all their
dayes, than they could find in their hart to minish their hord / they
haue such fantasy to loke theron / yea & some men for fere lest theves
shuld stele it fro them / be their own theves & stele it fro them selfe,
while they dare not so mich as ⌐let it lye where them selfe may loke
25 theron⌐ but put it in a pot, & hide it in the grownd, & there let it lye
safe, till they dye / & sometyme / vij / yere after / from which place
if the pot had bene stolen away five yere before his deth / all the same
five yere that he livid after, wenyng alway that his pot lay safe still
what had he bene the porer while he neuer occupied it after /

---

1 richesse] riches Z; set by] *faulty* t A   3 8] viij^{th} L   4 riches] rychesse *1557*   5 there
thereof] there *om.* Z   6 fantasye] fansye L   7 nay)] *parenth. ed.*, nay / A; garnishid
in] garnished with L *1553 1573*   8 Hit] hit A, It Z   9 deliciouse] ci *interl.* B; vitayle]
victual *1553 1573*   10 fare,] feare A: *canc. and* fare, *interl.* B   11 there] *interl.* A
13 & the payne] & *om. 1553 1573*   15 Beside] beside A: B *wr. over* b B, Besydes *1553
1557 1573*; that riches] the riches *1573*   17 richesse] riches Z; richesse] ryches Z; a
thing] thinges L *1553*   21 hart] hartes L   22 fantasy] fansye L   23 fro] from L
1553 1573; fro] from L *1553 1573*; selfe] selvys L   24 selfe] selvys L

Vincent

By my trowth vncle not one penye for aught that I perceve.

The litle comoditie of fame being desirid but
for worldly pleasure /

The / 9 / chapitre /   5

Antony

Let vs now consider good name / honest estimacion, & honourable
fame / for these / 3 / thinges are of their ⌐own¬ nature one / & take
their difference in effect, but of the maner of the comen spech in di-
uersite of degrees / for a good name may a man haue be he neuer so   10
pore / honest estimacion in the comen takyng of the peple, belongeth
not vnto any man but hym that is taken for one of some countenaunce
& havour, & among his neighbours had in some reputacion. [f. 151]
In the word of honourable fame, folke conceve the renome of greate
estates / mich & farre spoken of by reason of their laudable actes.   15
Now all this gere vsid as a thing plesaunt & commodiouse for this
present life / plesaunt yt may seme to hym that fastenith his fantasye
therein / but of the nature of the thing it selfe, I perceyve no greate
comoditie that it hath / I say of the nature of the thing it selfe / because
it may be by chaunce some occasion of commoditie / as yf it happe   20
that for the good name the pore man hath / or for the honest estimacion that a man of some havour & substaunce standith in among his
neighbours / or for the honourable fame wherwith the greate estate
is renomed / yf it hap I say / that any man beryng them the bettre
will therfor / do them therfor any good / And yet as for that, like as   25
it may some tyme so happ / & some tyme so happeth in dede / so may
it happe some time, on the tother side & on the tother side so it some

---

5 9] ix^th L   6 Antony] *misplaced before summary A*   9 spech] *final* e *added B*   13 havour]
behauour *L 1553 1573*; neighbours] neigbours *A*; reputacion.] *period ed.*   14 renome]
renowme *L 1553 1573*   15 farre] *interl. B above canc.* faree *A: first* e *wr. over* r? *A*
17 fantasye] fansye *L*   21 ex *canc. A before* estimacion   24 renomed] renowmed *L*
1553 1573; the] *om. 1553 1573*   25 will therfor / do them therfor] *first* therfor *om. L 1553*
26 so *interl. A before* tyme, *then canc. A*; happeth] happeth it *L 1573*   27 some time]
interl. A; tother ... tother] other ... other *1553 1573*

tyme happeth in dede, that such folke are of some other envied &
hatid / & as redely by them that envie them & hate them take harme,
as they take by them that love them good /

But now to speke of the thing it selfe in his own proper nature, what
5 is it but a blast of a nother mans mouth, as sone passid as spoken /
wheruppon he that settith his delite, fedeth hymselfe but with wynd /
wherof be he neuer so full, he hath litle substaunce therin / And many
tymes shall he mich deceve hymselfe / for he shall wene that many
prayse hym that neuer speke word of hym / and they that do / say it
10 much lesse than he weneth, & far more seldome to / for they spend not
all the [f. 151ᵛ] day he may be sure in talkyng of hym alone / And
who so commend hym most, will yet I wene in euery foure & twenty
houres winke & forget hym ones / besides this that while one talketh
well of hym in one place / A nother sittith & sayth as shrewdely of
15 hym in a nother / And fynally some that most prayse hym in his
presence, behynd his bak mok hym as fast, & lowd lawgh hym to
scorne, & some tyme slyly to his own face to / And yet are there some
folis so fed with this fond fantasye of fame, that they reioyce & glory,
to thinke how they be contynually praysed all abowt / as though all
20 the world did nothing els day nor night, but euer sit & sing *sanctus* /
sanctus / *sanctus* vppon them.

Of flatery /

The xᵗʰ chapitre /

And into this pleasaunt fransie of mich folishe vaynglory be there
25 some men brought some tyme, by such as themselfe do in a maner hyre
to flater them, & wold not be content yf a man shuld do otherwise /
but wold be right angry, not onely yf a man told them trouth, whan
they do nought in dede / but also if they prayse it but slenderly /

Vincent

30 Forsoth vncle this is very truth / I haue bene ere this & not very

9 say it] saye yet *Z*　　14 well] *second* l *added B?*　　15 most] *om.* L *1553*　　18 fantasye]
fansye *L*　　19 how they] how how they *A*　　21 *second* sanctus *lacks* c *A*　　23 xᵗʰ] x
1553 1557 1573　　25 themselfe] theym selvys *L*, themselues *1553 1573*

long agoo, where I saw so propre experience of this poynt, that I must
stopp your tale for so long while I tell you myn.

Antonye

I pray you Cosyn tell on /

Vincent 5

Whan I was first in Almayne vncle, it happid me to be somwhat
favorid with a greate man of the church, & a greate state, one of the
greatest in all that countrey there / & in dede who so euer might spend
as mich as he might in one thing & other, were a right great estate in
any country [f. 152] of christendome / But gloriouse was he very 10
far above all measure / & that was greate pitie / for it did harm, and
made hym abuse many greate giftes that god had givyn hym / Neuer
was he saciate of heryng his own prayse /

So happyd it one day that he had in a greate audience, made an
oracion in a certeyne maner / wherin he likyd hymselfe so well / that 15
at his dener he sat hym thought on thornes / till he might here how
they that satt with hym at his borde, wold commend it / And whan
he had sit musyng a while devising as I thought after, vppon some
pretty proper way to bryng yt in withall / at the last for lacke of a bettre
(lest he shuld haue lettyd the mater to long) he brought it evyn blont 20
forth / and askyd vs all that sat at his bordes end (for at his owne
messe in the myddes there sat but hym selfe alone) how well we likyd
his oracion that he had made that daye / But in fayth vncle whan
that probleme was ones proponid / till it was full answerid, no man
I wene / ete one morsell of mete more / euery man was fallen in so 25
diepe a studye / for the findyng of some exquisite prayse / For he that
shuld haue brought out ┌but┐ a vulgare & a comen comendacion,
wold haue thought hym selfe shamid for euer / Than said we our
sentences by row as we sat / from the lowest vnto the highest / in good
ordre / as it had bene a greate mater of the comen well in a right 30

---

9 great estate] greate state L *1553 1573*   16 dener] y *wr. over first* e B   18 sit] sitten
1573; while] h *interl.* A; vppon] on *1553 1573*   19 at the last] the *om.* L *1553 1573*
20 to long] over longe L; long)] *parenth. wr. over* / B; blont] *canc. and* blontly *interl.* B,
bloontly Ƶ   22 myddes] myddest *1553*   23 he had made] had *om.* L *1553*   25
wene /] / *canc.* B; mete] mete / A : / *canc.* B; man] *interl.* A   30 well] *canc. and* wele *interl.*
B, welth L, wayle *1553*, weale *1557 1573*

solempne counsayle / Whan it came to my part (I will not say it vncle
for no bost) me thought / by our lady for my part I quyt my selfe
metely well / & I likyd my selfe the bettre because my thought my
wordes beyng but a stranger, went yet with some grace in the Almayne
5 tonge, wherin [f. 152ᵛ] lettyng my laten alone, me listid to shew my
connyng / And I hopid to be likyd the bettre, because I saw that he
that sat next me & shuld say his sentence after me / was an vnlernid
preest / for he cold speke no laten at all / But whan he came forth
for his part with my lordes commendacion, the wily fox had be so
10 well accustumyd in court with the crafte of flatery, that he went beyond me to to far / And than might I se by hym, what excelence a
right meane wit may come to, in one crafte, that in all his whole life
studith & besieth his wit about no mo but that one / But I made after
a solempne vowe to my selfe, that yf euer he & I were matchid together
15 at that borde agayne / whan we shuld fall to our flatery, I wold flater
in laten, that he shuld ⌐not⌐ contend with me no more / for though
I could be content to be out runne of an horse / yet wold I no more
abide it to be outrunne of an Asse / But vncle here beganne now the
game / He that sat hiest, & was to speke last, was a great beneficed
20 man / & not a doctour onely / but also somewhat lernid in dede in
the lawes of the church / A world it was to see how he markid euery
mans word that spake before hym / And it semyd that euery word,
the more proper that it was, the worse he likyd / for the combraunce
that he had to study out a bettre to passe it / The man evyn swet
25 with the labour, so that he was fayne in the while now & than to
wipe his face / How be it in conclusion whan it came to his course, we
that ⌐had⌐ spoken before hym, had so taken vpp all among vs before,
that we had not left hym one wise word to speke ⌐after.⌐

Antony

30   Alas good man among so many of you, some good felow shuld
[f. 153] haue lent hym one /

---

1 Whan] whan A   1–2 vncle for no bost] for no boste Uncle *1553 1573*   2 bost)]
parenth. wr. over | B; thought /] | *canc.* B   3 metely] very L *1553*   5 listid] lusted *1553*
9 fox] fox | A: | *canc.* B; had be] hadde beene L *1553 1573*   10 in court] in the courte
1553   11 excelence] excellencie L *1553 1573*   14 vowe to] vowe vnto *1557*   16 not]
added by B *at end of line*   17 an horse] a horse L *1553 1573*   19 last] *om. 1557*
23 proper that] that *om. 1557*; likyd] liked it *Z*   27 vpp all] all vp *1553 1573*
28 after.] *added by* E *at end of line, period added by* B *after* speke, after *om.* L *1553*

Vincent

It neded not as happ was vncle / for he found out such a shyfte,
that in his flatryng he passid vs all the mayny /

Anthonye

Whye what sayd he Cosyn?   5

Vincent

By our Lady vncle not one word / But like as I trow *Plinius* tellith,
that whan Apelles the paynter in the table that he payntid of the
sacrifice & the deth of Iphigenia, had in the makyng of the sorowfull
countenaunces of the other noble men of Grece that beheld it, spent 10
owt so mich his crafte & his connyng / that when he came to make
the countenaunce of kyng Agamemnon her father which he reseruid
for the last, lest yf he had made his visage before he must in some of
the other after, either haue made the visage lesse dolorouse than he
could, & therby haue forborne some part of his prayse / or doyng 15
the vttermost of his crafte, might haue happid to make some other
loke more hevily for the pitie of her payne than her own father / which
had bene yet a far greater faute in his payntyng / Whan he came I
say to the makyng of his face therfor last of all, he could devise no
maner of new hevy chere or countenaunce for her father / but that he 20
had made there all redy in some of the tother a mich more hevy
before / And therfor to the entent that no man shuld see what maner
countenaunce it was that her father had / the paynter was fayne to
paynt hym holdyng his face in his handkercher.
    The like pageant in a maner plaid vs there this good auncient [f. 25
153ᵛ] honourable flaterer / for whan he saw that he could find no
wordes of prayse that wold passe all that had bene spoken before all
redy / the wily fox wold speke neuer a word, but as he that were ravishid vnto havyn ward, with the wonder of the wisedome & eloquence

---

3 mayny] ay *wr. by B over illeg. letter* (a.?)   5 Cosyn?] *question-mark ed.*   8 Apelles]
Timanthes *1573*   10 other] *om.* L *1553*   11 his crafte] of hys craft L *1553 1573*; his
connyng] his *om.* L; connyng /] / *canc. and comma added B*   12 he reseruid] ye reserued
1553; reseruid] v *wr. over* u B   16 vutt *canc. A before* vttermost   18 came] *interl.* B
over canc. abbreviation   20 chere or] cheare and ᵹ   21 tother] other *1553 1573*; a mich]
a *om. 1553*   22 the entent] thentent ᵹ   25 there] here *1573*   27 wordes] woorde
1553 1573   28 he that were] that *om. 1553 1573*   29 havyn] e *wr. over* a B

that my lordes grace had vttrid in that oracion, he fet a long sigh with an oh fro the bottom of his brest, & held vpp both his handes, & lyft vpp his hed, & cast vpp his yien into the welkyn, and wept /

Antony

5   Forsoth Cosyn he playd his part very properly /
But was that great prelates oracion Cosyn any thing prayse worthy / for you can tell I see well / For you wold not I wene play as Iuuenall meryly describeth the blynd senatour, one of the flaterers of Tyberius the Emperour / that among the remenaunt so magnified the greate
10   fissh that the emperour had sent for them to shew them which this blynd Senatour Montanus I tro they callid hym, merveylid of as mich as any that mervaylid most, & many thynges he spake therof, with some of his wordes directid therunto, lokyng him selfe toward his left side, while the fishe lay on his right side / you wold not I trow Cosyn
15   haue taken vppon you to prayse it so / but yf you had herd it.

Vincent

I herd it vncle in dede / & to say the truth it was not to disprayse / howbeit surely / somwhat lesse prayse might haue seruid it by more a greate deale than the halfe / But this am I sure / had it bene the worst
20   that euer was made / the prayse had not bene the lesse of one here / For they that vsid to prayse him to his face / neuer considerid how mich the thing deseruid / but how ⌜gret⌝ [f. 154] a lawd and prayse them selfe could give his good grace.

Antonye

25   Surely Cosyn (as Terence sayth) such folke make men of foles evyn starke mad / & mich cause haue their lordes to be right angry with them /

---

2 ho *canc. A before* oh; fro] from *Z*; lyft] lyfted *1553 1573*   3 cast vpp his yien] cast both hys yien vp *1553 1573*; wept /] *period before* / *B*   5 Cosyn] *om.* L *1553 1573*   9 the Emperour] themperoure L *1553 1573*   10 the emperour] themperoure L *1553*   11 tro] *final* w *added B*   13 his left] the lyfte *1553 1573*   15 prayse] pray *A*, se *added B*, prayse *Z*   17 vncle in dede] in dede vncle L   25 sayth)] sayth / *A*; folke] folkes L *1553 1573*

Vincent

God hath in dede, & is I wene / But as for their lordes vncle, yf
they wold after wax angry with them therfor, they shuld in my mynd
do them very greate wrong, whan it is one of the thinges that they
specially kepe them for / For those that are of such vayngloriouse 5
mynd (be they lordes / or be they meaner men) can be mich bettre
contentid to haue their devices commendid than amendid / and require they their seruauntes & their frend, neuer so specially to tell
them the very trewth, yet shall they bettre please them / yf he speke
them fayre than yf he tellith them truth / for they be in the case that 10
Martialis spekith of in an Epigrame vnto a frend of his, that required
his iugement how he likyd his versis / But he prayed hym in any wise
to tell hym evyn the very truth. To whom martiall made answere in
this wise /

The very trewth of me thow doost requere   15
The very trewth is this my frend dere
The very trewth thow woldeste not gladly here.

And in good faith vncle the selfe same prelate that I told you my
tale of / I dare be bold to swere it I know it so surely / had on a tyme
made of his own drawyng a certeyne tretice, that shuld serue for a 20
leige betwene that countrey & a greate prince / In which treatice hym
selfe thought that he had devisid his articles so wisely, & enditid them
so well, that all the world wold alow them / wheruppon [f. 154ᵛ]
longyng sore to be praysid, he callid vnto hym a frend of his a man
well lernid & of good worship, & very well expert in those maters, as 25
he that had be diuers tymes Embassiatour for that countrey, & had
made many such treatices hym selfe. Whan he toke him the treatice,
& that he had redd it / he askyd hym how he likyd it / and said / But
I pray you hartely tell me the very trouth / and that he spake so
hartely / that the tother had went he wold ⌐fayn⌐ haue herd the 30

---

7 contentid] content *1553 1573*   8 seruauntes] seruaunt *Z*   9 shall they] shall he *Z*
10 tellith] tell *L 1553 1573*   11 Martialis] Martyall *L*, Martial *1573*; required]
requireth *1553*   13 truth.] *period ed.*   15–17 *Set as prose 1553*   16 dere] *period added B*
16–17 dere The] so dere, That *L*, dere, that the *1553*   20 le *canc. A before* tretice;
tretice] Treatie *1573*   21 leige] leage *Z*; that countrey] the countreye *1553*; treatice]
Treatie *1573*   22 enditid] endicted *L 1557*, indicted *1553*, indited *1573*   26 had be]
had been *Z*   27 selfe.] *period ed.*; *after* selfe *A fills out line with five flourishes*; treatices]
Treaties *1573*; treatice] Treatie *1573*   29 hartely tell] hartely *om. 1553*

trowthe / And in trust therof, he told hym a fawte therin at the heryng wherof, he sware in greate anger / By the masse thow art a very fole / The tother afterward told me, that he wold neuer tell hym trowth agayne /

5   Antonye

Without question Cosyn I can not greatly blame hym. And thus them selfe make euery man mokk them, flater them, & deceve them / those I say that are of suche vayngloriouse mynd. For yf they be content to here the truth, let them than make mich of them that tell
10 them the trouth, & withdraw their eare from them that falsely flater them / & they shalbe more trewly seruid than with xx^{te} requestes praying men to tell them trew.

Kyng Ladislaus our lord assoile his soule, vsyd mich this maner among his seruauntes / Whan one of them praysid any dede of his
15 or any condicion in him / yf he perceyvid that they said but the truth / he wold let it passe by, vncontrollid / But whan he saw that they set a glose vppon it for his prayse of their own makyng beside / than wold he shortly say vnto them: I pray the good felow whan thow say grace at my bord, neuer bring in gloria patry without a Sicut erat / Eny
20 act that euer I did, yf thow report it agayne to myn honour with a gloria patry / neuer report it, but with a sicut erat / that is to wit, evyn as it was & none otherwise / And lift me not vpp with no lies / for [f. 155] I love yt not.

If men wold vse this way with them that this noble kyng vsid, it
25 wold mynish much of their false flatery / I can well alow that men shuld commend (kyping them within the bondes of trewth) such thinges as they se prayse worthy in other men, to give them the greater corage to thencrease therof / For men kepe still in that poynt one condicion of children, that prayse must prukke them

---

1 therin at] therin. At B (*period added*, a *alt. to* A), therein. At *1553 1573*, therein, at *1557*
3 tother] other *1553 1573*; trowth] the trewth L   7 selfe] selvys L   9 of them] them
canc. and those *interl.* B, of those Z   10 them the trouth] the *om.* L *1553*; eare] eares L;
from] fro *1557*; tell them *canc.* A *before* falsely   11 seruid] v *wr. over* u B; than] Z,
that A; xx^{te}] *dot over* e *indicates intended* i   12 trew] trueth *1553 1573*   14 one of them]
any of them *1553 1573*   15 the truth] the *om.* L *1553*   16–17 set a] sette to a L *1553 1573*
18 the good] ye good L, thee good *1553 1573*; say] st *added* B, sayest Z   19 patry] y
canc. and i *ins. after* r B; without a] a *om.* L; Eny] Euery L *1553*   21 patry] y *canc. and*
i *ins. after* r B; wit] wete *1553*   26 kyping] e *wr. over* y B; bondes] bounds L *1573*;
trewth)] trewth / A   29 prukke] y *wr. over* u B

forth / But bettre it were to do well & loke for none / how be it they
that can not fynd in their hart to commend a nother mans good dede /
shew them selfe either enviouse, or els of nature very cold and dull /

But out of question, he that putteth his pleasure in the prayse of the
people, hath but a fond fantasye / for if his fynger do but ake of an 5
hote blayne, a greate many mens mouthes blowyng out his prayse,
will scantly do hym among them all halfe so much ease, as to haue
one boy blow vppon his fynger /

The litle commoditie that men haue of romes, offices,
& aucthorite / yf they desire them but for their   10
worldly comoditie /

The xj chapitre

Lett vs now consider in likewise, what greate worldly welth ariseth
vnto men, by greate offices / romes, & aucthoritie / to those worldly
disposid people I say / that desire them for no bettre purpose / for 15
of them that desire them for bettre we shall speke after a non.

The greate thing that they chiefe like all therin, is that thcy may
bere a rule / commaund, & controll other men, & live vncommaundid
& vncontrollid them selfe / And yet this commoditie toke I so litell
hede of, that I neuer was ware it was so greate / till a good frend 20
of ours merily told me [f. 155ᵛ] ones, that his wife ones in a greate
angre tawght it hym. For whan her husband had no list to grow
greatly vpward in the world / nor neither wold labour for office of
aucthorite / & ouer that forsoke a right worshipfull rome whan it
was offrid hym / she felle in hand with hym / he told me / and all 25
to ratid hym / and askyd hym / what will you do, that you list not to
put forth your selfe as other folke do / will you sitt still by the fier &
make goslynges in the asshis with a stikke as children do / wold god

---

2 hart] hartes *L*   3 selfe] selvys *L*   5 fantasye] fansye *L*   6 many mens] mayny of
mens *L 1553*   8 one boy] one litle boye *L 1553 1573*; blow] to blowe *1553 1573*
12 xj] xjᵗʰ *L*   16 a non] *words connected B*   18 a rule] a *om. L*; controll] controlled *1553*
19 selfe] selves *L*   21 merily told me] told me merely *L*   22 list] lust *1553*
23 vpward] *divided* vp-ward: *extra* wa *canc A after* vp   25 / he told me /] *parentheses wr.*
over virgules B   26-27 that you list not to put forth your selfe as other folke do] *om. L*
1553   27 folke] folkes *1573*

I were a man, and loke what I wold do / why wife quoth her husband
what wold you do / ⌐what?¬ by god go forward with the best / for as
my mother was wont to say (god haue mercy on her soule) it is euer
more bettre to rule than to be rulid / And therfor by god I wold not
5 I warrant you be so folish to be rulid where I might rule / By my
trouth wife quoth her husband in this I dare say you say trouth / for
I neuer found you willyng to be rulid yet.

Vincent

Well vncle I wot where you be now well inough / she is in dede a
10 stowte master woman / And in good fayth for ought that I can see,
evyn that same womanysh mynd of hers / is the greast commodite
that men reken vppon in romes & offices of aucthorite /

Antonye

By my trowth, & me thinketh very few there are of them, that
15 atteyne any greate comoditie therin / For first there is in euery kyngdome but one, that can haue an office of such aucthorite / that no man
may commaund hym or controll hym / none officer can there stand in
that case / but the kyng hym selfe, which onely vncontrollid or vncommaundid [f. 156] may controll & commaund all / Now of all the
20 remenaunt, eche is vnder hym / And yet beside hym, almost euery
one is vnder mo commaunders & controllers to / than one / And some
man that is in a greate office, commaundith fewer thinges & lesse
labour to many men that ⌐are¬ vnder hym / than some one that is
ouer hym commaundith hym alone.

25   ## Vincent

Yet it doth them good vncle, that men must make courtesy to them,
& salute them with reuerence, & stand barehed before them, or vnto
some of them knele peradventure to.

---

2 best] best of them L *1553 1573*   3 say (god)] / *before parenth. A*; soule)] *parenth. added B*
3–4 euer more] *om. 1553,* more *om. 1573*   6 trouth] very trowth L   9 now] *om. 1553*
11 greast] greatest *Z*   17 none] No *1573*; there] *interl. A*   18–19 vncommaundid]
1557 1573, commaundid *A L 1553*   23 than] that? *A*: n *wr. over* t? *B*   26 to them]
vnto them L   27 barehed] bare headed *1553*; or vnto] or to L *1553 1573*

Antonye

Well Cosyn in some part they do but play at gleke, receve reuerence / & to their cost pay honour agayne therfor / for except as I said /
onely a kyng, the greaest in aucthorite vnder hym, receyuith not so
much reuerence of no man / as accordyng to reason hym selfe doth 5
honour to hym / nor .xx. mens courtesies do hym not so mich pleasure,
as his own ones knelyng doth hym payne yf his knee happe to be sore /

And I wist ones a great officer of the kynges say / and in good faith
I wene he sayd but as he thought / that xx^te men standyng barehed
before hym, kept not his hed halfe so warm, as to kepe on his own 10
cappe / Nor he toke neuer so mich ease with their beyng barehed
before hym / as he caught ones grefe, with a cough that came vppon
hym, by standyng barehed long before the kyng /

But let it be, that these commodities be somwhat such as they be /
yet than consider whither that any incommodities be so ioynid ther- 15
with, that a man were almost as good lakke both as haue bothe.

Goeth all thing euermore as euery one of them wold haue yt / That
[f. 156^v] were as herd as to please all the people at ones with one
weder / while in one house the husband wold haue fayre weder for
his courne, & his wife wold haue rayne for her lekes / So while they 20
that are in aucthorite be not all euermore of one mynd / but sometyme
variaunce among them, either for the respect of profitt, or for conten-
cion of rule / or for mayntenaunce of matres, sundry partis for their
sundry frendes / it can not be, that both the parties can haue their
own mynd / nor often are they content, which see their conclusion 25
quayle / but tenne tymes they take the missing of their mynd more dis-
plesauntly, than other pore men do / And this goth not onely to men
of meane aucthorite, but vnto the very greattest. The princes them
selfe, can not haue you wot well all their will. For how were it possible / while eche of them almost wold yf he might, be lord ouer all the 30
remenaunt / Than many men vnder their princes in aucthorite / are
in that case, that privy malice & envie many bere them in hart, falsely
speke them full fayre, & prayse them with their mouth / which whan

3 cost] cost / A: / canc. B   4 greaest] greatest Z; receyuith] v wr. over u B   8 officer]
orig. officers, s canc. A   10 kept] kepe 1557   11 toke neuer] neuer toke Z   13 kyng /]
/ canc. and period added B   19 weder] weather Z; weder] weather Z   23 partis] orig.
parties, s canc. and s wr. over e A, partes Z   24 the] om. L; parties] partes L 1553 1573
29 selfe] selvys L; wot] interl. A   32 in that case] in the case L 1553 1573; falsely] that
falsely 1573   33 full] om. L 1553 1573; mouth] mouthes L 1553 1573

there happeth any greate fall vnto theym, ball & barke & byte vppon
them like dogges.

Fynally the coste & charge / the dainger & perell of warre, wherin
their part is more than a pore mans is / sith the mater more dependith
5 vppon them / and many a pore ploughman may sit still by the fire,
while they must arise & walke. And some tyme their authorite fallith
by chaunge of their masters mynd / And of that se we dayly in one
place [or] other ensamples such & so many, that the parable of the
philosopher can lakke no testimonye / which likenid the seruauntes
10 of greate princes vnto the counptours, with which men do cast a
compt / For like as that counptour that standith sometyme for a ferthing, is sodenly [f. 157] set vpp & standith for a thowsand pownd / and
after as sone set down efte sone beneth, to stand for a ferthing agayne /
so fareth it lo sometyme with those that seke the way to rise & grow
15 vpp in authorite, by the favour of greate princes / that as they rise vpp
high, so fall they down agayne as low.

How be it though a man escape all such adventures, & abide in
greate authorite till he dye / yet than at the lest wise euery man must
leve it at the last / And that which we call at last, hath no very long
20 tyme to it / Let a man reken his yeres that are passid of his age, ere
euer he can gett vpp alofte, and let hym whan he haue it furst in his
fyst, reken how long he shalbe like to live after / & I wene that than
the most part shall ⌐haue littill cause to reioyce / they shall⌐ se the
tyme likely to be ⌐so⌐ short / that their honour & authorite by nature
25 shall endure / beside the manifold chaunces wherby they may lese it
more sone / And than whan they see that they must nedes leve it,
the thing which they did mich more set their hart vppon than euer
they had resonable cause, what sorow they take therfor, that shall I
not nede to tell you / And thus it semeth vnto me Cosyn in good fayth,
30 that sith in the havyng the profit is not grete, & the displeasures neyther smalle nor few / & of the lesyng so many sundry chaunces / &
that by no meane a man can kepe it long / and that to part therfrom

---

1 ball] baule *1553 1573*   6 arise] ryse L *1553 1573*   7 chaunge] chaunce *A*: g *wr. over*
second c *B*, the chaunge L *1553*, chaunge *1557 1573*   8 or] *Ƶ*, & *A*   11 as that] as the
L *1553 1573*   13 down efte sone] downe, and eftesone *1573*   14 fareth] *divided* fa-reth:
extra re *canc. A after* fa   19 at last] at least *1553*   21 haue] th *wr. over* ue *B*, hath *Ƶ*;
furst] u *wr. over illeg. letter B*   24 so] *wr. in space between words B*; *extra* that *canc. B after*
short   25 chaunces] *one minim missing in* un *A, redundant superl.* a *A*   27 hart] hartes L
31 chaunces /] | *wr. over comma B*

is such a paynfull grief / I can see no very greate cause / for which
as an high worldly commoditie, men shuld greatly desier it.

That these outward goodes desirid but for worldly welth, be not onely litle good for the body, but are also mich harme for the soule /

The xij chapitre

And thus far haue we considerid hitherto, in these outward [f.
157ᵛ] goodes, that are callid the giftes of fortune / no ferther but the
slender commoditie that worldly myndid men haue by them. But now
yf we consider ferther, what harm to the soule they take by them,
that desire them but onely for the wrechid welth of this world /
than shall we well perceve / how far more happy is he that well leseth
them / than he that evill fyndeth them.

These thinges though they be such as are of their own nature indeferent / that is to wit of them selfe, thinges neither good nor bad / but
are mater that may serue to the tone or the tother, after as men will
vse them / yet nede we litle to dowt yt / but that they that desire them
but for their worldly pleasure, & for no ferther godly purpose / the
devill shall sone turne them from thinges indeferent vnto them, &
make them thinges very nought / For though that they be indeferent
of their nature / yet can not the vse of them litely stand indeferent /
but determynatly must eyther be good or bad / and therfor he that
desireth them but for worldly pleasure, desiereth them not for any
good / & for bettre purpose than he desiereth them / to bettre vse is
he not likely to put them / and therfor not vnto good, but consequently
to nought.

As for ensample, first consider it in riches, he that longeth for them
as for thing of temporall commoditie, & not for any godly purpose /
what good they shall do hym S paule declareth where he writith vnto
Tymothe: *Qui volunt diuites fieri, incidunt in tentationem, & in laqueum*

---

6 xij] xijᵗʰ L; / before xij A   11 wrechid] whrechid A: *first* h *canc.* B; world] worke *1553*
15 selfe] selvys L   16 tone . . . tother] one . . . other *1573*   17 w *canc.* A *before* nede
21 litely] *divided* lite-ly A: ght *wr. over* te B   22 and] a *alt. to* A B   23 worldly]
wordly A   27 riches] richesse *1557*   28 thing] thynges Z

*Diaboli, & desideria multa inutilia & noxia, quae mergunt homines in inter-
itum & perditionem* / They that long to be rich, fall into temptacion
[f. 158] & into the grynne of the devill, & into many desires vnprofitable & noyouse, which drowne men into deth & into perdition. And
5 the holy scripture sayth also, in the xx^th chapiter of the proverbis /
Qui congregat thesauros impingetur ad laqueos mortis / He that gathereth
treasours, shalbe shovid into the grynne of deth / so that where as by
the mouth of S. paule god sayth that they shall fall into the devilles
grynne / he sayth in the tother place, that they shalbe pusshid and
10 shovid in by violence / And of trouth while a man desierith richesse
not for any good godly purpose, but for onely worldly welth / it must
nedes be, that he shall haue litle conscience in the gettyng / but by
all evill wayes that he can invent, shall labour to get them / & than
shall he either negardly hepe them vpp to gether (which is you wot
15 well dampnable) or wastfully misse spend them about worldly pompe
pride & glotony, with occasion of many synnys mo. And that is yet
mich more dampnable /

As for fame & glory desired but for worldly pleasure / doth vnto
the soule inestimable harme / for that settith mens hartes vppon high
20 devisis & desieres of such thinges as are immoderate & outragiouse /
⌜&⌝ by helpe of false flateres / puff vpp a man in pride, & make a
brotle man lately made of earth / & that shall agayne shortly be laid
full low in earth / & there lye & rott & turn agayne into earth / take
hym selfe in the meane tyme for a god here vppon earth, & wene to
25 wynne hym selfe to be lord of all the earth /

This maketh batayles betwene these greate princes, & with mich
trowble to much peple, & greate effucion of bloude, [f. 158ᵛ] one
kyng to loke to reyne in five realmes, that can not well rule one / for
how many hath now this greate Turke / and yet aspirethe to mo / And
30 those that he hath, he ordreth evill & yet hymselfe worse /

Than offices & romes of authorite, yf men desire them only for

1 noxia] nociua *1557 1573*   4 drowne] drownde *L*   5 xx^th] xxj^th *L*, .xxi. *1553 1557*,
om. *1573* (Cap. 21. *in margin 1573*); chapiter] Booke *1573*   6 ad laqueos] in laqueos *L*,
in laqueus *1553*   7 shovid] showued *1553*; grynne] grinnes *Z*   9–10 and shovid] or
showued *L 1553*   10 richesse] riches *Z*   11 worldly] om. *1553*   13 that] than *1553*
14 (which] *parenth. wr. over* | *B*   15 dampnable)] *parenth. added B*; *flourish after* damp-
nable | *A*   21 flateres] flatterers *Z*   22 brotle] bryttel *L 1553*, brittle *1573*; earth /]
comma wr. over | *B*   24 vppon earth] vpon the earth *L 1553*   25 earth /] *period
before* | *B*   27 bloude] u? *blotted by B*   30 worse] moche worse *L*

their worldly fantasies / who can loke that euer they shall occupy
them well / but abuse their authorite / & do therby greate hurt / for
than shall they fall from indifferency & maynteyn false matters of
their frendes / bere vpp their seruauntes & such as depend vppon
them, with beryng downe of other innocent folke / & not so able to do 5
hurt as easy to take harm / Than the lawes that are made agaynst malefactours, shall they make as an old philosopher said, to be mich like
vnto Cobwebbes, in which the litle knettes & flyes stikk still & hang
fast / but the greate humble bees breke them & flye quyte thorow /
And than the lawes that are made as a buckler in the defence of 10
innocentes, those shall they make serue for a swerd, to cutt & sore
wound them with, & therwith wound they their own soules sorer /
And thus you see cosyn, that of all this outward goodes, ⸢which men
call the goodes⸣ of fortune, there is neuer one that vnto them which
long therfor, not for any godly purpose / but onely for their worldly 15
welth, hath any greate commoditie to the body / & yet are they all in
such case besides that, very dedly destruccion vnto the soule.

Whither men desire these owtward goodes for their
owne worldly welth / or for any good vertuouse purpose /
this persecusion of the Turke agaynst the fayth, will   20
declare / and the comfort that both twayne may take
in the lesing them thus /

The xiij Chapitre

Vincent

Veryly good vncle this thing is so playnly trew, that no man may by 25
any good reason deny it / But I wene vncle also, that [f. 159] there

---

1 fantasies] fansyes *L*   3 maynteyn] *B Z*, maynten^ance *A*: ce *and superscript* a *canc. and*
yn *wr. over* nn *B*   5 &] *om. 1573*   7 philosopher] lo *interl. A*   8 knettes] *first* e *alt.*
to a *B*, gnattes *L 1553*, knattes *1557*, gnats *1573*   11 serue] v *wr. over* u *B*; / *canc. B*
after serue   11–12 sore wound] sore wounded *1553*   13 this] these *Z*   17 very]
the very *L*   19 owne] onely *Z*   23 xiij] xiijth *L*; / *after* xiij *A*   25 by] with *Z*
26 But] & *1573*

will no man say nay / for I se no man that will for very shame confesse, that he desireth riches / honour, & renome, offices / & romes
of authorite / for his own worldly pleasure / for euery man wold
fayne seme as holy as an horse / & therfor will euery man say / & wold
5 it were bilevid to, that he desireth these thinges (though for his
own worldly welth a litle so) yet principally to merit therby / thorow
doing some good therwith.

Antonye

This is Cosyn very sure so / that so doth euery say / But first he that
10 in the desire therof, hath his respect therin vnto his worldly welth /
as you say but a litle so / so mich as hym selfe weneth were but a
litle / may sone preve a greate deale to mich. And many ⌜men⌝ will
say so to, that haue in dede their principall respect therin vnto their
worldly commodytie, & vnto godward therin litle or nothing at all &
15 yet they pretend the contrary / & that vnto their own harm / *quia
deus non irridetur* / god can not be mokkyd /
And some peradventure know not well their own affeccion them
selfe / but their lieth more imperfeccion secret in their affeccion, than
them selfe are well ware of, which onely god beholdith / & therfor
20 sayth the profet vnto god / *Inperfectum meum viderunt oculi tui* / myn
Imperfeccion haue thyn yeen beholden / for which the prophete prayeth / *Ab occultis meis munda me domine*: Fro myn hydde sinnis clense thow
me good Lord.
But now Cosyn this tribulacion of the Turke, if he so persecute vs
25 for the fayth, that those that will forsake their fayth shall kepe their
goodes / and those shall lese their goodes that will not leve their fayth:
this maner of persecucion lo, shall like a towch stone [f. 159ᵛ] trye
them, & shew the faynid fro the trew myndid, & tech also them that
wene they mene bettre than they do in dede, bettre to descerne them

---

i for] f *alt. to* F B   2 renome] renowne L *1553*, renoume *1557*, renowme *1573*   3 own]
onely Ƶ; wold] *orig.* will, o *wr. over* i *and* d *over final* l A   4 an horse] a horse L *1553*
1573   5 were] were so Ƶ   6 own] *om.* Ƶ   7 good therwith] good dede therwith
L *1553*   9 euery say] euery man say Ƶ   10 the] *om.* L; worldly] worldly / A   13 in
dede their] *om. 1557*; their] *interl.* A *above orig.* his (*canc.* A *and* B)   14 welth *canc.* A *and*
B *before* commodytie; therin] *om.* Ƶ   16 deus] dominus *1557*   18 selfe] selvys L
19 selfe] selvys L; ware of] *wr. together* A, B *adds vertical line after* ware   21 thyn]thy L
1553; yeen] eies *1573*   22 Fro] From L *1553*; myn] my L *1553 1573*   28 fro] from
L *1553 1573*; tech] *final* e *added* B

selfe / For some there are that wene they mene well / while they frame
them selfe a conscience, & euer kepe still a greate heape of superfluouse substaunce by them / thinkyng euer still that they will bethinke
them selfe vppon some good dede / wheron they will well bestow it
ones / or that els their executours shall / But now yf they lye not 5
vnto them selfe / but kepe their good for any good purpose to the
pleasure of god in dede / than shall they in this persecucion, for the
pleasure of god in kepyng of his fayth, be glad to depart fro them /
  And therfor as for all these thinges, the losse I mene of all these owtward thinges that men call the gifte of fortune / this is me thinketh in 10
this Turkes persecucion for the fayth, consolacion greate & sufficyent /
that sith euery man that hath them, either settith by them for the
world or for god / he that settith by them for the world, hath as I haue
shewid you litle profit by them to the body, & greate harme vnto the
soule / & therfor may well (yf he be wise) rekyn that he wynneth by 15
the losse / all though he lost them but by some comen chaunce / And
mich more happy than while he leseth them by such a meritoriouse
meane / And on the tother side, he that kepeth them for some good
purpose, entendyng to bestow them for the pleasure of god / the losse
of them in this turkes persecucion for kepyng of the fayth, can be no 20
maner grief vnto hym / sith that by his so partyng fro them, he bestoweth them in such wise vnto goddes pleasure, that at [f. 160] the
tyme whan he leseth them, by no way could he bestough them vnto
his high pleasure bettre / For though it had be peradventure bettre,
to haue bestowed them well before / yet sith he kept them for some 25
good purpose / he wold not haue lefte them vnbestowed yf he had foreknowen the chaunce / but being now preventid so by persecution, that
he can not bestow them in that other good way that he wold / yet
while he partith fro them, because he will not part fro the fayth /
though the devilles eschetour violently take them from hym / yet 30
willyngly giveth he them to god /

---

1 selfe] selvys *L* 2 selfe] selvys *L* 4 selfe] selvys *L* 5 that] *om. L 1553 1573*; now]
om. L 1553 6 selfe] selves *L*; their good] theyr goodes *Z* 8 in kepyng] in the keping
L 1553 1573; glad to] glad for to *1553 1557*; fro] from *L 1573* 9 these] those *L 1553
1573*; these] those *1553 1573* 10 gifte] giftes *Z* 14 vnto] to *L* 15 wise)] *parenth.
added B*; rek *canc. A before* rekyn 21 fro] from *Z* 22–23 the tyme] that tyme *1553 1573*
24 had be] hadde beene *L 1553 1573* 26 vnbestowed] w *wr. over illeg. letter* (u?) *B*
29 fro] from *L 1553 1573*; fro] from *L 1553 1573* 31 giveth he] he geueth *L 1553 1573*

A nother cause for which eny man shuld be content to forgo his goodes in the Turkes said persecucion

The / 14 / chapiter /

Vincent

5   I can not in good fayth good vncle say nay to none of this. And in
dede vnto them that by the Turkes ouer runnyng of the cuntrey, were
happid to be spoylid & robbid, & all their substaunce moveable &
vnmoveable byreft & lost all redy, their persons onely fled & safe /
I thinke that these consideracions (considerid therwith that as you
10 lately said their sorow could not amend their chaunce) might vnto
them be good occasion of comfort / & cause them as you said, make
a vertue of necessitie / But in the case vncle that we now speke of /
that is to wit, where they haue yet their substaunce vntouchid in their
own handes / & that the kepyng or the ⌐losyng,¬ shall hang both in
15 their owne handes by the Turkes offre vppon the reteynyng / or the
renouncyng of the christen fayth / here vncle I fynd it as you said, that
this temptacion [f. 160ᵛ] is most sore & most perilouse / for I fere me
that we shall find few of such as haue much to lese / that shall fynd in
their hartes so sodenly to forsake their good, with all those other
20 thinges afore rehersid / wheruppon their worldly welth dependith /

Antonye

    That fere I mych Cosyn to / but therby shall it well as I said aper /
that semed they neuer so good & vertuose before, & flaterid ⌐they¬
them selfe with neuer so gay a glose of good and graciouse purpose
25 that they kepe their good for / yet were theire hartes inwardly in
the depe sight of god not sound & sure such as they shuld be, & as
peradventure some had them selfe went they had be / but like a puff
ring of parice holow light & counterfayte in dede /

---

3 14] xiiijᵗʰ L   8 byreft] by reft A, *words connected* B   10 chaunce)] *parenth. added* B;
might] I mighte *1553*   11 make] to make *1573*   13 wit] wete *1553*   14 losyng,]
wr. in margin B   19 *extra* to forsake *canc.* B *before* their; good] es *added* B, goodes Z
20 their] all theyr L *1553 1573*   22 aper] *final* e *added* B   24 selfe] selvys L
25 kepe] kept Z; good] es *added* B, goodes Z   27 selfe] selves L; had be] had bene L
1573   27–28 puff ring] pursering L *1553 1573*   28 parice] s *wr. over* ce B, parvys L

And yet they being evyn such / this wold I fayne aske one of them /
And I pray you Cosyn take you his person vppon you / & in this case
answere for hym / what lettith you wold I aske (for we will take no
small man for a sample in this part / nor hym that had litle to lese /
For such one were me thinke so far from all frame / that wold cast 5
away god for a litle that he were not worthy to talke with) what
lettith I say therfor your lordship that you be not gladly content
without any deliberacion at all / in this kynd of persecucion / rather
than to leve your fayth / to let go all that euer you haue at ones.

Vincent   10

Sith you put it vncle vnto me, to make the mater the more playne /
that I shuld play that greate mans part that is so welthy and haue so
mich to lese / albeit I can not be very sure of [f. 161] a nother mans
mynd / nor what a nother man wold say / yet as far as myn own mynd
can coniecture / I shall answere in his person what I wenc wold be 15
his let /
And therfor to your question I answere, that there lettith me the
thyng that your selfe may lightly gesse, the lesyng of the manyfold
commodities which I now haue / richesse / and substaunce / landes
and great possessions of enheritauns / with greate rule and aucthorite 20
here in my countrey / all which thinges the greate Turke grauntith
me to kepe still in pease / and haue them enhauncid to / so that I
will forsake the faythe of christ / ye I may say ⌈to⌉ you / I haue a
mocion secretly made me ferther, to kepe all this yet bettre chepe /
that is to witt, not be compellid vtterly to forsake christ / nor all the 25
whole christen fayth, but onely some such partes therof as may not
stond with macometes law / & onely grauntyng machomete for a
trew prophete, & serving the Turke truly in his warres agaynst all
christen kynges: I shall not be lettid to prayse christ also, & to call
hym a good man, & worship hym and serve hym to.   30

1 evyn] om. L 1553 1573   3 lettith you wold I aske] letteth, would I aske you L 1553
1573; (for] parenth. wr. over | B   4 part /] comma before | B   5 wold] he would L
6 with)] parenth. wr. over | B   9 leve] interl. A above lese (canc. A and B)   11 vncle]
interl. A; the more] the om. L 1553 1573   12 haue] hath Z   13 lese] lose 1553 1573
18 lesyng] losing 1553 1573   19 richesse] Rytches L 1553 1573   23 christ /] period
before | B   25 witt] wete 1553   27 macometes] Machomettes L, Machomets 1553
1573, Mahomettes 1557; machomete] Machomett L, Machomet 1553 1573, Mahomete
1557

Antonye

Nay nay my lord / Christ hath not so greate nede of your Lord-
shippe, as rather than to lese your service, he wold fall at such coven-
auntes with you / to take your service at halfes, to serve hym & his
5 enymy both / he hath given you playne warnyng all redye by S. paule,
that he will haue in your servyce no partyng felow: *Que societas lucis
ad tenebras / Christi ad Belial /* what feleship is there betwene light &
darknes, betwene christ & Beliall / And he hath also playnly shewid
you hymselfe, by his own mouth / *Nemo potest duobus dominis seruire /*
10 no man [f. 161ᵛ] may serve two lordes at ones / he will haue you bileve
all that he tellith you / and do all that he biddeth you, & forbere all
that he forbiddeth you, without any maner excepcion / Breke one
of his commaundementes & breke all / forsake one poynt of his fayth,
& forsake all / as for any thanke you get of hym for the remanaunt /
15 And therfor yf you devise as it were indentures betwene god & you,
what thing you will do for hym / & what thing you will not do / as
though he shuld hold hym content with such servis of yours as your
selfe list to appoynt hym / yf you make I say such indentures, you shall
seale both the partes your selfe / and you gete therto none agrement
20 of hym /

   And this I say, though the Turke wold make such an appoyntment
with you as you speke of, & wold whan he had made it kepe it / where
as he wold not I warrant you leve you so / whan he had ones brought
you so ferforth / but wold litle & litle after ere he lefte you, make you
25 denye christ all together, & take machomete in his stede / & so doth
he in the begynnyng / whan he will not haue you beleve hym to
be god / For surely yf he were not god / he were no good man
neyther / while he playnely said / he was god.

   But though he wold neuer go so far forth with you / yet christ will
30 (as I said) ⌐not⌐ take your service to halfes / but will that you shall
love hym with all your whole hart / And because that while he was
livyng ⌐here⌐ xvᶜ yere agoo, he forsaw this mynd of yours that you

---

4 halfes] halves *L*   6 lucis] luci *1557*   7 Christi ad Belial] Que autem conuentio
Christi ad Belial *1557 1573*   12 maner] manor of *L*   14 thanke] thanks *1557*; of
hym] *om. L 1553 1573*   16 hym /] / *canc. and comma added B*   18 list] lust *1553*; to
appoynt] to *canc. B, om. 1557*   19 both the] the *om. L*; none] no *1553*   23 so /] / /
canc. and comma added B   25 &] *canc. and* And *interl. B*   28 said /] / *canc. B*
30 said)] *parenth. ins. before* /B   30 halfes] halves *L*   32 xvᶜ] xv, hundreth *L*, fiftene
hundreth *1553*, fiftene hundred *1573*

haue now, with which you wold fayne serve hym in some such fashion
as you might kepe your worldly substaunce styll / but rather forsake
his seruice than ⌈put⌉ all your substaunce from you / he tellith you
playne xv^c yere agoo his own mouth, that [f. 162] he will no such
seruice of you / sayng / *Non potestis seruire Deo & mammone* / you can 5
not serve both god & your riches together / And therfor this thing
stablishid for a playne conclucion which you must nedes graunt / yf
you haue fayth / and yf you be gone from that grownd of fayth all
redye / than is all our disputacion you wot well at an end / For wherto
shuld you than rather lese your goodes than forsake your fayth / yf 10
you haue lost your fayth & let it go all redye / This poynt I say therfor
put first for a grownd betwene vs both twayne agreed / that you
haue yet the fayth still / and entend to kepe it alwaye still in your
hart / and are but in dowte whither you will lese all your worldly
substaunce, rather than forsake your fayth in your onely word / now 15
shall I replye to the poynt of your answere / wherin you tell me the
lothnesse of your losse / & the comfort of the kepyng, lettith you to
forgo them, & moveth you rather to forsake your fayth /

I let passe all that I haue spoken of the small commoditie of them
vnto your body, & of the great harm that the havyng of them do to 20
your soule / And sith the promise of the Turke made vnto you for
the kepyng of them, is the thing that moveth you & maketh you thus
to dowt / I aske you first wherby you wote, that whan you haue done
all that he will haue you do agaynst christ to the harm of your sowle /
wherby wote you I saye, that he will kepe you his promise in these 25
thinges that he promiseth you, concernyng the retaynyng of your
welbelovyd worldly welth / for the pleasure of your bodye /

Vincent

What surety can a man haue of such a greate prince but his promise,
which for his own honour it can not become hym to breke ? [f. 162^v] 30

---

2 substaunce] *minim lacking in* un, *superfluous superscript a* A; styll /] / *wr. over comma* B; but
rather] & rather *1573*   3 put] *interl.* B *above canc.* pull A; tellith] told L   4 xv^c]
.xv hundreth L *1553*, fiftene hundred *1573*   5 seruire Deo] deo seruire Z; mammone]
hook added to e B   6 riches] richesse *1553 1557*   7 conclucion] si *wr. over* c B; graunt/]
/ *canc.* B   9 all our] al your *1553 1573*   16 your answere] your *canc. and* the *interl. and
then canc.* B (*corrections partly erased*)   17 your losse /] your *canc. and* the *interl.* B, comma
before / B, the losse Z; the kepyng] the *om. 1553*   20–21 do to your] doth to your *1573*
21 soule /] / *canc. and period added* B   22 maketh] Z, make A   26 promiseth]
promysed L   30 breke ?] *question-mark ed.*

Antonye

I haue knowen hym & his father afore hym to / breke mo promises
than five as grete as this is that he shuld make with you. Who shall
come & cast in his teth & tell hym, it is a shame for hym to be so ficle
5 & so false of his promise / And than what careth he for those wordes,
that he woteth well he shall neuer here / not very mich / although they
were told hym to / Iff you might come after & complayne your grefe
vnto his own person your selfe / you shuld fynd hym as shamfast as a
frend of myn a merchaunt found ones the Sowdane of Siry / to whome
10 being certayne yeres about his merchaundice in that countrey, he
gave a greate some of money for a certeyne office mete for hym there
for the while / which he scant had hym grauntid & put in his hand /
but that ere euer it was awght worth vnto hym, the Sowdane sodaynly
sold it to a nother of his own sect, & put our hungaryen out / Than
15 came he to hym & humbly put hym in remembraunce of his graunt
passid his own mowth, & signid with his own hand / whervnto the
Sowdane answerid hym with a grymme countenaunce / I will thow
wit it losell, that neyther my mowth nor myn hand shalbe master ouer
me, to bynd all my body at their pleasure / but I will so be lord &
20 master ouer them both, that what so euer the tone say or the tother
wryte / I wilbe at myn own libertie to do what my list my selfe, & aske
them both no leve / And therfor go gete the hens out of my countrey
knave /

Wene you now my lord, that Sowdane & this Turke being both
25 of one false sect / you may not fynd them both like false [f. 163] of their
promise /

Vincent

That must I nedes iubard / for other surety can there none be had /

---

2 afore] a fore *A*: *words connected B*, before *1553 1573*; hym to / breke] him, to breake *L*
1553, him to, breake *1557 1573*   3 shuld make] shoulde here make *Z*   4 cast in]
cast it in *Z*   10 merchaundice] d *wr. over* t *A*   12 hym grauntid] graunted him *1573*
13 ere euer] or euer *1553*; it was awght] it wer ought *L 1553 1573*; sodaynly] l *wr. over*
first y *A*   16 signid] singnid *A*   18 myn] my *L 1553 1573*   19 I will] I *om. L*
20 tone] one *1553 1573*; tother] other *1553 1573*   21 myn] my *1553*; my] me *Z*; list]
lust *1553*   22–23 And therfor go gete the hens out of my countrey knave /] *om. L 1553*
22 countrey] countries *1557 1573*   28 iubard] ieobarde *L*, ieoparde *1553*, ieopard *1573*

Anthony

An vnwise iuberdyng to put your soule in perell of dampnation, for the kepyng of your bodely pleasures, & yet without surety therof must iubard them to /

But yet go a litle ferther lo / Suppose me that you might be very 5 surc that the Turke wold breke no promise with you / Are you than sure Inough to retayne all your substaunce still /

Vincent

Yea than /

Anthony   10

What yf a man shold aske you how longe.

Vincent

How long / as long as I live /

Antonye

Well let it be so than / But yet as farre as I can see though the 15 greate Turke favour you neuer so mich / & lett you kepe your goodes as long as euer you live / yet yf it happe that you be this day fiftye yeare old / all the favour he can shew you, can not make you one day yonger to morow / but euery day shall you wax elder than other, & than within a while must you for all his favour lese all /   20

Vincent

Well a man wold be glad for all that, to be sure not to lakk while he livethe /

Antonye

Well than yf the greate Turke give you your good / can there than 25 in all your life none other take them from you agayne.

---

2 iuberdyng] *abbrev. form canc. and* iuberdyng, *interl.* B, ieobardyng L, ieoparding *1553 1573*, iubarding *1557*   4 iubard] ieobard L, ieoparde *1553*, iubarde *1557*, ieopard *1573* 5 you] ye *1553 1573*   7 your substaunce] our substaunce *1573*   17 this day] at thys daye L *1553 1573*   18 favour he] fauour that he L *1553 1573*   26 none] no *1553 1573*

Vincent

Verely I suppose no /

Anthony [f. 163ᵛ]

May he not lese this countrey agayne vnto christen men, & you
5 with the takyng of this way, fall in the same perell than, that you
wold now eschew /

Vincent

Forsoth I thinke that yf he get it ones, he will neuer lese yt agayne
in our dayes /

10   Anthonye

Yis by goddes grace / but yet yf he lese it after your dayes, there
goeth your childrens enheritaunce away agayne / But be it now
that he could neuer lese it / could none take your substaunce from
you than /

15   Vincent

No in good fayth none /

Anthonye

No none at all / not god /

Vincent

20   God / what yis perdie / who dowteth of that /

Antonye

Who / Mary / he / that dowteth whether there be any god or no /
And that there lakketh not some such, the prophet testifieth, where he
saith / *Dixit insipiens in corde suo non est deus* / the fole hath said in his
25 hart there is no god. With the mouth, the most folysh will forbere

---

5 you] ye *1557*   6 eschew /] *question-mark before* / *B*   8 neuer lese] neuer after lese
1573; yt agayne] it after again *1557*   18 god /] *question-mark ins. before* / *B*   20 God /]
question-mark ins. before / *B*   22 Who /] *question-mark ins. before* / *B*; Mary / he /] *virgules*
canc. B   24 insipiens] incipiens *A*: s *wr. over* c *B*

to say it vnto other folke / but in the hart they let not to say it softly
to them selfe / And I fere me there be many mo such foles than euery
man wold wene there were / & wold not let to saye it openly to, yf
they forbare it not more for drede or shame of men, than for any fere
of god / But now those that are so frantique folysh, as to wene there 5
were no god / and yet in their wordes confesse hym, though that / as
s. paule sayth / in their dedes they deny hym / we shall let them
passe till it please god shew hym selfe vnto them / eyther inwardly
by tyme by his mercifull grace, orels owtwardly (but ouer late for
them) by his terrible [f. 164] iudgement /   10

But vnto you my lord, sith you beleve & confesse (like as a wise man
shuld) that though the Turke kepe you promise in lettyng you kepe
your substaunce / because you do hym pleasure in the forsakyng of
your fayth / yet god / whose fayth you forsake / & therin do hym
displeasure / may so take them from you, that the grete Turke with 15
all the power he hath, is not hable to kepe you them / why will you be
so vnwise with the losse of your sowle, to please the greate Turke for
your goodes / while you wote well that god whom you displease
therwith, may take them from you to /

Besides this, sith you beleve there is a god / you can not but byleve 20
therwith that the greate Turke can not take your good from you without his will or sufferaunce / no more than the devill cold from Iob /
And thinke you than / that yf he will suffre the Turke take away your
good / albeit that by the kepyng & confessing of his fayth you please
hym / he will whan you displease hym by forsakyng his fayth, suffre 25
you of those goodes that you get or kep therby, to reioyce or enioy
any benyfite in /

Vincent

God is graciouse / & though that men offend hym, yet he suffreth
them many tymes to live in prosperite long after /   30

---

2 selfe] selves *L*   3 wene] wene / *A*: / *canc. B*; let to] to *wr. over it A*   4 forbare] a
wr. over e *A*; or shame] of shame *L 1553 1573*, or of shame *1557*   6 though] though /
A: / *canc. B*; that /] / *canc. B*   7–8 them passe] hym passe *1553*   8 god shew] god
to shewe *L 1553 1573*; eyther] *om. L*   9 by tyme] betyme *L 1553*; (but] / but *A*: / *canc.
and parenth. added B*   10 them)] *parenth. added B*   14 god /] / *canc. B*   15 from] fro
1557   16 hable] h *canc. B*, able *Z*; you them] you, the *1553*, you: then *1573*   22 from]
fro *1553 1557 1573*   26 kep] *final* e *added B*; or enioy] and enioy *L 1553 1573*   27 in]
canc. B, om. Z; question-mark after *benyfite B*   30 many tymes] *interl. A*

Anthonye

Long after / nay by my trouth my lord that doth he no man, for how
can that be that he shuld suffer you live in prosperite long after / whan
your whole life is but short in all together, & eyther almost halfe therof
5 or more than halfe you thinke your selfe I dare say / spent out all redy
before / Can you burn out halfe a short candell / & than haue a long
one left of the remenaunt / There can not be in this world a worse
mynd, than that a man to delite & take comfort in any commoditie
that he taketh by sinfull [f. 164ᵛ] meane / For it is the very strayte
10 way toward the takyng of boldnes & corage in synne / And fynally to
fall into infidelite, & thinke that god careth not / nor regardeth not
what thinges men do here, nor what mynd we be of /

But vnto such myndid folke, spekyth holy scripture in this wise:
Noli dicere peccaui, & nihil mihi accidit triste / patiens enim redditor est
15 *dominus* / say not I haue synnyd, & yet there hath happyd me no harm,
for god suffreth before he strike / but as saynt Austeyne sayth / the
lenger that he taryeth or he stryke, the sorer is the stroke whan he
streketh /

And therfor yf ye will well do, rekyn your selfe very sure, that whan
20 you dedly displease god for the gettyng or the kepyng of your goodes,
god shall not suffer those goodes to do you good / but eyther shall he
take them shortly from you / or suffer you to kepe them for a litle
while to your more harm / and after shall he whan you lest loke therfor, take you away from them / And than what a hepe of hevynes will
25 there entre into your hart / whan you shall see that you shall so
sodeynly go from your goodes, & leve them here in the earth in one
place / & that your bodye shalbe put in the erth in a nother place /
and (which than shalbe most hevines of all) whan you shall fere (& not
without greate cause) that your soule shall first forthwith / and after
30 that at the fynall iudgment your body to, be driven downe depe toward

---

2 man,] *comma ed., period B*   7 remenaunt /] *question-mark ins. before / B*; be] *canc. and interl.
after* world *B*; in this world] *interl. A*; be in this world a] in this world be a *Z*   8 that
a man] that *om. 1573*   10 And] *canc. and* & *interl. B*   12 thinges] es *added B?*, thing
L 1553 1573   15 there hath] hath there *L 1553 1573*; no] none *1557*   17 lenger]
longer *1553 1573*; or] ere *L 1573*   18 streketh] y *wr. over first* e *B*   19 ye] you *L
1553 1573*   20 goodes] good *1573*   23 lest] *final* e *added B*   24 a hepe] an heape
L 1553 1573   25–26 so sodeynly] sodainly so *1553*   26 the earth] thearth *L*
27–28 / and] (and *A: parenth. canc. before* and, *added before* which *B*   28 all)] all / *A:
parenth. wr. over / B*

the centre of the earth into the very pitt & doungeon of the devill of
hell, there to tarry in turment world without end / What goodes of
the world can any man Imagyne, wherof the pleasure & commoditie
cowld be such in a m^{le} yere, as were able to recompence that intollerable payne, that there is to be suffrid in one yere / yee or one daye /   5
or one hower eyther / And than what a madnes it is for the pore
pleasure of your worldly goodes of so few yeres, to cast your selfe both
bodye & sowle into the euerlastyng fyer of hell / wherof there is not
minyshid the mountenaunce of a moment [f. 165] by the lying there
the space of an hundred m^{le} yeres.   10

And therfor our saviour in few wordes, concludid & confutid all
those folyes of them / that for the short vse of this worldly substaunce,
forsake hym & his faythe, & sell their sowles vnto the devill for euer /
where he sayth / *Quid prodest homini si vniuersum mundum lucretur, anime
vero suae detrimentum patiatur* / what avaylith yt a man yff he wanne   15
all the whole worlde & lost his soule / This were me thinketh cause &
occasion inough to hym that had neuer so mich part of this world in
his hand / to be content rather to lese yt all, than for the reteynyng /
or encresyng of his worldly goodes, to lese & destroye his soule /

Vincent   20

This is good vncle in good fayth very trew / And what other thing
any of them that wold not for this be content / haue for to alledge in
reason for the defence of their folye / that can I not ymagyne / nor
list in this mater to play their part no lenger / but I pray god give me
the grace to play the contrary parte in dede / And that I neuer for any   25
good or substaunce of this wrechid worlde, forsake my fayth toward
god / neyther in hart nor tong, as I trust in his grete goodnes I neuer
shall /

---

1 centre] centrye *L*, centry *1553 1557*; the earth] thearthe *L*; very] *canc. and* fyry *interl.*
B, fyrye *L 1557*, fiery *1553 1573*   3 the world] this world Z 4 m^{le}] thousande Z
5 yee or one] or in one *1553*, yea in one *1573*   6 or one hower] or in one howre *1573*;
And than] yea & then *1553*; it is] s *wr. over* t *and* t *wr. over* s *B*, is it Z; the pore] that
poore *1553*   8 the euerlastyng] theverlastyng *L*   10 hundred] hundredred *A: extra*
red *canc. B*, hundreth *L 1553*; m^{le}] ^{le} *canc. B, then* l *interl. and canc. B*, thousande Z; a
interl. and canc. after in *B*   12 those] these Z 14 anime] *hook added to* e *B?*   15 suae] ae
wr. over e *B?*   16 worlde] worldle *A:* le *canc. B*   18 reteynyng /] / *canc. B*
24 list] lust *1553*; in this] not in this *1557 1573*; lenger] longre *1553 1573*   26 good]
es *added B*, goodes Z; substaunce] substaunce / *A:* / *canc. B*; worlde] worldle *A:* le *canc. B*

This kynd of tribulacion trieth what mynd men haue to
their goodes / which they that are wise, will at the fame
therof se well & wisely laid vp safe before

The / 15 / chapitre /

5   Anthonye

Me thinketh Cosyn that this persecution / shall not onely as I said
before / trye mens hartes when it commeth, & make them know their
owne affeccions / whither they haue a corrupt gredy covetouse mynd
or not / but also the very fame and expectacion therof, may tech
10 them this lesson ere euer the thing fall ⌐vppon them⌐ it selfe / to their
no litle frute / yf they haue the wit & the grace to take it in tyme while
they may / for now may [f. 165ᵛ] they find sure places to ley their
tresour in, so that all the Turkes armye shall neuer fynd it out /

Vincent

15   Mary ⌐vncle⌐ that way ⌐they⌐ will I warrant you not forget, as nere
as their wittes will serue them / But yet haue I knowen some, that
haue ere this thought that they had hid there money safe & sure
inough / diggyng it full depe in the grownd / & haue missid it yet
whan they came agayne, & haue found it diggid out & caried a way
20 to their handes /

Antony

Nay / fro their handes I wene you wold say / And it was no merveyle / for some such haue I knowen to / but they haue hid their
goodes folyshly / in such place as they were well warnid before, that
25 they shuld not / And that were they warnid by hym that they well
knew for such one, as wist well inough what wold come theron /

---

2 that] that / A: / canc. B   3 wisely] wisely / A: / canc. B   4 15] xvᵗʰ L   5 Anthonye]
om. 1553   12 for] f alt. to F B   13 tresour] treasures L 1553 1573; all] interl. A
15 they] interl. B above canc. I A   17 & sure] om. L   18 diggyng it] it om. 1553 1573
19 found] foundid A: id canc. B   22 you] ye 1557   26 such one] suche a one L

Vincent

Than were they more than madde / But ⌐dyd⌐ he tell them to, where
they shuld haue hid yt to haue it sure?

Antony

Yee by saynt mary did he / for els had he told them but halfe a tale /   5
but he told them an whole tale / biddyng them that they shuld in nowise hide their tresour in the grownd / and he shewid them a good
cause / for their thefes vse to dig it out & stele it away /

Vincent

Why / where shuld they hide it than said he / for thefis may happ   10
to fynd it out in any place.

Anthonye

Forsoth he counsaylid them to hyde their tresour in hevyn and there
lay it vpp / for there it shall lye safe / for thether he said there can no
thefe come / till he haue left his theft & be waxen a trew man first /   15
And he that gave this counsaile wist what he said well inough / for it
was our saviour hym selfe, which in the sixt chapitre of / s / mathew
sayth / *Nolite* [f. 166] *thesaurizare vobis thesauros in terra, vbi erugo & tinea
demolitur, & vbi fures effodiunt & furantur / Thesaurizate vobis thesauros in
caelo / vbi neque erugo neque tinea demolitur / & vbi fures non effodiunt nec*   20
furantur. Vbi enim est thesaurus tuus, ibi est & cor tuum / hord not vpp your
tresures in earth, where the rust & the ⌐mothe⌐ fret yt out, & where
theves dig it out & stele it away / But hord vpp your tresures in hevyn,
where neyther the rust & the ⌐mothe⌐ fret them out / & where thevis

---

3 sure?] *question-mark ed.*   6 an whole] a whole *L 1553 1573*   7 and] a *alt. to* A B
8 their thefes] *canc. and* there thevys *interl.* B, ther thevys *L,* there theues *1553,* ther theues
1557, there theeues *1573;* away] *orig.* way: *first* a *added* A?   10 thefis] *canc. and* thevys
interl. B, thevys *L,* theues *1553 1557,* theeues *1573*   14 there can] can there *L*   17 sixt]
om. 1573 (Matth. 6 *in margin*); chapitre] Gospel *1573*   19 furantur] furatur *A: bar added
over* a *B;* Thesaurizate] h *interl.* B; vobis] autem vobis *1557 1573*   20 vbi neque] vbi
nec *1557*   21 furantur.] furatur *A: bar added over* a *B, period ed.;* Vbi] vbi *A;* vpp] vpp
for *A,* for *canc.* B; your] for you *L 1553 1573*   22 mothe] *wr. by B in blank space left by*
A, moates *L,* mothes *1553*   24 rust &] & *canc. and* nor *interl.* B, nor *Z;* mothe] *wr. by B
in blank space left by A,* moates *L*

dig them not owt / & stele them away / for where as is thy tresour
there is thyne hart to /

Iff we wold well consider these wordes of our saviour christ, we
shuld as me thinke nede no more counsayle at all, nor no more com-
5 fort neyther, concernyng the losse of our temporall substaunce in this
Turkes persecution for the fayth / For here our lord in these wordes
techeath vs, where we may lay vpp our substaunce safe before the
persecucion come.

Yff we put it into the pore mens bousoms, there shall it ly safe / For
10 who wold go serch a beggers bag for money / yf we delyuer it to the
pore for christes sake, we delyuer yt vnto christ hym selfe / And than
what persecutour can there be so strong, as to take it out of his hand /

Vincent

These thinges are vncle vndowttely so trew, that no man may with
15 wordes wrastle therwith / but yet euer there hangith in a mans hart
a lothnesse to lakke a lyvyng /

Antonye

There doth in dede / in theyrs that eyther neuer or but seldome
here any good counsayle theragaynst / and whan they here it harken
20 ⌜it⌝ but as though they wold an idle tale / rather for a pastyme, or for
the maner sake, than for any substaunciall entent & purpose to folow
good aduertisement & take any frute therby / But verely yf we wold
not onely lay our eare, but also our hart therto / & consider [f. 166ᵛ]
that the saying of our saviour christ is not a poetes fable / nor an harp-
25 ers song / but the very holy word of almyghtye god hym selfe / we wold
& ⌜well⌝ we might / be full sore ashamid in our selfe & full sory to /
whan we felt in our affeccion those wordes to haue in our hartes no
more strength & wayght / but that we remayne still of the same dull
mynd as we did before we hard them /
30   This manner of ours / in whose brestes the great good counsayle
of god no bettre setleth, nor takith no bettre rote, may well declare

---

1 owt / &] / *canc.* B, & *canc. and* nor *interl.* B, nor Ƶ; thy] they A : *canc. and* thy *interl.* B
2 thyne] y *wr. over* e A, thy L *1553 1573*   4 thinke] thynketh L   6 Turkes] Thurkes
A, h *canc.* A   9 be *canc.* A *before* ly   14 vndowttely] vndoubtedly L *1553 1573*,
vndoutedlye *1557*   20 though] *canc.* A?, *om.* Ƶ   20–21 for the maner] the *om.* L *1553*
21 substaunciall] B Ƶ, substaunce A : iall *wr. over final* e B; & purpose] or purpose *1553 1573*

vs, that the thornes & the breres & the brambles of our worldly substaunce, grow so thicke & spryng vpp so ⌐high⌐ in the grownd of our
hartes / that they strangle (as the gospell sayth) the word of god that
was sowen therin / And therfor is god very good lord vnto vs, whan he
causeth like a good husband man his folke come on feld (for the 5
persecutours be his folke to this purpose) & with their hokes & their
stokkyng yrons, grubbe vpp this wikkyd wedes & busshis of our erthly
substaunce, & carry them quyte away from vs / that the word of god
sowen in our hartes, may haue rome therin / & a glad round abowt
for the warme sonne of grace to come to it & make it grow / / for 10
surely those wordes of our savyour shall we fynd full trew / *vbi thesaurus
tuus ibi est* ⌐&⌐ *cor tuum* / where as thy tresour is / there is also thyne
hart / yf we laye vpp our tresours in earth / in earth shalbe our
hartes / yf we send our tresour into hevyn / in hevyn shall we haue
our hartes. And surely the greaest comfort that any man may haue in 15
his tribulacion / is to haue his hart in hevyn /

Yff thyne hart were in dede out of this world & in hevyn, all the
kyndes of torment that all the world cold devise, coud put the to no
payne here / / let vs than send our hartes hens thether, in sich maner
as we may, by sendyng thither our worldly substaunce [f. 167] hens / 20
& let vs neuer dowte yt / but we shall (that ones done) fynd our hartes
so conuersaunt in hevyn, with the glad consideracion of our folowyng
the graciouse counsayle of christ, that the comfort of his holy spirite inspirid vs therfor / shall mitigate, minish, asswage, & in maner quench,
the greate furious fervour of the payne that we shall happen to haue 25
by his lovyng suffraunce / for our ferther merite in our tribulacion /
And therfor like as ⌐if⌐ we saw, that we shuld be within a while dryven
out of this land & fayne to flye into an other / we wold wene that
man were madde which wold not be content to forbere his goodes

---

1 the brambles] the *om. L 1553*; brambles] *second* b *interl.* B   2 high in] thicke in *A* : thicke
canc. and high *wr. over* in *B, in interl.* B, high in *Z*   3 hartes /] hartes (*A* : / *wr. over parenth.*
B; (as] / as *A* : *parenth. wr. over* / B; sayth)] sayth / *A* : *parenth. wr. over* / B   5 folj *canc.*
A before folke; come] to come *Z*; on feld] afield *1553 1573*; (for] / for *A* : *parenth. wr.*
over / B   7 this] these *Z*   9 glad] glade *1557 1573*   11 those] these *L 1573*; vbi]
vbi est *1557*   12 thy] they *A* : y *canc. and* y *wr. over* e B; thyne] thy *L 1553 1573*
13 tresours] treasure *Z*   14 hartes] *Z*, hates *A*   15 greaest] greatest *Z*   16 his
tribulacion] this tribulacion *1553 1573*   17 thyne] thy *L 1553 1573*   18 the world]
this world *Z*; the] them *1553*   20 hens /] hence, please god *L 1553 1573*   21 (that] /
that *A* : *parenth. wr. over* / B   24 in maner] in a maner *Z*   25 happen] happe *1553*
1573   27 *comma added and erased after* therfor B   28 flye] flee *L 1553 1573*

here for the whyle / & send them into that land before hym, where he
saw he shuld live all the remenaunt of his lyfe / so may we verely
thinke our selfe ⌜much⌝ more madde (seyng that we be sure / it can not
be long, ere we shalbe sent spyte of our teeth out of this world) yf the
5 feare of a litle lak or the love to see our goodes here about vs / & the
lothnes to part from them for this litle while which we may kepe
them here, shalbe hable to let vs fro the sure sendyng them before vs
into the tother world / in which we may be sure to live welthely with
them / yf we send them thyther / or els shortly leve them here behind
10 vs / & than stand in greate ieobardy there, to live wreches for euer /

Vincent

In good fayth good vncle / me thinketh that concernyng the losse
of these owtward thinges / these consideracions are so sufficyent comfortes / that for myne own part / saue onely grace well to remember
15 them, I wold me thinke desire no more.

A nother comfort / & corage agaynst the losse of
worldly substaunce /

The xvj^th Chapitre /

Antonye

20 Mych lesse than this may serve Cosyn / with callyng & trustyng
[f. 167^v] vppon goddes helpe / without which mich more than this,
can not serve / But the fervour of the christen fayth so sore fayntith
now adayes & decayeth / commyng from hote vnto luke warm, & fro
luke warm all most to kay cold / that men must now be fayne / as at
25 a fire that is almost out, to lay many dry stykkes therto / & vse mich
blowyng therat / but els wold I wene by my trouth, that vnto a warme

---

2 saw he] sawe that he L _1553_; lyfe /] | _canc. and colon added_ B   3 thinke our] thinke yet
oure _Z_; _comma after_ madde B; (seyng] _parenth. added_ B   7 hable] h _canc._ B, able
_Z_; fro] from L _1553 1573_; the sure] that sure _1553 1573_; sendyng them] sendyng of
theym L   9 them /] | _canc._ B   10 greate] greate | A: | _canc._ B   12 good vncle]
good _om._ L _1553 1573_; thinketh] thinke _1553 1573_   14 myne] my _1553_; saue] v _wr._
over u B   15 thinke] thyncketh L   18 xvj^th] xvi _1553 1557 1573_   19 Antonye] _om._
_1553_   23 fro] from _Z_   26 therat /] _period before_ | B; but] B _wr. over_ b B

faythfull man, one thing alone wherof we spake yet no word, were comfort inough in this kynd of persecucion, agaynst the losse of all his goodes /

Vincent

What thing may that be vncle / 5

Antony

In good fayth Cosyn evyn the bare remembraunce of the pouertie that our saviour willyngly suffred for vs / for I verely suppose, that yf there were a greate kyng / that had so tender a love to a servaunt of his, that he had to help hym out of daynger / forsaken & left of all his 10 worldly welth & royaltye, & become pore & nedy for his sake / that seruaunt could scant be founden that were of such an vnkynd villayne corage / that yf hym selfe cam after to some substaunce / wold not with bettre will lese it all agayne / than shamfully to forsake such a master / 15

And therfor (as I say) I do surely suppose, that yf we wold well re-membre & inwardly consider, the greate goodnes of our saviour toward vs / ᒋnotᒋ yet being his pore sinfull seruauntes, but rather his aduersaries & his ennymyes / & what welth of this world that he will-yngly forsoke for our sake, beyng in dede vniuersall kyng therof / & so 20 havyng the power in his own hand to haue [f. 168] vsid it yf he had wold / in stede wherof (to make vs rich in hevyn) he livid here in ned-enes & pouertie all his life / and neyther wold haue authorite, nor kepe neyther landes nor goodes / the depe consideracion & ernest aduise-ment of this one point alone / were able to make any kynd christen 25 man or woman, well content, rather for his sake agayne to give vpp all that euer god hath lent them (& lent them hath he all that euer they haue) than vnkyndly & vnfaythfully to forsake hym. And hym they forsake / yf that for feare they forsake the confessyng of his christen fayth / And therfor to fynish this pece with all, concernyng the dred 30

2–3 all his goodes] his *om. L 1553,* all worldly gooddes *L* 9 a love] a *om. Z*
10 daynger /] | *canc. and comma added B* 11–12 that seruaunt] the seruant *1573*
12 founden] found *L 1553 1573* 16 (as] *parenth. ed. (faulty virgule? A);* surely] verely
L 1553 17 saviour] sauiour Christ *1553 1573* 18 vs /] | *wr. over comma B;* not *interl.*
B above canc. & A 24 goodes /] | *canc. and colon added B* 25 alone] alole *A : canc. and*
alone, *interl. B* 29 confessyng] confession *1553 1573* 30 fynish] s *wr. over c? B*

of lesyng our owtward worldly goodes / let vs consider the slender
comoditie that they bring, with what labour they be bought / how
litle while they abide with whom so euer they abide longest / what
payne their pleasure is menglid with all / what harme the love of them
5 doth vnto the soule / what losse is in the kepyng / Christes fayth re-
fusid for them / what wynnyng in the losse / yf we lese them for
goddes sake / how mich more profitable they be well given than evill
kept / And fynally what vnkyndnes yt were / yf we wold not rather
forsake them for christes sake / than vnfaythfully forsake christ for
10 them / which while he livid for our sake, forsoke all the world / beside
the suffryng of shamfull & paynefull deth / wherof we shall speke
after / Iff we these thinges I say / will consider well / & will pray god
with his holy hand to prent them in our hartes / & will abide & dwell
still in the hope of his helpe / his trouth shall as the prophet sayth
15 so compas vs about with a pavice, that we shall not nede to be aferd /
Ab incursu & demonio / *meridiano* / of this incursion of this mid day
divill / this open playne persecucion of the Turke, [f. 168ᵛ] for any
losse that we can take by the berevyng from vs of our wretchid worldly
goodes / for whose short & small pleasure in this life forborne / we shal-
20 be with hevenly substaunce euerlastyngly recompensid of god in
ioyfull blys & glory /

Of bodely payne / and that a man hath no cause to take
discomfort in persecution, though he fele hym selfe in an
horrour at the thinkyng vppon bodely payne /

25   The 17 chapiter

Vincent

Forsoth vncle, as for these owtward goodes, you haue so farforth
said / that albeit no man can be sure / what strength he shall haue / or

3 abide longest] be longest *1553 1573*   5 kepyng /] / *canc. B*   6 losse /] / *canc. B*
12 after /] / *canc. and colon added B*   15 aferd] afrayd *1553 1573*   20 euerlastyngly] *divided* euerlast-tyngly *A*   21 glory /] / *canc. and period added B*   22 no] not *1553*   24
vppon bodely] vpon the bodely *L 1553*   25 17] xvijᵗʰ *L*; chapiter] chap *A*: iter *wr. over
abbrev. sign B*   28 sure /] / *canc. and comma added B*; haue /] / *canc. and comma added B*

how faynt / & how feble / he may hap to fynd hym selfe whan he shall
come to the poynt / & therfor I can make no warauntise of my selfe /
seying that / s. / peter so sodenly fayntid / at a womans word / & so
cowerdly forsoke his master / for whom he had so boldely fought
within so few howers before / & by that fall in forsakyng, well per-   5
ceyvid that he had bene to rash in his promise, & was well worthy to
take a fall ⌐for⌐ puttyng so full trust in hym selfe / yet in good fayth me
thinketh now (and god shall I trust helpe me to kepe this thought
still) that yf the Turke shuld take all that I haue vnto my very shirt /
except I wold forsake my fayth / & offer it me all agayne, with five   10
tymes as mich therto to fall into his sect: I wold not ones stike therat /
rather to forsake it euery whit / than of christes holy fayth to forsake
any poynt / But surely good vncle, whan I bethynke me ferther on the
greefe & the payne that may tourne vnto my flesh: here fynd I the
feare that forceth myne hart to tremble /   15

Antonye

Neyther haue I cause therof to mervayle / nor you cosyn cause to
be dismayid therfore / The great horrour & the fere that our saviour
had in his own flesh agaynst his paynfull passion, [f. 169] maketh me
litle to mervayle / & I may well make you take that comfort to / that   20
for no such maner of grudgyng felt in our scntiall partes the flesh
shrinkyng at the mcditacion of payne & deth / your reason shall give
ouer / but resist it & manly master it / & though you wold fayne fle
from the paynfull deth, & be loth to come therto / yet may the meditacion of his gret grevous agony move you / & hym selfe shall yf you so   25
desire hym, not fayle to worke with you therin / & get & give you the
grace, that you shall submit & conforme your will therin vnto his /
as he did his vnto his father / and shall thervppon be so comfortid with
the secret inward inspiracion of his holy sprite / as he was with the

---

1 faynt /] / canc. B; feble /] / canc. B   4 cowerdly] e alt. to a B; boldely] Z, bodely A
5 before] afore L 1553 1573   6 bene] be 1557; to rash] to om. 1553 1573   7 selfe /]
/ canc. and colon added B   8 me to kepe] me too, kepe 1553   9 shirt /] / canc. B   10 wold
forsake] wold om. L 1553   11 stike] shryncke L   12 holy] om. L   13 any poynt]
any one poynt L 1553 1573   15 myne] my L 1553 1573; tremble /] period after / B
17 therof to mervayle] to meruayle therof L 1553 1573   18 the fere] the om. Z   20 I
may] I om. L 1553 1573; to] second o added B   21 grudgyng] gendring 1553; our] y ins.
before our B, your Z; sentiall] sensual Z   22 shrinkyng] shrinketh 1553   23 though]
thoug A; fle] flye 1557   26 t canc. A after hym   29 sprite] spirite 1557 1573

personall presence of that Angell / that after his agony came & comfortid hym / that you shall as his trew deciple folow hym / & with
good will without grudge / do as he did / & take your crosse of payne
& passion vppon your bak / & dye for the truth with hym, & therby
5 rayne with hym crownid in eternall glory / And this I say to give you
warnyng of the thing that is trewth / to thentent whan a man feleth
such an horrour of deth in his hart, he shuld not therby stand in outragiouse feare that he were fallyng / for many such man standeth for
all that feare / full fast / & fynally bettre abyde the brunt / whan god
10 is so good vnto hym as to bring hym therto & encorage hym therin /
than doth some other, that in the begynnyng feleth no feare at all /
And yet may it be, & most often so it is / for god havyng many mansions, & all wonderfull welthfull in his fathers house, exalteth not euery
good man vp to the glory of a martire / but forseyng their infirmyte /
15 that though they be of good will before, & peradventure of right good
corage to / wold yet play saynt Peter yf they were brought to the
poynt, & therby bryng their soules into the perell of eternall dampnacion / he prouideth otherwise for them before they come therat / and
either fyndeth a waye that men shall not [f. 169ᵛ] haue the mynd to
20 lay any handes vppon them / as he found for his disciples / whan hym
selfe was willyngly taken / or that yf they set hand on them, they shall
haue no power to hold them / as he found for / s. / Iohn thevangelist,
which let his shete fall fro hym / whervppon they caught hold, & so
fled hymselfe naked away & escapid fro them / or though they hold
25 hym & bryng hym to prison to / yet god sometyme deliuereth them
thens, as he did saynt Peter / And sometyme he taketh them to hym
out of the prison into hevyn, & suffreth them not to come to their
turment at all / as he hath done by many a good holy man / And some
he suffreth to be brought into the tourmentes / and yet suffreth them
30 not to dye therin, but lyve many yeres after and dye their naturall
deth / as he did by Romanus that shuld haue bene beheddid as Eusebius tellith / *Blonidina & apud Divus Ciprianus quidam & relictus pro mortuo* /

1 that Angell] the Angel *1573*   2 deciple] is *wr. over* e *B*   6 thentent] the entente *1557*
8 *comma erased after* feare *B*; many such] manye a suche *1557 1573*; man] men *L 1553*
9 abyde] abydeth *Z*   12 for] *parenth. ins. before* for *and then canc. B* (/ *assumed beneath heavy
cancellation*); for god] that God *1573*   22 thevangelist] the Euangelist *1573*   23 fro]
from *L 1553 1573*; hym /] / *canc. B*   24 escapid] scaped *L 1553 1573*; fro] from *L 1557*
26 thens,] *comma ed.: period B*   29 tourmentes] tormente *1553*; yet suffreth] yet he suffereth
L 1553 1573   31 by] *om. L 1553*   31–32 Romanus ... mortuo] *canc. B, om. Z in this
place, but 1557 puts in margin (p. 1235, col. 2):* Romanus that shoulde haue ben beheaded

Saynt Iohn thevangelist & by many a nother mo / as we may well
see both by sundrye storys & in the pistles of S. Cipriane also /

And therfor which way god will take with vs, we can not tell / But
surely yf we be trew christen men / this can we well tell, that without
any bold warrantyse of our selfe / or folysh trust in our own strength / 5
we be bound vppon payne of dampnacion, that we be not of the contrary mynd / but that we will with his help / how loth so euer we fele
our flesh therto / rather yet than forsake hym or his fayth afore the
worlde (which yf we do he hath promisid to forsake vs afore his father
& all his holy company of hevyn) rather I say than we wold so do / we 10
wold with his help endure & sustayn for his sake, all the turmentry
that the devill with all his faythles tourmentours in this world wold
devise / And than whan we be of this mynd / & submit our will vnto
his, & call & pray for his grace: we [f. 170] can tell well inough, that
he will neuer suffre them to put more vppon vs / than his grace will 15
make vs hable to bere / but will also with their temptacion prouide
for vs a sure wayc / For / *fidelis est deus* sayth saynt paule / *qui non patitur
vos temptare / supra id quod potestis sed dat etiam cum tentatione prouentum vt
possitis ferre* / God is (sayth thappostell) faythfull, which suffreth you
not to be temptid above that you may bere / but giveth also with the 20
temptacion a way out / for eyther / as I said he will kepe vs out of their
handes (though he before suffrid vs to be fearid with them to prove
our fayth with all) that we may haue by thexamynacion of our own
mynd some comfort in hope of his grace / & some feare of our own
fraylty, to drive vs to call for grace / or els yf we fall in their handes / 25

---

as Eusebius telleth. *and then in italic (p. 1236, col. 1) 1557 puts in margin:* Blomdina, &
apud .S Cipr. quidam relictus pro mortuo. *1573 puts in margin (f. 168ᵛ):* Euseb. hist lib.
3. c 25. De Blandina et alijs. Hist. Eccl. lib. 5. Cap. 2; *see Introduction* 32 Divus
Ciprianus] D& Cipr *A*

---

1 thevangelist] the Euaungelyste *1557 1573* 2 both by] bothe in *L 1553 1573*; pistles]
Epistles *1553 1573* 5 warrantyse] l *before* y *canc. A*; selfe /] / *canc. B*; our own strength]
own *om. L 1553 1573* 6 bound] bounden *1557* 9 worlde] worldle *A*: le *canc. B*;
(which) *parenth. wr. over* / *B* 10 his holy] the holy *L 1553 1573*; hevyn)] *parenth. wr.
over* / *B* 12 wold] could *1573* 16 hable] h *canc. B*, able *L 1557 1573*, all *1553*
17 for vs] vs for *1553*; est deus] est *om. L 1553 1573*; patitur] patiatur *1557* 17–19 *A
abbreviates*: pat vos temptare / s id quod pot sed dat etiam cū tent prou vt possitis ferre, *B
cancels all this except* quod *and* sed dat etiam cū, *and interlineates* patitur vos tentari supra id ...
potestis ... tentatione prouentum 18 temptare] tentari *Z* 18–19 vt possitis ferre]
om. Z 19 (sayth thappostell)] *parenth. added B*, the Apostle *Z* 21 eyther /] / *canc. B*
22 suffrid] suffre *L 1553 1573* 23 thexamynacion] the examinacion *1553 1573*

so that we fall not fro the trust of hym, nor cease to call for his helpe /
his truth shall (as the prophet sayth) so compase vs about with a
pavice, that we shall not nede to fere this incursion of this mydday
devill / for eyther shall these Turkes his tourmentours that shall entre
5 this land & persecute vs / eyther they shall I say / not haue the power /
to towch our bodies at all / or els the short payne that they shall put
vnto our bodies, shall tourne vs to eternall profitt / both in our soules
& in our bodyes to / And therfor Cosyn to begyn with / let vs be of
good comfort / For sith we be by our fayth very sure, that holy scrip-
10 ture is the very word of god / & that the word of god can not be but
trew / & that we see that both by the mowth of his holy prophet / &
by the mouth of his blessid apostell also, god hath made vs so faythfull promises, both that he [f. 170ᵛ] will not suffer vs to be temptid
above our power / but will both prouide a way out for vs / & that he
15 will also round about so compasse vs with his pavice / & defend vs,
that we shall haue no cause to fere this midday devill with all his
persecucion / we can not now / but be very sure (except we be very
shamfully cowardouse of hart, & toward god in fayth out of measure
faynt / & in love lesse than luke warm / or wexen evyn kay cold) we
20 may be very sure I say, that eyther god shall not suffre the Turkes
to invade this land / or yf they do, god shall prouide such resistens,
that they shall not ⌈prevayle. Or if they⌉ prevayle, yet / yf we take
the way that I haue told you / we shall by their persecucion take litle
harme / or rather none harm at all / but that that shall seme harme /
25 shall in dede be to vs none harm at all / but good / For yf god make vs
& kepe vs good men as he hath promisid to do / yf we pray well
therfor / than saith holy scripture / *Bonis* ⌈*omnia*⌉ *cooperantur in bonum* /
vnto good folke, all thinges turne them to good /

   And therfor Cosyn, sith that god knowith what shall happen & not
30 we / let vs in the meane while with a good hope in the help of goddes
grace, haue a good purpose with vs of sure standyng by his holy fayth
agaynst all persecucions / From which yf we shuld (which our lord
forbed) hereafter eyther for fere or payne / for lak of his grace lost in

---

1 fro] from *L*   4 for] f *alt. to* F *B*; his tourmentours] his *om. 1573*   10 very word]
very *om. L 1553*   10–11 but trew] but verye true *L 1553 1573*   11 both] *om. 1557*
13 promises] *final* s *canc. B,* promyse *Z*   15 pavice /] | *canc. B*   17 now /] | *canc. B*
19 cold)] *parenth. wr. over* | *B*   22 if they] if thei do *L 1553 1573*; yet /] | *canc. B*
24 none] no *L 1553 1573*   25 none] no *L 1553 1573*   26 pray well] well *om. 1553*
1573   27 *comma added after* Bonis *and then canc. B*   29 happen] happe *1553 1573*
33 for lak] or for lacke *1573*; his] *om. L 1553 1573*; lost] least *1557*

our own defaute / mishap to declyne / yet had we both wonne the
well spent tyme in this good purpose before, to the minyshment of
our payne / & were also mich the more likely that god shuld lift vs
vp after our fall, & give vs his [f. 171] grace agayne / how beit yf
this persecucion come, we be by this meditacion & well contynued 5
entent & purpose before, the bettre strengthid & confirmid, & mich
the more likely for to stand in dede / And yf it so fortune (as with
goddes grace at mens good prayours & amendment of our evill lives
it may fortune full well) that the Turkes shall eyther be well withstanden & vanquyshid / or peradventure not invade vs at all / than 10
shall we perdye by this good purpose, get our selfe of god a very good
chepe thanke /

And on the tother side, while we now thinke theron (as not to thinke
theron in so great liklyhed therof / I wene no wise man can) yf we
shuld for the feare of worldly losse / or bodely payne framid in our 15
own myndes / thinke that we wold give ouer / & ⌐to⌐ save our goodes
& our lives / forsake our saviour by denyall of his fayth / than whither
the Turkes come or come not / we be gone from god the while / And
than yf they come not in dede / or come & be driven to flight, what a
shame shuld this be to vs before the face of god, in so shamfull coward- 20
ouse wise to forsake hym for fere of that payne / that we neuer felt /
nor neuer was falling toward vs /

Vincent

By my trouth vncle I thanke you / me thinketh that though you
neuer said more in the mater, yet haue you evyn with this that you 25
haue / of the feare of bodely payne in this persecusion spoken here all
redy, mervelousely comfortid myn hart.

Antonye [f. 171ᵛ]

I am glad Cosyn / yf your hart haue taken comfort therby / But &

---

1 both] *interl. A*   4 agayne /] | *canc. and period added B*   13 the tother] *L 1557*, the
other *1553 1573*, the to thether *A* (o *wr. over first* e *of* thether *B*); theron (as] theron / [*end
of line*] as *A, parenth. added before as B*   14 liklyhed] lykelihode *L 1553 1573*, lykelyhood
1557; can)] *parenth. wr. over* | *B*   16 to] *interl. B above canc. so A*; goodes] good *1553*
17 lives /] | *canc. and comma added B*; whither] whither | *A*: | *canc. B*   18 Turkes] Turke
L 1553 1573; from] fro *1557*   19–20 what a shame] what at a shame *1573*   21 neuer]
neyther *L 1553*   22 toward] towardes *1553 1573*   24 thinketh] thynke *1553 1573*
27 myn] my *L 1573*

yf you so haue / give god the thanke & ⌜not⌝ me / for that worke is
his & not myne / for neyther am I able any good thing to say / but
by hym / nor all the good wordes in the world / no not the holy wordes
of god hym selfe / & spoken also with his own holy mowth, can be
5 hable to profit the man with the sownd entryng at his eare / but yf the
spirite of god therwith inwardly worke in his soule / but that is his
goodnes euer redy to do / except the let be thorough the vntowardnes
of our own froward will /

⌜Of⌝ Comfort agaynst bodely payne / & first agaynst
10   captiuite /

The / 18 / chapitre

And therfor now beyng somwhat in comfort & corage before,
wherby we may the more quyetly consider euery thing / which is
somewhat more hard & deficile to do / whan the hart is before taken
15 vpp & oppressid with the trowblouse affeccion of hevy sorowfull feare /
Let vs examyne the weyght & the substaunce of those bodely paynes
as the sorest part of this persecucion which you rehersid before / which
were yf I remember you right / tharldome / imprisonment / paynfull
& shamfull deth / And first let vs (as reason is) begyn with the tharl-
20 dome / for that was as I remember the first / /

Vincent

I pray you good vncle say than somewhat therof / for me thinketh
vncle that captyuite is a mervelouse hevy thing namely whan they
shall (as they most comonly do) cary vs far from home into a straunge
25 vncouth lande /

---

2 say /] / canc. B   3 wordes] Z, workes A; the world] is wr. over e B, this world L 1553
1573   5 hable] h canc. B, able Z; / but] period before / B; capital B wr. over / and b B
11 18] xviij^th L   15 trowblouse] trowlouse A   16 the substaunce] the om. L 1553 1573;
those] these 1553 1573   18 tharldome] thraldome Z   19 let vs] interl. A; (as] A writes
caret before as, B cancels old caret and inserts new caret before parenth.   19–20 tharldome]
thraldome Z   20 was as I] as om. 1553 1573; remember] Z, rember A   24 they most]
Z, the most A; do)] parenth. wr. over / B

Antonye

I can not say nay / but that grife it is cosyn in dede / but yet as vnto
me not halfe so mich as it wold be / yf they could cary me out into
any such vnknowen countrey / that god could not wit where, nor fynd
the meane to come at me / But in good fayth cosyn now yf my trans- 5
migracion into a straunge countrey / shuld be any grete [f. 172] gryef
vnto me / the fawt shuld be mych in my selfe / for sith I am very sure,
that whether so euer men convey me / god is no more verely here than
he shalbe there / yf I get (as I may yf I will) the grace to set my hole
hart vppon hym / & long for nothyng but hym / yt can than make me 10
no greate mater to my mynd / whether they cary me hense or leve me
here / And than yf I fynd my mynd mich offendid therwith, that I
am not still in myne own countrey / I must consider that the cause
of my gryefe, ys myn own wrong Imaginacion / wherby I begile my
selfe with an vntrew perswacion, wenyng that this were myn own 15
countrey / where as of trouth it is not so. For as S. paule sayth / *Non
habemus hic ciuitatem manentem sed futurum inquerimus* / We haue here no
cyte nor dwellyng countrey at all / but we seke for one that we shall
come to / And in what countrey so euer we walke in this world, we
be but as pilgryms & wayfaryng men / And yf I shuld take any 20
countrey for myn owne / it must be the countrey to which I come,
& not the countrey from which I came /

That countrey that shalbe to me than for a while so straunge, shall
yet perdye be no more straunge to me / nor lenger strange to me
neyther, than was myne owne natyve countrey when I came first 25
into yt / And therfor yf that poynt / of my beyng farre from hens, be
very grevouse to me, & that I fynd it a grete payne that I am not
where I wold be / that gryefe shall grete part grow, for lak of sure
settyng & setlyng my mynd in god where it shuld be / which faute
of myne / whan I mend, I shall sone ease my greefe / 30

---

2 grife] e *wr. over* i B, some grief *Z*   4 land *canc. A and B before* countrey; could] would
L 1553; wit] wete *1553*   5 meane to come] meane how to come *1573*   9 (as . . . will)]
parentheses wr. over virgules B; my] myne *1557*   10 vppon hym] on him *L 1553 1573*;
make me] me *om. Z*   13 still in] stil here in *Z*; myne] my *1553*   14 myn] my *L*;
wherby] wherby / *A*: / *canc.* B   15 perswacion] si *wr. over* c B   16 countrey /] / *canc.
and comma added B*; For] for *A*   17 ciuitatem manentem] manantem ciuitatem *1557*;
futurum inquerimus] futuram inquirimus *Z*   18 seke] loke *1573*   21 myn] my *1553
1573*; be the countrey] be that countrey *L 1553 1573*   22 from] fro *1557*   24 me /]
/ *canc. and comma added B*   26 poynt /] / *canc.* B   28 sure] sure / *A*: / *canc.* B

Now as for all other gryefes & paynes that are in captivite tharldome & bondage / I can not denye but many there are & [f. 172ᵛ]
grete. Howbeit they seme yet somwhat (what sey I somwhat?) I may
say a greate deale / the more because we take our formare liberty /
5 for more a great dele than in dede yt was / let vs therfor consider / the
mater thus /

Captivitie, bondage, or tharldome, what is it / but the violent restraynt of a man, beyng so subdued vnder the domynyon rule & power
of an other / that he must do what the tother lyst to commaund hym,
10 & may not do at his libertie such thinges as he lyst hym selfe /

Now whan we shalbe caried away with a Turke, & be fayne to be
occupied about such thinges as he list to set vs / here shall we lament
the losse of our libertie, & thinke we bere an hevy burden of our
servile condicion / & so to do we shall haue I graunt well many tymes
15 greate occasion / But yet shuld we I svppose set therby somwhat the
lesse / yf we wold remember well, what lybertie that was that we lost /
& take it for no larger than yt was in dede / For we reken as though
we might before do what we wold / But therin we deceve our selfe /
for what fre man ys there so fre, that can be suffred to do what hym
20 lyst / In many thinges god hath restraynid vs by his high commaundment / so many that of those thinges which els we wold do / I wene
yt be more than the halfe / howbeit because (god forgive vs) we let
so litle therfor / but do what we list / as though we hard hym not /
we reken our libertie neuerthelesse for that /

25 But than is our libertie much restraynid by the lawes made by
men, for the quyet & politike gouernaunce of the peple / And these
wold I wene let our libertie but a litle neyther / were yt not for feare
of the paynes that fall thervppon / / [f. 173]

Loke then whether other men that haue aucthorite ouer vs / com-

---

1 all other] al the other *1557 1573*   1–2 tharldome] thraldom Ƶ   3 Howbeit]
howbeit *A*; (what] *parenth. wr. over | by* B, *then canc. and comma added* B   4 greate] r
interl. A?; take] o *wr. over* a B, tooke Ƶ   7 tharldome] thraldome Ƶ; it /] | *canc. and
comma added* B   9 other /] | *canc. and comma added* B; lyst] lust *1553*   10 do at his
libertie such] at hys libertie dooe suche L *1553 1573*; libertie] libtie *A*; lyst] lust *1553*
12 list] luste *1553*   14 we shall haue I graunt well] I graunte well we shall haue L
1553 1573   16 rember *canc. A before* remember   18 we deceve] deceyue we *1553 1573*
20 lyst] lust *1553*   20–21 commaundment] commaundementes L   21 so many] &
so many *1573*   22 than] than / *A*: | *canc.* B   23 list] lust *1553*; therfor /] | *canc.* B
24 neuerthelesse] *separated by verticals*: neuer the lesse B   28 of the paynes] the *om. 1553*;
that fall] that maye fal L *1553*

maund vs neuer no bysines which we dare not but do / & therfor do
yt full oft full sore agaynst our willes / of which thinges some service is
sometyme so paynfull & so perilouse to / that no lord can lightly commaund his bondman worse / nor seldome doth commaund hym halfe
so sore /   5

Let euery fre man that rekenyth his libertie to stand in doyng what
he lyst, consider well these poyntes / and I wene he shall than fynd
his libertie mich lesse than he toke yt before. And yet haue I left ontowchid the bondage that almost euery man is in, that bosteth hym
selfe for fre / the bondage I meane of synne / which to be a very   10
bondage / I shall haue our saviour hym selfe to bere me good record /
for he sayth / *qui facit peccatum, seruus est peccati* / he that commyttith
synne, ys the thrall or bondman of synne / And than yf this be thus /
(as it most nedes be so, sith god sayth it is so) who ys there than that
may make so mich bost of his libertie / that he shuld take it for so sore   15
a thing & so straunge, to become thorow chaunce of warre bond
vnto a man / while he is alredy thorow synne / become willingly thrall
& bond vnto the devill /

Let vs loke well how many thinges & of what vile wrechid sort the
divell dreveth vs to do dayly, thorow the rash brades of our blynd   20
affeccions / which we be for our fawtfull lakk of grace fayne to folow,
& are to feble to refrayne / & than shall we fynd in our naturall
fredome our bond seruice such, that neuer was there any man lord of
any so vile a villayne, that euer wold for very sham, commaund hym
so shamfull seruice / And let vs in the doyng of our seruice to the   25
man that we be [f 173ᵛ] slave vnto / remember what ʳweˈ were wont
to do about the same tyme of the day, while we were at our fre libertie
before, & were well likely yf we were at libertie, to do the like agayne /
& we shall peradventure perceve / that it were bettre for vs to do this
bysynes than that /   30

Now shall we haue great occasion of comfort, yf we consider that
our seruitude (though in the compt of the world yt seme to come by

---

4 *extra* doth *canc. B before* commaund; doth] dooeth *1553*   7 lyst] lust *1553*; these
poyntes] the pointes L *1553*   8 yt before] it for before Z   12 qui] Omnis qui *1557*
1573; he that] Euery man that *1557 1573*   13 tharll *canc. A before* thrall; or bondman]
or the bondman *1553 1557 1573*   14 nedes] / *canc. A and B after* nedes; nedes be so]
nedes so be *1553 1573*   20 brades] *canc. and* braydys *interl. B*   24 sham] *final* e *added*
B; such *canc. A and B after* hym   25 th *erased after* in A; our] A *first writes* the, *then cancels*
th *and writes* o *over* e   29 perceve /] / *canc. and comma added B*

chaunce of warre) cometh yet in very dede vnto vs by the prouidente
sond of god / & that for our greate good / yf we will take yt well / both
in remission of synnes, & also mater of our merite /

    The greest grief that is in bondage or captivite, ys this as I trow /
5 that we be forcid to do such labour, as with our good will we wold
not / But than agaynst that griefe *Senek* techeth vs a good remedy /
Semper da operam, ne quid inuitus facias / Endevour thy selfe euermore,
that thow do nothyng agaynst thy will / But that thing that we se we
shall nedes do / let vs vse alwey / to put our good will therto /

10   Vincent

    That is vncle sone said / but it is hard to do /

                                    Antonye

    Our froward mynd maketh euery good thing hard / & that to our
own more hurt & harme / But in this case yf we wilbe good christen
15 men, we shall haue greate cause gladly to be content, for the great
comfort that we may take therby / while we remember, that in the
pacient & glad doyng of our seruice vnto that man for goddes sake,
accordyng to his high commaundment by the mowth of saynt paule /
serui obedite dominis / we shall haue our thanke & our reward of god /
20 Fynally / yf we remember the grete humble meknes of our [f. 174]
saviour crist hym selfe / that he beyng very almightie god, *humiliauit*
semet ipsum formam serui accipiens / humblid hymselfe, & toke the forme
of a bond man or slaue / rather than his father shuld forsake vs / we
may thinke our selfe very vnkynd kaytyfes & very frantyke foles to /
25 yf rather than to endure this worldly bondage for a while, we wold
forsake hym, that hath by his owne deth, deliuerid vs out of euerlastyng bondage of the devill, & will for our short bondage, give vs euerlastyng libertie /

---

1 prouidente] prouidence *A*: t *wr. over* c *B*   2 sond] send? *A*: o *wr. over* e? *B* (*see note*),
hand *1553 1573*, sounde *1557*   3 mater] for matter *L*   4 greest] t *ins. after first* e *B*,
greatest *Ƶ*   6 Senek] Seneca *1573*   7 facias] c *wr. over illeg. letter B*   8 But that]
but the *1573*   9 alwey] e *alt. to* a *B*   13 to our] vnto our *L 1553 1573*   17 vnto
that] vnto the *1573*   19 dominis] dominis carnalibus *1557 1573*; our reward] our
whole reward *Ƶ*   23 slaue] v *wr. over* u *B*, a slaue *1553 1573*; vs /] | *canc. and colon
added B*   24 selfe] selves *L*; vnkynd] vndynd *A*: k *wr. over first* d *B*   25 to endure]
to *om. L 1553*   27 bondage] bondage | *A*: | *canc. B*

Vincent

Well fare you good vncle this is very well said / albeit that bondage
is a condicion that euery man of any corage wold be glad to eschew &
very loth to fall in / yet haue you well made yt open, that it is a thing
neyther so straunge nor so sore / as it before semid vnto me / and 5
specially farr from such as any man that any wit hath, shuld for fere
therof shrinke from the confession of his fayth / And now therfor I
pray you somewhat speke of your prisonement / /

Of Imprisonment & comfort theragaynst

The / 19 / chapitre / 10

Antonye

That shall I cosyn with good will / And first yf we wold consider
what thing ymprisonment ys of his owne nature / we shuld not me
thinketh haue so greate horrour therof / for of yt selfe yt is perdie / but
a restraynt of lybertie which letith a man from goyng whether he 15
wold /

Vincent

Yes by saynt mary vncle me thinketh it is mich more sorow than
so / for beside the let & restraynt of libertie / yt [f. 174ᵛ] hathe many
mo displeasures, & very sore greifoo, knyt & ioynid therto. 20

Antony

That is Cosyn very trew in dede / & those paynes a mong ⌈many⌉
sorer than those, thought I not ⌈after⌉ to forget / Howbeit I purpose
now to consider first imprisonment / but as ymprisonment onely /
without any ⌈other⌉ incommodite beside. For a man may ⌈be⌉ 25

---

4 made yt] yt om. L 1553   5 sore /] / canc. B   7 from] fro 1553 1573; fayth /] / canc.
and period added B   8 of your prisonement] of impriesonment Z   10 19] xixᵗʰ L
12 wold] coulde 1557   13–14 me thinketh] me thinke 1573   14 perdie /] / canc. and
comma added B   15 period added B after lybertie   20 ioynid] adioyned Z; therto]
therunto L 1553 1573   23 purpose] purposed L 1553 1573   25 incommodite]
commoditie 1553; beside.] period ed.

perdye ymprisonid, & yet not set in the stokkes nor colorid fast by the
necke / & a man may be let walke at large where he will, & yet a payre
of feters fast rivettid on his legges / for in this countrey (ye wot well) &
in Civill & portingale to, so go all the slaves /

5   Howbeit because that for such thinges mennes hartes hath such
horrour therof / albeit ⌈that⌉ I am not so madd as to go about to prove
that bodely payne were no payne / yet sith that because of these
maner of paynes, we so specially abhorre the state & condicion of
prisoners / we shuld me thinketh well perceve / that a greate part of
10 our horrour, groweth of our own fantasie / yf we wold call to mynd &
consider the state & condicion of many other folke / in whose state &
condicion we wold wish our selfe to stand / takyng them for no prisoners at all, that stand yet for all that in mich part of the selfe same
poyntes that we abhorre ymprisonment for / let vs therfor consider
15 these thinges in order /
And first as I thought to begynne, because those other kindes of
gryefes that come with ymprisonment, are but accidentes therunto,
& yet neyther such kyndes of accidentes, as eyther be proper thervnto,
but that they may almost all, fall vnto a man without yt / nor are not
20 such accidentes thervnto, as are vnseparable therfro, but that ymprisonment may fall to a man & none of all them therwith / we will / I
say / therfor begynne with the consideryng, what manner payne or
incommoditie we shuld rekyn ymprisonment to be, of hym selfe & of
his owne nature alone / And than in the course of our communicacion,
25 you shall as you lyst encrease & aggreue the cause of your horrour,
with the terrour of those paynfull accidentes /

Vincent [f. 175]

I am sorye that I ded interupt your tale / For you were about I se
well ⌈to⌉ take an orderly way therein / And as your selfe haue devisid,
30 so I besech you procede / for though I rekyn ymprisonment mich the
sorer thing, by sore & hard handlyng therin / yet reken I not the

---

4 Civill] Cycylye L, Cicile *1553*, Cyuil *1557*, Siuile *1573*; go all] goe there all Z
5 mennes] second e *interl. A?*; hath such] haue such *1573*   9 thinketh] thinke *1553 1573*;
of] *superscript* r *above* o *canc. A*   10 fantasie] fansye L   16 *parenth. begun before* as A
18 eyther be] be eyther L *1553 1573*   20 thervnto] therinto *1553*   21 fall to] fall
vnto L   23 incommoditie] commoditie *1553 1573*; hym selfe] it selfe *1573*   25 lyst]
lust *1553*   27 Vincent] Antony *1553 1573*   28 ded] y *wr. over* e B

prisonment of yt selfe any lesse than a thing very tediouse / all were
it vsid in the most favorable maner that yt possible might / for vncle
yf it were a great prince that were taken prisouner vppon the feld, &
in the hand of a christen kyng, which vse in such case (for the consideracion of their former estate / & mutable chaunce of the warre) 5
to shew much humanytie to them / & in very favorable wise entreate
them / for these infidel Emperours handle oft tymes the princes that
they take more vilanously than they do the porest men / as the great
Tamberlane kept the grete Turke when he had taken hym / to tredd
on his bak alwaye while he lept on horse backe / But as I beganne to 10
say by the sample of a prince taken prisoner / were the ymprisonment
neuer so favorable / yet were it in my mynd no litle griefe in it selfe,
for a man to be pynnyd vpp, though not in a narrow chamber but
although his walke were right large / & right fayre gardyns to therin /
yt could not but grive his hart / to be restraynyd by an other man 15
within certeyne limytes & bowndes, & lese the libertie to be where
hym list /

Antonye

This ys Cosyn well considerid of you / for in this you perceve well,
that ymprisonment ys of hym selfe & his own very nature alone, 20
nothyng els but the retaynyng of a mans persoune, within the circute
of a certen space narower or larger as shalbe lymytyd vnto hym,
restraynyng his libertie fro the further goyng into any other place /

Vincent

Very well said as me thinketh / 25

Antony

Yet forgat I Cosyn to aske you one question /

---

1 prisonment] inpriesonment *1553*, imprisonment *1573*; were] where *A*: h *canc. B?*
2 possible] possibly *1573*   4 (for] *parenth. ed.*   5 estate] state *L 1553 1573*; & mutable]
and the mutable *L 1553 1573*; chaunce] chaunge *1553*   7 extra Emperourse *canc. A*
after infidel; oft] often *Ƶ*   8 they] the *A*, y *added B*   11 the ymprisonment] thymprysonment *L*   15 grive] e *wr. over* i *B*   17 list] lust *1553*   20 hym selfe] it selfe
1573   21 persoune] persounes *A*: nes *canc. and* u *alt. to* n *B* (*final* s *canc. A?*); which
canc. B before within   22 space] splace *A*, l *canc. A*, *word canc. and* space, *interl. B*; vnto]
vn *canc. B*, to *Ƶ*; hym,] *second comma canc. B*   23 fro] from *L 1553 1573*; further] farther
L 1553   25 Very] *orig.* Verely: y *wr. over second* e *and* ly *canc. A* (*correction clarified B*)

Vincent [f. 175ᵛ]

What is that vncle /

Antonye

This lo / yf there be ij men kept in / 2 / seuerall chambers of one
5 greate castell / of which / 2 / chambers the tone is mych more larger
than the tother / whither be they prisoners both, or but the tone that
hath the lesse rome to walke in /

Vincent

What question is it vncle / but that they be prisoners both / as I
10 said my selfe before / although the tone lay fast lokkyd in the stokkes,
& the tother had all the whole castell to walke in.

Antony

Me thinketh verely Cosyn that you say the trouth / And than yf
inprisonment be such a thing as your selfe here agre it is / that is to
15 wit but a lak of libertie to go yf we lyst / now wold I fayne wit of you /
what any one man you know that is at this day owt of prison /

Vincent

What one man vncle / mary I know almost none other / for surely
prisoner am I none acquentid with / that I remember /

20   Antony

Than I see well you visite pore prisoners seld.

Vincent

No by my trowth vncle / I cry god mercye / I send them sometyme
myne almoise / but by my trouth I loue not to come my selfe where
25 I shuld see such mysery /

---

5 larger] large *1557 1573*   6 be they] be the *1553*   10 in the stokkes] the *om. 1553 1573*
11 tother] tother / *A*: / *canc. B*   14 inprisonment] prisonment *Z*   15 whither *interl.*
B above yf (*uncanc.*), whither *Z*; lyst] lust *1553*   19 none] none / *A*: / *canc. B*   21 see]
interl. A above canc. perceve   23 my] *om. 1557*   24 myne] my *1553 1573*; almoise]
allmoyse *L*, almose *1553 1573*, almes *1557*

Antonye

In good fayth Cosyn Vincent though I say it before you / you haue
many good condicions / but surely though I say it before you to, that
condicion ys none of them / which condicion yf you wold amend,
than shuld you haue yet the mo good condicions by one / & perad- 5
venture the mo by three or foure / for I assure you it is hard to tell,
how mich good to a mannys soule the personall visytyng to pore pry-
soners doth.

But now sith you can name me none of them that are in prison / I
pray you name some one of all them, that you be as [f. 176] you say / 10
better acquentid with / men I meane that are out of prison / for I
know me thinketh as few of them as you know of the tother /

Vincent

That were vncle a straunge case / for euery man is vncle out of
prison, that may go where he will / though he be the porest begger in 15
the Towne / And in good fayth vncle (because you reken imprisonment so small a mater of yt selfe) the pore beggar / that is at his liberty
& may walke where he will, is as me semeth in better case, than is a
kyng kept in prison, that can not go but where men give hym leve /

Antonye   20

Well Cosyn whyther euery way walkyng begger be by ⌐this⌐ reson
out of pryson or no / we shall consider ferther when ye will / but in
the meane while / I can by this reason se no prince that semeth to
be out of prison / for yff the lakke of libertie to go where a man will
be ymprisonment / as your selfe say yt is / than is the great Turke by 25
whome we so feare to be put in prison / in prison all redy hymselfe /
for he may not go where he will / for & he might, he wold into portyngale / Italy / spayne / fraunce / Almaigne & England / & as far on
a nother quarter to / both *preter Iohns* land & the *graund Cams* to /

---

4 amend] mend *L*   6 the mo by] by mo than *L 1553 1573*   7 to] *canc. and* of *interl.*
B, of *Z*   9 you] ye *1557*   10 name some] name me some *1557*; say /] / *canc. B*
12 thinketh] thynke *1553 1573*   14 vncle] *om. L*   15 where] whither *1553*   16 (be-
cause] *parenth. ed.*, / because *A*   17 h *canc. after* of *A*   22 ferther] farder *L*; ye] you *Z*
25 say] sayeth *L*   27 & he] yf he *L*   28 & as] & *interl. A*   29 graund] greate *L*;
Cams] Canys *L*, Canis *1553*, Canes *1557*, Chams *1573*

Now the beggar that you speke of / yf he be as you say he ys / by
reason of his libertie to go where he will / in much better case than a
kyng kept in prison / because he can not go but where men give hym
leve / than is that beggar in better case, not onely than a prince in
5 prison / but also than many a prince owt of prison to / for I am sure
there is many a beggar that may without lett, walke ferther vppon
other mens grownd than many a prince at his best libertie may walke
vppon his own / And as for walkyng out abrode vppon other mens:
that prince might [f. 176ᵛ] happ to be said nay & holden fast, where
10 that beggar with his bagg & his staffe shuld be suffred to go forth &
hold on his waye / But for as much Cosyn / as neyther the beggar nor
the prince, ys at fre libertie to walke where they will / but that yf
they wold walke in some place / neyther of them both shuld be suffrid
but men wold withstand them / & say them nay / therfor yf imprison-
15 ment be (as you graunt yt is) a lak of libertie to go where we lyst / I
can not se but as I say, the beggar & the prince whom you reken both
at libertie, be by your own reason ⌐restraynyd⌐ in prison both.

Vincent

Ye but vncle both the tone & the tother haue way ynough to
20 walke / the tone in his own grownd, the tother in other mens or in the
comon high waye / where they may walke till they be both wery of
walkyng ere any man say them naye.

Antony

So may Cosyn that kyng, that had as your selfe put the case, all
25 the whole castell to walke in / and yet you say not nay / but that he is
prisoner for all that / though not so strayghtly kept / yet as verely
prisoner as he that lieth in the stokkes /

Vincent

But they may go at the lest wise to euery place that they nede, or

---

1 ys /] / *canc. and comma added B*   2 will /] / *canc. and comma added B*   4 no *canc. after*
not *A*   5 owt of prison] out of a prison *1573*; for] f *alt. to* F *B*   10 shuld] would
1553 1573   14–15 imprisonment] priesonment *L 1553 1573*   15 lyst] lust *1553*
16 but] (but *A*   19 both] *om. L 1553 1573*   20 in other] in *om. L 1553*   26 as]
(as *A: parenth. canc. B*   29 lest wise] least waies *1553*

that is commodiouse for them / & therfor they do not will to go but
where they may go / And therfor be they at libertie to go where they
will /

Antony

Me nedeth not Cosyn to spend the tyme about the impugnyng 5
euery part of this answere / for lettyng passe by / that though a prisoner were with his keper brought into euery place where nede re-
quirid / yet sith he might not when he wold, ⌐go where he wold⌐ for
his onely pleasure / he were ye wot well a prisoner styll. And lettyng
passe ouer also this, that it were to this beggar [f. 177] nede, & to this 10
kyng commodiouse / to go into diuers places where neyther of them
both may come / And lettyng passe also, that neyther of them both
is lightly so temperatly determynid / but that they both fayne so wold
do in dede / yf this reason of yours put them out of prisone / & set
thcm at libertie & make them free, as I will well graunt yt doth / yf 15
they so do in dede / that is to wit yf they haue no will to go / but
where they may go in dede / than let vs loke on our other prisoners
enclosid within a castell / and we shall fynd that the straytest kept
of them both / yf he get the wisedome & the grace to quyet his own
mynd, & hold hym selfe content with that place / & long not like a 20
woman with child for her lustes to be gaddyng out any where ⌐els, is
by the same reson of yours, while his will is not longyng to be any
where⌐ els / he is I say at his fre libertie to be where he will / & so
is out of prison to /

And on the tother side / yf though his will be not longyng to be any 25
where els / yet because that yt his wlll so were, he shuld not so be
suffred / he is therfor not at his fre liberte but a prisoner still / so sith
your fre beggar that you speke of, & the prince that you call out of
prison to / though they be (which I wene / very few be) by some
speciall wisedome so temperatly disposid, that they haue not the will 30
to be but where they see they may be suffred to be / yet sith that yf
they wold haue that will, they cold not than be where they wold /
they lakke theffect of fre libertie / & be both twayne in prison to /

---

5 impugnyng] *divided* impugn-nyng *A*: *extra* n *at end of line canc. B*   6 by /] / *canc. and
comma added B*; though] *divided* tho-ugh *A*: *canc. and* though *interl. B*   9 ye] you *L 1553
1573*   13 determynid /] / / *A*   16 dede /] dede) *A*; go /] / *canc. B*   20 content]
content / *A*: / *canc. B*   29 (which] *parenth. added B*   32 not] not / *A*: / *canc. B*
33 theffect] the effect *1557*

Vincent

Well vncle yf euery man vniuersally be by this reson in prison alredy, after the very proprietie of ymprisonment / yet to be imprisonid in this speciall maner, which maner is onely comenly callid
5 imprisonment, [f. 177ᵛ] is a thing of greate horrour & feare, both for the straightnes of the kepyng, & the hard handlyng that many men haue therin / of all which griefes & paynes & displeasures in this other generall imprisonment that you speke of, we fele nothing at all / And therfor euery man abhorrith the tone, & wold be loth to come into
10 it / & no man abhorrith the tother, for they fele none harm nor fynd no fawt therin / wherfor vncle in good fayth though I can not fynd answeres convenient wher with to avoyd your argumentes / yet to be playne with you & tell you the very trewth / my mynd fyndeth not yt selfe satisfied in this poynt / but that euer me thinketh that these
15 thinges wherwith you rather convince & conclude me than enduce a credence & perswade me / that euery man is in prison all redye / be but sophisticall fantasies / & that / except those that are comenly callid prisoners / other men are not in any prison at all /

Antony

20 Well fare thyne hart good Cosyn Vincent / There was in good fayth no word that you spake syns we talkyd of these matters, that halfe so well liked me as this that you speke now / For yf you had assentid in wordes / & in your mynd departyd vnperswadid / than yf the thing be trew that I say / yet had you lost the frute / & yf it be peradventure
25 false & my selfe decevid therin / than while I shuld wene that yt liked you to / you shuld haue confyrmyd me in my folye / for in good fayth Cosyn such an old fole am I, that this thing, in the perswadyng wherof vnto you I had went I had quyt me well / & whan I haue all done apperith to your mynd but [f. 178] a tryfle / & a sophisticall
30 fantasye / my selfe haue so many yeres taken for so very substanciall

---

3 very] y *wr. over* e *A*: y *clarified B*; proprietie] proprety *L*, property *1553 1573*   4 onely]
interl. A   8 imprisonment] inprisonment *1573*   10 none] no *L 1553 1573*   11 good]
om. L 1553 1573   14 that euer] that *om. L 1553 1573*   16 me /] | *canc. and comma
added B*   17 fantasies] fansyes *L*; that /] | *canc. B*   18 any] *om. L 1553 1573*
20 thyne] thy *1553 1573*   21 we talkyd] we fyrst talked *1557*; these] those *1553 1573*
22 as this] as these *Z*   24 say /] | *canc. and comma added B*; frute | &] | *canc. and period added
B*, & *canc. and* And *interl. B*   26 for] f *alt. to* F *B*   30 fantasye] fansye *L*

trewth / that as yet my mynd can not give me to thinke it any
other / Wherfor lest I play as the french prest playd, that had so long
vsid to say *Dominus* / with the second silable long / that at last he
thought it must nedes be so / & was ashamyd to say it short / to thentent you may the bettre perceve me / or I the bettre my selfe / we shall 5
here betwene vs a litle more consider the thing. And hardely spet well
on your handes & take good hold, & give yt not ouer agaynst your
own mynd / For than were we neuer the nere /

Vincent

Nay by my trouth vncle that I intend not / nor nothyng dyd yet 10
syns we began / & that may you well perceve by some thinges, which
without any greate cause / save for the ferther satisfaccion of myne
owne mynd, I repetid & debatyd agayne /

Antonye

That guyse Cosyn hold on hardely styll / for in this matter I pur- 15
pose to give ouer my part / except / I make your selfe perceve / both
that euery man vniuersally ys a very prisoner in very prison playnly /
without any sophisticacion at all / And that there is also no prince
lyvyng vppon earth, but he is in worse case prisoner by this generall
ymprisonment that I speke of / ⌐than is many a lewd simple wrech by 20
that speciall imprisonment that you speke of.¬ And ouer this that in
this generall imprisonment that I speke of, men are for the tyme that
they be therin, so sore handlyd, & so hardly, & in such paynefull
wise, that mens hartes haue with reson great cause, as sore to abhorre
this hard handlyng that is in this ymprisonment, as the tother that is 25
in that.

Vincent

By my trowth vncle / these thinges wold I fayne se well provid. [f.
178ᵛ]

---

3 that at last] that *om. 1553,* at the last *1553 1573*   4–5 thentent you] thentent that
you *Z*   5 bettre] bettre / *A*: / *canc. B*   10 I intend] entended I *1553,* entende I *L*
1557 1573   12 cause /] / *canc. and comma added B;* satisfaccion] satysfyeng *L;* myne]
mynd *A*: nd *first canc. B, then whole word canc. and* myne *interl. B*   16 except /] / *canc. B*
17 playnly /] *divided* playn-ly: *canc. and* playnly *interl. B,* / *canc. B*   20 of /] *caret wr. over* /
and comma added B   21 imp *canc. B before* speciall; imprisonment] prisonment *L 1553*
23 paynefull] *Z,* paynefully *A*   25 tother] other *1553 1573*

Antonye

Tell me than Cosyn first, by your trouth, yf there were a man
attayntid of treason or felonye / & after iudgment given of his deth /
and that it were determynid that he shuld dye / onely the tyme of his
5 execucion delayed till the kynges ferther pleasure knowen / & he thervppon delyuerid to certeyne kepers, & put vpp in a sure place, out of
which he could not scape: were this man a prisoner or no /

Vincent

This man quoth he / ye mary that he were in very dede, yf euer any
10 man were /

Antonye

But now what yf for the tyme ⌐that were⌐ meane betwene his
attaynder & his execucion, he were so favorably handlyd, that he were
suffred to do what he wold as he was while he was abrode / & to haue
15 the vse of his landes & his goodes, & his wife and his children licence
to be with hym / & his frendes leve at liberty to resort vnto hym /
⌐& his servantes not forboden to byde abowt him / and adde⌐ yet
therunto, that the place were a grete castell royall / with parkes &
other pleasures therin a very greate circuyte about / yea add yet & ye
20 wyll that he were suffred to go & ride also / both whan he wold &
whyther he wold / onely this one poynt alway prouidid & foresene /
that he shuld euer be surely sene to & safely kept fro scapyng / so that
toke he neuer so much of his own mynd in the meane while all other
wayes saue scapyng / yet he well knew that scape he could not / & that
25 whan he were callid for / to deth & execucion he shuld / Now Cosyn
Vincent what wold you call this man / a prisoner, because he is kept
for execucion / or no prisoner, because he is in the meane while so
favorably handlid & suffred to do all that he wold saue scape / And
I bid you not here be hastye in your answere / but advise yt well,

---

2 first] *om. L 1553 1573*   2–3 man attayntid] man first attainted *1573*   3 or felonye]
or of felony *Z*   6 to] vnto *1553*   9 he /] | *canc. and question-mark added B*   15 goodes,] |
after comma B   17 byde] abide *Z*; ad *canc. B before* adde; yet] And yet *A*: And *canc. B*
after insertion   19 *period after* therin *B*; y *canc. A after* yea   20 wyll] y *wr. over* e *A*;
also /] | *canc. and comma added B*   21 foresene /] | *canc. and comma added B*   22 fro]
from *L 1553 1573*   25 for /] | *canc. and comma added B*; to deth & execucion] to exequcion,
and to death *Z*

that you graunt no such thing in hast, as you ⌜wold⌝ after mislike by leysure, & thinke your selfe deceyvid /

Vincent

Nay by my trouth vncle this thyng nedeth no study ⌜at all⌝ in my mynd / but [f. 179] that for all this favour shewid hym / & all this 5 libertie lent hym / yet beyng condempnid to deth / & beyng kept therfor / & kept with such sure watch layd vppon hym that he can not escape / he is all that while a very playne prisoner styll /

Antonye

In good fayth Cosyn me thinketh you say very trew / But than one 10 thing must I yet desire you Cosyn to tell me a litle ferther / yf there were a nother layd in prison for a fray / & thorow the gaolers displeasure, were boltid & fettrid & laid in a low dongeon in the stokkes, where he might hap to lye peradventure for a while, & abide in the meane season some payne, but no daynger of deth at all / 15 but that out agayne he shuld come well ynough / whyther of these two prisoners stode in worse case / he that hath all this favour, or he that is thus hardly handlyd /

Vincent

By our lady vncle I wene the most part of men yf they shuld nedes 20 chose, had leuer be such prisoners in euery poynt, as he that so sorely lieth in the stokkes / than in euery poynt such as he / that at such libertie walketh about the parke /

Antony

Consider than Cosyn whether this thyng seme any sophistry to 25 you that I shall shew you now / for yt shalbe such as semeth in good

1 graunt] *minim lacking in* un   4 thyng] tyng *A*: th *wr. over* t *B*; at all] *om. L 1553*
5–6 this libertie] hys libertie *L 1553 1573*   6 condempnid] condenpnid *A*   6–7 kept
therfor] therfore kept *L 1553 1573*; therfor] *final* e *added B*; & kept] *om. L 1553*, add kept
1557   8 escape] scape *L 1553 1573*   10 Cosyn] *om. L*   12 gaolers] Iailors *L 1553*
1573   14 for a while] for *om. L 1553*   16 whyther] whiche *1557*   18 handlyd /]
question-mark *ins. before* | *B*   21 rather *interl. B above* leuer (*uncanc.*); soryly *interl. B above*
sorely (*uncanc.*), soryly *L*   22 *comma after* such *B*; he /] | *canc. B*   25 thyng] tyng *A*:
th *wr. over* t *B*

fayth substanciall trew to me / And yf it so happen that you thinke
otherwise / I wilbe very glad to perceve which of vs both is begild /
For yt semeth to me Cosyn first, that euery man commyng into this
world here ⌐vppon yerth,⌐ as he is creatid by god / so cometh he
5 hether by the prouydence of god / / ys this any sophestry first or not /

Vincent

Nay verely / this is very substanciall trewth /

Antony

Now take I this also for very trewth in my mynd, that there com-
10 meth no man nor woman hyther into the erth / but ⌐that⌐ ere ⌐ever⌐
they come quik into the world out of the mothers wombe / god con-
dempneth them vnto deth by his own sentence & iugement, [f. 179ᵛ]
for the orígynall synne that they bryng with them / contractid in the
corruptid stokke of our forfather Adam / ys this Cosyn thinke you
15 verely thus or not /

Vincent

This is vncle very trew in dede /

Antonye

Than semeth this trew further vnto me / that god hath put euery
20 man here vppon earth, vnder so sure & vnder so safe kepyng, that of
all the whole people lyvyng in this ⌐wyde⌐ world / there is neyther
man woman nor child, wold they neuer so fayne wander about &
seke yt, that possible can fynd any way, wherby they may scape fro
deth / ys this Cosyn a fond ymagynyd fantasy, or ys it very trewth in
25 dede /

---

1 substanciall] substauncially L 1553 1573; be canc. A and B after it; happen] happe L 1553
1573   4 here] here / A: caret wr. over / B   5 god //] period placed before virgules B; ys]
canc. and Is interl. B   10 the erth] thearth L 1553   11 quik] om. L 1553   13 the
orígynall] thorigynall 1557   14 forfather] e interl. after for B; Adam /] / canc. and period
added B; ys] I wr. over y B; Cosyn] canc. and interl. before verely B; Cosyn thinke you] thinke
you Cosin Z   15 thus] true L 1553; not /] / canc. and question-mark added B   19 further]
farther L 1553 1573; here] here / A: / canc. B   20 earth] thearth B (th interl.), thearth
L 1553 1557, the earth 1573   21 wyde] wild A: canc. and wyde interl. B, wide Z
22 fayne] canc. and farre interl. B, farre Z   23 possible] possibly Z; fro] from L 1553
1573   24 fantasy] fansye L

Vincent

Nay this ys none ymagynacion vncle / but a thing so clerely provid
trew, that no man is so madd to say nay /

Antonye

Than nede I no more Cosyn / for than is all the mater playne & 5
open evident trewth / which I said I toke for trewth / which is yet more
a litle now, than I told you before, whan you toke my profe yet but for
a sophisticall fantasye / & said that for all my resonyng that euery man
is a prisoner / yet you thought that except these whom the comon
people call prisoners, there is els no man a very prisoner in dede / 10
And now you graunt your selfe agayne for very substanciall open
trewth / that euery man is here (though he be the greest kyng vppon
earth) set here by the ordenaunce of god in a place (be it neuer so
large) a place I say yet (and you say the same) out of which no man
can escape / but that therein ys euery man put vnder sure & safe kep- 15
yng to be redely fet forth whan god callith for hym, & that than he
shall surely dye / And is not than Cosyn by your own grauntyng before, euery man a ⌜very⌝ prisoner / whan he is put in a place to be
kept to be brote forth / when he wold not, & hym selfe wot not
whyther / [f. 180]   20

Vincent

Yes in good fayth vncle I can not but well perceve this to be so /

Antony

This were you wot well trew, although a man shuld be but taken by
the arme, & in fayre maner lede out of this world vnto his iudgment / 25
But now while we well know that there is no kyng so grete, but that
all the while he walkith here / walke he neuer so lose / ride he with

---

2 none] no L 1553 1573   3 nay] naye to yt L   6 trewth /] | canc. and comma added B
6–7 yet more a litle now] more a litle yet now 1553; litle] litle / A: | canc. B   8 fan-
tasye /] | canc. and comma added B, fansye L   9 prisoner /] | canc. and comma added B; these]
those L 1553 1573   10 els] interl. A, om. 1573   11 open] om. L 1553 1573   12 trewth
/] | canc. and comma added B; he be] vertical line after he B; greest] greatest Ƶ   13 god
in] god here in 1553   14 same)] parenth. wr. over | B   15 escape] scape L 1553 1573
19 brote] canc. and brought interl. B; forth /] | canc. B   20 whyther /] question-mark ins.
before | B   24 although] athough A: lt wr. over t B   25 arme] armye A: e canc. and
e wr. over y, then whole word canc. and arme, interl. B   27 with] interl. A

neuer so strong an armye for his defence / yet hym selfe is very sure /
though he seke in the meane season some other pastyme to put yt out
of his mynd / yet is he very sure / I say / that escape he can not / & very
well he knowith that he hath alredy sentence given vppon hym to
5 dye / and that verely dye he shall / & that hym selfe though he hope
vppon long respitt of his execution / yet can he not tell how sone / &
therfor but yf he be a fole, he can neuer be without feare, that eyther
on the morow or on the selfe same day / the griesly cruell hang man
deth / which from his first comyng in, hath euer hovid a lofe & lokyd
10 toward hym, & euer lyen in a wayte on hym, shall amyd a mong all
his rialtye & all his mayne strength, neyther knele before hym / nor
make hym any reuerence / nor with any good maner desier hym to
come forth / but rygorowsely & fiercely gripe hym by the very
brest, & make all his bones ratle / & so by long & diuerse sore tor-
15 mentes strike hym starke dede in this prison / & than cause his bodye
to be cast into the grownd in a fowle pytt within some corner of the
same, there to rott & be eaten with wretchid wormes of the earth /
sendyng yet his sowle owt ferther vnto a more fearefull iudgment,
wherof at his temporall deth his successe ys vncerteyne / And therfor
20 though by godes grace not out of good hope / yet for all that in the
meane while in very sore [f. 180ᵛ] dreade & feare / & peradventure
in perell inevitable of eternal fyer /

Me thinketh therfor Cosyn that / as I told you, this kepyng of euery
man in this wrechid world for execucion of deth, it is a very playne
25 ymprisonment in dede / And that (as I say) such, that the gretest kyng
ⸯisⸯ in this prison in mych worse case in all his welth, than many a
man is by the tother ymprisonment that is therin sore and hardly
handeld / for where some of those lye not there attayntid nor condempnid to deth / the greest man of this world & the most welthye,
30 in this vniuersall prison ys laid in, to be kept vndowtydly for deth /

1 sure /] | canc. and comma added B   3 escape] scape L 1553 1573; he can not] can he
not 1557 1573   6 sone /] period wr. over | B; &] canc. and And interl. B   9 losse? canc.
A before lofe   10 lyen] lye 1553; a mong] a canc. B, a om. 1557   11 rialtye] royaltie
L 1553 1557, roialtie 1573; hym /] | canc. and comma added B   17 with wretchid] with
the wretched Z; the earth] thearth L   19 vncerteyne /] | canc. and period added B
22 inevitable] vneuitable L 1553 1573; fyer] fyre too Z   24 it] canc. B, om. Z
25 ymprisonment] illeg. letter canc. A after first n; say)] say | A: parenth. wr. over | B
27 tother] other 1553 1573   28 handeld] handell A: d wr. over last l B   29 greest]
greatest Z

Vincent

But yet vncle in that case is the tother prisoner to / for he is as
sure that he shall dye to perdye /

Antonye

This is very trew Cosyn in dede / & well obiectid to / But than you 5
most consider, that he is not in daynger of deth, by reson of that
prison into which he is put peradventure but for a light fray / but his
daynger of deth, is by the tother ymprisonment by which he is
prisoner in the greate prison of this whole earth / in which prison all
the princes therof be prisoners as well as he / Yf a man condempnid 10
to deth, were put vpp in a large prison / & while hys execucion were
respitid, he were for fityng with his felowes, put vp in a strayt place
part of the same / he is in daynger of deth in that strayt prison / but
not by the beyng in that / for therin he is but for the fraye / but his
dedly ymprisonment was the tother / the larger I say, into which he 15
was put for deth / So the prisoner that you speke of, is beside that narrow prison / a prisoner of the brode world, & all the princes therof
ᵀtherinᵀ prisoners with hym / And by that ymprisonment, both they
and he in like daynger of deth / not by that strayt ymprisonment that
is commonly callid ymprisonment, [f. 181] but by that ymprison- 20
ment / which because of the large walke men call ᵀitᵀ libertie / And
which prison you therfor thought but a fantasy sophisticall to proue yt
any prison at all / But now may you me thinketh very playnly perceve,
that this whole earth / ys not onely for all the whole kynd of man a
very playné prison in dede / but also that euery man without excep- 25
cion, evyn those that are most at their libertie therin, & reken them
selfes grete lordes and possessioners of a very grete parcell therof /
& therby wax with wantones so forgetfull of theire own state, that

---

3 dye to] to *om. 1557*   5 This] That *L 1553 1573*; obiectid to] obiected too *1553 1557*
5–6 you most] must you *L 1553 1573*   8 tother] other *1553 1573*   10 he /] *period
before | B*; Yf] yf *A: canc. and* If *interl. B*; condempnid] condenpnid *A*   12 fityng] *canc.
and* fyghtyng *interl. B*; strayt] strayter *L*   13 in that strayt] in the strait *1573*
13–14 but not] but now *1557*; he is] is he *Z*   15 tother] other *1553 1573*   16 skeke
canc. A before speke   21 it] *added in margin at end of line B; period ? canc. B after* libertie;
And] *canc. and* & *interl. B*   22 therfor thought] thought therfore *L 1553 1573*; fantasy]
fansye *L*   24 earth /] | *canc. and comma added B*   26–27 them selfes] es *canc. B*, theym
selvys *L*, themself *1557*, themselues *1573*   27 a] *canc. B, om. Z*; pecys *interl. B above*
parcell *(uncanc.)*, pieces *Z*   28 theire] i *interl. A*; *virgule erased after* state

they wene they stand in greate welth / do stand for all that in dede, by
the reason of that ymprisonment in this large pryson of the whole
earth, in the selfe same condicion that other do stand / which in the
narrow prisons which onely be callid prisons, & which onely be
5 reputid prisons in the opynion of the comen people, stand in the most
ferefull & in the most odyouse case, that ys to witt condempnid all
redy to deth /

And now Cosyn, yf this thyng that I tell you, seme but a sophisticall
fantasye to your mynd / I wold be glad to know what moveth you so
10 to thinke / For in good fayth as I haue told you twyse, I am no wiser
but that I verely wene, that the thing ys thus of very playne trowth
in ⌜very⌝ dede /

The xxth Chapitre /

Vincent

15   In good fayth vncle, as for this farforth, I not onely can make with
any reason no resistence there agaynst, but also se very clerely
⌜provyd,⌝ that yt can be none otherwise / but that euery man is in this
world a very prisoner, sith we be all put here into a sure hold to be
kept till we be put to execucion, as folke alredy condempnid ⌜all⌝
20 vnto deth / But yet vncle that strayt kepyng / coleryng / boltyng / &
stokkyng / with lying in straw or on the cold grownd / which maner
[f. 181ᵛ] of hard handlyng is vsid in these speciall prisonmentes that
onely be callid commonly by that name / must nedes make that ymprisonment which onely berith among the people that name, mych
25 more odyouse & dredfull, than the generall imprisoning wherwith

---

2 that] *canc. and* theyr *interl.* B, theyr Ƶ   3 stand /] / *canc. and comma added* B   5 the
opynion] thopynyon L   9 fantasye] fansye L   10 twyse,] *second comma canc.* B
13 xxth] xx *1553 1557 1573*   15 this] thus Ƶ; oe *canc. A before* onely   16 caret *wr. over*
comma after* clerely B   17 provyd] *om.* L *1553;* otherwise /] / *canc. and comma added* B   19
put to] vn *interl. before* to B, putte to L *1553 1573*   19–20 all vnto] vn *canc.* B, all to Ƶ
21 / which] *parenth. wr. over* / B   22 prisonmentes] *superscript* i *canc.* A *after first* n
23 callid commonly] commonlye called L *1553 1573;* name /] *parenth. wr. over* / B
24 onely berith among the people] only among the people beareth *1553 1573*   25 im-
prisoning] *superscript* t *canc.* A *above second* n (A *first wrote* imprisonmᵗ: m *then changed to* in *by
dotting first minim),* impriesonment *1553 1573;* wherwith] *superscript* t *canc.* A *above first* w

we be euery man vniuersally prisounyd at large / walkyng where we
will round about the ⌐wide⌐ world / in which brod prison out of those
narrow prisons, ther is with the prisoners no such hard handlyng
vsyd /

Antonye 5

I said I trow Cosyn, that I purposid to proue you ferther yet, that
in this generall prison / the large prison I meane of this whole world,
folke be for the tyme that they be therin / as sore handled & as hardly,
& wrenchid & wrongid & brakyd in such paynefull wise, that our
hartes (save that we consider it not) haue with reason good & gret 10
cause to grudge agaynst and (as ferforth as perteynyth onely to the
respect of payne) as much horrour to conceve agaynst the hard handlyng that is in this prison, as the tother that is in that /

Vincent

In dede vncle trouth it is that this you said you wold prove / 15

Antonye

Nay so mich said I not Cosyn / but I said I wold yf I cold / & yf I
could not / than wold I therin give ouer my part / But that trust I
cosyn I shall not nede to do, the thing semeth me ⌐so⌐ playne / for
Cosyn not onely the prince & kyng / but also though he hath both 20
angels & devilles that are gaylours vnder hym / yet the chiefe gaylour
ouer this whole brode prison / the world is (as I take it) god / & that I
suppose ye will graunt me to /

Vincent

That will I not vncle denye / 25

---

1 large /] | *canc. and comma added B*   2 wide] *interl. B above canc.* wild *A*, wide *Z*   3 ther is]
s *canc.*, e *wr. over* i *and is interl. B*, there is *Z*   7 prison /] | *canc. and comma added B*
8 therin /] | *canc. and comma added B; comma erased after* handled   9 wrongid] wrongen
L 1553 1573   10 hartes (save] hartes | *(end of line) A, parenth. added B*   11 agaynst]
agaynst | *A*, thereagainst *L 1573*; (as] | as *A*: *parenth. wr. over* | *B*; as perteynyth onely]
onely as pertayneth *1553*   20 kyng /] | *canc. and comma added B*; not onely the prince
& king | but also though he] though the prynce and King *L*, though the prince and
Kynges *1553*; hath] haue *Z*   21 vnder hym] over theym *L* (over *canc. and* vnder *interl.*
by second hand L), ouer hym *1553*   22 (as] *parenth. ed.*   23 ye] you *L 1553 1573*

Antonye

Yf a man be (Cosyn) comyttid to prison for no cause but to be kept,
though there be neuer so greate charge vppon hym / yet his keper yf
he be good & honest, ⌐is¬ neyther so cruell that wold payne the man
5 of malice / nor so covetouse that wold put hym to payne to make hym
[f. 182] seke his frendes to pay for a peny worth of ease / els yf the
place be such that he be sure to kepe hym ⌐safe¬ otherwise / or that he
can get suretye for the recompence of more harm than he seeth he
shuld haue yf he scapid / he will neuer handle hym in any such hard
10 fassion, as we most abhorre ymprisonment for / But mary yf the place
be such as the keper can not otherwise be sure / than is he compellid
to kepe hym after the rate the straighter /

And also yf the prisoner be vnruly & fall to fityng with his
felows, or do some other maner of shrewid tournes / than vseth the
15 keper to punyssh hym sondry wise, in some of such fashions as your
selfe haue spoken of.

So is it now Cosyn that god the chiefe gaylour (as I say) of this
brode prison the world / ys neyther cruell nor covetouse / And this
prison is also so sure & so subtilly bildyd, that albeit that yt lyeth open
20 on euery side without any wall in the world / yet wander we neuer
so ferre about therin, the way to get out at / shall we neuer fynd /
so that he nedeth not to coler vs nor to stokk vs for any fere of scapyng awaye. And therfor / except he see some other cause than our
onely kepyng for deth, he lettith vs in the meane while (for as long as
25 he list to respit vs) walk about in the prison, & do therin what we will,
vsyng our selfe in such wise / as he hath by reason & revelacion fro
tyme to tyme told vs his pleasure /

And hereof yt cometh lo / that by reason of this favour for a tyme,
we wax (as I said) so wanton / that we forget where we bee / wenyng

---

2 (Cosyn)] *parentheses added B*; to] vn *interl. B before* to, vnto Z 3 there be] there lye
L 1553 1573; yet] yet yf *L*   6 frendes to] frendes, and to Z 7 safe] *interl. B above
canc.* selfe *A*, safe Z 13 fityng] *canc. and* fyghting *interl. B*   14 tournes] turne *L 1553
1573*   15 punyssh] *first* s *wr. over* i? *B*   17 say)] say / *A*: *parenth. wr. over* / *B*
19 bildyd] *orig.* bildyll, d *wr. over first* l *and second* l *canc. A*   20 on] vpon *L 1553
1573*, he neither nedeth *1557*   23 therfor /] / *canc. and comma added B*   25 list] luste
1553; walk] wall *A*: *final* l *alt. to* k *B*   26 wise /] / *canc. and comma added B*; fro] from
L 1553 1573   28 lo /] / *canc. and comma added B*   29 (as] *parenth. added B*

that we were lordes at large / where as we be in dede yf we wold consider yt / evyn sely pore whrechis in prison / for of very trouth our
very prison this earth is / And yet therof we cant vs out / part by cove-
nauntes that we make among vs / & part by [f. 182ᵛ] fraude, & part
by violence to / diuerse partes diuersly to our selfe / & chaunge the 5
name therof / fro the odyouse name of prison, & call yt our own land
& our lyvelod /

Vppon our prison we bild our prison: we garnysh yt with gold &
make yt gloriouse / In this prison they bye & sell / in this prison they
brall and chide / in this they run together & fight / in this they dyce / 10
in this they carde / In this they pipe & revell / In this they sing &
dawnce / And in this prison many a man reputid right honest lettith
not for his pleasure in the darke prively to play the knave /

And thus while god our kyng & our chiefe gaylour to / suffreth vs
and lettith vs alone / we wene our selfe at libertye / & we abhorre the 15
state of those whom we call prisoners, takyng our selfe for no prisoners
at all.

In which false perswasion of welth & forgetfulncs of our own
wretchid state (which ys but a wandryng about for a while in this
pryson of this world, till we be brought vnto the execucion of deth) 20
where we forget with our foly both our selfe & our gaole, & our vnder
gaolers Angelles & devilles both / & our chiefe gaolour god to / god
that forgettith not vs, but seeth vs all the while well inough, & beyng
sore discontent to to se so shrewde rule kept in the gaole / beside that
he sendith the hangman deth to put to execucion here & there some- 25
tyme by the thowsandes at ones / he handeleth many of the remenaunt / whose execucion he forberith yet vnto a further tyme / evyn

1–2 wold consider] woulde well consyder L 1553 1573   2 whrechis] r interl. A; for] f alt.
to F B; very] om. L 1553 1573   3 cant] caute 1553; out /] | canc., comma added and then
erased B   3–4 part by covenauntes] partely by couenauntes 1553 1573   6 therof /] | canc.
B; fro] from L 1553 1573   6–7 land &] lande or L 1553   8 Virgule wr. after bild B;
bild our prison: we] buylde oure prison, we L 1553, bild: our prison we 1557, build, our
prison we 1573; garnysh yt] yt canc. B, om. 1557 1573 (see note)   9 extra this canc. B before
prison   10 in this they] In this pryson they L 1553 1573; dyce /] | wr. over comma B
12 letth canc. A and B before lettith   15 selfe at] selvys at L   16 selfe for] selvys for L,
selues for 1553 1573   18 perswasion] w wr. over u? B   19 (which] / which A: parenth.
wr. after | B   20 the execucion] thexecucion L 1557   21 where] yl wr. over er B, whyle Ƶ
23 beyng] begyng A: canc. and beyng interl. B   24 to to se] one to om. Ƶ   25 here] he
A: canc. and here interl. B   25–26 sometyme] some tymes 1553 1573   27 / whose]
parenth. wr. over | B; tyme /] parenth. wr. over | B

as hardly, & punysheth them as sore in this comen prison of the
world / as there are any handlid in those specyall prisons which for
the hard handlyng vsid (you say) therin, your hart hath in such
horrour & so ⌐sore⌐ abhorreth.

5   Vincent

The remenaunt will I not agayne say / for me thinketh I se it so in
dede / but that god our chiefe gaylour in this world, vseth [f. 183]
⌐eny⌐ such prisonly fasshion of punyshment / that poynt most I nedes
deny / for I neyther see hym ley any man in the stokkes, or strike fet-
10 ters on his legges / or so much as shete hym vpp in a chamber
eyther /

Antonye

Ys he no mynstrell Cosyn that playeth not on an harp? maketh
no man melodye but he that playeth on a lute / he may be a mynstrell
15 & make melodye you wot well with some other instrument, some
strange fashionid peradventure that neuer was seen before / God our
chiefe gaylour as hym selfe is invisible / so vseth ⌐he⌐ in his punyshmentes invisible instrumentes / & therfor not of like fasshion as the
tother gaolers do / but yet of like effect / & as paynfull in felyng as
20 those / for he layeth one of his prisoners with an hote feuer, as evyll at
his ease in a warm bed / as the tother gaoler layth his on the cold
grownd / he wryngeth them by the browes with a mygrem / he collereth them by the neck with a quyncy / he bolteth them by the armes
with a paluesey, that they can not lyft theire handes to their head /
25 he manacleth their handes with ⌐the⌐ gowt in their fyngers / he wringeth them by the legges with the cramp in their shynnes / he byndeth

2 world /] | canc. and comma added B   4 so sore] second so canc. after so and sore interl. B
6 agayne say] gayne saye Z; thinketh] thynke 1553 1573   7 dede / but] B wr. over / and
b, period added after dede B   8 eny] onely A: canc. and eny interl. B, any Z (catchword f.
182ᵛ: onely canc. and eny wr. before B?); most I] I must L 1553 1573   10 or so much]
and so muche L 1553; shete] shytt B (y wr. over first e and t over second e), shutte L 1553,
shet 1557, shut 1573   13 an harp] a harpe L 1553 1573   14 no man melodye] no
manne no melodie L 1553 1573; mynstrell] final l added B?   17 invisible /] | canc. and
comma added B   17–18 punyshmentes] punyshemente 1553 1573   19 of] interl. A
20 those /] | canc. and period added B; for] f alt. to F B   21 bed /] | canc. and comma added B;
on] in A: o wr. over i B, vpon L 1553 1573   22 them] hym 1553   23 he bolteth]
he om. 1553   24 theire] i interl. A; head] heades L 1553 1573   26 the cramp] a
crampe 1553 1573

them to the bed bord with the crik in the bakke / & layeth one there
a long, & as vnhable to rise as though he lay by the feet fast in the
stokkes /

Some prisoner of a nother gaole syngeth ⌜&⌝ dawnceth in his ij
feters, & fereth not his fete for stumblyng at a stone / [while] goddes 5
prisoner that hath his one fote feterid with the gowte lieth gronyng /
on a cowch / & quaketh and crieth out yf he fere there wold fall on
his fote no more but a quysshion / And therfor Cosyn (as I said) yf
we consider yt well / we shall fynd this generall prison of this whole
earth, a place in which the prisoners [f. 183ᵛ] be as sore handlid as 10
they be in the tother / And evyn in the tother / some make as mery
⌜to,⌝ as there do some in this that are very mery at large out of that /

And surely like as we wene our selfe out of prison now / so yf there
were some folke born & brought vpp in a prison / that neuer cam on
the wall / nor lokyd out at the dore / nor neuer herd of other world 15
abrode / but saw some for their shrewed turnes done among them selfe,
lokkid vpp in some strayter rome, & herd them onely callid prisoners
that were so servid / & them selfe euer callid free folke at large / the
like opynion wold they haue there of them selfe ⌜than,⌝ that we haue
here of our selfe now / And whan we take our selfe for other than 20
prisoners now / as verely be we now deceyvid, as those prisoners shuld
there be than.

Vincent

I can not vncle in good fayth say nay / but that you haue performyd
all that you haue promisid / But ⌜yet⌝ sith that for all this there apper- 25
ith no more / but that as they be prisoners, so be we to / & that as
some of them be sore handlyd, so be some of vs to / sith we wote well
for all this that whan we come to those prisons, we shall not fayle to be
in a strayter prison than we be now, & to haue a dore shit vppon vs

1 layeth one there] lyeth on there *1553*   2 vnhable] h *canc.* B, vnable L *1553 1573*; by
the feet fast] by fast the feete *1557*   4 *caret wr.* by B *over comma after* syngeth; &] *om.* Z
5 while] Z, which A   6 hath his] hath but hys L *1553 1573*; gronyng /] | *canc.* B
8 quysshion] cusshion L *1557*, cushion *1553 1573*; said)] *parenth. ed.,* said | A   11 tother]
other *1553 1573*; tother] other *1553 1573*   15 nor lokyd] or loked *1553*; out at] out of
1553 1573   16 saw some] saue some *1553*; for their shrewed] their *om.* Z   17 in some
strayter] some *om.* Z   20 selfe for] selvys, for L   21 we now deceyvid] we deceiued
now L *1553 1573*   26 more /] | *canc. and comma added* B   29 shit] shutte L *1553*, shet
1557, shut *1573*

where we haue none shit on vs now: this shall we be sure of at the
lest wise / yf there come no worse / And than may there come worse
ye wot well, yt cometh there so comonly / wherfor for all this, it is
yet litell merveyle / though mens hartes grudge mich there agaynst.

<h6>5   Antony</h6>

Surely Cosyn in this you say very well / Howbeyt somwhat had
your wordes towchid me the nerer / yf I had sayd that ymprisonment
were no displeasure at all / But the thing that I say Cosyn for our
comfort therin ys, that our fantasy frameth vs a false opynion, by
10 which we deceyve our selfe [f. 184] and take yt for sorer than yt is /
And that do we, by the reson that we take our selfe before for more fre
than we be, & prisonment for a stranger thyng to vs than yt is in dede.
And thus ferforth / as I said haue I prouid very trouth in dede / But
now the yncommodities that you repete agayne, those I say that are
15 proper to thinprisonment of their own nature / that is to wit to haue
lesse rome to walke in, & to haue the dore shyt vppon vs: these are me
thinketh so very slender & sleyght / that in so greate a cause / as to
suffer for goddes sake / we might be sore ashamyd so mich as ones to
thinke vppon them /
20   Many a good man there is you wot well / whych without any force
at all / or any necessite wherfor he shuld so do, suffreth these ij thynges
willyngly of his own choyse, with mich ⌈other⌉ hardnes more / holy
monkes I meane of the charterouse order / such as neuer passe their
selles / but onely to the church set fast by their celles / & thence to
25 their celles agayne / & saynt Brygittes order / & s. clares mich like /
& in ⌈a⌉ maner all ⌈close⌉ religiouse howses / And yet Ancres & ancresses most especyally / all whose whole rome is lesse than a metely
large chamber / And yet are they there as well content many long

---

1 shit] shutte L *1553*, shette *1557*, shut *1573* (*these sp. variants not recorded hereafter*)
2 worse /] / *canc. and period added* B   3 ye] you L *1553 1573*   4 merveyle /] / *canc. and
comma added* B   6 very] wery A   9 therin] therin / A: / *canc.* B; fantasy] fansy L
12 thny *canc.* A *before* thyng   13 very trouth in dede] trueth in very dede *Z*   14 that
canc. A *and* B *after* those   15 thinprisonment] thymprysonment L, themprisonment
1553, the imprisonment *1573*; their] i *interl.* A   17 thinketh] thynke *1553 1573*;
cause /] / *canc.* B   20 there is] *interl.* A; you wot] ye wot *1557*; any force] any *om.*
L *1553 1573*   21 all /] / *canc.* B; shuld so do] so shoulde dooe L *1553*   22 hardnes] hardines *1553*   25 s.] s / A; clares] Claryce L *1553*, Claris *1557*   26 close] those A : *canc. and*
close *interl.* B, close *Z*   27 especyally] especyall L, specyall *1553*, specially *1573*; all] a *alt.*
to A B

yeres together / as are other men (& bettre to) that walke about the
world / And therfor you may see that the lothnes of lesse rome, &
the dore shit vppon vs / while so many folke are ⌐so well⌐ content
therwith, & will for goddes love live so to chuse, ys but an horrour
enhauncid of our own fantasye.   5

And in dede I wist a woman ones that came into a [f. 184ᵛ] prison,
to visit of her charite a pore prisoner there, whom she found in a
chamber / to say the trouth metely feyre / & at the lest wise it was
strong ynough / But with mattes of straw the prisoner had made yt
so warme / both vnder the fote & round about the walles, that in these 10
thinges for kepyng of his helth, she was on his behalfe glad & very
well comfortid / But a mong many other displeasures that for his sake
she was sory for / one she lamentid much in her mynd / that he shuld
haue the chamber dore vppon hym by nyght made fast by the gaoler
that shuld shit hym in / For by my trouth quod she / yf the dore shuld 15
be shit vppon me, I wold wene yt wold stopp vpp my breeth / At that
word of hers / the prisoner laughed in his mynd / but he durst not
laugh a lowde nor say nothing to her / For somewhat in dede he stode
in awe of her / & had his fyndyng there mich part of her charite for
almoyse / but he could not but laugh inwardly / while he wist well   20
inogh that she vsid on the inside to shit euery night full surely her
own chamber to her, both dore & wyndowes to / & vsid not to open
them of all the long night / And what difference than as to the stop-
pyng of the breth, whether they were shit vpp within or without / And
so surely cosyn these two thynges that you speke of, are neyther nother 25
of so greate weyght, that in christes cause ought to move a christen
⌐man⌐ / and the tone of the twayne is so very a childish fantasye, that
in a ⌐mater almost⌐ of .iij. chypps / but yf yt were in chaunce of fire,
neuer shuld move any man.

As for those other accidentes of hard handlyng therin / so madd am 30

---

1 (&] *parenth. added B*   2 see that] see wyth *1553*   4 but an] an *om. 1553*   5 fantasye]
fansye *L*   8 chamber /] | *canc. and comma added B*; the lest] the *om. L*   9 mattes] the
mattes *1553*   11 for kepyng] for the kepynge *Z*   13 sory] *Z*, sorow *A*; one] once
1553; he] she *L 1553*   14 dore] shyt *interl. and canc. B after* dore; dore vppon] doore
shutte vppon *L 1553 1573*; nyght made] night, & made *1573*   15 my] *orig.* me: y *wr.*
over e *A*   20 almoyse] allmoyse *L*, almose *1553 1573*, almes *1557*   24 were] we *A*:
canc. and were *interl. B*, were *Z*   27 fantasye] fansye *L*   28 mater] maner *A*: *canc.*
and mater almost *interl. B*, matter almoste *Z*; chypps /] | *canc. and comma added B*   29
neuer] neyther *1553 1573*; man] man, so moche as to thyncke therof *L*, manne as muche
as thynke thereof *1553 1573*

I not to say they be no griefe / but I say that our feare may Imagyne
them mich greater greife than they be. [f. 185] And I say / that such
as they be, many a man endureth them, yee & many a woman to /
that after fare full well / And than wold I wit what determynacion we
5 take, whither for our saviours sake to suffre some payne in our bodies /
sith he suffred in his blessid body so greate payne for vs / or els to give
hym warnyng to be at a poynt / rather vtterly to forsake hym, than
suffer any payne at all. He that cometh in his mynd vnto this latter
poynt / from which kynd of vnkyndnes god kepe euery man / comfort
10 ⌐he⌐ none nedeth / for he will flye the nede / & counsayle I fere avaylith hym litle / & yf grace be so farre gone from hym. But on the tother
syde / yf rather than forsake our saviour, we determyne our selfe to
suffre any payne at all / I can not than see, that the feare of hard
handlyng shuld any thyng styk with vs, & make vs so to shrynke, as
15 we rather wold forsake his fayth than to suffre for his sake so mich as
ymprisonment / sith the handlyng ys neyther such in pryson, but that
many men many yeres / & many women to, live therewith & sustayne
yt / & after ward yet fare full well / & yet that yt may well fortune,
that beside the very bare ymprisonment / there shall happ vs no
20 hard handlyng at all / nor that same happely but for a short whyle
neyther / & yet beside all this peradventure not ⌐at⌐ all / & specially
sith which of all these wayes shalbe taken with vs, lieth all in his will,
for whome we be content to take yt / & which for that mynd of ours,
favoreth vs, & will suffer [f. 185ᵛ] no man to put more payne vnto vs,
25 than he well woteth we shalbe well able to bere / For he will give vs
the strength therto hym selfe, as you haue hard his promise all redy /
by the mouth of S paule / *fidelis deus qui non patitur vos tentari supra id*
quod potestis ferre sed ⌐*dat etiam cum tentatione prouentum*: God⌐ ys faythfull,

---

1 our feare] *repeated by A, first occurrence canc. A and B, that interl. B after* say *and canc. B,*
that interl. A before second our feare   2 be.] *period ed.*; say /] | *canc. B*   3 to /] | *canc.*
and comma added B   7 warnyng to be] warning and be *Z*   8 He] he *A*: H *wr. over*
h *B*; in his] in thys *L 1553*   9 / from . . . man /] *parentheses wr. over virgules B*   10
nedeth /] | *canc. B*; flye] flee *1557 1573*   11 litle /] | *canc. and comma added B*; & yf] &
canc. B, om. Z   12 than forsake] than to forsake *1557*   14 so to] to to *1557*   17 men
many yeres] in many yeares *1553*; women] womey *A*: y *canc. and* n *added B*   18 *extra*
afterward *canc. B after* yet   19 ymprisonment /] | *canc. and comma added B*; happ]
happen *1553 1573*   19–20 no hard] none harde *1557*   25 give vs] vs *om. L 1553*
26 redy /] | *canc. B*   27 fidelis deus] Fidelis autem deus est *1557*; patitur] patietur
1557 1573   28 sed] sed &c God *A*: &c God *canc. B after* sed *and passage interl. as above,*
with abbrev. pro canc. B after tentatione

which suffreth you not to be temptid aboue that you may bere / but giveth also with the temptacion a way out / But now yf we haue not lost our fayth al redye, before we come to forsake it for feare: we know very wel by our fayth, that by the forsakyng of our fayth, we fall into the state to be cast into the prison of hell / & that can we not tell how 5 sone / but as it may be that god will suffre vs to live a while here vppon earth / so may it be that he will throw vs in that dungeon byneth before the tyme that the Turke shall ones aske vs the question / And therfor yf we fere ymprisonment so sore / we be mich more than madd, that we fere not moost for the more sore / for out of that prison shall 10 no man neuer get / & in this other shall noman abyde but a while.

In prison was Ioseph while his bretheren were at large / & yet afterward were his brethren fayne to seke vppon hym for brede /

In prison was danyell, & the wild lions about hym / & yet evyn here god kept hym harmlesse, & brought hym safe out agayne /   15

Yf we thinke that he will not do the likewise for vs / let vs not dout but he will do for vs eyther the like or better / for bettre [f. 186] may he do for vs, yf he suffer vs there to dye / S Iohn the baptist was (you wote well) ⌈in prison⌉ while herode & herodias sat full mery at the fest, & the daughter of herodias delytid them with her daunsyng / 20 till with her daunsyng / she daunsid of S. Iohns hed / & now sittith he with great fest in hevyn at goddes bord / while herode & herodias full hevely sytt in hell burnyng both twayne / & to make them sport withall, the devill with the damysell daunce in the fire afore them.   25

Fynally Cosyn to finish this piece with, our saviour was hym selfe taken prisoner for our sake, & prisoner was he caried, & prisoner was he kept / & prisoner was he brought forth before Annas, & prisoner from Annas caried vnto Cayphas / ⌈than prisoner was he⌉ caried from Cayphas vnto Pilate / & prisoner was he sent from Pilate 30

---

7 in that] into the L *1553*, into that *1557 1573*; comma after dungeon B   9 ymprisonment] impriesonmentes *1553*   10 that] if *interl.* B above that (*uncanc.*), if L *1553 1573*; moost for the more sore] for *canc. and* farre *interl.* B, most the more sore L *1553*, moste, farre the more sore *1557*, most the far more sore *1573*   12–13 afterward] ward *canc.* B, after *Z*   15 here] there *Z*   16 likewise] like *1573*   19 well)] *parenth. wr. over* / B 20–21 daunsyng / till] / *canc. and comma added* B   21 daunsyng / she] / *canc.* B   22 bord] bordes *A*: es *canc. A?,* boarde *Z*   27 taken] take L *1557*   29 than prisoner was he] *transferred by B from position in next line before* sent from Pilate (*A has* / *after* than)   30 he sent from] sent fro *1557*

to kyng herode / prisoner from herode vnto Pilate agayne / & so kept
as prisoner to thend of his passhion /

The tyme of his ymprisonment I graunt well was not long / but as
for hard handlyng (which our hartes most aborre) he had as mich in
5 that short while / as many men among them all in mich lenger tyme /
And surely than yf we consider of what estate he was / & therwith
that he was prisoner in such wise for our sake / we shall I trow (but
yf we be worse than wrechid bestes) neuer so shamfully play the vnkynd cowardes, as for fere of ymprisonment sinfully to forsake hym /
10 nor so folysh neyther, as by forsakyng of hym, to give hym the
occasion agayne [f. 186ᵛ] to forsake vs / & with the avoydyng of an
easier prison, fall into a worse / & in stede of a prison that can not kepe
vs long, fall into that prison out of which we can neuer come / where
the short prisonment wold wynne vs euerlastyng lybertie /

15   The feare of shamfull & paynfull dethe /

                    The xxjᵗʰ chapitre /

                          Vincent

For soth vncle / our lord reward you therfor / yf we fearid not ferther
beside ymprisonment / the terrible dart of shamfull & paynfull deth /
20 as for ymprisonment I wold veryly trust, that remembryng these
thinges which I haue here hard of you ⌐rather⌐ than I shuld forsake
the fayth of our saviour, I wold with help of grace neuer shrynke
therat / But now are we comen vncle with moch worke ⌐at the last,⌐
vnto the last & vttermost poynt of the drede, that maketh / *incursum*
25 *& demonium meridianum* / this incursion of this mydday devyll / This
open invasion of the Turke, & his persecucion agaynst the fayth, seme

1 kyng] kynd *A*: g *wr. over* d *B*; prisoner] and prysoner *L*   2 thend] the ende *1553*
1557 1573; passhion /] *canc. and* passion. *wr. at end of line B*   4 aborre] abhorre *Z*
5 while /] / *canc. and comma added B*; lenger] longer *1553 1573*   7 (but] / *canc. and parenth.
added B*   8 be *wr. over* w *A*; bestes)] *parenth. wr. over* / *B*   10 forsakyng] r *interl. B*
10–11 the occasion] thoccasion *L 1557*   12 of a prison] a *om. 1557*   13 where] whereas
1573   16 xxjᵗʰ] xxi *1553 1557 1573*   19 the] that *L 1553*   20 ymprisonment]
prysonment *L*; these] those *1553 1573*   21 here hard] hard here *L*   23 comen] come
L 1553; caret *wr. over comma after* worke *B*   24 incursum] r *interl. A*   25 devyll /] /
canc. and period added B; This] this *A*: T *wr. over* t *B*

so terrible to mens myndes, that all though the respect of god vaynquysshe all the remenaunt of the trowbles that we haue hetherto
pervsid / as losse of goodes, landes, & libertie / yet when we remember
the terrour of shamfull & paynfull deth, that poynt so sodaynly puttith
vs in oblivion of all that shuld be our comfort / that we fele all men I 5
fere me for the most part / the fervour of our fayth wax so cold, &
our hartes so faynt, that we fele our selfe at the poynt to fall evyn
therfro for feare.

Antonye

To this I say not nay Cosyn, but that in dede in this poynt is the 10
sore pynch / And yet you see for all this, that evyn this poynt [f. 187]
to, taketh encrease & mynyshment of dred, after the difference of
the affcccions that are before fixed & rotid in the mynd / so fer forth
that you se some man, sct so much by his worldly substaunce, that he
lesse fearcth the losse of his lyfe, than the losse of landes / ye some man 15
shall you see that abideth dedly tourment, & such as some other had
lever dye than indure / rather than he wold bryng forth the money
that he hath hydde /

And I dout not but you haue herd of many by right antique
storics, that some for one cause / some for other, haue not lettid 20
willyngly to suffre deth / diuerse in diverse kyndcs / & some both with
dispightfull rebuke & paynfull tourment to / And therfor as I say /
we may see, that thaffeccions of menys myndes toward thencrease or
decreace of dreade, maketh mich of the matter /

Now are the affeccions of mens myndes ymprintid by diuers 25
meanes / one way by the meane of the bodely sensis, movid by such
thinges pleasaunt or displeasaunt, as are outwardly thorow sensible

---

1 to] vn *interl. B before* to, vnto *Z*   1–2 vaynquysshe] vanquisheth *L 1553 1573*
2 trowbles] trowles *A*: b *interl. B*, trouble *1557*; hetherto] to *added B?*   3 remember]
remenber *A*: n *alt. to* m *B*   6 part /] | *canc. and comma added B*   7 fele] *canc. and*
fynde *interl. B*, fynde *Z*; selfe] selvys *L*   12 encrease &] encrease or *Z*; dred] *final* e
added B   17 lever] rather *L 1553*; indure] abyde and endure *L*; forth] *canc. and* owt *interl.*
B, oute *Z*   19 antique] autentyque *L*, antentiue *1553*, autentike *1557 1573*   20 cause
/] | *canc. and comma added B*; other] an other *1573*   22 dispightfull] dispighfull *A*
23 thaffeccions] s *canc. B*, the affeccion *L 1553 1573*, thaffeccion *1557*; menys] *bar added*
over e *B, then word canc. and the interl. B*, the *Z*; myndes] es *canc. and* e *wr. after* d *B*,
mynde *Z*; impryntyd by diuers meanys *interl. B after* myndes, *then canc. B* (*see note*);
thencrease] the encrease *1553 1573*   24 of dreade] of the dreade *L 1553*   25 the
affeccions] thaffeccions *1557*; mens] *bar added over* e *B*   26 meane of the] *om. L 1553*

worldly thinges, offred & obiectid vnto them. And this maner of
recevyng of ympression of affeccion, is comen vnto men & bestes / A
nother maner of recevyng affeccions, ⌈is⌉ by the meane of reason,
which both ordenately tempereth those affeccions that the bodely
5 five wittes ymprent / and also disposeth a man many tymes to some
spirituall vertues, very contrary to those affeccions, that are fleshly &
sensuall / And those resonable dispositions bene the affeccions
spirituall, & propre to the nature of man, & above the nature of best /
Now ⌈as⌉ our goostly ennymye the devill, enforseth hym selfe to make
10 vs lene vnto the sensuall affeccions and bestly / So doth almighty god
of his goodnes by his holy spirite, inspire vs good mocions, with ayd &
help of his grace [f. 187ᵛ] toward the tother affeccions spirituall / And
by sundry meanes instructith our reason to lene vnto them / & not
onely to receve them as ingendred & plantid in our soule, but also in
15 such wise water them with the wise advertisement of godly counsayle
& contynuall prayour, that they may be habitually radicate &
surely take depe rote therin / & after as the tone kynd of affeccion or
the tother bereth the strength in our hart / so be we stronger or febler
agaynst the terrour of deth in this cause /
20   And therfor will we Cosyn assay to consider, what thinges there are
for which we haue cause in reason to mayster that affeccion ferefull
& sensuall & though we can not clene avoyd it & put it away: yet in
such wise to brydle yt at the lest / that yt run not out so farre like an
hed strong horse, that spite of our teeth yt cary vs out vnto the
25 devill / /
    Let vs therfor now consider & well way this thyng that we drede so
sore / that is to witt shamfull & paynfull deth /

---

1 worldly] Z, wordly A; obiectid] abiected 1553   2 of ympression] the impressyon L
1553 1573, thimpression 1557; affeccion] final s added B, affeccions Z   3 is] added in
margin at end of line B, as ⟨A⟩ canc. B at beginning of next line   7 bene the] be L, the om. Z
8 best] es added B, beastes Z   10 lene] leve A: canc. and lene interl. B; vnto] to 1553
1573; bestly /] colon ins. before / B; So] canc. and so interl. B   12 And] canc. and & interl. B
15 with the wise] the om. 1553 1573   22 period added after sensuall B; &] canc. and And
interl. B   23 lest /] / canc. and comma added B   26 well way] waie wel L 1553 1573
27 sore /] / canc. and comma added B; deth /] chapter-heading follows as part of paragraph A

Off deth considerid by hym selfe alone,
as a bare levyng of this life onely /

The xxij Chapitre /

And first I perceve well by these two thinges that you ioyne vnto
deth / that is to wit shamfull & paynfull / you wold esteme deth so 5
mich the lesse / yf he shall come alone, without eyther shame or
payne /

Vincent

Without dowt vncle a great deale the lesse / But yet though he shuld
come without them both by hym selfe / what so euer I wold, I wot 10
well many a man wold be for all that very loth to dye.

Antonye

That I beleve well Cosyn & the more pytie it is / for that affeccion
happeth in very few / but that eyther the cause is, lake of fayth, lak of
hope / or fynally lak of witt / They that belive [f. 188] not the life to 15
come after this, & wene them selfe here in welth: are loth to leve
this / for than they thinke they lese all / And therfor cometh the
manyfold folysh vnfaythfull wordes, which are so rife in ᣔoverᣔ many
mouthes / This world we know, & the tother we know not / And that
some say in sport, & thinke in ernest / The devill ys not so blak as he ys 20
payntid / & let hym be as blak as he will, he is no blaker than a crow
with many such other folish fantasies of the same sort.
    Some that belyve well ynough / yet thorow the lewdnes of lyving,
fall out of good hope of salvacion / & than though they be loth to dye /
I very litle merveyle / how be yt some that purpose to mend, & wold 25

1 Off deth] *canc. at end of line and* Of deth *interl. at beginning of next line* B   3 xxij] xxijᵗʰ L
5 deth /] / *canc. and comma added* B   6 shall] shuld B (u *wr. over* a *and* d *wr. over final* l),
should Z   14 few /] / *canc. and comma added* B; lake] e *canc.* B   15 hope /] / *canc. and
comma added* B; witt /] / *canc. and period added* B   17 therfor] *canc. and* therof *interl.* B,
therof Z   18 rife in over] rife in oʳ A: *canc. and* ryfe in over *interl.* B; many]
mennys B (e *wr. over* a *and* s *added*)   18–19 over many mouthes] ouer many mennes
mouthes L 1553 1573, our manye mouthes 1557   19 tother] other 1553 1573   22
fantasies] fansyes L   25 merveyle /] / *canc. and period added* B

fayne haue some tyme lefte them lenger to bestow somwhat bettre, may peradventure be loth to dye also by & by. And that maner lothnes / albeit a very good will gladly to dye, & to be with god were in my mynd so thankfull / that yt were well hable to purchase as full
5 remission both of synne and payne as peradventure he were like yf he livid to purchase in many yeres penaunce / yet will I not say / but that such kynd of lothnes to dye, may be before god alowable / Some are there also that are loth to dye, that are ⌈yet⌉ very glad to dye, & long for to be dede /

10   Vincent

That were vncle a very straunge case /

                                        Antonye

The case I fere me Cosyn falleth not very often / but yet some tyme yt doth / as where there is any man of that good mynd that / S /
15 paule was, which for the longyng that he had to be with god, wold fayne haue bene ded / but for the profit of other folke, was content to live here in payne, and [f. 188ᵛ] differ & forbere for the while his inestimable blysse in hevyn. ⌈Cupio dissolui & esse cum Christo: bonum autem mihi manere propter vos.⌉ But of all these kyndes (Cosyn) of folkes
20 that are loth to dye / except the first kynd onely that lakketh fayth / there is I suppose none / but that except the fere of shame or sharp payne ioynid vnto deth, shold be the lett, wold els for the bare respect of deth alone, let to depart hens with good will / in this case of the fayth / well wyttyng by his fayth, that his deth taken for the
25 fayth, shuld clense hym clene of all his synnys, & send hym strayte to hevyn / And some of these (namely the last kynd) are such, that shame & payne both, ioynyd vnto deth, were vnlikely to make them

---

1 lefte them lenger] left the lenger *1553*   3 / albeit] *parenth. wr. over | and comma B*; *comma after* were *B*   4 thankfull /] | *canc. and comma added B*; hable] h *canc. B*, able *L 1553 1573*   6 penaunce /] *parenth. wr. over | B*   7 alowable /] alowed *canc. A and B before* alowable, | *canc. and period added B*; *err. heading* Vincent *canc. A before* Some are 8 very] *om. L 1553*   18–19 Cupio . . . propter vos] desiderium habens dissolui & esse cum Christo, multo magis melius parmanere autem in carne necessarium propter vos *1557 1573*   19 (Cosyn)] *parentheses added B*; kyndes (Cosyn) of folkes] kyndes of folkes Cosin *L 1553*, kindes of folke, Cosin *1573*   20 fayth /] | *canc. and comma added B*   21 none /] | *canc. and comma added B*; except] (except *A*: *parenth. canc. B*   23–24 case of the] the *om. L 1553*   26 these] those *L 1553*

loth deth ⌐or fere deth so sore, but that they wold suffer deth⌐ in this
case with good will, sith they know well, that the refusyng of the
fayth for any cause in this world (were the cause neuer so good in
sight) shuld yet seuer them fro god / with whom save for other folkes
profitt, they so fayne wold bee / And charite can it not be, for the 5
profitt of the whole world dedly to displease hym that made yt / Some
are there I say also, that are loth to dye for lak of witt / which albeit
that they belive the world that is to come, & hope also to come
thyther / yet they love so mich the welth of this world / & such thinges
as delight them therin, that they wold fayne kepe them as long as euer 10
they might evyn with toth & nayle / And whan they may be suffred
in no wise to kepe it no lenger / but that deth taketh them therfro /
than yf yt may be no bettre / they will agree to be (as sone as they be
hens) hawnsid vpp in hevyn & be with god by & by /

These folke are as very nydeot folys, as he that had kept from his 15
childhed a bagge full of chery stones, & cast such a fantasy therto,
that he wold not go from it for a bigger bagge fillid [f. 189] full of
gold.

These folke fare Cosyn as Esope tellith a fable that the snayle dyd /
For whan Iupiter (whom the poetes fayne for the greate god) 20
invitid all pore wormes of the earth to a greate solempne feaste that
it pleasid hym (I haue forgote vppon what occasion) vppon a tyme
to prepare for them / the snayle kept her at home, & wold not come
therat / And whan Iupiter askyd her after wherfor she came not at
his fest / where he said she shuld haue bene welcome, & haue faren 25
well, & shuld haue seen a goodly palice / & bene delited with many
goodly pleasures / she answerid hym that she lovid no place so well
as her own howse / with which answere Iupiter waxed so angry, that
he said, sith she lovid her house so well / she shuld neuer after go
from home / but shuld alway bere her howse vppon her bak whcre 30

---

1 loth] *final* e *added* B; loth deth] loth deth in this A: in this *canc.* B *and added at end of*
interl. passage   2 *comma canc.* B *after* case   4 sight)] *parenth. wr. over* / B; fro] from Z
5 it] *interl.* A   6 yt /] / *canc. and period added* B   11 toth] *final* e *added* B   14 hawnsid]
hawsed L *1553 1573*; in hevyn] into heauen L *1553 1573*   16 childhed] childheld A,
chyldehodde Z; fantasy] fansy L   17 full] evin full L   19 folke] folkes L *1553*;
tellith a] telleth in a Z   20 (whom] *parenth. ed.,* / whom A   21 all pore] al the
poore Z; the earth] thearth *1553*; to a] vnto a Z   22 hym (I] hym) I A: *err. parenth.*
canc. and new parenth. added B; forgote] forgotten L *1553 1573*; occasion)] occasion / A:
parenth. wr. over / B   29 lovid] loueth *1553 1573*   well /] / *canc. and comma added* B
30 alway bere] alway after beare *1557*, euer after beare *1573*

so euer she went / ⌈And⌉ so hath she done euer syns as they say / and at
the lest wise I wot well she doth so now, & hath done as long tyme
as I can remembre /

Vincent

5   Forsoth vncle I wold wene the tale were not all faynid / For I thinke
verely that so much of your tale is trew /

Antonye

Esope ment by that faynid fable, to towch the foly of suche folke,
as so set their fantasye vppon some smale simple pleasure, that they
10 can not fynd in their hart to forbere it / neyther for ⌈the⌉ pleasure of
a bettre man / nor for the gaynyng of a bettre thing / by which their
fond froward fasshyon, they sometyme fall in greate indygnacion, &
take therby no litle harm /
        And surely such christen folke as by their folysh affeccion [f. 189ᵛ]
15 which they haue set like the snayle vppon their own howse here in
this earth / can not for the lothnes of levyng that howse, fynd
in their hart with their good will to go to the greate fest that god
prepareth in hevyn, & of his goodnes so gentelly calleth them to / be
like I fere me (but yf they mend that mynd in tyme) to be servid as
20 the snayle was, & yet mich worse to / For they be like to haue theire
howse here the erth bound fast vppon their bakes for euer / & not
walke therwith where they will as the snayle crepith about with hers /
but lye fast bound in the myddes with the fowle fire of hell about
them /
25 For into this foly they bryng them selfe by their own faute / as the
dronken man bryngeth hymselfe into dronkenes / wherby the evill
that he doth in his dronkenes ys not forgiven hym for his foly / but
to his payne ymputid to his faute /

---

1 And] as *A*: *canc. and* And *interl. B*   9 fantasye] fansye *L*   10 hart] heartes *L 1553*
1573   15–16 in this earth] in *om. Z*   17 g *canc. A after* good   18 gentelly] y *wr. over*
second e *B*   19 (but] / but *A*: *parenth. wr. over* / *B*; tyme)] *parenth. added B*   26 dronken]
droken *A*

Vincent

Surely vncle this semeth not vnlikely / & by their faute they fall in
such foly in dede / And yet yf this be foly in dede / there are than
some folke foles that wene them selfe right wise /

Antonye   5

That wene them selfe wise / mary I neuer saw fole yet / that
thought hym selfe other than wise / For as it is one sparke of sobrenes
left in a dronken hed, whan he perceve hym selfe dronk & gettith
hym fare to bedd / so yf a fole perceyve hym self a fole, that poynt
is no foly / but a litle sparke of witt / But now Cosyn as for these kynd 10
of folys, sith they be loth to dye for the love that they bere to their
worldly fantasyes, which they shuld by their deth leve behynd them
& forsake / they that wold for that cause rather forsake the fayth than
dye / wold rather forsake it than lese their worldly goodes, though
there were offred them no perell of deth att all / & than as towchyng 15
those that are of [f. 190] that mynd, we haue you wot well said as
much as your selfe thought sufficient this after none here before /

Vincent

Verely vncle that is very trew / & now haue you rehersid as far as I
can remembre / all the other kyndes of them that wold be loth to dye, 20
for any other respect than the grevouse qualities of shame & payne
ioynid vnto deth / And of all these kyndes except the kynd of
infidelitie / whom no comfort can help / but counsayle onely to
thatteynyng of fayth / which fayth must be to the receyvyng of comfort
presupposid & had redy before, as you shewid in the begynnyng of 25
our comunicacion the first day that we talkyd of the mater / but els I
say (except that one kynd) there is none of the remenaunt of those
that were before vntouchid, which were likely to forsake their fayth

2 fall in] fall to L 1553, fal into 1573   8 perceve] th added B, perceyueth Z   9 fare]
ai wr. over a B; self] sell A: f wr. over l B   10 foly /] | canc. and comma added B; these]
those L 1553 1573   11 folys] fooles L 1553 1573, folies 1557   12 fantasyes] fansyes L
14 lese] sel 1553   15 period after all B; &] canc. and And interl. B   19 vncle that is]
that is vncle L 1553 1573   22 these] those L 1553 1573   23 whom] when 1557
24 thatteynyng] the atteyning 1557; fayth /] | wr. over period B

in the persecucion for the feare and dreade of deth / save for those
grevouse qualities (payne I meane & shame) that they se well wold
come therwith. And therfor vncle I pray you give vs some comfort
agaynst those twayne / For in good fayth yf deth shuld come without
5 them, in such a case as this is, wherin by the lesyng of this life we
shuld find a farre bettre / myn own reason giveth me that ⌐save for
the¬ tother griefes goyng before the chaung / there wold no man
that witt hath any thyng styk at all /

Antonye

10   Yes peradventure sodanly, before they gather there wittes vnto
them & therwith well way the mater / But they Cosyn that will
consider the mater well / reason growndid vppon the foundacion of
fayth, shall shew them very great substanciall causes, for which the
drede of those grevouse qualities that they see shal come with deth /
15 shame I meane & payne also, shall not so sore [f. 190ᵛ] abassh
them, as sinfully to dreve them therfro / for the profe wherof let vs
first begynne at the consideracion of the shame /

Off shame that ys ioynid with the deth in the persecucion for the fayth /

The xxiijth Chapitre

How can any faythfull wise man drede the deth so sore, for any
respect of shame, whan his reason & his fayth together, may shortly
make hym perceyve, that there is therin no piece of very shame at
all / for how can that deth be shamfull, that is gloryouse / or how can
25 that be but gloriouse to dye for the fayth of christ, yf we dye both for
the fayth & in the fayth ioynid with hope & charite / while the scrip-

---

1 in the] in this Z   2 shame)] shame / A: parenth. wr. over / B   5 wherin by] wherby L 1553 1573   6–7 save for the] sure? / for A: canc. B and save for the interl. B
7 tother] other 1553 1573; chaung] final e added B   13 selfe canc. A and B before very
18 Off shame] Of the shame Z   20 xxiijth] xxiii 1553 1557 1573   21 the deth] that
death L 1553   24–25 can that] can it Z   25 yf] (yf A: parenth. canc. B

ture so playnly sayth / *preciosa in conspectu domini mors sanctorum eius* /
preciouse is in the sight of god the deth of his sayntes / Now yf the
deth of his saintes be gloriouse in the sight of god: yt can neuer be
shamfull in very dede / how shamfull so euer yt seme here in the
sight of men / For here we may see and be sure, that not at the 5
deth of saynt Stephyn onely, to whom yt likyd hym to shew hymselfe
with the hevyn open ouer his hed / but at the deth also of euery man
that so dieth for the faytli, god with his hevenly companye beholdith
his hole passion & verely loketh on /

 Now yf it were so Cosyn that ye shuld be brought thorow the brode 10
high strete of a greate long cytie / And that al along the way that ye
were goyng, there were on the tone side of the way a rable of raggid
beggers & mad men that wold despise you & desprayse you, with all
the shamfull names that they could call you, & all the raylyng
wordes that they could say to you / & that there were than all along 15
the [f. 191] tother side of thc same strete where you shuld come by,
a goodly company standyng in a fayre range arow, of wise &
worshipfull folke, alowyng & commendyng you / mo than fivetene
tymes as many as that rable of Raggid beggers & raylyng mad men
are / wold you let your way by your will, wenyng that you went vnto 20
your shame, for the shamfull gestyng & raylyng of those mad
folysh wretchis / or hold on your way with a good chere & a glad
hart, thinkyng your selfe mich honoryd by the lawde & approbacion
of that other honourable sort /

Vincent   25

 Nay by my trowth vncle there is no dowght, but I wold mich regard
the comendacion of those commendable folke / & not regard a rish the
raylyng of all those Ribaldes.

---

1 sanctorum] *Z*, santorum *A*   10 were so] so were *L 1553 1573*; ye] you *L 1553 1573*
11 al] *second* l *added B*; along] *canc. and* a longe *interl. B*; ye] you *L 1553 1573*   13
despise] s *wr. over* c? *B*; despise you] you *om. 1557*   14 raylyng] *canc. and* vilanous *interl.*
B, villanous *Z*   15 to you] vnto you *L*   16 tother] other *1553*   18 alowyng]
allowing you *L 1553*   19 rable of] of *om. 1553*   20 you went] ye went *1557*   23
extra your *canc. A after* thinkyng   26 but I] but that I *L*   27 regard a] regarde of a
L 1553 1573; rish] s *wr. over illeg. letter B*, russhe *L*   28 those] these *L 1553 1573*;
Ribaldes] ragged rybbauldes *L*

Antonye

Than Cosyn can there no man that hath fayth, accompt hym selfe
shamid here, by any maner deth that he suffreth for the fayth of
christ / while how vile & how shamfull so euer yt seme in the sight
5 here of a few worldly wrechis, it is alowed & approvid for very
preciouse & honourable, in the sight of god / & of all the gloriouse
company of hevyn / which as perfitly stand & behold it / as those
pevish people do / & are in nomber mo than an hundreth to one /
And of that hundreth, euery one an hundreth tymes more to be
10 regardid and estemyd, than of the tother an hundreth such whole
rabels / And now yf a man wold be so mad, as for fere of the rebuke
that he shuld haue of such rebukefull bestes, he wold be ashamyd to
confesse the fayth of christ / than with fleyng ⌈from⌉ a shadow [f. 191ᵛ]
of shame / he shuld fall into a very shame & a dedly paynfull shame
15 in dede / for than hath our saviour made a sure promise / that he will
shew hym selfe ashamid of that man before the father of hevyn & all
his holy angelles / saying in the ix chapter of S Luke / *Qui me
erubuerit & meos sermones, hunc filius hominis erubescet ⌈quum⌉ venerit in
maiestate sua & patris & sanctorum Angelorum* / he that is ashamid of me
20 & of my wordes: of hym shall the sonne of man be ashamid / when
he shall come in the maiestie of hym selfe & of his father & of his
holy angelles / And what maner a shamfull shame shall that be than /
Yf a mans chekes glowe sometyme for shame in this world / they
will fall on fier for shame / whan christ shall shew hym selfe ashamid
25 of them there /

To suffre the thing for Christes fayth / that we worldly wrechid folys
wene were vilany & shame, the blessid apostles rekenid for greate
glory / for they when they were with despite & shame scourgid, &
there apon commaundid to speke no more of the name of christ /

---

5 it] wr. at end of line B: It (A) canc. B at beginning of next line   6 god /] | canc. and comma
added B; & of all] of canc. B, om. Z   7 perfitly] perfectly L 1553 1573; it /] | canc. and comma
added B; those] these L 1553 1573   8 do] added B?   8–9 hundreth . . . hundreth]
hundred . . . hundred Z   9 euery one an hundreth] euery one a hundred 1557, euery
one an hundred 1573   10 hundreth] hundred Z   14 shame canc. A and B after dedly
15 promise /] | canc. and comma added B   17 ix] ixth L; in the . . . Luke] om. 1573 (Luc
9. in margin)   18 quum] quan A: canc. and quum interl. B   20 of my] of canc. B,
the holy L 1553 1573   22 than /] | canc. and question-mark added B   23 Yf] yf A;
shame /] | canc. and comma added B   26 sake canc. A and B after Christes   27 apostles]
apostes A: es added B with A's abbrev. treated as an l; for] f alt. to F B

went ther way fro the councell ioyfull & glad, that god had vouch-
safed to do them the worship, to suffer shamfull despite for the name
of Ihesu / And so proude were they of that shame & velenouse payne
put vnto them / that for all the forbeding of that greate cowncell
assemblid, they seacid not euery day to prech out the name of 5
Ihesu still, not in the temple onely (out of which they were fett &
whyppid for the same before) but also to dowble it with, went prechyng that name about from howse to howse to / [f. 192]

I wold sith we regard so greatly thestimacion of worldly folke,
we wold among many naughty thinges that they vse / regard also 10
some such as are good / for it is a maner among them in many
places, that some by handy craft, some by merchauntdice / some by
other kynd of lyvyng arise & com forward in the world / and commonly
folke are in youth set forth to convenient masters, vnder whome they
are brought vpp & grow / but now when so euer they fynd a servant 15
such as he disdayneth to do such thinges as he that is his master did
while he was seruaunt hym selfe / That seruaunt euery man
accomptith for a prowde vnthrifte, neuer like to come to good
profe /

Let vs lo marke & consider this, & way well therwithall, that our 20
master christ / not the master onely, but the maker to of all this
whole world, was not so prowde to disdayne for our sakes, the most
vylanouse & most shamfull deth after the worldly compt that then was
vsid in the world / & the most despightfull mokkyng therwith,
ioynid to most grevous payne / As crownyng hym with sharp thorne 25
that the bloud ran downe about his face / than they gaue hym a
reade in his hand for a septer, & knelyd downe to hym & salutid

---

1 ther] *canc. and* theyr *interl. B*; fro] from *L*   3 velenouse] *illeg. letter canc. after* vele *and*
n *interl. B?*   5 seacid] *canc. and* ceasyd *interl. B*; prech] *final* e *added B*   7 whyppid]
i *wr. over* y *B?*; before)] *parenth. wr. over* / *B*   9 thestimacion] the estimation *1573*; folke]
folkes *L 1553*   10 vse /] / *canc. and comma added B*   11 good /] / *canc. and period added*
B; for] f *alt. to* F *B*   12 merchauntdice /] *superfluous superscript* a *above* un *A*, / *canc. and*
comma added B   13 arise] rise *1573*; world /] / *canc. and period added B*; and] a *alt. to* A *B*
14 in youth] inowe *L 1553*; they] y^{ey} *A: canc. and* they *interl. B*   15 are brought] be
brought *Z*; but] B *wr. over* b *B*; *period added after* grow *B*; now when so euer] when-
soeuer nowe *L 1553*   16 as he disdayneth] he *om. L 1553 1573*; service *canc. A and*
B *after* to do such   17 That] T *canc. and* t *ins. before* h *B*   18 accomptith] compteth *L*
20 lo marke] so marke *1553 1573*   21 christ /] / *canc. and comma added B*; maker to] to
om. L 1553   22 not so] nor so *1573*   23 worldly] ly *added A?*; compt] accompte *L*
1553 1573   26 bloud] o *wr. over* u *B*   27 reade] a *canc. A?*; septer] s *wr. over illeg.*
letter B

hym like a kyng in skorne, & bett than the rede vppon the sharp
thornes abought his holy hed. Now ⌜sayth⌝ our saviour / ⌜that⌝ the
deciple or seruaunt is not above his master / And therfor sith our
master enduryd so many kyndes of paynfull shame / very prowd
5 beastes may we well thynke our selfe / yf we [f. 192ᵛ] disdayne to do
as our master did / And where as he thorow shame assendid into
glory / we wold be so madd that we rather will fall into euerlastyng
shame both before hevyn & hell, than for feare of a short worldly
shame, to folow hym into euerlastyng glory / /

10   Off paynfull deth to be suffrid in the Turkes
                              persecucion for the fayth

                           The / 24 / chapitre /

                               Vincent

   In good fayth vncle / as for the shame, ye shall nede to take no
15 more payne / for I suppose surely that any man that hath reason in his
hed / shall hold hym selfe satisfied with this / But of trewth vncle all
the pynch is in the payn / for as for shame, I perceve well inough /
a man may with wisedome so master it / that it shall nothyng move
hym at all / so farforth that it is almost in euery countrey becom a
20 comen proverbe / that shame is as it is taken / But by god vncle
all the wisedome in this world, can neuer so maister payne, but that
payne wilbe paynefull spight of all the wit in this world /

                               Antonye

   Trouth it is Cosyn, that no man can with all the reason he hath,
25 in such wise chaunge the nature of payne, that in the havyng of

---

2 abought] a bought A; hed.] period ed.; sayth] interl. B over canc. sith (A)   3 deciple]
is wr. over e B; or seruant] or the seruaunt L 1553   4 vee canc. A and B before very
5 selfe] selvys L   8 than] Than A: T canc. and t ins. B; worldly] Z, wordly A   12 24]
xxiiijᵗʰ L   16 trewth] th added B   17 / for] f alt. to F B, period wr. over / B; inough /]
now Z, / canc. and comma added B   18 master] interl. B over A's abbreviation (canc. B)
19 / canc. and comma erased after countrey B; becom] becomen 1557   20 proverbe /] /
canc. and comma added B   24 it is] is it L 1553 1573

payne he fele it not / for but yf it be felt yt is perdye no payne / And
that is the naturall cause Cosyn / for which a man may haue his legge
stryken of by the kne & greve hym not / yf his hed be of but halfe
an hower before / But reason may make a reasonable man, though he
wold not be so folysh as causeles to fall therin, yet vppon good causes 5
eyther of gaynyng some kynd of [f. 193] great profitt / or avoydyng
of some greate losse / or eschewyng therby the suffryng of far greater
payne / not to shryng therefro & refuse yt to his more hurt & harm /
but for his far greater avantage & commoditie, content & glad to
sustayne yt / And this doth reason [alone] in many cases, where it 10
hath mich lesse help to take hold of, than it hath in this mater of
fayth / for well you wotte, to take a sower & a bitter ⌐pocion¬ is great
gryefe and displeasure / And to be lawncid & haue the flessh cut /
is no litle payne / now whan such thinges shalbe mynistrid vnto a
child / or to some childysh man eyther / they will by their own willes, 15
rather let their siknes or their sore grow vnto their more griefe, till yt
be become Incurable, than abide the payne of the curyng in tyme /
& that for faynt hart / ioynid with lak of discrecion / But a man
that hath more wisedome, though he wold with out cause no more
abide the payne willyngly, than wold the tother / yet sith reason 20
shewith hym what good he shall haue by the suffryng / and what
harm by the refusyng: this maketh hym well content & glad also
for to take it / /

Now than yf reason alone be sufficient to move a man to take
payne for the gaynyng of some worldly rest or pleasure, & for the 25
avoydyng of a nother payne throwgh peradventure more / yet
endurable but for a short season / [why] shold not reason growndid
vppon the sure fowndacion of fayth, & holpen also forward with

2 Virgule canc. B after And that; Cosyn /] / canc. and comma added B   3 not /] / canc. and
comma added B   4 before] afore 1557   6 kynd] kindes 1553   7 of some] of om. 1553
1557 1573; some greate losse] some kynde of great losse Z; greater] great 1553   8
shryng] shrynke Z; the canc. A before his   9 avantage] aduauntage Z   10 yt /] / canc.
and period added B; alone] Z, alow A   12 pocion] interl. B above canc. portion A,
pocion Z   13 gryefe] divided gry-efe A: canc. and grefe interl. B; & haue] and to haue
L 1553 1573   14 payne /] / canc. and period added B; now] N wr. over n B   16 grow
vnto] growe on to L 1553 1573   16–17 yt be become] be om. Z, it be come L 1553 1557,
it become 1573   20 tother] other 1553 1573   22–23 also for to take] for om. L 1553
1573   25 some canc. A and B after payne for; some] om. 1557   25–26 the avoydyng]
thauoyding 1557   26 throwgh] canc. and (though interl. B, thoughe Z   27 endur-
able] durable 1573; season /] parenth. wr. over / B; why] Z, whit A

ayd of goddes grace / as it euer is vndowtedly, whan folke for a good
[f. 193ᵛ] mynd in goddes name comen together theron, our saviour
saying hym selfe / *Vbi sunt duo vel tres congregati in nomine meo ibi & ego
sum in medio eorum* / where there are two or three gatherid together
in my name, there am I also evyn in the very myddes of them / why
shuld not than reason I say thus fortherid with fayth & grace, be mych
more able, first to engendre in vs such an effeccion / and after by
long & depe meditacion therof, so to contynew that affeccion, that it
shall tourne into an habituall fast & depe rotid purpose, of pacient
suffryng the paynfull deth of this body here in earth, for the gaynyng
of euerlastyng welthy lyfe in hevyn, & avoydyng of euerlastyng
paynefull deth in hell /

Vincent

By my trouth vncle wordes can I none fynd, that shuld haue any
reason with them / fayth alway presupposid as you protestid in the
begynnyng for a grownd / wordes I say can I none fynd wherewith I
might reasonably counterplede this that you haue said here alredy.
But yet ⸢I⸣ remember the fable that Esope tellith, of a greate old hart,
that had fled from a litle byche, which had made sute after hym &
chasid hym so long that she had lost hym, & as he hopid more than
halfe given hym ouer / by occasion wherof having than sometyme
to talke, & metyng with a nother of his felowes / he fell in deliberacion
with hym what were best for hym to do / whether to run on styll &
fly ferther from her / or tourne agayne & fight with her. Whervnto
the tother hart advisid hym to flye no ferther, lest the bych might
happen to fynd hym agayne, at such tyme as he shuld with the labour
of farther flying, befallen out of breth, & therby all out of strength
to, & so shuld he be kyld lying where he could not stere hym / where
as yf he wold tourne & fight, he were in no perell at all. For the man

---

1 / as] *parenth. wr. over* / *B*; euer is] is euer ready *L 1553 1573*   2 comen] commen *L
1553*, common *1573*   5 them /] *parenth. wr. over* / *B*   6 fortherid] farthered *L*, forthered
1553 1557, furthered *1573*   7 able] hable *1557*; first to engendre in vs] to engendre in
vs first *L 1553 1573* (*L has canc.* fyrst *before* to)   10 here] *interl. A*   19 byche] y *wr.
over* e? *A*   22 *comma after* with *B*   24 fly] flee *1573*; Whervnto] *cap. ed.*   25 tother]
other *1553 1573*; flye] flee *1573*; might] *Z*, migh *A*   26 happen] hap *L 1553 1573*
27 of farther] of hys farther *L 1553*; flying] flyeng *L*, fleing *1557 1573*; befallen] *vertical
line after* be *B*; breth] *final* e *added B*   28 stere] styrre *B* (y *wr. over first* e, re *wr. over final*
e), styrr *L*, stire *1553*, styrre *1557 1573*

with whome she honteth is more than a myle behynd her / & she is
but a litle body scant halfe so mich as thow / & thy hornes may thrust
her thorow before she can touch thy flesh by more then ten tymes her
toth [f. 194] length / By my trouth quoth the tother hart I like your
councell well, and me thinketh that the thing is even sothely such as   5
you say / But I fere me whan I here ones that vrchyn bich bark / I
shall fall to my fete & forget all together / But yet & you will go
back with me / than me thinke we shalbe strong inough agaynst that
one bich betwene vs both / Wherunto the tother hart agreed / & so
they both apoyntid them theron / ✛ But evyn as they were about   10
to buske them forward to it / the bych had fownd the fote agayne, &
on she come yarnyng toward the place / whom as sone as the hartes
herde / they to go both twayne apace /

   And in good fayth vncle evyn so I fere yt wold fare by my selfe &
many other to / which thowgh we thinke it reason that you saye / &   15
in our myndes agree that we shuld do as you say / ye & do peradventure thinke also, that we wold in dede do as ye say: yet as sone as we
shuld ones here these hell howndes / these Turkes come yalpyng &
ballyng vppon vs / our hartes shuld sone fall as clene from vs, as
those other hartes flye from the howndes.   20

✛ ⌐(here it must be known of some man that can skyll of huntyng,
whither that we mystake not our termys / for than are we vtterly
shamyd ye wot well. And I am so connyng, that I cannot tell whither
among them, a bych be a bych or no. But as I remember she is no
bych, but a brache. This is a hye poynt in a low howse. Beware of   25
barkyng / for there lakkyth a nother huntyng term. At a fox it is

1 honteth] *canc. and* huntyth, *interl.* B   3 by more] be more *1553*   4 By my trouth]
Nowe by my trowth L *1573*, nowe but by my truth *1553*; tother] other *1553*   5 think-
eth] thinke *1553 1573*   8 me thinke] me thyncketh L   9 tother] other *1553 1573*
10 theron] thereupon L *1553*   12 come] o *alt. to* a B, came Ƶ; yarnyng] gerning *1557*
13 apace /] *period before* / B   14 fere yt wold] feare me would yt L, feare me, it woulde
1553 1573   16–17 as you say / ye & do peradventure] as yow saye, and paradventure
doo L, as ye say, yea & dooe peraduenture *1557*   17 as ye say] as you saye L *1553 1573*
18 these hell] those hell *1557*; howndes /] / *canc. and comma added* B   18–19 yalpyng
& ballyng] yelpyng and bawlyng L *1573*, yelpyng and bauling *1553*, yalping & balling
1557   20 flye] flee *1557 1573*; from] fro *1557*; howndes] *divided* how-ndes A: *canc. and*
howndes *wr. in space at end of paragraph* B   21–296/2 (here it must be known . . . no mater
of a fart)] *om. 1557, included in* L *1553 1573 as part of text after* apoyntid them theron (*line
10*) : no parenth., *separate paragraph* L, *no parenth., no paragraph 1553, in parenth. without paragraph
1573; see Introduction*   21 man] *orig.* men?: e? *alt. to* a B   22 that we] he *canc. before*
we B   24 *illeg. letter canc. before* or no B   25 This is] thys ys lo, L; a hye] an high L
1553 1573

callyd cryeng. I wot not what they call it at a hart / but it shall make
no mater of a fart)[1]

Antonye

Cosyn in those dayes that Esope spekith of / though those hartes
5 & other brute bestes mo, had (yf he sayth soth) the power to speke &
talke / & in ther talkyng power to talke reason to / yet to folow reason
& rule them selfe therby / therto had they neuer geven them the
powre / And in good fayth Cosyn / as for such thynges as perteyne
toward the conductyng of resonable men to salvacion / I thinke with-
10 out help of grace, mennys reasonyng shall do litle more / But than
are we sure as I said before / that as for grace yf we desire yt / god is
at such reasonyng alway present, & very redy to give yt / & but yf that
men will afterward willyngly cast it away / he is euer still as redy to
kepe yt / & fro tyme to tyme glad to encrese it / And therfor byddith
15 vs our lord by the mowth of the prophet, [f. 194^v] that we shuld not
be like such brutish & vnreasonable bestes, as were those hartes,
& as are our horses & mules / *Nolite fieri sicut equus & mulus* ⌈*in*⌉ *quibus
non est intellectus* / be not you like an horse & a mule that hath none
vnderstandyng / And therfor Cosyn let vs neuer drede / but that yf
20 we will apply our myndes to the gatheryng of comfort & corage
agaynst such persecucions, & here reason, & let it synke into our hart /
& cast it not out agayne / vomyt yt not vpp / nor evyn there choke it
vpp & styfle it, with pamperyng in & stuffyng vp our stomakes with
a surfyt of worldly vanyties / god shall so well worke therwith / that
25 we shall fele strength therin / & not in such wise haue all such shamfull
cowardyse hartes, as to forsake our saviour, & therby lese our own
salvacion & run into eternall fire for fere of dethe ioynid ⌈ther⌉
with, though bytter & sharp / yet short for all that, & in a maner a
momentary payne /

---

1 a hart /] an hart L *1553 1573, period wr. under or over* | B   2 of a fart] *om. 1573; parenth.
wr. over period* B   5 sayth] saye Z   10 more /] | *canc. and period added* B   11 before
/] | *canc. and comma added* B, afore Z   14 fro] from L *1553 1573*   16 be like] *vertical line
after* be B   17 our] *canc.* B, *om.* Z; in quibus] in *om. 1557 1573*   18 none] no L *1553
1573*   21 synke] syncke depe L; hart] hartes L   22 vomyt yt not vpp] *om.* L *1553;*
choke] *interl.* B *above canc.* choike A   24 vanyties /] | *canc. and colon added* B   25 fele
strength] fynde great strength L *1553 1573*   26 cowardyse] cowardous Z; as] *interl.* B
above canc. As A; lese] lose *1557*   28 *Virgule canc.* B *after* though

Vincent

Euery man vncle naturally grogeth at payne & is very loth to come
at it /

Antonye

That is very trowth / nor no man holdyth any man to go run into   5
it / but that yf he be taken & may not flye / Than we say that reason
playnly tellyth vs, that we shuld rather suffer & endure the lesse &
shorter here, than in hell the sorer & so farre the lenger to /

Vincent

I hard vncle of late where such a reason was made as you make me   10
now / which reason semeth vndoughtid and vnevitable vnto me /
Yet hard I late as I say a man answere it thus / He said that yf a man
in this persecution shuld stand still in the confession of his fayth, &
therby fall into paynfull tourmentry / he myght peradventure happ
for the sharpnes & bitternes of the payne, to forsake our saviour [f.   15
195] evyn in the myddes, & dye there with his synne, & so be dampnid for euer / where as by the forsakyng of the fayth in the begynnyng
betyme / & for the tyme, & yet not but in word nether, kepyng yt still
neuer the lesse in his hart / A man may save hym selfe from that paynfull deth, & after aske mercy, & haue yt, & live long & do many good   20
dedes, & be savid as S peter was /

Antonye

That mans reason Cosyn, is like a three fotid stole, so tottryng on
euery side, that who so sitt theron may sone take a fowle fawlle / For
these are the three fete of this tottcryng ⌜stole/⌝ fantasticall feare /   25
false fayth / false flattryng hope / First it is a fantasticall feare, that the
man conceyvith that yt shuld be perelouse to stand in the confession
of the fayth at the begynnyng / lest he might afterward thorowgh the
bitternes of payne, fall to the forsakyng, & so dye ⌜there⌝ in the payne

---

2 grogeth] grudgeth *Z*   3 at] *canc. and* to *interl.* B, to *Z*   5 holdyth] *canc. and* byddyth
interl. B, biddeth *Z*   6 flye /] e *wr. over* y B, flee *Z, comma wr. before* / B; Than] *canc.
and* than *interl.* B   8 shorter] the shorter *Z*; lenger] longar *L*   24 fawlle] *canc. and*
fall. *interl.* B   26 it is] this is *L 1553 1573*   28 begynnyng /] / *canc. and comma added* B

therwith owt of hand, & therby be vtterly dampnid / as though ⌐that⌐
yf a man with payne were ouercome, & so forsoke his fayth / god
could not or wold not aswell give hym grace to repent agayne, &
thervppon give hym forgivenes / as hym that forsoke his fayth in the
5 begynnyng, & did set so litle by hym / that he wold rather forsake
hym than suffer for his sake any maner payne at all / As though the
more payne that a man takith for goddes sake / the worse wold god be
to hym /

Yff this reason were not vnreasonable: than shuld our savyour not
10 haue said as he did / *Ne terreamini* / *ab hijs qui occidunt corpus et post hac*
non habent amplius quid faciant / be not a ferd of them that kyll the
bodye, & after that haue nothing that [f. 195ᵛ] they can do farther /
For he shuld by this reason haue said: dreade & fere them that may
slee the body / for they may by the tourment of paynefull deth / but
15 yff thow forsake me betymes in the begynnyng, & so save thy life &
get of me thy pardon & forgivenes after / make thee peradventure
forsake me to late, & so to be dampnid for euer /

The second fote of this totteryng stole / is a false fayth / for it is but
a faynid fayth, for a man to say to god secretly that he beleveth hym /
20 trustith hym / & lovith hym / & then openly where he shuld to goddes
honour tell the same tale, and therby prove that he doth so / there to
goddes dishonour as mich as in hym is / flatter goddes enymyes, &
do them pleasure & worldly worship, with the forsakyng of goddes
fayth before the world / & is eyther faythles in his hart to / or els wot-
25 eth well that he doth god this dispight evyn before his own face / for
except he lak fayth, he can not but know that our lord is euery where
present / & while he so shamfully forsakith hym, full angrely lokith
on /

The third fote of this tottering stole / is false flateryng hope, for sith
30 the thing that he doth when he forsakith his fayth for feare, is by the

---

1 th *canc. A before* therwith   2 with payne] by payne *Z*   5 set] *interl. A*; hym /] /
canc. and comma added B   6 the] the the *A*   8 hym/] / *canc. and period added B*   10–11
Ne terreamini . . . quid faciant] Nolite timere eos qui corpus possunt occidere, & vlterius
non habent quod faciunt. *L 1553*, Nolite timere eos qui occidunt corpus, & post haec non
habent amplius quid faciant. *1573*   11 be not a ferd of] Feare not *Z*; that kyll] that
may kil *Z*   14 slee] slaye *Z*   16 thee] *second* e *canc. B*   17 so to be] to *om. L 1553*
1573   19 beleveth hym /] / *canc. and comma added B*; trustith hym /] / *canc. and comma*
added B   21 so /] / *canc. and comma added B*; there] *interl. B above canc.* There *A*   22
is /] / *canc. and comma added B*; flatter] doth he flatter *L 1553*   24 & is] and he is *1573*
27 forsakith] forsake *1553*   29 hope,] *comma ed., period B*; for] f *alt. to* F *B*

mowth of god vppon the payne of eternall deth forboden / though
the goodnes of god forgiveth many folke the fawte / yet to be
ᵗheᵗ bolder in offendyng, for the hope of forgivyng, is a very false
pestylent hope, wherwith a man flatterith hym selfe toward his own
distruccion / /   5

He that in a sodayne brayde for fere / or other affeccion, vnadvisidly falleth / & after in laboryng to rise agayne, comforteth hym selfe
with hope of goddes gracyous forgivenes: walketh in the redy way toward his salvacion / But he that with [f. 196] the hope of goddes
mercye to folow, doth encorage hym selfe to synne, & therwith offen- 10
dith god first / I haue no power to shet the hand of god fro givyng out
his pardone where he lyst / nor wold yf I cold / but rather help to pray
therfor. But yet I very sore fere, that such a man may mysse the grace
to requyre yt, in such effectuall wise as to haue yt grauntid / Nor I
can not sodaynly now remembre any sample or promise expressid in 15
holy scripture, that the offender in such a kynd, shall haue the grace
offred after in such wise to seke for pardon, that god hath by his other
promises of remission promysid to penytentes, bownden hymselfe to
graunt yt / But this kynd of presumpcion vnder the pretext of hope,
semeth rather to draw nere on the tone side / as dispayre doth on the 20
tother side / toward the abomynable synne of blasphamye / agaynst
the holy goost / a gaynst which synne / concernyng yether the
Impossibelite / or at the lest the greate difficultie of forgivenes, our
saviour hath shewid hym selfe in the xij^{th} chapiter of saynt mathew &
in the iij chapiter of S marke / where he sayth, that blasphamye 25
agaynot the holy goost shall neuer be forgyven, nether in this world /
nor in the world to come / And where the man that you spelto of, take
in his reason a sample of S. Petre which forsoke our saviour & gate
forgivenes after / let hym consider agayne on the tother side, that he
forsoke hym not vppon the boldnes of any such synfull trust / but 30

1 deth] dampnacion L; forboden] forbidden 1573   3 the bolder] the om. 1557   6
fere /] | canc. B   7 hym selfe] them self 1553   11 fro] from L   12 lyst] luste 1553
17 after] om. L 1553; hath] om. 1557   18 to penytentes] to the penitentes L 1553 1573;
bownden] bounde L 1553 1573   19 vnder the] the om. Z   21 abomynable] abhom-
inable L 1553; blasphamye /] | canc. B   22 synne /] | canc. and comma added B; yether]
y canc. B   22–23 the Impossibelite /] thimpossibilitie 1553, | canc. and comma added B
23 the greate] the om. L 1553   24 xij^{th}] xii. 1553 1557 1573   25 iij chapiter] thyrde
(chapiter om.) L 1553 1573   26 this world /] | canc. B   27 speke] spake L 1553 1573;
take] o wr. over a B, toke L 1553 1573, tooke 1557   29 on] in A: o wr. over i B, on Z

was ouercome & vanqueshid vppon a sodayne feare / And yet by
the forsakyng, S. petre wanne but litle / for he did but delay his
trowble but a litle while you wott well / for beside that he repentid
forthwith very sore, that he [f. 196ᵛ] had so done / & wept therfor by
5 & by full bitterly / he cam forthe at the whitsontide ensewyng, & confessid his master agayne, & sone after that he was ymprisonid therfor /
& not seasyng so / was thervpon sore scourgid for the confession of
his fayth / and yet after that ymprisonid agayne afresh / & beyng
from thens deliuerid, stintid not to preach on still / vntill that after
10 many fold labours travayles & trobles he was at Rome crucified &
with cruell tourment slayne.

And in likewise I wene I might in a maner well warrant, that there
shuld no man which denyeth our saviour ones, & after attayneth remission / escape thorow that denying one peny the better chepe / but
15 that he shall ere he come in hevyn, full sewerly pay therfor /

Vincent

He shall peradventure vncle afterward worke it owt in the frutefull
workes of penaunce prayour & almes dede, done in trew fayth & dew
charitie, & attayne in such wise forgivenes well ynough /

Antony

20

All his forgivenes goeth Cosyn / you se well, but by perhappes. But
as yt may be perhappes ye / so may it be perhappes nay / and where
is he than / And yet you wot well by no maner happ, he shall neuer
happ fynally to scape fro deth / for feare of which he forsoke his fayth /

Vincent

25

No but he may dye his naturall deth, & escape that violent deth /

---

1 ouercome] ouercomen *1557*   1–2 by the] by that *1573*   3 but a litle] but *canc. and*
for *interl.* B, for a litle *Z*; for beside] *wr. together* A, *vertical line after* for B   4 had
so done] so had doone *Z*; wept] *superscript letter above* p *canc.* B   7 scourgid] r *interl.* A
13 shuld] shall *Z*   14 escape] scape *L 1553 1573*   15 sewerly] *canc. and* surely *interl.*
B; therfor] *final* e *added* B   17 vncle afterward worke it owt] worke it out afterward
Uncle *1553*, Uncle, worke it out afterward *1573*   18 almes] allmoyse *L*, almose *1553*
1573; dede] dedes *L*   21 Cosyn /] *parentheses wr. around* Cosyn B   21–22 But as] but
A: B *wr. over* b B   23 yet you wot well] you wote wel yet *L 1553*   24 fro] from *L*;
deth /] / *canc. and comma added* B; wher *canc.* A *before* feare   26 escape] scape *Z*; that]
the *L*

& then he savith hym selfe fro mich payne, & so wynneth therwith
mych ease / For euermore a violent ⌐deth¬ is paynfull.

Antonye

Peradventure he shall not avoyd a violent deth therby / for god is
without dowt displeasid / & can bryng hym shortly to a deth as 5
violent by some other way / /

Howbeit I see well that you reken that who so dieth a naturall
deth / dieth like a wanton even at his ease / you make me remembre
[f. 197] a man that was ones in a galey subtill with vs on the see /
which while the see was sore wrought, & the waves rose very high, & 10
he came neuer on the see before, & lay tossid hether & thether / the
pore sowle gronyd sore, & for payne he thought he wold very fayne
be ded / & euer he whishid / wold god I were on land, that I myght
dye in rest / The waves so trowblid hym there with tossyng hym vpp &
downe to & fro / that he thought that trowble lettyd hym to dye / 15
because the waves wold not let hym rest. But yf he might get ones
to land, he thought he shuld than dye there even at his ease /

Vincent

Nay vncle this is no dowt, but that deth is to euery man paynfull /
but yet is not the naturall deth so paynfull, as ys the violent / 20

Antonye

By my trouth Cosyn, me thinketh that the deth which men call
comonly naturall, ys a violent deth to euery man whom yt fetcheth
hens beforce agaynst his will / And that ys euery man, which whan
he dieth ys loth to dye / & fayne wold yet live lenger yf he might / 25

Howbeit how small the payne ys in the naturall deth Cosyn, fayne
wold I wit who hath told you / As far as I can perceve, those folke
that comonly depart of there naturall deth, haue euer one desease &
sicknes or other / wherof yf the payne of that whole weke or twayne
in which they lye pynyng in their bed, were gatherid together into so 30

1 fro] from Z   6 other] r added B   7 naturall] final l added B?   8 even at] euen
al at L 1553 1573   11 before] afore Z   13 whishid] canc. and wyshyd, interl. B   20
as ys the] ys om. L 1553 1573   24 beforce] before A: ce wr. over final e by B, then word canc.
and by force interl. B, by force Z   25 lenger] longer 1557 1573   27 far as] as om. 1573
28 there] yr wr. over re B; desease] y wr. over first e B   29 that] the 1573   30 into so]
in so L 1553

short a tyme as a man hath his payne that dieth a violent deth / It
wold I wene make dowble the payne that that is / so that he that
naturally dieth, ofter suffreth more payne / than lesse / though he
suffreth it in a lenger tyme / And ⌐than¬ wold many a man be more
5 loth to suffre so long lyngeryng in payne, than with a sharper to be
soner rid.

And yet lieth many a man mo dayes than one, in well nere [f. 197ᵛ]
as great payne contynually, as is the payne that with the vyolent deth
riddith the man in lesse than halfe an howre / except a man wold
10 wene, that where as the payne ys greate to haue a knyfe to cut his
flesh on the owtside fro the skynne inward, the payne wold be mich
lesse yf the knyfe myght begyn on the inside & cut fro the myddes
outward / /

Some we here in their deth bed complayne, that they thinke they
15 fele sharpe knyfes cut atwo their hart strynges / Some crye out &
thynke they fele within the brayne pan, their hed prickyd even
full of pynnys / And they that lye in a plurisie, thynke that euery
tyme they cough, they fele a sharpe swerd swapp them to the hart /

The consideracion of the paynes of hell, in which we
20 fall / yf we forsake our saviour, may make vs set all the
paynfull deth of this world at ⌐right¬ nowght /

The / 25 / chapiter

How be it what shuld we neade to make any such comparison,
betwene the naturall deth & the violent / for the matter that we be
25 in hand with here / we may put yt out of dowt, that he which for the
fere of the violent deth forsakith the fayth of christ, putteth hym selfe

---

1 *extra* dyeth *canc. A and B after* that   2 that is] that *canc. and* it *interl. B,* it is *Ƶ; virgule*
canc. after so *and placed before* so *B*   3 payne /] | *canc. B;* lesse /] | *canc. and comma added*
B   4 suffreth] suffer *Ƶ;* lenger] longer *1553 1573*   5 loth] *final* e *added B*   10 to cut]
to *om. L 1553 1573*   11 on the] in the *L 1573*   12 begyn on the inside] on the inside
beginne *L 1553 1573;* fro] from *L*   13 *period after* outward *B*   14 bed] beddes *L 1553*
1573   15 Some crye] And some crye *L 1553*   17–18 that euery tyme they cough] at
euerye time that they coughe *L 1553,* that euery time that they cough *1573*   18 swerd]
sword *L 1553 1573,* sweorde *1557*   19 paynes] paine *1553 1573*   20 fall /] | *canc. B*
21 deth] deathes *L*   22 25] xxvᵗʰ *L;* chapiter] piter *added B*   25 we may] we *om. L*
1553 1573   25–26 for the fere] the *canc. B, om. Ƶ*

in the perell, to fynd his naturall deth more paynefull a thowsand
tymes / for his naturall deth ⌐hath⌐ his euerlastyng payne so sodaynly
knyt vnto it, that ther is not one moment of an hower betwene, but
thend of the tone is the begynnyng of the tother that after neuer shall
haue end / And therfor was yt not without great cause, that Christ 5
gave vs so good warnyng before, when he said / as S Luke in the xij
chapitre rehersith / *Dico autem vobis amicis meis, ne terreamini ab hijs qui
occidunt corpus, et post hac non habent amplius quid faciant / Ostendam autem
vobis quem timeatis / Timete eum qui postquam occiderit,* [f. 198] *habet potest-
atem mittere in gehennam / ita dico vobis hunc timete /* I say to you that 10
are my frendes, be not aferde of them that kill the body / & which
whan that ys done, are able to do no more / But I shall shew you
whom you shuld feare / Feare hym which when he hath kyllid, hath
in his power forther to cast hym whom he kylleth into euerlastyng
fyre / So I say to you be aferd of hym / 15

God meaneth not here, that we shuld nothyng dreade at all any
man that can but kyll the bodye / but he meanyth that we shuld not
in such wise dreade any such, that we shuld for dreade of them displease hym, that can euerlastyngly kyll both body & soule, with a
deth euer dying & that yet neuer dye / And therfor he addith & repet- 20
ith in thend agayne, the feare that we shuld haue of hym & sayth
Ita dico vobis hunc timete / So I say to you fere hym / /

Oh good ⌐god⌐ Cosyn, yf a man wold well waye those wordes, &
let them syncke as they shuld do downe depe into his hart, & often
bethynke hym selfe theron / yt wold I dowt not be able ynough to 25
make vs set at nowght, all the greate Turkes threttes, & esteme hym
not at a straw / but well content to endure all the payne that all the
world wold put vppon vs, for so short while as all they were able to
make vs dwell therin / rather then by the shrynkyng fro those paynes

4 thend] the ende *1553 1557 1573*; neuer shall] shall neuer *L 1553 1573*   5 g *canc. A
after* great   6 xij] xij^th *L*   6-7 in the xij chapitre] *om. 1573* (Luc. 12. *in margin*)
7 rehersith] hehersith *A*: *canc. and* rehersyth, *interl. B*; Dico autem] autem *om. L 1553 1573*;
hijs] iis *1553 1573*   8 quid] quod *L 1553*; autem] *interl. A*   9 habet] habet: catchword f. 197^v, alt. to* habet *B*   11 frendes] fendes *A*: re *wr. over first* e *B*; aferde] afrayd
L 1553 1573   12 able] hable *1557*; sa *canc. A and B before* shall   13 shuld] shal *1553*;
Feare hym which] Feare hym that, which *L 1553*, Feare him, that *1573*   14 forther]
farther *Z*   15 aferd] afraid *1573*   20 that yet] that shall yet *Z*   21 thend] the
end *1553 1557 1573*   23 those] these *L 1553 1573*   25 able] hable *1557*   27 not
at] at *om. 1573*; but well] but be well *L*   28 wold put] could put *Z*; able] hable *1557*
29 fro] from *L 1553 1573*

though neuer so sharpe, yet but short / to cast our selfe into the payne
of hell, an hundred thowsand tymes more intollerable / & whereof
there shall neuer come an end / A wofull deth is that deth in which
folke shall euermore be dyyng & neuer can ones be ded / wherof the
5 scripture sayth *vocabunt mortem et mors fugiet ab eis* / They shall call &
cry for deth, and deth shall flye from them / [f. 198ᵛ]

Oh good lord, yf one of them were now put in choyse of the
bothe / they wold rather suffre the whole yere together, the most
terrible deth that all the Turkes in Turkey could devise, than the
10 deth that ⌐they⌐ lye in for the space of halfe an howre. In how wrechid
foly fall than those faythlesse or feble faythed folke, that to avoyd the
payne so farre the lesse & so short, fall in the stede therof, into payne
a thowsand thowsand tymes more horrible, & of which terrible tourment they be sure they shall neuer haue end.

15 This mater Cosyn lakkith as I belive, ⌐but⌐ eyther full fayth or sufficient myndyng / for I thinke on my fayth / yf we haue the grace
verely to belive yt, & often to thynke well theron / the fere of all the
Turkes persecucion (with all this myd day devill / were able to make
them do in the forcyng vs to forsake our fayth) shuld neuer be able
20 to tourne vs /

Vincent

By my trowth vncle I thynke yt be as you say / for sewerly yf we
wold as often thynke on these paynes of hell, as we be very loth to do /
& seke vs pevysh pastymes of purpose to put such hevy thinges out of
25 our thought / this one poynt alone, were hable ynough to make I
thynk many a martyre /

---

2 hundred] hundreth *L 1553*   3 end /] / *canc. and period added B*   5 vocabunt mortem]
Desiderabunt mori *1557 1573*; mors fugiet] fugiet mors *1557*   6 flye] flee *1573*; from]
fro *1557*   7 in choyse] in the choise *L 1553 1573*   7–8 of the bothe] the *om. 1573*
10 an *canc. A and B before* halfe; howre.] *period ed.*; w *canc. A and B before* how   11 those]
these *1553 1573*   16 fayth /] / *canc. and comma added B*; all this] al that this *1573*; devill /] / *canc. and comma added B*;
comma erased before* with *B*; all this] al that this *1573*; devill /] / *canc. and comma added B*;
able] hable *1557*   19 fayth)] *parenth. wr. over comma B*; able] hable *1557*   22 yt be
as] it is as *Z*; sewerly] *canc. and* surely *interl. B*, sure *1553 1573*   23 often] oft *1573*;
paynes of] paynes in *L*   25 hable] h *canc. B*, able *L 1553 1573*

The consideracion of the ioyes of hevyn, shuld make vs
for Christes sake, abyde & endure any paynfull deth /

The / 26 / Chapiter /

Antony

Forsoth Cosyn yf we were such as we shuld be, I wold scant for very 5
shame, in exortacion to the kepyng of Christes [f. 199] fayth speke of
the paynes of hell / I wold rather put vs in mynd of the Ioyes of heven /
the pleasure wherof we shuld be more glad to gete / than we shuld be
to flye & escape all the paynes in hell /

But sewerly god in that thing wherin he may seme most rygorouse / 10
is very mercyfull to vs / & that is (which many men wold litle wene)
in that he prouidid hell / For I suppose very surely Cosyn, that many
a man & woman ᴵto,ᴵ of whome there now sitt some / & more shall
hereafter sit full gloriously crownid in hevyn / had they not first bene
afrayd of hell, wold toward heven neuer haue set fote forward /   15

But yet vndowtidly were yt so, that we could as well conceyue in
our hartes the mervelowse ioyes of heven, as we conceyve the ferefull
paynes of hell / howbeyt sufficiently we can conceyve nether nother /
but yf we wold in our ymagynacion, draw as mych toward the per-
ceyvyng of the tone, as we may toward the consideracion of the 20
tother / we shuld not fayle to be far more movid & styrid to the
suffryng for christes sake in this world, for the wynnyng of the hevenly
ioyes / than for tho eschewyng of all those infernall paynes / But for
as mych as the fleshly plesures be far lesse plesaunt than the fleshly
paynes be paynfull: Therfor we fleshly folke that are so drownd in 25

---

3 Chapiter] iter *added ed.*; 26] xxvj^th *L*   6 *comma after* fayth *B*   8 gete /] / *canc. and
comma added B*   9 flye] flee *1557 1573*; escape] scape *L 1553 1573*; hell /] / *canc. and
period added B*   10 rygorouse /] / *canc. and comma added B*   11 very] *canc. and* mervelouse
interl. B, merueilous *Z*; to vs] vnto vs *L*; is (which] *reversed parenth. canc. and parenth. added
B before* which   12 hell /] / *canc. and period added B*   13 to,] *added in margin B, om. L
1553*; now sitt some] sit some nowe *L 1553 1573*; some /] / *canc. and comma added B*; more]
mo *L 1573*   18 we can *canc. A and B before* sufficiently   19 wold] coulde *Z*   20
tone, as we may toward the consideracion of the] *om. 1553*   21 shuld] would *Z*
22 the] ose *wr. over* e *B*, those *L 1553 1573*, these *1557*   23 the eschewyng] theschewing
L 1557   24 lesse] lasse *A*: e *wr. over* a *B*; plesaunt] *superfluous superscript* a *above* un *A*
25 paynes be] paines are *Z*; Therfor] T *canc. and* t *ins. B*

these flesshly pleasures, & in the desire therof, that we can all most
haue no maner savour or taste in any pleasure spirituall, haue no
cause to mervayle, that our fleshly affeccions be more abatid &
refraynid by the dreade & terrour of hell / than affeccions spirituall
5 Imprintid in vs & prickid forward with desire & Ioyfull hope of
hevyn / / [f. 199ᵛ]

    Howbeit yf we wold somwhat sett lesse by the filthy voluptuouse
appetites of the flesh, & wold by withdrawing from them with helpe
of prayour throw the grace of god, draw nere to the secret inward
10 pleasure of the spirite, we shuld by the litle sippyng that our hartes
shuld haue here now, & that sodayne tast therof / haue such an estymacion of the Incomperable & vncogitable Ioy that we shall haue
(yf we will) in hevyn by the very full drawght therof / wherof it is
wrytten / *Satiabor quum apparuerit gloria tua* / I shalbe satyatt satisfied &
15 fullfild whan thy glory good lord shall apere / that ys to witt with the
fruytyon of the sight of goddes gloryouse maiestye face to face / That
the desire expectacion & hevenly hope therof, shall more encorage
vs, & make vs strong to suffre & susteyne for the love of god & salvacion of our sowle / than euer we could be movid to suffre here worldly
20 payne, by the terrible drede of all the horrible paynes that dampnid
wrechys haue in hell / /

    Wherfor in the meane tyme for lacke of such experimentall tast,
as god giveth here sometyme to some of his speciall seruauntes, to
thentent we may draw toward spirituall exercise to / for which
25 spirituall exercise / god with that gifte as with an ernest peny of there
hole reward after in heven, comfortith them here in earth / Let vs not
so mich with lokyng to haue describid what maner of Ioyes they
shalbe, as with heryng what our lord telleth vs in holy scripture / how
mervelouse greate they shalbe, labour by prayour to conceve in our

---

1–2 all most haue] haue almost *L 1553 1573*   2 maner] manour a *L*; or taste] to taste
L 1553   4 dreade] *divided* dre-ade *A*: ade *canc. and* de *added to* dre *B*   5 with desire]
with the desier *Z*   8 by withdrawing] *Z*, be withdrawen *A*: y *wr. by B over* e *of* be
9 nere] *final* r *added B*, nerer *L 1573*, neuer *1553 1557*   10 shuld] shall *1557*   12 In-
comperable] *first* e *alt. to* a *B*   14 quum] quan? *A, bar wr. above second* u, *cancelling
superscript* a *B*   14–15 & fullfild] or fulfilled *Z*   15 apere] aperee *A*: *canc. and* apere
interl. B   16 mag *canc. A before* maiestye; That] *canc. and* that *interl. B*   19 movid]
made *1557*   20 all the] the *om. L 1553*   21 *period after* hell *B*   22 experimentall]y
wr. over i *B*   24 toward spirituall] toward that spyrytuall *L*, toward the spritual *1553
1557 1573*   25 there] yr *wr. over* re *B*   27 Ioyes] I *wr. over* i *A*   28 scripture /] /
canc. and comma added B

hartes such a fervent longyng for them, that we may for attaynyng to them, vtterly set at nought all fleshly delight, all worldly pleasures / all erthly losses, all bodely tourment and payne /

Howbe yt some thinges are there in scripture expressid, of the maner of the pleasures & Ioyes that we shall haue in hevin as where / 5 *fulgebunt Iusti sicut sol, & qui erudiunt ad iustitiam* [f. 200] *tanquam scintille in arundineto discurrent* / Ryghteus men shall shyne as the sone, & shall run about like sparkes of fyre among redes / /

Now tell some carnall myndid man of this maner pleasure / & he shall take litle pleasure therin, & say he careth not to haue hys flesh 10 shyne he / nor like a sparke of fire to skyp a bowt in the skye /

Tell hym that his bodye shalbe Impassible, & neuer fele harm / yet yf he thinke than therwith, that he shall neuer be an hungred nor a thurst / & shall therby forbere all his pleasure of eatyng & drynkyng, & that he shall neuer haue lust to slepe / & therby lese the pleas- 15 ure that he was wont to take in sloggyng / and that men & women shall there live together as angelles without any maner mynd or mocyon vnto the carnall act of generacion, & that he shall therby not vse there his old filthy voluptuouse facyon / he will say he is bettre at ease all redy, & wold not give this world for that / for as saynt paule sayth / 20 *Animalis homo non ⌐percipit¬ ea quae sunt spiritus dei / stultitia est enim ei /* But when the tyme shall come, that these fowle filthy pleasures shalbe so taken from hym, that yt shall abhore his hart ones to thinke on them / wherof euery man hath a mong a certayne shadow of experience in a fervent griefe of a sore paynful siknes, while the stomake 25 can scant abide to loke vppon any meate / and as for actes of the tother fowle filthy lust / ys redy to vomyt yf yt hap hym to thynke theron / whan men shall I saye / after this life fele that horrible abhomynacion in there hart at the remembraunce of those voluptuouse

<hr>

1 the *canc. A and B before* attaynyng   2 pleasures /] / *canc. and comma added B*   3 torment] tormentes L *1553 1573*; payne /] / *canc. and period added B*   6 fulgebunt] *Z,* fulgebit *A*   6–7 scintille] L *1553 1557,* scintilli *A,* scintillae *1573*   7 Ryghteus] o *interl. before* u *B*; shyne] *divided* shy-ne *A*: ne *canc. and added to* shy *B, then whole word canc. and* schyne *interl. B*; sone] *bar wr. above* o *B*   8 sparkes] sparckles *Z*   11 shyne he] shine hye *1553*; sparke] sparckle *L*   15 lust] list *L 1557*   16 sloggyng] slugging *L 1557 1573* 21 percipit] *interl. B above canc.* recipit *A,* percipit *Z*; stultitia est enim] stultitia enim est *Z*; ei /] illi. *B* (e *canc.,* 1 *wr. over / and* li. *added*), illi *Z*; *after the Latin 1557 1573 add:* A carnal man feleth not the things that be of the spirite of God, for it is foolishnes to him.   25 in a fervent] in the feruent L *1553 1573*   26 for actes] for the actes *Z* 27 ys redy] he ys ready *L*; hap] happen *1553 1573*   28 saye /] / *canc. B*   29 hart] hartes *L*; those] these *Z*

pleasures, of which abomynacion siknes hath here a shadow / for
which voluptuouse pleasures he wold here be loth to chaunge with the
Ioyes [f. 200ᵛ] of hevyn / when he shall I say / after this life haue his
fleshly pleasures in abhomynacion / & shall of those hevenly ioyes
5 which he set here so lytle by / haue there a glymeryng / though far
from a perfitt sight / Oh good god, how fayne will he than be / with
how good will & how glad / will he than give this whole world yf yt
were his / to haue the felyng of some litle part of those Ioyes / And
therfor let vs all that can not now conceve such delight in the con-
10 sideracion of them as we shuld: haue often in our eyen by readyng /
often in our eares by heryng / often in our mouthes by rehersyng /
often in our hartes by meditacion & thynkyng / Those ioyfull wordes
of holy scripture / by which we lerne how wonderfull howge & greate
those spirituall hevenly Ioyes are / of which our carnall hartes hath so
15 feble & so faynte a felyng / & our dull worldly wittes so litle hable to
conceyve so mych as a shadow of the right Imagynacion / A shadow
I say / for as for the thyng as it is / that can not onely no fleshly
carnall fantasy conceyve / but ouer that no spirituall gostly person
peradventure nether that here is here lyvyng styll in this world.
20 For sith the very substaunce essentiall of all the celestiall Ioy, standith in blessid beholdyng of the gloriouse godhed face to face / there
may no man presume or loke to attayne yt in this life / for god hath
so said hym selfe / *Non videbit me homo & viuet* / there shall no man
here lyvyng behold me. And therfor we may well know, that for
25 the state of this life, we be not onely shyt from the fruytion of the
blysse of hevyn, but also that the very best man livyng here vppon
earth (the best man I meane beyng no more but a man) can not I
wene attayne the right Imagynacion therof / but those [f. 201] that are
very vertuouse, are yet in a maner as far therfro as the borne blynd
30 man fro the right Imagynacion of colours.

---

1 hath here] hath been *L 1553*   2 be loth] *vertical line after* be *B, final* e *added to* loth *B*
5 which he set] which be set *1557*   6 perfitt] perfecte *L 1553*; lord *canc. B before* god
7 glad /] | *canc. B*   8 his] is *A*: h *added B*   9 that can] that we can *1573*; not] *om.*
L 1553 1573; now conceve] conceiue nowe *L 1553 1573*   10 *comma canc. after* them *B*;
eyen] yies *L 1553*, eyes *1573*   11 hartes *canc. A and B before* eares   12 Those] T *canc.*
and t *ins.* B, *then whole word canc. and* those *interl.* B; thynkyng / Those] thinking vpon those
L 1553 1573, thynking those *1557*   14 spit *canc. A and B before* spirituall; Io *canc. A before*
hevenly; hath] haue *1573*   15 hable] h *canc.* B, able *Ƶ*   18 fantasy] fansye *L*
19 / *canc.* B *after* peradventure; here lyvyng] here *om.* Ƶ   20 very] Ƶ, vey *A*; Ioy] Ioyes
1553 1573   27 meane] meane) *A, parenth. canc.* B   28 attayne] attayn to *L*
29 *comma after* therfro *B*   30 colours] coloʳs *A*: *canc. and* colours *interl.* B

The wordes that S. paule rehersith of the prophet Esay, prophecy-eng of Christes incarnacion, may properly be veryfied of the Ioyes of hevyn / *Nec oculus vidit, nec auris audiuit, nec in cor hominis ascendit, que preparauit deus diligentibus se* / For sewerly for this state of this world, the Ioyes of hevyn are by mans mowth vnspekeable / to mans eares 5 not audible / to mens hartes vncogitable / so farforth excell they all that euer men haue hard of / all that euer men can speke of / and all that euer any man can by naturall possibilitie thinke on / And yet where the Ioyes of hevyn be such preparid for euery savyd sowle / our lord sayth yet by the mowth of S Iohn, that he will give his holy 10 martires that suffer for his sake, many a speciall kynd of Ioy. For he sayth / *vincenti dabo edere de ligno vite* / To hym that ouercometh, I shall give hym to eate of the tree of lyfe / And also he that ouercom-eth shalbe clothid in whyte clothes / and I shall confesse hys name be-fore my father & before his Angelles / And also he sayth: feare none 15 of those thynges that thow shallt suffre &c ⌐but¬ be faythfull vnto the deth / and I shall give the ⌐the¬ crowne of lyfe. He that ouercometh shall not be hurt of the second deth / he sayth also / *vincenti dabo manna absconditvm, & dabo illi calculum candidum. Et in calculo nomen nouum scriptum quod nemo scit nisi qui accipit* / To hym that ouercometh will I 20 give manna secret & hid / & I will give hym a white suffrage, & in his suffrage a new name wrytten, which no man knowith but he that receyveth it /

They vsid of old in Grece / where saynt Iohn did wryte, to elect & chose men vnto honourable romes / & euery mans assent was callid 25 his suffrages / which in some place ⌐was¬ by the voyces / [f. 201ᵛ] in some place by handes / & one kynd of thos suffrages, was by certeyne thynges that are in laten ⌐callyd¬ / *calculi* / because that in some places they vsid therto round stones / Now sayth our lord that vnto

3 Nec oculus vidit] Oculus non vidit *1557 1573*; auris] aures *A*: i *wr. over* e *B*   4 for this state] for the state *L 1553 1573*   5–6 by mans mowth vnspekeable / to mans eares not audible] by mannes eares not audible, to mannes mouthe vnspeakable, to mannes eares not audible, *1553*   6 mens hartes] mannes hearte *L 1553 1573*   7 men] man *A*: e *wr. over* a *B*; and] And *A*: A *alt. to* a *B*   8 possibilitie] possibititie *A*; thinke] *divided* thin-ke *A*: ke *canc. and* k *added to* thin *B*   9 be such] being such *L 1553*   11 For] for *A* 12 vite] *hook added to* e *B*   14 ch *canc. A and B before* clothid   15 he sayth] he *om. L 1553*   16 thow shallt] you shal *L 1553*   17 the the] the, yᵉ *L*, them the *1553*, thee the *1557 1573*   19 absconditvm] absconditam *A*: v *wr. over second* a *B*; candidum.] *period ed.* 21 suffrage] a *wr. over* r? *A*   24 where saynt] where as Saynte *L 1553*   25 chose] close *A*: l *alt. to* h *B*   26 suffrages] suffrage *1573*   27 place] places *L 1553 1573*; thos] this *A*: o *wr. over* i *B*   29 stol *canc. A and B before* stones

hym which ouercometh, he will give a white suffrage / for those that
were white, signified approvyng / as the blacke signifieth reprovyng /
& in those suffrages did they vse to wryte the name of hym to whome
they gave theire voyce / And now sayth our lord that vnto hym that
5 ouercometh, he will in the suffrage give hym a new name, which no
man knowith but he that receyvith yt /

He sayth also / he that ouercometh, I will make hym a piller in the
temple of my god / & he shall go no more out therof / & I shall wryte
vppon hym the name of my god / & the name of the Citie of my god
10 the new Iherusalem, which descendith from hevyn fro my god / and I
shall wryte on hym also my new name /

Iff we shuld dilate & were hable to declare these speciall gyftes,
with yet other mo specyfied in the second & the third chapitre of
thapocalyps / there wold yt apere, how farr those hevenly Ioyes, shall
15 surmount above all the comfort that euer came in the mynd of any
man lyvyng here vppon earth.

The blessid Apostell ⌐S.¬ Paule, that suffrid so many perelles & so
many passions, he that sayth of hym selfe that he hath bene, *In
laboribus pluribus in Carceribus abundantius, in plagis supra modum &c* / in
20 many labours, in prysons ofter than other, in strypys above mesure,
at poynt of deth often tymes, of the Iewes had I five tymes fourty
strypes saue one / Thryes haue I bene beten with roddes, ones was I
stonyd [f. 202] Thryes haue I bene in shippe wrake / A day & a nyght
was ⌐I¬ in the depth of the see / In my iourneyes ofte haue I bene in
25 perell of flodes, in perell of theves / in perelles by the Iewes / in perelles by the paynymes / In perelles in the Citie / In perelles in
desert / In perelles in the see / perelles by false bretheren / In labour &
mysery / In many nightes watch / In hungre & thyrst / In many
fastynges / In cold & nakednes beside those thynges that are outward,
30 my dayly instant labour, I meane my care & solicitude about all the

---

2 signifieth] signified *Z*   3 those] these *L 1553 1573*   4 vnto hym] to him *Z*   10 fro
my] from my *L 1553 1573*   11 on hym] vpon him *L 1553 1573*   12 shuld] would *Z*;
hable] h *canc. B*, able *L 1553 1573*   13 the third] the *om. 1553 1573*   14 thapocalyps]
the Apocalips *L 1553 1573*; those hevenly] these heauenly *L 1553 1573*   17 S. Paule]
S. *om. L 1553*   19 pluribus] bus *interl. B*; Carceribus] Carcerib *A*; supra modum] *om.*
1573   22 Thryes] T *canc. and* t *ins. B*   23 Thryes] T *canc. and* t *ins. B*   25 theves /]
| *canc. and comma added B*; perelles] peril *1557*   25 Iewes /] | *canc. and comma added B*   26
paynymes /] | *canc. and comma added B*; Citie / In] Citie / I *A*, n *added B*   27 see / perelles]
see, in perylles *L 1573*, sea. In perilles *1553*   28 hungre] er *wr. over* re *B*

Churches / And yet sayth he more of his tribulacions, which for the
length I let passe / This blessid apostle I say for all the tribulacions
that hym selfe suffred in the contynuaunce of so many yeres, &
calleth yet all the trybulacions of this world, but light & as short
as a moment in respect of the wayghty glory that yt after this world 5
wynneth vs: *Id enim quod in presenti est momentaneum et leue tribulacionis*
nostre supra modum, in sublimitate eternum glorie pondus operatur in nobis
non contemplantibus nobis quae videntur sed quae non videntur, ⌐*que enim*
videntur⌐ *temporalia sunt, quae autem non videntur aeterna sunt* / This same
short & momentary trybulacion of ours, that is in this present tyme, 10
worketh within vs the weyght of glory above measure / *in sublimitate* on
hygh we beholdyng not those thynges that we see / but those thynges
that we see not / For those thynges that we see, be but temporall
thynges / but those thynges that are not seen are eternall / /
 Now to this greate glory, can there no man come hedlesse. Our 15
hed is Christ / & therfor to hym must we be Ioynid / & as [f. 202ᵛ]
membres of his must we folow hym / yf we will come thither. He is
our Guyde to guyde vs thyther & is entryd in before vs / and he therfor that will enter in after, *Debet sicut ille ambulauit et ipse ambulare* / the
same way that Christ walkyd, the same way must he walke / And 20
what was the way by which he walkid into hevyn / hym selfe shewith
what way it was, that his father had providid for hym, where he said
vnto the two deciples goyng toward the Castell of Emaues *Nesciebatis*
quia oportebat Christum pati, & sic introire in regnum suum? knew you not
that Christ must suffre passion, & by that way entre into his kyng- 25
dome? Who can for very shame desire to entre into the kyngdom
of Christ with ease, whan hym selfe entrid not into his own without
payne /

---

1 And] A *alt. to* a B 1–2 the length] the *om. L 1573* 2 passe /] *colon added after* / B;
This] T *canc. and* t *ins.* B 3 the] thos B (os *wr. over* e), these Ʒ; &] *canc.* B, *om.* Ʒ 4
yet all] it all *1557*; & as short] as *om. L 1553 1573* 6 tribulacionis] c *alt. to* t B, tribulaciones (e *wr. over final* i) L 7 glorie] *hook added to* e B 8 videntur] ridentur A: v
wr. over first r B 11 in sublimitate] in sublymyte L, in sublimitie *1553* 12 not those
thynges] not these thynges *1557* 15 hedlesse] *marked as two words* B 21 hevyn /]
question-mark ins. before / B 22 his] he A: is *wr. over* e B 23 deciples] is *wr. over first*
e B; Emaues] s *wr. over second* e *and final* s *canc.* B 23–24 Nesciebatis quia oportebat
Christum pati, & sic introire in regnum suum] Nonne haec oportuit pati Christum & ita
intrare in gloriam suam *1557 1573* 24 knew] Know L *1573*; you] ye L *1553 1573*
26 the] *interl.* A *above* his (*canc.* A *and* B)

The consideracion of the paynefull deth ⌐of⌐ Chryst, is
sufficient to make vs content to suffre paynefull deth
for his sake

The xxvijth Chapitre

5   Surely Cosyn as I said before in beryng the losse of worldly goodes,
in suffryng of captyuytie thraldome & Imprisonment, & in the glad
susteyning of worldly shame, that yf we wold in all those poyntes,
dyepely pondre the sample of our saviour hym selfe / It were of yt
selfe alone sufficyent, to encorage euery kynd christen man &
10   woman, to refuse none of all those calamytees for his sake / So say I
now / for paynefull deth also, that yf we could & wold with dew compassion, conceyve in our myndes a right Imagynacion & remembraunce of Christes byttre paynefull passion, of the many sore blody
strokes ⌐that⌐ the cruell tourmentours with roddes & whyppes gaue
15   hym vppon euery part of his holy tendre body / the scornefull crowne
of sharp [f. 203] thornes beten down vppon his holy hed, so strayght
& so diepe, that on euery part his blyssid blode yssued owt & stremyd
down / his lovely lymmys drawen & strechid out vppon the crosse to
the Intollerable payne of his forebeten & sorebeten vaynes and syn-
20   ewes / new felyng with the cruell strechyng & straynyng payne far
passyng any crampe, in euery part of his blyssid body at ones / Than
the greate long nayles cruelly dryven with hamers thorow his holy
handes and fete / & ⌐in⌐ this horryble payne lyft vpp & let hang with
the payce of all his body beryng down vppon the paynfull woundid
25   places so grevously percyd with nayles / & in suche tourment /
without pitie, but not without many dispightes / suffred to be pynyd
& paynid the space of more than three long howres / tyll hym selfe
willyngly gave vpp vnto his father his holy soule / after which yet
to shew the myghtenes of their malice after his holy soule departid /
30   perced his holy hart with a sharp spere / at which issued out the holy
blode & water, wherof his holy sacramentes haue Inestymable secrete

---

1 *second* of] for *A*: *canc. and* of added at end of line *B*   4 xxvijth] last, *L 1553 1573*, xxvii *1557*
5 before in] beford in *A*: *canc. and* before, in the *interl. B*, the *canc. B*; in beryng] in the
bearing *L 1553*   7 susteyning] susteyng *A*   19 the Intollerable] thintolerable *L 1557*
25 tourment /]] / *canc. B*   26 dispith *canc. A and B before* dispightes   30 perced] they
perced *1557 1573*

strength / yf we wold I say remembre these thinges in such wise, as
wold god we wold / I verely suppose that the consideracion of his
incomparable kyndnes, could not fayle in such wise to inflame our
kay cold hartes, & set them on fire in his love / that we shuld fynd
our selfe not onely content, but also glad & desierouse to suffre deth 5
for his sake / that so mervelously lovyngly lettid not to sustayne so
farre passyng paynfull deth for ⌐ours⌐.

Wold god we wold here to the shame of our cold affeccion, agayne
toward god for such fervent love & Inestimable kyndnes of god toward vs / wold god we wold I say but consider, what hote affeccion 10
many of thes fleshly lovers [f. 203ᵛ] haue borne & dayly do, to those
vppon whome they dote. How many of them haue not lettid to iubard
their lives / & how many haue willyngly lost their lives in dede,
without eyther great kyndnes shewid them before / And afterward
you wot well they could nothyng wynne / but evyn that yet contentid 15
& satisfied their mynd ⌐that by⌐ their deth, their lover shuld clerely
see / how faythfully they lovid / the delite wherof imprintid in their
fantasy / not asswagid onely, but conterpaysid also they thought, all
their payne / Off these affeccions, with the wonderfull dolorouse ef-
fectes folowyng theron, not onely old written stories, but ouer that I 20
thinke in euery countrey christen & hethen both experience giveth
vs profe inough / And ys it not than a wondrefull shame for vs / for the
drede of temporall deth, to forsake our savyour, that willyngly suffred
so paynefull deth, rather than he wold forsake vs / considering that
beside that / he shall for our suffryng so highly reward vs with euer- 25
lastyng welth / /

Oh yf he that is content to die for his love, of whome he lokith after
for no reward, & yet by ⌐his⌐ deth goeth from her, might by his deth be
sure to come to her, & euer after in delite & pleasure to dwell with
her: such a lover wold not let here to dye for her twyse / And how 30

---

2 verely suppose] verely thinke & suppose *L 1553 1573*   3 fayle in such wise] in such
wise faile *L 1553 1573*   6 mervelously] meruelous *Z*   7 ours] *wr. by B in space at end
of ¶*   11 bon *canc. A before* borne; do, to] doe beare to *L 1553 1573*   12 How] how *A*
13 haue willyngly lost] *Z*, haue willyngly haue lost *A*   14 And] *canc. and & interl. B*
15 yet] *canc. and it interl. B*, it *Z*   17 see /] | *canc. and comma added B*   18 fantasy]
fansye *L*   22 ys it] yt is *A*: s *wr. over t and t wr. over s B*, is it *Z*   24 rather] rathar
A: e *wr. over second a B*   25 beside that] *om. 1553*; that /] | *canc. and comma added B*
26 *question-mark after* welth *B*   27 his love] her loue *L 1553 1573*   28 by his] bys *A*: s
canc. and his interl. B, by hys *Z*; *extra* might by his deth *canc. B after* deth

cold lovers be we than vnto god / yf rather than dye for hym ones,
we will refuse hym & [forsake him] for euer, that both dyed for vs
before / & hath also prouidid, that yf we dye here for hym, we shall
in hevyn euerlastyngly both live & also reigne with hym / for as
5 saynt Peter sayth *Si compatimur et conregnabimus*: yf we suffre with
hym we shall reigne with hym / [f. 204]

How many Romaynes / how many noble corages of other sundry
countreys, haue willyngly geven their own lives, & suffre greate dedly
paynes & very paynfull dethes, for their countreys, & the respect of
10 wynnyng by their dethes, the onely reward of worldly renome &
fame / And shuld we than shrynke to suffre as much, for eternall
honour in hevyn & euerlastyng glorye / The devill hath also some so
obstynate heretiques, that endure willyngly paynfull deth for vayne
glory / & is it not than more than shame, that Christ shall see
15 his Catholiques forsake his fayth / rather than suffre the same for
hevyn & very glory /

Wold god as I many tymes haue said, that the remembraunce of
Christes kyndnes in suffryng his passion for vs / the consideracion of
hell that we shuld fall in by forsakyng of hym / the Ioyfull meditacion
20 of eternal lyfe in hevyn that we shall wynne, with this short temperall
deth patiently taken for hym, had so dyepe a place in our brest as
reason wold they shuld, & (as yf we wold do our devour toward yt &
labour for yt / & pray therefor) I verely thinke they shuld / For than
shuld they so take vpp our mynd, & ravish yt all an other way, that as
25 a man hurt in a fray, feleth not sometyme his wound / nor yet is not
ware therof, till his mynd fall more theron / so farforth that some
tyme an other man shewith hym that he hath lost an hand, before
that he perceveth it hym selfe: so the mynd ravishid in the thinkyng
[f. 204ᵛ] diepely of those other thinges, Christes deth / hell & hevyn,
30 were lykly to mynish & put away of our paynefull deth, foure partes
of the felyng, eyther of the feare or the payne. For of this am I very

---

1 vnto god] to god *L*   2 forsake him] *Z*, forsakyng *A*   5 Paule *interl. B above* Peter
(*uncanc.*), Paule *Z*; Si compatimur et conregnabimus] *om. L 1553 1573*; : yf] *colon ed.*
8 suffre] suffred *Z*   10 renome] renowme *L 1573*, renowne *1553*, renoume *1557*
12 also some] some also *L 1553 1573*; glorye /] *question-mark ins. before | B*   13 will-
yngly] wittingly *Z*   14 is it] it is *A*: s *wr. over* t *and* t *wr. over* s *B*, is it *Z*   16 glory /]
| *canc. and question-mark added B*   22 (as] *parenth. added B*   23 yt /] | *canc. and comma
added B*; therefor)] *parenth. wr. over | B*; thyng *canc. A and B before* thinke   27–28 before
that] that *om. Z*; perceveth] perceiue *Z*   29 deth /] | *canc. and comma added B*   31 or
the payne] or of the paine *1553 1573*

sure / yf we had the fyfteneth part of the love to Christ, that he both
had and hath to vs: all the payne of this Turkes persecucion, could
not kepe vs from hym / but that there wold be at this day, as many
martires here in Hungarye, as haue bene afore in other countreys of
old.   5

And of this poynt put I nothing dowt, but that yf the Turke stode
evyn here with all his whole armye about hym, & euery one of them
all, were redy at our hand, with all the terrible tourmentes that they
cold ymagyne, & but yf we wold forsake the fayth were settyng their
tourmentes to vs, & to thencrese of our terrour, fell all at ones in a   10
showt with trumpettes / taberettes, & tumbrelles, all blowyne vp at
ones, & all their gonnes let go there with, to make vs a ferefull noyse /
yf yon shuld sodaynly than on the tother side, the grownd quake &
ryve atwayne, & the devilles rise out of hell, & shew themselfe in such
vgly shappe as dampnid wretchis shall see them / & with that hydy-   15
ouse howlyng that those hell howndes shuld shrich / lay hell open on
euery side round about our fete, ⌐that⌐ as we stode / we shuld loke
downe into that pestilent pitt & se the swarme of sely soules in the
terrible tourmentes there: we wold wax so ferd of that sight, that as
for the Turkes hoste, we shuld scantly remembre we saw them /   20

And in good fayth for all that, yet thinke I farther this / that yf there
myght than apere the glory of god, the Trynitie in his high mervelouse
maiestie, our saviour in his glorious manhod sittyng on his Trone,
with his Immaculate mother & all that gloriouse companye [f. 205]
callyng vs there vnto them / & that yet our way shuld lye thorow mer-   25
velouse paynfull deth before we could come at them: vppon the
sight I say / of that glory, there wold I wene be no man that ones wold
shrinke therat / but euery man wold run on toward them in all that
euer he might, though there lay for malice to kyll vs by the way, both
all the Turkes tourmentours, & all the devilles to / And therfor Cosyn,   30

1 fyfteneth] xv *1557*   1–2 he both had] he hath had L *1553*   2 to vs] vn *interl. B*
before to, vnto vs *Ƶ*; payne] paynes A: s *canc. A*   4 bene] be *1553 1557*; afore] afore
tyme L   5 old.] *period ed., flourish A*   6 nothing] no *1553 1573*   7 one] *canc. B,*
om. Ƶ   7–8 of them all] all *om.* L *1553*   10 thencrese] the encrease *1553 1573*;
at] a A: t *added B*   11 trumpettes /] | *canc. and comma added B*; blowyne] *final e? alt. to*
n, *then canc. B*; at] a A: t *added B*   12 noyse] noyse withall L   13 yon] *canc.*
and there interl. B, there *Ƶ*; tother] other *1553 1573*   16 shrich] *final* e *added B*
17 stode /] | *canc. B*   19 ferd] frayde *1553 1573*; that sight] the sight *1553 1573*
21 yet] yt A: e *interl. after* y B, yet Ƶ   22 the glory] the great glory Ƶ   23 manhod]
manhold A, manhed *1557*   30 devilles to] to *om. 1557*

let vs well consider these thynges, & let vs haue sure hope in the helpe
of god / & than I dowt not, but that we shalbe sure, that as the prophet sayth, the truth of his promise shall so compace vs with a
pavise, that of this incursion of this mydday devill / this Turkes perse-
5 cucion / we shall neuer nede to fere / for eyther yf we trust in god well,
& prepare vs therfor / the Turke shall neuer medle with vs / or els
yf he do, harm shall he none do vs / but in stede of harme inestimable
good / Off whose graciouse helpe wherfor shuld we so sore now
dispayre (except we were so madd men, as to wene that eyther his
10 power or his mercye were woren out alredy) whan we see so many a
thowsand holy martyres by his holy helpe, suffred as mich before, as
any man shalbe put to now / or what excuse can we haue by the
tendernes of our flesh, whan we can be no more tendre, than were
many of them / among whome were not onely men of strength, but
15 also weke women & children / /

And sith the strength of them all stode in the help of god, and that
the very strongest of them all, was neuer able of them selfe / and
with goddes helpe the feblest of them all, was strong ynough to stand
agaynst all the world / let vs prepare our selfe with prayour, with our
20 whole trust in his helpe, without any trust in our own strength / Let
vs thinke theron & prepare vs in our mynd therto long before / let vs
therin conform our will vnto his / not desieryng to be brought vnto the
perell of persecution. For it semeth a prowde hyigh mynd, to desire
martirdome / but desiryng help & strength of god yf he suffre vs to
25 come to the stresse, eyther beyng sought, founden, & brought out
agaynst [f. 205ᵛ] our willes / or els beyng by his commaundment /
for the comfort of our cure bounden to abide /

Let vs fall to fastyng, to prayour, to Almes dede in tyme / & give
that vnto god that may be taken from vs / yf the devill put in our

---

2 than I] I than *L 1553 1573*; but that we] that *om. L 1553 1573*   3 truth] *final e
added B*; vs with] vs abowt with *L*   4 devill /] / *canc. and comma added B*   4-5 persecucion /] / *canc. and comma added B*   5 / for] f *alt. to* F *B, period placed before* / *B*   6
Turke] Turkes *1553*   9 so ma *canc. A and B before* men   10 alredy)] *parenth. wr. over* / *B*
12 shalbe] should be *1553*; / or] or *canc. and* Or *interl. B, period placed before* / *B*   14 we
canc. A after whome (r *seems to be added to* we *by B and canc.*)   15 *period after* children *B*
17 able] hable *1557*; and] And *A*: A *alt. to a B*   20 extra any *canc. B before* trust
21 mynd] myndes *L 1553 1573*   25 founden] founde *L 1553 1573*; & brought] or
broughte *L 1553 1573*   26 or els] *om. L 1553*; commaundment /] / *canc. and comma
added B*   27 bounden] bownd *L*   28 Almes] allmoyse *L*, almose *1553 1573*   29
vs/] / *canc. and period added B*

mynd the savyng of our land & our goodes / let vs remembre that
we can not save them long / yf he fere vs with exile, & flying from
our countrey, let vs remembre that we be borne in the brode world,
& not like a tre to styk still in one place, & that wether so euer we go
god shall go with vs / /   5

Iff he threten vs with captyuyte / let vs tell hym agayne, bettre ys
to be thrall vnto man a while for the pleasure of god, than by displeas-
yng god, be perpetuall thrall vnto the devill / If he thret vs with
Imprisonment / let vs tell hym we will rather be mans prisoners a
while here in earth / than by forsakyng the fayth, be his prisoners 10
euer in hell /

Iff he put in our myndes the terrour of the Turkes / let vs consider
his false slayte therein / For this tale he tellith vs to make vs forget
hym / But let vs remembre well that in respect of hymselfe, the Turke
is but a shadow / nor all that they all can do, ⌐can⌐ be but a flye byt- 15
yng in comparison of the myschiefe that he goeth about / The Turkes
are but his tourmentours, for hymselfe doth the dede / our lord sayth
in the Apocalyps / *Diabolus mittet aliquos vestrum in Carcerem vt tentemini* :
The devill shall send some of you to prison, to tempt you / he sayth
not that men shall / but that the devill shall hym selfe / for without 20
question the divelles own dede it is, to bryng vs by his temptacion with
feare & force therof, into eternall dampnacion / And therfor sayth
S. Paule / *Non est nobis colluctatio aduersus carnem & sanguinem* ⌐sed⌐ *&c.*
Our wrestlyng is not agaynst flesh & bloud &c. Thus may we see that
in such persecucions, it is the mydday devill hym selfe that maketh 25
such incursion vppon vs, by the men that are his ministers to make
vs fall for feare / For till we fall, he can neuer hurt vs. And therfor
sayth S. Peter / *Resistite Diabolo et fugiet a vobis* / Stand agaynst the
devill, & he shall flye fro you / for he neuer runneth apon a man to
seas on hym with his clawes, [f. 206] tyll he see hym down on the 30

---

2 flying] fleyng *L*, fleing *1553*, fleeing *1573*   3 in the] into the *Z*   4 wether] h *interl.*
after w *B*   6–7 bettre ys to] better is it to *Z*   7 god] of god *L 1553 1573*   11 euer]
for euer *L 1553 1573*   13 slayte] sleight *Z*   15 flye] e *wr. over* y *B*, flea *L 1553 1573*,
fle *1557*   18 Diabolus mittet] Ecce, missurus est diabolus *1557 1573*; vestrum] ex vobis
1557 1573; tentemini:] *colon ed.*   23 sed &c.] *period ed.*   24 bloud &c.] *period ed., after*
bloud *1573 adds* but against the Princes & Powers, & Ghostly enemies that be rulers of
these darknesses.; we see] you see *L 1553*   25 *comma after* selfe *B*   26 incursion] in-
cursioon *A*: *first* o *canc. A?*   28 S. Peter] Saynte James *1557 1573*; Reso *canc. A before*
Resistite   29 flye] flee *1557 1573*; fro] *final* m *canc.* B (*partly erased by A*), from *Z*

grownd willyngly fallyn hym selfe / for his fasshion ys to set his seruauntes agaynst vs, & by them to make vs for feare or for Impacyence
to fall / And hym selfe in the meane while compasseth vs, runnyng &
roryng like a rampyng lyon ⌐abowt vs,¹ lokyng who will fall, that he
5 than may devoure hym / *Aduersarius vester Diabolus* sayth S. Peter
sicut leo rugiens circuit querens quem deuoret / your adversary the devill
lyke a roryng lyon, runnyth about in circuite, sekyng whome he
may devoure / The devill it is therfor, that yf we for fere of men will
fall, is redy to rone vppon vs & devoure vs. And is it wisedome than,
10 so mych to thinke vppon the Turkes, that we forgete the devill / What
mad man is he, that whan a lion were about to devoure hym, wold
vouchsafe to regarde the bytyng of a lytle fistyng curre / Therfor whan
he roreth out vppon vs by the threttes of mortall men / let vs tell hym
that with our inward yie, we see hym well ynough, & intend to stand
15 & fight with hym evyn hand to hand. Iff he thretten vs that we be to
weyke / let vs tell hym that our capten Christ is with vs, & that we
shall fight with his strength that hath vainquyshid hym all redy /

And let vs fence vs with fayth, & comfort vs with hope, & smyte
the devill in the face with a firebrond of charitie / For surely yf we
20 be of that tendre lovyng mynd, that our master was / & not hate them
that kill vs, but pytie them & pray for them, with sorow for the perell
that they worke vnto them selfe / that fire of charitie throwne in his
face, stryketh the devill sodaynly so blynd, that he can not see where
to fasten a stroke on vs /

25   Whan we fele vs to bold / remembre our own feblenes / whan we
fele vs to faynt / remembre Christes strength / In our fere let vs remembre Christes paynfull agonye, that hym selfe wold for our comfort
suffre before his passion, to thentent that no fere shuld make vs dispayre / & euer call for his help, such as hymselfe lyst to send vs / &
30 than nede we neuer to dowt / but that eyther [f. 206ᵛ] he shall kepe
vs from the paynfull deth / or shall not fayle so to strength vs in yt,
that he shall ioyously bryng vs to hevyn by yt / & than doth he much

---

1 fallyn] fallyng *A*: g *canc. B*; selfe /] *| canc. and period added B*; for] f *alt. to* F *B*   4 caret
wr. by B over comma after lyon   6 sicut] tanquam *1557 1573*   7 he] we *1557*   9 rone]
ronne *B (bar added above* o); is it] it is *A*: s *wr. over* t, t *wr. over* s *B*, is it Z   10 devill /]
| *canc. and question-mark added B*   12 fistyng] fityng *A*: ist *wr. over it B*, fysting Z; curre
/] | *canc. and period added B*   20 that tendre] the tender *L 1553 1557*   22 vnto them]
to them *L 1553 1573*   24 sa *canc. A before* fasten   25 *comma after* remembre *B*   28
thentent] the entent *1557*   29 lyst] lust *1553*   30 nede we] we nede *L 1553 1573*;
dowt /] | *canc. and comma added B*   31 deth /] | *canc. and comma added B*

more for vs than yf he kept vs fro yt / For as god did more for pore
Lazare, in helpyng hym pacyently to dye for hungre at the rychmans
dore / than yf he had brought hym to the dore all the rich glotons
dyner / so though he be graciouse to a man whom he deliuerith out of
paynfull trowble / yet doth he mych more for a man / yf thorow right 5
paynfull deth, he delyuer hym from this wrechid world into eternall
blysse / From which who so euer shrynke away with forsakyng his
fayth, & falleth in the perell of euerlastyng fire: he shalbe very sure to
repent yt ere yt be long after / For I wene that whan so euer he falleth
sik next, he will wish that he had be kyllid for Christes sake before / 10
What foly ys it than for feare to flye fro that deth, which thow seest
thow shallt shortly after wish thow hadest dyed / yee I wene almost
euery good Christen man, wold very fayne this day that he had
bene for Christes fayth cruelly kyllid yister day / evyn for the desire
of hevyn, though there were none hell / but to feare while the payne 15
ys comyng, there is all our lett / but than yf we wold remembre hell
payne on the tother side, into which we fall while we flye fro this /
than shuld this short payne be no let at all / And yet shuld we be more
prikyd forward, yf we were faythfull by dyepe consideryng of the
ioyes of hevyn, of which thapostle sayth: *Non sunt condigne passiones* 20
huius temporis ad futuram gloriam que reuelabitur in nobis / the passiones
of this tyme, be not worthy to the glory that ys to come, which shalbe
shewid in vs / We shuld not I wene Cosyn nede mych more in all this
whole mater, than that one text of saynt Paule, yf we wold consider
yt well / For surely myn own good Cosyn, remembre that yf yt were 25
possible for me and you alone, to suffre as mych trowble as the whole
world doth together / all that were [f. 207] not worthy of yt selfe, to
bryng vs to the ioy which we hope to haue euerlastyngly / And therfor I pray you let the consideracion of that Ioy, put out all worldly

---

1 fro] from *L 1553 1573*   2 hungre] *divided* hun-gre *A: canc. and* hunger *interl. B*
7 so] o *wr. over illeg. letter B*   7–8 his fayth] of hys fayth *L 1553 1573*   10 be kyllid]
been killed *L 1553 1573*; before /] *period and extra / added B*   11 flye] flee *1557 1573*;
fro] from *Z*   14 sake *canc. A and B after* Christes; evyn] evyng *A:* g *canc. B*   15 / but]
B *wr. over /and* b *B, period added before / B*; none hell] no hell *L 1553 1573*   16 *extra* the
payne *canc. B before* ys; lett /] *Z,* bett *A,* / *canc. and period added B*; but] B *wr. over* b *B*
17 tother] other *1553 1573*; flye] flee *1557 1573*; fro] from *L*   18 all /] / *canc. and period*
added B   20 thapostle] the Apostle *Z*; condigne] *hook added to* e *B,* digne *L 1553*;
passiones] passionis *A:* e *wr. over second* i *B*   21 reuelabitur] *second* e *wr. over illeg. letter B*;
passiones] s *wr. over* e, *final* s *canc. B*   22 worthy to] worthy of *1573*; ce? *canc. A before*
come   23 We] we *A*   25 myn] my *1553*   29 conside *canc. B before* consideracion

trowble out of your hart / and also pray that yt may do the same in
me / And evyn thus will I good Cosyn with these wordes, make a sodayne end of myn whole tale, & bid you fare well / For now begynne
I to fele my selfe somewhat werye /

5   Vincent

Forsoth good vncle this is a good end / & it is no mervayle though
you be waxen wery / For I haue this day put you to so mych labour,
that savyng for the comfort that your selfe may take of your tyme so
well bestowed / & for the comfort that I haue my selfe taken (& mo
10 shall I trust) of your good counsayle given / or els wold I be very sory
to haue put you to so mych payne. But now shall our lord reward &
recompence you therfor / and many shall I trust pray for you / For,
to thentent that the mo may take profit by you, I purpose vncle as my
pore witt and lernyng will serve me, to put your good counsayle in
15 remembrauns, not in our own langage onely, but in the Almayne
tong to. And thus praying god to give me & all other that shall reade
yt, the grace to folow your good counsayle therin: I shall commytt you
to god /

Antonye

20   Syth you be myndid Cosyn to bestow so mych labour theron, I wold
yt ⌐had⌐ happid you to feche the counsayle at some wyser man, that
could haue given you bettre / But bettre men may set mo thynges,
& bettre also therto / And in the meane tyme, I besech our lord to
breth of his holy spirite into the readers brest, which inwardly may
25 tech hym in hart, without whome litle availeth all that all the
mowthes of the world were able to tech in mens eares / And thus good
Cosyn fare well, till god bryng vs together agayne, eyther here or in
hevyn / Amen /

Finis

---

3 myn] my L *1553 1573*   3–4 begynne I] I begin *1553 1573*   10 of your good] for
your good *1553 1573*; or] *canc. B, om.* Z   11 But now] and now L *1553*   13 thentent]
the intente *1557*   15 own] *om.* L *1553 1573*   23–24 to breth] to *om. 1557*; breth]
final e *added B*; into the] in the L *1553*   29 Finis] *om.* L

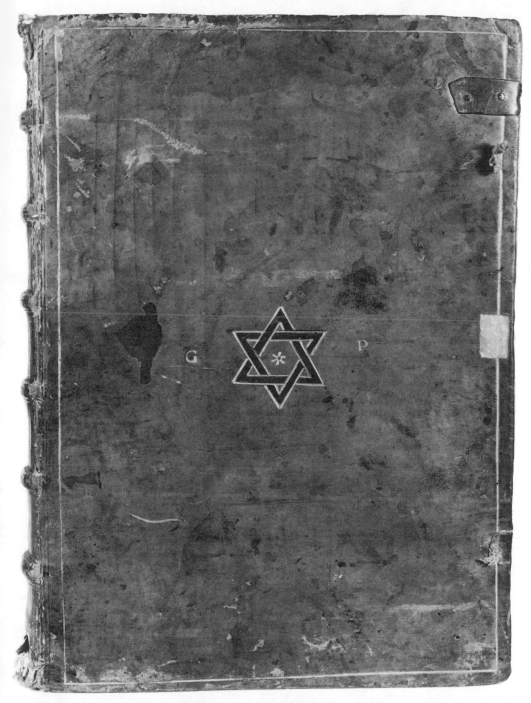

PLATE VI. Front Cover of the Corpus Christi College MS of *A Dialogue of Comfort* (reduced)

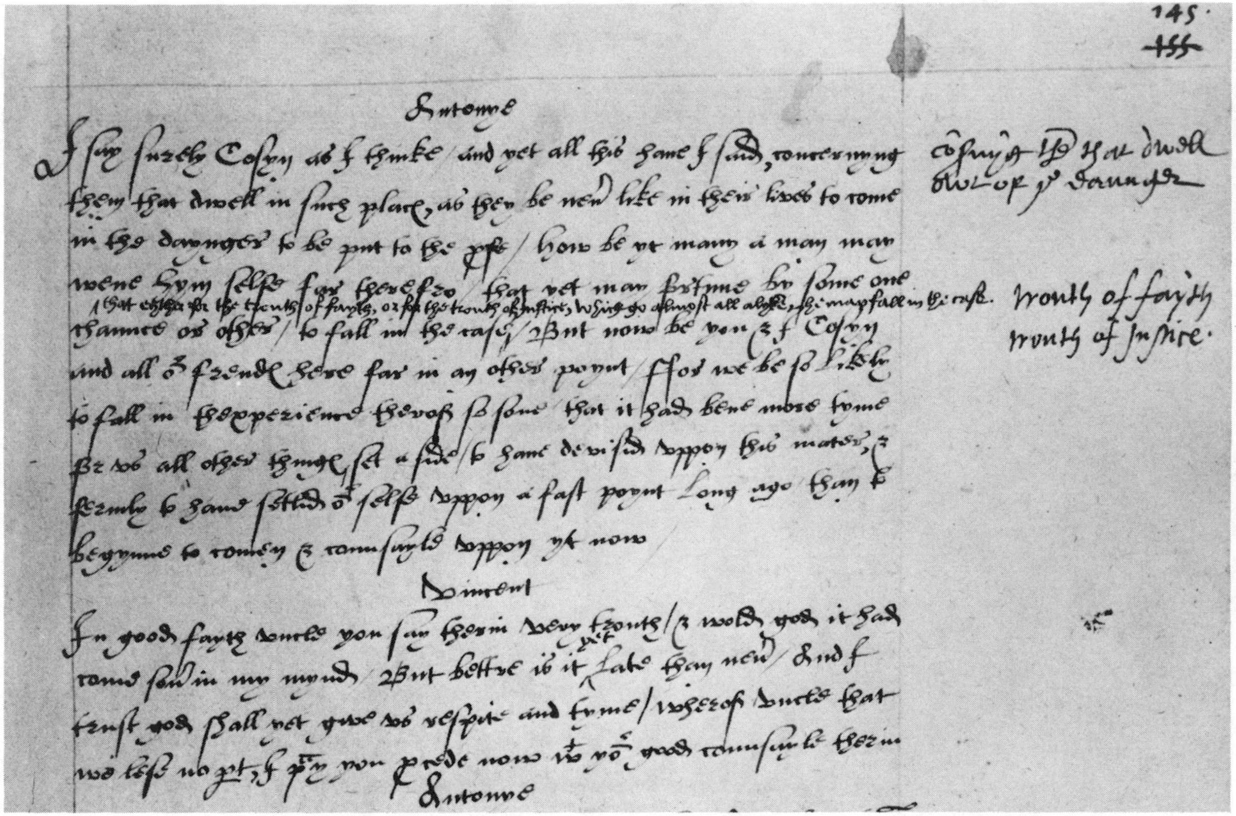

PLATE VII. Corpus Christi College MS: fol. 145 (detail: reduced)

than those faythles, or feble faythed folke', ꝑ to avoyd
the payn so fals the lesse', and so shorte', fall in ꝭ stede
therof in to payn', a thowsand thowsand tymes more'
horryble', and of whych terryble torment they be
sure', they shall never have end.

Thus matter Cosyn lacketh no I beleve', but eyther full
fayth, or suffycyent myndyng. Ffor I thynke on my
fayth yf we have the grace verely to beleve yt, and
offen to thynke well theroy, the feare' of all ꝭ cruell
ꝑsequutyon, wyth all that mych dampe devyll were' able
to make theym doo in the forsyng vs to forsake' owr
fayth, shold never be able to turne' vs. **Vyncent**.
By my trowth vncle', I thynke yt vs as yow saye, Ffor
surely yf we would as offen thynck on these' paynes in hell
as we be very lothe to doo, and seke' vs pevyshe' pastymes
of purpose', to putt suche heavy thyng owt of owr thought,
thys one poynte alone, were' able ynough to make I
thynke' many a martyr,

The consyderacon of the ioyes of heaven,
shold make vs for chryst sake, abyde and endure
any paynfull death, The xxxvijᵗͪ Chapyter
~ ~ **Anthony** ~

Forsoth Cosyn yf we were' suche, as we should be
I would seint for very shame, in exhortacyon to ꝭ
kepyng of chryst fayth, speake' of the paynes of hell. I
would rather putt vs in mynd, of the ioyes of heaven
the pleasure' wherof we should be more glad to gett, than
we should be to flye and scape all the paynes in hell
But surely god in that thyng wherin he maye' seme' most

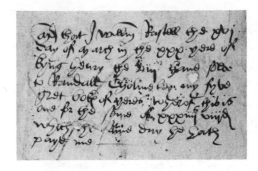

A. Rastell's memorandum of sale of the Year Books (reduced)

B. Marginalia in the Year Books, probably by Rastell (Hen. VI, 19, fol. 38; Hen. VIII, 12, fol. 1)

C. Footnote by *B* in the Corpus Christi MS, fol. 194 (reduced)

D. Interlineation by *B* in the Corpus Christi MS, fol. 188ᵛ (reduced)

PLATE IX. Examples of Handwriting by William Rastell (?)

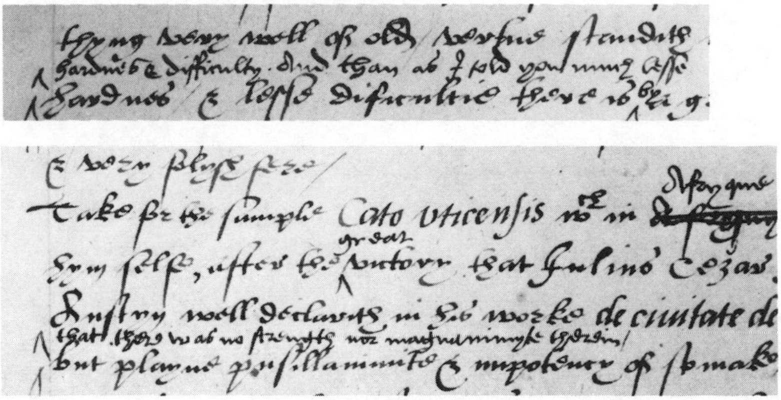

A. Interlineations by *B* in the Corpus Christi MS, fols. 60, 101ᵛ (reduced)

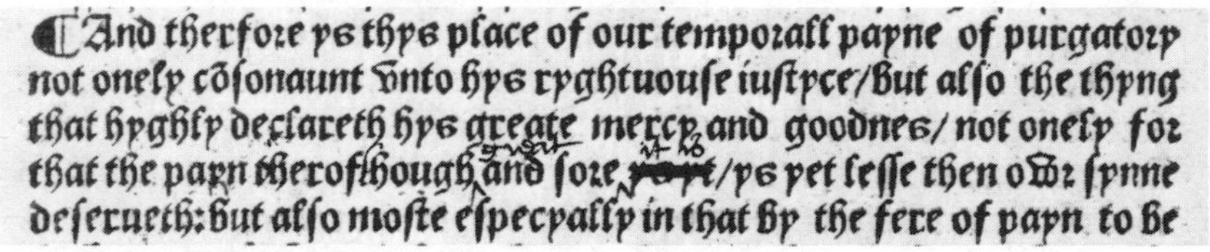

B. Interlineation in the printer's copy of More's *Supplycacyon*, fol. 24ᵛ (reduced)

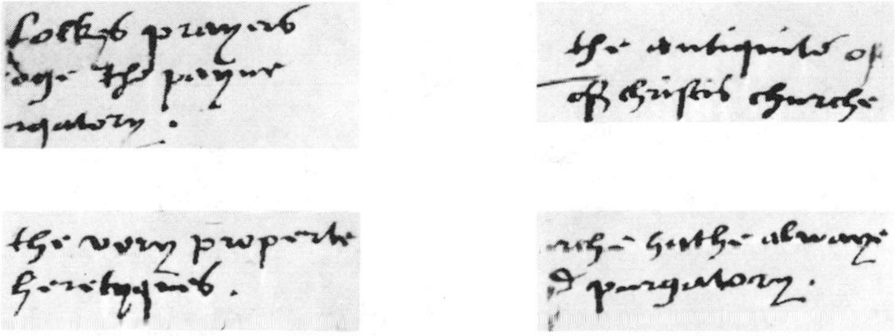

C. Marginalia in the printer's copy of More's *Supplycacyon*, fols. 13, 24ᵛ, 31ᵛ, 35 (reduced)

D. William Rastell's signatures in the Year Books

PLATE X. Examples of Handwriting by William Rastell (?)

SVLIMAN·OTOMAN·REX·TVRC·X·

PLATE XI. Suleiman the Magnificent: engraving by Agostino Veneziano, 1535 (reduced)

Cum Priuilegio

IMAGO SVLEYMANNI TVRCARVM IMP. IN ORIENTE, VNICI SELIMY FILII, QVI AN. DO. M.D.XX. PATRI IN IMPERIO SVCCESSIT: QVO ETI: AM ANNO CAROLVS. V. MAXÆMYLIANI CÆSARIS NEPOS AQVISGRANI IN OCCIDENTE CORONATVS EST CHRISTIAN: IMP: A MELCHIO: RE LORICH FLENSBVRGENSI, HOLSATIO, ANTIQVITATIS STVDIOSISS. CONSTANTINOPOLI, AN.M.DLIX, MEN. FEB, DIE XV, VERISSIMÈ EXPRESSA.

PLATE XII. Suleiman the Magnificent: engraving by Melchior Lorch
after a drawing made in 1559 (reduced)

PLATE XIII. Lady Jane Dormer, Duchess of Feria, by Alonso Sánchez Coello, 1563
(reduced)

COMMENTARY

COMMENTARY

The following bibliography and list of abbreviations includes the titles of all works cited frequently in the Commentary and in the Introduction. The titles of works referred to only once or occurring only in a brief cluster of references are given in full as they occur. Works frequently cited in the Commentary are referred to by short title only, both the first time they occur and in all subsequent references. Unless noted to the contrary, quotations from classical authors are taken from the readily available texts of the Loeb edition, which are cited here with the permission of the Harvard University Press. The abbreviations used to designate classical texts are those employed in *The Oxford Classical Dictionary* (Oxford, 1949), cited as *OCD*. Passages from More's English works not yet edited for the *Complete Works* are cited from the English Works of 1557 (*EW*), except for the text of the *Apology*, where references are to the edition by A. I. Taft (1930). Quotations from More's *De Tristitia Christi* (formerly referred to as the "*Expositio Passionis*") are taken from the new edition of the holograph manuscript of this work (ed. Clarence Miller, Vol. 14 in the *Complete Works*), now in press and scheduled for publication in 1976. A table of corresponding pages, which allows the reader to correlate the present text with the text of *A Dialogue of Comfort* in the 1557 *English Works*, is provided in Appendix C. The marginalia in the Corpus Christi MS., in *EW*, and in John Fowler's edition of the *Dialogue of Comfort* (Antwerp, 1573) are given in Appendix A. References to Erasmus' *Adagia* follow the system developed by Margaret M. Phillips, *The 'Adages' of Erasmus* (Cambridge, 1964), p. xiii. Thus "Adag. I. II. lvii" refers to the first thousand, second hundred, number 57, and enables the reader to locate the adage in any of the collected editions as well as in the *Opera Omnia* (Leyden, 1703–1706). Cross references within the Commentary are selective in nature and may be supplemented by reference to the Index.

Scriptural references pose a particular problem. In *A Dialogue of Comfort* More frequently seems to quote scripture with an eye not only to the particular verse cited, but also to the immediate context in which the verse appears. A number of these contextual allusions are obvious enough to anyone familiar with the Bible. Others, however, are more suggestive than certain. The temptation to pursue these possible dimensions of meaning in the Commentary has been difficult to resist. In the notes that follow, however, only the most obvious echoes have been called to the reader's attention, without further comment; numerous others have been passed over in silence. The reader is referred to the discussion of this general problem in the Introduction. Scriptural references are in all cases to *Biblia Sacra, Vulgatae Editionis Sixti V. et Clementis VIII. Jussu Recognita atque Edita* (London, 1865), with the exception of the Psalms, which in this edition do not follow the normal numbering of the Vulgate. References to the Psalms, therefore, are taken from *Biblia Sacra iuxta Vulgatam Clementiam*, ed. A. Colunga and L. Turrado (Madrid, 1959). When More's quotations do not differ from the Vulgate, a simple reference to chapter and verse is provided; when variation occurs, the quotation has been checked against the *Biblia Latina* of 1498, which in most passages agrees with the Vulgate. In those cases where the *Biblia Latina* differs from the Vulgate the *Biblia* reading is also noted. More's quotations from the Psalms, where they differ from the Vulgate, have also been checked against the text of the *Psalter* that comprises part of his *Prayer Book*. With all biblical quotations, full use has been made (and our debt here is gratefully acknowledged) of G. Marc'hadour, *Thomas More et la Bible* (Paris, 1969) and the same author's *The Bible in the Works of St. Thomas More*, 5 vols. (Nieuwkoop, 1969–71).

All references in the Corpus Christi, 1557 and 1573 marginalia, listed in Appendix A, have been checked against the Commentary. Where the marginal reference is incorrect, the error has been noted. Where the marginal reference is unnecessary or redundant (as in certain scriptural references), it has been passed over in silence. References to volumes 2, *15*, *23*, *24*, and *26* in the *Patrologia Latina* are from the 1845 edition. The pagination in later reissues of these volumes varies from that of the original edition.

One final word of caution: in using these or any other glosses one should always keep in mind the somber warning of Don Quixote: "'A wise friend of mine,' said Don Quixote, 'was of the opinion that no one should weary himself by writing glosses; and the reason, he said, was that the gloss could never come near to the text; and that often, or most times, the gloss was a long way from the intention and purpose of the theme set; and, furthermore, that the rules for glossing were too stringent, for they allowed no interrogations, nor '*said he*' nor '*shall say*', nor making verbs of nouns, nor changing the verse; with other restrictions and limitations by which glossers are bound'" (trans. J. M. Cohen, II, xviii).

BIBLIOGRAPHY AND SHORT TITLES

Adams, R. P., *The Better Part of Valor: More, Erasmus, Colet and Vives on Humanism, War, and Peace, 1496–1535*, Seattle, 1962.
Aesopi Phrygis, et Aliorum Fabulae, ed. L. Valla, Erasmus, Angelus Politianus, et al., Lugduni, 1540. Cited as *Fabulae*.
Aesopi Phrygis Vita et Fabellae, cum latina interpretatione, Basel, 1517.
Allen. *See* Erasmus.
Aquinas, Thomas, *Summa Theologica*, 3 vols., Cambridge, 1964. Cited as *ST*.
Arbesmann, Rudolph, "The Concept of Christus Medicus in St. Augustine," *Traditio, 10* (1954), 1–28.
Aristotle's De Anima and the Commentary of St. Thomas Aquinas, tr. K. Foster and S. Humphries, London, 1951.
Bacon, Roger, *De Retardatione Accidentium Senectutis*, ed. A. G. Little and E. Worthington, Oxford, 1928.
Batman, Stephen, *Batman vppon Bartholome, his Booke De Proprietatibus Rerum*, London, 1582. Cited as "Batman."
Battenhouse, Roy, *Marlowe's Tamburlaine*, Nashville, Tenn., 1941.
Baumer, F. L., "England, the Turk, and the Common Corps of Christendom," *American Historical Review, 50* (1944), 26–48.
Bergenroth, G. A., ed., *Calendar of Letters, Despatches, and State Papers ... Between England and Spain, Preserved ... at Simancas and Elsewhere* [1485–1553], 13 vols., London, 1862–1954. Cited as *Spanish Calendar*.
Bernard de Clairvaux, *Lent with Saint Bernard: A Devotional Commentary on Psalm Ninety-one*, tr. and ed. by a Religious of C.S.M.V., London, 1953.
Beza, Theodore, *Novum D. N. Iesu Christi Testamentum*, n. p., 1557.
[*Biblia*] *cum glosa ordinaria et expositione lyre literali et morali: necnon additionibus ac replicis ...* 6 vols., John Peter and John Froben, Basel, 1498. Bible text interlined with the Gloss of Anselmus Laudunensis, the Glosses of Walafrid Strabo and others, the Postillae and Moralitates of Nicholas de Lyra, the Additiones of Paulus de Sancta Maria (Bishop of Burgos, 1354–1435), with Matthias Doring's replies. Cited as *Biblia Latina*.
Biblia Sacra iuxta Vulgatam Clementinam, ed. A. Colunga and L. Turrado, Madrid, 1959.
Biblia Sacra, Vulgatae Editionis, Sixti V. et Clementis VIII. Jussu Recognita atque Edita, London, 1865. Cited as "Vulgate."

Bibliotheca Sanctorum, 12 vols., Istituto Giovanni XXIII, Pontificia
Università Lateranense, Rome, 1961–69.
Blackburn, E. B., "The Legacy of 'Prester John' by Damião á Goes and
John More," *Moreana*, *14* (1967), 37–98.
Bodin, Jean, *Heptaplomeres*, ed. L. Noack, Paris, 1857.
Boland, Paschal, *The Concept of Discretio Spirituum in John Gerson's De
Probatione Spirituum and De Distinctione Verarum Visionum a Falsis*, Wash-
ington, D.C., 1959.
Bridgett, T. E., *Life and Writings of Blessed Thomas More*, London, 1891.
Briquet, Charles M., *Les Filigranes: Dictionnaire Historique des Marques du Papier*,
4 vols., Geneva, 1907. Facsimile, ed. A. Stevenson, Amsterdam, 1968.
Byrom, H. J., "Richard Tottell—His Life and Work," *The Library* (4th
Series), *8* (1927–8), 199–232.
The Cambridge Modern History, ed. A. W. Ward, G. W. Prothero, and
S. Leathes, 13 vols., London, 1902–11.
Castelli, Alberto, tr. and ed., *Il Dialogo del Conforto nella Tribolazioni*, Roma,
1970. Cited as "Castelli."
The Catholic Encyclopedia, 15 vols., New York, 1907–12.
Cavanaugh, John, "The Saint Stephen Motif in Saint Thomas More's
Thought," *Moreana*, *8* (1965), 59–64.
Cavendish, George, *The Life and Death of Cardinal Wolsey*, ed. Richard S.
Sylvester, London, 1959, *EETS*, Original Series, no. 243. Cited as
"Cavendish, *Life of Wolsey*."
Caxton's Aesop, ed. R. T. Lenaghan, Cambridge, Mass., 1967. Cited as
"Caxton."
Chambers, R. W., *Thomas More*, London, 1935. Cited as "Chambers,
Thomas More."
Chew, Samuel C., *The Crescent and the Rose*, New York, 1937.
Creasy, Edward S., *History of the Ottoman Turks*, ed. Zeine N. Zeine, Beirut,
1961.
CW. See More.
Daniel, N. A., *Islam and the West: The Making of an Image*, Edinburgh, 1960.
Dante Alighieri, *Opere*, ed. E. More and P. Toynbee, Oxford, 1924.
Davis, D. B., *The Problem of Slavery in Western Culture*, Ithaca, N.Y., 1966.
Delcourt, Joseph, *Essai sur la langue de Sir Thomas More*, Paris, 1914.
Cited as "Delcourt."
DNB. Dictionary of National Biography, 63 vols., London, 1885–1900.
DTC. Dictionnaire de théologie catholique, 15 vols., Paris, 1908–50.
Du Cange, Charles Du Fresne, *Glossarium Mediae et Infimae Latinitatis*,
ed. L. Favre, 10 vols., Paris 1937–38.
Dyce. See Skelton.
Einstein, Lewis, *The Italian Renaissance in England*, New York, 1913.
Erasmus, Desiderius, *The Colloquies of Erasmus*, ed. Craig Thompson,
Chicago, 1965.
———, *Opera Omnia*, ed. J. Clericus, 10 vols., Leyden, 1703–06. Cited as
"Erasmus, *Opera*."

———, *Opus Epistolarum Des. Erasmi Roterodami*, ed. P. S. Allen, H. M. Allen, *et al.*, 12 vols., Oxford, 1906–58. Cited as "Allen."

EW. See More.

Fabule Esopi cum Commento, London, 1503.

Fischer-Galati, S., *Ottoman Imperialism and German Protestantism, 1521–1555*, Cambridge, Mass., 1959.

Flete, William, "Remedies against Temptations," ed. E. Colledge and N. Chadwick, *Archivio Italiano per la Storia della Pieta, 14* (1968), 201–40.

Fowler, John, ed., *A Dialogue of Cumfort against Tribulation*, Antwerp, 1573. Cited as "Fowler" or *1573.*

Fumée, M., *The Historie of the Troubles of Hungarie*, tr. R. C., Gentleman, London, 1600. Cited as "Fumée."

Galen, *Opera Omnia in Medicorum Graecorum Opera quae extant*, ed. C. G. Kühn, 26 vols., Lipsiae, 1821–30. Cited as "Galen, *Opera*."

Gerson, Jean, *Oeuvres Complètes*, ed. P. Glorieux, 3 vols., Paris, 1960–.

———, *Opera Omnia*, ed. M. L. Ellies du Pin, 5 vols., Antwerp, 1706. Cited as "Gerson, *Opera*."

Gibson, R. W. and Patrick, J. Max, *St. Thomas More: A Preliminary Bibliography of His Works and of Moreana to the Year 1750*, New Haven, 1961. Cited as "Gibson."

Gilson, Étienne, *The Mystical Theology of St. Bernard*, tr. A. H. C. Downes, London, 1940.

Green, Paul D., "Suicide, Martyrdom, and Thomas More," *Studies in the Renaissance, 19* (1972), 135–55.

Hackett, Benedict, "William Flete," *The Month, 26* (1961), 68–80.

Hallett, Philip E., ed., *A Dialogue of Comfort against Tribulation*, London, 1937. Cited as "Hallett."

Harpsfield, Nicholas, *The Life and Death of Sir Thomas More*, ed. E. V. Hitchcock, *EETS*, Original Series, no. 186, London, 1932. Cited as "Harpsfield."

Hazlitt, W. Carew, ed., *Brand's Popular Antiquities of Great Britain, Faiths and Folklore; a Dictionary of National Beliefs, Superstitions, and Popular Customs*, 2 vols., London, 1905.

Heresies. See More.

Hervieux, Léopold, *Les Fabulistes Latins: depuis le Siècle d'Auguste jusqu'à la fin du Moyen Age*, 5 vols., Paris, 1893–99.

Inalcik, Halil, *The Ottoman Empire: The Classical Age, 1300–1600*, tr. N. Itzkowitz and C. Imber, London, 1973.

The Interpreter's Bible, ed. G. A. Buttrick, *et al.*, 12 vols., New York and Nashville, 1952–57.

Jovius, Paulus, *A Shorte Treatise vpon the Turkes Chronicles*, tr. Peter Ashton, London, 1546. Cited as "Jovius."

Jungmann, Joseph A., S. J., *The Mass of the Roman Rite: Its Origins and Development*, tr. Francis A. Brunner, 2 vols., New York, 1951–55.

Juvenal, *Satyrographi Opus*, ed. J. B. Ascensius, Venice, 1523.

à Kempis, Thomas, *The Imitation of Christ*, tr. Richard Whitford, ed. E. J. Klein, New York, 1941.

Kidd, B. J., *Documents Illustrative of the Continental Reformation*, Oxford, 1911.

Kuhn, Joaquin, "The Function of Psalm 90 in Thomas More's *A Dialogue of Comfort*," *Moreana*, *22* (1969), 61–67.

à Lapide, Cornelius, S. J., *Commentarii in IV. Evangelia*, 2 vols., Augustae Vind and Herbipoli, 1747.

LP. Letters and Papers, Foreign and domestic, of the Reign of Henry VIII, ed. J. S. Brewer, James Gairdner, and R. H. Brodie, 21 vols., London, 1862–1932.

Luther, Martin, *Works*, ed. Jaroslav Pelikan, H. T. Lehmann, *et al.*, 55 vols., Saint Louis and Philadelphia, 1955–71.

Lycosthenes, Conrad, *Prodigiorum ac Ostentorum Chronicon*, Basel, 1557.

Malleus Maleficarum, Lugduni, 1584. Tr. M. Summers, London, 1948.

Manzalaoui, Mahmoud, "'Syria' in the *Dialogue of Comfort*," *Moreana*, *8* (1965), 21–27.

Marc'hadour, G., *The Bible in the Works of St. Thomas More*, 5 vols., Nieuwkoop, 1969–71. Cited as "Marc'hadour, *The Bible*."

———, *Thomas More et la Bible*, Paris, 1969.

———, "Three Tudor Editors of Thomas More," in *Editing Sixteenth Century Texts*, ed. R. J. Schoeck, Toronto, 1966, pp. 59–71. Cited as "Marc'hadour, Editing."

———, "Review of *Il Dialogo del Conforto nelle Tribolazione*, tr. and ed. Alberto Castelli," *Moreana*, *29* (1971), 83–91.

Miles, Leland, ed., *A Dialogue of Comfort against Tribulation*, Bloomington and London, 1965. Cited as "Miles."

———, "Patristic Comforters in More's *Dialogue of Comfort*," *Moreana*, *8* (1965), 9–20.

More, Thomas, *The Apologye of Syr Thomas More, Knyght*, ed. A. I. Taft, *EETS*, Original Series, no. 180, London, 1930. Cited as "Taft, *Apologye*.

———, *The Complete Works of St. Thomas More*: Vol. 2, *The History of King Richard III*, ed. R. S. Sylvester; Vol. 3, Part 1, *Translations of Lucian*, ed. C. R. Thompson; Vol. 4, *Utopia*, ed. Edward Surtz and J. H. Hexter; Vol. 5, *Responsio ad Lutherum*, ed. John Headley and tr. Sister Scholastica Mandeville; Vol. 8, *Confutation*, ed. L. Schuster, R. Marius, J. Lusardi, and R. J. Schoeck; Vol. 13, *Treatise on the Passion*, etc., ed. Garry Haupt; Vol. 14, *De Tristitia Christi*, ed. Clarence Miller; New Haven and London, 1963–. Cited as *CW 2*, *CW 3*, *1*, *CW 4*, *CW 5*, *CW 8*, *CW 13* and *CW 14*.

———, *The Correspondence of Sir Thomas More*, ed. Elizabeth F. Rogers, Princeton, 1947. Cited as "Rogers."

———, *The Dialogue Concerning Heresies*, London, J. Rastell, 1529. Cited from the 1557 *English Works* (*EW*).

———, *The Latin Epigrams of Thomas More*, ed. L. Bradner and C. A. Lynch, Chicago, 1953. Cited as *Epigrams*.

————, *Omnia, quae hucusque ad manus nostras pervenerunt, Latina opera*, Louvain, 1565.

————, *St. Thomas More: Selected Letters*, ed. Elizabeth F. Rogers, New Haven and London, 1961. Cited as *SL*.

————, *Sir Thomas More, Selections*, ed. H. M. Allen and P. S. Allen, Oxford, 1924.

————, *Thomas More's Prayer Book*, ed. Louis L. Martz and R. S. Sylvester, New Haven and London, 1969. Cited as *Prayer Book*.

————, *The Workes . . . in the English Tonge*, London, 1557. Cited as *EW* or *1557*.

Navagero, Andreas, *Opera*, ed. G. Antonio Volpi, Padua, 1718.

New Catholic Encyclopedia, 15 vols., New York, 1967.

Newton, Thomas, *A Notable Historie of the Saracens . . . Drawen out of Augustine Curio and sundry other good Authours*, London, 1575. Cited as "Newton."

NT. New Testament (generic reference.)

OCD. Oxford Classical Dictionary, Oxford, 1961.

ODEP. Oxford Dictionary of English Proverbs, Oxford, 1960.

OED. The Oxford English Dictionary, 13 vols., Oxford, 1961.

O'Shea, W. J., *The Worship of the Church*, London, 1957.

OT. Old Testament (generic reference).

Pace, Richard, *De Fructu qui ex Doctrina Percipitur*, ed. and tr. F. Manley and R. S. Sylvester, New York, 1967, *Renaissance Text Series*, 2. Cited as "Pace, *De Fructu*."

Patrides, C. A., "'The Bloody and Cruell Turke': the Background of a Renaissance Commonplace," *Studies in the Renaissance*, *10* (1963), 126–35.

Paulus Diaconis, *History of the Langobards*, tr. W. D. Foulke, New York, 1906.

Perry, B. E., ed., *Aesopica*, Urbana, Ill., 1952.

PG. Patrologiae Cursus Completus: Series Graeca, ed. J. P. Migne, 161 vols., Paris, 1857–66. Cited as *PG* by volume and column.

PL. Patrologiae Cursus Completus: Series Latina, ed. J. P. Migne, 221 vols., Paris, 1844–1903. Cited as *PL* by volume and column.

Reynolds, E. E., *St. Thomas More*, London, 1953.

————, *The Field Is Won*, London, 1968.

Ro. Ba., *The Lyfe of Syr Thomas More*, ed. E. V. Hitchcock and P. E. Hallett, *EETS*, Original Series, no. 222, London, 1950.

Rogers. *See* More.

Roper, W., *The Lyfe of Sir Thomas Moore, Knighte*, *EETS*, Original Series, no. 197, London, 1935. Cited as "Roper."

Schoeck, R. J., "Thomas More's *Dialogue of Comfort* and the Problem of the Real Grand Turk," *English Miscellany*, *20* (1969), 23–37.

Schwoebel, Robert, *The Shadow of the Crescent*, Nieuwkoop, 1967. Cited as "Schwoebel."

Seneca, Lucius Annaeus, *Opera Omnia*, ed. M. N. Bouillet, 9 vols., Paris, 1827–32.

Skelton, John, *The Poetical Works*, ed. Alexander Dyce, 2 vols., Boston, 1856. Cited as "Dyce."

SL. See More.

Slessarev, Vsevolod, *Prester John*, Minneapolis, 1959.

Southern, R. W., *Western Views of Islam in the Middle Ages*, Cambridge, Mass., 1962.

Spanish Calendar, See Bergenroth.

ST. See Aquinas.

Stapleton, Thomas, *The Life . . . of Sir Thomas More*, tr. Philip E. Hallett, London, 1928. Cited as "Stapleton."

State Papers, King Henry the Eighth, Published under the Authority of his Majesty's Commission, 11 vols., London, 1830–52. Cited as *State Papers, Henry VIII.*

STC. A Short-Title Catalogue of Books Printed in England, Scotland and Ireland, 1475–1640, London, 1926.

The Subtyle Fables of Esope in Englysshe, London, 1551.

Surtz, E. L., S. J., *The Works and Days of John Fisher*, Cambridge, Mass., 1967.

Sylvester, Richard S., ed., *St. Thomas More: Action and Contemplation, Proceedings of the Symposium Held at St. John's University, October 9–10, 1970*, New Haven and London, 1972.

Taft, *Apologye. See* More.

Tilley, M., *A Dictionary of the Proverbs in England in the Sixteenth and Seventeenth Centuries*, Ann Arbor, 1950. Cited as "Tilley."

Topsell, Edward, *The History of Four-footed Beasts, Serpents, and Insects*, London, 1658.

Tractatus quidam de Turcis, Nuremberg, 1474.

Verlinden, Charles, *L'Esclavage dans L'Europe Medievale*, vol. 1 of ongoing series, Brugge, 1955–.

Vogt, G. M., "Gleanings for the History of a Sentiment: *Generositas Virtus, non Sanguis*," *Journal of English and Germanic Philology*, 24 (1925), 101–24.

Whiting, B. J. and H. S., *Proverbs, Sentences and Proverbial Phrases from English Writings Mainly before 1500*, Cambridge, Mass., 1968. Cited as "Whiting."

3/1 **comfort.** It is essential to recall the derivation of this word from the Latin *confortare*, "to strengthen," for the basic meaning which More assigns to "comfort," whether as a noun or verb or in other forms, relates to this derivation, in the primary and now obsolete senses defined by the *OED:* "comfort," *v.* 1 "To strengthen (morally or spiritually); to encourage, hearten, inspirit, incite." The secondary meanings of "relief or aid in want, pain, sickness, etc.," "relief or support in mental distress or affliction; consolation, solace, soothing" ("comfort," *sb.* 4, 5) are also present, but usually as related to the root.

More himself seemed to think of "comfort" more specifically as an attribute of hope. Cf. Antony's formal definition of the term toward the end of Book I (below, 68/12–16): "comfort . . . is properly taken by them that take it right / rather for the consolacion of good hope, that men take in their hart / of some good growing toward them / than for a present pleasure with which the body is delitid & tyklyd for the while." Cf. also More's letter to Margaret cited below, 22/15–20 and n. and his comment on Gal. 5:22–23 in the *Confutation:* "by these thynges as very good tokens of grace the spyryte of god bereth recorde vnto our spyryte, that is to wyt geueth our spyryte the comforte of good hope, as longe as we so do, that we be the sonnes of god" (*CW 8*, 757/23–26). In other contexts More speaks of the Holy Spirit as the "Paraclete," which he translates in one of its traditional meanings as "Comforter"; see below, n. to 5/3–7. For the *consolatio* tradition and the importance of the theological virtue of hope to the overall structure and meaning of *A Dialogue of Comfort*, see the Introduction.

3/2–6 **made by . . . Englysh.** In his final speech in *A Dialogue of Comfort* Vincent promises to put Antony's counsel in remembrance "not in our own langage onely, but in the Almayne tong to" (320/15–16), thus linking Hungary and Germany, Turk and Protestant, and glancing at a progress or *translatio* of heresy and persecution for the faith. This concluding device would seem to have been prepared for earlier in Book III where Vincent mentions having visited Germany and speaks of his proficiency in both German and Latin: "my wordes beyng but a stranger, went yet with some grace in the Almayne tonge, wherin lettyng my laten alone, me listid to shew my connyng" (214/3–6). In his polemical works More commonly associated the Protestants of Germany with the Turks (e.g., *Supplication, EW*, sig. v₂v, and *Confutation, CW 8*, 266/9–19), but if he had intended to imply in *A Dialogue of Comfort* a progress of persecution westward toward England under the Great Turk Henry VIII, he seems to have altered the pattern here in the title by dropping German and substituting French instead. The change adds to the verisimilitude of the work since French or Italian would have been a more normal channel in the ordinary course of Renaissance translation into English. It also tends to universalize the book, making it applicable to all people throughout Europe and not just those under the immediate pressure of persecution.

3/7 **Antony & Vyncent.** This heading is crowded uncomfortably into the space between the title and the beginning of the dialogue. The hand is certainly not *A* and probably not *B;* its peculiar formation of the capital letter "A" is similar to that found in the marginal comment "Anna" on fol. 77ᵛ. This hand has therefore been designated as *E?* See the Introduction. The manuscript originally began without any names of speakers.

For speculation on the names, see Marc'hadour, *Thomas More et la Bible,* p. 334, and his review of Castelli in *Moreana, 29* (1971), 83–91. In general Marc'hadour associates Antony with St. Anthony the Great: "a bridge between the church of the martyrs and that of the confessors, he inflicted upon himself the hardships that an earlier generation had endured in imperial jails or mines. And in sixteenth-century Christendom, the time had come for confessors to face again the threat of martyrdom" (*Moreana, 29* [1971], 88). Marc'hadour associates Vincent with the Latin *vincere,* "to be victorious" or "to overcome," and points particularly to the verses in Rev. referring to martyrs, e.g. 2:7: "Vincenti dabo edere de ligno vitae" and 2:17: "Vincenti dabo manna absconditum," which More quotes frequently toward the end of Book III (below, 309/18–310/16).

3/15–16 **to lyft . . . lyfe.** Marc'hadour notes that the phrase may be a bitterly ironic echo of the *Sursum corda* of the mass and Col. 3:1–2: "Igitur, si consurrexistis cum Christo: quae sursum sunt quaerite, ubi Christus est in dextera Dei sedens: quae sursum sunt sapite, non quae super terram." "With hallowed words in his mouth," Marc'hadour continues, "the worldly comforter is actually keeping the heart of his sick friend glued to the earth" (*The Bible,* Part IV, p. 129).

3/25–26 **as he . . . dayes.** It is impossible to say precisely what campaigns Vincent has in mind here since Hungary was famous throughout Europe for waging almost continuous war with the Turks for over a century. In 1470, for example, when Antony would presumably have been in his early twenties (see below, n. to 7/29–30), "the Turkes army entred into *Hungarie* spoyling and robbing as farre as Zagabria, and carried away with them .10000. Prisoners." In 1473 they invaded Hungary again and "spoyled al the Cities neere the water side." In 1476 King Matthias captured a "strong Forte" from the Turks "at the Ryuer of Saue." In 1479 Mahomet II invaded the country once again and captured "a great multitude" of Christian prisoners. In 1492, when Antony would have been in his forties, King Matthias captured Sabatrum from the Turks, and in 1493 the Turks led another army into Hungary "by whom were slayne vii.M. Hungarians: and for testimony of this spoyle and ouerthrow geeuen to the Christians, they sent many Christian mens Heades with their noses cut of and in loathsome wise disfigured, to *Constantinople*" (Newton, fols. 132ᵛ–136). After the 1490s the Hungarians lived in relative peace until the invasion of Suleiman the Magnificent in 1521. Cf. below, 109/29–110/1 and n.

4/2 **very . . . orphanes.** *B*'s emendation of "very" to "sory" (followed by
Ƶ) is persuasive, especially in view of the alliteration with "sort." Yet a
scribe would not easily misread one word for the other, and "very" is
frequently used throughout *A Dialogue of Comfort* in the sense of "true" or
"truly." See exactly the same usage at 285/15, "very nydeot folys"; also
70/30, "very comfort"; 130/9, "very strength"; 192/30, "very batayle";
263/17, "a very prisoner in very prison playnly"; 277/27, "so very a
childish fantasye." In the case of 4/2 the definition of the *OED* ("very,"
A. *adj.* I. 1) is especially appropriate: "Really or truly entitled to the
name or designation . . . properly so called or designated."

4/7 **Cosyn.** I.e., nephew; cf. above, 3/9. The *OED* ("cousin," *sb.* 1)
defines this obsolete use of the term as "a collateral relative more distant
than a brother or sister; a kinsman or kinswoman, a relative; formerly
very frequently applied to a nephew or niece."

4/12 **deth . . . hell.** The traditional four last things of the church. Cf.
More's unfinished treatise on the subject (written about 1522) entitled *A
Treatyce (vnfynshed) vpon these wordes of holye Scrypture, Memorare nouissima, &
in eternum non peccabis. Remember the last thynges, and thou shalt neuer synne* (*EW*,
sig. e₄v–fg₈). Possibly because of the subject matter, the *Four Last Things*
contains a great many verbal parallels to *A Dialogue of Comfort* and similar
references and allusions, more than in any of More's other works except
those written in the Tower.

4/15–17 **for as . . . long.** Cf. "a yonge man may die soone, and an olde
manne cannot live long, but within a litle while die the tone may, the
tother muste" (*Four Last Things, EW*, sig. e₈). The saying probably has
its source in Cicero's *De Senectute*, from which More quotes directly in
the next sentence. Cf. 19, 68: "At sperat adulescens diu se victurum,
quod sperare idem senex non potest." Cf. also below, 86/7–10, where
Antony again repeats the statement and connects it with the "very trew
proverbe / that as sone commeth a yong sheps skyn to the market as an
old."

4/17–19 **as Tullye . . . more.** In *Sen.* 7, 24, Cicero mentions the farmers
of the Sabine country, who are never absent from their fields during
planting and harvest: "Quamquam in aliis minus hoc mirum est, nemo
enim est tam senex qui se annum non putet posse vivere; sed idem in eis
elaborant, quae sciunt nihil ad se omnino pertinere: 'serit arbores, quae
alteri saeculo prosint.'" More cites the same passage for the same purpose
in his *Four Last Things, EW*, sig. e₈.

4/21–23. **fyer . . . grace.** In the common physiology of the Renaissance,
each man was believed to be supplied with a fixed amount of vital
moisture, which was held in delicate balance with his vital heat. Old age
was explained as a drying up of this vital moisture through its interaction
with vital heat, which feeds on it. The bodies of the aged, therefore, were

regarded as brittle and dry. Cf. "calor naturalis in humiditate existit naturali, et ab ea nutritur; et cum humiditas illa dissoluitur, calor minuitur et debilitatur" (Roger Bacon, *De Retardatione Accidentium Senectutis*, ed. A. G. Little and E. Worthington [Oxford, 1928], p. 86; see also Batman, IV, 4, 6, and *Twelfth Night*, I, iii, 65–72). More combines this with the traditional image of God's grace as dew falling on the soul in the secrecy of night, which goes back as far as Hos. 14:5 and Isa. 45:8. See, for example, *PL 202*, 721; *PL 168*, 201; *PL 184*, 264–65; and *De Tristitia*, *CW 14*, 415–16. For a similar metaphor of grace as the vital moisture in the body of the church, see *Heresies*, *EW*, sig. m₆v. Marc'hadour, *The Bible*, Part IV, pp. 135–36, cites a number of parallels from Fisher, but Fisher's development of the imagery is not quite the same as More's. As Marc'hadour observes, More's "well-known fondness for biological imagery contrasts with Fisher's preference for the realm of vegetation."

4/23–24 **by which ... heven.** Marc'hadour, *The Bible*, Part III, p. 113, notes a submerged allusion to Phil. 1:23: "desiderium habens dissolvi, et esse cum Christo," which Aquinas defines as the ultimate degree of charity or the love of man for God (*ST*, II–II, Q. 24, a. 9). For More's direct use of the passage, see below, 284/14–19 and n.

4/24–5/3 **Now ... not I.** In a letter written in the Tower, More quotes from a letter of Margaret's, "Good Father strenght my frayltie with your deuoute prayers," and he continues, "The father of heauen mote strenght thy frailtie, my good daughter and the frayltie of thy fraile father too ... That you feare your owne frailtie Marget, nothinge mislyketh me. God geue vs both twaine the grace, to dispayre of our owne self, and whole to depende and hange vpon the hope and strenght of God" (Rogers, p. 545).

5/3–7 **And he ... hym selfe.** John 14:16, 18, 25–26: "Et ego rogabo Patrem, et alium Paraclitum dabit vobis, ut maneat vobiscum in aeternum ... Non relinquam vos orphanos: veniam ad vos ... Haec locutus sum vobis, apud vos manens. Paraclitus autem Spiritus sanctus, quem mittet Pater in nomine meo, ille vos docebit omnia, et suggeret vobis omnia, quaecumque dixero vobis." Cf. also John 15:25–27. Lines 7–8 ("made ... hymselfe") conflate John 14:16 with Matt. 28:20: "Et ecce ego vobiscum sum omnibus diebus, usque ad consummationem saeculi." *Paraclete* in Greek means "advocate" or "pleader" and refers to the Holy Spirit as comforter or intercessor. Cf. *Confutation*, *CW 8*, 377/5–7: "If the spyryt of god gouernynge the chyrche, and ledynge it in to all trouth, put vs not in surety and certaynte of the trouth: howe coud he be to vs as he is named *paracletus*, that is a comforter." See also *Heresies*, *EW*, sigs. m₃–m₃v. Commenting on John 14:16, the *Biblia Latina*, 5, sig. R₄v, notes: "iste consolator non auferetur a vobis: sicut subtrahitur humanitas mea per mortem: sed eternaliter erit vobiscum hic per gratiam: sed in futuro per gloriam." Antony plays the verses against Vincent's previous reference to him as one who had been as it were "a naturall father" (4/5), who would leave his kindred after his death "a sort of very comfortles orphanes" (4/2).

5/23–25 **to stable ... see.** Cf. Rogers, pp. 538 and 560–61; *De Tristitia, CW*, *14*, 49 and 265.

5/28–29 **or els ... within.** Cf. 1 John 2:27 and John 14:26. See also *Confutation, CW 8*, 259/15–21 and 889/23–890/6.

6/6–14 **Therfor ... drounnyng.** According to Harpsfield (pp. 133–34), More's "principall drifte and scope [in the *Dialogue of Comfort*] was to stirre and prepare the mindes of englishe men manfully and couragiously to withstande, and not to shrinke at, the imminent and open persecution which he fore[sawe], and immediately folowed, against the vnitie / of the Churche and the catholike fayth / of the same." For the traditional image of the ship, see *Utopia, CW 4*, 98/25–28, and *Supplication, EW*, sigs. t$_8$ and v$_8$. It is also related to the Christian image of the ship of the church or the individual soul. Cf. Augustine: "Ecce in eo quod terrebat, naves natant, et non mergentur. Naves Ecclesias intelligimus; commeant inter tempestates, inter procellas tentationum, inter fluctus saeculi, inter animalia pusilla et magna. Gubernator est Christus in ligno crucis suae" (*PL 37*, 1380–81; see also Ambrose, *PL 14*, 387–88). The "cruel Turke" of l. 10 is Suleiman the Magnificent. For the historical background, see the Introduction.

7/1–2 **And yet ... Turkey.** In the marginalia written in his *Psalter* while he was in prison, More notes opposite Ps. 68:6–20: "in tribulacione dicendum fidelibus a Hungaris inualcscentibus turcis et multis hungarorum in turcarum perfidiam desciscentibus (to be said in [time of] tribulation by the faithful among the Hungarians when the Turks grow strong and many Hungarians fall away into the false faith of the Turks)" (*Prayer Book*, pp. 114–15, 197).
The reference in l. 3 ("confeteryd with hym") is probably to John Zapolya, one of the rival claimants to the Hungarian throne, who was suspected of being in league with the Turks. See below, n. to 8/3. More may indeed have met a representative of Zapolya, for he was attending upon Wolsey when the cardinal conferred with Zapolya's ambassador in 1527. When Wolsey questioned him, the ambassador denied "that his master had intelligence with the Turke, and had treated and practesed with him," though he admitted "that there be presently with his master two Ambassadours, sent from the Turke, who doo continually sollicite and presse him to a confederacion with the Turke: neverthelcs, abhorring that, and trusting to thayde of other Christen Princes, by good meanes delayeth and puttith over the answer" (*State Papers, Henry VIII*, *1*, 201–02, July 5, 1527). The reference in l. 4 ("this quarter") is to the vicinity of Budapest; see below, 124/15.

7/15–18 **our sauiour ... them.** Luke 23:28–30. Jesus is speaking to the women of Jerusalem, who wept for Him while He was carrying the cross:

"Filiae Jerusalem, nolite flere super me, sed super vos ipsas flete, et super filios vestros. Quoniam ecce venient dies, in quibus dicent: Beatae steriles, et ventres, qui non genuerunt, et ubera, quae non lactaverunt. Tunc incipient dicere montibus; Cadite super nos: et collibus: Operite nos." More translates *vallibus* ("valleys") rather then *collibus* ("hills"), the reading of the Vulgate. The prophecy is generally taken to refer to the end of the world, and in the early sixteenth century the Turkish threat was widely believed to signal the beginning of those days. For an entire treatise on the subject of the Turks and the Apocalypse, drawing the analogy point by point, see for example, *Tractatus quidam de Turcis*, printed by Conrad Zininger at Nuremberg in 1474. Despite the oblique allusion here, however, More makes it clear later in Book III (193/24–194/13) that he believes the last days are not yet come. The reference to Luke 13 in the marginalia of *1557* is incorrect.

7/29–30 **Grece . . . his.** In 1445 Amurath II took the Isthmus of Corinth and all the Peloponnesus. Mahomet II completed the conquest; in 1452 he sacked Athens and in the following year took Constantinople and most of the Greek Isles. For the symbolic impact of the fall of Greece on the men of the early Renaissance, cf. "The famous and renowmed Citie of *Athens*, the Uniuersitie and Nurce of all worthy Artes & Disciplines, was conquered and rased to the ground by this most cruel Tyrant the Turk, who in some places therof digged vp the very foundacions, for extreeme hatred that he bore to learning. He threw all the Bookes and Monuments that he could finde, into dyrtie Sinkes and filthiest places in the citie, and to be put to the vilest vses that could be. And if any man seemed to lament it, the same partye was streight wayes put to death" (Newton, fol. 131). For an extensive account of the fall of Constantinople and its impact on the West, see Schwoebel, pp. 1–24.

This sentence provides the best evidence of Antony's age. He was apparently born about 1445–1450 and thus would be about 80 years old at the fictional time of the dialogue. For a discussion of the ages of both Antony and Vincent, see Mahmoud Manzalaoui, "'Syria' in the *Dialogue of Comfort*," *Moreana*, *8* (1965), 21–27.

7/30–8/1 **The gret . . . to.** Kansuh Ghuri, Sultan of the Circassian Mamelukes of Syria and Egypt. In a religious war between the Sunnite and Shüte branches of Mohammedanism, Selim I invaded Persia and defeated the Shütes under Shah Ishmail on the plain of Chaldiran (1514). He then turned on Syria and Egypt under the pretext of an alliance between the Shah of Persia and the aged Kansuh Ghuri. The Mameluke army met the Ottomans in a battle fought near Aleppo (August 1516). Kansuh Ghuri was killed while trying to escape, and the surviving Mamelukes retreated to Cairo. Selim immediately occupied all the major Syrian cities and marched to Egypt, where he defeated Ashraf Tuman Bey, the successor to Kansuh Ghuri, in a battle at Reydaniya near Cairo (January 1517). Tuman Bey was captured and hung. The fall of Egypt was followed

shortly thereafter by the surrender of the remaining Mameluke strongholds in Arabia and North Africa.

More's reference to Syria rather than Egypt is something of a distortion
since Cairo was the capital of the Mameluke Empire, and Egypt was
therefore its center. See Mahmoud Manzalaoui's article on the subject in
Moreana, 8 (1965), 21–27. More probably has in mind the fact that the
first defeat in Syria led to the almost immediate collapse of the remainder
of the empire.

8/1–2 **Than . . . realme.** Belgrade was captured by Suleiman the Magnificent on August 29, 1521, shortly after he had attained the throne.
Located on the southern frontier and well known as "a sure fortresse and
defense, not onlye of Hungary, but also of all Christentie" (Jovius, fol.
103ᵛ; see also Newton, fol. 136), Belgrade had been unsuccessfully be-
sieged a number of times in the past, notably by Amurath II in 1442 and
Mahomet II in 1456. For the situation and defenses of the town, cf.
Fumée, p. 14: "On this side the river Sauus, is the castle of Zemlen, and
betweene that and the towne of Belgrade, is the mouth of Sauus, which in
that place, by reason of the entrance therof into Danubius, maketh it a
large and deepe current, which is enioyed by the towne of Belgrade, so
much renowmed for famous battailes, being fought in that place against
the Turke. . . . The Hungars call this Fortresse Nandor-Albe, and some
Albe-grecque: the ancients call it Taurinum, and at this day it is called
Greichsunneisneburg. It is placed vpon a steepe Rock, which on that side
Hungarie is seene, and at the foote thereof is the towne, hauing on the one
side Sauus, and on the other Danubius." Schwoebel (pp. 43–50) has a full
and graphic account of Mahomet II's unsuccessful siege of the city in 1456.

8/2–3 **And syns . . . kyng.** Louis II (1506–26), the only son of Vladislav
II and Anne de Candale of France. According to report he was born with
no skin on his body but survived with the help of physicians "who by their
art succoured and helped the want and defect of nature" (Fumée, p. 32).
In 1521 he was declared of age to rule and in the following year married
Maria of Austria. Paulus Jovius and most modern historians speak of him
as "a young man not all of the wyttyest, ne yet (because he was young) of
any experience" (fol. 103). In the Renaissance, he tended to be senti-
mentalized because of his youth and his early death. Cf. Andreas Navagero's epitaph in *Lusus*, *XL* (*Opera*, ed. G. Antonio Volpi [Padua, 1718]):

> Danubii ad ripas primo Rex flore juventae,
>   Caesus pro patria, cum patria hic jaceo.
> Nec queror, immiti quod sim prostratus ab hoste,
>   Sed quod me Reges deseruere pii:
> Qui, dum alia ex aliis inter se praelia miscent,
>   Et me, & se rabidis hostibus objiciunt.

Fumée describes him as a "comely young Prince, tall and well formed,
excelling any of his age. He was of a sweet and milde spirite, not anything

crooked or way-ward . . . He was greatly delighted in managing of Horses, and to beare armes, to hunt, and all other exercises worthie and commendable in a young man . . . Notwithstanding all these goodly vertues, he was in contempt and dislike among the greatest of his court, who abusing his young yeares did pill and spoyle his estate, whilest they lived in all excessive lust and pleasure" (p. 7). He was killed on August 29, 1526, at the Battle of Mohács, along with many of the Hungarian nobility. After the battle, his body was found "in a great whirle, or rift of earth, above Mohacz . . . the which meadow was then ouerflowed . . . with Danubius: in that place he was stifled with his horse vnder the water, being armed as he was at the battaile" (Fumée, p. 31). Suleiman went on to sack Buda, which was left undefended, and retired from Hungary in the same year, before the onset of winter.

8/3 **And now . . . vs.** After the death of Louis II, who died without issue, the Hungarian throne was claimed by John Zapolya, Voivode of Transylvania, and Ferdinand, Archduke of Austria and the brother of Charles V. Hungary was an elective monarchy. After the battle of Mohács, the surviving nobility of Hungary and the Council of Soldiers assembled in Diet (the *Rhakos*) at Alberegalis to elect a new king. "In this assemblie Iohn the Vayuode not finding any Competitour, with the generall consent and good liking of every one, was chosen King, and crowned with the auncient crowne of golde, (which then was in the coustodie of *Peter Peren*) by *Paul* Archbishop of Strigonium, and by *Stephen Broderic* Bishop of Vacchy, who afterward was chosen Chaunceller of Hungarie; and by these two he was annoynted" (Fumée, pp. 38–39). Ferdinand, meanwhile, claimed the throne by right of inheritance. Ferdinand's sister Maria was the wife of Louis II, and he himself had married Louis' sister Anne. After defeating Zapolya indecisively in 1527, Ferdinand had himself crowned king by the Archbishop of Strigonium, the same man who had crowned Zapolya (Fumée, pp. 36–46; see also *State Papers, Henry VIII, 1*, 205–06; *5*, 600–01, 572–73, 582). Antony's remark sets the date of his conversation as sometime after Ferdinand's coronation in 1527 but before Suleiman's invasion of Hungary in 1529.

8/4 **the third dogg.** Suleiman the Magnificent. The expression is proverbial, related ultimately to Aesop's fable of the Dog and his Shadow (*Fabule Esopi cum commento* [London, 1503], sig. B₄). The fable was repeated by Phaedrus, *Fabulae*, I, 4 (Hervieux, *1*, 8), and appeared in almost every other subsequent collection of fables. Cf. More's own variant in his epigram *De Cane Venante* (*Epigrams*, no. 116, p. 55). Tilley, D 545, quotes George Gascoigne (1573): "whiles two dogges do strive for a bone, the third may come and carie it away."

    After being defeated by Ferdinand in 1527, Zapolya retired to Poland and sent his envoy, Jerome Lasczky, to the court of the Turk, asking for assistance to regain the throne and promising "a reasonable tribute"; and "in token of true fidelitie and alleageance . . . he would yeeld himselfe to bee his subiect" (Fumée, pp. 42–43). Ferdinand attempted to ratify a truce, but Suleiman invaded Hungary in the spring of 1529. By September he was at the gates of Vienna.

8/5–8 What shuld . . . hym. Rhodes had long been a bulwark against the Turk. Defended by the Christian Knights of St. John of Jerusalem, it successfully resisted the siege of Mahomet II, the conqueror of Constantinople, but finally fell to Suleiman in December 1522 after a five-month siege. As ll. 8–15 indicate, More is being bitterly ironic when he says that "all cristendome was not hable to defend that strong Towne," for it was notorious at the time that Rhodes fell primarily because of Christian disunity. Even the pope was condemned for his part in the affair: "Nowe although certayne monethes were past, sithe this siege began, yet not wistanding no ayde ne succour was sent to the Rhodyens from anye prince." Cardinal Medici asked Pope Hadrian to send some galleys he had at his disposal. "But this our most holye father, which latelye ascended to the Apostolical seate, smally regarding or yet stickyng to this theyr godly and profitable counsayle, had not the grace of the holy goste, to fauoure and further this vyage, for the relyefe and ayde of the silly Rhodiens . . . Wherefore the Rhodyens altogether hopeles, & in vtter dispayre of reskue . . . yelded themselues to the Turke" (Jovius, fols. 106–107ᵛ; see also Newton, fol. 136).

8/8–15 Howbeyt . . . content. A common opinion of the time. Paulus Jovius' remarks are typical: "This opinion [that the Turks can be defeated] wer not far from the truthe, if the Christien princes were so wholy of one mynde and consent, that at the firste rumour of the Turkes commyng they wolde assemble and gather together power and strengthe of men able to resist and withstand hym. But certes we can skante truste that this shall happen, for no man wyll perswade hym selfe that the Turke wyl come, vntil at length he be come so nere, that all prouision and purueyaunce, hym to withstande, is to late and of none effecte: Lyke as we se it fare in his warres agaynste the Rhodes, Belgrade and Bude" (fols. 138–139). Cf. also More's words to Eustace Chapuys concerning the "blindness" of Christian princes who refused in 1531 to aid the emperor in driving back the Turk, "so cruel and implacable an enemy" (*Spanish Calendar, 4*, ii, 114).

8/20–9/5 for surely . . . rish. An anticipation of the argument that concludes the *Dialogue*; cf. below, 302/19–311/28 and, in particular, 315/6–30. Lines 2–3 ("me thought . . . tumbrelles") perhaps recalls (ironically) Ps. 150 or Lauds, the official morning prayer of the church: "Laudate Dominum in sanctis ejus . . . Laudate eum in sono tubae; laudate eum in psalterio, et cithara. Laudate eum in tympano, et choro; laudate eum in chordis, et organo. Laudate eum in cymbalis bene sonantibus; laudate eum in cymbalis jubilationis" (150:1, 3–5). The image is repeated more graphically below, 315/6–12.

9/3 **tumbrelles.** "Timbrels," percussion instruments held in the hand. Cf. 315/11, below. The *OED* ("timbrel," *sb.*¹) notes that "More's spelling appears to be due to confusion with the earlier word *tumbrel, sb.*, which was also sometimes written *timbrel.*"

9/12 **treacle.** The ancient *theriaca*, a universal antidote against snakebite, poison, and malignant disease. Pliny mentions it in his *Nat. Hist.*, *20*, 24, 100, and Galen wrote two books on the subject (*Opera*, *14*, 210–310). For contemporary Renaissance opinions, see Pace's *De Fructu*, pp. 62–64. Pace calls it "illius celebrantissimi & salutiferi in primis medicaminis." The image was a favorite of More's, used throughout his works; *e.g.*, *Four Last Things*, *EW*, sigs. e₄v, e₅; *Supplication*, *EW*, sig. t₅; and *Confutation, CW 8*, 37/34, etc.

9/12 **desperat dreade.** The word "desperat" is used with perhaps a conscious awareness or at least a suggestion of the root meaning of the word: *desperare*, a state of being without hope. For More's definition of comfort as "the consolacion of good hope," see below, 69/12–15, and above, n. to 3/1.

9/17 **The first chapiter.** More seems to have believed that literary dialogue should imitate as far as possible the natural flow of conversation: it should not be divided up into chapters since men do not ordinarily speak in chapters. In the *Debellation* More quotes the introduction to Saint-German's *Salem and Bizance:* "I shal cause it to be written here after in this dialogue worde for worde, as it is come to my handes, and then thou shalt wyth good will haue it. And thou shalte vnderstande that hys aunswere begynneth at the nexte chapiter hereafter ensuyng, and continueth to the place where I shall shew thee that it endeth." More then comments: "Consider good readers that thys introduccion he dothe not bringe in, as a rehearsall of a communicacion hadde before, but as a communi[ca]cion present. And then let hym shewe me where euer he hath herde in his lyfe any twoo men in theire talking togither, deuide their present communicacion into chapters. This is a point not onely so farre fro yᵉ nature of a dialogue, but also from all reason, that a very childe woulde not I weene haue handeled the thyng so childishelye" (*EW*, sig. N₇).

In the *Utopia*, where there are no chapters, the Dialogue of Counsel is divided from Raphael's Discourse in Book II by a natural pause for dinner. The Books in *A Dialogue of Comfort* are similarly divided by natural breaks in the conversation prepared for in the text itself, but the chapter divisions are not prepared for. They simply occur. They are also highly irregular, ranging from some a sentence or so in length (e.g., III, 4, and II, 3) to others that flow on for twenty or thirty pages (II, 16, 17).

More's *Dialogue of Heresies*, which he wrote carefully over the period of a year, is divided into chapters as well as books, presumably because of the argumentative, polemical nature of the work. The same may be true of the first book of *A Dialogue of Comfort*, but the chapter divisions in the last two books are so erratic that they raise serious doubts. See the discussion of this whole problem in the Introduction.

9/22–10/15 **naturall ... all.** "Naturall wise men" refers to those who relied only on their natural faculties, unaided by the supernatural gift of divine revelation (*Heresies, EW*, sig. o₃v, and *Confutation, CW 8*, 581/20–21). Cf. *Four Last Things, EW*, sig. e₇: "What profite and commoditye commeth vnto mans soule by the meditacion of death, is not onelye marked of the chosen people of god, but also of such as wer the best sorte among gentiles & painims. For some of the olde famous philosophers, whan thei wer demaunded what facultie philosophy was, answerd that it was the meditacion or exercise of death. For like as death maketh a seuerance of the body & the soul, whan thei by course of nature must nedes depart a sonder, so (said thei) dothe the study of philosophy, labor to seuer the soule fro the loue & affeccions of the body while thei be together."

10/13 **exirtyng.** This is probably a variant spelling of "exhorting": cf. 75/22, "exortith"; 152/12, "exorteth." Though such a variant is not recorded by the *OED*, the possibility is supported by the recognized variant "confirm" for "conform" used several times in *A Dialogue of Comfort* (see 68/18, 74/10). *B's* emendation to "excyting," followed by *Z*, does not exactly fit the context.

10/15–12/4 **Howbeit ... damnacion.** The medical imagery and the metaphor of Christ as a physician who cured the deadly wounds of sin are essentially Augustinian. Though used occasionally by other early fathers, such as Arnobius, Lactantius, Tertullian, and Ambrose, it was Augustine who developed the theme and gave it its traditional form. See Rudolph Arbesmann, "The Concept of *Christus Medicus* in St. Augustine," *Traditio, 10* (1954), 1–28. Arbesmann identifies over fifty instances of the concept in Augustine's works. The following are most immediately relevant: *Enarr. in Ps.*, 102, 5, and 130, 7 (*PL 37*, 1319–1320 and 1708); *Serm.* 175, 8, 9 (*PL 38*, 949); and *In Joh. Evang.* 3, 2, and 25, 16 (*PL 35*, 1396 and 1604). Cf. also More's *De Tristitia, CW 14*, 95, and *Poisoned Book, EW*, sig. V₇.

11/10 **in corners.** A phrase frequently used by More. It apparently means secret, out-of-the-way places. Cf. *Richard III, CW 2*, 86/3–4; Rogers, p. 441; and Taft, *Apologye*, pp. 178 and 186.

11/11 **blynd bayerdes.** "Bayard" was the name of a magic horse in medieval romance, the gift of Charlemagne to Rinaldo; the name was later used mock-heroically for the name of any horse. "Alluded to in many phrases and proverbial sayings, the origin of which was in later times forgotten, and 'Bayard' taken as the type of blindness or blind recklessness" (*OED*). Cf. *Confutation, CW 8*, 337/20: "be bold vppon yt lyke blynde bayarde," and *Heresies, EW*, sig. q₆v.

11/21–23 **honora ... necessitie.** Ecclus. 38:1. The Vulgate reads *etenim illum creauit* rather than *enim ordinauit eum.* For a discussion of the variants, see Marc'hadour, *The Bible,* Part I, p. 197.

11/26 **dedly woundes.** Original sin was traditionally described as a wound. Cf. Aquinas: "Haec ... originalis justitia subtracta est per peccatum primi parentis ... Et ideo omnes vires animae remanent quodammodo destitutae proprio ordine, quo naturaliter ordinantur ad virtutem; et ipsa destitutio vulneratio naturae dicitur" (*ST,* I-II, Q. 85, a. 3; see also Cyprian, *PL 4,* 625–26, and Augustine, *PL 36,* 353, and *PL 35,* 1604).

12/5 **The second chapiter.** For the omission of this chapter in *CC,* see the Introduction.

12/30–32 **Omne ... lightes.** Jas. 1:17. The verse occurs at the end of a passage (1:1–16) that speaks of the necessity of faith in times of trial and persecution. For the significance of the context of this and the quotations from scripture immediately following, through 13/5–6, see the Introduction.

13/3–5 **Credo ... beliefe.** Mark 9:23. Spoken by the father of a child possessed by an evil spirit, which Jesus cast out: "Jesus autem ait illi: Si potes credere, omnia possibilia sunt credenti. Et continuo exclamans pater pueri cum lacrymis aiebat: Credo, Domine, adjuva incredulitatem meam" (9:22–23). The disciples had tried previously to deliver the boy themselves, but they were unable to. The same story is told in Matt. 17:14–20 and Luke 9:38–42 but without the particular quotation More uses. From this point on to the end of his speech Antony weaves the three accounts together.

13/5–6 **Domine ... fayth.** Luke 17:5. The Vulgate reads: "Et dixerunt Apostoli Domino: Adauge ... " The passage immediately preceding this verse speaks of the impossibility of avoiding temptations or the inducements to sin (*scandala*) and the necessity to forgive one's enemies through whom temptations come (1:1–4). In his *Psalter* More annotated a number of the Psalms "pro rege" (*Prayer Book,* pp. 47, 48, 104, 119, 147) and said that it is necessary for a meek man in tribulation "maledicentibus benedicere et libenter pati ... ([to] bless those who speak evil of him and suffer willingly)" (pp. 75, 194). Cf. below, n. to 22/15–20.

13/7 **Chrystes saying.** Luke 17:6: "Dixit autem Dominus: Si habueritis fidem, sicut granum sinapis, dicetis huic arbori moro: Eradicare, et transplantare in mare: et obediet vobis." The parable of the mustard seed, to which More refers below, 13/13–18, is related in Matt. 13:31–32, Mark 4:30–32, and Luke 13:18–19.

13/11–13 **but that ... rowme.** Cf. ll. 8–12 of More's famous prayer in his *Book of Hours:* "Lytle & litle vttrely to caste of the world / And ridde my mynd of all the bysynes therof / Not to long to here of eny worldely thyngis / But that the heryng of worldely fantesyes may be to me displesaunt" (*Prayer Book*, pp. 6–7, 185).

13/18–23 **and then . . . hillocke.** Mark 11:21–23; Matt. 17:19–20. Mark reads: "Et recordatus Petrus, dixit ei: Rabbi, ecce ficus, cui maledixisti, aruit. Et respondens Jesus ait illis: Habete fidem Dei. Amen dico vobis, quia quicumque dixerit huic monti: Tollere, et mittere in mare, et non haesitaverit in corde suo, sed crediderit, quia quodcumque dixerit fiat, fiet ei." The passage in Matthew refers to the mustard seed, but not the heart; it is also connected with the story of the boy who was possessed by a demon the disciples were unable to cast out. See above, 13/3–5.

14/17–20 **for first . . . letarge.** A traditional metaphor for sin. Augustine (*De Civitate Dei*, XV, vi) and Aquinas (*ST*, I-II, Q. 81, a. 4) use it for original sin, whereas More's use is similar to Bernard's, for whom *languor animi* (at times called *mentis hebetudo, inertia spiritus*) described the "state of the soul in the absence of the beloved" (*PL 183*, 1026; see Etienne Gilson, *The Mystical Theology of Saint Bernard*, trans. A. H. C. Downes [London, 1940], pp. 104, 239, 262). Cf. also *Four Last Things, EW*, sig. e₅–e₅v.

15/8–15 **But this . . . Barnarde.** *In Adventu Domini, Sermones de Tempore*, I, i (*PL 183*, 35): "Quibus assimilabimus homines generationis hujus, aut quibus comparabimus illos, quos videmus a terrenis et corporalibus consolationibus avelli separarique non posse? Profecto similes sunt his qui submersi periclitantur in aquis. Nimirum videas eos tenentes tenere, nec ulla ratione deserere quod primum occurrerit manibus, quidquid sit illud, licet tale sit aliquid, quod omnino prodesse non possit, ut sunt radices herbarum, caeteraque similia. Nam et si qui ad eos forte veniant ut subveniant, nonnunquam solent apprehensos involvere secum: adeo ut jam nec sibi, nec illis auxilium ferre praevaleant. Sic pereunt in hoc mari magno et spatioso, sic pereunt miseri; dum peritura sectantes, amittunt solida, quibus apprehensis emergere et salvare possent animas suas "

15/29–30 **petite . . . haue.** John 16:24. The passage reads: "Amen, amen dico vobis: si quid petieritis Patrem in nomine meo, dabit vobis . . . Petite, et accipietis, ut gaudium vestrum sit plenum" (16:23–24). The parallel passages in Mark 11:24 and Matt. 7:7–8 do not use the particular forms of the words More quotes. The passage in Mark, however, follows immediately after Christ's saying that faith can move mountains (11:21–23), to which More referred at the end of the previous chapter (13/18–23).

17/22–26 **Saynt paule . . . apostle.** The story of Paul's conversion is told in Acts 9:1–20 and repeated in Acts 22:4–16 and 26:9–18. He was cured "in body and sowle" by Ananias, who caused the scales of blindness to fall from his eyes and baptized him (9:18).

17/28–18/6 **The prowd . . . agayne.** Exod. 7–9. Although the Pharaoh agreed to let the people of Israel go after the plagues of blood and frogs (8:8) and again after the plagues of gnats and flies (8:28), he did not confess "himselfe for a synner" until after the plague that killed the cattle, the plague of boils, and the plague of hail (9:27–28). He also repented temporarily after the plagues of locusts and darkness (Exod. 10).

20/8–14 **and many . . . end.** More seems to imply that he will treat this "sorest tribulacion of all" as a separate category at the very end of the work, and he does so, by inference, throughout Book III. He approaches the problem explicitly in chapters 25 and 26 (302/19–311/28), in comparing the pains of hell with the joys of heaven.

21/3–4 **of which . . . Romaynes.** Rom. 7–8. The following verses are especially relevant: "Condelector enim legi Dei secundum interiorem hominem: Video autem aliam legem in membris meis, repugnantem legi mentis meae, et captivantem me in lege peccati, quae est in membris meis. Infelix ego homo, quis me liberabit de corpore mortis hujus? Gratia Dei per Jesum Christum Dominum nostram. Igitur ego ipse mente servio legi Dei: carne autem legi peccati" (7:22–25).

21/9–18 **For the . . . pacyently.** Cf. Rogers, p. 543, a letter of 1534: "I assure you Margaret on my faith, I neuer haue prayde God to bringe me hence nor deliuer me fro death, but referring all thing whole vnto his onely pleasure, as to hym that seeth better what is best for me than my selfe dooth. Nor neuer longed I since I came hether to set my fote in mine owne howse, for any desire of or pleasure of my howse, but gladlie wolde I sometime somewhat talke with my frendes, and specially my wyfe and you that pertein to my charge. But sith that God otherwise disposeth, I committe all wholy to his goodnes."

21/24–29 **And therfor . . . best.** Cf. Samuel Johnson, *The Vanity of Human Wishes*, 351–56:

> Still raise for good the supplicating voice,
> But leave to heav'n the measure and the choicc,
> Safe in his pow'r, whose eyes discern afar
> The secret ambush of a specious pray'r.
> Implore his aid, in his decisions rest,
> Secure whate'er he gives, he gives the best.

21/30–22/1 **as he . . . people.** 2 Kings 24:1–16. After David repented of his "high pride" in counting the number of his people, God offered him the choice of three punishments: seven years of famine, three months of flight from his enemies, or three days of pestilence. David chose by saying he would place himself in the hands of God rather than in the hands of men, and the Lord sent the angel of pestilence. But before the destruction of Jerusalem was complete, He relented.

22/15–20 **the blessid . . . hym.** Cf. 2 Cor. 12:7–10: "datus est mihi stimulus carnis meae, angelus satanae, qui me colaphizet. Propter quod ter Dominum rogavi ut discederet a me: Et dixit mihi: Sufficit tibi gratia mea: nam virtus in infirmitate perficitur. Libenter igitur gloriabor in infirmitatibus meis, ut inhabitet in me virtus Christi. Propter quod placeo mihi in infirmitatibus meis, in contumeliis, in necessitatibus, in persecutionibus, in angustiis pro Christo: Cum enim infirmor, tunc potens sum" (12:10). In his commentary on these verses in his *NT*, Erasmus agrees with Ambrose that Paul's *sore tribulacion* consisted of persecution by evil men (*insectationem malorum hominum*): "Quod autem hoc loco infirmitatem sentiat, non morbum corporis, sed afflictionem ab inimicis illatam" (*Opera, 6,* 793–94). Cf. above, n. to 13/5–6.

In a letter to Margaret dated from the Tower, 1534, More writes: "God geue vs both twaine the grace, to dispayre of our owne self, and whole to depende and hange vpon the hope and strenght of God." He then refers to this passage from Paul, commenting on it at length, and concluding: "it well semeth, that the temptacion was so stronge (what so euer kind of temptacion it was) that he was very fearde of falling, throwgh the feblenesse of resisting that he began to feele in hym self. Wherfore for his comfort God answered (*Sufficit tibi gratia mea*) puttinge hym in suretie, that were he of hym selfe neuer so feble and faint, nor neuer so lykely to fall, yet the grace of God was sufficient to kepe hym vp and make him stand. And our Lord sayd ferther, (*Virtus in infirmitate proficitur*). The more weke that man is, the more is the strenght of God in his saueguard declared. And so S. Paule saith (*Omnia possum in eo qui me confortat*). Surely Megge a fainter hearte than thy fraile father hath, canst you not haue. And yet I verily trust in the great mercye of God, that he shall of his goodnesse so staye me with his holy hand, that he shall not finally suffer me to fall wretchedlie from his fauour" (Rogers, pp. 545–46). For a discussion of the underlying contextual significance of this and the scriptural quotations immediately following, through 34/22–26, see the Introduction.

22/26–30 **Nos ... groninges.** Rom. 8:26. The Vulgate reads *nam* for *Nos autem* and *sicut* for *vt*. The verse is clearly linked to the previous quotation from 2 Cor. (22/15–20) by the direct reference to the Holy Spirit's assistance with which it begins: "Similiter autem et Spiritus adjuvat infirmitatem nostram: nam quid ... " For More's later use of this passage, again linking it with the idea that God's grace is sufficient for human weakness, see below, nn. to 248/27–28 and 319/20–23.

23/7–8 **Si ... vs.** Rom. 8:31. Scribe *A* has apparently misread an abbreviation as *dominus*. *B* corrects to *deus* in accordance with the Vulgate, but leaves *nobiscum*, where the Vulgate reads *pro nobis* (cf. the correction in *1573*).

25/4–24 **These ... otherwise.** Cf. *Heresies, EW,* sig. n₃. For "by the ...

passion" (25/13), cf. *Confutation, CW 8*, 91/12–21, 409/34–410/13, 580/23–31, 633/35–634/7, 841/1–11, and 848/37–849/8, where More explains that penance alone is insufficient. See also below, 36/22–31, 95/10–14, and 319/25–28.

26/7 **vertew of necessitie.** Cf. Whiting, V 43, and Tilley, V 73. See also Erasmus, *Adag.*, "Necessarium malum," sig. m_4v (I. V. xxvi).

26/9–22 **Consider . . . man.** The story of Achan is told in Joshua 7. He stole from among the forbidden things of the Lord ("aliquid de anathemate" [7:1]), and God gave the victory to the men of Hai. The discovery of the thief "by lottes" is described in verse 14. More quotes verse 19. The Vulgate reads *Domino deo* for *deo* (cf. the correction in *1573*), *confitere* for *confiteri* (cf. the correction in Z), and *ne* for *& ne*. More uses the same example in *Heresies, EW*, sig. p_2, to illustrate the value of penance and open confession and again links it with the story of the good thief as he does immediately below (26/26–31).

26/26–31 **Consider . . . salvacion.** Luke 23:33, 39–43. There is no scriptural evidence to suggest that the good thief hung on Christ's right hand. The gospels merely say that the two thieves were crucified on either side of Jesus, one on the right and one on the left. Tradition placed the good thief on the right since the left was regarded as "sinister." See, for example, Rabanus Maurus, *Commentaria in Matthaeum*, VIII, 4 (*PL 107*, 1158); C. à Lapide, *2*, 228; *Heresies, EW*, sig. n_6; and *Confutation, CW 8*, 216/27.

28/6–11 **Nullius . . . vs.** 1 Cor. 4:4. The Vulgate reads *Nihil enim mihi* for *Nullius mihi*. Paul is speaking specifically of the judgment of God as opposed to the judgment of man. Cf. "Mihi autem pro minimo est ut a vobis judicer, aut ab humano die: . . . qui autem judicat me, Dominus est. Itaque nolite ante tempus judicare, quodusque veniat Dominus" (4:3–5). The verse in the second quotation (ll. 9–10) is from John 1:8. The Vulgate reads *quoniam* rather than *quia*.

28/26–29 **Iff . . . plaster.** Cf. *Four Last Things, EW*, sig. e_4v.

29/5 **crosse.** The sense of "adversity, misfortune, trouble" (*OED*, "cross," *sb.* 10) turns into a nautical metaphor, where the cross becomes a mast on which the "low saile" (l. 6) of humility is set. John Donne notes the same similarity in "The Crosse": "The Mast and yard made one, where seas do tosse" (l. 20). Cf. Jerome: "Navis per maria, antenna cruci similata afflatur" (cited in C. à Lapide, *1*, 534).

29/8–20 **Some yong . . . nek.** For the story, cf. *Four Last Things, EW*, sig. e_8, and below, 307/26–28. The language, and the situation, recall one of Skelton's "Dyuers Ballettys and Dyties Solacyous" (Dyce, *1*, 23):

> The auncient acquaintance, madam, betwen vs twayn,
>   The famylyaryte, the formar dalyaunce,

> Causyth me that I can not myself refrayne
> But that I must wryte for my plesaunt pastaunce:
>
> . . . .
>
> . . . a rumer begynnyth for to ryse,
> How in good horsmen ye set your hole delyght,
> And haue forgoten your old trew louyng knyght. (ll. 1-4, 13-15)

The color of the kite's claw (l. 16) was yellowish-white. Cf. Skelton, *The Tunnyng of Elynour Rummyng* (Dyce, *1*, 108):

> Her kyrtell she did vptucke
> An ynch aboue her kne,
> Her legges that ye myght se;
>
> . . . .
>
> As fayre and as whyte
> As the fote of a kyte.

For "lay in her lapp" (l. 18), a common euphemism in the Renaissance for sexual intercourse, cf. *Hamlet*, III,ii, 108; "Lady, shall I lie in your lap?" The primary meaning of "breke . . . stomak" (ll. 18-19) is "reveal one's inmost thoughts" (*OED*, stomach, *sb.* 6. b.), but More uses the phrase to mean "vomit" at the same time that he glances at the sexual connotation (reveal to him the bottom of her stomach).

29/21-30 **Did . . . hym.** See above, 22/15-20 and n. The reference is to 2 Cor. 12:1-10. Paul speaks of "a man" (obviously himself) who was taken up to the third heaven, where he heard things which no one can utter. He then adds: "Et ne magnitudo revelationum extollat me, datus est mihi stimulus carnis meae." (12:7). Paul does not say that God allowed him to remain in torment for any great length of time. More perhaps believed this to be implied by the fact that he called upon God three times for relief and by God's reply, "Sufficit tibi gratia mea" (12:8). Cf. "our lord agayne shewed hym that it was not good for hym to lacke it [the tribulation] so soone, nor to haue it so sodenly taken away from hym / but shewed him that his grace was suffycyent" (*Confutation, CW 8*, 454/ 6-9). In all his comments on the passage More emphasizes the value of tribulation in humbling pride; cf. *Confutation, CW 8*, 445/20-24, and 454/ 1-14; Rogers, pp. 545-46.

31/14-19 **as it . . . had.** 2 Cor. 12:1-10, cited above, 29/21-30, and Job 6, 23, 31.

32/8 **pacion.** The word is used with some precision to recall Christ's passion, for Christ was commonly believed to be the first martyr, "nempe martyrum omnium antesignanum et ducem," as More called him in the *De Tristitia, CW 14*, 55. Martyrdom itself was thought to be a reenactment or in some mysterious way a participation in Christ's archetypal suffering and death. Bernard, for example, speaks of Christ as "flos campi, martyr, martyrum corona, martyrii forma" (*Sermones in Cantica, PL 183*, 1010; see also *PL 183*, 1074). In the *De Tristitia*, More imagines Christ saying to all men who are called to martyrdom and are afraid: "En ego te in uia ista tam formidolosa precedo. Meae uestis fimbriam apprehende. Inde uirtutem exire senties / qui hunc animi tui in metus uanos effluentem sanguinem sistet salubriter / et animum reddet alacriorem / quippe quum recordaberis quod meis inheres uestigijs" (p. 105). See also *Ibid.*, *CW 14*, 217–247; Rev. 1:5 and 3:14; Augustine, *PL 38*, 1449 and 1454; and the meditation on the Way of the Cross that concludes *A Dialogue of Comfort*, below, 312–20.

32/13–14 **Onerosi . . . you.** Job 16:2. The Vulgate (cf. the correction in *1573*) reads: "consolatores onerosi omnes vos estis."

32/17–19 **so yf . . . glorye.** Cf. 2 Cor. 4:17: "Id enim, quod in praesenti est momentaneum et leve tribulationis nostrae, supra modum in sublimitate aeternum gloriae pondus operatur in nobis." See also *De Tristitia*, *CW 14*, 101–05; and Augustine, Sermo 328 (*PL 38*, 1454).

33/2–7 **But now . . . glory.** Cf. *De Tristitia*, *CW 14*, 181–83: "Nam et martyres in celum dicimus protinus a morte conscendere." See also below, 284/24–26. The belief was traditional; cf. Augustine, Sermo 329 (*PL 38*, 1454–1455): "Empti sunt fideles et martyres: sed martyrum fides probata est: testis est sanguis"; Sermo 326 (*PL 38*, 1449). Aquinas equates martyrdom with the plenary absolution of baptism and the full deliverance therefore of the punishment due to both venial and mortal sins (*ST*, III, Q.68, a. 2, and III, Q.87, a. 1).

34/6–14 **Non . . . folkes.** The scriptural references in this passage run as follows: Rom. 12:19; Matt. 5:40, where More has telescoped the verse somewhat; and a conflation of Phil. 2:4 and 1 Cor. 10:24. The syntax and most of the phrasing in the final quotation is from Philippians: "Non quae sua sunt singuli considerantes, sed ea quae aliorum"; 1 Corinthians adds only the *quaerere*: "Nemo quod suum est quaerat, sed quod alterius."

34/22–26 **Bcati . . . hevyn.** Matt. 5:7. The Vulgate (cf. the correction in *1573*) reads *quoniam ipsi* rather than *quia*. The second quotation is from Matt. 5:10.

37/8–18 **but yet . . . dede.** Because of the nature of the work, More is careful in *A Dialogue of Comfort* to avoid polemics, allowing controversy over such doctrines as purgatory and justification by faith alone to come up only occasionally, as here. For More's earlier defense of purgatory see, for example, his *Supplication*, *EW*, sigs. t₄v-y₆, and *Confutation*, *CW 8*, 289/ 6–22; for his attack on the protestant doctrine of faith, *Confutation*, *CW 8*, 312/25–313, 486–560, 658/5–15, and Taft, *Apologye*, pp. 36–43.

38/3–5 **The first . . . fayth.** The reference is vague, and More may intend the "communicacions" to be taken simply as rumors that never came to pass. Certainly none of the events of 1527–29, the fictitious date of *A Dialogue of Comfort*, would seem to fit. The protestant princes of Germany were actively engaged shortly before that time in uniting against the Catholics for mutual protection, first in the League of Torgau (May 1526) and afterward in the Diet of Speier (June 1526). In order to unify Germany against the Turks, however, the Diet of Speier voted to put the problem of Luther aside until a general council should meet. See below, n. to 38/10–13. The most celebrated attempt at compromise between Protestant and Catholic was the Augsburg Confession (June 1530), drawn up by Philip Melanchthon in an attempt to formulate protestant opinion and at the same time reconcile Protestants and moderate Catholics who felt the need of reform. Melanchthon based the Confession on the Schwaback Articles, Luther's own agreement among Protestants, but because of his fear of war with Charles V, he attempted to minimize the differences between Lutherans and Catholics against the Zwinglians.

More perhaps refers to events of the year 1534–35, when he was actually writing *A Dialogue of Comfort*. At that time Lutherans and Catholics, haunted by memories of the Peasants' Revolt (1525), had momentarily drawn together to eradicate the growing number of protestant sects, such as the Anabaptists at Münster and the dissenters at Lübeck. Writing in prison in 1534–35, during a time of religious persecution in his own country, More could not have been innocent of the irony of the statement.

38/6–9 **The second . . . it.** A reference, perhaps, to the Peace of Cadan (June 29, 1534), which reaffirmed the Peace of Nürnberg (1532) between the Emperor Charles V and the Protestant League of Schmalkalden, signed by nine princes and twenty-four cities. The Peace of Nürnberg stressed the need for Christian unity against the Turk: "Et quoniam causa controversiae religionis, multis laboribus frustra susceptis, non potuit ad aliquam concordiam reduci, ad animum revocavimus, id quod res est, non posse crudelitati ac tyrannidi Turcicae validus resisti quam si in Imperio communis ac firma pax constituatur." It called an end, therefore, to all war over religion, urging instead "true friendship and Christian charity": "nemo propter religionis vel ullam aliam causam alteri bellum indicat, inferat, ipsumve spoliet, capiat, invadat, obsideat, neque ad haec facienda per se vel per alium cuiquam inserviat, arces, urbes, oppida, castella, pagos, villas vel praedia insidiis occupet aut contra voluntatem alterius violenter adimat, dolove malo, incediis vel alia ratione alteri damnum det. Neque ullis istiusmodi machinatoribus, consilio, auxilio vel alio modo opem ferat, neque eos sciens hospitio excipiat, victum potum aut receptum praebeat aut toleret: sed unusquisque alterum vera amicitia et Christiana cavitate complectatur" (*Documents Illustrative of the Continental Reformation*, ed. B. J. Kidd [Oxford, 1911], pp. 302–03).

38/7 **contencions . . . prohibitid.** *1573* attempted to normalize the usage here by reading "contentious dispicions . . . are prohibited," but the printer has turned an "n" to print "dispicious" (fol. 25).

38/10–13 **The Third . . . Turke.** Early in 1529 it was well known that
Suleiman was preparing his army for a new thrust through Hungary to
Austria. More refers to the various imperial diets that attempted to unite
Germany to meet the threat. At the Diet of Innsbruck (March 1529) the
German Princes promised 120,000 Rhenish guilders for defense against
the Turk, and at the reconvened Diet of Speier (May 1529), a 16,000-man
army and 4,000 cavalry. The Diet of Augsburg (1530) and the Peace of
Nürnberg (1532) were further attempts at unity.

In spite of the diets and their official promises, however, Germany was
unable to raise any unified defense, and Antony's statement must be taken
as somewhat satiric. The Turkish army swept across the plains of Hungary
and on September 20, 1529, laid siege to Vienna. Charles V was occupied
in Italy and left the city relatively defenseless. At Linz, Ferdinand believed
that Suleiman intended to winter in Vienna and spend the next few years
conquering Germany. Unable to capture the city before the onset of
winter, however, Suleiman raised the siege on October 15, 1529, and
retreated through Austria, using "vnspeakeable crueltie: of some he cut
of their noses, some he put out their eyes, of some he cut of their priuy
members, of women they cut their pappes, Virgins they rauished, and of
women great with childe they rypped their bellyes and brent the children:
beside this, all along as they went, they brent Corne, Trees, Houses and
all that was combustible, to make the countrey desolate" (Newton, fol.
136ᵛ).

38/16–19 **of his . . . selfe.** The long omission in *1573* was caused by a
printer's error: "in the defence" comes in the last line on fol. 25, with the
catchword "of"; the printer, at some point in the process, jumped ahead
to pick up "of" in "of the contrary" (fol. 25ᵛ).

38/27–29 **And I . . . hell.** In his polemical works More frequently makes
use of the idea that belief in purgatory helps keep a man from hell. He
modifies it here somewhat and makes it more temperate in accord with
his more conciliatory mood. Cf. *Confutation, CW 8*, 288/26–31: "Tyndale.
What am I the better for the bylyefe of purgatorye? More. In good fayth
not the better of an halfpeny, whyle ye byleue yt no better then ye do.
But surely if ye byleued yt well / ye myghte be bothe the better for purgatorye and yᵉ farther from hell." See also *Supplication, EW*, sigs. t₅ and
y₅ᵛ-y₆.

38/29–39/3 **And as . . . selfe.** Cf. "For in Saxony firste and among al the
Lutherans there be as many heades as many wittes. And all as wise as
wilde geese. And as late as thei began, yet bee there not onely as many
sectes almoste as men, but also the maisters them selfe chaunge theyr
mindes and theyr oppynions euery daye and wote nere where to hold
them. Boheme is also in yᵉ same case. One faith in the towne, another in
the fielde. One in Prage, another in the next towne. And yet in Prage it
self one faith in one strete, another in yᵉ next. So that if ye assigne it in

Boheme, ye must tell in what town. And if ye name a towne, yet muste ye tel in what strete" (*Heresies*, *EW*, sig. m₆). See also *Treatise on the Passion*, *EW*, sig. OO₄v, and *Confutation*, *CW 8,* 342/8–343/5. The idea of such a diversity of opinion was of course abhorrent to More's own belief in one catholic, universal church based on tradition as well as revelation.

39/12–13 **but is . . . dewtie.** Cf. Luke 17:10: "Servi inutiles sumus: quod debuimus facere, fecimus."

39/22–23 **while . . . workes.** Cf. Mark 9:40 and Matt. 5:3–11, 16:27, 25:31–46. The strongest support for More's position, however, comes from the words of the apostles. Cf. Jas. 2:24: "Videtis quoniam ex operibus justificatur homo, et non ex fide tantum?" See also 1 Cor. 3–8 and Heb. 6:10.

40/1–3 **fides . . . charite.** 1 Cor. 13:13, the conclusion of Paul's celebrated description of charity (13:4–14).

40/3 **greaest.** This spelling, without the "t", occurs eight times in *A*, and is only once changed by *B*. It appears to reflect a colloquial usage. See 126/21, 220/11, 221/4, 241/15, 254/4, 267/12, 268/29.

41/6–14 **nor haue . . . yt.** The first reference to Paul is from Heb. 13:14: "Non enim habemus hic manentem civitatem, sed futurus inquirimus." The second (ll. 8–10) is from 1 Cor. 9:24–25: "Nescitis quod ii, qui in stadio currunt, omnes quidem currunt, sed unus accipit bravium? Sic currite ut comprehendatis. Omnis autem, qui in agone contendit, ab omnibus abstinet: et illi quidem ut corruptibilem coronam accipiant: nos autem incorruptam."

41/29–42/1 **ve vobis . . . laughyng.** Luke 6:25. and Eccles. 3:4. The Vulgate reads "Tempus flendi; et tempus ridendi."

42/4 **There . . . repyng to.** Eccles. 3:2. "Tempus nascendi, et tempus moriendi. Tempus plantandi, et tempus evellendi quod plantatum est."

42/8–13 **Euntes . . . handes.** Ps. 125:6.

42/18 **our . . . thrise.** Christ wept over the dead Lazarus (John 11:35) and over the city of Jerusalem (Luke 19:41). See also Heb. 5:7.

42/26–31 **Ducunt . . . recevith.** Job 21:13 and Heb. 12:6. In the latter the Vulgate reads *autem* rather than *Et*. The entire passage in Hebrews extends the idea developed in the text; cf. particularly the reference to martyrdom at 12:3–4.

42/31–43/2 **per multas . . . god.** Acts 14:21. The Vulgate reads *intrare* rather than *introire*. More may have picked up the latter word from his next biblical quotation (Luke 24:26; below, n. to 43/4–6). Paul says this after being stoned and left for dead at Lystra.

43/3 **castell of Emaus.** In the Vulgate, Emmaus is called a "castellum," which gave rise to the Middle English "castle" (meaning "town" or "village") as a translation of the biblical word. More uses the term also at 311/23 and in the *Treatise on the Blessed Body* (*EW*, sig. LL₆v).

43/4–6 **An nesciebatis . . . kyngdome.** Luke 24:26. The Vulgate reads: "Nonne haec oportuit pati Christum, et ita intrare in gloriam suam?" More's *oportebat Cristum pati* comes from Luke 24:46. See Marc'hadour, *The Bible*, Part II, p. 137. The disciples did not recognize the risen Christ and were telling Him of His own death and resurrection.

43/6–7 **And wold . . . selfe.** John 15:19–20: "quia vero de mundo non estis, sed ego elegi vos de mundo, propterea odit vos mundus. Mementote sermonis mei, quem ego dixi vobis: Non est servus major domino suo. Si me persecuti sunt, et vos persequentur." See also Matt. 10:24–25 and John 13:16.

43/7–9 **wold we . . . payne.** Cf. *Heresies*, *EW*, sig. k₄: "what ease also cal you this, yᵗ we be bounden to abide all sorowe and shameful death & al martirdome vppon pain of perpetual damnacion for the profession of our faith. Trowe ye that these easy wordes of his easy yoke & light burdein wer not aswel spoken to his apostles as to you, & yet what ease called he them to. Called he not them to watching, fasting, praying, preching, walking, hunger, thurst, colde, & heate, beating, scourging, prisonment, painful & shamefull death. The ease of his yoke standeth not in bodily ease, nor the lightnes of his burden standeth not in the slacknes of any bodily payn (except we be so wanton, yᵗ wher himself had not heauen without pain, we loke to come thither with playe) but it standeth in the swetenes of hope, wherby we fele in our pain a pleasaunt taste of heauen." Cf. Roper, pp. 26–27: "If his wife or any of his children had bine diseased or troubled he wold say vnto them: 'We may not look at our pleasure to go to heauen in fetherbeds: it is not the way, for our lord himself went thither with great payne and by many tribulacions, which was the path wherein he walked thither; for the servaunt may not looke to be in better case then his master.'"

43/10–12 **Qui vult . . . me.** The phrasing is a combination of Matt. 16:24 and Luke 14:27. Matthew reads: "Si quis vult post me venire, abneget semetipsum, et tollat crucem suam, et sequatur me." Luke adds the phrase "meus esse discipulus." See also Luke 9:23 and Mark 9:34.

43/16–22 **and it . . . tribulacions.** Heb.12:6 and Acts 14:21, cited above, 42/26–43/2.

45/16–23 **Ad probaticam . . . eares.** John 5:2–4: "Est autem Ierosolymis probatica piscina, quae cognominatur Hebraice Bethsaida, quinque porticus habens. In his jacebat multitudo magna languentium, caecorum, claudorum, aridorum, expectantium aquae motum. Angelus autem Domini descendebat secundum tempus in piscinam: et movebatur aqua.

Et qui prior descendisset in piscinam post motionem aquae, sanus fiebat a quacumque detinebatur infirmitate." The words *probatica piscina* are usually translated as "a pool by the Sheep Gate." More's information that the pool was used to wash sheep for sacrifice is derived from traditional glosses such as Bede's *In S. Joannis Evangelium Expositio* (*PL 92*, 690–91): "Et bene piscina eadem probatica vocatur:... quippe Graece *oves* dicuntur ... Vulgo autem probatica, id est, pecuaria piscina fertur appellata, quod in ea sacerdotes hostias lavare consueverant"; see also Erasmus, *Opera, 6,* 357–58, and C. à Lapide, *2,* 316, who cites Jansenius and Jerome. More's identification of the stirring of the waters with the coming of grace in the soul was also traditional. Cf. Bede: "Multitudo languentium ... significat eorum catervas qui, legis verba audientes, suis se hanc viribus implere non posse dolebant, atque ideo dominicae auxilium gratiae totis animi affectibus implorabant." The waters were also associated allegorically with Christ's passion and therefore with baptism and penance; see Bede, *loc. cit.,* and C. à Lapide, *2,* 318, who cites Tertullian, Ambrose, and Augustine.

45/30–46/11 **as the ... do.** "More is speaking of those spiritual advisers who will not warn great men that they are courting destruction by persisting in their obstinate ways. He is thinking, there can be little doubt, of King Henry VIII, and his subservient clergy, who are leaving the duty of withstanding the king, to him, Thomas More, a mere layman" (Chambers, *Thomas More,* p. 58). In the *De Tristitia* More compares the bishops of the church to the apostles, who slept during Christ's agony in the garden: "Cur non hic contemplentur episcopi sompnolentiam suam qui sicut in apostolorum succedunt locum sic utinam uirtutes eorum perinde nobis referrent ut et authoritatem libenter amplectuntur / et ignauam istam illorum dormitantiam representant. Nam plerique serendis in populo uirtutibus et asserendae ueritati dormiunt / dum inimici Christi / serendis uicijs aeradicandae fidei hoc est quoad in ipsis est apprehendendo christo iterumque crudeliter crucifigendo peruigilant" (*CW 14,* 259 61) Cf Roper, p. 78: "And surely daughter, it is greate pitye that any Christian prince should by a flexible Councell ready to follow his affections, and by a weake Cleargie lacking grace constantly to stand to their learninge, with Flatterye be so shamefully abused."

46/17 **colletes.** The prayers in the mass, varying with the day, between the gloria and the epistle, as well as the secrets and post-communions.

47/7–18 **Salamon ... welth.** For Solomon, see 3 Kings 10:14–29 and 3:3–14. The reference to 2 Kings 10 in the marginalia of *1557* is a misprint. Job's wealth is recounted in Job 1:1–3. More quotes Job 42:10. The Vulgate reads: "Et addidit Dominus omnia quaecumque fuerant Job, duplicia." Job's long life is mentioned in Job 42:16: "Vixit autem Job post haec, centum quadraginta annis." For Abraham, see Gen. 13:2.

47/17–20 **yee . . . bosome.** Luke 16:22. Abraham's bosom was taken by Augustine to be a place of peace, "locus quietis, in quo post mortem recipiebantur, & etiamnum recipiuntur imitatores fidei & pietatis Abrahae: qui ante Christum limbus patrum, post Christum est caelum, quod est paradisus Beatorum" (*De Anima et ejus Origine*, IV, 16, cited in C. à Lapide, *2*, 188). Lapide adds that Abraham "in limbo patrum caeterorum videtur fuisse primus & princeps" (*loc. cit.*). More follows Augustine's gloss in *Four Last Things, EW*, sig. fg₅v, where he contrasts the bosom of Abraham, or Limbo, with the bosom of Christ: "There dyed he [Lazarus] wᵗout grudge, without anxietie, with good wyll and glad hope, whereby he went into Abrahams bosom. Nowe if thou do the lyke, thou shalt go into a better bosome, into heuen into yᵉ bosom of our sauior Christ."

48/8–12 **Et facit . . . recevith.** Matt. 5:45. The Vulgate reads "qui solem suum oriri facit." The context speaks of the need to love those who persecute you and accuse you falsely (*calumniantibus*). For More's previous use of the passage, see above, 34/6–26. The second reference (ll. 11–12) is to Heb. 12:6.

48/13–14 **multa . . . also.** Ps. 31:10. The remainder of the verse reads: "sperantem autem in Domino misericordia circumdabit." Like all the psalms referred to in the next three quotations (48/19–49/8), Psalm 31 is essentially a plea for strength by the just man who trusts in the Lord: "Tu es refugium meum a tribulatione, quae circumdedit me; Exsultatio mea, erue me a circumdantibus me" (31:7). In his *Psalter* More wrote opposite this verse, "tri (tri[bulation])," and opposite verse 5, which reads "Delictum meum cognitum tibi fecit: Et iniustitiam meam non abscondi," he wrote, "confessio peccati (confession of sin)" (*Prayer Book*, pp. 61–62, 193).

48/19–21 **Multiplicate . . . hast.** Ps. 15:4. In his *Psalter* More wrote opposite this verse, "tribulationis utilitas (the usefulness of tribulation)" (*Prayer Book*, pp. 41, 191). Like Psalm 31, Psalm 15 is also a plea for strength, beginning, "Conserva me, Domine, quoniam speravi in te." Opposite verses 8–10 More wrote in his *Psalter*: "solacium in tribulatione (comfort in tribulation)" (*Prayer Book*, pp. 42, 191). The verses read: "Providebam Dominum in conspectu meo semper: quoniam a dextris est mihi, ne commovear. Propter hoc laetatum est cor meum, et exultavit lingua mea: insuper et caro mea requiescet in spe. Quoniam non derelinques animam meam in inferno: nec dabis sanctum tuum videre corruptionem." It will be recalled that, as a young man, More had translated Pico della Mirandola's commentary on this psalm (*EW*, sigs. b₁–b₂v).

48/29–49/3 **homo . . . them.** Ps. 48:12 and 20; the verse is used as a refrain. Opposite verses 1–2 ("Audite haec, omnes Gentes . . . "), More wrote in his *Psalter*, "Inuitatio (Invitation)"; opposite verse 14 ("Sicut oves in inferno positi sunt: mors depascet eos"), he wrote "demones (demons)"; and opposite verses 16–17, he wrote "diuitum miseranda superbia (the pride of the rich is to be pitied)." Verses 16–17 read: "Ne timueris cum dives factus fuerit homo: et cum multiplicata fuerit gloria domus ejus. Quoniam cum interierit, non sumet omnia: neque descendet cum eo gloria ejus" (*Prayer Book*, pp. 87–88, 195). See also below, 74/4.

49/5–8 **Non ... iniquitie.** Ps. 124:3. More's concern with the just man who trusts in God, which underlies this series of quotations from the psalms (48/13–49/8), is brought here to the surface of the text itself.

49/15 **mete for the shote.** The meaning is "determine the success of the various shots." The *OED* defines "mete" (*v.* 2.b), with this instance as the first example, as "To measure distances for shooting at a mark; hence, to aim at." But since Vincent has obviously "shot" (made his various objections) already, the word "mete" means here "to measure the closeness of the arrows to the center of the target." Cf. ll. 15–18, "and consider how nere toward or how far of your arrows ar from the prik." The "prick" is here the bull's-eye of a target (see *OED*, "prick" *sb.* IV. 10), while the "marke" (l. 14) refers to the target in general (cf. below, 159/15 and n.). Vincent has "shot" without really seeing the "marke," which is only now "set vp well in our sight" (l. 15) by Antony. (Cf. "no greate merveyle though I shote wide, while I somwat mystake the marke" [ll. 21–22]). "Mete" is used in a similar sense at 49/21, 49/25, 50/13, and 56/17, "shote" at 49/25 and 56/17.

The spelling of the MS, "shote," at 49/15 raises a problem that the *OED* ("shoot," *sb.*[1]) explains: "In the early 16th c. the spellings *shote* and *shoote* are both ambiguous, so that only the shade of meaning can determine whether the word is *shoot* (rhyming with *root*) f. the pres. stem of the vb., or the older *shote* (rhyming with *throat*)." The *OED* gives a separate entry for the noun "shote," meaning (2), "The action or an act of shooting with a bow, gun, etc., also the missiles discharged," but concedes that "in some or all of the later instances, the word may be a mere graphic or dialectical variant of *shoot sb.*[1] or *shot sb.*[1]" At 49/15, B evidently took the word to be "shot," for he cancelled the "e" of "shote." *L, 1553,* and *1557* read "shoote"; *1573* reads "shoot." The *OED* gives this passage as its first example under "shoot" *sb.*[1]1: "An act of shooting ... a discharge of arrows, bullets, etc." In any case the word here signifies both the act of shooting and the actual shot (arrow) registered on the target.

49/20 **your.** B writes "my" above, but does not cancel "your"—his usual way of suggesting a choice when doubtful. The other texts divide equally here: *L* and *1553* read "your"; *1557* and *1573* read "my." The latter makes more obvious sense, but "your" may indicate a way of counting up the results by giving over the losing arrows to Antony.

50/4 **further.** B emends to "furnysh" and is followed by Z. But More uses "further" in a similar way (meaning "help forward, assist") at 56/11. Cf. also "fortherid," 294/6.

50/8 **lye.** *A* wrote "kye" (fol. 39), which seems to be a scribal slip for "lye" in this context (cf. "lieth", l. 9). Antony seems to be following out the archery metaphor of the whole sentence; that is, "I lye the same" means "I agree with you"—but the point is wide of the mark in any case. *B* cancels "sith I kye" and makes an elaborate interlineation: "I think lo that syth I say:" which is followed by *Z*. Here is one of the places where *B* seems to be engaging in creative editing.

52/12 **as they . . . Ninive.** After he was released from the whale, Jonah obeyed God's command and went to Nineveh to preach repentance, for God had promised otherwise to destroy the city in forty days. The people listened, put on sackcloth and ashes, and the Lord turned aside the destruction He had designed for them. More refers specifically to the third chapter of Jonah. Cf. below, 95/27–29.

52/12–13 **as the . . . did.** In 2 Kings 12:1–24 Nathan was sent to warn David of his sins in taking Bathsheba and killing her husband, Uriah the Hittite. David repented and the Lord spared him but killed the child of his adultery. For David's repentance in 2 Kings 24:1–16 for counting the number of his people, see above, n. to 21/30–22/1. The reference to 3 Kings 12 and 24 in the marginalia of *1573* is a misprint. Cf. *Heresies, EW,* sig. s₄v, and *Confutation, CW 8,* 210/16–18.

53/6 **As for Salamon was.** See the *OED,* "as" (B. VII. 33. b.): "After *as for,* a pronoun was formerly omitted."

53/6–16 **Salamon . . . selfe.** Solomon's wealth is recounted in 3 Kings 10:14–27 (see above, n. to 47/7–18); his early favor with God in 3 Kings 3:3–14; and the number and nationality of his wives in 3 Kings 11:1–3. He is said to have had seven hundred wives and three hundred concubines. In his old age his heart was corrupted by his wives, and he worshipped Astarte, Moloch, Chamos, and Moab (11:4–9). The commandment forbidding multiple wives was given in Deut. 17:17. Marriage to foreign wives was forbidden in Exod. 34:14–16, under the heading of the first commandment; the prohibition was repeated in Deut. 7:3–4 and again in 3 Kings 11:2 in reference to Solomon.

53/16–22 **and of . . . sure.** The biblical accounts of Solomon break off before his death by saying that the rest of his deeds have already been recounted in other works—in the Book of the Acts of Solomon, the works of Nathan the Prophet, the Books of Ahia the Silonite, and the Vision of Addo the Seer (3 Kings 11:41; 2 Par. 9:29–31). Hence More's doubts. The Bible simply says: "Dormivitque Salomon cum patribus suis, et sepultus est in Civitate David patris sui" (3 Kings 11:43; 2 Par. 9:31). For David's repentance, see above, 52/12–13 and n.

53/26–54/6 **As for . . . bosome.** For Job and Abraham, see above, nn. to 47/7–18 and 17–20.

54/8 **but that yet it.** *A* reads "but that it it." *B* cancels the first "it," but this seems likely to be an example of the *A* scribe's frequent habit of spelling "yet" as "it" or "yt." (See textual footnotes to 32/1, 69/16, 70/7, 94/2, 158/17, 178/5, 315/21.) The phrase "but that yet" is characteristic of More.

54/8–18 **Was it . . . them.** In Gen. 12:1 Abraham was told to leave the land of his birth and go to a country the Lord would show him. Although he remained all his life a stranger and sojourner in Canaan, God repeatedly promised him that his seed would inherit the land (Gen. 12:7; 15:18; 17:8; 28:4). The trouble with Lot is recounted in Gen. 13:5–11. Their servants quarreled because there was not enough pasture for the herds of both Abraham and Lot. After separating from Abraham, Lot settled in Sodom, which was attacked by four kings. More's reference to three kings is a mistake. Gen. 14:1–2, 8–9, makes it clear that four kings attacked the kings of the five cities of the plain: "Et egressi sunt rex Sodomorum et rex Gomorrhae rexque Adamae et rex Seboim necnon et rex Balae, quae est Segor; et direxerunt aciem contra eos in valle silvestri; scilicet adversus Chodorlahomor regem Elamitarum et Thadal regem gentium et Amraphel regem Sennaar et Arioch regem Ponti: quattuor reges adversus quinque." The "five cities," then, were Sodom, Gomorrah, Adama (Admah), Seboim, and Bala (also known as Segor or Zoar). The phrase "five cities" is derived from the "pentapolis" of Wisdom 10:6–7, where the destruction of the cities is recalled: "Haec iustum a pereuntibus impiis liberavit fugientem, descendente igne in Pentapolim, quibus in testimonium nequitiae fumigabunda constat deserta terra, et incerto tempore fructus habentes arbores, et incredibilis animae memoria stans figmentum salis." But Segor was not destroyed; it was saved by the appeal of Lot (Gen. 19:21–22). For the story of the destruction and Abraham's attempt to save the cities by pleading with the Lord see Gen. 18–19.

54/19–22 **His hart . . . tyme.** In Gerar, Abraham was afraid he would be killed because of his wife and pretended that she was his sister. (She was, in fact, his half-sister [Gen. 20:12]). Abimelech took her, but after the Lord appeared to him in a dream, he restored her untouched to Abraham (Gen. 20:1–16). The wealth Abraham was given for his trouble consisted of "oves et boves, et servos et ancillas," as well as "mille argenteos" (Gen. 20:14, 16).

54/23 **long.** This word is crowded into a space beneath the ruling at the top of the page; the hand appears different from *A*, but the difference may be caused by the crowding. It is certainly not *B*.

54/23–55/4 **What . . . than.** Abraham's "mone" to God because he had no child of his own is to be found in Gen. 15:2–3. He sired Ishmael on a servant, Hagar the Egyptian, whom Sarah had given him to take as wife since she herself was unable to conceive. When Sarah later gave birth to Isaac, she asked Abraham to cast out Hagar and Ishmael. Abraham was grieved, but the Lord consoled him, and he sent them out into the wilderness of Beersheba (Gen. 16:1–16). For "child of promiscion," a favorite Pauline phrase, cf. Gal. 4:28: "Nos autem, fratres, secundum Isaac promissionis filii sumus." See also Rom. 9:8 and Gal. 3:29. The reference here is to the covenant with Abraham which was to be passed on through Isaac. John Frith uses the phrase in the same way in *A pistle to the Christen reader* prefacing *The Revelation of Antichrist* (Antwerp, 1529, sig. B₁v): "We (deare brothren) are the children of promission as Isaac was / not the sonnes of the bond woman as Ismael." Isaac's life was "vnlokyd for" because of the extreme old age of his parents (Gen. 21:1–7). The story of the sacrifice of Isaac is told in Gen. 22:1–15. Abraham's feelings are not mentioned, hence More's surmise.

54/27 **was.** *A* reads: "& was yet no grefe than whan he was cast out the mother & the child both." *B*'s emendation of "yet" to "it" seems acceptable (*A* probably misreading "yt" as "yet"); but *B*'s emendation of "was" to "must" seems doubtful, even though it makes good sense. It seems quite possible that More, with the emphasis on "Ismaell" in the previous clause, wrote "he was cast out," and then added parenthetically —"the mother & the child both."

55/6–8 **Than . . . willyngly.** Cf. *Confutation, CW 8,* 301/10–13.

55/16–33 **an other . . . payne.** Luke 16:19–31. The "other rich man" was Dives, at whose gate Lazarus lay, full of sores. In describing Dives' torment in hell More refers specifically to 16:24: "Et ipse clamans dixit: Pater Abraham, miserere mei, et mitte Lazarum ut intingat extremum digiti sui in aquam ut refrigeret linguam meam, quia crucior in hac flamma." The "fyry cowch" is More's own ironic addition, suiting the punishment to the crime. It refers to the ancient custom of reclining while fcasting. More quotes Luke 16:25 and 16:19. The story is told by Christ, hence More's reference to Christ's description (l. 25). Cf. also below, 319/1–4.

57/23–29 **wherfor . . . vpp.** 1 Cor. 5:1–5 and 2 Cor. 2:1–11. More quotes 2 Cor. 2:7. The Vulgate reads (cf. the correction of *1573*): "ne forte abundantiori tristitia absorbeatur." More's identification of the fornicator mentioned in 1 Cor. 5 with the sinner referred to in 2 Cor. 2 is dependent upon tradition, such as the comment in the *Glossa Ordinaria, PL 114,* 553. They are no longer believed to be the same man; see *The Interpreter's Bible* (New York, 1952–57), *10,* 294.

58/5–11 **& not . . . seeth not.** For the phrase "not sine affectione" (l. 5), see 2 Tim. 3:2–3 "homines seipsos amantes . . . non obedientes, ingrati,

scelesti, sine affectione, sine pace," and cf. Rom. 1:28–32. For "he that
... not" (ll. 10–11), see 1 John 4:20.

In l. 6 *B* writes "hart" above the last two letters of "affeccions," with
a caret below. This seems to be a suggested substitution (to read "tender
hart") and not an insertion, which would make no sense. All other texts
read "affeccyons here." Apparently at some point in the manuscript
tradition "hart" was interpreted as an error for "here."

58/15–18 **when ... hym.** Acts 12:5: "Et Petrus quidem servabatur in
carcere. Oratio autem fiebat sine intermissione ab Ecclesia ad Deum pro
eo." More refers to Peter's imprisonment by Herod during the Passover.
He was delivered by an angel who woke him at night, struck the chains
from his hands, led him into the city, and then disappeared.

58/20–21 **Salua ... tempest.** Matt. 8:25. The Vulgate reads: "Domine,
salva nos ... " Jesus replied: "Quid timidi estis, modicae fidei? Tunc
surgens, imperavit ventis et mari, et facta est tranquillitas magna" (8:26).

58/21–23 **And now ... helpe.** More refers to the "extraordinary" processions of the church as opposed to the "ordinary" proccssions on
certain fixed days of the liturgical year, such as Candlemas, Palm Sunday,
and Corpus Christi Day. In the Roman ritual extraordinary processions
are regarded as a form of public supplication promulgated by local
bishops in times of great need or distress, such as war, famine, pestilence,
or any other calamity (*pro quacunque tribulatione*). The litany of the saints
and a special supplication proper to the occasion are usually recited as
the procession proceeds. In the medieval church there were a great
number of such extraordinary forms, associated primarily with petitions
for good weather and abundant harvests. See *The Catholic Encyclopedia*, s.v.
"Processions."

59/17–60/6 **Some ... hym.** For More's concern with sleeplessness see his
Tower letter to Margaret: "I am of nature so shrinking from paine, that
I am allmost afeard of a philip, yet in all the agonies that I haue had,
wherof before my coming hether (as I haue shewed you ere this) I haue
had neither small nor few, with heauy fearfull heart, forecasting all such
peryls and paynfull deathes, as by any maner of possibilitie might after
fall vnto me, and in such thought lyen longe restles and wakyng, while my
wyfe had went I had slept, yet in anye such feare and heauy pensifenes
(I thanke the mightie mercie of God) I neuer in my minde entended to
consent, that I woulde for the enduring of the vttermost, doe any such
thinge as I shoulde in mine owne conscience ... thinke to be to my self,
such as shoulde dampnably cast me in the displeasure of God" (Rogers,
pp. 546–47; see also p. 530).

60/6–8 **& biddeth ... hony.** Exod. 3:8: "liberem eum de manibus
Aegyptiorum, et educam de terra illa in terram bonam, et spatiosam, in

terram quae fluit lacte et melle." The Exodus was traditionally alle-
gorized as the freedom of the soul from its bondage to sin and its departure
through death to heaven. Cf. Dante's letter to Can Grande (*Opere*, ed.
E. More and P. Toynbee [Oxford, 1924], p. 416), and *Treatise on the
Passion, EW*, sig. NN₃v: "the thraldome of the chyldren of Israel vnder
king Pharao and thegipcians, signifieth the bondage of mankynde vnder
the prynce of thys darke world, the dyuell and hys euyl spirites . . . And
by al the course after of the people conuayed from the red sea, by the
deserte towarde the land of byhest . . . is there sygnified and fygured, the
long payneful wandering of men in the wylde wylderness of this wreched
world ere we can get hence to heauen."

61/1–2 **peccator . . . contymneth.** Prov. 18:3. The Vulgate reads:
"Impium, cum in profundum venerit peccatorum, contemnit." The verse
continues, "sed sequitur eum ignominia et opprobrium," as More
indicates in the next paragraph (61/5 ff.). Evidently *A* made some error
in the letters "mn" of "contymneth" (l. 2) (probably missing a minim, so
that the letters looked like "nu"); someone, probably *E*, has heavily
written "mn" over the "nu"(?); then "contemneth" has been interlineated (above the cancelled original word) by the same hand (*E*) as that
in the marginalia on this folio. The rest of this interlineation "& settyth
nought" is by *B*.

61/6 **serue,.** A short black line above the comma makes the punctuation
appear to be a semi-colon, but this is apparently only an accidental pen-
stroke. Semi-colons are not used elsewhere in the MS.

61/27 **fansies . . . fantasies.** The words are interchangeable, both in the
CC MS and in the other texts, "fancy" being simply a contraction of
"fantasy," as the *OED* makes clear in its account of both these words. The
basic meaning is derived from scholastic psychology: "Mental apprehension of an object of perception; the faculty by which this is performed"
(*OED*, "fantasy," *sb.* 1). From here the sense moves to that of "illusory
appearance" (2), or "delusive imagination" (3), and then on into (4):
"Imagination: the process or the faculty of forming mental representations
of things not actually present." More also uses the word occasionally in
the sense of "caprice, changeful mood" (6), and also "inclination, liking,
desire" (7). More uses virtually the entire range of possibilities recorded
under the interesting *OED* account of "fantasy." For the scholastic interpretation, see *Aristotle's De Anima and the Commentary of St. Thomas Aquinas*,
trans. K. Foster and F. Humphries (London, 1951), III, iii, 696, p. 390.
Cf. below, 109/27–28.

62/7–23 **Some . . . slayne.** 1 Kings 28:3–19. The reference to 1 Kings 27
in the 1557 and 1573 marginalia is an error. When the Philistines came
with a large army and camped at Shunen, Saul became afraid and consulted the Lord. But God did not answer him, "neque per somnia, neque

per sacerdotes, neque per prophetas" (28:6). Saul therefore sought out
the Witch of Endor, who raised up the dead Samuel. Samuel told Saul
that his army would be defeated and that he would die, which is the
"evill answere" More refers to (62/22). In 28:3 Saul is said to have
removed (*abstulit*) the magicians and soothsayers from the land. In 28:9,
however, he is said to have wiped them out or destroyed them (*eraserit*).
Saul presumably acted in accord with the command of Lev. 20:27: "Vir,
sive mulier, in quibus pythonicus vel divinationis fuerit spiritus, morte
moriantur: lapidibus obruent eos: sanguis eorum sit super illos." Necromancy, in the literal sense of consultation of the dead, was forbidden in
Deut. 18:10–11. God's prohibition against witchcraft is given in Lev.
19:31, and 20:6, 27. See also *Heresies, EW*, sig. i₁. Saul had previously
incurred God's anger for not destroying all the possessions of the Amale-
kites, which is what More refers to in 62/14–15. Samuel told him: "Pro
eo ergo quod abjecisti sermonem Domini, abjecit te Dominus ne sis rex"
(1 Kings 15:23). Saul repented, but God did not forgive him. David was
anointed king, and Saul began to be tormented by an evil spirit from the
Lord (15:24–16:14).

62/23–27 **And as . . . law.** 1 Par. 10:13: "Mortuus est ergo Saul propter
iniquitates suas, eo quod praevaricatus sit mandatum Domini quod
praeceperat, et non custodierit illud: sed in super etiam pythonissam
consulerit." In his Tower works More frequently turned to Saul as an
exemplum of lack of trust in God. Cf. *De Tristitia, CW 14*, 153: "ne quum
quippiam precamur quod non impetramus animo concidamus ut Rex
Saul sortilegus." See also *Devotions, EW*, sigs. VV₃v (mismarked XX₃v)
and VV₄v.

63/1–17 **And . . . god.** More parodies witchcraft and sympathetic magic,
piling one typical absurdity on another. Although distinctions were made
between witches of the sort More describes and those who effected their
cures by compacts with the devil, both were condemned for interfering
with God's intentions. Cf. *Malleus Maleficarum*, II, ii: "to approach such
women [witches who work through sympathetic magic] in order to be
cured is all the more pernicious because they seem to bring greater
contempt upon the Faith than others who effect their cures by means of a
merely tacit compact with the devil. For they who resort to such witches
are thinking more of their bodily health than of God, and besides that,
God cuts short their lives to punish them for taking into their own hands
the vengeance for their wrongs. For so the Divine vengeance overtook
Saul, because he first cast out of the land all magicians and wizards, and
afterwards consulted a witch" (ed. and trans. Montague Summers
[London, 1948], p. 160). As the quotation indicates, the cause of Saul's
death, the warning More draws from it, and its application to witches in
general were also commonplaces in treatises on magic and demonology.

63/10 **sower.** *B* emends to "sowce," and this reading (and spelling) is followed by $\mathcal{Z}$. The *OED* lists "sowce" as a variant spelling of "souse," which can mean (v^1 I. 1.) to steep "in some kind of pickle, especially one made with vinegar or other tart liquor." The *OED* does not record "sowce" as a variant spelling for "sauce"—though this verb is perhaps a possibility (see *OED*, "sauce" *v.* 2. b. "to qualify with a mixture of bitterness"). But no emendation seems necessary: "siropes," as the *OED* makes clear (see the examples under "syrup") were associated with bitter, or sour medicines.

63/16 **their soles.** This is the original reading of *A*; "soles" is a possible spelling for "souls" in the sixteenth century, but no other example of this spelling occurs in *CC*. *B* may well be right in emending the word to "foles" (cf. 63/1), changing "their" to "there," and inserting "many," to read: "there many foles," a reading followed by *L* and *1557*, while *1553* and *1573* agree on the last two words (see textual footnote).

64/20–22 **they ... taken.** For the distinction between the categories of good, bad, and indifferent in traditional ethics, see below, 223/14–26 and n.

65/23 **patereth.** More uses the word in its etymological sense: "To repeat the Paternoster or other prayer, esp. in a rapid, mechanical, or indistinct fashion: to mumble or mutter one's prayers" (*OED*, *Patter*, v^1, 1).

65/27 **a long ... mattyns.** Matins refers to the night office of the church, formerly held at midnight. The service was notable for its length. For major feasts it consisted of nine psalms and nine readings in the Roman liturgy, twelve psalms and twelve readings plus three *OT* canticles in the monastic liturgy. In both liturgies a responsory followed each reading. By a "payre" of matins More may mean the entire service repeated twice. He most likely refers to it, however, in a collective sense, as in a pair of steps or a pair of trousers. Cf. "And so in a payre of matyns it is much work to happen on the meane. And than to saye theim to shorte is lacke of deuocion. And to saye theim to seryously is somwhat supersticiouse. And therfore the best waye were in my mynd, to saie none at all" (*Heresies*, *EW*, sig. o₄v).

65/28–29 **vij ... anelyng.** The seven penitential psalms (6, 31, 37, 50, 101, 129, and 142 in the Vulgate), recited after confession in the liturgy of extreme unction. Recitation of the seven psalms usually included the litany as well; see *Confutation*, *CW 8*, 11/20–21, and below, n. to 155/20–21.

66/9–22 **Grete ... father.** Phil. 2:8–11. The Vulgate (cf. the correction in $\mathcal{Z}$) reads *confiteatur* rather than *confitiatur*. The history of commentary on the verses More quotes is extremely complex, involving the Arian heresy and extended philosophical distinctions between form and substance and appearance and reality. Erasmus gives an excellent survey in his *NT*, concluding that Jesus was both God and man: "Loquitur [Paul] enim de

Christo, quatenus erat homo . . . Deus erat, homo erat. Deum celavit, hominen exhibuit usque ad sepulturam : . . . hominem abjectum, hominem damnatum Christus agere non potuit, nisi fuisset homo" (*Opera, 6,* 867–68). See also Peter Lombard, *Collectanea in Epistolas D. Pauli (PL 192,* 233–38) ; Theodore Beza, *Novum D. N. Iesu Christi Testamentum* (n. p., 1557), fol. 289; and More's own repeated references in the *De Tristitia, CW 14,* 87–93, 149–53, *et passim.*

66/27–29 **not his . . . neyther.** I.e., "Christ's act of washing His apostles' feet did not have the same degree of merit as His passion; His sleep did not have the same degree of merit as His watch and prayer (in Gethsemane); perhaps even His prayers were not all of the same degree of merit." The term "maundy," used in More's time for the commemorative ceremony of washing the feet of the poor on Maundy or Holy Thursday, is derived from the Latin *mandatum* or commandment, the first word of the antiphon sung at the ceremony: "Mandatum novum do vobis: ut diligatis invicem, sicut dilexi vos." Cf. *Confutation, CW 8,* 196/13, 313/4, and 376/26.

67/4–10 **The first . . . crosse.** For Christ's prostration of Himself, see Matt. 26:36–44; the bloody sweat is from Luke 22:44. The prayer is recorded in both gospels; the version in Luke reads: "Pater, si vis, transfer calicem istum a me: Veruntamen non mea voluntas, sed tua fiat." The prayers on the cross occur in Luke 23:34: "Pater, dimitte illis: non enim sciunt quid faciunt," and Luke 23:46: "Pater, in manus tuas commendo spiritum meum." The reference to Acts 26 in the 1557 marginalia is an allusion to Paul's account of his conversion as given in his trial before Agrippa; it is not a gloss on More's text.

68/18 **confirmyd.** "conformed" *Z.* This is one of many examples of the variant spellings noted by the *OED* under "conform" *v*: "In 14–16 c. there was considerable confusion between *conform* and *confirm; conferm, -firm, -fyrm* being often written for *conform* . . . This prob. points to a (? dial.) pronunciation." The other texts obliterate this usage by normalizing to "-form." For other instances see 71/4, 16; 74/5, 10, 12, 15.

69/11–19 **Melius . . . gladnes.** Eccles. 7:3. The Vulgate (cf. the correction in *Z*) reads *hominum* rather than *homo;* the reading *homo* in *A* may have resulted from the scribe's failure to expand an abbreviation in his copytext. The second quotation (l. 17) is from Eccles. 7:5.

69/24–29 **Now . . . waywardnes.** Cf. Deut. 33:26–29, 20–30; Exod. 32:9–14.

69/29–70/2 **and therfor . . . perfeccion.** Cf. Gal. 3:24–25: "Itaque lex paedagogus noster fuit in Christo, ut ex fide justificemur. At ubi venit fides, jam non sumus sub paedagogo." The metaphor of the *paedagogus* was extended in traditional glosses, such as Jerome's: "Paedogogus parvulis assignatur, ut lasciviens refrenetur aetas, et prona in vitia corda teneantur, dum tenera studiis eruditur infantia, et ad majores philosophiae ac regendae reipublicae disciplinas, metu poenae coercita praeparatur. Non tamen paedogogus magister et pater est, nec haereditatem et scientiam paedogogi is qui eruditur, exspectat; sed alienum custodit filium paedogogus, ab eo postquam ille ad legitimum capiendae haereditatis tempus advenerit, recessurus" (*Commentariorum in Epistolam ad Galatos Libri Tres*, II, iii [*PL 26*, 368]). See also *Glossa Ordinaria, PL 114*, 577.

More (70/1) quotes Heb. 7:19. The Vulgate reads *Nihil enim* for *Nihil* and *adduxit* for *duxit*.

70/14–18 **the wordes . . . mirth.** Eccles. 7:3 and 7:5, quoted above at 69/11–19.

70/18–21 **wherto . . . hevynes.** Prov. 11:28: "Qui confidit in divitiis suis, corruet." More seems to have linked this verse with Prov. 14:11, "Domus impiorum delebitur," which occurs in the passage from which he quotes. The quotation is from Prov. 14:13, but it has nothing to do with wealth, as More implies. The contrast is between the wicked and the just, the wise man and the fool.

70/22–25 **ve . . . comfortid.** The first quotation is from Luke 6:25. The Vulgate reads *ridetis nunc* (*Biblia Latina*, "nunc ridetis") rather than *ridetis*. Cf. above, 41/29–31. The associative link with the passage from Ecclesiastes on the dangers of wealth immediately above (70/18–21) was probably provided by Luke 6:24: "Verumtamen vae vobis divitibus, quia habetis consolationem vestram." But in a larger sense the context of the entire passage is significant: Christians are blessed when men hate them and cast them out; they should love their enemies and those who bring false accusations against them.

The second quotation is from the parallel passage in Matt. 5:5, the sermon on the mount. The Vulgate reads *ipsi* rather than *illi*.

70/26–28 **Mundus . . . ioy.** John 16:20. The Vulgate reads *mundus autem* for *Mundus* and *contristabimini* for *dolebitis*. Jesus tells the disciples they must suffer persecution for His sake and speaks in a veiled fashion of His own death. He then offers them this consolation, using the image of a woman who gives birth in anguish that later turns to joy (John 15:18–16:4, 16–22).

71/28–29 **as many . . . hym.** More probably has in mind the various occasions in which David offended the Lord and repented, such as 2 Kings 12:13–18 and 2 Kings 24:10, as well as the penitential psalms attributed to David, such as Ps. 50, and those in which he affirms that his love for God is greater than all earthly power and wealth (e.g., Ps. 51 and Ps. 18).

72/6–7 **he doth . . . welth.** I.e., "the rich man diminishes the amount of his worldly wealth to the extent that he uses it to do good deeds" (so that these deeds partake more of tribulation than of wealth [cf. ll. 16–17]).

72/19 **aperes.** *A* reads "aperee"; the final "e" is cancelled by *B* and the penultimate "e" is corrected in a way that seems designed to clarify the original "e." The other texts all read "appeare" and make sense out of the passage by adding another "doth" before "doth in" (see textual footnote to 72/18). But it seems preferable to assume that "aperee" is a scribal slip for "aperes" and thus to avoid the clumsy duplication of "doth."

74/4 **Confitebimur . . . ei.** Ps. 48:19: "We will praise you when you benefit him." The Vulgate (cf. the correction in Z) reads *confitebitur* for *Confitebimur*. The reference to Ps. 28 in the 1573 marginalia is an error. For More's earlier use of this psalm and the marginalia in his *Psalter*, see above, 48/29–49/3 and n.

74/7–9 **For . . . difficulty.** A common idea among a variety of philosophers. Cf. Seneca, *Prov.*, V, 9–10: "Quare tamen deus tam iniquus in distributione fati fuit, ut bonis viris paupertatem et vulnera et acerba funera ascriberet? . . . Ut efficiatur vir cum cura dicendus, fortiore fato opus est. Non erit illi planum iter; sursum oportet ac deorsum eat, fluctuetur ac navigium in turbido regat. Contra fortunam illi tenendus est cursus; multa accident dura, aspera, sed quae molliat et complanet ipse. Ignis aurum probat, miseria fortes viros." See also Aristotle, *Eth. Nic.*, II, iii (1105*a*, 9–13), and Erasmus, *Adag.*, "Aspera vita, sed salubris," sig. Nnn₃ (III. X. xxvii).

74/17–30 **And . . . agayne.** Job 1:9–12; Luke 6:32–35, and Matt. 5:44–47.

76/6–12 **Quia . . . biddeth.** Ps. 33:19. The Vulgate reads *Juxta est Dominus iis* rather than *Quia deus iuxta est ijs*. The references to Ps. 32 in the 1557 marginalia and to Ps. 31 in the 1573 marginalia are in error. The entire psalm forms an interesting comment on this concluding statement of Book I. (Eight verses, including verse 19, are marked by More with a marginal line in his *Psalter;* see *Prayer Book*, pp. 65–66.) It is the song of a just man who prayed to God for help in his fear and tribulation and whose prayers were answered. It would seem to be related to the catena of quotations from the Psalms above, 48/13–49/5, and looks forward to the use of Psalm 90 in Books II and III. Cf. "Clamaverunt iusti, et Dominus exaudivit eos: et ex omnibus tribulationibus eorum liberavit eos . . . Mors peccatorum pessima: et qui oderunt justum delinquent. Redimet Dominus animas servorum suorum: et non delinquent omnes qui sperant in eo" (Ps. 33:18, 22–23).

The reference at ll. 11–12 is to James 5:14: "Infirmatur quis in vobis? inducat presbyteros Ecclesiae, et orent super eum, ungentes eum oleo in nomine Domini."

76/25–28 **for charite . . . out.** In this passage More refers to 1 Pet. 4:8; Rom. 10:11, where Paul paraphrases Prov. 29:25 or Ecclus. 2:11; and John 6:37. As the 1557 and 1573 marginalia indicate, 1 Pet. 4:8 is similar to Prov. 10:12.

78/24–26 **It . . . talke.** Cf. Juvenal, *Sat.*, X, 188–245; Horace, *Ars P.* 169–76.

78/25 **a rostid crabb.** A reference to the common practice of putting roasted crab-apples in bowls or cups of ale. Cf. Shakespeare, *Love's Labor's Lost*, V, ii, 925: "When roasted crabs hiss in the bowl"; also Puck's words in *A Midsummer Night's Dream*, II, i, 47–50.

79/24 **ofter.** *A* reads "other," which may be right, in the sense of "further, additional" (*OED* "other," *adj.* A. 5). *B*'s emendation has been accepted with some hesitation.

80/1–2 **a close religion.** I.e., an enclosed, cloistered religious order or house (see *OED*, "religion" 2), where the nuns are never allowed to leave the convent. Cf. *Richard III, CW* 2, 3/11–12, where More renders the phrase "an house of close Nunnes" as "in monasterio monialium inclusarum."

80/7 **locutory.** Literally, "the speaking place": the grate at which nuns of contemplative orders are allowed to speak to visitors. In contemporary Carmelite monasteries it consists of an iron grille covered with a screen of black cloth. The room is still known as the "speak room."

81/1–18 **there . . . halfe.** Hallet (p. viii) sees this story as a personal anecdote involving More himself and Dame Alice. The evidence is inconclusive, as is the case with all such anecdotes in *A Dialogue of Comfort*, but the identification here seems reasonable and the anecdote entirely in keeping with what we know of More's relationship with his second wife. Erasmus, who never learned to like her, called her a *mater familias*, "acrem et vigilantem," whom More had learned to handle through a kind of playful seriousness (Allen, *4*, 19). More's custom seems to have been to project on their relationship the stock characters and situations of medieval anti-feminism, which makes it difficult to say whether he is drawing directly on that vast reservoir of oral and written tradition or whether the anecdotes he relates had some basis in fact. In this particular anecdote, More seems to emphasize the question of the kinswoman's identity by having Antony guess who she was (l. 20).

81/20–22 **I wold . . . talke.** The sense is obscure. At first one might think Antony is saying that she is far from the worst of wives in this regard; but the syntax does not bear this out. He seems rather to be saying that in spite of her merry words, he wishes there were no women among his kindred with this habit, even though they hindered their husbands less. *1553* was apparently puzzled too and revised the passage rather ineffectively to read: "but yet the fewer of that kinde, the quieter is the many (for all her mery wordes) that thus woulde let her husbande to talke" (sig. F₃).

82/16–18 **Salamon . . . sorow.** Prov. 31 : 6–7.

82/18–21 **saynt . . . dedly.** *ST*, II-II, Q. 168, a. 2. Arguing whether there is any virtue in play ("Utrum in ludis possit esse aliqua virtus"), Aquinas replies to Ambrose and Chrysostom that "ludicra verba et facta" are necessary to refresh the mind: "Sicut . . . fatigatio corporalis solvitur per corporis quietem, ita etiam oportet quod fatigatio animalis solvatur per animae quietem. Quies autem animae est delectatio, ut supra habitum est cum de passionibus ageretur." He then goes on to identify the virtue found in play as Aristotle's εὐτραπελία. In his *Eth. Nic.* Aristotle spoke of εὐτραπελία as wittiness: "Those who joke in a tasteful way are called ready witted, which implies a sort of readiness to turn this way and that" (IV, viii, 3 [1128 *a*]). The word εὐτραπελία is derived from τρέπειν, "to turn." Aquinas translated it as *bona conversione*, that is, a good turn of mind: "Et dicitur aliquis eutrapelus a bona conversione, quia scilicet bene convertit aliqua dicta vel facta in solatium."

83/4–5 **my selfe . . . more.** A pun perhaps on More's surname. Cf. Erasmus' description of More in his letter to Ulrich von Hutten of July 23, 1519: "Iam inde a puero sic iocis est delectatus vt ad hos natus videri possit, sed in his nec ad scurrilitatem vsque progressus est, nec mordacitatem vnquam amauit" (Allen, *4*, 16). Cf. *Heresies, EW,* sig. h₁v, and *Apology, EW,* sig. N₄.

84/5–15 **Cassianus . . . reherse.** The story is told, not in the *Collationes,* but in Cassianus' *De Coenobiorum Institutis,* V, 31 (*PL 49*, 247–48). A number of details are also wrong. The aged monk was not delivering a sermon; he was engaged in a discussion of spiritual affairs. And the point of the story is different from More's. The old monk uses it to show how the devil delights in merry tales: "Hic idem senex otiosarum fabularum diabolum esse fautorem, ac spiritalium collationum impugnatorem semper existere, his declaravit indiciis. Nam cum fratribus quibusdam de rebus necessariis ac spiritalibus disputaret, eosque videret lethaeo quodam sopore demergi, nec posse ab oculis suis pondus somni depellere; otiosam repente fabulam introduxit. Ad cujus oblectationum cum eos evigilasse confestim, erectas aures suas habere vidisset, ingemiscens ait: Nunc usque de rebus coelestibus loquebamur, et omnium vestrum oculi lethali dormitione deprimebatur; at cum otiosa fabula intromissa est, omnes expergefacti torporem somni dominantis excussimus. Vel ex hoc ergo perpendite quisnam Collationis illius spiritalis fuerit impugnator, aut quis hujus infructuosae atque carnalis insinuator existat. Ille etenim esse manifestissime deprehenditur, qui malis adgaudens, vel istam fovere, vel illam impugnare non desinit."

84/24–29 **How . . . on.** Cf. the prayer More wrote in his *Book of Hours* (*Prayer Book*, pp. 18–19, 186): "To abstayn from vayne confabulations / To estew light folysh myrth & gladnesse / Recreationys not necessary / to cutt off / of worldely substauns frendys libertie life and all / to sett the losse at right nowght for the wynnyng of christ."

86/2 **yt.** *B*'s emendation to "yet" is probably right, but "yt" is preserved here for two reasons: (1) to provide an example of the approximately eight cases where *A* seems to write "it" or "yt" for "yit" ("yet") (the *OED* records the spelling "yt" for "yit" in the fifteenth century); (2) the word in this particular instance may be a loose and general use of the pronoun.

86/7–8 **ther . . . old.** Tilley, L 39 and S 293; *ODEP*, p. 53.

86/8–10 **yet . . . long.** Cf. above, 4/15–17 and n.

88/10 **tercian.** A form of fever in which the onslaughts occur every third (that is, every alternate) day (*OED*).

88/4–90/7 **that straunge . . . to.** According to Harpsfield this is a personal anecdote. The fever was More's own, and the young girl was Margaret Giggs, "a woman furnished with muche vertue and wisdome, and with the knowledge of the latine and greeke tonge, yea, and physicke too, aboue many that seeme good and cunning phisitians" (pp. 90–91). Born around 1505, she was reared and educated with More's own children. Her parents are unknown, though her mother may have been Margaret More's wet nurse. The Basel sketch by Holbein (1527) pictures her at the age of twenty-two. Early in 1526 she married John Clement, former tutor to More's children. He had also served as Wolsey Lecturer in Rhetoric and Reader in Greek at Oxford and studied medicine at Louvain and Siena, receiving his M.D. at Siena in March 1525. In February 1527/28 he was admitted as a member of the College of Physicians and shortly afterward was appointed physician to the court. More was visiting the Clements on Sunday, April 12, 1534, when he was summoned to appear the next day before the commissioners at Lambeth. During the last months of More's imprisonment, Margaret Clement secretly fed the Carthusians chained to posts and left to die "by the hand of God." She was the only member of the family present at More's death and helped bury his body in the chapel of St. Peter ad Vincula in the Tower. She died in exile at Mechlin in Brabant on July 6, 1570, two years before her husband.

Antony says the fever occurred "more than fiften yeres agoo" (88/9–10); if we assume that More is dating from the time of writing (1534–35), the event would have occurred around 1520, when Margaret was about fifteen years old. But whatever real knowledge she had of medicine probably came later, after her marriage to Clement. More says she was taught physic by a "kynsman of hers" (89/12–13); the phrase is perhaps

meant to be a joking allusion to their marriage. More seems to be creating a
pleasant fiction out of real events here.

89/21–24 **a worke . . . same.** See Galen, *De differentiis febrium*, Book II,
Chap. 6: "De febre epiala qua simul febricitant, ac rigent . . ." ("Of the
fever called 'epiala' in which at one and the same time they feel feverish
and have chills"). The quotation is taken from the Latin translation by
Laurentius Laurentianus, of which six separate editions appeared
between 1512 and 1526. Since the Cologne edition of 1526 is marred by
misprints, quotations have been taken from the well-printed Paris
edition of 1535, edited by Simon Thomas. The opening of chapter 6
makes the point clearly: "Hoc genere continetur febris epiala proprie
nominata, quoties simul febricitant ac rigent: & utrunque sentiunt,
eodem tempore in quauis corporis parte." That is, as Antony says, "They
feel both hot and cold at the same time in every part of the body." The
controversy over this alleged kind of fever described by Galen is made
clear in the interesting edition of the *De differentiis febrium* published at
Lyons in 1514, with the "antiqua traductio" followed by the new translation by Nicolaus Leonicenus, along with an extensive commentary by
Thomas de Garbo. At the front of this volume appears an "Index dubio-
rum" in which one of the questions is: "An in empiala simul in eisdem
partibus sentiatur calor et frigus," followed by a reference to folio xc,
part of the long commentary on Book II, Chap. 6. (The spelling "empiala"
is picked up from the old translation and carried in the chapter headings;
but "epiala" is correct.) Folios 89ᵛ–91 of this edition carry a long account
of the problems concerning this kind of fever "in qua simul et semel in
omni parte corporis sentitur calor et frigus." Another edition of Garbo's
commentary appeared in Venice, in 1521. For editions of Galen available
to More in Latin see Richard J. Durling, "A Chronological Census of
Renaissance Editions and Translations of Galen," *Journal of the Warburg
and Courtauld Institutes,* 24 (1961), 230–305.

But in referring to a work "redy to be sold in the boke sellers shopps,"
More may be making a sly reference to a work in which Margaret Giggs's
husband had a part: the Greek *editio princeps* of Galen, which was published
in five volumes at Venice by the Aldine Press in 1525. John Clement is
mentioned in the preface to volume five (sig. A₃) and thanked for his
assistance, along with two other Englishmen, Odoardus and Roseus:
"Sed quando tu unus velut Imperator bellum hoc patrare tam difficile &
arduum non poteras & grati est animi fateri cui debeas: agent etiam
gratias graeci latinique restitui Galeni Clementi, & Odoardo, & Roseis
Brittanis, qui te veluti Centuriones acerrime victoria hac consequenda
plurimam adiuvere, etc." (cited by Headley in *Responsio, CW 5,* 798–99).
From this brief acknowledgement, it is impossible to tell the extent of
Clement's work on Galen, but More's reference to *De Differentiis Febrium*
is probably designed as a compliment to him, even though Erasmus
thought the edition a bad one (Allen, *6,* 142, and *2,* 198).

90/7 **that . . . her.** I.e., "that compliment is well spent upon her." See the *OED*, "ware" v^2: "to spend, lay out," especially usage d., which illustrates the phrases "To be well, or ill, wared."

90/13–15 **& shall . . . ioyfull.** In his *Four Last Things* More attributes the saying to Augustine, not Jerome, but without indicating its location: "Lo the holy doctor sainct Austine, exhortyng penitentes and repentant synners to sorow for theyr offences, sayeth vnto them. Sorowe (saith this holy man) and be glad of thy sorow" (*EW*, sig. e₅v). The basis of the quotation is to be found not in Augustine's works, but in the pseudonymous *Liber de Vera et Falsa Poenitentia*, XIII, 28: "Ubi enim dolor finitur, deficit et poenitentia. Si autem poenitentia finitur, quid relinquitur de venia? Tamdiu enim gaudeat et speret de gratia, quandiu sustentatur a poenitentia. Dixit enim Dominus, *Vade, et amplius noli peccare* (*Joan.* VIII, 11). Non dixit, ne pecces; sed, nec voluntas peccandi in te oriatur. Quod quomodo servabitur, nisi dolor continue in poenitentia, custodiatur? Hinc semper doleat, et de dolore gaudeat, et de doloris poenitentia, si contigerit, semper doleat. Et non sit satis quod doleat, sed ex fide doleat, et non semper doluisse doleat" (*PL 40*, 1124). In the Middle Ages this work was almost universally attributed to Augustine—by Peter Lombard, Vincent de Beauvais, Gratian, Aquinas, and others. More again attributes it to Augustine in the *Confutation*, *CW 8*, 867/30–34; but Erasmus and others denied that it was his, partly because Augustine himself is cited in chapter XVII as one of the authorities used in the text. The treatise is now believed to date from the twelfth century.

90/21–22 **And did . . . come.** In view of his extensive use of Psalm 90 later in the work, More may have been thinking specifically of Jerome's comment on Psalm 90:4. The psalm speaks of God's shadowing men under His wings. Jerome comments: "Exaltabitur in cruce, extendet manus, et proteget nos" (*Breviarum in Psalmos* [*PL 26*, 1098]). The same idea is repeated by N. de Lyra in his *Postilla* on Psalm 90:4: "brachiis in cruce protensis in modum alarum" (*Biblia Latina, 3*, sig. I₆v).

90/22–25 **And envy . . . all.** Luke 23:39–43, which More combines with the conclusion of the parable of the lost sheep in Luke 15:7.

91/18–23 **As . . . haue.** More paraphrases 1 Cor. 15:9–10. In the Vulgate (cf. the corrections in *1557* and *1573*) the quotation reads *abundantius illis omnibus* rather than *plus omnibus*.

91/26–92/3 **And hireth . . . mornyng.** See Matt. 20:1–16.

92/9–16 **They . . . life.** Cf. *Supplication*, *EW*, sigs. x₂–x₂v: "suche heretikes haue perswaded vnto som men all readye, that . iii. or . iiii. woordes ere they dye shall sufficyentely serue them to bring them streight to heauen. Wher as besydes the feare that they shoulde haue lest they shall lacke at last yᵉ grace to turne at all, and so for faulte of those iii. or. iiii. wordes fall to the fyre of hell, if they belieue therwᵗ the thing yᵗ trueth is besyde, that is to wit that though thei hap to haue the grace to repente & be forgeuen the synne and so to be deliuered of the endlesse payne of hel, yet they shall not so frely be deliuered of purgatorye."

Stories in which the devil carries off what is assigned to him in anger are fairly common. Caesarius of Heisterbach, for example, tells two such *exempla*—one about a woman whose husband told her to go to the devil, and the devil immediately entered her ear; the other about a boy whose father told him to go to the devil, and the devil came and carried him off (*Dialogue of Miracles*, V, xi-xii, trans. H. von E. Scott and C. C. Swinton Bland [London, 1929], *I*, 331-32). The stories turn on the popular belief that a curse is effective when it comes from the heart. A reverse variant appears in Chaucer's *Friar's Tale*, 1539-70, where the devil is given an opportunity to carry off a horse and a cart of hay that are stuck in the mud, but declines since he knows that the carter did not mean what he said: "The carl spak oo thing, but he thoughte another" (1568).

92/14 **in a soden flight.** The phrase is ambiguous, but "flight" seems primarily to refer to the man's emotional, not physical, state. See the *OED*, "flight" *sb.*¹ 4: "A state of flutter or agitation; a trembling, fright ... *in flight:* in a state of perturbation," (with two examples of this usage from More).

92/25-93/17 **But ... folye.** More paraphrases common protestant opinion on repentance and fasting, but in keeping with the tone and decorum of *A Dialogue of Comfort* refrains from direct attack. For his polemical treatment of these subjects, see the *Confutation*, *CW 8*, 62/17-73/17, and 400/34-403/17. Tyndale rejected the sacrament of penance in its entirety, but argued particularly against the concept of satisfaction, the belief that the penitent must perform some actual penance assigned by the priest, such as fasting or good deeds, to show his true repentance. Tyndale held that Christ Himself is sufficient satisfaction for men's sins and that they are forgiven simply by confessing to Him. See *CW 8*, n. to 66/15. In the *Confutation* (*CW 8*, 63/29-31) More also accused Tyndale of believing that fasting served only to tame the flesh, but the opinion was Luther's, not Tyndale's. See Luther's *Treatise on Good Works, 1520*, trans. W. A. Lambert, rev. J. Atkinson, in *Luther's Works* (Philadelphia, 1966), *44*, 74-75; and *CW 8*, n. to 64/2-3.

Saxony (93/13) at this time was made up of Meissen, Thuringia, and Saxe-Wittenburg. Under Luther's protector, Frederick the Wise, it was the stronghold and seminary of the Reformation.

93/25-27 **nor Luther ... habite.** Luther married Katherine von Bora, a former Cistercian nun, on June 13, 1525. In canon law the marriage of a monk and a nun was regarded as incest. More uses the marriage in his polemical works as a recurrent image of Luther's "very beastly bitchery." Cf. *Heresies*, *EW*, sig. l₈v, and *Confutation*, *CW 8*, 925/10-926/37 *et passim*. There are more than sixty references to the theme in the *Confutation* (*CW 8*,

n. to 41/30–31). In keeping with the tone of *A Dialogue of Comfort,* More restrains his usual sense of outrage and uses the marriage simply as a memorable date (because of its notoriety). In "religiouse men out of their habite" More refers to monks who left their order and forsook their order's garb.

93/28–94/17 And . . . passion. The sermon may be intended as a parody of some specific individual, but the sentiments were widely held and the style is typically evangelical. Cf. Tyndale's *Mammon,* sig. C₆, "Iff thou woldist obtayne heven with the merytes and deservinges of thyne awne workes / so dyddist thou wronge / yee and shamedist the bloud of Christ / and vnto the were Christ deade in vayne." See also Luther's *Sermon at Erfurt, 7 April 1521,* trans. and ed. J. W. Doberstein, in *Luther's Works* (Philadelphia, 1959), *51,* 63–66, 113. For "for he . . . synnes" (94/7–9), cf. 1 Cor. 1:30.

94/22–28 And . . . downe. Cf. *Confutation, CW 8,* 63/34–64/3: "For ellys yf there were no suche [fasting days] / the moste parte of the people whyche now in yᵉ comon fastes do tame the flesshe . . . wolde fynde very few dayes therfore of theyr owne mynde, & many not one thorow the hole yere as ye now se it in Saxony, where they that were woont to faste many, faste now neuer a one."

95/10–14 They . . . do. See above, 25/13 and n.

95/15–17 And . . . hym. Luke 14:27; Matt. 16:24. Cf. also Luke 9:23, and see below, n. to 109/2–7.

95/19–96/10 I wold . . . fastyng. For a similar scriptural catena on fasting made up of many of the same examples, see the *Confutation, CW 8,* 66/33–71/23.

95/20–24 Moyses . . . folish. Exod. 34:28. Moses fasted forty days and forty nights when he received the ten commandments. In the *Confutation, CW 8,* 67/2–4, More adds the comment that Moses' fast was a penance for the sin of his people in worshiping the golden calf (Exod. 33). In 3 Kings 19:1–8 Jezebel sent a messenger to Elias (More's "hely"), threatening his life. Elias went out into the wilderness and slept. An angel awoke him and told him to eat the food set before him. After eating twice, Elias did not eat again for forty days. Christ's fast occurred during the temptation in the wilderness (Luke 4:1–2) and was traditionally regarded as the origin of Lent, prefigured by Moses and Elias and imitated first by the apostles and then by the entire church. Cf. "ut quadragesimale jejunium Christianis ex Apostolica traditione servandum, inchoaret, & suo exemplo sanctiret & quasi consecraret. Ita S. Ignatius epist. 7. & passim alij Patres" (C. à Lapide, *1,* 99). See also St. Leo, *PL 54,* 633.

95/24–96/2 Kyng . . . therfor. 3 Kings 21:17–29. Ahab was told by Elias that he would be destroyed and the bodies of those belonging to him eaten by dogs and the birds of the air, whereupon Ahab tore his garments and fasted in repentance, and the Lord put off the evil He had intended for him. More refers specifically to 3 Kings 21:27. The reference to 3 Kings 12 in the 1557 marginalia is a misprint. Jonah prophesied that in forty days Nineveh would be overthrown. The king listened, put on sackcloth and ashes, and published a proclamation calling for a general fast for man and beast (Jonah 3:7–8). Cf. *Confutation*, *CW 8*, 67/5–22, 69/35–70/5, and above, 52/12. Anna's fasts in the Temple are related in Luke 2:36–38. The 1557 marginalia refers to Anna, the mother of Samuel, in 1 Kings 1, but she is not the widow More had in mind. The reference to Luke 3 in the 1573 marginalia is also incorrect.

96/2–3 **Saint . . . neyther.** In a list of his tribulations Paul mentions, "in vigiliis multis, in fame, et siti, in jejuniis multis, in frigore, et nuditate" (2 Cor. 11:27). In 1 Cor. 4:10–11 he speaks of the "fools" of Christ: "Usque in hanc horam et esurimus, et sitimus, et nudi sumus, et colaphis caedimur, et instabiles sumus." As with Anna in the previous example, More has moved away from those who fasted as penance for sin to those who willingly suffered tribulation for the love of God.

96/5 **prophetes.** As indicated by *B*'s change to "profyttes" (followed by *Z*), the meaning here is almost certainly "profits," i.c., benefits other than "temperaunce."

96/9–10 **Nisi . . . fastyng.** Mark 9:28. Cf. above, 13/3–5 and n.

96/14–22 **Scindite . . . water.** The first quotation is from Joel 2:13. The second (l. 16) is from Ps. 50:19. The reference to Ps. 56 in the marginalia of *1557* is an error. More marked the verse with a flag in his *Psalter* (*Prayer Book*, p. 92). The psalm is a plea for mercy and deliverance from death. Cf. above, 35/3–7 and n. The final quotation (ll. 19–20) is from Ps. 6:7, which is also a plea for deliverance. Opposite verse 2 ("Domine, ne in furore tuo arguas me, neque in ira tua corripias me") More wrote in his *Psalter*: "Imploratio ueniae pro peccatis (a prayer imploring pardon for one's sins)" (*Prayer Book*, pp. 29, 189).

97/17–23 **Howbeit . . . do.** Ps. 144:9. The Vulgate reads: "Suavis Dominus universis: et miserationes eius super omnia opera eius." The second quotation (ll. 19–20) is from Ps. 102. More combines verse 14, "Quoniam ipse cognovit figmentum nostrum. Recordatus est quoniam pulvis sumus" and verse 3, "Qui propitiatur omnibus iniquitatibus tuis: qui sanat omnes infirmitates tuas." Opposite Ps. 102:1 ("Benedic, anima mea, Domino"), More wrote in his *Psalter*, "Inuitatio ad agendas gratias (an invitation to give thanks)," and opposite verses 10–11, "misericordia dei (the mercy of God)" (*Prayer Book*, pp. 163–64, 201).

More's translation of *figmentum* as "erthen vessell" (a phrase probably borrowed from 2 Cor. 4:7) is very free; the literal meaning of the word is "shape" or "frame." He was led to it perhaps by the reference in the

verse to *pulvis* or "dust" and the relationship between *figmentum* and *figulus*
or "potter," both of which go back to the same root (*fingere*, "to form or
fashion"). The metaphor of God as potter is of course a commonplace; cf.
Confutation, CW 8, 794/16–17, *De Tristitia, CW 14*, 549. The last clause of
the translation ("& shall not exact," etc.) is More's own addition, derived
from 1 Cor. 10:13 and 2 Cor. 12:9. See above, 22/15–20 and n.

97/27–98/1 **And . . . sorow.** The attribution to Jerome is incorrect. See
above, 90/13–15 and n.

98/13–14 **& none . . . hevyn.** Rev. 21:27: "Non intrabit in eam aliquod
coinquinatum."

98/16–19 **the counsaile . . . flesh.** More probably refers to *The Imitation
of Christ*, formerly attributed to Gerson. Cf. the early English editions by
Pynson (1503) and de Worde (1528?), the translation by Whitford (1530),
and More's *Confutation, CW 8*, 37/30–31. It is now attributed to Thomas à
Kempis. There are a number of passages More may have had in mind
since the idea is fairly commonplace, but the most probable is the following
from II, xii, "Of the way of the cross and how profitable patience is in
adversity": "The more the flesh is punished with tribulation, the more is
the soul strengthened daily by inward consolation. And sometimes the
soul shall feel such comfort in adversities, that for love and desire to be
conformed to Christ crucified, it would not be without sorrow and trouble;
for the more that it may suffer for his love here, the more acceptable shall
it be to him in the life to come" (trans. Richard Whitford, ed. Edward J.
Klein [New York, 1941], pp. 86–87). Cf. also I, xiii (pp. 20, 23), *et passim*.
For somewhat similar statements in Gerson's own works, see *Opera, 3*,
1125, and *1*, 151–52.

98/25 **new men.** Upstarts: heretics such as Luther and Tyndale. The
phrase was used pejoratively in the Renaissance to signify those who had
broken away from established custom either in thought, politics, eco-
nomics, or manners. Machiavelli was a new man, as were Paracelsus,
Giordano Bruno, and Shakespeare's Iago. See Lewis Einstein, *The Italian
Renaissance in England* (New York, 1913), *passim*. The term as More uses
it is a translation of the Roman *novus homo*, which referred to the first
member of a family to hold high political office and later came to assume
the more general meaning of one newly ennobled, a parvenu or upstart.
See Cicero, *Rep.* I, i, 1, and *Off.* I, 39, 138; Juvenal, 8, 237.

99/11 **sett cokke a hope.** The *OED* ("cock-a-hoop" 1) cites this passage
and defines the term as "to turn on the tap and let the liquor flow; hence,
to drink without stint; to drink and make good cheer with reckless prodi-
gality." See the *OED* for a long account of possible origins of the phrase.

100/13–22 **For . . . fight.** Cf. the total texture of More's annotations in
his *Psalter*. The majority of the notes are directed either *contra demones* or

refer to temptation or tribulation. More's contrast in ll. 18–22 between the devil's "traynes" and his "open fight" in persecution is derived from the exegetical tradition of Psalm 90. Drawing on the light-dark imagery in verses 5–6 of the psalm, most commentators separate the four temptations described there into those that are secret and subtle, working through ignorance, obscurity, and darkness (*occulta*), and those that are blatant and overt, occurring in the full light of knowledge (*aperta*). See, for example, The Interlinear Gloss (*Biblia Latina, 3,* sigs. I₅v–I₆) and Paulus Burgensis (*Biblia Latina, 3,* sig. K₁); see also below, 107/18–23 and n., 166/18–167/8 and n. All commentators agree that the temptation of the noonday devil is the most vehement and severe. Following Augustine, More later identifies this temptation as open persecution for the faith (below, 200/5–8 and n.).

101/5–7 **vnder ... eius.** Matt. 10:36. *1573* adds the translation: "A mans owne familiar frindes are his enemies" (fol. 69ᵛ); but this does not quite make the point: the enemies are "members of his own household."

101/10–13 **omne ... temptacions.** Jas. 1:2. The Vulgate (cf. the corrections in *1557* and *1573*) reads *fratres mei* rather than *fratres*. The verse goes on to speak of the necessity for steadfastness in times of trial.

101/18–22 **Non ... ayer.** Eph. 6:12. The Vulgate (cf. the corrections in *1557* and *1573*) reads *potestates, adversus mundi rectores tenebrarum* for *potestates tenebrarum.* For the relationship between the devil and the men who are his agents, see below, 317/12–27, where More again refers to the same passage. Though More's translation of *colluctatio* as "wrestelyng" is correct, Paul goes on to develop the image of warfare, assuming the whole armor of God. The passage is linked with the previous quotation from James by a similar emphasis on standing fast on the evil day (6:11, 13–14).

101/25–27 **Nemo ... game.** 2 Tim. 2:5. The Vulgate (cf. the corrections in *1557* and *1573*) reads *non coronatur* for *Nemo coronabitur* and *nisi* for *nisi qui.* The *Biblia Latina* has *non coronabitur nisi qui.*

101/27–29 **saynt ... therto.** Cf. *Meditationes de Cognitione Humanae Conditionis,* XII, 34 (*PL 184,* 504): "Daemonum officium est suggestiones malas ingerere: nostrum est illis non consentire. Nam quoties resistimus, diabolum superamus, angelos laetificamus, Deum honorificamus. Ipse enim nos hortatur ut pugnemus, adjuvat ut vincamus: certantes in bello spectat, deficientes sublevat, vincentes coronat." Bernard makes a number of such statements. Cf., for example, *Sermones in Cantica, Sermo* XVII (*PL 183,* 858); *Sermones de Tempore et de Sanctis, In Quadragesima Sermo V* (*PL 183,* 179), and *Liber de Modo Bene Vivendi,* LXVII (*PL 184,* 1298).

101/29–102/3 **And ... reward.** Jas. 1:2, cited above, 101/10–13. More picks up the idea of crowning an athlete in the preceding quotation from 2 Tim. 2:5 and links it with the crown of life mentioned in Jas. 1:12:

"Beatus vir, qui suffert tentationem: quoniam cum probatus fuerit, accipiet coronam vitae, quam repromisit Deus diligentibus se."

102/10–15 **fortitudo . . . craftes.** The first quotation is from Ps. 117:14. The Vulgate reads *mea* for *mea est* (cf. the correction in *Z*) and *et factus* for *factus* (cf. the corrections in *1557* and *1573*). The second quotation (ll. 12–13) is from Jas. 1:5. The Vulgate reads: "Si quis autem vestrum indiget sapientia, postulet a Deo . . . et dabitur ei." Cf. also Matt. 7:7. The third quotation (ll. 13–14) is a summary in paraphrase of Eph. 3:18 which More evidently meant to expand, as *CC* indicates by leaving a half-line of blank space between the Latin and the translation (see the textual footnote to l. 14). Eph. 3:18 reads: "Ut possitis comprehendere cum omnibus sanctis, quae sit latitudo, et longitudo, et sublimitas, et profundum." The context makes it clear that the wisdom More speaks of is the wisdom of love. Writing to the Ephesians from prison, Paul prays that Christ may dwell in their hearts through faith founded on charity ("per fidem . . . in caritate radicati, et fundati" [3:17]). Then follows the verse More refers to.

102/22–24 **Iustus . . . hand.** Ps. 36:24. The Vulgate reads *Cum ceciderit justus* for *Iustus si ceciderit* and *manum suam* for *manum* (cf. the corrections in *1557* and *1573*). The psalm contrasts the destruction of the wicked with God's protection of the just. Opposite verse 1, "Noli aemulari in malignantibus: neque zelaveris facientes iniquitatem," More wrote in his *Psalter*: "ne quis invideat improborum prosperitati (let no one envy the prosperity of the wicked)" (*Prayer Book*, pp. 70, 194). The conclusion of the psalm speaks of God as the refuge of those who hope in Him, anticipating the introduction of Psalm 90 immediately below: "Salus autem justorum a Domino: et protector eorum in tempore tribulationis. Et adjuvabit eos Dominus, et liberabit eos: et eruet eos a peccatoribus, et salvabit eos: quia speraverunt in eo" (36:39–40). Most of this psalm is marked with flags and marginal lines in More's *Psalter*.

102/25–103/2 **The prophet . . . hevyn.** Ps. 90:1. The quotation of the opening verse marks the beginning of More's complex exposition of Psalm 90, which forms the basis for the remainder of the work. Opposite this verse More has written in the margin of his *Psalter*: "de protectione dei (concerning the protection of God)" (*Prayer Book*, pp. 150, 201). Verses 2–7 are marked by an unusually heavy marginal line, with special wavy lines marking verses 3 and 5, and the word "demones" written opposite verse 6. Verse 9 is marked by a flag and marginal line, verse 13 by a flag.

Verses 11-12 of Psalm 90 were quoted by Satan in his second temptation of Christ in the wilderness, the temptation to suicide on the pinnacle of the temple (Matt. 4:5–7); the psalm was therefore regarded as instructing man in resistance against diabolical temptation in the wilderness of this world: "Iste psalmus est de quo Dominum nostrum, id est, Christum diabolus ausus est tentare. Audeamus ergo ut instructi possimus resistere tentatori non in nobis praesumentes, sed in eo qui prior tentatus est, ne nos in tentatione vinceremur . . . Quia quisquis sic imitatur Christum ut patienter toleret hujus vitae tentationes, tribulationes et molestias corporales et spem omnem in eo ponit, ita ut nec illecebra capiatur, nec timore frangatur: hic est qui exemplo Domini sui habitat in adjutorio Altissimi, et in protectione Dei coeli commorabitur" (Pseudo-Bede, *In Psalmorum Librum Exegesis, PL 93*, 930; this is in part a paraphrase of Augustine, *PL 37*, 1149-50). See also Jerome, *PL 26*, 1166; Cassiodorus, *PL 70*, 650; and Bernard, *PL 183*, 186. The psalm was also associated with persecution for the faith, the fear of torture, demonic illusion, and the virtue of hope informed by charity. See the detailed notes to the psalm below, *passim*.

In the liturgy of the church, Ps. 90 is regarded as the special prayer of Compline and as such is recited daily in the divine office throughout the year (except from Holy Thursday to Good Friday) so as to compose the mind for sleep and ward off the temptations of the devil. It is also the special psalm of Lent, which commemorates Christ's temptation in the wilderness. In the mass for the first Sunday in Lent, for example, the whole psalm is used for the gradual and tract; the gospel is the account of Christ's temptation in Matthew. The entire psalm is used on only one other occasion in the liturgy: in the *Ordo ad servitium peregrinorum*, the traditional service for pilgrims beginning their journey. For the importance of these liturgical associations to the *Dialogue of Comfort*, see Joaquin Kuhn's article on the subject in *Moreana, 22* (1969), 61-67.

103/3–103/12 **Surely . . . hym.** More's emphasis on faith and hope is derived from the exegetical tradition on Psalm 90. Augustine stresses hope: "Ergo qui sic imitatur Christum, ut toleret omnes molestias hujus saeculi, spes ejus in Deo sit, ut nec illecebra capiatur, nec timore frangatur, ipse est qui habitat in adiutorio Altissimi" (*Enarratio in Psalmum XC*, I, 3 [*PL 37*, 1151; see also 1163, *et passim*]). Bernard identified this hope more specifically as the theological virtue and, combining it with faith and charity, used it to form the central thesis of his course of seventeen lenten sermons delivered to the monks of Clairvaux between 1138 and 1153: "Nempe germana, fidei, speique cognatio est; ut quod illa futurum credit, haec sibi incipiat sperare futurum. Merito proinde Apostolus fidem sperandarum rerum substantiam esse definit (*Hebr.* 11:1): quod videlicet non credita nemo sperare, non plus quam super inane pingere possit. Dicit ergo fides: Parata sunt magna et inexcognitabilia bona a Deo fidelibus suis. Dicit spes: Mihi illa servantur. Nam tertia quidem charitas: Curro mihi, ait, ad illa" (*PL 183*, 221; see also 186, 188, 219). After Bernard, this remained the standard interpretation of the Psalm. Nicholas de Lyra, for example, reads it in its moral or doctrinal dimension (*moraliter*) as referring to "quolibet fideli in domino sperante spe formata charitate" (*Biblia Latina, 3*, sig. I₆v), and Paulus Burgensis in his *Addi-*

tiones to de Lyra's *Postilla* identifies this hope as vehement love: "notandum quod vbi in translatione nostra habent: sperauit in hebr. habent hasach: quod signat amorem non solum simpliciter: sed etiam vehementia amoris. . . . Et vt ostenderet quod hec dilectio non est fundata in aliqua vana seu falsa cognitione: idcirco dicit: . . . cognouit nomen meum, scilicet per veram fidem (*Biblia Latina, 3,* sig. K₁v).

103/14–16 **scapulis . . . trust.** Ps. 90:4.

103/17–22 **for as . . . tribulacion.** Cf. above, 100/13–22.

103/18 **concident.** Although the *OED* gives no example of this form, it seems possible that More may have used such a Latinism (from *concidere*), instead of "coincydent" as *B* and *Z* read. It is curious that the *OED* does not list any examples of "coincident" or related forms earlier than 1563. The word "concidence" is listed, but with only one example from 1656.

103/22–28 **In . . . betwene.** Cf. the image of fervent heat in Augustine's commentary on the noonday devil in *Enarratio in Psalmum XC,* I, 8–10: "Quare autem in meridie? Quia multum fervet persecutio: majores aestus dixit meridiem . . . Coepit fervere sol, coepit fervere aestus . . . casum ferventis caloris nimiae persecutionis" (*PL 37,* 1154–56). Bernard adds the idea that men are shaded from that heat by God's wings: "sub his umbraculum salubre refrigerat nos, et repellit nimium solis fervorem" (*In Psalmum XC,* IV, 3 [*PL 183,* 194]). See also N. de Lyra (*Biblia Latina, 3,* sig. I₆v). Cf. More's use of the word "refrigerate" (l. 25).

103/32–104/4 **as the . . . wynges.** Both Jerome and Augustine develop the image of the hen protecting her young in their commentaries on Psalm 90 (*PL 26,* 1095; *PL 37,* 1152–53). Augustine also introduced the image of the hawk or kite: "Si gallina protegit pullos suos sub alis suis; quanto magis tu sub alis Dei tutus eris, et adversus diabolum et angelos ejus, quae aereae potestates tanquam accipitres circumvolitant, ut infirmum pullum auferant" (*PL 37,* 1152; see also Bernard, *PL 183,* 194).

104/7–13 **Hieruselem . . . not.** Matt. 23:37. The Vulgate reads *congregare filios tuos* rather than *congregare te.* More's translation, which varies from his Latin, substitutes "thy sones" for "you" and thus corresponds with the Vulgate. The quotation is from Jesus' diatribe against the scribes and pharisees in which He foretells His own death. Jerome and Augustine both use this same passage in their commentary on Psalm 90:4 to arrive at the image of the hen protecting its young (*PL 26,* 1098; *PL 37,* 1152–53).

104/18 **Those . . . walkith.** *B* emends to "chekyns . . . walke" and *Z* follows. But perhaps More used "chekyn" here in a collective or plural sense. The *OED* allows this possibility: see "chicken" 1.c. In this case "walkith" might follow.

104/25–27 **Pone . . . will.** The verse is not from the psalms, as More's ascription to "the prophet" might seem to indicate, but from Job 17:3.

105/3–6 **sub . . . reioyce.** Ps. 62:8. The Vulgate (cf. the corrections in *1557* and *1573*) reads *in velamento* rather than *sub vmbra*. Opposite verse 2 ("Sitivit in te anima mea") More wrote in his *Psalter*, "desiderium in deum (longing for God)"; opposite verse 4 ("Quoniam melior est misericordia tua super vitas: labia mea laudabunt te") he wrote "in tribulatione et timore mortis (in tribulation and fear of death)" (*Prayer Book*, pp. 105, 197). Verses 7–8 are marked by a flag and marginal line. The reference to Ps. 2 in the 1557 marginalia is incorrect.

105/17–23 **Scuto . . . day.** Ps. 90:5–6.

106/8–11 **with a . . . selfe.** Bernard, *In Psalmum XC*, V, 2 (*PL 183*, 196): "Non incongrue sane scuto comparatur gratia divinae protectionis, quod in superiori parte amplum et latum est, ut caput humerosque custodiat; in inferiori vero strictius, ut minus oneret, maxime quod graciliores sint tibiae, nec tam facile vulnerentur, sed nec adeo periculosum sit illis in partibus vulnerari. Sic omnino sic militibus suis Christus ad inferiora tuenda, id est carnem, magnam, ut ita dixerim, strictitatem atque penuriam rerum temporalium donat; nec vult eos illarum multitudine praegravari, sed ut victum et vestitum habentes, quemadmodum, ait Apostolus, his contenti simus (1 *Tim.* 10:13); in superioribus vero ampliorem latitudinem, et abundantiam gratiae spiritualis."

106/12–18 **And . . . aboute.** Cf. Jerome, *Breviarium in Psalmos* (*PL 26*, 1098): "Scutum nostrum rotundum est, hoc est, ex omni parte nos sepit. Non solum scutum est, sed et murus." Cf. also Augustine on the incomprehensible nature of God's shield and the inadequacy of language to describe it: "Quae sunt alae, hoc est scutum; quia nec alae sunt, nec scutum. Si aliquid horum proprie esset, numquid alae scutum esse possent, vel scutum alae? Sed quia figurate per similitudines dici omnia ista possunt, ideo et alae et scutum esse potuerunt" (*PL 37*, 1153).

106/18 **continently.** This is the only example of the word "continently" in the *OED* with the meaning "continuously, without interruption." However, the *OED* records many examples of the adjectival form, "continent," with the meanings "continuous, uninterrupted, or connected with," though never in this context of a continuous literary text; the reading does have etymological justification, from the Latin *continere* (intr.): "to hold together, be continuous" (see *OED*, "continent" *a.* II). *B*, evidently puzzled by the word, changed it to read "incontinently," i.e., "at once, immediately" (see the textual footnote); but the wording of *A* is accepted by *Z*.

107/4–8 **By . . . wikednes.** Cf. Bernard, *In Psalmum XC*, VI, 1 (*PL 183*, 197): "Solet in divinis Scripturis adversitas designari per noctem." More quotes Job 34:25. The Vulgate reads *enim* for *enim deus*. Elihu is speaking of God's total control over the universe and the lives of the just and the unjust.

107/10–17 **therfor ... feare.** Cf. Augustine, *In Psalmum XC*, I, 1: "Sic ergo et tu molestias hujus saeculi cum pateris, quas facit diabolus, sive aperte per homines, sive occulte sicut Job, sis fortis, sis tolerans; habitans in adjutorio Altissimi" (*PL 37*, 1150). More's identification of night fear with impatience is independent of any of the traditional commentaries on the psalm, though it may owe something to Bernard, who associates it with the struggle against the flesh (*certamen de molestiis corporis*). Bernard continues: "Nocturnus plane et tenebrosus timor; sed facile hunc radius veritatis exsuperat. Ingerit enim oculis cordis nunc quidem peccata quae fecimus; ut, quemadmodum de se propheta ait, etiam nos in flagella parati simus, annuntiantes iniquitatem nostram, et cogitantes pro peccato nostro (*Ps. 37*: 18, 19), nunc vero aeterna supplicia quae meruimus, ut in eorum comparatione quae evadimus, universa quae patimur delicias reputemus" (*In Psalmum XC*, VI, 1 [*PL 183*, 197]). Cf. also More's numerous references to patience and demons in his *Psalter* (*Prayer Book*, pp. 54–55, 96–97, 105, 111, *et passim*).

107/18–23 **the tone ... persecucion.** Augustine and Jerome both pick up the light-dark imagery in Psalm 90 and associate the night with ignorance (*PL 26*, 1099; *PL 37*, 1153–54). The reference to persecution is dependent specifically on Augustine, who interprets all four temptations in Psalm 90 as various degrees of persecution for the faith.

107/23–108/1 **A nother ... is.** Cf. Bernard *In Psalmum XC*, VI, 1–2: "Bene autem dicitur non timendum a timore nocturno, et non dicitur a nocte; quia non ipsa afflictio tentatio est, sed magis timor ipsius ... timor ipse tentatio est" (*PL 183*, 197).

108/1–6 **Posuisti ... meate.** Ps. 103:20–21. The Vulgate reads *ipsa* for *illa, silvae* for *siluarum* (cf. the corrections in *1557* and *1573*) and *ut rapiant, et quaerant* for *quaerentes*. More's identification of the lion whelps with the devil in the next few paragraphs is dependent on other passages in scripture such as 1 Pet. 5:8: "adversarius vester diabolus tanquam leo rugiens circuit, quaerens quem devoret." It also looks back to traditional commentaries on Ps. 90:13 such as that of Bernard (*PL 183*, 238). See below, n. to 318/5–8. More perhaps uses the lion throughout *A Dialogue of Comfort* as an oblique allusion to the king. See 110/30–111/3 and 317/24–318/17. In the medieval-renaissance system of correspondences the lion and king were regarded as analogous since both were the prime representatives of their respective species. Symbolic transfers from one to the other were therefore commonplace. Cf. More's advice to Cromwell on how to handle Henry VIII: "ever tell him what he owght to doe, but never what he is able to doe. So shall you shewe yourself a true faithfull servant and a right worthy Councelour. For if a Lion knewe his owne strength, harde were it for any man to rule him" (Roper, pp. 56–57).

108/15 **body ... soule.** See below, n. to 109/12–13.

108/19–21 **for . . . leve.** Cf. Job 2:3–8 and 4:10–11.

109/2–7 **And . . . fier.** Matt. 10:28, Luke 12:4–5. Part of Christ's warning to His disciples that they will suffer persecution for His name's sake. More adds the reference to the lion whelps. Matthew reads: "Et nolite timere eos, qui occidunt corpus, animam autem non possunt occidere: sed potius timete eum, qui potest et animam, et corpus perdere in gehennam." The entire passage, from Matt. 10:17 to 10:39, is of key importance to *A Dialogue of Comfort*. More returns to it repeatedly. A portion of it has been quoted above, 101/5–7; see also below, 165/2, 198/5–8, and 247/9–10.

109/12–13 **And . . . soule.** Cf. 2 Cor. 5:1–4; 1 Cor. 15:40–50, 53; Rom. 7:23–25. See also *De Tristitia, CW 14*, 605, where More again speaks of the body as the garment of the soul and makes the same association with Matt. 10:28 as he does immediately above. The passage in the *De Tristitia* is part of More's commentary on the young man in Mark 14:51–52 who would have been taken with Jesus except that he left his cloak behind and ran away naked. The clothing image is developed extensively throughout the entire section (*CW, 14*, 551–681).

109/22–24 **the prophet . . . wode.** Ps. 103:20, quoted above at 108/1–6.

109/27–28 **For . . . thefe.** Cf. *Four Last Things, EW*, sig. e₈, and Shakespeare, *Midsummer Night's Dream*, V, i, 21–22: "Or in the night, imagining some fear, / How easy is a bush supposed a bear." For More's use of "fancy," see above, n. to 61/27.

109/29–110/1 **I remember . . . than.** For the capture of Belgrade see above, n. to 8/1–2. Antony probably refers to one of the many campaigns between 1470 and 1490, when Hungary was ruled by the warlike Matthias Corvinus. See below, 124/15 and n.

110/30–111/3 **for . . . asse.** More combines Ps. 103.20 21 with Aesop's fable of the Ass in the Lion's Skin. See above, 108/1–6 and n. In the fable the ass put on a lion's skin and frightened all the beasts in the forest but gave himself away at last with his braying. The story was repeated by Avianus and from there passed into various medieval collections; cf. Caxton, p. 179; Hervieux, *3*, 267, and *4*, 422. See also Erasmus, *Adag.*, "Induitis me leonis exuvium," sig. I₂v (I. III. lxvi).

112/6–10 **loke . . . yt.** Matt. 25:14–30; the parable of the fearful servant who knew his master to be a hard man and therefore buried his one talent of gold in the ground. When his master returned, he gave the talent back to him with no addition and was cast out "in tenebras exteriores." See also Luke 19:12–28.

112/15 **scripelous.** The forms "scripelous" and "scrupelous," "scriple" and "scruple," etc., were interchangeable in More's time. The *OED* gives

separate entries for these various forms (cf. "scripulous" and "scrupulous")
and explains their presumed origin: in the Latin variants *scrupulum*,
scripulum (see *OED* "scruple," *sb*¹). *B* sometimes changes "i" to "u," and
the other texts tend to eliminate the form with "i."

113/13–14 yet ... without. I.e., "the scrupulous man commits these
(venial) sins, despite the fact that he considers them mortal, especially
since they are the kind that no one goes very long without committing."

114/1–13 More ... large. Cf. *Heresies*, *EW*, sigs. o₄–o₄v, where More
tells the story of a lawyer who fell from the study of law to the study of
scripture and became so overly scrupulous that he thought it was a sin to
say his prayers anywhere outside his room. Eventually wearying himself
with his fears, he then fell into the opposite device: "And vnder pretexte
of loue and libertie waxed so dronke of the new must of lewd lightnes of
mynde & vayn gladnesse of harte, which he toke for spirituall consolacion,
that what so euer him self lysted to take for good, that thought he forthwith approued by god." More notes that the man's scrupulosity "was
more peuyshe and painful, than euill and synful."

The clause "or synne ... venially" (ll. 4–5) means "he will commit a
mortal sin, since he consents to a deed which his (scrupulous) conscience
tells him is a mortal offense, even though objectively it is only venial."

In an article in *The Month*, *26* (1961), 68–80, Benedict Hackett argues
for the possible influence of William Flete's *De Remediis contra Temptaciones*
(1359) on *A Dialogue of Comfort* and cites specifically a passage on scrupulosity which he believes parallels this particular passage in More. In their
edition of Flete's *De Remediis* (*Archivio Italiano per la Storia della Pieta*, *14*
[1968], 220), E. Colledge and N. Chadwick note that More is not tran-
scribing from any of the thirty-seven surviving Latin or English MSS or
printed editions in the passage cited by Hackett and suggest that he is
probably paraphrasing from memory. Castelli, however (p. 150), quotes
an equally parallel passage from Gerson (*Opera*, *3*, 581). The idea was
probably a commonplace of late medieval, early renaissance spirituality.

114/15 mother mawd. More uses the name in quite a different context
in the *Confutation*, *CW 8*, 725/6–7: "And so I see well Tyndale meneth for
his mother, some old mother mawde, some baudy chyrche of heretykes."
Here he calls her "a good old woman." The name may also have been
chosen, however, because of its partial rhyme with "Audley." It is
Audley's version of the story that More retells here. See below, n. to
114/24–27.

114/21–23 plinius ... therof. Pliny, *Ep.*, III, 5, quoting the words of
his uncle, Pliny the Elder: "Nihil enim legit, quod non excerperet;
dicere etiam solebat nullum esse librum tam malum, ut non aliqua parte
prodesset."

114/24–27 I remember ... Fox. Early, less elaborate versions of Mother

Maud's Tale appear in the *Fabulae* of Odo de Ceritona and various other medieval collections reprinted in Hervieux, *2*, 313, *4*, 255, and in *Aesopica*, ed. B. E. Perry (Urbana, Ill., 1952), pp. 644–45. See also *Fabulae*, p. 265.

More's direct source, however, seems to have been a conversation between his step-daughter, Alice Alington, and Sir Thomas Audley, Lord Chancellor of England during the time of More's imprisonment. In a letter to Margaret Roper dated August 17, ⟨1534⟩, Alice explained that Audley had come to hunt deer in her park, and during the visit she asked him to intercede for her father. Audley "merueyled that my father is so obstinate in his owne conceite . . . He saide I woulde not haue your father so scrupulous of his conscience." He then told her a shorter version of the fable More retells here, of "a lion, an asse, and a wolfe and of their confession." "Fyrste the lion confessed him that he had deuoured all the beastes that he coulde come by. His confessor assoyled him because he was a kinge and also it was his nature so to doe. Then came the poore asse and saide that he toke but one strawe owte of his maisters shoe for hunger, by the meanes whereof he thought that his maister did take colde. His confessor coulde not assoile this great trespace, but by and by sente him to the bisshoppe. Than came the wolfe and made his confession, and he was straightely commaunded that he shoulde not passe vi^d at a meale. But whan this saide wolfe had vsed this diet a litle while, he waxed very hungrye, in so much that on a day when he sawe a cowe with her calfe come by him he saied to himselfe, I am very hungrye and fayne would I eate, but that I am bounden by my ghostely father. Notwithstandinge that, my conscience shall iudge me. And then if it be so, than shall my consciens be thus, that the cowe dothe seme to me nowe but worthe a groate, and than if the cowe be but worthe a groate than is the calfe but worth ii^d. So did the wolfe eate bothe the cowe and the calfe." Alice got nothing more from Audley, "nor I wiste not what to saye for I was abashed of this aunswere" (Rogers, pp. 511–13).

When Margaret next visited her father in the Tower, she showed him the letter. More read it over twice and commented on the fable in a way that indicates that he had not heard it before, observing that it was probably not by Aesop since it has to do with confession: "For in Grece before Christes daies they vsed not confession, no more the men than, than the beastes nowe." He also identified himself correctly as the over-scrupulous ass: "But by the folish scrupelous asse . . . my Lordes other wordes of my scruple declare, that his Lordship meryly meant that by me: signifieng (as it semeth by that similitude) that of ouersight and folye, my scrupulous conscience taketh for a great perilous thing towarde my soule, if I shoulde swere this othe, which thinge as his Lordship thinketh, were in dede but a trifle" (Rogers, pp. 514–20). For those who knew the circumstances, this elaborate retelling of Audley's fable by the man the fable was designed to accuse would have given it an added, ironic dimension of meaning. The date of Alice Alington's letter, one might add, is the only piece of contemporary external evidence we have concerning the time of composition of any portion of *A Dialogue of Comfort*.

114/27–115/6 **The pore . . . redy.** Shrovetide (l. 27) is the Sunday, Monday and Tuesday preceding Ash Wednesday, a period when members of the church were urged to go to confession so as to prepare themselves for lenten penance (F. A. Gasquet, *Parish Life in Medieval England* [London, 1909], pp. 168–69). The ass is well within the stipulated time, but the wolf delays until Lent is almost over.

Benedicite (l. 2) was the standard formula for the beginning of confession. The term was originally a form of greeting: "Vox salutationis apud monachos praesertim, qua inferior superiorem salutat et adit" (Du Cange, *Glossarium Mediae et Infimae Latinitatis* [Paris, 1937–38]). Du Cange cites *Reinardus Vulpes*, IV, 1491, and adds in a note that it was also used by laymen. Cf. Shakespeare, *Romeo and Juliet*, II, iii, 31, and *Measure for Measure*, II, iii, 39.

"Clensing days" (l. 5) refers to the period of Shrovetide. Instead of being allowed to go to communion, lenten penitents had a special prayer said over them, which remains in the missal as *Oratio super populum*. The prayer was originally intended to be said in every mass during Lent, but Gregory the Great confined it to weekdays only (W. J. O'Shea, *The Worship of the Church* [London, 1957], pp. 248–49).

115/25–26 **father Raynart.** The name alludes to the unscrupulous hero of the popular medieval beast epic, *Reinardus Vulpes*. The earliest versions were written in Latin, but the most extensive and best known was the French cycle, *Roman de Reynard*, an English version of which was published by Caxton in 1481. See N. F. Blake's edition, London, Early English Text Society, 1970.

116/3–12 **Nay Nay . . . do.** Fasting was required every day in Lent except Sunday, which was a day of abstinence, when no meat was permitted. On weekdays the fast was not broken until after vespers. The fox's opinions parody protestant views. Cf. the Saxon preacher's sermon above, 94/12–13: "leve I besech you these invencions of men, your folysh lenton fastes & your pevish penance."

116/7 **mone . . . water.** A proverbial expression meaning unreal, illusory things that cannot be attained. Tilley, M 1128, cites Shakespeare, *Love's Labor's Lost*, V, ii, 208: "Thou now requests but moonshine in the water."

116/23 **passe . . . selfe.** Cf. 117/12. The phrase is not quite clear. It seems to mean "exceed in reference to himself."

117/9–10 **measure . . . meane.** Cf. Whiting, M 454; Tilley, M 804. See also Erasmus, *Adag.*, "Dimidium plus toto," sig. z₃v (I. IX. xcv) and "Neque pessimus, neque primus," sig. Ttt₂ (IV. III. xxii).

118/2–17 **as a . . . good.** Harpsfield (p. 94) identifies this as an anecdote

about Dame Alice and comments: "Which merye conceyted talke, though
nowe and then it proued true in verye deede, Sir Thomas More could
well digest and like in her and in his children and other." More extends
the joke by having his fictional characters discuss it in such a way as to
break down the fiction. The anecdote draws on the archetype of the
shrewish wife in the medieval anti-feminist tradition. Cf. the saying of
More's father: "whan he heareth folke blame wyues, & say that there bee
so manye of them shrewes: he sayeth that they dyffame them falselye. For
he sayth plainly y^t there is but one shrewde wyfe in the worlde: but he
sayth in dede that eueri man weneth he hath her, & that that one is his
owne" (*Heresies, EW*, sig. q$_1$). See also *Heresies, EW*, sig. n$_7$v, and Rogers,
pp. 310–11.
   The clause "Than will you make me make my worde good" means "If
you tell her, then my story will be proven true." The implication is that as
a result, her husband would receive a fresh taste of the lady's renewed
shrewishness.

119/10–11 **& I . . . to.** I.e., "even if I should die because of the way in
which my sinful soul is tending."

119/15–16 **specially . . . fote.** An ambler is a horse that lifts both legs
on the same side at the same time and thus provides a smooth ride. A
trotter moves his legs diagonally and proceeds in a half-walk, half-run.
The technical terms are ironic, however, since the horse is half-dead and
ambles only because it can hardly stand up.

120/5 **cheuerell poynt.** A lace or cord made out of kidskin, a material
noted for its quality of stretching; the "point" was used to attach hose to a
doublet, to lace up a bodice—in general, to fasten clothing (see *OED*,
"point" *sb*. II. 5).

120/11–12 **while . . . charibdis.** Cf. Erasmus, *Adag.*, "Evitata Charybdi
in Scyllam incidi," sig. M$_2$v (I. V. iv). Cf. also *De Tristitia, CW 14*, 91,
and below, 148/3–8. Scylla was the name of a rock off the coast of Sicily
and of the sea monster with six heads and twelve feet that inhabited it.
Charybdis was a whirlpool on the opposite side of the same strait. The
story is told in the *Odyssey*, XII, 85–110, 234–59.

121/1–3 **& than . . . all.** The passage as it stands is confusing. In order
to provide "were" with a subject, *1553* emends "than" to "that" but *1573*
makes the understood syntax explicit by adding "it" after "were." *B*
cancels the virgule after "helth" to make clear the relation of the clauses:
"than [i.e., then] were [it] good for his helth that" etc. The second "that"
is redundant and should probably be omitted in accord with *B* and *Z*
(see textual footnote).

123/4–5 **with . . . selfe.** Cf. the account of the citizen of Winchester,
whom More cured of "greivous tentations of desperation." Chambers
calls Ro. Ba.'s version of it "one of the great stories of the world": "there

come to hym a Citizen of Winchester, who had bene once with Sir Thomas before, and it was vpon this occasion. This poore man was greivouslie vexed with verie vehement and greivous tentations of desperation, and could never be ridd of it either by counsaile or prayer of his owne or of his friendes. At last a good friend of his brought hym to Sir Thomas, being then Chauncellour; who taking compassion of the poore mans miserie, gaue hym the best counsell and advice he could, but it would not serue. Then fell he to his prayers for hym, earnestlie beseeching Almightie god to rid the poore man of his trouble of mynde. He obtained it; For after that the Hampshire man was never troubled with it anie more, so long as he could come to Sir Thomas More. But after he was imprisoned, and could haue no accesse vnto hym, his tentation began againe, more vehement and troublesome then ever before; so he spent his daies with a heavie hart, and without all hope of remedie. But when he hard that Sir Thomas was condemned, he poasted from Winchester, hoping at least to see hym as he should goe to execution; and so determined to speake with hym, come what would of it. And for that cause, he placed hym selfe in the way, and at his comming by he thrust through the throng, and with a loud voice said, 'Maister More, doe you knowe me? I pray you, for our Lordes sake, help me. I am as ill troubled as ever I was.' Sir Thomas aunswered, 'I remember thee full well. Goe thy waies in peace, and pray for me, and I will not faile to pray for thee.' And from that tyme after, so long as he lived, he was never troubled with that manner of tentation" (*The Life of Syr Thomas More*, ed. E. V. Hitchcock and P. E. Hallett, *EETS*, 222 [London, 1950], pp. 260–61).

124/15 **Buda . . . dayes.** Buda was the fortress and surrounding town on a high bluff of the Danube, opposite the town of Pest, on the low west bank of the river. In a letter to Henry VIII dated August 22, 1527, Ferdinand of Austria signs himself "in castris nostris ad civitatem nostram Regiam Budensem infra Pest positis" (*State Papers, Henry VIII*, 5, 601). The two towns were incorporated into the present city of Budapest in 1872.

Vladislav II (1471–1516), son of Casimir, King of Poland, was elected to the Hungarian throne in 1490, after the death of Matthias Corvinus. He was popularly known as "Dobzse Laszlo" from his habit of saying "dobzse" ("all right") to everything. He died at Buda on March 13, 1516, after having ruled for twenty-one years. He was succeeded by his ten-year-old son, Louis II.

125/23 **good man.** This may be used as "goodman": i.e., the head of a household, a husband.

126/20–23 **But . . . woman.** Vladislav's queen was Anne de Candale, niece of Louis XII of France and sister of Gaston de Foix. She had two children, Anne, who married Ferdinand of Austria, and Louis, the future Louis II.

128/13 **fede.** Cf. "fode" *Z*. Either word can mean "beguile, lead on under false pretenses" (*OED*, "feed" *v.* 1.b). As the *OED* says ("fode" *v.*), "the occasional use of *to feed forth* instead of *to fode forth* . . . seems to show that the word ["fode"] was sometimes so interpreted in 15–16th c."

128/27 **she toke . . . tribulacion.** See textual footnote for this line. *1553* adds "but for a maruelous mery mortall temptacion." This addition seems to be related to the way in which *L* adds "but" after "tribulacion" and then leaves a half-page blank. Some other manuscript seems to have filled out the phrase in imitation of 131/23: "but in a perilous mery mortall temptacion."

129/9–25 **But . . . hevyn.** *Collationes*, II, 5 (*PL 49*, 529–30). Cassianus tells the story of the old monk Hero, who secluded himself and fasted excessively against the advice and commands of his superiors. After refusing to join his brothers at the feast of Easter, he was visited for his presumption by an "angel of Satan as an angel of light," who commanded him to throw himself headlong into a bottomless well. He died three days later still unconvinced that he had been deluded by the devil. More's recollection of the story is generally correct except for a few details. The old monk did not have any revelations his fellows feared would prove to be illusions of the devil. He simply changed abruptly after forty-five years in the monastery: "ante paucos admodum dies illusione diabolica a summis ad ima dejectum, quem quinquaginta annis in hac eremo commoratum." Nor was he told that his suicide was God's will and that he would go straight to heaven. He knew only that an angel of light had commanded him to throw himself into the well as a test of virtue: "Cujus rei fidem, ut experimento suae sospitatis evidentissime comprobaret, supradicto se puteo nocte intempesta illusus injecit, magnum scilicet virtutis suae meritum probaturus, cum inde exisset illaesus."

130/9–10 **very . . . prudence.** Cf. Aquinas, *ST*, I–II, Q. 58, a. 4: "Dicendum quod virtus moralis potest quidem esse sine quibusdam intellectualibus virtutibus, sicut sine sapientia, scientia et arte; non autem potest esse sine . . . prudentia. Sine prudentia quidem esse non potest moralis virtus, quia moralis virtus est habitus electivus." Aquinas defined prudence as "right reason about things to be done" (*recta ratio agibilium*); it was regarded therefore as the necessary ingredient and directing principle of all other moral virtues. See *ST*, I–II, Q. 58, a. 5 and Q. 61, a. 2.

130/15 **Afryque.** The various layers of revision here are very hard to decipher. It is certain that *A* wrote "a fry" and left a small blank space for letters that he evidently could not make out. The *E* hand has apparently created a capital "A," connected the first two letters, and added "uyke" in the blank space. This creates the curious spelling "Afryuyke." Someone, possibly *B*, has then written a heavy "q" over the first "y," but this makes the situation worse. *B* therefore cancels the whole mess and writes "Afryque" above.

130/15–22 **Take . . . selfe.** After Pompey's forces were defeated by Caesar in the battle of Pharsala (48 B.C.), Cato led a remnant of the army to Africa and occupied Utica. He held the city until the last of his forces were evacuated by sea; then he committed suicide, having spent his last night reading Plato's *Phaedo.* His death was widely praised by Plutarch, *C. Min.,* 65–70; Dio Cassius, *Hist. Rom.,* 42, x–xiii; Cicero, *Off.,* I, xxxi, *Tusc.,* I, xxx; and others. In *De Civ. D.,* I, xxiii (*PL 41,* 36–37), Augustine argues that suicide is not praiseworthy, as pagans often believe. Lucretia and Cato are their most celebrated examples. But Cato's own friends did not agree: "imbecillioris quam fortioris animi facinus esse censuerunt, quo demonstraretur non honestas turpia praecavens, sed infirmitas adversa non sustinens." Augustine then gives the real reasons for Cato's suicide, love for his son and envy of Caesar's glory: "Quid est ergo, nisi quod filium quantum amavit, cui parci a Caesare et speravit et voluit; tantum gloriae ipsius Caesaris, ne ab illo etiam sibi parceretur, ut ipse Caesar dixisse fertur, invidit; aut, ut aliquid nos mitius dicamus, erubuit?"

132/11 **dirige.** A funeral song or lament. *Dirige* was the first word in the first antiphon of matins in the Office for the Dead; taken from Ps. 5:9. Cf. *Heresies, EW,* sig. r₅; *Supplication, EW,* sig. x₈v.

132/17–21 **Or . . . much.** Cf. Rogers, p. 171; *Debellation, EW,* sig. T₈v. Augustine consistently believed that all lies were sins no matter how innocent or trivial. In his treatise *De Mendacio,* for example, he lists eight kinds of lie arranged in order from the most grievous ("in doctrina religionis") to the most innocent ("quod et nulli obest, et ad hoc prodest, ut ab immunditia corporali aliquem tueatur"). All are sins, but in varying degrees: "In his autem octo generibus tanto quisque minus peccat cum mentitur, quanto emergit ad octavum; tanto amplius, quanto devergit ad primum. Quisquis autem esse aliquod genus mendacii quod peccatum non sit putaverit, decipiet se ipsum turpiter" (*PL 40,* 505–16). See also *Contra Mendacium ad Consentium,* ii (*PL 40,* 520–21); *Enchiridion,* I, xviii, 6, and I, xxii, 7 (*PL 40,* 240–43). Jerome, on the other hand, did not take the clear-cut position More attributes to him. His most consistent opinion seems to have been that falsehoods of all sorts are opposed to God's truth; cf. *PL 24,* 232; *22,* 946. At one point, however, in his *Commentarii in Epistolam ad Galatas,* I, ii, Jerome implies that "simulation" for a good cause is justifiable: "Utilem vero simulationem, et assumendam in tempore, Jehu regis Israel nos doceat exemplum, qui non potuisset interficere sacerdotes Baal, nisi se finxisset velle idolum colere, dicens: *Congregate . . . mihi omnes sacerdotes Baal: si enim Achab servivit Baal in paucis, ego serviam in multis* (IV *Reg.* x, 18). Et David quando mutavit faciem suam coram Ablimelech, et dimisit eum, et abiit (I *Reg.* xxi, 13). Nec mirum, quamvis justos homines, tamen aliqua simulare pro tempore, ob suam et aliorum salutem, cum et ipse Dominus noster non habens peccatum, nec carnem peccati, simulationem peccatricis carnis assumpserit, ut condemnans in carne peccatum, nos in se faceret justitiam Dei" (*PL 26*, 339–40).

More probably refers to Jerome because of Augustine's dispute with him over this interpretation. In his *De Mendacio* Augustine mentions it twice and refutes it there and in a number of letters (*PL 40*, 492, 517; *PL 33*, 112, 285). More may also have been thinking of a passage in Jerome's *Contra Rufinum* where he quotes Origen and Plato to the effect that one may lie "quasi condimento atque medicamine," as when heads of state are forced to lie "vel contra hostes, vel pro patria et civibus." Because of his rhetoric and the length of the quotation, Jerome seems to agree with this, but he is clearly being ironic: "scripsit in libris, quos ad perfectos et ad discipulos loquebatur: docetque magistris mentiendum, discipulos autem non debere mentiri" (*PL 23*, 412). For the Platonic-Stoic theory of the officious lie and the opinions of Erasmus and More, see *Utopia, CW 4*, 40/23–29, 100/3–29, 291–92, and 374–75. Aquinas, not Jerome, is usually set against Augustine as the defender of certain kinds of lies under certain conditions; see *ST*, II–II, Q. 110.

132/25–133/1 **Nolite ... light.** 1 John 4:1; 2 Cor. 11:14. The Vulgate reads *ipse enim satanas* rather than *Angelus sathane* in the latter passage. Both quotations are used by Gerson as the texts for his *De Probatione Spirituum*; see below, 133/7–8. Gerson also connects these texts with the noonday devil from Psalm 90: "*Angelus sathanae transfigurat se in Angelum lucis* ... sic ut fiat daemonium meridianum, dum pro tenebris errorum quas ad tempus celare permittitur, lucem veritatis claram se fingit afferre" (*Opera, 3*, 37). The connection of the noonday devil with the problem of the discernment of spirits is derived from Bernard's interpretation of Psalm 90, where the noonday devil is identified as a form of ignorance in which lovers of the good are persuaded that evil is the good they seek: "Quos enim perfectos boni noverit amatores, malum eis sub specie boni non mediocris, sed perfecti persuadere conatur" (*PL 183*, 199). Bernard then goes on to quote 2 Cor. 11:14 and give some examples from the gospels of the questioning of spiritual apparitions. For the interpretation of the noonday devil More develops later, see below, n. to 200/5–8. In Book III More follows Augustine and interprets it as open persecution for the faith. By linking the noonday devil with temptation by devilish illusion, Bernard and Gerson perhaps pointed to still another, more subtle form of attack in which a man's faith and the depth of his love for God were used against him. For More's own self-doubts about the position he had taken, see the Introduction.

More's interest in the discernment of spirits is also illustrated by the part he played in the case of Elizabeth Barton, the Holy Maid of Kent. See Chambers, *Thomas More*, pp. 294–98. In February 1534, More was charged with misprision of treason for allegedly listening to her prophesies and revelations concerning the king and then failing to denounce them.

In his letter to Cromwell dated ⟨March ? 1534⟩, defending himself, More explained that at first he was unwilling to pass judgment on her (Rogers, p. 481), but after her public confession at St. Paul's Cross in November 1533, he denounced her as "a false deceyvinge ypocrite" by whose example "euerye other wretche maye take warninge, and be ferde to sett forthe theire owne devilishe dissimuled falshed, vnder the maner and color of the wonderfull worke of God" (Rogers, p. 486).

133/2–3 **the bettre . . . own.** I.e., "It will be better if he cites these texts himself, but if he doesn't do so, then you should bring in the text yourself."

133/5–8 **wherof . . . spirituum.** Cf. the list of authorities in Gerson's *De Probatione Spirituum* (*Opera*, *3*, 38): "Hoc Gregorius in Dialogo: hoc Augustinus in Confessionibus de seipso & Matre: hoc Hugo de Arca animae, cum pluribus aliis." Gerson himself wrote two major treatises on the subject: *De Probatione Spirituum* and *De Distinctione Verarum Visionum a Falsis* (*ibid.*, 37–59). The two go over much the same material, but the *De Distinctione* treats it in terms of a dominant money metaphor (false visions are counterfeit), whereas the *De Probatione Spirituum* is informed by a metaphor of dream and waking (false visions are like dreams). More refers to both treatises under the title of the *De Probatione Spirituum*, which he used more than the other. Although More appears to be following the *De Probatione Spirituum* point by point in the next few pages, he is actually constructing a formula of his own for spiritual discernment, based on Gerson. See detailed notes to specific passages below and Paschal Boland, *The Concept of Discretio Spirituum in John Gerson's De Probatione Spirituum and De Distinctione Verarum Visionum a Falsis* (Washington, D.C., 1959). More seems to have had a copy of Gerson's works with him in the Tower, or at least Gerson's harmony of the Gospels, the *Monatessaron*, which he used as the text for his *De Tristitia Christi*, written in the last few months of his life. See *De Tristitia, CW 14*, 623.

133/9–10 **As . . . fantasticall.** Cf. *De Probatione Spirituum* (*Opera*, *3*, 39): "consideretur imprimis persona suscipiens visiones si sit boni & discreti judicii, rationis naturalis, quia laeso cerebro turbatur judicium rationis. Si laesus phantasias patiatur, non magnopere quaerendum est a quo spiritu veniant melancholicae illusoriaeque visiones, ut patet in phreneticis, in aegrotis variis, qui vigilantes se talia videre putant, audire, gustare &c. qualia somniantes patiuntur." Gerson returns later to the problem of distinguishing between reason and phantasy in his twelfth *Consideratio*: "unde spiritus veniat, aut quo vadet" (*ibid.*, 42).

133/11–18 **Whether . . . brest.** This is related to Gerson's first point in *De Probatione Spirituum*, "persona suscipiens visiones," though Gerson mentions pride only in passing as one of the possible manifestations of religious mania. It does not have for him the importance it does for More. More also adds most of the psychological complexity—the wiliness that springs from pride and the concomitant mistrust and paranoia. Gerson notes only the curious paradox that pride of this sort should originate in humility. His discussion, however, comes very close to the problem of spiritual pride that More faced in prison: "Hoc super omnia conveniet observare ne latet interior superbia spiritualis, quam Bernardus vere nominat subtile malum, quoniam & de humilitatione sua nascitur, de sordibus & cilicio, de jejuniis & virginitate; immo & de sua morte suoque contrario trahit originem. Quid igitur erit tutum a superbia, cum nec ipsa virtus tuta sit ab ea? Est autem superbia quaedam in intellectu, dum non vult subjici alieno judicio, sed innititur proprio: Quaedam in voluntate, dum renuit obedire; & haec citius deprehenditur; ideoque facilius corrigitur quam prima" (*Opera, 3,* 39).

133/19–23 **Or . . . wonders.** More probably has in mind Gerson's third major point in *De Probatione Spirituum,* the *quare,* or *why* (i.e., the reason) the person to whom the revelations are given reveals them: "persona cui visiones hujusmodi reciantur, habeat se prudenter & cautissime: praesertim in principio consideret acriter quare movetur haec persona, secretum suum pandere . . . Cave ergo quisquis eris auditor aut consultor ut non applaudas tali personae, non obinde laudes eam, non mineris quasi Sanctam dignamque revelationibus atque miraculis" (*Opera, 3,* 40). Later in the same section Gerson notes: "Porro dici non potest quantum haec curiositas, vel cognoscendi futura & occulta, vel miracula vivendi vel faciendi, fefellit plurimos, & a vera Religione frequenter averterit" (*ibid.,* 41).

133/24–29 **Also . . . church.** The first of these—withdrawal and isolation —is apparently More's own psychological observation; it is not mentioned by Gerson. The second—singularity of opinion—is treated at length by Gerson under the general heading of *quid,* or the overall truthfulness of the vision itself: "Probatio spirituum respicit . . . visionum qualitatem si vera sunt omnia, etiam usque ad minimam propositionem, quoniam in spiritu veritatis falsitas non est; in spiritu autem mendacii mille quandoque sunt veritates apertae, ut in unica latenti falsitate decipiat . . . Si rursus excedant hae visiones communem intelligendi modum, vel in Scriptura sacra positum, vel in ratione naturali vel morali collactum; quia si non, videretur illud adscribi frustra revelationi" (*Opera, 3,* 40; see also 38).

133/30–134/3 **Many . . . withall.** Cf. "Probatio spirituum considerat causam quare fieri dicuntur visiones, praesertim quo sine nedum proximo, nedum aperto, sed occulto & longinquo. Potest itaque finis primus apparere bonus & salubris & devotus, ad aedificationem aliorum, qui tandem prolabetur in multiplicius scandalum, dum vel non respondebunt ultima primis, vel aliud fictumque deprehendetur in personis fuisse, quod reputabatur sanctitatis & devotinis" (*Opera, 3,* 41).

134/10–17 **Orels . . . hevyn.** The example is related to Cassianus' account of the old monk, Hero, above, 129/9–25.

135/21–22 **And . . . these.** These are More's own categories though they are ultimately based on Gerson's. Hence the air of scholastic logic. More's first item, "the man," corresponds to Gerson's *quis* or "persona suscipiens visionis." The second corresponds to Gerson's *quid* or "visionem qualitatem si vera sunt omnia." The third, "the law of God," is not one of Gerson's major distinctions, though he mentions it at the very beginning: "Probare *spiritus si ex Deo* sunt contingit multipliciter. Uno quidem modo per modum artis & doctrinae generalis, sicut per eruditionem sacrarum Scripturarum, diligenti pioque studio acquisitam." Gerson seems to be thinking of specific passages in scripture, however, and not the word of God as a whole, for he goes on: "Sunt nimirum Scripturae in quibus putamus nos fidem habere, continentes artem falsos Prophetas a veris & ab illusionibus revelationes cognoscendi" (*Opera, 3,* 37–38; see also 40).

136/4–7 **for . . . shew.** Cf. Matt. 7:15–17: "Attendite a falsis prophetis . . . a fructibus eorum cognoscetis eos. Numquid colligunt de spinis uvas, aut de tribulis ficus? Sic omnis arbor bona fructus bonos facit: mala autem arbor malos fructus facit." See also *De Probatione Spirituum* (*Opera, 3,* 39).

136/13–15 **sith . . . man.** Exod. 20:13, the sixth commandment; Deut. 5:17. For the reference to Augustine, see *De Civitate Dei,* I, xx (*PL 41,* 34–35): "Neque enim frustra in sanctis canonicis Libris nusquam nobis divinitus praeceptum permissumve reperiri potest . . . Nam et prohibitos nos esse intelligendum est, ubi Lex ait, *Non occides* . . . restat ut de homine intelligamus, quod dictum est, *Non occides*: nec alterum ergo, nec te. Neque enim qui se occidit, aliud quam hominem occidit." Cf. also *De Patientia, PL 40,* 617.

137/12–17 **May . . . therof.** Cf. "Alius invenitur modus [probatio spirituum] per inspirationem intimam, seu internum saporem, sive per experimentalem dulcedinem quandam, sive per illustrationem a montibus aeternis effugantem tenebras omnis dubietatis. Hoc autem est manna absconditum, & nomen novum in calculo scriptum, quod nemo novit, nisi qui acceperit" (*De Probatione Spirituum, Opera, 3,* 38). A few sentences later Gerson speaks of this inward knowledge as "donum Spiritus sancti."

137/19–22 **And . . . therof.** For the metaphor of waking and dreaming, which More begins here and extends through the next ten paragraphs, cf. Gerson, who uses it to conclude his discussion of the inspiration of the Holy Spirit: "Itaque sicut nemo novit quae sunt spiritus, nisi spiritus; ita nemo cognoscit infallibili certitudine ea quae per solam experimentalem notitiam vel sentimentum interius & sensum aguntur in alterius animo. Quemadmodum ergo tradere regulam generalem quae distingueret infallibiliter inter visionem somnialem & illam quae fit in vigilia, nullus facile posset, propter varias similitudines inter utrasque visiones; multo magis in proposito" (*Opera, 3,* 38).

137/24–27 **& than ... them.** The old monk in Cassianus (129/9–25), whom More has here confused with the example of the "secret frend," above, 134/10–17.

138/25–139/2 **Goddes ... slepe.** Cf. More's own reputation for joking with a straight face: "Habet & nasum, quum uult, etiam inter nasutissimos, quem tam artificiose etiam detrahit, ut eo detracto, nullum faciei desit lineamentum" (Pace, p. 104). In Latin *nasus* means not only "nose," but also "wit" or "derision." Cf. Martial, I, xlii, 18; V, xix, 17.

139/13–15 **yet ... confesse it.** Cf. *De Probatione Spirituum (Opera, 3,* 38): "Scit nihilominis homo vigilans se certitudinaliter & experimentaliter videre, quamvis non ignoret se habuisse in somniis visiones valde vicinas & similes suae vigiliae; adeo quod somnium suum narrare somniando quandoque videatur, quamvis dicat Seneca 'esse vigilantis somnium narrare.'"

139/18–27 **And ... knowith.** Cf. "Scit similiter homo spiritualis in vigilia verae lucis divinae positus, videre se diuina quae videt, vere sentire, odorare & sapere. Quare? quia vigilat. Potest nihilominus recogitare ex se vel aliis nonnumquam ponitur in quodam somnio naturalis conditionis aut diabolicae illusionis, qui dum sic se habet & quoddammodo dormit ad diuina, putare potest quod vigilet ad ea, sic que falli" (*De Probatione Spirituum, Opera, 3,* 38). See also Gerson's *De Distinctione Verarum Visionum a Falsis, ibid.,* 52–53.

140/12–15 **as he ... phelisties.** Gen. 22:1–14; Judges 16:28–30. Augustine uses the same examples in his section on suicide in *De Civitate Dei,* I, xxi (*PL 41,* 35), concluding: "His igitur exceptis, quos vel lex justa generaliter, vel ipse fons justitiae Deus specialiter occidit jubet; quisquis hominem vel se ipsum, vel quemlibet occiderit, homicidii crimine innectitur." For More's acknowledgment of his indebtedness to Augustine here, see below, 141/23.

141/6–18 **In Sampson ... Sampson.** It is not clear in Judges 16 that Sampson was commanded by God to kill himself, though he prays to God for strength to revenge himself on his enemies (16:28). See the next note. More quotes either Judges 14:6 or 15:14. The phrasing is the same in each, though the Vulgate reads *Spiritus Domini* rather than *virtus domini.*

141/23–142/3 **S. Austyn ... chastite.** *De Civitate Dei,* I, xxvi (*PL 41,* 39): "Sed quaedam, inquiunt, sanctae feminae tempore persecutionis, ut insectatores suae pudicitiae devitarent, in rapturum atque necaturum se fluvium projecerunt; eoque modo defunctae sunt, earumque martyria in catholica Ecclesia veneratione celeberrima frequentantur. De his nihil temere audeo judicare. Utrum enim Ecclesiae aliquibus fide dignis testificationibus, ut earum memoriam sic honoret, divina persuaserit auctoritas, nescio: et fieri potest ut ita sit. Quid si enim hoc fecerunt, non humanitus deceptae, sed divinitus jussae; nec errantes, sed obedientes? sicut de Samsone aliud nobis fas non est credere. Cum autem Deus jubet, seque jubere sine ullis ambagibus intimat; quis obedientiam in crimen vocet? . . . tantummodo videat, utrum divina jussio nullo nutet incerto." More combines this passage with Augustine's discussion of the rape of Lucrece in *De Civ. D.*, I, xix. Augustine's general position is that Lucrece or any woman who is raped remains chaste. So long as she does not submit willingly, she is not touched by another's sin: "An forte huic perspicuae rationi, qua dicimus corpore oppresso, nequaquam proposito castitatis ulla in malum consensione mutato, illius tantum esse flagitium qui opprimens concubuerit, non illius quae oppressa concumbenti nulla voluntate consenserit" (*PL 41*, 32). See also *PL 41*, 40, and Aquinas, *ST*, II–II, Q. 124, a. 4: "Utrum mors sit de ratione martyri."

143/27 **the comen tale.** As might be expected, no source has been discovered for More's tale of the carver and his wife.

146/12 **Here must the.** The blank space left by *A* after "the" indicates that the original scribe found a word here that he could not decipher. *B* solves the problem by simply altering "the" to "they," and drawing a line across the blank space (the other texts follow).

146/23–29 **And . . . knowen.** All three are types of repentant sinners who fell through weakness of the flesh: Magdalene in her prostitution (Luke 7:36–50), David in his lust for Bathsheba (I Kings 11–12), and St. Peter in his denial of Christ through fear (Matt. 26:69–75). More spoke of his own fear of pain and death in the Tower as sensual in nature: "albeit (myne owne good daughter) that I founde my selfe (I cry God mercie) very sensuall and my fleshe much more shrinkinge from payne and from death, than me thought it the part of a faithfull Christen man . . . yet I thanke our Lorde, that in that conflict, the Spirite had in conclusion the maistry" (Rogers, p. 542). St. Peter in particular seems to have assumed a special meaning for More in the months preceding his execution. References accumulate in his letters and his other Tower works. They are particularly prevalent in Book III below. See Rogers, pp. 531 and 546; *De Tristitia, CW 14*, 159–75.

147/19–22 **if a . . . perell.** Cf. Augustine's account of the physician Vindiciamus, below, 173/9–21 and n.

148/3–8 **And . . . tother.** Cf. above, 120/11–12 and n.

148/25–149/16 **One . . . bynd hym.** For More's experience in counseling potential suicides, see above, n. to 123/4–5.

149/22–24 **Aduersarius . . . devour.** 1 Pet. 5:8. The Vulgate (cf. the corrections in *L* and *1553*) reads *tanquam* rather than *quasi*.

150/2-7 **but also ... temptacion.** In the physiology of More's day, "complexcions" refers to the makeup or combination of a person's four humors: blood, phlegm, choler, and melancholy. Differences of personality and temperament were ascribed to varying proportions of humors in the body. Health was defined as a reasonable balance of one's four humors: "the conflict of the diuers qualifyed elementes tempered in our body, continually laboring ech to vanquish other, & thereby to dissolue the whole, though it be as sore against the continuance of our nature, & as sore laboreth to the dissolucion of y^e whole body as other sicknes do, yet we neither cal it sicknes, nor the meat y^t resisteth it we cal no medicin, & that for none other cause, but for the continuall familiaritie that we haue therewith" (*Four Last Things, EW*, sig. f$_1$). See also *Utopia, CW 4,* 172/23-174/3. All sublunary compounds were thought to be inevitably subject to dissolution simply because of their constituent contrariety. Cf. "Non ... invenitur corruptio, nisi ubi invenitur contrarietas; generationes enim et corruptiones ex contraviis in contraria sunt. Unde corpora caelestia, quia non habent materiam contrarietati subjectam, incorruptibilia sunt" (Aquinas, *ST*, I-I, Q. 75, a. 6; see also Plato, *Phd.* 78c; Cicero, *Tusc.*, I, xxix, 71).

150/8-13 **Now ... anger.** Cf. "Pure blood & whole togethers is not but in young folke: for Phisitians say that bloud wasteth by age" (Batman, IV, 7). The word "colour" (l. 12) is, of course, a variant spelling of "choler," "the venemous qualytie whereof" was believed to breed "euill passions ... and also prouoketh to the worke of Venus" (Batman, IV, 10). Choler was also believed to produce "boldnes and hardinesse, mouing and lyghtnesse, & stirreth to wrath and desire of reuenge ... And so choloricke men be generally wrathful, hardie and unmeeke, light, unstable, vnmercifull" (*loc. cit.*).

150/13-28 **so where ... all.** Cf. Batman, IV, 11: "By the qualytie of the humor [of melancholy], the patient is faint, and fearfull in hearte without cause: and so all that haue this passion, are fearefull ... and oft sory ... and so if we aske of such heauie folkes what they feare, or wherefore they be sorye, they haue none answere ... And therefore he dreameth dreadfull darke dreames, and very ill to see, & of stinking sauour and smell, of which is bred *Passio melancholia.*" The word "maliciouse" (l. 20) has been changed to "melancolyous" by *B*, and the change is followed by *Z*; the same emendation is made by *B* and *Z* at 151/10. But "maliciouse" makes excellent sense in both places, being evidently used in the medical sense of "malignant, virulent," current in More's day (see the *OED*, "malicious" *a.* 5). It seems unlikely that *A* would have missed the word twice; *B*'s emendation is apparently prompted by the use of "malencolious" at line 14. Cf. "evill humours," 151/19, 24.

152/11-14 **for which ... soule.** Jas. 5:14-15: "Infirmatur quis in vobis? inducat presbyteros Ecclesiae, et orent super eum, ungentes eum oleo in nomine Domini: Et oratio fidei salvabit infirmum, et alleviabit eum Dominus: et si in peccatis sit, remittentur ei." The verb *inducat* is echoed in More's paraphrase by the imperative *induce*, which is used in its Latin meaning of "bring in." In his polemical works More frequently quotes this verse in defense of the sacrament of extreme unction. See Marc'hadour, *The Bible*, Part III, pp. 157, 149–52. Cf. also Roper's account of More's prayers for Margaret and her miraculous recovery from the sweating sickness after "bothe phisitions and all other there dispaired of her recouerye, and gave her ouer" (pp. 28–29).

153/2–6 **You ... out.** Cf. Mark 1:23–26 and 9:25–27; Matt. 8:28–32; Luke 4:33–35.

153/28–30 **the payne ... purgatory.** The reference again is probably to *The Imitation of Christ*; see above, 98/16–19 and n. Cf. I, xii, "Of temptations to be resisted" and II, xii, "Of the way of the cross" in Richard Whytford, trans., *The Folowynge of Chryste*, ed. E. J. Klein (New York, 1941), pp. 20–23, 87, 89. Castelli (p. 193) cites Gerson, *Opera, 3*, 170–71, but the idea was a commonplace of the period. More makes the same statement a number of times in his works without referring to any authority. Cf. *Heresies, EW*, sigs. p₂–p₂v; *Confutation, CW 8*, 214/5–215/8, 289/6–15; and the famous prayer written in his *Psalter*: "Gyve me thy grace good lord/ ... gladly to bere my purgatory here" (*Prayer Book*, pp. 185–86).

154/3–14 **Resist ... may.** Cf. below, 288/12–16 and 292/24–294/12. For the importance of reason to the overall meaning and structure of *A Dialogue of Comfort*, see the Introduction. Cf. also More's letter to Margaret dated from the Tower, 1534: "the Spirite had in conclusion the maistry, and reason with helpe of faith finally concluded, that for to be put to death wrongefully for doinge well ... is a case in which a man may leese his head and yet haue none harme" (Rogers, p. 542). See also *Devotions, EW*, sig. VV₃v (mismarked XX₃v), and *De Tristitia, CW 14*, 57–65.

154/21 **yf it were.** This must mean "as if it were." *L* and *1553* solve the problem by reading "though it were but a fote brode."

155/3–5 **but sometyme ... thereon.** Cf. More's prayer written in his *Psalter* (*Prayer Book*, p. 185): "Gyve me thy grace good lord / To sett the world at nought ... / Lytle & litle vttrely to caste of the world / And ridde my mynd of all the bysynes thereof."

155/20–21 **or yf ... folow.** The litany of the saints; "suffrages" are short intercessory prayers. "As found in the Sarum Breviaries of the time of More ... [the litanies] varied for each day of the week, though with some features in common. The number of saints explicitly named was much greater than at present" (T. E. Bridgett, *Life and Writings of Blessed Thomas More* [London, 1924], p. 61 n.). It was More's custom when visited by Margaret in the Tower to recite with her the seven penitential psalms and the litany "ere he fell in talke of any worldly matters" (Roper, pp. 75–76; Rogers, p. 515). Harpsfield adds: "When he was at home, as his custome was dayly, beside his priuate prayers, with his children to say the seuen psalmes, letanie and suffrages folowing" (p. 75). For the relation between the seven psalms and the litany, see above, n. to 65/28–29.

155/21–156/1 **which . . . borne.** During a time of flood and pestilence at Rome in 590 A.D., St. Gregory decreed a day of intercession consisting of public prayer and processions. (In the early church public processions which included chanted prayers were also known as litanies.) The procession was made up of seven columns: priests, monks, nuns, children, laymen, widows, and married women. All were to proceed on different routes and meet at a certain point. Because of its formation, this became known as the *Litania Septiformis* and included the Litany of the Saints (cf. *Heresies, EW*, sig. r₃). For a detailed description, see Paulus Diaconis, *De Gestis Langobardum*, III, xxiv (*PL 95*, 526); the earliest account occurs in Gregory of Tours, *Historia Francorum*, X, i (*PL 71*, 528–29). Medieval authors, such as Walafrid Strabo, *De Rebus Ecclesiasticis*, xxviii (*PL 114*, 962), saw this custom as the origin of the litany. Modern scholars agree with More, however, that the origins are obscure. References to Christian litanies appear as early as the fourth century A.D. in the epistles of St. Basil and the sermons of St. John Chrysostom.

156/1–3 **And . . . hand.** Cf. *De Triplici Genere Bonorum, Sermones de Diversis*, XVI, 3–4 (*PL 183*, 580–81): "A sanctis vero angelis auxilium quaerendum est, et occultis suspiriis, et frequentia lachrymarum: ut illi supereminenti majestati preces nostras offerant, referant gratiam, qui administratorii spiritus sunt, missi propter nos, ut haereditatem capiamus salutis." For saints, cf. *In Festo Omnium Sanctorum, Sermo* v (*PL 183*, 480): "Sane ut eam [gloriam] nobis sperare liceat, et ad tantam beatitudinem aspirare, summopere nobis desideranda sunt suffragia, quoque sanctorum, ut quod possibilitas nostra non obtinet, eorum nobis intercessione donetur." See also *Meditationes Piissimae De Cognitione Humanae Conditionis* (*PL 184*, 495–96).

156/3–7 **Yf . . . vndone.** Again in keeping with the decorum of the work, More refrains from direct attack on protestant rejection of the theory of intercession. See above, 92/25–93/17 and n.; *Heresies, EW*, sigs. n₂v–n₃.

156/17–26 **Speciall . . . malo.** Cf. More's annotations in his *Psalter* against temptations and demons (*Prayer Book*, pp. 189–202 *passim*). The first quotation is from Ps. 67:2: "Let God arise, and let his enemies be scattered, and let those who hate him flee from his face." Opposite this verse More wrote: "contra demonum insidias et insultus (against the snares and insults of the demons)" (*Prayer Book*, pp. 111, 197). The two quotations that follow (ll. 23 and 25–26) are from Matt. 4:10: "Begone, Satan," Christ's words in the temptation in the wilderness; and Matt. 6:13: "and lead us not into temptation, but deliver us from evil," the ending of the Our Father.

157/4 **A sagitta ... die.** Ps. 90:6: "From the arrow that flies by day."

157/17–26 **for ... day.** Ps. 90:5–6. Cf. N. de Lyra, who glosses the arrow that flies by day as "superbia" (*Biblia Latina*, *3*, sig. I₆v), and Bernard, who interprets it as "vana gloria," or the vain desire for praise: "Nox praecessit: ut filius lucis et diei honeste ambulans, time sagittam. Leviter volat, leviter penetrat: sed dico tibi, non leve infligit vulnus, cito interficit. Nimirum sagitta haec vana gloria est: non est unde haec impugnet pusillanimes et remissos ... Difficile prorsus, ni fallor, homo verbis laudantium hominem in vita sua abduci poterit altum sapere, si se intus ad lucem veritatis solicita consideratione discutiat" (*In Psalmum XC*, VI, 3 [*PL 183*, 198]). More seems to think of pride, however, not as the desire for praise, but more specifically and more personally perhaps as worldly prosperity. He thus tends to combine it with Bernard's interpretation of the third temptation in Psalm 90 as "cupiditas," or the desire for the honors and riches of this world (*loc. cit.*). Following Bernard, N. de Lyra glossed the third temptation as "luxuria" (*loc. cit.*). See below, 166/18–167/8 and n.

158/11–13 **& ouer ... Antes.** For the image, cf. Roper's anecdote (p. 35): "that some of vs, as highe as we seeme to sitt vppon the mountaynes, treading heretikes vnder our feete like antes. . . . "

158/25–159/10 **Quid ... hell.** Sap. 5:8–9, 12–14, where the scene is not hell, but the time of judgment. More quotes from the speech of the wicked, who persecuted the man of God in this life and drove him to an early death surrounded by his enemies (4:7–18). They then see him in glory and come to understand the vanity of their lives (5:1–14). More refers to the same general passage again at 307/6–8, where he describes the glory of the righteous. See the Introduction.

159/15 **marke ... prikke.** A "marke" in archery means any kind of target; "butte" has the same general meaning, but refers specifically to "a mound or other erection on which the target is set up" (*OED*, "butt" *sb.*⁴ II. 2); "prikke" refers to a particular kind of round target containing a bull's-eye, and, more specifically, to the bull's-eye itself (*OED*, "prick" *sb.* IV. 10). Cf. above, 49/15 and n.

159/17, 27 **a copp high.** *1573* gives a clue to the meaning by hyphenating "cop-hie" in both places. See the *OED*, "cop" *sb.*² ("The top or summit of anything"), where the phrase "cop-height" ("a great height") is listed, with an example from 1591: "That Envie, though she shoote on cop-height, cannot reach her." More's phrase seems to be related to "a-high" ("an high," "on high"), "to a height" (*OED*, "high" *a.* and *sb.*² III. 18). To shoot up "a copp high" would thus mean to shoot up to the very peak or top of the arrow's flight, to shoot as high as possible.

159/26–160/4 **For ... hell.** Part of the taunt of the people of Israel over the King of Babylon in Isaiah 14, traditionally interpreted as an account of the fall of Lucifer; see *Treatise on the Passion, EW*, sig. LL₈. More combines verses 13 and 14: "In caelum conscendam, super astra Dei exaltabo solium meum, sedebo in monte testamenti, in lateribus Aquilonis. Ascendam super altitudinem nubium, similis ero Altissimo." For the associations with the passage from Sapientia quoted above (n. to 158/25–159/10), see the Introduction.

160/21–24 **to towch . . . desier.** For pitch, cf. Ecclus. 13:1. The proverb was common in the renaissance. Tilley, P 358, cites Shakespeare, *I Henry IV*, II, iv, 454: "This pitch, as ancient writers do report, doth defile; so doth the company thou keepest." See also *Treatise on the Passion, EW*, sig. MM₂v and, for variants, Tilley, H 549, S 972, T 236, and T 602.

For flax, cf. Tilley, F 278, and Eras., *Adag.*, "Oleum camino addere," sig. E₂v (I. II. ix). In most of its versions the proverb is directly connected with the temptations of the flesh and the inflammable nature of youth, which More introduces as the last item in the series. Tilley cites Lyly, *Euphues and his England* (1580): "Wine to a young blood, is in the spring time Flaxe to a fire" and John Davies, *English Proverbs* (1611): "Fire and flax differ, not to make fire, Like men and women that burne in desire." See also Tilley, F 351.

For the serpent, cf. Erasmus, *Adag.*, "Columbrum in sinu fovere," sig. Rrr₂v (IV. II. xl).

161/24 **thadmendment.** Possibly a scribal error, but also possibly an unusual form; see the *OED* ("ad-" *pref.* 2) for the frequent use of "ad-" for "a-" in the sixteenth century.

162/4–9 **Beatus . . . timerouse.** The first quotation is from Prov. 28:14. The verses immediately following refer to an impious king who, like a roaring lion, impoverishes his people and crushes them with false accusations (*per calumniam*). The second quotation (l. 5) is from 1 Cor. 10:12. The Vulgate reads *qui se existimat stare* rather than *stat*. The next verse continues: "Tentatio vos non apprehendat nisi humana; fidelis autem Deus est, qui non patietur vos tentari supra id, quod potestis, sed faciet etiam cum tentatione proventum, ut possitis sustinere." See above, n. to 22/15–20. The final reference (l. 9) is to Ecclus. 7:9.

163/29 **his bare . . . agayne.** Cf. Shakespeare, *King Lear*, V, ii, 9–11: "Men must endure / Their going hence, even as their coming hither: / Ripeness is all."

164/15–23 **Let . . . god.** Reminiscent of More's own "new building": "And because he was desirous for godlye purposes sometyme to be solitary, and sequester himself from worldly company, A good distaunce from his mansion house builded he a place called the newe buildinge, wherein there was a Chappell, a library, and a gallery; In which, as his vse was vppon other dayes to occupy himself in prayer and study together, So on the Fridaie there vsually contynewed he from morning till evening, spending his time only in devoute praiers and spirituall exercises" (Roper, pp. 25–26).

165/2–3 **Inimici . . . famyliers.** Matt. 10:36.

165/24–30 **And . . . mater.** Ps. 90:6.

166/11–17 **Qui . . . darkenessis.** Ps. 90: 1, 5–6.

166/18–167/8 **Negocium . . . goodes.** Augustine identified all four temptations as varying degrees of persecution for the faith and, following Jerome (*PL 26*, 2000), took the light-dark imagery as metaphors for sins committed in ignorance as opposed to those committed in the full light of knowledge: "Quid est timendum in nocte, et quid in die? Cum quisque ignorans peccat, tanquam in nocte peccat: cum autem sciens peccat tanquam die peccat. Duo ergo illa leviora; ipsa sunt graviora, quae repetita sunt . . . Quae sunt leves tentationes? Quae non sic instant, non sic urgent, ut cogant, sed possunt cito declinata transire" (*Enarratio in Psalmum XC*, I, 7 [*PL 37*, 1153–54]). More shifts the metaphor from knowledge to grace. Like Augustine, he distinguishes various degrees of temptation, but unlike Augustine, he focuses here on darkness, in keeping with the nature of the third temptation, "perambulans in tenebris."

More's identification of *Negotium* as "bisines," or excessive concern for worldly things, is in part a literal translation of the word and in part derived from Bernard's commentary on Psalm 90. Bernard interpreted the third temptation as "cupiditas," or the pursuit of worldly honor and wealth: "Quis, putas, erit hic proditor? Plane cupiditas, radix iniquitatis . . . Contempsit vanam gloriam [Bernard's second temptation], ait, quoniam vana est: forte solidius aliquid affectaret, forte honores, forte divitias. Quantos hoc negotium perambulans in tenebris trudi fecit in tenebras exteriores" (*In Psalmum XC*, VI, 4 [*PL 183*, 198]). Following Bernard, N. de Lyra glossed *Negotium* simply as "luxuria" (*Biblia Latina*, *3*, sig. I₆v). More's first category, the pursuit of pleasure, would seem to look back to de Lyra's "luxuria" and his second, the pursuit of worldly goods, to Bernard's "cupiditas." Cf. More's "covetice," below, 167/22–23.

167/11–12 **Qui . . . goth.** John 12:35. Jesus' reply to those who ask him who is the Son of Man: "Adhuc modicum, lumen in vobis est. Ambulate dum lucem habetis, ut non vos tenebrae comprehendant." Then follows the passage More quotes.

167/14 **mase.** A "maze" is still made out of hedge in some English gardens, as at Hampton Court Palace. More seems to be referring to such a pleasurable maze (cf. "plesaunt," 168/4).

168/5–12 **Ducunt . . . destruccion.** Job 21:13 and 1 Tim. 6:9. The passage in Timothy continues: "Radix enim omnium malorum est cupiditas: quam quidam appetentes erraverunt a fide, et inseruerunt se doloribus multis" (6:10).

168/16–23 **The covetouse ... be.** Luke 12:13–21. The parable of the rich fool. More quotes from the conclusion, verse 20. The Vulgate reads *repetunt* rather than *tollent* (*B*'s addition).

168/31–169/7 **that ... therfor.** Harpsfield again identifies this as a personal anecdote concerning Dame Alice, using the story to show that More was not put down by his wife's sharp tongue but repaid "home againe often time such kinde of talke" (p. 94).

169/10–11 **Lassati ... wikkednes.** Sap. 5:7. From the speech of the unrighteous at judgment referred to above, 158/25–159/10.

169/17–19 **So ... halfe.** For a similar idea, cf. *Four Last Things* (*EW*, sig. fg₇): "Wonder it is yᵗ the worlde is so mad, that we had leuer take sinne with pain, than vertue with pleasure. For as I said in yᵉ beginning and often shal I say, vertue bringeth his plesure, and vice is not wᵗout pain. And yet speake I not of the world to come, but of the life present. If vertue wer al painfull, and vice al pleasant, yet sith deth shal shortly finish both yᵉ pain of the tone and the pleasure of the tother, gret madnes wer it, if we would not rather take a short pain for the winning of euerlasting pleasure, than a short plesure for the winning of euerlastyng pain. But now if it be true as it is in dede, that our sin is painful and our vertue pleasant, how much is it than a more madnes, to take sinnefull paine in thys world, that shall win vs eternal pain in hell, rather than pleasant vertue in this world, that shall win vs eternall plesure in heauen?"

170/29–171/3 **Qui ... god.** 1 Tim. 6:9, cited above, 168/7–12. The second quotation (ll. 31–32) is from Mark 10:25; see also Luke 18:25 and Matt. 19:24. The passage from Mark goes on to say that those who accept persecution and give up their home, family, and lands will have their reward (10:29–30). Erasmus in his *NT* has an extended discussion of the *camel/cable crux* which More refers to here. According to Erasmus, Jerome, following Origen, took κάμηλον to refer to the animal. Theophylactus disagreed, believing that a nautical cable made more sense (*quudiui*) in relation to the eye of a needle. Erasmus agrees with Jerome and the Vulgate for the very reason that the image of the animal is more absurd: "Nam quod istos offendit, qui ex camelo funem faciunt nauticum, nempe quod absurdum videatur camelum duci per foramen acus, hoc ipsum pro nobis facit: siquidem Christus hoc exemplum velut ἀδύνατον proposuit. Velut enim omnino videri impossibile, ut camelus, ingens animal ac tortuosum, per foramen acus transeat" (*Opera, 6,* 102). More, however, was apparently unable to make up his mind. He usually gives both interpretations whenever he quotes the verse. See below, 171/18–19; *Four Last Things, EW,* sig. fg₅v; and Rogers, p. 452.

171/8–9 **the havyng ... thereto.** The distinction is essentially Augustinian; see below, n. to 209/20–24.

171/15 **richesse.** The occasional use of this older form, both in *CC* and in

1557, is probably more than a variant in spelling. It seems to denote the older word, still current in More's day, that lies behind the modern word "riches." The *OED* explains that "riches" is a variant of "richesse" ("wealth"), "assuming the form of a pl., and finally construed as such." The various spellings here show the word in the process of this transition. For the use in *1557* see, for example, the textual footnotes at 172/22, 23, 26.

171/16–29 **Diuitie . . . god.** The first quotation is from Ps. 61:11. Opposite verses 2 and 3 ("Nonne Deo subjecta erit anima mea? Ab ipso enim salutare meum. Nam et ipse Deus et salutaris meus; susceptor meus, non movebor amplius"), More wrote in his *Psalter:* "patientia in tribulacione vel non committam tale peccatum amplius (patience in tribulation, or I shall not commit such a sin again)." Opposite verse 6 ("Veruntamen Deo subjecta esto, anima mea, quoniam ab ipso patientia mea"), he again noted: "patientia" (*Prayer Book*, pp. 104–05, 196–97). The whole psalm is concerned with the need to hope in God, as a protection against fear (cf. "A timore" in the printed heading of Ps. 61 in More's *Psalter*).

More goes on to paraphrase very closely Mark 10:23–27. At first Jesus said that it was hard (*difficile*) for a rich man to enter heaven. Later, after his image of the camel, he said that it was impossible: "Apud homines impossible est, sed non apud Deum: omnia enim possibilia sunt apud Deum" (10:27). In ll. 26–27 More quotes verse 24; the Vulgate (cf. the corrections in *L, 1553* and *1573*) reads *in regnum* rather than *regnum*.

172/18–19 **Ambrose . . . them.** More is apparently mistaken. The passage occurs not in Ambrose, but in Zeno's "De Justitia," *Tractatus*, I, iii (*PL 11*, 287): "paupere quotidie moriente oppressione, fame, frigore, injuria, amicum tibi excolis aurum: custodis argentum: vestem pretiosam ornamentaque superba et supervacanea pro sacrosancto habes, sicut idolum: te per momenta componis, dives in publico, ditior in secreto: nec intelligis, quia homini inopia morienti, tantis opibus qui cum possit subvenire, non subvenit, ipse eum videtur occidere?"

Ambrose has a good bit to say about the relief of poverty, but nothing as stark as the statement More attributes to him. His usual idea is that all men are unified in Christ; in giving to the poor therefore we are giving to Christ Himself. Cf. *Expositio in Psalmum CXVIII*, X, 26 (*PL 15*, 1340): "Vides ergo quia multas Christi imagines ambulamus? Caveamus ne coronam imagini detrahere videamur, quam unicuique Christus imposuit. Caveamus ne aliquid detrahamus iis quibus debemus adjungere. Sed quod pejus est, non solum non honestamus pauperes, sed etiam dehonestamus, destruimus, persequimur; et ignoramus quod has Dei imagini congeramus injurias, cum factos ad imaginem Dei putamus esse laedendos. Qui enim irridet pauperem, exacerbat eum qui fecit illum. Set aderit ille qui dicat *Esurivi et non dedistis mihi manducare* . . . Propterea caveamus diligentius, ne cui vel minimo contumeliam irrogemus, ne ipse Domino in illis minimis contumeliosi fuisse videamur." See also the similar remarks in *Expositio in Lucam*, VIII, 18 (*PL 15*, 1875), which Fowler uses as a gloss in the 1573 edition of *A Dialogue of Comfort,* and *De Officiis,* II, 28 (*PL 16,* 140), cited by Castelli (p. 211).

172/24 **as Abraham did.** Cf. above, 47/16–20 and 54–56.

173/9–21 **Holy . . . before.** *Epistola 138, Ad Marcellinum* (*PL 33,* 526–27): "magnus ille nostrorum temporum medicus Vindicianus, consultus a quodam, dolori ejus adhiberi jussit quod in tempore congruere videbatur; adhibitum sanitas consecuta est. Deinde post annos aliquot eadem rursus corporis causa commota, hoc idem ille putavit adhibendum; adhibitum vertit in pejus. Miratus recurrit ad medicum, indicat factum: at ille ut erat acerrimus, ita respondit, *Ideo male acceptus es, quia ego non jussi;* ut omnes qui audissent, parumque hominem nossent non eum arte medicinali fidere, sed nescio qua illicita potentia putarent. Unde cum esset a quibusdam postea stupentibus interrogatus, apuerit quod non intellexerant, videlicet illi aetati jam non hoc se fuisse jussurum. Tantum igitur valet ratione atque artibus non mutatis, quid secundum eas sit pro temporum varietate mutandum." Cf. above, 147/19–22, and *Four Last Things, EW,* sig. e₄v.

173/30–174/10 **than . . . hand.** Cf. above, 44/9–46/11, and n. to 45/30–46/11. More quotes Ezek. 3:18; cf. also Ezek. 33:8, 9.

174/18–26 **Qui . . . disciple.** Luke 14:33 and 14:26. In the first quotation the Vulgate reads *renunciat* rather than *renunciauerit.* The passage goes on to speak of the imitation of Christ in following the Way of the Cross: "Et qui non bajulat crucem suam, et venit post me, non potest meus esse discipulus" (Luke 14:27).

175/8–9 **There . . . mansions.** John 14:2.

175/11 **veryly.** This is the reading of *B* and *Z,* but the "very" of *A* is perhaps possible, as an adjective, meaning "true."

175/11–15 **Hit . . . rich.** Cf. Luke 6:20–21: "Beati pauperes: quia vestrum est regnum Dei. Beati, qui nunc esuritis: quia saturabimini."

175/15–20 **by . . . tabernacles.** Luke 16:9. In More's translation (ll. 18–19) "make you frendes of the wikked riches," the word "of" indicates cause or means: "by means of" (cf. "*de*" in the Vulgate and *OED,* "of" *prep.* IV, VI). The verse occurs at the end of the parable of the unjust steward, who bought himself friends by writing off his master's debts.

175/26 **Lazarus & Abraham.** See Luke 16: 19–31, and above, 47/16–20 and 54/1–56/12.

176/7–29 **Zacheus . . . mich.** Luke 19:1–10. At 176/9–10 More translates verse 5: "Zachaee, festinans descende: quia hodie in domo tua oportet me manere," and at 176/26–29, verse 8: "Ecce dimidium bonorum meorum. Domine, do pauperibus: et si quid aliquem defraudavi, reddo quadruplum." Cf. *Treatise on the Blessed Body, EW,* sig. LL₇.

178/3–4 **Domini . . . tong.** Prov. 16:1.

178/18 **litle Zacheus.** Luke 19:3 mentions that Zachaeus was very short ("statura pusillus erat"); therefore he climbed the sycamore tree to see Jesus over the heads of the crowd.

178/22–26 **And . . . vttermost.** Cf. Exod. 22:1, 7, 9; Deut. 19:21; and Matt. 5:38–39: "Audistis quia dictum est: Oculum pro oculo, et dentem pro dente. Ego autem dico vobis, non resistere malo: sed si quis te percusserit in dextram maxillam tuam, praebe illi in alteram."

178/30–179/1 **Nihil . . . you.** Luke 3:13, the reply of John the Baptist to the publicans who came to be baptized and asked what they should do. The Vulgate reads *quam quod* rather than *quam*.

179/4–10 **Reddite . . . Abraham.** Mark 12:17. The Vulgate reads *Reddite igitur* (*Biblia Latina*, "Reddite ergo") rather than *Reddite*. More adds the phrase "refusyng all extorcion and brybery beside." The second quotation is from Luke 19:9, Jesus' words to Zachaeus after he promised to distribute his money. The Vulgate reads *Quia hodie salus domui huic facta est.*

179/20 **As for.** Pleonastic: "for."

179/23–25 **pauperes . . . vnto.** Jesus' reply to His disciples, who felt that the jar of costly ointment He was anointed with should have been sold and the money given to the poor. More quotes the version in Mark 14:7. The Vulgate reads *et cum volueritis* for *quibus quum vultis* and *illis benefacere* for *benefacere*. In Matthew 26:11 and John 12:8 the last clause is omitted. See also *Supplication, EW,* sig. t₆v.

179/30–180/13 **But . . . after.** This defense of capitalism would seem to contradict More's earlier economic egalitarianism in *Utopia*. But *Utopia* was never a practical program of social reform. In its totality the work presents two carefully counterbalanced socio-cconomic systems: the capitalism of Europe and the communism of Utopia, the real and the visionary. Each of these states is incomplete without the other, and the result is a complexity of vision and ironic brilliance that makes extrapolation risky. In the present case More is speaking of Europe alone without the *persona* of Hythlodaeus to offer the possibility of an alternative vision. Cf. *CW 4,* cv-cxxiv, cxxiv-cxxvi. For the general problem of inconsistencies in More, see Chambers, *Thomas More,* pp. 256–67, 359–72.

180/29–181/4 **as it . . . many.** The fable of the goose that laid the golden eggs was widely attributed in the Renaissance to Avianus, not Aesop. Avianus reworked into Latin distichs forty-two of the Greek fables of Babrius, dating from the first century A.D. Renaissance translations of Babrius' *Tetrasticha,* such as the one included in the Froben edition of Aesop (*Fabulae,* p. 241), substitute a hen for the goose, as does More:

> Ouum aureum Gallina semel peperit.
> Quidamque auarus deceptus animo
> Eam occidit aureum accepturus
> Sed spes perdidit maius fortunae donum.

Avianus' fable changes the hen to a goose; see *Fabulae*, p. 144, and Caxton, p. 190.

181/11–12 **omni . . . nothyng.** The phrasing is a combination of Luke 6:30 (*Omni autem petenti te, tribue*) and Matt. 5:42 (*Qui petit a te, da ei*).

181/14–18 **But . . . aske the.** The blank spaces have been left approximately as they appear in *A*, so that the reader may see the problems facing the editors, whether early or late. It is remarkable that *B*, who filled in most of the other blanks in *CC*, made no effort at all to cope with the problems here. *L* makes reasonably good sense, preserving the first blank space, but omitting the other, longer space, embellishing with the word "holy" (followed by *Z*), changing "christ sayth" to "Christe saye" (*Z*), re-punctuating and capitalizing to clarify: "But verely cosyn that sayng hath (as .Sayncte   sayth other places in scrypture hath) nede of enterpretacyon, For as holy .S. Awstyn saith, Though Chryste saye, gyve every man that asketh the, he sayth not yet gyve theym all that they wyll aske the" (fol. 111). *1553* makes a guess at St. Paul and revises accordingly: "But verely Cosin, that saying hath, as S. Paule saith, and other places in Scripture, neede of interpretacion. For as holy .S. Austen saith: Though Christ say, geue euerye man that asketh the: he saith not yet, geue them al that they wil aske thee" (sig. M₆ᵛ). *1557* prefers Augustine, in spite of the awkward repetition: "But verely cosin, that saying hath (as saint Austine saith other places in scripture hath) nede of interpretacion. For as holy saint Austine saith: though Christ say, Geue euery man that asketh thee, he saith not yet, geue them all that they will aske thee" (sig. GG₈). *1573*, comparing *1553* and *1557*, cannot decide between Paul and Augustine and therefore avoids the issue entirely: "But verily, Cosin, that saying hath (as other places in Scripture, haue) neede of interpretation. For as holy S. Austin saith: Though Christ say: Giue euery man that asketh thee, he saith not yet, giue them al that they wil aske thee" (fol. 124ᵛ).

The uncertainties in *CC* may indicate some difficulties in More's holograph that the scribe could not resolve: perhaps some revisions and interlineations that made the position of some phrases uncertain. The scribe clearly thought that "as saynt Austyn sayth" was meant to be followed by a quotation from Augustine, but he also took the phrase "Though christ sayth" as beginning another sentence. The early editors seem surely to be right in bringing these two phrases together, for More appears to be referring to a specific passage in Augustine: *De Sermone Domini in Monte*, II, xx (*PL 34*, 1263–64): "*Omni petenti, inquit; non, omnia petenti; ut id des quod dare honeste et juste potes. Quid si enim pecuniam petat, qua* innocentam conetur opprimere? quid si postremo stuprum petat? Sed ne multa persequar quae sunt innumerabilia, id profecto dandum est quod nec tibi nec alteri noceat." More omits the harm to others, concentrating only on the harm to oneself.

But is *1557* right in filling the first blank with a reference to Augustine? In his polemical works More consistently uses Augustine as his authority on the need for the interpretation of scripture. Cf. *Heresies, EW,* sig. k$_8$r-v; *Confutation, CW 8,* 287/23–284/4, 331/5–15, 354/4–7; and Rogers, p. 49. The idea is common in Augustine. Cf., for example: "Verbi Dei altitudo exercet studium, non denegat intellectum. Si enim omnia clausa essent, nihil esset unde revelarentur obscura. Rursus si omnia tecta essent, non esset unde alimentum perciperet anima, et haberet vires quibus posset ad clausa pulsare" (*PL 38,* 849). See also *PL 41,* 332–33; *PL 34,* 38; and *PL 36,* 136.

But then why would More himself have left a blank for such an obvious allusion? One suspects that in fact he did not leave a blank, but that the scribe was puzzled by the two references to Augustine in such close succession, and decided to leave the first reference blank. Rastell, knowing More's reliance on Augustine, could well have supplied the name by his own intuition.

181/21–182/1 **Our . . . asketh.** More paraphrases Luke 6:27–30.

182/5–6 **si esurierit . . . mete.** Rom. 12:20, where Paul paraphrases Prov. 25:21. The Vulgate reads *ciba illum: si sitit, potum da illi* rather than *da illi cibum.*

182/11–13 **Qui . . . infidell.** 1 Tim. 5:8, which reads in full: "Si quis autem suorum, et maxime domesticorum curam non habet, fidem negavit, et est infideli deterior."

183/4–7 **By . . . children.** Cf. Exod. 20:12, the fourth commandment, and 2 Cor. 12:14: "Nec enim debent filii parentibus thesaurizare, sed parentes filiis."

184/19–28 **But . . . hipocryte.** Cf. Roper, p. 48: "This Lord Chancelour, albeit he was to god and the world well knowen of notable vertue . . . yeat, for the avoiding of singularity, wold he appeare none otherwise then other men in his apparell and other behaviour. And albeit outwardly he appeared honorable like one of his callinge, yeat inwardly he no such vanityes esteeming, secreatly next his body ware a shirte of heare."

184/29 **as did . . . hester.** The passage More refers to specifically occurs in the Greek additions to the Book of Esther in the Apocrypha. Before going to the king to plead for her people, Esther was seized with anxiety and prayed, explaining to God how she detested her place next to the king and all her outward signs of glory: "Tu scis necessitatem meam, quod abominer signum superbiae et gloriae meae, quod est super caput meum in diebus ostentationis meae, et detester illud quasi pannum menstruatae, et non portem in diebus silentii mei . . . et nunquam laetata sit ancilla tua, ex quo huc translata sum usque in praesentem diem, nisi in te Domine Deus Abraham. Deus fortis super omnes, exaudi vocem eorum, qui nullam aliam spem habent, et libera nos de manu iniquorum, et erue me a timore meo" (14:16–19).

185/11–15 **which . . . nought.** Luke 10:38–42. More refers specifically to verses 41–42: "Martha, Martha, sollicita es et turbaris erga plurima. Porro unum est necessarium. Maria optimam partem elegit, quae non auferetur ab ea." In traditional interpretations, such as Richard of St. Victor's *Expositio in Cantica Canticorum*, 8 (*PL 196*, 428), Martha was taken as a type of the active life and Mary, the contemplative. Ever since the days of Tertullian (*De Pudicitia*, xi [*PL 2*, 1001]), the Latin Church identified Mary of Bethany, the sister of Martha and Lazarus, with Mary Magdalene and the penitent woman in Luke 7:37–50. See Gregory the Great, *PL 76*, 1189, and *Glossa Ordinaria, PL 114*, 229. The Greek Church, following Origen (*PG 13*, 1721–26), regarded them as three separate. individuals. The unity of the three Marys was beginning to be questioned in More's time by Lefèvre d'Étaples and others. See E. L. Surtz, *The Works and Days of John Fisher* (Cambridge, Mass., 1967), pp. 5–7, 274–89. More, however, held to the traditional view. See *Treatise on the Passion, EW*, sig. NN₇v; *Treatise on the Blessed Body, EW*, sig. LL₆v; and *Supplication, EW*, sig. v₄v.

188/7–22 **I was . . . hand.** Letters from merchants were one of the most common means of receiving news from within the Turkish Empire. Cf. Jean Bodin, *Heptaplomeres*, ed. L. Noack (Paris, 1857), pp. 10–11: "Hic CORONAEUS litteras quas Corcyraeo mercatore acceperat mihi pro Phaedone legendas dedit, quibus ea continebantur, quae Constantinopoli gesta fuerant in circumcisione primogeniti Turcarum regis, qui principium, qui legatorum conventus, quae fiequentia peregrinorum, qualis pompa ludorum Circensium, quae convivia, quae largitiones, quantas rerum omnium apparatus et quo quaeque ordine gesta fuisset." See also Schwoebel, p. 35. The Italian city states, particularly Venice and Genoa, were major centers of trade with the East, and were commonly accused of being in league with the Turks. See Schwoebel, pp. 179–81.

188/23–189/2 **The Turke . . . together.** The Turkish cavalry was made up of native Turks, feudal retainers, and vassals to the sultan, who served only in time of war. The infantry constituted a standing army of special troops taken as children in war or received as tribute and trained to the military life. In their early stages of training they were known as *ajami oghlanlars*. At the age of twenty-five they became *yani chari*, or Janissaries, which means *the new soldiers*. The Janissaries were not allowed to leave camp, marry, or exercise a trade. At the beginning of Suleiman's reign they numbered around 12,000 men and were notoriously difficult to control. At the conquest of Rhodes, for example, they mutinied and ran riot, refusing to observe the terms of surrender. After lying in idleness in 1523–24, they broke out in mutiny again at Constantinople: "The Janissaries began to murmur at their Sultan's forgetfulness of war, and at last they broke out into open brigandage, and pillaged the houses of the principal ministers. Solyman returned to Constantinople, and strove to quell the storm by his presence. He boldly confronted the mutinous troops, and cut down two of their ringleaders with his own hand; but he was obliged to pacify them by a donative, though he afterwards partly avenged himself by putting to death many of their officers" (E. S. Creasy, *History of the Ottoman Turks* [Beirut, 1961], pp. 162–64). The need to put his troops into action was one of the immediate causes of Suleiman's invasion of Hungary in 1526.

189/6 **visage.** "An assumed appearance; an outward show": *OED*, "visage" *sb.* 8, where this passage is cited, among other examples. The reading of Z has been adopted with considerable hesitation; the reading of *A*, "viage," which *B* did not change, may well be right, since "viage" carried the meaning of "a military enterprise" in the sixteenth century. See the *OED*, "voyage" *sb.* 2, where the phrases "martial voyaige" (1549) and "voyage of warre" (1584) are cited. More's use of "vyage" at 188/11 could be used to explain a scribal misreading in the second instance—or to support the reading itself.

189/13–14 **For . . . dogges.** A reference to the supporters of John Zapolya, who was suspected of being in league with the Turk. See above, n. to 7/1–12. For the fable of the sheep and the dogs, cf. Erasmus, *Adag.*, "Ovem lupo commisisti," sig. K₃v (I. IV. x). Erasmus cites Cicero's *Third Phillipic:* "'Etenim in concione dixerat se custodem futurum urbis, usque ad calendas Maias, ad urbem exercitum habiturum. O praeclarum custodem, ovium ut aiunt, lupum! custos ne urbis, an direptor & vexator esset Antonius?' Unde quadrare videtur, quoties inimico negocium committitur, quique nobis pessime velit: propterea quod lupus & agnus genuino quodam odio diffident." See also Tilley, W 602. More probably confused the proverb with Aesop's fable of the war between the sheep and the wolves, in which the sheep took the dogs as allies. The wolves were beaten and sued for peace on condition that the dogs be given to the wolves. The wolves then killed the dogs and ate the sheep. See Caxton, pp. 114–15, and "De Lupis et Ovibus" in *Fabulae*.

189/21–26 **For . . . therin.** Suleiman protested that he was not interested in annexing Hungary, but only in exacting tribute and in seeing that there was a native Hungarian king on the throne. After the death of Louis II, he is said to have affirmed "with an oth, that he was not come to expell him out of his kingdome, but onely to reuenge his men of the inuries which the Hungars had done them, greatly complaining for the death of *Lewis*, the which had taken from him all means wherby in effect he might shew the truth of his words, the which were, that he would haue placed him againe in his fathers kingdome, vnder certaine good conditions of an honest and reasonable tribute" (Fumée, p. 37). With Louis dead, Suleiman chose Zapolya. When Suleiman invaded Hungary again in the spring of 1529, Zapolya met him at Belgrade and formally swore his allegiance, acknowledging himself as a Turkish tributary (Fumée, p. 44). The Ottomans eventually annexed a large portion of Hungary in 1547. A paraphrase may help to clarify the use of "he" and "hym" in ll. 22–26: "The Turk will wait to see the result before he fully shows his intentions; but in the end, if he is able to get the country for Zapolya, you shall see the Turk so deal with the situation that he shall not fail to get the country from Zapolya, and that very quickly, before he allows Zapolya to settle himself securely in control of the country."

190/3–9 **He . . . lyst.** Commonly believed because of the theocratic nature of the Ottoman Empire; see, for example, Schwoebel, p. 187. During the reign of Suleiman, a code of law was drawn up by Ibrahim Haleby of Aleppo composed of the *Koran*, the *Sunnas*, or early sayings and deeds of the Prophet, the "apostolic laws," and the *Kiyas*, or canonical decisions of the four great Imams. This code, known as the *Multeka-ul-ubhar*, or "Confluence of the Seas," called for the conquest of unbelievers as one of the primary duties of Islam: "they must be converted to Islam, subjected to tribute, or destroyed by the sword. The fulfillment of this religious duty was the end and purpose of the Ottoman power, to which its institutions were designed and excellently adapted" (J. B. Bury, "The Ottoman Conquest" in *The Cambridge Modern History*, *1* [New York, 1902], 98).

190/10–12 **Out . . . regresse.** A common feature of the Turkish wars. After the defeat of Louis II at Mohàcs, Suleiman returned to Turkey when the coming of winter put an end to the campaign: "His soldiers were laden with the richest plunder; and they drove before them a herd of 100,000 Christians, men, women and little children destined for sale in the Turkish slavemarkets" (Creasy, p. 166). Earlier, in 1470, the Turks are reported to have taken 10,000 Hungarian prisoners, and in 1479 they again made away with "a great multitude of Christian Prisoners" (Newton, fol. 132ᵛ).

190/21–22 **Chio . . . morea.** Chios is one of the Greek Isles, about ten miles off the coast of Asia Minor. Candy or Candia is another name for Crete. The Morea is the Peloponnesus, that portion of Greece below the Isthmus of Corinth.

190/24–29 **in all . . . withall.** The cruelty of the Turks was of course proverbial. After the battle of Mohàcs, for example, the Turkish cavalry was said to have been sent to "put all to fire and sword whom they met betweene Danubius and the Lake of Balator, euen vnto Iauarine," and

Hungarian mothers buried alive their suckling babes for fear their crying would betray them. A few weeks later, the Turks found a group of Hungarian refugees holed up at Maroth in a narrow mountain valley. After breaking their barricade of wagons with artillery, the Turks killed almost all the defenders and their wives and children. "The great heapes of bones, which is to be seene at this day, in that place, doth sufficiently witnes the greatnes of the massacre, the which, as those few reporte that escaped, was 25000. persons one and other." The total number of Hungarians killed or captured in the summer of 1526 was reported to have been "wel neere 200000" (Fumée, pp. 33–35).

190/30–191/6 **There lo . . . cheving.** "There" refers to Greece. More is speaking of the Turkish system of *kharâj* and *devshirme*. According to Janus Lascaris, in his *Informatione impresa contro a Turchi* (1508), three hundred thousand Christian families in Greece were required to pay a special tax known as the *kharâj*. Those who paid it were sometimes allowed to keep their horses and even carry a scimitar. Christians who served in the territorial guard were free of the tax, and the younger generation, Lascaris lamented, tempted with exemption from the *kharâj*, were learning to abjure their faith and turn renegade (cited in Schwoebel, pp. 161–63). Greek Christians were further caught between the *kharâj* and the system of *devshirme* or levying of tribute children. Teodoro Spandugino, in his *Geneologie du grant Turc à present regnant* (1519), observed that Christians in Greece married their children early since only unmarried children between the ages of eight and fifteen were included in the levies, but the early marriages only increased the size of their families and their assessment in the *kharâj* (Schwoebel, pp. 209–11). The system of *devshirme* was devised by the Turks primarily to supply the army with Janissaries. See above, n. to 188/23–189/2. Besides becoming Janissaries, tribute children were also chosen to serve in the seraglio, as functionaries and officials in the Turkish government, or as members of a special group of cavalry who formed the Sultan's private bodyguard. There is a considerable body of literature written by children captured in war and victims of the *devshirme* who escaped and returned to Europe. See Schwoebel's bibliography, p. 228. One of the most famous of these is the *Tractatus de Condicionibus et Nequicia Turcorum*, written by George of Hungary in 1480 and intended as a guide to survival. It deals particularly with the subtle pressures and inducements of the Turks to force the children to renounce Christ (Schwoebel, p. 208).

192/1–3 **For . . . boystuouse.** More had used this same image earlier in his *Richard III*; cf. *CW* 2, 44/22–23 and n. For "boystuouse," see *ibid.*, 57/25.

192/12–14 **For . . . is.** The question of title to the Hungarian throne arose on the death of Louis II in August 1526. See above, 8/3. It was not settled until 1538, when both contenders agreed to partition the country.

192/22-193/2 **it hath . . . vnknowen.** This is not mentioned in any of the standard renaissance histories of Hungary. Conrad Lycosthenes in his authoritative work on the subject notes only that after the death of Louis II two "parelia" were seen in the skies over Hungary, indicating the three kings who would contend for the throne: Ferdinand, John Zapolya, and Suleiman (*Prodigiorum ac Ostentorum Chronicon* [Basel, 1577], p. 531). The only comparable allusion to children's games we have been able to locate occurs in W. Carew Hazlitt's edition of *Brand's Popular Antiquities of Great Britain* (London, 1905), *1*, 113, which cites an article from *The Craftsman*, February 4, 1738 (pp. 80-81). The article notes that in the seventeenth century, at the time of the Civil War in England, children's games were observed to parody the behavior of those involved in political events. Though the games were looked upon as foreshadowings of events to come, this was true only because the children mysteriously sensed what was happening and imitated the actions of those who were actually working to bring about the Revolution. For the *dirige*, see above, n. to 132/11.

193/29 **wher . . . yet.** The Turkish threat to Europe in the late fifteenth and early sixteenth century was commonly interpreted as the fulfillment of the prophecies concerning the end of the world. See above, n. to 7/15-18.

193/32-194/6 **Filius . . . comyng.** Luke 18:8, the end of the parable of the importunate widow, whom Christ likens to the elect. The Vulgate (cf. the corrections in *1557* and *1573*) reads *veniens* rather than *quum venerit*. The parable follows hard on Christ's revelations concerning the end of the world in Luke 17:22. The reference to the Apocalypse (194/3) is to Rev. 3:18-a, but More in ll. 4-7 paraphrases Matt. 24:22: "Et nisi brevitati fuissent dies illi, non fieret salva omnis caro: sed propter electos breviabuntur dies illi." "Rev. 1" in the 1573 marginalia is an error.

194/2-3 **as who say.** "That is to say."

194/8-10 **tokens . . . strayght.** See Rev. 3:9: "Ecce dabo de synagoga Satanae, qui dicunt se Iudaeos esse, et non sunt, sed mentiuntur: ecce faciam illos ut veniant, et adorent ante pedes tuos: et scient quia ego dilexi te." At the end of Book III (309/6-310/16, below), More again returns to this section of Revelation and identifies the elect with the holy martyrs, who suffer on earth for Christ's sake and enter in glory into heaven.

194/9 **the comyng . . . iewes.** The conversion of the Jews, as prophesied by Paul in Romans 11:1-32. See the *OED* ("come," *v.* IX. 59. f.) for the phrase "come in," meaning "to submit, yield, give in one's adhesion."

It is possible that there is also an allusion here to the prophecy that the Jews will return to a restored Jerusalem: see Isaiah 54–55.

195/7–8 **halfe . . . ernest.** Cf. Erasmus, *Adag.*, "Joca seriaque," sig. Cc₄v (II. I. xxiv), and "Jocandum ut seria agas," sig. Bbbb₃v (IV. VIII. xxxix); Whiting, G 21 and S 641. See also *Confutation, CW 8*, 263/1, 950/24–25, and Taft, *Apologye*, p. 194.

195/18–21 **the tone . . . sect.** Although Ferdinand invaded Hungary with a German-Bohemian army and defeated Zapolya in 1527, his base of operations remained in Austria. When Suleiman invaded Hungary in 1529, for example, "he marched directly to Buda, which was forsaken by the citizens, as soone as euer they heard of the report of his comming; and so it came vnder the gouernment of the enemie, without any resistance: only the Fortresse was kept by 700. Germanes, who very couragiously for a time did their endeuour to defend it" (Fumée, p. 45). Suleiman fought briefly at Ofen and immediately advanced to Vienna, where the major struggle with Ferdinand took place. More is mistaken, however, in implying that Zapolya was still in the country at the time. After being defeated by Ferdinand in 1527 near the castle of Thoccay in Transylvania, he escaped to Poland, where he negotiated with Suleiman for the restoration of his throne. It was not until the Turkish invasion of 1529 that Zapolya returned to native Hungarian soil, meeting Suleiman for the first time at Belgrade. At the meeting, Suleiman promised "with ease to reconquer all that which vniustly had been taken from him, and that by the iustice of his forces, which being done, he would liberally render it to him againe" (Fumée, p. 44). Cf. above, 7/1–3.

196/13–14 **the fawte . . . fall.** Matt. 26:33–35, 69–75. See also Mark 14:29–31, 66–72; Luke 22:33–34, 54–62; John 13:36–38; 18:25–27. Cf. below, 196/27–28, and above, n. to 146/23–29.

197/11–21 **But . . . man.** Cf. More's remarks to Margaret concerning equivocation in taking the Oath of Succession: "Verely, Daughter, I neuer entend . . . to pynne my soule at a nother mans backe . . . Some may do for fauour, and some may doe for feare . . . And some may be peraduenture of that minde, that if they say one thing and thinke the while the contrary, God more regardeth their harte than their tonge, and that therfore their othe goeth vpon that they thinke, and not vpon that they say, as a woman resoned once, I trow, Daughter, you wer by. But in good faith, Marget, I can vse no such waies in so great a matter . . . I dare not do it, mine owne conscience standing against it" (Rogers, p. 521). Chambers (*Thomas More*, p. 310) suggests that the woman who argued in favor of equivocation was Dame Alice. Margaret herself is said to have taken the oath with mental reservations (*EW*, sig. YY₅, marginal gloss).

198/5–7 **Fynally . . . fayth.** Cf. Matt. 10:32–33: "Omnis ergo, qui confitebitur me coram hominibus, confitebor et ego eum coram Patre meo, qui in caelis est: Qui autem negaverit me coram hominibus, negabo et ego eum coram Patre meo, qui in caelis est." See also Mark 8:38 and Luke 12:9, and cf. above, n. to 109/2–7.

198/9 **condicionally.** There may be an allusion here to a conditional proposition in logic: "consisting of two categorical clauses, the former of which, expressing a condition introduced by *if* . . . is called the *antecedent* (in Grammar *protasis*), the latter, stating the conclusion, is called the *consequent* (apodosis)." (*OED*, "conditional" *a.* II. 5, with an example from More's *Confutation*.) The two "yf" clauses before and after the word represent examples of the antecedent in this context.

199/8–10 **eyther . . . alyke.** Cf. above, 31/10–33/26.

199/12 **more.** Used in the sense of "rather" (cf. "than," l. 14).

200/5–8 **The . . . meridiano.** Ps. 90:6. More's interpretation of the noonday devil as open persecution for the faith is taken from Augustine's *Enarratio in Psalmum XC*, I, 7–9 (*PL 37*, 1153–56). This was the standard gloss, adopted by Cassiodorus (*PL 70*, 652), Pseudo-Bede (*PL 93*, 974–75), Paulus Burgensis (*Biblia Latina*, *3*, sig. K₁), and the Interlinear Gloss (*Biblia Latina*, *3*, sig. I₆), among others. Nicholas de Lyra and Bernard represent a different tradition. Bernard interpreted the noonday devil as a form of ignorance in which lovers of the good are persuaded that evil is the good they seek, as in the case of demonic illusion. See above, n. to 132/25–133/1.

200/8–22 **And . . . he is.** For the gradation among the four temptations in terms of degrees of severity and degrees of ignorance and knowledge, see Augustine and Jerome, cited above, nn. to 107/18–23 and 166/18–167/8. Augustine develops the idea that the incursion of the noonday devil is an assault specifically on those who are firm in their faith and know that they are called to a future life: "noverunt se ad futuram spem vocatos . . . norunt ista: sed quando coeperit persecutor instare vehementius, agere minis, poenis, tormentis, aliquando cedunt, et scientes tanquam in die cadunt" (*Enarratio in Psalmum XC*, I, 7 [*PL 37*, 1154]).

201/1–2 **lyke . . . lyon.** Cf. above, n. to 108/1–6, and below, n. to 318/5–8.

201/3–11 **This . . . turment.** According to Augustine, the temptation of the noonday devil was the most vehement and perilous temptation of all because it used the body and the frailty of human nature to destroy the spirit. It was a form of persecution in which a person was tortured and repeatedly tortured until he gave way: "Quicumque confessus se fuerit christianum, torqueatur, et tamdiu torqueatur, donec neget se esse christianum. Comparate sagittam volantem per diem, et daemonium meridianum. Sagitta volans per diem quid erat? Qui se confessus fuerit christianum, feriatur. Quis fidelis eam mortis celeritate non declinaret?

Illud autem, Si se confitetur christianum, non occidatur; sed torqueatur, donec neget; si se negaverit, dimittatur: daemonium meridianum erat" (*Enarratio in Psalmum XC*, I, 8 [*PL 37*, 1155]). More does not insist upon this aspect of Augustine's interpretation, though it underlies Book III and accounts for a considerable portion of the structure and meaning of *A Dialogue of Comfort*.

201/18–19 **of necessite . . . vertue.** Cf. above, n. to 26/7.

202/18–26 **In . . . other.** Cf. Harpsfield's account of the "principall drifte and scope" of the *Dialogue of Comfort*, above, n. to 6/6–14. The phrase "alies within a litle" (202/24) means "close relatives."

202/27–28 **Vnicuique . . . neighbour.** Ecclus. 17:12. The Vulgate reads: "Et mandavit illis unicuique de proximo suo."

204/18–20 **& not . . . now.** More once again refers to Peter's assertion that he would die with Christ rather than deny Him, and his later betrayal through fear (Matt. 26:33–35, 69–75). See above, 196/13–14 and n. to 146/23–29.

204/29 **love longyng.** All other texts place a comma after "love," to make "longyng" the beginning of a participial phrase; but it seems better to take "love longyng" as a noun-phrase. See the *OED*, "love-longing": "The longing felt by those who are in love." The *OED* provides striking examples of the phrase from Chaucer, Drayton, and others.

206/5 **substaunce.** See the *OED* ("substance," 17.b) for the meaning "maintenance, subsistence." The reading is not changed by *B*, but all other texts read "sustenaunce." This looks like an editorial change made because of the repetition of "substaunce" in the next line.

206/19–22 **And . . . lost.** The Mameluke Empire of Syria and Egypt fell to the Ottoman Turks in the summer of 1516. See above, n. to 7/30–8/1. The fictitious date of the *Dialogue of Comfort* is 1527–28, eleven or twelve years after Syria and Egypt fell, not twenty or thereabout. More seems to have dated from the actual time of composition in 1534–35.

206/27–207/3 **what . . . yron.** A common idea of More's. Cf. *Utopia, CW 4*, 150/16–23, and *Treatise on the Passion, EW*, sig. LL₈v.

207/23–24 **Grece . . . to.** Greece fell in 1453, Syria in 1516. See above, 7/29–30 and n.

207/26–208/2 **yf . . . land.** Despite the reference to Plato, More uses the idea in a popular sense, as though the world soul were simply the sort of thing that would endow the inanimate earth with consciousness and reason. In Plato the concept is much more abstract and obscure, with little analogy to human experience. Cf. *Timaeus*, 34A–37C, where the world soul is described as coeval with the world body, extending from center to circumference, enclosing the body both inside and out. Circular in form and complete within itself, it is composed of various intermediate degrees of existence, sameness and difference, compounded and arranged according to musical proportion. In 36E–37B Plato explains its reasonable nature and the discourse proper to it in almost opaque terms.

208/3–11 **ah . . . agoo.** Cf. Roper, pp. 83–84. When Dame Alice visited More in the Tower and asked him why he preferred to remain shut up in prison "amongst mise and rattes" when he might be at home in his good house in Chelsea with his family and all his possessions, he replied: "I see no greate cause why I should much Ioye either of my gay house or of any thinge belonginge therunto; when, if I shoulde but seuen yeares lye buried vnder the ground, and then arise and come thither againe, I should not faile to find some therein that wold bid me get me out of doores, and tell me it were none of mine. What cause haue I then to like such an house as wold so soone forgett his master?" Cf. also *Epigrams*, no. 3, p. 7.

208/15–20 **In . . . crowne.** A variant of the ancient *topos, generositas virtus, non sanguis.* Cf. Chaucer's *Wife of Bath's Tale*, 1109–1206; Dante, *Convivio*, IV, 3, 10, 14–15. See also *Hamlet*, V, i, 223–38; IV, iii, 23–34; and *Picus, EW*, sig. a₁–a₁v. For excellent surveys of the idea, see George M. Vogt, "Gleanings for the History of a Sentiment: *Generositas Virtus, non Sanguis*," *JEGP, 24* (1925), 101–24, and Lewis Einstein, *The Italian Renaissance in England* (New York, 1913), pp. 61–68.

208/22 **antique.** The reading of *A* and *1557* has been retained, but "autentique," the reading of *L, 1553,* and *1573,* may be right. It would be easy to misread one word for the other, if "autentique" were abbreviated. Cf. below, 281/19.

209/20 **either . . . come.** More has in mind the Augustinian distinction between the use (*uti*) of worldly things and the enjoyment or love of them (*frui*) for their own sake. See below, n. to 223/14–26.

210/6–12 **It . . . holsome.** Similar reflections occur in Lucian's *Cynicus*, which More translated. Cf. *CW 3*, 1, 17/7–8, 13–14: "uestes illae uariae nihilo magis quicquam queant calefacere . . . Praeterea omnigenae illae circa edulia curae, nihilo magis alunt, quin tabefaciunt potius corpora, ijsdemque morbos ingenerant." Cf. also *Utopia* (*CW 4*, 132/29–134/10).

210/25–29 **but put . . . after.** Cf. More's early work, "A mery Jest" (*EW*, sig. ₵₁v): "First fayre and wele, / Therof much dele, / He dygged it in a pot, / But then him thought, / That way was nought, / And there he left it not."

212/4–5 **But . . . mouth.** A favorite image of More's, used throughout his works. Cf. the beginning of the prayer written in his *Book of Hours* (*Prayer Book*, pp. 3–4, 185): "Gyve me thy grace good lord . . . not to

hange vppon the blaste of mennys mowthis." See also *Four Last Things,*
EW, sig. fg₂; *Heresies, EW*, sig. s₄; Taft, *Apologye*, p. 77.

212/19–21 **as though . . . them.** I.e., as though they were God. Cf. Isa.
6:1–3, where God is described on His throne surrounded by seraphim,
who sing: "Sanctus, sanctus, sanctus, Dominus Deus exercituum, plena
est omnis terra gloria ejus." See also Rev. 4:8. The phrase is also used at
the beginning of the consecration in the mass.

213/6–216/3 **Whan . . . wept.** Harpsfield (pp. 34–35) identifies this
"greate man of the church" as Cardinal Wolsey: "Truely, this Cardinall
did [not] heartily loue Sir Thomas More, yea, he rather feared him then
loued him. And albeit he were adorned with many goodly graces and
qualities, yet was he of so outragious aspiring, ambitious nature, and so
fedd with vaineglory and with the hearing of his owne praise, and by the
excesse thereof fallen, as it were into a certaine pleasant phrenesie, that
the enormious fault ouerwhelmed, defaced and destroyed the true commendation of all his good properties. He sore longed and thirsted after the
hearing of his owne praise, not onely when he had done some thinges
commendable, but euen when he had sometimes done that that was
naught in deede." He then goes on to quote More's anecdote as an
example of "this vaineglorious, scabbed, itching follye to heare his owne
prayse." Harpsfield adds that More himself was present at the occasion.
For Wolsey's love of pomp and splendor (213/10–11), see Cavendish's
description (pp. 18–21) of "the order of his howse & officers," totaling
more than four hundred attendants and servants. The list includes such
items as "A yoman of his Stirrope . . . xij Syngyng prestes . . . xij syngyng
Childerne . . . A riding Clarke / a Clarke of the hamper / A Chaffer of
waxe / Then had he A Clarke of the Chekke as well to chekke his Chap-
pleyns as hys yomen of the Chamber . . . iiijᵒʳ Mynstrelles / A keper of
his Tentes . . . And a Clarke of the Grean clothe."

213/21–22 **bordes . . . alone.** It seems the situation involved a long table,
at which the great man sat alone in the middle, while the others were
seated together at one end. There is a certain irony in the use of the word
"messe" here, since it was often used to indicate "each of the small
groups, normally of four persons (sitting together and helped from the
same dishes), into which the company at a banquet was commonly
divided" (*OED*, "mess" *sb.* II. 4). For Wolsey's isolation at his dining
table, cf. Cavendish (p. 26), "my lord Cardynall syttyng vnder the clothe
of estat / And hauyng all his seruyce all alone."

214/16–18 **for . . . Asse.** Related to the proverb "Ab equis ad asinos,"
which Erasmus explains: "Ubi quis a studiis honestioribus ad parum
honesta deflectit . . . Quadrabit item, ubi quis e conditione lautiore ad
abjectiora devenerit" (*Adag.*, sig. S₁ [I. VII. xxix]). See also Tilley,
H 713.

214/20-21 **not a . . . church.** I.e., not only a theologian, but also learned in canon law.

215/7-24 **But . . . handkercher.** *Nat. Hist.*, XXXV, xxxvi, 73-74. The painter was not Apelles, but Timanthes (cf. the correction in *1573*), who lived in Cythnus and later in Sicyon in the late fifth century B.C. The *Iphigenia* was his most famous work: "Nam Timanthis vel plurimum adfuit ingenii. eius enim est Iphigenia oratorum laudibus celebrata, qua stante ad aras peritura cum maestros pinxisset omnes praecipueque patruum et tristitiae omnem imaginem consumpsisset, patris ipsius voltum velavit, quem digne non poterat ostendere . . . atque in unius huius operibus intelligitur plus semper quam pingitur et, cum ars summa, ingenium tamen ultra artem est." Apelles of Cos (*fl.* 332-329 B.C.) was the most renowned painter of antiquity. Pliny says that his pictures of horses were so lifelike that other horses would neigh at them, and he was able to paint things, like thunder and lightning, that could not be painted (XXXV, xxxvi, 79-96).

216/7-14 **as Iuuenall . . . side.** *Sat.* IV, 119-21. Juvenal describes a large fish that was caught and presented to the emperor. The emperor could not find a platter large enough to cook it in, so he called a meeting of important men to decide what to do with it. This emperor, whom Juvenal describes as a "bald-headed Nero," was identified in More's time (as he is today) as Domitian, not Tiberius: "In hac quarta satyra: ut calderinus scribit: poeta accusaturus domitianum crudelitatis gulae & auaricie a crispino orditur" (Juvenal, *Satyrographi Opus*, ed. J. B. Ascensius [Venice, 1523], fol. 47ᵛ). Moreover, although a certain Montanus was present at the emperor's meeting, he was not the blind senator who made the remarks More refers to. Juvenal calls him "mortifero . . . Catullo," identified by Calderinus and Ascensius as Catullus Messalinus. Messalinus was a well-known *delator* or informer, hence the title, *mortifero*. He is mentioned by Pliny in his *Ep.*, IV, 22, as one "qui luminibus orbatus ingenio saevo mala caecitatis addiderat: non verebatur, non erubescebat, non miserebatur; quo saepius a Domitiano non secus ac tela, quae et ipsa caeca et improvida feruntur, in optimum quemque contorquebatur." See also Tacitus, *Agr.*, 45. Juvenal ends by calling him a "caecus adulator" (116). More refers specifically to ll. 119-21: "Nemo magis rhombum stupuit: nam plurima dixit / In laevum conversus: at illi dextra iacebat / Belua."

216/25-26 **as Terence . . . mad.** I.e., "such folk turn fools into madmen." Cf. *Eun.*, II, 254. Gnatho the parasite tells how he flatters everyone: "quidquid dicunt laudo; id rursum si negant, laudo id quoque; / negant quis: nego; ait: aio." Parmeno the slave then makes the remark More quotes: "scitum hercule hominem! hic homines prorsum ex stultis insanos facit."

217/10–17 **for . . . here.** Martial, *Epig.*, VIII, lxxvi: "'Dic verum mihi, Marce, dic amabo; / nil est quod magis audiam libenter.' / sic et cum recitas tuos libellos, / et causam quoties agis clientis, / oras, Gallice, me rogasque, semper. / durum est me tibi quod petis negare. / vero verius ergo quid sit audi: / verum, Gallice, non libenter audis."

217/18–218/4 **And . . . agayne.** Chambers suggests that this also is a personal anecdote (*Thomas More*, pp. 161–62). Following Harpsfield (cf. above, n. to 213/6–216/3), he identifies the prelate as Cardinal Wolsey and the friend as More himself. Stapleton (pp. 136–37) tells of a similar occasion in which Wolsey called More a fool. Shortly after More joined the Privy Council, Wolsey proposed the creation of a new office of Supreme Constable of England in the hopes that he would be the one to fill it. More spoke strongly against the proposal, and it was defeated. Stapleton continues: "The Cardinal was angry and thus addressed More: 'Are you not ashamed, Mr. More, being the lowest of all in place and dignity, to dissent from so many noble and prudent men? You show yourself to be a stupid and foolish Councillor.' 'Thanks be to God,' replied More instantly, 'that the King's Majesty has but one fool in his Council.'"

218/13 **Kyng Ladislaus.** Vladislav II. See above, n. to 124/15.

218/19 **neuer . . . erat.** The first words of the lesser doxology, "Gloria Patri, et Filii, et Spiritu Sancto," usually followed by: "sicut erat in principio et nunc et semper et in saecula saeculorum, amen."

219/20–220/10 **till . . . woman.** Harpsfield (pp. 94–95) again identifies this as a personal anecdote: "This wife, when she saw that Sir Thomas More, her husbande, had no list to growe greatly vpward in the world, nor neyther would labour for office of authoritie, and ouer that forsooke a right woorshipfull rowme when it was offered him, she fell in handc with him and all too rated him."

221/4–13 **nor . . . kyng.** The homely realism is typical of More's spirituality. Cf. *Utopia, CW 4,* 168/2–5: "Nam quid naturalis & uerae uoluptatis affert nudatus alterius uertex, aut curuati poplites, hoccine tuorum poplitum dolori medebitur? aut tui capitis phrenesim leuabit?" Cf. also above, 219/4–8.

222/8–16 **the parable . . . low.** The "philosopher" is Polybius, and the metaphor appears in his *Hist.*, V, xxvi, 12–13. Early in the reign of Philip of Macedonia, a subordinate named Apelles gave out that the king was still too young to govern and took more and more authority into his own hands. Philip humbled Apelles by inviting him to Corinth, and after allowing him to enter the city with great pomp, had him turned away from the door of the royal residence by a servant who told him that the king was busy at the moment. After waiting in the courtyard, bewildered and abashed, Apelles eventually withdrew, and by the time he reached lodgings of his own, his followers had all deserted him. Then follows the comparison More quotes. Burton uses the same metaphor from Polybius for the same purposes in his *Anatomy of Melancholy*, ed. F. Dell and P. Jordan-Smith (New York, 1927), p. 94.

223/14–26 **These . . . nought.** More's distinctions between the categories of good, bad, and indifferent and the proper use of worldly things are traditional and fundamentally Augustinian. These categories were first developed by the Stoics. Cf. Seneca, *Ep.* 82, 9–13, and J. Lipsius, *Manductiones ad Stoicam Philosophiam*, II, xxiii, in Seneca, *Opera Omnia*, ed. M. N. Bouillet (Paris, 1827), *1*, cliij–clviij. They were adopted by Augustine in his *De Sermone Domini in Monte*, II, 18 (*PL 34*, 1297), and from there passed on into the main stream of Christian ethics. Cf. Aquinas, *ST*, I–II, Q. 18, a. 8: "si objectum actus includat aliquid quod conveniat ordini rationis erit actus bonus secundum suam speciem, sicut dare eleemosynam indigenti. Si autem includat aliquid quod repugnat ordini rationis erit malus actus secundum speciem, sicut furari, quod est tollere aliena. Contingit autem quod objectum actus non includit aliquid pertinens ad ordinem rationis, sicut levare festucam de terra, ire ad campum, et hujusmodi; et tales actus secundum speciem suam sunt indifferentes."

More develops the distinction, basic to Augustinian ethics, between *uti* (to use) and *frui* (to delight in). Augustine's ethic is essentially an ethic of love. The things of this world may be used (*uti*) to allow man to arrive at God, but they must not be loved or delighted in (*frui*) for their own sake. Cf. *De Doctrina Christiana*, I, iv (*PL 34*, 20): "Frui enim est amore alicui rei inhaerere propter seipsam. Uti autem, quod in usum venerit ad id quod amas obtinendum referre, si tamen amandum est. Nam usus illicitus, abusus potius vel abusio nominandus est . . . sic in hujus mortalitatis vita peregrinantes a Domino (II Cor. v. 6), si redire in patriam volumus, ubi beati esse possimus, utendum est hoc mundo, non fruendum; ut invisibilia Dei, per ea quae facta sunt, intellecta conspiciantur (Rom. I, 20), hoc est, ut de corporalibus temporalibusque rebus aeterna et spiritualia capiamus." See also *PL 34*, 26, 32–33; *PL 38*, 958; and *PL 40*, 19–20. Cf. above, 209/20–24, and Taft, *Apologye*, pp. 86–87.

223/30–224/7 **Qui . . . deth.** I Tim. 6:9 and Prov. 21:6. More's reference in the text to Prov. 20 is a mistake, as is the marginal note in *CC*. In Prov. 21:6 the Vulgate reads: "Qui congregat thesauros lingua mendacii vanus et excors est, et impingetur ad laqueos mortis." For the reference to I Tim., cf. above, 168/5–12, 170/29–171/3 and n., 171/10.

224/4 **noyouse, which drowne.** The phrasing suggests that More may intend a pun here on "noyouse," meaning "annoying" or "vexatious," and the French "noyer," to drown.

225/6–9 **Than . . . thorow.** Attributed to Anacharsis by Plutarch in his *Life of Solon*, v, and to Solon by Diogenes Laertius (I, ii, 59). In the

Renaissance it was generally thought to be by Anacharsis. Cf. *The Garden of Pleasure*, trans. James Sanford (1573), cited in Tilley, L 116, and the note to Erasmus, *Adag.*, "Arenearum telos texere," sig. L₃ (I. IV. lxvii). Generally, however, it was taken to be a common proverb. Cf. Erasmus, *loc. cit.*; Pace, *De Fructu*, p. 32.

226/4 **holy as an horse.** Cf. *Heresies, EW*, sig. i₈v: "theyr parishe prieste . . . as lene & as pore and as haulting as his hors, & as holy to." The expression was apparently proverbial. Cf. Tilley, H 629, and Whiting, H 500.

226/15–16 **quia . . . mokkyd.** Gal. 6:7, where the Vulgate reads *deus* for *quia deus*.

226/20–21 **Inperfectum . . . beholden.** Ps. 138:16.

226/20–24 **Ab . . . Lord.** Ps. 18:13. The Vulgate omits "domine" here, but More probably transferred the word from verse 15, "Domine, adiutor meus etc."

228/11–12 **make . . . necessitie.** Cf. above, n. to 26/7.

228/27–28 **puff . . . dede.** The *OED* ("puff," *sb.* 9. b) cites this passage as the first example of the use of "puff ring" and defines it as "a counterfeit ring made hollow instead of solid." The word "parice" probably refers to "plaster of Paris," the fine white plaster made out of gypsum; the term was current in More's day (see the *OED*, "Plaster of Paris"). *L*'s alteration to "purse rynge" (followed by *1553* and *1573*) is offered by the *OED* as the only example of this usage, defined as "a ring, or one of the two sliding rings, closing a silk or leather purse" (*OED*, "purse-ring" 1); the citation comes from an edition of 1847. *L* also reads "parvys" for "parice". If this is not simply a wrong or unusual spelling, *L* may be interpreting the word as "parvis"—"the enclosed area or court in front of a building, esp. of a cathedral or church"; cf. *OED*, "parvis" 1, where it is noted: "The parvis of St. Paul's in London was a noted place of resort, esp. for lawyers." This is the sort of place where a "purse-ring" might often be seen(?).

230/6–10 **Que . . . ones.** The first quotation is from 2 Cor. 6:14–15. More has telescoped the verses. The Vulgate (cf. the corrections in *1557* and *1573*) reads: "Aut quae societas luci ad tenebras? Quae autem conventio Christi ad Belial?" The second quotation is from Matt. 6:24. The passage in 2 Corinthians distinguishes between believers and unbelievers, Christians and infidels. In Matthew, however, the two masters are God and Mammon, going back to Vincent's statement in the preceding paragraph (229/17–30) that one might be tempted to compromise his faith through a desire to retain his worldly possessions. The reference to Mammon, present only in context here, emerges fully below, 231/5 and 239/18–240/2. The 1557 and 1573 marginalia refer to Luke 6, but this is merely an allusion to the Sermon on the Mount (Luke 6:20–38); it is not a gloss on More's text.

231/5 **Non . . . together.** Matt. 6:24. Cf. above, 230/6–10 and n.

232/8–23 **you . . . knave.** The source of this anecdote is unknown, but an analogue, in which parts of the body are similarly separated from the person they belong to, occurs in *Heresies, EW*, sig. i₄, where More tells the story of a poor man whose wife engaged in sexual activity with a priest. The husband accused the priest publicly, but since he was unable to prove it, he was sentenced by the bishop's court to stand up in church on Sunday and say, "mouth thou lyest." On the appointed Sunday the husband stood up as directed, put his hand to his mouth, and said, "mouth mouth thou lyest." Then he put his hands over his eyes and said, "eyen eyen . . . by the masse ye lye not a whitte."

233/17–18 **fiftye yeare old.** At the time of writing More himself was about fifty-six years old.

234/24–25 **Dixit . . . hym.** Ps. 13:1 and Ps. 52:1. The citation of Ps. 32 in the 1573 marginalia is in the nature of an editorial allusion; it is not a gloss on More's text.

235/7 **s. paule . . . hym.** Titus 1:16: "Confitentur se nosse Deum, factis autem negant: cum sint abominati, et incredibiles, et ad omne opus bonum reprobi."

235/22 **no more . . . Iob.** Cf. Job 1:12.

236/14–16 **Noli . . . strike.** Ecclus. 5:4. The Vulgate reads: "Ne dixeris: peccavi; et quid mihi accidit triste? Altissimus enim est patiens redditor."

236/16–18 **Austeyne . . . stroketh,** *Epistola* CXXXVIII, ii, 14 (*PL 33,* 531): "Haec si Deus pollere permittat, tunc indignatur gravius; haec si impunita dimittat, tunc punit infestius. Cum vero evertit subsidium vitiorum, et copiosas libidines inopes reddit, misericorditer adversatur." See also *PL 38,* 935; *PL 33,* 392; and *Treatise on the Passion, EW,* sig. MM₃v.

237/14–19 **Quid . . . soule.** Matt. 16:26. The Vulgate reads *Quid enim* rather than *quid.* See also Mark 8:36 and Luke 9:25.

239/18–240/2 **Nolite . . . to.** Matt. 6:19–21. The Vulgate (cf. the corrections in *1557* and *1573*) reads *Thesaurizate autem* rather than *Thesaurizate.* See above, n. to 231/5.

240/14 **vndowttely.** The *OED* lists the adverb "undoubtly" with examples from 1487 and 1539.

240/24–25 **the saying . . . selfe.** The contrast between poetry and scripture was traditional. Cf. Dante, *Convivio,* II, i, 2–4. Aquinas explains the basis for the distinction in *ST*, I, Q.1, a. 10: "Dicendum quod auctor Sacrae Scripturae est Deus, in cuius potestate est ut non solum voces ad significandum accommodet, quod etiam facere potest, sed etiam res ipsas. Et ideo cum in omnibus scientiis voces significent, hoc habet proprium ista scientia, quod ipsae res significatae per voces etiam significant aliquid."

240/30–241/4 **This . . . therin.** Matt. 13:3–9, the parable of the sower and the seed. More refers specifically to Jesus' explanation of the parable in Matt. 13:22: "Qui autem seminatus est in spinis, hic est, qui verbum audit, et sollicitudo saeculi istius, et fallacia divitiarum suffocat verbum, et sine fructu efficitur." Cf. also Luke 8:24.

241/11–13 **vbi . . . hart.** Matt. 6:21. Cf. above, 239/18–240/2, and n. to 231/5.

243/25–28 **kynd . . . vnkindly.** The context here develops a broad range of meanings in the word "kynd" and its opposite, beginning with "natural," "in accordance with the nature" (of a Christian), and spreading out to include "generous," "affectionate," "loving," "grateful"—and their opposites.

244/28–245/13 **albeit . . . poynt.** Cf. "And yet I knowe well for all this mine owne frailtie, and that Saint Peter which fered it much lesse than I, fell in such feare sone after, that at the worde of a simple gyrle he forsoke and forsware our Sauiour. And therfore am I not (Megge) so mad, as to warraunt my selfe to stande. But I shall praye, and I praye the mine owne good daughter to praye with me, that it may please God that hath geuen me this minde, to geue me the grace to kepe it" (Rogers, p. 543; see also pp. 516, 530–31, 546–47). Cf. above, 146/23–29 and n. For the reference to Peter at 245/3–7, see Matt. 26:69–75, Mark 14:66–72, and Luke 22:54–62. None of the gospels say that Peter literally fainted. More uses the word in the archaic sense of "turned fainthearted." John 18:10, 26, is the only gospel that identifies Peter as the man who fought and cut off Malchus' ear when Christ was betrayed by Judas. All the others say simply that it was one of those who was with Jesus. Peter's "rash promise" is given in its strongest form in Luke 22:33: "Domine, tecum paratus sum et in carcarem et in mortem ire."

245/18–20 **The great . . . mervayle.** Cf. *De Tristitia Christi, CW 14,* 233–37: "cuipiam ex martyribus adhibita fuisse et plura et maiora tormentorem genera / adde etiam, si placet diuturniora quam Christo / . . . ? Cuius enim unquam tam acerba fuit anxietas ut toto ex corpore / guttatim in terram sanguineus sudor efflueret? . . . quo et futurorum martyrum fundendum in terram sanguinem figuraret / et simul eos qui ad supplicij meditationem trepidaturi forent / ne timorem suum ruina presagium interpretantes / desperatione succumberent / tam nouo tam miro tam immensae anxietatis exemplo solaretur." See also *ibid.*, *CW 14*, 87–93, 245, and above, 66/9–22 and n.

245/24–246/5 **yet . . . glory.** Besides the meditation on Christ's crucifixion that concludes *A Dialogue of Comfort*, cf. More's extensive commentary and meditation on the agony in the garden in his *De Tristitia*. The most detailed account of Gethsemane is given in Luke 22:39–46. At 245/27 More paraphrases Christ's prayer: "Pater, si vis, transfer calicem istum a me: Veruntamen non mea voluntas, sed tua fiat" (Luke 22:42). The angel is mentioned only in Luke 22:43: "Apparuit autem illi Angelus de caelo, confortans eum." The angel appeared immediately after Jesus submitted His will to the Father. At 246/2–5 More paraphrases Luke 9:23. See above, 174/18–26 and n.

246/5–18 **And . . . therat.** Cf. *De Tristitia, CW 14*, 61–67: "Quin seruator noster christus / etsi (quum uitari non potest) mortem potius iubet tolerari / quam ut eius metu desciscamus ab ipso (desciscimus autem si coram mundo fidem eius abnegamus) tantum tamen abest ut iubeat eam uim nos nature facere ne mortem quicquam metuamus / ut etiam (ubi citra dispendium cause datur facultas) indulgeat fugiendi supplicij libertatem . . . At istud fortitudinis tam ardum et accliue fastigium / misericors deus nos non iubet scandere / eoque nec tutum temere cuius eo prorumpere / unde se referre pedetentim non potest." See also *ibid., CW 14*, 229–41. For the reference to many mansions at 246/12–13, see John 14:2.

246/18–21 **and . . . taken.** John 18:8–9. When the crowd who had come to take Him told Him they were seeking Jesus of Nazareth, Jesus replied, "Dixi vobis ego sum: si ergo me quaeritis, sinite hos abire." John adds that this was to fulfill the words He had spoken: "Quia quos dedisti mihi, non perdidi ex eis quemquam." Matthew (26:56) and Mark (14:50) say merely that "discipuli omnes, relicto eo, fugerunt." Cf. More's commentary in the *De Tristitia, CW 14*, 431–39, and 625.

246/21–24 **or . . . them.** Mark 14:51–52: "Adulescens autem quidam sequebatur eum amictus sindone super nudo: et tenuerunt eum. At ille, rejecta sindone, nudus profugit ab eis." Ambrose, Chrysostom, Gregory, and a number of the early fathers identified this young man as John. Others thought he was James and still others, a servant in the house where the last supper was held. See Erasmus, *Opera*, 6, 207–08, and C. à Lapide, *1*, 625. In the *De Tristitia, CW 14*, 565–87, More summarizes the tradition and concludes that the young man was not John, but a servant, since one of the apostles would have been clothed in something more than a linen sheet.

246/24–26 **or . . . Peter.** Acts 12:6–11. Cf. above, 58/15–18 and n.

246/26–28 **And sometyme . . . man.** In view of the reference below (246/32) to St. Blandina of Lyons, it may be significant to note the summary that Eusebius gives at the close of his account of the persecutions in

Gaul (*Historia Ecclesiastica*, V, iv, *PG 20*, 459). Here Eusebius says there is no need for him to give the detailed lists of those who suffered for the faith in Gaul, among them being certain Christians who died in prison ("alii in carcere exanimati sunt"), and certain "confessors" who survived the persecutions: "Quid item opus est referre numerum confessorum qui postea superfuerunt?"

246/28–32 **And some . . . tellith.** In this reference to St. Romanus of Caesarea, as in the subsequent reference to St. Blandina of Lyons, More's memory has failed him, with regard to the manner of their deaths. Neither one died a natural death: Romanus was strangled and Blandina's throat was cut. Nevertheless, both were examples of saints who endured incredible torments and whose threatened executions were not immediately carried out. As the passage from Eusebius cited below indicates, Romanus was sent back to prison after his tongue had been cut out, and he spent a long time there before he was strangled. St. John the Evangelist (247/1) is the perfect example to make More's point here; the other two were quite properly cancelled by *B*.

There is another kind of inaccuracy in the reference to Romanus "that shuld haue bene beheddid." Romanus of Caesarea (d. A.D. 303) was a deacon of the church in Palestine who urged his fellow Christians in Antioch not to sacrifice to pagan gods in token of their renunciation of the faith; he was therefore taken prisoner and condemned to death by burning, not beheading. More perhaps confused this threatened execution with that suffered by St. Romanus of Rome, who, after his conversion by St. Lawrence, was beheaded for his faith in A.D. 258 (see *Bibliotheca Sanctorum*, *11*, 326–27). In any case, Romanus of Caesarea's sentence was never carried out, for as he was about to be burned, according to Eusebius, there was a delay in the proceedings, and Romanus stoutly demanded his fire. For his boldness the Emperor Galerius ordered his tongue to be cut out: "Quibus dictis accitus coram imperatore sistitur, novo quodam supplicii genere plectendus, linguae scilicet abscissione. Quod quidem supplicium cum fortissime pertulisset, reipsa omnibus declaravit, iis qui quemlibet cruciatum pro pietate sustinent, semper praesto adesse divinam virtutem, quae et dolores eorum imminuat, et animos ipsorum confirmet. Comperta igitur novitate supplicii, nequaquam conterritus vir fortissimus, ultro protendit linguam, promptissime eam descendam carnificibus praebens. Post quod supplicium contrusus in carcerem, ac diutissime ibidem maceratus, tandem cum imperatoris vicennalia jam adessent, et ex solemni more universis qui in custodia tenebantur indulgentia publice per praeconem annuntiata esset, solus ad quatuor usque puncta distentos habens pedes, in ipso jacens nervo, fractis laqueo faucibus, martyrio sicut optaverat exornatus est" (*PG 20*, 1467, 1470). The story in Prudentius (*Peristephanon, Hymnus X* [*PL 60*, 444–530]) is considerably different: in his version the fire is actually started for the execution, but a rainstorm miraculously stops it.

246/32 **Blonidina . . . mortuo.** I.e., "Blandina and in St. Cyprian a certain one also left for dead." St. Blandina was martyred at Lyons in the reign of Marcus Aurelius. In the first attempt to execute her, she was tortured in relays until her torturers became exhausted and released her. Sometime later, in a second attempt, she was suspended on a stake and exposed to wild beasts in the arena, but the beasts would not touch her, and so she was sent back to prison for a time. Finally, on a third occasion, she was again brought into the arena, where she was scourged, set upon by wild beasts, roasted, and tossed by a bull; at last her throat was cut, in imitation of a sacrificial victim. Sanctus, Maturus, Attalus, and others who were with her survived similar torments. See Eusebius, *Historia Ecclesiastica*, V, i (*PG 20*, 407–34).

In *Epistola* **XXXV**, Cyprian mentions a certain Numidicus, who was left for dead after having been burned and stoned with a group of martyrs in Africa during the Decian persecution. He was later found half-alive by his daughter, who dug him out and revived him: "Ipse semiustulatus et lapidibus obrutus et pro mortuo derelictus, cadaver patris inquirit, semianimis inventus et extractus et refocillatus" (*PL 4*, 333–34).

In *A* the spelling of "Blonidina" looks at first to be "Blomdina," and so *1557* reads it in transferring this name to the margin of the text; but a dot over the third minim seems clear in the MS. *1573* correctly gives "Blandina" in the marginal reference. For "Divus" *A* reads "D&" but the "&" must be a scribal misreading of the abbreviation. For this whole passage see the Introduction and textual footnotes.

247/1–2 **Saynt . . . also.** During the persecutions of Domitian John is said to have been brought to Rome and thrown into a cauldron of boiling oil before the Latin Gate; he supposedly emerged unharmed: "Apostolus Joannes, posteaquam, in oleum igneum demersus, nihil passus est, in insulam relegatur" (Tertullian, *De Praescriptionibus*, xxxvi [*PL 2*, 48–50]). He died years later, full of age, at Ephesus (Eusebius, *Historia Ecclesiastica*, III, xxxi [*PG 20*, 279]). According to other accounts, however, John did not die, but was translated directly to heaven. Cf. *Heresies*, *EW*, sig. n₄v: "the bodye shrined or not maketh no doute of the saynt. No man douteth of our lady. No man douteth of saint Iohn the euangelist, though their bodies be not founden."

For Cyprian, cf. *Epistola* **VIII**, as well as the accounts of Celerinus and Aurelius in *Epistola* **XXXIV** and **XXXIII** (*PL 4*, 255, 329–33, 325–29). See also Eusebius, *Historia Ecclesiastica*, IV, xv, and V, i–ii (*PG 20*, 355–58, 407–36, *passim*). Fowler and Miles refer to similar stories in Theodoret, *Ecclesiastical History*, III, 16, and III, 3.

247/9–10 **which . . . hevyn.** A combination of the phrasing in Matt. 10: 33 and Luke 12:9. Matthew reads: "Qui autem negaverit me coram hominibus, negabo et ego eum coram Patre meo qui in caelis est." Luke is essentially the same, but substitutes for *Patre meo, qui in caelis est* the phrase *Angelis Dei* (More's "holy company of hevyn"). See above, 101/3–7, and n. to 109/2–7.

247/17–21 **fidelis . . . way out.** 1 Cor. 10:13. The Vulgate reads *fidelis autem* for *fidelis, Deus est* for *deus, patitur* for *patitur, tentari* for *temptare, faciet* for *dat,* and *sustinere* for *ferre.* Note the various attempts at correction in *B* and *Z.* Paul is speaking of the children of Israel, who turned away from God during their journey through the wilderness, denied their faith, and worshipped false gods.

248/23–25 **we . . . good.** Cf. More's famous remark to Margaret (Rogers, p. 542): "to be put to death wrongefully for doinge well . . . is a case in which a man may leese his head and yet haue none harme."

248/27–28 **Bonis . . . good.** Rom. 8:28: "Scimus autem quoniam diligentibus Deum omnia cooperantur in bonum, iis, qui secundum propositum vocati sunt sancti." This verse seems to have been associated in More's mind with the idea that God's grace is sufficient in weakness, referred to in the quotation from 1 Corinthians immediately above, 247/17–21. More makes the same association earlier at 22/15–23/8.

251/16–19 **Non . . . come to.** Heb. 13:14. The Vulgate reads *Non enim* rather than *Non* and *inquirimus* (cf. the correction in *Z*) rather than *inquerimus.* Cf. above, n. to 41/6–14. More was also no doubt aware of the context, which speaks not only of pilgrimage, but also of martyrdom in imitation of Christ.

253/12–13 **qui . . . synne.** John 8:34. Jesus' reply to the Jews who said they were of the seed of Abraham and had never been in bondage.

253/20 **rash brades.** Cf. *Richard III* (*CW 2,* 91/22–24): "And parceiuing . . . the dukes pride now & then balke oute a lytle breide of enuy."

253/24 **villayne.** In this context the word keeps close to its basic meaning: "a low-born base-minded rustic" (*OED,* "villain" *sb.* 1).

254/2 **sond.** See the *OED,* "sand" *sb.*[1] 1: "The action of sending; that which is sent, a message, present; (God's) dispensation or ordinance." No example of the usage is recorded here later than 1525. *L* accepts "sond," but *1553* does not, emending to "hand," a reading followed by *1573. 1557* reads "sounde," a variant spelling of "sand," "sond." *A* seems to have written "send," which *B* alters to "sond" ("o" is written so heavily by *B* over the original letter that one cannot be absolutely certain about the "e"). One should note then that the *OED* also lists the noun "send," also meaning "the action of sending; dispensation (of God)"; but the only example given is a Scottish usage of 1551 ("send," *sb.*[1]1).

254/6–8 **But . . . will.** *Ep.,* LXI, 2. Seneca, however, is speaking not of slavery, but of the need to accept death willingly and cheerfully: "Ante senectutem curavi, ut bene viverem, in senectute, ut bene moriar; bene autem mori est libenter mori. Da operam, ne quid umquam invitus facias. Quicquid necesse futurum est repugnanti, volenti necessitas non est. Ita dico: qui imperia libens excipit, partem acerbissimam servitutis effugit, facere quod nolit . . . Itaque sic animum conponamus, ut quicquid res exiget, id velimus et in primis ut finem nostri sine tristitia cogitemus. Ante ad mortem quam ad vitam praeparandi sumus . . . Ut satis vixerimus, nec anni nec dies faciunt, sed animus. Vixi, Lucili carissime, quantum satis erat; mortem plenus exspecto."

254/18-23 **accordyng . . . slaue.** Eph. 6:5-8: "Slaves, obey your masters." The second quotation (ll. 21-22) is from Phil. 2:7-8. More telescopes the verses, which read: "sed semetipsum exinanivit formam servi accipiens, in similitudinem hominum factus, et habitu inventus ut homo. Humiliavit semetipsum factus obediens usque ad mortem, mortem autem crucis."

255/8 **your prisonement.** "Your idea of imprisonment," or, less precisely, the usage of *OED*, "your" 5: "Used more or less vaguely of something which the person or persons addressed may be expected to possess, or have to do with in some way." The other texts omit "your" and read "imprisonment" ("ymprysonment" *L*); it is true that "ym" might have been read as "yʳ" but *B* finds no difficulty here, and the colloquial use of "your" is quite in line with the style of the speaker. See also the use of "prisonment" at 276/12 and 280/14.

256/2-4 **a man . . . slaves.** Personal slavery persisted throughout the Middle Ages in those areas of Europe that bordered on the Moslem empire. See Charles Verlinden, *L'Esclavage dans L'Europe Medievale* (Brugge, 1955), *1*, 136. Neither Moslems nor Christians officially objected to slavery *per se*. By the end of the thirteenth century slavery had died out in most sections of Western Europe, but the Spanish and Portuguese continued to hold both Moslems and Black Africans as slaves for centuries after the Christian reconquest of the Iberian peninsula. The African slave trade increased during the later fifteenth century under Prince Henry the Navigator, and portions of southern Spain and Portugal became major trading centers, particularly Seville. During the same period the slave trade in Eastern Europe was stimulated by the fall of Constantinople in 1453 (David B. Davis, *The Problem of Slavery in Western Culture* [Ithaca, N.Y., 1966], pp. 98-101). See also Verlinden, pp. 794-95, 835; Marlowe's *Jew of Malta;* and Cervantes' account of Don Quixote's freeing the galley slaves of their shackles.

257/8-10 **as the . . . backe.** After defeating Bajazeth I in a battle fought near Ankara on July 20, 1402, Tamburlaine is said to have kept him in a cage for almost a year, feeding him with scraps from his table and occasionally using him as a mounting block. Cf. Marlowe, *I Tamburlaine*, IV, ii, 1-30. The idea of using a conquered king as a footstool was, however, not entirely original with Tamburlaine. Lactantius, *De Mortibus Persecutorum*, v (*PL 7*, 202) reports that the Roman Emperor Valerian was also used as a mounting block by Sapores, King of Persia: "Nam Rex Persarum Sapor, is qui eum ceperat, si quando libuerit aut vehiculum ascendere, aut equum, inclinare sibi Romanum jubebat, ac terga praebere, et imposito pede supra dorsum ejus, illud esse verum dicebat (triumphi genus) exprobrans ei cum risu, non quod in tabulis aut parietibus Romani pingerent." Fowler's reference in *1573* (see Appendix B) to "Sabellic, aenead 9. lib. 9" is to Marcus Antonius Coccius Sabellicus, *Enneades ab Orbe Condito ad Inclinationem Romani Imperii*, first published in 1498 and expanded in 1504. See Castelli, p. 304. The information was available in almost any European history of the period, however; see Roy Battenhouse, *Marlowe's Tamburlaine* (Nashville, Tenn., 1941), p. 138.

258/13–16 **And ... prison.** For the idea of the world as a prison, which More begins here and develops over the next twenty or so pages, cf. *Epigrams*, no. 101, p. 51, and *Four Last Things, EW*, sig. fg$_2$v. The idea, of course, was a commonplace as old as Plato's allegory of the cave in the *Republic*. It forms the basis of Boethius' *De Consolatione Philosophiae* and was still current as late as Shakespeare's *Richard II* (V, v, 1–41) and *Hamlet* (II, ii, 239–50). The fact that More was probably in prison when he wrote these pages gives the topos an added dimension of meaning.

259/29 **both ... to.** Prester John was the ruler of a legendary Christian kingdom beyond Persia and Armenia, in India or Ethiopia. First mentioned in the twelfth century *Chronicle* of Bishop Otto of Freisingen, by the mid-sixteenth century Prester John's kingdom had come to be identified specifically with Ethiopia. In August 1439, as a result of the interest of Pope Eugenius IV and the Council of Florence, emissaries were sent bearing letters to Thomas, Emperor of India and Prester John, Emperor of Ethiopia. By the beginning of the sixteenth century Portuguese exploration had penetrated the Indian Ocean and confirmed the presence of Eastern Christians in Ethiopia and on the Malabar Coast. In 1514 the Negus of Ethiopia requested a military alliance with King Manuel of Portugal and the acceptance of the Ethiopian Church as a member of Western Christendom. For further information and bibliography, see J. Headley's survey of the subject in *Responsio, CW 5*, 929–31. More's son John had translated an account of Prester John's land by the Portuguese humanist Damião á Goes. It was printed by William Rastell in 1533. For facsimiles of both the original and translation, see Elizabeth Brooke Blackburn, "The Legacy of 'Prester John' by Damião á Goes and John More," *Moreana, 14* (1967), 37–98.

More uses the reference to Prester John as a gesture of geographical immensity and completeness, encompassing both the known, European nations of the West and the vast, legendary kingdoms of the East. Cf. Shakespeare, *Much Ado*, II, i, 234–35, 237–40: "Will your Grace command me any service to the world's end? . . . I will fetch you a toothpicker now from the furthest inch of Asia; bring you the length of Prester John's foot; fetch you a hair off the great Cham's beard." More also perhaps alludes to the long dream of Western Christendom of establishing relations with this Eastern segment of the church so as to outflank and encompass Islam. Cf. Vsevolod Slessarev, *Prester John* (Minneapolis, 1959), pp. 5, 80–92. Thus, if the Great Turk were to proceed in either direction, East or West, he would find himself hemmed in by Christian lands.

The Great Khan (of which *Cam*, l. 29, is an obsolete form) was a title used variously for the Emperor of China or the rulers of the Tartars and Mongols.

263/2–4 **as . . . short.** The story is apparently a combination of two anecdotes that follow one another on the same page in Pace's *De Fructu*, p. 102. One has to do with an illiterate English priest who, for thirty years, had been saying *mumpsimus* in the mass instead of *sumpsimus*: "Et quum moneretur a docto, ut errorem emendaret, respondit se nolle mutare suum antiquum mumpsimus, ipsius nouo sumpsimus." The other anecdote is about a French priest who used to say *quesúmus domíne* in prayer, with the accents on the wrong syllables. When this was called to his attention, he replied, "Nos Gallici . . . non cúramus de quantítate syllabarum, haec quoque omnia peruerso proferens accentu." Erasmus seems to be the earliest source for the *mumpsimus-sumpsimus* story (1516); see Allen, *2*, 323; *3*, 40.

264/2ff. **Tell me etc.** For the example of the prisoner condemned to death, which runs to the end of the chapter, cf. *Four Last Things, EW*, sigs. f₁v. and fg₂v.

264/9 **quoth he.** See the *OED*, "quoth a" *interj.*: "The phrase 'said he?', used with contemptuous or sarcastic force in repeating a word or phrase used by another; hence = indeed! forsooth!"

271/21–22 **yet . . . god.** Cf. *Four Last Things, EW*, sig. fg₂v: "The prison is large and many prisoners in it, but the gailor can lese none, he is so present in euery place, that we can crepe into no corner out of his sight. For as holy Dauid saith to this gailor whither shal I go fro thy spirit, & whither shal I fle fro thy face: as who saith nowhither."

272/2–12 **Yf . . . straighter.** A paraphrase may help to unravel the rather complicated syntax of this passage: "If a man is imprisoned for no other reason than to be kept there (i.e., not to extract information from him, etc.), even though there are very serious charges against him, an honest jailer will neither torture the man out of maliciousness, nor be so greedy as to torture him so that his friends will pay for more humane treatment. Besides, if the prison is such that the jailer can be sure that his prisoner is securely kept, or that he can get a bond or assurance to be more than compensated for any harm which might come to him should the prisoner actually escape, then he would never treat the prisoner in the severe fashion which makes us hate imprisonment. Yet if the prison is not so secure, the jailer must take more rigorous precautions in so far as the situation demands it."

273/7 lyvelod. *L* follows this spelling exactly; the other texts have "liuelode." This was the normal usage in More's day: see *OED* "liveli-hood[1]": "In the 16th c. the spelling was gradually assimilated . . . to that of *Livelihood*[2]."

273/8–9 Vppon . . . gloriouse. The lack of punctuation in *A* creates a difficulty in interpretation: "Vppon our prison we bild our prison we garnysh yt with gold & make yt gloriouse /" *B* places a virgule after "bild" and cancels the first "yt" to read: "Vppon our prison we bild / our prison we garnysh with gold." This reading is followed by *1557* (with colon after "bild") and by *1573* (with comma after "build"). The present text is based on the reading of *L* and *1553*, where a comma is placed after the second "prison"; the comma has been replaced with a colon, to clarify the interpretation. More seems to be developing the idea of man's habitation as a prison within a prison.

276/22–25 holy . . . like. The Carthusian order was founded by St. Bruno in 1084 at the hermitage of the Grande Chartreuse near Grenoble. The English *Charterhouse* is a corruption of the French *Chartreuse* (see the *OED*, "Charterhouse," for a full explanation). The Carthusians are the most rigorous of all the contemplative orders. In his youth, while considering a religious vocation, More is said to have given "himself to devotion and prayer in the Charter house of London, religiously lyvinge there, without vowe, about iiij[er] yeares" (Roper, p. 6). E. E. Reynolds, however, in *The Field is Won* (London, 1968), pp. 32–33, suggests that Cresacre More's record of family tradition is more nearly correct: that More was "dwelling near the Charterhouse, frequenting their spiritual exercises," rather than residing within. On April 20, 1535, the priors of the Charterhouses of London, Beauvale, and Axholme were arrested for refusing to subscribe to the Act of Supremacy. Their trial served as a precedent for More's own. For his remarks to Margaret as he saw the priors being led to execution, see Roper, pp. 80–81, and Rogers, pp. 550–51.

The Brigittines or Order of the Most Holy Savior was founded by St. Bridget of Sweden in 1370. The order follows a semi-cloistered Augustinian rule. Founded primarily for nuns, monks were later added to provide spiritual assistance. Before the Reformation the houses were dual, presided over by an abbess. The only Brigittine monastery in England in More's time was at Syon, near Islesworth on the Thames, established by Henry V in 1415. More frequently visited Syon, and it was there he questioned Elizabeth Barton, the Holy Maid of Kent (see above, n. to

132/25–133/1). Dr. Richard Reynolds of the Brigittine monastery at Syon was executed for treason along with the Carthusians on May 4, 1535.

The Poor Ladies or Poor Clares were founded in 1212 by St. Clare, friend of St. Francis of Assisi. More had dedicated his *Life of Pico* (1510) as a New Year's gift to Joyeuce Leigh, who had entered the convent of the Poor Clares, known as the Minories, outside the walls of London. The Leighs were friends and fellow-parishioners of More's at St. Stephen Walbrook.

277/6–24 **I wist . . . without.** Harpsfield identifies this as a personal anecdote and links it with Roper's famous account of Dame Alice's visit to the Tower (cf. above, n. to 208/3–11). Harpsfield concludes that, like Job's wife, Dame Alice was an instrument of the devil: "yet could not this woman any thing infringe or breake the constant settled good purposes of this worthy man, her husbande, no, not in his extreme aduersitie; no more then blessed Jobes wife could shake and ouerturne any part of his good patience. And yet surely no stronger nor mightier temptation in all the worlde is there then that proceedeth from the wife. And therefore some thinke and write that though the deuill might haue, by the wordes of his Commission geuen to him from God, destroyed also Jobes wife as well as he did his children, yet did the wretched, malitious caytiffe full wilily spare her, to make her his instrument to the destruction of her husbandes patience" (pp. 98–99). A number of details in the anecdote itself lend support to Harpsfield's identification, particularly the fact that the prisoner knew the intimate details of the woman's sleeping arrangements, though she was supposed to be only a casual acquaintance. If the anecdote is in fact autobiographical, it supplies the only glimpse we have of the interior of More's cell and the actual conditions of his confinement. The reference to the prisoner's dependence on the lady's charity for his "fyndyng" alludes perhaps to Dame Alice's contributions to More's support in the Tower. Cf. her letter to Cromwell of May 1535: "The cause of my wrytyng, at this tyme, is to certyfye your especiall gud Maistershypp of my great and extreme necessyte; which, on and besydes the charge of myn owne house, doe pay weekly 15 shillings for the bord-wages of my poure husband, and his servant; for the mayntaining whereof, I have ben compellyd, of verey necessyte, to sell part of myn apparell" (Rogers, pp. 554–55).

277/28 **in a . . . chypps.** "In such a trivial matter—hardly worth three chips." The emendation of *B* (followed by *Z*) has been adopted with some hesitation, for the reading of *A* could be construed as making sense: "in a maner of .iij. chypps": that is, "in a fashion worth only three chips."

278/27–279/2 **fidelis . . . out.** 1 Cor. 10:13. For the Vulgate variants (cf. the corrections in *1557* and *1573*), see above, n. to 274/17–21. Cf. also above, 22/15–20.

279/12–13 **In prison . . . brede.** Gen. 39–45.

279/14–15 **In ... agayne.** Dan. 5–6.

279/18–25 **Iohn ... them.** Matt. 14:1–2, Mark 6:17–29. John the Baptist was imprisoned by Herod for telling him that he had sinned in taking his brother's wife, Herodias. Herod wished to put him to death, but he was afraid of the people until Salome, the daughter of Herodias, danced and so pleased him that he promised her whatever she desired. She requested the head of John the Baptist and gave it to her mother. Cf. *Epigrams*, nos. 210 and 211, pp. 93–94. The analogy between Herod's feast and Henry VIII's enchantment by Anne Boleyn was commonly noted. Cf. Stapleton, pp. 81–82: "The marriage of Anne Boleyn took place after his [More's] resignation, and while he was living a private life, for in his official capacity he would never approve of it. A friend of his was one day telling him that she was leading a life of continual pleasure at Court, with dances day and night, and that nothing could be more gay than life now was there. More replied: 'These dances of Anne Boleyn are bringing with them another game of quite a different kind. Her dances are playing with our heads like footballs ...' The event very soon showed the truth of this prediction. For, as we shall hereafter more fully show, by Anne's instigation many good men were beheaded, notably John Fisher, Bishop of Rochester, and Thomas More himself (for Henry VIII, like another Herod, was enchanted by her dancing)." See also *Appendix I: The Rastell Fragments*, in Harpsfield, p. 235.

279/26–280/2 **our ... passhion.** More combines the gospel accounts. Most of the sequence is taken from John 18:13–14, 24, 28. Luke 23:1–16 adds the detail that Christ was taken from Pilate to Herod and back again to Pilate. See also Matt. 26 and 27, Mark 14 and 15.

281/23 **myndes.** Scribe *B* has interlineated "impryntyd by diuers meanys" after "myndes," and has then cancelled the phrase, apparently because he found it after "myndes" at ll. 25–26 below. This occurrence suggests that *B*, in comparing the text with another MS, picked up the wrong line and thought the phrase had been omitted at l. 23, but then discovered his mistake and cancelled his error. One should note that the spelling of the cancelled phrase is different in its use of "y" from that in ll. 25–26.

281/25–282/8 **Now ... best.** In scholastic psychology the sensible soul (common to both beasts and man) received the impressions from the various senses and combined them by means of the phantasy into an image of the thing perceived. The rational soul on the other hand belonged to man alone. It was immortal and therefore not entirely dependent on the body: "Yea, and the more it drowneth it selfe into the bodie, the more slowly and lesse perfectly it understandeth. And the more it withdraweth from the bends and liking of the flesh, the more easilye and cleerely it understandeth" (Batman, III, 9–13). Cf. *Four Last Things, EW,* sig. fg₆v, with its remarkable anticipation of the imagery in Marvell's *Dialogue between the Soul and Body*. See also Aquinas, *ST*, I, Q. 76, a. 3, and Burton, *Anatomy of Melancholy*, I, i, 2, 5–9.

282/22–25 **& though ... devill.** Cf. *Four Last Things, EW*, sig. fg₆v. The image of the horse goes back to Plato's famous metaphor of the charioteer (*Phaedrus*, 246 and 253 f.).

283/19–21 **This ... crow.** More apparently intends the reference to this world and the next to be taken as a commonplace or proverbial expression similar to the ones that follow. It is not listed in any of the standard compilations of proverbs. In the sayings concerning the devil and the crow More combines two common proverbs; see Tilley, D 255 and C 844.

284/14–19 **as where ... vos.** Phil. 1:23–24. The Vulgate reads: "Coartor autem e duobus: desiderium habens dissolvi, et esse cum Christo, multo magis melius: Permanere autem in carne, necessarium propter vos" (cf. the corrections in *1557* and *1573*). The *Biblia Latina* has "Coartor ... et cum Christi esse: multo magis enim melius: permanere ... necessarium est propter vos." At ll. 18–19 More evidently gave no biblical quotation in Latin; the quotation is added by *B* and appears also in this form in *L* and *1553*. *1557* corrects the Latin in accord with the Vulgate, and is followed by *1573*. For discussion of the widespread currency of the form (with "cupio") used here and elsewhere in More's works, see the essay by G. Marc'hadour in *Editing Sixteenth Century Texts*, ed. R. J. Schoeck (Toronto, 1966), pp. 63–64.

Cf. More's comment on the verses (cited in this form) in a letter to Margaret in the Tower (Margaret had referred to the passage in a previous letter): "surely if God geue vs that, he geueth vs and will geue vs therwith, all that euer we can well wishe. And therfore good Marget, when you praye it, pray it for vs both: and I shall on my parte the lyke, in such maner as it shall lyke our Lorde to geue me poore wretch the grace, that lykewise as in this wretched worlde I haue been very gladde of your company and you of mine, and yet wolde if it might be ... so we may reioyce and enioy ech others company, with our other kynesfolke, alies and frendes euerlastingly in the glorious blysse of heauen" (Rogers, p. 545).

284/24–26 **well ... hevyn.** Cf. above, n. to 33/2–7.

285/5–6 **And ... yt.** Cf. Luke 9:25: "Quid enim proficit homo, si lucretur universum mundum, se autem ipsum perdat, et detrimentum sui faciat?" Cf. above, n. to 43/10–12 and 109/2–7.

285/15–18 **as he ... gold.** Cherry stones were collected by children and used in a game in which the pits were thrown into a hole. See the *OED*, "cherry-pit". More frequently compares bags of cherry stones to gold. Cf. *Supplication, EW*, sig. y₄v; *Four Last Things, EW*, sig. fg₄v; *Confutation, CW 8*, 492/19.

285/19–286/3 **as Esope . . . remembre.** The occasion More forgot was
a wedding feast, and it was the turtle who was punished, not the snail:
"Iupiter nuptias celebrans, omnia animalia accipiebat: sola vero testudine
tarde profecta, admirans causam tarditatis, rogauit eam, quamobrem
ipsa ad coenam non accesserat. Cum haec dixisset, Domus chara, domus
optima: iratus ipsi, damnauit ut domum baiulans circumferret" (*Fabulae*,
pp. 84–85). For a similar fable of how the snail got its shell, see *Aesopi
Phrygis Vita et Fabellae* (Basel, 1517), p. 236; see also p. 197 and Erasmus,
Adag., "Domus amica, domus optima," sig. Ddd₂ (III. III. xxxviii).

286/14–20 **And surely . . . to.** The marginal references in *1557* allude to
Jesus' parable of the wedding feast in Matt. 22:1–4 and Luke 14:7–14.

289/1–2 **preciosa . . . sayntes.** Ps. 115:15. The psalm is a song of thanks-
giving for deliverance from the fear of tribulation and death.

289/5–9 **For . . . on.** Acts 7:55–58. At his trial before the high priest, St.
Stephen said he saw the heavens open and Jesus standing at the right
hand of God. But the people covered their ears at his blasphemy and took
him outside the city and killed him. Cf. *Devotions, EW*, sig. VV₃v (mismarked XX₃v): "Si quis vel vnum conspicere posset ex daemonibus illis,
qui magno numero nos expectant, vt in aeternum crucient, omnes
mortalium hominum minas, vnius terrore floccifaceret, & quanto magis
floccefaceret si videre posset coelos apertos, et Iesum stantem, sicut vidit
beatus Stephanus." Cf. also below, 315/6–30, and 1 Cor. 4:9. References
to St. Stephen became increasingly frequent for More as he drew closer
to the time of death. Cf., for example, the allusion in his speech to the
commissioners at his trial, reported by Roper, p. 96. See also John
Cavanaugh, "The Saint Stephen Motif in Saint Thomas More's Thought,"
Moreana, 8 (1965), 59–64.

290/2–11 **Than . . . rabels.** Cf. Rogers, p. 528: "to this shall I say to the,
Marget, that in some of my causes I nothing doubte at all, but that
though not in this realme, yet in Christendome aboute . . . they be not
the fewer parte that are of my minde . . . But go we now to them that are
dead before, and that are I trust in heauen, I am sure that it is not the
fewer parte of them that all the time while they liued, thought in some of
the thinges, the way that I thinke nowe. I am also, Margaret, of this thinge
sure ynough, that of those holy doctours and saintes, which to be with God
in heauen long ago no Christen man douteth, whose bookes yet at this day
remayne here in mens handes, there thought in some such thinges, as I
thinke now."

290/17–22 **Qui . . . angelles.** Luke 9:26. For the parallel passage in
Matthew and the general significance of these verses to More, see above,
n. to 198/5–8.

290/27–291/8 **the blessid . . . howse to.** Acts 5:17–42. The apostles were
imprisoned in Jerusalem for preaching and healing the sick. After being

freed by an angel, they were captured again at the Temple and taken before the council presided over by the high priest. The council ordered them to cease preaching, but they answered that it was more important to obey God than man (5:29). The council then wished to kill them but were dissuaded by a Pharisee named Gamaliel. See esp. 5:40–42: "Et convocantes Apostolos, caesis denunciaverunt ne omnino loquerentur in nomine Jesu, et dimiserunt eos. Et illi quidem ibant gaudentes a conspectu concilii, quoniam digni habiti sunt pro nomine Jesu contumeliam pati. Omni autem die non cessabant in templo et circa domos, docentes et evangelizantes Christum Jesum."

291/24–292/6 **the most ... did.** The scourging at the pillar is related in Matt. 27:27–31 and Mark 15:16–20. At 292/2–6 More refers to Matt. 10:24–25: "Non est discipulus super magistrum, nec servus super dominum suum. Sufficit discipulo, ut sit sicut magister ejus: et servo, sicut dominus ejus." The parallel passage in John adds, "Si me persecuti sunt, et vos persequentur" (15:20). See also John 13:16 and Luke 6:40.

292/20 **shame ... taken.** Tilley, S 274. See also Erasmus, *Adag.*, "Ubi timor, ibi & pudor," sig. G₁ (I. II. lxiv), and "Lucrum pudori praestat," sig. Kkk₂v (III. VII. xiv).

294/3–5 **Vbi ... them.** Matt. 18:20. The Vulgate reads *Ubi enim* for *Vbi*, and *ibi* for *ibi & ego*.

294/18–295/13 **But ... apace.** The fable is not by Aesop and does not, so far as we have been able to discover, appear in any of the standard collections of fables, renaissance or modern. The story may well be More's own creation. Cf. the apparently original fable which he has Cardinal Morton tell in *Richard III* (*CW 2*, 93 and 269).

295/11 **fownd the fote agayne.** "Picked up the track, recovered the scent." See the *OED*, "feute": "The traces or track (of an animal)," with the latest example from Malory: "He saw a black brachet sekyng ... as it had ben in the feaute of an hurt dere." The *OED* notes the variant spellings "foute" and "fute," but not "fote" (*A 1553 1573*) or "foote" (*L 1557*). The *OED* is in error when it cites this passage in More as an example of "find" (*v.* 4), in the sense, "to gain or recover the use of (one's limbs, powers, etc.)."

295/12 **yarnyng.** L "yernyng"; *1553, 1573* "yerning"; see the *OED*, "yearn" *v.*¹4: "Of hounds: To cry out eagerly, give tongue," with examples from Skelton and Heywood. *1557* reads "gerning"; if this is not a misprint, it indicates that *1557* did not understand the usage, and emended to the verb "gern"; see the *OED*, "girn" *v.*¹1: "To show the teeth in rage, pain, disappointment, etc.; to snarl as a dog," where this passage is cited from *1557*, among other examples.

295/21–296/2 **here it ... fart.** For discussion of the significance of this passage, see the Introduction.

295/21 **can skyll of.** "Has knowledge of"; from the verb "can," "to know," and the noun "skill." See the *OED*, "can" *v.*¹ I. 1. c, and "skill" *sb.*¹5.

295/25 **brache.** "A kind of hound which hunts by scent; in later Eng. use, always feminine, and extended to any kind of hound; a bitch-hound" (*OED*, "brach"). Cf. Edward Topsell, *The History of Four-footed Beasts, Serpents, and Insects* (London, 1658), p. 118: "There are in *England* and *Scotland*, two kinds of hunting Dogs, and no where else in all the world; the first kinde they call in *Scotland*, Ane Rache, and this is a foot-smelling creature, both of wilde Beasts, Birds, and Fishes also, which lie hid among the Rocks; the female herof in *England*, is called a Brache."

295/25 **This . . . howse.** Like most of the humanists, More had a low opinion of hunting. Cf. *Utopia*, *CW 4*, 170/11–12: "quae suauitas esse potest, ac non fastidium potius in audiendo latratu, atque ululatu canum? aut qui maior uoluptatis sensus est, cum leporem canis insequitur, quam quum canis canem?" See also *CW 4*, 457, and Erasmus' *Colloquy* on hunting, trans. Craig R. Thompson (Chicago, 1965), pp. 42–43.

295/26–296/1 **At a . . . hart.** Evidently this means "at the hunting of a fox," "at the hunting of a hart."

296/17–19 **Nolite . . . vnderstandyng.** Ps. 31:9. The Vulgate (cf. the corrections in *1557* and *1573*) reads *quibus* rather than *in quibus*. More annotated this psalm in his *Psalter;* see above, n. to 48/13–14.

297/12–21 **He said . . . was.** See above, n. to 201/3–11, on the noonday devil. Cf. also below, 319/7–15 and n., and Rogers, p. 530. For More's own fear of torture, see Rogers, pp. 516, 531, 542, 549–50.

298/1–8 **as though . . . hym.** Cf. Rogers, p. 531: "Mistruste him, Megge, wil I not, though I feale me faint, yea, and though I shoulde fele my feare euen at poynt to ouerthrowe me to, yet shall I remember how S. Peter, with a blast of winde, began to sinke for his faint faith, and shall doe as he did, call vpon Christ and praye him to helpe. And than I trust he shall set his holye hande vnto me, and in the stormy seas, holde me vp from drowning. Yea and if he suffer me to play S. Peter ferther, and to fall full to the grownd, and swere and forsware too (which our Lorde for his tender passion kepe me fro, and let me leese if it so fall, and neuer winne therby:) yet after shall I trust that his goodnes will cast vpon me his tender pyteous eie, as he did vpon S. Peter, and make me stande vp againe and confesse the trouth of my conscience afresh, and abide the shame and the harme here of mine owne faulte." See also Rogers, pp. 543, 546–47, 549–50; *De Tristitia*, *CW 14*, 99–109 and 247–51; and above, 102/15–21.

298/10–12 **Ne . . . farther.** Luke 12:4. The Vulgate reads *haec* rather than *hac*, and *quod* rather than *quid*. The quotation, which appears only partially here, emerges fully at the beginning of the next chapter, below,

303/7–15. The corrections in *L*, *1553*, and *1557* are a conflation of Luke 12:4 and the parallel passage in Matt. 10:28.

298/29–299/1 **for . . . forboden.** Cf. Matt. 10:32–33, Luke 12:8–9.

299/19–27 **But . . . come.** Matt. 12:31–32; Mark 3:28–29; Luke 12:10. The passage in Mark reads: "Amen dico vobis, quoniam omnia dimittentur filiis hominum peccata, et blasphemiae, quibus blasphemaverint: Qui autem blasphemaverit in Spiritum sanctum, non habebit remissionem in aeternum, sed reus erit aeterni delecti." In Luke, the quotation occurs in the same passage More refers to immediately above, 298/10–12.

At 299/19–21 More refers to the traditional definition of the sin against the Holy Spirit as both presumption and despair. Following Peter Lombard (*In 2 Sent.*, d. 43, I, 2), Aquinas, for example, identifies six varieties of sin against the Holy Spirit: "desperatio, praesumptio, impoenitentia, obstinatio, impugnatio veritatis agnitae et invidentia fraternae gratiae." Despair is a denial of God's mercy just as presumption is a denial of his justice: "Avertitur enim homo ab electione peccati ex consideratione divini indicii, quod habet institiam cum misericordia, et per spem, quae consurgit ex consideratione misericordiae remittentis peccata et praemiantis bona, et haec tollitur per desperationem; et iterum per timorem, qui consurgit ex consideratione divinae iustitiae punientis peccata; et hic tollitur per praesumptionem, dum scilicet aliquis praesumit se gloriam posse adipisci sine meritis, vel veniam sine poenitentia" (*ST*, II–II, Q. 14, a. 2).

The reference to Luke 3 in the 1573 marginalia is not a gloss on More's text; it is an allusion to the descent of the Holy Spirit on the souls of all Christians through the sacrament of baptism. See Luke 3:16, 21–22.

300/3–11 **beside . . . slayne.** Cf. Matt. 26:75: "Et recordatus est Petrus verbi Jesu, quod dixerat: Priusquam gallus cantet, ter me negabis. Et egressus foras, flevit amare." See also Mark 14:72 and Luke 22:62. At Pentecost, when the Holy Spirit descended on the apostles in tongues of fire, Peter went out and preached to the multitudes that gathered, calling upon them to repent and be baptized in the name of Christ (Acts 2:1–38). Shortly afterward, he was arrested for preaching and taken before the high priest, who let him off with a warning (Acts 4:1–22). His disregard of the warning and subsequent scourging is related in Acts 5:12–42, which More refers to above, 290/17–291/8. For his second imprisonment and deliverance, see Acts 12:1–11. The tradition that Peter was crucified upside down at Rome was first recorded by Tertullian in his *Adversus Gnosticos Scorpice*, 15 (*PL 2*, 151): "orientem fidem Romae primus Nero cruentavit. Tunc Petrus ab altero cingitur, cum cruci astringitur." See also Eusebius, *Historicae Ecclesiasticae*, II, i (*PG 20*, 215).

301/9 **galey subtill.** See the *OED*, "subtile," *a.* 3. b: "Of ships: Narrow, slender. Cf. OF *galere subtile*," with a good example of the usage from Caxton. Such a ship would have a terrible roll.

301/24 **beforce.** *A* wrote "before," which makes little sense here. *B* first wrote "ce" over "e" and then cancelled the word, writing "by force" above (the interlineation is followed by ζ). The unusual reading is kept here because it suggests that More may have written "beforce," as elsewhere he has evidently used the spelling "be" for "by."

301/26–302/18 **Howbeit . . . hart.** Cf. *Four Last Things, EW,* sig. e₇: "If thou couldeste nowe call to thy remembraunce, some of those sicknes that haue most grieued thee & tormented thee in thy dayes, as eueri man hath felt some, & than findest thou that some one disease in some one part of thy body . . . haue put thee to thine own minde to no lesse torment, than thou shouldest haue felt if one had put vp a knife, into the same place, and wouldest as thee than semed, haue bene content with such a chaunge think what it wil be than, whan thou shalt fele so many such paines in euery part of thy bodi breaking thy vaines & thy life stringes, wᵗ like pain & grief, as though as manye kniues as thy body might receiue, shold eueriwhere enter & mete in the middes." Cf. also above, 274/16–275/11, and Rogers, pp. 542–43.

303/7–15 **Dico . . . hym.** Luke 12:4–5. The Vulgate reads *haec* for *hac* (cf. the corrections in *L* and *1553*). See above, 298/10–12 and n. The reference to Luke 2 in the *CC* marginalia is an obvious mistake.

304/5–6 **vocabunt . . . them.** Rev. 9:6. The Vulgate reads: "Et in diebus illis quaerent homines mortem, et non invenient eam: et desiderabunt mori, et fugiet mors ab eis" (*Biblia Latina,* "ab illis"). The verse refers to those who, at the end of the world, do not have the seal of God on their foreheads. They will be tortured by locusts from hell for five months, stung as by scorpions, but unable to die.

306/14–15 **Satiabor . . . apere.** Ps. 16:15, the last verse of the psalm. The earlier verses are a plea to God for vindication and protection similar in imagery to Psalm 90. Stalked by his enemies as by a young lion and driven to bay, the psalmist calls upon God for deliverance, contrasting himself with his enemies, who find their reward in this life. In his *Psalter* More noted opposite verse 5 ("Perfice gressos meos"), "petit ne titubet in tentatione (he prays that he may not falter in [the time of] temptation)" and opposite verse 8 ("A resistentibus dexterae tuae custodi me"), "oratio christiani popoli [*sic*] contra potentiam turchorum (a prayer of the Christian people against the power of the Turks)" (*Prayer Book,* pp. 43, 44, 191).

306/26–29 **Let us . . . shalbe.** The 1557 and 1573 marginalia refer to Isa. 64:4, which Paul quotes in 1 Cor. 2:9–10. Cf. n. to 307/21, and 309/3–4 and n. The reference to Paul is incorrectly given in both marginalia as 1 Cor. 4.

307/6–8 **fulgebunt . . . redes.** Sap. 3:7. The Vulgate reads *Fulgebunt iusti,* as do the ζ texts, rather than the *fulgebit Iusti sicut sol* of *A.* "Sicut sol" in *A* comes from Matt. 13:43 ("Tunc iusti fulgebunt sicut sol in regno Patris eorum") which is echoing *Sap.* 3:7. More adds the phrase *qui erudiunt ad iustitiam* from Dan. 12:3 but does not translate it.

307/21 **Animalis . . . ei.** 1 Cor. 2:14. See textual footnote for the translation added by *1557*. The Vulgate reads *Animalis autem* rather than *Animalis*. This passage from 1 Cor. underlies the surface of the text for the next few pages. More alludes to it in 308/8–16 and quotes from it directly at 309/3–4, below. The passage is concerned with the discrepancy between the secret wisdom of God and the knowledge of the rulers of this world, who crucified Him. See 1 Cor. 2:1–8.

307/26–28 **and as . . . theron.** Cf. above, 29/8–20 and n.

308/8–16 **And . . . Imagynacion.** Cf. 1 Cor. 2:9–10: "Quod oculus non vidit, nec auris audivit, nec in cor hominis ascendit, quae praeparavit Deus iis, qui diligunt illum: Nobis autem revelavit Deus per spiritum suum." The allusion emerges fully below, 309/3–4.

308/21 **face to face.** Echoing 1 Cor. 13:12: "Videmus nunc per speculum in aenigmate, tunc autem facie ad faciem."

308/23–24 **Non . . . me.** Exod. 33:20. God's reply to Moses, who asked to see His face.

309/3–4 **Nec . . . se.** 1 Cor. 2:9: "The eye has not seen, nor has the ear heard, nor has it risen in the heart of man what God has prepared for those who love him." See above, 308/8–16. The Vulgate reads *Quod oculus non vidit* rather than *Nec oculus vidit*, and *Deus iis, qui diligunt illum* rather than *deus diligentibus se*. Paul paraphrases Isa. 64:4, where Isaiah prays to God to descend with power and might and make Himself known to His adversaries. The reference to Isa. 6 in the 1557 and 1573 marginalia is a misprint.

309/12–310/16 **vincenti . . . oarth.** The first quotation is from Rev. 2:7. At 309/13–15 More refers to Rev. 3:4–5: "Sed habes pauca nomina in Sardis, qui non inquinaverunt vestimenta sua: et ambulabunt mecum in albis, quia digni sunt. Qui vicerit, sic vestietur vestimentis albis, et non delebo nomen ejus de libro vitae, et confitebor nomen ejus coram Patre meo, et coram angelis ejus." Cf. also Matt. 10:32–33, which More refers to constantly throughout *A Dialogue of Comfort*. At 309/15–18 More paraphrases Rev. 2:10–11, omitting the reference to imprisonment and temptation: "Nihil horum timeas quae passurus es. Ecce missurus est diabolus aliquos ex vobis in carcerem, ut tentemini: et habebitis tribulationem diebus decem. Esto fidelis usque ad mortem, et dabo tibi coronam vitae. Qui habet aurem, audiat quid spiritus dicat Ecclesiis: Qui vicerit, non laedetur a morte secunda." More quotes the omitted portion later at 317/18–19. The quotation at 309/18–23 is from Rev. 2:17. See above, 3/7 and n. Erasmus gives virtually the same information on suffrage in his *NT:* "Olim calculis ferebant suffragia. Unde albo lapillo notari dicuntur quae probantur, atro quae damnantur. Et in suffragiis, nomen ejus, cui favebatur, calculo inscribebant" (*Opera, 6,* 1096). Cf. also *CW 3,* 1, 2–3 (More's 1506 dedication of his Lucian translations to Ruthall), "honorifico calculo mecum suffragatus est." The word *calculus* means small stone or pebble. The final reference at 310/7–11 is to Rev. 3:12.

310/18–311/14 **In ... eternall.** 2 Cor. 11:23–28. More quotes only a portion of the passage and translates the remainder. Cf. above, 96/2–3 and n. The second quotation is from 2 Cor. 4:17–18.

311/15–17 **Now ... thither.** At his trial in June 1535, More was sentenced to be hanged on the gallows at Tyburn, "cut down while still alive, ripped up, his bowels burnt in his sight, his head cut off, his body quartered and the parts set up in such places as the King shall designate" (Stapleton, p. 195). The king later commuted the sentence to beheading on Tower Hill. The reference to Christ is from Col. 1:18: "Et ipse est caput corporis Ecclesiae." See also Eph. 1: 22–23; Eph. 4: 15–16; *Confutation, CW 8,* 398/36–37, 855/2–4, 907/26; and Rogers, p. 498. A glance of grim humor in the word "hedlesse" is not beyond More's wit. The word may also carry the secondary meaning of "heedless" (i.e., without the reasoning and meditation which Antony has been describing).

311/17–26 **He ... kyngdome.** 1 John 2:6; Luke 24:26. In the second quotation, the Vulgate (cf. the corrections in *1557* and *1573*) reads: "Nonne haec oportuit pati Christum, et ita intrare in gloriam suam." See above, 43/4–6 and n. Cf. *De Tristitia, CW 14,* 105: "En, ego te in uia ista tam formidolosa precedo. Meae uestis fimbriam apprehende. Inde uirtutem exire senties / qui hunc animi tui in metus uanos effluentem sanguinem sistet salubriter / & animum reddet alacriorem / quippe quum recordaberis quod meis inheres uestigijs."

311/26–28 **Who ... payne.** Cf. above, 43/7–9 and n.

312/13–313/1 **of the ... strength.** Cf. Matt. 27:27–50; Mark 15:16–37; Luke 23:11, 26–46; and John 19:1–30. The scourging and crowning with thorns are omitted from Luke, which is probably why the reference to Luke is separated from the others in the 1557 and 1573 marginalia. The reference to the spear that pierced Christ's side is taken from John 19:24. The water and blood were traditionally believed to represent the mingling of water and wine in the eucharist. Cf. *Treatise on the Passion, EW,* sigs. PP$_8$v–QQ$_1$ and *Confutation, CW 8,* 319/29–32. Christ's blood was also associated with the waters of baptism, which cleanse away original sin through the merits of Christ's passion.

312/19 **forebeten.** It is not clear whether this word means "beaten previously" or whether it is a usage of "forbeat," "to beat severely." The

OED records no example of "forbeat" after 1470, but More may well have used it. On the other hand in the next line the phrase "new felying," i.e. "feeling anew (once again)," would seem to support the former meaning.

314/5–6 **Si ... hym.** Rom. 8:17. The Vulgate reads: "si tamen compatimur, ut et conglorificemur." More returns to Rom. 8:13–39 a number of times in *A Dialogue of Comfort.* See above, 22/26–30 and n., 248/27–28 and n., and below, 319/20–23.

315/6–30 **And of ... to.** Cf. above, 8/20–9/5, and 289/5–24 and n.

316/27 **for ... cure.** I.e., "for the strengthening of those for whom we are spiritually responsible."

317/18–19 **Diabolus ... you.** Rev. 2:10. The Vulgate (cf. the corrections in *1557* and *1573*) reads "missurus est diabolus aliquos ex vobis" rather than "Diabolus mittet aliquos vestrum." This is the portion More omitted in his paraphrase of the passage at 309/15–18. See above, n. to 309/18–310/16. The reference to Rev. 3 in the 1573 marginalia is incorrect.

317/23–24 **Non ... bloud &c.** Eph. 6:12. The portion of the passage More suppresses refers to the rulers of this world of shadows and the need to withstand them on the evil day: "sed adversus principes, et potestates, adversus mundi rectores tenebrarum harum, contra spiritualia nequitiae, in caelestibus. Propterea accipite armaturam Dei, ut possitis resistere in die malo, et in omnibus perfecti stare" (6:12–13). See above, 101/18–22 and n., 254/18–23.

317/24–27 **Thus ... feare.** For men as agents of the devil, see above, 101/18–22, 108/1–6, 110/30–111/3 and n.; *De Tristitia, CW 14,* 537–57; *Devotions, EW,* sig. VV₄v.

317/28–29 **Resistite ... you.** Jas. 4:7. The Vulgate reads *resistite autem* for *Resistite.* In attributing the verse to Peter rather than James, More may have confused it with 1 Pet. 5:9: "Cui (the devil) resistite fortes in fide." Both verses begin with the same imperative. Moreover, 1 Pet. was already in More's mind since he quotes from it immediately below, 318/5–8. In one of his *Devotions,* written, according to Rastell, in the Tower in 1534, More quotes Jas. 4:7 in the same sentence with 1 Pet. 5:9, combining them and at the same time distinguishing between them (*EW,* sig. VV₃v [mismarked XX₃v]). The marginal glosses in *1557* and *1573* correctly attribute this passage to James.

318/5–8 **Adversarius ... devore.** 1 Pet. 5:8. The Vulgate (cf. the corrections in *1557* and *1573*) reads *tamquam* for *sicut.* For the lion-king metaphor, see above, 108/1–6 and n., 110/30–111/3 and n., and 149/22–24. For the emphasis on fear, which begins at 317/23, cf. *Devotions, EW,* sig. VV₃v (mismarked XX₃v): "Aduersarius vester diabolus tanquam leo rugiens, circuit querens quem deuoret. Barnardus. Gratias ago magno illi leoni de tribu Iuda: rugire iste potest, mordere non potest. Quantumcumque minetur, non simus bestiae, vt nos prosternat vacuus ille rugitus. Vere bestia est verae rationis expers, qui tam pusillanimis est, vt solo timore cedat, qui sola futuri laboris exaggeratione victus ante conflictum, non telo sed tuba prosternitur. Non dum restitistis vsque ad sanguinem ait strenuus ille dux, qui leonis huius nouerat vanum esse rugitum. Et alius, Resistite inquit diabolo, & fugiet a vobis: resistite fortes in fide. Eos qui spe in deum relicta, fugiunt ad humanum auxilium, perituros praedicit cum suo auxilio."

The passage in Bernard, which More follows very closely, occurs in the commentary on Psalm 90 (*In Psalmum XC*, xiii [*PL 183*, 238]). Bernard is speaking of the lion in Psalm 90:13: "Super aspidem et basiliscum ambulabis. Et conculcabis leonem et draconem." In his next sermon (*XIV*), a continuation of the commentary on Psalm 90:13, Bernard associates the four beasts with the four temptations mentioned in verses 5 and 6. Thus he interprets the asp (*timore nocturno*) as desires of the body, the basilisk (*sagitta volante in die*) as vainglory, and the dragon (*negotio perambulante in tenebris*) as cupidity (*PL 183*, 241–43). Bernard also identifies these three allegorical animals with the three temptations of Christ in the wilderness (Matt. 4:1–11). The lion, however, causes him some difficulty. In terms of his overall pattern of fours, Bernard seems to imply that the lion is to be associated with the noonday devil, which he had interpreted earlier as evil masking itself as good (*PL 183*, 199). Jesus, he argues, could never have been taken in by this temptation. Bernard, therefore, seems to revert to Augustine's interpretation of the Psalm (*PL 37*, 1155) and associates the lion with Christ's Passion and the vehemence of all persecution: "Siquidem adversus Dominum post trinam confusionem hanc, non jam serpentina calliditate, sed crudelitate usus est leonina, usque ad contumelias, ad flagella, ad alapas, ad mortem, et mortem crucis. Sed manifeste etiam leonem te conculcavit Leo de tribu Juda. Sic et adversum nos, fratres, ut in caeteris omnibus viderit sese frustratum, toto jam furore persecutionem suscitat, qualis non fuerit ab initio, ut vehementia tribulationis regnum coeleste sperantibus intercludat" (*PL 183*, 242). Combining Augustine and Bernard, More directly associates the lion with the noonday devil (317/25). Cf. also Augustine, *PL 37*, 1168.

1 Pet. 5:8 was frequently used as a gloss on Psalm 90:13. Augustine, for example, in his *Enarratio in Psalmum XC*, II, 9 (*PL 37*, 1168) says that it was written "Exhortans martyres." See also *Glossa Ordinaria* and Paulus Burgensis, *Biblia Latina*, *3*, sigs. I$_6$v and K$_1$. The passage in 1 Pet. continues: "Cui resistite fortes in fide: scientes eandem passionem ei, quae in mundo est, vestrae fraternitati fieri. Deus autem omnis gratiae, qui vocavit nos in aeternam suam gloriam in Christo Jesu, modicum passos ipse perficiet, confirmabit, solidabitque" (5:9–10).

318/12 **fistyng.** A contemptuous epithet (from "fist," *v.*² to fart): see the

OED, "fisting" *ppl. a.* This is *B*'s emendation (followed by $\mathcal{Z}$), perhaps based on common usage of the term. But the reading of *A* ("fityng," i.e., "fighting") would also make sense, and may be right.

318/26–29 **In ... dispayre.** Cf. *De Tristitia, CW 14*, 43–71.

318/29–32 **& than ... yt.** Cf. above, 22/15–20 and n.

319/1–4 **For ... dyner.** Luke 16:19–25. Cf. above, 55/14–56/10. Abraham told Dives in hell: "Fili, recordare quia recepisti bona in vita tua, et Lazarus similiter mala: nunc autem hic consolatur, tu vero cruciaris" (16:25).

319/7–15 **From ... hell.** Cf. Rogers, pp. 542–43: "And I thanke our Lorde (Megge) since I am come hether I sett by death euery daye lesse than other. For thoughe a man leese of his yeres in this worlde, it is more than manyfolde recompensed by cominge the sooner to heauen. And thoughe it be a paine to die while a man is in health yet see I very fewe that in sickenes dye with ease. And finally, very sure am I that when so euer the tyme shal come that may happe to come, God wote how sone, in which I shoulde lye sicke in my death bed by nature, I shal than thinke that God had done much for me, if he had suffred me to dye before by the colowr of such a lawe. And therfore my reason sheweth me (Margaret) that it wer gret foly for me to be sory to come to that death, which I wolde after wyshe that I had dyed." Cf. also *Devotions, EW*, sigs. VV₃–VV₃v (mismarked XX₃–XX₃v) and above, 297/12–21.

319/20–23 **Non ... in vs.** Rom. 8:18. The verse follows Paul's statement in Rom. 8:17 that to be heirs of Christ men must suffer with Him in order to be glorified with Him. See above, 314/5–6 and n. Since this is the last scriptural reference in *A Dialogue of Comfort*, it takes on an additional weight and significance, as More himself indicates (ll. 23–24) when he says that one does not "nede mych more" than this one verse "in all this whole matter."

319/25–28 **For ... euerlastyngly.** Cf. above, 25/13, and n. to 25/4–24.

320/15–16 **Almayne tong.** I.e., so that it would also be of use to those who suffer for the faith in Germany at the hands of the heretics. See above, n. to 3/2–6. For More's habitual association of heretic and Turk in his polemical works, see *Heresies, EW*, sigs. r₆-r₆v, s₆-s₆v; *Supplication, EW*, sig. v₂v; *Confutation, CW 8*, 94/27–29, 253/12–19, 266/9–10, 466/29–467/2; and *Treatise on the Passion, EW*, sig. OO₆v.

APPENDIX A

Marginalia in the
Corpus Christi Manuscript and in the Early Editions

APPENDIX A

The marginalia in the texts of *CC*, *1557*, and *1573* are presented in full. Compositors' or scribes' contractions and abbreviations, with the exception of yᵉ and yᵗ in the printed texts, have been silently expanded, and accidental printer's errors (inverted letters, etc.) have been silently corrected. Scribal cancellations in *CC* are not recorded. The use of initial capital letters in the printed marginalia is inconsistent but as this reflects an incomplete type font in the printshop rather than the intention of the annotator, the capitalization has been normalized. Periods at the end of the notes in *1557* and *1573* have been silently dropped, except in the case of abbreviated source references. The question mark, often doubling for an exclamation point, is retained.

In the *CC* marginalia, square brackets denote editorial conjectures in places where readings have been cut away at the edge of the page; angle brackets denote places where two hands occur within a single comment. See the Introduction for a discussion of the various hands in the *CC* marginalia.

Although the longer notes are frequently hyphenated in the original texts, they are printed here without any division. The presence of the small hand-sign with its finger pointing at pertinent sentences in the text is also indicated. In a number of instances (particularly so in *1557*), the marginalia slipped slightly in the process of printing; the positions listed here are those in the original editions—no adjustments have been made. The prefatory matter to the edition of 1573 is given separately in Appendix B below.

PART I

Marginalia in the Corpus Christi Manuscript

5/1	Simjlitude	8/1	Belgrade
5/6	god	8/5	Roodes
5/11	the holy trinyte	8/15	vnkyndnes
6/29	Hand-sign	8/26	not[1]
7/29	Grece	9/12	as a triacle
7/30	Soudan of Syry	10/6	tribulation

[1] The annotator's abbreviation for "Nota"; used frequently in the *CC* marginalia.

447

10/12   the philosophers
10/21   the fynall ende
10/26   [t]he very speciall meane
10/27   [g]racyouse help & ayde [o]f god
11/2   some good drugges
11/24   a good petityon
14/12   example
14/15   ij kynd of folke
14/17   of thes that wyll not ar[e] also ij sortes
14/20   letarge
14/23   slouthe
14/25   fumysh
15/4   Ire
15/6   on sort that for worldly comforte
15/9   .s. barnard.
15/11   example
15/18   Hand-sign
15/21   ij sort that desyr comfort of god[1]
15/26   fyrst concyderation
16/4   faythe
16/6   not here
16/13   not
16/17   referryng the maner of comfort vnto god can not fayle to spede
16/23   a good faythe
16/26   example
16/31   not
17/8   woo may be to them th[at] [lack?] that mynd[2]
17/9   Wavy line along margin
17/20   tribulation for a a [sic] meane of amendment
17/25   god heled s paule by hys mynyster Ananias
17/29   pharow
18/6   hys tribulation occasi[on] of profyt / & hys help occasion of harme
18/13   the very tribulation it s[elf]
18/26   slouthe Impatience hope of wordly [sic] comfort
19/1   to pray to god
19/27   not euery case

19/30   tribulations of many sondry kyndes
20/12   Hand-sign
20/18   hunger syknes
20/28   when wold a man she[w] hym self content to dy[e]
21/1   the rebellyon of sensua[lity]
21/5   We may not pray this kynd of tribulation to be taken vtterly from vs
21/9–11 Line drawn along inner margin
21/9   we may boldly pray for our sowle helthe for faythe, for hope & for charite
21/17   gladly
21/18   paciently
21/31   Dauyd
22/6   Not
22/13   Hand-sign
22/16   .s. paul
23/1   pray for ayde and comfort
23/4   thys mynd commyth [of] god
23/22   [e]uery tribulation medicynable [o]r may become medicynable [o]r is better then medicynable
24/4   syknes that foloweth surfet
24/5   prisonment for our crym[e]
24/11   profyt of patyens
25/11   thys worldly tribulation
25/18   god punyshth not on thyng twyse
25/21   the great goodnes of god passeth
25/26   confesse the fawlt
25/31   our lord
26/9   Acham
26/24   ⟨Acham⟩ thys theffe made ⟨a good medycyn⟩ of hy[s] well deseruyd payn
26/27   the converted thefe that hange on the ryght hand of christ
28/18   a double medycyn
28/21   tribulation medycynable to cure the syns passed & purchasith remyscion of the payne dew therfor
28/24   tribulation medicinable in that

---

[1] The word "seid" is written over "ij" by another hand.
[2] The second "that" is cancelled and "lakyth" written above by another hand.

	it preseruethe vs fro the synne in to whyche we wer elles lyke to fall		of derision to the enymyes off crist
28/26	a good medicyn	38/2	iij thynges
28/27	Hand-sign	38/3	1
28/31	god forseyng how myche weight of worldly welthe a man may be able to bere	38/6	2
		38/10	.3.
29/8	a yong lovely lady	38/16	yn defence of hys name
29/12	god louyng her more tenderly	38/17	yn truthe of hys fayth
29/25	his remedy ayenst pride was a paynfull tribulation	38/22	Hand-sign
		38/23	purgatorye
29/29	Not	38/24	Hand-sign
29/31	tribulation is a dowbl[e] medy- cyn bothe a cur[e] for the syn passed & [a] preseruatiue fro the syne [that] is to come	39/6	Wavy lines drawn along margin
		39/9	not
		39/14	Not
		39/18	for fayth alone & nothyng for workes
30/6	Not	39/22	Hand-sign
31/1	Hand-sign	39/33	charite
31/20	Not	40/10	the effecte
32/3	Hand-sign	41/8	*non habemus hic ciuitatem manentem*
32/21[1]	σ̄	42/21	of wepyng
32/28	dyeth for Christes sak	43/10	σ̄
32/30	thouroughe the meryt of Cristes passion	43/16	σ̄
		43/21	σ̄
33/8	a Martyr	44/22	lucre
33/26	to abyd by the trouth	44/23	fere
34/14	defend a pore wydow	45/14	Not
34/19	tribulations better then only medicynable	45/23	the pole of penance
		45/30	the mother with the chyld
35/2	godes nerer cause of faith ayenst the turke	46/9	freres
		47/1	Hand-sign
35/19	twayne	47/7	Salamon
35/27	pray to god for grace to pacy- ence	47/10	Iob
		47/16	Abraham
36/9	hell	48/25	goodes of the worl[d]
36/11	purgatorye	48/29	Some in welhe [*sic*] fall to folye
36/18	penance ⟨by our gostly fath- [er]⟩	49/4	Some with tribulation fall to synne
		49/8	σ̄
36/20	deuocyon	49/10	in ethe estat welthe or tribula- tion may be matter of vertue or vice.
36/22	the lyberall goodnes of god thouroughe the merite of cristes passion		
		49/11	the poynt that standyth here in question Whether contynuall welth in thys world be a fear- full signe
36/27	the liberall good[nes] of god		
36/29	Not		
37/10	.1.	49/14	Hand-sign
37/15	.2.	49/27	.1.
37/25	variances of our fayth is cavse		

[1] Presumably an abbreviation for "Nota," which was often written as "Nσ̄" in the fifteenth and sixteenth centuries. Cf. below at 43/10, 16, 21; 49/8; 95/10; etc.

50/1	.2.
50/4	.3.
50/6	.4.
50/8	last bolte
50/19	tribulation is euery such thyng as greuethe the man ether in body or in mynd
50/20	a prike or a thorne
50/22	the prike that priketh the mynd passethe the greff of the body
51/9	tribulacions yn temptation of the devyll / the world & the fleshe
51/15	to hym that feryth god the tribulation off temptation is paynfull
51/21	Wavy line along margin
51/24	the Ruffell of hys desyr
51/27	payne in resistyng
51/32	an interuption of prosperouse welthe
52/1	non man prayeth to kepe in contynuall prosperite
52/9	the chyrche aduisythe euery man to fast to watche to pray
52/12	Dauyd
52/16	tribulation
52/18	payn payne
52/20	the church aduisithe euery man to take tribulation for hys syn
52/26	yf ease of body or mynd inquieted
52/27	temptation
52/28	voluntary affliction
52/29	Not
53/6	Salamon
53/26	Iob
54/1	Abraham
54/7	Abraham had not syche contynall [sic] prosperite .1.
54/9	it trobuled hym⟨[t]o leve hys countray⟩ in to a straunge land to go .2
54/13	3 ⟨loth & abraham depart company⟩ because their seruantes cowd not agree
54/15	4 ⟨takyng of loth⟩ was trobull to abraham
54/17	⟨[d]estruction of the .v. cytes⟩
54/20	was no smale trobull to abraham .5.
54/20	⟨abimelech⟩ to have hys wyff .6.
54/24	that he many a day no chyld of hys owne body .7.
54/26	trobull to Abraham to cast ⟨Ismael⟩ owt mother and chyld bothe .8.
55/1	.9. ⟨Isaac⟩ was no small trobull to the father when he bownd hym
55/6	Lazarus
55/8	obedyence wyllyngly
57/5	god that techeth
57/8	famyn
57/11	pestilence
57/15	fastyng
57/16	prayng
57/18	wakyng
58/1	Hand-sign
58/8	Not pytye of thyr
58/10	.s. Ihon
58/12	payn of our neybo[r]
58/16	the hole chyrche pr[ayd]
58/25	Hand-sign
60/5	holsome
60/7	Hand-sign
60/12	[t]hys callyng of god
60/21	turne to the fleshe
61/6	no soft bede wyll serue
61/12	Hand-sign
61/28	fantisyes of their owne lewde lyff
62/7	Saule
62/14	Samuell
62/19	becavse he was not hard with god he made sute to the devyll
62/24	paralipomenon
62/25	for lak of trust in god
63/3	a cape or hose to a wyse woman otherwyse called a wytche
63/11	v. leves of valerian
64/14	a man may hathe wordly [sic] w[elth] & go to god
64/15	a man may be myserab[le] [&] lyve in tribulation & go to [the] devyll
64/16	a man may please god by [paci]ence in aduersite

64/17   a man may please god by [thankes] gyvyng in pros-perite.

64/20   prosperite⎤ nether good [nor] aduersite ⎦ badd off t[heir] owne nature

64/23   a questyon why prehemy-[nance] shold be geven to tribula[tion]

65/12   Hand-sign

65/19   that is not desperat or a dull beste

66/3   god requyryth not in syche case long prayors

66/6   The Martyrs

66/10   as man crist merite not for vs only but for hymself also.

66/24   Not

66/26   mavndy ⟨passion⟩

66/27   slepe ⟨watche⟩

66/28   prayour

67/2   crist prayd in bytter ag[ony]

67/4   fyrst

67/5   when he thrise fell prostrate

67/9   second

67/10   the paynfull prayers that he made vppon the crosse

67/15   ij very devout & fervent prayers

67/22   prayour in tribulation effect-[ual] & most strong

67/28   Not

67/29   Wavy line drawn along margin

68/12   Comfort Ryght

68/17   that pacyently taketh

68/18   god rewardeth the sufferer

68/22   Long wavy line drawn along margin

68/22   though the welthy ma[n] thanke god for the fa[vor] yet god promysethe hy[m] no reward yn heven

68/24   Not

68/25   off comfort of go[ds] fauour & remissi[on] of Synnes

68/27   comfort that commythe of tri-bula[tion]

69/3   contynuall welth perelouse

69/5   on cawse of comfort [in] tribu-lation

69/6   on cause of comfort

69/8   scriptur commendyth tribula-tion of more profit

69/11   Ecclesiastes

69/13   a nother cause

69/17   the hart of wyse men

69/20   Wavy line drawn along margin

69/21   wordly [sic] merthe commen-dy[d] in scriptur.

69/24   prosperite to the children of Israell

69/26   Wavy line drawn along margin

69/30   moyses *pedagogu*[s]

70/1   the old law

70/3   another reason

70/12   tribulation

70/15   Ecclesiastes

70/20   *extrema gaudij*

70/24   *beati qui lugent*

70/26   *Mundus gaudebit*

70/30   in matter of very comfor[t] tribulation is a [sic] farre abo[ve] prosperite as the day is abov[e] the nyght

71/1   in occasion of merit & re[ward] tribulation hath prehemin-en[ce]

71/4   tribulation meritith in pacyence & in obedient [sic]

71/6   Riches

71/7   Aucthorite

71/12   Hand-sign

71/13   good wyll

71/18   tribulation occacyon of the pacientes desert

71/27   secretly levethe in a contrit hart & a lyf penytencyall

71/28   to Dauyd worldly welthe no welthe to hyme

72/18   in those good dedes the prero-grative [sic] of tribulation

72/23   after portion

73/1   the portion in euery goo[d] dede don the mattor is al[l] [one]

74/13   thankes geven for tribulation

74/24   the pacyence of Iob

75/7   Wavy line drawn along margin

75/8   fast fayth

75/11   tribulation a especyall gyfte of god.

75/12   I

75/13   2[1]
75/14   3
75/15   4
75/16   5
75/17   .6.
75/17   .7.
75/18   .8.
75/19   .9.
75/20   .10.
75/21   .11.
75/21   .12.
75/22   13.
75/23   14.
75/24   .15.
75/26   first by pacyence
76/6   god
76/9   especyally trust in god
76/12   .S. Iames
76/12   confession
76/20   he that is lothe to leve thys wretched world
76/23   a longyng to be with god
76/25   charite couerythe a multit[ude] of Synis
79/29   A none & her brother
81/2   a Tale
82/16   Salamon
82/18   .s. Thomas
83/10   fyrst our chieff comfort of god & with hym contynew & with hym end. (Line drawn along margin)
83/19   Not (Line drawn along margin)
83/24   drede of hell
83/30   it is in the soule somwha[t] as it is in the body
84/1   Hand-sign
84/5   *Cassianus*
84/10   a merry tale
84/22   better wold I wyshe but I can not helpe it
84/26   sawce not our meate
84/27   let vs pray (Line drawn along margin)
85/1   Not
85/5   begyn by faythe & to fayth by praor

85/20   the snof of a candell (Line drawn along margin)
85/23   Line drawn along margin
86/20   1
86/21   2
86/22   3
88/3   Hand-sign
88/17   In on on [*sic*] Instant bo[th] hote and cold at o[nes]
89/22   *Galenus de differen[tiis] februm.*
90/12   he that is contryt shall [be] both sad & gla[d]
90/14   S. Iherom.
90/19   [the] goodnes of godes excellent mercy
92/17   grace commyth but a[t] gods wyll
92/20   Not
93/13   In Saxony
93/20   wemen wax mannyshe
93/28   a religiouse man
94/20   Hand-sign
95/8   Not
95/10   σ‾
95/16   bere the cross
95/20   Moises
95/22   hely
95/23   our sauyour chryst
95/23   the apposteles fasted lent
95/24   .K. Achas
95/27   the Nynyvites
95/29   Anna
96/2   .s. Paule
96/7   fastyng of on man m[ay] do good to an other
97/17   *misericordia*
97/19   nouit *figmentum suum*
97/25   σ‾
97/27   σ‾
98/2   σ‾
98/7   faynt fayth or dull diligence
98/10   drede
98/11   love
98/17   Gerson
98/19   Line drawn along margin
98/21   affliction of the flesh
98/22   with faythfull pray[er]

---

[1] Sequence originally numbered 1–14; then 2 is added and following numbers are changed.

100/6	temptacion	130/22	Hand-sign
100/7	persecution	131/7	fyrst
100/15	temptacion to good men is tri- bulation	131/23	a mery mortall tempta[tion]
		133/8	*Io. Gerson de probatione spirituum.*
100/17	diferens	137/20	syght of a thing wakyng
101/13	a game of wreste[lyng]	137/21	syght of a thyng slepyng
101/24	Not	139/23	Hand-sign
102/8	Strenght	143/28	A Cervers wyff
102/9	wysdom	146/13	Hand-sign
102/22	Not	146/22	Hand-sign
103/9	by fast fayth and sure hope dwell in godes helpe	147/24	similitude
		148/3	Symilitude
103/19	Hand-sign	148/10	Hand-sign
103/32	similitud	149/1	Not
107/11	nyght feare	150/3	Hand-sign
107/18	nyghtes feare	150/8	warme lusty bloude
107/19	1	150/12	hote blode & color.
107/20	Hand-sign	150/14	[d]ull malencoly humors
107/23	2	150/16	Hand-sign
108/11	of god	150/24	Not
108/15	the body	151/16	Counsell
108/16	⟨the soule.⟩ which is the sub- stance of man	151/17	Prayour
		152/12	.S. Iames
108/18	⟨faythfully⟩ in adiutorio altis- simi	152/21	Not
		153/15	Hand-sign
108/24	lake of fayth and good hope	154/1	3 thinges
108/29	spirituall vnderstandyng & the eye of our faythe	154/2	In resystyng
		154/3	In contempnyng
109/12	the body the garment of our soule	154/3	Inuocation of helpe
		154/14	symilitude
109/13	fayntnes of our fayth	154/15	a hyghe brydg[e]
109/19	⟨similitud⟩ of a old rayne beten cloke	154/22	devyll
		155/5	T
109/30	a Tale	155/11	Hand-sign
110/1	belgrade	155/15	fynall fight is by Invocacion of helpe vnto god prayng for hym selff & desieryng other to pray for hym
110/26	a fayre long hedge		
113/1	a tale		
113/27	Not		
114/14	Mother Mavde	155/18	yn the seruyse of the Masse
121/5	Not	155/20	the Letany
122/23	Not	155/26	C yeres befor .S. gregory
124/15	Buda	156/1	.s. bernard
124/16	a fendyshe woman	156/2	pray to Avngelles & sayntes
125/9	a Carpenter	156/18	psal. .6.7.
126/20	the quens grace	156/28	good cowncell & prayour ver- tuose bysenes & vertuose companye & faythfull hope of godes helpe
129/15	wole gath(?) (at bottom edge of folio 100ᵛ)		
130/4	⟨from pryd to⟩ pusillanimite		
130/9	very strenght can not be with- out prudence	157/20	the arrow of pryde
		158/4	example

454

158/7 worldly welthe is [a] short wynter day
159/17 example
159/22 hell
160/17 the deuylles temptation vnto pride is a great tribulation
160/27 dedly desyr of ambitious glorye
160/28 Line drawn along margin
161/10 Not
161/10 pusillanimite in the day of prosperite
161/14 Not
161/26 Hand-sign
162/8 ouermych fere perilouse
162/10 tempere feare with good hope
162/13 symony
162/16 blesse hym self
162/22 Not pityfullnes
162/26 euery pore begger hys felow.
163/8 the knot
163/23 Hand-sign
163/28 a christen man
164/6 Not
164/12 resort to confession
164/15 secret solitary place
164/24 Not invisibly presen[t]
164/26 remembrance of the benefyttes of god
164/31 wordly [sic] frendes
166/18 ⟨Negocium⟩ the name of a devyll
166/21 ij tymes of darknesse
166/24 ij tymes of darknesse in the soule
167/3 [y]ᵉ deuyl called besenes
167/6 1
167/7 2
167/14 a round mase
167/21 the bely
167/22 partes beneth the bely
167/23 couetys
167/24 a centre or mydle place
167/27 hell
168/4 flesly folke
168/7 couetuose men
168/13 Hand-sign
168/27 Hand-sign
169/1 a mery tale
169/2 Line drawn along margin
169/18 ⟨Not⟩ man byethe hell

169/22 wittes
169/30 very good folkes
170/17 tempted & not follow
170/18 Not (Line drawn along margin)
171/9 the affection that the haver vnlefully berethe
171/10 qui volunt diuetes fieri
171/27 hard for them then [sic] put theire trust & confidence in their monye to entre into heven
172/18 .s. Ambrose
173/9 .s. Austeyne tellyth of a phisicion
173/17 in the sekenes difference or in the man hymself or in the place or the tyme of the yere
174/4 curattes bownden
174/28 our sauour meanythe that none can be hys dyscyple but yf he love hym above all hys kynne
175/6 to gyve awaye all or that no man shuld be riche
175/9 many mansions
175/21 riches & pouerty comparid
176/2 a mynd to dispose it well
176/7 Zacheus
176/21 temerariouse Iudgment
177/21 it is alway good to do som good dede owt of hand
178/18 Zacheus
179/30 men of ryches
180/3 Line drawn along margin
181/1 a golden egge
181/21 .6. cap. .s. luke
182/11 Hand-sign
182/14 by nature
182/15 by lawe
182/26 a gest a way faryng man
183/2 not
183/4 our parentes
183/7 convenyently
183/11 yf to muche wold make them nowght the father shold gyve lesse
183/15 honour father & mother
183/20 vrgent necessite of a stravnger
183/21 Hand-sign
184/16 for a glory
184/19 vayne folyshe pride
184/29 quene hester

185/4   kepyng a good houshold
185/11   Mary Mawdelene
185/30   god is more mercyfull to mans
         imperfection
189/13   Esope
192/2   similitude of the see
192/5   the name of the Turke
192/7   glad to fynd fawlt at euery state
         of christedome
192/12   the title of crowne yn question
192/15   neweltes
192/23   boda
192/32   tokens
194/2   faythe in the erthe?
194/9   commyng yn of the Iewes
194/17   not
195/15   Pacience
195/22   turkes naturall
195/25   pray styll & call vnto god
195/30   appoynt a for hand with godes
         help what they entend to do
         yf the worst fall.
196/9   perilouse
196/12   rather suffer dethe
196/16   forsake god in dede
196/22   in wrytyng
197/3   the offence of .s. Peter
197/8   example of a pore begger
197/12   all the perell is yf he wyll for-
         sake christ with hys mouth.
197/14   by thys mynd he falleth in to
         dedly syn
197/18   habit of fayth cold
197/23   mery medycyne for the tothe
         ache
198/5   christ spake often
198/9   condicyonally
198/9   actually
198/10   habitually
198/14   remembre the payne that Cryst
         sufferd & hartely pray for
         grace
198/20   percever in good hope
198/23   euery curat theyr
198/29   thourough syche actuall medi-
         tation he shall confirme a
         sure habit of spirituall fayth-
         full strenght
199/4   consernyng them that dwell
         owt of the daunger

199/9   trouth of fayth
199/9   trouth of Iustice.
200/1   the iiij^{th} temptation which is
         persecution for the faythe
200/8   thys is the most perilouse
200/23   *Demonium meridianum*
200/29   thys kynd of persecution is not
         a wyly temptation but a
         furiouse feare
201/1   in other temptations he stelyth
         on lyke a fox but here he
         commyth lyke a roryng lyon
201/5   yn prosperite he allurythe man
         delectably to syn
201/6   yn aduersite he vseth to pul a
         man to murmore & Impatienc
201/8   both twayn
201/12   losse, siknes, dethe.
201/15   necessite a man must of fyn
         force
201/18   of necessite to make a vertue
201/22   wher a man is taken & in hold
201/26   a meruelouse occasyon to fall in
         to the syn that the deuyll
         wold dreve hym to.
202/13   reherse the greffes & I shall
         gyve you cowncell
203/4   all the harmes in generall
203/7   man made of the body & the
         soule
203/11   Soule
203/13   inordinat love and affection
         that the soule beryth to the
         body
203/15   Bodye
203/17   delyght that the soule hathe to
         the body
203/23   losse of mony plate or other
         moveable substance offices,
         authorite landes of enherit-
         ance
204/1   nedines pouerte, the payne of
         lackyng shame of beggyng
204/8   for the body losse of liberte,
         labour Imprisonment payn-
         full & shavmfull dethe
204/20   .s. peter
204/29   a desyre & love longyng to be
         with god
205/3   alas our faynt and feble fayth

206/3   with our love to god less than luke warm
206/3   of the losse off the goodes of fortune
206/6   worldly substance, offices honour, authorite
206/9   Hand-sign
206/13 experience prouyth
206/15 what shall a good man greatly reiose in that that he dayly seeth most habunde yn the handes of many that be nawght
206/20 the great Sowdan of Syry
207/6   vnsewrtye of landes & possessions
207/13 what dyfference to vs whether our substavnce be moveable or vnmoveable?
207/23 Grece, Syry
207/24 the land lost or the mony was found
207/27 plato
207/28 the grownd on whyche a prince bildyth hys palice
208/3   Line drawn along the margin
210/1   the lytle commodite of richesse
210/15 Riches
211/12 honest estimacion
211/18 of the nature
212/5   a blast of wynd
216/8   Iuuenall
217/11 martiall
218/13 Kyng Ladislaus
218/20 *Sicut erat*
218/29 prayse
219/6   a hote blayne
219/21 a mery tale
221/2   gleke
221/20 lekes
221/32 Hand-sign
222/9   parable of a philosopher
222/14 to rise to Avthorite by the fauour of princes
224/5   *prouerb. 20 capr.*
224/18 fame & glory
224/26 batteylles betwen great princes
226/20 *Imperferfectum* [*sic*] *meum viderunt oculi tui*

227/10 the gyft of fortune
227/30 the devilles eschetour
228/28 a puff ryng of paris
229/24 not
230/5   .s. paule
230/10 beleve all that he tellyth yow
230/11 do all that he byddythe yow
230/11 forbere all that he forbyddythe yow
230/12 with owt eny maner exception
230/14 Hand-sign
230/18 endentures
231/4   xv^c yeris
231/7   a plaine conclusion
231/13 the faythe
231/25 promyse
232/9   a marchaunt
235/2   Hand-sign
235/8   ynwardly
235/9   outwardly
235/18 god Not
235/18 whom yow displease
235/22 sufferance of god
236/6   a short candell
236/15 Hand-sign
236/16 .s. Augustine
237/1   Hand-sign
237/27 nether in hart nor to[ng]
239/17 .6. cap. mathew.
240/6   Not
240/23 not only our eare but a[lso] our hart.
241/1   thornes & breers
241/15 the greatest comfort in tribulation is to have hys hart in heven
241/23 Line drawn along the margin
242/5   Not
242/25 Simili
243/8   powerte of our sauyour
243/9   example of a great kyng
243/11 Hand-sign
243/25 Not
243/29 forsak chryst
245/29 Not
246/17 Not
246/22 .s. Ihon euangelyst
247/2   epistles of .s. Cipriane
247/8   Hand-sign

247/16 not
247/17 .s. paule
248/15 Hand-sign
248/31 a good purpose
249/1   Hand-sign
249/8   Not
249/19 not
250/5   but yf the sprite of god
251/21 Not
251/29 settyng & setlyng yn god
252/7   Captiuyte
252/19 What freman?
253/3   not
253/12 Synne
253/17 wyllyngly thrall & bonde
253/26 Hand-sign
254/1   by the prouidence of god
254/7   *Senek*
254/13 froward mynd
254/25 Not
255/15 a restraynt
256/4   yn Ciuill
256/10 our own fantesie
256/18 accidentes
257/9   Tamberlane
257/20 ymprisonment of hym self & hys own nature.
260/10 begger
272/18 god the cheff gaylour is neyther cruell nor covetouse
272/29 wax wanton
273/8   vppon our prison
273/18 a false persuasion of welthe
274/20 an hotte feuer
274/22 a mygrem
274/23 a quyncy
274/24 a paulsey
274/25 the goute
274/26 the crampe
275/1   the crike in the bak
275/6   gowt
275/14 folk borne & brought vp in prison
277/6   a woman
277/17 the prisoner laughed
278/13 the feare of hard handlyng
279/12 Ioseph
279/14 Danyell
279/26 our sauyour was taken prisoner.

281/23 the affection of the mynd
281/26 1 by the bodely sensis
282/2   affections commen vnto m[en] and bestes
282/3   2
282/7   Reasonable dispositions ben calle[d] affections spirituall
282/13 Hand-sign
283/4   Dethe chavmfull & paynfull
283/14 lak of faythe hope wytt
283/18 folyshe vnfaythful wordes
284/3   good wyll gladly to dye
284/14 .s. Paule
285/7   for lak of wytt
285/17 chery stonis
285/19 Snayle
286/21 Hand-sign
286/26 the dronken man
287/6   fole
287/23 Infidelite no comfort can helpe but counsel[l] only
288/12 reason groundyd vpp[on] the foundacyon of fayt[h]
290/2   no man that hauth fa[yth]
290/6   precyouse & honorab[le] in the sight of god
290/17 ix cap. .s. luke
290/29 Hand-sign
291/20 Not
291/25 crownyng
291/26 a rede
292/1   skorne
292/1   bett the rede
292/20 prouerbe
293/1   Hand-sign
293/10 reason
293/12 bitter pocyon
293/13 to be lavnced
293/15 a childyshe man
293/18 a man that hathe wysdo[m]
293/24 reason alone
293/27 reason grownded vpo[n] faythe
294/6   [r]eason furtheryd with faythe [&] grace
294/18 a great old hart
296/7   Not
296/10 grace
296/24 worldly vanytes
297/23 a iij foted stole

297/25 fantasticall feare
297/26 false faythe
297/26 false flateryng ho[pe]
298/4   Not
298/10 *Lucae. 12*
298/18 a false fayth 2.
298/29 3
298/30 false flatteryng hope
299/19 presumpcion
299/24 12 cap. .s. Mathew
299/25 3 cap. .s. Marke
301/9   a man that was o[nes] yn a
        galey
302/17 plurisie
303/6   2. cap. .s. luke
303/19 Not
304/5   Not
304/15 full fayth
304/16 sufficient myndyng
305/15 afrayd of hell
305/25 fleshly folke
306/22 experymentall tast
306/25 [a]s an ernest peny
307/12 body Impassib[le]
307/25 paynfull siknes
308/7   Hand-sign
308/10 by readyng
308/11 by heryng
308/11 by rehersyng
308/12 by meditation

308/16 a shadow
308/20 [t]he substance essentiall of [a]ll
        the celestiall Ioye
309/26 suffrages
310/7   a piller
310/13 2 & 3 ca. *Apoca.*
310/27 perelles by false brether[en]
311/5   Not
311/16 our hed is Christ
311/26 Hand-sign
312/31 holy sacrament
314/13 obstinat heretiques
314/18 christ passion
314/19 hell
314/20 heven
314/26 Simili
316/16 strengh stod in the help of god
316/23 it semeth a proud my[nd]
316/28 fastyng, prayer almes dede
317/1   land or goodes
317/2   exile
317/6   captiuite
317/26 the mydday deuill
318/12 Horizontal line
318/16 our capten Christ
318/19 charite
318/25 bold
318/26 feare
319/29 concyderation of euerla[sting]
        Ioy

PART II

Marginalia in the 1557 *English Works*

[1] *1557* reads *Hieremo.*

PART III

Marginalia in the 1573 Edition

469

178/30 Luc. 3
179/4   Marc. 12
179/8   Luc. 19
179/21 Pore folke shal there neuer lack
        Matth. 26. Marc. 14
179/30–180/1 There must nedes be
        som rich men
180/27 The riche mans substance is the
        poore mans liuing
181/1   The hen that laied golden
        egges
181/21 This place of S Luke truly ex-
        pounded
182/5   Rom. 12
182/11 Tim. 5
182/13 To these must we first giue
182/16 Dutie to seruants
182/21 Hand-sign
182/27 Note
183/5   2. Cor. 12
183/7   Duetie to children
183/8   Note wel
183/13 Duetie to Parents
183/19 Note
183/26 Discretion in giuing almose
184/15 A damnable state in riches
184/20 Would God there wer many
        such
184/23 A perfect good state in riches
184/25 In al external actions good men
        must somewhat yeeld to
        worldly fashions
184/29 Hester. 14
185/11 Luc. 10
185/20 A second, and lesse perfect
        state in riches
185/26 Hand-sign
186/8   How riches may be kept with
        saluation.
188/9   There be mo great Turkes than
        one
188/20 Why nouelties are somtimes
        blowen abrode
189/13 Note the parable, & beware the
        woulf
189/21 This is the right practise of
        heretiks
190/4   The Turkes othe
190/14 Haue not other Turks done al
        the same to?

190/25 Why Christien Catholike folke
        be spared some times, and in
        some Countreies
191/3   Hand-sign
191/20 Note this practise practised also
        now
192/1   A good similitude
192/3   Hand-sign
192/5   The worst folk do most find,
        and least amend faultes
192/13 A depe point of wisedom for
        rulers to consider
192/23 Hand-sign
193/3   Note the like bold fauour borne
        to ye Gewes in Flanders
193/6   Note wel this point & consider
        the sequele bothe in Turkish
        treacherie & in Protestants
        practises and proceedings
193/23 For al ye Turkes and Heretiks
        can do, Christendom &
        Catholike faith shal spring vp
        againe
193/32 Luc. 18
194/3   Apocal. 1. Matth. 24
194/12 Both Turkes & heretiks shal
        haue a fal at last
194/16 Turks & heretiks are Gods
        scourge
195/2   An heauie hearing in dede
195/8   These Turks haue had, and
        haue now their day
195/20 Marke what ensueth, when
        Christen Princes vse turks
        and heretiks aide
195/28 Good to foresee and forecast
        the worst
196/13 Iohan. 13. Luc. 22
196/24 One or two Doctors mind is not
        alway to be trusted
197/18 Such cold and faint faith is to
        common now
197/23 A medicine for the toth-ache
198/2   Men wink sometime & cannot
        slepe
198/5   Matth. 10. Luc. 12
198/9   If heretiks think they must dy
        for their faith, what must
        Christen Catholikes think &
        do for theirs?

198/23 Note this duetie of Curates and others

199/6 How many are now fallen in the case, yea and fallen to?

199/9 Persecution for Faith or Justice, muche alike

200/8 This temptation most perilous &c.

200/16 Who seeth not now yᵉ rage of this furious mid-day diuel?

200/31 1. Pet. 5

201/1–2 A ramping Lion in dede

201/14 Hand-sign

202/24 A good care for kinsfolk & frinds

202/27 Eccles. 17

203/2 O how charitably said?

203/13 The harme of yᵉ soule

203/23 Al these losses and harmes men haue and suffer now

204/14 How true is this tried now?

204/20 Luc. 22

204/23 The feruent faith of old time

205/3 The faint and feble faith now

205/12 Hand-sign

206/5 The goods of fortune

206/17 What great Turkish Bassawes do mount aloft now?

206/24 God send once that day

206/28 Hand-sign

207/6 Land and possessions

207/16 Money better than land sometime

207/22 Hand-sign

207/26 A proper fiction

208/7 Landed mens State

208/17 This case hath fallen to some kings, and to many Gentlemen

209/13 Hand-sign

210/7 Gay apparail

210/10 Delicate fare

210/22 Horders & hiders of monie

210/28 Hand-sign

211/10 A good name

211/11 Honest estimation

211/14 Honourable Fame

212/2 Enuie & hate folow fame

212/19 O glorious fooles

213/7 A notable example of flatterie

213/10 Hand-sign

214/10 Flatterie accustomed in Court

215/7 Natural. Hist. lib. 35. cap. 10

215/26 Flatterie wel assembled to Painting

216/7 Satyr. 4

216/11 Montanus

216/25 In Eunucho

217/5 Flattrers kept and fed for the nonce

217/13 Martialis. lib. 8. ad Gallicum

217/20 Another example

218/8 Tellers of trueth litle made of

218/13 Ladislaus

218/19 Gloria patri with a sicut erat

218/26 Lawful praising

219/14 Offices & Roumes

219/21 A mery tale

220/1–2 Women loue rule

220/10 Ambition is in dede but womannish

220/16 Commanders commodities

221/9 Hand-sign

221/15 Commanders incommodities

221/32 Priuie malice in Court

222/10 Princes seruants be but Counters

222/16 Who is vp aloft now?

222/21 A sure rekening

223/21 Things indifferent be not so in vse

223/30 1. Timoth. 6

224/6 Cap. 21

224/12 Note

224/24 See these earthly Gods now

224/26 The roote of warres

225/4 Bearing and bolstring

225/6 Abusing of lawes

225/10 Hand-sign

226/4 Eche man would feine holy

226/12 Very true

226/16 Gal. 6

226/20 Psal. 138

226/22 Psal. 18

226/27 Persecution is a touchestone

227/15 Note this cumfort

227/30 The diuels Escheators

228/18 Few such found, the more pity

228/26 Gods sight pearceth depe

229/5 Yet how many such are now?

---

[1] See the textual notes to p. 295 for Fowler's rearrangement of the text at this point.

APPENDIX B

Prefatory Matter in
the 1573 Edition

APPENDIX B

Prefatory Matter in the 1573 Edition

To the
*Right Honourable and Excellent Ladie,
the Ladie Iane, Duchesse of Feria.*[1]

WHereas I was so bold the last yere, to dedicate to your Honour, a litle Treatise[2] of mine owne translating, not worthie in dede to come foorth vnder the name of so Noble a Patronesse, whereby I might seme, not to applie any dede or gift of mine toward the honour or seruice of your Grace, but rather to vse the name of your honourable Personage for the better commendation and setting foorth of that smal labour of mine: to amend that fault and boldnes committed than, I thought good now, to present vnto your Grace, not any better gift of mine owne (as being yet not hable to giue any that is owght worth) but surely an excellent gift of an other mans deuise and making, which both hath done, doth, and shal do much good to many other good [*₂v] folke, and to your Noble Grace also. For though I know right wel, that the same hath bene sene and perused of your Honor many times before now, and that you haue yet, and many yeares haue had the same lying by you:[3] yet both by my selfe, and by other also, I know, that how oft so euer a man haue read the same, yet as oft shal he nede to reade it againe. And though he both haue and do stil reade it againe and againe, he shal yet take profit more and more by it, and alwaies shal haue nede, while he liueth here, to haue oft recourse therevnto. And that may wel appeare in this present case of your Honour, who in this long moorning for the lacke and losse of your right worthie and most Noble Husband, my good Lord the Dukes Grace,[4] cannot, I suppose, any where finde the like ease of your heauines and cumfort for the sole and sad estate of your vertuous widowhod, as here out of this Booke may be taken, bothe for that, and for any other worldly woes and afflictions.

These six or seuen yeres haue I bene desirous, to haue so good a Booke come forth againe in some smaller volume then it was in before, being in deede not so handsome[5] for the priuate vse and commoditie of the Reader, as I trust it shalbe now. But it hath not bene my chance through one let or other, to [*₃] accomplish that desire of mine, til now. And that is in deede the chiefe thing that I haue done therein, which I may accompt as mine: I meane, in that I haue brought it into this smal volume, and withal, by conferring of sundry Copies together, haue restored and corrected many places, and thereby made it muche more plaine and easie to be vnderstood of the Reader. Al which smal labour of mine I beseke your Honour to accept in good part, as of him that would be right glad, not only by this or any other meane to testifie alway my good hart and affection toward the noble Duke, both while he liued and stil after his deceasse, but also to doo likewise to your Grace, and to your Noble Sonne⁶ (being his Fathers owne Heire both of Estate and worthy Qualities) any such seruice, as my poore habilitie can any wise atchieue. And thus commending myselfe in al humble maner vnto your Grace, I shal remain, as before, bound alway to pray for the good health and long life of your Honour, and of your no lesse deare than noble Sonne, whom in his Fathers place I take stil for my good Lord also. From Antwarp, the last of September. An. 1573.

Your Graces most
humble Seruitour.
Iohn Fouler. [*₃v]⁷

(ORNAMENT) [*₄]

To the Reader

IF the whole life of man be a continual warfare vpon earth, as Gods owne word⁸ doth witnesse, & as our owne experience doth daily proue the same, and that man himselfe borne of a woman, is in dede a wo man, that is, ful of wo and miserie, euen from the very first hower of his birth, to the very last moment of his life,⁹ at which time he suffreth the extremest wo and most pinching paine of al, in parting from his owne natural bodie, that he naturally loueth so wel: how great nede haue we, to prouide and haue ready alway some good armour and weapon in this our long warfare,¹⁰ & not to be without some relief & succour against so many miseries as we be subiect vnto?

To make any particular discourse of al the sundrie sorowes and woes that appertaine to eche state, both of men and women, of yong and old, sicke and whole, rich and poore, high and low, subiect and Prince, & King and Quene and al: it would be to long a busines, and shal not nede at this [*₄v] present, referring the knowledge and remembrance thereof to eche person in his degree, as he daily and howrely feeleth the same.

For though that some there be, that neither feele nor know their owne miseries, and yet liue in most miserie of al, whereof the common Prouerb¹¹ saith, that such as are in hel, thinke there is none other heauen, & as in very dede many folke of this world take and wene this to be their heauen, bycause they know none other yet (and other shal they neuer know here, but by faith)[12] yet, be we neuer so blind in seeing & knowing our owne most miseries, we haue for al that other miseries bysides so many and so great, that there is no creature so happie here on earth, but that one way or other, at some time or other, he seeth & feeleth sorow and wo inough. And though that perhap to other folke he seeme to liue in al worldly wealth and blisse, yet himselfe knoweth best, what him ayleth most, and as another Prouerbe[13] also saieth, Eche man knoweth wel, where his owne shoe wringeth him.

And albeit that commonly the best folke suffer most afflictions in this world, as being most hated of the world, & best beloued of God, who reserueth for them in another world the crowne of eternal Blisse,[14] and for the euilles that they endure here, doth reward them with good thinges there: yet [*5] the common sort of folke, yea and the very woorst and most wicked to, haue likewise their kinds of afflictions and miseries, & do not lacke their worldly woes, which vexe them otherwhiles euen at the very hearts as much, and more, than any other tribulations either inward, or outward, do molest the mindes of the vertuous and good.

If then miseries be so common & so general vnto al, what ought al folke generally to prouide for, but remedie and cumfort against the same? And, if the infection of this pestilent maladie of man be suche & so sore, that it letteth none scape long without it, but visiteth ech bodie by some meane or other, where euer they dwel, and what aier so euer they liue & reast in: what great cause haue we, that cannot auoid this contagious aier, but must nedes leade our liues in it, and thereby fal sicke now and then, to seeke some good preseruatiues against such an vniuersal plague, or at least some good Comfortatiues for the hart & braines and principal partes of vs, that we be not so striken vpon the sodaine, but that we may temper the rage of this dissease, and ouercome the danger of it, to the recouery of our health and final saluation?

I would verily beleue, these thinges wel pondered, that is, both the general estate of mans miserie and paine, and the great [*5v] necessitie of cumfort which as generally followeth therewithal: that, whereas many bookes haue and do come foorth daily, that tend toward some benefit or other vnto man, yet scant any can appeare, the profit whereof is so great and extendeth so far, as of this.

The inuention in dede of the Authour seemeth to respect some particular cases, which was of him wonderful wittily deuised, appliyng his whole discourse to that peece of Christendome, to wit, the land of Hungarie, which hath bene these many yeares (and yet is) sore persecuted and oppressed by Turks.[15] But vnder this particular case of Turks persecution he generally comprehendeth al kinds of afflictions and persecutions both of body and mind, that may any way be suffred, either by sicknes or health, by frind or fo, by wicked & wrongful oppressors, by Miscreants and Turks, and the very fiends and diuels of hel also. And that was done for this entent (as it may wel seeme) that vnder this one kind of Turkish persecution, the benefit of yᵉ booke might be the more common to al Christen folke, as the which could iustly of none be reiected nor reprooued, but if themselues were very Turkes to, or woorse. And yet I trow, no Turke is so cruel and fel, that wil or can let a poore Christen man in the mids of al his afflictions put vpon him by [*₆] the same Turke, to seeke & vse some cumfort in his case, such as he may.

Howbeit this Booke is also such, and so generally profitable, & so charitably written and deuised to the behoof of al, that both good & bad, Christen and Heathen, Iew & Gentile, and the very Turkes to, in that they be mortal men, and subiect to worldly miseries, may, if they would reade and vse it, pike out many good counsels and cumforts, whereby to ease themselues also in their most aduersities. For sometime the chaunce is turned, and it fortunes as wel the Turkes to be taken prisoners by the Christen, as the Christen are taken & persecuted by them.

And surely if Turkes vnderstood the language, and perceaued wel the general commoditie of the Booke, what soeuer the common sort and furious multitude of them would do for their accustomed malice and enuie against al benefit of the Christen: yet (no doubt) a man should find some good number of them, so tractable and indifferent, that would for their owne sakes in considering of their owne nede, and the general condicion of al men, neither gainsay their Christen captiues to seeke them some ease in their miserie, nor yet refuse themselues, to vse (from among the reast) such cumforts here and there as may serue there owne turnes. For we see, that euen in the [*₆v] mids of their owne Countreies they suffer many Christen folke to dwel, paying certaine tributes and taxes for their safegard and sufferance to liue therc.¹⁶ And in other Countreies also which they newly subdue and win from the Christians, they do not so dispeople the whole lands and maine Countreies, but that they let many thousands dwel there stil, professing openly and freely their faith, with Churches & Chappels allowed for them: this only prouided, that they agnise the Turke to be lord of the land, and themselues to liue in quiet & ciuil subiection under him.

But blessed be God, that the Turkes themselues, though they haue ouer-runne already almost al Hungarie, and thereto wonne Cypres of late,¹⁷ are farre ynough of from vs yet: and would God al their Turkish fasshions and persecutions were as farre of from vs to, & that Christian Charitie did raigne more truly and plentifully in the hartes of al that beare the name of Christians in Christendome. For then a great part of the cumforts that are in this Booke, should not greatly nede, nor we should not greatly neede neither to feare, least any Christen folke would shew themselues so vnchristen, as to find fault or mislike with the vse & free hauing of the same among al men, whereas the matter & Argument thereof toucheth al men so nere. [*₇]

How be it very few shalbe found here in our Quarters (by al likelyhod) that haue so much degenerated from the nature of true Christianitie, as expressely to dissannul or dissalow the same, least they might thereby seeme, not only to be no Christians at al, but rather right Renegats, which are in dede much worse than any natural Turks.

For as for al such as professe the Gospel and fauour the truth of Gods word, they must nedes of fine force, both thinke wel hereof, and also allow and commend the reading and pervsing of the same among al good Christen people, whereas there is in maner nothing therin, but that is taken out of the very Scripture, out of Gods owne written word, & altogether treateth of faith, and of the principal points thereof. Wherefore (to conclude) there is no more to say, but only to wish vnto al men generally, that as their owne nede and aduersitie shal moue them to seeke for some ease & cumfort in their case: if it be their chance to light vpon this Booke, they may so loke thereon, and find such benefit and reliefe thereby, as may be most to Gods pleasure and quiet of their mindes. [*₇v]

Iohan. Fouleri Bristoliensis in D. Th. Mori
effigiem, Hexastichon.[18]

Effigiem quamcunque tui sic fingimus, at non
Tam facile est mores fingere, More, tuos.
Quam vellem Pictor mihi tam perfectus adesset;
Pingere qui vere posset vtrumque simul.
Tum quoque qui vitam tota, mortemque referret.
Ille magis multo doctus Apelle[19] foret.

The same in English Meter.
As Painters Art can skill, o Moore,
    Thy face here may we see:
Thy manners yet and vertues al
    To shew, hard would it be.
Would God some Painter might be had
    So perfect in his skill,
That truly face and manners both
    Could set foorth al at wil.
And then thy whole life, and thy death
    Could draw and make vs see.
Apelles learned hand could not
    Be better skild, than he.

NOTES

[1] Jane Dormer, Duchess of Feria, was born near Aylesbury in Buckinghamshire on January 6, 1538. Her mother died when she was four, and she was reared by her paternal grandmother, Jane, Lady Dormer. Her mother's father, Sir William Sidney, was the tutor and "governor" of Prince Edward (later Edward VI) and often brought Jane to play with him when he was at Ashbridge, near the Dormer home. She was later sent to the court of Queen Mary and remained with her during her entire reign, being described in the expense accounts for the queen's funeral as a gentlewoman of the Privy Chamber. A poem by Richard Edwards in praise of eight Ladies of Mary's Court (Howard, Dacars, Baynam, Arundel, Mancell, Dormer, Coke, and Briges) describes her thus: "Dormer is a darlinge and of suche lively hewe / that who so fedes his eyes on her may sone her bewte rue" (Leicester Bradner, ed., *The Life and Poems of Richard Edwards, Yale Studies in English*, 74 [New Haven, 1927], pp. 102, 94–95). She married Don Gomez Suarez de Figueroa y Cordova, Duke of Feria, a member of Philip II's council of state and captain of the Spanish guard. The marriage was opposed by her uncles, who thought the Spaniard was too old, too grave, and too foreign, but it was strongly supported by both Philip and Mary. Mary died, however, before the marriage could take place, and Jane left the court to live with her grandmother at the Savoy, in London. According to family tradition, the marriage took place there on December 29, 1558. The Duke of Feria refused on religious grounds to attend Queen Elizabeth's coronation and shortly afterward, because of deteriorating conditions, was commanded by Philip to leave the country. He departed with a group of English priests and religious—friends and relations of the Dormer family—about the end of May 1559. Lady Jane, who was pregnant at the time, remained at the Spanish embassy in London until suitable arrangements for her departure could be made. At the end of July 1559, Don Juan de Ayala arrived to escort her to Flanders. She was joined by her husband at Bruges and on September 28, 1559, gave birth to a son at Mechlin, in the house of Cardinal Granville. In March 1560, she proceeded with her husband to his principal estate at Zafra, in Estramadura. In 1571, the duke was appointed governor of the Spanish Netherlands but died before taking office. After her husband's death, Lady Jane petitioned Philip II to be allowed to settle in Flanders. The request was supported by Mary, Queen of Scots, and a number of English Catholics already established in the Low Countries, including Maurice Chauncey, Prior of the Carthusians; William Allen, founder of the English College at Douay; and Thomas Stapleton, author of *Tres Thomae*. The petition was denied, however, and Lady Jane remained at Zafra for the rest of her life. She took the habit of the third order of St. Francis and devoted herself to managing her husband's estates, aiding English exiles and prisoners in Spain, and building and restoring monasteries and churches. She never remarried. In her last years she wore a death's head fastened to her rosary and, like John Donne, had her coffin made and kept it with her in the house. She died at Madrid on January 23, 1612, attended by Father Cresswell, Provincial of the Jesuits in England, and was buried at Zafra in the church of St. Clara. Two portraits of Lady Jane hang in the Long Gallery of Burton Constable Hall, East Yorkshire. One, attributed to Zucchero, depicts her as a young woman in court dress; the other portrays her in the mourning garb of Spanish widows of the period, clutching a prayerbook and rosary.

Fowler's connection with the duchess may have been through her grandmother,

Jane, Lady Dormer, who accompanied her to the Low Countries in 1559 and settled in Louvain. She remained there until her death in 1571.

Most biographical accounts of Lady Jane go back to a manuscript life written in 1643 by Henry Clifford. Clifford had entered the service of the duchess in 1603. The tone is extremely adulatory and has affected all subsequent biographical work, including the sketch in the *DNB* and the most recent monograph on the subject by Sister Mary Cecily Dowling (*The Lady Jane Dormer Duchess de Feria 1538–1615*, Bridlington, 1970). The Clifford manuscript, still in the possession of the Dormer family, was edited by Joseph Stevenson, S.J., in 1887.

[2] Fowler probably refers to his translation from the Spanish of *A Brief Fourme of Confession* (*STC* 11181), to which he added More's *Treatise to Receive the Blessed Body of our Lord*, selections of his prayers and meditations, and "certaine Praiers . . . taken out of his Treatice vpon the Passion." Although the volume was published at Antwerp in 1576, the dedicatory letter to the Duchess of Feria is dated at Louvain, April 2, 1572, and is addressed primarily to her grief at the loss of her husband. The Duke of Feria died on September 8, 1571. It would appear that Fowler either dedicated *A Brief Fourme* to the duchess in 1572 and failed to publish until 1576 or (most likely) that there was a first edition of *A Brief Fourme* published in 1572, which is now lost. In the dedication to *A Brief Fourme*, Fowler also refers to "a brief Latin Chronicle . . . somewhat augmented . . . [by] my self," which he had previously dedicated "vnto that Noble Impe your Graces moste deare and onely Sonne" (sig. a₄r). Franklin B. Williams' *Index of Dedications and Commendatory Verses in English Books before 1641* (London, 1962), p. 55, lists only two works dedicated to Lady Jane, *A Brief Fourme* and *A Dialogue of Comfort*.

[3] Before Fowler's own edition, *A Dialogue of Comfort* was available in Tottel's quarto of 1553 or in Rastell's folio of 1557. Fowler's edition was printed in a small octavo, in keeping with his expressed desire to have the book "come forth againe in some smaller volume."

[4] El Conde Don Gomez Suarez de Figueroa y Cordova died after a brief illness on September 8, 1571, bequeathing to his wife "his soul, his honour, and his heir," along with a debt of 300,000 ducats. He is said to have been "open-handed, not always discriminating as to the recipients of his charity, and in some cases ready to give away what he did not possess" (Dowling, p. 29). By skillful management of his estate, Lady Jane cleared the debt before her son came of age. During his lifetime the duke held important positions of state under Philip II, frequently serving as his personal ambassador. In 1571 he was appointed governor of the Spanish Netherlands but died before taking office. He was an early supporter of the Jesuits in Spain and was instrumental in convincing Philip to allow a Jesuit Province to be established in the Netherlands. His interest in the Jesuits was probably aroused by his brother, Francis de Figueroa, who was a member of the Order. The duke was also a generous patron of other religious foundations, establishing the monastery of Our Lady de Monte-Virgine, near Villalva, and repairing at his own expense the houses of St. Onophrio de la Lapa and Our Lady del Rosario. In his dedication to *A Brief Fourme*, Fowler speaks of the duke's "liberalitie and passing Freenes in succouring poore Gentlemen and other in necessitie, . . . his Religious Deuotion toward God and his Catholique Churche, his faithful counsel to his Prince, his true and readie seruise in publike affaires at sundry times employed, [and] his valour and prowesse in Martial feates wel tried" (sig. a₃r).

⁵ "easy to handle"; see the *OED*, "handsome," *a.*1.

⁶ Don Lorenzo de Figueroa y Cordova, Marquis of Villalva, who was twelve years old at his father's death. He was born on September 28, 1559, at Mechlin. A second son, Pedro, was born in 1563, but he lived to be only three months old. After his father's death, Don Lorenzo was given the Encomienda of Seguera de la Sierra by the king and was sent for religious training to the Order of Santiago at Usles. In later life he served as ambassador to Philip II in some French affairs, became viceroy of Sicily, and died of a summer illness at Messina in 1611.

⁷ Catholic scholar and printer. Born at Bristol in 1537 and educated at the Winchester School and New College, Oxford, where he received his B.A. in 1556/57 and his M.A. in 1560. He married Alice Harris, the daughter of John Harris, Thomas More's secretary, and Dorothy Colley, Margaret Roper's maid. After the accession of Queen Elizabeth, Fowler left England and set up a printing press at Louvain, later moving it to Antwerp and Douay. He printed a number of important works by exiled English Catholics. Besides the 1573 edition of *A Dialogue of Comfort*, Fowler's own works include a translation of Peter Frarinus' *Oration against the unlawfull Insurrections of the Protestantes of our Time under pretence to reforme Religion* (Antwerp, 1566); *Ex Universa Summa . . . S. Thomae Aquinatis desumptae Conclusiones* (Antwerp, 1570); a translation of *A Brief Fourme of Confession*, to which Fowler added selections from More's works (Antwerp, 1576); *A Psalter for Catholics*; and epigrams and other verses. Anthony à Wood describes him as "well skill'd in the Greek and Latin tongues, a tolerable poet and orator, and a theologist not to be contemn'd. So learned he was also in criticisms, and other polite learning, that he might have passed for another Robert or Henry Stephens." He died at Namur in February 1578/79, and was buried near the body of John Harris in the church of St. John the Evangelist.

⁸ Job 7:1: "Militia est vita hominis super terram: et sicut dies mercenarii, dies ejus." Fowler's marginal glosses have been incorporated into the footnotes to the present text.

⁹ Job 14:1: "Homo natus de muliere, brevi vivens tempore, repletur multis miseriis."

¹⁰ Cf. Eph. 6:11: "Induite vos armaturam Dei, ut possitis stare adversus insidias diaboli."

¹¹ Tilley, H 410; Whiting, H 334.

¹² Echoing, as Fowler's gloss suggests, Heb. 11:3, "Fide intelligimus etc."

¹³ Tilley, M 129, who quotes Erasmus, *Similia*, 574E: "Ut nemo sentit qua parte stringat calceus, nisi qui indutus est." See also Whiting, S 266.

¹⁴ Fowler's marginal reference to Isa. 6 is to Isaiah's vision of God enthroned in glory, surrounded by seraphim (6:1–4). The reference to 1 Cor. 2 is to Paul's quotation of Isa. 64:4 in 1 Cor. 2:9: "Sed sicut scriptum est: quod oculus non videt nec auris audivit, nec in cor hominis ascendit, quae praeparavit Deus iis qui diligunt illum." Neither quotation refers specifically to a crown. The metaphor was probably taken from such verses as Jas. 1:12: "Beatus vir qui suffert tentationem, quoniam cum probatus fuerit, accipiet coronam vitae, quam repromisit Deus diligentibus se." See also 1 Pet. 5:4; Rev. 2:10.

15 At the time Fowler was writing, the Turks had occupied more of Europe than they had at the date of More's death. On the death of Zapolya in 1540, Ferdinand had invaded Hungary once again and offered to pay the Turks a yearly tribute of 100,000 gulden for the grant of the entire kingdom. Suleiman instead transformed Buda into a Turkish province under the control of a Pasha. It remained in Ottoman hands for 145 years. Fighting was renewed in 1543–44 and once again in 1551–52. In 1564 Ferdinand died and was succeeded by Maximilian II, who refused to ratify the Turkish tribute. War broke out once again. Suleiman died at the siege of Szigeth, and his successor, Selim II, inherited the Hungarian struggle. Fighting continued until February 17, 1568, when Maximilian signed a treaty of peace for eight years, agreeing to pay the Turks a yearly tribute of 30,000 ducats as a "gift of honor." From 1568 to 1593 fighting in Hungary consisted largely of border clashes. The major Turkish thrust had shifted to the Mediterranean.

16 "About three-fifths of the revenue [of the Ottoman empire at the beginning of the sixteenth century] were produced by the *kharaj* or capitation tax levied on all unbelieving subjects with the exception of priests, old men, and children under ten. It does not seem to have been oppressive; it was generally paid with docility; and the duties on exports and imports were so reasonable that commerce, which was mainly in the hands of Christians, was in a flourishing condition" (J. B. Bury, "The Ottoman Conquest" in *The Cambridge Modern History*, ed. A. W. Ward, *et al.* [London, 1902–11], I, 102). For further information on the Turkish system of kharâj, see the Commentary, above, n. to 190/30–191/16.

17 Famagosta, the last Venetian stronghold on Cyprus, fell to the Turks on August 1, 1571, after an eleven-month siege. The magistrates of the city and three hundred Christians were massacred after the surrender. Those who attempted to escape by ship to Crete were captured, dispossessed of all their property, and condemned to the galleys. Marcus Antonius Bragadenus, the commander of the garrison, had his nose and ears chopped off and, after being exhibited at various points throughout the city, was flayed alive. See R. Carr, trans., "The Narration of the warres of *Cyprus*" in *The Mahumetane or Turkish Historie* (London, 1600), sigs. Ff₁–Ff₂. Venice officially surrendered Cyprus to the Turks in March 1573.

18 An epigrammatic poem made up of six lines of verse. Fowler's translation is also a hexastichon in fourteeners, printed because of the length of the lines in ballad meter of six and eight.

19 Most renowned painter of antiquity. Famous for his mythological scenes and portraits of Philip and Alexander. Died at Cos, probably in the third century B.C. The tone of his pictures is said to have been produced by a secret varnish.

APPENDIX C

Table of Corresponding Pages:
The Corpus Christi Manuscript, The English
Works (1557), and The Yale Edition

APPENDIX C

Table of Corresponding Pages

Folio Numbers in Corpus MS	Page Numbers in 1557 Edition	Page Numbers in Yale Edition
1	1139	3
1^v	1139	3–4
2	1139–1140	4–5
2^v	1140	5
3	1140	6
3^v	1140	6–7
4	1140–1141	7
4^v	1141	7–8
5	1141	8–9
5^v	1141	9
6	1142	9–10
6^v	1142	10
7	1142	10–11
7^v	1142–1143	11–12
[f.8–f.9^v]*	1143	12–14
10	1144	14–15
10^v	1144	15
11	1144	15–16
11^v	1144–1145	16
12	1145	16–17
12^v	1145	17–18
13	1145	18
13^v	1145–1146	18–19
14	1146	19
14^v	1146	19–20
15	1146	20–21
15^v	1146	21
16	1146–1147	21–22
16^v	1147	22

* Fols. 8–9^v are lacking in the Corpus MS. See the Introduction.

Folio Numbers in Corpus MS	Page Numbers in 1557 Edition	Page Numbers in Yale Edition
17	1147	22–23
17ᵛ	1147	23–24
18	1147–1148	24
18ᵛ	1148	24–25
19	1148	25
19ᵛ	1148	25–26
20	1148	26
20ᵛ	1148–1149	26–27
21	1149	27–28
21ᵛ	1149	28
22	1149	28–29
22ᵛ	1149–1150	29
23	1150	29–30
23ᵛ	1150	30–31
24	1150	31
24ᵛ	1150	31–32
25	1150–1151	32–33
25ᵛ	1151	33
26	1151	33–34
26ᵛ	1151–1152	34–35
27	1152	35
27ᵛ	1152	35–36
28	1152	36
28ᵛ	1152–1153	36–37
29	1153	37–38
29ᵛ	1153	38
30	1153	38–39
30ᵛ	1153–1154	39
31	1154	39–40
31ᵛ	1154	40–41
32	1154	41
32ᵛ	1154–1155	41–42
33	1155	42–43
33ᵛ	1155	43
34	1155	43–44
34ᵛ	1155–1156	44–45
35	1156	45
35ᵛ	1156	45–46
36	1156	46

Folio Numbers in Corpus MS	Page Numbers in 1557 Edition	Page Numbers in Yale Edition
36ᵛ	1156	46–47
37	1156–1157	47–48
37ᵛ	1157	48
38	1157	48–49
38ᵛ	1157	49
39	1157–1158	49–50
39ᵛ	1158	50–51
40	1158	51
40ᵛ	1158	51–52
41	1158	52
41ᵛ	1158–1159	52–53
42	1159	53–54
42ᵛ	1159	54
43	1159	54–55
43ᵛ	1159–1160	55
44	1160	55–56
44ᵛ	1160	56–57
45	1160	57
45ᵛ	1160–1161	57–58
46	1161	58
46ᵛ	1161	58–59
47	1161	59–60
47ᵛ	1161–1162	60
48	1162	60–61
48ᵛ	1162	61
49	1162	61–62
49ᵛ	1162	62
50	1163	63
50ᵛ	1163	63–64
51	1163	64–65
51ᵛ	1163	65
52	1163–1164	65–66
52ᵛ	1164	66
53	1164	66–67
53ᵛ	1164	67
54	1164–1165	67–68
54ᵛ	1165	68
55	1165	68–69
55ᵛ	1165	69

Folio Numbers in Corpus MS	Page Numbers in 1557 Edition	Page Numbers in Yale Edition
56	1165	69–70
56ᵛ	1165–1166	70
57	1166	70–71
57ᵛ	1166	71
58	1166	71–72
58ᵛ	1166–1167	72
59	1167	72–73
59ᵛ	1167	73
60	1167	73–74
60ᵛ	1167–1168	74–75
61	1168	75
61ᵛ	1168	75–76
62	1168	76
62ᵛ	1168–1169	76–77
63	1169	77–78
63ᵛ	1169	78
64	1169	78–79
64ᵛ	1169–1170	79
65	1170	79–80
65ᵛ	1170	80
66	1170	80–81
66ᵛ	1170	81–82
67	1170–1171	82
67ᵛ	1171	82–83
68	1171	83–84
68ᵛ	1171	84
69	1171–1172	84–85
69ᵛ	1172	85
70	1172	85–86
70ᵛ	1172	86–87
71	1172–1173	87
71ᵛ	1173	87–88
72	1173	88
72ᵛ	1173	89
73	1173	89–90
73ᵛ	1173–1174	90–91
74	1174	91
74ᵛ	1174	91–92
75	1174–1175	92–93

Folio Numbers in Corpus MS	Page Numbers in 1557 Edition	Page Numbers in Yale Edition
75ᵛ	1175	93
76	1175	93–94
76ᵛ	1175	94–95
77	1175	95
77ᵛ	1175–1176	95–96
78	1176	96
78ᵛ	1176	96–97
79	1176	97–98
79ᵛ	1176–1177	98
80	1177	98–99
80ᵛ	1177	99
81	1177–1178	100
81ᵛ	1178	100–101
82	1178	101
82ᵛ	1178	101–102
83	1178	102–103
83ᵛ	1178–1179	103
84	1179	103–104
84ᵛ	1179	104–105
85	1179	105
85ᵛ	1179–1180	105–106
86	1180	106–107
86ᵛ	1180	107–108
87	1180–1181	108
87ᵛ	1181	108–109
88	1181	109
88ᵛ	1181	109–110
89	1181–1182	110–111
89ᵛ	1182	111
90	1182	111–112
90ᵛ	1182–1183	112–113
91	1183	113–114
91ᵛ	1183	114–115
92	1183	115
92ᵛ	1183–1184	115–116
93	1184	116–117
93ᵛ	1184	117
94	1184–1185	117–118
94ᵛ	1185	118–119

Folio Numbers in Corpus MS	Page Numbers in 1557 Edition	Page Numbers in Yale Edition
95	1185	119–120
95^v	1185	120
96	1185–1186	120–121
96^v	1186	121–122
97	1186	122–123
97^v	1186–1187	123–124
98	1187	124–125
98^v	1187	125
99	1187	126
99^v	1187–1188	126–127
100	1188	127–128
100^v	1188	128–129
101	1188–1189	129–130
101^v	1189	130–131
102	1189	131
102^v	1189	131–132
103	1189–1190	132–133
103^v	1190	133–134
104	1190	134
104^v	1190–1191	134–135
105	1191	135–136
105^v	1191	136–137
106	1191–1192	137–138
106^v	1192	139
107	1192	140
107^v	1192–1193	141
108	1193	141–142
108^v	1193	142–143
109	1193–1194	143–144
109^v	1194	144–145
110	1194	145–146
110^v	1194	146
111	1194–1195	146–147
111^v	1195	147–148
112	1195	148–149
112^v	1195–1196	149–150
113	1196	150–151
113^v	1196	151–152
114	1196–1197	152–153

Folio Numbers in Corpus MS	Page Numbers in 1557 Edition	Page Numbers in Yale Edition
114ᵛ	1197	153–154
115	1197	154
115ᵛ	1197–1198	154–155
116	1198	155–156
116ᵛ	1198–1199	156–157
117	1199	157–158
117ᵛ	1199	158–159
118	1199	159–160
118ᵛ	1199–1200	160
119	1200	160–161
119ᵛ	1200	161–162
120	1200–1201	162–163
120ᵛ	1201	163–164
121	1201	164
121ᵛ	1201–1202	164–165
122	1202 (misnumbered as 1124)	165–166
122ᵛ	1202	166–167
123	1202–1203	167–168
123ᵛ	1203 (misnumbered as 1205)	168–169
124	1203	169
124ᵛ	1203	169–170
125	1203 1204	170–171
125ᵛ	1204	171
126	1204–1205	171–172
126ᵛ	1205	172–173
127	1205	173–174
127ᵛ	1205	174–175
128	1205–1206	175–176
128ᵛ	1206	176
129	1206	176–177
129ᵛ	1206–1207	177–178
130	1207	178
130ᵛ	1207	178–179
131	1207–1208	179–180
131ᵛ	1208	180

Folio Numbers in Corpus MS	Page Numbers in 1557 Edition	Page Numbers in Yale Edition
132	1208	180–181
132ᵛ	1208	181–182
133	1208–1209	182–183
133ᵛ	1209	183
134	1209	183–184
134ᵛ	1209–1210	184–185
135	1210	185–186
135ᵛ	1210	186
136	1210–1211	186–187
136ᵛ	1211	187–188
137	1211	188
137ᵛ	1211	189
138	1211–1212	189–190
138ᵛ	1212	190
139	1212	190–191
139ᵛ	1212	191–192
140	1212–1213	192
140ᵛ	1213	192–193
141	1213	193
141ᵛ	1213	193–194
142	1213–1214	194–195
142ᵛ	1214	195
143	1214	196
143ᵛ	1214–1215	196–197
144	1215	197–198
144ᵛ	1215	198–199
145	1215–1216	199–200
145ᵛ	1216	200–201
146	1216–1217	201–202
146ᵛ	1217	202–203
147	1217–1218	203–204
147ᵛ	1218	204–205
148	1218	205–206
148ᵛ	1218–1219	206–207
149	1219	207–208
149ᵛ	1219	208–209
150	1220	209–210
150ᵛ	1220	210–211
151	1220–1221	211–212

Folio Numbers in Corpus MS	Page Numbers in 1557 Edition	Page Numbers in Yale Edition
151ᵛ	1221	212–213
152	1221–1222	213–214
152ᵛ	1222	214
153	1222	214–215
153ᵛ	1222–1223	215–216
154	1223	216–217
154ᵛ	1223	217–218
155	1223–1224	218–219
155ᵛ	1224	219–220
156	1224	220–221
156ᵛ	1224–1225	221–222
157	1225	222–223
157ᵛ	1225–1226	223–224
158	1226	224
158ᵛ	1226	224–225
159	1226–1227	225–226
159ᵛ	1227	226–227
160	1227–1228	227–228
160ᵛ	1228	228–229
161	1228	229–230
161ᵛ	1228–1229	230–231
162	1229	231
162ᵛ	1229	232
163	1229–1230	232–234
163ᵛ	1230	234–235
164	1230–1231	235–236
164ᵛ	1231	236–237
165	1231–1232	237–238
165ᵛ	1232	238–239
166	1232	239–240
166ᵛ	1232–1233	240–241
167	1233	241–242
167ᵛ	1233–1234	242–243
168	1234	243–244
168ᵛ	1234–1235	244–245
169	1235	245–246
169ᵛ	1235–1236	246–247
170	1236	247–248
170ᵛ	1236	248–249

Folio Numbers in Corpus MS	Page Numbers in 1557 Edition	Page Numbers in Yale Edition
171	1236–1237	249
171ᵛ	1237	249–251
172	1237–1238	251–252
172ᵛ	1238	252
173	1238–1239	252–253
173ᵛ	1239	253–254
174	1239	254–255
174ᵛ	1239–1240	255–256
175	1240	256–258
175ᵛ	1240	258–259
176	1240–1241	259–260
176ᵛ	1241	260–261
177	1241–1242	261–262
177ᵛ	1242	262
178	1242	262–263
178ᵛ	1242–1243	264–265
179	1243	265–266
179ᵛ	1243	266–267
180	1243–1244	267–268
180ᵛ	1244	268–269
181	1244–1245	269–270
181ᵛ	1245	270–272
182	1245	272–273
182ᵛ	1245–1246	273–274
183	1246	274–275
183ᵛ	1246	275–276
184	1246–1247	276–277
184ᵛ	1247	277–278
185	1247	278
185ᵛ	1247–1248	278–279
186	1248	279–280
186ᵛ	1248	280–281
187	1248–1249	281–282
187ᵛ	1249	282–283
188	1249–1250	283–284
188ᵛ	1250	284–285
189	1250	285–286
189ᵛ	1250–1251	286–287
190	1251	287–288

Folio Numbers in Corpus MS	Page Numbers in 1557 Edition	Page Numbers in Yale Edition
190ᵛ	1251–1252	288–289
191	1252	289–290
191ᵛ	1252	290–291
192	1252	291–292
192ᵛ	1252–1253	292–293
193	1253	293–294
193ᵛ	1253–1254	294–295
194	1254	295–296
194ᵛ	1254	296–297
195	1254–1255	297–298
195ᵛ	1255	298–299
196	1255	299–300
196ᵛ	1255–1256	300–301
197	1256	301–302
197ᵛ	1256–1257	302–303
198	1257	303–304
198ᵛ	1257	304–305
199	1257–1258	305–306
199ᵛ	1258	306–307
200	1258	307–308
200ᵛ	1258–1259	308
201	1259	308–309
201ᵛ	1259	309–310
202	1259–1260	310–311
202ᵛ	1260	311–312
203	1260	312–313
203ᵛ	1260	313–314
204	1261	314
204ᵛ	1261	314–315
205	1261–1262	315–316
205ᵛ	1262	316–317
206	1262–1263	317–318
206ᵛ	1263	318–319
207	1263–1264	319–320

GLOSSARY

GLOSSARY

The glossary is not a complete concordance, but it does contain words occurring in *A Dialogue of Comfort* whose forms and meanings are not easily recognizable. In general, if a word occurs more than twice, only the first instance, followed by "*etc.*," is cited. Cross references have been supplied for unusual variant spellings. The abbreviation "*See n.*" refers the reader to the Commentary, where the particular word or phrase is discussed. Unusual spellings of proper names have been included. No attempt has been made, however, to record systematically such normal sixteenth-century spelling variants as *y* for *i*, *ys* for *is* or *es*, *s* for *c* or *c* for *s*, *c* for *t* in *-cion*, *en* for *in*, etc. The reduced definite article *th-*, which is often combined in the text with a following noun or pronoun beginning with a vowel (e.g., *thentent* "the intent"), is ignored in the glossary.

abassh *v.* confound 288/15

abatid *pp.* subdued, cast down 306/3

abbredge *v.* shorten, cut in duration 194/5

a bed *adv.* in bed 29/11, 45/31

abhominable *adj. See* **ab(h)omynable**

abhomynacion *n. See* **ab(h)omynacion**

abhore *v. See* **ab(h)or(r)e**

abide, abyde *v.* stand firm 17/29 *etc.*; remain 72/21 *etc.*; put up with 94/26, 142/2; *abide by* remain true to 32/6 *etc.*; *pt.* **abode** 95/30

abiect *n.* outcast, one cast off 16/23

ab(h)omynable, ab(h)ominable *adj.* detestable, loathsome 57/24 *etc.*

ab(h)omynacion *n.* abhorrence, loathing 150/18 *etc.*

ab(h)or(r)e *v.* dread, shrink from 280/4; disgust 307/23

abou(gh)t, a bought, a bowt *prep.* about, around 61/16 *etc.*; on account of 232/10

above *prep.* beyond 97/22 *etc.*

abrode *adv.* abroad, outside, from without 5/27 *etc.*; out 90/21

ab(o)undaunce *n.* abundance 65/1; quantity, amount 151/23

abuseth *v. pr. 3 s.* takes bad advantage of 151/10 *etc.*

abyde *v. See* **abide**

Acam *n.* Achan 26/9

accidentes *n. pl.* accessories, non-essential qualities 256/17 *etc.*; incidents, occurrences 277/30

accompt, a compt *n.* account, reckoning 25/24, 222/10–11

accompt *v.* reckon, consider 71/22 *etc.*

accustume *v. refl. accustume them . . . in* accustom themselves to 198/26; *pp.* **accustumyd** trained, familiarized 214/10

Achas *n.* Ahab 95/24

a compt *n. See* **accompt**

acquentid, acquentyd *ppl. a.* familiar, customary 29/11 *etc.*

acquietyng *vbl. n.* bringing to rest, quieting, pacification 184/12

adayes *adv. now adayes* at present 242/23

admendment *n.* amendment, correction 161/24. *See n.*

aduertise *v.* notify, inform 195/23

aduertisement, advertisement *n.* advice, instruction 240/22, 282/15

aduisement *n.* consideration, pondering 243/24–25

adventure, aduenture, a venture *n.* chance occurrence, accident 222/17 *etc.*;

at adventure, at a venture recklessly 31/20; at random 117/1, 147/17; *stand at his own aduenture* take his own chances, shift for himself 45/29

adventure *v.* venture, hazard oneself 99/14, 135/1

advertisement *n.* See **aduertisement**

advise *n.* advice, counsel 120/22 *etc.*

advise *v.* ponder, consider 264/29

a(y)er *n.* air 101/22 *etc.*

aferd(e), a ferd *adj.* afraid 93/22 *etc.* See *also* **ferd**

affeccion(e), affection(e), effeccion, effection *n.* state of mind, mental inclination 83/23 *etc.*; attachment 171/9; *pl.* emotions, feelings, passions 51/13 *etc.*; *affeccion of* disposition toward 205/13

a flote *adv.* afloat 6/13

a flyght *ppl. a.* afflicted, distressed 9/9

afore *adv.* previously, already, before 3/9 *etc.* See *also* **fore**

a fore *prep.* before 18/28 *etc.*

afore hand *adv.* beforehand 9/11

aforesaid *ppl. a.* previously spoken 37/5

aforth *v.* supply, provide 116/28

Afryque *n.* Africa 130/15

after *adv.* afterwards 8/27 *etc.*

after *conj. after as* according to the way in which 64/22 *etc.*

after *prep.* according to 36/30 *etc.*

agayne *adv.* in return 39/15 *etc.*

agayne *prep.* against 151/20 *etc.*; *mych part agayne.* See **mich**

agayne say *v.* deny, disagree with 274/6

agaynward *adv.* on the contrary, on the other hand 71/11

aggreue *v.* make more serious, aggravate 256/25

agrevid *ppl. a.* weighed down, distressed 187/19

agrice *v.* shudder with terror, be horrified 198/14

ague *n.* acute or violent fever 147/23

ake *v.* ache 219/5

alacrite *n.* alacrity, cheerful readiness 65/4

albeit that *conj.* although, granted that 3/13 *etc.*

alfe *n.* half 177/24

alies *n. pl.* relatives, kin 202/24

all *conj.* although, even if 33/7 *etc.*

allectiue *n.* attraction, allurement 201/9;

pl. **allectives, allectyves** 200/10, 201/4–5

alledge *v.* bring forth, plead as an excuse 237/22

allmoise *n.* See **al(l)moise**

all redy(e) *adv.* already 6/16 *etc.*

allway, allwey *adv.* See **al(l)way**

Almayne *adj.* German 214/4, 320/15

Almayne, Almaigne *n.* Germany 213/6, 259/28

al(l)moise, almoyse, almouse *n. pl.* alms 72/8 *etc.*

a lofe *adv.* at a distance 268/9

a long *adv.* at full length 275/2

a low *adv.* low, downward 96/18

alow *v.* allow, concede 9/10 *etc.*; commend, approve, praise 217/23 *etc.*

althyng *adv.* wholly, completely, altogether 202/18

al(l)way, al(l)wey *adv.* always 20/26 *etc.*

amblers *n. pl.* 119/15. See *n.*

amend *v.* fix, rearrange 60/22

amendes *n. pl.* restitution 178/25

a mendid *ppl. a.* amended, improved, recovered 86/5

among *adv.* occasionally, now and again 59/20, 188/18

amyd *adv.* in the midst 268/10

Ancres *n. pl.* See **ankers**

ancresses *n. pl.* anchoresses, female hermits 276/26–27

and *conj.* if 43/16 *etc.*; *& yf,* if 278/11

anelyng *n.* sacrament of extreme unction, anointing 65/29

angre *n.* anger 124/1 *etc.*

angre *v.* anger, make angry 124/17

an hungred, an hungerd *ppl. a.* hungry 117/17, 307/13

ankers, Ancres *n. pl.* anchorites, male hermits 129/16, 276/26

anone, a non *adv.* at once, immediately 117/19 *etc.*

any thyng *adv.* in any measure, to any extent 6/18 *etc.*

a pace, apace *adv.* with speed, quickly 48/19 *etc.*

a part *adv.* separately 20/13

ap(p)er(e) *v.* seem 3/17 *etc.*; appear 31/14 *etc.*

apocalips, Apocalyps *n.* Book of Revelation 194/3 *etc.*

apon *prep.* upon 24/6 *etc.*

ap(p)oynt *v.* direct, prescribe 21/22, 179/1; arrange, settle 128/2 *etc.*; bestow, grant 230/18; *pt. refl.* **apoyntid** (**them**) resolved, made up their minds 295/10

apperteynyth *v. pr. 3 s.* is proper or appropriate 161/22

appetite *n.* desire 16/25 *etc.*

appoyntid *ppl. a.* arranged, previously determined 128/5, 159/2

appoyntment *n.* purpose 159/15; decision, resolution 196/13 *etc.*; covenant 230/21

appoyntynges *vbl. n. pl.* purposes 159/14

aquiete *v.* quiet, calm 121/19

are *adv. See* **er(e)**

Aron *n.* Aaron 18/3

arow *adv.* in a row, one after another 289/17

array *n.* military order 110/5

as *conj.* that 3/23 *etc.*; where 70/17 *etc.*

askith *v. pr. 3 s.* deserves, merits 34/10

asonder, a sondre, a sundre *adv.* asunder, apart 6/27, 189/1; scattered, dispersed 177/18

asperite *n.* harshness, severity 204/25

assaut, assawt *n.* assault 107/21 *etc.*

assawte *v.* assault 153/15–16

assay *n.* trial, testing 3/24 *etc.*; *pl.* attempts 155/10

assay *v.* test, try, attempt 60/22 *etc.*

assendid *v. pt.* ascended 292/6

assistyng *pr. p.* present in 121/18

assoyle, assoile *v.* absolve from sin, pardon 109/30, 218/13

asspire *v.* breathe (into) 198/27

asswage *v.* assuage, mitigate 6/18 *etc.*

a sundre *adv. See* **asonder**

at *prep.* from 43/11 *etc.*; in 67/20 *etc.*; before 47/20; *at rouers. See* **rouers**

a thurst *ppl. a.* thirsty 307/14

attaynder *n.* condemnation 264/13

attayne (**to**) *v.* reach 10/27; happen 203/12

attayntid *ppl. a.* convicted 264/3, 268/28

atteynyng, attaynyng (**to**) *vbl. n.* acquiring, obtaining 287/24, 307/1

atwayne *adv.* apart, asunder 315/14

atwo *adv.* in two 302/15

auaile, avayle *v.* benefit, profit 12/14 *etc.*

auct(h)orit(i)e, aut(h)orite, aucthoryte *n.* authority, power, influence 44/12 *etc.*

audience *n.* formal hearing or interview 213/14

aught *pron. See* **ought**

austerite *n.* austerity 131/1

Austyn(e), Austen, Austeyne *n.* Augustine 130/16 *etc.*

availe *n.* benefit, profit 34/5

avantage *n.* advantage 169/16

avaunt *v.* be off, depart 155/7

avoyd *v.* refute, disprove 262/12

a way *adv.* away 5/2 *etc.*; *can away with* can endure, tolerate 83/32–84/1

awght *pron. See* **ought**

a worke *adv.* set . . . *a worke. See* **set(t)**

axe *n. See* **chipp(e) axe**

ayer *n. See* **a(y)er**

bace *adj. See* **base**

bageard *n.* badger 115/17

bak(k)(e) *n.* back 43/12 *etc.*

bake *adv.* back 118/21 *etc.*

ball *v.* bawl, howl 222/1

ballyng *ppl. a.* bawling, barking, howling 295/19

banke *n. See* **pyn banke**

bare *adj.* mere, simple, without addition 32/29 *etc.*

base, bace *adj.* low, lowly, inferior 26/32 *etc.*

Bassawes *n. pl.* Bashaws, Turkish nobles 206/17

batayl(e) *n.* battle 62/11 *etc.*

bay *n.* position of a hunted animal when unable to flee further 140/23

bayerdes *n. poss.* 11/11. *See* n.

be *v. pr. pl.* are 6/5 *etc.*; *pp.* **be, byn** 80/2 *etc.*

be, bi *prep.* by 72/15 *etc.*

become *v.* befit, be suitable for 231/30

bed bord *n.* flat slab of board beneath a mattress 275/1

bedes *n. pl.* rosary beads 115/27

be fall *v.* happen, take place 203/3

beforce *adv.* by force 142/6, 301/24

before *adv.* already, previously 12/13 *etc.*

begil(e) *v.* beguile, deceive 28/11 *etc.*; *pp.* **bygilid, begild** 200/15, 266/2

begynne *v.* begin 256/22; *pp.* **begon(n)e** 89/12 *etc.*

behalfe *n. in that behalfe* in that matter 73/22

behed *v.* behead 55/3; *pp.* **beheddid** 246/31

behoueable *adj.* profitable, advantageous 22/28

beleve, belive *n.* belief 37/25, 109/8

beleve, belive, bileve, byleve *v.* believe 5/9 *etc.*

bely *n.* belly 167/21 *etc.*

benefice *n.* ecclesiastical living, income from certain church offices 161/26

beneficed *ppl. a.* holding a benefice or ecclesiastical living 214/19

beneth, byneth *adv.* beneath, below 106/10 *etc.*

bent *n.* incentive, encouragement 175/28

bere *v.* bear, carry 29/1 *etc.*; hold, possess 191/4 *etc.*; endure 247/16 *etc.*; *bere a rule* bear authority, possess power 219/18; *bere . . . in hand* maintain 99/6; *bere in mynd* remember 84/15; *bere . . . record. See* **record**; *bere . . . vpp* lift up, exalt 158/9–10 *etc.*; *pt.* **bare** 210/19; *pp.* **born(e)** 192/5 *etc.*

berevyng *vbl. n.* taking away 244/18

beried, beryed *pp.* buried 53/18, 194/14

berive *v.* deprive, rob 142/6; *pp.* **birevid, byreft, byrevyd** 115/9 *etc.*

beryng *vbl. n.* enduring 312/5; *beryng downe* oppressing 225/5

besech *v.* beseech 36/2 *etc.*

beseme *v.* suit 11/15

beset *v.* bestow, devote 4/13

beshrew *v.* invoke evil upon, curse 125/20

besid(e) *adv. See* **biside**

besid(e) *prep.* besides, in addition to 131/24; outside of, irrelevant to 160/7

besieth *v. pr. 3 s. besieth his wit about* occupies himself with, is concerned about 214/13

besines *n. See* **bissines**

be(e)st *n.* beast 65/19 *etc.*

bestly *adj.* beastly 29/13, 51/14

bestough *v.* bestow 227/23

besy, bisy, bysy *adj.* concerned, solicitous 16/31 *etc.*; feverishly active, excessively worldly 167/9

besynes *n. See* **bissines**

betaken *pp.* handed over, given up 191/13

bethinke, bethynke *v. refl.* collect one's thoughts 59/21 *etc.*; consider 164/7; *pt. and pp.* **bethought** 8/26 *etc.*

bethynkyng *vbl. n. bethynkyng vs of* considering, reflecting upon 85/2

betith *v. pr. 3 s.* beats 48/12; *pt.* **bett** 292/1; *pp.* **bet(t)en, betyn** 46/1 *etc.*

betwene *prep. passe betwene. See* **passe**

be tyme, betyme, by tyme *adv.* early, without delay 297/18; in good time, before it is too late 29/4, 235/9

betymes *adv.* early, soon, speedily 102/21, 298/15

bewrap(p)id *ppl. a.* enveloped, involved 60/18, 204/5

bewtie *n.* beauty 10/2 *etc.*

bewychid *pp.* bewitched 169/23

bi *prep. See* **be**

bich *n. See* **bych(e)**

bid, byd *v.* ask, command 11/20 *etc.*; *pt.* **bode** 26/11 *etc.*; *pp.* **bidden, bode** 121/20, 197/28. *See also* **forbed(e)**

bild *v.* build 180/21 *etc.*; *pp.* **bildyd** built 272/19

bileve *v. See* **beleve**

billes *n. pl.* prescriptions 11/5

birevid *pp. See* **berive**

biside, besid(e), by side *adv.* besides, in addition 30/10 *etc.*

bisily *adv. See* **bysily**

bisprent *ppl. a.* besprinkled, strewn 95/26

bissines, bisynes, besines, besynes, bysynes, bysines *n.* activity, occupation 57/18 *etc.*; feverish activity, excessive concern for worldly matters 105/21 *etc.*

bisy *adj. See* **besy**

bitter, bittre, byttre *adj.* painful, grievous 67/3 *etc.*

bitterly *adv.* grievously, with strong emotion 94/19

bittre *adv.* full of affliction, painfully, grievously 200/9

blak *adj.* black 60/1 *etc.*; *comp.* **blaker** 283/21

blaspamye *n.* blasphemy 201/7

blayne *n.* blister, inflammation 219/6

blo(w)de, bloud *n.* blood 11/26 *etc.*; descendants 208/1; *let . . . bloud. See* **let(t)**

blont *adv.* bluntly 213/20

blys *n.* bliss 244/21

bode *v. pt. and pp. See* **bid**

bold *adj.* audacious, presumptuous 22/22 *etc.*

boldnes *n.* presumption 299/30

bolles *n. pl.* bowls, balls used in game of bowls 115/28

bolt *n.* arrow 49/19, 50/8

bolteth *v. pr. 3 s.* fastens, fetters 274/23

boltyng *vbl. n.* fettering, imprisonment with fetters 270/20

bond *adj.* slavish, pertaining to bondage 253/23

bond *n.* slave 253/16, 18; *pl.* bounds, limits 218/26

bondman, bond man *n.* one in bondage, slave 253/4 *etc.*

bone *n.* boon, favor 36/8, 165/13

bord(e) *n.* table used for meals 213/17 *etc.* *See also* **bed bord**

born(e) *pp. See* **bere**

bost *n.* boast 214/2, 253/15

bost *v.* boast 207/30, 253/9

boteth *v. pr. 3 s. yt boteth no man* it is fruitless for anyone 14/26

bounden, bownden *pp.* confined, obligated 97/19 *etc.*

bousoms *n. pl.* bosoms 240/9

Bowda *n. See* **Buda**

boysteouse, boystuouse *adj.* rough, violent 29/6, 192/3

boystuously *adv.* boisterously, roughly, violently 132/4

brache *n.* hound which hunts by scent 295/25

brades *n. pl. See* **brayde**

brake *v. pt. See* **breke**

brakyd *pp. See* **breke**

brall *v.* wrangle, quarrel 273/10

brayde *n.* attack, assault 199/6; *pl.* **brades** outbursts of passion 253/20

brayne pan *n.* skull 302/16

brede *n.* bread 279/13

brede *n.* breadth 5/12

brede *v.* dwell, flourish 13/17

brefely *adv.* briefly 105/11

breke *v.* break 57/5 *etc.*; *breke . . . her stomak* 29/18–19. *See n.*; *pt.* **brake** revealed one's mind, disclosed one's thoughts 127/20; *pp.* **brakyd** broken, 271/9; *brake . . . my fast* had my breakfast 157/12

brere *n.* briar 50/20, 241/1

breth *v.* breathe 320/24

brod(e) *adj.* broad 103/24 *etc.*

brosyng *vbl. n.* bruising 102/21

brote *pp.* brought 267/19; **brought (in)** deceived 94/23

brotle *adj.* brittle, perishable 224/22

browes *n. pl.* foreheads 274/22

brydle *v.* curb, check, restrain 282/23

bryge *n.* bridge 92/12

brymme *adj.* strongly current, much spoken of 6/19; fierce, raging 152/28

brynke *n.* edge, perimeter 167/26

buck(e)ler *n.* small round shield 106/8, 225/10

Buda, Bowda *n.* Hungarian city 124/15, 192/23. *See n.*

bugge *n.* object of terror, bogey 60/1

bumblyng *ppl. a.* buzzing, humming; (also perhaps) bungling, blundering 167/5

burdenouse *adj.* burdensome 31/16, 32/13

burdeyne *n.* burden 83/21

buske *v. refl.* betake oneself, hasten 83/29, 295/11

but (if, yf) *conj.* unless 7/7 *etc.*; **but onely** except 93/5

butte *n.* archery target 159/15

by *prep.* through, by means of 8/24 *etc.*; during 38/22; *by that* because 175/15; *By my trouth. See* **trouth**

by(e) *v.* buy 116/27, 169/6; *pr. 3 s.* **bieth** 169/18

by & by *adv.* immediately, at once 159/3 *etc.*

bych(e), bich *n.* female dog 294/19 *etc.*

byde *v.* remain, stay 264/17

bygilid *pp. See* **begil(e)**

byhold *v. pt.* beheld 169/1

byhest *n. land of byhest* promised land 60/8

byleve *v. See* **beleve**

byn *pp. See* **be**

byndeth *v. pr. 3 s.* obliges, requires 6/7

byndid *pp.* bound 63/13

byneth *adv. See* **beneth**

byneth *prep.* beneath 55/17, 167/22

byrevyd, byreft *pp. See* **berive**

bys *prep.* by his 313/28

by side *adv. See* **biside**

bysily, bisily, bysyly *adv.* busily, actively 158/5 *etc.*; mischievously, insidiously 167/3 *etc.*

bysines *n. See* **bissines**

bysy *adj. See* **besy**

bysyly *adv. See* **bysily**

bysynes *n. See* **bissines**
byttre *adj. See* **bitter**
by tyme *adv. See* **be tyme**

cable rope *n.* thick rope by which a ship's anchor is fastened 171/2, 19
cach *v.* gain, derive 38/1
cakebrede *n.* bread made in flattened cakes 69/27
Cams *n. poss.* Cham's, Khan's 259/29. *See n.*
can *v.* know 117/8; *can skyll of* have skill in, have knowledge of 295/21. *See n.*
candy *n.* Candia, Crete 190/21. *See n.*
cannid *pp. cannid . . . thanke* expressed thanks, thanked 185/12–13
cant *v.* divide, parcel out 273/3
carde *v.* play cards 273/11
careles *adj.* negligent, indifferent 14/19; unconcerned, without apprehension 92/20
carter *n.* one who drives a cart 208/19
Carvers *n. poss.* of a woodcarver 143/27
case *n.* condition, situation 5/4 *etc.; put . . . case* suppose, propose a hypothetical situation 196/11 *etc.; pl. casis of . . . conscience* practical questions about which the conscience may be in doubt 147/4
cast *n. at the last cast* at the last shift, in extremities, near to death or ruin 91/2
cast *v.* consider, ponder, deliberate 8/30 *etc.;* send forth 59/20 *etc.; cast in his teth* reproach or upbraid him 232/4; *cast so ferre perell* anticipate such a perilous outcome 125/8
castell *n.* village 43/3, 311/23. *See n.*
castyng *vbl. n.* thrusting 151/11; *castyng bakke* weakening, relapse 78/19
casuall *adj.* subject to chance, precarious 207/7
causeles *adv.* without cause, without reason 293/5
Cayphas *n.* Caiaphas 279/29, 30
cellerer *n.* officer in a monastery in charge of the cellar or provisions 185/28
chapleyns *n. pl.* chaplains 46/9
charge *n.* care, responsibility 183/4; *at his . . . charge* at his expense or cost, *i.e.* in his employ, in his service 188/23–24
chargyd (**with**) *ppl. a.* responsible (for) 183/1

charibdis, charibdes *n.* Charybdis 120/12 *etc.*
charterouse *adj.* Carthusian 276/23
chasteseth *v. pr. 3 s.* chastises 43/20 *etc.*
chaunce *n.* event, happening, occurrence 125/25 *etc.*
chaung *n.* change 52/2 *etc.*
chekes *n. pl.* cheeks 290/23
chekyn(s), chikyns *n. pl.* chickens 103/32 *etc.*
chepe *adj.* inexpensive, easily obtained 249/12
chepe *n. bettre chepe, better chepe* more cheaply 116/28 *etc.*
chere *n.* countenance, expression of the face 215/20
chery *adj.* cherry 285/16
chese, chose, chuse *v.* choose 22/1 *etc.; to chuse adv. phr.* by choice 277/4
cheuerell *n. cheuerell poynt* 120/5. *See n.*
cheving *vbl. n.* outcome, fortune 191/16
chiefe *adv.* chiefly, mainly 219/17
chikyns *n. pl. See* **chekyn(s)**
childhed *n.* childhood 198/26, 285/16
Chio *n.* Chios 190/21. *See n.*
chipp(e) axe *n.* small hand axe 125/10, 23
chone *pron. See* **euery chone**
chose *v. See* **chese**
choyse, choise *n.* choice 21/31 *etc.*
chuse *v. See* **chese**
chypps *n. pl. mater . . . of .iij. chypps* matter of trifling consequence 277/28
Cicile *n.* Sicily 188/14
Cipris *n.* Cyprus 190/21
Civill *n.* Seville 256/4
claues *n. pl.* claws 104/1
clene *adj.* complete 55/31
clene *adv.* wholly, completely 8/26 *etc.*
clenly *adj.* morally or spiritually clean 158/20
clensing *ppl. a. clensing dayes* 115/5. *See n.*
clere *adv.* completely, entirely 185/24
clipid *pp.* encompassed, closely surrounded 107/15
cloke *n.* cloak 109/20
clokketh *v. pr. 3 s.* clucks, calls 104/17, 20
clokkyng *vbl. n.* clucking, calling 104/19
close *adj.* enclosed, cloistered 80/1, 276/26. *See n.; kepe . . . close* stay concealed, unobserved 133/19
close *n.* enclosed field 119/5

cloth *n.* woolen fabric 210/8

clymyd *v. pt.* climbed 176/7

cofer *n.* coffer, treasure chest 210/20

cokke *n. sett cokke a hope* let the liquor flow 99/11. *See n.*

cold *v.* could 83/5 *etc.*

cole *v.* cool 55/19

coler *v.* collar, grab or fasten by the neck 272/22; *pr. 3 s.* **collereth** 274/22–23; *pp.* **colorid** 256/1

coleryng *vbl. n.* imprisonment with a collar around the neck 270/20

collacion(s) *n.* discourse, treatise, title of work of Cassian 84/5–6, 129/11

collereth *v. pr. 3 s. See* **coler**

colletes *n. pl.* collects, short prayers 46/17. *See n.*

colorid *pp. See* **coler**

colour *n.* semblance, appearance, plausible reason 73/19 *etc.*; choler, bile, one of the four humors 150/12

comaundid *pp.* commanded 57/24

combraunce *n.* encumbrance, burden 214/23

combrid, combred, cumbred *ppl. a.* encumbered, burdened 30/4 *etc.*

comen *adj.* public, communal 20/21 *etc.* *See also* **comen weale**

com(m)en *pp.* come 26/22 *etc.*

comen *v. comen . . . vppon* discuss, consider 199/15

comendacion *n.* approval 289/27

comen weale, comen well *n.* public welfare, general good 162/22; body politic, state 113/30

comfort, c(o)umfort(e) *n.* strength, encouragement, consolation 3/1 *etc. See n.*

comfortable, confortable, c(o)umfortable *adj.* strengthening, consoling, encouraging 3/20 *etc.*

comfortles, cumfortles *adj.* without consolation or encouragement 4/2 *etc.*

comfortyng *vbl. n.* giving strength or encouragement 4/9 *etc.*

commendid *pp.* recommended, approved 141/4

commodiouse *adj. See* **com(m)odiouse**

commodite, commodytie *n. See* **comoditie**

communycacion, com(m)unicacion *n.* conversation, discussion 38/3 *etc.*

communid *v. pt.* talked together, conversed 79/1

commytt *v.* entrust 320/17

com(m)odiouse *adj.* beneficial, advantageous 209/7 *etc.*

comoditie, commodite, commodytie *n.* advantage, benefit 41/1 *etc.*

companid *pp.* accompanied 39/33

comparid (with) *pp.* made comparable to 49/2–3

compas(se) *n.* ring, circle 106/23; enclosed space 193/31; time span 208/23

compas(s)(e) (about) *v.* encompass, surround 105/19–20 *etc.*

compasyng *ppl. a.* encompassing, enclosing 106/24

complayne *v. trans.* bewail 232/7; *pr. 3 s.* **compleynyth** laments 21/4

complexcions *n. pl.* temperaments, combinations of the four bodily humors 150/2. *See n.*

comprehendith *v. pr. 3 s.* includes, describes in summary 105/11–12

compt *n.* reckoning, estimation 253/32, 291/23. *See also* **accompt**

comptith, countith *v. pr. 3 s.* regards, reckons 8/6, 25/31; *pt.* **counptid** 59/19

comyng *vbl. n. comyng in* submission, yielding, conversion 194/9

conceve *v.* form a mental idea of 211/14; *pt.* **concevid in** decided on, devised 22/1

conceyte *n.* conception, notion, imagining 112/5

concident *adj.* coincident, of the same nature 103/18. *See n.*

conclude *v.* overcome in argument, confute 237/11, 262/15

condecendid *v. pt. condecendid vnto* concurred, agreed with 179/11

condempn *v.* condemn 93/17 *etc.*

condempnid *ppl. a.* condemned 265/6 *etc.*

condicion *n.* personal quality 218/15 *etc.*

condicionally *adv.* a term of logic 198/9. *See n.*

conduce *v.* lead, conduct 120/16

confesse *v.* avow, declare 198/6

confession *n.* declaration, avowal 255/7

confeteryd *pp.* confederated, allied 7/3

confirme *v.* conform 68/18 *etc.*; *pp.* **confirmid, confyrmyd** strengthened 249/6, 262/26

confirmyng *vbl. n.* conforming, agreement 71/4, 74/12

confirmyte, conformyte *n.* conformity, compliance 71/16 *etc.*

conflyte *n.* conflict 21/1

conformable *adj.* disposed to conform or agree 175/30

conformyte *n. See* **confirmyte**

confortable *adj. See* **comfortable**

confoundid *pp.* utterly defeated, brought to ruin 76/26–27

confucion *n.* confounding, refutation 47/13

coniurere *n.* conjurer, medium 62/30

connyng *adj. See* **con(n)yng**

connyng *n.* wisdom, knowledge 90/3, 99/3

conserue *v.* preserve, keep safe 198/29

consideracion *n. consideracion of* regard for 130/24; *with the . . . consideracion of* due to the fact of 241/22; *pl.* motives, reasons 120/27

consonaunt *adj.* in agreement 143/11

constrewed *pp.* interpreted 39/25

contempnyng *vbl. n.* scorning 154/1

contrary wise *adv.* on the other hand, on the contrary 154/6

contrepayse *v.* counterbalance, compensate for 210/13; *pt.* **conterpaysid** 313/18

contumelies *n. pl.* insolent reproaches, contemptuous treatment 191/16

contymneth *v. pr. 3 s.* scorns, views with contempt 61/2

contynently *adv.* immediately, without interruption 106/18. *See n.*

contynew *v.* continue 83/11, 86/3

contynuaunce *n.* duration, period 311/3

conuersaunt *adj.* dwelling, actively present 195/23, 241/22

convenient *adj.* suitable, proper, appropriate 5/28 *etc.*

conveniently, convenyently *adv.* suitably, properly, appropriately 36/31 *etc.*

convince *v.* overcome, overpower 262/15

con(n)yng, cunnyng *adj.* wise, knowledgeable, learned 44/14 *etc.*

copp *n.* top, summit; *a copp high* to a great height 159/17, 27. *See n.*

courage, corage *n.* spirit, disposition, inclination 82/15, *etc.*; encouragement 242/16 etc.; *out of corage* contrary to

boldness 107/25; applied to persons: *noble corages* noble spirits 314/7

corage *v.* encourage, strengthen 148/16

corn *n.* grain of any kind 168/17

corners *n. pl. in corners* privily, without notice 11/10. *See n.*

corps *n.* body 8/6 *etc.*

corsis *n. pl.* dead bodies 192/24

cosyn, cosin *n.* relative 4/7 *etc. See n.*

cote *n.* coat 34/9, 109/21

coumfort(e) *n. See* **comfort**

coumfortable *adj. See* **comfortable**

councell, counceyle, counsaile *n.* counsel, advice, direction 3/21 *etc.*; *pl.* **counsaylles** 10/31

counptid *v. pt. See* **comptith**

counptour *n.* counter, anything used in counting or keeping account 222/10, 11

countenaunce *n.* estate, position, standing 211/12

counterfayte *adj.* counterfeit, bogus 228/28

counterplede *v.* plead in opposition 294/17

countith *v. pr. 3 s. See* **comptith**

countremen *n. pl.* countrymen 7/11

course *n.* turn, time for action 102/1; *out of course* out of sequence, not according to the pattern 88/11

covitice, covetice *n.* excessive desire for wealth, covetousness 167/22 *etc.*

cowardice *n.* cowardly state of mind 111/26

cowardouse, cowardyse *adj.* cowardly 249/20–21, 296/26

crabb *n.* crab-apple 78/25

craft(e) *n.* trickery 95/7 *etc.*; skill, profession 117/8 *etc. See also* **lech crafte**

credence *n.* trustworthiness, credibility 89/15; belief 262/16 *etc.*

crepe *v.* creep 48/18

crik *n.* painful muscle spasm 275/1

crosse *n.* trouble, misfortune, adversity 29/5

cumbred *ppl. a. See* **combrid**

cumbreth *v. pr. 3 s.* encumbers, burdens 113/16

cumfort *n. See* **comfort**

cumfortable *adj. See* **comfortable**

cumfortles *adj. See* **comfortles**

cunnyng *adj. See* **con(n)yng**

curat *n.* one entrusted with the care of souls, parish priest 198/23; *pl.* **curattes** 174/4

cure *n.* care, concern 202/28

curtsy *n.* courtesy 38/26

curtuouse *adj.* courteous 45/25

customable, custumable *adj.* customary, usual 4/9 *etc.*

custome *v. refl.* accustom (oneself) 15/16

custumably *adv.* customarily, usually 206/9

custumers *n. pl.* customs agents 176/14

cyt(i)e *n.* city 251/18, 289/11

daies, dayes *n. pl.* days 38/24 *etc.*; *clensing dayes. See* **clensing**; *erly dayes* early in the day 46/2–3

daingour, dayngour *n.* danger 154/17, 172/15

dam(p)nacion *n.* damnation 11/18 *etc.*

dampnable *adj.* damnable, worthy of damnation 156/16 *etc.*

dampnid *ppl. a.* damned, condemned to hell 39/27 *etc.*

danyell *n.* Daniel 279/14

darke *adj.* obscure 107/19

dayes *n. pl. See* **daies**

dayngour *n. See* **daingour**

deale *n.* part, bit, amount 51/29 *etc.*

debate *n. at debate* at odds, in controversy 127/17, 24

decaying *vbl. n.* causing to deteriorate 162/21

decease, desease *n.* disease 3/10 *etc.*

de(s)cerne *v.* discern 147/19, 226/20

declare *v.* make clear, elucidate, reveal 23/16 *etc.*

declyne *v.* turn away, fall 249/1

ded *v. pt.* did 53/30

deddly *adv. See* **ded(e)ly**

dede *n. in very dede* indeed, in fact 51/30, 56/26

dedly *adj.* deadly, mortal 11/18 *etc.*

ded(e)ly, deddly *adv.* gravely, mortally 175/1 *etc.*

defaut(e) *n.* fault, failure, neglect 161/23 *etc.*

def(f)erence, diference, differens(e) *n.* difference 66/26 *etc.*

deficile *adj.* difficult 250/14

deflorid *pp.* deflowered, ravished 141/25

defoylyng *vbl. n.* defiling, violation 142/3

degrees *n. pl.* social status 211/10

delatyng *vbl. n.* enlargement, expansion 194/9

delectacion *n.* delight, enjoyment 170/20

delite *n.* delight 61/17 *etc.*

deliteth *v. pr. 3 s.* delights 4/19, 33/11; *pt.* **delytid** 279/20; *pp.* **delited** 285/26

deliuere *n.* deliverance, release 23/1

delyuerd *v. pt.* delivered 58/18

demaunded *v. pt.* asked 23/17

demeaned *v. pt.* managed, employed 179/30

dener *n.* dinner 117/4 *etc.*

departeth (with) *v. pr. 3 s.* parts with, disposes of 72/8

d(i)epe *adv.* deeply 59/18 *etc.*

depravyng *pr. p.* vilifying, slandering 135/27

deprehendid *pp.* detected 26/15, 146/5

depurid *ppl. a.* purified, cleansed 185/24

dere *adj.* expensive, costly 119/15

dere *adv.* at great cost 169/7

descerne *v. See* **de(s)cerne**

desease *n. See* **decease**

desert *n.* merit 71/18

desperat(e) *adj.* hopeless 9/12 *etc. See n.*

despightfull, dispightfull *adj.* insulting, opprobrious 281/22, 291/24

despite, dispight *n.* scorn, disdain 290/28, 291/2; contemptuous or scornful action 67/14 *etc.*

desprayse *n.* blame, censure, disparage 289/13

det *n.* debt 33/6

determynacion *n.* decision 278/4

determynatly *adv.* definitely, distinctly 223/22

determyne *v. refl.* decide, resolve 278/12; *pp.* disposed 261/13

detract *v.* disparage, speak evil of 42/23

devise *n.* contrivance 128/26; *pl.* **devises, devisis, devices** opinions, notions 61/20 *etc.*

devise *v.* imagine, conjecture 36/32, 230/15; invent, contrive 79/25, 217/22; plan, plot 127/27 *etc.*; meditate, deliberate 199/13; *pt.* **dyvisid** considered, planned 8/21

devisyng, devysyng *vbl. n.* invention, contriving 11/9, 188/25; meditation, deliberation 205/10

devour *n.* duty, utmost or best endeavor 57/4 *etc.*

dew *adj.* due, proper 25/9 *etc.*

dewellyng *n.* dwelling 41/17

dewtie *n.* duty 4/28 *etc.*; tax, levy 176/15, 179/4

diepe *adv. See* **d(i)epe**

diepely *adv. See* **dyepely**

diference, differens(e) *n. See* **def(f)erence**

differ *v.* defer, put off 284/17

diffidence *n.* mistrust, misgivings 133/14

dilate *v.* extend, spread 190/5; discourse at length, expatiate 310/12

diligence *n. do ... diligence* make an earnest effort 148/1, 186/12

dilucion *n.* delusion 137/26

diologes *n. pl.* dialogues 79/26

dirige *n.* service for the dead, song of lament 132/11, 192/25. *See n.*

disburden *v.* unburden, relieve 151/26

discharge *v.* free 25/15, 69/6; *pp.* dischargid of freed of responsibility for 183/2-3

discomfit *pp.* defeated, routed 62/23

discomfort, discumfort *n.* discouragement, distress 14/13, 69/6

discomfortable, discumfortable, dyscomfortable *adj.* causing discouragement 25/5 *etc.*; comfortless, miserable 107/9-10 *etc.*

discomfortyng *pr. p.* depriving of courage, disheartening, dismaying 3/15

discommendith *v. pr. 3 s.* finds fault with, disapproves of 70/12

discontinued *pp.* interrupted 40/19

discontynuaunce *n.* interruption, absence 52/2

discrecion *n.* sound judgment 293/18

discrete *adj.* discerning, judicious 115/10

discretely *adv.* with discernment, appropriately 115/21-22

discumfortable *adj. See* **discomfortable**

discumfortles *adj.* undistressed, undismayed 17/10

disdaynouse *adj.* disdainful, scornful, contemptuous 161/1-2

disgressing *pr. p.* digressing 160/12

disparsyng *pr. p.* dispersing 190/10

dispayre *v.* despair 45/12 *etc.*

dispepled *ppl. a.* depopulated 190/27

dispice *v.* despise, scorn 96/19

dispicions *n. pl.* discussions, disputations 31/16, 38/7

dispight *n. See* **despite**

dispightfull *adj. See* **despightfull**

dispituously *adv.* contemptuously, spitefully 67/16

displeasures *n. pl.* discomforts, troubles 168/30-31

displesaunt *adj.* displeasing 48/5; unpleasant, disagreeable 78/13, 79/1

displesauntly *adv.* without pleasure 153/21-22; in an offended or displeased manner 221/26-27

disposid *ppl. a.* inclined 69/21 *etc.*

disputacion *n.* controversial argument, discussion 231/9

dissemblid *v. pt.* pretended not to notice 84/9

dissimulyng *pr. p.* disguising 200/14

distemperaunce *n.* bodily or mental disorder 152/3, 4

diuers(e), divers, dyuers *adj.* various, many 15/7 *etc.*

diuersitie *n.* perversity, erring nature 83/14

diuersly *adv.* in various ways, in several ways 30/3, 273/5

dolorouse *adj.* sorrowful, distressed 215/14

dome *n.* doom, judgment 193/29

dore *n. at dore* from the door 46/6; *out at dore* out of doors 81/8

dought *v. See* **dowt**

dout, dovt, dowt *n.* hesitation 31/26; doubt 132/12 *etc.*

dowble *adv.* doubly, twice 134/27

dowble *n. the dowble* twice as much 181/27

dowce *adj.* sweet, pleasant, soothing, gentle 146/9

dowt, dou(gh)t(e) *v.* be apprehensive, fear 7/27 *etc.*; be uncertain, doubt 16/1 *etc.*; hesitate 33/8, 121/19

draweth *v. pr. 3 s.* tends, leads 70/18; *pp.* **drawn** 130/23

drawght *n.* drinking 306/13

drawyng *vbl. n.* composition 217/20

dred *pp.* dreaded 205/25

drefull *adj.* dreadful 61/9

dresse *v.* prepare 185/14

dreve *v.* drive 107/23 *etc.*; *pt.* **drave** 147/ 15, 156/22; *pp.* **driven, dryven** deduced, concluded 40/12; forced 162/22; *dryve furth* pass the time 26/3

drinke *v. drinke out* drink throughout 92/7

drounnyng *vbl. n.* drowning 6/14

dry *adj.* witty, ironical 81/9

dryft(e) *n.* scheme, design 61/23, 112/10

dryve *v. See* **dreve**

dryvill *v.* slaver, dribble 78/26

ducates *n. pl.* gold coins 127/20, 180/23

dulcely *adv.* sweetly 198/26

dulnes *n.* depression, gloom 69/23 *etc.*

dumpes *n. pl.* mental depressions, fits of melancholy 6/17

dumpish *adj.* sad, melancholy, dejected 131/9

durst *v. pt.* dared 89/17 *etc.*

dyce *v.* play at dice 273/10

dyepely, diepely *adv.* deeply, in depth 312/8 *etc.*

dyscencions *n. pl.* dissentions 8/11

dyscomfortable *adj. See* **discomfortable**

dyvisid *v. See* **devise**

dyvisyng *vbl. n.* consideration 8/23

ech(e) *adj.* each 8/12 *etc.*

effeccion, effection *n. See* **affeccion(e)**

effectuall *adj.* effective 11/15 *etc.*

effectually *adv.* adequately, explicitly 20/ 14; strongly, powerfully 26/5

effucion *n.* shedding 224/27

efte sone *adv.* again, soon afterwards 222/ 13

egall *adj.* equal, neutral 64/21

egally *adv.* equally 180/7

eileth *v. pr. 3 s.* ails 113/5

either *adv. either other* either one or the other 152/4

eke *adv.* also, moreover 47/16

electes *n. pl.* those chosen by God for salvation 194/5

eleccion *n.* election, choosing 25/19

ell *n.* unit of length, roughly equivalent to a yard 66/7

el(le)s *adv.* else, otherwise 6/21 *etc.*

elvish *adj.* peevish, troublesome 113/5

Emau(e)s *n.* Emmaus 43/3, 311/23

Embassiatour *n.* ambassador, emissary 217/26

enbrace *v.* embrace 90/22

encomber *v.* burden, impose upon 64/7

encre(a)se *n.* increase 47/12 *etc.*

encre(a)se *v.* increase 8/14 *etc.*

end *n. vpp an end. See* **vpp**

endevour *v. refl.* make an effort, exert (oneself) 254/7

enditid *pp.* put into words, composed 217/ 22

enformyd *v. pt.* informed, instructed 117/ 32

enforseth *v. pr. 3 s. refl.* exerts (himself), strives 282/9

engendre *v.* conceive, give rise to, generate 205/12, 294/7; *pr. 3 s.* **engendreth, ingendreth** 152/4, 161/6; *pp.* **ingendred** conceived, begotten 282/14

enhaunce *v.* raise, elevate 29/2, 23; increase 229/22; intensify 277/5

enioynid *pp.* imposed, prescribed 36/18

ensample *n.* example 42/21 *etc.*

ensewyng *pr. p.* following 300/5

entent *n.* purpose, intention 240/21, 249/6; *to the entent that, to thentent (that)* in order that 184/5 *etc.*

enterchaungid *pp.* exchanged, alternated 79/23

enterparlyng *vbl. n.* sharing in a conversation 79/24

entre *n.* entry, opening 134/7

entreate *v.* treat, handle 257/6

entrid *v. pt.* entered 75/21

environ *v.* surround 106/18, 22

eny *adj.* any 17/11 *etc.*; *eny thing* to any extent, at all 133/9

en(n)ymye *n.* enemy 106/16 *etc.*; *pl.* **enymis, ennimies** 141/24 *etc.*

er(e), are *adv.* before 3/26 *etc.*

erely *adv.* early 127/21

erly *adj. erly dayes. See* **daies**

ernest *adj. ernest peny* pledge, foretaste 306/25

er(e)nest *n.* seriousness 195/8 *etc.*; *good ernest* actual fact 118/13

Esay *n.* Isaiah 309/1

eschetour *n.* confiscator 227/30

Esop(e) *n.* Aesop 180/29 *etc.*

estate *n.* person of high social rank 206/18 *etc.*; state of life, social status 257/5 *etc.*

esteme, estime *v.* value, account, consider 101/11 *etc.*; *pp.* **estemid, estemyd** 129/16 *etc.*

estimacion, estymacion *n.* reputation, esteem 146/7 *etc.*; appreciation 306/11–12

ete *v. pt.* ate 213/25

eth *adj.* easy 170/22

euery *pron.* each 35/11; everyone, everybody 226/9

euery chone *pron.* each one 191/15

evill *adv.* wickedly, badly 223/13, 224/30

evyll *adj. evyll at his ease* ill at ease, uncomfortable 274/20–21

evyn *adj.* even 66/8

except *conj.* unless 12/17 *etc.*

excitith *v.* moves, stirs 75/18

exirtyng *pr. p.* exhorting, rousing to action 10/13

exort *v.* exhort, encourage 57/3 *etc.*

exortacion *n.* exhortation 26/16 *etc.*

expense *n.* expenditure 87/20

experience *n.* demonstration 213/1

experimentall *adj.* experienced 306/22

expres *adj.* explicit 179/4

expres(s)ly *adv.* explicitly 20/21, 56/1

expresse *v.* make explicit 19/29, 21/14

exquisyte, exquisite *adj.* choice, dainty 210/10; ingeniously devised, uncommon 213/26

extenuate *v.* weaken the force of, mitigate 204/25

extorcion *n.* extortion, exaction by force 34/15

extorsiously *adv.* by reliance on extortion 178/11

Eye *int.* ay, oh 113/5

eyen *n. pl. See* **yee**

eyther *adj. eyther sort* each kind, both kinds 48/7

facultie *n.* branch of knowledge, profession 121/4

facyon *n. See* **fass(h)ion**

faire *adv. See* **fa(i)re**

fall *n.* overthrow 17/23 *etc.*; transgression, lapse into sin 146/14; occurrence, calamity 222/1

fall *v.* happen 14/21 *etc.*; become, grow 161/8 *etc.*; *fall at hand* be about to happen, be near at hand 3/17–18; *fall in hand with* consider, deal with 147/17–18, 202/8; *fall in . . . mind* come to mind 5/21, 153/19–20; *fall in our way* come to our attention 19/23; *fall in* be drawn into 188/25; *fall in vnto* fall in with, join 192/1; *fall . . . theron* become aware of it 314/26; *fall to* have recourse to 18/10 *etc.*; *fall to fedyng* begin eating 187/7; *fall to my fete* take to my heels, flee 295/7; *fall to them* become theirs 171/6; *pr. 3 s. falleth . . . vnto* comes as a possession 170/26–27; *pt. felle in hand* argued 219/25; *pp. fall in* under way 80/24

fals *adj.* false 6/30 *etc.*

fame *n.* rumor, report 238/2, 9

famely *n.* family 6/16

famyliers *n. pl.* intimate friends or associates 165/3

famyn *n.* famine 57/8

fansies *n. pl.* delusions, caprices 18/30; fantasies 61/27

fantasticall *adj.* irrational, imagined 113/7 *etc.*

fantasy(e) *n.* delusion, desire, caprice 61/18 *etc. See n.*; fondness, liking 149/4 *etc.*

farcid *pp.* stuffed 131/11, 188/19

fa(i)re, fayre *adv.* completely, fully 14/21; directly, straight 187/6, 287/9; courteously, kindly 146/9

far(r)e, fer(r)(e) *adv.* far 6/11 *etc.*

fare *v.* behave, act 46/8; *pp.* **faren** feasted 285/25

far(r)forth, forforth, ferforth, fer forth *adv.* far 270/15; *how farrforth* how much 87/24; *thus, so farforth* to such an extent 27/25 *etc.*

farther forth, fertherforth *adv.* in advance (of) 110/10; *no fertherforth* nothing further 179/7

fass(h)ion, facyon *n.* bearing, demeanor 131/12, 307/19; habit, custom 318/1

fast *adj.* steadfast, firm 13/31 *etc.*; certain, without question 52/22

fast *adv.* firmly, tightly 15/12 *etc.*; close, very near 276/24

fat *adj.* rich, overabundant 29/9

fatigacion *n.* exhausting toil 82/21

faut(e), fawt(e) *n.* fault, sin 11/6 *etc.*

favor *v. favorid with* in the good regard of 213/7

favour *n.* preference, inclination 206/9

fawtfull *adj.* culpable 253/21

fayle *v.* come to an end 175/19

fayn(e) *adj.* obliged, constrained 18/12 *etc.*

fayne *adv.* gladly, willingly 15/5 *etc.*

fayne *v.* fabricate 134/2; pretend 132/21 *etc.*

faynid, fayned *ppl. a.* imaginary, invented 79/26 *etc.*

faynt(e) *adj.* weak 12/23 *etc.*

fayntith *v. pr. 3 s.* grows weak, declines 242/22; *pt.* **fayntid** turned fainthearted 245/3

fayntnes *n.* weakness 102/20, 109/13

fayre *adv. See* **fa(i)re**

faythed *ppl. a. feble faythed* of weak faith 304/11

faytour *n.* imposter, cheat 183/26

fealyng *pr. p. See* **fele**

fearid *ppl. a.* frightened 247/22. *See also* **ferd**

fe(o)ble, fieble *adj.* weak, feeble 13/22 *etc.*

feche *v. See* **fet(ch)**

fede *v. fede . . . forth* beguile, lead on under false pretences 128/13–14

feld *n.* field 201/20 *etc.*

fele *v.* feel, experience 5/17 *etc.*; *pr. p.* **fealyng** 26/4

feleship *n.* fellowship, group 176/17, 230/7

fell *adj.* fierce, cruel 127/16

fell *n.* skin 29/15

felle *v. pt. felle in hand. See* **fall**

felow *n.* equal, peer 162/27 *etc.*

fence *v.* shield, protect 111/6, 318/18; *pp.* **fensid** 108/16

fend *n.* fiend, devil 63/20, 100/19

fendich *adj.* wicked 124/16

feoble *adj. See* **fe(o)ble**

fer(r)(e) *adv. See* **far(r)e**

ferd *ppl. a.* afraid 78/16 *etc. See also* **aferd(e), fearid**

fere *n.* fear 113/7 *etc.*; *not all out of fere of* not without some apprehension about 129/17

fere *v.* frighten 317/2; *refl.* be afraid 46/8, 173/28

ferforth, fer forth *adv. See* **far(r)forth**

ferther, forther *adj.* further 4/4 *etc.*

fertherforth *adv. See* **farther forth**

ferthing *n.* farthing, penny 180/24 *etc.*

fervent *adj.* burning, intense 29/14 *etc.*

fervour *n.* intensity 28/17 *etc.*

feryouse *adj.* furious, fierce, raging 9/2

fest *n.* feast, celebration 69/14 *etc.*

fet(ch), feche *v.* get, take, receive 3/11 *etc.*;

bring 301/23; *pt.* **fet** brought forth 216/1; *pp.* **fet(t)** 267/16, 291/6

feyre *adj.* fair 277/8

feystrid *pp.* festered 63/8

ficle *adj.* fickle, changeable 232/4

fieble *adj. See* **fe(o)ble**

fier *n. See* **fyer**

fiers *adj.* fierce 125/17

file *v.* defile 43/20, 160/21

firebrond *n.* piece of wood kindled at the fire 318/19

fistyng *ppl. a.* breaking wind; used as a term of contempt: *fistyng curre* 318/12

fityng *vbl. n.* fighting 269/12, 272/13

fivetene *adj.* fifteen 289/18

flateres *n. pl.* flatteries 224/21

flatt *adj.* plain, unqualified 195/8

fle *v.* flee 111/15 *etc.*; fly 157/27, 158/5; *pr. p.* **fleyng** flying 105/21, 157/19

fleshly *adj.* worldly 168/4; carnal, sexual 160/24

fletyng *vbl. n.* departing, shifting or moving away 100/10

flex *n.* flax 160/21

flight *n.* fright, agitation 92/14. *See n.*

flode *n.* flood, river 92/13

floke *n.* flock 5/9

flokmele *adv.* by groups, in droves 83/29

floure *v.* flower, flourish, thrive 194/13

flyngyng *ppl. a.* raging, rampant 63/20

flyt *v.* flee, depart 23/5, 134/8

fo(o) *n.* foe 182/8, 183/20

fodid *v. pt.* postponed by evasive excuses 115/1

fole *n.* fool 61/19 *etc.*; *pl.* **folis, folys** 69/18 *etc.*

foly(e) *n.* folly, madness 4/19, 82/3

fond *adj.* foolish 41/21 *etc.*

for *conj. for that* because 25/28 *etc.*

for *prep.* as 14/9 *etc.*; because of 124/19, 287/11; *for to* to 68/10

forbare *v. See* **forbere**

forbed(e) *v.* forbid 122/20 *etc.*; *pp.* **forboden** 38/8 *etc. See also* **bid**

forbeding *vbl. n.* prohibition 291/4

forbere, forbare *v.* abstain from, refrain from 82/2 *etc.*; spare, dispense 144/19; do without 180/24 *etc.*; put off, delay 273/27; *pt.* **forbare** 57/25 *etc.*; *pp.* **forborne** gone without 215/15, 244/19

forboden *pp. See* **forbed(e)**

forborne *pp. See* **forbere**

force, forse *n. no forse* it does not matter 116/17; *of fyne force* by constraint, from absolute necessity 201/15

forceth *v. pr. 3 s.* cares, is concerned 191/12

fore *adv.* previously, already 71/11 *etc. See* also **afore**

forebeten *ppl. a.* previously beaten, *or, perhaps,* severely beaten 312/19. *See n.*

foreknowen *pp.* foreseen 227/26–27

foreweried *pp.* worn out, exhausted 168/29

forforth *adv. See* **far(r)forth**

forgate *v. pt.* forgot 127/15; *pp.* **forgotone** 90/9

forgo *v.* give up, do without 228/2, 231/18

forseyng *pr. p.* foreseeing 28/31

For sooth, Forsoth, for soth *adv.* truly, indeed 13/28 *etc.*

forswere *v. refl.* perjure 95/5

forsweryng *vbl. n.* denial, repudiation 201/23

forth *adv.* further 77/9; *fede . . . forth. See* **fede**. *See also* **farther forth**

forther *adj. See* **ferther**

forther *adv.* further 303/14

fortherid *pp.* assisted, helped forward 294/6

forthynkyng *vbl. n.* repenting 96/13

fortres *n.* fortress, fortified town 8/2

fortune *v.* happen, chance 7/14 *etc.*

for(th)with *adv.* immediately, at once 80/10 *etc.*

fostryng *vbl. n.* nourishing, supporting 108/27

fote *n.* foot 54/11 *etc.*; track, scent 295/11. *See n.*; *pl.* fete 146/22 *etc.*; *fall to my fete. See* **fall**

fotid *ppl. a.* footed 297/23

frame *n.* order, regularity 229/5

frame *v.* shape, form, devise 112/6 *etc.*

fransie, frenesey *n.* rage, mad fury 15/1; folly, mania 212/24

frantik(e), frantyke *adj.* insane, lunatic 128/5 *etc.*

frantique *adv.* insanely, madly 235/5

fray(e) *n.* disturbance, brawl, fight 265/12 *etc.*

frayle *adj.* weak, unable to resist temptation 4/19 *etc.*

fray(e)lt(i)e *n.* frailty, weakness 26/5 *etc.*

fremde *adj.* strange, unrelated 183/18

frend *n.* friend 3/10 *etc.*

frenesey *n. See* **fransie**

freres *n. pl.* friars 3/13, 46/9

fret *v. fret out* gnaw away, eat, devour 239/22, 24

freting *vbl. n.* becoming vexed 87/10

fro *prep.* from 4/12 *etc.*

froward *adj.* unruly, perverse 45/26 *etc.*

frowardly *adv.* perversely 111/21

fruicion, fruytyon, fruytion *n.* enjoyment, pleasurable possession 204/30 *etc.*

frustrate *ppl. a.* useless, ineffectual 12/16

frute *n.* fruit, benefit 136/5 *etc.*

frut(e)full *adj.* fruitful, profitable 90/17 *etc.*

frut(e)les *adj.* fruitless, barren 92/20 *etc.*

ful(l) *adv.* fully, completely, very 15/2 *etc.*

fulfill *v.* fill fully 34/28; realize, satisfy 52/5

fumyng *vbl. n.* showing anger or impatience 87/10

furderaunce *n.* furtherance, advancement 188/21

furiouse *adj.* mad, raging 124/27

furth *adv.* forth 13/18 *etc.*

further *v.* help forward, assist 50/4, 56/11

fvmysh *adj.* irascible, hot tempered 14/25

fyer, fier *n.* fire 4/21 *etc.*

fynd *v.* provide for, support 116/20

fyndyng *vbl. n.* support, maintenance 277/19

fyne *adj. of fyne force. See* **force**

gaddyng *pr. p.* wandering idly 261/21

galey *n. galey subtill* galley-subtile, narrow flat ship propelled by sails and oars 301/9

galien, galyen *n.* Galen 89/22, 23

galped *v. pt.* vomited; *galped vp the goost* gave up the ghost, died 62/4–5

gameners *n. pl.* gamesters, gamblers 62/4

gaole *n.* jail 273/21, 24

gaolour *n. See* **gaylour**

garnysh *v.* embellish, ornament 273/8; *pp.* **garnishid** elegantly clothed 210/7

garr *v.* make, cause 29/4

gat(e) *v. pt.* got, earned 74/25; received 299/28

gay *adj.* plausible, specious 228/24

gaylour, gaolour *n.* jailer 271/21 *etc.*; *pl.* **gaylours, gaolers** 271/21 *etc.*

genisis *n.* Genesis 54/25

gentelly *adv.* generously, courteously 286/
18

gentill *adj.* well-born, belonging to the
gentry 190/14

gere *n.* property, possessions 62/30, 211/16;
sustenance 118/24; clothing, attire 163/11

gesse *v.* guess 81/2 *etc.*

gest *n.* guest 182/26

gestyng *vbl. n.* scoffing, jeering, mocking
289/21

geue, geve, gyve *v.* give 12/10 *etc.*; suggest
(to) 76/24, 194/25; misgive 114/5 *etc.*;
give ouer, geve ouer cease, leave off 111/18;
give up, surrender 245/22–23 *etc.*; *pr. 3 s.
as far as my mynd giveth me* as well as I can
remember 129/22; *pt. gave ouer his hold*
let go, failed to persevere 32/16; *pp.*
geuen, gevyn, geven, gyuyn 3/21 *etc.*

geverne *v.* govern, control 178/4

gevyng *vbl. n.* giving 3/12 *etc.*; *gevyng vpp
his rekenyng* rendering his account 164/
18–19

ghostely *adj. See* **go(o)stly**

gide *v.* guide 10/28

giglot *n.* one excessively given to merriment
83/4

g(u)ise, guyse *n.* habit, practice 3/15 *etc.*

give *v.* tell, suggest to 76/24

glad *n.* glade, clearing 241/9

gleke *n.* a card game 221/2

glistryng *vbl. n.* glittering 207/2

gloriouse *adj.* ostentatious, haughty 213/
10

glose *n.* flattering interpretation 218/17,
228/24

glosyng *vbl. n.* interpreting, explaining
away 136/17

glotony *n.* gluttony 115/21, 116/2

glymeryng *vbl. n.* inkling, faint notion
308/5

go *v.* walk 264/20; *go ... to worke. See* **warke**;
goeth about sets to work (at), seeks 194/16

Goddes *n. poss. Goddes lord* surely 138/25

godhed *n.* divine essence, deity 106/10,
308/21

godly *adj.* divine, spiritual 26/8 *etc.*

god ward, godward *adv.* to *god ward*,
vnto godward toward God, with respect
to God 39/9 *etc.*

gonnes *n. pl.* guns 315/12

good *n.* goods, property 62/31

goodly *adj.* splendid, admirable 8/3

goodly *adv.* properly, fittingly 26/6, 146/10

goost *n.* ghost, spirit 101/22; *galped vp the
goost. See* **galped**

goostly *adj. See* **go(o)stly**

gose *n.* goose 115/19, 116/25

goslynges *n. pl.* figures of goslings or
young geese 219/28

gossep *n.* familiar acquaintance, friend
47/1

go(o)stly, ghostely *adj.* spiritual 10/28
etc.; *go(o)stly father* confessor, spiritual
director 36/18–19 *etc.*; *gostly person* devout
person, a member of some ecclesiastical
order 308/18

gowt *n.* gout 274/25

gracious(e), gracyouse *adj.* conferring
grace 5/16 *etc.*; endowed with grace,
righteous 170/7

graciously *adv.* through divine grace 38/
16 *etc.*

grate *n.* grill work, allowing communication but not entry 80/6, 10

gre *adj.* great 31/8; *super.* **greast(e),
gre(a)est** greatest, most important 40/3
etc.

greef(e), gre(i)fe, grife, gryef(e) *n.* suffering 10/7 *etc.*; pain 10/15; illness 78/7,
221/12; grievance 232/7

grenne *n. See* **grynne**

gret(e) *adj.* great 91/5 *etc.*

greve, grive *v.* grieve, vex, trouble 10/9
etc.

griesly *adj.* horrible, terrifying 268/8

grife *n. See* **greef(e)**

grogeth *v. pr. 3 s. See* **gru(d)ge**

groneth *v. pr. 3 s.* sighs, yearns 22/25

groninges *n. pl.* sighs, yearnings 22/30

grote *n.* groat, small coin 62/31 *etc.*

grow *v.* come 73/17; *grow vppon* arise from
31/25; *pr. p. growing toward them* accruing
to them, arising for their benefit 68/14

growge *n. See* **gru(d)ge**

grownd, ground(e) *n.* ground, foundation,
basis 12/10 *etc.*

grownden *pp.* ground, sharpened 128/10

grubbe *v.* dig (up) by the roots 241/7

grudgyng *vbl. n.* complaint, protest 245/21

gru(d)ge, growge *n.* complaint 12/2 *etc.*;
scruple, murmuring of conscience, un-
easiness of mind 115/7

gru(d)ge v. complain 74/23 etc.; trouble, vex 117/20, 119/6; pr. 3 s. **grugeth, grogeth** 28/7, 297/2

gryef(e) n. See **greef(e)**

grynne, grenne n. snare, trap 168/10 etc.

guge n. judge 34/16

guise, guyse n. See **g(u)ise**

gyuyn pp. See **geue**

gyve v. See **geue**

habite n. garb worn by members of a religious order 93/27

hable adj. able 8/7 etc.

habound v. abound 206/16

habraham n. Abraham 50/5

habundantly adv. abundantly 184/21

hand n. bere . . . in hand. See **bere**; fall at hand, fall, felle in hand. See **fall**; in hand in process 188/21–22; under one's care 147/19; out of hand at once, immediately, without premeditation 177/21 etc.; set to . . . hands. See **set(t)**; to their hands without exertion on their part 238/20

handeleth v. pr. 3 s. treats, deals with 273/26; pp. **handel(y)d** 7/10 etc.

handkercher n. handkerchief 215/24

handlyng vbl. n. treatment 59/10 etc.

handy craft n. manual skill, manual occupation 291/12

hangeth v. pr. 3 s. hangeth vppon depends upon 53/26; pr. p. 192/16

hap(p)(e) v. happen (to), occur (to), chance 32/4 etc.; come by chance 22/8

hap(p)ely, happly adv. by chance, perhaps 7/4 etc.

happ(e) n. event, chance occurrence 89/16 etc.; chance, luck, fortune 90/3, 99/13

hard adj. severe, difficult 82/13, 178/24; ouer the hard eares over the very ears 45/23

hard v. pt. See **here**

hardely adv. scarcely, barely 178/22; harshly, severely 7/10; certainly, by all means 30/8 etc.; boldly, vigorously 263/6

hardnes n. hardship 276/22

hardy(e) adj. bold, intrepid 123/16, 124/6

harken v. consider, pay attention to 240/19; pt. **herknid** 84/11

harmlesse adj. free from harm, unharmed 279/15

hart n. male deer, stag 294/18 etc.

hart, hert n. heart 3/16 etc.

hartely adv. sincerely, earnestly 38/27 etc.

harty(e) adj. heartfelt, sincere 73/25, 164/28

hasardours n. pl. gamblers, dicers 95/5

hast n. haste 48/21 etc.

haue v. haue vpp take up, consider 187/29; haue none of care nothing for, have nothing to do with 58/9

havour n. estate, substance, wealth 211/13, 22

havour vbl. n. haver, one who has 171/9

havyn ward adv. See **hevyn ward**

hawnsid pp. raised, lifted 285/14. See also **enhaunce**

heare n. See **he(a)re**

hede n. heed, care 63/5, 121/11; toke hede to took care of 114/15

hedlesse adj. headless 311/15

hedling adv. head first, headlong 92/14

hed strong adj. headstrong, uncontrolled 282/24

hele n. heel 50/24

helid, helyd pp. healed 11/17, 17/25

helm n. handle, helve 125/12

hely n. Elijah 95/22

heng, hong v. pt. hung 26/26 etc.

hens(e) adv. hence, from here 3/26 etc.

hepe n. heap, quantity 5/23 etc.; pl. **heps** 6/15, 7/13

heping, hepyng vbl. n. gathering, amassing 8/18, 175/27

herd adj. hard 221/18

he(a)re n. hair 94/21 etc.

here v. hear 7/3 etc.; pt. **hard, herd** 9/6 etc.; pp. **hard** 5/20 etc.

here before adv. heretofore, in time past 4/26

herein adv. in this matter 9/13, 64/4

heres n. pl. ears 94/18

herknid v. pt. See **harken**

hervest n. harvest 42/8

heryng vbl. n. matter to hear 7/25 etc.; hearing 306/28 etc.

hester n. Esther 184/29

hete n. heat 103/22, 25

hether adv. hither, to or towards this place 6/19 etc.; up to this time, until now 179/27

hevely adv. grievously, seriously 4/25 etc.

hevy adj. grievous, burdensome 7/25; oppressive 32/13; sorrowful 90/12 etc.

hevy *adv.* grievously, heavily 7/13 *etc.*

hevynes, heuynes, hevenes, hevines *n.* sorrow, depression, grief 6/15 *etc.*

hevyn ward, havyn ward *n.* to *hevyn ward* in gaining heaven 21/11, 39/4–5; *vnto havyn ward* toward heaven 215/29

heynouse *adj.* heinous, grievous 24/6

hierico *n.* Jerico 26/10

hierom(e), Iherome *n.* Jerome 90/14 *etc.*

hierusalem, Iherusalem *n.* Jerusalem 104/10 *etc.*

high *adj.* extreme 6/24 *etc.*; *super.* **hiest** highest 103/1 *etc.*

hillocke *n.* small hill 13/23

his *adj.* its 39/6 *etc.*

hit *pron.* it 19/8 *etc.*

hokes *n. pl.* agricultural implements with cutting blades 241/6

hold *n.* support 54/1; captivity 201/22, 270/18

holdyth *v. pr. 3 s.* obliges, requires 297/5

hole *adj.* whole, entire 7/30 *etc.*

hole *adv.* wholly, completely 15/2 *etc.*

holp(e) *v. pt.* helped, aided 143/28, 173/10; *pp.* **holpen** 147/26, 293/28

holsom(e) *adj.* wholesome, salutary 4/22 *etc.*

homicide *n.* murderer 141/30

honest *adj.* honorable 191/4, 209/19 *etc.*

hong *v. pt. See* **heng**

honteth *v. pr. 3 s.* hunts 295/1

hopid *v. pt.* hoped 294/20

hord *v.* hoard, store 239/21, 23

horson *n.* son of a whore (term of reproach) 125/17 *etc.*

hosteler *n.* stableman 41/23

honerly *adv.* lightly, inattentively 63/19

hovid *pp.* lingered, remained 268/9

Howbeit though *conj.* although, even though 10/31

Howbeyt, Howbe it, How be it *adv.* nevertheless, yet 8/8 *etc.*

howge *adj.* vast, immense 308/13

humble bees *n. pl.* bumble bees 225/9

humour *n.* vital fluid, disposition 150/9 *etc. See* n.

husband man *n.* tiller of the soil 241/5

huswivis *n. poss.* housewife's 116/27

hyndred *pp.* hindered 56/12

icordyng *ppl. a.* according, corresponding 101/27

iebard, iubard, iuberd *v.* endanger, risk 45/9 *etc.*

ieobardy, iuberdy *n.* jeopardy, peril 148/1, 242/10

Iherome *n. See* **hierom(e)**

Iherusalem *n. See* **hierusalem**

Ihesu *n.* Jesus 291/3, 6

illucion, illusyon *n.* false vision 129/6 *etc.*

illudid *pp.* tricked, deluded 139/24

imaginacion *n.* image 6/23 *etc.*

immediatly, immedyatly *adv.* directly, without intermediary 16/27, 203/8–9

impacience, impacyence *n. See* **inpacyence**

impacient *adj.* unwilling to endure hardship 111/20 *etc.*

Impassible *adj.* not subject to suffering 307/12

importune *adj.* importunate, vexatious 77/6

impugnyng *vbl. n.* assailing, opposing as erroneous 261/5

in *prep.* into 20/24 *etc.*; on 44/15 *etc.*

incedent *adj.* naturally pertaining or attached (to) 100/13

incommodit(i)e *n.* disadvantage, discomfort 161/29, 255/25; *pl.* **incommodities, yncommodities** 221/15, 276/14

inconvenience *n.* harm, misfortune 113/25–26

indeferent *adj.* indifferent, morally neutral 64/21 *etc.*

indentures *n. pl.* terms of a contract 230/15, 18

Indifferency *n.* impartiality 225/3

induce *v.* bring in, summon 152/13

indygnacion *n.* angry or contemptuous treatment 286/12

infamid *ppl. a.* branded with infamy 176/16

ingendred *pp. See* **engendre**

ingendreth *v. pr. 3 s. See* **engendre**

ino(u)gh, inow, ynough *adv.* enough 44/17 *etc.*

inordinate *adj.* immoderate, excessive 52/3

inough, inow, ynough *adj.* enough 42/21 *etc.*

inpacyence, impacyence, impacience *n.* lack of endurance, refusal to bear hardships 12/2 *etc.*

inperfeccion *n.* imperfection 69/25
inprisonment *n.* imprisonment 258/14
inquietid *pp.* disturbed, disquieted 52/26
insinuate *v.* suggest indirectly 132/12
instant *adj.* urgent 310/30
instaunce *n.* entreaty 36/28
instingte *n.* prompting, impulse 141/31
interpawsyng *pr. p.* pausing, resting 78/
　12–13, 79/19
interprise *n.* enterprise, undertaking 6/20
invacion *n.* invasion 105/22
invencion *n.* discovery 134/24
invent *v.* find, discover 224/13
inward *adj.* interior 51/10 *etc.*
inwardly *adv.* from within, by inspiration
　6/3 *etc.*
Iosue *n.* Joshua 26/16
ioy *v.* rejoice 70/27
ioynid *pp.* joined 152/2
Ismaell *n.* Ishmael 54/26
iubard, iuberd *v. See* **iebard**
iuberdy *n. See* **ieobardy**
iuberdyng *vbl. n.* jeopardizing, risk 233/2
iuge *v.* judge, decide 34/18 *etc.*
iugeler *n.* trickster, magician 136/7
iug(e)ment *n.* judgment 4/12, 164/1
iust *adj.* suitable, proper 159/23

kay *n.* key 210/19; strategic position, stronghold 193/6. *See also* **key cold**
kaytyfes *n. pl.* wretches 254/24
keen *n. pl. See* **kyne**
kenne *v.* know, recognize 29/4
kep(e) *v.* keep 235/12 *etc.*; *kepe . . . close.*
　See **close**; *pr. p.* **kyping** 218/26
keuer *v.* cover 7/18
key cold, kay cold *adj.* cold as a key,
　without fervor, apathetic 13/8 *etc.*
ki(gh)tes *n. poss. See* **kyght**
knave *n.* unprincipled rogue 29/12, 273/
　13
knettes *n. pl.* gnats, small insects 225/8
knolege *n.* knowledge 10/19 *etc.*; acknowledgement 26/28
knolege *v.* acknowledge, admit 186/1
knott *n.* binding condition 163/8
knyt *pp.* bound, united 152/2 *etc.*
kyght, kyte *n.* kite, bird of prey 103/33,
　104/1; *poss.* **ki(gh)tes** 29/16, 104/19
kynd *a.* natural 243/25. *See n.*
kynd *n.* race 269/24

kyne, keen *n. pl.* cattle 119/18, 19
kyping *pr. p. See* **kep(e)**

labour *v. trans.* work for 18/25; *refl.* exert
　oneself, work strenuously 64/8
laid *v. pt. and pp. See* **lay(e)**
lak(k)(e) *n.* lack 10/19 *etc.*
lak(k)(e) *v.* lack 65/2 *etc.*
lappid *pp.* covered 117/18
large *adj.* permissive 114/11, 120/2; unrestrained, improper 193/4; *more at large*
　in greater depth, more completely 24/25
late *adv.* recently 62/28
laues *n. pl.* laws 192/8
laufull, le(i)full *adj.* permissible, lawful
　16/18 *etc.*
laufully *adv.* permissibly, lawfully 20/19,
　83/8
launce *v.* lance, pierce 57/13; *pp.* **lawncid**
　293/13
lawd(e) *n.* praise 216/22, 289/22
lawdid *ppl. a.* praised 191/1
lawncid *pp. See* **launce**
lay(e), ley *v.* propose, put forth 12/15 *etc.*;
　prostrate, lay low 274/20; *lay my life*
　wager my life 98/20; *pt.* **laid, layd** 18/1
　etc.; *pp.* **laid, layd** imputed 56/1; *layd vp*
　stored up 6/12
lay *v. pt. See* **ly(e)**
Lazare *n.* Lazarus 54/4 *etc.*
lech(e) *n.* doctor, healer 148/10 *etc.*
lech crafte *n.* leechcraft, medical science
　or treatment 63/9
lede *pp.* led 267/25
lefe *n.* leave, permission 126/12
leftyng *pr. p. See* **lift**
le(i)full *adj. See* **laufull**
leige *n.* league, pact 217/21
leke *v. See* **like**
lekes *n. pl.* herbs, similar to onions 221/20
leme *n.* flame 85/23
lene *adj.* lean, thin 117/2, 118/25
lene *v.* lean 5/2 *etc.*; *lene to* rely on 94/16;
　lene vnto incline towards, be attracted by
　282/10, 13
lenger *comp. adv.* longer 29/10 *etc.*
lenton *adj.* Lenten 94/13, 95/23
les *comp. adv.* less 75/17; *super.* **lest(e)**
　least 20/9 *etc.*
lese *v.* lose 6/31 *etc.*
lesing *vbl. n. See* **lesyng**

lesse *n. the lesse of* a shorter time by 76/15

lessid *pp.* lessened, decreased 76/17

lest *super. adj.* least 27/1 *etc.*; *at the lest wise.* *See* **wise**

lest(e) *super. adv. See* **les**

lest *n. at the lest* at least 86/9 *etc.*

lest *v.* last, persevere, continue 29/10

lesyng, lesing *vbl. n.* losing 20/10 *etc.*

let(t) *n.* obstacle, hindrance 75/7 *etc.*

let(t) *v.* hesitate 31/17 *etc.*; hinder, prevent 78/22 *etc.*; *pp.* **let** hindered, prevented 65/11 *etc.*; *let your way* stop your journey 289/20; *lettid with* held up by 188/7; *pr. p.* leaving 214/5

let *v.* allow; *let . . . bloud* allow blood to escape 57/12

letany *n.* litany 155/20

letarge *n.* lethargy, torpor 14/20

leuer, lever *comp. adv.* rather, more willingly 115/18 *etc.*

leve *n. get leve* be permitted 34/11, 74/22; *give . . . leve* permit 108/21, 259/19

leve *v.* leave 4/2 *etc.*; leave off, stop 6/2 *etc.*

leves *n. pl.* leaves 63/11, 12

levyng *vbl. n.* leaving 174/12, 283/2

lewd(d) *adj.* ignorant, low 11/11 *etc.*

lewdnes *n.* wickedness 283/23

ley *v. See* **lay(e)**

licence *n.* permission 264/15

licence *v.* allow, permit 136/19

lien *pp. See* **ly(e)**

lift *v. lift . . . vpp* exalt, praise 218/22; *pr. p.* **leftyng** lifting 130/27; *pp.* **lyft** 84/11, 312/23

light *v.* fall, come to rest 49/24 *etc.*; alight, land 150/01; *pr. 3 s. lightith his mynd* raises his spirits 82/14–15; *pp.* lightened, cheered 76/16

light(e)ly *adv.* easily, readily 22/13 *etc.*; triflingly, frivolously 114/22; in all probability 132/1, 261/13

lightsome *adj.* light-hearted, cheerful 131/9, 157/24

lightsomely *adv.* clearly, lucidly, manifestly 200/24

like, lyke *adj.* alike, the same, of equal value 30/9 *etc.*; likely, probable 9/8 *etc.*

like, lyke *adv.* likely 222/22; *like as* just as 5/21 *etc.*; *like vnto* in the same way as 27/26

like, leke, lyke *v.* please 6/8 *etc.*; *refl.* be pleased with oneself 184/17 *etc.*

liklyhod, likelyhed *n. See* **lyklyhod**

lik(e)wise as *conj. See* **lykewise as**; *in likewise* in the same manner 55/23

list *n.* desire 65/10, 219/22

list, lyst *v.* choose, wish, desire 39/7 *etc.*; *me lyst* pleases me 82/3–4; *pt. me listid* I desired 214/5

litell, litle *n. litle & litle* little by little, gradually 132/11–12 *etc.*; *within a litell* within a short time or space, nearly, almost 126/18 *etc.*

lo *int.* see, behold 25/4 *etc.*

locutory *n.* a grill at which the inmates of a monastery may speak with those outside 80/7

loke *v.* look 6/3 *etc.*; look for, expect 85/18 *etc.*; take care 63/14; *loke (vn)to* attend to, care for 89/4–5 *etc.*; *loke what* whatever 162/17

lokyng *vbl. n.* looking 4/11 *etc.*

londes *n. pl.* lands 150/1

lose *adv.* freely 267/27

losell *n.* rascal, scoundrel 232/18

loth *adj.* unwilling, reluctant 22/10 *etc.*

Loth *n.* Lot 54/12, 14

loth *v.* loathe 285/1

lothnes(se) *n.* unpleasantness, harmfulness 231/17 *etc.*; reluctance, disinclination 240/16 *etc.*

love longyng *n. phr.* longing felt by one in love 204/29. *See* **n.**

lucre *n.* wealth 11/8 *etc.*

lumpish *adj.* gloomy, sluggish 150/4

lust *n.* desire 29/1 *etc.*, vigor, good health and spirits 157/24

lusteth *v. pr. 3 s.* desires 41/11

lusty(e) *adj.* lustful, lecherous 29/17 *etc.*; vigorous, eager 82/20; healthy 149/12

ly(e) *v. lye the same* take the same position, be of the same opinion 50/8; *pr. 3 s. lieth . . . wide* is beside the point 50/9; *pt.* **lay, ley** 14/20 *etc.*; *pp.* **lien, lyen** 46/1, 268/10

lyft *pp. See* **lift**

lyke *adj. See* **like**

lyke *adv. See* **like**

lyke *n.* equal 6/6

lyke *v. See* **like**

lykewise as, lik(e)wise as *conj.* just as 11/27 *etc.*

lyklyhod, liklyhod, likelyhed *n.* probability, likelihood 6/5 *etc.*
lykyng *ppl. a.* healthy, "in condition"
149/12
lymmes, lymmys *n. pl.* limbs 67/11,
312/18
lyst *v. See* **list**
lyvelod *n.* livelihood 273/7
lyvid *pp.* lived 3/22 *etc.*

Macedonye *n.* Macedonia 190/22
Machomete, Mahumet(e) *n.* Moham-
med 7/1 *etc.*; *poss.* **Mac(h)ometes** 193/5
etc.
maistreys *n. pl. play maistreys* perform
conjuring feats or magic tricks 136/8
make *v. make shifte. See* **shift(e)**; *make
toward* go toward, head in the direction
of 49/24; *intr.* (*for pass.*) *put . . . to make*
request to be made 180/19
malefactour *n.* evil doer, malefactor
32/27, 225/6–7
malencolious, melancolyous *adj.* melancholy, gloomy 150/14 *etc.*
malignite *n.* wickedness, evil 159/7
mameryng *vbl. n.* state of doubt, hesitation 93/25
maner *n.* manner, proper behavior,
custom 4/9 *etc.*; kind (of) 4/20 *etc.*; sense
4/21 *etc.*; method, way 16/8 *etc.*; appearance 123/6; state of mind 149/18; *after
the maner of* of the same nature as,
similar in behavior to 69/28–29; *euery
maner kynd* every kind of 52/23; *for the
maner sake* for the sake of appearances
115/18; *in* (*a*) *maner* so to speak, very
nearly 64/26, 93/25; *in this* (*some, no*)
maner wise in this (some, no) way 63/2
etc.; *maner thyng* kind of thing 56/22
manerly *adv.* becomingly, properly 117/33
manhed *n.* manhood, state of being human
11/25, 106/11
mannyshe *adj.* man-like, masculine 93/20
manslawter *n.* manslaughter 32/23
manteyne *v.* maintain, support 57/20–21,
183/16
mark(e) *n.* indication, sign 134/3, 5; distinction 136/3; target 49/14 *etc.*
marke *v.* heed 83/25; notice, observe 51/7
etc.
markyng *vbl. n.* noticing, noting 142/23

Martialis, martiall *n.* Martial 217/11, 13
mary *int.* indeed, to be sure 32/2 *etc.*
mase *n.* maze, labyrinth 167/14 *etc.*
mastres *n.* mistress 81/8 *etc.*
match *v.* equal 185/7; *pt.* joined, associated
183/1
matches *n. pl.* equals 73/29
matres *n. pl.* matters, state of affairs 221/23
mattyns *n. pl.* matins, morning prayers;
payre of mattyns 65/27. *See* n.
maundy *n.* footwashing at the Last Supper
66/27. *See* n.
mawdeleyns *n. poss.* Magdalen's 185/11
mawgre *prep.* in spite of; *mawgre my tethe*
in spite of everything I could do 76/23
mayne *adj.* vigorous, mighty 268/11
mayntenaunce *n.* support, upholding,
abetting 32/3 *etc.*
mayny *n. all the mayny* the whole company
215/3
meane *adj.*¹ low, undistinguished 94/3;
meane wittid of inferior intelligence 39/24
meane *adj.*² (*with regard to time or season*)
intermediate, intervening 54/22 *etc.*
meane *n. See* **me(a)ne**
measure *n.* moderation 117/9; *above all
measure* beyond all limits 213/11; *out of
measure* immoderately, extremely 248/18
meate *n. See* **me(a)te**
medell, medill, medle *v.* deal (with),
concern oneself with 53/4 *etc.*
medicinable, medicynable *adj.* possessed of healing properties, curative
23/12 *etc.*
medisyn, medycyn *n.* medicine 11/4 *etc.*
meke *adj.* meek 25/14, 26/27
meke *n. refl.* humble (oneself) 146/20
mekely *adv.* meekly 26/8, 20
mek(e)nes *n.* meekness 45/21, 254/20
melancolyous *adj. See* **malencolious**
member *n.* section, part 24/24; *pl.* **membres** male genitalia 191/11
mencion *n. maketh mencion* mentions, calls
to mind 69/28
mendid *pp.* amended, reformed 206/24
mendyng *ppl. a.* healing, improving 85/18
me(a)ne *n.* means 10/26 *etc.*
mene *v.* mean 182/1 *etc.*; *pt.* **ment** 33/16,
48/4
menglid *pp.* mingled, mixed 70/20, 244/4
menisshing *vbl. n. See* **mynyshyng**

merchauntdice *n.* merchandising, engaging in trade 291/12

mere *adj.* absolute, perfect 39/6

merely, meryly *adv.* merrily 138/25 *etc.*

meritith (in) *v. pr. 3 s.* acquires merit (through) 71/4; *pt.* **meritid, merytid** acquired merit, was deserving 66/10, 24

mervelouse *adj.* astonishing 136/22 *etc.*

mervelouse, mervilouse *adv.* wondrously, to an astonishing degree 19/3 *etc.*

mery *adj.* amusing, animated, jesting 81/7 *etc.*; joyful 121/21 etc.

meryly *adv. See* **merely**

merytid *pp. See* **meritith**

messe *n.* a serving of food, course of dishes 213/22. *See n.*

mete *adj.* suitable, appropriate 85/16 *etc.*

mete *adv.* suitably, favorably 148/23, 189/10

me(a)te *n.* food 57/9 *etc.*

mete *v.* measure relative closeness of arrows to a mark 49/15, 50/13; *pt.* **met** 49/25

me thynke, my thynke *v. refl.* it seems to me 13/28 *etc.*; *pt.* **me thought** 8/28 *etc.*

met(e)ly *adv.* fairly, tolerably, moderately 65/14 *etc.*; appropriately 85/20

metyng *vbl. n.* measuring 49/21, 56/17

mich, mych *adj.* much 57/22 *etc.*; **mych part agayne** to a great extent against 94/3; *comp.* **more** greater 39/3, 64/11; *super.* **most** greatest 67/19, 101/6

mich, mych(e), moch *adv.* much 53/7 *etc.*

mind *n. See* **mynd**

minish, minysh *v. See* **mynish**

minishyng *vbl. n. See* **mynyshyng**

minister, mynister *v.* provide 150/5, 203/16; *pp.* **ministred** administered, applied 147/21

minyshment *n. See* **mynyshment**

misch(i)efe *n.* evil plight, misfortune 6/21, 125/1

miscreant *adj.* unbelieving 53/15

misfortuneth *v. pr. 3 s.* happens unfortunately 165/9

mishap(p) *v.* have the misfortune 151/2, 170/13

mislike *v. See* **myslike**

mislikyng (of) *vbl. n.* aversion (to) 98/12

misse, mysse *v.* be without, lack, fail to obtain 16/14 *etc.*

misse content *v. impers. it shall not misse content hym selfe* it will not distress him 132/14

misse happe *n.* ill fortune 120/14

misse iugyng *pr. p.* misjudging 135/27

misse like *v. See* **myslike**

misse report *v.* slander, speak falsely of 184/28

misse spend *v.* misspend 224/15

misse vse *v. refl.* misconduct oneself, misbehave 161/11

missing *vbl. n. missing of their mynd* failure to attain their desires 221/26

m¹ᵉ *adj.* thousand 237/4, 10

mo *adj.* more 4/21 *etc.*

moch *adv. See* **mich**

mocion *n. See* **motion**

mok(k) *v.* mock 212/16, 218/7; *pr. p.* *mokkyng stokke. See* **stok(k)e**; *pp.* **mokkyd, mokqued,** 155/12, 226/16

mone *n.* complaint, lamentation 54/25

mone *n.* moon 110/8, 116/7

moneth *n.* month 78/7

mo(u)ntayn *n.* mountain 7/17, 13/20

more *comp. adj. See* **mich**

morea *n.* Morea, the Peloponnesus 190/22. *See n.*

morn *v.* mourn 45/5, 52/10

morow *n. the morow* the following day 167/19

most *super. adj. See* **mich**

most *v.* must 10/25 *etc.*

motion, mocion *n.* inclination, prompting 73/14 *etc.*; proposal 229/24

mountenaunce *n.* amount, extent 237/9

move *v.* bring up, put forward 19/25 *etc.*; prompt, incite 19/1 *etc.*

moveable *adj. moveable substans. See* **substans**

movyng *vbl. n. by the movyng of them selfe* on their own initiative, by their own will 142/21

Moyses, moyses *n.* Moses 18/2 *etc.*

murm(o)ur *v.* grumble, express discontent 74/23 *etc.*

murmure *n.* muttered complaint 12/2 *etc.*

mutable *adj.* inconstant, changeable 257/5

mych *adj. See* **mich**

mych(e) *adv. See* **mich**

myddes *n.* middle, midst 213/22 *etc.*

mygrem *n.* migraine, severe headache 274/22

mynd, mind *n.* judgment, opinion 4/14; attitude, intention 17/2 *etc.*; *as far as my mynd giveth me. See* **geue**; *bere in mynd. See* **bere**; *fall in . . . mind. See* **fall**; *missing of their mynd. See* **missing**; *to my mynd* in my opinion 27/12–13

mynd *v.* intend 16/13 *etc.*

myndid *ppl. a.* inclined, disposed, determined 97/25 *etc.*

myndyng *vbl. n.* consideration 113/26, 304/16

mynish, mynysh, minysh, minish *v.* diminish, reduce 37/10 *etc.*

mynister *v. See* **minister**

mynstrell *n.* minstrel 274/13, 14

mynyshment, minyshment *n.* diminishing, lessening 16/9 *etc.*

mynyshyng, mynishyng, menisshing, minishyng *vbl. n.* diminishing, lessening 47/3 *etc.*

myschevose *adj.* harmful 15/3

myslike, mislike, misse like *v.* dislike, be displeased with 96/12 *etc.*

mysse *n.* want, loss 5/17

mysse *v. See* **misse**

my thinke *v. refl. See* **me thinke**

nakidly *adv.* simply, without elaboration 173/6

name *n. by name* especially, particularly 56/1

namely *adv.* particularly, especially 30/28 *etc.*

naturall *adj.* constituted by nature 4/5 *etc.*; of this world as opposed to spiritual, guided by God 9/22 *etc.*; native 195/22

naturall *adv.* by nature, normally 133/9

naturally *adv.* by natural processes 302/3

nature *n. of the nature selfe* of its own nature, naturally 107/9

naughty *adj.*; morally bad, wicked 291/10

nayle *n. with toth &* *nayle. See* **toth**

necessitie *n.* need 11/25 *etc.*; *of necessitie* necessarily 71/30

necromancy *n.* black magic 62/10

nede *v.* be necessary; *nede not* is not necessarily so 37/14; is not necessary 156/4

nedeles *adv.* unnecessarily 79/9

ne(a)des *adv.* necessarily 12/20 *etc.*

nedilles, nedlys *n. poss.* needle's 171/2, 19

nedines, nedenes *n.* poverty, neediness 204/1 *etc.*

nedith *v. pr. 3 s. nedith* not is unnecessary 92/22

negardly *adv.* parsimoniously, stingily 224/14

nekke *n.* neck 79/28

nere *adv.* nearer 263/8

nerer *comp. adj.* more pertinent, more germane 35/2

ne(y)ther *adj.* ne(y)ther nother. *See* **nother**

neuer *adv. neuer so greate* (*sore, etc.*) as great (sore, etc.) as possible 35/26 *etc.*

neuerthelesse *adv.* no less, not at all diminished 252/24

new *adv.* anew, over again 312/20

newelties *n. pl.* new or unusual activities, novelties 188/25, 192/15–16

next *adj.* nearest 101/6

neybour *n.* neighbor 58/4 *etc.*; *pl.* **neibours, neybors** 7/6, 46/25

Ninive, Nynive *n.* Nineveh 52/12, 95/27

noman *pron.* no one, nobody 8/12, 25

none *adj.* not any, no 53/17

none *n.* noon 165/29 *etc.*

none *n.* nun 79/29

nose *n.* socket of a candle stick 85/21, 23

noselid *pp.* trained, educated, nurtured 94/26

nother *adv.* neither 42/24

nother *pron.* other 35/19; *ne(y)ther nother* neither the one nor the other 71/27 *etc.*

nothing, nothyng *adv.* not at all 19/7 *etc.*

nought *adj.* bad, wicked 18/6 *etc.*

nought, nowght *n. set nought by, set at nought* scorn, despise 60/28 *etc.*

nowise *adv.* (in) no way, not at all 98/4 *etc.*

noyouse *adj.* vexatious, troublesome 224/4

nydeot *adj.* idiotic, mindless 285/15

nygh *adv.* near 201/14

Nynive *n. See* **Ninive**

obieccion *n.* objection 33/17 *etc.*

obiected *pp.* presented to the sight or other senses 282/1

obprobrious *adj.* insulting, abusive 191/20

occasion *n.* opportunity 133/2 *etc.*; *take occasion. See* **take**

occupie, occupy *v.* invest 112/10; hold, have possession of 210/29; use, employ 225/1

odyouse *adj.* odious, hateful 270/6, 273/6

of *adv.* off, away 7/29 *etc.*

of (**f**) *prep.* because of 4/25 *etc.*; from, out of 4/25 *etc.*; on, in 9/13 *etc.*; for 15/16 *etc.*; by 196/22; by means of 175/18; *of them selfe* by themselves 36/21

offre *n.* proposing, suggestion 133/3, 176/13

offrid *pp.* offered 10/11

ofter *comp. adv.* more often 19/24 *etc.*

on *prep.* in 14/20 *etc.*

onely *adj.* single, sole 95/13 *etc.*

onely *adv.* alone 262/4

ones *adv.* once 18/1 *etc.*

ontowchid *pp.* untouched, unmentioned 253/8–9

oower *poss. adj. See* **o(o)wer**

open *adj.* evident 24/7 *etc.*

open *v.* explain 23/16 *etc.*

or(e) *adv.* before 76/25 *etc.*

ordenately *adv.* in an orderly manner, within orderly limits 282/4

order *n. take such order* take such steps, arrange matters in such a way 165/20

ordeynid *pp.* prepared, made ready 43/9

ordred *pp.* managed, brought under control 145/14

ordreth *v. pr. 3 s.* administers, governs 224/30

ordynaunce *n.* command, law 21/6

orels *adv.* or else 52/5 *etc.*

orisons *n. pl.* prayers 20/21

othe *n.* oath 190/3

other *pron.* one another, each other 0/11 *etc.*; others 155/16; *either other. See* **either**

otherwise *adv.* with regard to other points, in other respects 47/10, 81/17; in other ways, by other means 63/19

ouer, over *adv.* too, overly 120/2 *etc.*

ouer *prep.* beyond, in addition to 5/21 *etc.*

ouer charge *v.* overburden 29/1

ouer litle *adj.* too little 36/2

ouer mich *adj.* too much 162/6

ouermuch *adv.* too much, excessively 161/10

ouer sight, ouersight *n.* oversight, thoughtlessness 78/15; rash imprudence, lack of perception 196/14

ouerwhelm *v.* cover completely, bury 7/17

ought, aught, awght *pron.* anything whatever 22/23 *etc.*

ought *v. pt.* owned, possessed 208/11

out *adv. drinke, slepe out. See* **drinke, slepe**; *out will my sowle* my soul will leave 86/3–4

out of *prep.* because of 108/22 *etc.*; outside of 120/7 *etc.*

outragiouse *adj.* excessive, immoderate 246/7–8

over *adv. See* **ouer**

o(o)wer *poss. adj.* our 6/13 *etc.*

owncle *n.* uncle 93/23

outewardly *adv.* outwardly 176/23

pacience, pacyence *n.* endurance, forbearance 14/26 *etc.*

pacientes *n. poss.* patient person's 71/18

pacion *n. See* **pass(h)ion**

pageant *n.* specious performance, trick 215/25

paluesey *n.* palsy, disease of the nervous system causing paralysis and trembling 274/24

pangid *v. pt.* grieved, anguished 55/5, 168/29

paralypomenon *n.* Paralipomenon, Books of Chronicles 62/24

parcell *n.* part, portion 269/27

parciall *adj.* partial, favorable 83/6

pardie *int. See* **perdy(e)**

parice *n.* Paris 228/28. *See n.*

parishons *n. pl.* parishioners 198/23

parsonage *n.* benefice or living of a parish priest 161/26

part *n.* party, side in a dispute 38/8 *etc.*

partld *pp.* divided, shared 79/23

party, partie *n.* person in question 133/9, 11; *pl.* **parti(e)s** parts 6/20, 138/17; factions 221/23, 24

partyng *ppl. a. partyng felow* sharer, partner 230/6

pase *n.* pace 119/16

passe *n.* completion, resolution 99/26, 125/8

passe *v.* depart, leave 276/23; surpass, exceed 25/21 *etc.*; pass over, pass by 87/17; *passe betwene* pass through, endure 205/2; *pp.* **passed, passid** past 3/9 *etc.*

pass(h)ion, pacion *n.* suffering, pain 32/8 *etc.*

passyng *adj.* surpassing, preeminent 35/3

pate *n.* head 32/16

patereth *v. pr. 3 s.* recites rapidly and mechanically 65/23. *See n.*

pavice, pavise, pauice *n.* convex shield large enough to cover the whole body 103/28 *etc.*

payce *n.* weight 312/24

payne *v.* punish, torture 272/4

paynym *adj.* pagan 9/19

paynym *n.* pagan 178/19, 310/26

payre *n.* pair 115/27 *etc.*; *payre of mattyns* 65/27. *See n.*

pease *n.* peace 229/22

pease *n. not worth a pease* not worth a pea, of little value 95/11

pece *n.* piece 125/10 *etc.*

pens *n. pl.* pence 116/24

penury(e) *n.* destitution, indigence 67/29, 175/12

penytentiall *adj.* of penitence 71/27–28

peradventure *adv.* perhaps 26/2 *etc.*

percase *adv.* perhaps, perchance 51/22 *etc.*

perced *v. pt.* pierced 312/30; *pr. p.* **persing** 158/9

percever *v.* persevere 7/10, 121/21; *pt.* **perseverd** remained 53/8–9

perdy(e), perdie, pardie *int.* by God, indeed 47/10 *etc.*

perell *n. See* **perill**

perfit(t) *adj.* perfect 12/31 *etc.*

perfitly *adv.* surely, certainly 290/7

performe *v.* perform, carry out 197/2

perhappes *n.* mere possibility 300/21

perill, perell *n.* peril 3/17 *etc.*; *cast so ferre perell. See* **cast**

perseverd *v. pt. See* **percever**

persing *pr. p. See* **perced**

perswacion *n.* conviction, assurance 251/15

pesable *adj.* peaceable 191/2

pestylent *adj.* pernicious, deadly 299/4

petites *n. pl.* young schoolboys 70/1

peuyshnes *n.* foolishness 93/19

pevesh, pevish, pevysh *adj.* foolish, senseless 15/17 *etc.*; worthless 119/20

pharow *n.* pharaoh 17/29

phelisties, philisties *n. pl.* Philistines 140/15 *etc.*

phisicion, phisition *n.* physician, doctor 11/2 *etc.*; *pl.* **phisitiens** 120/24

phisike *n.* medical treatment, medicine 63/2 *etc.*

pich *n.* pitch, tar 160/21

pilleth *v. pr. 3 s.* pillages, robs 191/4

pipe *v.* blow or play on a pipe 273/11

pismeres *n. pl.* ants 158/13

pistles *n. pl.* epistles, letters 247/2

plage *n.* plague 17/29 *etc.*

plaster *n.* external curative application 28/29, 57/12

play *v. play maistreys. See* **maistreys**

playne *adv.* plainly, clearly 70/30

plede *v.* plead 144/2

plentie, plentye *n.* abundance, fullness 6/11 *etc.*

plurisie *n.* pleurisy, inflammation of the membranes around the lungs 302/17

pocion *n.* potion, medicine 293/12

pole *n.* pool 45/17, 23

politike *adj.* judicious, prudent 252/26

poppe *n. at a poppe* in an instant, suddenly 168/6

por(e) *adj.* poor 34/14 *etc.*; *comp.* **porer** 184/17

porcion *n.* portion, particular part 72/6 *etc.*; *after the porcion, for the porcion* with regard to the part 72/16, 23

port *n.* carriage, bearing 160/29; importance, position 206/21

portingale, portyngale *n.* Portugal 256/4, 259/27–28

portuouse *n.* portable breviary 46/21

posill *n.* maid 112/20

possessioners *n. pl.* owners 269/27

potestates *n. pl.* potentates, rulers 101/21

poticaryes, poticaries, potycaries *n. pl.* apothecaries, pharmacists 11/4 *etc.*

pourge *v.* purge, cleanse 76/25, 98/19

powltre *n.* poultry dealer 116/29; *poss.* **powlters** 116/25

praers *n. pl.* prayers 46/21

praty *adj.* pretty 85/24

pray *n.* prey 108/8, 118/22

prayse *v.* appraise 119/24

praysid *pp.* praised 75/13

precise *adj.* overly particular 22/23, 193/23

precise *adv.* exactly, perfectly 52/31

precisely *adv. See* **presisely**

preest *n. See* **prest(e)**

prehemynaunce, pre(h)emynence *n.* pre-eminence, first position 64/23 *etc.*

prent *v.* imprint 244/13

prerogatyue *n.* prerogative, precedence, superiority 68/31, 72/19

prescribe *v.* dictate, direct 21/20

prescribyng *vbl. n.* dictating, ordering 22/2

presens *n.* presence 6/29

presisely, precisely *adv.* definitely, exactly 21/13 *etc.*

prest(e), preest *n.* priest 3/13 *etc.*

pretely *adv.* quietly, without fanfare 49/19

preter Iohns *n. poss.* Prester John's 259/29. *See n.*

prety *adv.* rather, fairly 213/19

preve, proue *v.* prove 226/12; test, try 132/26, 142/7

pricke *n. See* **prik(k)(e)**

pricketh *v. pr. 3 s. See* **prukke**

prickid *pp. See* **prukke**

prickyng *ppl. a.* piercing, wounding 159/24

prik(k)(e), pricke *n.* target in archery, center of target 49/17 *etc.*; puncture, scratch 50/20; prod, stimulus 50/21, 118/21

priketh *v. pr. 3 s. See* **prukke**

prikkid *v. pt. See* **prukke**

prik(k)yd *pp. See* **prukke**

prisonement *n.* imprisonment 255/8

prisounyd *pp.* imprisoned 271/1

prively *adv.* privately, secretly 127/22 *etc.*

privy *adj.* hidden, secret 221/32

proces(se) *n.* narrative, discourse 14/1 *etc.*

procure *v.* persuade, prevail upon 95/28

profe *n.* proof 47/13 *etc.*; result, outcome 189/23; test 199/6 *etc.*; *come to good profe* become successful, turn out well 291/18–19

profet *n.* prophet 226/20

prollyng *pr. p.* prowling, searching 118/24

promiscion *n.* promise 55/1

pronite *n.* propensity, inclination 165/6

pronosticacion *n.* portent, omen 194/21

prophet *n.* profit 176/11; *pl.* 96/5

proponid *pp.* proposed, raised 173/6 *etc.*

propre, proper *adj.* apt, appropriate 213/1; characteristic, inherent 256/18, 282/8

proprietie *n.* nature, essence 262/3

protestid *v. pt.* asserted, declared 294/15

proue *v. See* **preve**

prouicion *n.* provision, allowance 183/9

prouocacion *n.* incitement, instigation 162/16

prouokyd *pp.* summoned to a fight 101/31

provedent *adj.* provident, watchful 29/24

providyd *v. pt.* took care 54/20

prukke *v.* urge, incite 218/29; *pr. 3 s.* **pri(c)keth** stings, vexes 50/22, 60/18; *pt.* **prikkid** 118/19 *etc.*; *pr. p.* **prickyng** 67/13; *pp.* **prik(k)yd, prickid** 110/13 *etc.*; *was ... prikkyd forth* had ridden ahead 110/13–14

publicane *n.* publican, tax gatherer 176/14, 178/19

puff *v. puff vpp* inflate, flatter 131/13, 224/21

puff ring *n.* hollow counterfeit ring 228/27–28. *See n.*

pulyng *pr. p.* whining, crying childishly 112/18

pulyng *vbl. n.* crying faintly 112/25

purchase *v.* gain, obtain 84/30

pure *adj.* mere, simple 66/31

purgacions *n. pl.* purgings, cleansings 151/26

purpose *n. of purpose to* in order to 304/24

purpose *v.* intend 33/15 *etc.*

purposynges *n. pl.* purposes, intentions 159/13

pursew *v.* pursue 142/5

pusillanimite *n.* lack of fortitude, faintheartedness 111/10 *etc.*

put *v. put ... case. See* **case**; *put forth* advance, further 219/27; *put ... to make. See* **make**; *pp.* proposed 315/6; *put vnto* inflicted on 25/19

pyk *v. pyk out* glean, absorb 114/22–23

pyn banke *n.* instrument of torture, the rack 61/8

pynch *n.* difficulty, critical point 281/11, 292/17

pynched *ppl. a.* straitened in means, in financial distress 73/8

pynne *n. of a pynne* in the least, at all 51/26; *pl.* **pynnys** pins 302/17

pyn(n)yd *ppl. a.* transfixed, pinned 312/26; *pynnyd vpp* penned up, imprisoned 257/13

pynyng *pr. p.* suffering, afflicted 301/30

pyteouse, pytuouse *adj.* full of pity, compassionate 58/5, 162/18

quake *v.* shake, tremble, vibrate 315/13; tremble with fear 275/7

quarter, quartre *n.* region, locality 7/4 *etc.*

quayle *v.* give way, break down 221/26

quenes *n. poss.* queen's 126/20

quiet *adv. See* **quyt(e)**

quik(ke) *adj.* alive, lively 82/20 *etc.*

quiknes, quyckenes *n.* liveliness, animation 10/3, 113/29

quod *v. pt.* quoth, said 81/9 *etc.*

quyncy *n.* inflammation of the throat 274/23

quysshion *n.* cushion 275/8

quyt(e), quiet *adv.* completely, utterly 4/21 *etc.*

quyt *v. pt. refl.* acquitted (oneself), conducted (oneself) 214/2; *pp.* **quyt** 262/28

rabels *n. pl.* mobs, crowds 290/11

radicate *ppl. a.* rooted, firmly established 282/16

rampyng *ppl. a.* standing erect, rearing, showing fierceness 201/2, 318/4

range *n.* line, order 289/17

rate *n.* estimate, standard 36/30 *etc.*; quantity, amount 72/6 *etc.*; *after the rate* proportionately, according to the amount 68/19, 272/12

ratid *v. pt.* chided, scolded; *all to ratid* reproved vehemently 219/25–26

ratle *v.* rattle 29/14

ravenour *n.* plunderer 116/19

ravish *v.* carry off, transport in spirit 215/28–29 *etc.*

ravyn *n.* rapine, robbery 117/4 *etc.*

raylyng *ppl. a.* reviling, abusive 289/14, 19

raylyng *vbl. n.* abuse, scorn 289/21, 28

ray(g)ne *v. See* **reyne**

reason *n. of reason* reasonably, with good reason 69/7

rebukefull *adj.* deserving of rebuke, disgraceful, shameful 290/12

receyptes *n. pl.* prescriptions 11/7

reche *adj.* rich 54/6 *etc.*; *super.* **rechest** richest 47/8

reches *n. pl.* riches 10/1 *etc.*

recidivacion *n.* relapse, backsliding 148/15

recomfort *v.* encourage, console 38/2

recompence *n.* compensation, requital, repayment 93/10 *etc.*

recompence *v.* requite, compensate for 237/4, 320/12; *pp.* **recompensid, recumpensid** 47/5, 244/20

record *n. bere … record* bear witness, testify 253/11

re(a)de *n. See* **ride**

rede *v.* read 47/6 *etc.*; *pp.* **red(d)(e)** 9/15 *etc.*

redely *adv.* readily 212/2

redy *adv.* already 116/26

redye *adj.* likely, conducive 71/17

refer(re) *v.* commit, entrust 16/7 *etc.*

referryng *vbl. n.* assigning, committing 10/21 *etc.*

refrayne *v. trans.* restrain, hold back 29/19 *etc.*

refrigerate *v.* cool 103/25

regard *n. in the regard of* in comparison with 158/11–12

regard *v. not regard a rish. See* **rish**

regresse *n.* return, re-entry 190/12

rehersall *n.* mention 203/11

reherse *v.* recount, relate, tell 40/25 *etc.*

rehersid *ppl. a.* recounted, told 109/22

rehersyng *vbl. n.* relating, telling, repeating 8/18, 308/11

reken, rekyn *v.* consider, estimate 4/27 *etc.*

rekenyng *vbl. n.* consideration, reasoning 5/1 *etc.*; estimate, expectation 76/28

relefe *n.* relief 182/28

relent *v.* soften, dissolve 98/11, 21

relese *n.* release 36/29

releve *v.* relieve 172/18, 180/2

religion *n.* religious house, convent 80/2. *See n.*; religious order 185/24

religiouse *adj. religiouse man, religiouse person* one bound by monastic vows, a monk or friar 93/26 *etc.*

reliques *n. pl.* surviving traces, residue 21/2

remanaunt *n. See* **rem(e)na(u)nt(e)**

remembra(u)ns, remembraunce *n.* memory 6/12 *etc.*

remembrid *ppl. a.* mentioned 18/14 *etc.*

remiscion, remission *n.* forgiveness, pardon 28/22 *etc.*

remit *v.* resign, surrender 21/25

rem(e)na(u)nt(e), remnent, remanaunt *n.* rest, remainder 7/2 *etc.*

remors *n.* remorse 59/20

renegate *adj.* apostate 191/17

Renegates *n. pl.* apostates 191/14

reney *v.* deny, renounce 190/16

renome *n.* renown, fame 211/14 *etc.*

reno(w)med *pp.* renowned, celebrated 74/26, 211/24

renued *ppl. a.* renewed 164/14

reprouid *pp.* disproved, rejected 146/4

reprovyng *vbl. n.* disapproval 310/2

repute *v.* consider, regard 10/22 *etc.*

requier, requere, require, requyre *v.* ask, request 11/24 *etc.*

requyryng *vbl. n.* requesting, desiring 16/16

reseruid *v. pt.* postponed, put off 77/10, 215/12; *pp.* remaining, excepted 172/8

reseruyng *vbl. n.* holding back 175/1

resonyng *vbl. n.* reasoning 155/3, 204/25

resort(e) *v.* proceed, direct attention 27/13 *etc.*; betake oneself, make one's way 69/10 *etc.*; enter, arrive 190/18

respect *n.* consideration, regard 13/12 *etc.*; *in respect of* in comparison with 9/4 *etc.*

respit *v.* postpone, delay 269/12, 272/25

respitt *n.* respite, delay 268/6

rest *n. In rest* as for the remainder 190/17

restraynt *n.* confinement 252/7-8; curtailment 255/15, 19

retaynyng *vbl. n.* restraining, holding in custody 257/21

reteyne *v.* engage, hire 182/22

revenouse *adj.* ravenous 104/1

revolvid *v. pt.* turned over, pondered 82/10

rewle *n.* rule 97/19

reyne, ray(g)ne *v.* reign 195/17 *etc.*

reyse *v.* raise 62/12

r(o)iall *adj.* sumptuous, befitting a king 55/26, 208/17

rially *adv.* regally, splendidly 55/27

rialtie, rialtye *n.* pomp, splendor 184/16, 268/11

Ribaldes *n. pl.* knaves, rascals 289/28

richesse *n.* wealth 171/15 *etc. See* n.

riddith *v. pr. 3 s.* dispatches, disposes of 302/9; *pp.* **rid** 302/6

ride, re(a)de *n.* reed 5/2 *etc.*

riggid *ppl. a.* dressed 163/1

right *adv.* very 28/2 *etc.*; rightly, correctly 72/5

rightouse, ryghteus *adj.* righteous 18/4 *etc.*

ripe *adj.* properly informed, fully deliberated 178/12

ripe *v.* bring to a head 57/13

rish *n.* rush; *not regard a rish* care nothing for, take no account of 9/5, 289/27

roiall *adj. See* **r(o)iall**

rok(ke) *n.* rock 111/4, 8

rokkyd *pp.* rocked 132/2

ro(w)me *n.* office, position 161/27 *etc.*; room, space 13/13 *etc.*

Roodes *n.* Rhodes 8/5

rore *v.* roar 108/5 *etc.*

rote *n.* root 240/31, 282/17

rotid *pp.* rooted 281/13, 294/9

rouers *n. pl. at rouers* indiscriminately, at will 162/20

rowme *n. See* **ro(w)me**

rude *adj.* raw, unfinished 207/2

rude *adv.* harshly, discordantly 111/3

ruffle *n.* disturbance, perturbation 51/24

rule *n. bere a rule. See* **bere**

run *v. run together* join in combat 273/10

ryghteus *adj. See* **rightouse**

ryve *v.* split, crack 315/14

saciate, satyatt *adj.* satiated, filled to repletion 213/13, 306/14

sad *adj.* serious 83/2

saddly *adv.* seriously 139/1

safe gard(e), savegard *n.* safeguard, protection 102/12 *etc.*

sake cloth *n.* sackcloth 95/25

salute *v.* address, greet 220/27

sample *n.* example 33/18 *etc.*

Sapience *n.* Book of Wisdom 158/22

sat *v. pt. sat . . , on thornes. See* **thornes**

satyatt *adj. See* **saciate**

save *conj.* except 271/10

savegard *n. See* **safe gard(e)**

savour *n.* relish, delight 84/27 *etc.*

say *v. say well by* speak well of 74/28; *as who say* that is to say 194/2-3

scant *adv.* scarcely, barely, hardly 13/22 *etc.*

scantly *adv.* scarcely, hardly 6/17, 97/12

scape *v.* escape 140/26 *etc.*

scapyng *vbl. n.* escaping 264/22 *etc.*

scole *n.* school 46/2 *etc.*

scott *n.* reckoning, payment for entertainment 99/12

scriple *n.* scruple 114/3, 120/22

scrip(e)lous(e), scrupelous *adj.* scrupulous, overly fastidious 112/15 *etc. See n.*

scrupulosit(i)e *n.* scrupulousness, overly rigid conscience 112/19, 121/25

scrye *n.* clamor 110/3

Scurer *n.* scout, advance guard 110/5, 22

seame *v. See* **se(a)me**

seas *v.* seize 317/30

sease *v.* cease 153/24, 300/7; *pt.* **seasid, seacid** stopped, stilled 58/21 *etc.*

season *n. in season* at the proper time, opportunely 29/13

sede, seed *n.* seed 42/6 *etc.*; progeny, descendents 54/10

see *n.* sea 5/25 *etc.*

seke *v.* seek 3/11 *etc.*; *seke vpp* look for, try to find 177/17; *seke vppon* approach, apply to 279/13

sekyng *vbl. n.* seeking, search 6/2

seld *adj.* rare, infrequent 84/25

seld(e), silde *adv.* seldom, infrequently 80/19 *etc.*

selfe *adj. of the nature selfe. See* **nature**

selles *n. pl.* cells 276/24

sely *adj. See* **silly**

se(a)me *v.* seem 205/26; *semeth me, me semeth* it seems to me 18/25–26 *etc.*

Senek *n.* Seneca 254/6

sensible *adj.* perceptible by the senses 281/27

sensibly *adv.* with the senses, intensely 88/17

sentence *n.* opinion, judgment 97/5 *etc.*

sentiall *adj.* sensual, pertaining to the senses 245/21

servile *adj.* enslaved 252/14

servis *n.* service 230/17

set *ppl. a. godly set* fixed upon God, directed toward God 72/2

set(t) *v.* set down 39/25; *set a worke* put to work, rouse to action 167/5 *etc.*; *set at nought. See* **nought**; *set . . . by* value, depend upon 75/17 *etc.*; *set therby* value that 41/11, 252/15; *set . . . therto* add to that 39/17, 44/26–27; *pp. set down* lowered in value 222/13; *set to . . . handes* become seriously involved 8/9–10; *set vpp* raised in value 222/12

settyng *vbl. n. settyng . . . aworke* putting to work 185/5

seuer *v.* separate 6/27

seuerall *adj.* separate, individual 258/4

sew *v.* sue, appeal 6/7

sewer *adj. See* **suer**

sewerly, sur(e)ly *adv.* surely, certainly 140/22 *etc.*; securely 277/21, 282/17

sexten *n.* officer in a church in charge of bell-ringing, grave-digging *etc.* 185/29

sey(i)ng *pr. p.* seeing 45/11 *etc.*

shadow *n.* obscure indication, foreshadowing 307/24 *etc.*

shadow *v.* overshadow, cover 103/15, 106/2

sham *n.* shame 253/24

shamfast *adj.* bashful 82/3; ashamed 232/8

sharpe *adj.* acute, precise 39/27; strict 94/1; intense, severe 200/9 *etc.*

sharpid *pp.* sharpened 125/17

sheld *n. See* **shild**

shent *pp.* reproached, scolded 112/26

sheps *n. poss.* sheep's 86/8

shet(e), shit *v.* shut 299/11; *shete . . . vpp* enclose 274/10, 277/24; *pp.* **shit, shyt** 275/29 *etc.*; shut off, barred 308/25

shete *n.* sheet 246/23

shewid *v. pt.* showed 117/14 *etc.*; told, gave an account of 127/14; *shewid vnto* brought to the attention of 173/13

shift(e), shyfte *n.* expedient, contrivance 145/12 *etc.*; *make shifte* succeed with difficulty, manage with effort 207/17; *make . . . shyftes* make efforts, try all means 171/14

shift(e) *v.* manage 8/13; move 119/16

shild, sheld *n.* shield 107/15, 108/17

shirle *adj.* shrill, piercing 94/2

shirle *adv.* shrilly, piercingly 94/18, 95/9

shit *v. See* **shet(e)**

shogge *v.* shake, rouse (from sleep) 132/4, 143/23

shoke *v. pt.* shook 115/27

sholders *n. pl. See* **shulder**

shortly *adv.* curtly 218/18

shote *n.* act of shooting, shot registered on the target 49/15 *etc.*

shote *v.* shoot 49/15 *etc.*

shreven, shrevyn *ppl. a.* confessed, absolved 118/4 *etc.*

shrewd(e)ly *adv.* severely, harshly 112/26; maliciously 212/14

shrewed, shrewid, shrewde *adj.* shrewish, given to railing or scolding 118/2 *etc.*; of evil nature, with evil consequences 92/8; wicked, malicious 272/14 *etc.*

shrewdnes *n.* shrewishness, ill-temper 118/5, 11

shrewis, shrewes *n. pl.* rascals, villains 191/19, 193/4

shrich *v.* shriek, screech 315/16

shrift(e) *n.* confession 114/27 *etc.*

shroftide *n.* Shrovetide, the three days preceding Ash Wednesday 114/27. *See n.*

shryng *v.* shrink, recoil 293/8

shulder *n.* shoulder 103/28; *pl.* **sholders, shulders** 103/15 *etc.*

shyfte *n. See* **shift(e)**

shyt *pp. See* **shet(e)**

sibbe *adj.* akin, related 208/10

sich *adj.* such 241/19

side *n. on his side* on his part, as part of his argument 133/2; *vppon that side* in that direction, in that vein 134/28

sik(e), syk *adj.* sick 3/14 *etc.*

sik(e)nes, syknes *n.* sickness 3/11 *etc.*

silable *n.* syllable 263/3

silde *adv. See* **seld(e)**

silly, sely *adj.* deserving of pity, helpless 20/11 *etc.*; harmless, foolish 111/3

similitude *n.* comparison 137/24

simony *n.* traffic in ecclesiastical offices 162/13

singularite *n.* peculiarity, eccentricity 133/27

singuler *adj.* singular, exceptional 131/3

sin(ne)s *adv. See* **syns**

sins, syns *conj.* after 85/13; before 7/31

siropes *n. pl.* liquid medicines 63/10

Siry *n. See* **Syry**

sith, syth *conj.* since, because, seeing that, inasmuch as 4/1 *etc.*; *sith that* because 64/26

skyll *n. can skyll of. See* **can**

slee *v.* slay 298/14

sleight, slayte *n.* trickery, deceit, stratagem 80/12 *etc.*

slender *adj.* weak, slight 223/9 *etc.*

slenderly *adv.* weakly, slightly 212/28

slepe *n.* sleep 66/27

slepe *v. slepe out* sleep throughout 92/6

sleyght *adj.* slight 205/13

sloggyng *vbl. n.* lying about idly, being slothful 307/16

slonke *v. pt.* crept furtively 62/4

slougge *v.* be lazy 45/31

slowth, slouth *n.* sloth, laziness 14/23 *etc.*

smoth *adj.* smooth, placid 45/25

smyte *v.* strike, cut 125/19

snofe *n.* snuff, wick 85/20, 21

so *conj.* so long as, provided that 38/29

sobrenes *n.* soberness 287/7

soden, sodayn(e) *adj.* sudden 92/14 *etc.*

sode(y)nly, soda(y)nly *adv.* suddenly 8/22 *etc.*

so(w)le *n.* soul 8/24 *etc.*

solempne *adj.* formal, grand 155/25 *etc.*

soleyne *adj.* sullen, unsociable 160/29

sol(l)icitude *n.* care, concern 174/13 *etc.*

solicityng *pr. p.* tempting, alluring 51/9

some *n.* sum 127/27, 232/11

sond *n.* dispensation, ordinance 254/2. *See n.*

sondry, sundrye *adj.* sundry, various 65/18, 66/26; *sondry wise* in various ways 272/15

sone *adv.* soon, quickly 3/19 *etc.*; *comp.* **son(n)er** 45/1, 197/28

sone *n.* son 104/12 *etc.*

song *pp.* sung 132/2

sooth *n. See* **so(o)th**

sophisticacion *n.* sophistry, specious reasoning 263/18

sophisticall *adj.* specious, sophistic 262/17 *etc.*

sore *adj.* severe, extreme 22/16 *etc.*, *comp.* **sorer** 18/1, 109/1; *super.* **sorest** 20/11

sore *adv.* severely, extremely, harshly, grievously 6/6 *etc.*; *comp.* **sorer** 225/12

sorebeten *ppl. a.* severely beaten 312/19

sort(e) *n.* group, band 4/2 *etc.*

so(o)th *n.* truth 13/28 *etc. See also* **For sooth**

sothely *adv.* truly 174/9, 295/5

sotill, subtill *adj.* subtle, crafty 80/12 *etc.*; *galey subtill. See* **galey**

souperlesse *adj.* supperless 92/8

soupid *v. pt.* supped, ate 81/6

sourges *n. pl.* heavy waves, billows 5/24

Sowdan(e) *n.* Sultan 7/30 *etc.*

sower *v.* sour, cause acidity 63/10

sowne *n.* sound 84/8

538   A DIALOGUE OF COMFORT

sowne v. *sowneth to* have a connection with, refer to 70/14, 16

sowper n. supper 117/4

soylid pp. resolved, explained 64/6; absolved 118/1

spec(i)all adv. especially 108/29 etc.

spech n. speech 211/9

specyally adv. especially 83/14 etc.

spede n. success, result, outcome 62/20 etc.

spede v. intrans. fare, succeed, attain one's end 16/19 etc.; trans. take care of 187/22; pp. **sped** furthered, brought to success 156/3

spedely adv. speedily 174/15

spent v. pt. *spent owt* used up 215/10–11

spet(t) v. spit 133/17, 263/6

spight, spite n. See **spyte**

sponefull n. spoonful 36/25

spoylid pp. despoiled 228/7

spoylyng vbl. n. despoiling 6/25

sprongen pp. sprung, risen 110/21, 166/25

spryt(e), sprit(e) n. spirit 5/6 etc.

spyte, spite, spight n. *spight of* despite, in spite of 292/22; *spyte, spite of our teeth* despite our utmost efforts 242/4, 282/24

stable v. stabilize, make secure 5/23

stablyshid, stablishid pp. established, founded 121/25–26, 231/7

stager v. stagger 102/20

stak v. pt. See **styk(e)**

stand, stond v. stay, remain 8/26 etc.; stand firm 32/17 etc.; *stand in* consist of 130/6; *stand vnto* be inclined to 21/29; *stand with* be compatible with 47/14, 184/14; pt. **stode** 4/29 etc.

standyng vbl. n. standing firm, remaining faithful 198/21

state n. wealth, estate 213/7; institution, element, rank 192/7; pl. poss. nobles', lords' 46/9

staye n. support 4/4

staye v. secure, steady 6/13; support, sustain 7/23

stede n. stead, place 21/16 etc.; *in more stede or lesse* in better or worse circumstances 12/24

stedeth v. pr. 3 s. aids, helps 83/32

stele v. steal 90/23 etc.; pr. p. approaching stealthily 110/4

stere v. refl. move about, bestir oneself 294/28

steres n. pl. stars 159/29

sterke adv. completely, utterly 17/23

stike v. See **styk(e)**

stikke n. See **styk(k)(e)**

stintid v. pt. ceased 300/9

stirid pp. removed, taken away 207/10

stode v. pt. See **stand**

stok(k)e n. provisions, aggregate of goods 180/17; generation, line of descent 266/14; *mokkyng stokke* laughing stock, butt for ridicule 141/9; pl. the stocks 258/10 etc.

stokk v. put into the stocks 272/22

stokkyng ppl. a. *stokkyng yrons* agricultural implements used for uprooting 241/7

stokkyng vbl. n. imprisonment in the stocks 270/21

stole n. stool 185/14 etc.

stomak(e) n. disposition, inclination, spirit 82/15 etc.; appetite 78/5; *breke . . . her stomak* 29/18–19. See n.

stond v. See **stand**

stones n. pl. testicles 191/10

stope v. *stope at* bow before, give in to 18/1

store n. supply 9/11

stowte adj. formidable 220/10

straighter adv. See **strayghtly**

straightnes n. strictness, rigorousness 262/6

stranger n. foreigner 214/4

straw n. *not at a straw* extremely little, not at all 303/27

strayght adv. See **strayt(e)**

strayght n. time of severe hardship or difficulty 194/10

strayghtly adv. strictly, rigorously 260/26; comp. **straighter** 272/12; super. **straytest** 261/18

straynneth v. pr. 3 s. forces, constrains 173/1

strayt(e) adj. strict, rigorous, within narrow bounds 114/12 etc.; straight, direct 236/9; comp. **strayter** 275/17, 29

strayt(e), strayght adv. tightly 169/1 etc.; at once, directly 129/25, 284/25

straytest adv. See **strayghtly**

straytid ppl. a. forced into a narrow space, subjected to hardships 193/30

streke v. pt. See **strik(e)**

streng(h)th v. strengthen 5/23 etc.

stresse n. hardship, affliction, trial 316/25

strik(e), stryke *v.* strike 127/22 *etc.*;
fasten 274/9; *strik . . . into* make (one)
fall suddenly into 29/10; *pt.* **streke** 17/23
strive *v.* contend, dispute 34/9 *etc.*
strypes, strypys *n. pl.* lashes, wounds
from whipping 310/20, 22
studiouse *adj.* requiring careful attention
78/13
study(e) *n.* state of mental perplexity,
anxious meditation 213/26; *mater of
some study* matter requiring so much
thought 64/9
stye *v.* mount, ascend 159/29
styff *adj.* resistant 17/27
styk(k)(e), stikke *n.* stick, fagot 4/21 *etc.*
styk(e), stike *v.* scruple, demur, take
exception 156/4 *etc.*; be deterred by
205/2; *styk with* cause to hesitate 278/14;
pt. **stak** stuck 56/18
styll *adv.* continuously, always 79/22 *etc.*
stynt *n.* measure, extent 36/32
styre *v.* stir, incite, provoke 10/28 *etc.*
substance *n. See* **substans**
substanciall *adj.* solid, sound 202/2 *etc.*
substanciall *adv.* thoroughly, soundly
120/16, 266/1
substans, substa(u)nce *n.* possessions,
goods, estate 47/17 *etc.*; maintenance,
subsistence 206/5; *moveable substans* personal as opposed to real property, chattel
180/12 *etc.*; *substaunce . . . vnmoveable* real
property, land and possessions attached
to the land 207/13–14, 228/7–8
subtill *adj. See* **sotill**
successe *n.* outcome, result 268/19
suer, sure, sewer *adj.* sure, certain 25/15
etc.; trustworthy, reliable 5/3; assured,
confident 5/7; secure 264/6
suertie, suerty(e) *n. See* **surety(e)**
suffer, suffre *v.* allow, permit 8/12 *etc.*;
endure 27/28 *etc.*
suffrage *n.* a vote, usually of assent
(specifically an object used to indicate a
vote) 309/21 *etc.*; *pl.* 309/26; intercessory
prayers 155/21 *etc.*
suff(e)raunce *n.* endurance, forbearance
10/23 *etc.*; permission 107/11; *sufferaunce
of* toleration of, allowing of 190/12
suffryng *vbl. n.* enduring 130/21
sure *adj. See* **suer**
sure *adv.* securely 189/26

surety(e), suerty(e), suertie *n.* safety,
certainty 104/3 *etc.*; pledge, bond 272/8
surfet, surfyt *n.* gluttony, overindulgence
24/5 *etc.*; *pl.* **surfittes** illnesses arising
from intemperance 210/11
sur(e)ly *adv. See* **sewerly**
surmount (above) *v.* surpass, rise above
206/18, 310/15
sustayne, susteyne *v.* endure, undergo,
submit to 25/29 *etc.*
sute *n.* pursuit, chase 294/19; *make sute*
petition, supplicate 62/19, 156/2
swapp *v.* strike, smite 302/18
sware *v. pt.* swore 125/17, 128/19
swarve *v.* swerve, turn aside 204/17
swerd *n.* sword 225/11, 302/18
swet *v. pt.* sweat 214/24
swete *adj.* sweet 94/10 *etc.*
swe(a)te *n.* sweat 67/7, 94/20
sybbe *n.* relation 123/11
syk *adj. See* **sik(e)**
syknes *n. See* **sik(e)nes**
syncke *v.* sink, penetrate 303/24
syns, sin(ne)s *adv.* subsequently 8/2 *etc.*
syns *conj. See* **sins**
syns *prep.* since, ever since, from the time
of 78/4 *etc.*
Syry, Siry *n.* Syria 7/31 *etc.*
syth *conj. See* **sith**

taberettes *n. pl.* small drums 315/11
tabernacles *n. pl.* dwelling places 175/20
table *n.* surface on which a picture is
painted; hence the picture itself 215/8
take *v.* *take . . . for* consider 132/19 *etc.*;
take in worth consider valuable, worth-
while 52/17 *etc.*; *take occasion* take advantage of an opportunity 133/1; *take such
order. See* **order**; *pt.* **toke** 26/10 *etc.*; *toke
his time* saw his opportunity, took his cue
125/15–16; *toke hym selfe for so sure* was so
sure of himself 146/18; *pp.* **take** 80/4
takelyng *n.* rigging, nautical apparatus
57/31
takyng *vbl. n.* estimate, opinion 211/11;
capture 54/15
talis, talys *n. pl.* tales 60/2, 83/3
tallages *n. pl.* taxes levied upon feudal
dependants by their lords 191/5
tapsters *n. poss.* tapster's, of one who draws
ale in a tavern 41/23

tar(r)y(e) v. abide, remain 23/6 etc.; wait 45/18

teare v. tear 96/15; pp. **toren** 96/17

tech(e) v. teach 5/28 etc.; pp. **towght, tawght** 6/4, 219/22

techers n. pl. teachers 5/27

tedious adj. irksome, disagreeable 45/26

tell conj. until 117/24

temerariouse adj. reckless, rash 176/20

temper v. adapt, make suitable 148/13; moderate 162/10; pp. **temprid** mixed, diluted 84/2

temperatly adv. in moderation, with self-restraint 261/13, 30

temperaunce n. state of proper control 93/7 etc.

tempestious adj. tempestuous 5/24

temprid pp. See **temper**

temptid pp. tested, put to the trial 141/6

tender adj. weak, frail 66/1

tercian n. type of fever 88/10. See n.

terrowre n. terror 8/28

testie adj. irritable 14/25

testifie v. trans. witness to, proclaim 32/7

te(e)th, tethe n. pl. See **toth**

tewne n. tune 192/25

than adv. then 6/26 etc.

thanke n. thankfulness, gratitude 25/21 etc.; cannid . . . thanke. See **cannid**

thankfull adj. beneficial 284/4

tharldome n. See **thra(u)ldome**

the pron. thee 101/29 etc.

their adv. there 45/6

thens forth adv. thenceforth, from that time forth 97/10

therat, there at adv. to that place 41/12 etc.; there, at that place 63/13 etc.; at it, at that 138/16 etc.

therby(e) adv. by it, by that 41/11 etc.; by that means 48/16 etc.; in that place 111/18

there as conj. in the place where 69/18

therede n. thread 110/11

therefro adv. from it, from that 199/7 etc.

therevppon adv. then, in that case 138/12

ther(e)for(e) adv. for it, for that 13/26 etc.; for this reason 96/2 etc.

ther(e)in, there in adv. in that way 12/27 etc.; by means of it 12/20 etc.; in it, in that 4/29 etc.

therof adv. of it, of which 8/6 etc.; for that 26/23; from it 173/12

theron adv. thereon, upon this 4/19 etc.

therto adv. for that purpose, in regard to that 18/25, 112/1; to this, to that 39/17 etc.

therunto adv. to it, to that 24/4 etc.

therwith adv. by that means 4/20 etc.; in addition, besides 6/30 etc.; in that case 51/7 etc.; with it, with that 125/18 etc.

therwithall adv. by means of that 132/11

thes adj. these 7/19 etc.

thether adv. thither, to that place 43/23 etc.

theyre, ther adj. their 30/8 etc.

thing n. all thing everything, all things 175/3

Thombe n. thumb 63/13

thornes n. pl. sat . . . on thornes was in a painful state of anxiety or suspense 213/16

thorow(gh), tho(u)rough, thowrow, throw(gh) prep. through, by means of 32/30 etc.

thra(u)ldome, tharldome n. bondage, servitude 6/28 etc.

thrall n. slave 253/13, 17

thre adj. three 24/2

thret n. threat 70/18

thret v. threaten 317/8

thris(s)e, thry(e)s adv. thrice 22/16 etc.

thurst pp. thrust 50/20

thynke v. me thynketh, my thynke it seems to me 3/18 etc.

tide n. time, occasion 118/23

to prep. in 109/13

to adv. too 6/31 etc.

tocheth v. pr. 3 s. See **towch**

toke v. pt. See **take**

token n. sign, symbol 13/1 etc.; symptom 120/28, 121/11

toll n. tax 176/15

tollid v. pt. told 31/19

tone pron. one 65/10 etc.

tong(e) n. tongue 22/26 etc.

toren pp. See **teare**

to(u)rn(e) v. turn, convert, change 7/5 etc.

toth n. tooth; with toth & nayle vigorously, fiercely 285/11; pl. **te(e)th, tethe** 108/14 etc.; spite, spyte of our teeth. See **spyte**; cast in his teth. See **cast**; mawgre my tethe. See **mawgre**

tother adj. other 8/29 etc.

touch v. See **towch**

touchyng *vbl. n.* treatment, discussion 67/23

tourne *n. See* **t(o)urne**

tournyng *vbl. n.* conversion 91/12

toward *prep.* regarding, in reference to 10/13 *etc.*; coming upon, threatening 149/11

towardnes *n.* willingness, docility 141/6

towch, touch *v.* mention, consider, treat in passing 15/8 *etc.*; *pr. 3 s.* **tocheth** pertains to 53/29, 143/16

towching, towchyng *prep.* regarding, concerning 141/5, 287/15

towch stone *n.* that which serves to test the genuineness or value of anything, criterion 226/27

towght *pp. See* **tech(e)**

translacion *n.* transferral of property, handing over 207/23

translatid *pp.* transferred 206/26

transmigracion *n.* removal, deportation 251/5–6

tratice *n. See* **tre(a)tice**

travayles *n. pl.* exertions, hardships 300/10

trayne *n.* trap, scheme designed to deceive 100/19 *etc.*

treacle *n.* remedy, antidote 9/12. *See n.*

tre(a)tice, tratice *n. pl.* treatises 133/7; *sing.* treaty 217/20 *etc.*

tretyng *vbl. n.* treatment 59/10

trew *adj.* true 5/19 *etc.*

trew *adv.* truly, truthfully 65/17

tributaries *n. pl.* those who pay tribute 190/21

tro(w) *v.* trust, believe, suppose 44/14 *etc.*

troble *v.* trouble 77/5 *etc.*; *pp.* **trowblid** 161/8

trone *n.* throne 159/30, 315/23

troubelouse, troubelows *adj.* troublesome, vexatious 45/26 *etc.*

trouth, trowth *n.* truth 37/12 *etc.*; *By my trouth* Upon my honor, indeed 199/2; *Of trowth* In truth, indeed 79/7

trow *v. See* **tro(w)**

trowblid *pp. See* **troble**

try(e) *v.* ascertain by testing 238/1, 7; *try ... owt* determine, ascertain 26/12, 40/12

tryumph *n.* victory rite 6/29

Tullye *n.* M. Tullius Cicero 4/17

tumbrelles *n. pl.* timbrels, tambourines 9/3, 315/11. *See n.*

turment *n.* torment 55/24 *etc.*

turmentry *n.* torment, torture 247/11

t(o)urne *n.* turn, favor, occasion 21/21, 74/24; *pl. shrewid tournes, shrewed turnes* injuries, acts of ill will 272/14, 275/16

twayne, tweyn(e) *adj.* two 5/23 *etc.*; both 89/5

tyklyd *pp.* gratified 68/15

tyme *n. tyme inough* early enough, in time 46/3

tymerouse, timerouse *adj.* timorous, fearful 111/23 *etc.*

Tymothe *n.* Timothy 223/30

typp *n.* tip 80/9

vaded *ppl. a.* faded, decayed 194/4

valerian *n.* an herb 63/11

valure *n.* value, cost 116/24

vaynquysshe *v.* vanquish, overcome 281/1–2; *pp.* **vainquyshid, vanqueshid** 300/1, 318/17

velenouse, vylanouse *adj.* atrocious, horrible 291/3, 23

veniall, venyall *adj.* pardonable, as opposed to deadly or mortal 113/12 *etc.*

venture *n. See* **adventure**

verely, veryly *adv.* truly, certainly 8/18 *etc.*

vertew *n.* virtue 21/11 *etc.*; *pl.* **vertuose** 127/16

vertues, vertuo(u)se *adj.* virtuous 32/4 *etc.*

very, vyry *adj. or adv.* true, truly 4/2 *etc. See n.*

viage, vyage *n.* voyage, journey 132/23 *etc.*; a military expedition or enterprise 188/11

vicion *n.* vision 136/22, 25

villayne *adj.* mean, base 243/12

vinishid *ppl. a.* vanished 159/6

visage *n.* outward appearance, pretence 189/6

visitacion *n.* divine manifestation 71/5

vitayle *n.* victuals, foods 116/19, 210/9

vnadvisidly *adv.* unexpectedly, without reflection 299/6–7

vnckle *n.* uncle 3/9 *etc.*

vnclennes *n.* uncleanliness, foulness 152/21

vncogitable *adj.* inconceivable, beyond thought 306/12, 309/6

542

A DIALOGUE OF COMFORT

vncontrollid *ppl. a.* undisputed, uncontested 218/16

vncouth *adj.* strange, unfamiliar 250/25

vndeceveable *adj.* incapable of deceiving 133/4

vnder *adv.* underneath, beneath 102/24

vnderstanden, vnderstonden *pp.* understood, comprehended 69/21 *etc.*

vndowtid, vndoughtid *ppl. a.* undoubted, certain 16/30 *etc.*

vndowttely *adv.* undoubtedly 240/14

vnevitable *adj.* inevitable 297/11

vngraciouse *adj.* wicked, graceless 62/10 *etc.*; rude, unmannerly 125/15

vnhable *adj.* unable, incapable 112/1, 275/2

vnhappy *adj.* causing trouble, miserable 125/14

vnknowen *ppl. a.* unperceived 127/22

vnkynd *adj.* unnatural 243/12 *etc.*

vnkyndly *adv.* unnaturally 243/28

vnkyndnes *n.* unnatural conduct 8/15

vnleifully *adv.* unlawfully 171/9

vnlokyd for *pp.* unexpected 55/2

vnmanerly *adv.* rude, devoid of manners 187/8

vnmete *adj.* unfit, unworthy 111/27

vnmoveable *adj. substaunce . . . vnmoveable. See* **substans**

vnoccupied *ppl. a.* idle, not put to use 112/7

vnperfit *adj.* imperfect 25/22 *etc.*

vnpossible *adj.* impossible 88/12

vnquiat *adj.* disquieted, disturbed 113/22

vnresonable *adj.* irrational, lacking reason 51/12–13

vnseparable *adj.* inseparable 5/11

vnsewertie *n.* uncertainty, insecurity 207/4

vnspeakable, vnspekeable *adj.* unutterable, inexpressible 22/29–30, 309/5

vnsufficient *adj.* insufficient 10/31

vnthrifte *n.* shiftless, dissolute person 291/18

vnto *prep.* toward 74/18 *etc.*

vntouchid *ppl. a.* not discussed, unmentioned 10/18 *etc.*

vntoward *adj.* inept, perverse 84/13

vntowardnes *n.* perversity, obstinacy 250/7

vnwar(e) *adv.* unknowingly, unwittingly 161/17 *etc.*

vnware *adj.* unaware 22/11; unknown, unperceived 176/25, 200/12

void *adj.* empty 36/3

void, voyde *v.* disappear 13/21; avoid 154/8

voise *n.* voice 43/25

vouchsafe *v.* be willing, agree 85/7

vpp *adv. haue vpp. See* **haue**; *lift . . . vpp. See* **lift**; *vpp an end* upright 205/15

vppon *prep.* from, out of 64/5; in reference to 116/23, 117/12

vrchene *n.* ill-tempered or mischievous young person 113/5

vrchyn *adj.* ill-tempered 295/6

vre *n. in vre* into use, to work 112/9

vse *v.* be accustomed 66/5 *etc.*; *pr. p. vsyng our selfe* behaving 272/26

vssher *n.* teacher acting under another 69/31

vth *n.* youth 191/6

vttermost, vtter must *n.* farthest extent, utmost, extreme 40/12, 108/25

vtward *adj.* outward, external 61/7

vulgare *adj.* ordinary 213/27

vyage *n. See* **viage**

vylanouse *adj. See* **velenouse**

vyry *adv. See* **very**

walke *v. walke . . . toward* tend in the direction of 192/17; *walke . . . wide* miss the point 34/4

wanne *v. pt.* won 237/15, 300/2

wantid *v. pt.* lacked, was without 141/13

wanton *adj.* undisciplined, rebellious 29/15 *etc.*; foolish, frivolous 83/3

wanton *n.* a person spoiled by excessive luxury and leniency 301/8

wanton(n)es *n.* wantonness, lawlessness 95/19, 269/28

war(r)a(u)nt *v.* promise, assure, guarantee 16/12 *etc.*

warauntise, warrantyse *n.* assurance, guarantee 245/2, 247/5

ware *adj.* aware 51/8 *etc.*; careful, wary 80/13, 120/10

wared *pp.* expended 90/7. *See n.*

warke, worke *n.* work, occupation 92/1 *etc.*; *go . . . to worke* deal with the question 85/14, 137/2–3; try to confuse 138/25; *set a worke. See* **set(t)**

warrant *v. See* **war(r)a(u)nt**

warrantyse *n. See* **warauntise**

wast *n.* waste 6/25

watch *n.* state of being awake 66/28 *etc.*

watch word *n.* password, customary greeting 80/7

water *n.* urine 63/2

wax(e), wex *v.* grow, become 3/17 *etc.*

way(e) *v.* weigh, consider 130/12 *etc.; pp.* **wayed, weyed** 73/3, 173/22

wayfaryng, way faryng *ppl. a.* traveling, journeying 182/25, 251/20

wayght *n.* weight, significance 240/28

way walkyng *ppl. a.* vagrant 259/21

wayward *adj.* self-willed, refractory 132/7, 135/27

waywardnes *n.* disobedience, intractability 69/29

weale, well *n.* welfare, well-being 22/25 *etc. See also* **comen weale**

weder *n.* weather 58/22 *etc.*

weke *n.* week 163/12 *etc.*

wekely *adv.* weekly 180/25

welkyn *n.* sky, heavens 216/3

well *n. See* **weale**

well spring *n.* source 180/27–28

welps *n. pl.* whelps 108/14

welth *n.* well-being, state of happiness and prosperity 71/1

welthe *adj.* wealthy 71/15, 72/20–21

welthfull *adj.* prosperous, flourishing 246/13

wene *v.* think, suppose, believe 12/21 *etc.; pp.* **went** 3/9 *etc.*

were *v.* wear 14/21

werely *adv.* wearily 113/29

wery *adj.* weary 115/17, 149/13

w(h)ether *adv.* whither, to what place 59/25 *etc.*

wex *v. See* **wax(e)**

wey *n.* way, manner 3/12

weyed *pp. See* **way(e)**

whan *adv.* when 20/28 *etc.*

what *adv.* why, for what reason 96/23

where *conj.* while on the contrary, whereas 65/13

where as *adv.* where 240/1

where as *conj.* whereas, since 8/16 *etc.*

wherels *conj.* in which otherwise 114/4

wherfor(e) *adv.* why, for what reason 9/20 *etc.*

wherin *adv.* from which 130/26; in which 11/19 *etc.*

wherinto *adv.* into which 147/14

wherof *adv.* to which 4/12, 120/27; of which, by which 9/26 *etc.*; from what 173/13

wherto *adv.* to which 155/13; to what end 70/16, 18

wherwith *adv.* through which, by which 5/15 *etc.*; at which point 110/4; with which 161/18 *etc.*

whet *v.* sharpen 119/4, 125/16

whight *adj.* white 207/1

while *n.* period of time 41/18 *etc.; the while* meanwhile 63/7 *etc.*

whit(t) *n.* bit, particle 186/10; *not . . . a whit* not in the least 109/26–27; *euery whit(t)* every bit, completely 174/32 *etc.*

whither, whyther *conj.* whether 51/24 *etc.*

whitsontide *n.* Whitsuntide, Pentecostal season 300/5

wholy, whole *adv.* wholly, completely 21/15 *etc.*

whrechid *adj.* distressed, unhappy 112/18

whysh *v. See* **wyssh**

whyther *conj. See* **whither**

whyther *pron.* which (of two) 195/16, 265/16

wich *n.* witch 62/12 *etc.*

wile, wyle *adj.* wily, clever 115/16 *etc.*

will *n. at will* at one's disposal 45/7; *by your will* voluntarily, of your own accord 289/20; *in will to* willing to 92/1–2

will, wyll *v. pr. 3 s.* wills, wishes, desires 57/16 *etc., pt modal* **wold** would 3/9 *etc.; pt. 2 s.* **woldest** 104/13, 105/18; *pp.* **wold** 243/22; *wold god* "oh that it were God's will" 4/26 *etc.*

winke, wynke *v.* close one's eyes 198/2, 212/13

wise, wyse *n.* way, manner, fashion 22/26 *etc.; at the lest wise* in any event, at the very least 42/20 *etc.; maner wise. See* **maner**; *sondry wise. See* **sondry**. *See also* **contrary wise, nowise**

wist *v. pt. See* **wit(te)**

wit(t)(e), wyt *n.* mental capacity, reason, intellect 9/14 *etc.; the bodely five wittes* the five senses 282/4–5

wit(te) *v.* know, realize 22/15 *etc.; pt.* **wist** 29/29 *etc.; pr. p.* **wyttyng** 284/24; *to wit(te)* namely 10/21 *etc.*

withall, with all *adv.* besides, moreover 47/7 *etc.*; therewith, in that case 45/27 *etc.*; with 190/29; *to begyn withall* to begin with 12/10

within *prep. within a while* within a short time 86/4; *within a litell. See* **litell**

without *conj.* unless 39/9 *etc.*

withstand, withstanden *pp.* withstood 122/25, 249/9–10

wittid *ppl. a. meane wittid* of little understanding 39/24

wittyngly *adv.* knowingly, consciously 186/9

wo(o) *n.* woe 54/21 *etc.*

wode *n.* wood, forest 109/24 *etc.*

wold *pt. modal, pp. See* **will**

woldest *pt. 2 s. See* **will**

woman(n)ysh *adj.* characteristic of women, womanly 93/19, 220/11

wonderfull *adj.* wondrous, astonishing 126/2 *etc.*

wonderfull *adv.* wondrously, exceedingly 83/23

wonderfully *adv.* marvellously, wondrously 8/13 *etc.*

wonderouse *adv.* exceedingly, extremely 45/3, 149/12

wont *ppl. a.* accustomed 3/13 *etc.*

woo *adj.* woeful 17/8

woo *n. See* **wo(o)**

woode *adj.* wild, furious 59/13

worke *n. See* **warke**

worke *v.* become stirred up 192/2; bring about, cause 311/11; *pt.* **wrought** 176/24

worship *n.* honor, distinction 10/2 *etc.*

worshipfull *adj.* distinguished, honorable 168/32 *etc.*

worth *n. take in worth. See* **take**

worth *v. wo worth the while* may evil befall the time 61/13

worthy *adj.* sufficient to merit, deserving 319/22, 27

wot(t)(e) *v.* know 4/15 *etc.*

wrake *n.* wreck 310/23

wrechidnes *n.* wretchedness 3/20

wrestelers *n. pl.* wrestlers 101/15

wrestell, wrastle *v.* wrestle, contend 101/17 *etc.*

wrest(e)lyng *vbl. n.* wrestling 101/14 *etc.*

wrestyng *vbl. n.* turning, twisting 67/11

wrethen *pp.* made into a wreath 144/18

wringeth *v. pr. 3 s. See* **wryngeth**

wrongid, wrongyn *pp. See* **wryngeth**

wroth *adj.* wrathful, angry 45/3 *etc.*

wrought *ppl. a.* stirred up, agitated 301/10

wrought *v. pt. See* **worke**

wry *v.* swerve, turn 60/20

wryngeth, wringeth *v. pr. 3 s.* presses, squeezes 274/22, 25–26; *pp.* **wrongyn, wrongid** 80/10, 271/9

wyle *adj. See* **wile**

wynke *v. See* **winke**

wyse *n. See* **wise**

wyssh, whysh *v.* wish 56/22, 185/21; *pt.* **whishid** 301/13

wyt *n. See* **wit(t)(e)**

wyttyng *pr. p. See* **wit(te)**

yalpyng *ppl. a.* yelping, barking 295/18. *See n.*

yarnyng *vbl. n.* giving tongue, baying 295/12

ye(e), yea *inter.* yes, indeed 10/29 *etc.*

ye(e), yie *n.* eye 108/30 *etc.*; *pl.* **eyen, yeen, yien** 6/22 *etc.*

yeld *v.* yield, give 74/28, 178/13

yere *n.* year 3/9, 4/18

yerth *n.* earth 266/4

yether *adv.* either 37/17, 299/22

yister day *n.* yesterday 127/13, 319/14

ymprent *v.* imprint 282/5; *pp.* **ymprintid** 281/25

ynch *n.* inch 66/7, 207/19

yncommodities *n. pl. See* **incommodit(i)e**

ynough *adj. See* **inough**

ynough *adv. See* **ino(u)gh**

yon *adv.* yonder, over there 315/13

yt *adv.* yet 86/2. *See n.*

INDEX

INDEX

In the Index, entries are given, wherever possible, in modern spelling. Biblical names appear in the spelling of the Authorized Version. Unusual sixteenth-century spellings of proper names are entered in the Glossary, which, in these cases, should be used in conjunction with the Index. The abbreviation "n." after an entry designates a name occurring only in a footnote.